THE STOCK MARKET DIRECTORY

THE STOCK MARKET DIRECTORY

JOHN R. DORFMAN

DOUBLEDAY & COMPANY, INC.
GARDEN CITY, NEW YORK
1982

Library of Congress Cataloging in Publication Data

Dorfman, John.
The stock market directory.

Includes index.
1. Corporations—United States—Finance—Directories.
2. Stocks—United States. I. Title.
HG4057.A233 338.7'4'0973 81-43558
AACR2

ISBN: 0-385-17286-9
Library of Congress Catalog Card Number 81-43558
First Edition

Printed in the United States of America

To my research assistants:

Winifred Conkling

Brenda Good

Steve Jarvis

Suzanne Kurman

David Shaffer

Herman Tull

CONTENTS

THE STOCK MARKET DIRECTORY

HOW TO BUY STOCKS

There is a perfect way to buy stocks. It is with a crystal ball.

Those of us who lack crystal balls must make do with the hundreds of books, scores of newsletters, and dozens of magazines and newspaper sections devoted to the subject. Some of us will thrive, others will take losses. The vast majority of us will, in the long run, do about as well as the market averages.

This book — as you can see at a glance — is organized as a reference source. It's not primarily designed to suggest what stocks you should buy, though it may give you some ideas. Rather, it's a place you can look up a stock you're considering to get another perspective on it. We hold no brief that our perspective is infallible. But we suspect that you may find here certain ideas you hadn't considered. And, since this book is written for the lay individual investor, the ideas you'll find here are expressed in plain English.

In addition to giving you some perspective on a large number of common stocks, this book is intended as a handy reference for anyone interested in the stock market or in facts on major American corporations. The information in the book has been gathered from sources we believe to be reliable, but it can't be guaranteed.

Also not guaranteed, despite what some tip sheet or pundit may tell you, is any single system for making money in stocks. That's why you shouldn't put money that you can't afford to lose into the stock market. Losing it would be painful; you don't *intend* to lose it — in fact you intend to increase it quite a bit — but if worst came to worst and you lost it, life would go on. Don't invest in the stock market until you have a reasonable amount of savings, and adequate insurance. Don't invest if you're heavily in debt. If you want absolute safety, put your money in a bank account, or certificates of deposit, or (with *almost* absolute safety) a money market fund.

If you have some money you can risk, the stock market is an excellent place to risk it. It's as exciting as the race track, arguably more rational, probably less fixed, and has odds weighted in your favor (the long-term trend is up) rather than against you. The stock market performs a socially useful function, helping to make capital available to industries that provide jobs, goods, and services. As this book is being written, the early 1980s look to be a good time for investors in stocks. The market is recovering from some rocky years and has shown no major gains for some time. Such times discourage many investors, but (as noted in the timeless adage, "buy low, sell high") are precisely the best sort of time to invest.

Are All Stocks Created Equal?

Why will the stock of one company sell for $80, and the stock of another company sell for $30, when both companies earned $5 a share last year? The answer lies in investors' ideas about the future. The first company may be fast-growing, dynamic, highly regarded. It may be in a popular field (robotics and genetic engineering being recent examples). The second company may be old and stodgy, or in an industry headed for a slump. By pricing the first stock higher, investors are saying that they expect its earnings a few years hence to be well above those of the second stock.

A real-life example will make the point clear. In 1980, General Mills had profits (earnings) of $170 million, or $3.90 a share. General Nutrition, a much smaller company specializing in vitamins and health foods, had profits of about $13 million, or $1.56 a share. Yet in the fall of 1981, investors were willing to pay $38 for each share of General Nutrition, versus only about $35 for each share of General Mills. The smaller company was growing fast, riding a fad (or a trend, depending on your point of view), and investors were betting that the trend would continue. Accordingly, they were willing to pay only 9 times the previous year's earnings figure for General Mills, but 23 times the previous year's earnings for General Nutrition.

The number we have just cited for each stock is the *price / earnings ratio.* You'll see the price / earnings ratio discussed often in this book, and in many other investment manuals and articles. It is a very important number, for several reasons. In short summary, the price / earnings ratio reflects the results of an instantaneous and continuous popularity poll. Stocks that are popular at the moment have high price / earnings ratios. Stocks that are unpopular have low ones.

The price / earnings ratio may be called the p / e ratio, or simply the PE. It is also called the stock's *multiple,* since the earnings times the multiple equal the stock's price at the moment.

The most common way to calculate the price / earnings ratio is to use the earnings for the previous twelve months and the stock's price as of the previous day. Stock brokers and analysts sometimes calculate the ratio using the earnings they expect for the current 12 months, or the coming 12 months, or even the year after next. This can be of some analytical value, but when you see such calculations you should remember that there is some guesswork involved.

My bias is generally in favor of buying stocks with low price / earnings ratios. Why, when these are the unpopular stocks? Precisely *because* they're the unpopular stocks. If an out-of-favor stock returns to favor, it can rise dramatically because the price / earnings ratio fattens up again. By contrast, when you buy a popular stock, with a high price / earnings ratio, you can lose money even if your company shows decent profit progress. This is what happened to people who bought the "glamour" stocks (i.e. very popular stocks with very high price / earnings ratios) in the late 1960s and early 1970s. Companies like McDonalds, IBM, and Xerox have nothing to be ashamed of in their corporate performance. But the stocks were big losers when investors, seeing that the companies' red-hot growth of previous years had cooled, punctured the high p / e ratios like balloons.

David Dreman, a stock market observer who writes a column in *Forbes* magazine, cites several studies that show the low p / e stocks have — on the average and in the long run — outperformed high p / e stocks. However, you can't simply pick a portfolio of low p / e stocks and think that your worries are gone. The classic cliché here is the buggy whip. When the automobile was coming in, stocks in buggy-whip or carriage producers might have had low multiples, but they still wouldn't have been bargains.

Are all stocks created equal? There is a highly respectable school of analysis that holds they are. This is the *efficient market theory.* It says that every fact known about a company is instantly factored into the stock price. The average investor, lacking inside information, always arrives too late to take advantage of any knowledge he's picked up from *Barron's,* or his stock-tip newsletter, or his uncle. By the time the newsletter publishes it, or the uncle hears it, it's old news and has already been reflected in the price of the stock. Under this theory, high p / e and low p / e stocks are of equal worth. The fast growth or good prospects of the high p / e stock are already reflected in its price. So are the slow growth or bad prospects of the low-multiple stock. You might as well flip a coin.

Or throw a dart. In fact, randomly selected portfolios (including those selected by throwing darts at a newspaper stock page) have usually been found in studies to perform as well as portfolios under professional management. If this is bad news, it has its bright side: You stand to do as well as the big guys. (Your main disadvantage as an individual is that you pay higher commissions to your broker per share than a big institution like a bank or an insurance company does.)

My own view about the efficient market theory is that the market is pretty efficient, but not perfectly so. It reflects incoming news fast, all right, but sometimes overreacts to that news, as well as to short-term economic conditions. And though the market (i.e. the totality of investors) sees the short-term outlook in sharp focus, it's sometimes blurry on long-term trends. People who correctly foresaw the energy shortage, for example, made tremendous profits in oil and drilling stocks in the late 1970s.

Is Debt Good or Bad?

An enduring controversy among stock pickers is how much debt is too much. The issue here is what the financial community calls *leverage.* The word leverage is sometimes used almost as a synonym for debt. More precisely it refers to an effect debt has on financial results. Debt magnifies the results.

You may be familiar with this effect if you bought a house around, say, 1970. You borrowed $40,000 to buy a $60,000 house. In 1980 you sold the house for $100,000. After paying back what was left of the $40,000 debt, you had a profit of more than $40,-000, on an initial investment of just $20,000. Wasn't it marvelous?

It was, but suppose you try it again and this time the real estate market turns sour. Suppose you borrowed $80,000 to buy a $100,000 house in 1980, and in 1990 wanted to sell it during a bad market where you could get only $87,000. Aside from all the interest you paid, you'd have a $13,000 loss on your $20,000 investment.

For companies, as for you, leverage magnifies results both ways. When things are going well, the use of debt greatly enhances per-share earnings. The company has made money using somebody else's money (either bank debt or bond debt, usually). You, as a stockholder, have put in perhaps only $1 for each $2 the company used. Yet you get the full benefit of the company's earnings per share (and, with some companies, dividends per share). Without the debt, earnings per share could only have been half as much. You're pleased that the company used leverage.

But now comes a down year. The company has to pay its fixed expenses, as usual — not the least of which is interest on that debt. If the company loses money, the loss per share is twice as great as it would have been had the company avoided debt and financed itself solely through the issuance of common stock.

In the real world, it's rare these days to find a company with no debt, though there are still some. Even Disney and IBM, two traditionally debt-free companies, issued some bonds and had some debt in their capital structure during the 1970s. The average company these days probably has about 25 to 30 percent of its total capital in the form of debt. And it's not unusual to find companies whose debt is 50 percent or more of total capital. Whether an above-average debt is a danger sign depends in part on whether the company is growing vigorously and in part on what industry the company is in.

My bias, generally, is in favor of companies that have relatively little debt. It's true that debt (within the bounds of prudence) is a logical strategy in inflationary times, since borrowed money is paid back with ever-cheaper dollars. However, it's by no means clear that inflation is a permanent condition, even though people have come to feel it is. Traditionally, high and lasting inflation results sooner or later in a severe economic slump and deflation. Meanwhile, the cost of servicing debt is a real cost, and in some years a painful cost, for many companies. And the claims of debt holders (banks and bond holders, mainly) come before those of common stock holders. You, as a stockholder, don't get credited with a penny of earnings or a dime of dividends until the debt has been serviced.

How Profits Are Measured.

Understanding a little bit about leverage helps you understand the meaning of common measures of a company's profitability. Perhaps the best-known measure is raw dollars — e.g. Coca-Cola earned $481 million in 1981. The next best-known figure is the earnings per share, obtained simply by dividing the raw dollar total by the number of shares outstanding. For Coca-Cola, it was $3.62 per share in 1981, up twenty cents from the year before. It's easy to look at a stream of earnings-per-share figures and see whether the company lately has been headed up or down.

Those ways of looking at profitability, however, are merely a bare beginning. To see in more detail how investors look at profitability, let's shift from Coca-Cola to a hypothetical corporation, XXX Corp., whose profits happen to fall into nice, round numbers. XXX Corp. earned $100 million in profits last year. But that doesn't tell you whether the shareholders are happy. That depends in part, of course, on whether $100 million is up or down from the previous years, and by how much.

Whether the stockholders are happy also depends on how many of them are dividing up the pie — in this case, the $100 million pie. If XXX is a closely held private corporation with, say, five shareholders, each of the five is probably very pleased with his (her) $20 million in profits. But if XXX is a large, publicly owned corporation with 20 million shareholders, each holder may or may not be pleased with his $5 share of profits.

It depends in large part on how much money the stockholders put up in the first place. Suppose that XXX has $500 million in capital. Half the capital is in the form of debt and was raised by XXX's selling bonds. Then the stockholders would have put up only $250 million, and they'd be extremely pleased. The return on stockholders' equity, in this simplified example, would be 40 percent, a return so high it's hardly ever seen. That high return was made possible by a rather high level of debt — 50 percent of total capital. This level of debt involves some risks, since if business turns sour, the debt interest would still have to be paid.

Return on total capital measures how much profit a company makes as a percentage of all the capital it has to work with. In our example, it was 20 percent, which is well above average. (The recent average return on total capital for major American corporations was around 12 percent.) Return on total capital is a good measure of a company's operating efficiency.

Return on stockholders' equity measures the profits a company makes as a percentage of the capital put up by stockholders. (It takes account only indirectly of capital from the issuing of bonds, preferred stock, or the taking out of bank loans.) In our XXX example, return on equity was 40 percent, a figure rarely achieved in real life. About 15 percent has been the recent average for major corporations. A 20 percent return on equity is considered quite good, 12 percent fair, and less than 10 percent mediocre to poor.

In real life, too, the arithmetic is much more complicated. Stockholders' equity, in practice, includes not only the money originally paid by stockholders for their shares at the time those shares were first issued by the company; it also includes the sum of the amounts plowed back into the business each year by the company.

Suppose that XXX Corp. originally issues $250 million worth of stock. Then, in its first year of operation, it makes $100 million in profits. It might pay $40 million in taxes, pay out $20 million in dividends to shareholders, and plow $40 million back into the business. This last $40 million is called *retained earnings.* Stockholders' equity is the sum of all past retained earnings plus the amount originally obtained by issuing stock. In XXX's case, stockholders' equity after one year of operation would amount to $290 million.

If you're a stockholder, you're naturally interested in the return on stockholders' equity. But remember it's only one of several ways to measure a company's profitability.

You might divide profits by the company's assets, giving you, logically enough, the *return on assets.* This way of measuring profits is used chiefly to evaluate banks. A return of $.50 per $100 of assets is considered passable for a bank; $1 per $100 of assets is considered outstanding.

You might divide profits by the current market value of the company's stock — or (on a smaller scale but with the same result) profits per share by the current price per share. This gives you what's called the *earnings yield* (though it could just as logically be called the return on market value). If you stop to think about it, you'll discover that this figure is the reciprocal of the price / earnings ratio, discussed earlier in this chapter. For example, a fast-growing young company might have profits of $1.00 per share and a stock price of $25 per share. In this case the p / e would be a heady 25, and the earnings yield would be a relatively small 4%.

Another, and quite familiar, way to measure profits is to divide profits by the company's sales. What this gives us is simply the *profit margin.* If you buy a coat for $80 and sell it for $100, your profit margin is 20 percent (simplified, as usual). If you buy a million coats for $80 each and sell them for $100 each, your sales were $100 million and profits were $20 million, but your profit margin is just the same — 20 percent. Some businesses — supermarkets and discount department stores, for example — traditionally have low profit margins, around 1 or 2 percent. Others — oil field services, for example — traditionally have high profit margins. What is most significant in analyzing a stock is to watch the trend in profit margins and the size of profit margins relative to competitors'.

Reviewing quickly, you'll see that we've touched on seven ways of measuring profitability: (1) the raw profit total in dollars; (2) profits per share; (3) return on total capital; (4) return on stockholders' equity; (5) return on assets; (6) earnings yield; and (7) profit margin. There are more, which won't be mentioned here. No single measure is perfect; it often helps to look at several measures.

Keep in mind that wherever we've said "profits," the word "earnings" can be substituted. They mean the same thing. Keep in mind, too, that a company's trend, and its standing relative to competitors, are often at least as important as the numbers viewed in isolation.

Up to now, we've talked about measuring the company's profits. What about yours?

Measuring Your Return.

When you own a stock, your own personal profit can come from two sources — a capital gain (an increase in the price of the stock) and dividends you receive. If you own a stock that yields 5 percent a year in dividends and also goes up in price 7 percent a year, then your *total return* from the stock (dividends plus capital appreciation) is 12 percent a year.

You can, of course, have a negative return, since the price of a stock can go down as well as up. In some cases, dividend payments will offset your capital losses. You might (say, on a high-yielding utility stock) have a capital loss but a positive total return because of high dividends.

Dividends are cash payments to shareholders made at the discretion of the company's board of directors. They are your most tangible reward for being a part-owner of the company.

A stock's *dividend yield* is the company's current yearly dividend divided by the current stock price. A stock with a dividend yield of 5½ percent is paying you roughly as much cash as you'd get by keeping the same amount of money in a passbook savings account at a bank. (The stock, of course, also gives you a chance for a capital gain.) In this book, I generally use the terms "small" or "modest" for a yield of 3 percent or less; "moderate" for a yield of 3–6 percent; "substantial" for a yield of 6–9 percent; and "high" for a yield above 9 percent.

In this book or elsewhere, you may hear talk about a *payout ratio.* That means the percentage of profits a company pays out in dividends. Often, the payout ratio will be between 25 percent and 50 percent. However, it's possible for a company to pay out more in dividends than it made in profits that year. In this case, the payout ratio goes above 100 percent. Such a high payout ratio is a sign of a company in trouble trying to maintain investor confidence and / or stand by its shareholders during a difficult period. Obviously, no company can long maintain a payout ratio of that magnitude.

In pure theory, when you buy a stock, its value is based on the future stream of dividend payments to you. In practice, people buy stocks at least as much for capital gains as for dividends. Some fast-growing young companies don't pay dividends at all. And some well-established companies (such as Teledyne) don't pay them on principle. In fair part, this is because of the tax laws. Dividends are ordinarily subject to regular income tax, just like your salary. (However, the first $100 in dividends you get each year from U.S. corporations is normally exempt.) Capital gains, on the other hand, are favorably taxed. Under recent law, you are taxed only on 40 percent of the money you make from a long-term (i.e. more than one year) capital gain. In other words, if you buy a hundred shares of a stock on January 1, 1983, for $1,000 and sell them on February 5, 1984, for $2,000, you are taxed on only 40 percent of the gain — that is, $400. Your actual tax might be about $100 to $200, depending on your tax bracket.

Given this tax structure, a good case can be made that you should take as much of your profit as possible in the form of capital gains, not dividends. However, a bird in the hand is probably worth more than one in the bush. Dividends are here and now. Capital gains, lovely as they are, are probably a bit harder to predict than dividends.

A total return figure is shown in this book for almost every stock discussed. This figure includes both capital gains and dividends. It does not weight them according to tax consequences. We consider the showing of a total return (for two selected periods — roughly the last five years and the last ten) to be an unusual feature of this book.

The Use of Judgment.

It is not clear whether this book, or any other, will give you an unusual ability to pick stocks successfully. As mentioned earlier, economists and academics have made a good case that success in the stock market is a matter of luck or chance. A fast-growing company will sell for a high multiple of earnings, a slow-growing company for a low multiple. Thus, as with horses at the race track (where the fastest horses must carry the heaviest saddles), all the stocks offer a roughly equal chance of making you money.

In the long run, most people will do just about as well as the market averages (the Dow Jones, the Standard & Poor's 500, etc.). That in itself, by the way, is not necessarily something to sneeze at.

But I do believe that there may be an opportunity for thoughtful individuals to better the averages a bit. For the stock market not only instantly reflects the known facts, it sometimes overreacts to them. Thus a person with clear judgment may buy a stock when it's undervalued. And a far-seeing individual may see a product or industry coming to fill a need before others are quite aware that the need exists.

You, as an investor, will evolve your own preferences, if you haven't already done so. My own preference is generally for stocks that meet three criteria: (1) rising earnings; (2) a relatively low price / earnings ratio; and (3) relatively low debt, as a proportion of total capital. I do not believe that stocks that meet these criteria will necessarily be "winners," nor that stocks which do not meet them will necessarily be "losers." But I regard the criteria as a useful screening device, a good starting point for analysis.

Speaking of starting points, this book is itself a starting point. It is a reference source primarily for the beginning investor (though we hope that it also contains insights that experienced investors will find helpful). When you become seriously interested in the stock market, or when you are seriously considering buying an individual stock, it may be helpful to you to consult some additional sources.

Among encyclopedic sources, I particularly like *The Value Line Investment Survey.* Also useful are *Standard & Poor's Stock Reports,* and *Moody's Handbook of Common Stocks.* It also pays to see what's been written about a company in the major business magazines. I heartily recommend *Forbes.* * With varying degrees of heartiness, I also recommend *Fortune, Financial World, Business Week,* and *Barron's.* These publications are indexed in *Business Periodicals Index* and in the *F&S (Funk & Scott) Index*.

How to Use This Book.

Some understanding of the structure of this book may help you use the book effectively. We provide basic information on roughly 1,500 stocks, includ-

* After this book was written, but before it was published, the author joined the staff at *Forbes* as associate editor.

ing (to the best of our knowledge) every stock listed on the New York Stock Exchange as of January 1, 1982. For approximately 500 stocks, we also offer an analysis or "profile," describing factors to consider when you are contemplating a purchase of the shares. The 500 profiled stocks fall into three broad groups — large companies, highly profitable companies, and companies of great investor interest.

Here is a rundown on information provided in a standard format for almost every company:

Company name — the correct and legal name.

Ticker symbol — shown in parentheses. All stocks are on the New York Stock Exchange except for a few specifically designated as American Stock Exchange or Over the Counter.

Year founded — refers, in most cases, to the date the company was incorporated in its present form. Where a company has indicated a preference, we sometimes use the date business operations were started, even if it was before incorporation.

Address — this provides you with a convenient way to write the company (if you wish to get a copy of its annual report, for example).

Summary description — tells in four words or less the company's basic line of business.

Fuller description — tells, in one to three sentences of plain English, just what the company does.

Number of employees — rounded to the nearest or next-lowest 1000, at author's discretion; this is provided only for the 500 profiled companies.

Major subsidiaries, brands — a fairly comprehensive listing of other companies, or brand names, a company owns. These are listed in each company entry. At the back of the book there is an index of subsidiaries and brand names that can help you understand at a glance who owns what.

Sales — the company's total dollar intake in 1981* from the sale of all goods and services. In parentheses is the annual percentage trend in sales for the past five years. The trend is upward unless specifically shown as downward with a minus sign.

Earnings — the company's profits for 1981.* In parentheses is the annual percentage trend in profits for the past five years. The trend is, again, upward unless a minus sign is shown.

What happened to a $10,000 investment — in this section, we assume that you had invested $10,000 in the company at the beginning of 1972 or at the beginning of 1977. We then report on what your money would have earned you in dividends and in capital gains or losses.† Adding together the two figures we give your hypothetical total return — and render it easily understandable by expressing it as an annual percentage.

We lay no claim to having written the country's most comprehensive financial manual. Many reference materials, some of them mentioned above, have more details. Our aim was to write a volume that would be clear and helpful to the lay person.

Nor do we claim to have the latest, most current information. This book takes the long view — which is probably the appropriate viewpoint for individual investors, who generally are best off if they "buy and hold." Frequent trading may not increase your chances of picking winning stocks, but it will certainly increase your brokerage commissions. Still, since much of the information here was gathered in 1981, you should check newspapers, your broker, and other reference materials before you commit money to a specific stock.

Our underlying purpose is to provide a springboard into the fascinating world of investing in stocks. If we whet your appetite for more information, we're pleased. If we help you to make some money, we're delighted.

JOHN R. DORFMAN

* Or for the most recent 12-month period available when figures were compiled in early 1982.

† All numbers are adjusted for any stock splits that occurred during the period.

Information has been obtained from sources believed to be reliable, but cannot be guaranteed.

COMPANY PROFILES

A

AAR CORP. (AIR). Founded 1955. Headquarters: 2100 Touhy Ave., Elk Grove Village IL 60007. **AVIATION.** Provides repairs, maintenance, and other products and services for business and commercial aviation. **MAJOR SUBSIDIARIES, BRANDS:** AAR Del Monte; AAR Western Skyways.

Sales: $132.5 million (trend 16.0% a year).
Earnings: $3.61 million (trend 18.3% a year).
What happened to a $10,000 investment

Purchase Date	*Purchase Price*	*Price on 12-31-81*	*Dividends Paid*
12-31-71	$10.33	$7.62	$1,723.09
12-31-76	$ 6.69	$7.62	$1,959.55

Purchase Date	*Cap. Gains (– Losses)*	*Total Return*	*Rate of Return*
12-31-71	$–2,616.64	$–893.55	–.93%
12-31-76	$ 1,396.05	$ 3,355.61	5.96%

* * *

ACF INDUSTRIES, INC. (ACF). Founded 1899. Headquarters: 750 Third Ave., New York NY 10017. **RAILROAD CARS.** ACF is the second-largest U.S. railroad car manufacturer (after Pullman) and is also active in leasing railroad cars. Other operations include valve making (mainly for the oil exploration industry), specialty plastics, oil and gas exploration, and auto parts (chiefly carburetors). 13,000 employees. **MAJOR SUBSIDIARIES, BRANDS:** Amcar (railroad cars); WKM Valve; Carter Automotive Group; ACF Petroleum Co.; Polymer Corp. (plastics).

Sales: $1,044.6 million (trend 13.6% a year).
Earnings: $44.76 million (trend 9.1% a year).
What happened to a $10,000 investment

Purchase Date	*Purchase Price*	*Price on 12-31-81*	*Dividends Paid*
12-31-71	$34.33	$40.87	$5,745.64
12-31-76	$35.12	$40.87	$3,234.16

Purchase Date	*Cap. Gains (– Losses)*	*Total Return*	*Rate of Return*
12-31-71	$1,905.34	$7,650.98	5.85%
12-31-76	$1,637.01	$4,871.17	8.26%

PROFILE: Despite ACF's slow growth, investors were willing to pay as much as 10 times earnings for this stock in 1981. Why? Probably because they figured things couldn't get much worse at two of ACF's major divisions, railroad car manufacturing (Amcar) and auto parts (Carter Automotive Group).

In fact, 1981 was the worst year for railroad car orders in several decades — an ironic state of affairs considering that Wall Street has been looking forward to a rail boom (mainly to carry increasing amounts of coal). High interest rates have been the kiss of death to this business, which normally accounts for well over half of ACF's sales. As the rates decline, sales should pick up again.

Sales of auto parts, mainly carburetors, have of course been hurt by a prolonged slump in auto sales throughout 1980 and 1981 (1979 was no great shakes either). The slack at ACF has been taken up in part by the valves unit, which sells mainly to oil drillers.

The balance sheet shows a lot of debt (recently 47 percent of capital), but that's somewhat deceiving. Much of it is low-interest debt on which company-owned railroad cars are collateral. Profitability has been unexciting for the past decade, and profit margins have slowly been falling. Dividends have been paid each year since 1951; the yield in recent years has ranged between 5 and 7 percent.

* * *

AMF, INC. (AMF). Founded 1900. Headquarters: 777 Westchester Ave., White Plains NY 10604.

RECREATIONAL AND INDUSTRIAL PRODUCTS. AMF is best known for its "leisure products," from bowling equipment and volleyballs to motorcycles and yachts. About one third of sales, however, come from industrial equipment, including timers, filters, pipe coatings, process machinery, and oil field inspection devices. 29,000 employees. **MAJOR SUBSIDIARIES, BRANDS:** AMF bowling equipment; Voit balls and sporting equipment; Alcort, Crestliner, Hatteras, and Slickcraft boats; Head sports equipment; Ben Hogan golf equipment; Cuno filters; Paragon timers; Potter & Brumfield relays; Tuboscope oil field products; Scientific Drilling International; Geo Space Corp.

Sales: $1,534.0 million (trend 8.8% a year).
Earnings: $56.54 million (trend 11.6% a year).
What happened to a $10,000 investment

Purchase Date	*Purchase Price*	*Price on 12-31-81*	*Dividends Paid*
12-31-71	$48.25	$27.75	$2,509.84
12-31-76	$21.37	$27.75	$2,914.62

Purchase Date	*Cap. Gains (− Losses)*	*Total Return*	*Rate of Return*
12-31-71	$−4,248.70	$−1,738.86	−1.89%
12-31-76	$ 2,982.46	$ 5,897.08	9.71%

PROFILE: AMF's performance has been lackluster for several years. Name almost any indicator you want, and you'll find that AMF has performed, not terribly, but below average in that respect. Profits have ranged between $1 and $3 a share for the entire decade from 1970 to 1980, and if you look at the figures it's hard to discern much of a trend. Question: Is this a cyclical growth company, or just plain cyclical? As for the stock price, it soared to a peak around $67 in 1972, but ended the 1980s in the $20 range, the same price AMF shares had during the late 1960s.

Why, then, doesn't Wall Street penalize the stock with a low price / earnings multiple? In early 1981, the stock traded at about 8 times earnings, which was just about the average multiple. There are at least three reasons.

First, those were depressed earnings. When a recession ends, people are expected to pick up their spending for leisure products, and corporations are expected to spend more on process equipment.

Second, some people were hoping that W. Thomas York, who took over as chairman in 1978, would make good on his intention to improve profit margins and decrease cyclicality.

Third and most important, AMF has been moving into oil field services, an area that's been profitable in the past few years. AMF's Tuboscope subsidiary has had hot demand for its pipeline coatings and inspection equipment. And AMF has been seeking to acquire additional oil-field-service subsidiaries. In 1981 it acquired Scientific Drilling International and Geo Space Corp., which makes seismic exploration equipment.

* * *

AM INTERNATIONAL (AIN). Founded 1924. Headquarters: 1900 Ave. of the Stars, Los Angeles CA 90067. **OFFICE EQUIPMENT.** Formerly Addressograph-Multigraph Corp.; makes copiers, word processors, small business computer terminals, newspaper printing equipment. In 1982 it filed for protection under Chapter 11 of the bankruptcy code. **MAJOR SUBSIDIARIES, BRANDS:** ECRM; Micro-Data. Jacquard Systems was still owned in 1981, but its sale was planned; Addressograph was sold in 1981.

* * *

APL CORP. (APL). Founded 1959. Headquarters: 1 Linden Pl., Great Neck NY 11021. **PAPER PRODUCTS.** Makes paper towels, tissues, napkins, bags, paperboard boxes; plastic products, particularly bottles; and vitamins. **MAJOR SUBSIDIARIES, BRANDS:** Colortex; Foods Plus; Orchid.

Sales: $134.8 million (trend 5.5% a year).
Earnings: $−6.52 million.
What happened to a $10,000 investment

Purchase Date	*Purchase Price*	*Price on 12-31-81*	*Dividends Paid*
12-31-71	$10.62	$4.25	$4,752.94
12-31-76	$14.25	$4.25	$2,631.58

Purchase Date	*Cap. Gains (− Losses)*	*Total Return*	*Rate of Return*
12-31-71	$−6,000.00	$−1,247.06	−1.32%
12-31-76	$−7,017.54	$−4,385.96	−10.90%

* * *

ARA SERVICES, INC. (ARA). Founded 1959. Headquarters: Independence Sq. W., Philadelphia PA 19106. **FOOD SERVICE.** ARA is a diversified service company providing food services, health care services, distribution and transportation services, and laundry services. 79,000 employees. **MAJOR SUBSIDIARIES, BRANDS:** Smith's Transfer

Corp.; National Living Centers; Geriatrics Inc.; Work Wear.

Sales: $2,915.9 million (trend 18.5% a year).
Earnings: $45.84 million (trend 7.1% a year).
What happened to a $10,000 investment

Purchase Date	*Purchase Price*	*Price on 12-31-81*	*Dividends Paid*
12-31-71	$103.67	$26.87	$1,246.95
12-31-76	$ 50.25	$26.87	$1,653.73

Purchase Date	*Cap. Gains (− Losses)*	*Total Return*	*Rate of Return*
12-31-71	$−7,407.56	$−6,160.61	−9.13%
12-31-76	$−4,651.74	$−2,998.01	−6.88%

PROFILE: This company, which most people have never heard of, is one of the fifty or so largest employers in the United States. It provides cafeteria and vending machine food, buses kids to school, washes people's laundry, and runs nursing homes. Unlike many industries, the service sector of our economy is extremely diversified — so much so that ARA, with an estimated 3 percent of the market (according to Merrill Lynch in 1979) is the nation's biggest service company.

John A. Jensen, a Merrill Lynch analyst, was sweet on the stock in 1979. He wrote, "Question: How can investors participate in the $52 billion service sector of the economy, which is accounting for a growing portion of GNP? Answer: Through ARA shares."

Jensen conceded that ARA is vulnerable to changes in the economy. And how! At the end of 1979, ARA employed some 112,000 people — more than Boeing or McDonald's. At the end of 1980, the employment total was about 79,000. Profits were close to flat, in dollars unadjusted for inflation. Nor has ARA's long-term record of profit growth been inspiring; profits have grown, but more slowly than those of the average company. Another problem: What *The Wall Street Journal* in 1981 called the company's "history of many legal scrapes" with the Federal Trade Commission, Securities and Exchange Commission, and other regulatory agencies.

ARA stock has had a long slide down, from a peak of almost $125 a share in 1972 to a 1980 low of less than $25. Nevertheless, the company is profitable, and there comes a point when a stock has been oversold. That point may have come for ARA in the early 1980s as the p / e ratio was down to about 5.

* * *

ASA LIMITED (ASA). Founded 1958. Headquarters: 54 Marshall St., Johannesburg 2001 South Africa. **INVESTMENT CO.** ASA is a closed-end investment company that invests mainly in South African gold mines.

Sales: $65.1 million (trend 53.9% a year).
Earnings: $63.09 million (trend 56.1% a year).
What happened to a $10,000 investment

Purchase Date	*Purchase Price*	*Price on 12-31-81*	*Dividends Paid*
12-31-71	$ 8.56	$43.50	$22,043.80
12-31-76	$20.62	$43.50	$ 7,854.55

Purchase Date	*Cap. Gains (− Losses)*	*Total Return*	*Rate of Return*
12-31-71	$40,802.92	$62,846.72	21.97%
12-31-76	$11,090.91	$18,945.45	23.68%

* * *

AVX CORP. (AVX). Founded 1972. Headquarters: 60 Cuttermill Rd., Great Neck NY 11021. **ELECTRONICS.** Makes ceramic capacitors for computers, telecommunications equipment, and other uses.

Sales: $141.1 million (trend 39.6% a year).
Earnings: $8.02 million (trend 56.8% a year).
What happened to a $10,000 investment

Purchase Date	*Purchase Price*	*Price on 12-31-81*	*Dividends Paid*
12-31-71	$N/A	$13.87	$ N/A
12-31-76	$ 4.75	$13.87	$2,480.00

Purchase Date	*Cap. Gains (− Losses)*	*Total Return*	*Rate of Return*
12-31-71	$ N/A	$ N/A	N/A%
12-31-76	$19,210.53	$21,690.53	25.95%

* * *

ABBOTT LABORATORIES (ABT). Founded 1900. Headquarters: Abbott Park, North Chicago IL 60064. **HEALTH CARE.** Makes pharmaceuticals, blood testing equipment, vitamins, veterinary products. 28,000 employees. **MAJOR SUBSIDIARIES, BRANDS:** Erythrocin, Similac, Isomil, Sucaryl, Murine.

Sales: $2,038.2 million (trend 16.5% a year).
Earnings: $214.41 million (trend 24.8% a year).
What happened to a $10,000 investment

Purchase Date	Purchase Price	Price on 12-31-81	Dividends Paid
12-31-71	$ 8.06	$27.25	$3,996.12
12-31-76	$12.28	$27.25	$1,937.91

Purchase Date	Cap. Gains (— Losses)	Total Return	Rate of Return
12-31-71	$23,798.45	$27,794.57	14.22%
12-31-76	$12,188.30	$14,126.21	19.26%

PROFILE: Abbott emphasizes specialty products and foreign markets. It likes to carve out niches rather than try to compete across the board with larger pharmaceutical firms. That strategy has been successful: Abbott is number one in infant formulas (Similac), number two in intravenous solutions (despite a scandal in the early 1970s when contaminated solutions allegedly caused several deaths), and number two in eye drops (Murine). Intravenous solutions and infant formulas have each accounted for about 20 percent of sales, antibiotics for about 10 percent. More than a quarter of Abbott's profits have come from international operations, which are going strong.

Profits have grown, not explosively but consistently. During the 1970s, profits rose every year. The specialty-niche strategy has paid off in fat profit margins, almost always above 10 percent. It's not unusual for Abbott's profit margins to top the health care industry. Another plus: The company has kept the balance sheet free of excessive debt.

These positive factors are nothing to sneeze at; neither have they gone unnoticed. Abbott's stock price usually has built into it an expectation of continued progress. The stock has consistently sold for at least a dozen times current earnings, sometimes considerably more. If you fancy this stock, watch the p / e ratio to be sure you're not buying too dear. This is a stock you buy for capital gains, not income. Dividends have been paid each year since 1926, but are likely to be in the 2-to-3 percent range.

* * *

ACME-CLEVELAND CORP. (AMT). Founded 1916. Headquarters: PO Box 5617, Cleveland OH 44101. **MACHINERY.** Makes metal cutting tools, machine tools, metal casting equipment. **MAJOR SUBSIDIARIES, BRANDS:** Cleveland Twist Drill; Namco Controls; LaSalle Machine Tool; Nobur.

Sales: $400.7 million (trend 17.5% a year).
Earnings: $10.93 million (trend 36.8% a year).
What happened to a $10,000 investment

Purchase Date	Purchase Price	Price on 12-31-81	Dividends Paid
12-31-71	$14.25	$21.12	$6,294.74
12-31-76	$ 9.50	$21.12	$5,500.00

Purchase Date	Cap. Gains (— Losses)	Total Return	Rate of Return
12-31-71	$ 4,824.56	$11,119.30	7.76%
12-31-76	$12,236.84	$17,736.84	22.63%

* * *

ADAMS DRUG CO., INC. (ADG). Founded 1933. Headquarters: 75 Sabin St., Pawtucket RI 02860. **DRUGSTORES.** Adams operates close to 400 retail outlets, most of them drugstores, under several names. **MAJOR SUBSIDIARIES, BRANDS:** Adams; Brooks; Nescott; Optel; Sun; Whelan.

Sales: $207.1 million (trend 9.2% a year).
Earnings: $3.13 million (trend 6.9% a year).
What happened to a $10,000 investment

Purchase Date	Purchase Price	Price on 12-31-81	Dividends Paid
12-31-71	$N/A	$4.50	$ N/A
12-31-76	$ 3.25	$4.50	$615.38

Purchase Date	Cap. Gains (— Losses)	Total Return	Rate of Return
12-31-71	$ N/A	$ N/A	N/A%
12-31-76	$3,846.15	$4,461.54	7.66%

* * *

ADAMS EXPRESS CO. (ADX). Founded 1854. Headquarters: 201 N. Charles St., Baltimore MD 21201. **INVESTMENT CO.** Adams Express is a publicly traded, closed-end investment company.

* * *

ADAMS-MILLIS CORP. (ALL). Founded 1928. Headquarters: 225 N. Elm St., High Point NC 27261. **TEXTILES.** Makes hosiery and yarn. **MAJOR SUBSIDIARIES, BRANDS:** TexElastic Corp.

Sales: $77.4 million (trend 4.4% a year).
Earnings: $2.21 million (trend 29.7% a year).
What happened to a $10,000 investment

Purchase Date	*Purchase Price*	*Price on 12-31-81*	*Dividends Paid*
12-31-71	$10.87	$5.87	$1,425.29
12-31-76	$ 4.25	$5.87	$2,352.94

Purchase Date	*Cap. Gains (– Losses)*	*Total Return*	*Rate of Return*
12-31-71	$–4,597.70	$–3,172.41	–3.74%
12-31-76	$ 3,823.53	$ 6,176.47	10.10%

* * *

ADVANCED MICRO DEVICES, INC. (AMD). Founded 1969. Headquarters: 901 Thompson Pl., Sunnyvale CA 94086. ELECTRONICS. Company makes integrated circuits for use in computers and other electronic equipment.

Sales: $309.4 million (trend 54.9% a year).
Earnings: $24.68 million (trend 76.8% a year).
What happened to a $10,000 investment

Purchase Date	*Purchase Price*	*Price on 12-31-81*	*Dividends Paid*
12-31-71	$N/A	$17.62	$0.00
12-31-76	$ 5.61	$17.62	$0.00

Purchase Date	*Cap. Gains (– Losses)*	*Total Return*	*Rate of Return*
12-31-71	$ N/A	$ N/A	N/A%
12-31-76	$21,410.89	$21,410.89	25.72%

* * *

AETNA LIFE AND CASUALTY CO. (AET). Founded 1853. Headquarters: 151 Farmington Ave., Hartford CT 06156. INSURANCE. Aetna is the country's third-largest property and casualty insurance company, sixth-largest life insurance company, and largest stock company selling insurance as its primary business. 37,000 employees. MAJOR SUBSIDIARIES, BRANDS: Aetna Life Insurance Co.; Aetna Casualty & Surety Co.; Standard Fire Insurance Co.; Automobile Insurance Co. of Hartford; American Reinsurance Co.

Sales: $13,142.7 million (trend 16.9% a year).
Earnings: $508.30 million (trend 37.7% a year).
What happened to a $10,000 investment

Purchase Date	*Purchase Price*	*Price on 12-31-81*	*Dividends Paid*
12-31-71	$20.75	$44.25	$5,826.51
12-31-76	$23.75	$44.25	$3,665.96

Purchase Date	*Cap. Gains (– Losses)*	*Total Return*	*Rate of Return*
12-31-71	$11,325.30	$17,151.81	10.50%
12-31-76	$ 8,631.58	$12,297.54	17.40%

PROFILE: Lots of businesses are cyclical, but few are so cyclical as the property and casualty insurance business, in which Aetna is a major player and the largest you can buy stock in directly. (Allstate and State Farm are bigger, but Allstate is owned by Sears, and State Farm is a mutual company that doesn't sell stock.) The feast or famine cycle of the industry is reflected in a boom-or-bust mentality on the part of investors. So, the price of Aetna stock fluctuates fairly widely. If you buy it low and have the guts to hold on, you can make some money.

Aetna is also, at times, an income stock. In the early 1970s the dividend yield was less than 3 percent, but in the early 1980s it was above 7 percent. Come rain or hurricanes, the company has paid some dividends each year since 1934.

In the life insurance business, Aetna ranks about number six, but its larger competitors (like Prudential and Metropolitan) are mutual companies, so Aetna is the biggest life insurer you can buy stock in. Life insurance and group health insurance premiums, together with the property and casualty business, make Aetna the biggest multiple-line insurance company.

Size is, of course, no guarantor of profitability. Aetna recently has been showing a return on capital somewhat better than the average for the industry, but not dramatically so.

In 1982, Aetna announced plans to acquire Geosource Inc., a Houston-based oil-services firm (in which it already had a 29 percent stake) for some $638 million.

* * *

H. F. AHMANSON & CO. (AHM). Founded 1928. Headquarters: 3731 Wilshire Blvd., Los Angeles CA 90010. BANKING. Owns Home Savings & Loan Association, the largest savings and loan association in the country; also active in insurance. 4,000 employees. MAJOR SUBSIDIARIES, BRANDS: Home Savings & Loan Association; Bankers National Life Insurance Co.

Sales: $1,371.1 million (trend 19.7% a year).
Earnings: $48.08 million (trend 6.6% a year).
What happened to a $10,000 investment

Purchase Date	*Purchase Price*	*Price on 12-31-81*	*Dividends Paid*
12-31-71	$ N/A	$15.12	$ N/A
12-31-76	$16.37	$15.12	$3,114.50

Purchase Date	*Cap. Gains (— Losses)*	*Total Return*	*Rate of Return*
12-31-71	$ N/A	$ N/A	N/A%
12-31-76	$−763.36	$2,351.15	4.31%

PROFILE: You may never have heard of H. F. Ahmanson, but you may have heard of its biggest subsidiary, Home Savings & Loan Association, the largest savings and loan in the country. Home Savings is in California, so Ahmanson's fortunes depend to a substantial degree on the state of the real estate (particularly individual home) market on the West Coast. As with all bank stocks, its fortunes will also go up and down depending on the course of interest rates.

Ahmanson also owns a half dozen or so small insurance companies, and one medium-sized one, Bankers National Life, acquired recently. But its main business remains banking. Home Savings, with more than a hundred offices in California, accounted for more than 90 percent of revenues in 1980.

Ahmanson's operating results in recent years have been unspectacular. Like many thrift institutions, it's been squeezed between a rock (rising cost of attracting funds) and a hard place (a fixed return on the funds it's lent out, chiefly residential mortgages). In November 1980 Ahmanson announced that Home Savings would not write any more conventional long-term mortgages with fixed interest rates. It is demanding that regulators allow it to write variable mortgages that give it adequate protection against future interest-rate squeezes, and hence a chance to make a good profit. The company will probably prevail: It's long been considered a leader among thrift institutions. The question is, how soon? If you're considering buying these shares, be aware that they're more volatile than most. You must be prepared to buy on a down cycle and hold for a considerable time.

* * *

AILEEN, INC. (AEE). Founded 1948. Headquarters: 331 E. 38th St., New York NY 10016. **CLOTHING.** Makes women's and girls' clothing. **MAJOR SUBSIDIARIES, BRANDS:** Aileen; Aileen Girl; Aileen Teen; Aileen Sport; Red i; You and i.

Sales: $71.4 million (trend −1.6% a year).
Earnings: $2.92 million (trend −1.8% a year).
What happened to a $10,000 investment

Purchase Date	*Purchase Price*	*Price on 12-31-81*	*Dividends Paid*
12-31-71	$21.37	$2.62	$0.00
12-31-76	$ 3.87	$2.62	$0.00

Purchase Date	*Cap. Gains (— Losses)*	*Total Return*	*Rate of Return*
12-31-71	$−8,771.93	$−8,771.93	−18.92%
12-31-76	$−3,225.81	$−3,225.81	−7.49%

* * *

AIR PRODUCTS & CHEMICALS, INC. (APD). Founded 1940. Headquarters: PO Box 538, Allentown PA 18105. **INDUSTRIAL GASES, CHEMICALS.** Produces industrial and medical gases, gas handling equipment, and chemicals. 16,000 employees.

Sales: $1,570.1 million (trend 14.2% a year).
Earnings: $126.04 million (trend 16.3% a year).
What happened to a $10,000 investment

Purchase Date	*Purchase Price*	*Price on 12-31-81*	*Dividends Paid*
12-31-71	$11.82	$37.62	$2,897.79
12-31-76	$34.68	$37.62	$ 864.73

Purchase Date	*Cap. Gains (— Losses)*	*Total Return*	*Rate of Return*
12-31-71	$21,828.52	$24,726.31	13.26%
12-31-76	$ 848.76	$ 1,713.49	3.21%

PROFILE: Air Products has long been regarded on Wall Street as a company that stays within its defined specialty and knows what it's doing. What it does is to sell gases and chemicals, mainly to big users — oxygen by the ton to steel mills and chemical companies, for example, or hydrogen to the National Aeronautics and Space Administration (NASA) under a twelve-and-a-half-year contract.

Unlike some of its gases, the stock is not particularly volatile. It has been priced consistently over the years at a p / e multiple moderately above the average stock market multiple at the time. In 1972, for example, when the average stock sold for about 19 times earnings, Air Products sold for 21. In early 1980, when the average stock sold for about 8 times earnings, Air Products sold for 11.

Meanwhile, those earnings (in the case of Air Products, not the average stock) have been going up at the creditable rate of about 16 percent a year.

The recession of 1980–81 slowed down the growth, but the company continued to spend heavily on capital equipment right through the recession, to be poised to take advantage of any boom that developed. In particular, the company was ready for heavy involvement in synthetic fuels, chiefly the production of natural gas from coal.

In 1982, the company announced that it planned to acquire Stearns-Roger Corp., an engineering and construction firm based in Denver, for some $230 million.

Two cautions. As with most growth stocks, you can't expect much in the way of dividends from Air Products. Also, keep an eye on the debt load, which has bulged somewhat with the company's ambitious expansion plans.

* * *

AIRBORNE FREIGHT CORP. (ABF). Founded 1968. Headquarters: 190 Queen Anne Ave. N., Seattle WA 98111. AIR FREIGHT. Company is a major domestic and international air shipment firm. MAJOR SUBSIDIARIES, BRANDS: Midwest Charter Express.

Sales: $286.6 million (trend 21.2% a year).
Earnings: $7.90 million (trend 19.7% a year).
What happened to a $10,000 investment

Purchase Date	*Purchase Price*	*Price on 12-31-81*	*Dividends Paid*
12-31-71	$11.42	$9.75	$5,065.69
12-31-76	$14.50	$9.75	$3,172.41

Purchase Date	*Cap. Gains (− Losses)*	*Total Return*	*Rate of Return*
12-31-71	$−1,459.85	$ 3,605.84	3.13%
12-31-76	$−3,275.86	$−103.45	−.21%

* * *

AKZONA INC. (AXO). Founded 1928. Headquarters: PO Box 2930, Asheville NC 28802. CHEMICALS. Akzona is a producer of man-made fibers (particularly polyester yarns and rayon), industrial chemicals, electronic products, salt, drugs and medical equipment, and leather products. 16,000 employees. MAJOR SUBSIDIARIES, BRANDS: American Enka (fibers); Armak (industrial chemicals); Brand-Rex (electronics products, including wire and cable); International Salt (highway and grocery salts); Organon (drugs and medical diagnostic equipment); Armira Corp. (leather products).

Sales: $1,054.0 million (trend 9.7% a year).
Earnings: $4.88 million (trend 9.5% a year).
What happened to a $10,000 investment

Purchase Date	*Purchase Price*	*Price on 12-31-81*	*Dividends Paid*
12-31-71	$33.50	$10.37	$3,022.39
12-31-76	$16.87	$10.37	$2,548.15

Purchase Date	*Cap. Gains (− Losses)*	*Total Return*	*Rate of Return*
12-31-71	$−6,902.99	$−3,880.60	−4.79%
12-31-76	$−3,851.85	$−1,303.70	−2.76%

PROFILE: Is Akzona a diversified fibers company or a mini-conglomerate? That's a hard question to answer. It's easier to answer the question of whether or not Akzona has been a good investment for the past decade. No, it hasn't.

Back in the late 1960s and very early 1970s, Akzona used to earn profits of more than $2 a share routinely. Lately, that mark has been passed only in 1979 and 1974. Back then it wasn't unusual for the stock to fetch $40 a share. Lately the yearly highs have been closer to $15.

Profit margins haven't been above 2½ percent since 1974. (They used to be around 5 percent at the start of the '70s.) The return on stockholders' equity hasn't been above 10 percent since 1974, a miserable showing more remarkable in that the return on equity is hyped by a good deal of debt. (Debt was recently more than 40 percent of total capital.)

In the early 1980s, many people on Wall Street thought that the synthetic fibers industry, Akzona's single largest product line, was in for a profit revival after several very tough years. That may well be right. But Akzona may not be the stock with which you want to ride that recovery.

Dividends have been paid each year since 1934, and the yield in recent years has usually been 6 to 7 percent. But that record has been maintained only by paying out, in several years, more in dividends than the company actually earned in profits.

* * *

ALA MOANA HAWAII PROPERTIES (ALA). Founded 1981. Headquarters: 1441 Kapiolani Blvd., Honolulu HI 96814. REAL ESTATE. Holds several Hawaiian real estate properties formerly owned by Dillingham Corp. The stated purpose of the corporation was to sell off the properties and thus liquidate itself. MAJOR SUBSIDIARIES,

BRANDS: Ala Moana Shopping Center and Office Building; Kaahumanu Shopping Center.

* * *

ALAGASCO, INC. (AGA). Founded 1929. Headquarters: 1918 First Ave. N., Birmingham AL 35295. **NATURAL GAS.** Distributes natural gas to about a third of a million people in central Alabama.

Sales: $311.5 million (trend 24.0% a year).
Earnings: $5.74 million (trend 4.9% a year).
What happened to a $10,000 investment

Purchase Date	*Purchase Price*	*Price on 12-31-81*	*Dividends Paid*
12-31-71	$17.12	$15.37	$7,664.23
12-31-76	$16.25	$15.37	$4,455.38

Purchase Date	*Cap. Gains (− Losses)*	*Total Return*	*Rate of Return*
12-31-71	$−1,021.90	$6,642.34	5.23%
12-31-76	$ −538.46	$3,916.92	6.83%

* * *

ALASKA INTERSTATE CO. (AKI). Founded 1966. Headquarters: 2200 Post Oak Tower, 5051 Westheimer Rd., Houston TX 77056. **ENERGY.** Explores for and produces oil, natural gas, and coal in United States and abroad (chiefly Indonesia); distributes natural gas in Alaska. **MAJOR SUBSIDIARIES, BRANDS:** Alaska Pipeline Co.; Alaska Gas and Service Co.; Delta Engineering; McAlester Fuel.

Sales: $261.7 million (trend 11.5% a year).
Earnings: $77.19 million (trend 46.5% a year).
What happened to a $10,000 investment

Purchase Date	*Purchase Price*	*Price on 12-31-81*	*Dividends Paid*
12-31-71	$10.69	$18.25	$2,229.24
12-31-76	$ 7.56	$18.25	$2,753.72

Purchase Date	*Cap. Gains (− Losses)*	*Total Return*	*Rate of Return*
12-31-71	$ 7,076.02	$ 9,305.26	6.80%
12-31-76	$14,132.23	$16,885.95	21.87%

* * *

ALBANY INTERNATIONAL CORP. (ABY). Founded 1895. Headquarters: PO Box 1907, Albany NY 12201. **PAPER PRODUCTS MACHINERY.** Manufactures equipment for paper products producers, makes a variety of fabrics and plastics, and produces pheromones for insect control. **MAJOR SUBSIDIARIES, BRANDS:** Conrel.

Sales: $365.5 million (trend 12.9% a year).
Earnings: $25.91 million (trend 30.4% a year).
What happened to a $10,000 investment

Purchase Date	*Purchase Price*	*Price on 12-31-81*	*Dividends Paid*
12-31-71	$ N/A	$27.50	$ N/A
12-31-76	$14.70	$27.50	$3,078.91

Purchase Date	*Cap. Gains (− Losses)*	*Total Return*	*Rate of Return*
12-31-71	$ N/A	$ N/A	N/A%
12-31-76	$8,707.48	$11,786.39	16.85%

* * *

ALBERTO-CULVER CO. (ACV). Founded 1961. Headquarters: 2525 Armitage Ave., Melrose Park IL 60160. **COSMETICS.** Manufactures hair care products, health and beauty aids. **MAJOR SUBSIDIARIES, BRANDS:** Alberto VO5; Alberto Balsam; FDS; Static Guard; Sugartwin; Frye footwear; Masury-Columbia Co.

Sales: $294.4 million (trend 15.2% a year).
Earnings: $6.02 million (trend 34.9% a year).
What happened to a $10,000 investment

Purchase Date	*Purchase Price*	*Price on 12-31-81*	*Dividends Paid*
12-31-71	$22.25	$12.62	$1,604.49
12-31-76	$ 7.50	$12.62	$2,453.33

Purchase Date	*Cap. Gains (− Losses)*	*Total Return*	*Rate of Return*
12-31-71	$−4,325.84	$−2,721.35	−3.13%
12-31-76	$ 6,833.33	$ 9,286.67	14.04%

* * *

ALBERTSON'S, INC. (ABS). Founded 1945. Headquarters: 250 Parkcenter Blvd., Boise ID 83726. **RETAILER.** Operates some 400 supermarkets and combination (food and drug) stores in 15 states in the West and South. 25,000 employees. **MAJOR SUBSIDIARIES, BRANDS:** Southco; Fazio's.

Sales: $3,039.1 million (trend 19.8% a year).
Earnings: $41.62 million (trend 23.8% a year).
What happened to a $10,000 investment

Purchase Date	Purchase Price	Price on 12-31-81	Dividends Paid
12-31-71	$ 5.40	$26.50	$6,671.74
12-31-76	$11.56	$26.50	$1,971.89

Purchase Date	Cap. Gains (— Losses)	Total Return	Rate of Return
12-31-71	$39,094.71	$45,766.46	18.75%
12-31-76	$12,918.92	$14,890.81	20.01%

PROFILE: Big, modern stores; an aggressive and nearly continuous program of modernization and expansion; movement toward "one-stop" shopping; combining food with drugs or other purchases — those have been some of the hallmarks of Albertson's approach in recent years. Another characteristic is regional autonomy: Decisions about what to buy and what to advertise are made by each store, under the supervision of some ten regional vice-presidents. Financial management is centered at the Idaho headquarters.

Albertson's ranks roughly eighteenth by sales among U.S. retailers, and about ninth among supermarkets. Sales and earnings have been growing fast, and the company has been consistently more profitable than average for the supermarket industry. But it looks somewhat better if you look at return on equity than if you look at return on total capital. That's because the chain carries a lot of debt — recently more than half of total capital. A hefty measure of debt is par for the course for a supermarket chain. However, in my opinion, a capital structure consisting of more than half debt is getting a bit lopsided. Some top competitors like Food Town and Bruno's have been able to expand profits rapidly without as much reliance on debt.

A fair chunk of the company is closely held. Recently, founder Joseph Albertson had about 24 percent of the stock, and West German supermarket magnate Theo Albrecht had about 10 percent.

* * *

ALCAN ALUMINUM LIMITED (AL). Founded 1928. Headquarters: 1 Place Ville Marie, Montreal Canada H3C 3H2. **ALUMINUM.** World's second largest aluminum producer, as of 1980.

Sales: $5,215.0 million (trend 18.0% a year).
Earnings: $541.94 million (trend 92.7% a year).
What happened to a $10,000 investment

Purchase Date	Purchase Price	Price on 12-31-81	Dividends Paid
12-31-71	$ 9.12	$23.25	$8,356.16
12-31-76	$11.81	$23.25	$4,677.25

Purchase Date	Cap. Gains (— Losses)	Total Return	Rate of Return
12-31-71	$15,479.45	$23,835.62	12.96%
12-31-76	$ 9,682.54	$14,359.79	19.49%

* * *

ALCO STANDARD CORP. (ASN). Founded 1952. Headquarters: Valley Forge PA 19482. **CONGLOMERATE.** Derives most of its revenues from warehousing and distribution of a wide variety of products; also involved in manufacturing (chemicals, rubber, and plastics, primarily) and in coal mining. **MAJOR SUBSIDIARIES, BRANDS:** Barnes & Tucker; Metalsource; Edward Phillips; Riekes Group; Unisource; Upshur Coals.

Sales: $2,521.7 million (trend 20.0% a year).
Earnings: $57.66 million (trend 10.2% a year).
What happened to a $10,000 investment

Purchase Date	Purchase Price	Price on 12-31-81	Dividends Paid
12-31-71	$8.37	$19.37	$5,656.72
12-31-76	$9.31	$19.37	$3,865.77

Purchase Date	Cap. Gains (— Losses)	Total Return	Rate of Return
12-31-71	$13,134.33	$18,791.04	11.15%
12-31-76	$10,805.37	$14,671.14	19.79%

* * *

ALEXANDER & ALEXANDER SERVICES INC. (AALS, Over-the-Counter). Founded 1922. Headquarters: 1211 Ave. of the Americas, New York NY 10036. **INSURANCE BROKER.** Alexander & Alexander is the second-largest U.S. insurance brokerage firm (after Marsh & McLennan). Also does actuarial and employee-benefit consulting. 7,000 employees.

Sales: $403.1 million (trend 28.1% a year).
Earnings: $56.40 million (trend 39.1% a year).
What happened to a $10,000 investment

Purchase Date	Purchase Price	Price on 12-31-81	Dividends Paid
12-31-71	$22.12	$25.50	$3,794.35
12-31-76	$19.06	$25.50	$3,504.26

Purchase Date	*Cap. Gains (– Losses)*	*Total Return*	*Rate of Return*
12-31-71	$1,525.42	$5,319.77	4.36%
12-31-76	$3,377.05	$6,881.31	11.04%

PROFILE: In size, Alexander & Alexander runs second to Marsh & McLennan, the behemoth of the U.S. insurance brokerage industry. But among the big U.S. brokers, Alexander & Alexander is consistently at the top of the heap in growth and profitability.

The red-hot growth rate (see figures above) is in large part a result of Alexander & Alexander's penchant for mergers. It seems that every time you turn around, the firm has just gobbled up another small or medium-sized brokerage house.

The profitability, up to now, has come with the territory. What brokers like A & A sell is primarily property and casualty insurance for businesses (about three quarters of revenues). Though commissions are negotiable in this realm, what amounts to a hefty commission for the broker is barely a drop in the bucket to many of the corporations purchasing the coverage.

However, rougher sledding may be ahead. The convergence of various types of financial corporations will probably mean increased competition in the coming years — maybe from stock brokerage houses, maybe from banks, perhaps even from the likes of Sears. And the insurance business, always international in scope, has become even more so. Marsh & McLennan has a leg up there: Its merger with C. T. Bowring (the largest British insurance broker) came through. A & A's proposed merger with the Sedgwick group (the second-largest British insurance broker) didn't.

Because of the company's fine track record, the stock more than doubled during the 1970s. The balance sheet here is very strong, with not a wisp of debt on it recently. Return on equity has been outstanding, often above 30 percent. Dividends have been paid yearly since the company was founded; the yield recently has been around 5-to-6 percent.

* * *

ALEXANDER'S, INC. (ALX). Founded 1955. Headquarters: 500 Seventh Ave., New York NY 10018. **RETAILER.** Runs a chain of some sixteen department stores in the Northeast and a string of women's specialty shops in the South. **MAJOR SUBSIDIARIES, BRANDS:** Alexander's; Margo's La Mode.

Sales: $523.6 million (trend 6.8% a year).
Earnings: $–9.57 million.
What happened to a $10,000 investment

Purchase Date	*Purchase Price*	*Price on 12-31-81*	*Dividends Paid*
12-31-71	$22.50	$10.12	$1,182.22
12-31-76	$ 7.12	$10.12	$2,385.96

Purchase Date	*Cap. Gains (– Losses)*	*Total Return*	*Rate of Return*
12-31-71	$–5,500.00	$–4,317.78	–5.50%
12-31-76	$ 4,210.53	$ 6,596.49	10.66%

* * *

ALLEGHANY CORP. (Y). Founded 1929. Headquarters: 350 Park Ave., New York NY 10022. **FINANCIAL SERVICES.** Alleghany Corp. is active in insurance, mortgage banking, mutual funds, and portfolio management for pension and endowment funds; also engages in trucking. **MAJOR SUBSIDIARIES, BRANDS:** Investors Diversified Services, Inc. (IDS); Jones Motor Co.

Sales: $1,165.6 million (trend 47.6% a year).
Earnings: $45.38 million (trend 45.9% a year).
What happened to a $10,000 investment

Purchase Date	*Purchase Price*	*Price on 12-31-81*	*Dividends Paid*
12-31-71	$ N/A	$48.50	$ N/A
12-31-76	$12.87	$48.50	$4,124.27

Purchase Date	*Cap. Gains (– Losses)*	*Total Return*	*Rate of Return*
12-31-71	$ N/A	$ N/A	N/A%
12-31-76	$27,669.90	$31,794.17	33.11%

* * *

ALLEGHENY INTERNATIONAL, INC. (AG). Founded 1929. Headquarters: 2 Oliver Plaza, Pittsburgh PA 15222. **SPECIALTY STEEL.** Makes specialty steel and alloys, industrial products, industrial gases. 19,000 employees. **MAJOR SUBSIDIARIES, BRANDS:** Titanium Metals Corp. of America (50% owned); Standard-Thomson Corp.; Chemetron Corp.; Liquid Air Corp. (33% owned); Wilkinson Match Co. (Wilkinson razor blades, Scripto pens, True Temper lawn and garden equipment); Sunbeam.

Sales: $923.5 million (trend 8.0% a year).
Earnings: $50.63 million (trend 17.9% a year).
What happened to a $10,000 investment

Purchase Date	Purchase Price	Price on 12-31-81	Dividends Paid
12-31-71	$12.50	$33.37	$9,218.67
12-31-76	$24.25	$33.37	$2,750.52

Purchase Date	Cap. Gains (− Losses)	Total Return	Rate of Return
12-31-71	$16,700.00	$25,918.67	13.64%
12-31-76	$ 3,762.89	$ 6,513.40	10.55%

PROFILE: In 1980, Allegheny Ludlum — since renamed Allegheny International — unloaded the operation it was best known for — the making of stainless steel — on Texas entrepreneur Clint Murchison, owner of the Dallas Cowboys. Chairman Robert J. Buckley was clearly delighted to be out of the stainless steel business, which had pushed and pulled the company through violent earnings swings over the years. Asked by a *Forbes* reporter if he'd sold off the junk and kept the cream of the specialty steel and alloys business, Buckley said, "You've done a very good job of homework." Then he quickly added, "But it isn't junk. . . . You're bringing tears to my eyes."

In fact, the steel corporation might work out okay as a private business for Murchison. But Wall Street was delighted that Allegheny had unloaded it; Allegheny stock rose 15 percent after the sale.

With stainless gone, what's left? A lot. Allegheny Ludlum will still be making specialty alloys, such as high temperature "superalloys" for jet aircraft engines. That business can be consistently profitable. It will continue making a lot of tubing for oil and gas pipelines. Through its 50-percent-owned subsidiary, Titanium Metals Corp. of America, it will be involved in making a variety of parts for jets and missiles.

To this collection, Allegheny in 1981 added Sunbeam, a major manufacturer of small appliances with an indifferent record in recent years. The cost was some $550 million in cash and stock. As he did with the stainless steel business, Buckley will probably sell the less profitable parts of Sunbeam, and keep the more profitable parts.

* * *

ALLEGHENY POWER SYSTEM, INC. (AYP). Founded 1925. Headquarters: 320 Park Ave., New York NY 10022. UTILITY. Provides electric power to portions of Pennsylvania, Maryland, and West Virginia.

Sales: $1,159.5 million (trend 12.2% a year).
Earnings: $103.75 million (trend 6.0% a year).
What happened to a $10,000 investment

Purchase Date	Purchase Price	Price on 12-31-81	Dividends Paid
12-31-71	$22.25	$16.12	$7,415.73
12-31-76	$22.25	$16.12	$4,035.96

Purchase Date	Cap. Gains (− Losses)	Total Return	Rate of Return
12-31-71	$−2,752.81	$4,662.92	3.90%
12-31-76	$−2,752.81	$1,283.15	2.44%

* * *

ALLEN GROUP INC. (ALN). Founded 1928. Headquarters: 534 Broad Hollow Rd., Melville NY 11747. AUTO EQUIPMENT. Makes diagnostic equipment for car engines, emissions systems, and other systems and manufactures a variety of accessories for cars and trucks, including citizens band radio antennas.

Sales: $348.5 million (trend 9.0% a year).
Earnings: $8.83 million (trend 17.1% a year).
What happened to a $10,000 investment

Purchase Date	Purchase Price	Price on 12-31-81	Dividends Paid
12-31-71	$12.18	$15.12	$4,514.14
12-31-76	$10.80	$15.12	$3,979.63

Purchase Date	Cap. Gains (− Losses)	Total Return	Rate of Return
12-31-71	$2,418.41	$6,932.55	5.41%
12-31-76	$4,004.63	$7,984.26	12.45%

* * *

ALLIED CORP. (ALD). Founded 1920. Headquarters: Park Ave. at Columbia Road, Morristown NJ 07960. CHEMICALS. Manufactures chemicals, produces oil and gas, processes uranium, makes fibers and electrical equipment. 49,000 employees. MAJOR SUBSIDIARIES, BRANDS: Union Texas Petroleum; Bio Logicals; Eltra Corp.; C & D Batteries; Prestolite; Bunker Ramo Corp.; Fisher Scientific Co.; Gyrex Corp. In early 1982, the company was in the process of acquiring a 50 percent interest in Supron Energy Corp.

Sales: $5,519.0 million (trend 18.4% a year).
Earnings: $266.00 million (trend 15.0% a year).
What happened to a $10,000 investment

Purchase Date	*Purchase Price*	*Price on 12-31-81*	*Dividends Paid*
12-31-71	$29.12	$43.87	$6,169.96
12-31-76	$40.25	$43.87	$2,571.43

Purchase Date	*Cap. Gains (− Losses)*	*Total Return*	*Rate of Return*
12-31-71	$5,064.38	$11,234.33	7.82%
12-31-76	$ 900.62	$ 3,472.05	6.14%

PROFILE: If you think of Allied simply as a chemical company, you're way behind the times. In recent years, chemicals have accounted for less than a third of its sales and less than a sixth of its earnings. More than a third of sales and the bulk of profits have come from energy operations, including oil and gas drilling (notably in the North Sea, but also elsewhere) and uranium processing. Accordingly, the company recently changed its name from Allied Chemical Corp. to Allied Corp.

Allied acquired Eltra Corp., a New York-based manufacturer of electrical products, in 1979. Electrical products now account for roughly 10 percent of sales. Fibers (chiefly nylon and polyester) account for close to a quarter of sales. The recent acquisitions of Bunker Ramo and Fisher Scientific add to diversity and growth prospects.

With all this diversification, you might think that Allied would be one of the least volatile of stocks. But that's not true. In fact, it acts to a large degree like an energy stock, going up or down depending on what the outlook is for the Arabs putting the squeeze on us again, or what the latest rumors are about oil strikes in the North Sea.

Though incorporated in 1920, Allied has been in operation since the late nineteenth century and has paid dividends every year since 1887. You can expect the dividend to be a shade below what you'd get in a passbook savings account.

The company is moderately leveraged, with about a third of its total capital in the form of long-term debt. It's kept that ratio fairly constant for the past decade.

* * *

ALLIED MAINTENANCE CORP. (ALM). Founded 1944. Headquarters: 2 Pennsylvania Plaza, New York NY 10121. **MAINTENANCE.** Maintains industrial plants, sports facilities, airports, aircraft, and office buildings; also has engineering and design operations.

Sales: $177.4 million (trend 11.9% a year).
Earnings: $7.22 million (trend 6.6% a year).
What happened to a $10,000 investment

Purchase Date	*Purchase Price*	*Price on 12-31-81*	*Dividends Paid*
12-31-71	$39.18	$23.25	$1,501.68
12-31-76	$12.37	$23.25	$2,610.10

Purchase Date	*Cap. Gains (− Losses)*	*Total Return*	*Rate of Return*
12-31-71	$−4,066.26	$−2,564.57	−2.92%
12-31-76	$ 8,787.88	$ 11,397.98	16.43%

* * *

ALLIED PRODUCTS CORP. (ADP). Founded 1968. Headquarters: 10 S. Riverside Plaza, Chicago IL 60606. **INDUSTRIAL, AGRICULTURAL EQUIPMENT.** Produces fasteners and a variety of metal parts for industrial operations and the auto industry; manufactures agricultural equipment, textiles. **MAJOR SUBSIDIARIES, BRANDS:** Bush Hog (agricultural equipment); FabricsAmerica (textiles).

Sales: $289.4 million (trend 5.4% a year).
Earnings: $−2.23 million.
What happened to a $10,000 investment

Purchase Date	*Purchase Price*	*Price on 12-31-81*	*Dividends Paid*
12-31-71	$13.25	$9.25	$3,101.86
12-31-76	$ 7.17	$9.25	$2,348.79

Purchase Date	*Cap. Gains (− Losses)*	*Total Return*	*Rate of Return*
12-31-71	$−3,018.87	$ 82.99	.08%
12-31-76	$ 2,906.98	$5,255.77	8.81%

* * *

ALLIED STORES CORP. (ALS). Founded 1928. Headquarters: 1114 Ave. of the Americas, New York NY 10036. **RETAILER.** Owns and operates more than 200 stores in some 28 states through more than 20 divisions, which operate semi-independently of the parent company. 54,000 employees. **MAJOR SUBSIDIARIES, BRANDS:** Jordan Marsh; Bon Marche; Maas Brothers; Stern's; Bonwit Teller; Plymouth Shops; Gertz; Joske's; Block's; Donaldson's; Pomeroy's; Garfinckel's; Brooks Brothers; Miller & Rhoads, Inc.

Sales: $2,267.7 million (trend 5.9% a year).
Earnings: $83.79 million (trend 9.9% a year).
What happened to a $10,000 investment

Purchase Date	*Purchase Price*	*Price on 12-31-81*	*Dividends Paid*
12-31-71	$16.75	$26.12	$5,619.40
12-31-76	$23.12	$26.12	$2,421.62

Purchase Date	*Cap. Gains (− Losses)*	*Total Return*	*Rate of Return*
12-31-71	$5,597.01	$11,216.42	7.81%
12-31-76	$1,297.30	$ 3,718.92	6.53%

PROFILE: Sharp financial management has been the characteristic of Allied under the scrutiny of Thomas M. Macioce, president since 1971. Macioce inherited a barely profitable hodgepodge of stores from his predecessors and has improved profitability by doing three things: (1) emphasizing high-profit items; (2) expanding successful stores and getting rid of unsuccessful ones; (3) keeping a tight rein on inventory.

If this sounds like a financial man's approach to running a chain of department stores, it is. In fact, some buyers at the component stores dislike the fact that they don't have freedom to buy what they want. Allied is run pretty much by the numbers.

But those numbers, not too impressive in the 1960s, looked increasingly sharp in the 1970s. While Allied's sales have advanced at a snail's pace (due to the pruning of stores), its profits have been going up about 10 percent a year — one of the better earnings growth records in the department store business. The profit margin has been about 3½ percent recently — which may not sound impressive, but is good for a retailer (the average department store has about a 2½ percent margin). The recent acquisition of Brooks Brothers shouldn't hurt profit margins a bit.

Macioce told *Forbes* magazine, "The gal in Harrisburg, Pa., reads *Vogue* just like the gal in New York. The rich farmers in Boise wear cashmere sweaters just as men wear them in New York."

* * *

ALLIED TELEPHONE CO. (AT). Founded 1954. Headquarters: Allied Telephone Building, Little Rock AR 72203. **COMMUNICATIONS.** Provides telephone service to portions of Arkansas, Missouri, Tennessee, Kentucky, Texas, and Oklahoma. Also makes telephone equipment for use in its own system and for sale to others. **MAJOR SUBSIDIARIES, BRANDS:** Southern Telephone Supply Co.

Sales: $116.3 million (trend 23.0% a year).
Earnings: $7.25 million (trend 21.4% a year).
What happened to a $10,000 investment

Purchase Date	*Purchase Price*	*Price on 12-31-81*	*Dividends Paid*
12-31-71	$ 9.52	$18.12	$5,063.51
12-31-76	$10.01	$18.12	$3,495.63

Purchase Date	*Cap. Gains (− Losses)*	*Total Return*	*Rate of Return*
12-31-71	$9,033.22	$14,096.73	9.19%
12-31-76	$8,114.04	$11,609.67	16.66%

* * *

ALLIS-CHALMERS CORP. (AH). Founded 1913. Headquarters: 1205 S. 70th St., Milwaukee WI 53201. **MACHINERY.** Makes agricultural machinery and industrial process equipment. 29,000 employees. **MAJOR SUBSIDIARIES, BRANDS:** American Air Filter; Siemens-Allis (50 percent); Fiat-Allis (19.8 percent).

Sales: $2,063.9 million (trend 8.0% a year).
Earnings: $45.63 million (trend 9.6% a year).
What happened to a $10,000 investment

Purchase Date	*Purchase Price*	*Price on 12-31-81*	*Dividends Paid*
12-31-71	$13.25	$15.87	$7,046.04
12-31-76	$26.25	$15.87	$2,923.81

Purchase Date	*Cap. Gains (− Losses)*	*Total Return*	*Rate of Return*
12-31-71	$ 1,981.13	$ 9,027.17	6.64%
12-31-76	$−3,952.38	$−1,028.57	−2.15%

PROFILE: David C. Scott, who has performed near-miracles with the big Milwaukee machinery manufacturer since he took over as chairman and president in 1968, was due to retire at the end of 1982. One big question Wall Street will be asking is how well his successors are performing compared to Scott, who dragged the company up from a poor financial situation and preserved its independence in the face of a welter of takeover bids.

If Allis-Chalmers was a sick bird when Scott took over, it was hardly a high-flying eagle at the start of the 1980s. Sales were creeping up only slowly. Profit margins were no better than average for a machinery company or a multi-industry company, and sometimes worse. Return on equity wasn't spectacular either.

But if you looked at the long haul, you could see

some major changes in the company's position. Quality control had been improved. Debt, which had been more than 50 percent of total capital as recently as 1973, had been pared down to 30 percent by 1980. Dividends, which had been meager for years (and which disappeared altogether in 1969, the year Scott slashed unprofitable operations right and left), had been gradually growing and had finally, as of 1979, reached the point where the stock offered a better dividend yield than a passbook savings account.

If the 1980s prove to be a time of "reindustrialization," Allis-Chalmers, with its processing equipment for sale to a wide range of industries, could be in very good shape. A rebound in sales of farm equipment could help, too. The kicker, which might possibly make Allis-Chalmers a hot stock, is its venture into plants that make clean natural gas out of high-sulfur coal.

* * *

ALLRIGHT AUTO PARKS, INC. (ALR). Founded 1962. Headquarters: 1625 Neils Esperson Bldg., Houston TX 77002. PARKING. Owns and operates more than 1,500 parking lots and parking garages in the United States and Canada.

Sales: $80.9 million (trend 12.6% a year).
Earnings: $5.55 million (trend 8.4% a year).
What happened to a $10,000 investment

Purchase Date	*Purchase Price*	*Price on 12-31-81*	*Dividends Paid*
12-31-71	$9.39	$22.17	$3,070.16
12-31-76	$4.04	$22.17	$4,253.36

Purchase Date	*Cap. Gains (– Losses)*	*Total Return*	*Rate of Return*
12-31-71	$13,602.40	$16,672.55	10.31%
12-31-76	$44,852.03	$49,105.39	42.67%

* * *

ALPHA PORTLAND INDUSTRIES, INC. (APC). Founded 1910. Headquarters: Alpha Building, Easton PA 18042. CEMENT. Company is a major producer of construction aggregates and portland cement. A significant share of Alpha Portland (33 percent as of early 1981) is owned by Power Test Corp.

Sales: $257.7 million (trend 6.5% a year).
Earnings: $–11.45 million.
What happened to a $10,000 investment

Purchase Date	*Purchase Price*	*Price on 12-31-81*	*Dividends Paid*
12-31-71	$17.25	$12.25	$3,136.23
12-31-76	$15.37	$12.25	$2,198.37

Purchase Date	*Cap. Gains (– Losses)*	*Total Return*	*Rate of Return*
12-31-71	$–2,898.55	$237.68	.24%
12-31-76	$–2,032.52	$165.85	.33%

* * *

ALUMINUM CO. OF AMERICA (AA). Founded 1925. Headquarters: 1501 Alcoa Bldg., Pittsburgh PA 15219. ALUMINUM. Alcoa is the world's largest miner and fabricator of aluminum, with about a quarter of the U.S. market and about a sixth of the world market. 47,000 employees. MAJOR SUBSIDIARIES, BRANDS: Alcoa; Wear-Ever; Cutco.

Sales: $5,147.6 million (trend 17.6% a year).
Earnings: $467.40 million (trend 50.7% a year).
What happened to a $10,000 investment

Purchase Date	*Purchase Price*	*Price on 12-31-81*	*Dividends Paid*
12-31-71	$14.54	$25.62	$6,711.75
12-31-76	$28.62	$25.62	$2,270.74

Purchase Date	*Cap. Gains (– Losses)*	*Total Return*	*Rate of Return*
12-31-71	$ 7,621.78	$14,333.52	9.30%
12-31-76	$–1,048.03	$ 1,222.71	2.33%

PROFILE: Ever hear of the Pittsburgh Reduction Co.? That's what Alcoa was called back in the late 1800s, before it was rescued from oblivion by a loan from the Mellon family, which still owns a minority interest. The history of the company between that loan and the end of World War II is a largely happy one, as Alcoa controlled about nine tenths of the aluminum supply in the United States. Under pressure from Canadian nationalism and U.S. antitrust authorities, Alcoa lost its super-dominant position in 1946. Now it runs the risk of playing second fiddle to Alcan, its Canadian spin-off.

To understand why, you must realize that in aluminum production, the name of the game is electricity: Any major aluminum plant will use as much electricity as thousands of homes, and industry people speak in terms of the cost of electricity per pound of aluminum produced. Canada's abundant hydroelectric power plants give Alcan cheap energy and a big edge. So before you buy stock in Alcoa or any other U.S. producer, you should compare the company's performance (and its stock's price / earnings multiple) with Alcan's recent stats.

Among U.S. producers, Alcoa has been in recent years not only the biggest, but also the most profitable and the fastest growing. In both growth and profitability, though, Alcan has taken the lead, and it may overtake Alcoa in size as well. No fools, Alcoa's management has responded by building new aluminum production facilities in places like Brazil, where power is cheap.

Dividends, paid yearly since 1939, are traditionally modest.

* * *

AMALGAMATED SUGAR CO. (AGM). Founded 1915. Headquarters: First Security Bank Bldg., Ogden UT 84401. **SUGAR.** Refines and markets beet sugar; also engages in wet corn milling.

Sales: $349.6 million (trend 13.8% a year).
Earnings: $17.77 million (trend −11.4% a year).
What happened to a $10,000 investment

Purchase Date	*Purchase Price*	*Price on 12-31-81*	*Dividends Paid*
12-31-71	$26.87	$48.50	$9,544.19
12-31-76	$35.25	$48.50	$3,446.81

Purchase Date	*Cap. Gains (− Losses)*	*Total Return*	*Rate of Return*
12-31-71	$8,046.51	$17,590.70	10.68%
12-31-76	$3,758.87	$ 7,205.67	11.46%

* * *

AMAX INC. (AMX). Founded 1887. Headquarters: AMAX Center, Greenwich CT 06840. **MINING.** AMAX is the world's leading producer of molybdenum and also produces coal, potash, aluminum, silver, zinc, copper, lead, nickel, tungsten, cobalt, magnesium, oil, and natural gas. 17,000 employees. **MAJOR SUBSIDIARIES, BRANDS:** Alumax (50 percent); Anamas (50 percent); Rosario Resources; Adobe Oil & Gas (30 percent); Hecla Mining (21 percent). AMAX is 17 percent owned by Standard Oil Co. of California.

Sales: $2,949.2 million (trend 27.7% a year).
Earnings: $447.68 million (trend 33.1% a year).
What happened to a $10,000 investment

Purchase Date	*Purchase Price*	*Price on 12-31-81*	*Dividends Paid*
12-31-71	$18.83	$47.25	$7,575.24
12-31-76	$39.83	$47.25	$2,240.59

Purchase Date	*Cap. Gains (− Losses)*	*Total Return*	*Rate of Return*
12-31-71	$15,088.50	$22,663.73	12.57%
12-31-76	$ 1,861.92	$ 4,102.52	7.12%

PROFILE: AMAX mines practically everything under the sun (well, under the ground), but its specialty is molybdenum, of which it mines about half the world's supply. Molybdenum, a gray metal used to add strength to steel alloys, provided more than a third of AMAX's sales and close to two thirds of its profits in one recent year. So, if you contemplate buying AMAX stock, you'd do well to study up on the next few years' outlook for molybdenum.

Most of AMAX's molybdenum mining is done in Colorado, in two huge mines, one (the Climax Mine) near Leadville, the other (the Henderson Mine) near Empire. The Henderson Mine is remarkable because of the care, length of time, and expense that AMAX put into environmental safeguards and consultation with environmental groups. The company claims it will continue to work closely with environmental groups in the future.

That's praiseworthy, but what else is there to recommend AMAX stock? Diversity, for one thing. AMAX mines so many materials (see summary above) that it's unlikely it will have a bad year in all areas at once. Dividends have been paid each year since 1937.

In recent years, though, AMAX has turned in only about an average performance for a mining company. Profit margins are good and earnings have grown all right, but the debt load is a shade heavy for a mining enterprise. And mining companies as a group have been growing more slowly than the average U.S. company, at least from about 1975 to 1980.

Merger speculation may surface periodically. In 1981, Standard Oil of California made, and later withdrew, a $4 billion merger proposal.

* * *

AMDAHL CORP. (AMH, American Stock Exchange**).** Founded 1970. Headquarters: 1250 E. Arques Ave., Sunnyvale CA 94086. **COMPUTERS.** Makes large computers compatible with IBM equipment. 4,000 employees.

Sales: $394.4 million (trend 39.9% a year).
Earnings: $15.22 million (trend .9% a year).
What happened to a $10,000 investment

Purchase Date	*Purchase Price*	*Price on 12-31-81*	*Dividends Paid*
12-31-71	$ N/A	$29.50	$ N/A
12-31-76	$19.37	$29.50	$812.90

Purchase Date	*Cap. Gains (— Losses)*	*Total Return*	*Rate of Return*
12-31-71	$ N/A	$ N/A	N/A%
12-31-76	$5,225.81	$6,038.71	9.91%

PROFILE: Whether you should own Amdahl stock depends in large part on what you think about a man who no longer works for Amdahl and about a company half a world away.

The man is Gene Amdahl, who founded the company in 1970 and who shaped its basic approach: try to offer equipment with computing power exceeding that of IBM's machines, but able to communicate with IBM's external storage devices. In 1979, Dr. Amdahl left Amdahl. If you buy this stock, you're betting that Amdahl can thrive without its founder.

The company half a world away is Fujitsu, which has always been a major supplier to Amdahl, a major investor in Amdahl, and, some would say, the force that truly controls Amdahl. Fujitsu sees itself as being in a global battle for computer supremacy with IBM. In the United States, it has chosen to compete through Amdahl for the large-computer market. (In minicomputers, Fujitsu has teamed up with TRW.) Amdahl has about 20 percent of the U.S. large computer market, and Fujitsu has 25 percent of Amdahl (with warrants that allow it to boost its control to 32 percent of the stock). Access to Fujitsu's technology is one of the big factors in Amdahl's success. If you think the Japanese are going to surpass the U.S. in computer and semiconductor technology, the most convenient way to express your belief in the stock market is by buying Amdahl.

But the Japanese connection is by no means an unmixed blessing. Amdahl twice made strong moves toward mergers (first with Memorex, then with Storage Technology) that Wall Street thought would be beneficial to it. The negotiations faltered, apparently because Fujitsu insisted on terms that the potential partners balked at.

In its short life (since 1976) as a publicly traded stock, Amdahl has been very volatile (matching its earnings history). Be aware of this as a potential buyer; and keep in mind too that the stock usually sells at a high multiple of earnings and pays low dividends.

* * *

AMERACE CORP. (AAE). Founded 1946. Headquarters: 555 Fifth Ave., New York NY 10017. **INDUSTRIAL, TRANSPORTATION COMPONENTS.** Amerace is a diversified manufacturer of components for industrial processes, aerospace, automotive, and consumer products. Hoses, fasteners, timers, switches, wiring devices, and other components are among its basic products.

Sales: $326.4 million (trend 10.5% a year).
Earnings: $8.59 million (trend 8.9% a year).
What happened to a $10,000 investment

Purchase Date	*Purchase Price*	*Price on 12-31-81*	*Dividends Paid*
12-31-71	$21.25	$17.25	$5,816.47
12-31-76	$18.37	$17.25	$3,461.22

Purchase Date	*Cap. Gains (— Losses)*	*Total Return*	*Rate of Return*
12-31-71	$−1,882.35	$3,934.12	3.37%
12-31-76	$ −612.24	$2,848.98	5.14%

* * *

AMERADA HESS CORP. (AHC). Founded 1920. Headquarters: 1185 Ave. of the Americas, New York NY 10036. **OIL.** Explores for, drills for, refines, and markets petroleum products, in the United States and abroad. 8,000 employees. **MAJOR BRAND:** Hess gasoline.

Sales: $7,869.0 million (trend 19.4% a year).
Earnings: $540.24 million (trend 35.1% a year).
What happened to a $10,000 investment

Purchase Date	*Purchase Price*	*Price on 12-31-81*	*Dividends Paid*
12-31-71	$17.13	$24.12	$2,476.90
12-31-76	$14.74	$24.12	$2,410.63

Purchase Date	*Cap. Gains (— Losses)*	*Total Return*	*Rate of Return*
12-31-71	$4,080.89	$6,557.79	5.17%
12-31-76	$6,365.32	$8,775.95	13.43%

PROFILE: The company was doing well, but the stock died . . . or nearly so. Investors were thrilled when Hess Oil & Chemical Corp., traditionally a refiner and marketer subject to violent earnings swings, merged with Amerada Petroleum in 1969. They bid the price of the stock up to a peak of 37 times earnings in 1972. Then the stock market started declining, and Amerada Hess fell much harder than most. The instant miracles investors had expected from the merger hadn't happened. From 1973 through 1980, the stock sold for from 4 to 6 times earnings.

Yet much of what investors hoped for has happened, only more slowly than they anticipated. Exploration and production are now full partners with refining and marketing. The huge cost of the 1969 merger, which at first resulted in a ballooning of debt, has been gradually absorbed. While debt was close to 50 percent of capital in 1970, it was down to about 30 percent in 1980.

Earnings swings are still volatile at Amerada Hess, but in the early 1980s financial analysts were beginning to conclude that the stock was severely undervalued. The mere worth of the company's oil reserves in the ground (carried on the books at a fraction of true value) was probably far more than the stock price. If you contemplate buying Amerada Hess, that's one key factor you should check. If the stock is still undervalued, you may have to be patient to get a big return, but get it you will.

Check, too, on where the company is drilling these days. Investors have been scared because a fair chunk of drilling has been in the Middle East. However, the company does about half its drilling in the United States, and another major portion of it in the North Sea.

Dividends have traditionally been modest.

* * *

AMERICAN AGRONOMICS CORP. (AGR). Founded 1960. Headquarters: 4600 W. Cypress St., Tampa FL 33607. **ORANGES.** Manages orange groves, produces oranges and orange juice concentrate. **MAJOR SUBSIDIARIES, BRANDS:** American Orange Corp.; Charter Distributing Co.; Golden Grove Management; Juice Tree Inc.; National Papaya Co.; Syndyne Corp.

Sales: $49.5 million (trend 34.9% a year).
Earnings: $5.27 million (trend 69.1% a year).
What happened to a $10,000 investment

Purchase Date	*Purchase Price*	*Price on 12-31-81*	*Dividends Paid*
12-31-71	$.63	$4.75	$2,429.33
12-31-76	$.17	$4.75	$8,907.55

Purchase Date	*Cap. Gains (− Losses)*	*Total Return*	*Rate of Return*
12-31-71	$ 65,999.96	$ 68,429.29	22.87%
12-31-76	$268,666.52	$277,574.07	95.77%

* * *

AMERICAN AIRLINES, INC. (AMR). Founded 1934. Headquarters: PO Box 61616, Dallas-Fort Worth Airport TX 75261. **AIRLINE.** Third-largest U.S. airline (by operating revenues), with routes to roughly sixty cities in North America and the Caribbean. 37,000 employees. **MAJOR SUBSIDIARIES, BRANDS:** AA Development (real estate); AA Energy Corp. (oil and gas exploration).

Sales: $3,821.0 million (trend 17.5% a year).
Earnings: $−163.69 million.
What happened to a $10,000 investment

Purchase Date	*Purchase Price*	*Price on 12-31-81*	*Dividends Paid*
12-31-71	$40.75	$11.25	$196.32
12-31-76	$13.50	$11.25	$592.59

Purchase Date	*Cap. Gains (− Losses)*	*Total Return*	*Rate of Return*
12-31-71	$−7,239.26	$−7,042.94	−11.47%
12-31-76	$−1,666.67	$−1,074.07	−2.25%

PROFILE: American entered the 1980s flying like a jetliner with one engine out — it was in bad shape. In the latter half of the 1970s, according to *Forbes* magazine, its return on stockholders' equity was a meager 8.7 percent — worse than the average for the airline industry (11.3), and far worse than the average for all industries (15.8). The year 1980 was far worse than the previous years: American lost close to $100 million. And 1981 (see figures above) was the worst of all. The company had also taken a loss, albeit a smaller one, in 1970, 1973, and 1975.

The airline industry, of course, is famous for its ups and downs. If you buy a stock when it's grounded and it takes off again, you can make high-flying profits. But the risks are high enough to engender some fear of flying. And American, with a whopping debt load, is probably riskier than most airline stocks. Long-term debt was a towering 57 percent of capital in 1980, while common stock made up only 37 percent (the rest was preferred stock). That's a lot of debt to service before shareholders get a dime. And certainly this is no stock to buy for dividends. There were none in early 1981, and the payout hasn't crept above $.40 a share since 1970 (it was $.80 in 1968 through 1970).

Yet the stock may be attractive to speculative investors, because of the chance for a dramatic cyclical move. The big debt load that makes the stock risky also gives leverage to company earnings. In early 1981, for example, American Airlines stock sold for less than $9 a share — only about two times the company's 1978 earnings of $4.27 a share.

* * *

AMERICAN BAKERIES CO. (ABA). Founded 1924. Headquarters: 10 S. Riverside Plaza, Chicago IL 60606. **BAKED GOODS.** Makes and distributes baked goods and other food products. **MAJOR SUBSIDIARIES, BRANDS:** Cookbook; Dressel's; Langendorf; Merita; Mickey; and Taystee baked goods.

Sales: $535.6 million (trend 5.3% a year).
Earnings: $1.83 million (trend −20.0% a year).
What happened to a $10,000 investment

Purchase Date	*Purchase Price*	*Price on 12-31-81*	*Dividends Paid*
12-31-71	$10.31	$13.62	$5,005.92
12-31-76	$11.75	$13.62	$2,987.65

Purchase Date	*Cap. Gains (− Losses)*	*Total Return*	*Rate of Return*
12-31-71	$3,218.94	$8,224.86	6.19%
12-31-76	$1,595.56	$4,583.21	7.84%

* * *

AMERICAN BRANDS, INC. (AMB). Founded 1904. Headquarters: 245 Park Ave., New York NY 10167. **CONSUMER PRODUCTS.** Tobacco accounts for more than half of sales and earnings at American Brands, but the company has diversified into a wide range of consumer products, including food and toiletries. 55,000 employees. **MAJOR SUBSIDIARIES, BRANDS:** Carlton, Lucky Strike, Pall Mall, and Tareyton cigarettes; Jim Beam Bourbon; Duffy-Mott, Taylor and Sunshine food products; Acme and Wilson Jones office supplies; Acushnet golf balls; Master Lock; Swingline stapling equipment; Andrew Jergens toiletries; Gallagher Ltd.; Franklin Life Insurance Co.

Sales: $4,276.5 million (trend 11.2% a year).
Earnings: $380.41 million (trend 27.5% a year).
What happened to a $10,000 investment

Purchase Date	*Purchase Price*	*Price on 12-31-81*	*Dividends Paid*
12-31-71	$20.94	$36.75	$8,659.58
12-31-76	$22.87	$36.75	$5,148.63

Purchase Date	*Cap. Gains (− Losses)*	*Total Return*	*Rate of Return*
12-31-71	$7,552.24	$16,211.82	10.12%
12-31-76	$6,065.57	$11,214.21	16.23%

PROFILE: American Brands is the epitome of a safe, conservative income stock — unless everybody in America stops smoking at once. The company pays high dividends, pays a high percentage of its earnings in dividends, has pledged to keep dividends rising at least in step with inflation, and so far has made good on that pledge. For example, from 1968 to 1978, inflation amounted to 93 percent, while American Brands's dividends had risen 111 percent. To make things convenient for income-oriented stockholders, a dividend reinvestment plan is available.

Capital gains are possible too, but if the past is any guide, these are likely to be modest. (The stock's low in 1978, for example, was below its high in 1965.) Nobody seems to get very excited about American Brands. It has long carried a price / earnings ratio far below the average for all stocks. It's not likely to soar, but neither is it likely to fall much; the stock's well suited for conservative investment portfolios.

Decades ago, American Brands had a near-monopoly on the tobacco business. As recently as the end of World War II, it was still the number-one U.S. tobacco company. Now it's number four, trailing R. J. Reynolds, Philip Morris, and Brown & Williamson, and commanding only around 12 percent of the U.S. cigarette market. However, American Brands has done a better job of diversifying than many of its rivals. The latest acquisition, Franklin Life Insurance Co., bought in 1979, has been very profitable so far.

* * *

AMERICAN BROADCASTING COMPANIES, INC. (ABC). Founded 1949. Headquarters: 1330 Ave. of the Americas, New York NY 10019. **BROADCASTING.** Provides television and radio programs to about 200 TV and 1,700 radio stations; owns and operates 5 TV and 13 radio stations. Also publishes specialty (farm, hobby, and business) magazines. 12,000 employees. **MAJOR SUBSIDIARIES, BRANDS:** WABC TV and Radio, New York; WLS TV and Radio, Chicago; KABC TV and Radio, Los Angeles; WXYZ TV and Radio, Detroit; KGO TV and Radio, San Francisco; radio stations WMAL and WRQX in Washington, D.C., WPLJ in New York, WDAI in Chicago, KLOS in Los Angeles, WRIF in Detroit, KAUM in Houston, KSFX in San Francisco; and the following magazines: *Los Angeles, High Fidelity, Homes, Modern Photography, Prairie Farmer, Wallaces Farmer.*

Sales: $2,256.2 million (trend 15.7% a year).
Earnings: $146.30 million (trend 46.1% a year).
What happened to a $10,000 investment

Purchase Date	*Purchase Price*	*Price on 12-31-81*	*Dividends Paid*
12-31-71	$17.54	$34.25	$4,971.02
12-31-76	$26.33	$34.25	$2,367.09

Purchase Date	*Cap. Gains (− Losses)*	*Total Return*	*Rate of Return*
12-31-71	$9,524.94	$14,495.96	9.37%
12-31-76	$3,006.33	$ 5,373.42	8.98%

PROFILE: American Broadcasting has turned in a good performance in recent years, but has been rewarded with low ratings by the stock market. The stock plummeted from a high of more than $47 a share in 1979 to a low of $26 in 1980, and rebounded only moderately in 1981. Why?

Basically, there were three reasons why ABC fell out of favor on Wall Street. First, its remarkable upsurge to number one in the Nielsen ratings (a rank it maintained from 1976 to 1979) petered out, as traditional ratings leader CBS regained the lead in 1980.

Second, Wall Street has been looking suspiciously at the network broadcasters, fearing murderous competition from cable TV. The fear is that cable operators will outbid the networks for the best sports events, movies, and even entertainment series. Stock prices for cable TV stocks have soared, while those for the networks have languished. But, as often happens, securities analysts may have gone overboard in their judgment on this point.

Third, the recession of 1980–81 hurt the networks, including ABC, which saw its 1980 earnings decline from 1979 levels. If you're selling less beer, or fewer cars, you're going to be more tightfisted with advertising dollars — and of course advertising is the lifeblood of the networks.

If this stock is still in the basement when you read this, it could be an excellent buy. Over the latter half of the 1970s, ABC's profits grew at a sparkling rate of more than 25 percent, and its profit margin was the highest of the three major networks. Its balance sheet isn't loaded up with debt (though it has more debt than CBS). If good times come again, and the networks don't get left holding the bag by cable operators, the stock could double or better in a few years.

* * *

AMERICAN BUILDING MAINTENANCE INDUSTRIES (ABM). Founded 1955. Headquarters: 333 Fell St., San Francisco CA 94102. **MAINTENANCE.** Maintains industrial plants, office buildings.

Sales: $247.1 million (trend 13.0% a year).
Earnings: $5.25 million (trend 11.1% a year).
What happened to a $10,000 investment

Purchase Date	*Purchase Price*	*Price on 12-31-81*	*Dividends Paid*
12-31-71	$44.12	$20.50	$1,149.01
12-31-76	$10.62	$20.50	$3,237.65

Purchase Date	*Cap. Gains (− Losses)*	*Total Return*	*Rate of Return*
12-31-71	$−5,354.11	$−4,205.10	−5.31%
12-31-76	$ 9,294.12	$ 12,531.76	17.64%

* * *

AMERICAN BUSINESS PRODUCTS, INC. (ABP). Founded 1967. Headquarters: Suite 500, 2690 Cumberland Parkway, Atlanta GA 30339. **OFFICE SUPPLIES.** Manufactures business forms and office supplies; also engages in book and commercial printing. **MAJOR SUBSIDIARIES, BRANDS:** BookCrafters; Curtis 1000; Speedi-Print.

Sales: $186.5 million (trend 20.3% a year).
Earnings: $8.06 million (trend 32.8% a year).
What happened to a $10,000 investment

Purchase Date	*Purchase Price*	*Price on 12-31-81*	*Dividends Paid*
12-31-71	$10.47	$12.62	$2,742.07
12-31-76	$ 7.87	$12.62	$2,501.59

Purchase Date	*Cap. Gains (− Losses)*	*Total Return*	*Rate of Return*
12-31-71	$2,062.10	$4,804.17	4.00%
12-31-76	$6,031.75	$8,533.33	13.13%

* * *

AMERICAN CAN CO. (AC). Founded 1901. Headquarters: American Lane, Greenwich CT 06830. **CANS, CONSUMER PRODUCTS.** Makes containers including aluminum cans, paperboard boxes, and plastic film, as well as packaging machinery. Also sells consumer paper products and distributes other consumer products; has sideline in resource recovery (particularly metals), chemicals, and forest products. 55,000 employees. **MAJOR**

SUBSIDIARIES, BRANDS: Butterick Co. (mail order craft books, sewing patterns, and audiovisual materials); Pickwick International (records and tapes); Dixie cups and paper products; Aurora, Northern, Gala, and Bolt paper products; Fingerhut (mail order). Associated Madison Companies (insurance) was in the process of being acquired in early 1982.

Sales: $4,812.2 million (trend 11.5% a year).
Earnings: $82.30 million (trend 3.8% a year).
What happened to a $10,000 investment

Purchase Date	*Purchase Price*	*Price on 12-31-81*	*Dividends Paid*
12-31-71	$33.37	$34.37	$7,475.66
12-31-76	$39.25	$34.37	$3,490.45

Purchase Date	*Cap. Gains (– Losses)*	*Total Return*	*Rate of Return*
12-31-71	$ 299.63	$7,775.28	5.92%
12-31-76	$–1,242.04	$2,248.41	4.14%

PROFILE: Why would you want to own stock in a can company? Dividends, perhaps. In early 1981, American Can stock had a 10 percent dividend yield. That's better than you could get on high-grade corporate bonds for most of the 1970s.

American Can has traditionally returned a much bigger slice of profits to shareholders in the form of dividends than most companies do — more than 50 percent in most years. This is a mixed blessing, since dividends are more heavily taxed than capital gains. But if yield is your bag, this stock might merit consideration. The only cloud on the horizon has been the deterioration of profit margins in the late 1970s and early 1980s. Check the trend in the company's profit margin before you put any money into this stock.

For capital gains, the picture's far less rosy. You could have bought a share in American Can for $59 back in 1965, $40 in 1970, and $30 in 1980. Not encouraging.

Of course, the company is no longer just a can company. Management has been aggressively on the prowl for acquisitions (Pickwick International, Fingerhut, Butterick), and continues to be. (Associated Madison looks to be next). The forest products division is up for sale. Containers are still more than half the business, but probably won't be by the late 1980s. It appears that what American Can really would like to be is a conglomerate.

* * *

AMERICAN CENTURY TRUST (ACT). Founded 1969. Headquarters: 11 E. Forsyth St., Jacksonville FL 32202. **INVESTMENT CO.** American Century is a closed-end, unincorporated business trust, converted in 1979 from a real estate investment trust (REIT).

Sales: $4.2 million (trend –1.5% a year).
Earnings: $1.64 million.
What happened to a $10,000 investment

Purchase Date	*Purchase Price*	*Price on 12-31-81*	*Dividends Paid*
12-31-71	$N/A	$7.62	$ N/A
12-31-76	$ 2.25	$7.62	$888.89

Purchase Date	*Cap. Gains (– Losses)*	*Total Return*	*Rate of Return*
12-31-71	$ N/A	$ N/A	N/A%
12-31-76	$23,888.89	$24,777.78	28.31%

* * *

AMERICAN CYANAMID CO. (ACY). Founded 1907. Headquarters: Berdan Ave., Wayne NJ 07470. **CHEMICALS.** Makes chemicals, fertilizers, pesticides, medical products, Formica, and household chemicals including cleaners and toiletries. 44,000 employees. **MAJOR SUBSIDIARIES, BRANDS:** Lederle (drugs); Davis & Geck (medical supplies); Formica; Breck shampoo; CIE, Nina Ricci, Pierre Cardin and Shulton's Old Spice toiletries; Pine-Sol cleaner.

Sales: $3,453.9 million (trend 13.1% a year).
Earnings: $159.19 million (trend 3.3% a year).
What happened to a $10,000 investment

Purchase Date	*Purchase Price*	*Price on 12-31-81*	*Dividends Paid*
12-31-71	$34.25	$29.25	$4,350.66
12-31-76	$27.87	$29.25	$2,825.11

Purchase Date	*Cap. Gains (– Losses)*	*Total Return*	*Rate of Return*
12-31-71	$–1,459.85	$2,890.80	2.57%
12-31-76	$ 493.27	$3,318.39	5.90%

PROFILE: American Cyanamid has some hallmarks of a poorly run company. It has run into frequent trouble with regulators and consumerists regarding pollution and occupational safety issues. That's not particularly unusual for a chemical company, but American Cyanamid doesn't have too much to show for it in the way of profitability or growth.

By most measures customarily used to measure management performance — return on stockholders' equity, profit margin, growth in sales, growth in earnings, and return on total capital — American Cyanamid lagged behind the chemical industry as a whole in the latter part of the 1970s. The chemical industry, in turn, lagged behind American industry as a whole during the same period.

Mind you, the company doesn't lose money. It hasn't had a deficit year in longer than I can remember, and it has paid dividends every year since 1934. From 1975 to 1980, the dividends were consistently in the 5½-to-6 percent yield range.

Capital gains? Possible, but unlikely to be dramatic. During the last couple of decades, the stock has ranged from about $17 to about $48 a share. But there were times when you could have bought it for $30 in 1970, 1971, 1972, 1973, 1975, 1978, 1979, and 1980.

* * *

AMERICAN DISTRICT TELEGRAPH CO. (ADT). Founded 1901. Headquarters: 1 World Trade Center, New York NY 10048. **SECURITY SYSTEMS.** Provides commercial and residential security systems, including fire and burglar alarms. Also makes industrial process interruption signal devices for factories. **MAJOR SUBSIDIARIES, BRANDS:** Aritech Corp.

Sales: $375.0 million (trend 14.3% a year).
Earnings: $20.25 million (trend 9.2% a year).
What happened to a $10,000 investment

Purchase Date	*Purchase Price*	*Price on 12-31-81*	*Dividends Paid*
12-31-71	$57.75	$39.87	$1,449.70
12-31-76	$27.37	$39.87	$2,089.50

Purchase Date	*Cap. Gains (− Losses)*	*Total Return*	*Rate of Return*
12-31-71	$−3,095.24	$−1,645.54	−1.78%
12-31-76	$ 4,566.21	$ 6,655.71	10.74%

* * *

AMERICAN ELECTRIC POWER CO., INC. (AEP). Founded 1905. Headquarters: 2 Broadway, New York NY 10004. **UTILITY.** American Electric Power is a holding company; it owns seven utilities serving portions of seven Midwestern and central Eastern states. 23,000 employees. **MAJOR SUBSIDIARIES:** Appalachian Power; Indiana & Michigan Electric; Kentucky Power; Kingsport Power; Michigan Power; Ohio Power; Wheeling Electric.

Sales: $3,756.5 million (trend 17.1% a year).
Earnings: $348.38 million (trend 8.8% a year).
What happened to a $10,000 investment

Purchase Date	*Purchase Price*	*Price on 12-31-81*	*Dividends Paid*
12-31-71	$30.37	$16.25	$6,747.33
12-31-76	$25.50	$16.25	$4,270.59

Purchase Date	*Cap. Gains (− Losses)*	*Total Return*	*Rate of Return*
12-31-71	$−4,650.21	$2,097.12	1.92%
12-31-76	$−3,627.45	$ 643.14	1.25%

PROFILE: It's hard to find a stock whose price has declined with the remorseless consistency of American Electric Power. It sold in the $40s in the 1960s, in the $30s and upper $20s in the early 1970s, in the lower $20s at the end of the 1970s, and in the $15-to-$20 range in 1980 and early 1981. Check your newspaper for the current price.

Partly to compensate investors for the lack of capital gains, the stock offers an unusually high yield — above 13 percent in early 1981, for example. That yield is comparable with the yields on high-grade bonds. But with the stock's price record, it had better be.

The company has made a point of raising dividends each year, usually by about a nickel or a dime per share. This has resulted in an annual dividend increase in the range of 3 percent a year — far less than inflation, of course. But can American Electric Power keep up even this modest rate of increase? It's a real question, because earnings didn't grow at all during the late 1970s. By the end of that decade, the company was paying out an astonishing 95 to 96 percent of profits in the form of dividends.

Most utilities carry a heavy load of debt, but few labor under more of it than American Electric, which relies on debt for more than half its capital. One possible bright spot: The companies in the American Electric family rely on coal and nuclear power, not on oil.

* * *

AMERICAN EXPRESS CO. (AXP). Founded 1850, incorporated in 1965. Headquarters: American Express Plaza, New York NY 10004. **FINANCIAL SERVICES.** American Express is involved in charge cards, traveler's checks, brokerage, international banking services, travel agencies, insurance, and cable television. 41,000 employees. **MAJOR SUBSIDIARIES, BRANDS:** Fireman's Fund Insurance

Co.; Warner-Amex Cable (50 percent owned); Shearson Loeb Rhoades Inc. (brokerage); The Boston Co. (investment management).

Sales: $5,504.0 million (trend 17.1% a year).
Earnings: $375.00 million (trend 18.8% a year).
What happened to a $10,000 investment

Purchase Date	*Purchase Price*	*Price on 12-31-81*	*Dividends Paid*
12-31-71	$43.83	$44.12	$2,609.13
12-31-76	$40.62	$44.12	$2,067.69

Purchase Date	*Cap. Gains (– Losses)*	*Total Return*	*Rate of Return*
12-31-71	$ 66.54	$2,675.67	2.40%
12-31-76	$861.54	$2,929.23	5.27%

PROFILE: Despite the company's steady earnings growth, Wall Street wasn't charmed by American Express during the late 1970s. The company's price / earnings multiple shrank each year from 1973 to 1979, and the price of the stock declined. Why?

You could argue that the company's earnings weren't quite so good as they looked. It's true that accounting methods have helped to keep alive American Express's thirty-four-year string of operating-earnings increases. But I don't think that was the major problem.

I think people were looking not so much at what has happened as at what might happen. First, investors have come to realize how important Fireman's Fund is to American Express's results. It accounted for half of profits and more than half of revenues in 1979, for example. While it's a multi-line insurer, Fireman's Fund is biggest in property and casualty insurance, an area notorious for profit swings. Despite Fireman's Fund's insistence that it will be more stable than most property and casualty insurers, investors have been edgy.

They're also worried about the original heart of the company's operations — charge cards. Credit and charge cards are becoming more alike as time goes on, and investors feared that American Express's lion's share of the travel and entertainment sector would be nibbled away by MasterCard, Visa, Diner's Club, and a Carte Blanche revived by its new owner, Citibank. Competition has heated up in traveler's checks too.

Reasonable fears. But American Express is a solid factor in several industries, including the new one of cable television. The recent acquisition of Shearson Loeb Rhoades gives American Express a major position in the brokerage industry, and strengthens its stature as a "financial supermarket." There's a limit to how long a company can have rising earnings and a falling stock. For American Express, that limit may have been reached at the start of the 1980s.

* * *

AMERICAN FAMILY CORP. (AFL). Founded 1955. Headquarters: 1932 Wynnton Rd., Columbus GA 31999. **CANCER INSURANCE.** Sells cancer insurance policies and intensive-care health insurance policies in United States and abroad. Also owns six TV stations in the Midwest and South, several cable TV franchises in Texas, and a producer of audiovisual materials (chiefly training films). **MAJOR SUBSIDIARIES, BRANDS:** American Family Life Assurance Co.; American Learning Systems, Inc.

* * *

AMERICAN GENERAL BOND FUND, INC. (AGB). Founded 1970. Headquarters: 3910 Keswick Rd., Baltimore MD 21211. **INVESTMENT COMPANY.** Company is a closed-end bond fund investing in government and corporate bonds and notes. It is managed by a subsidiary of American General Corp.

* * *

AMERICAN GENERAL CONVERTIBLE SECURITIES, INC. (AGS). Founded 1972. Headquarters: 2727 Allen Parkway, Houston TX 77019. **INVESTMENT COMPANY.** Company is a closed-end fund investing chiefly in convertible bonds and convertible preferred stock. It is managed by a subsidiary of American General Corp.

* * *

AMERICAN GENERAL CORP. (AGC). Founded 1926. Headquarters: 2727 Allen Parkway, Houston TX 77019. **INSURANCE.** American General is a major life insurer and property / casualty insurer. It has sidelines in mutual fund management, real estate investing, and mortgage lending. 8,000 employees. **MAJOR SUBSIDIARIES, BRANDS:** American General Life Insurance Co.; Maryland Casualty. Owns fractions (between 5 and 10 percent) of American National Insurance; BMA Corp.; Liberty National; NLT Corp.; St. Paul Companies.

PROFILE: "Insurance conglomerate" would be a fair description of American General. It gets a bit over half its sales and earnings from life insurance and related lines. About 40 percent of sales and earnings come from the sale of property and casualty insurance. Recently, less than 5 percent has come from the company's other activities, which include mutual fund management, real estate, and mortgage lending. Consumer lending may be added to the mix soon, through the pending merger of Credithrift Financial Inc., a medium-sized Indiana-based loan firm. In a proposed billion-dollar merger, American General is also trying to take over NLT Corp., a life insurance firm based in Tennessee and profiled later in this volume.

The stock has done pretty well in recent years, because of fairly steady and fairly rapid earnings growth. The balance sheet is strong, with long-term debt recently less than 10 percent of capital. Dividends, paid each year since 1929, provide a moderate yield. And the price / earnings ratio has been low since the early 1970s, so you're not going out on much of a limb here.

In short, the stock is pretty well suited for conservative portfolios, based on the company's past record. An imponderable is the extent to which changes in the insurance business (including life insurance buyers' increasing preference for term insurance), tougher price competition, and the advent of new products may affect the company's traditional profitability.

* * *

AMERICAN HERITAGE LIFE INVESTMENT CORP. (AHL). Founded 1956. Headquarters: 11 E. Forsyth St., Jacksonville FL 32202. INSURANCE. Owns American Heritage Life Insurance Co.; also runs a real estate investment trust and a data processing service. MAJOR SUBSIDIARIES, BRANDS: American Heritage Life Insurance Co.; American Century Advisors; Florida Associated Services.

* * *

AMERICAN HOIST & DERRICK CO. (AHO). Founded 1882. Headquarters: 63 South Robert St., St. Paul MN 55107. HEAVY LIFTING EQUIPMENT. Manufactures and sells lifting and construction equipment. MAJOR SUBSIDIARIES, BRANDS: American Hoist of Canada, Ltd.; Farrell, Ozmun, Kirk & Co.; Waterous.

Sales: $538.6 million (trend 8.5% a year).
Earnings: $20.29 million (trend 11.2% a year).
What happened to a $10,000 investment

Purchase Date	*Purchase Price*	*Price on 12-31-81*	*Dividends Paid*
12-31-71	$10.80	$16.12	$7,669.03
12-31-76	$18.25	$16.12	$2,887.67

Purchase Date	*Cap. Gains (− Losses)*	*Total Return*	*Rate of Return*
12-31-71	$ 4,929.21	$12,598.24	8.49%
12-31-76	$−1,164.38	$ 1,723.29	3.23%

* * *

AMERICAN HOME PRODUCTS CORP. (AHP). Founded 1926. Headquarters: 685 Third Ave., New York NY 10017. CONSUMER PRODUCTS, DRUGS. American Home Products is involved in prescription and over-the-counter drugs and a wide variety of consumer products, produced by some 200 subsidiaries. 50,000 employees. MAJOR SUBSIDIARIES, BRANDS: Major consumer brands include Anacin; Aero-Shave; Black Flag; E. J. Brach; Chef Boy-ar-dee; Country Kitchen; Dristan; Ekco; Easy-Off; Gulden's; Old English; Preparation H; Sani-Flush; Woolite; and Wizard. Drugs and medical supplies are produced by five subsidiaries: Ayerst; Crometrics; Fort Dodge; Ives; and Wyeth.

Sales: $3,798.5 million (trend 11.1% a year).
Earnings: $445.89 million (trend 12.3% a year).
What happened to a $10,000 investment

Purchase Date	*Purchase Price*	*Price on 12-31-81*	*Dividends Paid*
12-31-71	$29.79	$36.50	$3,848.94
12-31-76	$32.25	$36.50	$2,348.84

Purchase Date	*Cap. Gains (− Losses)*	*Total Return*	*Rate of Return*
12-31-71	$2,251.75	$6,100.69	4.88%
12-31-76	$1,317.83	$3,666.67	6.45%

PROFILE: Can you describe American Home Products in four words? Sure, it's easy:

Secretive, profitable, and tightfisted.

The penchant for secrecy, a preference of longtime chairman William Laporte, is reflected in a variety of ways: no public relations department, no touting of the stock to analysts, a brand name but not the corporate name on the hundreds of products produced by American Home Products's subsidiaries. Even the telephone at corporate headquarters has long been answered by an operator who repeats the number instead of giving the company's name. All advertising — and there's plenty, since the company is the nation's third-biggest television advertiser after Procter & Gamble and General Foods — promotes the product, not the company.

The profitability has been steady. The company

was headed for its twenty-ninth straight year of increased profits in 1981. Profits haven't risen spectacularly — about 12 percent a year in the late 1970s — but they've risen right through recessions, as drug company profits often do. And that's what American Home Products is — a drug company with a gigantic sideline in consumer goods. Prescription drugs account for about 40 percent of sales and 60 percent of profits. Add in over-the-counter medications like Anacin and Dristan, and drugs account for more than half of sales and close to three-quarters of profits.

Tightfistedness has been another hallmark. The giant company is virtually free of long-term debt — a real rarity. It likes to keep a huge pile of cash around, both to invest and to have ready for acquisitions. The company lists close to a hundred subsidiaries in reports to the Securities and Exchange Commission and has additional subsidiaries deemed too small to list. Cost-cutting is a way of life at American Home Products.

The negative side of tightfistedness has been a reluctance to spend much (as a percentage of sales) on drug research. Much of the company's profit has come from merchandising products developed abroad in the United States. But the company may not be able to do that much longer, as foreign drug companies are now more likely to sell here directly.

* * *

AMERICAN HOSPITAL SUPPLY CO. (AHS). Founded 1922. Headquarters: 1 American Plaza, Evanston IL 60201. **HOSPITAL SUPPLIES.** American Hospital Supply Corp. manufactures, markets, and distributes health care products, chiefly to hospitals and laboratories. **MAJOR SUBSIDIARIES, BRANDS:** Bentley Laboratories; American Wells Corp.; McGaw Supply Ltd.; Pacific International.

Sales: $2,339.9 million (trend 15.5% a year).
Earnings: $123.10 million (trend 17.1% a year).
What happened to a $10,000 investment

Purchase Date	*Purchase Price*	*Price on 12-31-81*	*Dividends Paid*
12-31-71	$39.75	$38.37	$1,362.26
12-31-76	$30.75	$38.37	$1,258.54

Purchase Date	*Cap. Gains (– Losses)*	*Total Return*	*Rate of Return*
12-31-71	$–345.91	$1,016.35	.97%
12-31-76	$ 2,479.67	$3,738.21	6.56%

* * *

AMERICAN INTERNATIONAL GROUP, INC. (AIGR, Over-the-Counter). Founded 1967. Headquarters: 70 Pine St., New York NY 10005. **INSURANCE.** Holding company for several insurance subsidiaries writing property and casualty insurance and life insurance in the United States and abroad. 19,000 employees. **MAJOR SUBSIDIARIES, BRANDS:** American Home, New Hampshire, and National Union Insurance Groups.

Sales: $2,709.5 million (trend 24.7% a year).
Earnings: $282.17 million (trend 30.9% a year).
What happened to a $10,000 investment

Purchase Date	*Purchase Price*	*Price on 12-31-81*	*Dividends Paid*
12-31-71	$ N/A	$64.75	$ N/A
12-31-76	$25.33	$64.75	$538.41

Purchase Date	*Cap. Gains (– Losses)*	*Total Return*	*Rate of Return*
12-31-71	$ N/A	$ N/A	N/A%
12-31-76	$15,559.21	$16,097.62	21.15%

PROFILE: A well-run company and a solid growth stock. Since it went public in 1969, American International Group has increased its profits every year and increased them at a clip approaching 25 percent a year. A 15 percent a year profit increase, turned in consistently, is enough to qualify a stock as a growth stock in almost anybody's book. American International has made that look as easy as child's play.

It's done it, moreover, in a business (property and casualty insurance) where drastic fluctuations in profits are the rule. But American International doesn't march to the same drumbeat as typical U.S. insurers. To begin with, as its name implies, it is an international insurer: About half of all business (and slightly more than half of profits) usually comes from abroad. Secondly, it doesn't specialize in the typical home and auto risks, but aims at more specialized areas (liability insurance for corporate board members or shipments of valuable business property, for example) where there's less competition and potentially higher profit. Thirdly, in large part as a result of the first two traits, it prices its policies to make money on their own, not (as is common) as break-even or loss-leader operations intended to pull in money that can then be invested.

The stock has done well but, based on the company's outstanding track record, deserves to do even better. One exciting development on the horizon, as investment counselor John Train noted in *Forbes* in 1980, is a possible boom in U.S. dealings with China and other countries in the Far East. American International, unlike other insurance companies, already has a large and well-trained staff there.

* * *

AMERICAN MEDICAL INTERNATIONAL, INC. (AMI). Founded 1956. Headquarters: 414 N. Camden Dr., Beverly Hills CA 90210. **MEDICAL SERVICES.** Owns and operates hospitals in the United States and abroad, provides services to other hospitals on a contract basis. 16,000 employees. **MAJOR SUBSIDIARIES, BRANDS:** Hyatt Medical Enterprises.

Sales: $913.5 million (trend 27.7% a year).
Earnings: $53.15 million (trend 41.4% a year).
What happened to a $10,000 investment

Purchase Date	*Purchase Price*	*Price on 12-31-81*	*Dividends Paid*
12-31-71	$11.39	$26.17	$1,334.89
12-31-76	$ 4.48	$26.17	$2,958.92

Purchase Date	*Cap. Gains (− Losses)*	*Total Return*	*Rate of Return*
12-31-71	$12,965.41	$14,300.30	9.29%
12-31-76	$48,344.56	$51,303.48	43.71%

PROFILE: You could have picked up this stock for $3 as recently as 1976. In 1980 it hit $44 a share. Wanna jump on the train before it's too late?

Before you do, be aware that this train is a roller coaster. American Medical International had sold for $45 a share back in 1972. So this has been a stock in which you could turn $1,000 into more than $10,000 . . . or $10,000 into less than $1,000.

American Medical International is a hospital management company — the third largest one, after Humana and Hospital Corp. of America. (You should check out these competitors as well as AMI if you contemplate investing in this field.) The word "international" in its name is more a pointer for the future than a present fact: In fiscal 1980, more than 85 percent of both sales and earnings came from U.S. operations. However, AMI does own a few hospitals in Europe and South America, and it provides contract services for several more. Venezuela and Brazil particularly seem like growth areas, and the company's profit on foreign business has been higher than on domestic (about 13 percent versus 9 percent).

Contributing to the volatility of the stock is the big debt load the company habitually carries. From 1973 through 1980, debt never was less than half of total capital. Dividends are — you guessed it — modest. So, welcome to the roller coaster, but make sure you've got a strong stomach . . . for speculation.

* * *

AMERICAN MOTORS CORP. (AMO). Founded 1916. Headquarters: 27777 Franklin Rd., Southfield MI 48034. **AUTOS.** Makes cars, military trucks, postal delivery vehicles. 28,000 employees. **MAJOR SUBSIDIARIES, BRANDS:** A. M. General (military vehicles and post office light-delivery trucks); Jeep; Eagle; Concord; Spirit. Renault, the French government-owned automobile manufacturer, owned more than 46 percent of American Motors stock in early 1981, and had options that would boost its holdings to more than 50 percent.

Sales: $2,552.6 million (trend 4.7% a year).
Earnings: $−197.52 million.
What happened to a $10,000 investment

Purchase Date	*Purchase Price*	*Price on 12-31-81*	*Dividends Paid*
12-31-71	$7.25	$2.37	$379.31
12-31-76	$3.87	$2.37	$193.55

Purchase Date	*Cap. Gains (− Losses)*	*Total Return*	*Rate of Return*
12-31-71	$−6,724.14	$−6,344.83	−9.57%
12-31-76	$−3,870.97	$−3,677.42	−8.76%

PROFILE: In all but name, American Motors is now an arm of Renault of France. Renault would own more than half the stock if it converted its convertible bonds and exercised its warrants. Effectively, it controls the company.

That may reflect a decline in American industrial strength, but it's not necessarily bad news for American Motors stockholders. Renault cars will broaden AMC dealers' offerings, and Renault's marketing force abroad can help sell AMC cars, especially the ever-popular Jeeps.

But let's face it, American Motors has been hanging on by its fingernails for a long time. Its share of the U.S. auto market has ranged from 2 percent to 5 percent over the last decade — usually closer to the low end of that range. It had back-to-back losses in 1975 and 1976, and lost about $150 million in fiscal 1980, which was more than its accumulated profits in the previous three years.

As a result, the stock sold for a song in the early

1980s. The tune may be appealing to you if you're a speculator or a Francophile.

Hopes for the stock depend on three factors: Jeeps, military vehicles, and Renault's potential to revive the chronically ailing manufacturer. To some extent, the stock's performance may depend on U.S.-French relations. If they cool, it may be hard for the U.S. government to award a lot of fat contracts to A. M. General for military trucks or post office delivery vehicles — especially if U.S. auto manufacturers are still struggling to pull out of the red ink that bathed them at the start of the decade.

* * *

AMERICAN NATURAL RESOURCES CO. (ANR). Founded 1964. Headquarters: 1 Woodland Ave., Detroit MI 48226. **NATURAL GAS.** Explores for and distributes natural gas in the Great Lakes area, primarily Michigan and Wisconsin. Also has operations in trucking, gas storage for other utilities, oil exploration, and coal mining. 17,000 employees. **MAJOR SUBSIDIARIES:** Michigan Wisconsin Pipe Line Co.; Great Lakes Transmission Co. (50 percent owned).

Sales: $3,038.5 million (trend 24.1% a year).
Earnings: $118.24 million (trend 3.1% a year).
What happened to a $10,000 investment

Purchase Date	*Purchase Price*	*Price on 12-31-81*	*Dividends Paid*
12-31-71	$39.50	$42.25	$7,086.08
12-31-76	$43.87	$42.25	$3,573.79

Purchase Date	*Cap. Gains (— Losses)*	*Total Return*	*Rate of Return*
12-31-71	$ 696.20	$7,782.28	5.93%
12-31-76	$−370.37	$3,203.42	5.72%

PROFILE: Like most utilities these days, American Natural Resources has seen the handwriting on the wall (slowing demand, stiff regulation) and is moving to diversify. In American's case, the diversification has been into trucking, oil exploration, and coal mining.

All of that comes none too soon. In its "Annual Report on American Industry" dated January 5, 1981, *Forbes* magazine ranked American Natural Resources ninth out of ten gas pipeliners and distributors in return on stockholders' equity, and worst of the ten in growth of earnings per share. (Profits had been creeping up at a pace of 3.8 percent a year.)

Recently, more than 80 percent of the company's earnings had come from Michigan Wisconsin Pipe Line Co., the interstate pipeline arm. Less than 10 percent had come from the company's huge retail operation, Michigan Consolidated Gas Co., which supplies natural gas to more than a million customers in Detroit, Grand Rapids, and other parts of Michigan.

So, at the start of 1982, the management spun off the retail part of the business to a newly formed company called Primark Corp. The idea seemed to be that if Michigan Consolidated stood on its own, the Michigan Public Service Commission, which regulates rates charged by utilities in the state, would have to be kinder to it.

The spin-off might restore some luster to a stock that's been essentially stagnant for more than a decade.

* * *

AMERICAN PETROFINA, INC. (API, American Stock Exchange). Founded 1956. Headquarters: Fina Plaza, Dallas TX 75206. **OIL.** American Petrofina explores for and produces oil and natural gas; also produces petrochemicals. The company is majority-owned by Petrofina, S.A. of Belgium. 3,000 employees. **MAJOR SUBSIDIARIES, BRANDS:** Cosden Oil & Chemical Co.; Hercofina (25 percent-owned joint venture with Hercules Inc.); FINA gasoline.

Sales: $2,130.0 million (trend 15.7% a year).
Earnings: $104.28 million (trend 20.0% a year).
What happened to a $10,000 investment

Purchase Date	*Purchase Price*	*Price on 12-31-81*	*Dividends Paid*
12-31-71	$22.75	$55.25	$9,252.75
12-31-76	$34.25	$55.25	$3,781.02

Purchase Date	*Cap. Gains (— Losses)*	*Total Return*	*Rate of Return*
12-31-71	$14,285.71	$23,538.46	12.86%
12-31-76	$ 6,131.39	$ 9,912.41	14.77%

PROFILE: Though it ranks among the largest 200 U.S. industrial companies, according to *Fortune,* American Petrofina isn't, in a sense, an American company. The majority of the "class A" stock (which is what you'd buy) is owned by Petrofina, S.A., an international oil company based in Belgium. Petrofina, S.A. also owns 99 percent of the "class B" stock, which has fewer shares outstanding and has the privilege of electing most of the board of directors.

As with any foreign-controlled venture, there's

always the temptation to wonder whose interests will predominate. That worry may help account for the low price / earnings ratio here: The p / e hasn't been above 10 since 1972. The low multiple also reflects erratic profitability and a fairly slow growth rate.

The stock can be volatile. Witness this example: If you'd bought in 1971 and sold in 1980, you might have roughly broken even, or you might have doubled your money — depending on when in 1980 you sold.

The company carries a considerable debt load, recently around 40 percent of capital. Dividends, paid each year since 1958, have recently provided a moderate yield.

* * *

AMERICAN SAVINGS & LOAN ASSOCIATION OF FLORIDA (AAA). Founded 1950. Headquarters: 17801 N.W. Second Ave., Miami FL 33169. **SAVINGS AND LOAN.** American Savings & Loan Association of Florida is the third largest savings and loan association in Florida.

* * *

THE AMERICAN SHIP BUILDING CO. (ABG). Founded 1899. Headquarters: Hillsboro Bldg., 512 Florida Ave., Tampa FL 33601. **SHIPS.** The American Ship Building Co. is active in the construction and repair of ships, barges, and building products. **MAJOR SUBSIDIARIES, BRANDS:** Amship; NABRICO.

Sales: $197.0 million (trend 7.4% a year).
Earnings: $14.13 million (trend 14.0% a year).
What happened to a $10,000 investment

Purchase Date	*Purchase Price*	*Price on 12-31-81*	*Dividends Paid*
12-31-71	$12.95	$11.50	$2,764.89
12-31-76	$ 5.74	$11.50	$5,029.89

Purchase Date	*Cap. Gains (− Losses)*	*Total Return*	*Rate of Return*
12-31-71	$−1,120.29	$ 1,644.61	1.53%
12-31-76	$ 10,032.25	$15,062.14	20.17%

* * *

AMERICAN STANDARD INC. (AST). Founded 1929. Headquarters: 40 W. 40th St., New York NY 10018. **BUILDING AND TRANSPORTATION PRODUCTS.** American Standard makes railroad and trucking equipment, plumbing and other building products, mining equipment, security systems, and graphic design products. 49,000 employees.

Sales: $2,673.6 million (trend 11.5% a year).
Earnings: $156.79 million (trend 26.7% a year).
What happened to a $10,000 investment

Purchase Date	*Purchase Price*	*Price on 12-31-81*	*Dividends Paid*
12-31-71	$ 7.69	$29.75	$12,504.07
12-31-76	$14.25	$29.75	$ 5,447.37

Purchase Date	*Cap. Gains (− Losses)*	*Total Return*	*Rate of Return*
12-31-71	$28,699.19	$41,203.25	17.74%
12-31-76	$10,877.19	$16,324.56	21.36%

PROFILE: People still think of American Standard as a dull American company that makes toilets. In fact, under the chairmanship of William A. Marquard, a partially deaf, tough, and intelligent manager, American Standard has for several years been a rapidly growing international conglomerate.

Truck brakes and railroad equipment account for a bigger percentage of sales and profits than building products (including plumbing fixtures) do. While these two lines are the mainstays of the corporation, American Standard is also diversified into other areas, like mining equipment, security systems, and graphic design and printing. Foreign sales account for almost half of business.

Profit growth figures look glowing, but a simple statistical analysis of them can be deceiving. American Standard stumbled into trouble during the late 1960s, having expanded loosely and managed poorly. So, during the 1970s, it achieved tremendous earnings growth, but off a very small base.

Competitors are impressed with the job Marquard has done since 1971. One place it shows up is on the company's balance sheet. Long-term debt has been pared from almost 50 percent of capital in 1971 down to a healthy level of about 25 percent. The stock has climbed from a low of about $4 in 1974 to a high of about $43 in 1981. Yet it still sells at a conservative multiple; in fact, American Standard did not sell for more than 7 times earnings during the period 1973–80. In 1981, the p / e flared up to 11, but in early 1982 it was back down to 6. If investors get convinced that this is really a growth stock, holders of American Standard shares could get substantial capital gains to go with the quite decent dividend yield (about 8 percent in early 1982).

* * *

AMERICAN STERILIZER CO. (ASZ). Founded 1902. Headquarters: 2222 W. Grandview Blvd., Erie PA 16506. **HEALTH CARE.** American Sterilizer Co. designs, manufactures, and markets health care supplies and equipment. **MAJOR SUBSIDIARIES, BRANDS:** West Chemical Co.

Sales: $206.5 million (trend 6.3% a year).
Earnings: $9.86 million (trend 14.9% a year).
What happened to a $10,000 investment

Purchase Date	*Purchase Price*	*Price on 12-31-81*	*Dividends Paid*
12-31-71	$16.62	$11.37	$1,810.53
12-31-76	$ 7.12	$11.37	$2,259.65

Purchase Date	*Cap. Gains (− Losses)*	*Total Return*	*Rate of Return*
12-31-71	$−3,157.89	$−1,347.37	−1.44%
12-31-76	$ 5,964.91	$ 8,224.56	12.75%

* * *

AMERICAN STORES CO. (ASC). Founded 1947. Headquarters: 709 E. South Temple, Salt Lake City UT 84127. **RETAILER.** Operates more than 1,000 supermarkets, drugstores, and combination stores nationwide. 62,000 employees. **MAJOR SUBSIDIARIES, BRANDS:** Acme, Alpha / Beta, Hy-Lo, Rea & Derick, Skaggs, and Super Saver stores.

Sales: $6,419.9 million (trend 60.5% a year).
Earnings: $40.33 million (trend 26.5% a year).
What happened to a $10,000 investment

Purchase Date	*Purchase Price*	*Price on 12-31-81*	*Dividends Paid*
12-31-71	$15.50	$29.50	$3,005.38
12-31-76	$22.75	$29.50	$1,285.71

Purchase Date	*Cap. Gains (− Losses)*	*Total Return*	*Rate of Return*
12-31-71	$9,032.26	$12,037.63	8.22%
12-31-76	$2,967.03	$ 4,252.75	7.34%

PROFILE: Like an aggressive woman who stalks the man she wants, marries him, and then changes her name to his, Skaggs Companies took over American Stores in 1979 and adopted its name.

Whether Skaggs was wise remains to be seen. The combined company sells for a lower multiple of earnings than Skaggs did in the late 1970s. But that may not be due to the merger. Retailing stocks in general were in the doghouse at the turn of the decade because of the 1980–81 recession.

The combined company boasts more than 1,000 stores. More than 300 of these are Alpha / Beta stores, which divide their space evenly between a supermarket shopping area and a drugstore shopping area. This approach provides the convenience of what retailers (using the latest buzz word) like to call "one-stop shopping."

Weaker are the Acme supermarkets, concentrated in the Northeast, where competition among supermarkets is especially fierce and where profit margins are, therefore, especially low. At the turn of the decade, many of the Acmes were small or in need of modernization. American Stores was modernizing some, eliminating others. As of early 1981, analysts for the Value Line Investment Survey said they wouldn't be surprised if the number of Acmes were trimmed below the then-current total of 360.

Skaggs has had a good long-term record for profitability and growth. However, it remains to be seen how well it will be able to manage its enlarged empire and whether it will stumble under the big debt burden (about 55 percent of capital) it took on to finance the 1979 merger.

* * *

AMERICAN TELEPHONE AND TELEGRAPH CO. (T). Founded 1885. Headquarters: 195 Broadway, New York NY 10007. **UTILITY.** Provides phone service to about 80 percent of U.S. phones, transmits more than 500 million conversations a day. 1,000,000 employees. **MAJOR SUBSIDIARIES, BRANDS:** Bell Telephone Laboratories (research); Western Electric (equipment manufacturing); New York Bell Telephone Co.; Pacific Telephone Co.; Illinois Bell Telephone Co.; Southwestern Bell Telephone Co.; New England Bell Telephone Co.

Sales: $50,791.2 million (trend 11.8% a year).
Earnings: $5,929.00 million (trend 15.3% a year).
What happened to a $10,000 investment

Purchase Date	*Purchase Price*	*Price on 12-31-81*	*Dividends Paid*
12-31-71	$44.75	$58.75	$8,985.47
12-31-76	$63.50	$58.75	$3,811.02

Purchase Date	*Cap. Gains (− Losses)*	*Total Return*	*Rate of Return*
12-31-71	$ 3,128.49	$12,113.97	8.26%
12-31-76	$−748.03	$ 3,062.99	5.49%

PROFILE: AT&T has long been known as the classic "widows and orphans" stock, with safe, dependable dividends. It had also come to be regarded on Wall Street as a bit dull.

No more. In early 1982, the company reached a settlement of a long-standing antitrust suit brought by the U.S. Justice Department. The settlement calls for AT&T to divest its twenty-two local operating companies over the next five years or so. It will keep its long-distance network, Bell Laboratories, and Western Electric, and presumably will be allowed to compete in the broader realm of telecommunications and computers, portions of which had previously been barred to it. The stock market reacted favorably. AT&T has become somewhat less safe, since it faces heavy competition in worldwide telecommunications, but it has become a possible vehicle for significant capital gains.

In late 1981, the dividend yield here was above 9 percent. As a conservative investment in income-oriented accounts, AT&T stock competes with bonds, which are also bought for current yield. Bonds tend to go up when interest rates go down, and vice versa. So, therefore, do these shares, which therefore attract extra attention at times when interest rates are widely believed to be about to decline.

For years, AT&T was known for keeping its dividends rising faster than inflation — no mean trick during the 1970s. In 1980, though, dividends were the same as in 1979. There was a moderate increase in 1981, and it's probably too early to predict whether the "new" AT&T will alter its traditional stress on dividends.

* * *

AMERICAN WATER WORKS COMPANY, INC. (AWK). Founded 1936. Headquarters: 3908 Kennett Pike, PO Box 3539, Greenville, Wilmington DE 19807. **PUBLIC WATER SUPPLY.** American Water Works Company, Inc. owns companies providing water service and sewage treatment service; also provides consulting services to water utilities. **MAJOR SUBSIDIARIES, BRANDS:** Commonwealth Water Co.; Ohio-American Water Co.; Western Pennsylvania Water Co.

Sales: $261.1 million (trend 7.6% a year).
Earnings: $21.07 million (trend 8.2% a year).
What happened to a $10,000 investment

Purchase Date	*Purchase Price*	*Price on 12-31-81*	*Dividends Paid*
12-31-71	$14.37	$12.50	$5,370.43
12-31-76	$11.62	$12.50	$3,879.57

Purchase Date	*Cap. Gains (− Losses)*	*Total Return*	*Rate of Return*
12-31-71	$−1,304.35	$4,066.09	3.47%
12-31-76	$ 752.69	$4,632.26	7.91%

* * *

AMERON, INC. (AMN). Founded 1907. Headquarters: 4700 Ramona Blvd., Monterey Park CA 91754. **CONSTRUCTION PRODUCTS.** Ameron, Inc. manufactures concrete and steel pressure pipe systems, protective coatings and linings, lighting poles, and wire, rod, and other construction products. **MAJOR SUBSIDIARIES, BRANDS:** American Pipe and Construction International; Amercoat Protective Coatings; Nukem mortars and grouts; Bondstrand pipes and fittings.

Sales: $291.9 million (trend 8.0% a year).
Earnings: $11.72 million (trend 8.9% a year).
What happened to a $10,000 investment

Purchase Date	*Purchase Price*	*Price on 12-31-81*	*Dividends Paid*
12-31-71	$15.87	$27.25	$6,133.54
12-31-76	$16.87	$27.25	$3,407.41

Purchase Date	*Cap. Gains (− Losses)*	*Total Return*	*Rate of Return*
12-31-71	$7,165.35	$13,298.90	8.83%
12-31-76	$6,148.15	$ 9,555.56	14.35%

* * *

AMES DEPARTMENT STORES, INC. (ADD). Founded 1962. Headquarters: 2418 Main St., Rocky Hills CT 06067. **RETAILING.** Ames Department Stores, Inc. operates a chain of discount department stores in the Northeast, primarily in smaller cities and towns.

Sales: $307.4 million (trend 22.0% a year).
Earnings: $8.56 million (trend 20.3% a year).
What happened to a $10,000 investment

Purchase Date	*Purchase Price*	*Price on 12-31-81*	*Dividends Paid*
12-31-71	$9.01	$20.87	$1,366.28
12-31-76	$5.64	$20.87	$1,702.36

Purchase Date	*Cap. Gains (− Losses)*	*Total Return*	*Rate of Return*
12-31-71	$13,168.42	$14,534.70	9.39%
12-31-76	$27,036.26	$28,738.62	31.11%

* * *

AMETEK, INC. (AME). Founded 1930. Headquarters: 410 Park Ave., New York NY 10022. **SCIENTIFIC EQUIPMENT.** AMETEK, Inc., manufactures scientific equipment used in medical markets and industrial equipment used in the automotive and home industries.

Sales: $400.2 million (trend 13.5% a year).
Earnings: $21.66 million (trend 12.6% a year).
What happened to a $10,000 investment

Purchase Date	*Purchase Price*	*Price on 12-31-81*	*Dividends Paid*
12-31-71	$ 9.19	$33.50	$7,401.36
12-31-76	$14.37	$33.50	$3,147.83

Purchase Date	*Cap. Gains (– Losses)*	*Total Return*	*Rate of Return*
12-31-71	$26,462.59	$33,863.95	15.93%
12-31-76	$13,304.35	$16,452.17	21.48%

* * *

AMFAC, INC. (AMA). Founded 1918. Headquarters: 700 Bishop St., Honolulu HI 96813. **WHOLESALE.** AMFAC, Inc. is involved in wholesale distribution, as well as investments in hotels and resorts, real estate, and agriculture.

Sales: $1,922.4 million (trend 11.0% a year).
Earnings: $76.10 million (trend 21.5% a year).
What happened to a $10,000 investment

Purchase Date	*Purchase Price*	*Price on 12-31-81*	*Dividends Paid*
12-31-71	$35.25	$26.50	$2,808.51
12-31-76	$15.25	$26.50	$3,908.20

Purchase Date	*Cap. Gains (– Losses)*	*Total Return*	*Rate of Return*
12-31-71	$–2,482.27	$ 326.24	.32%
12-31-76	$ 7,377.05	$11,285.25	16.31%

* * *

AMP INC. (AMP). Founded 1941. Headquarters: Eisenhower Blvd., Harrisburg PA 17105. **ELECTRONICS.** AMP is a major manufacturer of electronic connectors and wiring devices. 18,000 employees.

Sales: $1,155.4 million (trend 23.6% a year).
Earnings: $131.27 million (trend 35.2% a year).
What happened to a $10,000 investment

Purchase Date	*Purchase Price*	*Price on 12-31-81*	*Dividends Paid*
12-31-71	$23.75	$50.87	$2,366.04
12-31-76	$28.25	$50.87	$1,430.09

Purchase Date	*Cap. Gains (– Losses)*	*Total Return*	*Rate of Return*
12-31-71	$11,421.05	$13,787.09	9.05%
12-31-76	$ 8,008.85	$ 9,438.94	14.22%

PROFILE: As you might expect from its name, AMP is in the electronics business. As you might expect from its business, company earnings are affected by the prevailing economic winds. As you might expect from *that,* the stock price moves around a fair amount. Are there no surprises here, then? Yes, there are a few.

One is the balance sheet. Investors have come to shrug off 30-percent-of-capital debt levels as routine. At AMP, debt was recently a mere 8 percent of total capital. In fact, with about $50 million in long-term debt, the company had on hand more than $100 million in cash and cash equivalents.

Another surprise is the growth rates (see above). Recessions slow AMP down a bit, all right, but not as much as you'd expect. And the underlying growth trend has been very strong.

All of this had not gone unnoticed on Wall Street, which has awarded AMP with an above-average price / earnings ratio (recently 15, when the average stock was selling for about 8). But then AMP is no stranger to high p / e ratios — it sold for as much as 55 times earnings in 1975.

AMP's connectors are used in computers, office equipment, and a wide variety of other industries. Almost exactly half of sales are outside the United States. Servicing and consultation are also provided.

Dividends have been paid yearly since 1951, but the yield is modest.

* * *

AMPCO-PITTSBURGH CORP. (AP). Founded 1929. Headquarters: 700 Porter Bldg., Pittsburgh PA 15129. **STEEL.** AMPCO-Pittsburgh manufactures metal products that are used in industry, railroads, and construction equipment. **MAJOR SUBSIDIARIES, BRANDS:** Pittsburgh Forgings Co.

Sales: $430.7 million (trend 32.1% a year).
Earnings: $15.08 million (trend 24.6% a year).
What happened to a $10,000 investment

Purchase Date	*Purchase Price*	*Price on 12-31-81*	*Dividends Paid*
12-31-71	$5.44	$14.75	$7,696.52
12-31-76	$9.94	$14.75	$2,528.29

Purchase Date	*Cap. Gains (— Losses)*	*Total Return*	*Rate of Return*
12-31-71	$17,125.75	$24,822.28	13.29%
12-31-76	$ 4,842.39	$ 7,370.68	11.68%

* * *

AMREP CORP. (AXR). Founded 1955. Headquarters: 16 W. 61st St., New York NY 10023. **HOUSING.** AMREP Corp. is involved in the construction of single-family homes and the sale of land and housing sites. **MAJOR SUBSIDIARIES, BRANDS:** Kable News Co.

Sales: $41.8 million (trend 5.8% a year).
Earnings: $2.06 million (trend 28.0% a year).
What happened to a $10,000 investment

Purchase Date	*Purchase Price*	*Price on 12-31-81*	*Dividends Paid*
12-31-71	$19.50	$7.25	$0.00
12-31-76	$ 2.12	$7.25	$0.00

Purchase Date	*Cap. Gains (— Losses)*	*Total Return*	*Rate of Return*
12-31-71	$—6,282.05	$—6,282.05	—9.42%
12-31-76	$ 24,117.65	$ 24,117.65	27.82%

* * *

AMSOUTH BANCORPORATION (ASO). Founded 1970; bank dates to 1872. Headquarters: 1400 First National-Southern Natural Building, Birmingham AL 35288. **BANKING.** Holding company for Alabama's largest bank and several smaller banks which it plans to merge into its flagship chain. **MAJOR SUBSIDIARIES, BRANDS:** First National Bank of Birmingham (largest bank in Alabama).

Sales: $281.5 million (trend 19.0% a year).
Earnings: $28.30 million (trend 11.4% a year).
What happened to a $10,000 investment

Purchase Date	*Purchase Price*	*Price on 12-31-81*	*Dividends Paid*
12-31-71	$20.19	$19.12	$5,576.48
12-31-76	$20.60	$19.12	$3,100.00

Purchase Date	*Cap. Gains (— Losses)*	*Total Return*	*Rate of Return*
12-31-71	$—527.72	$5,048.76	4.17%
12-31-76	$—716.02	$2,383.98	4.37%

* * *

AMSTAR CORP. (ASR). Founded 1966. Headquarters: 1251 Ave. of the Americas, New York NY 10020. **SUGAR.** Refines and markets sugar and related products; also makes industrial tools and equipment. 8,000 employees. **MAJOR SUBSIDIARIES, BRANDS:** Domino; Spreckels; Duff-Norton; Milwaukee Electric Tool.

Sales: $1,980.4 million (trend 11.7% a year).
Earnings: $72.28 million (trend 10.6% a year).
What happened to a $10,000 investment

Purchase Date	*Purchase Price*	*Price on 12-31-81*	*Dividends Paid*
12-31-71	$17.06	$25.87	$6,960.00
12-31-76	$23.25	$25.87	$2,984.09

Purchase Date	*Cap. Gains (— Losses)*	*Total Return*	*Rate of Return*
12-31-71	$5,164.84	$12,124.84	8.26%
12-31-76	$1,129.03	$ 4,113.12	7.13%

PROFILE: Buying this stock is like speculating in the commodities market. A couple of excerpts from financial magazines will give you the picture.

From *Business Week,* June 25, 1979: "Sugar's downturn has been long and steep. . . . The decline [from $.65 a pound in 1974 to $.15 in 1979] has had a devastating effect on Amstar. . . ."

From *Barron's,* November 10, 1980: "Among the so-called soft commodities, sugar has been this year's star performer. . . . The price of sugar has soared from 17 cents a pound last January to over 40 cents in the past month. . . . A chief beneficiary of this trend has been Amstar Corp. . . ."

As the song says, this door swings both ways. And while many sugar refiners and marketers have in recent years tried to diversify away from sugar to lessen the violent earnings swings associated with it, Amstar has not. It wouldn't be stretching the point too much to say that Amstar's attempts at diversification have been halfhearted. Its sidelines in industrial tools and equipment contributed only 14 percent of sales in fiscal 1980.

With violent earnings swings go violent price swings. Hardly a year goes by in which Amstar shares don't move up or down by at least 50 percent. In 1980, a good year for sugar prices, Amstar's share price more than doubled.

Clearly, if you can get on and off the roller coaster at the right moments, you can make money in this stock. But that's easier said than done. Weather and political variables are notorious for playing havoc with commodity prices.

* * *

AMSTED INDUSTRIES, INC. (AD). Founded 1968. Headquarters: 3700 Prudential Plaza, Chicago IL 60601. RAILROAD EQUIPMENT. Amsted Industries manufactures railroad components and construction products.

Sales: $837.1 million (trend 13.2% a year).
Earnings: $50.60 million (trend 13.0% a year).
What happened to a $10,000 investment

Purchase Date	*Purchase Price*	*Price on 12-31-81*	*Dividends Paid*
12-31-71	$ 9.56	$35.12	$13,301.96
12-31-76	$25.81	$35.12	$ 3,533.17

Purchase Date	*Cap. Gains (− Losses)*	*Total Return*	*Rate of Return*
12-31-71	$26,732.03	$40,033.99	17.47%
12-31-76	$ 3,607.75	$ 7,140.92	11.38%

* * *

ANALOG DEVICES, INC. (ADI). Founded 1965. Headquarters: Route 1, Industrial Park (PO Box 280), Norwood MA 02062. DATA SYSTEMS. Analog Devices produces components and subsystems for computerized control systems used in industrial automation and medical equipment.

Sales: $135.7 million (trend 35.3% a year).
Earnings: $9.44 million (trend 49.3% a year).
What happened to a $10,000 investment

Purchase Date	*Purchase Price*	*Price on 12-31-81*	*Dividends Paid*
12-31-71	$1.74	$17.50	$0.00
12-31-76	$3.25	$17.50	$0.00

Purchase Date	*Cap. Gains (− Losses)*	*Total Return*	*Rate of Return*
12-31-71	$90,418.69	$90,418.69	25.95%
12-31-76	$43,906.18	$43,906.18	40.06%

* * *

ANCHOR HOCKING CORP. (ARH). Founded 1928. Headquarters: 109 N. Broad St., Lancaster OH 43130. GLASS. Anchor Hocking Corp. produces glass tableware and glass products. MAJOR SUBSIDIARIES, BRANDS: Amerock Corp.; Phoenix Glass.

Sales: $857.5 million (trend 10.6% a year).
Earnings: $28.78 million (trend 6.0% a year).
What happened to a $10,000 investment

Purchase Date	*Purchase Price*	*Price on 12-31-81*	*Dividends Paid*
12-31-71	$20.75	$17.25	$4,681.12
12-31-76	$20.25	$17.25	$2,916.87

Purchase Date	*Cap. Gains (− Losses)*	*Total Return*	*Rate of Return*
12-31-71	$−1,686.75	$2,994.38	2.65%
12-31-76	$−1,481.48	$1,435.39	2.72%

* * *

ANDERSON, CLAYTON & CO. (AYL). Founded 1904. Headquarters: 1100 Louisiana, Houston TX 77002. FOODS. Anderson, Clayton is a major food processor and distributor of food products, cottonseed meal, and cottonseed oil. Also engages in warehousing, insurance, and manufacture of materials-handling equipment. 18,000 employees. MAJOR SUBSIDIARIES, BRANDS: Chiffon; Seven Seas; Igloo Corp.; Ranger Insurance Co.; American Founders Life Insurance Co.; Avoset Food Corp.

Sales: $1,929.6 million (trend 22.0% a year).
Earnings: $51.40 million (trend 9.1% a year).
What happened to a $10,000 investment

Purchase Date	*Purchase Price*	*Price on 12-31-81*	*Dividends Paid*
12-31-71	$10.88	$26.75	$6,843.75
12-31-76	$23.25	$26.75	$2,279.57

Purchase Date	*Cap. Gains (− Losses)*	*Total Return*	*Rate of Return*
12-31-71	$14,592.26	$21,436.02	12.14%
12-31-76	$ 1,505.38	$ 3,784.95	6.63%

PROFILE: Quiet, consistent, and a bit conservative. That's how Anderson, Clayton came through the 1970s.

Officers and directors, mainly members of the Clayton family, control an unusually large share (about 37 percent, as of 1981) of this company, which was once the giant of the cotton business and still does a big chunk of business in cottonseed processing. Processing of oilseeds (mainly cottonseeds) accounted for 36 percent of sales and about 22 percent of profits in fiscal 1980.

As Anderson, Clayton diversified out of cotton, starting in the 1950s, it went mainly into food processing. Sales of consumer foods (including Chiffon margarine, Seven Seas salad dressing, and imitation cheese products) accounted for 27 percent of sales recently.

The second wave of diversification was into insurance, which has recently accounted for about 15 percent of sales and profits.

While many companies have had to pay hefty interest charges on their debt loads, Anderson, Clayton has gone very light on debt (less than 10 percent of capital in fiscal 1978–80), and was able to add about $100 million of investment income to fiscal 1980 revenues. Even so, chairman T. J. Barlow has said he wants to take on more debt — perhaps up to about 30 percent of capital. The extra money would probably be used to finance another big acquisition. Having been rejected in the corporate singles bar by Gerber Products Co. and Stokely-Van Camp Inc., the company is generally believed to be still on the prowl.

About 40 percent of recent profits have come from Anderson, Clayton's extensive foreign operations, mainly in Mexico and Brazil.

* * *

ANGELICA CORP. (AGL). Founded 1968. Headquarters: 10176 Corporate Sq., St. Louis MO 63132. APPAREL. Angelica Corp. manufactures and distributes uniforms and protective clothing. MAJOR SUBSIDIARIES, BRANDS: Environmentals and Southern Service Co.; Life Uniform Shops.

Sales: $180.9 million (trend 12.3% a year).
Earnings: $8.96 million (trend 17.2% a year).
What happened to a $10,000 investment

Purchase Date	*Purchase Price*	*Price on 12-31-81*	*Dividends Paid*
12-31-71	$14.12	$22.50	$1,321.77
12-31-76	$ 6.87	$22.50	$1,869.09

Purchase Date	*Cap. Gains (− Losses)*	*Total Return*	*Rate of Return*
12-31-71	$ 5,929.20	$ 7,250.97	5.60%
12-31-76	$22,727.27	$24,596.36	28.18%

* * *

ANHEUSER-BUSCH COMPANIES, INC. (BUD). Founded 1925. Headquarters: 721 Pestalozzi St., St. Louis MO 63118. BEER. Anheuser-Busch is the country's biggest brewer; also has interests in the St. Louis Cardinals, theme parks, snack foods, real estate, and yeast and corn products. 17,000 employees. MAJOR SUBSIDIARIES, BRANDS: Budweiser, Busch, Classic Dark, Michelob, Michelob Light, Natural Light, and Wurzburger beers.

Sales: $3,295.4 million (trend 17.5% a year).
Earnings: $171.80 million (trend 20.7% a year).
What happened to a $10,000 investment

Purchase Date	*Purchase Price*	*Price on 12-31-81*	*Dividends Paid*
12-31-71	$56.25	$41.12	$1,360.00
12-31-76	$22.87	$41.12	$1,989.07

Purchase Date	*Cap. Gains (− Losses)*	*Total Return*	*Rate of Return*
12-31-71	$−2,688.89	$−1,328.89	−1.42%
12-31-76	$ 7,978.14	$ 9,967.21	14.83%

PROFILE: In the beer industry, the name of the game is market share. To borrow a term from basketball, the action gets pretty rough under the boards, and the elbows can be pretty sharp.

Anheuser-Busch, whose biggest brand is Budweiser, has long had the greatest part of this market. In the mid-1970s, Anheuser-Busch was losing market share to Philip Morris (Miller Beer), which was early to recognize the potential of light beer and also the appeal of having several brands on the shelves for consumers to choose from. It took Anheuser-Busch a while to learn those two lessons, but it learned them in spades and has been consolidating its position at the top of the industry since the late 1970s. Now both Anheuser-Busch and Philip Morris are gaining, and it's practically everybody else who's losing. Small brewers have been falling by the wayside for more than a decade now; they just can't compete with the big advertising dollars spent by the giants, and the total beer market isn't growing to speak of (about 3 percent a year).

Chairman August A. Busch III recognizes these trends. "The domestic beer business will one day become a cash cow," he has said, using the slang term for a high-volume but low-growth business. "We've got to make sure we provide the avenues for the other businesses to use the cash."

But what other businesses will those be? Though Busch says beer will account for only 70 percent of sales by 1990, it accounted for about 90 percent in 1980, and the company's diversification moves so far (into amusement parks and snack foods, for example) have been too tentative to give a clear picture of the company's future direction.

Meanwhile, the company is going full blast building new brewing capacity. To do so, it's borrowing heavily. Long-term debt was expected to equal 45 percent of capital by the end of 1981. In short, Anheuser-Busch is betting that it can keep on expanding its share (about 27 percent in 1981) of a beer market that isn't expanding.

* * *

ANIXTER BROS., INC. (ANX). Founded 1967. Headquarters: 4711 Golf Rd., Skokie IL 60076. ELECTRICAL PRODUCTS. Distributes electrical products to cable television and telephone industries. MAJOR SUBSIDIARIES, BRANDS: CATV.

Sales: $441.5 million (trend 24.7% a year).
Earnings: $18.93 million (trend 48.7% a year).
What happened to a $10,000 investment

Purchase Date	*Purchase Price*	*Price on 12-31-81*	*Dividends Paid*
12-31-71	$1.81	$15.62	$2,868.97
12-31-76	$1.81	$15.62	$2,386.21

Purchase Date	*Cap. Gains (− Losses)*	*Total Return*	*Rate of Return*
12-31-71	$76,206.90	$79,075.86	24.44%
12-31-76	$76,206.90	$78,593.10	54.70%

* * *

ANTA CORP. (ANA). Founded 1967. Headquarters: 101 N. Robinson, Oklahoma City OK 73102. ALUMINUM, HEALTH CARE, OIL. Anta is a relatively small conglomerate, which recently has derived most of its sales from aluminum manufacturing, although most of its profits from oil drilling. Also active in nursing-home operation. MAJOR SUBSIDIARIES, BRANDS: Bonray Drilling Corp. (oil and gas drilling); Four Seasons Nursing Centers; Nichols-Homeshield (aluminum).

* * *

ANTHONY INDUSTRIES, INC. (ANT). Founded 1959. Headquarters: 4900 Triggs St., City of Commerce, Los Angeles CA 90022. SWIMMING POOLS. Anthony Industries builds residential swimming pools, manufactures athletic apparel and fiberboard products. MAJOR SUBSIDIARIES, BRANDS: Hilton Athletic Apparel, Shakespeare Co., Simplex Industries.

Sales: $204.0 million (trend 21.0% a year).
Earnings: $3.16 million (trend 16.9% a year).
What happened to a $10,000 investment

Purchase Date	*Purchase Price*	*Price on 12-31-81*	*Dividends Paid*
12-31-71	$11.13	$6.75	$1,315.66
12-31-76	$ 5.02	$6.75	$2,916.68

Purchase Date	*Cap. Gains (− Losses)*	*Total Return*	*Rate of Return*
12-31-71	$−3,932.85	$−2,617.18	−2.99%
12-31-76	$ 3,450.21	$ 6,366.89	10.36%

* * *

APACHE CORP. (APA). Founded 1954. Headquarters: Foshay Tower, Minneapolis MN 55402. OIL. Apache Corp. is involved in oil and gas exploration and development.

Sales: $96.7 million (trend −11.3% a year).
Earnings: $17.21 million (trend 14.9% a year).
What happened to a $10,000 investment

Purchase Date	*Purchase Price*	*Price on 12-31-81*	*Dividends Paid*
12-31-71	$2.54	$19.50	$5,216.11
12-31-76	$3.67	$19.50	$2,542.53

Purchase Date	*Cap. Gains (− Losses)*	*Total Return*	*Rate of Return*
12-31-71	$66,912.74	$72,128.85	23.44%
12-31-76	$43,180.47	$45,723.00	41.00%

* * *

APACHE PETROLEUM CO. (APP). Founded 1980. Headquarters: Foshay Tower, Minneapolis MN 55402. OIL, GAS. Explores for and produces oil and natural gas. Company is structured as a limited partnership.

* * *

APPLIED MAGNETICS CORP. (APM). Founded 1957. Headquarters: 75 Robin Hill Rd., Goleta CA 93117. COMPUTER TAPE EQUIPMENT. Applied Magnetics is a leading maker of magnetic recording heads used with computer tape; also makes a variety of industrial equipment, particularly for assembly lines. The corporation has stated its intention to liquidate itself by selling off its subsidiaries and distributing the proceeds to shareholders; some parts of the corporation (notably Geo Space Corp.) have already been sold. MAJOR SUB-

SIDIARIES, BRANDS: Magnetic Head division; Key Electro Sonic division.

Sales: $73.9 million (trend 5.3% a year).
Earnings: $6.09 million (trend 34.0% a year).
What happened to a $10,000 investment

Purchase Date	*Purchase Price*	*Price on 12-31-81*	*Dividends Paid*
12-31-71	$11.14	$16.75	$0.00
12-31-76	$ 3.52	$16.75	$0.00

Purchase Date	*Cap. Gains (– Losses)*	*Total Return*	*Rate of Return*
12-31-71	$ 5,040.81	$ 5,040.81	4.17%
12-31-76	$37,548.36	$37,548.36	36.59%

* * *

ARCATA CORP. (ACA). Founded 1939. Headquarters: 2750 Sand Hill Rd., Menlo Park CA 94025. PRINTING, FOREST PRODUCTS. Arcata is the second largest U.S. printer. It has major sidelines in forest products and molded containers. 14,000 employees. MAJOR SUBSIDIARIES, BRANDS: Keyes Fibre Co., Chinet plastic tableware. In 1981, Arcata agreed in principle to be acquired by a new corporation to be set up by the investment banking firm Kohlberg, Kravis, Roberts & Co. However, as of early 1982 a merger agreement had not yet been approved by stockholders.

Sales: $763.0 million (trend 22.7% a year).
Earnings: $27.08 million (trend 19.1% a year).
What happened to a $10,000 investment

Purchase Date	*Purchase Price*	*Price on 12-31-81*	*Dividends Paid*
12-31-71	$19.37	$36.25	$3,140.65
12-31-76	$15.50	$36.25	$3,129.03

Purchase Date	*Cap. Gains (– Losses)*	*Total Return*	*Rate of Return*
12-31-71	$ 8,709.68	$11,850.32	8.13%
12-31-76	$13,387.10	$16,516.13	21.54%

PROFILE: Arcata's list of printing clients reads like a Who's Who of American publishing: Harlequin Enterprises, the *National Enquirer, Parade,* Pocket Books, *Reader's Digest, Sports Illustrated, Time, TV Guide, U.S. News & World Report,* Warner Books. Among printers, only R. R. Donnelly & Sons is larger.

Unfortunately, the printing business tends to be cyclical, and Arcata's other businesses — mainly forest products and molded containers (foam plastic and wood pulp) — tend to be even more so.

A long-term graph of Arcata's price action looks a bit like the trajectory of a yo-yo. From a 1974 low of $5 a share, the price climbed to $30 in 1980 — but it had been above $50 a share in the late 1960s. That's not all because of cyclicality. Arcata used to be Arcata Redwood Co. In the late 1960s, it lost more than half its redwood timberland to the National Park system. The company then branched out wildly in several directions — only to have its unsuccessful diversification efforts lopped off later like dead limbs. Now the company sticks mainly to printing (52 percent of fiscal 1980 profits) and forest products operations (29 percent of profits, though only 9 percent of sales). The molded containers business accounted for more than a quarter of sales in fiscal 1980, but less than a fifth of earnings.

One factor to watch is the steadily mounting debt load. Debt has marched up from about 13 percent of capital at the start of the 1970s to about 40 percent at the start of the 1980s. There's a lot of preferred stock out, too. Common stock is less than half of capital. That capital structure will tend to intensify any price movements — up or down.

In 1981, Arcata agreed to be acquired by a parent to be created for the purpose by Kohlberg, Kravis, Roberts & Co. (an investment banking organization). The tentative price was $37 a share, but the stock market apparently had some doubts whether the merger would go through, since the stock was trading a few dollars below that price.

* * *

ARCHER-DANIELS-MIDLAND CO. (ADM). Founded 1923. Headquarters: 4666 Faries Parkway, Decatur IL 62525. FOOD PROCESSING. Company is a leading processor of soybeans, corn, and other grains. 5,500 employees.

Sales: $3,647.5 million (trend 15.7% a year).
Earnings: $175.98 million (trend 21.7% a year).
What happened to a $10,000 investment

Purchase Date	*Purchase Price*	*Price on 12-31-81*	*Dividends Paid*
12-31-71	$ 2.91	$19.29	$3,399.11
12-31-76	$11.03	$19.29	$ 518.85

Purchase Date	*Cap. Gains (– Losses)*	*Total Return*	*Rate of Return*
12-31-71	$56,306.82	$59,705.93	21.43%
12-31-76	$ 7,477.34	$ 7,996.19	12.47%

PROFILE: What kind of hick would invest in a company that processes soybeans? Maybe the kind of hick who likes to see the price of a stock rise from about $4 a share in 1970 to about $40 a share in 1980.

There's a saying in the foods industry that profits rise as you get closer to the table. If that's true, Archer-Daniels-Midland should be in bad shape. It hardly sells anything to consumers; practically everything goes to other processors to be made ready for an end use as human or animal food. Yet the company's profits were rising at better than a 20 percent clip from 1975–80. If you peg inflation during that period at 10 percent, that means Archer-Daniels-Midland was enjoying 10 percent real growth, while the average big U.S. corporation had real growth of less than 4 percent.

Sales have grown more slowly than profits. The differential reflects the company's penny-pinching ways, which have paid off in the bottom line. Profit margins, traditionally low, have recently moved up to near the average for U.S. industry (about 5 percent), in large part as a result of high prices for corn sweeteners and success for the company's move into gasohol production.

In 1981 some analysts expected corn sweetener prices to weaken. (They'd risen in tandem with prices for a competitive commodity, sugar.) And the early 1981 price multiple was about 12 times the last year's earnings; analysts expected it to drop.

The multiple did fall—it was 7 in early 1982—and thereon hangs a moral. This is no hot stock, but it's a steady company. If you contemplate buying the stock, I suggest doing so at a time when the price / earnings ratio is no higher than the market multiple (i.e. the average p / e ratio for stocks as a group).

One other caveat: Don't buy this stock for dividends. The company prefers to plow profits back into the business.

* * *

ARIZONA PUBLIC SERVICE CO. (AZP). Founded 1920. Headquarters: 411 North Central Ave. (PO Box 21666), Phoenix AZ 85036. **UTILITY.** Arizona Public Service supplies electricity and natural gas to residents of Arizona.

Sales: $765.8 million (trend 16.9% a year).
Earnings: $118.23 million (trend 22.9% a year).
What happened to a $10,000 investment

Purchase Date	*Purchase Price*	*Price on 12-31-81*	*Dividends Paid*
12-31-71	$20.25	$19.37	$7,851.85
12-31-76	$19.62	$19.37	$4,820.38

Purchase Date	*Cap. Gains (– Losses)*	*Total Return*	*Rate of Return*
12-31-71	$–432.10	$7,419.75	5.71%
12-31-76	$–127.39	$4,692.99	8.00%

* * *

ARKANSAS BEST CORP. (AZB). Founded 1966. Headquarters: 1000 S. 21st St., Fort Smith AK 72902. **MOTOR CARRIER.** Arkansas Best Corp. is involved in interstate trucking; also furniture manufacturing. **MAJOR SUBSIDIARIES, BRANDS:** Container Carrier Corp.; Riverside Furniture Corp.

Sales: $340.5 million (trend 25.5% a year).
Earnings: $6.34 million (trend –1.0% a year).
What happened to a $10,000 investment

Purchase Date	*Purchase Price*	*Price on 12-31-81*	*Dividends Paid*
12-31-71	$22.98	$8.37	$1,930.90
12-31-76	$10.00	$8.37	$2,885.78

Purchase Date	*Cap. Gains (– Losses)*	*Total Return*	*Rate of Return*
12-31-71	$–6,355.31	$–4,424.41	–5.67%
12-31-76	$–1,625.01	$ 1,260.78	2.40%

* * *

ARKANSAS LOUISIANA GAS CO. (ALG). Founded 1928. Headquarters: Arkla Bldg. (PO Box 21734), Shreveport LA 71151. **NATURAL GAS.** Arkansas Louisiana Gas provides natural gas to residents of Arkansas, Louisiana, Texas, Kansas, and Oklahoma; also manufactures cement and air conditioners.

Sales: $974.5 million (trend 24.5% a year).
Earnings: $73.33 million (trend 13.0% a year).
What happened to a $10,000 investment

Purchase Date	*Purchase Price*	*Price on 12-31-81*	*Dividends Paid*
12-31-71	$4.52	$17.87	$9,895.03
12-31-76	$7.56	$17.87	$3,761.98

Purchase Date	Cap. Gains (− Losses)	Total Return	Rate of Return
12-31-71	$29,502.76	$39,397.79	17.32%
12-31-76	$13,636.36	$17,398.35	22.33%

* * *

ARLEN REALTY & DEVELOPMENT CORP. (ARE). Founded 1970. Headquarters: 888 Seventh Ave., New York NY 10019. **REAL ESTATE.** Arlen Realty is involved in the sale, management, and leasing of real estate.

Sales: $58.2 million (trend −46.5% a year).
Earnings: $8.53 million.
What happened to a $10,000 investment

Purchase Date	Purchase Price	Price on 12-31-81	Dividends Paid
12-31-71	$15.50	$1.12	$0.00
12-31-76	$ 3.37	$1.12	$0.00

Purchase Date	Cap. Gains (− Losses)	Total Return	Rate of Return
12-31-71	$−9,274.19	$−9,274.19	−23.07%
12-31-76	$−6,666.67	$−6,666.67	−19.73%

* * *

ARMADA CORP. (ABW). Founded 1926. Headquarters: 630 Buhl Bldg., Detroit MI 48226. **ELECTRICAL PRODUCTS.** Armada Corp. manufactures wire products. **MAJOR SUBSIDIARIES, BRANDS:** Hoskins Manufacturing Co.; Hoskins's Brookfield Wire Co.

Sales: $64.2 million (trend 12.0% a year).
Earnings: $.47 million (trend −1.6% a year).
What happened to a $10,000 investment

Purchase Date	Purchase Price	Price on 12-31-81	Dividends Paid
12-31-71	$8.25	$6.62	$0.00
12-31-76	$5.25	$6.62	$0.00

Purchase Date	Cap. Gains (− Losses)	Total Return	Rate of Return
12-31-71	$−1,969.70	$−1,969.70	−2.17%
12-31-76	$ 2,619.05	$ 2,619.05	4.76%

* * *

ARMCO INC. (AS). Founded 1917. Headquarters: 703 Curtis St., Middletown OH 45043. **STEEL.** Armco produces steel, oil field equipment, and fabricated metal products; it is moving into lending and insurance. 55,000 employees. **MAJOR SUBSIDIARIES, BRANDS:** Armco Finance Corp.; Ladish Co. (metal forging); NN Corp. (insurance).

Sales: $5,678.0 million (trend 14.5% a year).
Earnings: $259.20 million (trend 21.3% a year).
What happened to a $10,000 investment

Purchase Date	Purchase Price	Price on 12-31-81	Dividends Paid
12-31-71	$13.42	$28.25	$9,142.86
12-31-76	$21.67	$28.25	$3,323.08

Purchase Date	Cap. Gains (− Losses)	Total Return	Rate of Return
12-31-71	$11,055.90	$20,198.76	11.69%
12-31-76	$ 3,038.46	$ 6,361.54	10.35%

PROFILE: What a coincidence! Of the major steelmakers, Armco has been the most profitable in recent years. It has also gone furthest in diversifying away from steel.

At the start of the 1980s, Armco had reduced reliance on steel to the point where steel production accounted for less than two thirds of sales and only about half of profits. The biggest and most successful diversification move has been into oil field equipment, which lately has provided more than a quarter of profits. The newest push has been into finance and insurance. For years, Armco conducted lending operations (to other corporations) as a small sideline. Lately that's been expanded. In addition, in 1980 Armco acquired NN Corp., a property and casualty insurance company.

It would be no surprise if, by the end of the decade, steel accounted for less than half of Armco's revenues.

Armco boasts what is probably the strongest balance sheet of the major steel companies. Long-term debt was a trim 23 percent of capital at the start of 1980, down from about 34 percent ten years before.

Yet, what does it avail Armco to be in better shape than most steel companies? In the investment climate of the early 1980s, that's like being prettier than the town hag, or faster than a fellow on crutches. Even while topping its competitors in profitability, Armco has lagged well behind the average U.S. company in profit margins, profit growth, and return on equity.

* * *

THE ARMSTRONG RUBBER CO. (ARM). Founded 1912. Headquarters: 500 Sargent Dr., New Haven CT 06507. **TIRES.** The Armstrong Rubber Co. manufactures tires and inner tubes.

MAJOR SUBSIDIARIES, BRANDS: Arco Wheel; Richmond Converters, Inc.

Sales: $560.5 million (trend 8.8% a year).
Earnings: $16.09 million (trend 9.4% a year).
What happened to a $10,000 investment

Purchase Date	*Purchase Price*	*Price on 12-31-81*	*Dividends Paid*
12-31-71	$40.50	$32.75	$2,950.62
12-31-76	$20.75	$32.75	$2,867.47

Purchase Date	*Cap. Gains (– Losses)*	*Total Return*	*Rate of Return*
12-31-71	$–1,913.58	$1,037.04	.99%
12-31-76	$ 5,783.13	$8,650.60	13.28%

* * *

ARMSTRONG WORLD INDUSTRIES, INC. (ACK). Founded 1860. Headquarters: Liberty St., Lancaster PA 17604. **FURNISHINGS.** Armstrong is a major manufacturer of flooring, carpeting, furniture, and ceiling materials; also makes insulation, adhesives, and textiles. 22,000 employees. **MAJOR SUBSIDIARIES, BRANDS:** Thomasville furniture; Armstrong flooring; Evans-Black carpet.

Sales: $1,323.0 million (trend 9.7% a year).
Earnings: $48.12 million (trend 8.3% a year).
What happened to a $10,000 investment

Purchase Date	*Purchase Price*	*Price on 12-31-81*	*Dividends Paid*
12-31-71	$43.25	$16.75	$2,204.62
12-31-76	$27.50	$16.75	$1,918.18

Purchase Date	*Cap. Gains (– Losses)*	*Total Return*	*Rate of Return*
12-31-71	$–6,127.17	$–3,922.54	–4.86%
12-31-76	$–3,909.09	$–1,990.91	–4.34%

PROFILE: In case you wonder why the ticker symbol is ACK, the company used to be Armstrong Cork. But "ack" could also be the sound many investors have made as they've watched these shares slide from a 1971 high of more than $45 to a recent price of less than $17.

Earnings in dollars not adjusted for inflation peaked at $2.58 in 1979. It's not surprising that 1980 earnings were down (to $1.94), with the housing industry in a slump. But Armstrong's slide predates the recent housing slump and also predates the stock market debacle of 1974. The shares have been gradually declining for years, mainly because the company is in a fairly mature industry, has experienced slow earnings growth (struggling to keep pace with inflation), and faces lots of competition both from domestic manufacturers and from abroad. Profit margins, 6 to 7 percent at the beginning of the 1970s, have fallen into the 3-to-5 percent range lately. Return on equity has played ring-around-the-rosy with an uninspiring benchmark of 10 percent. The balance sheet has stayed strong, though, with long-term debt recently less than 15 percent of equity. The company also offers an above-average dividend yield, recently more than 7 percent. Dividends have been paid each year since 1934.

* * *

ARO CORP. (ARO). Founded 1965. Headquarters: 1 Aro Center, Bryan OH 43506. **INSTRUMENTS.** Aro is a leading maker of portable hydraulic and pneumatic tools. Among its products are oxygen systems for aerospace use and air-powered pumps used in paint spraying and other applications.

Sales: $84.9 million (trend 13.5% a year).
Earnings: $4.95 million (trend 13.0% a year).
What happened to a $10,000 investment

Purchase Date	*Purchase Price*	*Price on 12-31-81*	*Dividends Paid*
12-31-71	$12.23	$15.75	$6,156.62
12-31-76	$13.62	$15.75	$3,148.08

Purchase Date	*Cap. Gains (– Losses)*	*Total Return*	*Rate of Return*
12-31-71	$2,876.17	$9,032.79	6.65%
12-31-76	$1,565.90	$4,713.98	8.03%

* * *

ARROW ELECTRONICS (ARW). Founded 1946. Headquarters: 600 Steamboat Rd., Greenwich CT 06830. **ELECTRONIC PARTS.** Arrow Electronics distributes electrical and electronic components. **MAJOR SUBSIDIARIES, BRANDS:** Schuylkill Metals Corp.

Sales: $352.3 million (trend 34.1% a year).
Earnings: $8.02 million (trend 49.6% a year).
What happened to a $10,000 investment

Purchase Date	*Purchase Price*	*Price on 12-31-81*	*Dividends Paid*
12-31-71	$3.51	$16.25	$1,434.80
12-31-76	$1.81	$16.25	$2,787.61

Purchase Date	*Cap. Gains (− Losses)*	*Total Return*	*Rate of Return*
12-31-71	$36,264.65	$37,699.45	16.91%
12-31-76	$79,885.61	$82,673.22	56.10%

* * *

ARTRA GROUP, INC. (ATA). Founded 1933. Headquarters: 500 Central Ave., Northfield IL 60093. **PLASTICS, METALS.** ARTRA Group, Inc. manufactures plastic and metal machinery. **MAJOR SUBSIDIARIES, BRANDS:** Harvel Industries Corp.; Mueller Engineering and Manufacturing; Rhodes Plastics Corp.

Sales: $71.2 million (trend 15.4% a year).
Earnings: $−.45 million.
What happened to a $10,000 investment

Purchase Date	*Purchase Price*	*Price on 12-31-81*	*Dividends Paid*
12-31-71	$ 9.25	$23.87	$1,135.14
12-31-76	$13.25	$23.87	$ 637.74

Purchase Date	*Cap. Gains (− Losses)*	*Total Return*	*Rate of Return*
12-31-71	$15,810.81	$16,945.95	10.42%
12-31-76	$ 8,018.87	$ 8,656.60	13.28%

* * *

ARVIN INDUSTRIES, INC. (ARV). Founded 1919. Headquarters: 1531 13th St., Columbus IN 47201. **AUTO PARTS.** Arvin Industries, Inc. manufactures auto parts, metal coatings, and consumer products. **MAJOR SUBSIDIARIES, BRANDS:** Calspan Corp.; Roll Coater, Inc.

Sales: $428.8 million (trend 5.4% a year).
Earnings: $6.04 million (trend 1.3% a year).
What happened to a $10,000 investment

Purchase Date	*Purchase Price*	*Price on 12-31-81*	*Dividends Paid*
12-31-71	$16.63	$14.87	$4,369.52
12-31-76	$16.75	$14.87	$3,032.84

Purchase Date	*Cap. Gains (− Losses)*	*Total Return*	*Rate of Return*
12-31-71	$−1,053.29	$3,316.23	2.91%
12-31-76	$−1,119.40	$1,913.43	3.56%

* * *

ASARCO INC. (AR). Founded 1899. Headquarters: 120 Broadway, New York NY 10271. **MINING, SMELTING.** ASARCO is the largest U.S. metals smelter and a major mining company producing copper, silver, lead, zinc, gold, and other minerals. 12,000 employees. **MAJOR SUBSIDIARIES, BRANDS:** Owns fractions (from 33 to 52 percent) of Revere Copper & Brass (U.S.); M.I.M. Holdings Ltd. (Australia); Mexico Desarrollo Industrial Minero, S.A. (Mexico); Southern Peru Copper Corp. (Peru). M.I.M. Holdings owns roughly 12 percent of ASARCO.

Sales: $1,817.0 million (trend 13.5% a year).
Earnings: $216.47 million (trend 57.7% a year).
What happened to a $10,000 investment

Purchase Date	*Purchase Price*	*Price on 12-31-81*	*Dividends Paid*
12-31-71	$19.75	$25.75	$5,683.54
12-31-76	$16.75	$25.75	$3,373.13

Purchase Date	*Cap. Gains (− Losses)*	*Total Return*	*Rate of Return*
12-31-71	$3,037.97	$8,721.52	6.47%
12-31-76	$5,373.13	$8,746.27	13.39%

PROFILE: When you invest in a mining company, you can be sure of one thing: You'll have good years and bad years. Need proof? Look at ASARCO's earnings — better than $4 a share in 1973 and 1974, less than $2 the next four years (including a loss in 1977), and better than $8 in 1979 and 1980.

The stock, like the company, has its ups and downs. In 1980, to take one of many possible sample years, the high was $58.50, the low, $25.50. There are plenty of years in which the yearly high is at least double the low.

Clearly, then, this is a stock to be purchased when it's out of favor. Usually that means a time when the price of copper or silver (two of ASARCO's chief products) is down. Better yet, for buying in, is a time when both are down — such as 1981, when this book was written. Of course such years, while buyers' delights, make for poor sleeping in people who already own the stock.

Even dividend payments go up and down here, though dividends have been paid each year since 1936. The yield recently has been moderate. The balance sheet is in good shape with debt recently pared to below 20 percent of total capital.

ASARCO is the largest mining company that remains independent; many of the others have been snapped up by oil companies or conglomerates. It is the subject of periodic take-over rumors and occasional actual take-over attempts. None have succeeded to date, but this dimension adds further volatility to the stock.

* * *

ASHLAND OIL, INC. (ASH). Founded 1936. Headquarters: 1401 Winchester Ave., Ashland KY 41101. **OIL REFINER AND MARKETER.** Ashland refines and sells petroleum products (mainly to independent dealers); also is involved in highway construction, coal mining, and chemical production. 25,000 employees. **MAJOR SUBSIDIARIES, BRANDS:** Integon Life Insurance Co.; U.S. Filter Corp.

Sales: $9,262.1 million (trend 18.4% a year).
Earnings: $58.76 million (trend −6.5% a year).
What happened to a $10,000 investment

Purchase Date	*Purchase Price*	*Price on 12-31-81*	*Dividends Paid*
12-31-71	$15.83	$31.25	$8,600.00
12-31-76	$23.00	$31.25	$3,913.04

Purchase Date	*Cap. Gains (− Losses)*	*Total Return*	*Rate of Return*
12-31-71	$9,736.84	$18,336.84	10.98%
12-31-76	$3,586.96	$ 7,500.00	11.84%

PROFILE: Ashland's not terribly well known, and it's only about the seventeenth-largest oil company. Yet it's among the fifty or so largest corporations in the United States.

Ashland made a historic decision in the late 1970s, electing to become a refiner and seller of petroleum products, but not a producer of them. Selling off its production facilities netted Ashland about half a billion dollars, which it has used to trim the balance sheet a bit and to finance acquisitions. Truth to tell, Ashland had never produced more than about 20 percent of its own crude anyway. And it had no appetite to continue the kind of tremendous capital expenditures involved in playing the petroleum production ballgame these days.

Road building and chemicals are important sidelines to Ashland; they've contributed about a quarter of sales and earnings in recent years. Both are cyclical, and both were down in the recession of 1980–81.

A more serious concern is whether Ashland is caught between a rock and a hard place in petroleum refining. As everyone knows, crude is expensive to buy. (Ashland's selling of its own production operations only made this problem worse, of course.) Yet there's competition at the gas pump that recently has tended to keep prices for refined products down. If you plan to buy the stock, check the latest trend for profit margins.

* * *

ASSOCIATED DRY GOODS CORP. (DG). Founded 1916. Headquarters: 417 Fifth Ave., New York NY 10016. **RETAILING.** Owns and operates department stores and specialty stores specializing in women's clothing and home furnishings for the upper-income market. 50,000 employees. **MAJOR SUBSIDIARIES, BRANDS:** Lord & Taylor; L. S. Ayres; Denver Dry Goods; The Diamond; Goldwaters; Hahne & Co.; Joseph Horne; H & S Pogue; Powers Dry Goods; J. W. Robinson; Robinson's of Florida; Sibley, Lindsay & Curr; Stewart & Co.; Stewart Dry Goods; Stix, Baer & Fuller.

Sales: $1,952.2 million (trend 6.6% a year).
Earnings: $52.21 million (trend 2.9% a year).
What happened to a $10,000 investment

Purchase Date	*Purchase Price*	*Price on 12-31-81*	*Dividends Paid*
12-31-71	$58.25	$24.50	$2,218.20
12-31-76	$33.12	$24.50	$1,826.42

Purchase Date	*Cap. Gains (− Losses)*	*Total Return*	*Rate of Return*
12-31-71	$−5,793.99	$−3,575.79	−4.33%
12-31-76	$−2,603.77	$ −777.36	−1.61%

PROFILE: How are the mighty fallen. The stores that make up the Associated Dry Goods family used to be sales and profit leaders in their cities. Now most of them are also-rans. And even though these stores generally aim at the upper-income buyer, their profit margin (about 2.6 percent in 1980) is no better than average for a department-store chain.

The flagship store is Lord & Taylor, which was highly innovative and profitable under the leadership of Dorothy Shavers from the late 1920s through the late 1950s. Her successors have not displayed Shavers's flair for leadership or profitability. Even so, Associated would be tickled pink if most of its stores were doing as well as Lord & Taylor.

In the late 1970s, the chain's profits were flat (which means they were declining in real terms, after inflation) and sales were rising no faster than inflation. The stock, which had sold as high as $60 a share in 1968, had declined steadily for more than a decade. Even in 1974, a terrible year for the stock market, Associated Dry Goods sold as high as $30. In the early 1980s the price was hovering close to $20.

If you buy this stock, you're buying it for the rebound (and for dividends, which have yielded above passbook rates in recent years). The company, whose balance sheet is still strong, may decide to sell off some of its less profitable divisions and pour money into restoring luster to the better ones.

* * *

ATHLONE INDUSTRIES, INC. (ATH). Founded 1966. Headquarters: 200 Webro Rd., Parsippany NJ 07054. **SPECIALTY METALS.** Athlone Industries, Inc. manufactures stainless tool and alloy steels, industrial fasteners, and consumer products. **MAJOR SUBSIDIARIES, BRANDS:** Green River Steel Corp.; Jessop Steel Co.

Sales: $282.7 million (trend 5.2% a year).
Earnings: $10.40 million (trend .1% a year).
What happened to a $10,000 investment

Purchase Date	*Purchase Price*	*Price on 12-31-81*	*Dividends Paid*
12-31-71	$ 4.42	$28.62	$17,049.13
12-31-76	$14.25	$28.62	$ 4,140.35

Purchase Date	*Cap. Gains (– Losses)*	*Total Return*	*Rate of Return*
12-31-71	$54,811.32	$71,860.45	23.40%
12-31-76	$10,087.72	$14,228.07	19.36%

* * *

ATLANTIC CITY ELECTRIC CO. (ATE). Founded 1907. Headquarters: 1600 Pacific Ave., Atlantic City NJ 08404. **ELECTRICITY.** Provides electricity to southern New Jersey.

Sales: $358.4 million (trend 11.8% a year).
Earnings: $32.38 million (trend 6.4% a year).
What happened to a $10,000 investment

Purchase Date	*Purchase Price*	*Price on 12-31-81*	*Dividends Paid*
12-31-71	$22.25	$17.25	$7,473.08
12-31-76	$23.75	$17.25	$3,840.00

Purchase Date	*Cap. Gains (– Losses)*	*Total Return*	*Rate of Return*
12-31-71	$–2,247.19	$5,225.89	4.29%
12-31-76	$–2,736.84	$1,103.16	2.11%

* * *

ATLANTIC RICHFIELD CO. (ARC). Founded 1970. Headquarters: 515 S. Flower St., Los Angeles CA 90071. **OIL.** Explores for, produces, refines, and sells petroleum products; also produces chemicals and minerals. 52,000 employees. **MAJOR SUBSIDIARIES, BRANDS:** Arco; Anaconda Co.

Sales: $23,744.3 million (trend 25.5% a year).
Earnings: $1,650.12 million (trend 33.2% a year).
What happened to a $10,000 investment

Purchase Date	*Purchase Price*	*Price on 12-31-81*	*Dividends Paid*
12-31-71	$18.06	$46.87	$5,757.79
12-31-76	$28.87	$46.87	$2,597.40

Purchase Date	*Cap. Gains (– Losses)*	*Total Return*	*Rate of Return*
12-31-71	$15,951.56	$21,709.34	12.23%
12-31-76	$ 6,233.77	$ 8,831.17	13.49%

PROFILE: If you had to sum up Atlantic Richfield in two words, the two best would probably be "domestic oil." Among major oil producers, only Standard Oil Co. of Ohio is less dependent on foreign sources than Atlantic Richfield is. More than 90 percent of Atlantic Richfield's production comes from the United States, much of it from Alaska, where the company was the first to strike oil in Prudhoe Bay.

However, another two-word phrase also applies: "Full blast." Atlantic Richfield is pouring money into a dramatic five-year effort to expand its production. From 1980 through 1984 it expects to spend no less than $20 billion in the expansion effort, of which $4 billion is aimed at exploration.

That massive effort will probably tend to keep dividends down, but dividends have traditionally been modest here anyway. Capital gains is what buyers of this stock were always after, and in the late 1970s, it's what they got. Oil stocks in general moved up strongly, and Atlantic Richfield stock more than doubled, because its supplies were in the politically secure United States, not in the high-risk Middle East or even in medium-risk areas like Canada or Latin America.

Yet, despite the big run-up, Atlantic Richfield still sold in the early 1980s for a price earnings multiple only moderately higher than the stock market as a whole. If you think OPEC will tighten the screws on the United States in the coming years, and you don't mind the debt Atlantic Richfield is taking on in its expansion program, you may want to keep an eye on this stock and buy it during a price dip.

* * *

ATLAS CORP. (AZ). Founded 1929. Headquarters: 353 Nassau St., Princeton NJ 08540. **URA-**

NIUM. Atlas is a major producer of uranium. It has sidelines in plastics, shoe parts, and construction. **MAJOR SUBSIDIARIES, BRANDS:** Brockton Sole & Plastics; Camden Lime; Global Associates (55 percent owned); Western Sky Industries.

Sales: $94.1 million (trend 11.7% a year).
Earnings: $7.85 million (trend −2.5% a year).
What happened to a $10,000 investment

Purchase Date	*Purchase Price*	*Price on 12-31-81*	*Dividends Paid*
12-31-71	$11.25	$19.37	$0.00
12-31-76	$19.38	$19.37	$0.00

Purchase Date	*Cap. Gains (− Losses)*	*Total Return*	*Rate of Return*
12-31-71	$7,222.22	$7,222.22	5.59%
12-31-76	$ .00	$ .00	.00%

* * *

AUGAT, INC. (AUG). Founded 1936. Headquarters: 33 Perre Ave., PO Box 799, Attleboro MA 02703. **ELECTRONICS.** Augat, Inc. manufactures electromechanical components and provides related services for the electronics industry. **MAJOR SUBSIDIARIES, BRANDS:** Alco Electronic Products, Inc.; Isotronics Inc.; LRC Electronics Inc.

Sales: $157.3 million (trend 43.9% a year).
Earnings: $18.01 million (trend 47.3% a year).
What happened to a $10,000 investment

Purchase Date	*Purchase Price*	*Price on 12-31-81*	*Dividends Paid*
12-31-71	$6.43	$25.25	$2,094.23
12-31-76	$5.07	$25.25	$2,224.61

Purchase Date	*Cap. Gains (− Losses)*	*Total Return*	*Rate of Return*
12-31-71	$29,271.31	$31,365.54	15.26%
12-31-76	$39,835.53	$42,060.13	39.09%

* * *

AUTOMATIC DATA PROCESSING, INC. (AUD). Founded 1961. Headquarters: 405 Route 3, Clifton NJ 07015. **DATA PROCESSING.** Automatic Data Processing, Inc. provides data processing services such as payroll and financial statement preparation.

Sales: $558.4 million (trend 23.9% a year).
Earnings: $47.36 million (trend 21.3% a year).
What happened to a $10,000 investment

Purchase Date	*Purchase Price*	*Price on 12-31-81*	*Dividends Paid*
12-31-71	$18.41	$25.12	$836.67
12-31-76	$14.81	$25.12	$918.14

Purchase Date	*Cap. Gains (− Losses)*	*Total Return*	*Rate of Return*
12-31-71	$3,650.25	$4,486.93	3.78%
12-31-76	$6,962.03	$7,880.17	12.32%

* * *

AVCO CORP. (AV). Founded 1929. Headquarters: 1275 King St., Greenwich CT 06830. **CONGLOMERATE.** Avco is involved chiefly in consumer loans, insurance, and the manufacture of transportation equipment such as tank and aircraft engines. It also has operations in several other areas, including electronics, weapons systems, movies, food service, and farm equipment. 27,000 employees. **MAJOR SUBSIDIARIES, BRANDS:** Avco Financial Services; Paul Revere insurance companies; Lycoming Stratford engines.

Sales: $2,149.9 million (trend 32.5% a year).
Earnings: $104.04 million (trend 46.1% a year).
What happened to a $10,000 investment

Purchase Date	*Purchase Price*	*Price on 12-31-81*	*Dividends Paid*
12-31-71	$16.25	$20.12	$2,646.15
12-31-76	$13.25	$20.12	$3,245.28

Purchase Date	*Cap. Gains (− Losses)*	*Total Return*	*Rate of Return*
12-31-71	$2,384.62	$5,030.77	4.16%
12-31-76	$5,188.68	$8,433.96	13.01%

PROFILE: As befits a conglomerate built around a loan company, Avco is the most in debt of all major conglomerates. In the early 1980s, debt was a staggering 72 percent of total capital. There was also a bit of preferred stock hanging around, so that common stock accounted for only 24 percent of capital.

If you're a speculator looking for a "leveraged play" on a diverse set of operations, this stock may ring your chimes. If you're a risk-averse or middle-of-the-road investor, stay away.

Forbes magazine's "Annual Report on American Industry for 1980" (published in 1981) provides a dramatic example of the effect of Avco's leverage. Avco's return on total capital for the preceding five years was 7.9 percent, which ranked thirty-third among the forty-five conglomerates analyzed. Yet the return on stockholders' equity was 17.2 percent, which was good enough to rank fourth among the conglomerates.

The short-term outlook for Avco in the early 1980s was pretty bright: Falling interest rates could help the loan business, and increased defense spending could help aircraft parts, aircraft engines, and tank engines. (Avco supplies the engines for the XM-1 tank, built by Chrysler Defense Inc., which is being taken over by General Dynamics.)

Yet leverage remains a two-edged sword. If the outlook sours, the stock could fall further than most. Long-term shareholders will never forget the precipitous decline from $65 a share in the late 1960s to $2 a share in 1974. Avco's come a long way back since, and the company, under chairman James Kerr, is better managed than it was in its go-go willy-nilly acquisition days. Still, it's not a vehicle for the fainthearted or even the cautious.

* * *

AVERY INTERNATIONAL CORP. (AVY). Founded 1977. Headquarters: 415 Huntington Dr., San Marino CA 91108. **LABELS.** Avery International Corp. manufactures labels and labeling systems.

Sales: $618.7 million (trend 16.6% a year).
Earnings: $24.54 million (trend 32.5% a year).
What happened to a $10,000 investment

Purchase Date	*Purchase Price*	*Price on 12-31-81*	*Dividends Paid*
12-31-71	$27.62	$27.75	$1,607.24
12-31-76	$21.75	$27.75	$1,360.92

Purchase Date	*Cap. Gains (− Losses)*	*Total Return*	*Rate of Return*
12-31-71	$ 45.25	$1,652.49	1.54%
12-31-76	$2,758.62	$4,119.54	7.14%

* * *

AVNET, INC. (AVT). Founded 1955. Headquarters: 767 Fifth Ave., New York NY 10153. **ELECTRONICS DISTRIBUTION.** Avnet is the largest U.S. distributor of electrical and electronic components, particularly semiconductors. Also makes consumer electronics products and musical instruments. 12,000 employees. **MAJOR SUBSIDIARIES, BRANDS:** BIC / Avnet (stereo equipment); Channel Master (stereo and TV equipment); Guild Musical Instruments; Meisel Music Co.

Sales: $1,316.2 million (trend 17.7% a year).
Earnings: $68.00 million (trend 17.0% a year).
What happened to a $10,000 investment

Purchase Date	*Purchase Price*	*Price on 12-31-81*	*Dividends Paid*
12-31-71	$10.45	$46.12	$4,921.65
12-31-76	$16.02	$46.12	$2,226.89

Purchase Date	*Cap. Gains (− Losses)*	*Total Return*	*Rate of Return*
12-31-71	$34,119.54	$39,041.19	17.23%
12-31-76	$18,787.22	$21,014.11	25.40%

PROFILE: When the semiconductor business was hot, Avnet's growth rate was smoking. Sales grew from less than $300 million to more than $1 billion between 1971 and 1979. As the leading distributor of electronics components equipment, particularly semiconductors, Avnet could ride the wave.

In the past couple of years, with the semiconductor business only lukewarm, the company's mettle has been tested. It's come through pretty well. Earnings dropped off a bit in fiscal 1981, and return on equity was down too — but not too far. Meantime, the company in the past few years has trimmed its debt substantially — from about 40 percent of capital back in 1974 to about 11 percent recently.

Due to its favorable growth history, Avnet recently has commanded a price / earnings ratio above that of the average stock. For example, it was 11 in late 1981, when the average p / e was about 8. The p / e tends to be volatile, though. Avnet sold for as little as two times earnings in 1974, and as little as 5 times earnings in parts of 1980. Dividends have been paid yearly since 1961, but the yield is small.

In 1981, Avnet shed its wire-and-cable business (Carol Cable Co.) to concentrate on distribution and consumer electronics.

* * *

AVON PRODUCTS, INC. (AVP). Founded 1916. Headquarters: 9 W. 57th St., New York NY 10019. **COSMETICS.** Avon is the world's largest manufacturer of cosmetics, which it sells door-to-door along with costume jewelry. 34,000 employees; about 1 million door-to-door sales representatives. **MAJOR SUBSIDIARIES, BRANDS:** Tiffany & Co.; Geni; Avon Fashions. Merger pending with Mallinckrodt, Inc. (health care products, fragrances, specialty chemicals, and flavorings).

Sales: $2,569.1 million (trend 15.8% a year).
Earnings: $241.30 million (trend 12.5% a year).
What happened to a $10,000 investment

Purchase Date	*Purchase Price*	*Price on 12-31-81*	*Dividends Paid*
12-31-71	$100.37	$30.25	$2,091.16
12-31-76	$ 49.50	$30.25	$2,717.17

Purchase Date	*Cap. Gains (— Losses)*	*Total Return*	*Rate of Return*
12-31-71	$−6,986.30	$−4,895.14	−6.50%
12-31-76	$−3,888.89	$−1,171.72	−2.46%

PROFILE: You might not go so far as to say that the Avon lady has gotten dowdy. But this is a far different sort of stock than it once was.

In the 1960s and early 1970s what it was was a hot stock, with all the trimmings: skimpy dividends, fast growth, and a towering p / e ratio (over 50 in 1968–69 and in 1971–72). All that has changed. Avon's growth has slowed to a walk — though the company is trying to rekindle the old fire by going into foreign markets like Latin America. And all of a sudden, this is an income stock. Believe it or not, Avon was yielding close to 9 percent in dividends in early 1981. The price / earnings ratio started the 1980s in unfamiliar single-digit territory.

In short, Avon stock is now valued much more conservatively than it was and represents a much better buy. At recent yield levels, you need only modest capital appreciation to achieve a good total return.

Has Avon saturated the door-to-door cosmetics market? Probably not: The mild earnings downturn of the early 1980s can be attributed mainly to recession. Nevertheless, analysts don't figure that Avon's sales will continue to grow as they used to. Indeed, while Avon has stayed on top of the cosmetics industry in profitability, its sales and growth rates have been below the industry averages in recent years.

The company is probably ripe to diversify, and the 1979 acquisition of Tiffany & Co. may be the first in a string of diversification moves. Avon's balance sheet is in perfect shape to allow an ambitious acquisition program — the company has practically no debt at all.

* * *

AXIA INC. (AX). Founded 1891. Headquarters: 122 W. 22nd St., Oak Brook IL 60521. **TOOLS.** Axia (formerly Bliss & Laughlin Industries Inc.) manufactures construction tools and metal products. **MAJOR SUBSIDIARIES, BRANDS:** Ames Taping Tool Systems; BLK Steel Inc.; Goldblatt Tool Co.; Jensen Tools Inc.

Sales: $256.6 million (trend 14.2% a year).
Earnings: $18.51 million (trend 16.0% a year).
What happened to a $10,000 investment

Purchase Date	*Purchase Price*	*Price on 12-31-81*	*Dividends Paid*
12-31-71	$8.18	$18.75	$8,053.90
12-31-76	$9.53	$18.75	$4,448.07

Purchase Date	*Cap. Gains (— Losses)*	*Total Return*	*Rate of Return*
12-31-71	$12,916.63	$20,970.54	11.97%
12-31-76	$ 9,667.82	$14,115.90	19.25%

* * *

AYDIN CORP. (AYD). Founded 1967. Headquarters: 401 Commerce Dr., Fort Washington PA 19034. **MICROWAVE AND DATA COMMUNICATIONS.** Aydin Corp. manufactures microwave and data communications products such as satellite–earth communications equipment.

Sales: $102.9 million (trend 20.4% a year).
Earnings: $7.32 million (trend 42.8% a year).
What happened to a $10,000 investment

Purchase Date	*Purchase Price*	*Price on 12-31-81*	*Dividends Paid*
12-31-71	$ .42	$25.75	$0.00
12-31-76	$5.00	$25.75	$0.00

Purchase Date	*Cap. Gains (— Losses)*	*Total Return*	*Rate of Return*
12-31-71	$608,000.00	$608,000.00	51.04%
12-31-76	$ 41,500.00	$ 41,500.00	38.79%

B

BT MORTGAGE INVESTORS (BTM). Founded 1970. Headquarters: 1100 Franklin Ave., Garden City NY 11530. **MORTGAGE INVESTMENTS.** BT Mortgage Investors engages in long-term mortgage lending.

Sales: $6.5 million (trend −.1% a year).
Earnings: $−1.69 million.
What happened to a $10,000 investment

Purchase Date	*Purchase Price*	*Price on 12-31-81*	*Dividends Paid*
12-31-71	$25.62	$1.25	$2,796.10
12-31-76	$ 2.50	$1.25	$ 0.00

Purchase Date	*Cap. Gains (– Losses)*	*Total Return*	*Rate of Return*
12-31-71	$–9,512.20	$–6,716.10	–10.54%
12-31-76	$–5,000.00	$–5,000.00	–12.94%

* * *

BAIRNCO CORP. (BZ). Founded 1981. Headquarters: 200 Park Ave., New York NY 10017. **BEARINGS, LIGHTING.** Bairnco is a newly minted parent to Keene Corp., which has interests in bearings, lighting, filters, and other industrial products. Besides serving as a holding company for Keene, which created it, Bairnco is expected to make acquisitions, and possibly later spin some of these acquisitions off to stockholders. A tender offer has been made to stockholders of Lightolier Inc.

Sales: $210.1 million (trend 10.4% a year).
Earnings: $12.01 million (trend 24.7% a year).
What happened to a $10,000 investment

Purchase Date	*Purchase Price*	*Price on 12-31-81*	*Dividends Paid*
12-31-71	$5.44	$16.75	$3,034.48
12-31-76	$5.44	$16.75	$2,344.83

Purchase Date	*Cap. Gains (– Losses)*	*Total Return*	*Rate of Return*
12-31-71	$20,804.60	$23,839.08	12.96%
12-31-76	$20,804.60	$23,149.43	27.09%

* * *

BAKER INTERNATIONAL CORP. (BKO). Founded 1913. Headquarters: 500 City Parkway W., Orange CA 92668. **OIL DRILLING.** Provides oil field products and services to companies engaged in petroleum production. 19,000 employees. **MAJOR SUBSIDIARIES, BRANDS:** Reed Tool; Milchem.

Sales: $2,140.0 million (trend 30.6% a year).
Earnings: $224.99 million (trend 34.5% a year).
What happened to a $10,000 investment

Purchase Date	*Purchase Price*	*Price on 12-31-81*	*Dividends Paid*
12-31-71	$ 5.55	$38.25	$3,457.89
12-31-76	$11.31	$38.25	$1,270.72

Purchase Date	*Cap. Gains (– Losses)*	*Total Return*	*Rate of Return*
12-31-71	$58,957.75	$62,415.64	21.89%
12-31-76	$23,812.15	$25,082.87	28.53%

PROFILE: "We staked our careers on the price of crude going up in the early 1970s," chairman E. H. Clark told *Fortune* at the end of the decade. He guessed right, acquiring a collection of oil field service and products companies just in time for an OPEC-served feast. He guessed right again in the mid-1970s, pushing ahead with a major expansion in time for oil and gas price decontrol under the Carter and Reagan administrations. In fact, Clark's guesses have been so good that they deserve a better name — how about a shrewd sense of timing?

Baker International's reward has been to lead the oil field equipment pack in growth of both sales and profits during recent years. That's quite a pack to lead. And it was Baker, not its larger rivals (like Schlumberger, Halliburton, and Dresser Industries) that had the honor of providing the highest total return of any Fortune 500 company during the 1970s — about 20 percent a year. Had you put $10,000 into Baker International stock at the start of the decade, you would have had more than $61,000 at the start of the 1980s. Then, in 1980, you would have come close to doubling your money again.

How long can Baker keep this up? Probably for a good while. The company had racked up fourteen consecutive record years going into 1981. However, high expectations gradually got built into the price of the stock. In early 1981, for example, it sold for 21 times earnings. In late 1981 and early 1982, the stock took a tumble, reflecting lower oil prices.

* * *

BALDOR ELECTRIC CO. (BEZ). Founded 1920. Headquarters: 5711 S. Seventh St., Fort Smith AR 72902. **MOTORS.** Baldor Electric Co. manufactures electric motors; also markets grinders and buffers.

Sales: $146.5 million (trend 22.4% a year).
Earnings: $9.41 million (trend 31.8% a year).
What happened to a $10,000 investment

Purchase Date	*Purchase Price*	*Price on 12-31-81*	*Dividends Paid*
12-31-71	$N/A	$25.12	$ N/A
12-31-76	$ 3.75	$25.12	$2,551.02

Purchase Date	*Cap. Gains (– Losses)*	*Total Return*	*Rate of Return*
12-31-71	$ N/A	$ N/A	N/A%
12-31-76	$57,000.00	$59,551.02	47.39%

* * *

BALDWIN-UNITED CORP. (BDW). Founded 1977. Headquarters: 1801 Gilbert Ave., Cincinnati OH 45202. FINANCIAL HOLDING COMPANY. Baldwin-United provides financial services including insurance, savings and loans, mortgages, leasing; also manufactures Baldwin musical instruments. MAJOR SUBSIDIARIES, BRANDS: Baldwin; Gretsch; Sperry & Hutchinson Co. (S & H Green Stamps). In late 1981, Baldwin agreed to buy MGIC Investment Corp. (a major mortgage insurer) for approximately $1.2 billion.

Sales: $939.6 million (trend 52.8% a year).
Earnings: $59.83 million (trend 47.9% a year).
What happened to a $10,000 investment

Purchase Date	*Purchase Price*	*Price on 12-31-81*	*Dividends Paid*
12-31-71	$N/A	$62.50	$ N/A
12-31-76	$13.62	$62.50	$4,308.26

Purchase Date	*Cap. Gains (− Losses)*	*Total Return*	*Rate of Return*
12-31-71	$ N/A	$ N/A	N/A%
12-31-76	$35,871.56	$40,179.82	38.07%

* * *

BALL CORP. (BLL). Founded 1922. Headquarters: 345 S. High St., Muncie IN 47302. GLASS, PACKAGING. Ball Corp. produces glass, metal, and plastic containers and packaging supplies for industrial and technical uses.

Sales: $698.8 million (trend 13.4% a year).
Earnings: $24.40 million (trend 14.4% a year).
What happened to a $10,000 investment

Purchase Date	*Purchase Price*	*Price on 12-31-81*	*Dividends Paid*
12-31-71	$N/A	$33.62	$ N/A
12-31-76	$18.87	$33.62	$3,443.71

Purchase Date	*Cap. Gains (− Losses)*	*Total Return*	*Rate of Return*
12-31-71	$ N/A	$ N/A	N/A%
12-31-76	$7,814.57	$11,258.28	16.28%

* * *

BALLY MANUFACTURING CORP. (BLY). Founded 1968. Headquarters: 2640 W. Belmont Ave., Chicago IL 60618. GAMING EQUIPMENT. Bally is the world's largest manufacturer of slot machines and pinball machines, and a major manufacturer of other amusement arcade games. 9,000 employees. MAJOR SUBSIDIARIES, BRANDS: Midway Manufacturing; Park Place hotel and casino; Six Flags and Aladdin's Castle amusement parks.

Sales: $679.1 million (trend 29.9% a year).
Earnings: $54.94 million (trend 51.7% a year).
What happened to a $10,000 investment

Purchase Date	*Purchase Price*	*Price on 12-31-81*	*Dividends Paid*
12-31-71	$6.19	$29.12	$646.46
12-31-76	$8.06	$29.12	$434.11

Purchase Date	*Cap. Gains (− Losses)*	*Total Return*	*Rate of Return*
12-31-71	$37,070.71	$37,717.17	16.91%
12-31-76	$26,124.03	$26,558.14	29.60%

PROFILE: Gambling. That's what Bally's fortunes depend on. And that's what you're doing when you buy the stock.

Bally stock sold for less than $2 a share in the early 1970s. As recently as 1976, the high was around $8 (on a restated basis, after adjusting for splits). If you'd bought at the 1976 high, you could have quintupled your money by 1979, when the stock soared above $48. That capped a two-year surge touched off by the legalization of gambling in Atlantic City, New Jersey.

Then gambling stocks in general, and Bally too, receded. If you'd sunk $5,000 into Bally at its 1979 peak, you would have had only $1,979 left when the stock hit its 1980 low of $19 a share.

As you see, you don't have to roll dice or go to Las Vegas to gamble. While all gambling stocks are volatile, Bally's volatility is enhanced by its capital structure, which consists of roughly equal parts debt and common stock. Playing with somebody else's money always magnifies your results, up or down.

This is almost a pure capital gains play. Dividends had never been more than a dime a share through 1980, and aren't likely to go much higher soon. If you contemplate buying the stock, watch the p / e ratio, which has historically fluctuated between about 6 and 20. When it's on the high end, investors are sweet on gambling stocks — and that may be just the wrong time to buy.

* * *

BALTIMORE GAS & ELECTRIC. (BGE). Founded 1906. Headquarters: Gas & Electric Bldg., Charles Center, Baltimore MD 21203. UTILITIES.

Baltimore Gas & Electric provides residents of central Maryland with electricity and natural gas.

Sales: $1,226.4 million (trend 12.6% a year).
Earnings: $117.30 million (trend 9.2% a year).
What happened to a $10,000 investment

Purchase Date	*Purchase Price*	*Price on 12-31-81*	*Dividends Paid*
12-31-71	$32.62	$23.12	$6,684.29
12-31-76	$26.75	$23.12	$4,463.55

Purchase Date	*Cap. Gains (– Losses)*	*Total Return*	*Rate of Return*
12-31-71	$–2,911.88	$3,772.41	3.25%
12-31-76	$–1,355.14	$3,108.41	5.56%

* * *

BANCAL TRI-STATE CORP. (BNC). Founded 1972. Headquarters: 400 California St., San Francisco CA 94104. BANKING. BanCal Tri-State Corp. is the holding company of Bank of California, which operates in Washington and Oregon as well as California. MAJOR SUBSIDIARIES, BRANDS: The Bank of California, N.A.

Sales: $397.1 million (trend 12.9% a year).
Earnings: $17.91 million (trend 49.7% a year).
What happened to a $10,000 investment

Purchase Date	*Purchase Price*	*Price on 12-31-81*	*Dividends Paid*
12-31-71	$29.75	$25.50	$3,536.13
12-31-76	$15.37	$25.50	$2,965.85

Purchase Date	*Cap. Gains (– Losses)*	*Total Return*	*Rate of Return*
12-31-71	$–1,428.57	$2,107.56	1.93%
12-31-76	$ 6,585.37	$9,551.22	14.35%

* * *

BANDAG INC. (BDG). Founded 1957. Headquarters: Bandag Center, Mascatine IA 52761. TIRES. Bandag Inc. manufactures products used in making tread for bus and truck tires.

Sales: $330.9 million (trend 15.5% a year).
Earnings: $27.35 million (trend 8.1% a year).
What happened to a $10,000 investment

Purchase Date	*Purchase Price*	*Price on 12-31-81*	*Dividends Paid*
12-31-71	$26.75	$25.12	$1,177.57
12-31-76	$17.87	$25.12	$1,650.35

Purchase Date	*Cap. Gains (– Losses)*	*Total Return*	*Rate of Return*
12-31-71	$–607.48	$ 570.09	.56%
12-31-76	$ 4,055.94	$5,706.29	9.45%

* * *

BANGOR PUNTA CORP. (BNK). Founded 1932. Headquarters: 1 Greenwich Plaza, Greenwich CT 06830. AVIATION. Bangor Punta Corp. produces aircraft equipment, firearms, and sporting goods. MAJOR SUBSIDIARIES, BRANDS: Piper Aircraft; Smith & Wesson; Starcraft.

Sales: $800.0 million (trend 19.8% a year).
Earnings: $43.42 million (trend 27.1% a year).
What happened to a $10,000 investment

Purchase Date	*Purchase Price*	*Price on 12-31-81*	*Dividends Paid*
12-31-71	$6.50	$18.87	$3,308.21
12-31-76	$7.50	$18.87	$2,867.11

Purchase Date	*Cap. Gains (– Losses)*	*Total Return*	*Rate of Return*
12-31-71	$19,038.46	$22,346.67	12.46%
12-31-76	$15,166.67	$18,033.78	22.90%

* * *

THE BANK OF NEW YORK COMPANY, INC. (BK). Founded 1784. Headquarters: 48 Wall St., New York NY 10015. BANKING. The Bank of New York Co. provides banking, trust, and investment services for domestic and international businesses and individuals.

Sales: $1,101.9 million (trend 30.0% a year).
Earnings: $50.52 million (trend 9.7% a year).
What happened to a $10,000 investment

Purchase Date	*Purchase Price*	*Price on 12-31-81*	*Dividends Paid*
12-31-71	$43.25	$42.87	$5,482.08
12-31-76	$36.50	$42.87	$3,591.78

Purchase Date	*Cap. Gains (– Losses)*	*Total Return*	*Rate of Return*
12-31-71	$ –86.71	$5,395.38	4.41%
12-31-76	$1,746.58	$5,338.36	8.93%

* * *

BANK OF VIRGINIA CO. (BKV). Founded 1962. Headquarters: 7 N. Eighth St., PO Box 25970, Richmond VA 23260. BANK HOLDING COMPANY. Holding company for Bank of Virginia, formed from a union of nine banking institutions; has more than one hundred offices throughout Virginia. **MAJOR SUBSIDIARIES, BRANDS:** Bank of Virginia, Bank of Virginia International, General Finance Service Corp.

Sales: $282.1 million (trend 12.7% a year).
Earnings: $12.65 million (trend 13.9% a year).
What happened to a $10,000 investment

Purchase Date	*Purchase Price*	*Price on 12-31-81*	*Dividends Paid*
12-31-71	$23.50	$14.75	$4,102.13
12-31-76	$15.25	$14.75	$3,488.52

Purchase Date	*Cap. Gains (− Losses)*	*Total Return*	*Rate of Return*
12-31-71	$−3,723.40	$ 378.72	.37%
12-31-76	$ −327.87	$3,160.66	5.65%

* * *

BANKAMERICA CORP. (BAM). Founded 1930. Headquarters: Bank of America Plaza, San Francisco CA 94120. **BANK.** BankAmerica Corp. is the holding company for Bank of America, the country's largest bank (measured by assets); also owns a finance company and a computer leasing firm. 81,000 employees. **MAJOR SUBSIDIARIES, BRANDS:** Bank of America; Finance-America Corp.; Decimus Corp.

Sales: $12,074.5 million (trend 21.9% a year).
Earnings: $645.00 million (trend 18.0% a year).
What happened to a $10,000 investment

Purchase Date	*Purchase Price*	*Price on 12-31-81*	*Dividends Paid*
12-31-71	$17.72	$21.25	$5,355.91
12-31-76	$30.25	$21.25	$2,004.96

Purchase Date	*Cap. Gains (− Losses)*	*Total Return*	*Rate of Return*
12-31-71	$ 1,992.95	$ 7,348.85	5.66%
12-31-76	$−2,975.21	$−970.25	−2.02%

PROFILE: Bank of America, long the nation's largest bank, has had to share that billing during the 1970s with Citibank. First the New York upstart passed its California rival in profits and then, in 1980, passed it in total assets as well. But Bank of America appeared to have regained both crowns — at least for a while — in 1981.

The teetering of the title is a tribute to Citibank's aggressiveness and savvy, but it doesn't really reflect badly on Bank of America, which has been one of the nation's most profitable banks and whose own growth rates have been nothing to sneeze at.

The stock price hasn't gone much of anywhere in recent years — mainly because the prices of all bank stocks were in the basement during the late 1970s. They — and BankAmerica in particular — deserve better. This isn't a company whose profits will soar, but it has racked up a consistent record of steadily rising profits, in good times and bad. Slow and steady may win the race — especially at a time when the stock's price / earnings ratio is below 7, as it has been in recent years.

During the late 1960s and early 1970s, this stock sold for 12 to 20 times earnings. A return to a multiple of 10 times earnings, coupled with a continuation of the company's historic earnings growth, would see this stock selling at around $89 a share by 1985. Yet in early 1981 the price was only $26 a share.

Foreign operations provide more than a third of BankAmerica's income and help shield it against fluctuations in the U.S. economy.

In late 1981, BankAmerica announced its intention to acquire Charles Schwab Corp., which runs the nation's largest discount brokerage house, for about $53 million in stock. The acquisition, if it goes through, would allow BankAmerica to offer its customers a larger variety of financial services under one roof than it did before.

* * *

BANKAMERICA REALTY INVESTORS. (BRE). Founded 1970. Headquarters: Bank of America Center, Suite 4275, 555 California St., San Francisco CA 94104. **REAL ESTATE INVESTMENTS.** BankAmerica Realty Investors offers mortgage loans to shopping centers, office buildings, and apartments.

Sales: $27.2 million (trend .2% a year).
Earnings: $10.14 million (trend 46.6% a year).
What happened to a $10,000 investment

Purchase Date	*Purchase Price*	*Price on 12-31-81*	*Dividends Paid*
12-31-71	$26.37	$25.37	$4,519.43
12-31-76	$10.25	$25.37	$5,034.15

Purchase Date	*Cap. Gains (− Losses)*	*Total Return*	*Rate of Return*
12-31-71	$ −379.15	$ 4,140.28	3.53%
12-31-76	$14,756.10	$19,790.24	24.40%

* * *

BANKERS TRUST NEW YORK CORP. (BT). Founded 1966. Headquarters: 280 Park Ave., New York NY 10017. **BANK.** This corporation is the holding company for Bankers Trust Co., one of the nation's ten largest banks. 12,000 employees.

Sales: $3,693.3 million (trend 21.4% a year).
Earnings: $200.18 million (trend 26.5% a year).
What happened to a $10,000 investment

Purchase Date	*Purchase Price*	*Price on 12-31-81*	*Dividends Paid*
12-31-71	$27.37	$33.87	$5,704.11
12-31-76	$18.81	$33.87	$4,345.51

Purchase Date	*Cap. Gains (− Losses)*	*Total Return*	*Rate of Return*
12-31-71	$2,374.43	$ 8,078.54	6.10%
12-31-76	$8,006.64	$12,352.16	17.45%

PROFILE: In the early 1970s, Bankers Trust had an advertisement that twitted its New York City rival, Chase Manhattan. While Chase was advertising "You have a friend at Chase Manhattan," Bankers Trust proclaimed, "You'll find a banker at Bankers Trust."

The ad proved to be more prophetic than Bankers Trust realized. In the early 1980s, Bankers Trust pulled out of consumer banking to concentrate on being a banker's banker — a "wholesale" bank, dealing almost exclusively with large corporate clients in the United States and abroad. (Foreign operations now account for at least half of the bank's profits.)

In the process, Bankers Trust sold about 200 of its branch banks. Money from the sale (to several buyers) helped to improve the company's balance sheet, which was further improved by a stock sale in 1980.

In the mid-1970s, Bankers Trust ran into problems, mainly as a result of some unfortunate loans, especially to real estate ventures. The company remained profitable, but profits dipped. The stock market, which was sour on bank stocks anyway in the late 1970s, punished the company severely. The stock declined to the point where it was a ridiculous bargain, then rebounded at the start of the 1980s. Nevertheless, the stock remained cheap recently. In early 1981 the p/e multiple was about 3 — a hyperconservative valuation of a profitable company with growing earnings.

* * *

BANNER INDUSTRIES, INC. (BNR). Founded 1968. Headquarters: 24500 Chagrin Blvd., Cleveland OH 44122. **TRUCKING.** Banner Industries, Inc. manufactures motor freight carriers, industrial products. **MAJOR SUBSIDIARIES, BRANDS:** Commercial Lovelace Motor Freight, Inc.

Sales: $208.8 million (trend 17.3% a year).
Earnings: $4.77 million (trend 3.5% a year).
What happened to a $10,000 investment

Purchase Date	*Purchase Price*	*Price on 12-31-81*	*Dividends Paid*
12-31-71	$5.12	$12.12	$1,463.41
12-31-76	$5.87	$12.12	$1,021.28

Purchase Date	*Cap. Gains (− Losses)*	*Total Return*	*Rate of Return*
12-31-71	$13,658.54	$15,121.95	9.65%
12-31-76	$10,638.30	$11,659.57	16.72%

* * *

BARD, C. R. INC. (BCR). Founded 1972. Headquarters: 731 Central Ave., Murray Hill, NJ 07974. **HEALTH CARE PRODUCTS.** Bard produces disposable medical and general health care products; it is a leading manufacturer of urological supplies. **MAJOR SUBSIDIARIES, BRANDS:** Automated Screening Devices, Inc.; Davol Inc.

Sales: $246.5 million (trend 12.7% a year).
Earnings: $16.60 million (trend 11.1% a year).
What happened to a $10,000 investment

Purchase Date	*Purchase Price*	*Price on 12-31-81*	*Dividends Paid*
12-31-71	$33.25	$30.25	$ 810.47
12-31-76	$14.62	$30.25	$1,189.74

Purchase Date	*Cap. Gains (− Losses)*	*Total Return*	*Rate of Return*
12-31-71	$ −902.26	$ −91.79	−.09%
12-31-76	$10,683.76	$11,873.50	16.95%

* * *

BARNES GROUP, INC. (B). Founded 1925. Headquarters: 123 Main St., Bristol CT 06010. **METAL PARTS.** Barnes Group, Inc. manufactures precision metal parts such as mechanical springs; also distributes automotive parts. **MAJOR SUBSIDIARIES, BRANDS:** Central Metal Products Co.

Sales: $433.9 million (trend 17.2% a year).
Earnings: $24.26 million (trend 25.3% a year).
What happened to a $10,000 investment

Purchase Date	*Purchase Price*	*Price on 12-31-81*	*Dividends Paid*
12-31-71	$ 8.99	$18.12	$6,668.56
12-31-76	$12.58	$18.12	$3,033.14

Purchase Date	*Cap. Gains (− Losses)*	*Total Return*	*Rate of Return*
12-31-71	$10,163.09	$16,831.65	10.37%
12-31-76	$ 4,403.97	$ 7,437.11	11.76%

* * *

BARNETT BANKS OF FLORIDA, INC. (BBF). Founded 1877. Headquarters: 100 Laura St., Jacksonville FL 32231. BANK HOLDING COMPANY. Barnett Banks of Florida, Inc. is a holding company of nearly 150 banks in Florida.

Sales: $434.8 million (trend 19.8% a year).
Earnings: $38.04 million (trend 30.3% a year).
What happened to a $10,000 investment

Purchase Date	*Purchase Price*	*Price on 12-31-81*	*Dividends Paid*
12-31-71	$16.08	$22.75	$3,403.11
12-31-76	$10.33	$22.75	$3,154.84

Purchase Date	*Cap. Gains (− Losses)*	*Total Return*	*Rate of Return*
12-31-71	$ 4,145.08	$ 7,548.19	5.78%
12-31-76	$12,016.13	$15,170.97	20.28%

* * *

BARRY WRIGHT CORP. (BAR). Founded 1943. Headquarters: 680 Pleasant St., Watertown MA 02172. DATA PROCESSING. Barry Wright Corp. produces data processing supplies, computer accessories, and variable speed controls for AC motors. MAJOR SUBSIDIARIES, BRANDS: Wright Line Inc.

Sales: $124.5 million (trend 24.7% a year).
Earnings: $10.01 million (trend 42.2% a year).
What happened to a $10,000 investment

Purchase Date	*Purchase Price*	*Price on 12-31-81*	*Dividends Paid*
12-31-71	$2.28	$18.25	$7,046.58
12-31-76	$2.72	$18.25	$4,229.89

Purchase Date	*Cap. Gains (− Losses)*	*Total Return*	*Rate of Return*
12-31-71	$70,000.00	$77,046.58	24.16%
12-31-76	$57,126.44	$61,356.32	48.14%

* * *

BASIC RESOURCES CORP. (BAS). Founded 1957. Headquarters: 595 Madison Ave., New York NY 10022. HIGHWAY TOLL EQUIPMENT. Basic Resources Corp. manufactures highway toll equipment; also involved in printing and publishing and in oil and gas exploration. MAJOR SUBSIDIARIES, BRANDS: Aerostyle Ltd.; Emerson Plastronics; Philadelphia Printing Properties.

Sales: $29.1 million (trend 26.1% a year).
Earnings: $2.20 million (trend 38.6% a year).
What happened to a $10,000 investment

Purchase Date	*Purchase Price*	*Price on 12-31-81*	*Dividends Paid*
12-31-71	$5.36	$4.50	$0.00
12-31-76	$1.43	$4.50	$0.00

Purchase Date	*Cap. Gains (− Losses)*	*Total Return*	*Rate of Return*
12-31-71	$−1,600.01	$−1,600.01	−1.73%
12-31-76	$ 21,499.98	$ 21,499.98	25.79%

* * *

BAUSCH & LOMB INC. (BOL). Founded 1908. Headquarters: 1 Lincoln First Square, Rochester NY 14601. OPTICAL SUPPLIES. Bausch & Lomb Inc. produces optical supplies and scientific equipment. MAJOR SUBSIDIARIES, BRANDS: SOFLENS.

Sales: $582.7 million (trend 12.2% a year).
Earnings: $52.27 million (trend 26.3% a year).
What happened to a $10,000 investment

Purchase Date	*Purchase Price*	*Price on 12-31-81*	*Dividends Paid*
12-31-71	$44.31	$52.87	$1,436.39
12-31-76	$14.56	$52.87	$3,426.61

Purchase Date	*Cap. Gains (− Losses)*	*Total Return*	*Rate of Return*
12-31-71	$ 1,932.30	$ 3,368.69	2.95%
12-31-76	$26,309.01	$29,735.62	31.78%

* * *

BAXTER TRAVENOL LABORATORIES, INC. (BAX). Founded 1931. Headquarters: 1 Baxter Parkway, Deerfield IL 60015. DRUGS. Company is the largest maker of kidney dialysis equipment and intravenous feeding solutions; also produces blood therapy, respiratory therapy, and other medical products. 33,000 employees.

Sales: $1,374.4 million (trend 19.7% a year).
Earnings: $128.34 million (trend 23.4% a year).
What happened to a $10,000 investment

Purchase Date	*Purchase Price*	*Price on 12-31-81*	*Dividends Paid*
12-31-71	$17.87	$33.50	$968.53
12-31-76	$20.25	$33.50	$638.27

Purchase Date	*Cap. Gains (− Losses)*	*Total Return*	*Rate of Return*
12-31-71	$8,741.26	$9,709.79	7.02%
12-31-76	$6,543.21	$7,181.48	11.43%

PROFILE: Pity poor Baxter Travenol. Its sales and earnings growth rates in the late 1970s were only about average for a major drug firm. Its stock price hasn't moved much (except for temporary fluctuations) since 1974.

Malarkey. If you look past the indifferent stock price action of recent years you'll see an excellent company and a stock that represents potentially excellent value.

Sales and earnings have been going up about 21 percent a year for about the last twenty-five years. You'd have to search long and hard to find a company with that kind of record of consistent, first-rate growth. In recent years, the 21 percent figure has been about average for a drug company. But it's far above the growth rates experienced by companies in most other industries, who would give their eyeteeth to have 21 percent growth in selected years, let alone year in and year out.

Drug companies in general have good growth rates and are resistant to recession. That's why people are willing to pay a relatively high price relative to earnings for drug stocks. But a look at the historical record of Baxter Travenol's p / e ratio is very instructive. The stock sold for almost 60 times earnings in 1972 (an unrealistic level for any stock). Since then, the p / e ratio has come way down, even while actual earnings have continued to march up.

Foreign sales are about a third of Baxter Travenol's business and are expanding faster than U.S. sales. The company also conducts many of its manufacturing operations in Puerto Rico, taking advantage of tax breaks.

In 1980, Baxter Travenol started marketing a new portable dialysis system that allows kidney patients freedom of movement and treatment at a lower cost than with traditional kidney machines. Not all kidney patients can use it, but many can, and the new system should be a substantial contributor to profits.

* * *

BAY FINANCIAL CORP. (BAY). Founded 1979. Headquarters: 2 Faneuil Hall Marketplace, Boston MA 02109. REAL ESTATE. Bay Financial Corp. supervises real estate investments; also operates and develops real estate.

Sales: $20.9 million (trend 13.8% a year).
Earnings: $1.80 million (trend 142.0% a year).
What happened to a $10,000 investment

Purchase Date	*Purchase Price*	*Price on 12-31-81*	*Dividends Paid*
12-31-71	$27.25	$9.25	$2,106.42
12-31-76	$ 3.62	$9.25	$ 0.00

Purchase Date	*Cap. Gains (− Losses)*	*Total Return*	*Rate of Return*
12-31-71	$−6,605.50	$−4,499.08	−5.80%
12-31-76	$ 15,517.24	$ 15,517.24	20.61%

* * *

BAY STATE GAS CO. (BGC). Founded 1974. Headquarters: 120 Royall St., Canton MA 02021. GAS. Bay State Gas Co. distributes natural gas in Massachusetts, New Hampshire, and southern Maine. MAJOR SUBSIDIARIES, BRANDS: Northern Utilities, Inc.; Bay State Exploration, Inc.

Sales: $209.6 million (trend 17.8% a year).
Earnings: $7.75 million (trend 8.6% a year).
What happened to a $10,000 investment

Purchase Date	*Purchase Price*	*Price on 12-31-81*	*Dividends Paid*
12-31-71	$N/A	$19.25	$ N/A
12-31-76	$21.25	$19.25	$4,945.88

Purchase Date	*Cap. Gains (− Losses)*	*Total Return*	*Rate of Return*
12-31-71	$ N/A	$ N/A	N/A%
12-31-76	$−941.18	$4,004.71	6.97%

* * *

BAYUK CIGARS INC. (BYK). Founded 1920. Headquarters: 2150 S. Andrews Ave., PO Box 6000, Fort Lauderdale FL 33310. CIGARS. Bayuk Cigars Inc. manufactures and sells cigars. MAJOR

SUBSIDIARIES, BRANDS: Garcia Y Vega; Phillies; Webster.

Sales: $23.9 million (trend −4.7% a year).
Earnings: $2.92 million (trend 50.1% a year).
What happened to a $10,000 investment

Purchase Date	*Purchase Price*	*Price on 12-31-81*	*Dividends Paid*
12-31-71	$2.87	$11.75	$8,169.57
12-31-76	$2.37	$11.75	$7,073.68

Purchase Date	*Cap. Gains (− Losses)*	*Total Return*	*Rate of Return*
12-31-71	$30,869.57	$39,039.13	17.23%
12-31-76	$39,473.68	$46,547.37	41.41%

* * *

BEARINGS, INC. (BER). Founded 1928. Headquarters: 3600 Euclid Ave., Cleveland OH 44115. **BEARINGS.** Bearings, Inc. distributes ball, roller, thrust, and linear bearings; also related bearing devices and equipment.

Sales: $357.4 million (trend 14.1% a year).
Earnings: $14.19 million (trend 7.8% a year).
What happened to a $10,000 investment

Purchase Date	*Purchase Price*	*Price on 12-31-81*	*Dividends Paid*
12-31-71	$19.37	$35.25	$2,776.77
12-31-76	$31.62	$35.25	$1,207.91

Purchase Date	*Cap. Gains (− Losses)*	*Total Return*	*Rate of Return*
12-31-71	$8,193.55	$10,970.32	7.69%
12-31-76	$1,146.25	$ 2,354.15	4.32%

* * *

BEATRICE FOODS CO. (BRY). Founded 1924. Headquarters: 2 N. LaSalle St., Chicago IL 60602. **FOODS.** Beatrice produces some 9,000 products through some 400 subsidiaries. About three quarters of revenues are from food products, the remainder are from widely diversified enterprises. 84,000 employees. **MAJOR SUBSIDIARIES, BRANDS:** Tropicana; Fisher nuts; La Choy oriental foods; Meadow Gold and Louis Sherry ice cream; Samsonite luggage; Coca-Cola Bottling Co. of Los Angeles; Buckingham Corp. (importer of Cutty Sark scotch).

Sales: $8,772.8 million (trend 14.2% a year).
Earnings: $287.60 million (trend 13.8% a year).
What happened to a $10,000 investment

Purchase Date	*Purchase Price*	*Price on 12-31-81*	*Dividends Paid*
12-31-71	$21.62	$18.25	$3,700.58
12-31-76	$28.37	$18.25	$1,600.00

Purchase Date	*Cap. Gains (− Losses)*	*Total Return*	*Rate of Return*
12-31-71	$−1,560.69	$ 2,139.88	1.96%
12-31-76	$−3,568.28	$−1,968.28	−4.29%

PROFILE: In the stock market dance of the late 1970s and early 1980s, all the boys could hardly wait to get their hands on the high technology stocks. Companies like Beatrice were wallflowers. Nevertheless, it's an excellent stock to bring home to mother.

Beatrice (named after Beatrice, Nebraska, where the dairy that was the precursor of the present corporation was started in 1894) chalked up its thirtieth straight year of rising sales and earnings in 1981. The growth hasn't been dramatic, but it's been steady.

In recent years, the stock price has been stagnant. Earnings go up a bit each year. The p / e ratio deteriorates a bit each year. Standoff.

There's reason to think that the company, and (even more so) its stock may do better in the years ahead. A bitter wrangle in the executive suites — one of the most highly publicized intracorporate brawls of recent years — has been settled. James L. Dutt now seems firmly in charge as chairman, and his moves to date have almost universally impressed both insiders and outside analysts. One thing Dutt has done is to change the longstanding unspoken rule that Beatrice acquires companies, but doesn't sell them. Dutt has jettisoned some of the losers among the 400 or so subsidiaries (e.g. Harmon International and Southwestern Investment Co., with Airstream slated to go next), and has made it clear that he won't hesitate to kick out even money-making subsidiaries from the Beatrice family if their profits are growing at a snail's pace.

In short, steady earnings growth is likely to continue, and may even get a bit more brisk. Yet, the stock sells at a very conservative valuation (about 6 times earnings in early 1982). And the dividend yield is substantial (above 7 percent recently). The chances for an excellent total return in Beatrice shares over the next few years are good.

* * *

BECKMAN INSTRUMENTS, INC. (BEC). Founded 1935. Headquarters: 2500 Harbor Blvd., Fullerton CA 92634. INSTRUMENT MANUFACTURER. Beckman Instruments, Inc. manufactures analytical instruments and chemical products; also produces industrial instruments and precision electronic components. In 1981, Beckman agreed in principle to be merged into SmithKline Corp.

Sales: $618.1 million (trend 21.7% a year).
Earnings: $36.75 million (trend 27.3% a year).
What happened to a $10,000 investment

Purchase Date	*Purchase Price*	*Price on 12-31-81*	*Dividends Paid*
12-31-71	$10.41	$46.25	$1,823.42
12-31-76	$14.12	$46.25	$ 895.58

Purchase Date	*Cap. Gains (– Losses)*	*Total Return*	*Rate of Return*
12-31-71	$34,444.44	$36,267.87	16.55%
12-31-76	$22,743.36	$23,638.94	27.46%

* * *

BECTON, DICKINSON AND CO. (BDX). Founded 1906. Headquarters: Mack Centre Dr., Paramus NJ 07652. HOSPITAL SUPPLIES. Becton, Dickinson and Co. manufactures medical and hospital supplies; also involved in producing industrial safety equipment. MAJOR SUBSIDIARIES, BRANDS: Bard Parker (medical equipment); Bauer & Black (elastic goods).

Sales: $1,066.1 million (trend 16.1% a year).
Earnings: $77.10 million (trend 13.5% a year).
What happened to a $10,000 investment

Purchase Date	*Purchase Price*	*Price on 12-31-81*	*Dividends Paid*
12-31-71	$34.50	$47.75	$1,744.20
12-31-76	$33.75	$47.75	$1,208.89

Purchase Date	*Cap. Gains (– Losses)*	*Total Return*	*Rate of Return*
12-31-71	$3,840.58	$5,584.78	4.54%
12-31-76	$4,148.15	$5,357.04	8.96%

* * *

BEKER INDUSTRIES CORP. (BKI). Founded 1971. Headquarters: 124 W. Putnam Ave., Greenwich CT 06830. FERTILIZERS. Beker produces fertilizers and feed products for animals; has sideline in uranium extraction.

Sales: $295.2 million (trend 12.1% a year).
Earnings: $28.88 million (trend –6.8% a year).
What happened to a $10,000 investment

Purchase Date	*Purchase Price*	*Price on 12-31-81*	*Dividends Paid*
12-31-71	$N/A	$8.37	$N/A
12-31-76	$ 9.62	$8.37	$ 0.00

Purchase Date	*Cap. Gains (– Losses)*	*Total Return*	*Rate of Return*
12-31-71	$ N/A	$ N/A	N/A%
12-31-76	$–1,298.70	$–1,298.70	–2.74%

* * *

BELCO PETROLEUM CORP. (BPC). Founded 1959. Headquarters: 1 Dag Hammarskjold Plaza, New York NY 10017. OIL, NATURAL GAS. Belco Petroleum Corp. is involved in exploration, production, and sale of oil and natural gas. MAJOR SUBSIDIARIES, BRANDS: Hawley Fuel Corp.; Sonapco.

Sales: $836.9 million (trend 21.9% a year).
Earnings: $77.89 million (trend 31.4% a year).
What happened to a $10,000 investment

Purchase Date	*Purchase Price*	*Price on 12-31-81*	*Dividends Paid*
12-31-71	$4.98	$26.75	$5,669.92
12-31-76	$8.13	$26.75	$2,667.20

Purchase Date	*Cap. Gains (– Losses)*	*Total Return*	*Rate of Return*
12-31-71	$43,765.68	$49,435.59	19.51%
12-31-76	$22,890.61	$25,557.81	28.88%

* * *

BELDING HEMINWAY COMPANY, INC. (BHY). Founded 1947. Headquarters: 1430 Broadway, New York NY 10018. THREADS. Belding Heminway Company, Inc. produces industrial thread, specialty fabrics, and consumer sewing supplies. MAJOR SUBSIDIARIES, BRANDS: Belding Corticelli; Belding Lily; La Mode; Le Chic; Penn.

Sales: $121.3 million (trend 3.3% a year).
Earnings: $2.18 million (trend –2.2% a year).
What happened to a $10,000 investment

Purchase Date	*Purchase Price*	*Price on 12-31-81*	*Dividends Paid*
12-31-71	$13.36	$6.37	$2,091.92
12-31-76	$ 7.02	$6.37	$2,365.39

Purchase Date	*Cap. Gains (– Losses)*	*Total Return*	*Rate of Return*
12-31-71	$–5,227.43	$–3,135.51	–3.69%
12-31-76	$ –923.91	$ 1,441.47	2.73%

* * *

BELL & HOWELL CO. (BWH). Founded 1907. Headquarters: 7100 McCormick Rd., Chicago IL 60645. **INFORMATION SYSTEMS.** Bell & Howell Co. produces microfilm systems and related equipment, learning systems, reference materials, and electronic instruments.

Sales: $640.0 million (trend 9.4% a year).
Earnings: $19.22 million (trend 8.8% a year).
What happened to a $10,000 investment

Purchase Date	*Purchase Price*	*Price on 12-31-81*	*Dividends Paid*
12-31-71	$57.25	$19.25	$1,480.87
12-31-76	$18.75	$19.25	$2,448.00

Purchase Date	*Cap. Gains (– Losses)*	*Total Return*	*Rate of Return*
12-31-71	$–6,637.55	$–5,156.68	–6.99%
12-31-76	$ 266.67	$ 2,714.67	4.92%

* * *

BELL INDUSTRIES, INC. (BI). Founded 1959. Headquarters: 1880 Century Park E., Los Angeles CA 90067. **ELECTRONICS, BUILDING PRODUCTS.** Bell Industries manufactures and distributes electronics and computer equipment, building and construction products, transportation supplies, and graphic art supplies.

Sales: $191.0 million (trend 19.2% a year).
Earnings: $8.16 million (trend 22.0% a year).
What happened to a $10,000 investment

Purchase Date	*Purchase Price*	*Price on 12-31-81*	*Dividends Paid*
12-31-71	$4.37	$15.87	$2,628.57
12-31-76	$4.50	$15.87	$1,888.89

Purchase Date	*Cap. Gains (– Losses)*	*Total Return*	*Rate of Return*
12-31-71	$26,285.71	$28,914.29	14.55%
12-31-76	$25,277.78	$27,166.67	30.03%

* * *

BELL CANADA (BCA). Founded 1880. Headquarters: 1050 Beaver Hall Hill, Montreal, Quebec, Canada H3C 3G4. **TELECOMMUNICATIONS.** Bell Canada provides telephone service in Ontario and Quebec; also involved in the production of telecommunications equipment. **MAJOR SUBSIDIARIES, BRANDS:** Northern Telecom Ltd. (54.9% owned).

Sales: $5,053.0 million (trend 11.5% a year).
Earnings: $272.44 million (trend 4.8% a year).
What happened to a $10,000 investment

Purchase Date	*Purchase Price*	*Price on 12-31-81*	*Dividends Paid*
12-31-71	$15.46	$16.37	$7,798.21
12-31-76	$15.75	$16.37	$4,327.70

Purchase Date	*Cap. Gains (– Losses)*	*Total Return*	*Rate of Return*
12-31-71	$592.99	$8,391.20	6.28%
12-31-76	$396.83	$4,724.53	8.05%

* * *

BEMIS COMPANY, INC. (BMS). Founded 1858. Headquarters: 800 Northstar Center, Minneapolis MN 55402. **PACKAGING.** Bemis Company, Inc. manufactures and sells materials and equipment for the packaging industry. **MAJOR SUBSIDIARIES, BRANDS:** Curwood, Inc.; Hayssen Mfg.; Morgan Adhesives Co.; Western Litho; Pervel Industries.

Sales: $662.4 million (trend 3.7% a year).
Earnings: $15.64 million (trend 13.2% a year).
What happened to a $10,000 investment

Purchase Date	*Purchase Price*	*Price on 12-31-81*	*Dividends Paid*
12-31-71	$16.43	$24.37	$6,923.19
12-31-76	$22.75	$24.37	$3,076.92

Purchase Date	*Cap. Gains (– Losses)*	*Total Return*	*Rate of Return*
12-31-71	$4,836.95	$11,760.13	8.09%
12-31-76	$ 714.29	$ 3,791.21	6.64%

* * *

BENDIX CORP. (BX). Founded 1929. Headquarters: Bendix Center, Southfield MI 48037. **AUTO, AEROSPACE.** Bendix is a leading manufacturer of auto and aircraft components and of machine tools. 78,000 employees. **MAJOR SUBSIDIARIES, BRANDS:** Warner & Swasey; Autolite spark plugs; Fram filters.

Sales: $4,393.1 million (trend 7.5% a year).
Earnings: $204.50 million (trend 15.2% a year).
What happened to a $10,000 investment

Purchase Date	*Purchase Price*	*Price on 12-31-81*	*Dividends Paid*
12-31-71	$31.69	$58.75	$6,135.74
12-31-76	$44.62	$58.75	$2,841.46

Purchase Date	*Cap. Gains (– Losses)*	*Total Return*	*Rate of Return*
12-31-71	$8,539.97	$14,675.71	9.45%
12-31-76	$3,165.27	$ 6,006.72	9.87%

PROFILE: There's been no shortage of speculation in recent years about Bendix Corp. In 1980, the great fall spectator sport was discussing chairman Bill Agee's denial that a personal relationship played a part in his naming twenty-nine-year-old Mary Cunningham as vice-president for strategic planning. Once the issue became public, it created such a distracting flap that Cunningham left.

That left speculative-minded observers to wonder next about what Bendix would do with the mountain of cash it was piling up by selling off its forest products business for $435 million, its 20 percent stake in Asarco for about $250 million, and a few assorted other assets for a few more millions of dollars. "High technology" acquisitions would be given first consideration, said Agee. Many people thought funds would be poured into Bendix's profitable aerospace business. But in fact, the first thing Bendix did with the cash was to offer to buy back about four million shares of its own stock. That's often a good sign, since it signals management's confidence that the stock is undervalued, and it lessens the number of shares outstanding (resulting in higher earnings per share)

Investors might do well to speculate a bit less, though, and look harder at Bendix's track record. Recently, the company has been running a mean race, while dragging the equivalent of a lead ball. Fully half of Bendix's sales are in auto parts — a market that was quite depressed in 1979 through 1981. Despite that, Bendix not only stayed profitable, it continued to increase its earnings. Just think what the company might do when the auto industry finally rebounds.

Bendix is also in a position to participate fully in the reindustrialization of America, if and when that catch phrase becomes a reality. The 1980 acquisition of Warner & Swasey, coupled with Bendix's previous operations in machine tools, makes Bendix the nation's second-largest machine tool manufacturer after Cincinnati Milacron.

* * *

BENEFICIAL CORP. (BNL). Founded 1929. Headquarters: 1300 Market St., Wilmington DE 19899. **LOANS.** Beneficial is the nation's largest consumer loan company; has sidelines in insurance, banking, auto supplies, CB radios, and mail order merchandising. 25,000 employees. **MAJOR SUBSIDIARIES, BRANDS:** First Texas Financial Corp.; Western Auto Supply Co.; Midland International.

Sales: $1,323.2 million (trend 23.1% a year).
Earnings: $76.90 million (trend 3.3% a year).
What happened to a $10,000 investment

Purchase Date	*Purchase Price*	*Price on 12-31-81*	*Dividends Paid*
12-31-71	$45.00	$20.12	$3,441.67
12-31-76	$27.12	$20.12	$3,410.14

Purchase Date	*Cap. Gains (– Losses)*	*Total Return*	*Rate of Return*
12-31-71	$–5,527.78	$–2,086.11	–2.31%
12-31-76	$–2,580.65	$ 829.49	1.61%

PROFILE: A loan company is like a funnel. Money comes in at one end (mainly by the loan company's own borrowing, from banks and by bond issues) and goes out the other (in consumer loans). The profitability of the company depends on the spread between the interest rate on the incoming end and the interest rate on the outgoing end.

In a good year, the spread is big. For example, in 1979, *Forbes* magazine wrote an article about Beneficial under the headline: "Borrows at 9%, lends at 20%."

If things were always that way — and if it were that simple — a loan company would be a profit machine. However, it's not that simple. Beneficial has had good growth in recent years for a loan company, passing Household Finance Corp. to become the biggest consumer lender (though HFC is bigger overall). Yet, Beneficial has been less profitable than the average U.S. corporation. Its return on equity has been mediocre, its return on total capital miserable.

The difference between the two reflects the fact that Beneficial labors under a tremendous debt load of its own. Debt was recently 4.2 times equity (versus only about 2.4 in 1970–76). A big debt load is par for the course in a loan company, but anyone who wants to invest in a company with Beneficial's debt load must have a big appetite for leverage — and risk. What happens if consumer loan demand dries up, and Beneficial still has to keep paying interest on all that debt?

One problem Beneficial has had is a trio of turkeys acquired by the predecessors of chairman Finn Casperson (over his objections). Midland International, Western Auto Supply, and Spiegel have all required attention and have done very little for profits. There have been recurrent rumors that all three were up for sale; Spiegel, a big mail order house, is scheduled to go to a German buyer.

The bright spots for this stock, in the early 1980s, are the relatively low p / e ratio and the high dividend yield (about 9½ percent in 1981). The company has never chopped its dividend in recent memory. But there's always a first time.

* * *

BENGUET CORP. (BE). Founded 1903. Headquarters: 2259 Pasong Tamo Extension, Makati, Metro Manila, Philippines. MINING. Benguet mines gold, copper, and some silver in the Philippines; has sidelines in engineering, forest products, and trucking.

Sales: $236.0 million (trend 40.5% a year).
Earnings: $33.00 million (trend 31.5% a year).
What happened to a $10,000 investment

Purchase Date	*Purchase Price*	*Price on 12-31-81*	*Dividends Paid*
12-31-71	$6.75	$4.37	$ 937.78
12-31-76	$1.62	$4.37	$1,950.77

Purchase Date	*Cap. Gains (— Losses)*	*Total Return*	*Rate of Return*
12-31-71	$−3,518.52	$−2,580.74	−2.94%
12-31-76	$ 16,923.08	$ 18,873.85	23.62%

* * *

BERGEN BRUNSWIG CORP. (BBG, American Stock Exchange**).** Founded 1956. Headquarters: 1900 Ave. of the Stars, Los Angeles CA 90067. DRUG WHOLESALING. Bergen Brunswig is a major distributor of pharmaceuticals, laboratory supplies, and surgical supplies, 2,000 employees. MAJOR SUBSIDIARIES, BRANDS: Dataservice Co.

Sales: $867.5 million (trend 17.6% a year).
Earnings: $12.46 million (trend 52.2% a year).
What happened to a $10,000 investment

Purchase Date	*Purchase Price*	*Price on 12-31-81*	*Dividends Paid*
12-31-71	$7.55	$30.50	$1,163.17
12-31-76	$5.00	$30.50	$1,568.00

Purchase Date	*Cap. Gains (— Losses)*	*Total Return*	*Rate of Return*
12-31-71	$30,402.56	$31,565.72	15.31%
12-31-76	$51,000.00	$52,568.00	44.30%

PROFILE: This relatively small company is, quite simply, one of the most profitable corporations in the United States. In the introductory chapter of this book, we explained the concept of return on stockholders' equity and used a hypothetical example of a company with a 40 percent return on equity. We were quick to caution that a 40 percent return on equity is almost unheard of in real life.

But Bergen Brunswig has heard of it — and accomplished it no fewer than four times, in 1975, 1977, 1978, and 1979. What's more, the company just missed doing it again in 1980, when the return on equity was a still-sizzling 39 percent. The 1981 figure was "only" 22.5 percent—still a figure most companies would love to have.

Bergen Brunswig is primarily a distributor of drugs and medical supplies. In this realm, it competes with the far larger firm Foremost-McKesson, which is number one in size. (Bergen Brunswig is number two in the field.) But Foremost-McKesson has never achieved the kind of profitability, or the rapid growth, that Bergen Brunswig has.

One of the company's secrets is a computerized order entry system, which is quick and highly efficient. A subsidiary, Dataservice Co., markets computer billing services.

The balance sheet is trim, with long-term debt recently just over a quarter of total capital. Dividends were suspended from 1972 through 1978, resumed in 1979; the yield is small.

From an investor's point of view, the main flaw in this stock may be that the company's success is already well-enough known so that the stock carries a high multiple. In late 1981, for example, Bergen Brunswig sold for 15 times earnings; at the time, the average stock fetched about half that.

* * *

BERKEY PHOTO, INC. (BKY). Founded 1960. Headquarters: 1 Water St., White Plains NY 01601. PHOTOGRAPHY. Berkey Photo, Inc. processes film, imports and distributes photographic equipment, and manufactures photography-related supplies.

Sales: $186.4 million (trend .2% a year).
Earnings: $1.69 million (trend 32.4% a year).
What happened to a $10,000 investment

Purchase Date	*Purchase Price*	*Price on 12-31-81*	*Dividends Paid*
12-31-71	$16.37	$3.37	$152.67
12-31-76	$ 4.37	$3.37	$ 0.00

Purchase Date	*Cap. Gains (– Losses)*	*Total Return*	*Rate of Return*
12-31-71	$–7,938.93	$–7,786.26	–14.00%
12-31-76	$–2,285.71	$–2,285.71	–5.06%

* * *

BEST PRODUCTS CO., INC. (BES). Founded 1969. Headquarters: Parham Rd. at Interstate 95, Richmond VA 23227. CATALOG SHOWROOMS. Best is the nation's largest catalog showroom merchandiser. 4,000 employees.

Sales: $1,002.0 million (trend 27.9% a year).
Earnings: $24.25 million (trend 16.1% a year).
What happened to a $10,000 investment

Purchase Date	*Purchase Price*	*Price on 12-31-81*	*Dividends Paid*
12-31-71	$15.47	$18.25	$469.87
12-31-76	$16.17	$18.25	$449.69

Purchase Date	*Cap. Gains (– Losses)*	*Total Return*	*Rate of Return*
12-31-71	$1,795.33	$2,265.21	2.06%
12-31-76	$1,288.66	$1,738.35	3.26%

PROFILE: Best Products sold about $19 million worth of goods in 1970, the year after it incorporated. In 1981 it sold $1 billion.

Dramatic growth was the hallmark of Best's through the 1970s. It was among the handful of fastest-growing retailers in both sales and profits. In fact, its growth rates were matched only by a couple of dozen other major firms, in or out of retailing. The company also picked up a reputation for the unusual architecture of its showrooms, some of which feature jagged outside walls.

Sellers of consumer goods (other than food and medicine) tend to encounter tough going during recessions, and Best Products is no exception. Its earnings slid about 32 percent in 1974 and about 29 percent in 1980. Fiscal 1981 showed a moderate rebound, but profits were below 1978 and 1979 levels.

The price of the stock tends to bob and weave. You could have ridden it up from about $1 in 1970 to about $22 in 1973 (when, like many stocks, it sold for a ridiculously high p / e ratio — in Best's case, 57). Then you could have ridden it back all the way down to less than $1 the very next year. In the early 1980s the p / e, and the stock, were in the intermediate range.

One factor that accentuates the market swings is the fact that Best Products, like many young, rapidly growing firms, has chosen to finance its rapid expansion with a lot of borrowed money. Common stock provides less than half of the company's total capital. The debt load was starting to hurt in 1981, and the company had trimmed back some of its expansion plans.

* * *

BETHLEHEM STEEL CORP. (BS). Founded 1936. Headquarters: Martin Tower, Bethlehem PA 18016. STEEL. Bethlehem is the second largest U.S. steel company. It is also involved in mining (mainly for its own consumption), shipbuilding, and ship repair. It makes a broad range of steel products, but emphasizes heavy steel for construction, shipbuilding, and bridge building. 89,000 employees.

Sales: $6,743.0 million (trend 7.7% a year).
Earnings: $121.00 million (trend –5.2% a year).
What happened to a $10,000 investment

Purchase Date	*Purchase Price*	*Price on 12-31-81*	*Dividends Paid*
12-31-71	$29.25	$23.25	$5,846.15
12-31-76	$40.37	$23.25	$1,783.28

Purchase Date	*Cap. Gains (– Losses)*	*Total Return*	*Rate of Return*
12-31-71	$–2,051.28	$ 3,794.87	3.27%
12-31-76	$–4,241.49	$–2,458.20	–5.49%

PROFILE: Even though it has closed down several obsolete plants, shrinking its work force and its expenses, Bethlehem still faces tough going ahead. The American steel industry must compete against the modern low-cost facilities of foreign producers — notably the Japanese, but also to some extent the Germans and, in the future, the Brazilians. To hold the lion's share of the U.S. market, American firms don't have to be more efficient than the competition, just equally efficient (since domestic firms by and large have lower transportation costs). The average Bethlehem facility, according to a 1981 analysis by Value Line, is about eleven years old. According to a 1981 estimate by *Forbes* magazine, it would take about $3 billion to modernize the company's facilities enough to make them internationally competitive. But the combined profits for 1978–80 were $622 million. And the company judges neither new debt offerings nor a stock issue to be practical now. So it must stay in the ring with a $750 million modernization plan and slug it out as best it can.

Earnings "growth" during the 1970s was negative over most periods you might choose to look at. Since 1978, the stock has sold for anywhere between 3 and 10 times earnings. Dividends have been paid each year since 1939, and the yield was recently more than 7 percent. But four times in the past decade, it's taken more than half the company's profits to pay the dividend.

* * *

BIG THREE INDUSTRIES, INC. (BIG). Founded 1956. Headquarters: 3535 W. 12th St., Houston TX 77008. OIL EQUIPMENT. Big Three Industries, Inc. manufactures and services oil field equipment, produces industrial gases, and makes welding equipment.

Sales: $659.1 million (trend 24.9% a year).
Earnings: $86.60 million (trend 23.7% a year).
What happened to a $10,000 investment

Purchase Date	*Purchase Price*	*Price on 12-31-81*	*Dividends Paid*
12-31-71	$ 5.98	$28.25	$3,953.04
12-31-76	$15.99	$28.25	$1,172.50

Purchase Date	*Cap. Gains (– Losses)*	*Total Return*	*Rate of Return*
12-31-71	$37,274.93	$41,227.97	17.75%
12-31-76	$ 7,667.57	$ 8,840.07	13.51%

* * *

BINNEY & SMITH INC. (BYS). Founded 1864. Headquarters: 1100 Church Lane, Easton PA 18042. ART SUPPLIES. Binney & Smith Inc. manufactures crayons, water colors, clay, paste, oil and acrylic paints, brushes, and other art supplies. MAJOR SUBSIDIARIES, BRANDS: Binney & Smith Ltd.; Crayola; Liquitex.

Sales: $94.0 million (trend 10.6% a year).
Earnings: $5.84 million (trend 6.7% a year).
What happened to a $10,000 investment

Purchase Date	*Purchase Price*	*Price on 12-31-81*	*Dividends Paid*
12-31-71	$10.32	$25.12	$5,904.65
12-31-76	$10.40	$25.12	$3,850.00

Purchase Date	*Cap. Gains (– Losses)*	*Total Return*	*Rate of Return*
12-31-71	$14,345.93	$20,250.58	11.71%
12-31-76	$14,158.65	$18,008.65	22.87%

* * *

BISCAYNE FEDERAL SAVINGS & LOAN ASSOCIATION (BIS). Founded 1976. Headquarters: 1790 Biscayne Blvd., Miami FL 33132. SAVINGS AND LOANS. Biscayne Federal Savings & Loan Association operates savings and loan associations in south Florida; loans are primarily for single-family homes.

* * *

BLACK & DECKER MANUFACTURING CO. (BDK). Founded 1910. Headquarters: 701 E. Joppa Rd., Towson MD 21204. POWER TOOLS. Black & Decker is the world's largest manufacturer of portable power tools. 21,000 employees. MAJOR SUBSIDIARIES, BRANDS: Black & Decker; McCulloch Corp. (chain saws).

Sales: $1,431.0 million (trend 16.0% a year).
Earnings: $65.66 million (trend 12.8% a year).
What happened to a $10,000 investment

Purchase Date	*Purchase Price*	*Price on 12-31-81*	*Dividends Paid*
12-31-71	$25.80	$15.12	$1,961.35
12-31-76	$20.12	$15.12	$1,595.03

Purchase Date	*Cap. Gains (– Losses)*	*Total Return*	*Rate of Return*
12-31-71	$–4,137.89	$–2,176.54	–2.42%
12-31-76	$–2,484.47	$ –889.44	–1.85%

PROFILE: Like its power tools, Black & Decker has turned in a good, workmanlike job. But investors have been left feeling as if they'd been caressed by a power sander. It's a classic case of a company that turns in a good performance only to be booed off the stage by an audience expecting a great one.

Years of fast earnings growth (at a 15 percent a year clip) had led investors to tag Black & Decker with that magic label "growth stock" and a p / e ratio to match. In 1973, investors had bid the stock up to more than $40 a share, which was more than 40 times the company's earnings at the time. Then the stock price softened with the market as a whole — and collapsed further when Black & Decker had an off year in 1975. Through much of the late 1970s and early 1980s the stock traded in the teens and low twenties.

Meanwhile, Black & Decker has pretty much resumed its historic growth rate (though 15 percent a year earnings growth wasn't as impressive in the recent inflationary days as it used to be). The company, which is number one in consumer sales of power tools in the United States, has even stronger positions in several countries abroad. (It has about 90 percent of the market in Britain, for example.) Expanding foreign sales account for about 60 percent of the company's earnings.

Along with new markets, Black & Decker has been pushing ahead with new products, from portable cordless vacuum cleaners to operating-room saws. The balance sheet is nice and trim (only about 15 percent debt). If you can buy this stock at a time when its price doesn't reflect great expectations, it could be a very good investment.

* * *

BLACK HILLS POWER & LIGHT CO. (BHP). Founded 1941. Headquarters: 625 Ninth St., PO Box 1400, Rapid City SD 57709. ELECTRICITY. Black Hills Power & Light Co. provides western South Dakota, southeastern Montana, and northeastern Wyoming with electricity.

Sales: $62.9 million (trend 31.0% a year).
Earnings: $6.94 million (trend 26.9% a year).
What happened to a $10,000 investment

Purchase Date	*Purchase Price*	*Price on 12-31-81*	*Dividends Paid*
12-31-71	$16.12	$23.25	$9,054.26
12-31-76	$20.37	$23.25	$4,294.48

Purchase Date	*Cap. Gains (− Losses)*	*Total Return*	*Rate of Return*
12-31-71	$4,418.60	$13,472.87	8.91%
12-31-76	$1,411.04	$ 5,705.52	9.45%

* * *

JOHN BLAIR & CO. (BJ). Founded 1935. Headquarters: 717 Fifth Ave., New York NY 10022. ADVERTISING. John Blair & Co. is involved in national and regional advertising sales for radio and television; also owns several radio and television stations. MAJOR SUBSIDIARIES, BRANDS: Alden Press; American Printers and Lithographers; Blairsat, Inc.

Sales: $220.6 million (trend 20.4% a year).
Earnings: $11.64 million (trend 32.9% a year).
What happened to a $10,000 investment

Purchase Date	*Purchase Price*	*Price on 12-31-81*	*Dividends Paid*
12-31-71	$11.25	$24.62	$5,241.45
12-31-76	$ 7.50	$24.62	$5,835.51

Purchase Date	*Cap. Gains (− Losses)*	*Total Return*	*Rate of Return*
12-31-71	$11,888.89	$17,130.34	10.50%
12-31-76	$22,833.33	$28,668.84	31.06%

* * *

H & R BLOCK, INC. (HRB). Founded 1955. Headquarters: 4410 Main St., Kansas City MO 64111. TAX RETURN PREPARER. H & R Block, Inc., prepares federal, state, and local income tax returns; also owns an employment firm. MAJOR SUBSIDIARIES, BRANDS: Personnel Pool of America; Block Management Co.

Sales: $263.8 million (trend 16.6% a year).
Earnings: $37.66 million (trend 13.0% a year).
What happened to a $10,000 investment

Purchase Date	*Purchase Price*	*Price on 12-31-81*	*Dividends Paid*
12-31-71	$38.75	$38.25	$2,155.10
12-31-76	$23.25	$38.25	$2,486.45

Purchase Date	*Cap. Gains (− Losses)*	*Total Return*	*Rate of Return*
12-31-71	$−129.03	$2,026.06	1.86%
12-31-76	$ 6,451.61	$8,938.06	13.62%

* * *

BLUE BELL, INC. (BBL). Founded 1962. Headquarters: 335 Church Court, Greensboro NC 27401. CLOTHING. Blue Bell is a major manufacturer of casual and work clothing, particularly blue jeans. 30,000 employees. MAJOR SUBSIDIARIES, BRANDS: Wrangler; Big Ben; Maverick; Red Kap; Sandra Lou; Sedgefield; Jantzen Inc.

Sales: $1,427.2 million (trend 15.1% a year).
Earnings: $46.68 million (trend −2.3% a year).
What happened to a $10,000 investment

Purchase Date	*Purchase Price*	*Price on 12-31-81*	*Dividends Paid*
12-31-71	$20.31	$25.12	$4,671.26
12-31-76	$29.25	$25.12	$2,564.10

Purchase Date	*Cap. Gains (− Losses)*	*Total Return*	*Rate of Return*
12-31-71	$ 2,369.23	$7,040.49	5.47%
12-31-76	$−1,410.26	$1,153.85	2.21%

PROFILE: If you think ads for Wrangler jeans bear a resemblance to Winston cigarette advertisements, it's probably not a coincidence. In 1980 Blue Bell brought in Robert Odear, an executive with a track record for marketing Winstons and L'eggs panty hose, to head its Wrangler group in the United States. At the same time, Blue Bell gave Odear an increase in Wrangler's marketing budget, to about 3 percent of sales, the same percentage arch rival Levi Strauss spends.

Levi Strauss controlled about 33 percent of the jeans market in 1979 (according to research by the brokerage firm Dean Witter Reynolds), while Blue Bell, number two in jeans, had about 10 percent. A major part of Blue Bell's strategy is to try to increase its slice of the jeans market. At the same time, it has been cutting back its European operations, which have been disappointing in recent years, and diversifying a bit (e.g. by acquiring Jantzen swimwear in 1980).

When the dust settled on a 1980 power struggle within the company, two major officers and board members were gone, and a take-over bid from Allegheny Ludlum Industries had been rejected. The power was in the hands of president L. Kimsey Mann, who will turn sixty-five in 1983.

Though Blue Bell was incorporated in its present form in 1962, the company has been in existence since 1916 (originally as the Jellico Clothing Manufacturing Co., and after 1926 as the Blue Bell Overall Co.). The company hasn't suffered a loss year since 1924, and has paid dividends every year since 1923. Recently it has attracted considerable takeover interest, so the stock may fluctuate with merger rumors.

* * *

BOBBIE BROOKS, INC. (BBK). Founded 1939. Headquarters: 3830 Kelley Ave., Cleveland OH 44114. **WOMEN'S CLOTHING.** Bobbie Brooks, Inc. designs, manufactures, and sells women's apparel. **MAJOR SUBSIDIARIES, BRANDS:** Abby Michael; Bobbie Brooks; Bryn Mawr; Perception; Prologue Perception.

Sales: $190.4 million (trend 7.1% a year).
Earnings: $−1.20 million.
What happened to a $10,000 investment

Purchase Date	*Purchase Price*	*Price on 12-31-81*	*Dividends Paid*
12-31-71	$14.62	$2.25	$0.00
12-31-76	$ 3.50	$2.25	$0.00

Purchase Date	*Cap. Gains (− Losses)*	*Total Return*	*Rate of Return*
12-31-71	$−8,461.54	$−8,461.54	−17.07%
12-31-76	$−3,571.43	$−3,571.43	−8.46%

* * *

THE BOEING CO. (BA). Founded 1934. Headquarters: 7755 E. Marginal Way S., Seattle WA 98108. **AEROSPACE.** Boeing is the world's largest manufacturer of commercial jet planes and a major manufacturer of missiles and military planes. 98,000 employees. **MAJOR SUBSIDIARIES, BRANDS:** Boeing 727, 737, 747, 757 and 767 planes; Chinook and C-47 helicopters; Cruise and MX missiles.

Sales: $9,426.2 million (trend 22.7% a year).
Earnings: $600.50 million (trend 56.5% a year).
What happened to a $10,000 investment

Purchase Date	*Purchase Price*	*Price on 12-31-81*	*Dividends Paid*
12-31-71	$4.14	$22.50	$15,194.63
12-31-76	$9.94	$22.50	$ 5,474.86

Purchase Date	*Cap. Gains (− Losses)*	*Total Return*	*Rate of Return*
12-31-71	$44,362.42	$59,557.05	21.40%
12-31-76	$12,625.70	$18,100.56	22.95%

PROFILE: There were times in Boeing's history when the address "Marginal Way" seemed frighteningly appropriate. The company scraped out a profit by the skin of its teeth in 1969–71 and had to lay off thousands of workers, contributing to economic woe in the Seattle area. Today, however, Boeing looks awesome. Both Boeing investors and Seattle have reason to be pleased with the long-term outlook. The company dominates commercial aircraft production. It built some 60 percent of the planes now in use in the Western world and seems, if anything, to be increasing its market share. (Sales of commercial planes are divided about evenly between the U.S. and other countries.) And military business, which recently has accounted for about 20 percent of Boeing's sales, looks strong in the light of pledged increases in defense spending under the Reagan administration.

The short-term outlook is less favorable. Airlines, hurt badly by the recession, have cut back on plane orders.

The company's balance sheet is rock-solid, with less than 5 percent debt and no preferred stock, as of 1980. The price / earnings ratio in recent years has been conservative, ranging from about 5 to 8 in 1973–80.

Chairman T. (that's what they call him) Wilson, never timid, is pouring some $3 billion into production of a new generation of fuel-efficient planes. That may depress profits for a while, but Boeing is betting on big sales in the middle and late 1980s. Its biggest competition is the Airbus, built by a consortium of government-backed companies in West Germany, France, and Spain.

* * *

BOISE CASCADE CORP. (BCC). Founded 1931. Headquarters: 1 Jefferson Square, Boise ID 83728. FOREST PRODUCTS. Boise is a major manufacturer of paper, building materials, and other wood products; it owns a bit over 3 million acres of timberland and controls an additional 4.3 million or so. 35,000 employees.

Sales: $3,018.9 million (trend 15.3% a year).
Earnings: $136.01 million (trend 17.8% a year).
What happened to a $10,000 investment

Purchase Date	*Purchase Price*	*Price on 12-31-81*	*Dividends Paid*
12-31-71	$18.75	$34.25	$5,100.53
12-31-76	$33.62	$34.25	$2,230.48

Purchase Date	*Cap. Gains (– Losses)*	*Total Return*	*Rate of Return*
12-31-71	$8,266.67	$13,367.20	8.86%
12-31-76	$ 185.87	$ 2,416.36	4.42%

PROFILE: Back to basics. That's been the watchword at Boise for about a decade now, following a decade in which the company attempted to become a freewheeling, high-flying conglomerate.

The 1960s saw Boise, under then-chairman Robert Hansberger, fly off in several directions at once, to the merry tune of applause from Wall Street. Real estate, recreational vehicles, even South American utilities — nothing was forbidden, so long as it offered some promise of adding to sales and profits. Investors were tickled. They bid the stock up to a peak of $77 in 1969 and the p / e ratio up to a peak of about 44 in 1970. Then the coach turned back into a pumpkin. The company lost $37 million in 1971, the applause stopped, and in 1972 Hansberger departed. The stock hit a 1973 low of about $8.37 a share.

His successor and the current chairman, John B. Fery, has tried to undo the diversification program and to redirect Boise's energies back into its historic business, forest products. What's more, he has launched a major expansion plan (budgeted at $2.3 billion in capital spending for 1979–83) to try to lift Boise to the top of the forest products industry in size and profitability. (As of 1980, Boise was about the sixth largest forest products company in the United States. In profitability, it has been below average in recent years.)

Slowly, the company under Fery has been grinding out a comeback. The stock sold between $30 and $40 a share in most of 1975–81. Progress has been slowed by poor conditions in the building industry.

* * *

BORDEN, INC. (BN). Founded 1899. Headquarters: 277 Park Ave., New York NY 10017. FOODS, CHEMICALS. Borden is a major producer of dairy products and foods and a manufacturer of chemical products. 39,000 employees. MAJOR SUBSIDIARIES, BRANDS: Bama jellies; Borden milk and cheese; Colonial sugar; Cracker Jack; Drake's cake; Elmer's glue; Kava instant coffee; Lite-Line and Liederkranz cheeses; Old London snack foods; ReaLemon lemon juice; Sacramento tomato juice; Wise snack foods; Wyler's soups.

Sales: $4,595.8 million (trend 7.0% a year).
Earnings: $147.86 million (trend 8.7% a year).
What happened to a $10,000 investment

Purchase Date	*Purchase Price*	*Price on 12-31-81*	*Dividends Paid*
12-31-71	$27.62	$28.25	$5,497.74
12-31-76	$34.25	$28.25	$2,594.89

Purchase Date	*Cap. Gains (– Losses)*	*Total Return*	*Rate of Return*
12-31-71	$ 226.24	$5,723.98	4.63%
12-31-76	$–1,751.82	$ 843.07	1.63%

PROFILE: In 1970, Borden rang up sales of about $1.8 billion. In 1980 it sold $4.5 billion of food and chemicals. A growth stock? A darling of Wall Street?

Heck, no. In 1970 Borden stock ranged between $17 and $27 a share. In 1980 it ranged between $19 and $27. Hardly budged. The fact is, Borden's profit performance over the past decade has been nothing to break open a box of Cracker Jack about.

Its profitability and profit growth have both been below average. The return on stockholders' equity in recent years has been about 12 percent, compared with close to 16 percent for the average big company. No wonder Stanley Fishman, an analyst for Fahnestock & Co., said that many investors see Borden as a "sleeping giant."

In 1980, Borden announced a five-year, $1.5 billion change in direction. It's going to become more of a chemical company, less of a foods company. (In 1979, chemicals contributed only 24 percent of sales, but 40 percent of profits.) In both foods and chemicals, it hopes to sell off businesses that were a drag on profits and redeploy assets into faster-growth areas. The stated aim: to jack up return on stockholders' equity to 18 percent. In early 1981, Borden had already sold off Mystic tape, Lusterware, Sterling (plastic goods), and its phosphate operations. Next to go were fertilizers and bulk cheese. Such divestitures are expected to pay for a fair chunk of the five-year plan and to make Borden leaner (in sales) but more profitable. Money is to be poured into such nonglamorous but — Borden trusts — profitable areas as production of polyvinyl chloride resins and ammonia.

Borden has paid dividends every year since it was founded in 1899. The dividend yield has been above 4 percent since 1969 and was above 7 percent in early 1981.

* * *

BORG-WARNER CORP. (BOR). Founded 1967. Headquarters: 200 S. Michigan Ave., Chicago IL 60604. **DIVERSIFIED MANUFACTURER.** Borg-Warner's major operations are in industrial process equipment, transportation equipment, chemicals, air conditioning, and security. 57,000 employees. **MAJOR SUBSIDIARIES, BRANDS:** Blendex; Cycopac; Weston (specialty chemicals); York Air Conditioning; 18 percent interest in Hughes Tool Co.

Sales: $2,673.3 million (trend 11.2% a year).
Earnings: $126.10 million (trend 23.5% a year).
What happened to a $10,000 investment

Purchase Date	*Purchase Price*	*Price on 12-31-81*	*Dividends Paid*
12-31-71	$15.12	$26.50	$5,683.47
12-31-76	$15.25	$26.50	$3,436.07

Purchase Date	*Cap. Gains (– Losses)*	*Total Return*	*Rate of Return*
12-31-71	$7,520.66	$13,204.13	8.78%
12-31-76	$7,377.05	$10,813.11	15.79%

PROFILE: Borg-Warner is one of those companies you may never think about, but whose products you use without knowing it. Perhaps you drive to work in a car with a carburetor, transmission, or other parts built by Borg-Warner. At work, you might be cooled by a York air conditioner. Or, you might get into an accident on the way and go to the hospital, where you'd rest in a Borg-Warner-manufactured bed. Thus does Borg-Warner quietly roll up about $3 billion a year in sales.

Apparently, there's nothing here to ignite the imagination of investors, who have attached a very conservative multiple (from 4 to 7 in the eight years 1973–80) to Borg-Warner's stock. A nice clean balance sheet (less than 15 percent debt) and a good earnings trend (up about 20 percent a year recently) haven't been enough to set investors' greed glands going. The stock price hasn't changed much in over a decade.

Still, Borg-Warner has been showing a long-term earnings uptrend in the face of poor conditions in some of its principal markets. It's hard to sell chemicals during a recession, harder still to thrive on auto parts during the auto industry's most miserable time (1980–81) in decades. The next big cyclical upturn in the economy should give a significant boost to Borg-Warner's earnings and its stock.

* * *

BORMAN'S INC. (BRF). Founded 1969. Headquarters: 18718 Borman Ave., PO Box 446, Detroit MI 48232. **SUPERMARKETS, DRUGSTORES.** Borman's Inc. operates supermarkets and drugstores in Detroit; also involved in dairy production and film processing. **MAJOR SUBSIDIARIES, BRANDS:** Farmer Jack; Food Fair Mini Mart; Town Pride; Wesley's Quaker Maid.

Sales: $1,000.8 million (trend 12.3% a year).
Earnings: $.03 million (trend −48.0% a year).
What happened to a $10,000 investment

Purchase Date	*Purchase Price*	*Price on 12-31-81*	*Dividends Paid*
12-31-71	$7.87	$2.12	$ 571.43
12-31-76	$3.87	$2.12	$1,161.29

Purchase Date	*Cap. Gains (– Losses)*	*Total Return*	*Rate of Return*
12-31-71	$−7,301.59	$−6,730.16	−10.58%
12-31-76	$−4,516.13	$−3,354.84	−7.85%

* * *

BOSTON EDISON CO. (BSE). Founded 1886. Headquarters: 800 Boylston St., Boston MA 02199. UTILITY. Boston Edison Co. provides electricity to Boston and neighboring areas.

Sales: $886.4 million (trend 10.8% a year).
Earnings: $51.66 million (trend 18.3% a year).
What happened to a $10,000 investment

Purchase Date	*Purchase Price*	*Price on 12-31-81*	*Dividends Paid*
12-31-71	$39.87	$22.25	$6,274.61
12-31-76	$27.37	$22.25	$4,690.41

Purchase Date	*Cap. Gains (− Losses)*	*Total Return*	*Rate of Return*
12-31-71	$−4,420.06	$1,854.55	1.72%
12-31-76	$−1,872.15	$2,818.26	5.09%

* * *

BRANIFF INTERNATIONAL CORP. (BNF). Founded 1971. Headquarters: Braniff Blvd., Dallas-Fort Worth Airport TX 75261. AIRLINE. Until May of 1982, Braniff flew to some fifty U.S. cities and some twelve foreign countries (in Europe and South America), mainly from a hub at Dallas-Forth Worth. At that time, it filed for protection under federal bankruptcy laws and suspended operations. MAJOR SUBSIDIARIES, BRANDS: Braniff Airways.

Sales: $1,452.1 million (trend 21.0% a year).
Earnings: $−131.44 million.
What happened to a $10,000 investment

Purchase Date	*Purchase Price*	*Price on 12-31-81*	*Dividends Paid*
12-31-71	$15.41	$2.25	$1,051.09
12-31-76	$10.87	$2.25	$ 956.32

Purchase Date	*Cap. Gains (− Losses)*	*Total Return*	*Rate of Return*
12-31-71	$−8,540.16	$−7,489.07	−12.91%
12-31-76	$−7,931.03	$−6,974.71	−21.27%

PROFILE: It's not true that vultures circle Braniff planes as they ply the skies. But it is true that Braniff is a pretty sick airline.

Overambitious expansion plans in the late 1970s boomeranged, leaving Braniff awash in red ink. The company tried to add on bunches of new routes just as the recession was dampening demand and fuel costs were soaring. The airline was forced into a financial crash landing. It lost about $44 million in 1979, $128 million in 1980, and $160 million in 1981. As of 1981 it was weighed down by a crushing debt load — 80 percent of capital. In 1982, it finally threw in the towel and filed for protection under Chapter 11 of the federal bankruptcy code.

Predictably, when a company is in trouble, there will be executive suite upheavals and merger rumors. Both were rife at Braniff in the early 1980s. In what one Braniff executive called a "Christmas massacre," chairman Harding L. Lawrence was forced to resign in 1980, and president Russell Thayer was demoted. John Casey got the possibly dubious honor of picking up both titles—until he resigned in 1982, and was replaced by Howard Putnam.

Braniff had reacted to its woes by selling off airplanes to raise money and cutting back on routes and flight schedules. It "rented" its South American routes to Eastern. The company had been hoping for a merger to bail it out, but who would want to touch such a hot potato—unless Braniff's banks ease the way by forgiving some debts. Eastern Airlines, itself heavily leveraged, had indicated some interest. The two airlines with the strongest balance sheets, Delta and Northwest, had shown none.

* * *

BRIGGS & STRATTON CORP. (BGG). Founded 1909. Headquarters: 3300 N. 124th St., Wauwatosa WI 53222. ENGINES. Briggs & Stratton Corp. manufactures gasoline engines and automotive locks and keys. MAJOR SUBSIDIARIES, BRANDS: Briggs & Stratton Disc, Inc.; Briggs & Stratton Export Corp.; Farymann Diesel GmbH.

Sales: $569.0 million (trend 14.8% a year).
Earnings: $25.11 million (trend 2.8% a year).
What happened to a $10,000 investment

Purchase Date	*Purchase Price*	*Price on 12-31-81*	*Dividends Paid*
12-31-71	$17.81	$23.75	$6,021.05
12-31-76	$33.25	$23.75	$2,006.02

Purchase Date	*Cap. Gains (− Losses)*	*Total Return*	*Rate of Return*
12-31-71	$ 3,333.33	$ 9,354.39	6.83%
12-31-76	$−2,857.14	$−851.13	−1.76%

* * *

BRISTOL-MYERS CO. (BMY). Founded 1933. Headquarters: 345 Park Ave., New York NY 10022. TOILETRIES, DRUGS. Bristol-Myers is a major manufacturer of toiletries, over-the-counter and prescription drugs, and household consumer products. 34,000 employees. **MAJOR SUBSIDIARIES, BRANDS:** Clairol hair dyes; Ban deodorant; Bufferin and Excedrin pain relievers; Enfamil baby formula; Drano drain cleaner; Vanish toilet bowl cleaner; Windex window cleaner; Platinol and other anti-cancer agents.

Sales: $3,158.3 million (trend 11.5% a year).
Earnings: $268.00 million (trend 14.1% a year).
What happened to a $10,000 investment

Purchase Date	*Purchase Price*	*Price on 12-31-81*	*Dividends Paid*
12-31-71	$29.19	$53.12	$3,643.68
12-31-76	$34.19	$53.12	$1,971.48

Purchase Date	*Cap. Gains (− Losses)*	*Total Return*	*Rate of Return*
12-31-71	$8,201.28	$11,844.97	8.13%
12-31-76	$5,539.31	$ 7,510.79	11.86%

PROFILE: Household names? They've got 'em coming out of their ears at Bristol-Myers: Bufferin, Excedrin, Ban, Clairol, and Windex, to name only a few.

Bristol-Myers is, above all, a marketing company. It's a machine for generating new products — and for advertising the heck out of the ones it already has. That's a very simple formula . . . simple to state, anyway. But the skill is in the implementation.

Bristol-Myers has implemented it well enough to have achieved twenty-seven straight years of record profits going into 1981. In recent years, profits have been rising about 15 percent a year, a very respectable percentage for a big, established, diversified company. With its churning cornucopia of heavily advertised products, Bristol-Myers has been able to walk away smiling from a lot of product failures (Vote toothpaste, That Look shampoo, Trig deodorant), knowing that other products would pick up the slack.

Perhaps it's not surprising that the company applies the same approach, emphasizing marketing and diversity, in its prescription drug business. But that's an oddity in that business, where basic research and the search for a single big "blockbuster" drug are a common emphasis. Bristol-Myers has a lot of medium-selling drugs, no blockbusters. With typical marketing skill, it saw an opportunity in anti-cancer drugs when others didn't and is a leader in that field. Yet it still has no major reputation as a leader in research.

The stock usually sells at a p / e ratio higher than that of the market as a whole and pays modest dividends.

* * *

BRITISH PETROLEUM CO. LTD. (BP). Founded 1909. Headquarters: Britannic House, Moor Lane, London, England EC2Y 9BU. **OIL.** As the holding company for a number of oil companies, British Petroleum is involved in exploration, production, refining, shipping, and marketing of oil and natural gas.

Sales: $49,368.0 million (trend 27.1% a year).
Earnings: $3,428.00 million (trend 77.0% a year).
What happened to a $10,000 investment

Purchase Date	*Purchase Price*	*Price on 12-31-81*	*Dividends Paid*
12-31-71	$13.12	$23.75	$6,139.96
12-31-76	$13.87	$23.75	$4,373.05

Purchase Date	*Cap. Gains (− Losses)*	*Total Return*	*Rate of Return*
12-31-71	$8,095.24	$14,235.20	9.26%
12-31-76	$7,117.12	$11,490.16	16.53%

* * *

BROCK HOTEL CORP. (BHC). Founded 1969. Headquarters: 2209 W. 29th St., Topeka KS 66611. **HOTELS, RESTAURANTS.** Brock manages some fifty Holiday Inns in twenty states (making it the biggest manager of Holiday Inns except for Holiday Inns itself); also owns a majority interest in a pizza restaurant chain. **MAJOR SUBSIDIARIES, BRANDS:** Show-Biz Pizza Place (80 percent owned).

Sales: $104.3 million.
Earnings: $4.38 million.

* * *

BROCKWAY GLASS COMPANY, INC. (BRK). Founded 1907. Headquarters: McCollough Ave., Brockway PA 15824. **GLASS.** Brockway Glass Company, Inc. produces glass, plastic, and metal containers and manufactures glass tubing. **MAJOR SUBSIDIARIES, BRANDS:** Captainer Plastics Corp.; Crown Airways.

Sales: $698.5 million (trend 13.3% a year).
Earnings: $17.19 million (trend −5.1% a year).
What happened to a $10,000 investment

Purchase Date	*Purchase Price*	*Price on 12-31-81*	*Dividends Paid*
12-31-71	$15.92	$14.50	$5,283.77
12-31-76	$22.83	$14.50	$2,353.28

Purchase Date	*Cap. Gains (— Losses)*	*Total Return*	*Rate of Return*
12-31-71	$ −890.05	$ 4,393.72	3.71%
12-31-76	$−3,649.64	$−1,296.35	−2.74%

* * *

THE BROOKLYN UNION GAS CO. (BU). Founded 1895. Headquarters: 195 Montague St., Brooklyn NY 11201. NATURAL GAS. The Brooklyn Union Gas Co. distributes natural gas to Brooklyn, Staten Island, and parts of Queens. MAJOR SUBSIDIARIES, BRANDS: Fuel Resources Inc.; Gas Energy Inc.

Sales: $627.7 million (trend 17.0% a year).
Earnings: $28.08 million (trend 16.2% a year).
What happened to a $10,000 investment

Purchase Date	*Purchase Price*	*Price on 12-31-81*	*Dividends Paid*
12-31-71	$24.50	$24.50	$7,875.51
12-31-76	$19.62	$24.50	$5,449.68

Purchase Date	*Cap. Gains (— Losses)*	*Total Return*	*Rate of Return*
12-31-71	$ .00	$7,875.51	5.98%
12-31-76	$2,484.08	$7,933.76	12.39%

* * *

BROWN & SHARPE MANUFACTURING CO. (BNS). Founded 1969. Headquarters: Precision Park, North Kingstown RI 02852. TOOLS. Brown & Sharpe Manufacturing Co. makes precision measuring, metal cutting, and hydraulic machinery. MAJOR SUBSIDIARIES, BRANDS: Chamberlain Group Ltd.

Sales: $227.5 million (trend 23.3% a year).
Earnings: $14.50 million (trend 89.6% a year).
What happened to a $10,000 investment

Purchase Date	*Purchase Price*	*Price on 12-31-81*	*Dividends Paid*
12-31-71	$10.10	$18.50	$5,013.61
12-31-76	$ 7.29	$18.50	$5,804.57

Purchase Date	*Cap. Gains (— Losses)*	*Total Return*	*Rate of Return*
12-31-71	$ 8,309.28	$13,322.88	8.84%
12-31-76	$15,371.42	$21,176.00	25.53%

* * *

BROWN GROUP, INC. (BG). Founded 1913. Headquarters: 8400 Maryland Ave., St. Louis MO 63105. SHOES. Brown is a major manufacturer of women's, men's, and children's shoes; has sidelines in fabrics, casual clothing, and sports equipment. 26,000 employees. MAJOR SUBSIDIARIES, BRANDS: Brown Shoe Co. (Buster Brown, Air Step, DeLiso, Levi's For Feet, Naturalizer); Wohl Shoe Co. (Regal); BottomHalf; Cloth World; Eagle Rubber; Hedstrom Co.; Outdoor Sports Industries; Famous Footwear.

Sales: $1,220.9 million (trend 10.3% a year).
Earnings: $44.97 million (trend 25.3% a year).
What happened to a $10,000 investment

Purchase Date	*Purchase Price*	*Price on 12-31-81*	*Dividends Paid*
12-31-71	$25.67	$28.37	$4,272.73
12-31-76	$15.25	$28.37	$4,010.93

Purchase Date	*Cap. Gains (— Losses)*	*Total Return*	*Rate of Return*
12-31-71	$1,055.19	$ 5,327.92	4.36%
12-31-76	$8,606.56	$12,617.49	17.73%

PROFILE: This stock hasn't gone much of anywhere in more than a decade. It has consistently sold for a low multiple of earnings. Wall Street just hasn't been able to get very excited about the shoe business in general, or Brown in particular.

Nor has there really been too much to get excited about. *Forbes* magazine ranked Brown fifth among five shoe manufacturers in profitability for the period 1975–80. Sales and earnings have generally been rising, but more slowly than for the average company.

The diversifications — BottomHalf, Cloth World, Eagle Rubber, Hedstrom, and Outdoor Sports Industries — haven't really added too much to growth, profits, or even diversity. In fiscal 1979 the company still got 70 percent of its revenues and 75 percent of its profits from selling shoes.

One advantage Brown has over some other shoe manufacturers is that it sells about a third of its shoes in its own retail outlets. At least there's no question what brand those outlets will be pushing. To use its advertising dollars more effectively, Brown appears to be cutting back a bit on its plethora of brands (phasing out Pedwin and Roblee in 1980, for example) to concentrate more on its best-known and most successful ones. These include the famous Buster Brown line for children, the Regal line for men, and the successful Naturalizer line for women.

Dividends have been paid every year since 1923, and in recent years have been at a bit better than bank passbook rates.

* * *

BROWNING-FERRIS INDUSTRIES, INC. (BFI). Founded 1970. Headquarters: Browning-Ferris Bldg., 14701 St. Mary's, Houston TX 77079. WASTE DISPOSAL. Browning-Ferris Industries is involved in the disposal of solid and liquid wastes.

Sales: $552.9 million (trend 16.9% a year).
Earnings: $33.91 million (trend 19.6% a year).
What happened to a $10,000 investment

Purchase Date	*Purchase Price*	*Price on 12-31-81*	*Dividends Paid*
12-31-71	$28.75	$32.12	$1,304.35
12-31-76	$ 8.37	$32.12	$3,629.85

Purchase Date	*Cap. Gains (— Losses)*	*Total Return*	*Rate of Return*
12-31-71	$ 1,173.91	$ 2,478.26	2.24%
12-31-76	$28,358.21	$31,988.06	33.24%

* * *

BRUNSWICK CORP. (BC). Founded 1907. Headquarters: 1 Brunswick Plaza, Skokie IL 60077. CONGLOMERATE. Brunswick manufactures outboard motors, bowling and other recreational equipment, industrial and defense products. 28,000 employees. MAJOR SUBSIDIARIES, BRANDS: Mercury and Mariner outboard motors; Brunswick bowling equipment.

Sales: $1,199.7 million (trend 8.9% a year).
Earnings: $20.34 million (trend 3.5% a year).
What happened to a $10,000 investment

Purchase Date	*Purchase Price*	*Price on 12-31-81*	*Dividends Paid*
12-31-71	$37.12	$18.62	$1,434.34
12-31-76	$16.25	$18.62	$2,261.54

Purchase Date	*Cap. Gains (— Losses)*	*Total Return*	*Rate of Return*
12-31-71	$−4,983.16	$−3,548.82	−4.29%
12-31-76	$ 1,461.54	$ 3,723.08	6.53%

PROFILE: Remember Lot's wife, who looked back at Sodom and was turned into a pillar of salt? Brunswick suffered a somewhat similar fate. For more than a decade, it's been diversifying out of heavy reliance on consumer products and recreation. But there was one business in that realm that chairman K. Brooks Abernathy and Brunswick's board couldn't resist looking back at — and pouring money into. That was the outboard motor division.

After the Arab oil embargo of 1973, some people said the handwriting was on the wall for outboard motors. Abernathy, who came up through that division, didn't think so. Had outboard motors boomed again, his decision would have been hailed as courageous. As things turned out (at least so far), it's being hailed as dumb. The outboard motor division has been a terrible drain on Brunswick's profits recently. In fact, it's tremendous testimony to the health of Brunswick's other divisions that the corporation has been able to stay profitable overall.

In 1980 and 1981, management raised the dividend (as has been its habit at least once a year) in a show of confidence. The dividend yield, incidentally, has gradually risen from close to zero a decade ago to about 6 percent recently.

The real money-makers in this corporation in recent years have been the businesses Brunswick isn't known for — medical, industrial, and defense products. Among the defense products are aerial surveillance equipment, camouflage materials, and air-to-ground weapons.

In early 1982, Whittaker Corp. was buying Brunswick stock with a takeover in mind. Brunswick's management fought off the takeover by selling the medical division, which analysts think was Whittaker's chief target. However, Brunswick said that without the medical division, it might have to reduce or eliminate the dividend. The division had accounted for roughly a quarter of sales and more than 40 percent of profits.

* * *

BRUSH WELLMAN INC. (BW). Founded 1931. Headquarters: 17876 St. Clair Ave., Cleveland OH 44110. BERYLLIUM. Brush Wellman Inc. produces beryllium and beryllium-related products; also makes quartz products. MAJOR SUBSIDIARIES, BRANDS: S. K. Wellman.

Sales: $188.8 million (trend 20.2% a year).
Earnings: $18.18 million (trend 34.5% a year).
What happened to a $10,000 investment

Purchase Date	*Purchase Price*	*Price on 12-31-81*	*Dividends Paid*
12-31-71	$ 8.65	$34.62	$5,867.05
12-31-76	$11.10	$34.62	$3,716.22

Purchase Date	Cap. Gains (— Losses)	Total Return	Rate of Return
12-31-71	$30,028.90	$35,895.95	16.46%
12-31-76	$21,193.69	$24,909.91	28.41%

* * *

BUCYRUS-ERIE CO. (BY). Founded 1927. Headquarters: 1100 Milwaukee Ave., South Milwaukee WI 53172. **MINING, CONSTRUCTION MACHINERY.** Bucyrus-Erie Co. manufactures precision gears and gear drives used for mining and construction machinery; also manufactures railroad freight cars and steel castings. **MAJOR SUBSIDIARIES, BRANDS:** Bradfoote Gear Works, Inc.; Ruston-Bucyrus Limited.

Sales: $511.3 million (trend 6.5% a year).
Earnings: $48.23 million (trend 10.1% a year).
What happened to a $10,000 investment

Purchase Date	Purchase Price	Price on 12-31-81	Dividends Paid
12-31-71	$10.22	$16.25	$6,497.71
12-31-76	$27.12	$16.25	$1,533.64

Purchase Date	Cap. Gains (— Losses)	Total Return	Rate of Return
12-31-71	$ 5,901.74	$ 12,399.45	8.40%
12-31-76	$−4,009.22	$−2,475.58	−5.53%

* * *

BUNDY CORP. (BNY). Founded 1929. Headquarters: 333 W. Fort St., Detroit MI 48226. **STEEL TUBING.** Bundy Corp. produces small-diameter steel tubing, plastic hoses, and flexible metal hoses. **MAJOR SUBSIDIARIES, BRANDS:** Bundy of Canada; Dixon Industries.

Sales: $171.7 million (trend 11.0% a year).
Earnings: $7.47 million (trend −25.4% a year).
What happened to a $10,000 investment

Purchase Date	Purchase Price	Price on 12-31-81	Dividends Paid
12-31-71	$17.92	$8.75	$4,416.74
12-31-76	$12.25	$8.75	$3,395.92

Purchase Date	Cap. Gains (— Losses)	Total Return	Rate of Return
12-31-71	$−5,116.28	$−699.53	−.72%
12-31-76	$−2,857.14	$ 538.78	1.06%

* * *

BUNKER HILL INCOME SECURITIES, INC. (BHL). Founded 1973. Headquarters: 1000 E. Walnut St., PO Box 4602, Pasadena CA 91106. **INVESTMENTS.** Bunker Hill Income Securities, Inc. is a publicly traded investment company that invests primarily in long-term bonds.

* * *

BURLINGTON INDUSTRIES, INC. (BUR). Founded 1937. Headquarters: 3330 W. Friendly Ave., Greensboro NC 27410. **TEXTILES.** Burlington is the nation's largest manufacturer of textile products. 65,000 employees.

Sales: $3,262.9 million (trend 7.3% a year).
Earnings: $115.31 million (trend .7% a year).
What happened to a $10,000 investment

Purchase Date	Purchase Price	Price on 12-31-81	Dividends Paid
12-31-71	$34.37	$24.37	$4,055.27
12-31-76	$28.37	$24.37	$2,498.68

Purchase Date	Cap. Gains (— Losses)	Total Return	Rate of Return
12-31-71	$−2,909.09	$1,146.18	1.09%
12-31-76	$−1,409.69	$1,088.99	2.09%

PROFILE: For most periods during the past fifteen years or so, investing in Burlington Industries has been a formula for capital losses. The stock sold as high as $50 a share in 1966, $40 a share in 1972, $30 a share in 1977, and $20 a share in 1980. In early 1981 it was selling at $19 a share. The dividend yield, though good, has only roughly offset the capital losses.

Can Burlington go down any further? After all, the company is profitable, even if uninspiringly so. Dividends have been paid every year since 1931, six years before the company was incorporated in its present form. In early 1982, the stock was selling for a very conservative 5 times earnings. And the balance sheet is reasonably healthy, with long-term debt only about a third of capital.

Answer: It could go down further, but probably not much. The company has already absorbed much of the shock of rising wages due to unionization. Its recent stock price reflects a conservative multiple of earnings during a recession. The only way this stock can go down much more is for the economy to go completely sour.

But . . . there's no reason to expect this stock to do especially well, either. Textiles are not traditionally a high-growth business, and consumer spending is not likely to turn red-hot for quite a while. Wage costs will probably continue rising. And Burlington, though it's the biggest textile company, has been one of the less profitable in recent years. It's been a laggard stock in a laggard industry.

* * *

BURLINGTON NORTHERN INC. (BNI). Founded 1961. Headquarters: 176 E. Fifth St. St. Paul MN 55101. RAILROAD. Burlington Northern operates one of the nation's two longest railroad systems (CSX operates the other), with close to 30,000 miles of track in some twenty-five states in the Midwest, West, and South. Also has operations in natural resources recovery (oil, gas, and timber), in real estate, in trucking, and in air freight. 60,000 employees. MAJOR SUBSIDIARIES, BRANDS: Burlington-Northern Railroad; Burlington Northern Air Freight. (The company has announced plans to sell the air freight operation to Pittston Co.) Merged with the Saint Louis-San Francisco Railway Co. in 1980.

Sales: $3,953.6 million (trend 19.9% a year).
Earnings: $213.78 million (trend 33.3% a year).
What happened to a $10,000 investment

Purchase Date	*Purchase Price*	*Price on 12-31-81*	*Dividends Paid*
12-31-71	$24.62	$53.62	$3,526.90
12-31-76	$22.12	$53.62	$2,400.00

Purchase Date	*Cap. Gains (− Losses)*	*Total Return*	*Rate of Return*
12-31-71	$11,776.65	$15,303.55	9.73%
12-31-76	$14,237.29	$16,637.29	21.65%

PROFILE: Like Burlington Industries (see previous entry), Burlington Northern has in recent years been less profitable than the average company in its industry, and its industry has been less profitable than most industries. You might think, then, that Burlington Northern would have been a poor stock holding.

Quite the contrary. Railroads (unlike textiles) were darlings of Wall Street in 1979–80, and Burlington Northern has been one of the star performers. Investors, long sour on railroads because of their huge appetite for capital (track maintenance) and their need to operate in a highly regulated environment (government authorities must traditionally approve every detail of a company's rate structure) have gotten sweet on them once more. The main reason: energy. Railroads typically own lots of land, often land with coal or oil under it. And railroads haul two thirds of the nation's coal. So railroad stocks have become an energy — and in particular, a coal — play. The Burlington Northern, which is one of the nation's two largest in track mileage, and which has poured money into rejuvenating the track serving Western coalfields, epitomizes this trend.

Earnings have moved up smartly in the last couple of years, reflecting increased coal shipments and more favorable rate decisions from regulators. Hopes of deregulation have added to enthusiasm for the stock. As recently as 1979, you could buy Burlington Northern shares for about $18; in 1980, they hit a high of $77. The price / earnings ratio in 1982 was 8, about average for the stock market at the time.

* * *

BURNDY CORP. (BDC). Founded 1924. Headquarters: Richards Ave., Norwalk CT 06856. ELECTRICAL COMPONENTS. Burndy Corp. manufactures and sells electrical and electronic connectors. MAJOR SUBSIDIARIES, BRANDS: Berco Manufacturing Co.; Husky Products Inc.

Sales: $253.7 million (trend 16.4% a year).
Earnings: $24.21 million (trend 24.1% a year).
What happened to a $10,000 investment

Purchase Date	*Purchase Price*	*Price on 12-31-81*	*Dividends Paid*
12-31-71	$5.72	$19.25	$5,776.70
12-31-76	$9.62	$19.25	$2,441.56

Purchase Date	*Cap. Gains (− Losses)*	*Total Return*	*Rate of Return*
12-31-71	$23,640.78	$29,417.48	14.70%
12-31-76	$10,000.00	$12,441.56	17.55%

* * *

BURROUGHS CORP. (BGH). Founded 1905. Headquarters: Burroughs Pl., Detroit MI 48232. COMPUTERS. Burroughs is a major manufacturer of computers and information systems; also makes other office products. 57,000 employees. MAJOR SUBSIDIARIES, BRANDS: Memorex.

Sales: $2,857.2 million (trend 12.1% a year).
Earnings: $81.97 million (trend −5.1% a year).
What happened to a $10,000 investment

Purchase Date	*Purchase Price*	*Price on 12-31-81*	*Dividends Paid*
12-31-71	$76.37	$34.25	$1,594.11
12-31-76	$91.62	$34.25	$1,077.22

Purchase Date	Cap. Gains (− Losses)	Total Return	Rate of Return
12-31-71	$−5,515.55	$−3,921.44	−4.86%
12-31-76	$−6,261.94	$−5,184.72	−13.60%

PROFILE: In 1980, Burroughs suffered the snapping of what had seemed like an endless string of earnings gains. But trouble had been brewing for some time before that. Since about 1976, the company had gradually been losing market share, both in medium- and large-size computers (to Sperry's Univac, among others) and in small computers (to Digital Equipment and IBM, among others).

Burroughs was a pioneer in small computers, in advanced office equipment, and in distributed processing. But it failed to follow up its early lead in any of these areas. It was also common talk in the computer industry that Burroughs was run dictatorially by chairman Paul Mirabito, and that top-rank talent under him was thin.

All of that led in 1979 to Burroughs's decision to import W. Michael Blumenthal, who had just resigned as Treasury Secretary in the Carter administration, to be Mirabito's heir apparent. Blumenthal actually took over the reins as chairman in the fall of 1980, three months ahead of schedule. Two of his first moves were to order stiff write-offs on some unprofitable business and to preside over the acquisition of Systems Development Corp. (for $98 million), a promising company in the automated office equipment market. Most observers consider Blumenthal a tough and able manager. His coming on board gave the stock a temporary lift, but any lasting lift will have to depend on the results he achieves.

The company Blumenthal took over has a clean balance sheet, a full line of computers to fit customers of all sizes, and a good, though somewhat faded, reputation. The stock had declined from a 1972 peak of about $125 a share to a 1980 low of about $46 a share. If Blumenthal can make the company click again, holders of these shares should do extremely well.

A new element on the scene is Memorex, a long-ailing maker of computer peripheral equipment acquired in 1981. A reshaped Memorex could be helpful in fleshing out Burroughs's line of products and services.

* * *

BUTLER INTERNATIONAL, INC. (BTL). Founded 1968. Headquarters: 110 Summit Ave., PO Box 460, Montvale NJ 07645. **AVIATION SERVICES.** Butler International, Inc. is engaged in heavy specialized motor carrying, aviation services and fueling, and contract technical services. **MAJOR SUBSIDIARIES, BRANDS:** Butler Aviation International, Inc.; Butler Service Group, Inc.; International Transport, Inc.

Sales: $320.9 million (trend 28.0% a year).
Earnings: $8.90 million (trend 32.2% a year).
What happened to a $10,000 investment

Purchase Date	Purchase Price	Price on 12-31-81	Dividends Paid
12-31-71	$1.32	$10.75	$16,027.73
12-31-76	$2.78	$10.75	$ 6,767.63

Purchase Date	Cap. Gains (− Losses)	Total Return	Rate of Return
12-31-71	$71,319.75	$87,347.48	25.55%
12-31-76	$28,704.08	$35,471.71	35.38%

* * *

BUTTES GAS & OIL CO. (BGO). Founded 1954. Headquarters: 1221 Broadway, Suite 1900, Oakland CA 94612. **OIL, GAS.** Buttes Gas & Oil Co. is involved in the exploration, development, and production of domestic and foreign petroleum resources and some mineral resources; also provides contract offshore drilling services. **MAJOR SUBSIDIARIES, BRANDS:** Buttes Resources Co.; Progress Drilling & Marine, Inc.

Sales: $161.6 million (trend 8.7% a year).
Earnings: $11.26 million (trend −19.5% a year).
What happened to a $10,000 investment

Purchase Date	Purchase Price	Price on 12-31-81	Dividends Paid
12-31-71	$16.12	$16.25	$297.67
12-31-76	$20.37	$16.25	$235.58

Purchase Date	Cap. Gains (− Losses)	Total Return	Rate of Return
12-31-71	$ 77.52	$ 375.19	.37%
12-31-76	$−2,024.54	$−1,788.96	−3.87%

C

CBI INDUSTRIES, INC. (CBH). Founded 1889. Headquarters: 800 Jorie Blvd., Oak Brook IL 60521. **HOLDING COMPANY.** Parent of Chicago Bridge & Iron Co., metal plate fabricator; also involved in oil and offshore services, equipment for paper industry and water and waste treatment industries. **MAJOR SUBSIDIARIES, BRANDS:** Chicago

Bridge & Iron Co.; Circle Bar Drilling Co.; Sea-Con Services; Fairmac Realty Corp.

Sales: $682.3 million (trend 3.1% a year).
Earnings: $68.45 million (trend 7.3% a year).
What happened to a $10,000 investment

Purchase Date	*Purchase Price*	*Price on 12-31-81*	*Dividends Paid*
12-31-71	$17.16	$42.75	$5,626.52
12-31-76	$27.25	$42.75	$2,311.93

Purchase Date	*Cap. Gains (– Losses)*	*Total Return*	*Rate of Return*
12-31-71	$14,918.03	$20,544.55	11.81%
12-31-76	$ 5,688.07	$ 8,000.00	12.47%

* * *

CBS INC. (CBS). Founded 1927. Headquarters: 51 W. 52nd St., New York NY 10019. **BROADCASTING.** CBS operates nationwide television and radio networks; owns five TV stations and fourteen radio stations outright; is the world's largest manufacturer of phonograph records and a potentially major producer of video discs; and is also active in publishing, toy manufacturing, musical instrument manufacturing, and (to a minor extent) retailing. 32,000 employees. **MAJOR SUBSIDIARIES, BRANDS:** CBS TV and radio networks; WCBS TV and Radio (New York); WBBM TV and Radio (Chicago); WCAU TV and Radio (Philadelphia); KNXT TV and KNX Radio (Los Angeles); KMOX TV and Radio (St. Louis); WEEI Radio (Boston); KCBS Radio (San Francisco); Columbia, Epic, Jet, and Odyssey (records); Crest, Fawcett, Popular Library, and Holt, Rinehart & Winston (publishers); Fender-Rhodes, Gemeinhardt, Gulbransen, Lyon & Healy, Rogers, and Steinway (musical instruments); Leslie speakers; Child Guidance, Creative Playthings, Erector, Gabriel, Tinkertoy, and Wonder (toys); *Woman's Day, Mechanix Illustrated,* and *Field & Stream* (magazines); Pacific Stereo, SoundWorks (retail audio stores).

Sales: $3,962.9 million (trend 16.1% a year).
Earnings: $192.78 million (trend 8.9% a year).
What happened to a $10,000 investment

Purchase Date	*Purchase Price*	*Price on 12-31-81*	*Dividends Paid*
12-31-71	$46.62	$47.37	$4,373.19
12-31-76	$59.37	$47.37	$2,155.79

Purchase Date	*Cap. Gains (– Losses)*	*Total Return*	*Rate of Return*
12-31-71	$ 160.86	$4,534.05	3.81%
12-31-76	$–2,021.05	$ 134.74	.27%

PROFILE: CBS is a coherent conglomerate. Around the mighty network it has clustered a collection of distinguished companies (e.g. Steinway, Epic, Holt, Rinehart & Winston, Fawcett, Creative Playthings), all of which are tied to the concepts of communications or entertainment.

Earnings had been up eight years running before declining slightly in 1980 and 1981. In return on stockholders' equity, the company has far outpaced the average corporation, ranking in about the top 15 percent of major companies in recent years. The balance sheet has scarcely more debt than a concert Steinway has dust: Debt has recently been less than 10 percent of total capital. (That's considerably less debt than ABC carries, and far less than RCA, parent of NBC, has.) Sales and earnings in recent years have gone upward at a decent clip.

So where's the stock? In the doghouse. The share price has hovered around $50 for more than a decade. The price / earnings ratio in the early 1980s was around 7 — a lowly ratio indeed for a company with a track record like CBS's.

Investors, in my judgment, have been spooked in large part by fear that cable TV will take away lucrative big-ticket programming from the major networks. But that fear may have been blown out of all proportion. Certain cable TV stocks have been bid up to p / e ratios that make them highly speculative, while the major networks were priced very conservatively in 1980 and 1981.

Investors have also fretted about chairman William Paley's penchant for playing musical presidents. That, too, is a legitimate concern. But worries about succession and management are less important than the results the corporation achieves, and those have been highly creditable.

* * *

CCI CORP. (CCI). Founded 1959. Headquarters: PO Box 51500, Tulsa OK 74151. **MULTI-INDUSTRY HOLDING COMPANY.** Manufactures oil well servicing rigs; carriers for concrete, waste hauling, materials hauling; railroad signal, control, and communications systems; aerospace propulsion systems and controls. **MAJOR SUBSIDIARIES, BRANDS:** Crane Carrier Company; Safetran Systems Corp.; The Marquardt Co.

Sales: $267.3 million (trend 15.3% a year).
Earnings: $10.16 million (trend 28.6% a year).
What happened to a $10,000 investment

Purchase Date	*Purchase Price*	*Price on 12-31-81*	*Dividends Paid*
12-31-71	$4.87	$15.75	$0.00
12-31-76	$3.87	$15.75	$0.00

Purchase Date	*Cap. Gains (– Losses)*	*Total Return*	*Rate of Return*
12-31-71	$22,307.69	$22,307.69	12.44%
12-31-76	$30,645.16	$30,645.16	32.37%

* * *

CLC OF AMERICA, INC. (CLC). Founded 1962. Headquarters: 2 Allen Center, Suite 2200, Houston TX 77002. TRANSPORTATION. Operates barge lines; transports recreational vehicles; leases cars and trucks; sells and leases machinery and modular structures. MAJOR SUBSIDIARIES, BRANDS: Wisconsin Barge Line; CLC Barge Line; Consolidated Leasing Corp.; Morgan Drive Away.

Sales: $158.5 million (trend 8.1% a year).
Earnings: $7.53 million (trend 17.6% a year).
What happened to a $10,000 investment

Purchase Date	*Purchase Price*	*Price on 12-31-81*	*Dividends Paid*
12-31-71	$11.62	$11.25	$1,195.70
12-31-76	$ 4.87	$11.25	$1,476.92

Purchase Date	*Cap. Gains (– Losses)*	*Total Return*	*Rate of Return*
12-31-71	$ −322.58	$ 873.12	.84%
12-31-76	$13,076.92	$14,553.85	19.68%

* * *

CNA FINANCIAL CORP. (CAF). Founded 1967. Headquarters: CNA Plaza, Chicago IL 60685. INSURANCE. CNA is a major writer of both life insurance and property-and-casualty insurance. It is also involved in consumer loans. 12,000 employees. MAJOR SUBSIDIARIES, BRANDS: Continental Casualty (property and casualty insurance); Continental Assurance (life and health insurance); General Finance (consumer loans). The company is 84 percent owned by Loews Corp.

Sales: $2,966.3 million (trend 10.4% a year).
Earnings: $131.55 million (trend 55.4% a year).
What happened to a $10,000 investment

Purchase Date	*Purchase Price*	*Price on 12-31-81*	*Dividends Paid*
12-31-71	$N/A	$15.25	$1.37
12-31-76	$ 7.75	$15.25	$0.00

Purchase Date	*Cap. Gains (– Losses)*	*Total Return*	*Rate of Return*
12-31-71	$ N/A	$ N/A	N/A%
12-31-76	$9,677.42	$9,677.42	14.50%

PROFILE: Many insurance companies are banks at heart, depending in large part on profits from investing the "float" of money that passes through them. CNA Financial is a good example. Recently, it has "lost money" on its basic property and casualty insurance business, but come out ahead because of investment income. Net investment income has shown a steady climb from $144 million in 1971 to $410 million in 1980. However, a lasting and substantial decline in interest rates could interrupt this pattern.

CNA is unusually well balanced among various lines of insurance. Workmen's compensation is the single biggest line, accounting for more than half of property and casualty premiums at Continental Casualty. At Continental Assurance, health and accident policies bring in somewhat more money than life insurance.

An unusual feature of buying this stock is that you're buying into a small minority position. Loews Corp. (profiled later in this book) recently owned 87 percent of the common stock. Since many people expect a complete takeover, rumors concerning Loews' intentions can create moves in these shares.

CNA carries a relatively low price / earnings ratio (recently 4 to 7). Investors are disenchanted because the company hasn't been able to build up sustained earnings-growth momentum. Dividends were paid for seven years starting in 1968, then stopped after a disastrous 1974, when the company lost $207 million. The property-casualty insurance cycle can be a very nasty thing.

* * *

CNA INCOME SHARES, INC. (CNN). Founded 1973. Headquarters: CNA Plaza, Chicago IL 60685. INVESTMENT. Investment company with assets placed in investment-grade debt securities.

* * *

CPC INTERNATIONAL INC. (CPC). Founded 1959. Headquarters: International Plaza, Englewood Cliffs NJ 07632. FOODS. CPC is a major seller of branded grocery products worldwide, and the largest wet corn miller in the United States. 41,000 employees. **MAJOR SUBSIDIARIES, BRANDS:** Mazola corn oil and margarine; Skippy peanut butter; Hellman's mayonnaise; Argo and Kingsford corn starch; Karo and Golden Griddle syrup; Knorr soups; Thomas' English Muffins; Rit dyes; Niagara spray starch; Bosco chocolate flavoring.

Sales: $4,120.3 million (trend 9.3% a year).
Earnings: $197.40 million (trend 12.8% a year).
What happened to a $10,000 investment

Purchase Date	*Purchase Price*	*Price on 12-31-81*	*Dividends Paid*
12-31-71	$15.81	$35.50	$7,994.62
12-31-76	$23.75	$35.50	$3,250.53

Purchase Date	*Cap. Gains (− Losses)*	*Total Return*	*Rate of Return*
12-31-71	$12,450.59	$20,445.22	11.78%
12-31-76	$ 4,947.37	$ 8,197.89	12.72%

PROFILE: You can tell a lot about this company from its name. The initials derive from its old days as simply a corn products company. In the 1950s it decided to go into the more profitable business of branded consumer foods, where it's now a major power — fourth largest (after General Mills, General Foods, and Beatrice Foods) and second most profitable (after Kellogg). The "international" is no empty boast; more than half the company's sales and earnings come from outside the United States, and the company excels at modifying its products to suit local tastes in each country. Sales and profits are rising faster abroad than here, and probably will continue to do so.

Conservative is a word often applied to CPC. Its growth rates are decent, its profitability outstanding. New products, the life of the party at some consumer foods companies, are a rarity here. CPC prefers to stick with (and sometimes tinker with) its strong, established brands, which command consumer loyalty. The balance sheet is conservative, too. Debt, as of early 1981, was only about 16 percent of total capital. That makes CPC's return on equity (above 20 percent most years) all the more outstanding an accomplishment. The dividend yield, as of early 1981, was about 6 percent. Dividends have been paid each year since 1920, before the company took its current form and name.

* * *

CP NATIONAL CORP. (CPN). Founded 1928. Headquarters: 1355 Willow Way, Concord CA 94520. **UTILITY.** Electric, gas, telephone, and water utility operating in Oregon and other western states.

Sales: $109.9 million (trend 15.7% a year).
Earnings: $4.87 million (trend 10.7% a year).
What happened to a $10,000 investment

Purchase Date	*Purchase Price*	*Price on 12-31-81*	*Dividends Paid*
12-31-71	$18.25	$23.50	$8,743.01
12-31-76	$18.25	$23.50	$4,898.63

Purchase Date	*Cap. Gains (− Losses)*	*Total Return*	*Rate of Return*
12-31-71	$2,876.71	$11,619.73	8.02%
12-31-76	$2,876.71	$ 7,775.34	12.19%

* * *

CSX CORP. (CSX). Founded 1980 (but component railroad lines date back as far as 1827). Headquarters: PO Box C-32222, Richmond VA 23261. **RAILROAD.** CSX was formed by the 1980 merger of Chessie System and Seaboard Coast Line Industries; operates a 27,000-mile track system in some twenty-two states in the Southeast, Midwest, and Middle Atlantic. 77,000 employees. **MAJOR SUBSIDIARIES, BRANDS:** Component railroads include the Chesapeake & Ohio; Baltimore & Ohio; Seaboard; Louisville & Nashville; Clinchfield; and Western Maryland.

Sales: $4,841.3 million.
Earnings: $281.61 million.

PROFILE: If you think the future belongs to coal, this is one way to play it. As of 1981, CSX was one of the country's two longest railroads (it runs neck and neck with Burlington Northern) and the biggest coal carrier. Coal constituted about a quarter of its freight revenues, and CSX's component railroads moved close to 20 percent of the nation's coal shipments.

You don't absolutely have to believe in coal to want to bet on the railroads (though it helps). If you simply believe that gasoline will become extremely expensive, you may anticipate less business for the trucking industry, more for rail carriers. Since CSX was selling in early 1982 for only about 6 times earnings and offered a dividend yield a little above 6 percent, this is a fairly conservative investment.

The debt load's not too bad, but it's a factor to be reckoned with. As of early 1981, long-term debt was about 41 percent of capital. In light of railroads' tremendous appetite for money to maintain track, potential investors here should keep an eye on the balance sheet. CSX may be especially hungry for maintenance money, since one of the component lines, the Louisville & Nashville, had been poorly maintained for years.

The idea of railroads as an energy play has pushed share prices up and yields down. Until recently, a railroad like Chessie (which had paid dividends each year since 1922) yielded 6 to 8 percent in dividends alone. For tax reasons, most investors would be better off with capital gains anyway. They'll be there — if coal's day comes.

* * *

CTS CORP. (CTS). Founded 1896. Headquarters: 905 N. West Blvd., Elkhart IN 46514. **ELECTRONICS AND ELECTROMAGNETICS.** Produces electronics and electromagnetic components and subsystems sold mainly to manufacturers of electronic equipment. **MAJOR SUBSIDIARIES, BRANDS:** Keene Products, Inc.; CTS Microelectronics; CTS Knights.

Sales: $188.0 million (trend 8.4% a year).
Earnings: $10.31 million (trend 1.6% a year).
What happened to a $10,000 investment

Purchase Date	*Purchase Price*	*Price on 12-31-81*	*Dividends Paid*
12-31-71	$18.83	$28.75	$3,365.49
12-31-76	$19.50	$28.75	$2,051.28

Purchase Date	*Cap. Gains (− Losses)*	*Total Return*	*Rate of Return*
12-31-71	$5,265.49	$8,630.97	6.42%
12-31-76	$4,743.59	$6,794.87	10.93%

* * *

CABOT CORP. (CBT). Founded 1960. Headquarters: 125 High St., Boston MA 02110. **METALS, CHEMICALS, NATURAL GAS.** Cabot manufactures specialty metals; chemicals, particularly carbon black; and explores and drills for natural gas and oil. 7,600 employees. **MAJOR SUBSIDIARIES, BRANDS:** TUCO; Cab-O-Sil; Stellite; Kawecki Berylco.

Sales: $1,622.8 million (trend 30.9% a year).
Earnings: $110.17 million (trend 31.5% a year).
What happened to a $10,000 investment

Purchase Date	*Purchase Price*	*Price on 12-31-81*	*Dividends Paid*
12-31-71	$7.04	$24.87	$4,725.44
12-31-76	$7.15	$24.87	$3,629.15

Purchase Date	*Cap. Gains (− Losses)*	*Total Return*	*Rate of Return*
12-31-71	$25,325.44	$30,050.89	14.88%
12-31-76	$24,810.50	$28,439.65	30.90%

PROFILE: If you buy Cabot stock, you'll be in some exclusive company. Some 45 percent of the stock is owned by the Cabot family (who, according to a famous though not strictly accurate poem, "talk only to God.") Another 37 percent is held by institutions (banks, pension funds, and insurance companies mainly). That leaves 18 percent of the stock to be held by common folks like you and me.

Closely held companies tend to be more volatile than average, and Cabot is no exception. According to an estimate by the Value Line Investment Survey in 1981, Cabot stock is likely to move up or down about 40 percent more than the market as a whole.

No one who held the stock in recent years would have minded that at all. If you'd bought anywhere near the 1975 low and sold at somewhere near the 1980 high, you would have increased your money tenfold.

What had Wall Street loving Cabot lately was the company's move into natural gas (and, to a lesser extent, oil) exploration and drilling. Not until 1970 did the company get into that business; by 1980 it was contributing about a third of profits. With commendable honesty, president Robert Charpie told *Forbes* magazine that the company had a hard time deciding whether to get into the energy field. (This was some three years before the Arab oil embargo.) "In hindsight it looks smart, but we weren't so sure then," Charpie said.

Cabot's traditional business is carbon black, of which it remains the world's largest producer. The first diversification move was into specialty metals, which also paid off well. But it's gas that propelled this stock's ascent.

* * *

CADENCE INDUSTRIES CORP. (CDE). Founded 1937. Headquarters: 21 Henderson Dr., West Caldwell NJ 07006. **PUBLISHING, PHARMACEUTICALS.** Engages in publishing and publishing services, produces pharmaceuticals, manufactures and sells writing instruments, and operates movie theaters. **MAJOR SUBSIDIARIES, BRANDS:** Curtis Circulation Co.; Hudson Pharmaceutical; Hudson Vitamins; Marvel Comics; Perfect Subscription Co.; U.S. Pencil & Stationery; Saxon Theatre Corp.

Sales: $131.3 million (trend 9.0% a year).
Earnings: $3.02 million (trend 21.1% a year).
What happened to a $10,000 investment

Purchase Date	*Purchase Price*	*Price on 12-31-81*	*Dividends Paid*
12-31-71	$6.90	$7.75	$0.00
12-31-76	$3.57	$7.75	$0.00

Purchase Date	*Cap. Gains (– Losses)*	*Total Return*	*Rate of Return*
12-31-71	$ 1,224.13	$ 1,224.13	1.16%
12-31-76	$11,699.98	$11,699.98	16.76%

* * *

CAESARS WORLD, INC. (CAW). Founded 1958. Headquarters: 1801 Century Park E., Los Angeles CA 90067. GAMBLING. Runs hotel-casino combinations in Nevada and Atlantic City. 8,000 employees. MAJOR SUBSIDIARIES, BRANDS: Caesars Palace (Las Vegas); Caesars Tahoe (Lake Tahoe); Boardwalk Regency (Atlantic City).

Sales: $601.6 million (trend 40.5% a year).
Earnings: $35.04 million (trend 69.4% a year).
What happened to a $10,000 investment

Purchase Date	*Purchase Price*	*Price on 12-31-81*	*Dividends Paid*
12-31-71	$1.08	$8.75	$0.00
12-31-76	$ .94	$8.75	$0.00

Purchase Date	*Cap. Gains (– Losses)*	*Total Return*	*Rate of Return*
12-31-71	$70,769.23	$70,769.23	23.23%
12-31-76	$82,647.06	$82,647.06	56.09%

PROFILE: A gambling stock in every sense of the word. Step right up, ladies and gentlemen, and take a chance — if taking chances is your notion of investing.

Here is a stock that's guaranteed to give you action. You can double your money, or lose half of it, in weeks, not years. It's an unusual year in which this stock's high isn't at least 100 percent above its low.

On fundamentals, the big run-up in gambling stocks in general and Caesars World in particular in the late 1970s seemed to have left this stock overvalued. Its return on total capital for 1975–80, according to *Forbes* magazine, was a puny 7.4 percent a year — way under the average for American industry (11.1 percent). Yet over the same period, Caesars was one of the handful of top performing stocks on Wall Street!

Part of the trick was leverage. Caesars prefers to play with other people's money, not its own. Common stock has recently provided less than half of the company's capital; more than half is borrowed. So, any profits are magnified in their effect on per-share results.

Leverage is lovely when it's working in your favor, but in down years it works in reverse. Caesars' only down year recently was 1976, when it lost about $11 million (roughly equal to the previous three years' profits). But I'd hate to be holding this volatile stock when the next down year comes.

The other problem with using so much of other people's money is they don't loan it to you free. In fiscal 1980, Caesars was paying about $35 million a year in interest — more than 7 percent of its operating revenues and more than a third of its operating income.

Even though company earnings have held up, the stock — which had been available for $1 a share in 1977, then climbed to $36 in 1979 — had fallen back to around $7 in early 1982. One reason: New Jersey regulators suspected the company founders of ties to organized crime. The board of directors has responded by moving to buy out the founders. . . . As I said, it's a gambling stock.

* * *

CALLAHAN MINING CORP. (CMN). Founded 1912. Headquarters: 6245 N. 24th St., Phoenix AZ 85016. MINING. Operates silver / copper mine; involved in natural resources exploration; manufactures flexible tubing. MAJOR SUBSIDIARIES, BRANDS: K.R.M. Petroleum Corp. (30%); Caladay Project (73%); Pinnacle Exploration (80%).

Sales: $26.8 million (trend 11.6% a year).
Earnings: $8.28 million (trend 39.7% a year).
What happened to a $10,000 investment

Purchase Date	*Purchase Price*	*Price on 12-31-81*	*Dividends Paid*
12-31-71	$4.65	$13.50	$7,868.70
12-31-76	$8.45	$13.50	$3,819.71

Purchase Date	*Cap. Gains (– Losses)*	*Total Return*	*Rate of Return*
12-31-71	$19,021.01	$26,889.70	13.94%
12-31-76	$ 5,977.41	$ 9,797.13	14.64%

* * *

CAMERON IRON WORKS, INC. (CIW). Founded 1920. Headquarters: 13013 Northwest Freeway, Houston TX 77040. **OIL TOOLS, VALVES, FORGING.** Produces tools and equipment for the oil well industry; manufactures ball valves, forged products.

Sales: $929.0 million (trend 17.1% a year).
Earnings: $110.00 million (trend 23.2% a year).
What happened to a $10,000 investment

Purchase Date	*Purchase Price*	*Price on 12-31-81*	*Dividends Paid*
12-31-71	$ N/A	$46.75	$ N/A
12-31-76	$10.85	$46.75	$847.60

Purchase Date	*Cap. Gains (− Losses)*	*Total Return*	*Rate of Return*
12-31-71	$ N/A	$ N/A	N/A%
12-31-76	$33,071.02	$33,918.62	34.44%

* * *

CAMPBELL RED LAKE MINES LTD. (CRK). Founded 1944. Headquarters: 365 Bay St., Suite 600, Toronto, Ont., Canada M5H 2V9. **GOLD.** Operates gold mine in western Ontario.

Sales: $116.2 million (trend 33.4% a year).
Earnings: $48.15 million (trend 37.1% a year).
What happened to a $10,000 investment

Purchase Date	*Purchase Price*	*Price on 12-31-81*	*Dividends Paid*
12-31-71	$1.73	$14.75	$9,200.34
12-31-76	$4.12	$14.75	$2,794.95

Purchase Date	*Cap. Gains (− Losses)*	*Total Return*	*Rate of Return*
12-31-71	$75,301.20	$84,501.54	25.18%
12-31-76	$25,757.58	$28,552.53	30.98%

* * *

CAMPBELL SOUP CO. (CPB). Founded 1922. Headquarters: Campbell Place, Camden NJ 08101. **FOODS.** Campbell's is the country's largest manufacturer of canned soup, and a major seller of other food products including frozen entrées, vegetable juice, and canned spaghetti. Also operates candy shops and restaurants. 38,000 employees. **MAJOR SUBSIDIARIES, BRANDS:** Bounty; Campbell's; Franco-American; Godiva chocolates; Pepperidge Farm; Pietro's; Recipe pet food; Swanson; V-8; Vlasic.

Sales: $2,797.7 million (trend 11.9% a year).
Earnings: $129.72 million (trend 6.0% a year).
What happened to a $10,000 investment

Purchase Date	*Purchase Price*	*Price on 12-31-81*	*Dividends Paid*
12-31-71	$30.25	$28.62	$4,842.98
12-31-76	$39.37	$28.62	$2,198.10

Purchase Date	*Cap. Gains (− Losses)*	*Total Return*	*Rate of Return*
12-31-71	$ −537.19	$ 4,305.79	3.65%
12-31-76	$−2,730.16	$−532.06	−1.09%

PROFILE: Every single year from 1971 through 1979, you could (at some time during the year) buy Campbell's stock for $35 a share. That's dependability. That's constancy. That's — from the standpoint of investors — a disaster.

It's also a testimony to the irrationality of the stock market. For, during the same period, Campbell's profits went from $2.00 a share to about $4.00 a share. Dividends were paid consistently, return on stockholders' equity wasn't bad (about 15 percent recently), and the company's balance sheet was — and is — excellent.

Obviously, Wall Street was thumbing its nose at a solid, albeit cautious, company in a mature industry. Bring on the dancing girls! Bring on the semiconductors, oil drilling ventures, genetic engineering speculations!

Well, Campbell will probably never be faddish; hiking boots are better suited to its pace than go-go boots. But it does appear to be readying itself for some changes to seek faster growth. In 1980, for the first time in 111 years, it raised a significant amount of capital through a bond issue. Previously, the company had kept debt to an absolute minimum and generated all its funds internally. In 1981, it was widely speculated that Campbell was going to use the money thus raised to buy one or more companies, possibly outside the foods business. When this book went to press, that hadn't happened. Nor is there any track record to show how Campbell would do outside the foods business.

* * *

CAMPBELL TAGGART, INC. (CTI). Founded 1927. Headquarters: 6211 Lemmon Ave., Dallas TX 75222. **BAKERY.** Campbell Taggart operates the nation's second-largest chain of bakeries (after ITT Continental); also produces frozen foods (particularly Mexican) and operates a chain of Mexican restaurants. The company, through acquisitions, recently entered the food service field. 22,000 employees. **MAJOR SUBSIDIARIES, BRANDS:** Rainbo bread; El Chico restaurants; El Charrito frozen Mexican foods; Earth Grains, Colonial, and Manor breads and bread products; Bimbo (largest bakery company in Spain); Plus Vita (Brazil); Europate (France); Larry's Food Products (frozen meat portions and sandwiches for restaurants and cafeterias); Rod's Food Products (salad dressings, dips, and spreads, also for restaurants and cafeterias).

Sales: $1,113.1 million (trend 11.4% a year).
Earnings: $36.25 million (trend 14.6% a year).
What happened to a $10,000 investment

Purchase Date	*Purchase Price*	*Price on 12-31-81*	*Dividends Paid*
12-31-71	$10.15	$20.87	$5,450.36
12-31-76	$13.89	$20.87	2,625.60

Purchase Date	*Cap. Gains (– Losses)*	*Total Return*	*Rate of Return*
12-31-71	$10,570.26	$16,020.62	10.04%
12-31-76	$ 5,030.00	$ 7,655.60	12.04%

PROFILE: Let's say you want to own stock in a large bakery. The largest is ITT Continental (maker of Wonder Bread), but it is part of a conglomerate so large that the bakery portion may be dwarfed by unrelated businesses. In Campbell Taggart you get a pure foods play — bakery goods, Mexican food, and food service. Bread and bread-related products remain the staple here, but the diversifications (such as El Chico, Rod's Food Products, and Larry's Food Products) have lately been the faster-growing side of the business.

Why would you want to own stock in a bakery? Maybe for steady growth. Campbell Taggart in 1981 was cruising to its twelfth straight up year. The growth rate has been moderate and profitability has been a bit above average for a major U.S. corporation. Dividends have been paid every year since 1937 and provide a moderate yield. It's been the company's practice to pay out just over a third of profits in dividends.

In a 1981 profile of the company, *Fortune* magazine quoted Leonard Teitelbaum, a Merrill Lynch analyst, as crediting Campbell Taggart with the best cost control system he had ever seen. Every Wednesday, top company officials get a computer printout showing (among other things) the profit and loss at each of the bakeries the company owns (approximately sixty-four). The figures are compared with the week before and the year before and broken down into sixty product lines. For good measure, the computer throws in such tidbits as the amount of stale bread returned by supermarkets, the pounds produced per employee, and the waste per employee.

* * *

CANADIAN PACIFIC LTD. (CP). Founded 1881. Headquarters: 910 Peel St., PO Box 6402, Station A, Montreal, Que. Canada H3C 3E4. **TRANSPORTATION.** Operates Canadian transportation system, including railroad and airline as well as trucking, shipping, and telecommunications activities. **MAJOR SUBSIDIARIES, BRANDS:** The Soo Line Railroad.

Sales: $8,357.1 million (trend 19.5% a year).
Earnings: $486.40 million (trend 26.0% a year).
What happened to a $10,000 investment

Purchase Date	*Purchase Price*	*Price on 12-31-81*	*Dividends Paid*
12-31-71	$14.12	$35.12	$7,536.64
12-31-76	$16.75	$35.12	$3,939.28

Purchase Date	*Cap. Gains (– Losses)*	*Total Return*	*Rate of Return*
12-31-71	$14,867.26	$22,403.89	12.48%
12-31-76	$10,970.15	$14,909.43	20.03%

* * *

CANADIAN PACIFIC ENTERPRISES LTD. (ENT). Founded 1962. Headquarters: Place du Canada, Suite 1900, Montreal, Que. Canada H3B 2N2. **NATURAL RESOURCES.** Active through subsidiaries in oil and gas production, mining, steel manufacture, and other diversified operations, principally in Canada.

Sales: $5,594.9 million.
Earnings: $411.16 million.

* * *

CANAL-RANDOLPH CORP. (CRH). Founded 1855. Headquarters: 277 Park Ave., New York NY 10017. **REAL ESTATE.** This company's holdings include a large public stockyard and office buildings throughout the country. **MAJOR SUBSIDIARIES, BRANDS:** United Stockyards.

Sales: $36.8 million (trend .3% a year).
Earnings: $1.48 million (trend −5.5% a year).
What happened to a $10,000 investment

Purchase Date	*Purchase Price*	*Price on 12-31-81*	*Dividends Paid*
12-31-71	$15.50	$28.25	$5,464.52
12-31-76	$ 8.50	$28.25	$3,764.71

Purchase Date	*Cap. Gains (− Losses)*	*Total Return*	*Rate of Return*
12-31-71	$ 8,225.81	$13,690.32	9.01%
12-31-76	$23,235.29	$27,000.00	29.91%

* * *

CANNON MILLS CO. (CAN). Founded 1928. Headquarters: Kannapolis NC 28081. **TEXTILES.** Major textile manufacturer; products include towels, sheets, bedding, yarns, and fabrics. **MAJOR SUBSIDIARIES, BRANDS:** Cannon; Beacon Manufacturing Co.; Maiden Knitting Mills.

Sales: $659.6 million (trend 10.7% a year).
Earnings: $20.63 million (trend 10.2% a year).
What happened to a $10,000 investment

Purchase Date	*Purchase Price*	*Price on 12-31-81*	*Dividends Paid*
12-31-71	$17.86	$28.75	$5,320.10
12-31-76	$14.66	$28.75	$3,758.14

Purchase Date	*Cap. Gains (− Losses)*	*Total Return*	*Rate of Return*
12-31-71	$6,094.14	$11,414.24	7.91%
12-31-76	$9,612.39	$13,370.53	18.50%

* * *

CAPITAL CITIES COMMUNICATIONS, INC. (CCB). Founded 1946. Headquarters: 485 Madison Ave., New York NY 10022. **BROADCASTING, PUBLISHING.** Publishes newspapers and magazines; owns six television and fourteen radio stations; also controls more than fifty cable television systems. **MAJOR SUBSIDIARIES, BRANDS:** Fairchild Publications; WPVI-TV (Philadelphia); WTRK-TV (Houston).

Sales: $472.1 million (trend 22.7% a year).
Earnings: $70.78 million (trend 22.5% a year).
What happened to a $10,000 investment

Purchase Date	*Purchase Price*	*Price on 12-31-81*	*Dividends Paid*
12-31-71	$24.25	$73.75	$412.37
12-31-76	$28.19	$73.75	$310.42

Purchase Date	*Cap. Gains (− Losses)*	*Total Return*	*Rate of Return*
12-31-71	$20,412.37	$20,824.74	11.92%
12-31-76	$16,164.08	$16,474.50	21.50%

* * *

CAPITAL HOLDING CORP. (CPH). Founded 1904. Headquarters: Commonwealth Bldg., Louisville KY 40201. **INSURANCE.** Parent company for life and property-casualty insurance companies. **MAJOR SUBSIDIARIES, BRANDS:** Commonwealth Life Insurance Co.; Georgia International Life; Home Security Life; National Standard Life; National Trust Life; Peoples Life; Home Life Insurance of America.

Sales: $548.7 million (trend 8.2% a year).
Earnings: $89.52 million (trend 11.2% a year).
What happened to a $10,000 investment

Purchase Date	*Purchase Price*	*Price on 12-31-81*	*Dividends Paid*
12-31-71	$22.06	$22.25	$2,759.43
12-31-76	$22.25	$22.25	$2,049.44

Purchase Date	*Cap. Gains (− Losses)*	*Total Return*	*Rate of Return*
12-31-71	$84.99	$2,844.42	2.53%
12-31-76	$ .00	$2,049.44	3.80%

* * *

CARLING O'KEEFE LTD. (CKB). Founded 1930. Headquarters: 79 St. Clair Ave. E., Toronto, Ont. Canada M4T 1M6. **BEER, WINE.** Major Canadian brewer and winemaker; also involved in gas and oil exploration, owns football and hockey team. **MAJOR SUBSIDIARIES, BRANDS:** Carling Black Label, Carlsberg, Bass Ale.

Sales: $302.7 million (trend −5.1% a year).
Earnings: $14.92 million (trend 50.8% a year).
What happened to a $10,000 investment

Purchase Date	*Purchase Price*	*Price on 12-31-81*	*Dividends Paid*
12-31-71	$6.87	$4.25	$1,163.35
12-31-76	$3.12	$4.25	$ 953.92

Purchase Date	*Cap. Gains (− Losses)*	*Total Return*	*Rate of Return*
12-31-71	$−3,818.18	$−2,654.84	−3.04%
12-31-76	$ 3,600.00	$ 4,553.92	7.79%

* * *

CARLISLE CORP. (CSL). Founded 1917. Headquarters: 1700 DuBois Tower, Cincinnati OH 42502. **METAL, RUBBER, PLASTICS.** Produces industrial rubber, plastic, and metal products. **MAJOR SUBSIDIARIES, BRANDS:** Continental Plastics Co.; Graham Magnetics Inc.; Kraft Systems, Inc.; Malsbary Manufacturing Co.

Sales: $380.8 million (trend 28.0% a year).
Earnings: $25.78 million (trend 59.6% a year).
What happened to a $10,000 investment

Purchase Date	*Purchase Price*	*Price on 12-31-81*	*Dividends Paid*
12-31-71	$5.06	$28.75	$6,320.99
12-31-76	$3.78	$28.75	$5,950.41

Purchase Date	*Cap. Gains (− Losses)*	*Total Return*	*Rate of Return*
12-31-71	$46,790.12	$53,111.11	20.23%
12-31-76	$66,033.06	$71,983.47	52.32%

* * *

CARNATION CO. (CMK). Founded 1899. Headquarters: 5045 Wilshire Blvd., Los Angeles CA 90036. **FOODS.** Carnation is a leading producer of evaporated milk and other dairy products. It also produces tomato products and pet foods, and, through a subsidiary, school rings and yearbooks. 22,000 employees. **MAJOR SUBSIDIARIES, BRANDS:** Carnation evaporated milk and other dairy items; Coffee-mate; Bright Eyes, Buffet Chef's Blend, Friskies, and Mighty Dog pet foods; Herff Jones (school rings and yearbooks).

Sales: $3,236.2 million (trend 9.3% a year).
Earnings: $154.75 million (trend 11.3% a year).
What happened to a $10,000 investment

Purchase Date	*Purchase Price*	*Price on 12-31-81*	*Dividends Paid*
12-31-71	$30.87	$29.25	$3,332.59
12-31-76	$39.37	$29.25	$1,874.29

Purchase Date	*Cap. Gains (− Losses)*	*Total Return*	*Rate of Return*
12-31-71	$ −525.71	$ 2,806.88	2.50%
12-31-76	$−2,571.43	$−697.14	−1.43%

PROFILE: Prospectors on their way to Alaska's gold rush were the original consumers of Carnation's evaporated milk, which has remained a mainstay of the company. Founder Elbridge Amos Stuart supplied the milk out of a plant he bought from a bankrupt firm. His heirs owned most of the company's stock until recently, and it was only in 1980 that Carnation became listed on the New York Stock Exchange. The family still owns a big block of stock (around 40 percent in 1981). They've agreed not to sell it off faster than 9 percent a year (so as not to depress the stock price); meanwhile, the company is making offsetting purchases of its own shares.

The dividend yield, above 6 percent recently, is one attraction here. Dividends may not rise as fast in the future as they had in recent years, now that a family foundation is no longer the main recipient. However, some analysts expect the company to be more aggressive with new product introductions, such as the recent new pet food brands, Come 'N Get It and Fish Ahoy.

Profit margins have consistently been between 4 and 5 percent over the past decade, and profit growth has been moderate but consistent—twenty-nine straight up years through 1981. The balance sheet is in good shape, with long-term debt recently less than 15 percent of total capital. Basically, it's a conservative stock for people who like to sleep well at night. But the company has been a little too sleepy for Wall Street's taste. The 1980 high of $31 was a dollar below the high back in 1971.

* * *

CAROLINA CLINCHFIELD AND OHIO RAILWAY (CCL). Founded 1905. Headquarters: 3600 W. Broad St., Richmond VA 23261. **RAILROAD.** Small railroad company; operates under a leasing agreement with Seaboard Coast Line Railroad and Louisville & Nashville Railroad.

* * *

CAROLINA FREIGHT CARRIERS CORP. (CAO). Founded 1937. Headquarters: N.C. Highway 150 E., Cherryville NC 28021. **TRUCKING.** Involved in interstate transportation of motor freight. **MAJOR SUBSIDIARIES, BRANDS:** Cardinal Contract Carriers, Inc.; Motor Carrier Insurance, Ltd.

Sales: $240.7 million (trend 19.5% a year).
Earnings: $5.57 million (trend 45.6% a year).
What happened to a $10,000 investment

Purchase Date	*Purchase Price*	*Price on 12-31-81*	*Dividends Paid*
12-31-71	$17.37	$14.87	$2,028.78
12-31-76	$ 5.87	$14.87	$3,293.62

Purchase Date	*Cap. Gains (– Losses)*	*Total Return*	*Rate of Return*
12-31-71	$–1,438.85	$ 589.93	.57%
12-31-76	$ 15,319.15	$18,612.77	23.40%

* * *

CAROLINA POWER & LIGHT CO. (CPL). Founded 1926. Headquarters: 411 Fayetteville St., Raleigh NC 27602. **ELECTRIC UTILITY.** Provides electricity to major portions of North and South Carolina.

Sales: $1,075.6 million (trend 11.5% a year).
Earnings: $126.75 million (trend 11.2% a year).
What happened to a $10,000 investment

Purchase Date	*Purchase Price*	*Price on 12-31-81*	*Dividends Paid*
12-31-71	$25.25	$20.25	$7,099.01
12-31-76	$24.12	$20.25	$4,165.80

Purchase Date	*Cap. Gains (– Losses)*	*Total Return*	*Rate of Return*
12-31-71	$–1,980.20	$5,118.81	4.22%
12-31-76	$–1,606.22	$2,559.59	4.66%

* * *

CARPENTER TECHNOLOGY CORP. (CRS). Founded 1904. Headquarters: 101 W. Bern St., Reading PA 19603. **STEEL.** Manufacturer of high-alloy steel bars, wire, tubing, and custom shapes.

Sales: $570.7 million (trend 17.4% a year).
Earnings: $44.73 million (trend 19.2% a year).
What happened to a $10,000 investment

Purchase Date	*Purchase Price*	*Price on 12-31-81*	*Dividends Paid*
12-31-71	$ 9.62	$46.25	$11,311.69
12-31-76	$17.94	$46.25	$ 4,264.81

Purchase Date	*Cap. Gains (– Losses)*	*Total Return*	*Rate of Return*
12-31-71	$38,051.95	$49,363.64	19.50%
12-31-76	$15,783.97	$20,048.78	24.61%

* * *

CARSON PIRIE SCOTT & CO. (CRN). Founded 1854. Headquarters: 1 S. State St., Chicago IL 60603. **DEPARTMENT STORES.** Major Chicago area department chain. Also involved in airline catering, airport concessions, food service, and wholesale floor coverings. **MAJOR SUBSIDIARIES, BRANDS:** Carson International Inc.; Dobbs Houses, Inc.; Honey Bear Farm; Nordic Hills Country Club.

Sales: $582.1 million (trend 9.8% a year).
Earnings: $12.04 million (trend 8.2% a year).
What happened to a $10,000 investment

Purchase Date	*Purchase Price*	*Price on 12-31-81*	*Dividends Paid*
12-31-71	$10.66	$16.12	$6,366.36
12-31-76	$13.25	$16.12	$3,056.60

Purchase Date	*Cap. Gains (– Losses)*	*Total Return*	*Rate of Return*
12-31-71	$5,130.82	$11,497.18	7.95%
12-31-76	$2,169.81	$ 5,226.42	8.77%

* * *

CARTER HAWLEY HALE STORES, INC. (CHH). Founded 1897. Headquarters: 550 S. Flower St., Los Angeles CA 90071. **RETAILING.** Operates department and clothing stores, mainly for the upper-income market, as well as specialty stores. 54,000 employees. **MAJOR SUBSIDIARIES, BRANDS:** Neiman-Marcus; Bergdorf Goodman; John Wanamaker; Thalhimer's; The Broadway; Emporium Capwell; Holt, Renfrew; Weinstock's; Contempo Casuals; Waldenbook.

Sales: $2,632.9 million (trend 17.8% a year).
Earnings: $54.77 million (trend 11.4% a year).
What happened to a $10,000 investment

Purchase Date	*Purchase Price*	*Price on 12-31-81*	*Dividends Paid*
12-31-71	$31.00	$15.25	$2,605.90
12-31-76	$19.25	$15.25	$2,153.25

Purchase Date	*Cap. Gains (– Losses)*	*Total Return*	*Rate of Return*
12-31-71	$–5,080.65	$–2,474.74	–2.80%
12-31-76	$–2,077.92	$ 75.32	.15%

PROFILE: The wealthy buyers who shop in Neiman-Marcus and Bergdorf Goodman didn't get wealthy buying stock in their favorite stores' parent company. Except for astute short-term trading (or blind luck — and it's sometimes hard to distinguish the two), it's been very hard to turn a profit in this stock during the last decade.

Carter Hawley Hale entered the 1980s carrying a bit more debt than most department store chains. Common stock makes up about 50 percent of capital, long-term debt a bit more than 40 percent, a preferred stock the balance. Without that leverage,

Carter Hawley Hale's return on equity would have been below par for a department store chain in recent years. As it was, profitability was just above average. Ditto for profit margins: They were between 2½ and 3 percent in recent years — not very good for a store that sells to an upscale clientele.

Forbes, in 1980, attributed Carter Hawley Hale's problems to "the company's almost limitless fascination with buying up great old retailing names and trying to convert them into profitable businesses." Scolded writer John Merwin, "Just as turnaround efforts start paying off in one subsidiary, CHH goes out and buys another weak sister, dampening earnings."

The recession of 1980–81 didn't help retail stocks in general, or Carter Hawley Hale in particular. In early 1981, the stock was selling at about 7 times earnings, a modest p / e ratio. If several divisions catch fire at once, the stock could make a major move upward. But some changes in management approach might be needed to make that happen.

* * *

CARTER-WALLACE, INC. (CAR). Founded 1968. Headquarters: 767 Fifth Ave., New York NY 10022. PERSONAL PRODUCTS. Manufactures health care products, antiperspirants, and deodorants. **MAJOR SUBSIDIARIES, BRANDS:** Arrid; Rise; Sea & Ski.

Sales: $237.0 million (trend 7.8% a year).
Earnings: $11.55 million (trend 62.0% a year).
What happened to a $10,000 investment

Purchase Date	*Purchase Price*	*Price on 12-31-81*	*Dividends Paid*
12-31-71	$21.37	$9.75	$1,707.60
12-31-76	$ 7.50	$9.75	$2,133.33

Purchase Date	*Cap. Gains (− Losses)*	*Total Return*	*Rate of Return*
12-31-71	$−5,438.60	$−3,730.99	−4.56%
12-31-76	$ 3,000.00	$ 5,133.33	8.64%

* * *

CASCADE NATURAL GAS CORP. (CGC). Founded 1953. Headquarters: 222 Fairview Ave. N., Seattle WA 98109. NATURAL GAS. Washington and Oregon distributor of natural gas. **MAJOR SUBSIDIARIES, BRANDS:** Cascade Land Leasing Co.

Sales: $176.2 million (trend 12.9% a year).
Earnings: $4.12 million (trend 15.6% a year).
What happened to a $10,000 investment

Purchase Date	*Purchase Price*	*Price on 12-31-81*	*Dividends Paid*
12-31-71	$8.73	$8.87	$8,171.36
12-31-76	$8.21	$8.87	$4,623.98

Purchase Date	*Cap. Gains (− Losses)*	*Total Return*	*Rate of Return*
12-31-71	$161.14	$8,332.50	6.25%
12-31-76	$805.88	$5,429.86	9.06%

* * *

CASTLE & COOKE, INC. (CKE). Founded 1851. Headquarters: Financial Plaza of the Pacific, 130 Merchant St., Honolulu HI 96802. FOODS. Castle & Cooke is a major marketer of pineapples, bananas, tuna, and other foods in the United States and abroad. Also has interests in real estate, swimming pool supplies, and farm equipment. 37,000 employees. **MAJOR SUBSIDIARIES, BRANDS:** Dole pineapples and bananas; Bumble Bee tuna; Bud of California fresh produce; Royal Alaskan seafoods.

Sales: $1,733.5 million (trend 17.9% a year).
Earnings: $28.32 million (trend −6.6% a year).
What happened to a $10,000 investment

Purchase Date	*Purchase Price*	*Price on 12-31-81*	*Dividends Paid*
12-31-71	$ 8.55	$10.25	$6,786.97
12-31-76	$12.20	$10.25	$3,019.90

Purchase Date	*Cap. Gains (− Losses)*	*Total Return*	*Rate of Return*
12-31-71	$ 1,983.77	$8,770.74	6.50%
12-31-76	$−1,598.33	$1,421.57	2.69%

PROFILE: Only once in the decade 1971–80 did Castle & Cooke break the 15 percent barrier in return on stockholders' equity. Since the average corporation these days usually earns a return around that benchmark, it's natural to wonder if things are amiss at this major food firm.

An inspection of the record isn't reassuring. In the firm's best recent year, 1974, it earned close to 6 cents on each dollar of sales, but margins slid under 2 cents in 1979 and 1980. Earnings, while naturally erratic in the pineapple, banana, and seafood businesses, haven't shown much of a long-term uptrend. In both 1979 and 1980, the company paid well over $40 million in interest on its debt; profits in those years were $31 and $32 million. Debt was recently more than 40 percent of total capital, and it has been at that level since 1978. In an effort to chop that debt, the company recently scaled back its plans for capital spending.

At the end of 1979, *Forbes* magazine sniped, in a headline, "Bad luck? Or bad management?" The fact is that there's probably been some of both. As *Forbes* pointed out, the company has suffered from bad weather, high interest rates, and tough competition. But all of these thorns are a natural part of the forest that is Castle & Cooke's domain.

Dividends have been paid each year since 1896, and the dividend yield has recently been a substantial 6 to 7 percent. In recent years it's taken more than half of earnings to sustain this payout.

* * *

CATERPILLAR TRACTOR CO. (CAT). Founded 1925. Headquarters: 100 N.E. Adams St., Peoria IL 61629. **EARTH-MOVING MACHINERY.** Caterpillar is the largest U.S. manufacturer of earth-moving and construction machinery; also makes diesel and natural gas engines for trucks, boats, and factories. 89,000 employees. **MAJOR SUBSIDIARIES, BRANDS:** Solar Turbines International.

Sales: $8,597.8 million (trend 12.7% a year).
Earnings: $564.80 million (trend 8.1% a year).
What happened to a $10,000 investment

Purchase Date	*Purchase Price*	*Price on 12-31-81*	*Dividends Paid*
12-31-71	$31.50	$55.50	$5,079.35
12-31-76	$58.25	$55.50	$1,763.95

Purchase Date	*Cap. Gains (− Losses)*	*Total Return*	*Rate of Return*
12-31-71	$ 7,619.05	$12,698.40	8.54%
12-31-76	$−472.10	$ 1,291.85	2.46%

PROFILE: Thanks to some offhand remarks in the Nixon White House ("Will it play in Peoria?"), Peoria, Illinois has become something of a symbol of common, everyday America. And Caterpillar is certainly the economic heart of Peoria.

In light of this, it's instructive to note that more than half of Caterpillar's fiscal 1979 sales were to buyers outside the United States. To a very great extent, the economy has become a world economy.

During the recent recession, Caterpillar has seen its earnings bog down. But it's demonstrated its strength by expanding production capacity to meet an expected increase in demand for earth-moving equipment and heavy engines during the mid and late 1980s. It also managed to improve its balance sheet, no mean feat in bad times.

So, Caterpillar is well positioned for the years ahead. This fact hasn't gone unnoticed on Wall Street. In 1981, for example, while many heavy-industry companies were going for bargain-basement p / e ratios of 5 to 7, Caterpillar was selling for 9 to 10 times earnings.

The dividend yield is moderate. It was near 6 percent in early 1982.

Some analysts claim to have discerned a secondary oil play here (engines for oil drilling equipment). That's farfetched. The company is in the earth-moving business; engines will remain a sideline.

* * *

THE CECO CORP. (CCP). Founded 1956. Headquarters: 1400 Kensington Rd., Oak Brook IL 60521. **BUILDING PRODUCTS.** Engaged in concrete forming, operates steel mills, designs and manufactures fabricated building products.

Sales: $434.9 million (trend 13.5% a year).
Earnings: $16.01 million (trend 20.4% a year).
What happened to a $10,000 investment

Purchase Date	*Purchase Price*	*Price on 12-31-81*	*Dividends Paid*
12-31-71	$30.25	$19.25	$2,956.69
12-31-76	$17.25	$19.25	$2,108.70

Purchase Date	*Cap. Gains (− Losses)*	*Total Return*	*Rate of Return*
12-31-71	$−3,636.36	$−679.67	−.70%
12-31-76	$ 1,159.42	$ 3,268.12	5.82%

* * *

CELANESE CORP. (CZ). Founded 1918. Headquarters: 1211 Ave. of the Americas, New York NY 10036. **CHEMICALS, FIBERS.** Manufactures synthetic fibers, particularly acetate and polyester; also produces petrochemicals, plastics, and specialty chemicals. 46,000 employees. **MAJOR SUBSIDIARIES, BRANDS:** Arnel; Fortrel.

Sales: $3,348.0 million (trend 12.5% a year).
Earnings: $118.00 million (trend 23.7% a year).
What happened to a $10,000 investment

Purchase Date	*Purchase Price*	*Price on 12-31-81*	*Dividends Paid*
12-31-71	$71.50	$55.87	$3,930.07
12-31-76	$49.25	$55.87	$3,269.04

Purchase Date	*Cap. Gains (– Losses)*	*Total Return*	*Rate of Return*
12-31-71	$–2,185.31	$1,744.76	1.62%
12-31-76	$ 1,345.18	$4,614.21	7.88%

PROFILE: Who buys artificial fibers? Clothing makers, you say. Right, but that's only part of the story. Auto makers and the housing industry are big customers, too. That being the case, you might think that Celanese would rise and fall with the waves of the economy. Right again.

Business Week in 1979 blasted Celanese for being too vulnerable to recessions. "We have to become broader," the magazine quoted then-president John Macomber as saying, "to avoid these terrible ups and downs we seem to have habitually." But *Business Week* concluded that Celanese's diversification strategy "exists in name only." Celanese, it wrote, "is no more diversified today than it was prior to the last recession."

Indeed, earnings did nosedive roughly 25 percent in the recession year of 1980. But in the strange world of Wall Street, what counts in large part is how you did compared to expectations. A company whose earnings went up, but by less than expected, may see its stock plummet. A company whose earnings went down, but by less than expected, may see its stock rise. That's what seems to have happened with Celanese, whose stock didn't get above $50 a share in 1978 or 1979, but traded in the $60s during 1980 and early 1981.

If you're going to buy these shares, the ideal time is in the trough of a recession, to take advantage of the company's cyclicity. Of course, the trough is always easier to identify a couple of years after the fact, with benefit of hindsight.

Celanese has paid dividends each year since 1939, and the dividend in recent years has ranged between 5½ and 8 percent.

* * *

CENCO INC. (CNC). Founded 1948. Headquarters: 2809 Butterfield Rd., Oak Brook IL 60521. **DIVERSIFIED.** Involved in management of nursing homes, vitamin and food product distribution, waste treatment, consumer hardware, and specialty glass products.

Sales: $130.8 million (trend –5.9% a year).
Earnings: $6.48 million (trend 32.8% a year).
What happened to a $10,000 investment

Purchase Date	*Purchase Price*	*Price on 12-31-81*	*Dividends Paid*
12-31-71	$23.75	$12.75	$210.53
12-31-76	$ 3.12	$12.75	$ 0.00

Purchase Date	*Cap. Gains (– Losses)*	*Total Return*	*Rate of Return*
12-31-71	$–4,631.58	$–4,421.05	–5.67%
12-31-76	$ 30,800.00	$ 30,800.00	32.47%

* * *

CENTEX CORP. (CTX). Founded 1950. Headquarters: 4600 Republic National Bank Tower, Dallas TX 75201. **HOME BUILDING.** Large-scale developer of residential property, primarily building single-family homes. Also involved in cement manufacture and natural resources. **MAJOR SUBSIDIARIES, BRANDS:** J. W. Bateson Co.

Sales: $1,056.8 million (trend 24.9% a year).
Earnings: $62.40 million (trend 35.6% a year).
What happened to a $10,000 investment

Purchase Date	*Purchase Price*	*Price on 12-31-81*	*Dividends Paid*
12-31-71	$32.75	$25.25	$427.48
12-31-76	$12.37	$25.25	$694.95

Purchase Date	*Cap. Gains (– Losses)*	*Total Return*	*Rate of Return*
12-31-71	$–2,290.08	$–1,862.60	–2.04%
12-31-76	$ 10,404.04	$ 11,098.99	16.11%

* * *

CENTRAL & SOUTH WEST CORP. (CSR). Founded 1925. Headquarters: 2700 One Main Pl., Dallas TX 75250. **UTILITY.** Provides electricity in Texas, Oklahoma, Louisiana, and Arkansas. **MAJOR SUBSIDIARIES, BRANDS:** Central Power & Light; Public Service of Oklahoma; Southwestern Electric Power; West Texas Utilities.

Sales: $1,731.3 million (trend 17.5% a year).
Earnings: $185.01 million (trend 17.1% a year).
What happened to a $10,000 investment

Purchase Date	*Purchase Price*	*Price on 12-31-81*	*Dividends Paid*
12-31-71	$24.62	$13.87	$5,157.36
12-31-76	$16.87	$13.87	$4,207.41

Purchase Date	*Cap. Gains (– Losses)*	*Total Return*	*Rate of Return*
12-31-71	$–4,365.48	$ 791.88	.76%
12-31-76	$–1,777.78	$2,429.63	4.45%

* * *

CENTRAL HUDSON GAS & ELECTRIC CORP. (CNH). Founded 1926. Headquarters: 284 South Ave., Poughkeepsie NY 12602. **UTILITY.** Provides electric and gas service in mid-Hudson area.

Sales: $328.0 million (trend 14.9% a year).
Earnings: $19.77 million (trend 11.3% a year).
What happened to a $10,000 investment

Purchase Date	*Purchase Price*	*Price on 12-31-81*	*Dividends Paid*
12-31-71	$24.75	$18.25	$7,482.83
12-31-76	$20.75	$18.25	$4,934.94

Purchase Date	*Cap. Gains (– Losses)*	*Total Return*	*Rate of Return*
12-31-71	$–2,626.26	$4,856.57	4.04%
12-31-76	$–1,204.82	$3,730.12	6.55%

* * *

CENTRAL ILLINOIS LIGHT CO. (CER). Founded 1913. Headquarters: 300 Liberty St., Peoria IL 61602. **UTILITY.** Provides electricity and natural gas in central Illinois.

Sales: $394.8 million (trend 17.0% a year).
Earnings: $21.96 million (trend 13.8% a year).
What happened to a $10,000 investment

Purchase Date	*Purchase Price*	*Price on 12-31-81*	*Dividends Paid*
12-31-71	$27.50	$13.62	$5,956.36
12-31-76	$18.12	$13.62	$4,645.52

Purchase Date	*Cap. Gains (– Losses)*	*Total Return*	*Rate of Return*
12-31-71	$–5,045.45	$ 910.91	.88%
12-31-76	$–2,482.76	$2,162.76	3.99%

* * *

CENTRAL ILLINOIS PUBLIC SERVICE CO. (CIP). Founded 1902. Headquarters: 607 E. Adams St., Springfield IL 62701. **UTILITY.** Electric and gas utility serving sixty-five Illinois counties.

Sales: $502.4 million (trend 15.8% a year).
Earnings: $41.96 million (trend 14.2% a year).
What happened to a $10,000 investment

Purchase Date	*Purchase Price*	*Price on 12-31-81*	*Dividends Paid*
12-31-71	$19.62	$11.25	$6,512.10
12-31-76	$15.37	$11.25	$4,370.73

Purchase Date	*Cap. Gains (– Losses)*	*Total Return*	*Rate of Return*
12-31-71	$–4,267.52	$2,244.59	2.05%
12-31-76	$–2,682.93	$1,687.80	3.17%

* * *

CENTRAL LOUISIANA ENERGY CORP. (CEL). Founded 1934. Headquarters: 666 Jefferson St., PO Box 4331, Lafayette LA 70502. **NATURAL RESOURCES.** Operates intrastate gas pipeline; provides electric, gas, and water services; involved in natural resources exploration, gas processing, and oil refining. **MAJOR SUBSIDIARIES, BRANDS:** Louisiana Intrastate Gas; South Louisiana Production Co.; Mid Louisiana Gas Co.; Central Louisiana Electric.

Sales: $1,013.0 million (trend 45.2% a year).
Earnings: $81.67 million (trend 33.1% a year).
What happened to a $10,000 investment

Purchase Date	*Purchase Price*	*Price on 12-31-81*	*Dividends Paid*
12-31-71	$12.12	$34.25	$6,020.62
12-31-76	$14.12	$34.25	$3,044.25

Purchase Date	*Cap. Gains (– Losses)*	*Total Return*	*Rate of Return*
12-31-71	$18,247.42	$24,268.04	13.11%
12-31-76	$14,247.79	$17,292.04	22.24%

* * *

CENTRAL MAINE POWER CO. (CTP). Founded 1899. Headquarters: Edison Dr., Augusta ME 04336. **UTILITY.** Maine electricity supplier.

Sales: $335.3 million (trend 18.5% a year).
Earnings: $20.65 million (trend 15.5% a year).
What happened to a $10,000 investment

Purchase Date	*Purchase Price*	*Price on 12-31-81*	*Dividends Paid*
12-31-71	$17.25	$12.37	$8,318.84
12-31-76	$16.50	$12.37	$4,739.39

Purchase Date	*Cap. Gains (– Losses)*	*Total Return*	*Rate of Return*
12-31-71	$−2,826.09	$5,492.75	4.48%
12-31-76	$−2,500.00	$2,239.39	4.12%

* * *

CENTRAL SOYA CO. INC. (CSY). Founded 1934. Headquarters: 1300 Fort Wayne National Bank Bldg., Fort Wayne IN 46802. **FOOD PROCESSING.** Central Soya is a major soybean processor; also buys and sells grain and produces animal feed, processed foods, poultry, and eggs. 10,000 employees.

Sales: $1,975.0 million (trend −.6% a year).
Earnings: $19.90 million (trend .1% a year).
What happened to a $10,000 investment

Purchase Date	*Purchase Price*	*Price on 12-31-81*	*Dividends Paid*
12-31-71	$12.44	$12.25	$5,338.69
12-31-76	$14.37	$12.25	$2,671.30

Purchase Date	*Cap. Gains (– Losses)*	*Total Return*	*Rate of Return*
12-31-71	$ −150.75	$5,187.94	4.27%
12-31-76	$−1,478.26	$1,193.04	2.28%

PROFILE: When a major soybean processor decides to diversify, what does it go into? Animal feeds and processed food. Well, what were you expecting? Auto parts and spectrographic equipment?

The diversification move described above may not seem like a big change to a layman, but it seems mighty important to people who follow this big agribusiness company. You see, Central Soya is notorious for violent earnings swings. Sure, they say that about lots of companies, but I really mean *violent.* Like, $2.06 a share earnings in 1974, $1.19 in 1975. Or, $2.44 in 1976 followed by $0.80 in 1977. That, ladies and gentlemen, is volatility.

That is also why the stock's price / earnings ratio hugged the ground in 1979 through early 1981, when it was about 5. Investors aren't ready to pay any high multiple of earnings for this stock when they don't know whether the earnings will still be there tomorrow.

But the fact is that Central Soya turned in an unaccustomed four years in a row with earnings gains from 1977 through 1980. And many observers believed that the gross volatility of the past was now behind the company. "Perhaps an old dog can learn new tricks," mused *Financial World* in early 1981. Around the same time, *Barron's* wrote, "Central Soya Heads for Strong Year Amid Moves to Lessen Volatility." It quoted chairman Douglas Fleming as saying he wanted food and feed to provide the bulk of the company's sales and profits, lessening dependence on commodity operations and soybean processing. One trouble, though, is that it's precisely those unstable areas that contributed to the upswing in profits in 1977–80. Food and feed may be more stable, but it remains to be seen whether Central Soya can make them, in a major way, profitable.

* * *

CENTRAL TELEPHONE & UTILITIES CORP. (CTU). Founded 1909. Headquarters: O'Hare Plaza, 5725 E. River Rd., Chicago IL 60631. **UTILITY.** Operates independent telephone system; operates electric utilities in Colorado and Kansas.

Sales: $893.6 million (trend 20.3% a year).
Earnings: $91.25 million (trend 16.4% a year).
What happened to a $10,000 investment

Purchase Date	*Purchase Price*	*Price on 12-31-81*	*Dividends Paid*
12-31-71	$19.50	$33.12	$7,615.90
12-31-76	$25.12	$33.12	$3,681.59

Purchase Date	*Cap. Gains (– Losses)*	*Total Return*	*Rate of Return*
12-31-71	$6,987.18	$14,603.08	9.42%
12-31-76	$3,184.08	$ 6,865.67	11.02%

* * *

CENTRAL VERMONT PUBLIC SERVICE CORP. (CV). Founded 1929. Headquarters: 77 Grove St., Rutland VT 05701. **UTILITY.** Supplies electricity to much of Vermont and a portion of New Hampshire.

Sales: $90.7 million (trend 9.5% a year).
Earnings: $6.80 million (trend 11.7% a year).
What happened to a $10,000 investment

Purchase Date	*Purchase Price*	*Price on 12-31-81*	*Dividends Paid*
12-31-71	$16.62	$17.50	$8,890.23
12-31-76	$15.37	$17.50	$5,411.38

Purchase Date	*Cap. Gains (– Losses)*	*Total Return*	*Rate of Return*
12-31-71	$ 526.32	$9,416.54	6.86%
12-31-76	$1,382.11	$6,793.50	10.92%

* * *

CENTRONICS DATA COMPUTER CORP. (CEN). Founded 1968. Headquarters: 1 Wall St., Hudson NH 03051. **COMPUTER PRINTERS.** Major independent computer printer manufacturing company.

Sales: $120.8 million (trend 22.5% a year).
Earnings: $−24.54 million.
What happened to a $10,000 investment

Purchase Date	*Purchase Price*	*Price on 12-31-81*	*Dividends Paid*
12-31-71	$N/A	$13.37	$ N/A
12-31-76	$22.10	$13.37	$1,757.47

Purchase Date	*Cap. Gains (− Losses)*	*Total Return*	*Rate of Return*
12-31-71	$ N/A	$ N/A	N/A%
12-31-76	$−3,947.96	$−2,190.50	−4.82%

* * *

CENTURY TELEPHONE ENTERPRISES, INC. (CTL). Founded 1968. Headquarters: 520 Riverside Dr., Monroe LA 71201. **TELEPHONE COMPANY.** Independent telephone system serving eleven states; also sells construction supplies and communications equipment. **MAJOR SUBSIDIARIES, BRANDS:** United Supply.

Sales: $98.0 million (trend 17.7% a year).
Earnings: $5.65 million (trend 21.6% a year).
What happened to a $10,000 investment

Purchase Date	*Purchase Price*	*Price on 12-31-81*	*Dividends Paid*
12-31-71	$10.87	$6.75	$3,406.90
12-31-76	$ 6.50	$6.75	$4,476.92

Purchase Date	*Cap. Gains (− Losses)*	*Total Return*	*Rate of Return*
12-31-71	$−3,793.10	$−386.21	−.39%
12-31-76	$ 384.62	$4,861.54	8.25%

* * *

CENVILL COMMUNITIES, INC. (CVI). Founded 1960. Headquarters: North Haverhill Rd., West Palm Beach FL 33409. **REAL ESTATE.** Residential community developer primarily active in Florida. **MAJOR SUBSIDIARIES, BRANDS:** Pacific Coast Properties (80 percent).

Sales: $175.9 million (trend 41.7% a year).
Earnings: $20.90 million (trend 98.0% a year).
What happened to a $10,000 investment

Purchase Date	*Purchase Price*	*Price on 12-31-81*	*Dividends Paid*
12-31-71	$3.89	$32.37	$14,123.52
12-31-76	$7.58	$32.37	$ 7,010.07

Purchase Date	*Cap. Gains (− Losses)*	*Total Return*	*Rate of Return*
12-31-71	$73,249.92	$87,373.44	25.56%
12-31-76	$32,734.97	$39,745.04	37.83%

* * *

CERTAIN-TEED CORP. (CRT). Founded 1917. Headquarters: PO Box 860, Valley Forge PA 19482. **BUILDING PRODUCTS.** Manufactures roofing materials, millwork, doors and windows, fiberglass insulation products, and plastic piping.

Sales: $868.2 million (trend 9.9% a year).
Earnings: $.05 million (trend −62.2% a year).
What happened to a $10,000 investment

Purchase Date	*Purchase Price*	*Price on 12-31-81*	*Dividends Paid*
12-31-71	$22.75	$11.62	$2,979.56
12-31-76	$21.37	$11.62	$1,865.50

Purchase Date	*Cap. Gains (− Losses)*	*Total Return*	*Rate of Return*
12-31-71	$−4,890.11	$−1,910.55	−2.10%
12-31-76	$−4,561.40	$−2,695.91	−6.09%

* * *

THE CESSNA AIRCRAFT CO. (CEA). Founded 1927. Headquarters: 5800 E. Pawnee, Wichita KS 67201. **AIRCRAFT.** Cessna is a major producer and seller of small aircraft; also makes fluid power equipment. **MAJOR SUBSIDIARIES, BRANDS:** Cessna Finance Corp.; Cessna Fluid Power, Ltd.

Sales: $1,060.1 million (trend 16.9% a year).
Earnings: $60.57 million (trend 9.0% a year).
What happened to a $10,000 investment

Purchase Date	*Purchase Price*	*Price on 12-31-81*	*Dividends Paid*
12-31-71	$11.55	$21.75	$4,453.66
12-31-76	$13.75	$21.75	$2,341.12

Purchase Date	*Cap. Gains (– Losses)*	*Total Return*	*Rate of Return*
12-31-71	$8,824.88	$13,278.54	8.82%
12-31-76	$5,818.17	$ 8,159.30	12.67%

* * *

CHAMPION INTERNATIONAL CORP. (CHA). Founded 1937. Headquarters: Champion Plaza, Stamford CT 06921. **FOREST PRODUCTS.** Champion is a major producer of building materials, printing and writing paper, and paper and cardboard packaging. 43,000 employees. **MAJOR SUBSIDIARIES, BRANDS:** Hoerner Waldorf.

Sales: $3,752.7 million (trend 9.3% a year).
Earnings: $176.46 million (trend 30.7% a year).
What happened to a $10,000 investment

Purchase Date	*Purchase Price*	*Price on 12-31-81*	*Dividends Paid*
12-31-71	$30.37	$19.75	$3,674.07
12-31-76	$27.37	$19.75	$2,359.82

Purchase Date	*Cap. Gains (– Losses)*	*Total Return*	*Rate of Return*
12-31-71	$–3,497.94	$ 176.13	.17%
12-31-76	$–2,785.39	$–425.57	–.87%

PROFILE: If you think a paperless society is coming and we're all going to talk to each other on portable phones or communicate through computers only, then maybe you should skip this stock. If you take the view that paper is with us to stay, you may want to consider it carefully.

Champion in 1979 had such a heavy backlog of orders for its paper products that it launched into a major $3.2 billion, five-year expansion program, much of it devoted to the paper segment of the business. The company predicted it would have customers for its increased production even if the economy didn't do particularly well. In 1980, paper products contributed some 65 percent of Champion's profits, though only about 39 percent of its sales.

In the early 1980s, building materials and packaging (the latter mainly through the Hoerner Waldorf subsidiary, acquired in 1977) weren't doing so well, but the company expected them to recover with the economy as a whole.

Like Boise Cascade, Champion International listened to the experts in the 1960s and diversified away from forest products, only to be saddled with a parcel of semiprofitable businesses that didn't really fit. Andrew Sigler, chairman since 1974, has sold off all the barnacles and spearheaded the current expansion plan.

There was some talk that the company would generate most of the cash for the expansion drive internally, but that doesn't look likely. Keep an eye on the debt ratio, which will probably rise substantially from the 1980 level (about 31 percent of total capital). On the other hand, keep an eye on the p / e ratio, which in recent years has been attractively low (5–8), and on the dividend yield, which recently has been above passbook savings rates.

* * *

CHAMPION SPARK PLUG CO. (CHM). Founded 1910. Headquarters: 900 Upton Ave., Toledo OH 43661. **AUTOMOTIVE.** Manufacturers of spark plugs, windshield wipers, health care products, coating application equipment. **MAJOR SUBSIDIARIES, BRANDS:** The Anderson Co.; The DeVilbiss Co.; Baron Drawn Steel Corp.

Sales: $799.8 million (trend 13.2% a year).
Earnings: $36.90 million (trend –1.1% a year).
What happened to a $10,000 investment

Purchase Date	*Purchase Price*	*Price on 12-31-81*	*Dividends Paid*
12-31-71	$16.42	$7.50	$3,953.32
12-31-76	$12.87	$7.50	$2,928.16

Purchase Date	*Cap. Gains (– Losses)*	*Total Return*	*Rate of Return*
12-31-71	$–5,431.47	$–1,478.15	–1.59%
12-31-76	$–4,174.76	$–1,246.60	–2.63%

* * *

CHARTER CO. (CHR). Founded 1959. Headquarters: 21 W. Church St., Jacksonville FL 32202. **CONGLOMERATE.** Refines and sells petroleum products; also has major operations in insurance, printing, and publishing. 8,000 employees. **MAJOR SUBSIDIARIES, BRANDS:** Charter Oil; Dixie Vim, Billups, and Supertest gas stations; *Redbook, Ladies' Home Journal,* and *Sport* magazines.

Sales: $4,518.1 million (trend 39.7% a year).
Earnings: $43.58 million (trend 68.7% a year).
What happened to a $10,000 investment

Purchase Date	*Purchase Price*	*Price on 12-31-81*	*Dividends Paid*
12-31-71	$6.82	$8.12	$4,893.77
12-31-76	$3.75	$8.12	$7,520.00

Purchase Date	*Cap. Gains (– Losses)*	*Total Return*	*Rate of Return*
12-31-71	$ 1,904.76	$ 6,798.53	5.32%
12-31-76	$11,666.67	$19,186.67	23.89%

PROFILE: You may think of Charter as the company that paid Billy Carter to negotiate an oil deal with Libya. Or as the parent of the now-defunct Philadelphia *Bulletin.*

Or you may think of it as one of the great business success stories of the 1970s — a company that came from nowhere and, under the aggressive leadership of chairman-founder Raymond Mason, built itself into a conglomerate that is among the nation's largest companies.

As for me, I think of Charter as the "O" company. That's because, as *Business Week* pointed out in a 1980 article ("Charter piles debt on top of debt"), the company has gone to the well with so many preferred stock offerings, it has already worked its way up to the letter "O" in the alphabet to designate the various series.

You might think any company with the rocketing rise Charter has had would sell for a soaring multiple of earnings. Yet in the middle of 1980, Charter's p / e ratio was an unimaginably low 2. In part, that was due to statistical quirks. But in part, it bespeaks some investors' concerns that the whole enterprise may prove to be a house of cards.

In early 1981, common stock was about half of the company's capital and shrinking as a percentage of capitalization, while long-term debt was about 40 percent and rising. There were also a slew of warrants outstanding, plus that preferred stock. In short, stockholders may not be anywhere near the front of the line to receive future increases in operating earnings. The debt is mainly carried at high interest rates.

Despite Billy Carter's ministrations, the oil Charter gets from Libya comes dear (perhaps even dearer than the borrowed money). According to some analysts, Charter can rack up profits when oil supplies are tight, but may be hard-put to do so when petroleum products are reasonably abundant.

As befits the stock of a highly leveraged company that takes major business risks almost routinely, Charter stock is extremely volatile. In 1979, for example, the price ranged from about $5 to $50.

* * *

CHASE CONVERTIBLE FUND OF BOSTON, INC. (CFB). Founded 1971. Headquarters: 535 Boylston St., Boston MA 02116. **INVESTMENT COMPANY.** Investments are mainly convertible securities.

* * *

CHASE MANHATTAN CORP. (CMB). Founded 1969 (but bank dates to 1799). Headquarters: 1 Chase Manhattan Plaza, New York NY 10005. **BANK.** Chase Manhattan is the third-largest bank in the United States, measured by assets. It had more than 200 offices in New York state in 1980 and did business in more than 100 foreign countries. 33,000 employees.

Sales: $8,002.6 million (trend 21.9% a year).
Earnings: $337.34 million (trend 23.2% a year).
What happened to a $10,000 investment

Purchase Date	*Purchase Price*	*Price on 12-31-81*	*Dividends Paid*
12-31-71	$57.87	$53.87	$4,025.92
12-31-76	$30.62	$53.87	$4,146.94

Purchase Date	*Cap. Gains (– Losses)*	*Total Return*	*Rate of Return*
12-31-71	$–691.14	$ 3,334.77	2.92%
12-31-76	$ 7,591.84	$11,738.78	16.80%

PROFILE: What makes this bank different from other banks? Well, there's the multimillion dollar art collection at company headquarters in Manhattan — Rothkos, Cézannes and the like — prominently but tastefully displayed.

And there's the Rockefeller name. Before he retired in 1981, David Rockefeller had been at the helm for two decades. He owns 1.7 percent of the stock (as of 1980), and the Rockefeller family is believed to own about 5 percent in all (roughly $70 million worth).

The operating results have been somewhat less glamorous. By most measures, Chase has performed less well in recent years than most major banks — and, to its chagrin, less well than arch rival Citicorp. Particularly bad was the period 1974–78, when Chase's return ranged from $.23 to $.43 per $100 of assets. During the late 1970s, Chase's earnings growth rate was less than 5 percent a year. Take inflation into account, and that amounts to shrinking earnings. The bank has performed better in the last few years, but its showing still isn't among the best in the industry.

Even so, the stock may well be undervalued in the early 1980s. In early 1982, for example, it was selling at the bargain-basement rate of 4 times earnings. The price in early 1982 was about $56 a share, well below the 1972 peak of about $67. Yet earnings in the intervening decade had more than doubled.

The dividend yield has been around 7 percent since 1975; dividends have been paid every year since 1848.

* * *

CHELSEA INDUSTRIES, INC. (CHD). Founded 1964. Headquarters: 1360 Soldiers Field Rd., Boston MA 02135. MANUFACTURING. Manufactures plastics products; shoe products; webbing, tapes, and other narrow fabrics; milk protein derivatives for food processing.

Sales: $199.6 million (trend 2.8% a year).
Earnings: $4.15 million (trend 43.5% a year).
What happened to a $10,000 investment

Purchase Date	*Purchase Price*	*Price on 12-31-81*	*Dividends Paid*
12-31-71	$11.36	$9.50	$3,592.32
12-31-76	$ 6.02	$9.50	$4,174.19

Purchase Date	*Cap. Gains (− Losses)*	*Total Return*	*Rate of Return*
12-31-71	$−1,640.00	$1,952.31	1.80%
12-31-76	$ 5,773.58	$9,947.76	14.81%

* * *

CHEMICAL NEW YORK CORP. (CHL). Founded 1968 (but bank dates to 1824). Headquarters: 20 Pine St., New York NY 10015. BANK. Chemical Bank, the basic asset of this holding company, is the sixth largest bank in the United States. It had more than 250 offices in the New York area and more than 70 in foreign countries, as of 1980. 17,000 employees. MAJOR SUBSIDIARIES, BRANDS: Chemical Bank.

Sales: $4,299.9 million (trend 20.6% a year).
Earnings: $166.93 million (trend 11.8% a year).
What happened to a $10,000 investment

Purchase Date	*Purchase Price*	*Price on 12-31-81*	*Dividends Paid*
12-31-71	$56.25	$54.50	$5,491.56
12-31-76	$42.87	$54.50	$3,846.06

Purchase Date	*Cap. Gains (− Losses)*	*Total Return*	*Rate of Return*
12-31-71	$−311.11	$5,180.44	4.26%
12-31-76	$ 2,711.37	$6,557.43	10.61%

PROFILE: This stock has trended slowly downward ever since the holding company was formed in 1968. But it's difficult to see how it could go down much further than it had in the early 1980s.

In early 1982, Chemical shares sold for about $55, after having dipped as low as $33 in 1980. (The 1968 high was about $73.) At that price, Chemical was yielding between 7 and 8 percent in dividends. Its price / earnings ratio was an extremely conservative 4.

Granted, Chemical hadn't been tearing up the track. Its earnings had been rising slowly. But they had risen each year since 1976, and there has been a slow, steady long-term trend upward in earnings. If you're willing to buck Wall Street's preference for hares over tortoises, these shares might reward your patience.

It's hard to deny Chemical's credentials as an income stock. Dividends have been raised most years; in those occasional recent years when they haven't been raised, they've been kept constant. Dividends have been paid every year since 1827.

Consumer lending accounts for only about 4 percent of Chemical's return on assets, so the pullback in consumer borrowing that many economists expect for the mid-1980s shouldn't hurt this bank much. Business borrowing may well be strong, and Chemical has trimmed its bad-loan portfolio well. Anticipating the advent of interstate banking, Chemical has tried to gain a foothold in Florida by making overtures to Florida National Banks.

* * *

THE CHESAPEAKE CORP. OF VIRGINIA (CSK). Founded 1918. Headquarters: West Point VA 23181. PAPER. Manufactures paper, paperboard, corrugated containers, market pulp, prefabricated housing components, horticultural products.

Sales: $257.8 million (trend 14.9% a year).
Earnings: $23.44 million (trend 16.9% a year).
What happened to a $10,000 investment

Purchase Date	*Purchase Price*	*Price on 12-31-81*	*Dividends Paid*
12-31-71	$10.08	$27.50	$6,891.72
12-31-76	$14.62	$27.50	$2,723.08

Purchase Date	*Cap. Gains (− Losses)*	*Total Return*	*Rate of Return*
12-31-71	$17,272.73	$24,164.45	13.07%
12-31-76	$ 8,803.42	$11,526.50	16.57%

* * *

CHESEBROUGH-POND'S INC. (CBM). Founded 1955. Headquarters: 33 Benedict Pl., Greenwich CT 06830. **CONSUMER PRODUCTS.** Chesebrough-Pond's is a diversified manufacturer of consumer products including cosmetics and toiletries, packaged food, clothing, and hospital products. 19,000 employees. **MAJOR SUBSIDIARIES, BRANDS:** Vaseline; Q-Tips; Pond's skin cream; Cutex nail polish; Pertussin cough medicine; Ragu spaghetti sauce; Adolph's meat tenderizer; Health-tex children's clothing; G. H. Bass & Co. (Weejun loafers); Aviance, Cachet, Prince Matchabelli, and Wind Song perfumes and toiletries.

Sales: $1,377.5 million (trend 15.7% a year).
Earnings: $100.20 million (trend 15.7% a year).
What happened to a $10,000 investment

Purchase Date	*Purchase Price*	*Price on 12-31-81*	*Dividends Paid*
12-31-71	$29.62	$33.75	$2,977.22
12-31-76	$25.25	$33.75	$2,241.58

Purchase Date	*Cap. Gains (— Losses)*	*Total Return*	*Rate of Return*
12-31-71	$1,392.41	$4,369.62	3.69%
12-31-76	$3,366.34	$5,607.92	9.31%

PROFILE: Chesebrough-Pond's has an unorthodox but highly successful method of operation. It looks for a small company making a product for which there's substantial demand (often, an order backlog). It buys the company (paying too much, according to critics), expands production of the product, and markets it forcefully nationwide. Under Ralph Ward, chairman since the late 1960s, the strategy has worked again and again, even though Ward applies it in ways that often raise the eyebrows of more conventional marketers.

For one thing, Ward doesn't care if the target company is in an industry characterized as "mature" or "slow-growing." You could certainly have said that about spaghetti sauce, children's clothing, and shoes. Yet Chesebrough has made Ragu (acquired in 1969), Health-tex (1973), and G. H. Bass & Co. (1978) pay off handsomely.

Another eyebrow-raiser: Chesebrough will often take a bold action without prior market research. When Ragu's market dominance was challenged by a spicier competitor (Hunt & Wesson's Prima Salsa), Chesebrough went straight to market with an "Extra Thick and Zesty" version of Ragu. The highly successful Rave hair ("home permanent") spray was also put on the market without testing.

Since it was formed in 1955 by the merger of Pond's Extract Co. and Chesebrough Manufacturing Co., Chesebrough-Pond's has never had a down year. The stock, however, has been up and down, and the p / e ratio has expanded and contracted like an accordion. In early 1982, it was a moderate 10.

* * *

CHICAGO AND NORTH WESTERN TRANSPORTATION CO. (CNW). Founded 1972. Headquarters: 400 W. Madison St., Chicago IL 60606. **RAILROAD.** The Chicago and North Western operates some 8,000 miles of track in eleven Midwestern and Western states, carrying grain, coal, and other cargo. 15,000 employees.

Sales: $935.7 million (trend 14.5% a year).
Earnings: $39.03 million (trend 11.8% a year).
What happened to a $10,000 investment

Purchase Date	*Purchase Price*	*Price on 12-31-81*	*Dividends Paid*
12-31-71	$N/A	$21.75	$0.00
12-31-76	$ 1.50	$21.75	$0.00

Purchase Date	*Cap. Gains (— Losses)*	*Total Return*	*Rate of Return*
12-31-71	$ N/A	$ N/A	N/A%
12-31-76	$135,000.00	$135,000.00	70.72%

PROFILE: Those of us with a soft spot in our hearts for worker-owned ventures have to be pleased with the way things have gone lately at the Chicago and North Western. For a time it looked as if the workers were suckers in a wily deal pulled off by entrepreneur Ben Heineman, chairman of Northwest Industries. The workers bought the railroad for a song, at $50 a share (a total of less than $4 million), but they assumed a massive debt. Northwest got to keep the tax loss carry-forwards, which were also massive. Yet the deal turned out to be good for everyone. Lately it's looked especially sweet to the employee-owners, many now millionaires.

Each original share is now 198 shares, and each share was worth $27 in the fall of 1981. That means a worker who scraped together $1,000 to buy 20 shares in 1972 recently had 3,960 shares worth roughly $106,000. "When I retire, I'll buy some land in Texas and watch the armadillos," Jeff Green, a yardmaster, told *The Wall Street Journal.*

The stock was listed on the Big Board in 1981. Workers and former workers still own about 57 percent of the shares, and institutions hold another 19 percent or so. The stock has been hot partly because of hopes for coal traffic between Wyoming and Chicago, partly because the line is doing well with grain traffic, partly because management has been astute in cutting back track to make the line workable, and partly because of merger speculation.

Though the stock has done very well, it still carries a lot of risk. Long-term debt was recently about 56 percent of total capital. That's down from a ridiculous high of 85 percent a decade ago, but it's still a lot of debt. Using borrowed money always magnifies operating results per share, so the road does spectacularly in good years, but can look very bad in lean years. For example, the return on stockholders' equity was above 40 percent in 1980, below 3 percent in 1979.

No dividends have been paid on the stock since the company was spun off from Northwest Industries. It's possible that dividends may be started up soon, however.

* * *

CHICAGO MILWAUKEE CORP. (CHG). Founded 1927. Headquarters: 666 N. Lake Shore Dr., Chicago IL 60611. **HOLDING COMPANY.** Parent of Chicago, Milwaukee, St. Paul & Pacific Railroad; also involved in food service and distribution, metal fabrication, and concrete paving. **MAJOR SUBSIDIARIES, BRANDS:** The Milwaukee Road; Southern Boiler & Tank Works; Vulcan-Hart Corp.; Aslesen Co.

Sales: $111.1 million (trend −28.2% a year).
Earnings: $2.12 million (trend 15.1% a year).
What happened to a $10,000 investment

Purchase Date	*Purchase Price*	*Price on 12-31-81*	*Dividends Paid*
12-31-71	$ N/A	$66.62	$0.00
12-31-76	$ 7.50	$66.62	$0.00

Purchase Date	*Cap. Gains (− Losses)*	*Total Return*	*Rate of Return*
12-31-71	$ N/A	$ N/A	N/A%
12-31-76	$78,833.33	$78,833.33	54.78%

* * *

CHICAGO PNEUMATIC TOOL CO. (CGG). Founded 1901. Headquarters: 6 E. 44th St., New York NY 10017. **TOOLS.** Makes tools and equipment used in the transportation, mining, and construction industries. Also produces instruments and controls. **MAJOR SUBSIDIARIES, BRANDS:** The Jacobs Manufacturing Co.; The Allen Manufacturing Co.; Qualitrol Corp.; The Partlow Corp.; Allied Steel & Tractor Products; Fox Valley Instrument Co.; Norford Corp.; Dynapar Corp.; Hennessy Industries.

Sales: $474.2 million (trend 13.4% a year).
Earnings: $11.93 million (trend 2.4% a year).
What happened to a $10,000 investment

Purchase Date	*Purchase Price*	*Price on 12-31-81*	*Dividends Paid*
12-31-71	$42.50	$19.25	$4,705.88
12-31-76	$29.12	$19.25	$3,433.48

Purchase Date	*Cap. Gains (− Losses)*	*Total Return*	*Rate of Return*
12-31-71	$−5,470.59	$−764.71	−.79%
12-31-76	$−3,390.56	$ 42.92	.09%

* * *

CHOCK FULL O'NUTS CORP. (CHF). Founded 1932. Headquarters: 425 Lexington Ave., New York NY 10017. **FOOD PROCESSING, RESTAURANTS.** Produces line of frozen cakes and coffee products; operates chain of restaurants.

Sales: $118.7 million (trend −.9% a year).
Earnings: $3.21 million (trend .6% a year).
What happened to a $10,000 investment

Purchase Date	*Purchase Price*	*Price on 12-31-81*	*Dividends Paid*
12-31-71	$8.47	$10.50	$1,164.75
12-31-76	$3.25	$10.50	$1,692.31

Purchase Date	*Cap. Gains (− Losses)*	*Total Return*	*Rate of Return*
12-31-71	$ 2,400.70	$ 3,565.45	3.10%
12-31-76	$22,307.69	$24,000.00	27.73%

* * *

CHRIS-CRAFT INDUSTRIES INC. (CCN). Founded 1928. Headquarters: 600 Madison Ave., New York NY 10022. **TELEVISION, PLASTICS AND CHEMICALS.** Owns and operates a pair of television stations; manufactures plastic and chemical products. Chris-Craft no longer produces the boats for which the firm was named (boat division sold in 1980). **MAJOR SUBSIDIARIES, BRANDS:** Montrose Chemical Corp. of California (50%); KCOP (Los Angeles); KPTV (Portland OR).

Sales: $64.9 million (trend −4.4% a year).
Earnings: $4.12 million (trend 35.8% a year).
What happened to a $10,000 investment

Purchase Date	*Purchase Price*	*Price on 12-31-81*	*Dividends Paid*
12-31-71	$4.94	$35.71	$0.00
12-31-76	$5.61	$35.71	$0.00

Purchase Date	*Cap. Gains (− Losses)*	*Total Return*	*Rate of Return*
12-31-71	$62,333.96	$62,333.96	21.88%
12-31-76	$53,653.88	$53,653.88	44.80%

* * *

THE CHRISTIANA COMPANIES, INC. (CST). Founded 1953. Headquarters: 225 Broadway, San Diego CA 92111. COMMUNITY DEVELOPMENT. Developer and builder of planned communities; also involved in investment real estate and publishing.

Sales: $36.0 million (trend 13.2% a year).
Earnings: $2.52 million (trend 12.7% a year).
What happened to a $10,000 investment

Purchase Date	*Purchase Price*	*Price on 12-31-81*	*Dividends Paid*
12-31-71	$7.37	$7.62	$2,305.08
12-31-76	$3.25	$7.62	$5,230.77

Purchase Date	*Cap. Gains (− Losses)*	*Total Return*	*Rate of Return*
12-31-71	$ 338.98	$ 2,644.07	2.37%
12-31-76	$13,461.54	$18,692.31	23.47%

* * *

CHROMALLOY AMERICAN CORP. (CRO). Founded 1951. Headquarters: 120 S. Central Ave., St. Louis MO 63105. CONGLOMERATE. This highly diversified company gets the majority of its earnings from metal fabrication, shipping, and trucking. It is also actively involved in manufacture of farm equipment, textiles, clothing, and industrial products; it provides oil field services, and it runs a chain of art supply stores. 28,000 employees.

Sales: $1,518.0 million (trend 15.2% a year).
Earnings: $39.17 million (trend 17.5% a year).
What happened to a $10,000 investment

Purchase Date	*Purchase Price*	*Price on 12-31-81*	*Dividends Paid*
12-31-71	$19.25	$18.25	$4,553.25
12-31-76	$14.87	$18.25	$3,569.75

Purchase Date	*Cap. Gains (− Losses)*	*Total Return*	*Rate of Return*
12-31-71	$−519.48	$4,033.77	3.45%
12-31-76	$ 2,268.91	$5,838.66	9.63%

PROFILE: This conglomerate has some problems. One problem is that it is being dogged by an unfriendly take-over offer from Sun Chemical Corp., an outfit one third its size.

According to *Business Week,* Norman Alexander, the head of Sun Chemical, started buying Chromalloy stock in January of 1978, immediately after the death of Chromalloy's chairman, Joseph Friedman, in December 1977. Sun Chemical, which has previously tried, unsuccessfully, to take over Twentieth Century–Fox, Chemetron, and United Brands, has continued to accumulate Chromalloy stock. In early 1980, it owned close to 30 percent of the company.

It's not clear whether the merger possibility has had any major impact on Chromalloy's stock price. The stock had been selling for around 6 times earnings before Sun Chemical began buying, and the multiple had risen only to 9 in early 1981.

One reason the stock sells for a moderate multiple is that Chromalloy's earnings progress hasn't been much to boast about. In the late 1970s earnings were growing at less than 10 percent a year. In 1980, a recession year, earnings were down. Farm equipment did poorly, metal fabricating only fairly well. However, oil field services were booming, and transportation (particularly coal and grain shipments by barge) was doing very well.

Chromalloy has traditionally operated on an unusually low profit margin (often 3 percent or less), but many of the things it sells are big-ticket items. In most measures of financial performance, it's been about average for a conglomerate. Its debt load had been above average, but in recent years has been trimmed some through a program of selling off selected operations.

* * *

CHRYSLER CORP. (C). Founded 1925. Headquarters: 12000 Lynn Townsend Dr., Highland Park MI 48288. AUTOS. Chrysler is the third-largest U.S. auto maker; also manufactures chemicals, boat engines and motors, and powder metal products. 244,000 employees. MAJOR SUBSIDIARIES,

BRANDS: Chrysler; Plymouth; Dodge; owns 15 percent of Peugeot.

Sales: $9,225.3 million (trend −5.9% a year).
Earnings: $−1,738.80 million.
What happened to a $10,000 investment

Purchase Date	*Purchase Price*	*Price on 12-31-81*	*Dividends Paid*
12-31-71	$28.62	$3.37	$2,043.67
12-31-76	$20.37	$3.37	$ 957.06

Purchase Date	*Cap. Gains (− Losses)*	*Total Return*	*Rate of Return*
12-31-71	$−8,820.96	$−6,777.29	−10.71%
12-31-76	$−8,343.56	$−7,386.50	−23.54%

PROFILE: Chrysler ran deficits in 1970, 1974, 1975, 1978, 1979, 1980, and 1981. The 1979 and 1980 deficits combined were on the order of $2.8 billion, or more than twice the company's profits for the previous five profitable years. In early 1982, common stock accounted for a negligible percentage of the company's capital. Most was preferred stock and outright debt. Long-term debt was a staggering $2.4 billion. The company had issued one survival plan after another.

In 1982, it sold its profitable Chrysler Defense subsidiary (a major maker of tanks) to General Dynamics for some much-needed cash. Analysts were more optimistic than they had been that the company would survive. There were some signs that car sales were picking up.

For the investor, though, mere survival isn't the issue. Suppose the company really does have the cars America wants? Suppose the ads, with the virile voice and sturdy beat proclaiming "We're coming back" are right? Even then, even if the company makes a fair amount of money, a huge proportion of it will have to go for debt service and preferred stock dividends.

Of course, if people really come to think Chrysler's going to make it, some hardy soul will make quite a bit on these highly leveraged shares, which will leap up from the miserable $5 or so per share they commanded during much of the early 1980s. But are you that hardy soul? Only if you have a titanic tolerance for risk in your investments.

* * *

CHURCH'S FRIED CHICKEN, INC. (CHU). Founded 1952. Headquarters: 355 Spencer Lane, San Antonio TX 78284. **FAST FOOD RESTAURANTS.** This company sells fried chicken and other food items through neighborhood take-out stores. **MAJOR SUBSIDIARIES, BRANDS:** Church's Fried Chicken; G.W. Jr. Hamburgers.

Sales: $386.5 million (trend 24.0% a year).
Earnings: $38.10 million (trend 32.4% a year).
What happened to a $10,000 investment

Purchase Date	*Purchase Price*	*Price on 12-31-81*	*Dividends Paid*
12-31-71	$ 9.79	$28.87	$3,120.63
12-31-76	$11.58	$28.87	$2,356.83

Purchase Date	*Cap. Gains (− Losses)*	*Total Return*	*Rate of Return*
12-31-71	$19,499.30	$22,619.94	12.55%
12-31-76	$14,928.06	$17,284.89	22.23%

* * *

CINCINNATI BELL INC. (CSN). Founded 1873. Headquarters: 225 E. Fourth St., Cincinnati OH 45201. **TELEPHONE COMPANY.** Provides telephone service in parts of Ohio, Kentucky, and Indiana.

Sales: $318.6 million (trend 12.4% a year).
Earnings: $34.28 million (trend 16.0% a year).
What happened to a $10,000 investment

Purchase Date	*Purchase Price*	*Price on 12-31-81*	*Dividends Paid*
12-31-71	$22.50	$28.25	$8,344.44
12-31-76	$23.75	$28.25	$4,816.84

Purchase Date	*Cap. Gains (− Losses)*	*Total Return*	*Rate of Return*
12-31-71	$2,555.56	$10,900.00	7.65%
12-31-76	$1,894.74	$ 6,711.58	10.82%

* * *

THE CINCINNATI GAS & ELECTRIC CO. (CIN). Founded 1837. Headquarters: 139 E. Fourth St., Cincinnati OH 45202. **UTILITY.** Supplies electricity and natural gas to portions of Ohio, Indiana, and Kentucky. **MAJOR SUBSIDIARIES, BRANDS:** The Union Light, Heat and Power Co.

Sales: $955.0 million (trend 14.7% a year).
Earnings: $69.18 million (trend 14.6% a year).
What happened to a $10,000 investment

Purchase Date	*Purchase Price*	*Price on 12-31-81*	*Dividends Paid*
12-31-71	$26.12	$15.75	$6,805.74
12-31-76	$22.87	$15.75	$4,222.95

Purchase Date	*Cap. Gains (− Losses)*	*Total Return*	*Rate of Return*
12-31-71	$−3,971.29	$2,834.45	2.53%
12-31-76	$−3,114.75	$1,108.20	2.12%

* * *

CINCINNATI MILACRON INC. (CMZ). Founded 1922. Headquarters: 4701 Marburg Ave., Cincinnati OH 45209. MACHINE TOOLS. Company is the leading U.S. machine tool manufacturer and a leader in industrial robots. Also makes plastic molding and extruding machinery, circuit boards, semiconductors, and other industrial products. 13,000 employees.

Sales: $816.4 million (trend 14.3% a year).
Earnings: $52.21 million (trend 49.5% a year).
What happened to a $10,000 investment

Purchase Date	*Purchase Price*	*Price on 12-31-81*	*Dividends Paid*
12-31-71	$6.96	$25.75	$5,113.77
12-31-76	$5.77	$25.75	$4,144.40

Purchase Date	*Cap. Gains (− Losses)*	*Total Return*	*Rate of Return*
12-31-71	$27,005.99	$32,119.76	15.46%
12-31-76	$34,620.94	$38,765.34	37.28%

PROFILE: If there's one thing that can build a fire under a stock, it's a Wall Street buzz word. If the stock ties in with not one but two buzz words, the fire can ignite the rocket fuel of investor enthusiasm to send the stock soaring into orbit.

That's what happened with Cincinnati Milacron, which sold between about $9 and $19 a share in 1978, and hit a 1980 high of about $57, before a three-for-two stock split in early 1981. The first buzz word was reindustrialization. Who better could capitalize on a pro-business attitude in Washington and expected tax incentives for business expansion (and capital spending) than the leading maker of machine tools? The second buzz word was robots. The company is the leader in industrial robot technology, with about one third of the (as yet small) market.

This is a good company, and one for which the outlook over the next few years is bright. But that bright outlook has already, to a considerable extent, been built into its stock price. (The p / e ratio in late 1980, for example, was 15, at a time when most stocks were selling for about half that multiple.) If you decide to invest here, think carefully first; it might be a bit like falling in love with the class prom queen. Though she might be a fine girl, there can be problems when you direct your affections at someone dozens of others are already in love with. You might also glance at her past. On a restated basis (adjusted for splits), the 1977 high and the 1966 high were both within a whisker of $7 a share.

* * *

CITICORP (FNC). Founded 1968 (but bank dates to 1812). Headquarters: 399 Park Ave., New York NY 10043. BANK. Citicorp is the holding company for Citibank, the second largest bank in the United States, measured by 1981 assets. It has some 300 branch offices in New York state, and close to 2,000 in some 92 foreign countries. 52,000 employees. MAJOR SUBSIDIARIES, BRANDS: Citibank; Carte Blanche.

Sales: $14,211.0 million (trend 25.8% a year).
Earnings: $507.00 million (trend 8.9% a year).
What happened to a $10,000 investment

Purchase Date	*Purchase Price*	*Price on 12-31-81*	*Dividends Paid*
12-31-71	$23.25	$25.25	$4,524.73
12-31-76	$32.75	$25.25	$1,984.73

Purchase Date	*Cap. Gains (− Losses)*	*Total Return*	*Rate of Return*
12-31-71	$ 860.22	$ 5,384.95	4.40%
12-31-76	$−2,290.08	$−305.34	−.62%

PROFILE: Citicorp, one of the two largest banks in the country, achieved that status by being innovative and tough. However, to listen to Citicorp officials talk (and to see them act), they have just begun to fight.

They fight with federal and state regulators over usury ceilings, over branch banking laws, over any obstacles that keep them from being able to establish the kind of nationwide banking system they envision, one in which banks would compete head to head on fair terms with money market funds and brokerage houses like Merrill Lynch.

While some banks (Bankers Trust is a good example) have trimmed consumer operations to concentrate on serving big corporate clients, Citibank has been going in the opposite direction. It has been making large-scale and expensive moves to serve consumers, not just in New York state but nationwide (when the expected day of nationwide banking arrives). It costs more in staff time to raise $1 million in deposits from 1,000 consumers than from one big corporate client, or to make a thousand $1,000 loans rather than one $1 million loan. In addition, consumers are notoriously fickle in shifting their funds. So investors are uncertain whether Citicorp's big gamble on the consumer will pay off and are penalizing Citibank with a low price / earnings multiple (about 5 in the early 1980s). Uncertainty about loans to foreign countries in shaky financial health has also dampened enthusiasm for this stock. Yet Citicorp's international loan portfolio is extremely well diversified, which lessens the risk.

Contrary to many people's opinion, high interest rates are generally bad for banks. They're particularly bad for banks that do a lot of consumer business (because state usury ceilings limit the return on loans, even though the bank's cost of funds may be high — hence margins are squeezed). So, Citibank's stock has been dealt a third blow by the high interest rates that prevailed in the early 1980s.

Three strikes and you're out? Hardly. Though this stock has been up, down, and mostly going nowhere in recent years, the company's management is widely respected, and the shares may be poised for a major move upward during the 1980s.

* * *

CITIES SERVICE CO. (CS). Founded 1910. Headquarters: 110 W. Seventh St., Tulsa OK 74102. **OIL.** Cities Service explores for, drills for, refines, and markets petroleum products. Also operates a natural gas pipeline, produces chemicals, and is engaged in mining coal and other minerals. 18,000 employees. **MAJOR SUBSIDIARIES, BRANDS:** Cities Service Gas Co.; Syncrude Canada Ltd. (18 percent owned).

Sales: $7,786.3 million (trend 18.3% a year).
Earnings: $477.50 million (trend 22.3% a year).
What happened to a $10,000 investment

Purchase Date	*Purchase Price*	*Price on 12-31-81*	*Dividends Paid*
12-31-71	$14.00	$46.25	$7,249.23
12-31-76	$19.83	$46.25	$3,176.45

Purchase Date	*Cap. Gains (− Losses)*	*Total Return*	*Rate of Return*
12-31-71	$23,043.34	$30,292.58	14.95%
12-31-76	$13,319.33	$16,495.78	21.52%

PROFILE: Cities Service is only the eighteenth largest U.S. oil company, yet it's among the fifty largest corporations in the country. Score one more for the power of oil.

Like other oil stocks, Cities Service had a brisk run-up in 1979 and 1980. With perfect timing, it would have been possible for a 1978 buyer to quadruple his money in two years. Yet the run-up left Cities Service selling at a relatively modest 8 times earnings. Why?

Partly, it's because the company refines more oil than it produces. Since it has to buy some oil on the OPEC-dominated open market, its profit margins get squeezed any time OPEC jacks up the price. Partly, it's because Cities Service's overall results have been less inspiring than those of other oil companies. *Forbes,* in its 1981 Annual Report on American Industry, put Cities Service forty-first out of forty-four primarily domestic oils in five-year return on equity. In sales growth it was thirty-sixth, in earnings growth thirty-second.

Still, Cities Service has a lot going for it on the production front. It's been pouring money into exploration and drilling lately, and it holds a tremendous fistful of domestic leases, covering 11 million acres. That puts it fifth in the industry in U.S. acreage, behind four giant rivals — Exxon, Standard Oil of Indiana, Gulf, and Shell. And Cities Service gets some 80 percent of its production from U.S. wells, a percentage many another oil company would love to have.

* * *

CITY INVESTING CO. (CNV). Founded 1904. Headquarters: 59 Maiden Lane, New York NY 10038. **CONGLOMERATE.** Activities include insurance, housing, printing, water heaters, steel containers, budget motels, food service, banking, and restaurant operations. 69,000 employees. **MAJOR SUBSIDIARIES, BRANDS:** The Home Group; The Home Insurance Co.; GDV Inc.; General Development Corp. (subsidiary of GDV); Guerdon Industries (mobile home subsidiary of GDV); Woods Brothers Homes (subsidiary of GDV); World Color Press; Rheem (water heaters, steel containers); Motel 6; Servomation; Southern California Savings & Loan Association; Red Barn restaurants.

Sales: $5,386.2 million (trend 22.0% a year).
Earnings: $102.05 million (trend 35.2% a year).
What happened to a $10,000 investment

Purchase Date	*Purchase Price*	*Price on 12-31-81*	*Dividends Paid*
12-31-71	$20.25	$22.75	$4,538.27
12-31-76	$13.25	$22.75	$4,603.77

Purchase Date	*Cap. Gains (− Losses)*	*Total Return*	*Rate of Return*
12-31-71	$1,234.57	$ 5,772.84	4.66%
12-31-76	$7,169.81	$11,773.58	16.84%

PROFILE: At some time during every year from 1973–79, you could buy this stock for only 4 times earnings (in some years, 3). Obviously, City Investing has not been a favorite on Wall Street. The stock hit a 1968 high of more than $39 a share, dipped to $4 in 1974 during the nadir of the recession, rose back to a 1980 high of about $30, and had settled back to $24 in early 1982. It's volatile partly because the results per share are magnified by leverage. The company has more debt than equity in its capital structure. At least it did in 1981 (when the ratio was 61 percent debt, 32 percent common stock, and 7 percent preferred stock). Rumor had it that the company would soon sell off some of its less essential subsidiaries to balance out the balance sheet a bit.

Recessions are bad for several of City's businesses, most notably housing. In the early 1980s, a down time for housing coincided with a low-profitability point in the so-called underwriting cycle, which affects property and casualty insurers. (The Home Group, though it sells life insurance, is a major factor in property and casualty.) A rebound in these two key areas (which account for roughly half of sales and earnings) could result in a major profit increase, and a significant rise in the stock price. But the timing is uncertain. Meanwhile, the $5 billion plus (sales) conglomerate was paying out something on the order of $200 million a year in interest on its debt.

With its stock so low, City is vulnerable to takeover attempts. Sharon Steel and Tamco Enterprises have both been nibbling at the stock; they recently owned about 10 percent apiece.

* * *

CLABIR CORP. (CLG). Founded 1977. Headquarters: 1455 E. Putnam Ave., Old Greenwich CT 06870. WEAPONS, FOOD. Clabir owns a half interest in the largest U.S. producer of tank ammunition; also owns a majority interest in a food company. MAJOR SUBSIDIARIES, BRANDS: General Defense Corp. (50 percent owned); Isaly Co., Inc. (83 percent owned; makes Klondike ice cream bars and owns Sweet William restaurants).

Sales: $107.5 million (trend 17.0% a year).
Earnings: $5.39 million (trend 33.8% a year).
What happened to a $10,000 investment

Purchase Date	*Purchase Price*	*Price on 12-31-81*	*Dividends Paid*
12-31-71	$N/A	$6.37	$ N/A
12-31-76	$ 1.18	$6.37	$3,225.77

Purchase Date	*Cap. Gains (− Losses)*	*Total Return*	*Rate of Return*
12-31-71	$ N/A	$ N/A	N/A%
12-31-76	$44,241.85	$47,467.62	41.87%

* * *

CLARK EQUIPMENT CO. (CKL). Founded 1916. Headquarters: Circle Dr., Buchanan MI 49107. FORKLIFTS, CONSTRUCTION EQUIPMENT. Clark is the world's largest maker of forklift trucks and a major manufacturer of general truck components (particularly axles and transmissions) and construction equipment. 22,000 employees.

Sales: $1,533.7 million (trend 4.3% a year).
Earnings: $53.51 million (trend 6.9% a year).
What happened to a $10,000 investment

Purchase Date	*Purchase Price*	*Price on 12-31-81*	*Dividends Paid*
12-31-71	$46.87	$27.25	$3,831.47
12-31-76	$42.37	$27.25	$2,383.48

Purchase Date	*Cap. Gains (− Losses)*	*Total Return*	*Rate of Return*
12-31-71	$−4,186.67	$ −355.20	−.36%
12-31-76	$−3,569.32	$−1,185.84	−2.49%

PROFILE: This big Michigan company resembles some of its own equipment: large, sturdy, and slow-moving. Sales growth in recent years has been clocked at the towing-tractor pace of about 4 percent a year. Earnings growth has been faster, but not fast enough to make anyone think about Clark as a growth company. So the stock hasn't gone much of anywhere. It usually sells at a conservative multiple of earnings and yields a healthy dividend (about 9 percent in early 1982). The dividend has been paid each year since 1933 and has been inched upward most years with the slow, assured pace of a forklift raising a delicate cargo.

The balance sheet is as solid as a truck axle (debt less than 20 percent of capital in 1980–81) and has remained so even in tough times like the recent recession. This is not a stock in which you're likely to lose a lot of money.

However, is it one in which you can make much? Clark could certainly get a big boost from an economic boom. All three major business lines (forklifts, construction equipment, and truck components) would benefit from a genuine boom. Earnings would rise, and the p / e ratio would probably rise too, providing the chance for a substantial capital gain.

The historical record, however, doesn't offer much precedent for big capital gains here. And, of course, there are lots of stocks that could do well in a genuine boom. Still, Clark might be a suitable pick for some conservative portfolios.

* * *

THE CLEVELAND-CLIFFS IRON CO. (CLF). Founded 1947. Headquarters: 1460 Union Commerce Bldg., Cleveland OH 44115. **IRON ORE.** Produces iron ore; also involved in marine transportation, minerals, and forest products.

Sales: $377.3 million (trend 16.9% a year).
Earnings: $50.23 million (trend 10.9% a year).
What happened to a $10,000 investment

Purchase Date	*Purchase Price*	*Price on 12-31-81*	*Dividends Paid*
12-31-71	$16.56	$30.75	$6,113.96
12-31-76	$35.37	$30.75	$1,922.26

Purchase Date	*Cap. Gains (– Losses)*	*Total Return*	*Rate of Return*
12-31-71	$ 8,566.04	$14,680.00	9.45%
12-31-76	$–1,307.42	$ 614.84	1.20%

* * *

THE CLEVELAND ELECTRIC ILLUMINATING CO. (CVX). Founded 1881. Headquarters: PO Box 5000, Cleveland OH 44101. **ELECTRIC UTILITY.** Provides electric power to city of Cleveland and elsewhere in northeastern Ohio.

Sales: $893.6 million (trend 12.1% a year).
Earnings: $97.67 million (trend 12.6% a year).
What happened to a $10,000 investment

Purchase Date	*Purchase Price*	*Price on 12-31-81*	*Dividends Paid*
12-31-71	$25.50	$16.25	$6,912.42
12-31-76	$23.08	$16.25	$4,158.84

Purchase Date	*Cap. Gains (– Losses)*	*Total Return*	*Rate of Return*
12-31-71	$–3,627.45	$3,284.97	2.88%
12-31-76	$–2,960.29	$1,198.56	2.29%

* * *

CLEVEPAK CORP. (CLV). Founded 1962. Headquarters: 925 Westchester Ave., White Plains NY 10604. **PAPER.** Produces recycled paperboard for container manufacturing. Also manufactures shipping case partitions, equipment for the packaging and textile industries, and industrial products.

Sales: $107.6 million (trend 9.4% a year).
Earnings: $2.25 million (trend –19.7% a year).
What happened to a $10,000 investment

Purchase Date	*Purchase Price*	*Price on 12-31-81*	*Dividends Paid*
12-31-71	$ 9.62	$7.25	$4,675.32
12-31-76	$12.62	$7.25	$2,376.24

Purchase Date	*Cap. Gains (– Losses)*	*Total Return*	*Rate of Return*
12-31-71	$–2,467.53	$ 2,207.79	2.01%
12-31-76	$–4,257.43	$–1,881.19	–4.08%

* * *

THE CLOROX CO. (CLX). Founded 1957. Headquarters: 1221 Broadway, Oakland CA 94612. **HOUSEHOLD PRODUCTS.** Manufactures bleach and other household products, produces specialty foods; operates restaurant chain. **MAJOR SUBSIDIARIES, BRANDS:** Clorox; Formula 409; Litter Green; Soft Scrub; Kingsford; Hidden Valley Ranch; B & B; Mr. Mushroom; Duraflame; Liquid-plumr; Twice as Fresh.

Sales: $714.0 million (trend –6.5% a year).
Earnings: $38.08 million (trend 4.7% a year).
What happened to a $10,000 investment

Purchase Date	*Purchase Price*	*Price on 12-31-81*	*Dividends Paid*
12-31-71	$29.87	$11.25	$2,013.39
12-31-76	$12.25	$11.25	$2,808.16

Purchase Date	*Cap. Gains (– Losses)*	*Total Return*	*Rate of Return*
12-31-71	$–6,234.31	$–4,220.92	–5.34%
12-31-76	$ –816.33	$ 1,991.84	3.70%

* * *

CLUETT, PEABODY & CO., INC. (CLU). Founded 1851. Headquarters: 510 Fifth Ave., New York NY 10036. **APPAREL.** Manufactures men's, women's, and children's wear. **MAJOR SUBSIDIARIES, BRANDS:** The Arrow Co.; J. Schoeneman; The Sanforized Co.; Spring City Knitting Co.; Arrow shirts; Lady Arrow; Gold Toe; Sanforized; Sanfor-Set; Saturdays in California; Donmoor; Duofold.

Sales: $738.6 million (trend 6.4% a year).
Earnings: $17.83 million (trend 8.0% a year).
What happened to a $10,000 investment

Purchase Date	*Purchase Price*	*Price on 12-31-81*	*Dividends Paid*
12-31-71	$22.87	$15.25	$2,585.79
12-31-76	$ 9.25	$15.25	$3,421.62

Purchase Date	*Cap. Gains (− Losses)*	*Total Return*	*Rate of Return*
12-31-71	$−3,333.33	$−747.54	−.77%
12-31-76	$ 6,486.49	$ 9,908.11	14.76%

* * *

COACHMEN INDUSTRIES, INC. (COA). Founded 1964. Headquarters: PO Box 30, Yoder Industrial Park, Middlebury IN 46540. RECREATIONAL VEHICLES. Manufactures and markets recreational vehicles, boats, and component parts. MAJOR SUBSIDIARIES, BRANDS: Shasta; Fan Coach; Viking Boat; Shadow Interiors Parts and Accessories Co.; Henco; Kenco; Sportscoach; Lux Co.

Sales: $125.3 million (trend .1% a year).
Earnings: $−7.58 million.
What happened to a $10,000 investment

Purchase Date	*Purchase Price*	*Price on 12-31-81*	*Dividends Paid*
12-31-71	$11.69	$8.50	$1,219.25
12-31-76	$16.62	$8.50	$ 736.84

Purchase Date	*Cap. Gains (− Losses)*	*Total Return*	*Rate of Return*
12-31-71	$−2,727.27	$−1,508.02	−1.62%
12-31-76	$−4,887.22	$−4,150.38	−10.17%

* * *

COASTAL CORP. (CGP). Founded 1972. Headquarters: 9 Greenway Plaza, Houston TX 77046. NATURAL GAS, OIL. Coastal explores for, produces, transmits, trades, refines, and markets natural gas and petroleum products. 6,000 employees.

Sales: $5,115.4 million (trend 22.0% a year).
Earnings: $100.33 million (trend 15.4% a year).
What happened to a $10,000 investment

Purchase Date	*Purchase Price*	*Price on 12-31-81*	*Dividends Paid*
12-31-71	$51.25	$35.37	$ 351.22
12-31-76	$13.62	$35.37	$1,321.10

Purchase Date	*Cap. Gains (− Losses)*	*Total Return*	*Rate of Return*
12-31-71	$−3,097.56	$−2,746.34	−3.16%
12-31-76	$ 15,963.30	$ 17,284.40	22.23%

PROFILE: Ghosts from the past took away Coastal's Texas gas pipeline in 1979. Though the company was incorporated in its present form in 1972, its history goes back to the mid-1950s, when it was founded (as Coastal States Gas Corp.) by Oscar Wyatt, Jr. One way Wyatt achieved rapid growth was to promise cities like Austin and San Antonio gas for a long time at a set price (about $.22 per thousand cubic feet). By the 1970s, Coastal was cringing at the practice of giving away gas at that price when unregulated intrastate prices had risen to close to $2.00 per thousand cubic feet. It cut back its low-priced shipments and got hauled into court by angry municipalities.

The end result was an agreement by Coastal to spin off the pipeline (now Valero Energy Corp.) to shareholders (excluding Wyatt) and customers — and to supply it with a certain amount of gas in the future at below-market prices.

According to *Business Week,* the pipeline had accounted for about a sixth of Coastal's profits, and Coastal has tried to make up for the loss by plunging deeper into the volatile and controversial field of oil trading. That step could make future earnings more erratic than past earnings have been.

A modest dividend has been paid since 1977, but the yield is only a token — less than 2 percent as of early 1982. Debt makes up more than half of the company's capital, adding to this stock's risk and volatility.

* * *

COCA-COLA CO. (KO). Founded 1919. Headquarters: 310 North Ave. N.W., Atlanta GA 30313. SOFT DRINKS. Coke is the world's leading producer of soft drinks and is also a major marketer of wine, orange juice, fruit drinks, coffee, and tea. 39,000 employees. MAJOR SUBSIDIARIES, BRANDS: Coca-Cola; Sprite; Tab; Fanta; Fresca; Minute Maid; Snow Crop; Hi-C; Taylor; Columbia Pictures.

Sales: $5,912.6 million (trend 16.3% a year).
Earnings: $422.11 million (trend 12.6% a year).
What happened to a $10,000 investment

Purchase Date	*Purchase Price*	*Price on 12-31-81*	*Dividends Paid*
12-31-71	$61.12	$34.75	$2,446.67
12-31-76	$39.62	$34.75	$2,453.00

Purchase Date	*Cap. Gains (− Losses)*	*Total Return*	*Rate of Return*
12-31-71	$−4,314.93	$−1,868.26	−2.05%
12-31-76	$−1,230.28	$ 1,222.71	2.33%

PROFILE: Coke sits on top of the soft drink industry, with a 35 percent share of the market in the United States and an even higher share in quite a few countries abroad. In the United States, Pepsi is number two with a 25 percent market share, and everybody else is scrambling for the remaining part of the pie. Coke and Pepsi have been increasing their shares, and the hot competition between them seems to be keeping both companies on their toes. In the early 1980s, most analysts felt the momentum was swinging toward Coke and away from Pepsi, after a few years in which the reverse had been true.

One thing Pepsi has that Coca-Cola doesn't is a highly profitable snack foods arm (Frito Lay). At Coca-Cola, soft drinks have recently accounted for about 76 percent of sales and about 86 percent of profits. Roberto C. Goizueta, the Cuban-born Coke executive who took over as chairman in 1981, is said to be dissatisfied with the performance of some of the non-soft-drink subsidiaries, especially coffee; he may ax a few. In 1982 he picked up a dynamic addition in Columbia Pictures.

The financial results of the corporation would make any accountant think of the slogan, "Have a Coke and a smile." Return on stockholders' equity has been above 20 percent. The balance sheet is clean as a model's teeth (6 percent debt and 94 percent equity in early 1981). Growth in sales and earnings has been steady and respectable, though not as fast as Goizueta wants.

And that's the rub on Wall Street, where Coca-Cola, as a well-known growth stock, often sold at more than 40 times earnings from 1971–73. The p / e multiple had come down to a moderate 9 in early 1982. The collapsing of the multiple has pulled the stock price down, even though the company's earnings have continued to rise. From a 1973 high of $75 a share, Coca-Cola fell to a 1974 low around $22, and has been fluctuating since in the $30 to $50 range.

* * *

COLE NATIONAL CORP. (CLE). Founded 1949. Headquarters: 29001 Cedar Rd., Cleveland OH 44124. **RETAIL OPTICAL PRODUCTS, GIFTS.** Operates leased departments in major department stores, selling eyeglasses, personalized gifts, and key duplication services. **MAJOR SUBSIDIARIES, BRANDS:** Child World; Craft Showcase; Things Remembered Stores.

Sales: $174.0 million (trend 10.3% a year).
Earnings: $6.78 million (trend 17.9% a year).
What happened to a $10,000 investment

Purchase Date	*Purchase Price*	*Price on 12-31-81*	*Dividends Paid*
12-31-71	$16.91	$18.50	$2,421.99
12-31-76	$ 9.50	$18.50	$2,282.11

Purchase Date	*Cap. Gains (− Losses)*	*Total Return*	*Rate of Return*
12-31-71	$ 940.85	$ 3,362.84	2.94%
12-31-76	$9,473.68	$11,755.79	16.82%

* * *

COLECO INDUSTRIES, INC. (CLO). Founded 1932. Headquarters: 945 Asylum Ave., Hartford CT 06105. **RECREATIONAL PRODUCTS.** Coleco manufactures above-ground swimming pools and accessories, toys, and games. **MAJOR SUBSIDIARIES, BRANDS:** Head to Head; Quiz Wiz; Lil Genius; Telstar Colortron Electronic Learning Machine.

Sales: $162.9 million (trend 13.3% a year).
Earnings: $13.06 million (trend 112.1% a year).
What happened to a $10,000 investment

Purchase Date	*Purchase Price*	*Price on 12-31-81*	*Dividends Paid*
12-31-71	$22.56	$6.87	$68.70
12-31-76	$ 5.25	$6.87	$ 0.00

Purchase Date	*Cap. Gains (− Losses)*	*Total Return*	*Rate of Return*
12-31-71	$−6,952.91	$−6,884.21	−11.01%
12-31-76	$ 3,095.24	$ 3,095.24	5.54%

* * *

COLEMAN CO., INC. (CLN). Founded 1928. Headquarters: 250 N. Saint Francis Ave., Wichita KS 67202. **CAMPING, RECREATION.** Coleman is a well-known maker of camping equipment, including stoves, lanterns, coolers, canoes, and trailers. Subsidiaries make sailboats, water skis, air rifles, heating and air-conditioning equipment. **MAJOR SUBSIDIARIES, BRANDS:** Crosman (air rifles); Hobie Cat (sailboats); O'Brien (water skis).

Sales: $300.5 million (trend 11.4% a year).
Earnings: $14.09 million (trend 10.4% a year).
What happened to a $10,000 investment

Purchase Date	*Purchase Price*	*Price on 12-31-81*	*Dividends Paid*
12-31-71	$30.62	$22.25	$2,223.67
12-31-76	$16.25	$22.25	$2,787.69

Purchase Date	*Cap. Gains (− Losses)*	*Total Return*	*Rate of Return*
12-31-71	$−2,734.69	$−511.02	−.52%
12-31-76	$ 3,692.31	$ 6,480.00	10.51%

* * *

COLGATE-PALMOLIVE CO. (CL). Founded 1923. Headquarters: 300 Park Ave., New York NY 10022. **TOILETRIES, HOUSEHOLD PRODUCTS.** Colgate is a major manufacturer of toiletries and cleaning products and is diversified into health care, foods, sporting goods, textiles, jewelry, and other areas. 49,000 employees. **MAJOR SUBSIDIARIES, BRANDS:** Colgate and Ultra Brite toothpastes; Palmolive and Irish Spring soaps; Dermassage; Ajax, Borax, Dynamo, Fab, and Fresh Start detergents and cleansers; Baggies; Handy Wipes; Curad bandages; Riviana Foods (Carolina Rice); Bancroft and Ram sporting goods; Respiratory Care, Medesonics, and NDM (health care); Kendall (specialty fabrics).

Sales: $5,130.5 million (trend 11.4% a year).
Earnings: $195.81 million (trend 9.8% a year).
What happened to a $10,000 investment

Purchase Date	*Purchase Price*	*Price on 12-31-81*	*Dividends Paid*
12-31-71	$19.54	$16.75	$4,286.91
12-31-76	$27.50	$16.75	$1,909.09

Purchase Date	*Cap. Gains (− Losses)*	*Total Return*	*Rate of Return*
12-31-71	$−1,428.57	$ 2,858.34	2.55%
12-31-76	$−3,909.09	$−2,000.00	−4.36%

PROFILE: A lot of investors think of Colgate-Palmolive as an also-ran, a decent enough company up against better competition. You can use companies' price / earnings ratios as an indication of investors' growth expectations. It tells you something that Colgate's p / e was 7 in early 1982, while Procter & Gamble's was 10, and Bristol-Myers's was 13.

Colgate entered the 1970s as a large company built around toothpaste and soap. It entered the 1980s as a much larger company, considerably diversified. Through acquisition, Colgate has moved into health care, textiles, pipeline coverings, food, and hobby products. The conglomeration adds up to what *Fortune,* in 1979, called a "large but untidy empire." So untidy was it that in 1980 Colgate unloaded a parcel of subsidiaries acquired by former chairman David Foster in the preceding eight years of diversification. The jettisoned included the racket division of Bancroft sporting goods; most of Lum's and Ranch House restaurants; Hebrew National (salami, et cetera); and, most importantly, Helena Rubenstein, an unprofitable cosmetics manufacturer that had been rumored to be on the auction block for a long time. But Keith Crane, who took over as chairman in 1979, has kept many of Foster's acquisitions, including the health care facilities (such as Respiratory Care, Medesonics, and NDM) that contributed 20 percent of the company's 1979 profits on only 14 percent of sales.

Colgate's return on stockholders' equity has been sub-par in recent years. In 1980 its profit margin was less than 3.8 percent, while rival Procter & Gamble's was 5.9 percent. The company is hoping that the recent divestitures will make it trimmer and more profitable. It's also banking on increased penetration of foreign markets (such as Mexico and Australia), which already account for more than half of sales and profits.

* * *

COLLINS & AIKMAN CORP. (CK). Founded 1927. Headquarters: 210 Madison Ave., New York NY 10016. **TEXTILES.** Manufactures textiles, apparel, carpeting, and yarn for consumer and automotive applications. **MAJOR SUBSIDIARIES, BRANDS:** Imperial Paper Co., Mastercraft Corp., Tennessee Tufting, Anderson Hosiery.

Sales: $603.9 million (trend 9.0% a year).
Earnings: $14.40 million (trend −4.7% a year).
What happened to a $10,000 investment

Purchase Date	*Purchase Price*	*Price on 12-31-81*	*Dividends Paid*
12-31-71	$30.62	$11.25	$1,808.98
12-31-76	$13.25	$11.25	$2,128.30

Purchase Date	*Cap. Gains (– Losses)*	*Total Return*	*Rate of Return*
12-31-71	$–6,326.53	$–4,517.55	–5.83%
12-31-76	$–1,509.43	$ 618.87	1.21%

* * *

COLLINS FOODS INTERNATIONAL, INC. (CF). Founded 1968. Headquarters: 12731 W. Jefferson Blvd., Los Angeles CA 90066. **FAST FOOD.** Owns, operates, and franchises fast food restaurants and wholesale food distribution centers. **MAJOR SUBSIDIARIES, BRANDS:** Sizzler Family Steak Houses. Operates (but does not own) approximately 200 Kentucky Fried Chicken outlets.

Sales: $265.2 million (trend 18.1% a year).
Earnings: $7.45 million (trend 17.7% a year).
What happened to a $10,000 investment

Purchase Date	*Purchase Price*	*Price on 12-31-81*	*Dividends Paid*
12-31-71	$11.53	$13.87	$ 865.04
12-31-76	$ 5.81	$13.87	$1,458.06

Purchase Date	*Cap. Gains (– Losses)*	*Total Return*	*Rate of Return*
12-31-71	$ 2,032.22	$ 2,897.26	2.58%
12-31-76	$13,870.36	$15,328.43	20.43%

* * *

COLONIAL PENN GROUP, INC. (CPG). Founded 1963. Headquarters: 5 Penn Center Plaza, Philadelphia PA 19181. **INSURANCE.** Specializes in personal lines of insurance for persons aged fifty and over; also involved in travel and temporary employment services and a retirement community.

Sales: $799.8 million (trend 18.4% a year).
Earnings: $53.13 million (trend 7.0% a year).
What happened to a $10,000 investment

Purchase Date	*Purchase Price*	*Price on 12-31-81*	*Dividends Paid*
12-31-71	$N/A	$15.25	$ N/A
12-31-76	$29.25	$15.25	$2,128.21

Purchase Date	*Cap. Gains (– Losses)*	*Total Return*	*Rate of Return*
12-31-71	$ N/A	$ N/A	N/A%
12-31-76	$–4,786.32	$–2,658.12	–5.99%

* * *

COLT INDUSTRIES INC. (COT). Founded 1911. Headquarters: 430 Park Ave., New York NY 10022. **INDUSTRIAL PRODUCTS.** Colt is a manufacturer of specialty steel, industrial products, power transmission equipment, fluid control systems, shock mitigation equipment, auto components, industrial coatings and seals, firearms, and aircraft landing gear. 33,000 employees. **MAJOR SUBSIDIARIES, BRANDS:** Crucible Steel; Elox; Fairbanks Morse; Garlock Inc.; Holley Carburetor; Menasco Inc.; Quincy Compressor; Trent Tube; Colt firearms.

Sales: $2,165.6 million (trend 17.0% a year).
Earnings: $96.11 million (trend 17.6% a year).
What happened to a $10,000 investment

Purchase Date	*Purchase Price*	*Price on 12-31-81*	*Dividends Paid*
12-31-71	$ 5.54	$28.12	$15,157.86
12-31-76	$18.17	$28.12	$ 3,362.38

Purchase Date	*Cap. Gains (– Losses)*	*Total Return*	*Rate of Return*
12-31-71	$40,751.88	$55,909.74	20.75%
12-31-76	$ 5,481.65	$ 8,844.03	13.51%

PROFILE: The name Colt, taken from the firearms division (which makes M-16 rifles) is a bit deceiving. During the Vietnam war, firearms accounted for close to a third of company earnings, but now it's probably 5 percent or less. What Colt Industries mainly does is supply industrial equipment, transportation equipment (aircraft landing gear and automobile carburetors), and specialty steel. The company is a conglomerate with a unified focus: serving heavy industry.

Chairman George Strichman has done a great deal for this company (formerly named Fairbanks Whitney) since he took over the reins in 1963. Then, the company was in deep financial trouble; recently debt was less than 30 percent of capital. Then, the company was subject to violent earnings swings; today there are still major cyclical swings, but the company's diversity acts as a shock absorber. And a fundamental uptrend has been clearly visible beneath the cycles.

Both Strichman and stockholders have been well rewarded. The chairman pulls down about $2.5 million a year. The stock price has risen from the $8-to-$17 range in the early 1970s to the $35-to-$55 range at the beginning of the 1980s. With astute (or lucky) timing, you could have quintupled your money here in a decade, disregarding dividends.

Dividends have been paid each year since 1968, and have been above bank passbook rates since 1974. The dividend yield in early 1982 was about 7 percent.

In 1981, Colt had its second-best year ever, despite the recession. Come a boom, the company could march to several years of record earnings.

Penn Central's unsuccessful attempt to take over Colt caused a temporary bulge in the stock price in 1981.

* * *

COLUMBIA GAS SYSTEM, INC. (CG). Founded 1906. Headquarters: 20 Montchanin Rd., Wilmington DE 19807. NATURAL GAS. Columbia Gas is one of the nation's largest providers of natural gas, which it transports via pipelines and sells to industrial, commercial, and residential customers, and to utilities. It also explores for and produces natural gas. 11,000 employees.

Sales: $3,636.5 million (trend 19.4% a year).
Earnings: $165.31 million (trend 8.8% a year).
What happened to a $10,000 investment

Purchase Date	*Purchase Price*	*Price on 12-31-81*	*Dividends Paid*
12-31-71	$32.62	$32.12	$6,798.47
12-31-76	$30.37	$32.12	$4,042.80

Purchase Date	*Cap. Gains (− Losses)*	*Total Return*	*Rate of Return*
12-31-71	$−153.26	$6,645.21	5.23%
12-31-76	$ 576.13	$4,618.93	7.89%

PROFILE: If you want natural gas in Maryland, Virginia, West Virginia, Ohio, Pennsylvania, Kentucky, the District of Columbia, or parts of New York, there's a good chance you'll get it either from Columbia or from someone who got it from Columbia.

Distributing natural gas is the company's stock in trade. To be sure, it also produces gas, but only enough to amount to about a sixth of the quantity it sells. It buys most of its gas from the original producers in the Gulf Coast and Southwest regions.

Several other major gas distributors are also profiled in this book. Among them: El Paso Co.; Empire, Inc.; InterNorth; Pacific Lighting; Peoples Energy Corp.; Tenneco; Texas Eastern; and United Energy Resources. If you want to invest in a gas distributor, you have plenty of choices, so shop and compare.

One factor to recommend Columbia recently has been its low price / earnings ratio. The multiple has been 7 or less during at least part of every year since 1973. At these prices, you know you're not buying glamour.

Another factor in Columbia's favor is the high dividend yield — often above 8 percent, and occasionally above 9 percent in recent years. Dividends have been paid each year since 1943, and raised each year for more than a decade.

Factors arguing against purchase of these shares include a mediocre return on equity in recent years, slow earnings growth, and a rather heavy debt load. Debt recently has been almost half of total capital.

* * *

COMBINED INTERNATIONAL CORP. (PMA). Founded 1949. Headquarters: 500 Combined Centre, Northbrook IL 60062. INSURANCE. Insurance holding company (formerly Combined Insurance Co. of America) specializing in accident, health, and life insurance sold through group presentations to employees.

Sales: $757.0 million (trend 14.1% a year).
Earnings: $95.61 million (trend 14.4% a year).
What happened to a $10,000 investment

Purchase Date	*Purchase Price*	*Price on 12-31-81*	*Dividends Paid*
12-31-71	$30.34	$24.25	$2,937.52
12-31-76	$14.37	$24.25	$4,347.83

Purchase Date	*Cap. Gains (− Losses)*	*Total Return*	*Rate of Return*
12-31-71	$−2,007.49	$ 930.02	.89%
12-31-76	$ 6,869.57	$11,217.39	16.24%

* * *

COMBUSTION ENGINEERING, INC. (CSP). Founded 1912. Headquarters: 900 Long Ridge Rd., Stamford CT 06902. POWER GENERATION, OIL FIELD EQUIPMENT. This company, long the leading supplier of steam power-generation equipment for electric utilities, has diversified into engineering, oil field equipment, and industrial products, including glass, building materials, and mineral processing equipment. 43,000 employees. MAJOR SUBSIDIARIES, BRANDS: Lummus Co. (engineering and construction); Gray Tool Co.; Vetco; Natco; Beaumont Well Works (oil drilling equipment).

Sales: $3,146.5 million (trend 13.4% a year).
Earnings: $116.67 million (trend 21.3% a year).
What happened to a $10,000 investment

Purchase Date	*Purchase Price*	*Price on 12-31-81*	*Dividends Paid*
12-31-71	$20.71	$37.25	$3,929.26
12-31-76	$16.75	$37.25	$3,164.18

Purchase Date	*Cap. Gains (− Losses)*	*Total Return*	*Rate of Return*
12-31-71	$ 7,987.93	$11,917.18	8.16%
12-31-76	$12,238.81	$15,402.99	20.50%

PROFILE: A shrewd and well-timed diversification program helped Combustion Engineering earn high marks on Wall Street in recent years. The stock more than tripled between 1978 and 1980, before settling back a bit in early 1981.

For years, Combustion Engineering was known mainly as a supplier of power generation equipment to electric utilities. That's not a growth market these days. But the company saw the handwriting on the wall from a distance and diversified into such lucrative fields as oil drilling equipment and petroleum plant retooling.

Not only is Combustion Engineering now among the largest dozen-or-so suppliers of oil and gas drill ing equipment, it occupies special (and hence profitable) niches within that industry. Gray Tool Co., acquired in 1976, specializes in extra-deep drilling for natural gas; Vetco in offshore drilling; Natco in stimulated recovery of heavy crude. Oilfield equipment contributed about 30 percent of profits in 1979 and may contribute about 40 percent in 1981, according to some analysts. The company is pouring money into these subsidiaries, and into the Lummus Co. engineering and construction arm, which has developed a major reputation in the retooling of oil refineries.

These lovely developments have not gone unnoticed: The 1978–80 price upsurge left the stock selling at a p / e ratio (about 11 to 15) at which favorable expectations were already built into the stock price. The dividend yield is modest (3 to 5 percent in recent years), but dividends have been paid every year since the company's incorporation in 1912.

* * *

COMDISCO, INC. (CDO). Founded 1971. Headquarters: 6400 Shafer Court, Rosemont IL 60018. **COMPUTERS.** Buys, sells, leases, finances new and used computer equipment, primarily IBM.

Sales: $287.8 million (trend 29.4% a year).
Earnings: $16.50 million (trend 44.9% a year).
What happened to a $10,000 investment

Purchase Date	*Purchase Price*	*Price on 12-31-81*	*Dividends Paid*
12-31-71	$N/A	$25.62	$ N/A
12-31-76	$ 1.69	$25.62	$4,676.37

Purchase Date	*Cap. Gains (− Losses)*	*Total Return*	*Rate of Return*
12-31-71	$ N/A	$ N/A	N/A%
12-31-76	$141,726.97	$146,403.34	73.32%

* * *

COMMERCE SOUTHWEST INC. (CSI). Founded 1978; flagship bank dates to 1889. Headquarters: 1525 Elm St., Dallas TX 75201. **BANKING.** Holding company for National Bank of Commerce and several smaller banks in the Dallas region. **MAJOR SUBSIDIARIES, BRANDS:** National Bank of Commerce (fifth largest bank in Dallas).

* * *

COMMODORE INTERNATIONAL LTD. (CBU). Founded 1976. Headquarters: 3330 Scott Blvd., Santa Clara CA 95050. **COMPUTER SYSTEMS.** Manufactures personal computers, microcomputer systems, computer components, and office equipment.

Sales: $186.5 million (trend 30.7% a year).
Earnings: $24.90 million (trend 82.3% a year).
What happened to a $10,000 investment

Purchase Date	*Purchase Price*	*Price on 12-31-81*	*Dividends Paid*
12-31-71	$N/A	$46.25	$0.00
12-31-76	$ .83	$46.25	$0.00

Purchase Date	*Cap. Gains (− Losses)*	*Total Return*	*Rate of Return*
12-31-71	$ N/A	$ N/A	N/A%
12-31-76	$545,000.00	$545,000.00	123.28%

* * *

COMMONWEALTH EDISON CO. (CWE). Founded 1913. Headquarters: 1 First National Plaza, Chicago IL 60690. **ELECTRIC UTILITY.** Supplies electricity to some 8 million customers in Chicago and northern Illinois. 16,000 employees.

Sales: $3,324.0 million (trend 13.7% a year).
Earnings: $287.09 million (trend 10.2% a year).
What happened to a $10,000 investment

Purchase Date	*Purchase Price*	*Price on 12-31-81*	*Dividends Paid*
12-31-71	$39.75	$19.87	$6,100.63
12-31-76	$31.62	$19.87	$4,031.62

Purchase Date	*Cap. Gains (− Losses)*	*Total Return*	*Rate of Return*
12-31-71	$−5,000.00	$1,100.63	1.05%
12-31-76	$−3,715.42	$ 316.21	.62%

PROFILE: What makes Commonwealth Edison different from other utilities? Its energy mix. A good guess for 1981 was that Commonwealth Edison got 45 percent of its electrical generation capacity from nuclear power (the highest percentage in the country), 45 percent from coal, and only about 10 percent from oil and gas. Company officials like to say that their utility uses the energy sources of the future, not those that are dwindling and subject to OPEC price hikes.

That's well and good, but the road to nuclear power has been paved with potholes. Financial potholes, in the case of Commonwealth Edison. Briefly, the problem is that nuclear power plants are extremely costly and time-consuming to build. In 1979, the company got caught in the middle of a $4.4 billion nuclear expansion program without enough money to finance it. The Illinois Commerce Commission was in no mood to help with rate hikes. So the company had to take on more debt, at high interest costs. (Debt is about half of total capital.) It had to issue more preferred stock (about 13 percent of capital, adding together recent and previous issues). And it had to sell more common stock, even though the stock price was low, and the action contributed to further dilution of per-share earnings. Belatedly, Illinois authorities granted a substantial rate increase in 1980, adding some light to a grim picture.

In the *Forbes* Annual Report on American Industry published in 1981, Commonwealth Edison ranked last among 23 Midwest utilities in revenue growth, twenty-first in return on stockholders' equity. The earnings growth rate was negative.

The stock has declined steadily for more than a decade. If the regulators' more favorable attitude holds up and Commonwealth Edison can complete its expansion program anywhere close to on schedule (and budget), a rebound, and a capital gain, are possible. But the chief appeal of the stock is the dividend yield, which was above 14 percent in early 1981. Utilities realize that most of their attractiveness to investors lies in their yield, and they'll go to considerable lengths to maintain it. In 1979, Commonwealth Edison paid out more in dividends than the sum of its after-tax profits.

* * *

COMMONWEALTH ENERGY SYSTEM (CES). Founded 1926. Headquarters: 675 Massachusetts Ave., Cambridge MA 02139. **UTILITIES.** Holding company for several utilities that supply electricity and gas in Massachusetts. The company changed its name in 1981 from New England Gas & Electric Association. **MAJOR SUBSIDIARIES, BRANDS:** Commonwealth Electric; Commonwealth Gas; Cambridge Electric Light; Com / Energy Steam; Com / Energy Exploration; Canal Electric.

Sales: $512.5 million (trend 10.0% a year).
Earnings: $22.89 million (trend 12.8% a year).
What happened to a $10,000 investment

Purchase Date	*Purchase Price*	*Price on 12-31-81*	*Dividends Paid*
12-31-71	$19.50	$14.87	$7,151.28
12-31-76	$16.12	$14.87	$4,936.43

Purchase Date	*Cap. Gains (− Losses)*	*Total Return*	*Rate of Return*
12-31-71	$−2,371.79	$4,779.49	3.98%
12-31-76	$ −775.19	$4,161.24	7.21%

* * *

COMMONWEALTH OIL REFINING CO., INC. (CWOP, Pacific Stock Exchange**).** Founded: 1953. Headquarters: 8626 Tesoro Dr., San Antonio TX 78217. **OIL.** Refines petroleum products; also produces petrochemicals. 1,500 employees. Company is 37 percent owned by Tesoro Petroleum.

PROFILE: Commonwealth Oil has been in Chapter 11 bankruptcy since 1978. It has paid no dividends since 1971. It lost money in five out of the six years from 1975 to 1980.

Why would anyone be interested in Commonwealth Oil shares? The answer's the same as with other continuing enterprises in bankruptcy: for speculation. When a stock's down this far (selling for less than $4 a share in early 1981 — this, mind you, for a Fortune 500 company), it can be expected either to topple into final liquidation or to give investors a capital gain worth talking about.

Emergence from bankruptcy is possible. Still, unless you've got a gambler's temperament — and a bankroll to match — you'd probably do best to avoid these shares. The immediate cause of the bankruptcy was a pair of ill-fated petrochemical-producing ventures undertaken with PPG and W. R. Grace. But a more fundamental problem is the erosion of the profitability in Commonwealth's basic strategy.

For years, the strategy worked: Buy crude oil cheap from Venezuela and refine it at a big Puerto Rican refinery (which, because of Puerto Rico's commonwealth status, enjoys certain tax advantages). Now that Venezuela has had its consciousness — and its oil prices — raised, with help from its OPEC sisters, the scheme seems anachronistic. But it's not clear with what new overall plan Commonwealth Oil could replace it.

* * *

COMMUNICATIONS SATELLITE CORP. (CO). Founded 1963. Headquarters: 950 L'Enfant Plaza S.W., Washington DC 20024. TELECOMMUNICATIONS. COMSAT provides international, domestic, and maritime satellite communications services. MAJOR SUBSIDIARIES, BRANDS: COMSAT General Corp.; Environmental Research & Technology, Inc.; Satellite Television Corp.

Sales: $299.7 million (trend 16.7% a year).
Earnings: $38.29 million (trend −2.0% a year).
What happened to a $10,000 investment

Purchase Date	*Purchase Price*	*Price on 12-31-81*	*Dividends Paid*
12-31-71	$64.50	$63.50	$2,168.99
12-31-76	$31.87	$63.50	$3,113.73

Purchase Date	*Cap. Gains (− Losses)*	*Total Return*	*Rate of Return*
12-31-71	$−155.04	$ 2,013.95	1.85%
12-31-76	$ 9,921.57	$13,035.29	18.16%

* * *

COMMUNITY PSYCHIATRIC CENTERS (CMY). Founded 1962. Headquarters: 517 Washington St., San Francisco CA 94111. HEALTH CARE. Operates acute psychiatric hospitals and kidney dialysis centers.

Sales: $59.4 million (trend 27.9% a year).
Earnings: $8.89 million (trend 39.5% a year).
What happened to a $10,000 investment

Purchase Date	*Purchase Price*	*Price on 12-31-81*	*Dividends Paid*
12-31-71	$2.08	$22.25	$4,432.00
12-31-76	$1.79	$22.25	$4,595.35

Purchase Date	*Cap. Gains (− Losses)*	*Total Return*	*Rate of Return*
12-31-71	$ 96,800.00	$101,232.00	27.24%
12-31-76	$114,186.05	$118,781.40	66.71%

* * *

COMPUGRAPHIC CORP. (CPU). Founded 1960. Headquarters: 200 Ballardvale St., Wilmington MA 01887. TYPESETTING EQUIPMENT. Manufactures, markets, and services photocomposition machines and related equipment for newspaper and printing market.

Sales: $278.1 million (trend 25.6% a year).
Earnings: $−6.66 million.
What happened to a $10,000 investment

Purchase Date	*Purchase Price*	*Price on 12-31-81*	*Dividends Paid*
12-31-71	$ 4.56	$10.12	$2,115.07
12-31-76	$16.31	$10.12	$ 576.25

Purchase Date	*Cap. Gains (− Losses)*	*Total Return*	*Rate of Return*
12-31-71	$ 12,191.78	$ 14,306.85	9.29%
12-31-76	$−3,793.10	$−3,216.86	−7.47%

* * *

COMPUTER SCIENCES CORP. (CSC). Founded 1959. Headquarters: 650 N. Sepulveda Blvd., El Segundo CA 90245. COMPUTER SERVICES. Computer Sciences is one of the major providers of computer software (i.e. programming) to the U.S. government and to private industry. 15,000 employees. MAJOR SUBSIDIARIES, BRANDS: Infonet.

Sales: $600.6 million (trend 22.9% a year).
Earnings: $24.72 million (trend 26.3% a year).
What happened to a $10,000 investment

Purchase Date	*Purchase Price*	*Price on 12-31-81*	*Dividends Paid*
12-31-71	$8.25	$13.12	$0.00
12-31-76	$7.25	$13.12	$0.00

Purchase Date	*Cap. Gains (− Losses)*	*Total Return*	*Rate of Return*
12-31-71	$5,909.09	$5,909.09	4.75%
12-31-76	$8,103.45	$8,103.45	12.60%

PROFILE: It used to be taken for granted that the way to make money in computers was to make computers. Hardware is still the heavy-revenue end of the industry, but software is becoming more important each year. Computer Sciences is a leading example of a company that has made it big in software. It will help design your company's computer system, take care of your computers, and provide the programs to make your computers do what you want them to. Or, it will plug you into a time-sharing network, letting you tap prepared programs through its well-known Infonet service.

Computer Sciences' corporate work is about evenly split between the United States and abroad, which gives the company good balance and growth potential. But more than half its revenues don't come from corporations at all. They come from the U.S. government, notably the Navy and the National Aeronautics and Space Administration (NASA). For that reason, it was a bitter blow when the company was temporarily banned from bidding on new government work after being indicted on charges of making false claims in regard to a General Services Administration (GSA) contract. The indictment was dismissed in February 1981, but the stock reacted severely and recovered only gradually in the aftermath.

Severe fluctuations in the stock price are nothing new here, though. The stock sold for more than $30 a share in 1969–70, dropped below $2 in parts of 1974–75, then rose to nearly $30 again before losing about half its value in the wake of the indictment. A high debt load has historically added to volatility. Debt was an incredible 90 percent of capital in 1971–72 and was more than 50 percent of capital until 1979. Recently it has been about 34 percent of capital, a figure that hardly raises anyone's eyebrows nowadays.

A token dividend was paid prior to 1969 but none have been paid since that year. Earnings growth (see figures above) has been excellent, and profitability has been outstanding. For five straight years recently the return on stockholders' equity has been above 30 percent. The stock usually sells for a multiple higher than that of most stocks, but the p / e is very volatile. It's ranged recently from 6 to 16.

* * *

COMPUTERVISION CORP. (CVN). Founded 1969. Headquarters: 201 Burlington Rd., Bedford MA 01730. **COMPUTER SYSTEMS.** Designs, manufactures, sells, and services computer products that automate product development and production processes.

Sales: $224.2 million (trend 59.0% a year).
Earnings: $23.32 million (trend 116.3% a year).
What happened to a $10,000 investment

Purchase Date	*Purchase Price*	*Price on 12-31-81*	*Dividends Paid*
12-31-71	$N/A	$32.50	$0.00
12-31-76	$ .69	$32.50	$0.00

Purchase Date	*Cap. Gains (– Losses)*	*Total Return*	*Rate of Return*
12-31-71	$ N/A	$ N/A	N/A%
12-31-76	$462,727.27	$462,727.27	116.23%

* * *

CONAGRA, INC. (CAG). Founded 1919. Headquarters: 200 Kiewit Plaza, Omaha NB 68131. **FOODS.** ConAgra is active in flour milling, poultry raising, animal feeds, pesticide and herbicide manufacture, pet foods, and consumer food products. 13,000 employees. **MAJOR SUBSIDIARIES, BRANDS:** Banquet foods; United Agri Products (pesticides and herbicides); Bow Wow dog food; Taco Plaza restaurants.

Sales: $1,376.8 million (trend 20.7% a year).
Earnings: $26.68 million (trend 13.8% a year).
What happened to a $10,000 investment

Purchase Date	*Purchase Price*	*Price on 12-31-81*	*Dividends Paid*
12-31-71	$3.70	$17.37	$7,771.62
12-31-76	$4.21	$17.37	$5,274.85

Purchase Date	*Cap. Gains (– Losses)*	*Total Return*	*Rate of Return*
12-31-71	$36,931.90	$44,703.52	18.52%
12-31-76	$31,287.13	$36,561.98	36.02%

PROFILE: This is an old milling company that has diversified into a number of food-related areas, most notably poultry raising.

Just as aluminum production is highly dependent on the cost of electricity (see Aluminum Co. of America), so poultry raising is crucially dependent on the price of grain. When grain prices are cheap or falling, beef and pork producers tend to do well. But when grain prices rise, chicken producers thrive, because the price gap between chicken and other protein sources tends to widen (or, alternatively, profit margins in selling chicken fatten). That's because chickens need far less feed per ounce of edible meat than cattle or pigs do.

ConAgra decided some years ago that the long-term trend in U.S. grain prices would be up. That's good both for the company's basic grain commodity business and for the chicken business. (The two together account for more than half of ConAgra sales.) So far, the forecast has been right on target.

The 1980 acquisition of Banquet Foods (from RCA) was probably correctly explained by *Business Week* as having been aimed more at acquiring Banquet's supply of chickens than at increasing penetration of consumer foods markets (which account for only 10 percent of ConAgra's sales). The acquisition made ConAgra the nation's fifth largest poultry producer.

Taco Plaza and Bow Wow dog food have been marginal. But an interesting ancillary business is "aquaculture," chiefly catfish farming, with shrimp farming possibly to follow.

* * *

CONE MILLS CORP. (COE). Founded 1895. Headquarters: 1201 Maple St., Greensboro NC 27405. **TEXTILES.** Manufactures corduroy and denim fabrics; also engages in custom finishing.

Sales: $729.9 million (trend 8.0% a year).
Earnings: $51.25 million (trend 13.5% a year).
What happened to a $10,000 investment

Purchase Date	*Purchase Price*	*Price on 12-31-81*	*Dividends Paid*
12-31-71	$11.12	$30.87	$11,159.55
12-31-76	$25.50	$30.87	$ 3,509.80

Purchase Date	*Cap. Gains (– Losses)*	*Total Return*	*Rate of Return*
12-31-71	$17,752.81	$28,912.36	14.55%
12-31-76	$ 2,107.84	$ 5,617.65	9.33%

* * *

CONNECTICUT GENERAL INSURANCE CORP. (CGN). Founded 1865. Headquarters: 900 Cottage Grove Rd., Bloomfield CT 06152. **INSURANCE.** Connecticut General is approximately the seventh-largest U.S. life insurance company. It is active in the sale of both group and individual life insurance, health insurance, and annuities, as well as property and casualty insurance. Connecticut General recently announced its intention to merge with INA Corp. The merged entity, to be called CIGNA Corp., would be the nation's fifth largest insurance company. 14,000 employees. **MAJOR SUBSIDIARIES, BRANDS:** Connecticut General Life Insurance Co. (life and health); Aetna Insurance Co. (property and casualty).

Sales: $5,279.4 million (trend 12.3% a year).
Earnings: $316.70 million (trend 18.8% a year).
What happened to a $10,000 investment

Purchase Date	*Purchase Price*	*Price on 12-31-81*	*Dividends Paid*
12-31-71	$31.67	$50.25	$2,915.09
12-31-76	$38.92	$50.25	$1,665.10

Purchase Date	*Cap. Gains (– Losses)*	*Total Return*	*Rate of Return*
12-31-71	$5,868.42	$8,783.51	6.51%
12-31-76	$2,912.21	$4,577.30	7.83%

PROFILE: Connecticut General is one of the "Hartford troika," the three largest stock life insurance companies in the country. In the sale of life insurance, it ranks either seventh or eighth, depending on what measure you use — neck and neck with crosstown rival Travelers. (Five of the top eight companies are mutual companies that don't sell stock.) In property and casualty insurance, it ranks about twenty-first, through its Aetna Insurance Co. subsidiary (not to be confused, if you can help it, with Aetna Life and Casualty Co., the biggest member of the Hartford troika, and in recent years the most profitable).

A decade ago, CG (as it sometimes calls itself in its commercials) was primarily a seller of individual life insurance. Though the company hasn't flat-out said so, it decided that was a no-growth or slow-growth business and has been concentrating on other areas. The main move has been to group insurance (life, health, and annuities), where CG has now carved itself a big chunk of business and a major reputation. The second-largest move has been into property and casualty insurance, and the company says it plans to continue to emphasize that area, despite the notorious profitability swings of the property and casualty business. It anticipates that P and C insurance — particularly auto insurance — is going to be increasingly a fringe benefit item in the future. Assuming that's so, CG figures its extensive experience in group business will stand it in good stead marketing group auto (or other P and C) policies.

The stock pays a modest dividend, has a low p / e ratio (5 to 9 in recent years), and has appreciated moderately since the holding company was formed in 1967.

The proposed merger with INA Corp. (profiled elsewhere in this volume) was still some distance from consummation when this book went to press.

* * *

CONNECTICUT NATURAL GAS CORP. (CTG). Founded 1848. Headquarters: 100 Columbus Blvd., Hartford CT 06103. UTILITY. Distributes natural gas in central Connecticut. MAJOR SUBSIDIARIES, BRANDS: Fuels, Inc.; Hartford Steam Service Co.; CNG Realty Corp.

Sales: $123.5 million (trend 13.2% a year).
Earnings: $3.97 million (trend 1.8% a year).
What happened to a $10,000 investment

Purchase Date	*Purchase Price*	*Price on 12-31-81*	*Dividends Paid*
12-31-71	$ N/A	$18.12	$ N/A
12-31-76	$18.75	$18.12	$4,400.00

Purchase Date	*Cap. Gains (− Losses)*	*Total Return*	*Rate of Return*
12-31-71	$ N/A	$ N/A	N/A%
12-31-76	$−333.33	$4,066.67	7.06%

* * *

CONRAC CORP. (CAX). Founded 1935. Headquarters: 3 Landmark Sq., Stamford CT 06901. ELECTRONICS. International manufacturer of electronic products and systems in four business segments: information display and control, aerospace, telecommunications, and architectural and industrial products.

Sales: $146.8 million (trend 8.2% a year).
Earnings: $4.31 million (trend −1.8% a year).
What happened to a $10,000 investment

Purchase Date	*Purchase Price*	*Price on 12-31-81*	*Dividends Paid*
12-31-71	$18.10	$27.75	$3,323.28
12-31-76	$18.73	$27.75	$2,067.95

Purchase Date	*Cap. Gains (− Losses)*	*Total Return*	*Rate of Return*
12-31-71	$5,332.17	$8,655.45	6.43%
12-31-76	$4,817.95	$6,885.90	11.05%

* * *

CONSOLIDATED EDISON CO. OF N.Y., INC. (ED). Founded 1884. Headquarters: 4 Irving Pl., New York NY 10003. UTILITY. Con Ed supplies electricity to almost all of New York City and to most of Westchester County, N.Y. It is the country's fifth largest electric utility company. 23,000 employees.

Sales: $3,947.2 million (trend 7.1% a year).
Earnings: $293.12 million (trend 4.2% a year).
What happened to a $10,000 investment

Purchase Date	*Purchase Price*	*Price on 12-31-81*	*Dividends Paid*
12-31-71	$25.87	$32.50	$7,547.83
12-31-76	$21.25	$32.50	$5,778.82

Purchase Date	*Cap. Gains (− Losses)*	*Total Return*	*Rate of Return*
12-31-71	$2,560.39	$10,108.21	7.24%
12-31-76	$5,294.12	$11,072.94	16.08%

PROFILE: One day in 1974, Consolidated Edison took the then unthinkable step of announcing it would skip a quarterly dividend payment. That decision was a watershed in the history of utility stocks. Or perhaps "bloodshed" should be the word. Faced with the thought that electric utilities might not be dividend-paying machines after all, investors lost enthusiasm for utilities in general and Con Ed in particular. Prices plummeted. It took Con Ed until 1980 to get back to its 1973 high of $26 a share.

There are good reasons why investors are cool to utilities these days. Many of them have high raw-material (e.g., oil) costs. Almost all have their rates strictly regulated by state commissions that are under heavy public pressure to keep rates down. And many are operating in mature markets where little growth in electrical demand is expected. All three of those negative factors apply here.

In late 1980 analyst Jeffrey Hoffman of Sanford C. Bernstein & Co. issued a favorable report on Con Ed, the central point of which was that since it was serving a mature market, it wouldn't face the heavy construction outlays some utilities have to deal with. He pointed out that while many utilities are adding to their already high debt loads, Con Ed is reducing its debt to about 50 percent of capital. And he predicted that, with the balance sheet in decent shape, Con Ed would hike its dividend payout ratio to about 70 percent (from about 57 percent in 1980). Valid points, all, but they add up to a parcel of minor virtues. If you buy this stock, you're buying it for its high yield (about 13 percent in early 1981) and hoping that the yield will be supplemented by modest capital gains — or at least not undercut by capital losses.

* * *

CONSOLIDATED FOODS CORP. (CFD). Founded 1941. Headquarters: 135 S. LaSalle St.,

Chicago IL 60603. **FOODS.** The company derives about three quarters of sales and earnings from consumer food products and food services. Also owns Hanes Group, the leading maker of panty hose, and three door-to-door sales companies. 89,000 employees. **MAJOR SUBSIDIARIES, BRANDS:** Sara Lee (frozen baked desserts); Booth (frozen fish); Popsicle; Shasta (soft drinks). Owns 65 percent of Douwe Egberts B.V., a major international coffee supplier based in the Netherlands. Door-to-door sales group includes Fuller Brush; Electrolux (vacuum cleaners); Oxford (industrial chemicals). Food service group includes Lawson's; Lyon's Restaurants; PYA / Monarch.

Sales: $5,614.1 million (trend 17.7% a year).
Earnings: $135.32 million (trend 13.5% a year).
What happened to a $10,000 investment

Purchase Date	*Purchase Price*	*Price on 12-31-81*	*Dividends Paid*
12-31-71	$43.37	$31.50	$3,362.07
12-31-76	$26.62	$31.50	$3,012.96

Purchase Date	*Cap. Gains (− Losses)*	*Total Return*	*Rate of Return*
12-31-71	$−2,737.75	$ 624.32	.61%
12-31-76	$ 1,830.99	$4,843.94	8.22%

PROFILE: Once upon a time, a foods company decided it wanted to be a conglomerate. Like the frog that tried to puff itself up to be bigger than an ox, it got into a lot of trouble.

Unlike the frog, Consolidated Foods didn't burst; it made a successful recovery. After the ill-fated acquisition binge of 1969–72, the task of recovery went to John Bryan, who became Consolidated's chairman in 1975 at the tender age of thirty-eight. "A management nightmare" was how Bryan described to *Financial World* the situation he inherited. As the magazine put it, "the company was into an incredible range of small, nonfood businesses — everything from furniture and motels to rental equipment and men's shirts, all of which operated autonomously and many of which skated on razor-thin profit margins." Out, over the next few years, went more than fifty subsidiaries.

When housecleaning was done, Bryan did some acquiring of his own, but on a more substantial scale. To the company's traditional food business, he added a 65 percent share of the big Dutch coffee firm, Douwe Egberts. Outside the food business, he paid $250 million to acquire Hanes, the nation's leading seller of panty hose, which was scoring a market triumph with L'eggs. Hanes has continued to add sales and earnings, despite the fact that the panty hose market as a whole has been shrinking in recent years.

Earnings and sales growth at Consolidated have been roughly average, which accounts for the stock's low p / e ratio (from 5 to 8 in recent years). But the stock offers a substantial yield (recently 6 to 7 percent), plus (as a food company) relative resistance to recessions.

* * *

CONSOLIDATED FREIGHTWAYS, INC. (CNF). Founded 1958. Headquarters: 601 California St., San Francisco CA 94108. **TRUCKING.** The nation's second-largest motor freight carrier, Consolidated Freightways also has a small but rapidly growing air freight subsidiary. 24,000 employees. **MAJOR SUBSIDIARIES, BRANDS:** CF Air.

Sales: $1,653.6 million (trend 22.4% a year).
Earnings: $41.90 million (trend 18.7% a year).
What happened to a $10,000 investment

Purchase Date	*Purchase Price*	*Price on 12-31-81*	*Dividends Paid*
12-31-71	$27.44	$39.50	$3,376.77
12-31-76	$26.50	$39.50	$2,298.11

Purchase Date	*Cap. Gains (− Losses)*	*Total Return*	*Rate of Return*
12-31-71	$4,396.36	$7,773.12	5.92%
12-31-76	$4,905.66	$7,203.77	11.46%

PROFILE: In 1981, Consolidated decided it would run trucks, not manufacture them. The company announced plans to sell its Freightliner Corp. subsidiary, the sixth- or seventh-largest maker of truck tractors, to Daimler-Benz. The move, which will certainly make this leading freight carrier run lighter, was enthusiastically greeted on Wall Street; the stock shot up seven points on the announcement.

Chairman Raymond O'Brien seems to have a clear strategic idea, based on the fact that the U.S. trucking industry is entering a new era of less regulation and more competition. He, like the other big trucking companies (including Roadway Express and Yellow Freight, which sandwich Consolidated in trucking revenue rankings), hopes to pick up market share at the expense of smaller firms. To this end, Consolidated has been pouring money into upgrading and enlarging its nationwide network of truck terminals (it had 291 in early 1981), even while the 1980–81 recession was draining current earnings. The company had the financial strength to make that bold move, since it had trimmed debt from more than 46 percent of capital in 1970 to about half of that going into the 1980s.

Selling Freightliner should allow Consolidated to continue that strategy without going heavily into debt again. And though the manufacturing arm of the company was profitable, it was less so than the freight business, contributing only 30 percent of 1979 profits on 45% of sales.

Watch the air freight operation, which chipped in 6 percent of profits on 3 percent of sales. According to *Forbes,* CF Air has been growing at the rate of 40 to 50 percent a year.

The stock pays moderate dividends (about 5 to 6 percent yield recently), and has paid dividends every year since 1962.

* * *

CONSOLIDATED NATURAL GAS CO. (CNG). Founded 1942. Headquarters: 4 Gateway Center, Pittsburgh PA 15222. NATURAL GAS. Wholesale, retail distributor of natural gas; also engaged in exploration.

Sales: $2,503.1 million (trend 20.1% a year).
Earnings: $113.01 million (trend 10.2% a year).
What happened to a $10,000 investment

Purchase Date	*Purchase Price*	*Price on 12-31-81*	*Dividends Paid*
12-31-71	$30.12	$50.75	$8,471.37
12-31-76	$36.50	$50.75	$4,115.07

Purchase Date	*Cap. Gains (– Losses)*	*Total Return*	*Rate of Return*
12-31-71	$6,846.47	$15,317.84	9.73%
12-31-76	$3,904.11	$ 8,019.18	12.50%

* * *

CONSUMERS POWER CO. (CMS). Founded 1910. Headquarters: 212 W. Michigan Ave., Jackson MI 49201. UTILITY. Supplies electricity to some 5 million people in the southern half of Michigan. 12,000 employees.

Sales: $2,304.0 million (trend 10.7% a year).
Earnings: $167.05 million (trend 16.7% a year).
What happened to a $10,000 investment

Purchase Date	*Purchase Price*	*Price on 12-31-81*	*Dividends Paid*
12-31-71	$31.50	$17.12	$6,758.73
12-31-76	$22.62	$17.12	$4,990.06

Purchase Date	*Cap. Gains (– Losses)*	*Total Return*	*Rate of Return*
12-31-71	$–4,563.49	$2,195.24	2.00%
12-31-76	$–2,430.94	$2,559.12	4.66%

PROFILE: Consumers Power's profits in 1980 were a few pennies per share below those of 1977 and significantly below those of 1976, the company's peak year. Long-term debt is slightly above half of total capital, and has been for several years.

Sounds bad? More precisely, it sounds like the typical utility these days. In short, sounds bad.

There are a couple of bright spots to report. As with most utilities, when you're looking for a silver lining, start with the dividend yield. The yield here has been above 10 percent since 1979, and pushed above 15 percent in 1981. That means you can get an acceptable rate of return even if the share price doesn't budge.

But utility stocks work like bonds, since they serve much the same purpose (current yield) in many investors' portfolios. When interest rates fall, bond prices rise (because their current yield looks more attractive than it had before). As virtual bond substitutes, utility stocks do likewise. Thus a sustained fall in interest rates will mean a capital gain for holders of these shares.

What else? Well, the power blend's not bad—mostly coal, with a fair amount of nuclear power thrown in. At least this utility's not oil-heavy.

And the stock is mighty cheap. It hasn't sold for more than 8 times earnings since 1974. Recently the p / e has often been as low as 5. Companies that are stable and profitable can't be bought much cheaper than that.

* * *

CONTINENTAL AIR LINES, INC. (CAL). Founded 1934. Headquarters: Los Angeles International Airport, Los Angeles CA 90009. AIRLINE. Continental provides airline service to more than thirty U.S. cities. It has been unprofitable in recent years, and since 1981 has been controlled (and 50.3 percent owned) by Texas Air Corp. In 1982 the two airlines announced plans for a total merger.

Sales: $992.0 million (trend 15.4% a year).
Earnings: $–20.70 million.
What happened to a $10,000 investment

Purchase Date	*Purchase Price*	*Price on 12-31-81*	*Dividends Paid*
12-31-71	$19.20	$4.37	$ 546.75
12-31-76	$ 6.87	$4.37	$1,527.27

Purchase Date	*Cap. Gains (− Losses)*	*Total Return*	*Rate of Return*
12-31-71	$−7,721.89	$−7,175.15	−11.87%
12-31-76	$−3,636.36	$−2,109.09	−4.63%

* * *

CONTINENTAL COPPER & STEEL INDUSTRIES, INC. (CCX). Founded: 1944. Headquarters: 12 Commerce Dr., Cranford NJ 07016. **METALS.** Makes specialty steel; wire and cable products. **MAJOR SUBSIDIARIES, BRANDS:** Hatfield Wire & Cable; Hanover Wire Cloth; Braeburn Alloy Steel; Aceros Anglos.

Sales: $165.5 million (trend 10.6% a year).
Earnings: $3.21 million (trend 61.8% a year).
What happened to a $10,000 investment

Purchase Date	*Purchase Price*	*Price on 12-31-81*	*Dividends Paid*
12-31-71	$4.60	$5.00	$2,938.78
12-31-76	$4.13	$5.00	$ 227.27

Purchase Date	*Cap. Gains (− Losses)*	*Total Return*	*Rate of Return*
12-31-71	$ 865.28	$3,804.06	3.28%
12-31-76	$2,099.97	$2,327.25	4.27%

* * *

CONTINENTAL CORP. (CIC). Founded 1853. Headquarters: 80 Maiden Lane, New York NY 10038. **INSURANCE.** Continental Corp. is a holding company with extensive operations in several facets of insurance and with activities in consumer lending. It is roughly the sixth-largest U.S. property and casualty insurer. 22,000 employees. **MAJOR SUBSIDIARIES, BRANDS:** Continental Insurance Co.; Ben Franklin Life Insurance Co.; AFCO Credit Corp.

Sales: $3,430.4 million (trend 10.2% a year).
Earnings: $191.88 million (trend 24.4% a year).
What happened to a $10,000 investment

Purchase Date	*Purchase Price*	*Price on 12-31-81*	*Dividends Paid*
12-31-71	$20.62	$26.37	$7,680.00
12-31-76	$27.37	$26.37	$3,570.78

Purchase Date	*Cap. Gains (− Losses)*	*Total Return*	*Rate of Return*
12-31-71	$ 2,787.88	$10,467.88	7.43%
12-31-76	$−365.30	$ 3,205.48	5.72%

PROFILE: In the you-can't-tell-the-players-without-a-scorecard department note this: Continental Corporation's main holding is Continental Insurance Co. Continental Insurance should not be confused with Continental Assurance or with Continental Casualty, two similarly named insurance companies. *They* belong to CNA Financial Corp. (see that entry), which in turn is 87 percent controlled by Loews Corp. (see that too, if you wish).

While those other Continentals are principally involved in life insurance (Continental Assurance) or workmen's compensation (Continental Casualty), Continental Insurance gets the single biggest chunk of its income from automobile insurance. It also insures homes and businesses, and does a fair piece of workmen's compensation as well. In addition, the parent Continental Corp. owns AFCO, a major finance company. It used to own Diner's Club, but sold it in 1981 to Citicorp for an undisclosed sum.

Earnings have been up and down, which is typical in the property and casualty insurance business. The company lost money on underwriting (i.e., the pure insurance side of the business) in 1975, 1976, 1979, and 1980. In all of those years the company ended up in the black, mainly because investment income more than offset the underwriting losses. (The investment portfolio is about half bonds, one third common stock; most of the rest is preferred stock.)

The balance sheet here is quite strong. Dividends have been paid each year for more than a century (since 1854, to be exact), and the yield recently has been been in the 8-to-10 percent range.

* * *

CONTINENTAL GROUP, INC. (CCC). Founded 1913. Headquarters: 1 Harbor Plaza, Stamford CT 06902. **PACKAGING.** Built around Continental Can Co., the nation's largest producer of metal cans, Continental Group is also involved in forest products, insurance, financial services, and natural gas transmission. 54,000 employees. **MAJOR SUBSIDIARIES, BRANDS:** Continental Can Co.; Continental Forest Industries; Life Insurance Co. of Virginia. In 1982, Continental was in the process of buying a 50 percent interest in Supron Energy Corp.

Sales: $5,119.5 million (trend 9.8% a year).
Earnings: $199.70 million (trend 12.2% a year).
What happened to a $10,000 investment

Purchase Date	*Purchase Price*	*Price on 12-31-81*	*Dividends Paid*
12-31-71	$32.12	$32.75	$6,194.55
12-31-76	$33.87	$32.75	$3,365.31

Purchase Date	*Cap. Gains (− Losses)*	*Total Return*	*Rate of Return*
12-31-71	$ 194.55	$6,389.11	5.06%
12-31-76	$−332.10	$3,033.21	5.44%

PROFILE: The can business, said a top Continental Group official in 1978, is "ripe for a technological breakthrough." Maybe so. But if so, maybe the nation's largest can company isn't sure that it will be the one to provide it. The company has been diversifying away from cans as if it thought they were the sort of mature, slow-growing business that everybody else thinks they are.

In 1979 Continental picked up Florida Gas Co., and natural resources chipped in 6 percent of that year's profits. In 1977 and 1978 Continental acquired a number of small insurance companies and one medium-sized one, Life Insurance Co. of Virginia. Financial services contributed 23 percent of 1979 earnings. Thus the company's recent diversifications are already providing close to a third of profits. Cans, meanwhile, are providing only a bit more than a third of profits, even though they account for more than half of sales. The main hope for increased can sales is outside the U.S., where Continental is concentrating on the European and Australian markets.

Back home, Continental is pleased with its forest products business. It owns about 1½ million acres of timberland and is a major producer of cartons, corrugated shipping containers, and paper bags.

The company has paid dividends each year since 1923, and had a dividend yield of more than 8 percent in early 1982.

* * *

CONTINENTAL ILLINOIS CORP. (CIL). Founded 1932. Headquarters: 231 S. LaSalle St., Chicago IL 60693. **BANK.** Corporation is the holding company for Continental Illinois National Bank & Trust Co., the largest bank in Chicago and seventh-largest in the U.S. 12,000 employees. **MAJOR SUBSIDIARIES, BRANDS:** Continental Illinois National Bank & Trust Co.

Sales: $4,716.1 million (trend 28.7% a year).
Earnings: $224.14 million (trend 13.7% a year).
What happened to a $10,000 investment

Purchase Date	*Purchase Price*	*Price on 12-31-81*	*Dividends Paid*
12-31-71	$19.31	$33.12	$6,759.87
12-31-76	$29.12	$33.12	$2,664.38

Purchase Date	*Cap. Gains (− Losses)*	*Total Return*	*Rate of Return*
12-31-71	$7,152.10	$13,911.97	9.11%
12-31-76	$1,373.39	$ 4,037.77	7.02%

PROFILE: Aggressive. That's the word everyone uses for Continental. It seeks out corporate loan clients more aggressively than other banks. It makes loans at lower interest rates. It makes decisions on loans faster. It structures loans more innovatively. It will lend to some companies that other banks won't deal with.

All of this has helped Continental achieve rapid growth, for which it was rewarded on Wall Street during the mid-1970s. While many bank stocks were standing still, Continental climbed from its 1974 low of about $12 to a 1978 high around $33. During the late 1970s and early 1980s, however, interest rates were very high. Continental had to pay stiff prices to attract funds, but since its loan portfolio was at relatively low interest rates its profit margins were squeezed harder than most banks'. The stock fluctuated in the $20s and low $30s from 1978 through early 1981. Its price / earnings ratio, never very high, was only about 5 in early 1981, admittedly a time when bank stocks in general were out of favor.

The fact remains that Continental has been more profitable than many banks in recent years. It has paid dividends each year since 1936, and was yielding more than 6 percent in dividends in early 1981.

* * *

CONTINENTAL TELEPHONE CORP. (CTC). Founded 1960. Headquarters: 56 Perimeter Center E., Atlanta GA 30346. **TELEPHONE COMPANY.** Major independent telephone holding company. **MAJOR SUBSIDIARIES, BRANDS:** American Satellite Corp. (50 percent owned); Executone, Inc.; Network Analysis Corp. (65 percent owned).

Sales: $1,267.7 million (trend 18.6% a year).
Earnings: $116.21 million (trend 18.5% a year).
What happened to a $10,000 investment

Purchase Date	*Purchase Price*	*Price on 12-31-81*	*Dividends Paid*
12-31-71	$22.37	$16.87	$5,041.34
12-31-76	$17.62	$16.87	$3,710.64

Purchase Date	*Cap. Gains (− Losses)*	*Total Return*	*Rate of Return*
12-31-71	$−2,458.10	$2,583.24	2.32%
12-31-76	$ −425.53	$3,285.11	5.85%

* * *

CONTROL DATA CORP. (CDA). Founded 1957. Headquarters: 8100 34th Ave. S., Minneapolis MN 55420. **COMPUTERS.** Control Data is approximately the fourth-largest U.S. computer manufacturer; it also owns a major finance company and some small savings and loan associations and insurance companies. 58,000 employees. **MAJOR SUBSIDIARIES, BRANDS:** Commercial Credit Co.; Ohio Scientific Co.

Sales: $2,765.6 million (trend 18.3% a year).
Earnings: $146.20 million (trend 32.0% a year).
What happened to a $10,000 investment

Purchase Date	*Purchase Price*	*Price on 12-31-81*	*Dividends Paid*
12-31-71	$22.81	$35.25	$515.07
12-31-76	$12.87	$35.25	$912.62

Purchase Date	*Cap. Gains (− Losses)*	*Total Return*	*Rate of Return*
12-31-71	$ 5,452.05	$ 5,967.12	4.79%
12-31-76	$17,378.64	$18,291.26	23.12%

PROFILE: Every computer manufacturer must decide how to distinguish itself from, and compete against, IBM. In Control Data's case, there are three clear points of differentiation.

First, Control Data is a major factor in supercomputers — gigantic units that, as of 1980, can process up to 800 million units of data per second. In recent years, only a handful of buyers (chiefly government and universities) would order such mammoth computers each year. But each sale brings in about $8 to $16 million. And the market may grow. As of early 1981, the only other company involved in supercomputers — and the leader, having stolen that crown from Control Data in the mid-1970s — was Cray Research.

Second, Control Data puts major emphasis on software. The Plato programs, developed for classroom use, have been modified to create programs that can be used for small-business bookkeeping. Control Data plans to sell the programming and hardware together at retail computer stores.

Third, Control Data is the only computer manufacturer that is heavily involved in the finance business. Its finance company, Commercial Credit, makes Control Data a less volatile company, but also, in some analysts' eyes, a less interesting one. That's one reason this stock carries a lower p / e multiple than many computer stocks do. (The multiple was 7 in early 1982, for example.) However, the credit subsidiary may offer a plus in marketing small-business computer systems, since the company will be able to offer hardware, software, and financing all in one package.

* * *

CONWOOD CORP. (CWD). Founded 1900. Headquarters: 813 Ridge Lake Blvd., Memphis TN 38138. **CHEWING TOBACCO.** Important factor in snuff and chewing tobacco. Also involved in popcorn, popcorn machines and equipment, and household products. **MAJOR SUBSIDIARIES, BRANDS:** Bull of the Woods, Old Taylor, Levi Garrett tobaccos; Honest and Dental brand snuffs; Hot Shot and Skram insecticides; Blevins Popcorn Co.

Sales: $161.6 million (trend 16.3% a year).
Earnings: $15.95 million (trend 20.1% a year).
What happened to a $10,000 investment

Purchase Date	*Purchase Price*	*Price on 12-31-81*	*Dividends Paid*
12-31-71	$8.16	$23.62	$8,260.54
12-31-76	$8.81	$23.62	$4,765.96

Purchase Date	*Cap. Gains (− Losses)*	*Total Return*	*Rate of Return*
12-31-71	$18,965.52	$27,226.05	14.05%
12-31-76	$16,808.51	$21,574.47	25.85%

* * *

COOK UNITED, INC. (CCF). Founded 1925. Headquarters: 16501 Rockside Rd., Maple Heights OH 44137. **RETAILING.** Cook owns several small chains of discount department stores, plus three specialized retail chains. 5,000 employees. **MAJOR SUBSIDIARIES, BRANDS:** Rink's, Cook's, Clark's, Ontario, Uncle Bill's (all discount department store chains); Consolidated Sales Co. (operates discount department stores, gas stations, and car washes); Stratford Jewelers and Distributors (catalog showroom); J. P. Snodgrass (clothing).

Sales: $427.9 million (trend 1.4% a year).
Earnings: $1.61 million (trend 5.9% a year).
What happened to a $10,000 investment

Purchase Date	*Purchase Price*	*Price on 12-31-81*	*Dividends Paid*
12-31-71	$14.28	$3.87	$827.89
12-31-76	$ 3.57	$3.87	$793.13

Purchase Date	*Cap. Gains (− Losses)*	*Total Return*	*Rate of Return*
12-31-71	$−7,285.56	$−6,457.67	−9.86%
12-31-76	$ 859.24	$ 1,652.37	3.11%

PROFILE: This struggling discount retailer has attracted interest among speculators because of the way it keeps climbing up off the mat after being floored. The stock is volatile, with the yearly high often double or triple the yearly low.

In 1974 Cook United lost close to $10 million. Its return on equity never climbed above 10 percent between 1972 and 1980. Earnings have seesawed, and debt is close to half of total capital. Dividends were stopped in 1974, started again in 1979. In 1981 the cash dividend was once again discontinued, though a stock dividend (often viewed as a meaningless gesture) was paid. Those with a bent for unkind phrasing might view the preceding description as the portrait of a dog.

But speculators may find there's bark as well as bite in these shares. In 1974, the year of Cook's only recent loss, the stock dropped below $1 a share. Since then it has sold as high as $9.50 (in 1979) and was selling in late 1981 for a bit over $6. Back in the late 1960s the shares used to go for more than $30. Sales have actually shrunk since then, a rare occurrence among major retailers.

Although it's listed on the Big Board, Cook United is almost a penny stock, with high risk but a speculative possibility of high total return.

* * *

COOPER INDUSTRIES, INC. (CBE). Founded 1929. Headquarters: 2700 Two Houston Center, Houston TX 77002. **CONGLOMERATE.** Cooper is involved in energy services (chiefly the manufacture of drilling equipment and compressors for gas pipelines), tools and other hardware, mining equipment, and aircraft maintenance. 25,000 employees. **MAJOR SUBSIDIARIES, BRANDS:** Boker Tree (knives); Crescent (wrenches); Funk (machinery); Gardner-Denver (mining and drilling equipment); Lufkin (measuring tapes); Nicholson (files); Rotor Tool; Weller (soldering irons); Wiss (scissors); Xcelite (screwdrivers); Crouse-Hinds (lighting and electrical products); Kirsch (drapery hardware).

Sales: $1,836.8 million (trend 31.8% a year).
Earnings: $130.75 million (trend 33.9% a year).
What happened to a $10,000 investment

Purchase Date	*Purchase Price*	*Price on 12-31-81*	*Dividends Paid*
12-31-71	$ 5.81	$51.50	$10,331.18
12-31-76	$20.12	$51.50	$ 2,260.87

Purchase Date	*Cap. Gains (− Losses)*	*Total Return*	*Rate of Return*
12-31-71	$78,602.15	$88,933.33	25.76%
12-31-76	$15,590.06	$17,850.93	22.73%

PROFILE: "We don't suffer from analysis paralysis like some companies," boasted a Cooper official in late 1980. In 1981, the company made two major acquisitions — Crouse-Hinds (electrical products) and Kirsch (drapery hardware). This will put Cooper in the rather select class of companies with annual sales over $2 billion (as of 1980, there were fewer than 300 such companies). As recently as 1978, before it bought Gardner-Denver Co., Cooper's sales were $782 million.

But this is not a company that prowls indiscriminately for merger partners. All three of the companies just mentioned came to Cooper as a "white knight" to rescue them from potential unfriendly takeovers. What's more, all three fit nicely with Cooper's established product lines. Gardner-Denver's drilling and mining equipment meshed well with Cooper's longstanding position in gas pipeline compressors. Crouse-Hinds and Kirsch fit well into the hardware distribution channels Cooper had already set up for its quality name-brand Crescent wrenches, Xcelite screwdrivers and the like.

Since the mergers will increase the number of shares outstanding, they'll lessen earnings per share for a year or two. Hence the stock dropped (nearly 25 percent) in late 1980 and early 1981. Even after the drop, it was selling for about 11 times earnings. The long-term trend in this stock has definitely been upward throughout the 1970s. The dividend yield in recent years has been from 2 to 3½ percent.

* * *

COOPER LABORATORIES, INC. (COO). Founded 1961. Headquarters: 3142 Porter Dr., Palo Alto CA 94304. **HEALTH CARE PRODUCTS.** Manufactures optical and dental products, drugs, and biomedical equipment. **MAJOR SUBSIDIARIES, BRANDS:** Sterdent Corp. (33 ⅓ percent owned);

Cavitron Corp. (34 percent owned); CooperVision; CooperCare.

Sales: $172.8 million (trend 15.9% a year).
Earnings: $20.78 million (trend 51.4% a year).
What happened to a $10,000 investment

Purchase Date	*Purchase Price*	*Price on 12-31-81*	*Dividends Paid*
12-31-71	$23.91	$28.25	$ 961.82
12-31-76	$11.25	$28.25	$2,044.44

Purchase Date	*Cap. Gains (– Losses)*	*Total Return*	*Rate of Return*
12-31-71	$ 1,813.63	$ 2,775.45	2.48%
12-31-76	$15,111.11	$17,155.56	22.12%

* * *

COOPER TIRE & RUBBER CO. (CTB). Founded 1914. Headquarters: Lima & Western Aves., Findlay OH 45840. **RUBBER.** Converts natural and synthetic rubbers into a variety of carbon black reinforced rubber products, including tires, inner tubes, and industrial rubber products. **MAJOR SUBSIDIARIES, BRANDS:** Cooper; Falls; Giant.

Sales: $324.0 million (trend 11.8% a year).
Earnings: $12.55 million (trend 10.4% a year).
What happened to a $10,000 investment

Purchase Date	*Purchase Price*	*Price on 12-31-81*	*Dividends Paid*
12-31-71	$8.37	$14.50	$4,749.25
12-31-76	$7.69	$14.50	$2,692.68

Purchase Date	*Cap. Gains (– Losses)*	*Total Return*	*Rate of Return*
12-31-71	$7,313.43	$12,062.69	8.23%
12-31-76	$8,861.79	$11,554.47	16.60%

* * *

COPPERWELD CORP. (COS). Founded 1915. Headquarters: 2 Oliver Plaza, Pittsburgh PA 15222. **METAL PRODUCTS.** Manufactures specialty tubing, alloy steel, and copper-covered steel rod, wire, and strand.

Sales: $460.7 million (trend 12.5% a year).
Earnings: $18.98 million (trend 1.1% a year).
What happened to a $10,000 investment

Purchase Date	*Purchase Price*	*Price on 12-31-81*	*Dividends Paid*
12-31-71	$ 8.99	$36.75	$12,273.36
12-31-76	$22.87	$36.75	$ 2,998.91

Purchase Date	*Cap. Gains (– Losses)*	*Total Return*	*Rate of Return*
12-31-71	$30,887.39	$43,160.75	18.18%
12-31-76	$ 6,065.57	$ 9,064.48	13.77%

* * *

CORDURA CORP. (CDU). Founded 1966. Headquarters: 2029 Century Park East, Suite 3210, Los Angeles CA 90067. **INFORMATION.** Publishes databases on various subjects for design engineers and purchasing agents; consultant on employee benefits. **MAJOR SUBSIDIARIES, BRANDS:** R. E. Harrington.

Sales: $26.9 million (trend –20.6% a year).
Earnings: $4.10 million (trend 34.5% a year).
What happened to a $10,000 investment

Purchase Date	*Purchase Price*	*Price on 12-31-81*	*Dividends Paid*
12-31-71	$24.25	$7.75	$ 865.98
12-31-76	$ 3.50	$7.75	$6,000.00

Purchase Date	*Cap. Gains (– Losses)*	*Total Return*	*Rate of Return*
12-31-71	$–6,804.12	$–5,938.14	–8.62%
12-31-76	$ 12,142.86	$ 18,142.86	22.99%

* * *

CORE INDUSTRIES INC. (CRI). Founded 1964. Headquarters: 1411 N. Woodward Ave., PO Box 3500, Birmingham MI 48012. **SPECIALTY PRODUCTS.** Manufactures electronic controls, fluid controls, construction equipment, and farm equipment.

Sales: $161.0 million (trend 11.0% a year).
Earnings: $13.71 million (trend 19.5% a year).
What happened to a $10,000 investment

Purchase Date	*Purchase Price*	*Price on 12-31-81*	*Dividends Paid*
12-31-71	$3.22	$13.37	$5,198.74
12-31-76	$4.56	$13.37	$2,686.59

Purchase Date	*Cap. Gains (– Losses)*	*Total Return*	*Rate of Return*
12-31-71	$31,508.62	$36,707.36	16.66%
12-31-76	$19,359.76	$22,046.34	26.23%

* * *

CORNING GLASS WORKS (GLW). Founded 1936. Headquarters: Houghton Park, Corning NY 14830. **GLASS.** Manufactures some 60,000 glass and ceramic products. 30,000 employees. **MAJOR SUBSIDIARIES, BRANDS:** Dow Corning (50 percent owned); Pittsburgh Corning (50 percent owned); Pyrex, Corning Ware, Corelle, Steuben Glass. In 1982, an acquisition of Met Path Inc. (a clinical laboratory) was in progress.

Sales: $1,529.7 million (trend 10.6% a year).
Earnings: $114.72 million (trend 25.1% a year).
What happened to a $10,000 investment

Purchase Date	*Purchase Price*	*Price on 12-31-81*	*Dividends Paid*
12-31-71	$74.20	$51.87	$2,260.11
12-31-76	$71.25	$51.87	$1,364.21

Purchase Date	*Cap. Gains (– Losses)*	*Total Return*	*Rate of Return*
12-31-71	$–3,008.76	$ –748.65	–.78%
12-31-76	$–2,719.30	$–1,355.09	–2.87%

PROFILE: This is one of the classic fallen growth stocks. Not that the company ever fell (nor did Xerox or IBM). It's the stocks that did.

In the late 1960s and early 1970s, investors were so entranced with the marvelous growth records of these companies that they bid the stock prices to extravagant levels. For the "nifty fifty," the "one-decision stocks," price / earnings ratios of 40, 50, or even 60 became the norm. As recently as 1971, Corning Glass sold at 53 times earnings. Forgotten was the canny Wall Street adage, "Even the tallest trees don't grow into the sky." Upon its rediscovery, stocks carrying lofty price / earnings ratios toppled, even when the companies continued to turn in creditable performances.

That's been the story with Corning Glass. In 1971 earnings were $2.11 a share. In 1980 they were $6.26. That represents a near-tripling of earnings in a decade, not bad work at all. But investors had been expecting miracles. The stock price in 1980 varied between $45 and $76 a share, far below its 1973 zenith of $126 or its 1971–72 high of $110.

In the early 1980s, selling at around 9 to 12 times earnings, Corning Glass may well be a bargain. It's a cyclical growth stock; company earnings will decline when a recession affects the auto industry, housing industry, and consumer spending. But the long-term earnings trend has been favorable.

Though incorporated in 1936, the company goes back further: It supplied glass to Edison for his light bulbs. Dividends have been paid yearly since 1881, but are traditionally moderate; the yield was around 5 percent in early 1981.

* * *

CORROON & BLACK CORP. (CBL). Founded 1928. Headquarters: Wall Street Plaza, New York NY 10005. **INSURANCE.** Major insurance brokerage house.

Sales: $150.7 million (trend 32.2% a year).
Earnings: $17.90 million (trend 35.8% a year).
What happened to a $10,000 investment

Purchase Date	*Purchase Price*	*Price on 12-31-81*	*Dividends Paid*
12-31-71	$16.37	$21.25	$5,870.69
12-31-76	$13.37	$21.25	$5,312.15

Purchase Date	*Cap. Gains (– Losses)*	*Total Return*	*Rate of Return*
12-31-71	$2,977.10	$ 8,847.79	6.54%
12-31-76	$5,887.85	$11,200.00	16.22%

* * *

COWLES COMMUNICATIONS, INC. (CWL). Founded 1936. Headquarters: 44 Seabreeze Blvd., Daytona Beach FL 32018. **PUBLISHING, BROADCASTING.** Owns a pair of television stations, and holds 2,600,000 Class A shares of The New York Times Co., about a 21 percent share. **MAJOR SUBSIDIARIES, BRANDS:** KCCI-TV (Des Moines, IA); WESH-TV (Orlando, FL).

Sales: $20.7 million (trend 15.1% a year).
Earnings: $6.24 million (trend 18.9% a year).
What happened to a $10,000 investment

Purchase Date	*Purchase Price*	*Price on 12-31-81*	*Dividends Paid*
12-31-71	$10.25	$31.50	$5,365.85
12-31-76	$12.50	$31.50	$3,548.00

Purchase Date	*Cap. Gains (– Losses)*	*Total Return*	*Rate of Return*
12-31-71	$20,731.71	$26,097.56	13.70%
12-31-76	$15,200.00	$18,748.00	23.52%

* * *

COX BROADCASTING CORP. (COX). Founded 1964. Headquarters: 1601 W. Peachtree St. N.E., Atlanta GA 30309. **BROADCASTING GROUP.** Owns and operates some twelve radio and five television stations; also active in cable television, movie production, and auto auctions. **MAJOR SUBSIDIARIES, BRANDS:** Bing Crosby Productions; KFI-AM and KOST-FM (Los Angeles); WIOD-AM and WAIA-FM (Miami); KTVU television (San Francisco-

Oakland); WSB (AM and FM radio and television, Atlanta); WPXI television (Pittsburgh); WLIF-FM (Baltimore); WWSH-FM (Philadelphia); WHIO (AM and FM radio and television, Dayton, OH); WSOC (AM and FM radio and television, Charlotte NC).

Sales: $309.2 million (trend 24.2% a year).
Earnings: $46.42 million (trend 27.5% a year).
What happened to a $10,000 investment

Purchase Date	*Purchase Price*	*Price on 12-31-81*	*Dividends Paid*
12-31-71	$9.47	$36.25	$1,564.25
12-31-76	$8.31	$36.25	$1,202.89

Purchase Date	*Cap. Gains (− Losses)*	*Total Return*	*Rate of Return*
12-31-71	$28,283.83	$29,848.08	14.83%
12-31-76	$33,609.02	$34,811.91	34.98%

* * *

CRAIG CORP. (CRA). Founded 1929. Headquarters: 921 W. Artesia Blvd., Compton CA 90220. **CONSUMER ELECTRONICS.** Imports, manufactures, and distributes consumer electronics products. **MAJOR SUBSIDIARIES, BRANDS:** Magnasync / Moviola, Dynatech Corp.

Sales: $113.9 million (trend −1.0% a year).
Earnings: $−1.94 million.
What happened to a $10,000 investment

Purchase Date	*Purchase Price*	*Price on 12-31-81*	*Dividends Paid*
12-31-71	$ 3.25	$6.62	$4,538.46
12-31-76	$15.12	$6.62	$ 909.09

Purchase Date	*Cap. Gains (− Losses)*	*Total Return*	*Rate of Return*
12-31-71	$ 10,384.62	$ 14,923.08	9.56%
12-31-76	$−5,619.83	$−4,710.74	−11.96%

* * *

CRANE CO. (CR). Founded 1865. Headquarters: 300 Park Ave., New York NY 10022. **CONGLOMERATE.** This company's diversified activities include manufacture of valves (of which it is the world's largest producer), pollution control equipment, cement, steel, and building products. 21,000 employees. **MAJOR SUBSIDIARIES, BRANDS:** Medusa Corp. (96 percent owned); CF&I Steel (96 percent owned); Huttig Sash & Door; Crane Canada Ltd.

Sales: $1,527.6 million (trend 8.1% a year).
Earnings: $42.51 million (trend −6.2% a year).
What happened to a $10,000 investment

Purchase Date	*Purchase Price*	*Price on 12-31-81*	*Dividends Paid*
12-31-71	$ 9.47	$36.25	$11,113.10
12-31-76	$26.49	$36.25	$ 2,711.15

Purchase Date	*Cap. Gains (− Losses)*	*Total Return*	*Rate of Return*
12-31-71	$28,295.53	$39,408.63	17.32%
12-31-76	$ 3,683.00	$ 6,394.15	10.39%

PROFILE: Not listed in the summary of Crane's basic businesses (above) is one of its favorite activities: playing the 5 percent game with considerable skill. The rules of the game are as follows. You buy a 5 percent interest in a corporation that looks like a good investment. This makes you a major stockholder and gives you an inside look at the company's operations. If things look promising, you increase your stake. At that point the target company figures you are out to take it over, and it buys back its shares or runs to a "white knight" which promises to acquire the company for a higher price and keep present management in place. You then sell off your shares for a handsome profit.

Longtime chairman Thomas Mellon (Tom) Evans, who owns some 11 percent of Crane's stock, has played this game successfully with Asarco, Chemetron, Cooper Range, Inspiration Consolidated Copper, Morrison-Knudsen, Zapata, and — most notably — Anaconda. Of course, it's not a game you want to play with a company you don't regard as fundamentally a good investment, because sometimes the flirtation goes all the way to the altar. That's what happened with Medusa Corp., one of the nation's leading cement companies. Acquired in 1979, it provided 19 percent of Crane's profits (on 16 percent of sales) that year.

The stock, which offers a moderate dividend yield (about 6 percent in early 1982), performed well over the past decade, rising from a 1971 high of $10.50 to a 1980 high of $47.50. The price tumbled in the recent recession, however, and was down to about $27 in early 1982. Adding to the company's wheeler-dealer image is a debt load of roughly 51 percent of capital, as of early 1981.

* * *

CRAY RESEARCH, INC. (CYR). Founded 1973. Headquarters: 1440 Northland Dr., Mendota Heights MN 55120. **COMPUTERS.** Cray is the leading manufacturer of the extremely large computers known as supercomputers. 700 employees.

Sales: $60.7 million (trend 197.0% a year).
Earnings: $10.90 million (trend 126.8% a year).
What happened to a $10,000 investment

Purchase Date	*Purchase Price*	*Price on 12-31-81*	*Dividends Paid*
12-31-71	$N/A	$36.50	$0.00
12-31-76	$ 2.43	$36.50	$0.00

Purchase Date	*Cap. Gains (− Losses)*	*Total Return*	*Rate of Return*
12-31-71	$ N/A	$ N/A	N/A%
12-31-76	$140,000.00	$140,000.00	71.88%

PROFILE: As of 1981, there are only two companies in the business of selling supercomputers—Cray and Control Data. There used to be just one, Control Data, before Seymour Cray left Control Data in 1972 to found his own company. By 1976, when Cray was opened up to public ownership, it was well on the way to taking over the field. Since then it has solidified its lead, but in 1980 and 1981 Control Data was taking steps to fight back, both through new products and through marketing. As a much larger company than Cray, Control Data may be able to engage in some vigorous price cutting, which Cray may be hard put to match, especially if it is to maintain its traditionally high profit margins (18 percent in 1979, for example).

Supercomputers are a high-margin, low-volume business. Cray installed ten supercomputers in 1980, and expected to install thirteen in 1981. Users have traditionally been found solely in the realms of government (defense, weather forecasting) and major universities (research labs). Now that prices are being chopped, in some cases, below the traditional $8 million and up, some major corporations will be added to the customer list.

Determined to maintain its technological edge, Cray spends extremely heavily on continued research. In *Business Week*'s annual report on research and development published in 1980, Cray topped the list both in R&D expenditures per employee ($11,399) and in R&D spending as a percent of sales (14 percent).

This is an exciting company and the stock has rocketed up from the $2 range in 1976 to a 1980 high of about $48 (adjusted for splits). In early 1982 it was selling for about $29. The company pays no dividends and has no current plans to pay any. The price reflects a glowing promise, but the investors who are banking on that promise were recently paying 20 to 40 times earnings for the stock. At that kind of p / e ratio, Cray Research has to be considered a speculative holding.

* * *

CREDITHRIFT FINANCIAL, INC. (CRD). Founded 1974. Headquarters: 601 N.W. Second St., Evansville IN 47708. FINANCE AND INSURANCE. Makes loans, secured and unsecured, purchases retail installment sales contracts, and issues credit insurance. **MAJOR SUBSIDIARIES, BRANDS:** Yosemite Insurance Co.; Great Falls Insurance Co.; The Morris Plan Co. of California; Evansville Morris Plan Co., Inc.; Thrift, Inc.

Sales: $216.2 million (trend 6.4% a year).
Earnings: $12.03 million (trend 29.0% a year).
What happened to a $10,000 investment

Purchase Date	*Purchase Price*	*Price on 12-31-81*	*Dividends Paid*
12-31-71	$11.75	$12.12	$3,297.87
12-31-76	$ 6.12	$12.12	$3,510.20

Purchase Date	*Cap. Gains (− Losses)*	*Total Return*	*Rate of Return*
12-31-71	$ 319.15	$ 3,617.02	3.14%
12-31-76	$9,795.92	$13,306.12	18.44%

* * *

CRITON CORP. (CN). Founded 1958. Headquarters: 10800 N.E. Eighth St., Bellevue WA 98004. AIRCRAFT PRODUCTS. Manufactures airplane interiors and aircraft components; also manufactures architectural, electronics, and defense products.

Sales: $140.8 million (trend 25.7% a year).
Earnings: $13.98 million (trend 41.2% a year).
What happened to a $10,000 investment

Purchase Date	*Purchase Price*	*Price on 12-31-81*	*Dividends Paid*
12-31-71	$3.33	$24.75	$0.00
12-31-76	$2.74	$24.75	$0.00

Purchase Date	*Cap. Gains (− Losses)*	*Total Return*	*Rate of Return*
12-31-71	$64,249.97	$64,249.97	22.20%
12-31-76	$80,304.05	$80,304.05	55.29%

* * *

CROCKER NATIONAL CORP. (CKN). Founded 1968; bank dates to 1870. Headquarters: 1 Montgomery St., San Francisco CA 94104. BANK. Corporation is holding company for Crocker National Bank, the nation's thirteenth-largest bank as of 1980. It is 51 percent owned by Midland Bank Ltd. of London; Midland is to acquire another 6 percent of the stock by 1985. 15,000 employees. **MAJOR SUBSIDIARIES, BRANDS:** Crocker National Bank.

Sales: $2,006.3 million (trend 21.5% a year).
Earnings: $90.03 million (trend 20.4% a year).
What happened to a $10,000 investment

Purchase Date	*Purchase Price*	*Price on 12-31-81*	*Dividends Paid*
12-31-71	$35.12	$30.62	$5,056.23
12-31-76	$28.25	$30.62	$3,348.67

Purchase Date	*Cap. Gains (− Losses)*	*Total Return*	*Rate of Return*
12-31-71	$−1,281.14	$3,775.09	3.25%
12-31-76	$ 840.71	$4,189.38	7.25%

PROFILE: One doesn't usually think of a bank as a turnaround situation, but the description applies to Crocker National. In 1974 it earned a miserable 20 cents or so per $100 of assets. Not coincidentally, that was the year Thomas R. Wilcox took over Crocker's reins after leaving Citibank (where he had lost out to Walter Wriston as chief executive officer). Wilcox slashed the payroll and revamped the loan portfolio (more corporate loans, fewer real estate loans), among other decisive actions. Now Crocker is generally highly regarded by the banking community, and earns a respectable 50 to 60 cents per $100 of assets. As for investor opinion — well, *all* banking stocks have been out of favor in recent years.

In late 1980 Crocker's stockholders agreed to let Midland Bank Ltd., Britain's third-largest bank, take a 57 percent interest in Crocker. Most analysts viewed the deal as favorable to Crocker, since it would provide the California bank with a substantial infusion of capital.

During the 1970s the stock fluctuated between a 1974 low of about $13 and a 1971 high of about $41. It was possible to make money off the fluctuations, but the buy-and-hold investor hasn't had much to be happy about. The dividend yield has ranged between 5 and 8 percent, and was about 8 percent in early 1982. Dividends have been paid every year since 1926.

If the mid-1980s see a decline in interest rates and a pickup in economic activity, bank stocks should revive. Especially if the infusion of British capital comes through, this one may do better than most.

* * *

CROMPTON & KNOWLES CORP. (CNK). Founded 1840. Headquarters: 345 Park Ave., New York NY 10154. **SPECIALTY CHEMICALS.** Manufactures dyes and other organic chemicals, cleaning and maintenance products; also textile and plastics extrusion machinery.

Sales: $241.8 million (trend 15.4% a year).
Earnings: $7.15 million (trend 16.8% a year).
What happened to a $10,000 investment

Purchase Date	*Purchase Price*	*Price on 12-31-81*	*Dividends Paid*
12-31-71	$12.08	$17.25	$5,252.44
12-31-76	$ 9.00	$17.25	$4,088.93

Purchase Date	*Cap. Gains (− Losses)*	*Total Return*	*Rate of Return*
12-31-71	$4,275.86	$ 9,528.30	6.92%
12-31-76	$9,166.67	$13,255.59	18.39%

* * *

CROWN CENTRAL PETROLEUM CORP. (CNP, American Stock Exchange**).** Founded 1937. Headquarters: 1 N. Charles St., Baltimore MD 21203. **OIL.** Crown Central is a medium-sized international oil company. It has a sideline in the life insurance business. 1,500 employees. **MAJOR SUBSIDIARIES, BRANDS:** Continental American Life Insurance Co.

Sales: $1,266.9 million (trend 22.7% a year).
Earnings: $19.15 million (trend 40.8% a year).
What happened to a $10,000 investment

Purchase Date	*Purchase Price*	*Price on 12-31-81*	*Dividends Paid*
12-31-71	$5.80	$15.25	$5,755.84
12-31-76	$9.34	$15.25	$3,167.13

Purchase Date	*Cap. Gains (− Losses)*	*Total Return*	*Rate of Return*
12-31-71	$16,281.77	$22,037.61	12.35%
12-31-76	$ 6,326.31	$ 9,493.44	14.28%

PROFILE: Between 1979 and 1981, you could have turned $5,000 into $20,000 by investing in Crown Central — or turned $20,000 into less than $6,000. The stock roared from $9 a share up to more than $41, then fell back all the way to around $11 before beginning a rebound.

What kind of stock is this? What accounts for such swings? Call it geography. Crown Central is based in Baltimore, but it gets close to three quarters of its oil from abroad, mainly Nigeria and secondarily Mexico. International political and economic conditions can be volatile, and the volatility hits harder at a medium-sized outfit like Crown Central than it does at a huge, diversified giant like Exxon or Mobil. So, earnings and profitability have seesawed.

Diversification moves, probably aimed at reducing the volatility of earnings, have included the 1980 acquisition of Continental American Life Insurance Co. and the acquisition of several producing oil wells in Oklahoma and Texas. But so far the diversification efforts amount to only pebbles for ballast.

The balance sheet contains a fair amount of debt. Long-term debt was recently about 33 percent of capital, but has sporadically been more than 40 percent.

Dividends, on again and off again, have been paid each year since 1976. Recently they have provided a moderate yield.

* * *

CROWN CORK & SEAL CO., INC. (CCK). Founded 1927. Headquarters: 9300 Ashton Rd., Philadelphia PA 19136. CANS, CAPS. Crown is the fourth-largest U.S. can manufacturer, as of 1980, and the world's largest manufacturer of caps and other closures. 16,000 employees. MAJOR SUBSIDIARIES, BRANDS: Crown Financial Corp.

Sales: $1,459.8 million (trend 13.2% a year).
Earnings: $73.20 million (trend 13.0% a year).
What happened to a $10,000 investment

Purchase Date	*Purchase Price*	*Price on 12-31-81*	*Dividends Paid*
12-31-71	$19.12	$30.25	$0.00
12-31-76	$21.62	$30.25	$0.00

Purchase Date	*Cap. Gains (− Losses)*	*Total Return*	*Rate of Return*
12-31-71	$5,816.99	$5,816.99	4.69%
12-31-76	$3,988.44	$3,988.44	6.94%

PROFILE: This is an eccentric and remarkable company. It sticks to a product — cans — widely viewed as a no-growth or slow-growth commodity, and turns in a record of steady earnings gains that would make a drug or computer company jealous. As of 1980, Crown had increased its profits every quarter (compared to the same quarter the year before) for twenty-four consecutive years. The stock pays no dividends; all the action is in capital gains. The company has virtually no debt — 98 percent of the capital was common stock as of early 1981. And, like Teledyne, Crown follows a policy of buying back its own stock whenever the price dips below book value. Management salaries aren't much, compared with those at other major corporations, and top managers are housed in spartan quarters above a can facility. But oh, those stock options!

The big question here is whether the person who wrought all these remarkable developments, longtime chairman John Connelly, will be around much longer. Born around 1905 (there's some dispute), he has to retire sometime, and Wall Street wonders whether his successors will be able to keep the company's remarkable act going. Wall Street, in any event, has never quite believed that a can and closure company could really produce such stellar earnings, so Crown doesn't usually sell at a very high multiple of earnings. In early 1981 its p / e ratio was 6. The stock hasn't seen a p / e above 10 since 1973.

Smart (should we say canny?) penetration of foreign markets has been a hallmark of Crown, and its foreign plants (which contribute about 40 percent of sales and profits) are managed exclusively by natives of their host countries.

* * *

CROWN ZELLERBACH CORP. (ZB). Founded 1924. Headquarters: 1 Bush St., San Francisco CA 94104. FOREST PRODUCTS. As of 1980, Crown Zellerbach was the sixth-largest U.S. forest products company. 31,000 employees.

Sales: $3,069.8 million (trend 11.0% a year).
Earnings: $88.30 million (trend 5.5% a year).
What happened to a $10,000 investment

Purchase Date	*Purchase Price*	*Price on 12-31-81*	*Dividends Paid*
12-31-71	$34.25	$29.25	$5,313.87
12-31-76	$45.25	$29.25	$2,287.29

Purchase Date	*Cap. Gains (− Losses)*	*Total Return*	*Rate of Return*
12-31-71	$−1,459.85	$ 3,854.01	3.31%
12-31-76	$−3,535.91	$−1,248.62	−2.63%

PROFILE: Crown Zellerbach ranks with the giants in forest products in terms of sales (about $3.3 billion in 1980) and in terms of acreage controlled (about 3.4 million acres). When it comes to profitability, though, this company has been an also-ran. In the *Forbes* Annual Report on American Industry published in 1981, Crown Zellerbach had the lowest profit margin — 3.2 percent — of twenty-two forest products companies ranked. The average forest products company showed a profit margin of 6 percent. Crown's five-year return on equity was only about 12 percent, versus more than 15 percent for its average competitor. And its return on equity in the most recent year had been a mere 8.7 percent — again, the worst of the twenty-two companies.

On the plus side, at least the company has been steadily profitable. Though profits have emulated a yo-yo, dividends have not. They've been paid each year since 1937, and each year in recent memory the company has kept them constant or rising. Dividend yield was about 5 percent in early 1981.

Despite the uninspiring profit record, this stock was selling at 13 times earnings in early 1981, a prestigious ratio at a time when the average stock commanded only a multiple of 8. What was tickling investors' fancy? The chance of oil or gas finds on some of those 3.4 million acres. From all indications, though, these hopes were mostly rumor and speculation. The company has no track record as a petroleum producer.

* * *

CRUM AND FORSTER (CMF). Founded 1907. Headquarters: 110 William St., New York NY 10038. INSURANCE. Property-casualty insurance holding company. MAJOR SUBSIDIARIES, BRANDS: Industrial Indemnity Co., Constitution Reinsurance Corp.

Sales: $1,931.8 million (trend 16.1% a year).
Earnings: $131.40 million (trend 38.9% a year).
What happened to a $10,000 investment

Purchase Date	*Purchase Price*	*Price on 12-31-81*	*Dividends Paid*
12-31-71	$15.56	$33.37	$5,863.45
12-31-76	$15.56	$33.37	$3,691.57

Purchase Date	*Cap. Gains (– Losses)*	*Total Return*	*Rate of Return*
12-31-71	$11,445.78	$17,309.24	10.57%
12-31-76	$11,445.78	$15,137.35	20.24%

* * *

CULBRO CORP. (CUC). Founded 1906. Headquarters: 605 Third Ave., New York NY 10016. CIGARS AND TOBACCO. Major producer of cigars, tobacco distributor, also involved in plastics, snack foods, consumer finance. MAJOR SUBSIDIARIES, BRANDS: Robert Burns, William Penn, White Owl; Cain's Marcelle Potato Chip Co., Fairmont Food Co.

Sales: $376.4 million (trend 5.5% a year).
Earnings: $5.58 million (trend –3.0% a year).
What happened to a $10,000 investment

Purchase Date	*Purchase Price*	*Price on 12-31-81*	*Dividends Paid*
12-31-71	$24.25	$20.25	$4,107.22
12-31-76	$21.25	$20.25	$1,821.18

Purchase Date	*Cap. Gains (– Losses)*	*Total Return*	*Rate of Return*
12-31-71	$–1,649.48	$2,457.73	2.22%
12-31-76	$ –470.59	$1,350.59	2.57%

* * *

CUMMINS ENGINE CO., INC. (CUM). Founded 1919. Headquarters: 1000 Fifth St., Columbus IN 47201. DIESEL ENGINES. Largest U.S. manufacturer of diesel engines for trucks, construction equipment, and industrial applications. 24,000 employees.

Sales: $1,666.6 million.
Earnings: $–10.99 million.
What happened to a $10,000 investment

Purchase Date	*Purchase Price*	*Price on 12-31-81*	*Dividends Paid*
12-31-71	$53.12	$35.50	$2,545.88
12-31-76	$48.50	$35.50	$1,779.38

Purchase Date	*Cap. Gains (– Losses)*	*Total Return*	*Rate of Return*
12-31-71	$–3,317.65	$–771.76	–.80%
12-31-76	$–2,680.41	$–901.03	–1.87%

* * *

PROFILE: Investors think of Cummins Engine as a manufacturer of big, powerful diesels. It is. Some go on to dismiss Cummins as a relic of the past, when trucks routinely cruised the nation's highways at 70 miles per hour. It isn't. Cummins is living very much in the present — and future. The very petroleum shortage that curtailed high-speed highway traffic has some positive implications for this company.

Diesel engines are much costlier than gasoline engines, but diesel fuel is considerably less expensive than gasoline. The result, as *Forbes* magazine pointed out in 1980, is that as gas prices rise, it may become profitable to equip smaller trucks with diesel engines. That would result in a huge increase in Cummins's market. However, the "oil glut" of 1981-1982 upset this scenario and caused the stock to slump.

Cummins apparently expects the glut to be temporary, and it's putting its money where its prediction is. Thus the company has been spending heavily on new capital equipment, even during the 1980–81 recession when revenues and profits were down. At the same time the company has continued to pay dividends, betting that it has the financial strength to tough out the short-run problems. It's not an easy proposition. To see how Cummins is managing this feat, keep an eye on the debt ratio. Long-term debt was less than 22 percent of capital in 1979. By early 1981 it had risen to 38 percent. But if the gamble pays off, it will produce handsome rewards for shareholders.

* * *

CURRENT INCOME SHARES, INC. (CUR). Founded 1972. Headquarters: 9595 Wilshire Blvd., Beverly Hills CA 90212. INVESTMENTS. Investment company holding primarily quality debt securities.

* * *

CURTISS-WRIGHT CORP. (CW). Founded 1929. Headquarters: 1 Passaic St., Wood-Ridge NJ 07075. DIVERSIFIED MANUFACTURE. Manufactures electrical generating equipment, nuclear and aerospace products.

Sales: $185.5 million (trend −7.4% a year).
Earnings: $39.29 million (trend 22.1% a year).
What happened to a $10,000 investment

Purchase Date	*Purchase Price*	*Price on 12-31-81*	*Dividends Paid*
12-31-71	$13.50	$41.25	$4,037.04
12-31-76	$17.25	$41.25	$2,376.81

Purchase Date	*Cap. Gains (− Losses)*	*Total Return*	*Rate of Return*
12-31-71	$20,555.56	$24,592.59	13.21%
12-31-76	$13,913.04	$16,289.86	21.33%

* * *

CYCLOPS CORP. (CYL). Founded 1908. Headquarters: 650 Washington Rd., Pittsburgh PA 15228. STEEL. Major manufacturer of stainless, tool, carbon and specialty steel; also owns home improvement and appliance stores. MAJOR SUBSIDIARIES, BRANDS: Busy Beaver Building Centers, Silo, Inc.

Sales: $979.0 million (trend 15.9% a year).
Earnings: $19.70 million (trend 7.2% a year).
What happened to a $10,000 investment

Purchase Date	*Purchase Price*	*Price on 12-31-81*	*Dividends Paid*
12-31-71	$15.17	$25.50	$6,775.82
12-31-76	$15.92	$25.50	$3,650.26

Purchase Date	*Cap. Gains (− Losses)*	*Total Return*	*Rate of Return*
12-31-71	$6,813.19	$13,589.01	8.96%
12-31-76	$6,020.94	$ 9,671.20	14.49%

D

DMG, INC. (DMG). Founded 1969. Headquarters: 5915 Ponce de Leon Blvd., Coral Gables FL 33146. REAL ESTATE. DMG manages and sells real estate acquired through foreclosures; also engages in some mortgage lending.

Sales: $4.4 million (trend −32.2% a year).
Earnings: $.20 million.
What happened to a $10,000 investment

Purchase Date	*Purchase Price*	*Price on 12-31-81*	*Dividends Paid*
12-31-71	$27.62	$3.50	$2,595.48
12-31-76	$ 1.50	$3.50	$ 0.00

Purchase Date	*Cap. Gains (− Losses)*	*Total Return*	*Rate of Return*
12-31-71	$−8,733.03	$−6,137.56	−9.07%
12-31-76	$ 13,333.33	$ 13,333.33	18.47%

* * *

DAMON CORP. (DMN). Founded 1961. Headquarters: 115 Fourth Ave., Needham Heights MA 02194. MEDICAL SERVICES. Damon Corp. operates clinical laboratories and manufactures medical products; also produces hobby and educational products.

Sales: $145.7 million (trend 1.1% a year).
Earnings: $−.01 million.
What happened to a $10,000 investment

Purchase Date	*Purchase Price*	*Price on 12-31-81*	*Dividends Paid*
12-31-71	$52.25	$8.75	$ 258.37
12-31-76	$ 8.25	$8.75	$1,212.12

Purchase Date	*Cap. Gains (– Losses)*	*Total Return*	*Rate of Return*
12-31-71	$–8,325.36	$–8,066.99	–15.16%
12-31-76	$ 606.06	$ 1,818.18	3.40%

* * *

DAN RIVER INC. (DML). Founded 1909. Headquarters: 107 Frederick St., Greenville SC 29606. **TEXTILES.** Dan River Inc. manufactures textiles for clothing, carpeting, and home furnishings. **MAJOR SUBSIDIARIES, BRANDS:** Dan River, Wunda Weve.

Sales: $607.7 million (trend 7.6% a year).
Earnings: $19.33 million (trend 17.1% a year).
What happened to a $10,000 investment

Purchase Date	*Purchase Price*	*Price on 12-31-81*	*Dividends Paid*
12-31-71	$8.50	$13.37	$7,223.53
12-31-76	$9.50	$13.37	$4,863.16

Purchase Date	*Cap. Gains (– Losses)*	*Total Return*	*Rate of Return*
12-31-71	$5,735.29	$12,958.82	8.67%
12-31-76	$4,078.95	$ 8,942.11	13.63%

* * *

DANA CORP. (DCN). Founded 1916. Headquarters: 4500 Dorr St., Toledo OH 43615. **TRUCK, CAR, AND INDUSTRIAL COMPONENTS.** Dana makes original equipment and replacement parts for cars and trucks; also makes a variety of components for industrial equipment and has a modest sideline in consumer finance. 37,000 employees. **MAJOR SUBSIDIARIES, BRANDS:** Diamond Financial Holdings Inc., General Ohio S&L Corp.

Sales: $2,524.0 million (trend 19.2% a year).
Earnings: $95.73 million (trend 12.8% a year).
What happened to a $10,000 investment

Purchase Date	*Purchase Price*	*Price on 12-31-81*	*Dividends Paid*
12-31-71	$16.73	$29.50	$6,091.95
12-31-76	$29.25	$29.50	$2,331.62

Purchase Date	*Cap. Gains (– Losses)*	*Total Return*	*Rate of Return*
12-31-71	$7,637.00	$13,728.95	9.03%
12-31-76	$ 85.47	$ 2,417.09	4.42%

PROFILE: Going into 1980, Dana had achieved eight straight years of record sales and profits. In 1980 that string snapped like a rubber band. Layoffs were severe, and attracted more attention than they would at most companies because Dana had long boasted excellent labor-management relations and a policy of no layoffs.

Still, things could have been a lot worse. After all, Dana's major customers, the car and truck manufacturers, were swimming in red ink. Dana, for all its problems, still showed a profit in 1980 (about $96 million, down from $164 million the year before). It not only continued paying dividends, it raised them. (This was important to many of the laid-off workers, who own often substantial amounts of Dana stock under the company's generous stock purchase plan.) In early 1981 the dividend yield was around 6 percent. Dana hasn't missed paying dividends since 1936.

The chief cause of the 1980 downturn was the same factor that had carried Dana happily through the 1974–75 recession — light trucks. Supplying parts for light trucks had grown to be more than a third of Dana's business, which left the company with egg on its face when buyers tired of the gas-hungry vehicles. "The light truck market took off like a Hula-Hoop — and us along with it," chairman Gerry Mitchell told *Fortune* magazine. "It's the last damn product we'll have like that."

Dana has already made considerable strides in diversifying. Industrial components are more than 20 percent of the business now, versus less than 10 percent in the preceding decade. Though attracting controversy over whether the company is straying outside its realm of expertise, in the long run the fledgling financial services operation may add a bit of stability to earnings. The balance sheet is still in good shape. Debt was 26 percent of capital in early 1981, up from 19.5 percent in 1978. There's no way this company can ever escape being cyclical. But except for 1980 it's weathered storms well. A kicker: the company says it has a device under development that can increase fuel efficiency of cars and trucks by 10 to 15 percent.

* * *

DANIEL INDUSTRIES, INC. (DAN). Founded 1965. Headquarters: 1 Riverway, Houston TX 77056. **OIL SYSTEMS.** Makes systems to measure oil and natural gas flow; also makes nuts, bolts, and pipeline valves. **MAJOR SUBSIDIARIES, BRANDS:** Daniel Valve Co., Daniel Oil Tools Co.

Sales: $155.8 million (trend 20.7% a year).
Earnings: $9.34 million (trend 12.7% a year).
What happened to a $10,000 investment

Purchase Date	*Purchase Price*	*Price on 12-31-81*	*Dividends Paid*
12-31-71	$2.00	$22.25	$3,773.83
12-31-76	$8.06	$22.25	$ 720.88

Purchase Date	*Cap. Gains (— Losses)*	*Total Return*	*Rate of Return*
12-31-71	$101,187.99	$104,961.82	27.66%
12-31-76	$ 17,609.93	$ 18,330.82	23.15%

* * *

DART & KRAFT, INC. (DKI). Founded 1980. Headquarters: Kraft Court, Glenview IL 60025. **FOODS, CONSUMER PRODUCTS.** Formed by the merger of Kraft Inc. and Dart Industries, the company is a major seller of food and consumer products, particularly cheese, food dressings, kitchen durables, and batteries. Also makes glass, chemicals, and plastics. 80,000 employees. **MAJOR SUBSIDIARIES, BRANDS:** Kraft cheeses and dressings; Miracle Whip; Parkay and Breakstone margarines and butters; Light 'N Lively dairy products; Breyers and Sealtest ice creams; Tupperware household goods; Duracell batteries (P. R. Mallory); Thatcher Glass; West Bend appliances; Wilsonart decorative laminates.

Sales: $9,411.5 million (trend 12.6% a year).
Earnings: $383.10 million (trend 19.4% a year).
What happened to a $10,000 investment

Purchase Date	*Purchase Price*	*Price on 12-31-81*	*Dividends Paid*
12-31-71	$46.75	$50.75	$5,139.68
12-31-76	$46.50	$50.75	$3,133.33

Purchase Date	*Cap. Gains (— Losses)*	*Total Return*	*Rate of Return*
12-31-71	$855.61	$5,995.29	4.81%
12-31-76	$913.98	$4,047.31	7.03%

PROFILE: When Dart merged with Kraft, Dart stockholders groused that they'd been stuck with a slow-growing pile of cheese, and that if Dart wanted a merger it could have done better elsewhere. After all, Tupperware, Dart's leading division, had incredible 30 percent profit margins and was growing twice as fast as Kraft. Dart as a whole was growing about half again as fast.

With characteristic bluntness, Dart chairman Justin Dart (now head of the executive committee for the new corporation, of which Kraft's John Richman is chairman) turned aside the criticism. "Tupperware won't go on growing at its present rate," he told *Fortune* magazine in 1980 shortly before the merger was consummated. "We're already in thirty-five countries. Where do we go next — Poland?" Dart added that the merger provided "diversification, security, stability."

That it does. The merger giant has a very strong balance sheet, with debt less than 20 percent of capital. It should be relatively resistant to recessions. People always have to eat, and a cheese sandwich with mayonnaise is as good a bet as any. And the company has growth prospects, aided by Dart's reputation for smart acquisitions.

The first acquisition target of the corporation post-merger was Hobart Corp., maker of the highly regarded KitchenAid dishwashers and other appliances, which was acquired in 1981.

The stock in early 1982 sold for a run-of-the-mill p / e multiple of 8, and yielded close to 7 percent.

* * *

DATA GENERAL CORP. (DGN). Founded 1968. Headquarters: 440 Computer Dr., Westboro MA 01580. **COMPUTERS.** Data General Corp. designs, manufactures, and sells general-purpose computer systems and related products and services. **MAJOR SUBSIDIARIES, BRANDS:** Eclipse, microNOVA, NOVA.

Sales: $736.9 million (trend 35.8% a year).
Earnings: $40.81 million (trend 18.7% a year).
What happened to a $10,000 investment

Purchase Date	*Purchase Price*	*Price on 12-31-81*	*Dividends Paid*
12-31-71	$18.17	$53.75	$0.00
12-31-76	$45.37	$53.75	$0.00

Purchase Date	*Cap. Gains (— Losses)*	*Total Return*	*Rate of Return*
12-31-71	$19,587.16	$19,587.16	11.46%
12-31-76	$ 1,845.73	$ 1,845.73	3.45%

* * *

DATA TERMINAL SYSTEMS, INC. (DTS). Founded 1970. Headquarters: 124 Acton St., Maynard MA 01754. **CASH REGISTERS.** Manufactures electronic cash registers and retail business control systems.

Sales: $118.3 million (trend 55.8% a year).
Earnings: $−2.95 million.
What happened to a $10,000 investment

Purchase Date	Purchase Price	Price on 12-31-81	Dividends Paid
12-31-71	$N/A	$10.75	$ N/A
12-31-76	$ 6.42	$10.75	$1,168.83

Purchase Date	Cap. Gains (– Losses)	Total Return	Rate of Return
12-31-71	$ N/A	$ N/A	N/A%
12-31-76	$6,753.25	$7,922.08	12.38%

* * *

DATAPOINT CORP. (DPT). Founded 1976. Headquarters: 7900 Callaghan Rd., San Antonio TX 78284. **COMPUTERS.** Datapoint Corp. manufactures processors that can distribute computer capability throughout an office; the various user stations share a software library.

Sales: $396.2 million (trend 42.0% a year).
Earnings: $48.76 million (trend 54.3% a year).
What happened to a $10,000 investment

Purchase Date	Purchase Price	Price on 12-31-81	Dividends Paid
12-31-71	$3.44	$51.25	$0.00
12-31-76	$7.31	$51.25	$0.00

Purchase Date	Cap. Gains (– Losses)	Total Return	Rate of Return
12-31-71	$139,090.86	$139,090.86	31.02%
12-31-76	$ 60,085.47	$ 60,085.47	47.61%

* * *

DAYCO CORP. (DAY). Founded 1966. Headquarters: 333 W. First St., Dayton OH 45402. **RUBBER, PLASTIC.** Dayco Corp. produces rubber, plastic, chemical, and industrial products.

Sales: $716.4 million (trend 12.9% a year).
Earnings: $8.45 million (trend 5.5% a year).
What happened to a $10,000 investment

Purchase Date	Purchase Price	Price on 12-31-81	Dividends Paid
12-31-71	$13.86	$11.37	$4,044.04
12-31-76	$12.54	$11.37	$1,915.96

Purchase Date	Cap. Gains (– Losses)	Total Return	Rate of Return
12-31-71	$–1,792.43	$2,251.61	2.05%
12-31-76	$ –928.01	$ 987.95	1.90%

* * *

DAYTON-HUDSON CORP. (DH). Founded 1902. Headquarters: 777 Nicollet Mall, Minneapolis MN 55402. **RETAILER.** Operates department stores, discount department stores, bookstores, jewelry stores, and clothing stores, mainly in the Midwest and South. 34,000 employees. **MAJOR SUBSIDIARIES, BRANDS:** B. Dalton (books); Target (discount stores); Dayton's, Hudson's, Diamond's, and John A. Brown department stores; Lechmere; Mervyn's; Dayton-Hudson Jewelers.

Sales: $4,033.5 million (trend 20.0% a year).
Earnings: $138.04 million (trend 22.6% a year).
What happened to a $10,000 investment

Purchase Date	Purchase Price	Price on 12-31-81	Dividends Paid
12-31-71	$18.31	$30.25	$2,584.30
12-31-76	$19.12	$30.25	$1,620.92

Purchase Date	Cap. Gains (– Losses)	Total Return	Rate of Return
12-31-71	$6,518.77	$9,103.07	6.69%
12-31-76	$5,816.99	$7,437.91	11.76%

PROFILE: Dayton-Hudson is far and away the nation's leading department store chain, according to the Forbes *Annual Report on American Industry* published in 1981. Its five-year average return on equity dwarfed that of its competitors, and at 24.3 percent was double the average. Its net profit margin, 4.4 percent, was the highest in the industry.

Why, then, has Dayton-Hudson been making a drastic shift in the way it does business? Answer: It believes that the traditional department store business is doomed, and that people will increasingly turn to specialized stores, discount stores, or top-of-the-line stores, depending on their income and needs.

Anticipating that inflation will continue to be severe, and that most people's budgets will continue to be tight, Dayton-Hudson has been pouring funds into its fast-growing discount operation, Target, which already had close to 150 stores in sixteen states in 1981. Target started out as a Midwestern chain, but is being expanded rapidly into the Southeast and Southwest, and is claiming about $900 million of a five-year (1981–85), $1.7 billion spending program. The other chief beneficiaries will be B. Dalton books and Mervyn's clothing stores; the traditional department stores will get the crumbs.

The expansion program will probably push Dayton-Hudson's debt load well above the level (30 percent of capital) that prevailed at the beginning of the decade. If the company is betting right about inflation, it will be paying off that debt with ever-cheapening dollars.

Dividends have been paid yearly since 1966. The dividend yield in recent years has been a modest 3 to 4 percent.

* * *

DAYTON POWER & LIGHT CO. (DPL). Founded 1911. Headquarters: Courthouse Plaza S.W., Dayton OH 45401. UTILITIES. The Dayton Power & Light Co. provides Dayton and the surrounding area with electricity and natural gas.

Sales: $650.0 million (trend 13.0% a year).
Earnings: $47.17 million (trend 8.6% a year).
What happened to a $10,000 investment

Purchase Date	*Purchase Price*	*Price on 12-31-81*	*Dividends Paid*
12-31-71	$24.87	$14.62	$6,793.97
12-31-76	$19.87	$14.62	$4,327.04

Purchase Date	*Cap. Gains (– Losses)*	*Total Return*	*Rate of Return*
12-31-71	$–4,120.60	$2,673.37	2.40%
12-31-76	$–2,641.51	$1,685.53	3.16%

* * *

DEAN FOODS CO. (DF). Founded 1929. Headquarters: 3600 N. River Rd., Franklin Park IL 60131. DAIRY PRODUCTS. Dean produces milk, cheese, yogurt and other dairy products, as well as other food products. Also operates some 300 Baskin-Robbins ice cream stores under franchise arrangement.

Sales: $611.7 million (trend 17.5% a year).
Earnings: $12.46 million (trend 21.2% a year).
What happened to a $10,000 investment

Purchase Date	*Purchase Price*	*Price on 12-31-81*	*Dividends Paid*
12-31-71	$3.33	$18.50	$8,457.45
12-31-76	$7.83	$18.50	$2,543.60

Purchase Date	*Cap. Gains (– Losses)*	*Total Return*	*Rate of Return*
12-31-71	$45,500.00	$53,957.45	20.39%
12-31-76	$13,617.02	$16,160.62	21.21%

* * *

DEAN WITTER REYNOLDS ORGANIZATION INC. (DWR). Founded 1973. Headquarters: 45 Montgomery St., San Francisco CA 94104. SECURITIES. Dean Witter Reynolds Organization Inc. deals in corporate, municipal, and government securities, is involved in investment banking, and operates an insurance company. MAJOR SUBSIDIARIES, BRANDS: Dean Witter Reynolds InterCapital Inc.; Surety Life Insurance Co.

Sales: $901.4 million (trend 36.8% a year).
Earnings: $53.14 million (trend 31.1% a year).
What happened to a $10,000 investment

Purchase Date	*Purchase Price*	*Price on 12-31-81*	*Dividends Paid*
12-31-71	$N/A	$49.50	$ N/A
12-31-76	$11.90	$49.50	$2,857.14

Purchase Date	*Cap. Gains (– Losses)*	*Total Return*	*Rate of Return*
12-31-71	$ N/A	$ N/A	N/A%
12-31-76	$31,596.64	$34,453.78	34.77%

* * *

DEERE & CO. (DE). Founded 1837. Headquarters: John Deere Rd., Moline IL 61265. FARM MACHINERY. Deere is the world's leading maker of tractors and other farm machinery; also makes forestry and construction equipment, lawn and garden equipment, and snowmobiles. 65,000 employees.

Sales: $5,446.7 million (trend 12.7% a year).
Earnings: $250.99 million (trend .0% a year).
What happened to a $10,000 investment

Purchase Date	*Purchase Price*	*Price on 12-31-81*	*Dividends Paid*
12-31-71	$12.81	$35.50	$9,096.59
12-31-76	$31.62	$35.50	$2,482.21

Purchase Date	*Cap. Gains (– Losses)*	*Total Return*	*Rate of Return*
12-31-71	$17,707.32	$26,803.90	13.92%
12-31-76	$ 1,225.30	$ 3,707.51	6.51%

PROFILE: Deere has consistently been a fine company, but whether it's a wise stock to buy varies from time to time. During the period from 1974 to 1979, Deere shares sold for less than 8 times earnings. A person who bought at the 1974 low (about $14, restated for splits) could have tripled his money by 1981; a person who'd bought at the 1974 or 1975 high (about $26) could have come fairly close to doubling it. It's not clear whether those sorts of capital gains will come as easily during the 1980s, since the quality of the company is now a bit more widely recognized and is more fully reflected in the stock price (the p / e was 12 in early 1981, 9 in early 1982).

The reasoning for buying the stock goes something like this: Worldwide demand for food will accelerate during the coming years. Crop failures worldwide will be at least as frequent in the future as in the past. To the United States will fall the bulk of the burden for feeding the free world. Domestic demand for agricultural equipment is therefore likely to be high. And Deere is not only the largest (with about a 33 percent market share) but also the most highly regarded of the farm equipment manufacturers. With an outstanding dealer network and a bent for making the large machines that can be the most profitable segment of the market, Deere should thrive.

It's a reasonable scenario, but farmers know better than anyone that it's an unpredictable world. The investor must check the price of Deere shares to see how much belief is built into the stock price at the moment.

The stock provides a moderate dividend, recently between 4 and 5 percent of the share price.

* * *

DELMARVA POWER & LIGHT CO. (DEW). Founded 1909. Headquarters: 800 King St., PO Box 231, Wilmington DE 19899. UTILITIES. Delmarva Power & Light Co. distributes electricity and natural gas in Delaware, Maryland, and Virginia.

Sales: $520.5 million (trend 13.5% a year).
Earnings: $39.53 million (trend 11.5% a year).
What happened to a $10,000 investment

Purchase Date	*Purchase Price*	*Price on 12-31-81*	*Dividends Paid*
12-31-71	$18.25	$12.62	$6,827.40
12-31-76	$14.12	$12.62	$4,856.64

Purchase Date	*Cap. Gains (− Losses)*	*Total Return*	*Rate of Return*
12-31-71	$−3,082.19	$3,745.21	3.23%
12-31-76	$−1,061.95	$3,794.69	6.65%

* * *

DELTA AIR LINES, INC. (DAL). Founded 1930. Headquarters: Hartsfield Atlanta International Airport, Atlanta GA 30320. AIRLINE. Delta is approximately the sixth-largest U.S. airline. Its routes connect its Atlanta hub with cities throughout the United States, and with Europe and the Caribbean. 37,000 employees.

Sales: $3,533.3 million (trend 18.6% a year).
Earnings: $146.47 million (trend 11.3% a year).
What happened to a $10,000 investment

Purchase Date	*Purchase Price*	*Price on 12-31-81*	*Dividends Paid*
12-31-71	$24.44	$24.62	$1,616.37
12-31-76	$19.25	$24.62	$1,324.68

Purchase Date	*Cap. Gains (− Losses)*	*Total Return*	*Rate of Return*
12-31-71	$ 76.73	$1,693.09	1.58%
12-31-76	$2,792.21	$4,116.88	7.14%

PROFILE: Delta is almost universally acknowledged to be the country's best-run and most profitable airline. Northwest may have a cleaner balance sheet, but Delta has put together a strong balance sheet, strategic planning for the future, a sensible plane procurement strategy, and consistent (for an airline) growth in a way no other airline can match.

It also is unusual in having no unions to negotiate with, and the management puts a lot of effort into keeping it that way. "Delta," said *The Wall Street Journal,* "promotes from within, pays better than most airlines and rarely lays off workers. . . . It's difficult to find workers with serious complaints."

In 1980, when many airlines were bathing in red ink, the New York *Times* headlined, "Prosperous Delta Air Expands . . . Line Gains as Industry Retrenches."

Time magazine said in 1981 that Delta "has won faithful business travelers for its efficient, on-time service. . . . Delta is well placed for the turbulent times ahead. Its 'hub and spokes' has become a wheel of fortune."

Even more bluntly, *Forbes* magazine wrote in 1980, "The nation's five biggest airlines — United, American, Pan Am, TWA and Eastern — are in deep, long-term trouble. The sixth largest is not. Guess who may be number one in 1990."

In light of all this favorable press, it may be surprising that Delta stock sold for only 10 times earnings in 1981, a modest premium to the market. Some investors may feel that Delta shines only because it's "the best of a bad lot." Airline earnings are notoriously volatile. Regulation is easing, but fuel costs continue to be a long-term question. Delta's dividend yield is modest (only about 2½ percent in early 1981). This much seems clear: If you're going to invest in any airline stock, don't pick a competitor without giving Delta a serious look.

* * *

DELTONA CORP. (DLT). Founded 1962. Headquarters: 3250 S.W. Third Ave., Miami FL 33129. **COMMUNITY DEVELOPMENT.** The Deltona Corp. develops major planned communities in several Florida locations. **MAJOR SUBSIDIARIES, BRANDS:** Imperial Lumber.

Sales: $193.7 million (trend 18.0% a year).
Earnings: $4.60 million (trend 77.2% a year).
What happened to a $10,000 investment

Purchase Date	*Purchase Price*	*Price on 12-31-81*	*Dividends Paid*
12-31-71	$27.62	$8.75	$0.00
12-31-76	$ 5.25	$8.75	$0.00

Purchase Date	*Cap. Gains (– Losses)*	*Total Return*	*Rate of Return*
12-31-71	$–6,832.58	$–6,832.58	–10.86%
12-31-76	$ 6,666.67	$ 6,666.67	10.76%

* * *

DELUXE CHECK PRINTERS, INC. (DLX). Founded 1920. Headquarters: 1080 W. County Rd. F, St. Paul MN 55112. **CHECK PRINTING.** Deluxe Check Printers, Inc., sells and prints checks, deposit slips, and other banking forms.

Sales: $428.5 million (trend 15.2% a year).
Earnings: $44.46 million (trend 14.7% a year).
What happened to a $10,000 investment

Purchase Date	*Purchase Price*	*Price on 12-31-81*	*Dividends Paid*
12-31-71	$14.37	$28.12	$3,180.87
12-31-76	$12.37	$28.12	$2,634.34

Purchase Date	*Cap. Gains (– Losses)*	*Total Return*	*Rate of Return*
12-31-71	$ 9,565.22	$12,746.09	8.57%
12-31-76	$12,727.27	$15,361.62	20.46%

* * *

DENNISON MANUFACTURING CO. (DSN). Founded 1962. Headquarters: 275 Wyman St., Waltham MA 02154. **STATIONERY.** Dennison Manufacturing Co. makes stationery products for industrial and consumer use; also produces merchandise identification and control systems.

Sales: $492.4 million (trend 15.0% a year).
Earnings: $23.30 million (trend 19.6% a year).
What happened to a $10,000 investment

Purchase Date	*Purchase Price*	*Price on 12-31-81*	*Dividends Paid*
12-31-71	$12.80	$22.25	$5,245.80
12-31-76	$11.69	$22.25	$4,141.18

Purchase Date	*Cap. Gains (– Losses)*	*Total Return*	*Rate of Return*
12-31-71	$7,386.62	$12,632.42	8.51%
12-31-76	$9,037.43	$13,178.61	18.31%

* * *

DENNY'S, INC. (DEN). Founded 1959. Headquarters: 14256 E. Firestone Blvd., La Mirada CA 90637. **RESTAURANTS.** Denny's, Inc., operates and franchises restaurants and doughnut stores in the U.S., Canada, Europe, Japan, and Mexico. **MAJOR SUBSIDIARIES, BRANDS:** Denny's restaurants; Winchell's Donut Houses.

Sales: $849.0 million (trend 18.8% a year).
Earnings: $26.92 million (trend 6.2% a year).
What happened to a $10,000 investment

Purchase Date	*Purchase Price*	*Price on 12-31-81*	*Dividends Paid*
12-31-71	$11.25	$29.25	$3,982.22
12-31-76	$24.87	$29.25	$1,491.46

Purchase Date	*Cap. Gains (– Losses)*	*Total Return*	*Rate of Return*
12-31-71	$16,000.00	$19,982.22	11.61%
12-31-76	$ 1,758.79	$ 3,250.25	5.79%

* * *

DENTSPLY INTERNATIONAL, INC. (DSP). Founded 1969. Headquarters: 570 W. College Ave., York PA 17405. **DENTAL SUPPLIES.** Dentsply International, Inc., manufactures dental supplies and equipment, and optical products.

Sales: $258.2 million (trend 20.0% a year).
Earnings: $6.10 million (trend –5.4% a year).
What happened to a $10,000 investment

Purchase Date	*Purchase Price*	*Price on 12-31-81*	*Dividends Paid*
12-31-71	$22.58	$17.12	$3,518.82
12-31-76	$30.50	$17.12	$1,383.61

Purchase Date	*Cap. Gains (– Losses)*	*Total Return*	*Rate of Return*
12-31-71	$–2,416.97	$ 1,101.85	1.05%
12-31-76	$–4,385.25	$–3,001.64	–6.89%

* * *

DESOTO, INC. (DSO). Founded 1956. Headquarters: 1700 S. Mt. Prospect Rd., Des Plaines IL 60018. PAINT. DeSoto, Inc., manufactures paint, industrial coatings, household cleaning products, furniture and fireplace furnishings. MAJOR SUBSIDIARIES, BRANDS: DeSoto Coatings Ltd.

Sales: $337.6 million (trend 5.4% a year).
Earnings: $11.29 million (trend 22.9% a year).
What happened to a $10,000 investment

Purchase Date	*Purchase Price*	*Price on 12-31-81*	*Dividends Paid*
12-31-71	$22.87	$12.25	$3,151.91
12-31-76	$14.25	$12.25	$3,410.53

Purchase Date	*Cap. Gains (− Losses)*	*Total Return*	*Rate of Return*
12-31-71	$−4,644.81	$−1,492.90	−1.60%
12-31-76	$−1,403.51	$ 2,007.02	3.73%

* * *

DETROIT EDISON CO. (DTE). Founded 1903. Headquarters: 2000 Second Ave., Detroit MI 48226. UTILITY. Supplies electricity to roughly 5 million people in the Detroit region; also supplies steam in the city of Detroit. 10,000 employees.

Sales: $1,812.5 million (trend 10.8% a year).
Earnings: $137.53 million (trend 13.9% a year).
What happened to a $10,000 investment

Purchase Date	*Purchase Price*	*Price on 12-31-81*	*Dividends Paid*
12-31-71	$21.25	$11.37	$7,071.76
12-31-76	$15.12	$11.37	$5,175.21

Purchase Date	*Cap. Gains (− Losses)*	*Total Return*	*Rate of Return*
12-31-71	$−4,647.06	$2,424.71	2.19%
12-31-76	$−2,479.34	$2,695.87	4.89%

PROFILE: A high dividend yield and low esteem: That's what Detroit Edison has in common with a lot of other utilities. The two are not unrelated. The actual dividend payment has barely budged for a decade and a half; it was $1.40 in 1966 and $1.60 a share in 1980. The dividend yield has soared because of that low esteem: the stock price has fallen so low that the dividend now looms larger as a percentage of the price. In 1981 the yield was about 14 percent, and the shares were selling at about 6 times earnings.

It's hard to see why Wall Street should award these shares a much richer multiple. Sales, earnings, and dividends have all been flat. The return on stockholders' equity has been between 9 and 10 percent in most recent years. Less than a third of the utility's electricity goes to private homes. Detroit's industries are big customers, and the leading customer — the auto industry — has, of course, been sick of late.

The balance sheet, as at many utilities, is weak. Long-term debt is just over half of total capital, and has been for several years.

The big attraction here, as with most utility stocks, is the high yield, coupled with the hope that declining interest rates will produce a capital gain. When interest rates decline, utility stocks (like bonds) generally rise.

* * *

DEXTER CORP. (DEX). Founded 1914. Headquarters: 1 Elm St., Windsor Locks CT 06096. SPECIALTY CHEMICALS. Dexter Corp. produces specialty chemicals and natural and synthetic fiber products.

Sales: $535.0 million (trend 30.5% a year).
Earnings: $25.72 million (trend 30.1% a year).
What happened to a $10,000 investment

Purchase Date	*Purchase Price*	*Price on 12-31-81*	*Dividends Paid*
12-31-71	$11.92	$24.62	$4,665.71
12-31-76	$16.33	$24.62	$2,653.04

Purchase Date	*Cap. Gains (− Losses)*	*Total Return*	*Rate of Return*
12-31-71	$10,664.34	$15,330.04	9.74%
12-31-76	$ 5,076.53	$ 7,729.57	12.13%

* * *

DI GIORGIO CORP. (DIG). Founded 1920. Headquarters: 1 Maritime Plaza, #2300, San Francisco CA 94111. FOOD PROCESSING. Di Giorgio Corp. is involved in food processing, grocery and drug distribution, timber manufacture, and real estate development. MAJOR SUBSIDIARIES, BRANDS: Borrego Springs Airline; Computer Accounting Management, Inc.; Di Giorgio Development Corp.

Sales: $888.2 million (trend 9.3% a year).
Earnings: $9.33 million (trend 61.5% a year).
What happened to a $10,000 investment

Purchase Date	*Purchase Price*	*Price on 12-31-81*	*Dividends Paid*
12-31-71	$15.12	$9.25	$2,937.19
12-31-76	$ 7.12	$9.25	$3,396.49

Purchase Date	*Cap. Gains (− Losses)*	*Total Return*	*Rate of Return*
12-31-71	$−3,884.30	$−947.11	−.99%
12-31-76	$ 2,982.46	$ 6,378.95	10.37%

* * *

DIAL CORP. (DFC). Founded 1897. Headquarters: 207 Ninth St., Des Moines IA 50307. **FINANCIAL SERVICE HOLDING CO.** Dial Corp. is the holding company for a consumer finance company and is also involved in insurance and in supplying computer services. **MAJOR SUBSIDIARIES, BRANDS:** Dial Financial Corp.; Centurion Life Insurance Co. In 1981 the company agreed to be merged into Northwest Bancorporation, subject to approval from regulators and shareholders.

Sales: $173.3 million (trend 14.6% a year).
Earnings: $17.16 million (trend 17.7% a year).
What happened to a $10,000 investment

Purchase Date	*Purchase Price*	*Price on 12-31-81*	*Dividends Paid*
12-31-71	$19.37	$48.25	$4,412.90
12-31-76	$12.87	$48.25	$4,446.60

Purchase Date	*Cap. Gains (− Losses)*	*Total Return*	*Rate of Return*
12-31-71	$14,903.23	$19,316.13	11.36%
12-31-76	$27,475.73	$31,922.33	33.20%

* * *

DIAMOND INTERNATIONAL CORP. (DN). Founded 1930. Headquarters: 733 Third Ave., New York NY 10017. **PACKAGING, FOREST PRODUCTS.** Diamond International is a large producer of plywood, lumber, corrugated packaging, pulp, paper products, labels, and cartons; also produces plastic and metal containers, wood housewares, and matches, and operates more than 100 building-supply stores. 18,000 employees. **MAJOR SUBSIDIARIES, BRANDS:** Brooks-Scanlon (forest products).

Sales: $1,282.6 million (trend 11.2% a year).
Earnings: $37.90 million (trend −1.9% a year).
What happened to a $10,000 investment

Purchase Date	*Purchase Price*	*Price on 12-31-81*	*Dividends Paid*
12-31-71	$36.25	$40.37	$5,330.41
12-31-76	$36.59	$40.37	$2,858.38

Purchase Date	*Cap. Gains (− Losses)*	*Total Return*	*Rate of Return*
12-31-71	$1,137.93	$6,468.33	5.12%
12-31-76	$1,034.16	$3,892.54	6.80%

PROFILE: First the good news, then the bad news, then the excitement.

The good news is that this packaging and forest products company is financially solid. In its corporate history, it has never missed a dividend. It has never lowered a dividend. Some years it takes some reaching to keep the streak alive. In 1980, for example, the company paid out 83 percent of its profits in dividends. The dividend yield in recent years has usually been in the 6-to-7 percent range. The balance sheet is better than average. Debt and preferred stock combined were less than 30 percent of capital as of early 1982.

The bad news is that the company's profits have been growing at a snail's pace in recent years. For example, 1974's record earnings of $4.01 a share weren't matched until 1978 ($4.17), and 1980 earnings exactly matched those of 1970 ($2.68 a share). Return on stockholders' equity hasn't been particularly good either. As for capital gains, there's been no fundamental uptrend in recent years, though there have been sharp fluctuations in the stock price.

That brings us to point three, the excitement. Those sharp jumps and dips in Diamond International's price have been mainly due to takeover speculation. At least two potential suitors are waiting on the porch. Cavenham Development Corp., the British company controlled by Sir James Goldsmith, owns 41 percent of the stock, and Goldsmith may take over the entire company, through a merger proposed in late 1981. Simpson Timber, a privately held company, owns another 9 percent.

* * *

DIAMOND SHAMROCK CORP. (DIA). Founded 1928. Headquarters: 717 N. Harwood St., Dallas TX 75201. **ENERGY, CHEMICALS.** Produces oil, gas, and coal; makes chlorine, plastics, agricultural and specialty chemicals. 12,000 employees. **MAJOR SUBSIDIARIES, BRANDS:** Falcon Seaboard (coal).

Sales: $3,143.0 million (trend 21.7% a year).
Earnings: $201.21 million (trend 11.5% a year).
What happened to a $10,000 investment

Purchase Date	*Purchase Price*	*Price on 12-31-81*	*Dividends Paid*
12-31-71	$10.12	$25.37	$10,666.67
12-31-76	$34.25	$25.37	$ 2,167.88

Purchase Date	*Cap. Gains (− Losses)*	*Total Return*	*Rate of Return*
12-31-71	$ 15,061.73	$25,728.40	13.58%
12-31-76	$−2,591.24	$ −423.36	−.86%

PROFILE: Energy is the siren song that beckons Diamond Shamrock chairman William Bricker. It was partly to be in the heart of oil and gas territory that he moved the company from Cleveland to Dallas in 1979. It was in the name of energy that he acquired, that same year, Falcon Seaboard Inc., a medium-sized coal producer, in a move that many analysts and board members criticized at the time (the price was about $330 million, or 24 times Falcon's earnings), but which many of the same people now see as smart. Energy accounted for about a third of Diamond Shamrock's earnings when it was formed in 1967 through the merger of Diamond Alkali Co. and Shamrock Oil & Gas Corp. By 1979 it was close to half, and by 1981 close to two thirds.

Late in 1980, Bricker announced that six of the components of the company's traditional chemical business were on the auction block. Some of these have been profitable, if only marginally so, but Bricker believes energy will provide higher profits. Being kept — at least for the time being — are some of the most profitable chemical lines, including chlorine production and production of specialty agricultural chemicals. Some people expect these, too, to be sold someday, but Bricker told *Business Week* at the end of 1980, "We have put up for sale all the businesses we intend to sell. Those who are waiting for another shoe to drop had better forget it."

The company has consistently paid dividends in the passbook savings range. In recent years the dividend yield has been 5 to 6 percent. The share price has been volatile.

* * *

DIEBOLD, INC. (DBD). Founded 1876. Headquarters: 818 Mulberry Rd. S.E., Canton OH 44711. **BANK SYSTEMS.** Diebold, Inc., manufactures bank security systems and automatic teller systems.

Sales: $346.9 million (trend 14.2% a year).
Earnings: $21.24 million (trend 28.7% a year).
What happened to a $10,000 investment

Purchase Date	*Purchase Price*	*Price on 12-31-81*	*Dividends Paid*
12-31-71	$30.05	$47.12	$1,168.34
12-31-76	$ 9.17	$47.12	$2,436.33

Purchase Date	*Cap. Gains (− Losses)*	*Total Return*	*Rate of Return*
12-31-71	$ 5,682.26	$ 6,850.59	5.36%
12-31-76	$41,409.09	$43,845.42	40.03%

* * *

DIGITAL EQUIPMENT CORP. (DEC). Founded 1957. Headquarters: 146 Main St., Maynard MA 01754. **COMPUTERS.** Digital Equipment is the nation's largest maker of minicomputers, and approximately the sixth-largest computer company overall. 57,000 employees.

Sales: $3,198.1 million (trend 33.0% a year).
Earnings: $352.14 million (trend 35.6% a year).
What happened to a $10,000 investment

Purchase Date	*Purchase Price*	*Price on 12-31-81*	*Dividends Paid*
12-31-71	$25.75	$86.50	$0.00
12-31-76	$53.87	$86.50	$0.00

Purchase Date	*Cap. Gains (− Losses)*	*Total Return*	*Rate of Return*
12-31-71	$23,592.23	$23,592.23	12.88%
12-31-76	$ 6,055.68	$ 6,055.68	9.93%

PROFILE: There's really only one question to ask about a company like this, and it's the question everybody asks: Can they keep it up?

Digital Equipment was one of the great growth companies of the 1970s. Sales grew from $135 million in 1970 to almost $2.4 billion in 1980. Profits grew from about $14 million in 1970 to about $250 million in 1980. And a share of Digital Equipment stock (adjusted for splits) grew from about $40 a share in early 1970 to a 1980 high of almost $99. Along the way, there were dips that might have permitted an alert investor to buy Digital Equipment shares for as little as $15 to $18 a share at various times in 1970, 1971, 1974, and 1975.

From an investor's point of view, the only trouble with this success story is that it's universally known. The stock always sells for a p / e multiple higher than the stock market as a whole. In 1971,

Digital shares actually sold for an incredible 81 times the company's then-current earnings! As recently as 1976, the multiple was above 30 times earnings. In the late 1970s and early 1980s, the stock market as a whole was more conservatively valued. In early 1982, the average stock sold for about 7 or 8 times earnings, Digital Equipment for 11.

The company's management structure has been as innovative as its products. Staff people have large amounts of flexibility and responsibility; the organization is highly democratic and decentralized (critics say too much so — but it's hard to find many critics when results are golden).

The company pays no dividends, and never has paid any. So if you buy in here, you're betting that the market for minicomputers will continue to grow, and that Digital Equipment will continue to reign as sovereign of that market. If you're right, you'll be rewarded, as investors in this stock have been in the past, by substantial capital gains.

* * *

DILLINGHAM CORP. (DHM). Founded 1902. Headquarters: PO Box 3468, Honolulu HI 96801. CONGLOMERATE. Dillingham Corp. is involved in construction, maritime activities, property development, and marketing of liquid propane gas. MAJOR SUBSIDIARIES, BRANDS: California Liquid Gas Corp.; Foss Launch & Tug Co.; Gordon H. Ball Inc.

Sales: $1,361.9 million (trend 9.0% a year).
Earnings: $32.90 million (trend 9.0% a year).
What happened to a $10,000 investment

Purchase Date	*Purchase Price*	*Price on 12-31-81*	*Dividends Paid*
12-31-71	$11.62	$13.25	$4,326.88
12-31-76	$ 9.37	$13.25	$3,146.67

Purchase Date	*Cap. Gains (– Losses)*	*Total Return*	*Rate of Return*
12-31-71	$1,397.85	$5,724.73	4.63%
12-31-76	$4,133.33	$7,280.00	11.56%

* * *

DILLON COMPANIES, INC. (DLL). Founded 1921. Headquarters: 700 E. 30th St., Hutchinson KS 67501. FOOD RETAILER. Operates more than 200 supermarkets and more than 300 convenience stores under several names; also has a small chain of department stores. 22,000 employees. MAJOR SUBSIDIARIES, BRANDS: Dillon's, City Market, Fry's Gerbes, and King Soopers supermarkets; Kwik Shops, Quik Stop Markets, and Time Saver convenience stores; Calhoun's department stores; Jackson's Ice Cream Co.

Sales: $2,498.7 million (trend 16.9% a year).
Earnings: $41.69 million (trend 9.8% a year).
What happened to a $10,000 investment

Purchase Date	*Purchase Price*	*Price on 12-31-81*	*Dividends Paid*
12-31-71	$ 8.74	$22.34	$6,410.41
12-31-76	$16.04	$22.34	$2,471.01

Purchase Date	*Cap. Gains (– Losses)*	*Total Return*	*Rate of Return*
12-31-71	$15,545.92	$21,956.33	12.32%
12-31-76	$ 3,923.30	$ 6,394.31	10.39%

PROFILE: If you don't live in the Southwest, chances are fairly good you have never heard of the Dillon Companies. Here are a few facts. (1) The company is among the 50 largest retailers in the United States (ranking 29th in 1981, according to *Fortune*). (2) Going into 1980, it had chalked up seventeen consecutive record earnings years. (3) It has consistently produced an annual return of more than 20 percent on stockholders' equity, well above average for retailers and for large corporations in general. (4) The return on equity wasn't achieved with mirrors; the company has less debt than most supermarket chains, though debt (at about 38 percent of capital in early 1981) isn't negligible. (5) The chain is based in Kansas and operates mainly in the Southwest, a high-growth area. (6) Directors, including members of the Dillon family, own about 21 percent of the stock as of 1981. Ray ("Ace") Dillon took over from his father as chairman in 1979, but said he plans to make a non-family member, Joseph Pichler (formerly a business school dean of University of Kansas) chief executive officer within a few years.

Though 1980 was an off year, snapping the seventeen-year string of earnings gains, it was still a profitable year — in fact, the chain's third-best. The trouble was that other chains, notably Safeway, tried to muscle into a bigger market share in Dillon's Southwestern territory by slashing prices. The price war lasted about nine months, hurt everyone's profits, and seems to have subsided: 1981 was a record year.

Dividends have been increased each year for more than two decades. The yield as of 1981 was about 5 percent.

* * *

WALT DISNEY PRODUCTIONS (DIS). Founded 1938. Headquarters: 500 S. Buena Vista St., Burbank CA 91521. ENTERTAINMENT. Operates two major amusement parks in Florida and California; produces motion pictures and television programming for family viewing; licenses and designs consumer products tying in with movie characters. 24,000 employees. MAJOR SUBSIDIARIES, BRANDS: Disneyland; Walt Disney World.

Sales: $1,005.0 million (trend 11.8% a year).
Earnings: $121.48 million (trend 12.4% a year).
What happened to a $10,000 investment

Purchase Date	*Purchase Price*	*Price on 12-31-81*	*Dividends Paid*
12-31-71	$61.37	$52.25	$520.66
12-31-76	$46.51	$52.25	$573.15

Purchase Date	*Cap. Gains (− Losses)*	*Total Return*	*Rate of Return*
12-31-71	$−1,485.64	$−964.97	−1.01%
12-31-76	$ 1,233.87	$ 1,807.02	3.38%

PROFILE: This is another of the great fallen growth stocks from the 1960s. As with IBM, Xerox, Corning Glass, and other members of what used to be called the "nifty fifty," the company has done well, but investors' dreams were punctured.

When you wish upon a star, there's almost no limit to the visions of profit growth you can conjure up. In 1972 and 1973, Disney sold for well over 50 times earnings most of the time. That sort of p / e multiple is predicated on the assumption of astronomic growth.

Instead, Disney's growth has been merely excellent. Earnings grew an average of 17 percent a year from 1967 to 1980. During that span, Disney increased its profits every single year.

Yet the stock fell from a 1973 high of $110 a share to a 1974 low of less than $16 a share. Since then, it's moved erratically. The share price in early 1982 was about $57; the p / e was about 17. That was more than twice the average p / e at the time.

Many investors probably think of Disney mainly in connection with films. The fact is, though, that in recent years it's been the theme parks that have provided the bulk of revenues and profits. One recurrent concern on Wall Street has been the potential vulnerability of the parks to gasoline shortages. It's a reasonable fear, but one that at least so far has never become a reality.

The stock pays a small dividend, but you wouldn't buy it for that: In 1981, for example, the dividend yield was around 2 percent. Oh, one more thing. The company recently has had absolutely no long-term debt.

* * *

DIVERSIFIED INDUSTRIES, INC. (DMC). Founded 1967. Headquarters: 1034 S. Brentwood Blvd., Richmond Heights MO 63117. METAL RECYCLING. Diversified Industries, Inc., recycles nonferrous metals and manufactures supplies for railroad freight car production.

Sales: $346.4 million (trend 12.6% a year).
Earnings: $5.73 million (trend 384.5% a year).
What happened to a $10,000 investment

Purchase Date	*Purchase Price*	*Price on 12-31-81*	*Dividends Paid*
12-31-71	$8.37	$2.62	$0.00
12-31-76	$1.37	$2.62	$0.00

Purchase Date	*Cap. Gains (− Losses)*	*Total Return*	*Rate of Return*
12-31-71	$−6,865.67	$−6,865.67	−10.95%
12-31-76	$ 9,090.91	$ 9,090.91	13.81%

* * *

DR PEPPER CO. (DOC). Founded 1923. Headquarters: 5523 E. Mockingbird Lane, PO Box 225086, Dallas TX 75265. SOFT DRINKS. Dr Pepper produces syrups and concentrates for Dr Pepper and Sugar Free Dr Pepper. In 1981 it reached an agreement in principle to acquire Canada Dry (beverages) from Norton Simon.

Sales: $333.2 million (trend 20.5% a year).
Earnings: $26.54 million (trend 16.7% a year).
What happened to a $10,000 investment

Purchase Date	*Purchase Price*	*Price on 12-31-81*	*Dividends Paid*
12-31-71	$20.12	$12.37	$2,355.78
12-31-76	$14.25	$12.37	$2,322.81

Purchase Date	*Cap. Gains (− Losses)*	*Total Return*	*Rate of Return*
12-31-71	$−3,850.93	$−1,495.16	−1.61%
12-31-76	$−1,315.79	$ 1,007.02	1.94%

* * *

DOME MINES LIMITED. (DM). Founded 1923. Headquarters: 365 Bay St., Toronto, Ont., Canada M5H 2V9. GOLD. Dome Mines Limited mines gold in Ontario and Quebec. MAJOR SUBSIDIARIES,

BRANDS: Dome Petroleum (26 percent owned); Campbell Red Lake Mines (majority owned); Sigma Mines (majority owned).

Sales: $201.4 million (trend 29.6% a year).
Earnings: $105.92 million (trend 45.8% a year).
What happened to a $10,000 investment

Purchase Date	*Purchase Price*	*Price on 12-31-81*	*Dividends Paid*
12-31-71	$1.51	$15.25	$5,519.59
12-31-76	$3.68	$15.25	$1,577.90

Purchase Date	*Cap. Gains (– Losses)*	*Total Return*	*Rate of Return*
12-31-71	$91,198.16	$96,717.75	26.71%
12-31-76	$31,473.09	$33,050.99	33.90%

* * *

DONALDSON COMPANY, INC. (DCI). Founded 1936. Headquarters: 1400 W. 94th St., Minneapolis MN 55431. **AIR CLEANERS.** Donaldson Company, Inc., makes filtration systems and air cleaners for engines and compressors.

Sales: $263.9 million (trend 17.5% a year).
Earnings: $12.63 million (trend 5.9% a year).
What happened to a $10,000 investment

Purchase Date	*Purchase Price*	*Price on 12-31-81*	*Dividends Paid*
12-31-71	$11.89	$23.25	$3,378.97
12-31-76	$12.83	$23.25	$2,011.69

Purchase Date	*Cap. Gains (– Losses)*	*Total Return*	*Rate of Return*
12-31-71	$9,556.07	$12,935.05	8.66%
12-31-76	$8,116.88	$10,128.57	15.02%

* * *

DONALDSON, LUFKIN & JENRETTE, INC. (DLJ). Founded 1959. Headquarters: 140 Broadway, New York NY 10005. **FINANCIAL SERVICES.** Donaldson, Lufkin & Jenrette offers financial services in the securities field to individuals, corporations, and government. **MAJOR SUBSIDIARIES, BRANDS:** Donaldson, Lufkin & Jenrette Securities; Pershing & Co., Inc.; Wood, Struthers & Winthrop, Inc.

Sales: $485.1 million (trend 52.0% a year).
Earnings: $8.75 million (trend 25.8% a year).
What happened to a $10,000 investment

Purchase Date	*Purchase Price*	*Price on 12-31-81*	*Dividends Paid*
12-31-71	$9.12	$16.25	$1,304.11
12-31-76	$4.37	$16.25	$1,714.29

Purchase Date	*Cap. Gains (– Losses)*	*Total Return*	*Rate of Return*
12-31-71	$ 7,808.22	$ 9,112.33	6.69%
12-31-76	$27,142.86	$28,857.14	31.19%

* * *

R. R. DONNELLEY & SONS CO. (DNY). Founded 1956. Headquarters: 2223 Martin Luther King Dr., Chicago IL 60616. **PRINTER.** Donnelley is the nation's largest printing company. 14,000 employees. **MAJOR SUBSIDIARIES, BRANDS:** Lakeside Press.

Sales: $1,111.3 million (trend 17.4% a year).
Earnings: $68.96 million (trend 14.4% a year).
What happened to a $10,000 investment

Purchase Date	*Purchase Price*	*Price on 12-31-81*	*Dividends Paid*
12-31-71	$23.12	$37.75	$3,334.05
12-31-76	$24.25	$37.75	$2,070.10

Purchase Date	*Cap. Gains (– Losses)*	*Total Return*	*Rate of Return*
12-31-71	$6,324.32	$9,658.38	6.99%
12-31-76	$5,567.01	$7,637.11	12.02%

PROFILE: Sometimes you wonder where R. R. Donnelley could turn for new business. It already prints most of the Sears and Penney's catalogs, a raft of telephone books, and such magazines as *Time, Sports Illustrated, Newsweek, TV Guide,* the New York *Times Magazine, Ladies' Home Journal, Redbook,* and *People.* In addition it prints books, with an emphasis on textbooks and encyclopedias, and lately has done a good deal of business in advertising inserts that are slipped into newspapers.

The company passed the $1 billion mark in sales in 1980, having tripled its sales during the past decade. Profits have risen a bit more slowly than sales but here, too, the upward march has been steady, with only occasional mild stumbles in bad recession years.

Sitting on top of the printing heap, with many new facilities at its disposal, Donnelley can charge a substantial price for its services. Profit margins usually range between 6 and 8 percent. The company has upped capital spending substantially, from about $24 million back in 1971 to around

$140 million in 1979 and in 1980. Yet the balance sheet hasn't been strained a whit.

In fact, Donnelley boasts one of the strongest balance sheets you'll see, with debt a mere speck on the horizon — recently only about 2 percent of total capital. Long-term debt is substantially less than cash on hand.

The price / earnings ratio (recently 7 to 11) is usually a bit above that of the average stock. Though the company in its present form was incorporated in 1956, dividends of the predecessor company and the current one have been paid without interruption since 1911. The yield for the past several years has been slightly over 3 percent.

* * *

DORSEY CORP. (DSY). Founded 1927. Headquarters: 400 W. 45th St., Chattanooga TN 37410. **PLASTIC / GLASS CONTAINERS.** Produces plastic and glass containers; also makes highway cargo trailers.

Sales: $466.0 million (trend 25.2% a year).
Earnings: $8.03 million (trend 23.4% a year).
What happened to a $10,000 investment

Purchase Date	*Purchase Price*	*Price on 12-31-81*	*Dividends Paid*
12-31-71	$16.25	$18.25	$2,584.62
12-31-76	$11.75	$18.25	$2,893.62

Purchase Date	*Cap. Gains (– Losses)*	*Total Return*	*Rate of Return*
12-31-71	$1,230.77	$3,815.38	3.28%
12-31-76	$5,531.91	$8,425.53	13.00%

* * *

DOVER CORP. (DOV). Founded 1947. Headquarters: 277 Park Ave., New York NY 10172. **ELEVATORS.** Dover Corp. produces elevators, oil field equipment, and industrial machinery.

Sales: $835.2 million (trend 21.4% a year).
Earnings: $73.21 million (trend 23.8% a year).
What happened to a $10,000 investment

Purchase Date	*Purchase Price*	*Price on 12-31-81*	*Dividends Paid*
12-31-71	$7.06	$33.25	$3,910.62
12-31-76	$9.44	$33.25	$2,164.24

Purchase Date	*Cap. Gains (– Losses)*	*Total Return*	*Rate of Return*
12-31-71	$37,079.65	$40,990.27	17.69%
12-31-76	$25,231.79	$27,396.03	30.19%

* * *

DOW CHEMICAL CO. (DOW). Founded 1947. Headquarters: 2030 Dow Center, Midland MI 48640. **CHEMICALS, PHARMACEUTICALS.** Dow derives the bulk of its revenue from the sale of basic chemicals. It is also active in specialty chemicals and packaging, and in 1980 acquired the prescription drug (Merrell) business of Richardson-Merrell. 56,000 employees. **MAJOR SUBSIDIARIES, BRANDS:** Merrell, Dow, Handi Wrap, Saran Wrap.

Sales: $10,626.0 million (trend 16.9% a year).
Earnings: $805.00 million (trend 6.2% a year).
What happened to a $10,000 investment

Purchase Date	*Purchase Price*	*Price on 12-31-81*	*Dividends Paid*
12-31-71	$19.72	$26.25	$5,394.61
12-31-76	$43.37	$26.25	$1,706.05

Purchase Date	*Cap. Gains (– Losses)*	*Total Return*	*Rate of Return*
12-31-71	$ 3,312.20	$ 8,706.81	6.46%
12-31-76	$–3,948.13	$–2,242.07	–4.95%

PROFILE: To the campus activists of the 1960s, Dow was the company that made napalm for use in Vietnam. To some analysts, it's the company that has acquired a reputation for shrewd anticipation of international economic trends. Still others, looking at the company's 1980 move into pharmaceuticals, see Dow as a company transforming itself.

The most important fact about Dow, however, is its status as a major international producer of basic chemicals. Truly a multinational company, Dow derives almost precisely half its sales and earnings from the United States, and half from abroad (mainly in Europe, Latin America, and Asia). Its high volume and efficient plant designs (the company designs its own installations) have enabled it to compete successfully in price with major German and Japanese firms. Though Dow is only the sixth largest chemical firm worldwide (second largest in the United States after Du Pont), it has been spending more on production equipment than most of its larger German rivals, and may therefore be very well positioned for soaring profits if a worldwide boom increases demand for chemicals.

The other side of the coin is that Dow could be

stuck with overcapacity if that boom doesn't materialize. The company carries a substantial amount of long-term debt (about 45 percent of capital as of early 1982) and might be forced to go even farther in that direction if its expansion moves prove premature.

To lessen dependence on its basic chemical business, Dow has been diversifying into specialty chemicals and consumer products, a trend exemplified by its 1980 acquisition of the prescription drug business of Richardson-Merrell for some $260 million.

Dividends have been paid each year since 1911 (before the company was incorporated in its present form). The yield in 1981 ranged between 5 percent and 7½ percent.

* * *

DOW JONES & COMPANY, INC. (DJ). Founded 1949. Headquarters: 22 Cortlandt St., New York NY 10007. PUBLISHING. Dow Jones & Company, Inc., publishes *The Wall Street Journal*, *Barron's*, and a chain of local newspapers. It operates a financial wire service (the Dow Jones news ticker), sells financial data bases, owns a textbook house, and owns a minority position in a cable TV company. MAJOR SUBSIDIARIES, BRANDS: Ottaway Newspapers Inc.; Richard D. Irwin Inc., *The Wall Street Journal; Barron's;* Cablevision (24 percent owned).

Sales: $530.7 million (trend 17.2% a year).
Earnings: $58.88 million (trend 17.6% a year).
What happened to a $10,000 investment

Purchase Date	*Purchase Price*	*Price on 12-31-81*	*Dividends Paid*
12-31-71	$21.31	$49.50	$2,948.97
12-31-76	$16.81	$49.50	$2,209.67

Purchase Date	*Cap. Gains (− Losses)*	*Total Return*	*Rate of Return*
12-31-71	$13,225.81	$16,174.78	10.10%
12-31-76	$19,442.38	$21,652.04	25.92%

* * *

DRAVO CORP. (DRV). Founded 1936. Headquarters: 1 Oliver Plaza, Pittsburgh PA 15222. ENGINEERING SERVICES. Dravo Corp. provides construction, design, and engineering services to businesses.

Sales: $1,113.9 million (trend 8.6% a year).
Earnings: $21.16 million (trend 16.0% a year).
What happened to a $10,000 investment

Purchase Date	*Purchase Price*	*Price on 12-31-81*	*Dividends Paid*
12-31-71	$ 9.83	$16.75	$7,027.12
12-31-76	$15.50	$16.75	$2,705.38

Purchase Date	*Cap. Gains (− Losses)*	*Total Return*	*Rate of Return*
12-31-71	$7,033.90	$14,061.02	9.18%
12-31-76	$ 806.45	$ 3,511.83	6.20%

* * *

DRESSER INDUSTRIES, INC. (DI). Founded 1956. Headquarters: 1505 Elm St., Dallas TX 75221. ENERGY SERVICES. Dresser makes drilling equipment for oil and natural gas fields, mining equipment, pipeline equipment, and a variety of capital goods. Also produces minerals used in steelmaking and other high-temperature industrial operations; makes industrial controls, tools, and abrasives. 55,000 employees.

Sales: $4,016.3 million (trend 15.2% a year).
Earnings: $261.10 million (trend 16.2% a year).
What happened to a $10,000 investment

Purchase Date	*Purchase Price*	*Price on 12-31-81*	*Dividends Paid*
12-31-71	$ 8.44	$33.25	$5,185.19
12-31-76	$21.12	$33.25	$1,230.77

Purchase Date	*Cap. Gains (− Losses)*	*Total Return*	*Rate of Return*
12-31-71	$29,407.41	$34,592.59	16.13%
12-31-76	$ 5,739.64	$ 6,970.41	11.16%

PROFILE: The man on the street probably thinks Dresser Industries makes furniture with four drawers to keep your clothes in. But this leading oil field service company is well known in energy circles — and on Wall Street. It also happens to be among the 100 largest industrial companies in the United States (as ranked by *Fortune*) and the 100 largest U.S. employers (as ranked by *Forbes*).

About half the company is concerned with oil field products and services (40 percent of sales and almost 50 percent of earnings in fiscal 1980). The rest is diversified, though many of the operations are energy-related. Since the oil field service segment has been chalking up the strong gains in recent years, some analysts have wondered why Dresser doesn't streamline itself down to those operations and sell off the rest. But chairman John James rejects that idea. "There are a lot of synergis tic sides to us that aren't apparent to the casual observer," he told *The Wall Street Journal* in 1981.

Dresser acquired its comparatively glamorous status on Wall Street fairly recently, with the vogue for energy-related stocks. From 1975 through 1979 the company's price / earnings ratio ranged from 5 to 11. In 1980 it went as high as 17, but by early 1982 it had sunk back to 5, as a (possibly temporary) oil glut depressed oil industry issues. If you contemplate buying the stock, check to see what sort of expectations are currently built into the stock price.

The balance sheet here is nice and trim, with debt recently only about 15 percent of capital. The dividend yield has been low in recent years.

* * *

DREXEL BOND-DEBENTURE TRADING FUND. (DBF). Founded 1971. Headquarters: 1500 Walnut St., Philadelphia PA 19102. **INVESTMENTS.** Drexel Bond-Debenture Trading Fund is a closed-end bond fund that invests primarily in investment-grade bonds, with some lower-quality bonds and convertibles composing up to about 25 percent of the portfolio.

* * *

THE DREYFUS CORP. (DRY). Founded 1947. Headquarters: 767 Fifth Ave., New York NY 10022.

FINANCIAL SERVICES. The Dreyfus Corp. provides financial investment services to individuals and institutions and manages mutual funds.

* * *

E. I. DU PONT DE NEMOURS & CO. (DD). Founded 1915. Headquarters: 1007 Market St., Wilmington DE 19898. **CHEMICALS.** Du Pont is the nation's leading maker of chemicals, and a leading maker of textile fibers. It also produces electronic components and firearms. 134,000 employees. **MAJOR SUBSIDIARIES, BRANDS:** Conoco; Remington firearms; Dacron, Freon, Kevlar, Lucite, Mylar, Qiana, Teflon.

Sales: $13,652.0 million (trend 13.8% a year).
Earnings: $706.00 million (trend 23.9% a year).
What happened to a $10,000 investment

Purchase Date	*Purchase Price*	*Price on 12-31-81*	*Dividends Paid*	*Cap. Gains (− Losses)*	*Total Return*	*Rate of Return*
12-31-71	$48.42	$37.25	$4,402.75	$−2,306.37	$2,096.39	1.92%
12-31-76	$45.04	$37.25	$2,793.71	$−1,729.88	$1,063.83	2.04%

PROFILE: The 1970s were disappointing for Du Pont, a company with a long and distinguished history of innovation. Earnings progress was erratic, slowed by a trudging performance from textile fibers, on which Du Pont had come to depend for about a third of its sales and earnings. The decade wasn't great for profits in the bulk, "commodity" chemicals either, as economic troubles in the United States and abroad held back demand.

The most profitable aspect of Du Pont's operations has been specialty chemicals. It is into this realm — and particularly life sciences — that Du Pont is now pouring substantial amounts of capital. (Capital expenditures were budgeted at about $1.5 billion in 1981 and again in 1982.) That means such things as agricultural chemicals, blood and body fluids analysis equipment, and, especially, genetic engineering. The public hasn't heard much about Du Pont's plunge into genetic engineering because, unlike such competitors as Monsanto, it hasn't chosen to buy into the highly publicized fledgling genetic engineering firms. Rather, following its own tradition, it's engaging in its own genetic engineering research.

Du Pont took a major step in 1981 when it acquired Conoco for some $7.6 billion, outbidding such other stalwarts as Mobil and Seagram. Since it issued new stock to pay for the merger, per-share earnings may be diluted for a while. (The merger also left Seagram holding about 18 percent of Du Pont's stock, since Seagram had already taken a significant stake in Conoco, and traded its Conoco shares for Du Pont shares.) Conoco's 1980 sales, at $18.8 billion, were larger than Du Pont's ($13.6 billion). The combined entity will be approximately the seventh largest U.S. corporation. It will be active in both oil and chemicals, and it's clear that the chemical divisions won't lack for petroleum base.

Some analysts have faulted Du Pont for having fallen into an assumption that a blockbuster product like nylon would come along every decade or so. In fact, Du Pont did develop a blockbuster for the 1970s — Kevlar, a synthetic fiber that's light but so strong it can be substituted for steel in a variety of uses. Kevlar didn't find market acceptance in the 1970s, but Du Pont is continuing to spend big on it, hoping for the product to come into its own in the 1980s.

This stock was out of favor in the late 1970s: It

sold for as little as 6 times earnings during much of 1978, 1979, and 1980. However, investors seemed to be sweetening on its prospects in the early 1980s. In parts of 1981, for example, the p / e ratio was up to 9. The dividend yield in recent years has varied between 4 and 7 percent.

* * *

DUKE POWER CO. (DUK). Founded 1917. Headquarters: 422 S. Church St., Charlotte NC 28242. UTILITY. Provides electric power to some 4 million people in portions of North and South Carolina. 19,000 employees.

Sales: $1,687.1 million (trend 11.5% a year).
Earnings: $252.48 million (trend 20.5% a year).
What happened to a $10,000 investment

Purchase Date	*Purchase Price*	*Price on 12-31-81*	*Dividends Paid*
12-31-71	$23.75	$20.62	$6,886.32
12-31-76	$22.25	$20.62	$4,148.31

Purchase Date	*Cap. Gains (− Losses)*	*Total Return*	*Rate of Return*
12-31-71	$−1,315.79	$5,570.53	4.53%
12-31-76	$ −730.34	$3,417.98	6.06%

PROFILE: Duke gets about two thirds of its generating power from coal, and almost all the rest from nuclear power. It is heavily committed to nuclear power for the future, planning to have eleven nuclear plants by the mid-1990s. (It had three active nuclear plants in 1980.)

Like Chicago's Commonwealth Edison, Duke has found that a commitment to nuclear power brings its share of headaches: public opposition, delays, and skyrocketing construction costs. Particularly in the wake of the Three Mile Island accident, safety worries must be given major consideration; along with such concerns come increased regulatory scrutiny and higher insurance rates.

Duke's long-term debt is about half of capital, which is a heavy debt load, though less than some other utilities carry. Reluctant to keep going back to the well for more debt (bond) financing in the late 1970s and early 1980s (mainly because interest rates were so high), Duke chose instead to issue additional stock six years running. The result was a major dilution of the stock; nevertheless, the company has managed to keep earnings per share, as well as dividends, rising.

Capital gains have been nonexistent for most Duke shareholders in recent years. Utility stocks compete with bonds for the investment dollars of conservative investors; these days, they must yield about as much as bonds to be attractive. In early 1981, Duke yielded more than 12 percent on its common stock, which was priced at a mere 5 times the company's recent earnings.

* * *

DUN & BRADSTREET CORP. (DNB). Founded 1930. Headquarters: 299 Park Ave., New York NY 10017. BUSINESS INFORMATION. Dun & Bradstreet Corp. provides business information such as credit ratings; also involved in broadcasting, publishing, and Moody's financial information services. MAJOR SUBSIDIARIES, BRANDS: Alcon Data Corp.; Funk & Wagnalls, Moody's Investor Service; Corinthian Broadcasting.

Sales: $1,176.1 million (trend 16.5% a year).
Earnings: $102.74 million (trend 20.7% a year).
What happened to a $10,000 investment

Purchase Date	*Purchase Price*	*Price on 12-31-81*	*Dividends Paid*
12-31-71	$34.12	$63.25	$3,838.83
12-31-76	$30.50	$63.25	$2,780.33

Purchase Date	*Cap. Gains (− Losses)*	*Total Return*	*Rate of Return*
12-31-71	$ 8,534.80	$12,373.63	8.39%
12-31-76	$10,737.70	$13,518.03	18.65%

* * *

DUQUESNE LIGHT CO. (DQU). Founded 1912. Headquarters: 435 Sixth Ave., Pittsburgh PA 15219. ELECTRICITY. Duquesne Light Co. provides southwestern Pennsylvania with coal-based electricity.

Sales: $689.5 million (trend 11.9% a year).
Earnings: $69.61 million (trend 2.7% a year).
What happened to a $10,000 investment

Purchase Date	*Purchase Price*	*Price on 12-31-81*	*Dividends Paid*
12-31-71	$24.62	$13.25	$7,061.93
12-31-76	$20.50	$13.25	$4,317.07

Purchase Date	*Cap. Gains (− Losses)*	*Total Return*	*Rate of Return*
12-31-71	$−4,619.29	$2,442.64	2.21%
12-31-76	$−3,536.59	$ 780.49	1.51%

* * *

DYCO PETROLEUM CORP. (DYC). Founded 1971. Headquarters: 1180 Shelard Tower, Wayzata Blvd. at Highway 18, Minneapolis MN 55426. OIL DRILLING. Dyco Petroleum Corp. is involved in the exploration and production of oil and natural gas; often involved in drilling partnerships with public investors.

Sales: $32.4 million (trend 58.3% a year).
Earnings: $8.50 million (trend 53.2% a year).
What happened to a $10,000 investment

Purchase Date	*Purchase Price*	*Price on 12-31-81*	*Dividends Paid*
12-31-71	$N/A	$25.25	$ N/A
12-31-76	$ 2.27	$25.25	$660.33

Purchase Date	*Cap. Gains (− Losses)*	*Total Return*	*Rate of Return*
12-31-71	$ N/A	$ N/A	N/A%
12-31-76	$101,154.89	$101,815.22	62.07%

* * *

DYNAMICS CORPORATION OF AMERICA. (DYA). Founded 1924. Headquarters: 475 Steamboat Rd., Greenwich CT 06830. DIVERSIFIED MANUFACTURING. Dynamics Corporation of America makes farm machinery, electrical and electronic appliances, metal products, and environmental systems.

Sales: $145.3 million (trend 6.9% a year).
Earnings: $12.33 million (trend 8.1% a year).
What happened to a $10,000 investment

Purchase Date	*Purchase Price*	*Price on 12-31-81*	*Dividends Paid*
12-31-71	$7.87	$7.25	$634.92
12-31-76	$5.75	$7.25	$869.57

Purchase Date	*Cap. Gains (− Losses)*	*Total Return*	*Rate of Return*
12-31-71	$−793.65	$−158.73	−.16%
12-31-76	$ 2,608.70	$ 3,478.26	6.15%

E

EG & G, INC. (EGG). Founded 1947. Headquarters: 45 Williams St., Wellesley MA 02181. TECHNICAL SERVICES. EG & G, Inc., provides technical services to government agencies and manufactures instruments used for nuclear and environmental testing. MAJOR SUBSIDIARIES, BRANDS: Almond Instruments Co.; Reynolds Electrical & Engineering; GES Pty. Ltd.

Sales: $613.1 million (trend 27.8% a year).
Earnings: $26.31 million (trend 30.6% a year).
What happened to a $10,000 investment

Purchase Date	*Purchase Price*	*Price on 12-31-81*	*Dividends Paid*
12-31-71	$11.62	$39.50	$1,625.81
12-31-76	$ 8.62	$39.50	$1,843.48

Purchase Date	*Cap. Gains (− Losses)*	*Total Return*	*Rate of Return*
12-31-71	$23,978.49	$25,604.30	13.54%
12-31-76	$35,797.10	$37,640.58	36.65%

* * *

E-SYSTEMS, INC. (EXY). Founded 1972. Headquarters: PO Box 226030, Dallas TX 75266. DEFENSE ELECTRONICS. E-Systems produces high-technology, non-consumer electronic systems and provides aircraft modification, overhaul and maintenance service for government and commercial users. MAJOR SUBSIDIARIES, BRANDS: Serv-Air; Air Asia; Garland; Melpar.

Sales: $442.2 million (trend 10.1% a year).
Earnings: $12.76 million (trend 7.8% a year).
What happened to a $10,000 investment

Purchase Date	*Purchase Price*	*Price on 12-31-81*	*Dividends Paid*
12-31-71	$ 5.19	$50.12	$12,808.52
12-31-76	$21.86	$50.12	$ 2,139.02

Purchase Date	*Cap. Gains (− Losses)*	*Total Return*	*Rate of Return*
12-31-71	$86,511.62	$99,320.14	27.02%
12-31-76	$12,934.17	$15,073.18	20.18%

* * *

EAGLE-PICHER INDUSTRIES, INC. (EPI). Founded 1916. Headquarters: 580 Walnut St., Cincinnati OH 45202. INDUSTRIAL PRODUCTS. Eagle-Picher Industries, Inc., manufactures heavy machinery, industrial products, and automobile parts.

Sales: $543.3 million (trend 10.5% a year).
Earnings: $21.30 million (trend 5.6% a year).
What happened to a $10,000 investment

Purchase Date	*Purchase Price*	*Price on 12-31-81*	*Dividends Paid*
12-31-71	$11.93	$14.25	$5,529.92
12-31-76	$19.44	$14.25	$2,145.34

Purchase Date	*Cap. Gains (− Losses)*	*Total Return*	*Rate of Return*
12-31-71	$ 1,942.85	$ 7,472.77	5.74%
12-31-76	$−2,668.81	$−523.47	−1.07%

* * *

EASCO CORP. (ES). Founded 1919. Headquarters: 201 N. Charles St., Baltimore MD 21201. TOOLS. Easco Corp. manufactures hand tools and industrial products and produces aluminum.

Sales: $357.3 million (trend 12.9% a year).
Earnings: $3.08 million (trend −9.6% a year).
What happened to a $10,000 investment

Purchase Date	*Purchase Price*	*Price on 12-31-81*	*Dividends Paid*
12-31-71	$15.14	$23.25	$5,360.92
12-31-76	$21.50	$23.25	$2,663.95

Purchase Date	*Cap. Gains (− Losses)*	*Total Return*	*Rate of Return*
12-31-71	$5,358.27	$10,719.19	7.56%
12-31-76	$ 813.95	$ 3,477.91	6.15%

* * *

EASTERN AIR LINES, INC. (EAL). Founded 1938. Headquarters: Miami International Airport, Miami FL 33148. AIRLINE. Eastern is approximately the fifth-largest U.S. airline by revenues. 40,000 employees.

Sales: $3,452.5 million (trend 16.3% a year).
Earnings: $−48.69 million.
What happened to a $10,000 investment

Purchase Date	*Purchase Price*	*Price on 12-31-81*	*Dividends Paid*
12-31-71	$22.62	$5.87	$0.00
12-31-76	$ 8.37	$5.87	$0.00

Purchase Date	*Cap. Gains (− Losses)*	*Total Return*	*Rate of Return*
12-31-71	$−7,403.31	$−7,403.31	−12.61%
12-31-76	$−2,985.07	$−2,985.07	−6.85%

PROFILE: This airline is in big trouble. Debt made up almost three quarters of its capital in the early 1980s, and it may need to borrow even more money in order to upgrade its fleet, which remains one of the oldest in the industry.

Former astronaut Frank Borman has received credit for the job he's done as Eastern's chairman, and he deserves it. The innovative wage incentive plan he sold to the company's unions, to almost everyone's surprise, has improved productivity. Under it, workers may earn up to 3½ percent less or more than their scheduled pay, depending on how the airline does in profitability. Borman has also modernized what was a fuel-guzzling fleet by adding newer and more efficient aircraft.

The problem is that productivity needs to be still higher, and the fleet, though better than it was, has a long way to go. The age of Eastern's average plane was about nine years, as of early 1981. Delta and American, by contrast, had an average fleet age of six years. Borman has talked about spending some $9 billion for new planes over the next dozen years or so, but it's not clear where that money will come from.

Eastern has lost money in three of the past ten years, and its profitable years have barely offset its unprofitable ones. No dividends have been paid since 1969. To make matters worse, the airline's pride, the Boston–New York–Washington shuttle, faces competition from a new shuttle entrant, New York Air.

* * *

EASTERN GAS & FUEL ASSOCIATES. (EFU). Founded 1929. Headquarters: 1 Beacon St., Boston MA 02108. UTILITIES. Eastern Gas & Fuel Associates operates coal mines in West Virginia and provides Massachusetts residents with natural gas. MAJOR SUBSIDIARIES, BRANDS: Algonquin Gas Transmission Co. (37 percent owned).

Sales: $1,002.7 million (trend 9.4% a year).
Earnings: $54.77 million (trend −6.1% a year).
What happened to a $10,000 investment

Purchase Date	*Purchase Price*	*Price on 12-31-81*	*Dividends Paid*
12-31-71	$14.19	$24.12	$4,119.11
12-31-76	$26.75	$24.12	$1,678.50

Purchase Date	*Cap. Gains (− Losses)*	*Total Return*	*Rate of Return*
12-31-71	$ 6,999.83	$11,118.95	7.76%
12-31-76	$−981.31	$ 697.20	1.36%

* * *

EASTERN UTILITIES ASSOCIATES. (EUA). Founded 1928. Headquarters: 99 High St., Boston MA 02110. ELECTRICITY. Eastern Utilities Associates generates and sells electricity in southeastern Massachusetts and northern Rhode Island.

Sales: $244.6 million (trend 10.3% a year).
Earnings: $8.99 million (trend 11.3% a year).
What happened to a $10,000 investment

Purchase Date	*Purchase Price*	*Price on 12-31-81*	*Dividends Paid*
12-31-71	$21.87	$11.37	$7,085.71
12-31-76	$18.25	$11.37	$4,383.56

Purchase Date	*Cap. Gains (− Losses)*	*Total Return*	*Rate of Return*
12-31-71	$−4,800.00	$2,285.71	2.08%
12-31-76	$−3,767.12	$ 616.44	1.20%

* * *

EASTMAN KODAK CO. (EK). Founded 1901. Headquarters: 343 State St., Rochester NY 14650. PHOTOGRAPHY. The world's leading maker of photographic equipment, Kodak also produces chemicals, plastics, and fibers. 129,000 employees. MAJOR SUBSIDIARIES, BRANDS: Kodak cameras and film; Eastman Chemicals; Ektachrome, Kodachrome, Ektra, and Colorburst photographic products.

Sales: $9,734.3 million (trend 14.4% a year).
Earnings: $1,153.58 million (trend 14.7% a year).
What happened to a $10,000 investment

Purchase Date	*Purchase Price*	*Price on 12-31-81*	*Dividends Paid*
12-31-71	$97.25	$71.12	$2,401.03
12-31-76	$86.25	$71.12	$1,626.67

Purchase Date	*Cap. Gains (− Losses)*	*Total Return*	*Rate of Return*
12-31-71	$−2,686.38	$−285.35	−.29%
12-31-76	$−1,753.62	$−126.96	−.26%

PROFILE: Things are clicking at Kodak again, after a lull. In the 1960s Kodak was one of the "one decision" stocks, also known as the nifty fifty. You "couldn't go wrong" buying these stocks, it was said.

As often happens on Wall Street, the conventional wisdom proved wrong. The investor who paid $151 a share for Kodak in 1973 saw his investment take a sickening slide all the way down to $41 in 1978. In part, Kodak was hit by the same change in the tide of opinion that sandbagged other great growth stocks like IBM and Xerox. People realized that these stocks couldn't grow astronomically forever, and they became unwilling to pay inflated multiples of earnings for them. Kodak, for example, sold at 37 times earnings in 1972, in contrast to only 8 to 11 times earnings in the last few years.

But part of the trouble was with Kodak itself. After growing rapidly and steadily through the 1960s, the company hit an earnings plateau from 1973 to 1977. Not until 1978 did earnings per share exceed the $4.05 a share earned in 1973. Kodak management has said that part of the trouble came from bringing too many new projects to the market at the same time, so that developmental expenses crimped earnings.

From 1978 through 1980, earnings growth resumed the fast pace traditional at Kodak: $5.59, $6.20, and $7.15 were the profit figures per share for those three years. In 1981, a recession year, profits were up, but less dramatically, to $7.66. Yet the p / e was still only about 9 in early 1982, and the stock pays a moderate dividend (about 4½ percent in early 1981) to boot.

Two added strengths are the company's towering reputation for research and its whistle-clean balance sheet, with long-term debt only about 3 percent of capital. For the prospective buyer of these shares, the main caution is to check and make sure that the p / e ratio hasn't reinflated to an extreme.

* * *

EATON CORP. (ETN). Founded 1916. Headquarters: 100 Erieview Plaza, Cleveland OH 44114. TRUCK COMPONENTS, ELECTRONICS. Eaton is a major manufacturer of components for trucks and (to a lesser extent) cars; also manufactures materials-handling equipment, particularly forklifts, and a variety of industrial process components and electronic equipment. 58,000 employees. MAJOR SUBSIDIARIES, BRANDS: Cutler-Hammer (electronics).

Sales: $3,176.5 million (trend 17.7% a year).
Earnings: $114.76 million (trend 20.1% a year).
What happened to a $10,000 investment

Purchase Date	*Purchase Price*	*Price on 12-31-81*	*Dividends Paid*
12-31-71	$27.83	$31.87	$4,880.24
12-31-76	$29.25	$31.87	$2,695.16

Purchase Date	*Cap. Gains (− Losses)*	*Total Return*	*Rate of Return*
12-31-71	$1,452.10	$6,332.34	5.03%
12-31-76	$ 897.44	$3,592.59	6.33%

PROFILE: If you know Eaton at all, you probably think of it as a maker of truck parts. That's fair enough. "Transportation products" accounted for about half of Eaton's sales in 1979 and close to two thirds of profits, according to Standard & Poor's. Truck parts alone are probably about 35 percent of sales, with the rest of the transportation area made up of parts for trailers and passenger cars.

But Eaton is determined to be not *just* a truck parts maker, and it's been steadily pushing diversification ever since 1975. That year profits fell to $1.77 a share from $3.46 the year before, and the company vowed, "Never again." As chairman E. M. DeWindt told *The Wall Street Journal* in 1980, "Everything we've done since 1974–75 has been to try to reduce the impact of downturns in the transportation business." Now, much of Eaton's business is in industrial process controls and other industrial products, plus electronics, where the company's Cutler-Hammer subsidiary is picking up some lucrative defense business. (It works on the space shuttle and Navy submarines, among other projects.)

The company employs a moderate amount of leverage, with long-term debt recently about 34 percent of capital. Dividends have been paid steadily and raised steadily; the yield has run from 5 to 7 percent in recent years. The company's not glamorous; its stock usually sells for a conservative multiple of earnings — between 5 and 8 in recent years.

* * *

ECHLIN MANUFACTURING CO. (ECH). Founded 1959. Headquarters: 175 N. Branford Rd., Branford CT 06405. AUTOMOTIVE EQUIPMENT. The Echlin Manufacturing Co. manufactures electrical, brake, and fuel systems for automobiles.

Sales: $415.7 million (trend 13.1% a year).
Earnings: $12.74 million (trend −5.1% a year).
What happened to a $10,000 investment

Purchase Date	*Purchase Price*	*Price on 12-31-81*	*Dividends Paid*
12-31-71	$15.62	$12.75	$1,881.60
12-31-76	$14.12	$12.75	$1,430.09

Purchase Date	*Cap. Gains (− Losses)*	*Total Return*	*Rate of Return*
12-31-71	$−1,840.00	$ 41.60	.04%
12-31-76	$ −973.45	$456.64	.90%

* * *

JACK ECKERD CORP. (ECK). Founded 1961. Headquarters: 8333 Bryan Dairy Rd., Clearwater FL 33518. DRUGSTORES. Eckerd's chain of 1,000 drugstores, the nation's second-largest drugstore chain, is concentrated in Florida, Texas, and five other Southern states. 25,000 employees. MAJOR SUBSIDIARIES, BRANDS: Eckerd Drug; Eckerd's Apparel; JByrons department stores; American Home Video Corp.

Sales: $1,752.5 million (trend 20.7% a year).
Earnings: $78.51 million (trend 18.7% a year).
What happened to a $10,000 investment

Purchase Date	*Purchase Price*	*Price on 12-31-81*	*Dividends Paid*
12-31-71	$18.83	$24.42	$1,784.07
12-31-76	$19.25	$24.42	$1,354.11

Purchase Date	*Cap. Gains (− Losses)*	*Total Return*	*Rate of Return*
12-31-71	$2,964.60	$4,748.67	3.96%
12-31-76	$2,683.98	$4,038.10	7.02%

PROFILE: The company has done phenomenally well, spinning off new stores like popping corn, chalking up record sales and profit growth rates (in the 20 percent a year range), and ranking as the nation's most profitable drug chain as well as its second largest.

The stock? Well, in recent years, you could make money in Eckerd stock — *if* you picked your purchase times to take advantage of fluctuations. Shares were as high as $28 to $29 in 1972 and 1973, as low as $6.75 in 1974. For most of the late 1970s the share price fluctuated between $15 and $20. In early 1982 it was around $19, having gone as high as $31.88 in 1981.

Why the relatively weak stock performance when the company has been achieving results any financial analyst (or investor) would drool over? It's that old bugaboo expectations. By the early 1970s everyone could see that Eckerd was a well-managed company on a fast track, located in fast-growth sunbelt states and keyed to the emerging trend toward one-stop shopping. The stock price in the early 1970s had already "discounted," or built in, expectations of the great things that were to come.

Nowadays investors are more conservative in bidding up stocks on expectations of future growth. Where Eckerd carried a p / e above 40 for much of the period 1971–73, it sold for only about 11 times earnings throughout 1981, a multiple only moderately higher than that prevailing at the time for the average stock (8).

Eckerd has a super-clean balance sheet, with barely a trace of debt (2 percent of capital). Its dividend yield in recent years has fluctuated between 2 and 5 percent.

The 1981 acquisition of American Home Video, a small company in a burgeoning market, was dilutive, but could be shrewd. Eckerd chairman Stewart Turley has gone on record as saying that the company can't wring 20 percent annual growth out of the drugstore business indefinitely. Clearly, Eckerd is dipping its toes into a new business with potential for explosive growth.

* * *

EDISON BROTHERS STORES, INC. (EBS). Founded 1922. Headquarters: 400 Washington Ave., PO Box 14020, St. Louis MO 63178. RETAILING. Edison Brothers Stores, Inc., operates retail specialty stores including women's shoe stores, men's and women's apparel stores, and do-it-yourself home centers. MAJOR SUBSIDIARIES, BRANDS: Bakers; Chandlers; Jeans West; Size 5-7-9 Shops; The Wild Pair.

Sales: $853.4 million (trend 12.6% a year).
Earnings: $42.38 million (trend 13.4% a year).
What happened to a $10,000 investment

Purchase Date	*Purchase Price*	*Price on 12-31-81*	*Dividends Paid*
12-31-71	$14.50	$25.25	$5,491.95
12-31-76	$19.92	$25.25	$2,882.01

Purchase Date	*Cap. Gains (– Losses)*	*Total Return*	*Rate of Return*
12-31-71	$7,413.79	$12,905.75	8.64%
12-31-76	$2,677.82	$ 5,559.83	9.24%

* * *

A. G. EDWARDS & SONS, INC. (AGE). Founded 1887. Headquarters: 1 N. Jefferson Ave., St. Louis MO 63103. SECURITIES AND COMMODITIES. A. G. Edwards & Sons, Inc., is a dealer and broker in securities and commodities.

Sales: $181.8 million (trend 22.2% a year).
Earnings: $23.70 million (trend 31.1% a year).
What happened to a $10,000 investment

Purchase Date	*Purchase Price*	*Price on 12-31-81*	*Dividends Paid*
12-31-71	$2.12	$21.12	$8,675.10
12-31-76	$3.21	$21.12	$4,416.50

Purchase Date	*Cap. Gains (– Losses)*	*Total Return*	*Rate of Return*
12-31-71	$89,427.17	$98,102.27	26.88%
12-31-76	$55,876.28	$60,292.78	47.70%

* * *

EL PASO CO. (ELG). Founded 1928. Headquarters: 2727 Allen Parkway, Houston TX 77019. GAS TRANSMISSION. El Paso derives the bulk of its revenues from natural gas transmission in the Southwest. It is also active in oil and gas exploration, petrochemical manufacturing, and to a small extent in coal mining. 8,000 employees.

Sales: $3,543.4 million (trend 23.3% a year).
Earnings: $108.89 million (trend 16.0% a year).
What happened to a $10,000 investment

Purchase Date	*Purchase Price*	*Price on 12-31-81*	*Dividends Paid*
12-31-71	$17.50	$24.87	$6,728.57
12-31-76	$14.87	$24.87	$4,420.17

Purchase Date	*Cap. Gains (– Losses)*	*Total Return*	*Rate of Return*
12-31-71	$4,214.29	$10,942.86	7.67%
12-31-76	$6,722.69	$11,142.86	16.15%

PROFILE: In 1980, the ax fell on El Paso. Algeria stopped delivering liquefied natural gas (LNG) to it for resale in the United States. There, with a single thump, went the business that had provided about 13 percent of the company's 1979 sales — and about 17 percent of profits.

Was the company crippled as a result? It didn't think so. It took a $365 million write-off for the discontinued LNG operation and proceeded to plow money more heavily into its other businesses. The stock market didn't think so either. Though El Paso in 1981 was trading well below its 1980 high of $30.50 a share, it was comfortably above the 1980 low of $15.75 a share.

It's a good bet that El Paso will now put much of its money into exploration and drilling — activities that were already more significant than some investors (who think of this as a pipeline company) realized. In 1979 oil and gas production accounted for only 3 percent of company revenues, but about 12 percent of profits. Both those figures can be expected to grow.

As for the pipeline operations, it may be worth noting that most of El Paso's volume goes not directly to consumers but to industrial users and utilities. That fact might be significant for future pricing, since regulators may be a bit more lenient with price increases that don't directly impact on consumers.

Dividends have been paid yearly since 1936 and the yield recently has ranged from 6 to 9 percent. One possible problem to watch is the debt load, recently about 55 percent of capital.

* * *

ELCOR CORP. (ELK). Founded 1962. Headquarters: 2100 Wilco Bldg., Midland TX 79701. ENGINEERING. Builds plants for the chemical and mining industries. Also manufactures roofing products and chrome plating, and processes equipment for the scrap metal recycling industry. MAJOR SUBSIDIARIES, BRANDS: Elk Corporation of America; Gory Associated Industries, Inc.; Chromium Corp.; Mosley Machinery Company, Inc.

Sales: $265.1 million (trend 25.2% a year).
Earnings: $1.96 million (trend −1.2% a year).
What happened to a $10,000 investment

Purchase Date	*Purchase Price*	*Price on 12-31-81*	*Dividends Paid*
12-31-71	$2.25	$9.25	$4,466.67
12-31-76	$7.25	$9.25	$1,317.24

Purchase Date	*Cap. Gains (− Losses)*	*Total Return*	*Rate of Return*
12-31-71	$31,111.11	$35,577.78	16.38%
12-31-76	$ 2,758.62	$ 4,075.86	7.08%

* * *

ELECTRONIC ASSOCIATES, INC. (EA). Founded 1945. Headquarters: 185 Monmouth Parkway, W. Long Branch NJ 07764. COMPUTERS. Electronic Associates, Inc. manufactures computer systems used in simulated testing and training programs.

Sales: $43.7 million (trend 8.9% a year).
Earnings: $1.76 million (trend 44.9% a year).
What happened to a $10,000 investment

Purchase Date	*Purchase Price*	*Price on 12-31-81*	*Dividends Paid*
12-31-71	$5.50	$6.75	$0.00
12-31-76	$2.62	$6.75	$0.00

Purchase Date	*Cap. Gains (− Losses)*	*Total Return*	*Rate of Return*
12-31-71	$ 2,272.73	$ 2,272.73	2.07%
12-31-76	$15,714.29	$15,714.29	20.79%

* * *

ELECTRONIC DATA SYSTEMS CORP. (EDS). Founded 1962. Headquarters: 7171 Forest Lane, Dallas TX 745230. INFORMATION SYSTEMS. Electronic Data Systems Corp. manufactures electronic data processing systems for government and corporate use. MAJOR SUBSIDIARIES, BRANDS: Centurion Computer Corp.

Sales: $448.6 million (trend 29.3% a year).
Earnings: $37.82 million (trend 22.1% a year).
What happened to a $10,000 investment

Purchase Date	*Purchase Price*	*Price on 12-31-81*	*Dividends Paid*
12-31-71	$23.06	$24.37	$1,643.36
12-31-76	$ 9.12	$24.37	$2,345.21

Purchase Date	*Cap. Gains (− Losses)*	*Total Return*	*Rate of Return*
12-31-71	$ 569.11	$ 2,212.47	2.02%
12-31-76	$16,712.33	$19,057.53	23.78%

* * *

ELECTRONIC MEMORIES & MAGNETICS CORP. (EMM). Founded 1969. Headquarters: 15760 Ventura Blvd., Encino CA 91436. MAGNETIC PRODUCTS. Electronic Memories & Magnetics Corp. manufactures magnetic equipment and materials used in computer memory systems; also makes other computer components.

Sales: $98.8 million (trend 2.9% a year).
Earnings: $1.94 million (trend −22.8% a year).
What happened to a $10,000 investment

Purchase Date	*Purchase Price*	*Price on 12-31-81*	*Dividends Paid*
12-31-71	$6.87	$3.25	$0.00
12-31-76	$3.50	$3.25	$0.00

Purchase Date	*Cap. Gains (− Losses)*	*Total Return*	*Rate of Return*
12-31-71	$−5,272.73	$−5,272.73	−7.22%
12-31-76	$ −714.29	$ −714.29	−1.47%

* * *

ELGIN NATIONAL INDUSTRIES, INC. (ENW). Founded 1968. Headquarters: 120 S. Riverside Plaza, Chicago IL 60606. **COAL.** Elgin National Industries, Inc., designs and builds coal preparation plants; also involved in the manufacture of watches. **MAJOR SUBSIDIARIES, BRANDS:** Clinch River Corp.; Roberts & Schaefer Co.; Bradley, Welby and Elgin watches.

* * *

ELIXIR INDUSTRIES. (EXR). Founded 1953. Headquarters: 17925 S. Broadway, Gardena CA 90248. **AUTOMOTIVE PARTS.** Elixir Industries manufactures component parts for recreational vehicles, mobile homes, and the automotive industry. **MAJOR SUBSIDIARIES, BRANDS:** Alum A Form; Plas-T-Cote; Travel Trim; Tru-Form Plastics.

Sales: $154.3 million (trend 2.2% a year).
Earnings: $2.25 million (trend −14.5% a year).
What happened to a $10,000 investment

Purchase Date	*Purchase Price*	*Price on 12-31-81*	*Dividends Paid*
12-31-71	$17.17	$8.50	$0.00
12-31-76	$ 8.25	$8.50	$0.00

Purchase Date	*Cap. Gains (− Losses)*	*Total Return*	*Rate of Return*
12-31-71	$−5,048.54	$−5,048.54	−6.79%
12-31-76	$ 303.03	$ 303.03	.60%

* * *

EMERSON ELECTRIC CO. (EMR). Founded 1890. Headquarters: 8100 W. Florissant Ave., St. Louis MO 63136. **ELECTRONICS.** Emerson Electric Co. is a major producer of electrical and electronic products. 54,000 employees.

Sales: $3,429.3 million (trend 18.3% a year).
Earnings: $273.27 million (trend 18.6% a year).
What happened to a $10,000 investment

Purchase Date	*Purchase Price*	*Price on 12-31-81*	*Dividends Paid*
12-31-71	$40.12	$45.37	$2,600.37
12-31-76	$34.50	$45.37	$2,028.99

Purchase Date	*Cap. Gains (− Losses)*	*Total Return*	*Rate of Return*
12-31-71	$1,308.41	$3,908.79	3.35%
12-31-76	$3,152.17	$5,181.16	8.71%

PROFILE: How does a company chalk up record earnings for twenty-three straight years while attracting little attention in the business press?

I don't know, but Emerson Electric has managed it. Part of the secret must be that the company is in the Midwest. Part of it may be that the company doesn't make a single, glamorous product like lasers or semiconductors, but rather makes a broad range of products for use by industry, consumers, and government.

One pundit who has noticed the company is Heinz Biel, vice-president of Janney Montgomery Scott and a columnist for *Forbes.* In early 1981 he wrote a glowing recommendation of the stock as undervalued at $38 a share. "I do not know," wrote Biel, "when the stock will break out of the rut of the past six years. . . . Investors in Emerson Electric may have to be patient a while longer, but the eventual reward seems all but inevitable."

In 1981 the company was expected to mark its twenty-fourth straight year of record earnings. It was selling during 1981 at a p / e ratio of about 11, a bit above the market but hardly exorbitant for a stock with its sort of track record. Debt was a mere 13 percent of capital, and return on stockholders' equity is around 20 percent most years. The dividend yield, traditionally modest, has been raised to a moderate 4 to 5 percent in recent years. Dividends have been paid each year since 1946 and raised each year since 1973.

* * *

EMERSON RADIO CORP. (EME). Founded 1977. Headquarters: 1 Emerson Lane, Secaucus NJ 07094. **RADIOS.** Emerson Radio Corp. manufactures and sells radios and stereos. **MAJOR SUBSIDIARIES, BRANDS:** Cardiac Resuscitator Corp. (80 percent owned).

Sales: $87.4 million (trend 28.4% a year).
Earnings: $−.25 million.
What happened to a $10,000 investment

Purchase Date	*Purchase Price*	*Price on 12-31-81*	*Dividends Paid*
12-31-71	$2.76	$12.25	$0.00
12-31-76	$3.51	$12.25	$0.00

Purchase Date	*Cap. Gains (– Losses)*	*Total Return*	*Rate of Return*
12-31-71	$34,455.67	$34,455.67	16.09%
12-31-76	$24,900.87	$24,900.87	28.40%

* * *

EMERY AIR FREIGHT CORP. (EAF). Founded 1946. Headquarters: Old Danbury Rd., Wilton CT 06897. **AIR FREIGHT.** Emery is a major carrier of U.S. air freight; also active in international air freight and domestic overnight express delivery of small packages. 4,000 employees. **MAJOR SUBSIDIARIES, BRANDS:** Blue Ribbon Insurance; Emery Ocean Freight.

Sales: $550.7 million (trend 18.2% a year).
Earnings: $21.56 million (trend 11.6% a year).
What happened to a $10,000 investment

Purchase Date	*Purchase Price*	*Price on 12-31-81*	*Dividends Paid*
12-31-71	$19.53	$12.75	$3,411.20
12-31-76	$18.69	$12.75	$2,445.48

Purchase Date	*Cap. Gains (– Losses)*	*Total Return*	*Rate of Return*
12-31-71	$–3,472.00	$ –60.80	–.06%
12-31-76	$–3,177.26	$–731.77	–1.51%

PROFILE: During the 1970s, Emery Air Freight's earnings more than quadrupled, from 38 cents a share in 1971 to $1.39 a share in 1980. The dividend exactly quadrupled, from 25 cents to $1. Revenues almost quintupled, from some $114 million to almost $553 million. Throughout the period Emery enjoyed a stunning return on equity, often in the area of 35 percent. In the *Forbes* tally of more than 1,000 companies' profitability from 1975–80, Emery ranked among the top twenty companies. What do you think happened to the stock price?

It went down.

That's right — despite the company's turning in one of American industry's outstanding performances for the decade, the price of an Emery share in early 1981 was about $16 as opposed to the 1973 high of $37.50. Even back in 1971, Emery shares went for as much as $19.50.

How can one explain such a freakish occurrence? In a nutshell, Emery was overvalued in the early 1970s (along with a host of other growth stocks), and it may well be undervalued today. The p / e ratio from 1971 to 1973 ranged from 32 to 56. In early 1981 it was 12. That's twelve times a recession year's earnings for an outstanding growth stock. The multiple of 12 was 50 percent higher than the stock market as a whole commanded at the time.

In the early 1980s it was possible to point to problems ahead for Emery. The biggest one was that the air freight business was no longer expanding in miles and tons (this may well have been a temporary setback), though it was still expanding in dollars.

Another problem: Emery's traditional strategy of "wet leasing" space on commercial aircraft was no longer viable. (As fuel costs soared, airlines cut back on their night flights.) So Emery was spending heavily to buy its own planes. That, in turn, might add substantially to the debt load of a company that had been debt-free as recently as 1977 and still had very little debt (less than 10 percent of capital) in late 1981.

The high cost of fuel itself was a third problem. Rolling these three problems together, some analysts doubted that Emery would be able to maintain its traditional high-dividend payout. (Emery has paid dividends each year since 1952. The stock yielded between 6 percent and 8 percent during 1981.) But even if the dividend should be cut, Emery shares offer the growth-oriented investor something worthy of consideration in the early 1980s.

* * *

EMHART CORP. (EMH). Founded 1902. Headquarters: 426 Colt Highway, Farmington CT 06032. **DIVERSIFIED MANUFACTURER.** Emhart (through the 1976 merger of USM Corp.) is the country's largest maker of machinery for shoe manufacturing. Also makes machines for the manufacture of glass, rubber, metal, and plastic products; fasteners, car components; electronic components; hardware; adhesives, coatings, and sealants; and a variety of other products. 37,000 employees. **MAJOR SUBSIDIARIES, BRANDS:** USM Corp.; Mallory Components Group.

Sales: $1,802.9 million (trend 30.4% a year).
Earnings: $66.70 million (trend 19.3% a year).
What happened to a $10,000 investment

Purchase Date	*Purchase Price*	*Price on 12-31-81*	*Dividends Paid*
12-31-71	$21.83	$32.12	$7,012.20
12-31-76	$29.10	$32.12	$3,652.92

Purchase Date	*Cap. Gains (— Losses)*	*Total Return*	*Rate of Return*
12-31-71	$4,713.73	$11,725.93	8.07%
12-31-76	$1,039.52	$ 4,692.44	8.00%

PROFILE: Emhart, said a leading investment service patronizingly in early 1981, has a "fairly good" earnings record. The truth is, most big American corporations would be glad to settle for the growth and profitability Emhart achieved during the past decade. Earnings ranged from $1.87 to $2.12 in 1971–73. They ranged from $4.30 to $5.77 in 1978–80.

And Emhart, it should be noted, does not dolly up its earnings figures to look good. If anything, it does the opposite, preferring an extremely conservative accounting basis. *Forbes* magazine in 1979 theorized that Emhart keeps its books so conservatively so as not to look too attractive to potential acquisitors. In the same vein, though the company's headquarters are in Connecticut, it is incorporated in Virginia. Why? Well, noted *Forbes* reporter Sharon Reier, in Virginia "the antitakeover laws are tough."

One thing that makes Emhart attractive to outsiders is its cash position. Just about all of its businesses are in mature industries. That doesn't inflame the lust of Wall Street — which is why Emhart sold at only 6 to 7 times earnings in 1981 (a multiple fairly typical of the period from 1974 on). But it means that Emhart generates tremendous cash flow. The company's balance sheet is extremely strong, with debt recently only about 6 percent of capital. "Cash cow" is the word analysts often apply to Emhart's shoe machinery operation (formerly USM Corp.). But it could really apply to the whole company.

The cash is amply shared with stockholders. The dividend (paid each year since 1902) has been raised each year since 1971. The yield, in early 1982, was more than 7 percent.

* * *

EMPIRE DISTRICT ELECTRIC CO. (EDE). Founded 1909. Headquarters: 602 Joplin St., Joplin MO 64801. **ELECTRICITY.** Empire District Electric Co. provides southwestern Missouri and surrounding areas with coal-generated electricity.

Sales: $87.9 million (trend 16.4% a year).
Earnings: $6.66 million (trend 16.0% a year).
What happened to a $10,000 investment

Purchase Date	*Purchase Price*	*Price on 12-31-81*	*Dividends Paid*
12-31-71	$19.67	$10.25	$6,839.00
12-31-76	$16.12	$10.25	$4,359.69

Purchase Date	*Cap. Gains (— Losses)*	*Total Return*	*Rate of Return*
12-31-71	$−4,788.14	$2,050.86	1.88%
12-31-76	$−3,643.41	$ 716.28	1.39%

* * *

EMPIRE INC. (EI). Founded 1963. Headquarters: 1700 S. Jefferson St., Lebanon MO 65536. **PROPANE DISTRIBUTOR.** Empire distributes propane and butane gas in most of the United States; also converts car and truck fleets to propane fuel, explores for and drills for oil and gas, and leases and sells high-reach equipment in the Southwest. 1,000 employees. **MAJOR SUBSIDIARIES, BRANDS:** Empire Machinery Corp.

Sales: $284.5 million (trend 31.7% a year).
Earnings: $−.36 million.
What happened to a $10,000 investment

Purchase Date	*Purchase Price*	*Price on 12-31-81*	*Dividends Paid*
12-31-71	$4.94	$14.75	$2,349.37
12-31-76	$4.59	$14.75	$2,416.33

Purchase Date	*Cap. Gains (— Losses)*	*Total Return*	*Rate of Return*
12-31-71	$19,873.42	$22,222.78	12.41%
12-31-76	$22,108.84	$24,525.17	28.12%

PROFILE: Empire is speculative because of the stock's volatility, high price-earnings ratio, and high debt load. It's a young, relatively small, rapidly growing, risk-taking company.

What do I mean by volatility? How about a trading range of $12 to $49.50 a share in 1981? This stock is not without risk.

But the underlying trend has definitely been up, at least since 1977 when the stock ranged between about $4.50 and $8 a share. Several forces have been working in the company's favor: the energy shortage, price decontrol of petroleum and natural gas, and the economy of propane compared to gasoline (propane has been about 75 percent cheaper). Fleet owners have been storming Empire's gates with requests to convert buses, trucks, and cars to the cheaper fuel.

Instead of diversifying when things looked bleak, Empire chairman Robert Plaster has wisely diversified while things are going well. His aim: to reduce Empire's extreme seasonal swings and volatility to manageable levels. The high-reach equipment leasing and sales venture is only one of a number of diversification moves that can be expected. The company made a pass at Biscayne Federal Savings & Loan Association of Miami, but backed out in the face of opposition and sold its holdings at a profit to Kaufman & Broad.

If you are thinking of investing here, check the latest p / e ratio (it gets inflated at times) and the debt ratio. Recently, debt was more than half of total capital. That's a lot of leverage — okay for people who want a lot of speculative action for their buck, but a bit much for more conservative investors.

* * *

ENGELHARD CORP. (EC). Founded 1938. Headquarters: Menlo Park, Box CN40, Edison NJ 08818. METALS. Engelhard is a leading fabricator of precious metals; also involved in mining kaolin and other minerals. 8,000 employees.

PROFILE: In 1981, the secretive but highly regarded colossus Engelhard Minerals & Chemicals Corp. split itself in two. One part became this corporation; the other, which is involved in commodities trading, became Phibro Corp., which is profiled elsewhere in this volume.

Both parts were and are profitable. Revenues of the metals and mining arm, Engelhard Corp., amounted to more than $3 billion in 1980, the year before the split-up. One of its major businesses is producing the components (including processed platinum) for catalytic converters to control pollution in automobile exhaust. Precious metals refining, precious metals recovery, and nonprecious minerals mining are also important activities here. The chief mineral produced is kaolin, which is used in various chemical processes and is a component of some high-grade paper coatings.

Engelhard has often been considered undervalued on Wall Street, to the point where the "undervalued" tag begins to seem a part of the name, as it does with certain baseball players. In 1981 the stock market began to show a bit more appreciation for these shares, bidding the p / e ratio up from 6 to about 9. The company's profitability has been above average, with a return on equity close to 20 percent. The balance sheet is strong, with debt recently less than 10 percent of total capital.

About 27 percent of the company is owned by Anglo American Corp. of South Africa.

* * *

ENNIS BUSINESS FORMS, INC. (EBF). Founded 1909. Headquarters: 107 N. Sherman St., Ennis TX 75119. BUSINESS FORMS. Ennis Business Forms, Inc., produces business forms and stationery supplies. MAJOR SUBSIDIARIES, BRANDS: Connolly Tool & Engineering Co.; Novo Script; Enline.

Sales: $84.0 million (trend 8.5% a year).
Earnings: $5.82 million (trend 19.5% a year).
What happened to a $10,000 investment

Purchase Date	*Purchase Price*	*Price on 12-31-81*	*Dividends Paid*
12-31-71	$5.17	$20.50	$4,876.77
12-31-76	$4.17	$20.50	$4,191.20

Purchase Date	*Cap. Gains (− Losses)*	*Total Return*	*Rate of Return*
12-31-71	$29,677.42	$34,554.19	16.12%
12-31-76	$39,200.00	$43,391.20	39.80%

* * *

ENSERCH CORP. (ENS). Founded 1942. Headquarters: 301 S. Harwood St., Dallas TX 75201. NATURAL GAS, OIL. Distributes natural gas in Texas and Oklahoma, and is involved in natural gas and oil exploration. MAJOR SUBSIDIARIES, BRANDS: Pool Co.; Ebasco Services; Lone Star Gas.

Sales: $2,694.9 million (trend 28.9% a year).
Earnings: $139.58 million (trend 21.5% a year).
What happened to a $10,000 investment

Purchase Date	*Purchase Price*	*Price on 12-31-81*	*Dividends Paid*
12-31-71	$12.11	$25.25	$6,992.66
12-31-76	$13.11	$25.25	$3,883.05

Purchase Date	*Cap. Gains (− Losses)*	*Total Return*	*Rate of Return*
12-31-71	$10,848.62	$17,841.28	10.78%
12-31-76	$ 9,258.47	$13,141.53	18.27%

* * *

ENSOURCE INC. (EEE). Founded 1981. Headquarters: 5575 DTC Parkway, Englewood CO 80111. NATURAL GAS. Explores for and produces oil and natural gas, mainly in the Gulf Coast and Rocky Mountain states. MAJOR SUBSIDIARIES, BRANDS: Opco Oil Development Inc.; Palo Petroleum Inc.

* * *

ENTERRA CORP. (EN). Founded 1981. Headquarters: 2 Radnor Corporate Center, 100 Matsonford Rd., Radnor PA 19087. ENERGY, FIRE PROTECTION. Company was formed in 1981 as a spin-off of certain operations from Philadelphia Suburban Corp. Its chief activity is renting equipment to oil and gas drillers. It also produces specialized fire-fighting equipment.

Sales: $338.0 million (trend 13.0% a year).
Earnings: $35.63 million (trend 18.6% a year).
What happened to a $10,000 investment

Purchase Date	*Purchase Price*	*Price on 12-31-81*	*Dividends Paid*
12-31-71	$10.31	$50.50	$8,164.85
12-31-76	$16.25	$50.50	$3,120.00

Purchase Date	*Cap. Gains (– Losses)*	*Total Return*	*Rate of Return*
12-31-71	$38,969.70	$47,134.55	19.04%
12-31-76	$21,076.92	$24,196.92	27.88%

* * *

ENTEX, INC. (ETX). Founded 1966. Headquarters: 1200 Milam St., PO Box 2628, Houston TX 77001. NATURAL GAS. Entex, Inc., distributes natural gas; also involved in oil and natural gas exploration, drilling, and savings and loan services. MAJOR SUBSIDIARIES, BRANDS: University Savings Association of Houston.

Sales: $981.6 million (trend 23.3% a year).
Earnings: $42.86 million (trend 16.5% a year).
What happened to a $10,000 investment

Purchase Date	*Purchase Price*	*Price on 12-31-81*	*Dividends Paid*
12-31-71	$2.96	$13.25	$13,470.15
12-31-76	$7.98	$13.25	$ 3,912.13

Purchase Date	*Cap. Gains (– Losses)*	*Total Return*	*Rate of Return*
12-31-71	$34,787.59	$48,257.74	19.27%
12-31-76	$ 6,614.00	$10,526.13	15.47%

* * *

ENVIROTECH CORP. (EVT). Founded 1969. Headquarters: 3000 Sand Hill Rd., Menlo Park CA 94025. INDUSTRIAL EQUIPMENT. Envirotech Corp. manufactures industrial processing and water treatment equipment and also makes mining machinery.

Sales: $383.0 million (trend 1.1% a year).
Earnings: $–5.96 million.
What happened to a $10,000 investment

Purchase Date	*Purchase Price*	*Price on 12-31-81*	*Dividends Paid*
12-31-71	$33.50	$15.87	$880.60
12-31-76	$34.25	$15.87	$773.72

Purchase Date	*Cap. Gains (– Losses)*	*Total Return*	*Rate of Return*
12-31-71	$–5,261.19	$–4,380.60	–5.60%
12-31-76	$–5,364.96	$–4,591.24	–11.57%

* * *

EQUIFAX INC. (EFX). Founded 1913. Headquarters: 1600 Peachtree St. N.W., PO Box 4081, Atlanta GA 30302. INFORMATION. Equifax Inc. provides businesses with consumers' credit records, employment records, and insurance-claim-related records; also performs market research.

Sales: $371.1 million (trend 10.1% a year).
Earnings: $10.53 million (trend 3.3% a year).
What happened to a $10,000 investment

Purchase Date	*Purchase Price*	*Price on 12-31-81*	*Dividends Paid*
12-31-71	$40.75	$23.25	$5,288.34
12-31-76	$29.50	$23.25	$3,847.46

Purchase Date	*Cap. Gains (– Losses)*	*Total Return*	*Rate of Return*
12-31-71	$–4,294.48	$ 993.87	.95%
12-31-76	$–2,118.64	$1,728.81	3.24%

* * *

EQUIMARK CORP. (EQK). Founded 1871. Headquarters: 2 Oliver Plaza, Pittsburgh PA 15222. BANKING SERVICES. Equimark Corp. is the holding company for Equibank, which provides banking services in southwest Pennsylvania. MAJOR SUBSIDIARIES, BRANDS: Equibank (banking); Nottingham Corp. (insurance).

Sales: $290.0 million (trend 8.6% a year).
Earnings: $7.63 million (trend –.9% a year).
What happened to a $10,000 investment

Purchase Date	*Purchase Price*	*Price on 12-31-81*	*Dividends Paid*
12-31-71	$18.92	$5.12	$4,565.66
12-31-76	$12.37	$5.12	$3,604.04

Purchase Date	*Cap. Gains (− Losses)*	*Total Return*	*Rate of Return*
12-31-71	$−7,290.75	$−2,725.09	−3.13%
12-31-76	$−5,858.59	$−2,254.55	−4.98%

* * *

EQUITABLE GAS CO. (EQT). Founded 1926. Headquarters: 420 Blvd. of the Allies, Pittsburgh PA 15219. NATURAL GAS. Equitable Gas Co. distributes natural gas to Pittsburgh and areas of West Virginia and Kentucky; also involved in natural gas liquids extraction. **MAJOR SUBSIDIARIES, BRANDS:** Equitable Gas-Energy; Kentucky Hydrocarbon Co.; Philadelphia Oil; West Virginia Gas Co.

Sales: $362.6 million (trend 20.8% a year).
Earnings: $34.06 million (trend 19.9% a year).
What happened to a $10,000 investment

Purchase Date	*Purchase Price*	*Price on 12-31-81*	*Dividends Paid*
12-31-71	$11.42	$35.75	$8,400.00
12-31-76	$12.37	$35.75	$4,422.90

Purchase Date	*Cap. Gains (− Losses)*	*Total Return*	*Rate of Return*
12-31-71	$21,313.87	$29,713.87	14.79%
12-31-76	$18,888.89	$23,311.78	27.21%

* * *

THE EQUITABLE LIFE MORTGAGE AND REALTY INVESTORS. (EQ). Founded 1970. Headquarters: 1 Federal St., Boston MA 02110. REAL ESTATE. The Equitable Life Mortgage and Realty Investors is engaged in real estate investments, diversified as to the type of investment, type of real property and location.

Sales: $47.1 million (trend 8.3% a year).
Earnings: $3.14 million (trend −16.6% a year).
What happened to a $10,000 investment

Purchase Date	*Purchase Price*	*Price on 12-31-81*	*Dividends Paid*
12-31-71	$29.25	$9.25	$6,871.79
12-31-76	$26.37	$9.25	$3,541.23

Purchase Date	*Cap. Gains (− Losses)*	*Total Return*	*Rate of Return*
12-31-71	$−6,837.61	$ 34.19	.03%
12-31-76	$−6,492.89	$−2,951.66	−6.76%

* * *

ESMARK, INC. (ESM). Founded 1885 as Swift & Co., reincorporated 1972 as Esmark. Headquarters: 55 E. Monroe St., Chicago IL 60603. CONSUMER PRODUCTS, SPECIALTY CHEMICALS. Esmark is a highly diversified company, involved mainly in manufacture of a variety of consumer products, and also in fertilizer production (including phosphate mining), processed meat, dental equipment manufacture, and specialty chemical manufacture. 45,000 employees. **MAJOR SUBSIDIARIES, BRANDS:** Swift & Co. (meats); Playtex International (household rubber products, bras, hosiery); International Jensen (car stereos); STP Corp. (car engine additives); Estech Inc. (a holding company within the larger holding company); Doric Co. (dental supplies).

Sales: $2,924.9 million (trend −4.4% a year).
Earnings: $55.86 million (trend −3.3% a year).
What happened to a $10,000 investment

Purchase Date	*Purchase Price*	*Price on 12-31-81*	*Dividends Paid*
12-31-71	$23.20	$51.50	$4,832.76
12-31-76	$28.60	$51.50	$2,588.81

Purchase Date	*Cap. Gains (− Losses)*	*Total Return*	*Rate of Return*
12-31-71	$12,198.28	$17,031.03	10.46%
12-31-76	$ 8,006.99	$10,595.80	15.55%

PROFILE: Esmark has undergone a major restructuring in recent years. But its moves seem more those of a company groping for an identity (and profitability) than those of a company executing a clearly defined plan.

In the beginning there was Swift & Co., one of the nation's largest meat packers. Over the years, it diversified. The name change to Esmark in 1972 confirmed that the company was now a conglomerate, not a meat packer. Unfortunately, the conglomerate failed to distinguish itself in either growth or profitability. In 1980 chairman Donald Kelly announced a dramatic shakeup. The company would sell off its most profitable subsidiary, Vickers Petroleum, which had provided 41 percent of the company's earnings (on only 14 percent of sales). Along with Vickers, Esmark would sell off the rest of its energy business (Doric Petroleum and TransOcean Oil), plus its original business, fresh meat packing.

As you might expect, it was easy to find buyers for the energy businesses, giving Esmark a big, if temporary, boost in profits and cash on hand. The meat packing business has been harder to get rid of, but was finally sold in mid-1981. The company will keep its other food operations (poultry, peanut butter, processed meats) under the Swift & Co. banner and hope for improvement in what has been a very poor profit showing.

Esmark's other three divisions (Estech, Playtex, and automotive) have been profitable, Playtex most of all. The company has been doing well in consumer products, in part by spending very heavily on advertising.

Of course, bras and car stereos are more vulnerable to recession than meat and oil. The new Esmark saw profits plummet to $2.61 a share in 1980 from $4.40 the year before. That's for the continuing operations. Selling off the energy divisions brought in a one-time gain of close to $20 a share, which will be used to reduce debt and finance acquisitions.

* * *

ESQUIRE, INC. (ESQ). Founded 1937. Headquarters: 488 Madison Ave., New York NY 10022. EDUCATIONAL MATERIALS. Esquire, Inc., manufactures educational print products, films, and multimedia products; also involved in music publishing and the manufacture of commercial and industrial light fixtures. *Esquire* magazine, which gave the company its name, was sold in 1977. MAJOR SUBSIDIARIES, BRANDS: Belwin-Mills Publishing Corp.; Craftlite; Globe Book Co.; Wide-Lite Corp.

Sales: $110.1 million (trend 9.5% a year).
Earnings: $7.93 million (trend 72.9% a year).
What happened to a $10,000 investment

Purchase Date	*Purchase Price*	*Price on 12-31-81*	*Dividends Paid*
12-31-71	$11.25	$28.37	$3,066.67
12-31-76	$ 8.50	$28.37	$2,482.35

Purchase Date	*Cap. Gains (– Losses)*	*Total Return*	*Rate of Return*
12-31-71	$15,222.22	$18,288.89	10.96%
12-31-76	$23,382.35	$25,864.71	29.10%

* * *

ESSEX CHEMICAL CORP. (ESX). Founded 1955. Headquarters: 1401 Broad St., Clifton NJ 07015. CHEMICALS. Essex Chemical Corp. manufactures chemical products; also produces Christmas decorations and electric generators. MAJOR SUBSIDIARIES, BRANDS: Essex Frank; Minerec Corp.; Racon Inc.

Sales: $152.1 million (trend 26.0% a year).
Earnings: $5.50 million (trend 18.1% a year).
What happened to a $10,000 investment

Purchase Date	*Purchase Price*	*Price on 12-31-81*	*Dividends Paid*
12-31-71	$3.20	$19.25	$9,806.54
12-31-76	$6.10	$19.25	$4,555.98

Purchase Date	*Cap. Gains (– Losses)*	*Total Return*	*Rate of Return*
12-31-71	$50,109.63	$59,916.17	21.47%
12-31-76	$21,583.03	$26,139.00	29.30%

* * *

ESTERLINE CORP. (ESL). Founded 1967. Headquarters: 1120 Post Rd., Darien CT 06820. AUTOMATION EQUIPMENT. Esterline Corp. manufactures electronic equipment, scientific instruments, and precision controls.

Sales: $243.4 million (trend 15.9% a year).
Earnings: $19.66 million (trend 54.5% a year).
What happened to a $10,000 investment

Purchase Date	*Purchase Price*	*Price on 12-31-81*	*Dividends Paid*
12-31-71	$4.50	$23.50	$5,382.72
12-31-76	$3.67	$23.50	$4,727.27

Purchase Date	*Cap. Gains (– Losses)*	*Total Return*	*Rate of Return*
12-31-71	$42,222.22	$47,604.94	19.14%
12-31-76	$54,090.91	$58,818.18	47.08%

* * *

ETHYL CORP. (EY). Founded 1887. Headquarters: 330 S. Fourth St., Richmond VA 23217. CHEMICALS. Ethyl makes both basic and specialty chemicals, including lead antiknock compounds for gasoline (of which it's the largest manufacturer). Also involved in plastics, aluminum products, insurance and (on a small but growing scale) coal, gas, and oil production. 16,000 employees. MAJOR SUBSIDIARIES, BRANDS: First Colony Life Insurance Co.

Sales: $1,740.6 million (trend 11.7% a year).
Earnings: $86.24 million (trend 9.5% a year).
What happened to a $10,000 investment

Purchase Date	*Purchase Price*	*Price on 12-31-81*	*Dividends Paid*
12-31-71	$12.44	$23.50	$7,501.51
12-31-76	$21.62	$23.50	$2,924.86

Purchase Date	*Cap. Gains (− Losses)*	*Total Return*	*Rate of Return*
12-31-71	$8,894.47	$16,395.98	10.19%
12-31-76	$ 867.05	$ 3,791.91	6.64%

PROFILE: "It's been terribly frustrating," Ethyl president Bruce Gottwald told *The Wall Street Journal* in 1979, "to have a good product and in a decade see it become a sacrificial lamb." The product is tetraethyl lead antiknock compound; some readers may remember when "fill it with ethyl" was synonymous with "fill it with premium." Antiknock compounds accounted for all of Ethyl's profits in the late 1950s, about 80 percent of profits during the late 1960s, and about 40 percent of profits (on 25 percent of sales) as recently as 1978. Now, unless the Reagan administration reverses the environmental protection trend that prevailed during the 1970s, it appears that business will soon shrivel to near nothing, because of a societal commitment to get lead out of the environment.

The loss of antiknock compounds is clearly nothing Ethyl welcomes, but is it the disaster it appears? If so, why was this stock selling at about 7 times earnings in early 1981? That's a low p / e ratio, to be sure, but the whole market was low — the average stock at the time had a p / e of about 8. The fact is that Ethyl long since saw the handwriting on the wall, and has been diversifying into other specialty chemicals, plastics, aluminum doors and windows, and coal production, to hit only the highlights. In 1981 it diversified further by acquiring First Colony Life Insurance Co.

"Ethyl Corp., a highflier until the 1970s, keeps reeling from environmental jabs." That was *The Wall Street Journal*'s headline in 1979. But Ethyl never flew terrifically high back then. (For example, 1966 earnings weren't duplicated until 1971.) And it's not doing so badly now. Earnings rose from $1.68 a share in 1971 to $4.49 in 1980. Over the same period, the stock rose from a 1971 high of $15 to a 1980 high of $36.50 a share. What's more, the company steadily pared its debt during the 1970s, from about 46 percent of capital to about 24 percent at the start of the 1980s. Dividends, paid yearly since 1957, offered a 5 percent yield in early 1981.

* * *

EVANS PRODUCTS CO. (EVY). Founded 1923. Headquarters: 1121 S.W. Salmon St., Portland OR 97208. **BUILDING SUPPLIES, MANUFACTURING.** Evans is a major retailer of building supplies to do-it-yourselfers and small contractors, and a major manufacturer and leaser of boxcars and truck trailers. Also involved in manufacture of prefabricated homes (sold partially finished), doors, windows, and cabinets; and in forest products. 18,000 employees. Evans has agreed in principle to be acquired by Sharon Steel Corp. **MAJOR SUBSIDIARIES, BRANDS:** Alamo Enterprises; Grossman's; Hubbard & Johnson; Lindsley; Moore's (building-supply stores).

Sales: $1,423.5 million (trend 16.0% a year).
Earnings: $36.43 million (trend 25.9% a year).
What happened to a $10,000 investment

Purchase Date	*Purchase Price*	*Price on 12-31-81*	*Dividends Paid*
12-31-71	$24.27	$17.50	$3,183.07
12-31-76	$13.25	$17.50	$4,830.19

Purchase Date	*Cap. Gains (− Losses)*	*Total Return*	*Rate of Return*
12-31-71	$−2,789.34	$ 393.73	.39%
12-31-76	$ 3,207.55	$8,037.74	12.52%

PROFILE: Too much diversification, too much emphasis on growth and not enough on profitability: That was Evans's problem in the early 1970s. Now the clutter has been trimmed back; the company is concentrating on building-supply stores and boxcar and truck trailer operations. Those operations rise and fall with the economy, but not as much as you might think. When people aren't buying new homes, they're more likely to spend money on remodeling the homes they have.

Still, Evans Products saw its earnings go down with a thump in 1980 ($2.96 a share versus $4.65 the year before). In 1981 they dropped still further, to $0.83 a share. What was hurting as much as the recession was sky-high interest rates. Fleet owners and railroads are less likely to buy or lease boxcars and trailers when interest rates are high; consumers are less likely to build homes. In addition, Evans is paying quite a chunk of interest on its own debt. In 1979 the company's profits after taxes were some $62 million; interest on debt was about $36 million. Debt, as of the end of 1979, was about 40 percent of capital. That's a lot, but a good deal less than the 65 percent debt load the company carried in 1974. "We were great believers in leverage," chairman

Monford Orloff ruefully told *Forbes* magazine in 1980.

Despite recent earnings problems, the stock didn't drop a great deal in 1980 or 1981. Recent and current problems were balanced against what looked like chances for a solid recovery over the next few years.

In 1982, Evans announced that it had agreed in principle to be taken over by Sharon Steel Corp., which in turn is 87 percent owned by NVF Co.

* * *

EX-CELL-O CORP. (XLO). Founded 1919. Headquarters: 2855 Coolidge Rd., Troy MI 48084. MACHINERY. Ex-Cell-O is a major manufacturer of machine tools, cutting tools, packaging machinery, construction equipment, and other industrial equipment. It also has operations in aerospace, auto parts, and weaponry. 16,000 employees.

Sales: $1,020.7 million (trend 23.6% a year).
Earnings: $50.40 million (trend 22.9% a year).
What happened to a $10,000 investment

Purchase Date	*Purchase Price*	*Price on 12-31-81*	*Dividends Paid*
12-31-71	$11.17	$22.37	$7,961.49
12-31-76	$17.17	$22.37	$3,353.59

Purchase Date	*Cap. Gains (— Losses)*	*Total Return*	*Rate of Return*
12-31-71	$10,037.31	$17,998.81	10.84%
12-31-76	$ 3,033.98	$ 6,387.57	10.38%

PROFILE: Ex-Cell-O has genuine diversification, but make no mistake about it, this is basically a machinery company. A wide variety of machinery (the items described above, plus a few more) accounted for more than half of sales recently, and more than two thirds of profits.

Of the company's other divisions, the most successful is aerospace — chiefly jet engine parts and aircraft fuel meters. In fall of 1981 the *Value Line Investment Survey* reported that Ex-Cell-O's aerospace division had already booked orders to the limit of its 1982 production capacity, and was taking orders for 1983 and 1984. This division recently has chipped in about a fifth of sales and earnings.

Less successful, not surprisingly, has been the auto parts group, which makes a variety of components from bumpers to windshield squirter systems. The auto industry has been in a prolonged slump; so, therefore, has this division, which recently accounted for a fifth of sales but only about 6 percent of company profits. An eventual rebound in auto sales should help. The weaponry (ordnance) division, which makes armored vehicles, is small, but expanding rapidly.

More important for Ex-Cell-O, though, is the projected boom in capital equipment spending by factories once the on-again, off-again recession stops dogging the American economy. Tax incentives for business spending on capital equipment are already in place.

Ex-Cell-O's balance sheet is strong, with long-term debt recently only about 13 percent of capital. Dividends have been paid yearly since 1936, and provide a moderate yield.

* * *

EXCELSIOR INCOME SHARES, INC. (EIS). Founded 1973. Headquarters: 20 Exchange Place, New York NY 10005. SECURITIES. Excelsior Income Shares, Inc., is a publicly traded investment company which invests in fixed-income securities.

* * *

EXXON CORP. (XON). Founded 1882. Headquarters: 1251 Ave. of the Americas, New York NY 10020. OIL. Exxon is the world's largest oil company. Also active in alternative energy sources (including coal, uranium, and synfuels), electrical equipment, petrochemical manufacture, and office equipment. 169,000 employees. MAJOR SUBSIDIARIES, BRANDS: Exxon (gasoline); Reliance Electric; Vydec (office equipment); Exxon Office Systems; Exxon Enterprises (high-technology venture capital); Imperial Oil (70 percent owned Canadian subsidiary).

Sales: $103,143.0 million (trend 17.8% a year).
Earnings: $5,650.09 million (trend 17.6% a year).
What happened to a $10,000 investment

Purchase Date	*Purchase Price*	*Price on 12-31-81*	*Dividends Paid*
12-31-71	$18.44	$31.25	$9,044.07
12-31-76	$26.81	$31.25	$4,027.97

Purchase Date	*Cap. Gains (— Losses)*	*Total Return*	*Rate of Return*
12-31-71	$6,949.15	$15,993.22	10.02%
12-31-76	$1,655.01	$ 5,682.98	9.42%

PROFILE: Exxon is already the world's largest corporation, as measured by sales, and the second-largest after AT&T in profits. So, where can it go from here?

Admittedly, sales and earnings aren't going to increase tenfold in the next few years; this is an ocean liner, not a speedboat. But there's plenty of room for upward movement of the stock, which was conservatively valued in the early 1980s.

In early 1981, for example, Exxon was selling for only 5 to 6 times the previous year's earnings, and was yielding 8 to 9 percent in dividends. That's the sort of valuation the market normally puts on a mature company in a no-growth industry. Is that what Exxon is?

Hardly. Exxon has tremendous oil reserves, in the United States as well as abroad. Oil is still the basic fuel of this country, and its price has, of course, been decontrolled. In addition, Exxon has major stakes in alternative energy sources, such as coal and uranium. If you think that, in the long run, energy will be in short supply, then Exxon has a scarce commodity in abundance.

Oil stocks in general had a big run up in 1979 and 1980 and Exxon participated, though less dramatically than some. Its price rose from a 1978 high of about $53 to a 1980 high of almost $89. The stocks were due for a correction, and one came with an oil glut in 1981. (By April of that year Exxon stock was down to $67.) But investors seemed to be overreacting to a temporary condition. They have also been hyper-cautious about the international oils. Sure, they're subject to expropriation and uncertainty abroad. But in Exxon's case, the stock price in early 1981 was far less than the asset value of its energy-producing properties in the United States alone.

The balance sheet is also strong here, with long-term debt a mere 16 percent of capital as of the early 1980s.

F

FMC CORP. (FMC). Founded 1928. Headquarters: 200 E. Randolph Dr., Chicago IL 60601. **MACHINERY, CHEMICALS, DEFENSE.** FMC makes materials-handling, oil-drilling, and construction machinery; produces industrial and agricultural chemicals; and builds defense products including Infantry Fighting Vehicles (IFVs), which resemble tanks but can carry more troops. 46,000 employees.

Sales: $3,482.2 million (trend 10.9% a year).
Earnings: $138.53 million (trend 7.1% a year).
What happened to a $10,000 investment

Purchase Date	*Purchase Price*	*Price on 12-31-81*	*Dividends Paid*	*Cap. Gains (− Losses)*	*Total Return*	*Rate of Return*
12-31-71	$25.25	$25.62	$4,505.94	$148.51	$4,654.46	3.90%
12-31-76	$24.50	$25.62	$2,775.51	$459.18	$3,234.69	5.77%

PROFILE: FMC is highly diversified — perhaps too much so. Recently chairman Robert Malott has started talking about jettisoning some of the divisions that aren't contributing enough to profits.

There are eight divisions altogether, but, according to an article in *Barron's* in late 1980, four of them are contributing the bulk of sales and a whopping 85 percent of profits. Those four are defense, oil-drilling equipment, agricultural chemicals, and industrial chemicals. Look for those four to stay. FMC will probably continue to churn out soda ash (of which it's the world's largest producer), hydrogen peroxide, phosphorus, fertilizer, insecticide, oil-drilling equipment, and Infantry Fighting Vehicles (IFVs). If the United States gets really serious about beefing up its conventional military forces, the IFVs (which are a combination troop carrier and tank) could become a gigantic business. The Soviets have been building them for a decade and a half, so the United States has a lot of catching up to do.

Possible candidates to be sold off are some of the company's machinery operations, such as materials-handling equipment and construction equipment. The Power Transmission Group was sold in 1981.

A leaner FMC might improve on the profitability record of recent years, which has been undistinguished. By most measures, FMC has been slightly less profitable than the average major corporation, although it has been consistently profitable. That's why its price / earnings ratio was only about 6 to 7 in 1981. Dividends have been paid regularly since 1935; the yield in recent years has been 5 to 6 percent.

* * *

FABERGÉ, INC. (FBG). Founded 1939. Headquarters: 1345 Ave. of the Americas, New York NY 10019. **BEAUTY PRODUCTS AND ENTERTAINMENT.** Produces perfumes, colognes, soaps, and other cosmetic items for men and women. Entertainment subsidiary distributes motion pictures. **MAJOR SUBSIDIARIES, BRANDS:** Babe, Brut, Aphrodesia, Tigress.

Sales: $248.2 million (trend 6.5% a year).
Earnings: $2.13 million (trend −4.2% a year).
What happened to a $10,000 investment

Purchase Date	Purchase Price	Price on 12-31-81	Dividends Paid
12-31-71	$17.87	$15.25	$2,327.27
12-31-76	$ 9.12	$15.25	$2,367.12

Purchase Date	Cap. Gains (− Losses)	Total Return	Rate of Return
12-31-71	$−1,468.53	$ 858.74	.83%
12-31-76	$ 6,712.33	$9,079.45	13.79%

* * *

FABRI-CENTERS OF AMERICA, INC. (FCA). Founded 1951. Headquarters: 23550 Commerce Park Rd., Cleveland OH 44122. **FABRIC RETAILING.** Operates large chain of retail stores which sell a variety of fabrics, draperies, and sewing notions. **MAJOR SUBSIDIARIES, BRANDS:** Jo-Ann Fabrics; House of Fine Fabrics; Showcase of Fine Fabrics.

Sales: $149.7 million (trend 13.7% a year).
Earnings: $4.01 million (trend 1.6% a year).
What happened to a $10,000 investment

Purchase Date	Purchase Price	Price on 12-31-81	Dividends Paid
12-31-71	$13.00	$11.87	$ 935.90
12-31-76	$ 9.37	$11.87	$1,013.33

Purchase Date	Cap. Gains (− Losses)	Total Return	Rate of Return
12-31-71	$−865.38	$ 70.51	.07%
12-31-76	$ 2,666.67	$3,680.00	6.47%

* * *

FACET ENTERPRISES, INC. (FCT). Founded 1975. Headquarters: 7030 S. Yale Ave., Tulsa OK 74177. **AUTO PARTS.** Manufactures filters, automotive components, environmental waste treatment systems, and bicycles. **MAJOR SUBSIDIARIES, BRANDS:** Campbell Filter Co.; Cal-Fact, Inc.; Scorpion (bicycles).

Sales: $141.2 million (trend 7.7% a year).
Earnings: $.60 million (trend −16.6% a year).
What happened to a $10,000 investment

Purchase Date	Purchase Price	Price on 12-31-81	Dividends Paid
12-31-71	$N/A	$5.25	$ N/A
12-31-76	$ 6.62	$5.25	$226.42

Purchase Date	Cap. Gains (− Losses)	Total Return	Rate of Return
12-31-71	$ N/A	$ N/A	N/A%
12-31-76	$−2,075.47	$−1,849.06	−4.01%

* * *

FAIRCHILD INDUSTRIES, INC. (FEN). Founded 1936. Headquarters: Germantown MD 20767. **AEROSPACE.** Fairchild is a major manufacturer of aircraft and aircraft components, about two thirds for the military. Also involved in work on the space program and in satellite communications. 11,000 employees. **MAJOR SUBSIDIARIES, BRANDS:** VSI Corp.; Swearingen Aircraft; American Satellite Corp. (50 percent owned); A-10 (fighter plane); Merlin, Metro (aircraft).

Sales: $906.2 million (trend 34.7% a year).
Earnings: $54.53 million (trend 84.1% a year).
What happened to a $10,000 investment

Purchase Date	Purchase Price	Price on 12-31-81	Dividends Paid
12-31-71	$4.35	$12.12	$6,988.51
12-31-76	$3.85	$12.12	$6,337.66

Purchase Date	Cap. Gains (− Losses)	Total Return	Rate of Return
12-31-71	$17,873.56	$24,862.07	13.30%
12-31-76	$21,493.51	$27,831.17	30.49%

PROFILE: Fairchild was one of the star performers in the dull stock market of the late 1970s. As recently as 1975, you could have picked up Fairchild for $2 a share. You could still get it for $3 a share in 1976, and for $4 a share in 1977. The 1978 high was about $14, the 1979 high near $22, and the 1980 high near $33. You might say the stock took off like a rocket.

Unfortunately, it had a hard landing. Fairchild was selling for a down-to-earth 4 times earnings in early 1982, when the price had dropped back to about $14. That was a modest p / e for a stock that had been experiencing the rapid profit growth Fairchild had, even though 1981 profits were down, after five up years. As for debt, Fairchild recently had long-term debt less than 20 percent of capital.

How could Wall Street allow a fast-growing outfit with a clean balance sheet to go for such a low multiple? Perhaps investors, knowing the company's history for volatility of earnings and share prices, were reluctant to pay too much for growth that might prove a chimera.

Fairchild makes the A-10 fighter plane, the latest

in a long line of anti-tank planes. So long as U.S. military spending is geared toward countering Soviet threats, there should be demand for anti-tank aircraft. However, orders for A-10s in 1982 were below those in 1981. The 19-seat Metro, used for small commercial flights, and the smaller Merlin, for private aviation, both are enjoying strong demand. In satellite communications, most analysts thought Fairchild did well in selling a half interest in its American Satellite Corp. to Continental Telephone, since the latter's experience in communications complements Fairchild's experience in aerospace.

* * *

FAMILY DOLLAR STORES, INC. (FDO). Founded 1969. Headquarters: 10401 Old Monroe Rd., Charlotte NC 28212. RETAIL STORES. Operates more than 400 stores in southeastern rural and urban communities that sell apparel, linens, auto supplies, housewares, and other general items.

Sales: $181.7 million (trend 21.2% a year).
Earnings: $9.12 million (trend 19.7% a year).
What happened to a $10,000 investment

Purchase Date	*Purchase Price*	*Price on 12-31-81*	*Dividends Paid*
12-31-71	$9.42	$15.00	$1,203.54
12-31-76	$4.25	$15.00	$2,478.43

Purchase Date	*Cap. Gains (− Losses)*	*Total Return*	*Rate of Return*
12-31-71	$ 5,929.20	$ 7,132.74	5.53%
12-31-76	$25,294.12	$27,772.55	30.45%

* * *

FAR WEST FINANCIAL CORP. (FWF). Founded 1959. Headquarters: 4001 MacArthur Blvd., Newport Beach CA 92660. SAVINGS AND LOANS. Parent to Far West Savings and Loan Association.

* * *

FARAH MANUFACTURING CO., INC. (FRA). Founded 1947. Headquarters: 8889 Gateway West, El Paso TX 79925. MEN'S CLOTHING. Manufactures clothing for men and boys which is sold in more than 4,000 stores across the United States and abroad.

Sales: $122.7 million (trend −6.7% a year).
Earnings: $3.81 million (trend 14.2% a year).
What happened to a $10,000 investment

Purchase Date	*Purchase Price*	*Price on 12-31-81*	*Dividends Paid*
12-31-71	$25.50	$9.87	$134.12
12-31-76	$ 5.75	$9.87	$ 0.00

Purchase Date	*Cap. Gains (− Losses)*	*Total Return*	*Rate of Return*
12-31-71	$−6,127.45	$−5,993.33	−8.74%
12-31-76	$ 7,173.91	$ 7,173.91	11.42%

* * *

FEDDERS CORP. (FJQ). Founded 1913. Headquarters: Edison NJ 08817. AIR CONDITIONING AND HEATING. Specializes in heat transfer products but also manufactures air conditioners and other equipment. MAJOR SUBSIDIARIES, BRANDS: Airtemp, Climatrol, Fedders.

Sales: $137.3 million (trend −7.2% a year).
Earnings: $−30.90 million.
What happened to a $10,000 investment

Purchase Date	*Purchase Price*	*Price on 12-31-81*	*Dividends Paid*
12-31-71	$42.37	$4.12	$353.98
12-31-76	$ 7.50	$4.12	$ 0.00

Purchase Date	*Cap. Gains (− Losses)*	*Total Return*	*Rate of Return*
12-31-71	$−9,026.55	$−8,672.57	−18.29%
12-31-76	$−4,500.00	$−4,500.00	−11.27%

* * *

FEDERAL CO. (FFF). Founded 1925. Headquarters: 1755-D Lynnfield Rd., Memphis TN 38117. POULTRY PRODUCTION. Processes broiler chickens and meat by-products, produces flour and operates a chain of more than 100 restaurants. MAJOR SUBSIDIARIES, BRANDS: White Lily Foods; Diana Fruit Preserving; National By-Products.

Sales: $1,099.9 million (trend 16.3% a year).
Earnings: $20.12 million (trend 1.5% a year).
What happened to a $10,000 investment

Purchase Date	*Purchase Price*	*Price on 12-31-81*	*Dividends Paid*
12-31-71	$ 6.56	$21.37	$11,038.10
12-31-76	$12.25	$21.37	$ 3,612.24

Purchase Date	*Cap. Gains (− Losses)*	*Total Return*	*Rate of Return*
12-31-71	$22,571.43	$33,609.52	15.87%
12-31-76	$ 7,448.98	$11,061.22	16.06%

* * *

FEDERAL EXPRESS CORP. (FDX). Founded 1971. Headquarters: 2387 Sprankel Ave., Memphis TN 38194. **AIR PACKAGE DELIVERY.** Federal Express is a pioneer and leader in the overnight delivery of small packages. 6,000 employees.

Sales: $589.5 million (trend 55.0% a year).
Earnings: $58.06 million (trend 67.6% a year).

PROFILE: A good, basic idea, superbly executed, has brought huge rewards to the founders of Federal Express — and to its investors. Since the stock went public at $6 a share in 1978, it has soared to a 1981 high of $72.25 with hardly a pause for breath. (In early 1982, the stock had settled back to around $50.)

The premise behind the company is simple. People sometimes need overnight delivery of important parcels, and will pay good money to get it. Packages are picked up at the sender's place of business or residence and flown to Memphis, where they are sorted and flown to their destination in time for delivery the next morning. The company uses a fleet of some 2,500 delivery vehicles and more than 50 owned planes, plus some additional leased ones. Recently service was added at selected hotels.

Fortune magazine rightly called Federal Express one of the ten top success stories of American business in the 1970s. However, one shouldn't automatically jump to the conclusion that the stock is a wise buy. There are some drawbacks to the purchase of the shares.

First, the company's success, and expectations for continued success, are already built into the stock price. In 1981, for example, the stock was selling at around 20 times the company's earnings for the previous year. That was about 2½ times the multiple the stock market awarded the average stock.

Second, there are no dividends, nor are there any prospects of them. For some investors that's no problem, but others prefer a dollop of income with their hoped-for capital gains.

Third, the debt load is not light — about 36 percent of capital in early 1982.

Fourth, competition is trying to climb on the bandwagon. It comes from Burlington Northern Air Freight, Emery Air Freight, Airborne Freight Corp., and the express mail delivery of the U.S. Postal Service.

Fifth, high fuel costs affect Federal Express, as they affect other air carriers.

Of these potential negatives, the most serious one is the high p / e ratio. Plenty of investors have lost money in excellent companies. (Ask the man who bought Xerox or IBM in the early 1970s.) You always have to ask how much of a price you're willing to pay for a red-hot record of growth.

* * *

FEDERAL-MOGUL CORP. (FMO). Founded 1899. Headquarters: PO Box 1966, Detroit MI 48235. **VEHICLE AND MACHINERY COMPONENTS.** Manufactures ball and roller bearings, precision forged products, sealing devices, aerospace components, and engine and transmission products. **MAJOR SUBSIDIARIES, BRANDS:** Huck Manufacturing Co.; Bower / BCA Bearings; National Oil Seals.

Sales: $721.2 million (trend 15.2% a year).
Earnings: $36.13 million (trend 52.4% a year).
What happened to a $10,000 investment

Purchase Date	*Purchase Price*	*Price on 12-31-81*	*Dividends Paid*
12-31-71	$13.44	$22.50	$6,746.05
12-31-76	$12.12	$22.50	$4,259.79

Purchase Date	*Cap. Gains (− Losses)*	*Total Return*	*Rate of Return*
12-31-71	$6,744.19	$13,490.23	8.92%
12-31-76	$8,556.70	$12,816.49	17.94%

* * *

FEDERAL NATIONAL MORTGAGE ASSOCIATION (FNM). Founded 1938. Headquarters: 3900 Wisconsin Ave. N.W., Washington DC 20016. **MORTGAGE DEALER.** Buys and sells mortgages from banks, savings and loan institutions, and other lenders. Preserves liquidity in the mortgage market. 1,000 employees.

Sales: $5,072.0 million (trend 16.1% a year).
Earnings: $14.21 million (trend −23.7% a year).
What happened to a $10,000 investment

Purchase Date	*Purchase Price*	*Price on 12-31-81*	*Dividends Paid*
12-31-71	$24.81	$8.50	$3,268.51
12-31-76	$17.25	$8.50	$2,869.57

Purchase Date	*Cap. Gains (− Losses)*	*Total Return*	*Rate of Return*
12-31-71	$−6,574.31	$−3,305.79	−3.93%
12-31-76	$−5,072.46	$−2,202.90	−4.85%

PROFILE: Fannie Mae, as the FNMA is commonly known, was founded as a government agency in 1938. It was designed to facilitate home ownership by providing mortgage lenders with a secondary market for mortgages, and it continues to serve that function. In 1954 it was converted to a semiprivate, semigovernmental agency. In 1968 it became 100 percent privately (investor) owned. But it still operates under government supervision. The President appoints five of the fifteen board members, and can remove any member of the board "for good cause." It's clear that Fannie Mae serves at least two masters, investors and the public at large.

Investors lately have been having a rough time of it. Between 1971 and 1980, Fannie Mae shares declined gently and irregularly, from a 1971 high of $25 to a 1980 high of $17.37. Though the stock isn't particularly volatile, it is sensitive to changes in interest rates. In the early 1980s interest rates were extremely high, which was murder on Fannie Mae since 97 percent of its capital comes from borrowing, while its income comes from a long-term mortgage portfolio, the return on which changes very slowly over time. About a third of Fannie Mae's borrowing is short-term, so recent sky-high interest rates have sent the enterprise into the red. It was barely profitable in 1980, and most analysts figured it would, at best, break even in 1981. Dividends — paid each year since 1956 and raised each year from 1970 to 1979 — were cut in 1980 and 1981, reducing the yield to about 2 percent in early 1982. There was some fear that the dividend might have to be eliminated.

Calling a turn in interest rate trends is notoriously difficult. However, if this country ever succeeds in getting inflation and interest rates under control, a long-term decline in interest rates would create a chance for a good total return in this stock.

* * *

FEDERAL PAPER BOARD CO., INC. (FBO). Founded 1916. Headquarters: 75 Chestnut Ridge Rd., Montvale NJ 07645. **PAPER AND PACKAGING.** Manufactures bleached pulps, bleached paperboard, lumber, recycled paperboard, folding cartons.

Sales: $476.1 million (trend 5.6% a year).
Earnings: $28.34 million (trend 11.8% a year).
What happened to a $10,000 investment

Purchase Date	*Purchase Price*	*Price on 12-31-81*	*Dividends Paid*
12-31-71	$12.31	$27.25	$6,639.59
12-31-76	$18.62	$27.25	$2,617.45

Purchase Date	*Cap. Gains (− Losses)*	*Total Return*	*Rate of Return*
12-31-71	$12,131.98	$18,771.57	11.15%
12-31-76	$ 4,630.87	$ 7,248.32	11.52%

* * *

FEDERAL SIGNAL CORP. (FSS). Founded 1969. Headquarters: 1415 W. 22nd St., Oak Brook IL 60521. **SIGNAL AND WARNING DEVICES.** Manufactures warning devices, communications systems, advertising sign displays.

Sales: $146.5 million (trend 16.5% a year).
Earnings: $9.92 million (trend 32.7% a year).
What happened to a $10,000 investment

Purchase Date	*Purchase Price*	*Price on 12-31-81*	*Dividends Paid*
12-31-71	$4.87	$23.12	$6,929.10
12-31-76	$5.73	$23.12	$4,689.73

Purchase Date	*Cap. Gains (− Losses)*	*Total Return*	*Rate of Return*
12-31-71	$37,443.29	$44,372.39	18.45%
12-31-76	$30,326.80	$35,016.53	35.11%

* * *

FEDERATED DEPARTMENT STORES, INC. (FDS). Founded 1929. Headquarters: 7 W. Seventh St., Cincinnati OH 45202. **RETAILER.** Federated is the nation's largest chain of department stores and also has discount store and supermarket operations. It is approximately the ninth-largest retailer in the United States. 112,000 employees. **MAJOR SUBSIDIARIES, BRANDS:** Bloomingdale's, Burdines, Abraham & Straus, Bullock's, Children's Place, Filene's, Foley's, Lazarus, I. Magnin, Rich's, Sanger-Harris, and Shillito's (department stores); Gold Circle, Richway (discount stores); Ralphs Grocery.

Sales: $6,300.7 million (trend 10.6% a year).
Earnings: $277.73 million (trend 10.2% a year).
What happened to a $10,000 investment

Purchase Date	*Purchase Price*	*Price on 12-31-81*	*Dividends Paid*
12-31-71	$51.62	$36.25	$2,422.28
12-31-76	$49.25	$36.25	$1,344.16

Purchase Date	*Cap. Gains (— Losses)*	*Total Return*	*Rate of Return*
12-31-71	$−2,978.21	$ −555.93	−.57%
12-31-76	$−2,639.59	$−1,295.43	−2.74%

PROFILE: "Carriage trade," "top of the line," and "classy" are some of the terms often used to describe Federated's stores, and Federated tries to keep the image polished. Many of the stores in the chain, all of which enjoy considerable autonomy, are masters of the sales place as showplace. Striking displays and (in newer stores, like the Burdines "Superstore" in Boca Raton, Florida) original architecture help to lift shoppers' spirits and loosen their wallets.

Both in profit margins (recently about 3½ to 4 percent) and in return on stockholders' equity, Federated has been among the top department store chains in recent years. Unfortunately, that isn't saying too much: Department stores in general have been lackluster performers. Federated shares have moved irregularly, but mostly down from 1976 on. The 1976 high was $60 a share, the price in 1981 about $35 a share.

However, the trend in retailing seems to be for consumers to prefer either trendy, high-quality stores or discount stores. This hurts stores in the middle (Sears being the classic example) but helps a chain like Federated, which owns discount stores as well as chic ones. In the next few years, Federated plans to pump a lot of money into expanding its discount operations.

The balance sheet here is solid; debt was less than 20 percent of total capital in the early 1980s. The price / earnings ratio in 1981 was around 7— a bit higher than that for most retailers, but still below the p / e (8) of the average stock at the time. The stock could do quite well when a major increase in consumer spending arrives.

* * *

FERRO CORP. (FOE). Founded 1919. Headquarters: 1 Erieview Plaza, Cleveland OH 44114. **RAW MATERIALS.** Produces raw materials for construction, appliances, and household furnishings. It is the world's largest producer of frit, which is used in making porcelain and enamel glazes.

Sales: $695.6 million (trend 16.5% a year).
Earnings: $29.02 million (trend 14.8% a year).
What happened to a $10,000 investment

Purchase Date	*Purchase Price*	*Price on 12-31-81*	*Dividends Paid*
12-31-71	$21.50	$28.25	$3,999.53
12-31-76	$20.83	$28.25	$2,633.60

Purchase Date	*Cap. Gains (— Losses)*	*Total Return*	*Rate of Return*
12-31-71	$3,139.53	$7,139.07	5.54%
12-31-76	$3,560.00	$6,193.60	10.12%

* * *

FIDELITY FINANCIAL CORP. (FDY). Founded 1969. Headquarters: 260 California St., San Francisco CA 94111. **LOANS.** Residential, commercial and consumer loans.

* * *

FIDELITY UNION BANCORPORATION. (FDU). Founded 1875. Headquarters: 765 Broad St., Newark NJ 07101. **BANKING.** A holding company that owns and operates six commercial banks in New Jersey and a small loan company. **MAJOR SUBSIDIARIES, BRANDS:** Fidelity Union Trust Co.; Garden State National Bank; Colonial First National Bank; First National Bank of New Jersey; Burlington County Trust Co.

Sales: $264.9 million (trend 20.7% a year).
Earnings: $23.36 million (trend 7.4% a year).
What happened to a $10,000 investment

Purchase Date	*Purchase Price*	*Price on 12-31-81*	*Dividends Paid*
12-31-71	$38.14	$25.12	$6,410.53
12-31-76	$32.75	$25.12	$4,045.80

Purchase Date	*Cap. Gains (— Losses)*	*Total Return*	*Rate of Return*
12-31-71	$−3,412.08	$2,998.45	2.66%
12-31-76	$−2,328.24	$1,717.56	3.22%

* * *

FIELDCREST MILLS, INC. (FLD). Founded 1953. Headquarters: 326 E. Stadium Dr., Eden NC 27288. **TEXTILES.** Manufactures textile products, carpets, rugs, bed and bath accessories. **MAJOR SUBSIDIARIES, BRANDS:** Fieldcrest; St. Marys; Karastan.

Sales: $527.2 million (trend 12.4% a year).
Earnings: $17.47 million (trend 15.9% a year).
What happened to a $10,000 investment

Purchase Date	*Purchase Price*	*Price on 12-31-81*	*Dividends Paid*
12-31-71	$34.75	$22.37	$4,690.65
12-31-76	$19.37	$22.37	$5,058.06

Purchase Date	*Cap. Gains (− Losses)*	*Total Return*	*Rate of Return*
12-31-71	$−3,561.15	$1,129.50	1.08%
12-31-76	$ 1,548.39	$6,606.45	10.68%

* * *

FIGGIE INTERNATIONAL. (FIG). Founded 1963. Headquarters: 4420 Sherwin Rd., Willoughby OH 44094. CONGLOMERATE. Figgie (formerly A-T-O) has operations in fire safety, construction, packaging, materials handling, recreation, and electronics. 17,000 employees. MAJOR SUBSIDIARIES, BRANDS: American LaFrance, Automatic Sprinkler Corp., Rawlings Sporting Goods, Fred Perry Sportswear, Rusco Electronic Systems, Thermometer Corp. of America.

Sales: $759.6 million (trend 9.7% a year).
Earnings: $18.79 million (trend 12.8% a year).
What happened to a $10,000 investment

Purchase Date	*Purchase Price*	*Price on 12-31-81*	*Dividends Paid*
12-31-71	$ 9.87	$17.75	$3,584.81
12-31-76	$10.25	$17.75	$2,517.07

Purchase Date	*Cap. Gains (− Losses)*	*Total Return*	*Rate of Return*
12-31-71	$7,974.68	$11,559.49	7.99%
12-31-76	$7,317.07	$ 9,834.15	14.68%

* * *

FILMWAYS, INC. (FWI). Founded 1968. Headquarters: 2049 Century Park East, Los Angeles CA 90067. ENTERTAINMENT AND PUBLISHING. Produces and distributes movies, publishes books and magazines, and works with network television programming. MAJOR SUBSIDIARIES, BRANDS: American International Pictures; Broadcast Electronics; Grosset & Dunlap; Ideal Publishing Co.; Pic-Mount.

Sales: $141.5 million (trend 7.9% a year).
Earnings: $−65.08 million.
What happened to a $10,000 investment

Purchase Date	*Purchase Price*	*Price on 12-31-81*	*Dividends Paid*
12-31-71	$4.58	$6.87	$1,500.13
12-31-76	$6.59	$6.87	$ 980.36

Purchase Date	*Cap. Gains (− Losses)*	*Total Return*	*Rate of Return*
12-31-71	$5,007.73	$6,507.86	5.14%
12-31-76	$ 437.57	$1,417.93	2.69%

* * *

FINANCIAL CORP. OF AMERICA. (FIN). Founded 1968. Headquarters: 6420 Wilshire Blvd., Los Angeles CA 90048. BANKING. Holding company for State Savings and Loan Association.

Sales: $178.4 million (trend 36.3% a year).
Earnings: $12.24 million (trend 67.3% a year).
What happened to a $10,000 investment

Purchase Date	*Purchase Price*	*Price on 12-31-81*	*Dividends Paid*
12-31-71	$1.89	$15.50	$6,932.06
12-31-76	$2.62	$15.50	$4,981.08

Purchase Date	*Cap. Gains (− Losses)*	*Total Return*	*Rate of Return*
12-31-71	$72,200.16	$79,132.22	24.45%
12-31-76	$49,065.50	$54,046.58	44.98%

* * *

FINANCIAL CORP. OF SANTA BARBARA. (FSB). Founded 1962. Headquarters: 7 W. Figueroa St., PO Box 1109, Santa Barbara CA 93102. BANKING. Holding company for Santa Barbara Savings and Loan Association.

* * *

FINANCIAL FEDERATION, INC. (FFI). Founded 1959. Headquarters: 615 S. Flower at Wilshire Blvd., Los Angeles CA 90017. SAVINGS AND LOANS. Owns eleven savings and loan associations with sixty-nine offices throughout California.

Sales: $228.4 million (trend 16.7% a year).
Earnings: $2.93 million (trend −11.5% a year).
What happened to a $10,000 investment

Purchase Date	*Purchase Price*	*Price on 12-31-81*	*Dividends Paid*
12-31-71	$13.57	$15.25	$3,370.25
12-31-76	$18.12	$15.25	$2,262.07

Purchase Date	*Cap. Gains (— Losses)*	*Total Return*	*Rate of Return*
12-31-71	$ 1,234.17	$4,604.43	3.86%
12-31-76	$−1,586.21	$ 675.86	1.32%

* * *

FIRESTONE TIRE & RUBBER CO. (FIR). Founded 1910. Headquarters: 1200 Firestone Parkway, Akron OH 44317. **TIRES.** Firestone is the second-largest tire manufacturer in the United States. 83,000 employees.

Sales: $4,361.0 million (trend 2.5% a year).
Earnings: $79.00 million (trend −5.7% a year).
What happened to a $10,000 investment

Purchase Date	*Purchase Price*	*Price on 12-31-81*	*Dividends Paid*
12-31-71	$26.87	$12.62	$3,360.00
12-31-76	$23.75	$12.62	$1,715.79

Purchase Date	*Cap. Gains (— Losses)*	*Total Return*	*Rate of Return*
12-31-71	$−5,302.33	$−1,942.33	−2.14%
12-31-76	$−4,684.21	$−2,968.42	−6.80%

PROFILE: A few headlines will tell the story. "Firestone becomes leaner and stronger by cutting capacity, jobs, product lines" (*The Wall Street Journal,* 1980). "I'm paid to be an s.o.b." (*Forbes* magazine in 1980, quoting John Nevin, who took over as Firestone's president in 1979). "Less means more at Firestone" (*Fortune,* 1980).

Leaner the company is, indeed. Nevin yanked it back as it was about to go, figuratively, over the cliff into a sea of debt. Had Firestone continued to churn out tires as planned (many of them, no doubt, destined to add to already huge piles in warehouses), its debt would have amounted to close to half of capital by the start of 1981. Instead, Nevin closed six U.S. plants (about a third of capacity in this country) and a slew of European operations that were unprofitable. The closed American plants were making bias-ply tires; Nevin is convinced radials will have about 80 percent of the market within a few years. By selling off assets, including a promising plastics business, Nevin got Firestone's debt load down to about 27 percent of capital in early 1981.

An import from Zenith, where he was chairman, Nevin is an outsider in Akron, and the least optimistic top manager in the tire industry. He thinks the gas shortage will last, people will drive less, and because radials need to be replaced less frequently than bias-ply tires, they'll replace tires less often. In short, he seems to see tires as a no-growth market. Given this attitude, it wouldn't be surprising to see Firestone diversify, once it has its financial house in order. In 1982, the company said it would like to buy Hertz, the rental car giant, from RCA.

* * *

FIRST ATLANTA CORP. (FAC). Founded 1968; bank dates to 1865. Headquarters: 2 Peachtree St. N.W., Atlanta GA 30303. **BANKING.** First Atlanta is the holding company for First National Bank of Atlanta, a pair of smaller banks, and some other subsidiaries that provide personal loans, commercial loans, and insurance. **MAJOR SUBSIDIARIES, BRANDS:** First National Bank of Atlanta (second-largest bank in Georgia); First Bank of Savannah; First National Bank of Dalton; Gulf Finance Corp. (personal loans); First Atlanta Factors Inc. (commercial loans); First Financial Life Insurance Co. (credit insurance); Tharpe & Brooks (mortgage banking).

Sales: $331.3 million (trend 13.8% a year).
Earnings: $24.02 million (trend 25.9% a year).
What happened to a $10,000 investment

Purchase Date	*Purchase Price*	*Price on 12-31-81*	*Dividends Paid*
12-31-71	$10.08	$17.42	$5,469.53
12-31-76	$ 9.22	$17.42	$3,322.89

Purchase Date	*Cap. Gains (— Losses)*	*Total Return*	*Rate of Return*
12-31-71	$7,284.85	$12,754.39	8.57%
12-31-76	$8,885.54	$12,208.43	17.30%

* * *

FIRST CHARTER FINANCIAL CORP. (FCF). Founded 1955. Headquarters: 9645 Wilshire Blvd., Beverly Hills CA 90212. **SAVINGS AND LOAN.** First Charter Financial is the holding company for American Savings and Loan Association, which, with more than 100 branch offices in California, is the nation's third-largest savings and loan. 2,000 employees. **MAJOR SUBSIDIARIES, BRANDS:** American Savings & Loan Association.

Sales: $953.6 million (trend 20.4% a year).
Earnings: $39.21 million (trend −1.2% a year).
What happened to a $10,000 investment

Purchase Date	*Purchase Price*	*Price on 12-31-81*	*Dividends Paid*
12-31-71	$21.84	$11.87	$1,716.96
12-31-76	$17.25	$11.87	$2,173.91

Purchase Date	*Cap. Gains (– Losses)*	*Total Return*	*Rate of Return*
12-31-71	$–4,562.96	$–2,845.99	–3.29%
12-31-76	$–3,115.94	$ –942.03	–1.96%

PROFILE: In 1981, when this book was written, First Charter Financial was heading for the first loss in its history. There seemed no way the iceberg could be avoided; the only question was how much damage there would be. In that regard, it appeared that the company would escape in better shape than most savings and loans.

The industry as a whole has been going through a rough time. Banking institutions make their money by taking in savings deposits at one rate and making loans at a higher rate. In the case of savings and loan associations, the loans are mainly (and in First Charter's case, almost exclusively) mortgage loans for residential construction. American Savings & Loan, First Charter's operating company, has about 84 percent of its loans in single-family homes; most of the rest are for apartment buildings. The rate that savings institutions have had to pay to attract funds has gone up and up. At American Savings & Loan, for example, passbook accounts recently accounted for only about 16 percent of deposits. The association had to raise most of its money through high-cost six-month money market certificates and jumbo certificates of deposit. But there's a limit to how high mortgage interest rates can be raised before people just plain stop buying houses.

One way the savings institutions have been trying to protect themselves from future interest rate swings is by issuing variable mortgages. First Charter is in the forefront of that trend. Recently, a third of its outstanding mortgages have been variable.

Dividend payments were started in 1977, and the yield recently has been moderate. However, the dividend hasn't been raised since 1978 and may have to be sliced.

* * *

FIRST CHICAGO CORP. (FNB). Founded 1969; bank dates to 1863. Headquarters: 1 First National Plaza, Chicago IL 60670. **BANK.** First Chicago is the holding company for First National Bank of Chicago, the nation's ninth-largest bank as of 1980. 10,000 employees. **MAJOR SUBSIDIARIES, BRANDS:** First National Bank of Chicago, First Chicago Realty Services, First Chicago Leasing Corp.

Sales: $3,414.8 million (trend 20.5% a year).
Earnings: $66.50 million (trend –4.2% a year).
What happened to a $10,000 investment

Purchase Date	*Purchase Price*	*Price on 12-31-81*	*Dividends Paid*
12-31-71	$19.37	$19.25	$5,144.52
12-31-76	$22.87	$19.25	$2,439.34

Purchase Date	*Cap. Gains (– Losses)*	*Total Return*	*Rate of Return*
12-31-71	$ –64.52	$5,080.00	4.19%
12-31-76	$–1,584.70	$ 854.64	1.65%

PROFILE: First Chicago in 1981 was still digging out from under a mountain of ill-advised loans made in the early 1970s. It was also working under its third management team in a decade. The first team, led by Gaylord Freeman, emphasized growth in loan volume, apparently at the expense of quality. (Like many banks, First Chicago suffered especially from bad real estate loans.) The second team, led by Robert Abboud, now president of Occidental Petroleum, slammed on the brakes and adopted a very conservative lending stance in order to improve the bank's balance sheet. Critics say that Abboud went overboard; he says he had no choice. The third team, led by Barry Sullivan (formerly of Chase Manhattan) as chairman, is charged with restoring morale and growth and finishing the mop-up process.

During the slamming-on-the-brakes years, First Chicago was surpassed as the Midwest's largest bank by its aggressive crosstown rival, Continental Bank. From 1972 to 1980, return per $100 of assets fell from 80 cents to 40 cents. The stock price fell from a 1974 high around $39 to an early 1982 price of about $19 a share. Earnings were fairly flat (ranging from $2.67 to $3.29 a share) from 1974 to 1979; they dropped to $1.59 a share in 1980, partly as the result of bad loan write-offs.

The stock has possible appeal as a turnaround situation. Dividends have been paid yearly since 1936, and the yield in recent years has been around 6 to 8 percent.

* * *

FIRST CITY BANCORP. OF TEXAS, INC. (FBT). Founded 1934. Headquarters: 1001 Main St., Houston TX 77002. **BANKING.** This holding company owns First City National Bank of Houston and forty other banks throughout Texas.

Sales: $1,061.4 million (trend 31.8% a year).
Earnings: $90.45 million (trend 27.2% a year).
What happened to a $10,000 investment

Purchase Date	*Purchase Price*	*Price on 12-31-81*	*Dividends Paid*
12-31-71	$12.25	$32.75	$4,974.30
12-31-76	$18.56	$32.75	$2,065.99

Purchase Date	*Cap. Gains (− Losses)*	*Total Return*	*Rate of Return*
12-31-71	$16,734.69	$21,708.99	12.23%
12-31-76	$ 7,643.10	$ 9,709.09	14.53%

* * *

FIRST CITY PROPERTIES INC. (FCP). Founded 1970. Headquarters: 8121 E. Florence Ave., Downey CA 90240. **REAL ESTATE.** First City Properties, formerly called State Mutual Investors, is a real estate investment trust (REIT).

Sales: $17.8 million (trend −2.5% a year).
Earnings: $.64 million (trend −35.5% a year).
What happened to a $10,000 investment

Purchase Date	*Purchase Price*	*Price on 12-31-81*	*Dividends Paid*
12-31-71	$23.50	$4.75	$2,502.13
12-31-76	$ 1.37	$4.75	$ 0.00

Purchase Date	*Cap. Gains (− Losses)*	*Total Return*	*Rate of Return*
12-31-71	$−7,978.72	$−5,476.60	−7.63%
12-31-76	$ 24,545.45	$ 24,545.45	28.14%

* * *

FIRST INTERSTATE BANCORP (WBC). Founded 1957. Headquarters: 707 Wilshire Blvd., Los Angeles CA 90054. **BANKING.** First Interstate is a holding company for twenty-one banks serving eleven Western states. 26,000 employees. **MAJOR SUBSIDIARIES, BRANDS:** First Interstate Bank of California, First Interstate Bank of Oregon, etc.

Sales: $3,296.2 million (trend 21.0% a year).
Earnings: $236.98 million (trend 27.6% a year).
What happened to a $10,000 investment

Purchase Date	*Purchase Price*	*Price on 12-31-81*	*Dividends Paid*
12-31-71	$23.58	$35.75	$5,185.88
12-31-76	$20.17	$35.75	$3,783.49

Purchase Date	*Cap. Gains (− Losses)*	*Total Return*	*Rate of Return*
12-31-71	$5,159.01	$10,344.89	7.36%
12-31-76	$7,727.27	$11,510.76	16.56%

PROFILE: This is the largest of seven bank holding companies that are permitted to own banks in more than one state. All seven got in under a "grandfather clause" in the Bank Holding Co. Act of 1956. Thus, First Interstate has a head start on what is widely believed to be the coming trend: interstate banking.

Among U.S. banking companies, Interstate recently ranked first in the number of branch offices (almost 900), ninth in assets, and eighth in deposits. It got its start as a spin-off from Bank of America. Bank of America was trying to become a nationwide colossus, but Congress and the antitrust laws intervened and it had to divest itself of its holdings outside California. Given the current glowing talk about Interstate's prospects, that piece of history seems ironic.

How much is a head start worth? That remains to be seen, since interstate banking hasn't begun in earnest yet. (Technically, the company must still run its twenty-one banks as independent entities.) First Interstate already allows customers of each of its banks to cash checks easily at the others, and has been integrating various management functions. To date, the company's profitability has been a shade better than that of the average bank, but nothing really spectacular. However, under new management (imported from — you guessed it — Bank of America), profitability has been improving in recent years. Return on equity has been upped to the 17–18 percent range and return on assets (for years around 50 cents per $100) has recently been about 70 to 80 cents per $100.

The company has paid dividends yearly since 1958, and offers a moderate yield well covered by earnings. As with almost all bank stocks, the p / e ratio has lately been modest — about 4 to 7 in recent years.

* * *

FIRST MISSISSIPPI CORP. (FRM). Founded 1957. Headquarters: 700 N St., Jackson MS 39205. **FERTILIZER AND INDUSTRIAL CHEMICALS.** Produces fertilizers and other agricultural products, industrial chemicals, and does some mining.

Sales: $357.7 million (trend 17.9% a year).
Earnings: $29.70 million (trend 16.8% a year).
What happened to a $10,000 investment

Purchase Date	*Purchase Price*	*Price on 12-31-81*	*Dividends Paid*
12-31-71	$ .42	$15.62	$27,016.11
12-31-76	$6.10	$15.62	$ 1,426.23

Purchase Date	*Cap. Gains (– Losses)*	*Total Return*	*Rate of Return*
12-31-71	$360,065.79	$387,081.89	44.51%
12-31-76	$ 15,614.75	$ 17,040.98	22.01%

* * *

FIRST NATIONAL BOSTON CORP. (FB). Founded 1970; bank dates to 1864. Headquarters: 100 Federal St., Boston MA 02110. **BANK HOLDING CO.** Owns First National Bank of Boston, the nation's seventeenth-largest bank and the largest in New England. 10,000 employees. **MAJOR SUBSIDIARIES, BRANDS:** First National Bank of Boston.

Sales: $2,333.3 million (trend 28.0% a year).
Earnings: $103.14 million (trend 21.4% a year).
What happened to a $10,000 investment

Purchase Date	*Purchase Price*	*Price on 12-31-81*	*Dividends Paid*
12-31-71	$33.75	$45.62	$5,771.85
12-31-76	$29.75	$45.62	$3,626.89

Purchase Date	*Cap. Gains (– Losses)*	*Total Return*	*Rate of Return*
12-31-71	$3,518.52	$9,290.37	6.79%
12-31-76	$5,336.13	$8,963.03	13.65%

PROFILE: The 1970s were not kind to First National Boston. It entered the decade earning about 88 cents on each $100 of assets, and left it earning 62 cents per $100 of assets in 1979. In between, there were a couple of years in which it earned less than 50 cents per $100 of assets, quite a poor showing.

The largest bank in New England also began the decade free of long-term debt, and left it with a debt ratio higher than average for a bank, about 39 percent of total capital.

Of course, without the leverage provided by that debt, the company's return on stockholders' equity would have looked not only uninspiring — as it did, ranging from 8 to 13 percent during the decade — but downright poor.

The 1980s may be much kinder to First National Boston — and will be, if 1980 was any indication. Earnings per share, which had already moved up in 1978 and 1979 from the depressed levels of the preceding three years, shot up to $8.30 (compared with $6.90 the year before and less than $4 in 1976–78). The bank earned a respectable 65 cents per $100 of assets, and trimmed back its debt to $400 million, the lowest level in six years.

Two of the reasons behind the improved showing are the economic revival that seems to be taking place in New England, and the bank's increased penetration of foreign markets — mainly in Latin America — which now account for more than 20 percent of earnings.

Most bank stocks were in the basement in the early 1980s, and First National Boston, with a p / e ratio of about 5, was in the sub-basement. If you think its rebound is going to continue, this stock could offer a good value.

* * *

FIRST NATIONAL STATE BANCORPORATION (FNS). Founded 1969. Headquarters: 550 Broad St., Newark NJ 07101. **BANKING.** Holding company for First National State Bank of New Jersey and five other banks. **MAJOR SUBSIDIARIES, BRANDS:** First National State Bank of New Jersey.

Sales: $297.8 million (trend 16.7% a year).
Earnings: $20.92 million (trend 10.7% a year).
What happened to a $10,000 investment

Purchase Date	*Purchase Price*	*Price on 12-31-81*	*Dividends Paid*
12-31-71	$32.26	$21.25	$6,097.41
12-31-76	$23.33	$21.25	$4,348.97

Purchase Date	*Cap. Gains (– Losses)*	*Total Return*	*Rate of Return*
12-31-71	$–3,413.29	$2,684.12	2.41%
12-31-76	$ –892.86	$3,456.11	6.12%

* * *

FIRST PENNSYLVANIA CORP. (FPA). Founded 1969. Headquarters: Centre Sq. Bldg., 16th & Market Sts., Philadelphia PA 19101. **FINANCIAL SERVICES.** A holding company. **MAJOR SUBSIDIARIES, BRANDS:** First Pennsylvania Bank.

Sales: $755.7 million (trend 11.1% a year).
Earnings: $–73.63 million.
What happened to a $10,000 investment

Purchase Date	*Purchase Price*	*Price on 12-31-81*	*Dividends Paid*
12-31-71	$37.25	$3.12	$2,759.73
12-31-76	$16.62	$3.12	$2,315.79

Purchase Date	*Cap. Gains (– Losses)*	*Total Return*	*Rate of Return*
12-31-71	$−9,161.07	$−6,401.34	−9.72%
12-31-76	$−8,120.30	$−5,804.51	−15.95%

* * *

FIRST PENNSYLVANIA MORTGAGE TRUST. (FPM). Founded 1970. Headquarters: 28 State St., Boston MA 02109. INVESTMENTS. An unincorporated business trust with investments in commercial and industrial properties, condominiums, and other residential areas.

Sales: $8.5 million (trend −1.6% a year).
Earnings: $.71 million.
What happened to a $10,000 investment

Purchase Date	*Purchase Price*	*Price on 12-31-81*	*Dividends Paid*
12-31-71	$27.25	$1.50	$2,447.71
12-31-76	$ 2.75	$1.50	$ 0.00

Purchase Date	*Cap. Gains (– Losses)*	*Total Return*	*Rate of Return*
12-31-71	$−9,449.54	$−7,001.83	−11.35%
12-31-76	$−4,545.45	$−4,545.45	−11.42%

* * *

FIRST UNION REAL ESTATE EQUITY & MORTGAGE INVESTMENTS. (FUR). Founded 1961. Headquarters: 55 Public Sq. Bldg., Cleveland OH 44113. REAL ESTATE INVESTMENTS. Invests mostly in shopping centers, office buildings, and other properties that produce income.

Sales: $48.4 million (trend 17.2% a year).
Earnings: $10.82 million (trend 24.5% a year).
What happened to a $10,000 investment

Purchase Date	*Purchase Price*	*Price on 12-31-81*	*Dividends Paid*
12-31-71	$7.83	$15.12	$9,463.83
12-31-76	$8.08	$15.12	$5,270.10

Purchase Date	*Cap. Gains (– Losses)*	*Total Return*	*Rate of Return*
12-31-71	$9,308.51	$18,772.34	11.15%
12-31-76	$8,711.34	$13,981.44	19.12%

* * *

FIRST VIRGINIA BANKS, INC. (FVB). Founded 1949. Headquarters: 6400 Arlington Blvd., Falls Church VA 22042. BANKING. A holding company that controls twenty-one banks, with the greatest concentration near Washington, D.C.

Sales: $158.0 million (trend 14.5% a year).
Earnings: $15.02 million (trend 18.1% a year).
What happened to a $10,000 investment

Purchase Date	*Purchase Price*	*Price on 12-31-81*	*Dividends Paid*
12-31-71	$11.25	$8.62	$4,215.56
12-31-76	$ 7.37	$8.62	$3,433.90

Purchase Date	*Cap. Gains (– Losses)*	*Total Return*	*Rate of Return*
12-31-71	$−2,333.33	$1,882.22	1.74%
12-31-76	$ 1,694.92	$5,128.81	8.63%

* * *

FIRST WISCONSIN CORP. (FWB). Founded 1929. Headquarters: 777 E. Wisconsin Ave., Milwaukee WI 53202. BANKING. Owns nineteen banks in Wisconsin. MAJOR SUBSIDIARIES, BRANDS: First Wisconsin National Bank of Milwaukee.

Sales: $513.8 million (trend 17.0% a year).
Earnings: $29.44 million (trend 23.4% a year).
What happened to a $10,000 investment

Purchase Date	*Purchase Price*	*Price on 12-31-81*	*Dividends Paid*
12-31-71	$34.62	$30.37	$5,163.90
12-31-76	$22.50	$30.37	$4,097.78

Purchase Date	*Cap. Gains (– Losses)*	*Total Return*	*Rate of Return*
12-31-71	$−1,227.44	$3,936.46	3.37%
12-31-76	$ 3,500.00	$7,597.78	11.97%

* * *

FISCHBACH CORP. (FIS). Founded 1924. Headquarters: 485 Lexington Ave., New York NY 10017. CONSTRUCTION CONTRACTOR. Electrical and mechanical contractor for construction. MAJOR SUBSIDIARIES, BRANDS: Fischbach and Moore (electrical contractor); Natkin & Co. (mechanical contractor).

Sales: $1,118.9 million (trend 13.0% a year).
Earnings: $22.22 million (trend 14.3% a year).
What happened to a $10,000 investment

Purchase Date	*Purchase Price*	*Price on 12-31-81*	*Dividends Paid*
12-31-71	$43.87	$38.25	$2,715.67
12-31-76	$30.25	$38.25	$2,338.84

Purchase Date	Cap. Gains (− Losses)	Total Return	Rate of Return
12-31-71	$−1,282.05	$1,433.62	1.35%
12-31-76	$ 2,644.63	$4,983.47	8.42%

* * *

FISHER FOODS, INC. (FHR). Founded 1908. Headquarters: 5300 Richmond Rd., Bedford Heights OH 44146. FOOD RETAILER. Operates two supermarket chains. MAJOR SUBSIDIARIES, BRANDS: Dominick's Finer Foods (in Chicago); Fazio's (in Ohio).

Sales: $1,413.0 million (trend −.5% a year).
Earnings: $6.59 million (trend −11.2% a year).
What happened to a $10,000 investment

Purchase Date	Purchase Price	Price on 12-31-81	Dividends Paid
12-31-71	$15.60	$13.25	$2,732.73
12-31-76	$11.87	$13.25	$2,273.68

Purchase Date	Cap. Gains (− Losses)	Total Return	Rate of Return
12-31-71	$−1,507.44	$1,225.29	1.16%
12-31-76	$ 1,157.89	$3,431.58	6.08%

* * *

FLEETWOOD ENTERPRISES, INC. (FLE). Founded 1950. Headquarters: 3125 Myers St., Riverside CA 92523. RECREATIONAL VEHICLES AND MOBILE HOMES. Manufactures recreational vehicles and mobile homes.

Sales: $427.6 million (trend .2% a year).
Earnings: $2.44 million (trend −23.4% a year).
What happened to a $10,000 investment

Purchase Date	Purchase Price	Price on 12-31-81	Dividends Paid
12-31-71	$36.25	$12.87	$ 868.97
12-31-76	$19.25	$12.87	$1,049.35

Purchase Date	Cap. Gains (− Losses)	Total Return	Rate of Return
12-31-71	$−6,448.28	$−5,579.31	−7.84%
12-31-76	$−3,311.69	$−2,262.34	−5.00%

* * *

FLEMING COS., INC. (FLM). Founded 1915. Headquarters: 6601 N. Broadway, PO Box 26647, Oklahoma City OK 73126. WHOLESALE FOOD DISTRIBUTING. Deals with the procurement, warehousing, order selection, and delivery of food and related products. The company also owns forty-eight retail supermarkets. MAJOR SUBSIDIARIES, BRANDS: Piggly Wiggly.

Sales: $2,817.0 million (trend 12.0% a year).
Earnings: $20.70 million (trend 10.8% a year).
What happened to a $10,000 investment

Purchase Date	Purchase Price	Price on 12-31-81	Dividends Paid
12-31-71	$11.75	$26.25	$6,885.11
12-31-76	$16.37	$26.25	$2,955.73

Purchase Date	Cap. Gains (− Losses)	Total Return	Rate of Return
12-31-71	$12,340.43	$19,225.53	11.32%
12-31-76	$ 6,030.53	$ 8,986.26	13.68%

* * *

FLEXI-VAN CORP. (FLX). Founded 1955. Headquarters: 330 Madison Ave., New York NY 10017. TRANSPORTATION EQUIPMENT LEASING. Leases cargo containers, chassis and over-the-road trailers internationally.

Sales: $190.8 million (trend 18.5% a year).
Earnings: $15.37 million (trend 36.4% a year).
What happened to a $10,000 investment

Purchase Date	Purchase Price	Price on 12-31-81	Dividends Paid
12-31-71	$14.64	$20.12	$2,595.26
12-31-76	$11.87	$20.12	$2,905.26

Purchase Date	Cap. Gains (− Losses)	Total Return	Rate of Return
12-31-71	$3,744.63	$6,339.89	5.03%
12-31-76	$6,947.37	$9,852.63	14.70%

* * *

FLIGHTSAFETY INTERNATIONAL, INC. (FSI). Founded 1951. Headquarters: Marine Air Terminal, La Guardia Airport, Flushing NY 11371. PILOT TRAINING. Trains pilots for private and commercial planes, technicians and crews for ocean vessels.

Sales: $51.3 million (trend 33.1% a year).
Earnings: $13.88 million (trend 33.8% a year).
What happened to a $10,000 investment

Purchase Date	Purchase Price	Price on 12-31-81	Dividends Paid
12-31-71	$1.06	$33.25	$3,578.74
12-31-76	$2.72	$33.25	$1,338.69

Purchase Date	Cap. Gains (− Losses)	Total Return	Rate of Return
12-31-71	$305,000.00	$308,578.74	41.36%
12-31-76	$112,142.86	$113,481.55	65.32%

* * *

FLOATING POINT SYSTEMS, INC. (FLP). Founded 1970. Headquarters: 3601 S.W. Murray Blvd., Beaverton OR 97005. COMPUTERS. Makes specialized computers, particularly for use in sophisticated X-ray and medical diagnostic equipment.

Sales: $42.4 million (trend 29.4% a year).
Earnings: $4.24 million (trend 32.3% a year).

* * *

FLORIDA EAST COAST RAILWAY CO. (FLA). Founded 1892. Headquarters: 1 Malago St., St. Augustine FL 32084. FREIGHT RAILROAD. Carries cars, rock, cement, sugar and other commodities over 859 miles of track in Florida.

Sales: $100.5 million (trend 17.6% a year).
Earnings: $19.22 million (trend 47.0% a year).
What happened to a $10,000 investment

Purchase Date	Purchase Price	Price on 12-31-81	Dividends Paid
12-31-71	$7.84	$18.25	$254.98
12-31-76	$6.87	$18.25	$290.91

Purchase Date	Cap. Gains (− Losses)	Total Return	Rate of Return
12-31-71	$13,266.93	$13,521.91	8.93%
12-31-76	$16,545.45	$16,836.36	21.83%

* * *

FLORIDA POWER & LIGHT CO. (FPL). Founded 1925. Headquarters: 9250 W. Flagler St., Miami FL 33152. UTILITY. Supplies electricity to major portions of Florida. 10,000 employees.

Sales: $2,347.3 million (trend 15.4% a year).
Earnings: $162.46 million (trend 9.8% a year).
What happened to a $10,000 investment

Purchase Date	Purchase Price	Price on 12-31-81	Dividends Paid
12-31-71	$36.31	$29.37	$5,001.03
12-31-76	$27.62	$29.37	$4,191.86

Purchase Date	Cap. Gains (− Losses)	Total Return	Rate of Return
12-31-71	$−1,910.50	$3,090.53	2.73%
12-31-76	$ 633.48	$4,825.34	8.19%

PROFILE: Like most utility stocks, this is one you should consider only for income, rather than for capital gains. True, the population growth in Florida means that Florida Power & Light may be experiencing a gradual rise in demand for electricity, while demand in most places is flat. That could lead to some earnings growth, and in turn, possibly, to some moderate capital gains. But don't count on it, and don't buy the stock for that.

The combination of yield and safety may appeal to conservative investors. The yield, as of 1981, was around 10 or 11 percent. You could get a bit more on some other utility stocks (in most cases, 12 to 14 percent), but some of them were on rather shaky ground financially. And, as mentioned above, few of them had any growth prospects.

In any other buisness, Florida Power & Light wouldn't be holding its balance sheet out with pride for the inspection of conservative investors. But a debt load of around half of total capital isn't considered bad for a utility these days.

The fuel mixture for power generation is fairly well balanced among various fuels. In 1979 it was a bit more than half oil, about a quarter nuclear, and a bit less than a quarter natural gas. Increased use of coal is planned, though, both through a major new generating facility designed to use coal, and through an experimental program for using an oil-and-coal mixture.

The stock has one other virtue, as of the early 1980s: It's cheap. The p / e ratio has been 6 or below during much of the period from 1977 through 1981.

* * *

FLORIDA POWER CORP. (FDP). Founded 1899. Headquarters: 3201 34th St. South, St. Petersburg FL 33711. UTILITIES. An electric utility company that serves areas in central and west coast Florida.

Sales: $970.2 million (trend 14.2% a year).
Earnings: $49.88 million (trend 1.4% a year).
What happened to a $10,000 investment

Purchase Date	Purchase Price	Price on 12-31-81	Dividends Paid
12-31-71	$23.12	$15.62	$5,148.65
12-31-76	$16.12	$15.62	$4,400.00

Purchase Date	*Cap. Gains (– Losses)*	*Total Return*	*Rate of Return*
12-31-71	$–3,243.24	$1,905.41	1.76%
12-31-76	$ –310.08	$4,089.92	7.10%

* * *

FLORIDA STEEL CORP. (FLS). Founded 1956. Headquarters: 1715 Cleveland St., Tampa FL 33606. **STEEL.** Manufactures primarily steel reinforcing bars. Also produces fabricated structural steel products and miscellaneous metals.

Sales: $319.5 million (trend 25.7% a year).
Earnings: $19.92 million (trend 64.3% a year).
What happened to a $10,000 investment

Purchase Date	*Purchase Price*	*Price on 12-31-81*	*Dividends Paid*
12-31-71	$6.94	$19.25	$5,443.24
12-31-76	$5.09	$19.25	$4,220.86

Purchase Date	*Cap. Gains (– Losses)*	*Total Return*	*Rate of Return*
12-31-71	$17,747.75	$23,190.99	12.75%
12-31-76	$27,791.41	$32,012.27	33.25%

* * *

FLOW GENERAL INC. (FGN). Founded 1975. Headquarters: 7655 Old Springhouse Rd., McLean VA 22102. **BIOMEDICAL RESEARCH.** Makes products for medical and biology research laboratories; also conducts contract research. **MAJOR SUBSIDIARIES, BRANDS:** Effects Technology, Inc.; Flow Laboratories; Mosely Associates, Inc.

Sales: $112.0 million (trend 22.5% a year).
Earnings: $7.96 million (trend 53.2% a year).
What happened to a $10,000 investment

Purchase Date	*Purchase Price*	*Price on 12-31-81*	*Dividends Paid*
12-31-71	$3.58	$27.75	$0.00
12-31-76	$1.21	$27.75	$0.00

Purchase Date	*Cap. Gains (– Losses)*	*Total Return*	*Rate of Return*
12-31-71	$ 67,441.86	$ 67,441.86	22.71%
12-31-76	$219,655.17	$219,655.17	87.16%

* * *

FLUOR CORP. (FLR). Founded 1924. Headquarters: 3333 Michelson Dr., Irvine CA 92730. **ENGINEERING.** Fluor is one of the nation's leading engineering and construction companies, with a specialty in oil, chemical, and synfuel plants. Also produces oil and coal, and in 1981 acquired St. Joe Minerals, a major producer of lead, zinc, coal, and precious metals. 25,000 employees (excluding St. Joe's). **MAJOR SUBSIDIARIES, BRANDS:** Daniel International; Peabody Coal (10 percent owned).

Sales: $4,826.3 million (trend 28.8% a year).
Earnings: $131.89 million (trend 20.1% a year).
What happened to a $10,000 investment

Purchase Date	*Purchase Price*	*Price on 12-31-81*	*Dividends Paid*
12-31-71	$ 4.41	$30.25	$6,955.57
12-31-76	$12.75	$30.25	$2,091.63

Purchase Date	*Cap. Gains (– Losses)*	*Total Return*	*Rate of Return*
12-31-71	$58,606.90	$65,562.47	22.41%
12-31-76	$13,725.49	$15,817.12	20.89%

PROFILE: Fluor is a magnificent company. But is it a magnificent stock? That's a separate question. The answer depends on when you buy it.

Certainly the stock was a superb investment vehicle for anyone wise enough to buy it in the mid-1970s. As recently as 1975 you could have bought Fluor shares for $5 each, which was about 5 times that year's earnings. If you'd sold at the 1980 high of $71, you would have reaped more than $1,400 for every $100 you invested.

Okay, that's an extreme example. Let's take 1978 instead. Fluor's high for the year was $14.50 a share. If you'd bought then, you could easily have quadrupled your money.

But that was a few years ago. Today the company is much better known, chiefly for its role as a leader in building synfuel plants. It was speculation over the potential for a boom in synfuels — to be spurred, investors thought, by government subsidies — that sparked the rise to $71 a share. Then two developments punctured the balloon. First, the Reagan administration said the heck with subsidies for synfuel development. Second, Fluor acquired St. Joe Minerals — another fine company, but one in a less glamorous industry (mining) than Fluor's (energy engineering). The merger, valued at between $2.5 and $3 billion, will dilute Fluor's earnings per share for a while. The two developments, combined, caused the stock to drop from the 1980 high of $71 to about $27 in early 1982.

Thus, a stock that sold for 26 times earnings in 1980 was recently selling for about 9 times earnings, a much less exorbitant price.

The balance sheet, preceding the merger, was extremely strong, with debt only 12 percent of capital. It should remain strong: St. Joe also has piles of cash.

The dividend yield is quite modest, ranging from 1 to 3 percent yield in recent years.

* * *

FOOTE, CONE & BELDING COMMUNICATIONS, INC. (FCB). Founded 1942. Headquarters: 401 N. Michigan Ave., Chicago IL 60611. **ADVERTISING.** Plans and creates advertising for radio, television, magazines, and newspapers and does promotion work.

Sales: $164.7 million (trend 24.7% a year).
Earnings: $11.36 million (trend 26.1% a year).
What happened to a $10,000 investment

Purchase Date	*Purchase Price*	*Price on 12-31-81*	*Dividends Paid*
12-31-71	$10.50	$28.25	$11,142.86
12-31-76	$15.75	$28.25	$ 4,984.13

Purchase Date	*Cap. Gains (− Losses)*	*Total Return*	*Rate of Return*
12-31-71	$16,904.76	$28,047.62	14.30%
12-31-76	$ 7,936.51	$12,920.63	18.04%

* * *

FORD MOTOR CO. (F). Founded 1919. Headquarters: The American Road, Dearborn MI 48121. **AUTOS.** Ford is the second-largest automobile manufacturer in the U.S. Also a major producer of trucks and military vehicles. 495,000 employees. **MAJOR SUBSIDIARIES, BRANDS:** Ford, Lincoln, Mercury; Ford Motor Credit Co.

Sales: $37,085.5 million (trend 10.6% a year).
Earnings: $−1,543.30 million.
What happened to a $10,000 investment

Purchase Date	*Purchase Price*	*Price on 12-31-81*	*Dividends Paid*
12-31-71	$56.20	$16.75	$4,594.31
12-31-76	$49.20	$16.75	$2,894.31

Purchase Date	*Cap. Gains (− Losses)*	*Total Return*	*Rate of Return*
12-31-71	$−7,019.57	$−2,425.27	−2.74%
12-31-76	$−6,595.53	$−3,701.22	−8.83%

PROFILE: Like all auto stocks, Ford is cyclical in the extreme. Earnings reached a cyclical peak of $5.06 a share in 1965, and fell to 65 cents a share in 1967. They rose to $7.30 a share at the next peak in 1973, then in 1975 fell to $1.95 in the next valley. Up again to a $14.16 crest in 1977. Since then, earnings have declined each year, to a loss of $12.83 a share in 1980, the company's first loss in more than three decades, and a huge loss in 1981.

Was 1980-81 just another downturn in a normal business cycle? Not really. Ford is hurting in ways that it hasn't in the past: It's losing market share to both General Motors and Japanese imports. Whereas Ford controlled about 25 percent of the U.S. auto market in 1972, it controlled only about 23 percent in the early 1980s. In early 1982, it skipped paying a dividend for the first time since the company went public in 1956.

So the company has some serious problems. But is it another Chrysler, teetering on the verge of bankruptcy, or another American Motors, needing a foreign merger partner to survive? Probably neither. The company may well be able to pull its way out of its troubles by becoming more efficient and by building smaller, more fuel-efficient cars. That requires a tremendous amount of retooling, and a breathtaking amount of money. The money probably won't be raised by issuing stock — that would dilute already weak earnings. Besides, with the stock selling in late 1981 at about $18 a share (versus close to $66 a share in 1973), it wouldn't be a sensible way to raise the cash. So the company, which traditionally has had a strong balance sheet (with long-term debt between 10 and 20 percent of capital) might have to take on a lot more debt.

One plus materialized in 1982, when the United Auto Workers traded an estimated $1 billion of benefit concessions for increased job security.

If one believes the U.S. can support at least two domestic car makers, there's a real question how much lower this stock could go. At the late 1981 price of $18, Ford was selling at far less than 2 times its 1977 earnings. The p / e hasn't been above 6 since 1976. Yet as recently as 1974 the stock sold for 14 times earnings. A long-term investor with a tolerance for some risk might be well rewarded here.

* * *

FOREMOST-MCKESSON, INC. (FOR). Founded 1928. Headquarters: Crocker Plaza, 1 Post St., San Francisco CA 94104. **DISTRIBUTION, FOOD PRODUCTION.** Foremost-McKesson is the nation's largest distributor of drugs, alcoholic beverages, and chemicals. It is also a major distributor of food products, and a producer of food products including dairy products, pasta, and bottled water. 16,000 employees. **MAJOR SUBSIDIARIES, BRANDS:**

Foremost (dairy products); Mueller (pasta); Dolly Madison (ice cream); Alhambra, Crystal, and Sparklett bottled water.

Sales: $4,132.6 million (trend 10.2% a year).
Earnings: $67.78 million (trend 18.6% a year).
What happened to a $10,000 investment

Purchase Date	*Purchase Price*	*Price on 12-31-81*	*Dividends Paid*
12-31-71	$24.62	$36.75	$4,249.75
12-31-76	$15.50	$36.75	$3,861.29

Purchase Date	*Cap. Gains (– Losses)*	*Total Return*	*Rate of Return*
12-31-71	$ 4,923.86	$ 9,173.60	6.73%
12-31-76	$13,709.68	$17,570.97	22.49%

PROFILE: Say you're a pharmacist with a drugstore to keep stocked. Do you order your prescription drugs directly from the many manufacturers? No; more than likely you deal with a distributor. The largest such distributor, and the only nationwide one, is Foremost-McKesson.

Much the same applies to buyers who need chemicals, or liquor store owners stocking their shelves. They too turn to distributors, and Foremost-McKesson is a major force in these markets also. All in all, distribution accounts for about two thirds of the company's sales and profits.

The remaining third or so comes from production, mainly of food products, especially dairy items. When you put together this blend of businesses, what you have is a company that is solid, stable, and slow-growing. The price / earnings ratio is often below that of the average stock. Profitability is about average. The balance sheet is a little bit on the leveraged side but has become less so over the years. The dividend yield is substantial— 6 to 7 percent in most recent years.

The company's newest business is chemical recycling, which may be a growth area. As of 1981 there were plans to build half a dozen chemical recycling plants.

* * *

FORT DEARBORN INCOME SECURITIES, INC. (FTD). Founded 1972. Headquarters: 126 S. State St., Room 800, Chicago IL 60603. INVESTMENTS. Primarily invests to create current income for its shareholders.

* * *

FORT HOWARD PAPER CO. (FHP). Founded 1919. Headquarters: 1919 S. Broadway, Green Bay WI 54304. PAPER PRODUCTS. Manufactures towels, tissues, paper napkins, and other paper items. MAJOR SUBSIDIARIES, BRANDS: Dolly Madison, Page, Edon, So-Dri, and Mardi Gras paper products.

Sales: $397.4 million (trend 14.2% a year).
Earnings: $68.70 million (trend 13.2% a year).
What happened to a $10,000 investment

Purchase Date	*Purchase Price*	*Price on 12-31-81*	*Dividends Paid*
12-31-71	$ 8.84	$40.50	$4,853.99
12-31-76	$18.25	$40.50	$1,767.12

Purchase Date	*Cap. Gains (– Losses)*	*Total Return*	*Rate of Return*
12-31-71	$35,795.05	$40,649.05	17.61%
12-31-76	$12,191.78	$13,958.90	19.09%

* * *

FOSTER WHEELER CORP. (FWC). Founded 1927. Headquarters: 110 S. Orange Ave., Livingston NJ 07039. ENGINEERING, CONSTRUCTION. Designs and builds power plants, oil refineries, chemical plants, and other industrial plants; also makes industrial and construction equipment. 17,000 employees.

Sales: $1,562.5 million (trend 11.1% a year).
Earnings: $59.36 million (trend 33.6% a year).
What happened to a $10,000 investment

Purchase Date	*Purchase Price*	*Price on 12-31-81*	*Dividends Paid*
12-31-71	$2.89	$14.62	$7,642.57
12-31-76	$5.22	$14.62	$3,075.45

Purchase Date	*Cap. Gains (– Losses)*	*Total Return*	*Rate of Return*
12-31-71	$40,659.76	$48,302.33	19.28%
12-31-76	$18,023.95	$21,099.40	25.47%

PROFILE: Foster Wheeler plays in a profitable, but tough, league. In construction and engineering, it goes head to head against such powerhouses as Fluor and Parsons. In the construction of steam generating plants, it ranks number three in size behind J. Ray McDermott and Combustion Engineering, but has been more profitable in most recent years than either.

The pattern of price action in recent years is very similar to that of Fluor. You could have picked up Foster Wheeler shares for less than $2 in 1974 or 1975, and ridden them up to a 1980 high of a bit more than $30, thus multiplying your holdings by a factor of 15, assuming ideal timing. Even without ideal timing, the person who bought in at the 1978 high of $10.12 a share had plenty of reason to be pleased.

But that's history, and investors must ask whether these shares are over- or undervalued at the time a purchase is contemplated. There was a correction in early 1981, when the shares backed down from $30 to $21. Even the latter price represented 13 times 1980 earnings, at a time when the average stock fetched only 8. This company, riding a decade of earnings increases, holding good prospects and a fat backlog, may be worth a premium price. But check the p / e and watch out if it begins to overheat.

The balance sheet is strong; debt recently was only about 15 percent of total capital. Dividends have been increased each year since 1973, but gradually. The rising stock price has left the dividend yield in the very modest 1–2 percent range.

* * *

FOTOMAT CORP. (FOT). Founded 1971. Headquarters: 64 Danbury Rd., Wilton CT 06897. PHOTOFINISHING. Operates a chain of more than 3,800 stores that develop camera film and sell film, video tape, and accessories.

Sales: $235.1 million (trend 14.0% a year).
Earnings: $.73 million (trend −38.7% a year).
What happened to a $10,000 investment

Purchase Date	*Purchase Price*	*Price on 12-31-81*	*Dividends Paid*
12-31-71	$ 5.75	$6.50	$2,452.17
12-31-76	$12.25	$6.50	$ 906.12

Purchase Date	*Cap. Gains (− Losses)*	*Total Return*	*Rate of Return*
12-31-71	$ 1,304.35	$ 3,756.52	3.24%
12-31-76	$−4,693.88	$−3,787.76	−9.08%

* * *

FOUR-PHASE SYSTEMS, INC. (FPS). Founded 1969. Headquarters: 10700 N. DeAnza Blvd., Cupertino CA 95014. COMPUTER SYSTEMS. Designer and manufacturer of data processing systems.

Sales: $197.2 million (trend 34.6% a year).
Earnings: $5.45 million (trend 43.2% a year).
What happened to a $10,000 investment

Purchase Date	*Purchase Price*	*Price on 12-31-81*	*Dividends Paid*
12-31-71	$ N/A	$40.25	$0.00
12-31-76	$16.87	$40.25	$0.00

Purchase Date	*Cap. Gains (− Losses)*	*Total Return*	*Rate of Return*
12-31-71	$ N/A	$ N/A	N/A%
12-31-76	$13,851.85	$13,851.85	18.99%

* * *

FOX-STANLEY PHOTO PRODUCTS, INC. (FSP). Founded 1905. Headquarters: 8750 Tesoro Dr., San Antonio TX 78286. PHOTOFINISHING. Provides photofinishing services, sells photographic products, greeting cards, and gift lines.

Sales: $153.5 million (trend 18.2% a year).
Earnings: $6.25 million (trend 17.2% a year).
What happened to a $10,000 investment

Purchase Date	*Purchase Price*	*Price on 12-31-81*	*Dividends Paid*
12-31-71	$17.12	$10.50	$2,496.35
12-31-76	$ 9.75	$10.50	$2,523.08

Purchase Date	*Cap. Gains (− Losses)*	*Total Return*	*Rate of Return*
12-31-71	$−3,868.61	$−1,372.26	−1.47%
12-31-76	$ 769.23	$ 3,292.31	5.86%

* * *

FOXBORO CO. (FOX). Founded 1914. Headquarters: 38 Neponset Ave., Foxboro MA 02035. ANALYTICAL INSTRUMENTS. Manufactures instruments and monitoring systems for controlling temperature, flow and density of materials, and other production processes.

Sales: $509.1 million (trend 11.2% a year).
Earnings: $32.05 million (trend 10.3% a year).
What happened to a $10,000 investment

Purchase Date	*Purchase Price*	*Price on 12-31-81*	*Dividends Paid*
12-31-71	$24.33	$52.37	$3,253.42
12-31-76	$33.00	$52.37	$1,772.73

Purchase Date	*Cap. Gains (− Losses)*	*Total Return*	*Rate of Return*
12-31-71	$11,523.97	$14,777.40	9.50%
12-31-76	$ 5,871.21	$ 7,643.94	12.03%

* * *

FREEPORT-MCMORAN INC. (FTX). Founded 1913. Headquarters: 200 Park Ave., New York NY 10017. **MINERAL PRODUCTION.** Produces sulfur and other minerals; explores for and produces oil and natural gas. **MAJOR SUBSIDIARIES, BRANDS:** Freeport Minerals Co.; McMoRan Oil and Gas Co.

Sales: $664.4 million (trend 16.9% a year).
Earnings: $147.40 million (trend 32.0% a year).
What happened to a $10,000 investment

Purchase Date	*Purchase Price*	*Price on 12-31-81*	*Dividends Paid*
12-31-71	$4.52	$23.87	$8,537.03
12-31-76	$7.30	$23.87	$3,247.49

Purchase Date	*Cap. Gains (− Losses)*	*Total Return*	*Rate of Return*
12-31-71	$42,835.66	$51,372.69	19.89%
12-31-76	$22,686.47	$25,933.95	29.15%

* * *

FRIGITRONICS, INC. (FRG). Founded 1967. Headquarters: 770 River Rd., Shelton CT 06486. **OPTICAL PRODUCTS.** Processes prescription optical products and distributes instruments for eye care.

Sales: $90.0 million (trend 15.3% a year).
Earnings: $4.83 million (trend 20.5% a year).
What happened to a $10,000 investment

Purchase Date	*Purchase Price*	*Price on 12-31-81*	*Dividends Paid*
12-31-71	$37.87	$17.62	$269.31
12-31-76	$17.50	$17.62	$525.71

Purchase Date	*Cap. Gains (− Losses)*	*Total Return*	*Rate of Return*
12-31-71	$−5,346.53	$−5,077.23	−6.84%
12-31-76	$ 71.43	$ 597.14	1.17%

* * *

FRUEHAUF CORP. (FTR). Founded 1918. Headquarters: 10900 Harper Ave., Detroit MI 48213. **TRUCK TRAILERS, AUTO PARTS.** Fruehauf is the world's largest maker of truck trailers, controlling about a quarter to a third of the U.S. market. Also involved in auto parts manufacture, shipbuilding, and aerospace. 33,000 employees. **MAJOR SUBSIDIARIES, BRANDS:** Kelsey-Hayes Co.

Sales: $2,081.7 million (trend 15.2% a year).
Earnings: $32.21 million (trend 9.9% a year).
What happened to a $10,000 investment

Purchase Date	*Purchase Price*	*Price on 12-31-81*	*Dividends Paid*
12-31-71	$38.87	$18.62	$5,080.39
12-31-76	$27.62	$18.62	$3,945.70

Purchase Date	*Cap. Gains (− Losses)*	*Total Return*	*Rate of Return*
12-31-71	$−5,209.00	$−128.62	−.13%
12-31-76	$−3,257.92	$ 687.78	1.34%

PROFILE: An energy play? This lumbering old maker of truck trailers an energy play? Well, you could make a case for it. Fruehauf is now working on a new generation of truck trailers that are lighter and can haul more cargo at a smaller fuel cost than those of years past. To boot, the Kelsey-Hayes subsidiary is a leading maker of small-car wheels, just what the market demands for the new generation of downsized cars.

Whether to buy this line of reasoning is an open question. But there's another case for Fruehauf — simply that, like almost all stocks in the automotive group, it's depressed and due for a rebound. In Fruehauf's case the stock price peaked way back in 1969, at about $48 a share. The recent low came in 1974, at about $13 a share. The stock made it back up to $40 in 1979, but was selling for only about $19 in late 1981. Earnings, naturally, are cyclical, but their underlying growth rate isn't bad. The late 1981 price was only 3 times 1979 earnings, and only about 7 times depressed 1980 earnings.

A possible negative is the balance sheet, where debt has been edging up in recent years and accounted for 43 percent of capital in early 1982. The debt load adds to the risk, but will also provide leverage for a dramatic rise in the stock price if things fall into place and car and truck-trailer sales take off in the mid-1980s.

Anyone willing to run this risk can console himself while waiting for a payoff by cashing the hefty dividend checks — assuming, of course, that they last. Fully 91 percent of 1980 profits were paid in dividends. But the company has paid dividends each year since 1960, and the yield in recent years has been 7 to 9 percent.

* * *

FUQUA INDUSTRIES, INC. (FQA). Founded 1929. Headquarters: 3800 First National Bank

Tower, Atlanta GA 30383. **MANUFACTURING.** Makes recreational goods, farm and home items. Petroleum distribution operations, which used to account for more than half of sales, were sold in 1981. Owns 40 percent of Pier 1 Imports, Inc.

Sales: $1,589.5 million (trend 34.7% a year).
Earnings: $30.22 million (trend 35.8% a year).
What happened to a $10,000 investment

Purchase Date	*Purchase Price*	*Price on 12-31-81*	*Dividends Paid*
12-31-71	$21.39	$21.25	$1,154.96
12-31-76	$11.50	$21.25	$2,008.70

Purchase Date	*Cap. Gains (− Losses)*	*Total Return*	*Rate of Return*
12-31-71	$ −63.60	$ 1,091.36	1.04%
12-31-76	$8,478.26	$10,486.96	15.42%

G

GAF CORP. (GAF). Founded 1929. Headquarters: 140 W. 51st St., New York NY 10020. **CHEMICALS, BUILDING MATERIALS.** GAF makes specialty chemicals, roofing, insulation, and flooring. 16,000 employees. **MAJOR SUBSIDIARIES, BRANDS:** Timberline and Sentinel (shingles); Gaftemp (insulation).

Sales: $677.2 million (trend −3.5% a year).
Earnings: $6.70 million (trend −14.8% a year).
What happened to a $10,000 investment

Purchase Date	*Purchase Price*	*Price on 12-31-81*	*Dividends Paid*
12-31-71	$23.25	$14.37	$2,524.73
12-31-76	$13.37	$14.37	$2,609.35

Purchase Date	*Cap. Gains (− Losses)*	*Total Return*	*Rate of Return*
12-31-71	$−3,817.20	$−1,292.47	−1.37%
12-31-76	$ 747.66	$ 3,357.01	5.96%

PROFILE: In case you ever wondered, GAF stands (or used to stand) for General Aniline & Film. The company went public under that name in 1965, and adopted the stock market abbreviation as its official name in 1968.

The manufacture of film happens to be one of nine operations put up for sale in 1980, leaving building materials and specialty chemicals as the two remaining activities. The idea was to strip the company down to its core operations, and to raise cash.

Cash is much needed, because the company had become top-heavy with debt. In early 1982 debt was a worrisome 55 percent of total capital. About a third of the rest was preferred stock, so holders of common stock were the third segment of a long line. The company nevertheless had kept the common stock dividend growing each year since 1972, even though this meant paying out dividends in 1980, when the company (primarily because of the massive restructuring, sell-offs, and write-offs of various divisions) lost $233 million, more than the sum of the profits in the preceding ten years. (The company had also lost $47 million in 1977.) The dividend yield, 5 to 7 percent in recent years, can't really be regarded as secure under these circumstances.

The stock price, which edged above $25 in 1972, hasn't been anywhere near that since. The stock hit a low of $6 a share in 1974, and was selling for $14 a share in late 1981. That price was about 7 times 1979 earnings. It was 6 times the peak earnings of $2.06 a share, which were achieved back in 1975.

Under these circumstances, the company must be praised for trying radical surgery. The results of the operation aren't in yet. Until they are, the stock is probably of interest only to speculators.

* * *

GATX CORP. (GMT). Founded 1916. Headquarters: 120 S. Riverside Plaza, Chicago IL 60606. **CAPITAL EQUIPMENT LEASING.** GATX Corp. provides capital equipment and related services to a variety of domestic and foreign industrial markets. **MAJOR SUBSIDIARIES, BRANDS:** Fuller Co.; GATX Tank Erection Corp.; General American Transportation Corp.

Sales: $992.7 million (trend 12.6% a year).
Earnings: $66.47 million (trend 10.5% a year).
What happened to a $10,000 investment

Purchase Date	*Purchase Price*	*Price on 12-31-81*	*Dividends Paid*
12-31-71	$53.75	$30.50	$3,527.44
12-31-76	$34.25	$30.50	$2,978.10

Purchase Date	*Cap. Gains (− Losses)*	*Total Return*	*Rate of Return*
12-31-71	$−4,325.58	$−798.14	−.83%
12-31-76	$−1,094.89	$ 1,883.21	3.51%

* * *

GCA CORP. (GCA). Founded 1958. Headquarters: 209 Burlington Rd., Bedford MA 01730. **CAPITAL EQUIPMENT.** GCA Corp. manufactures capital equipment for the semiconductor and metal processing industries; also makes laboratory equipment and performs research and development projects in environmental quality. **MAJOR SUBSIDIARIES, BRANDS:** GCA / Burlington Division; Precision Scientific; Mann (capital equipment).

Sales: $170.1 million (trend 32.9% a year).
Earnings: $13.10 million (trend 103.7% a year).
What happened to a $10,000 investment

Purchase Date	*Purchase Price*	*Price on 12-31-81*	*Dividends Paid*
12-31-71	$3.33	$27.37	$1,233.50
12-31-76	$2.33	$27.37	$1,762.14

Purchase Date	*Cap. Gains (− Losses)*	*Total Return*	*Rate of Return*
12-31-71	$ 72,125.00	$ 73,358.50	23.62%
12-31-76	$107,321.43	$109,083.57	64.12%

* * *

GEICO CORP. (GEC). Founded 1979. Headquarters: GEICO Plaza, Washington DC 20076. **INSURANCE.** GEICO Corp. sells automobile, homeowner, and fire insurance. **MAJOR SUBSIDIARIES, BRANDS:** Criterion Insurance Co.; Government Employees Insurance Co.; Government Employees Life Insurance Co. (65.3 percent owned); Government Employees Financial Corp. (55.15 percent owned).

* * *

GEO INTERNATIONAL CORP. (GX). Founded 1981. Headquarters: 1 Landmark Sq., Stamford CT 06901. **OIL FIELD SERVICES.** GEO International Corp. provides seismic services and drilling and production equipment and services for the oil and gas industries; also involved in nondestructive testing of products and services for energy-related markets, electronics, and industry. **MAJOR SUBSIDIARIES, BRANDS:** Geo Churchill, Inc.; Geo Drilling Fluids; Geo Vann, Inc.; Magnaflux Corp.

* * *

GF BUSINESS EQUIPMENT, INC. (GFB). Founded 1902. Headquarters: 229 E. Dennick Ave., Youngstown OH 44501. **OFFICE FURNITURE.** GF Business Equipment, Inc., manufactures office furniture and equipment; also makes parts for industrial and heavy construction equipment.

Sales: $168.7 million (trend 12.9% a year).
Earnings: $2.00 million (trend 20.3% a year).
What happened to a $10,000 investment

Purchase Date	*Purchase Price*	*Price on 12-31-81*	*Dividends Paid*
12-31-71	$9.25	$4.25	$1,481.08
12-31-76	$5.37	$4.25	$ 186.05

Purchase Date	*Cap. Gains (− Losses)*	*Total Return*	*Rate of Return*
12-31-71	$−5,405.41	$−3,924.32	−4.86%
12-31-76	$−2,093.02	$−1,906.98	−4.14%

* * *

GALVESTON-HOUSTON CO. (GHX). Founded 1936. Headquarters: 4801 Woodway Dr., Houston TX 77056. **OIL SERVICES.** Galveston-Houston Co. manufactures pipeline and oil processing equipment; also provides drilling and oil well services. **MAJOR SUBSIDIARIES, BRANDS:** Hensley Industries, Inc.; Texas Reamer Co.

Sales: $145.9 million (trend 50.7% a year).
Earnings: $10.58 million (trend 33.7% a year).
What happened to a $10,000 investment

Purchase Date	*Purchase Price*	*Price on 12-31-81*	*Dividends Paid*
12-31-71	$N/A	$28.25	$ N/A
12-31-76	$ 6.33	$28.25	$2,056.18

Purchase Date	*Cap. Gains (− Losses)*	*Total Return*	*Rate of Return*
12-31-71	$ N/A	$ N/A	N/A%
12-31-76	$34,605.26	$36,661.44	36.08%

* * *

GANNETT CO., INC. (GCI). Founded 1923. Headquarters: Lincoln Tower, Rochester NY 14604. **COMMUNICATIONS.** Gannett is the nation's largest newspaper chain, with more than 100 newspapers owned. It is also involved in broadcasting (owning some twenty radio and TV stations) and satellite communications, and is the nation's largest vendor of outdoor (billboard) advertising. 24,000 employees. **MAJOR SUBSIDIARIES, BRANDS:** Cincinnati *Enquirer,* Oakland *Tribune,* Combined Communications.

Sales: $1,215.0 million (trend 30.1% a year).
Earnings: $151.98 million (trend 33.5% a year).
What happened to a $10,000 investment

Purchase Date	*Purchase Price*	*Price on 12-31-81*	*Dividends Paid*
12-31-71	$19.17	$36.12	$3,883.48
12-31-76	$26.92	$36.12	$2,178.33

Purchase Date	*Cap. Gains (– Losses)*	*Total Return*	*Rate of Return*
12-31-71	$8,847.83	$12,731.30	8.56%
12-31-76	$3,421.05	$ 5,599.38	9.30%

PROFILE: "There is no reason why Gannett can't be the biggest communications company in the world," chairman Allen Neuharth told *Time* magazine in 1980. He probably means it. In the meantime Gannett is already the country's largest newspaper chain, largest seller of outdoor advertising, and one of the most profitable communications companies. Earnings have been up every year since 1966, which means they've risen through two sizable recessions — no mean trick for a communications company.

Wall Street has rewarded the company with a fairly high price / earnings ratio — 14 as of early 1981, a time when the average stock fetched only 8. In what was generally a dull decade for the stock market, Gannett doubled, from a 1971 high of $20 a share to an early 1981 price of a bit over $40.

To go with your hoped-for capital gains, there's a bit of a dividend. To paraphrase Hemingway, the dividend also rises — at least it has each year since 1971. However, the yield is modest — about 3 to 4 percent in recent years.

Time characterized Gannett papers as "invariably well packaged, smartly designed, and slickly promoted." Each paper enjoys considerable editorial autonomy. The chain generally sought out small and medium-sized papers away from urban areas. However, the 1979 merger with Combined Communications brought in some larger papers, such as the Cincinnati *Enquirer* and Oakland *Tribune.* In 1981 *Fortune* commented, "There aren't many good newspapers left to be gobbled up, so the largest of the chains is looking at new ventures, including communications satellites."

* * *

GAP STORES, INC. (GPS). Founded 1969. Headquarters: 900 Cherry Ave., PO Box 60, San Bruno CA 94066. **RETAIL CLOTHING.** Manufactures and sells blue jeans and related products to men, women, and children.

Sales: $369.8 million (trend 35.4% a year).
Earnings: $11.10 million (trend 19.6% a year).
What happened to a $10,000 investment

Purchase Date	*Purchase Price*	*Price on 12-31-81*	*Dividends Paid*
12-31-71	$N/A	$13.25	$ N/A
12-31-76	$ 9.62	$13.25	$1,324.68

Purchase Date	*Cap. Gains (– Losses)*	*Total Return*	*Rate of Return*
12-31-71	$ N/A	$ N/A	N/A%
12-31-76	$3,766.23	$5,090.91	8.58%

* * *

GAS SERVICE CO. (GSV). Founded 1925. Headquarters: 2460 Pershing Rd., Kansas City MO 64108. **NATURAL GAS.** Gas Service Co. distributes natural gas to Kansas City and areas of Kansas, Missouri, Oklahoma, and Nebraska.

Sales: $539.1 million (trend 19.6% a year).
Earnings: $5.63 million (trend 4.5% a year).
What happened to a $10,000 investment

Purchase Date	*Purchase Price*	*Price on 12-31-81*	*Dividends Paid*
12-31-71	$N/A	$9.87	$ N/A
12-31-76	$13.87	$9.87	$4,511.71

Purchase Date	*Cap. Gains (– Losses)*	*Total Return*	*Rate of Return*
12-31-71	$ N/A	$ N/A	N/A%
12-31-76	$–2,882.88	$1,628.83	3.06%

* * *

GEARHART INDUSTRIES, INC. (GOI). Founded 1955. Headquarters: 1100 Everman Rd., PO Box 1936, Fort Worth TX 76101. **OIL FIELD SERVICE.** Gearhart Industries, Inc. provides the petroleum industry with wireline services, measuring conditions inside wells. Also manufactures equipment used in oil production. **MAJOR SUBSIDIARIES, BRANDS:** Computalog Gearhart, Ltd.; Geotex Corp.; NEC Gas Analytical Services Ltd.; Petro Data, Ltd.

Sales: $239.2 million (trend 31.1% a year).
Earnings: $27.70 million (trend 33.6% a year).
What happened to a $10,000 investment

Purchase Date	*Purchase Price*	*Price on 12-31-81*	*Dividends Paid*
12-31-71	$1.27	$24.50	$6,256.79
12-31-76	$5.84	$24.50	$ 983.96

Purchase Date	*Cap. Gains (– Losses)*	*Total Return*	*Rate of Return*
12-31-71	$183,580.25	$189,837.04	34.92%
12-31-76	$ 31,925.13	$ 32,909.09	33.82%

* * *

GELCO CORP. (GEL). Founded 1957. Headquarters: 1 Gelco Dr., Eden Prairie MN 55344. **TRANSPORTATION MANAGEMENT.** Gelco Corp. rents and leases trucks, trailers, containers, automobiles, and modular buildings to businesses, industry, and government. **MAJOR SUBSIDIARIES, BRANDS:** CTI International, Inc.; Feld Truck Leasing Division; Gelco Fleet and Management Services Division; Transport International Pool, Inc.

Sales: $851.7 million (trend 41.5% a year).
Earnings: $48.22 million (trend 39.3% a year).
What happened to a $10,000 investment

Purchase Date	*Purchase Price*	*Price on 12-31-81*	*Dividends Paid*
12-31-71	$ 8.96	$20.25	$3,892.09
12-31-76	$10.92	$20.25	$2,885.50

Purchase Date	*Cap. Gains (– Losses)*	*Total Return*	*Rate of Return*
12-31-71	$12,604.65	$16,496.74	10.23%
12-31-76	$ 8,549.62	$11,435.11	16.47%

* * *

GEMINI FUND, INC. (GEM). Founded 1973. Headquarters: PO Box 1100, Valley Forge PA 19482. **INVESTMENT COMPANY.** Gemini Fund, Inc., is a publicly traded investment company which deals primarily in common stocks. Investors can buy either the current income portion of the portfolio or the capital gains portion.

* * *

GENENTECH, INC. (GENE, Over-the-Counter). Founded 1976. Headquarters: 460 Point San Bruno Blvd., S. San Francisco CA 94080. **BIOLOGICAL RESEARCH, GENETIC ENGINEERING.** Genentech seeks to develop gene-splicing techniques that have potential for commercial application, such as the production of synthetic human interferon and insulin. 250 employees.

PROFILE: When it went public in 1980, Genentech was the hottest new issue in history. Investors are almost always ravenous for small growth companies with new technologies that hold out the prospect of exponential growth. To many investors in 1980, genetic engineering seemed to be the equivalent of the philosopher's stone that would turn base metal into gold. Or, in Genentech's case, turn base organisms into factories to produce human insulin, interferon, and who knows what else? Genetic engineering was a new frontier, and brokerage houses were full of pinstriped pioneers.

So great was the initial demand for the stock that underwriters had to parcel out shares to brokers, who in turn had to ration them out to customers. On the first day of trading, the stock leaped from $35 to $89, then settled back to about $55 a share. At a time when the average stock was selling for 8 times earnings, Genentech was selling for about 4,000 times earnings, which were reported as a penny a share in 1979 (up from deficits of 14 cents and 17 cents a share the two previous years). In early 1982 the shares fetched about $35, more than 1,000 times the 1980 earnings of $0.03 a share.

Of course, people were buying the future. But *Forbes* magazine put things into some perspective when it observed that if Genentech's earnings grew 50 percent a year for ten straight years from the time the company went public, it would be earning $1.15 a share in 1990, assuming no more shares had been issued in the interim.

Like most new and popular growth companies, Genentech pays no dividends.

* * *

GENERAL AMERICAN INVESTORS CO., INC. (GAM). Founded 1927. Headquarters: 330 Madison Ave., New York NY 10017. **INVESTMENT COMPANY.** General American Investors Co., Inc., is a publicly traded investment fund with common stocks in oil, natural gas, insurance, electronics, publishing, and broadcasting; also a registered investment adviser. **MAJOR SUBSIDIARIES, BRANDS:** General American Advisers, Inc.

* * *

GENERAL AMERICAN OIL CO. OF TEXAS (GAO). Founded 1936. Headquarters: General American Oil Co. of Texas Meadows Bldg., Dallas TX 75206. **OIL AND NATURAL GAS.** General American Oil Co. of Texas is involved in exploration for the production of oil and natural gas in most of the major producing areas of the United States, offshore in the Gulf of Mexico, Canada, the United Kingdom and Netherlands Sectors of the North Sea. **MAJOR SUBSIDIARIES, BRANDS:** Stockton, Whatley, Davin & Co.

Sales: $315.5 million (trend 25.1% a year).
Earnings: $52.10 million (trend 21.1% a year).
What happened to a $10,000 investment

Purchase Date	*Purchase Price*	*Price on 12-31-81*	*Dividends Paid*
12-31-71	$ 8.51	$37.01	$3,034.63
12-31-76	$17.00	$37.01	$1,007.60

Purchase Date	*Cap. Gains (− Losses)*	*Total Return*	*Rate of Return*
12-31-71	$33,515.31	$36,549.94	16.63%
12-31-76	$11,778.76	$12,786.36	17.91%

* * *

GENERAL BANCSHARES CORP. (GBS). Founded 1946. Headquarters: 720 Olive St., St. Louis MO 63166. **BANK HOLDING COMPANY.** General Bancshares Corp. is a holding company for banks in Missouri, Illinois, and Tennessee.

Sales: $127.6 million (trend 18.2% a year).
Earnings: $10.36 million (trend 29.4% a year).
What happened to a $10,000 investment

Purchase Date	*Purchase Price*	*Price on 12-31-81*	*Dividends Paid*
12-31-71	$13.87	$20.12	$5,697.30
12-31-76	$11.25	$20.12	$3,608.89

Purchase Date	*Cap. Gains (− Losses)*	*Total Return*	*Rate of Return*
12-31-71	$4,504.50	$10,201.80	7.29%
12-31-76	$7,888.89	$11,497.78	16.54%

* * *

GENERAL CINEMA CORP. (GCN). Founded 1950. Headquarters: 27 Boylston St., Chestnut Hill MA 02167. **SOFT DRINK BOTTLER, MOVIES.** General Cinema Corp. bottles soft drinks and operates a movie theater chain; also owns a television station and several radio stations. **MAJOR SUBSIDIARIES, BRANDS:** Sunkist Soft Drinks.

Sales: $759.4 million (trend 17.9% a year).
Earnings: $33.36 million (trend 18.7% a year).
What happened to a $10,000 investment

Purchase Date	*Purchase Price*	*Price on 12-31-81*	*Dividends Paid*
12-31-71	$18.12	$36.50	$2,223.45
12-31-76	$13.31	$36.50	$2,234.74

Purchase Date	*Cap. Gains (− Losses)*	*Total Return*	*Rate of Return*
12-31-71	$10,137.93	$12,361.38	8.38%
12-31-76	$17,417.84	$19,652.58	24.28%

* * *

GENERAL DATACOMM INDUSTRIES, INC. (GDC). Founded 1969. Headquarters: 1 Kennedy Ave., Danbury CT 06810. **DATA COMMUNICATIONS.** General DataComm Industries, Inc., designs, manufactures, and services data communications equipment that transfers information between computers and other data processing equipment. **MAJOR SUBSIDIARIES, BRANDS:** General Data-Comm Systems, Inc.

Sales: $57.6 million (trend 31.8% a year).
Earnings: $1.84 million (trend 35.9% a year).
What happened to a $10,000 investment

Purchase Date	*Purchase Price*	*Price on 12-31-81*	*Dividends Paid*
12-31-71	$N/A	$8.62	$0.00
12-31-76	$ .52	$8.62	$0.00

Purchase Date	*Cap. Gains (− Losses)*	*Total Return*	*Rate of Return*
12-31-71	$ N/A	$ N/A	N/A%
12-31-76	$156,339.29	$156,339.29	75.47%

* * *

GENERAL DYNAMICS CORP. (GD). Founded 1952. Headquarters: Pierre Laclede Center, St. Louis MO 63105. **DEFENSE CONTRACTOR.** Builds aircraft, ships (including submarines), and missiles for U.S. military forces. Also involved in civilian aviation and telecommunications. 84,000 employees. **MAJOR SUBSIDIARIES, BRANDS:** F-16 (fighter plane); Trident and SSN-688 (submarines); Tomahawk (cruise missiles); American Telecommunications; Stromberg-Carlson. In 1982 General Dynamics agreed to acquire Chrysler's defense subsidiary, a major producer of tanks.

Sales: $4,742.7 million (trend 16.8% a year).
Earnings: $192.50 million (trend 20.2% a year).
What happened to a $10,000 investment

Purchase Date	*Purchase Price*	*Price on 12-31-81*	*Dividends Paid*
12-31-71	$ 4.35	$24.50	$4,482.76
12-31-76	$10.75	$24.50	$1,813.95

Purchase Date	*Cap. Gains (− Losses)*	*Total Return*	*Rate of Return*
12-31-71	$46,321.84	$50,804.60	19.78%
12-31-76	$12,790.70	$14,604.65	19.73%

PROFILE: This stock is volatile. It takes off like an F-16 fighter, sinks like a Trident submarine, and will give you quite a ride. It responds not only to stock market movements (which it usually magnifies), but to political news, foreign and domestic. It feuds with the Navy and the Air Force, even while it lives off them. In fact, General Dynamics is even more dependent now on military business (about 75 percent of sales in 1980) than it was a few years ago (around 66 percent). It is the nation's largest defense contractor.

Since 1974, investors have been glad to go along for the ride, ignoring the jolts, because the overall trend has definitely been up. You could have bought the stock for less than $3 a share in parts of 1974, sold it for more than $40 during parts of 1980 and 1981. In spring of 1981 the price came down to $31 a share, as investors realized that the Reagan administration might not get all the military dollars it wanted, and that a U.S. military buildup would in any event take some time. Furthermore, the stock was affected by temporary problems, to which the market probably (but typically) overreacted: setbacks on the Trident submarine program, and an expropriation tussle with Canada over a relatively small subsidiary, Asbestos Corp.

In 1981 the stock was selling for about 9 to 10 times earnings. It sold for a p / e as small as 2 in 1975, and as high as 17 in 1968. In keeping with its history of dips and surges, the company ran deficits in 1970 and 1978, but had rising earnings in every other year from 1970 to 1980. Dividends were resumed in 1979 after an eight-year hiatus. The dividend yield is modest, recently around 2 to 3 percent.

In the past decade the company has steadily pared down its debt, to the point where the balance sheet is scrubbed as clean as the deck of a Navy ship: Debt was recently only about 5 percent of total capital.

For investors who believe the U.S. military buildup will be a long-term phenomenon, this stock offers promise. Any purchases should be carefully timed, in light of the history of market fluctuations.

* * *

GENERAL ELECTRIC CO. (GE). Founded 1892. Headquarters: 3135 Easton Turnpike, Fairfield CT 06431. ELECTRONICS. GE produces a large variety of electronics products for consumers and industry. Also involved in mining, jet engine manufacture, credit, and construction of both nuclear and conventional power plant equipment. 404,000 employees. MAJOR SUBSIDIARIES, BRANDS: GE; Hotpoint; Utah International.

Sales: $24,959.0 million (trend 13.1% a year).
Earnings: $1,514.00 million (trend 19.2% a year).
What happened to a $10,000 investment

Purchase Date	*Purchase Price*	*Price on 12-31-81*	*Dividends Paid*
12-31-71	$62.62	$57.37	$3,393.21
12-31-76	$55.62	$57.37	$2,417.98

Purchase Date	*Cap. Gains (− Losses)*	*Total Return*	*Rate of Return*
12-31-71	$−838.32	$2,554.89	2.30%
12-31-76	$ 314.61	$2,732.58	4.95%

PROFILE: You probably think of GE as a company that brings you toasters, appliances, television sets, and a host of other doodads. True enough, but about two thirds of GE's sales aren't to consumers — they're to industry and government. The bulk of the company's money is made on such big-ticket items as power generating equipment, jet engines, coal, iron ore, plastics, and electronic equipment for industry.

In any given year GE stock tends to fluctuate about as much as the stock market does as a whole. The long-term trend, though, has been flat for more than a decade. GE keeps homing in on the $50 to $60 per share range. In much of 1981 it sold for around $61 a share, about the same price it sold for during parts of 1971.

Why such an uninspired stock market performance from a company whose earnings have gone up almost every year? Part of the trouble has been that the company founded by Thomas Edison had lost some of its reputation for innovation. In the 1970s it seemed to be more comfortable milking cash cows than creating new breeds. As the 1980s started, however, GE was beginning to regain a reputation for technological innovation. It was putting more money into high-technology research and development. It had bought a couple of high-technology subsidiaries, Intersil (semiconductors) and Calma (computer-aided design and manufacture). And it had appointed as its new chairman John F. Welch, Jr., a man known for supporting and understanding new technology.

Watching the flat trend in the stock price might conceal the fact that GE at $60 or so a share was a vastly better buy in the early 1980s than in the early 1970s. Back then the price / earnings ratio was about 20 to 25; recently it's been 7 to 10. The balance sheet, which has never been weak, is now extremely strong, with debt recently only about 11 percent of total capital. The dividend yield, recently

5 to 6 percent, is quite secure, and dividends have been paid every year since 1899.

* * *

GENERAL FOODS CORP. (GF). Founded 1922. Headquarters: 250 North St., White Plains NY 10625. PROCESSED FOODS. General Foods is the largest U.S. seller of coffee, and the nation's third-largest food processor in total revenues. 53,000 employees. MAJOR SUBSIDIARIES, BRANDS: Maxwell House, Sanka, Yuban, Brim, Maxim, Max-Pax (coffees); Oscar Mayer (packaged meats); Burger Chef (restaurants — the company plans to sell this division to Hardee's Food Systems, Inc.); Jell-O (gelatin); Birds Eye (frozen vegetables), Minute Rice; Post (cereals); Cycle, Full Course, Gaines, Gravy Train, Top Choice (pet foods); Kool-Aid (soft-drink mixes).

Sales: $6,601.3 million (trend 9.4% a year).
Earnings: $255.37 million (trend 12.3% a year).
What happened to a $10,000 investment

Purchase Date	*Purchase Price*	*Price on 12-31-81*	*Dividends Paid*
12-31-71	$35.87	$31.75	$4,089.20
12-31-76	$30.25	$31.75	$2,482.64

Purchase Date	*Cap. Gains (— Losses)*	*Total Return*	*Rate of Return*
12-31-71	$—1,149.83	$2,939.37	2.61%
12-31-76	$ 495.87	$2,978.51	5.35%

PROFILE: A diet consisting mainly of coffee, gelatin, Kool-Aid, hot dogs, and bologna might not be a nutritionist's delight, but it nourishes the financial tummy of General Foods, the nation's third-largest food processor (after Dart & Kraft, and Beatrice Foods). General Foods has been consistently profitable, and in recent years has consistently returned more than 15 percent on stockholders' equity.

Despite a reputation as a conservator of mature brands, the company has been keeping both sales and earnings advancing a half step ahead of inflation. Yet, it must have concluded that it couldn't keep on making progress by sticking with its stable of well-known brands, including such household names as Jell-O, Maxwell House, Kool-Aid, and Minute Rice. It has recently stepped up the pace of new product introductions, changed the salary-and-bonus system for executives to encourage product innovation, and made a major acquisition in Oscar Mayer.

Opinion was sharply divided on Wall Street as to the wisdom of the Oscar Mayer acquisition. "The wurst is yet to come," groaned *Forbes* magazine. "The price (about $464 million) is too high," suggested *The Value Line Investment Survey.* But General Foods wanted a counterweight to its coffee business, which a few years ago accounted for about 40 percent of sales. Coffee profits are highly erratic. So, of course, are profits from processed meats (they depend on hog prices, which in turn depend on corn prices). Cynics therefore said that General Foods now has feet on two banana peels instead of one. But the company is better balanced now; coffee and meat will probably each account for a bit under 25 percent of earnings in most years.

The stock hasn't gone much of anywhere in recent years, and since 1978 has carried quite a low price / earnings ratio — 6 in early 1981. That may make it a bargain, particularly for conservative investors who appreciate the strong balance sheet (only 14 percent debt recently) and the high dividend yield (recently above 7 percent).

* * *

GENERAL GROWTH PROPERTIES (GGP). Founded 1970. Headquarters: 1055 Sixth Ave., Des Moines IA 50306. REAL ESTATE INVESTMENT. General Growth Properties invests in real estate, mostly shopping centers.

Sales: $57.4 million (trend 10.9% a year).
Earnings: $2.06 million (trend 1.5% a year).
What happened to a $10,000 investment

Purchase Date	*Purchase Price*	*Price on 12-31-81*	*Dividends Paid*
12-31-71	$18.25	$18.25	$14,010.96
12-31-76	$22.25	$18.25	$ 9,204.49

Purchase Date	*Cap. Gains (— Losses)*	*Total Return*	*Rate of Return*
12-31-71	$ —.00	$14,010.96	9.15%
12-31-76	$—1,797.75	$ 7,406.74	11.72%

* * *

GENERAL HOST CORP. (GH). Founded 1911. Headquarters: 22 Gate House Rd., Stamford CT 06902. FOOD RETAILING. General Host Corp. operates specialty food stores, processes meat and related products, and imports salt products. MAJOR SUBSIDIARIES, BRANDS: Cudahy Foods Co.; Hickory Farms Sales Corp.; Hot Sam; Li'l General; Van de Kamp's Division (frozen foods).

Sales: $424.7 million (trend −5.1% a year).
Earnings: $11.42 million (trend 24.1% a year).
What happened to a $10,000 investment

Purchase Date	*Purchase Price*	*Price on 12-31-81*	*Dividends Paid*
12-31-71	$17.50	$19.75	$2,842.86
12-31-76	$12.25	$19.75	$2,877.55

Purchase Date	*Cap. Gains (− Losses)*	*Total Return*	*Rate of Return*
12-31-71	$1,285.71	$4,128.57	3.52%
12-31-76	$6,122.45	$9,000.00	13.70%

* * *

GENERAL INSTRUMENT CORP. (GRL). Founded 1937. Headquarters: 1775 Broadway, New York NY 10019. **ELECTRONICS.** General Instrument is the largest U.S. supplier of cable television equipment; also makes semiconductors and other electronic products, and produces equipment used in off-track betting and lottery operation. 24,000 employees. **MAJOR SUBSIDIARIES, BRANDS:** Jerrold Electronics; AmTote.

Sales: $825.1 million (trend 16.4% a year).
Earnings: $66.61 million (trend 58.9% a year).
What happened to a $10,000 investment

Purchase Date	*Purchase Price*	*Price on 12-31-81*	*Dividends Paid*
12-31-71	$6.29	$44.25	$1,351.39
12-31-76	$6.66	$44.25	$1,276.56

Purchase Date	*Cap. Gains (− Losses)*	*Total Return*	*Rate of Return*
12-31-71	$60,351.76	$61,703.15	21.77%
12-31-76	$56,456.41	$57,732.97	46.61%

PROFILE: This stock was one of the great stock market success stories of the past decade. Also one of the great stock market disasters of the past decade. In short, one of the great roller-coaster stocks of the past decade.

If you'd plunked $10,000 down for General Instrument Shares at their 1967 peak ($70.50 a share), your investment would have dwindled to less than $600 by 1974. But if you'd put in the same amount of money at the 1974 low of $4.12 a share, you could have sold out for more than $241,000 in 1980, when the price almost hit $100. In early 1982 the shares were selling for around $38, following a 3-for-1 split in 1981.

The price / earnings ratio has ranged from 65 (in 1969) to 4 (in 1976); in early 1982 it was about 13. Obviously, this is a stock about which investors' opinions and expectations can change rapidly.

With the exception of the 1974–75 recession years, the company's earnings have been in an uptrend since 1969. The rapid growth of cable TV, semiconductor technology, and gambling have all fed earnings — and the stock price. But the recent p / e multiple isn't faddish, and the company's balance sheet, with debt recently about 19 percent of capital, is a lot less leveraged than it was a decade ago when half of the capital was debt. The company has even settled down into the staid practice of paying dividends, starting in 1977. The dividends to date have been modest, and the dividend yield has been in the 1 to 2 percent range.

In short, this stock is still volatile, but probably less risky than it was a decade ago.

* * *

GENERAL MILLS, INC. (GIS). Founded 1928. Headquarters: 9200 Wayzata Blvd., Minneapolis MN 55440. **PROCESSED FOODS, CONSUMER PRODUCTS.** General Mills is a leading marketer of cereals and other processed foods. It has also diversified into restaurants, toys and games, clothing, and specialty retailing. 64,000 employees. **MAJOR SUBSIDIARIES, BRANDS:** Cheerios, Wheaties, Total (cereals); Betty Crocker (cake mixes); Gold Medal (flour); Bisquick (baking mix); Chef Saluto (frozen pizza); Red Lobster Inns, York Steak House (restaurants); David Crystal (Izod / Lacoste shirts); Ship 'n Shore (blouses); Monet (costume jewelry); Parker Brothers (games); Kenner, Craft Master (toys); Lionel (model trains); Wallpapers To Go.

Sales: $4,852.4 million (trend 12.9% a year).
Earnings: $196.60 million (trend 14.1% a year).
What happened to a $10,000 investment

Purchase Date	*Purchase Price*	*Price on 12-31-81*	*Dividends Paid*
12-31-71	$20.75	$35.87	$3,795.18
12-31-76	$34.37	$35.87	$1,399.27

Purchase Date	*Cap. Gains (− Losses)*	*Total Return*	*Rate of Return*
12-31-71	$7,289.16	$11,084.34	7.74%
12-31-76	$ 436.36	$ 1,835.64	3.43%

PROFILE: Everything is going right at General Mills except the stock price. The company's profits have been rising for eighteen years straight, and rising considerably faster than inflation. Following some unsuccessful diversification attempts in the 1950s, the company has in the 1960s and 1970s been one of the most successful diversifiers among major corporations, picking small, promising companies and helping them grow. The company is near the very top of the food-processing industry in profitability. It has paid dividends each year since 1898 (preceding incorporation), and has increased them each year since 1969. The recent yield was above 5 percent.

Yet the stock has been stagnant for a decade. The 1972 high was about $32; the 1980 high about $31. What gives?

In part, the trouble has been that Wall Street recently has knelt at the altar of rapid growth, for which it will pay almost any price, and has been indifferent to steady growth. In part, it's that none of General Mills's product lines are particularly glamorous. You don't buttonhole an attractive blonde at a cocktail party to explain that you've discovered this great stock, involved in cereal, blouses, and restaurants. In part, investors may be worried that too much diversification will flatten out results.

But all these worries seem, on inspection, to be either silly or unfounded. In recent years, selling at 5 to 9 times earnings, this stock appeared to be undervalued.

* * *

GENERAL MOTORS CORP. (GM). Founded 1916. Headquarters: 3044 W. Grand Blvd., Detroit MI 48202. **AUTOS.** General Motors is the nation's largest automobile manufacturer; also makes trucks, locomotives, and engines for aircraft and trains. 766,000 employees. **MAJOR SUBSIDIARIES, BRANDS:** Cadillac, Buick, Oldsmobile, Pontiac, Chevrolet; General Motors Acceptance Corp.; GMC (trucks). Opel, Holden, Vauxhall (imported cars and trucks).

Sales: $57,728.5 million (trend 10.7% a year).
Earnings: $−775.40 million.
What happened to a $10,000 investment

Purchase Date	*Purchase Price*	*Price on 12-31-81*	*Dividends Paid*
12-31-71	$80.50	$38.50	$5,527.95
12-31-76	$78.50	$38.50	$2,987.26

Purchase Date	*Cap. Gains (− Losses)*	*Total Return*	*Rate of Return*
12-31-71	$−5,217.39	$ 310.56	.31%
12-31-76	$−5,095.54	$−2,108.28	−4.63%

PROFILE: GM bestrides the auto world like a colossus, and its rivals are trembling in fear. GM not only has the biggest market share, it also has the greatest financial strength, is the farthest along in converting to small cars, and is spending the most on new plants. Many analysts believe that when the long-standing depression in the auto industry (which has spanned the years 1979–81) ends, General Motors will be the only company strongly positioned to take advantage of resurgent demand. Ford, Chrysler, and American Motors, it's argued, simply don't have the money to build the plants to produce vehicles in the numbers that will be needed.

Certainly, GM would like to believe that scenario. It is pouring at least $3 billion into new plants even while the red ink flows. In 1980 GM experienced its first full-year loss since 1921 — a loss of $762 million. That compares with a profit of $2.9 billion in 1979, and a peak profit of $3.5 billion the year before.

In the mid-1960s, GM shares sold for more than $100 each. Yet that was only about 13 times earnings, hardly an inflated multiple for the times. In late 1981, the average stock sold for about 8 times earnings; GM shares were selling for about $37 each. That was 39 times current earnings, but only 4 times 1979 earnings, and 1979 earnings were only the fourth-best in the company's history. There are no "sure things" in the stock market; however, a rebound in this stock seems about as close as you're likely to find.

The company's balance sheet remains strong. Debt, in early 1982, constituted only about 20 percent of capital — and even that was higher than normal, reflecting large expenditures on new plants. Dividends have been paid each year since the company's incorporation; the dividend yield was about 4 to 6 percent in 1981, reflecting dividend cuts the three previous years.

* * *

GENERAL NUTRITION, INC. (GNC). Founded 1955. Headquarters: 921 Penn Ave., Pittsburgh PA 15222. **VITAMINS.** Sells vitamins and dietary supplements through more than 1,000 company-owned outlets, as well as by mail. Also sells health foods and cosmetics. **MAJOR SUBSIDIARIES, BRANDS:** General Nutrition Centers.

Sales: $241.6 million.
Earnings: $12.78 million.

* * *

GENERAL PORTLAND INC. (GPT). Founded 1947. Headquarters: 12700 Park Central Pl., Dallas TX 75221. CEMENT. General Portland is a major U.S. cement producer. It has agreed to be acquired by Canada Cement LaFarge Ltd.

* * *

GENERAL PUBLIC UTILITIES CORP. (GPU). Founded 1969. Headquarters: 260 Cherry Hill Rd., Parsippany NJ 07054. UTILITY HOLDING CO. Owns three electric utilities that provide power to portions of Pennsylvania and New Jersey. 11,000 employees. MAJOR SUBSIDIARIES, BRANDS: Jersey Central Power & Light Co.; Metropolitan Edison Co.; Pennsylvania Electric Co.

Sales: $1,831.7 million (trend 13.3% a year).
Earnings: $20.59 million (trend −22.0% a year).
What happened to a $10,000 investment

Purchase Date	*Purchase Price*	*Price on 12-31-81*	*Dividends Paid*
12-31-71	$23.25	$6.75	$5,552.69
12-31-76	$19.50	$6.75	$2,394.87

Purchase Date	*Cap. Gains (− Losses)*	*Total Return*	*Rate of Return*
12-31-71	$−7,096.77	$−1,544.09	−1.66%
12-31-76	$−6,538.46	$−4,143.59	−10.15%

PROFILE: The nuclear accident at the Three Mile Island plant of the company's Metropolitan Edison subsidiary happened in March of 1979. The cost of cleaning up the damage and restoring the facility to operation was at first estimated at $400 million, then closer to $600 million, and by 1981 at about $1.4 billion. The company's insurance will cover $300 million of this tab.

Where is the company going to come up with the other $1.1 billion? Obviously it won't be easy. In the company's most profitable year ever, 1977, its profits came to a bit less than $184 million. But profits for 1980, in large part because of Three Mile Island, had dwindled to less than $64 million. At that rate it would take 100 percent of the company's profits for the next seventeen years to pay the tab — assuming the tab hadn't been swollen by delays, lawsuits, and other imponderables. Not surprisingly, regulators in Pennsylvania and New Jersey have so far refused to let the company jack up rates to cover the cleanup.

Of course, the lawsuits are flying. The company has sued Babcock & Wilcox, which built the reactor, for $500 million, and has sued the Nuclear Regulatory Commission for $4 billion. A presidential task force recommended that Uncle Sam pick up half the tab and provide loan guarantees for the other half. It seems likely that the company will have to go further into debt — and, like most utilities, it already had plenty (48 percent of capital in 1979).

The stock, which sold in the $20-to-$40 range in the late 1960s, had already dropped to the $10-to-$20 range in the 1970s, before the accident. In early 1981 it sold for about $4 or $5 a share. Dividends haven't been paid since 1979.

* * *

GENERAL REINSURANCE CORP. (GRN). Founded 1926. Headquarters: 600 Steamboat Rd., Greenwich CT 06830. REINSURANCE. General Reinsurance Corp. is a casualty and property reinsurer that handles almost all types of property and casualty risks. MAJOR SUBSIDIARIES, BRANDS: General Reinsurance Corp.; North Star Reinsurance Corp.; The Trident Group.

Sales: $1,104.3 million (trend 15.9% a year).
Earnings: $154.40 million (trend 33.1% a year).
What happened to a $10,000 investment

Purchase Date	*Purchase Price*	*Price on 12-31-81*	*Dividends Paid*
12-31-71	$41.16	$80.75	$1,312.98
12-31-76	$48.06	$80.75	$1,026.79

Purchase Date	*Cap. Gains (− Losses)*	*Total Return*	*Rate of Return*
12-31-71	$9,620.35	$10,933.33	7.67%
12-31-76	$6,801.04	$ 7,827.83	12.26%

* * *

GENERAL REFRACTORIES CO. (GRX). Founded 1922. Headquarters: 50 Monument Rd., Bala Cynwyd PA 19004. NON-METALLIC MINERALS. General Refractories Co. manufactures refractories, building and insulation products, and filtration products. MAJOR SUBSIDIARIES, BRANDS: Brohltal-Deumag A.G.; General Refractories Co. of Canada, Ltd.; Grefco, Inc.

Sales: $467.1 million (trend 9.3% a year).
Earnings: $.03 million (trend −45.8% a year).
What happened to a $10,000 investment

Purchase Date	*Purchase Price*	*Price on 12-31-81*	*Dividends Paid*
12-31-71	$8.12	$4.62	$615.38
12-31-76	$7.87	$4.62	$ 0.00

Purchase Date	*Cap. Gains (− Losses)*	*Total Return*	*Rate of Return*
12-31-71	$−4,307.69	$−3,692.31	−4.50%
12-31-76	$−4,126.98	$−4,126.98	−10.10%

* * *

GENERAL SIGNAL CORP. (GSX). Founded 1904. Headquarters: High Ridge Park, Stamford CT 06904. **INDUSTRIAL CONTROLS.** General Signal is a conglomerate of some forty companies, most of which produce controls or process equipment for the transportation industry, utilities, water treatment, or fluid control systems. 26,000 employees. **MAJOR SUBSIDIARIES, BRANDS:** Leeds & Northrup Co.; Kayex, Xynetics.

Sales: $1,521.7 million (trend 24.3% a year).
Earnings: $104.21 million (trend 34.6% a year).
What happened to a $10,000 investment

Purchase Date	*Purchase Price*	*Price on 12-31-81*	*Dividends Paid*
12-31-71	$17.37	$38.62	$4,211.80
12-31-76	$26.19	$38.62	$2,092.60

Purchase Date	*Cap. Gains (− Losses)*	*Total Return*	*Rate of Return*
12-31-71	$12,230.22	$16,442.01	10.21%
12-31-76	$ 4,749.40	$ 6,842.00	10.99%

PROFILE: This company has evolved from a railroad signal maker (it was General Railway Signal until the early 1960s) into a diversified maker of controls for industrial, utility, and transportation processes. At the helm for the past two decades has been Nathan (Nat) Owen, whose style has been to acquire companies he deems promising, and then leave them alone. In a 1980 portrait of Owen and the company, *Fortune* observed that this management style had made General Signal "court of first resort for companies that have decided to sell out or have been forced to" sell out because they were about to be the victim of a hostile takeover. As a well-known "white knight," General Signal gets to pick and choose between 100 to 200 potential acquisitions each year, according to *Fortune.*

The "leave 'em alone" strategy had produced decent but not spectacular results when, in the late 1970s, the company appeared to start exercising a bit more control from headquarters. Now (as of 1981) the return on equity is up to around 17 percent. What's even more impressive is the return on total capital, because the results aren't boosted by leverage. Long-term debt, as of early 1981, was a mere 11 percent of total capital.

The company has the good fortune to be respected, but not adored, on Wall Street. Too much adoration can push a company's p / e ratio to ridiculous heights, leading eventually to an uncomfortable fall. General Signal was never Wall Street's darling. Since 1974 the p / e ratio has stayed consistently in the 9–12 range.

Dividends have been paid each year since 1940, but they're modest. In recent years the yield has been 2 to 4 percent.

* * *

GENERAL STEEL INDUSTRIES, INC. (GSI). Founded 1928. Headquarters: 11 S. Meramec, St. Louis MO 63105. **STEEL.** General Steel Industries, Inc., produces iron and steel rolls, reflecting glass beads, screening, crushing, and conveying equipment; also designs railway suspension systems, applies protective coating for oil and water pipelines. **MAJOR SUBSIDIARIES, BRANDS:** Flex-O-Lite; Gaido-Lingle Division; Ludlow-Saylor; Standard Pipeprotection.

Sales: $82.3 million (trend 8.3% a year).
Earnings: $3.60 million (trend 11.2% a year).
What happened to a $10,000 investment

Purchase Date	*Purchase Price*	*Price on 12-31-81*	*Dividends Paid*
12-31-71	$5.07	$16.12	$2,565.86
12-31-76	$4.29	$16.12	$3,027.72

Purchase Date	*Cap. Gains (− Losses)*	*Total Return*	*Rate of Return*
12-31-71	$21,819.24	$24,385.10	13.15%
12-31-76	$27,546.70	$30,574.42	32.33%

* * *

GENERAL TELEPHONE & ELECTRONICS CORP. (GTE). Founded 1935. Headquarters: 1 Stamford Forum, Stamford CT 06904. **COMMUNICATIONS.** General Telephone is the country's second-largest telephone company, with some 18 million phones (versus 140 million for industry leader AT&T) in 31 states. Also involved in data transmission; manufacture of communications equipment; and electronics, including defense work. 227,000 employees. **MAJOR SUBSIDIARIES, BRANDS:** Telenet; GTE Electrical Products; GTE Communications Products.

Sales: $9,978.9 million (trend 11.7% a year).
Earnings: $587.00 million (trend 10.9% a year).
What happened to a $10,000 investment

Purchase Date	*Purchase Price*	*Price on 12-31-81*	*Dividends Paid*
12-31-71	$31.37	$32.25	$6,776.10
12-31-76	$31.87	$32.25	$3,946.67

Purchase Date	*Cap. Gains (– Losses)*	*Total Return*	*Rate of Return*
12-31-71	$278.88	$7,054.98	5.48%
12-31-76	$117.65	$4,064.31	7.06%

PROFILE: Can a small and heretofore unprofitable subsidiary restore pizazz to the stock of the nation's second-largest utility? Stockholders of GTE certainly hope so.

Image advertising (a description of a technological feat, followed by the slogan "Gee? No — GTE") may have broadened public knowledge of the company. But it hasn't done much for the stock, which languished at about $31 a share in late 1981, compared with a 1971 high of $35.62. The price / earnings ratio, never lofty, has descended to the 6 to 9 range in recent years. In early 1981, when the average stock sold for 8 times earnings, GTE sold for 7. Clearly, most investors don't have great expectations for this stock. The New York *Times* in 1980 called GTE "a company with a safe and solid business and a history of lackluster management."

To the rescue, perhaps, comes Telenet, a data transmission company acquired by GTE in 1978. Unprofitable so far, it has been given until 1983 by GTE management to prove itself — but holds the potential to be the touchstone of tremendous growth. Most analysts see tremendous potential both in transmission of data among computers and in "electronic mail," the rapid transmission of messages among the nation's offices. With Telenet, GTE holds an early lead in the electronic mail race, but faces potential competition from such titans as AT&T, ITT, Xerox, and Satellite Business Systems (a joint venture of IBM, Aetna Life & Casualty, and Comsat).

Absent a major growth in the volume of data transmission and electronic mail business, GTE will remain basically a phone company. Phone service provided about half of revenues and 85 percent of profits in 1979 — and that was before the divestiture of the company's consumer electronics operations. As a phone company, it's a local monopoly, subject to heavy (and sometimes heavy-handed) rate regulation.

This stock may have some appeal for those investors who want high yield with a possibility for growth, though the yield has not been as high as for some utilities. Dividends have been paid each year since 1936; in early 1982 the yield was about 9 percent.

* * *

GENERAL TIRE & RUBBER CO. (GY). Founded 1915. Headquarters: 1 General St., Akron OH 44329. **TIRES.** Though its base is in tires, General Tire is highly diversified. It is involved in aerospace, broadcasting, commercial aviation, soft drink bottling, plastics, and industrial equipment. 42,000 employees. **MAJOR SUBSIDIARIES, BRANDS:** Aerojet-General; RKO General; Frontier Airlines (60 percent owned).

Sales: $2,215.2 million (trend 4.7% a year).
Earnings: $40.43 million (trend −7.9% a year).
What happened to a $10,000 investment

Purchase Date	*Purchase Price*	*Price on 12-31-81*	*Dividends Paid*
12-31-71	$21.84	$21.50	$5,231.02
12-31-76	$23.78	$21.50	$2,853.53

Purchase Date	*Cap. Gains (– Losses)*	*Total Return*	*Rate of Return*
12-31-71	$−156.56	$5,074.45	4.19%
12-31-76	$−957.09	$1,896.44	3.53%

PROFILE: Recently, the non-tire businesses have been carrying the company. Earnings recently have been down substantially ($1.68 a share in 1980, for example, compared with $3.44 the year before and $4.89 a share in 1977, the company's best year), but there would have been red ink, not black, if the company were still dependent entirely on tires. General was the first tire company to embark on a major diversification program, and it's diversified more than any of its four larger competitors (Goodyear, Firestone, Goodrich, and Uniroyal). Recently, with the auto market depressed, tires have accounted for less than half of sales and only about a third of profits. Both figures can be expected to rise when normal times return to the auto industry.

The non-tire subsidiaries have problems, too. The RKO broadcasting arm has been told by the Federal Communications Commission to divest itself of at least three of its four television stations, in punishment for bribes made by the parent company a few years back. General has said it's being picked on unfairly, and hopes for a reversal of the decision from the FCC under the Reagan administration. Three legal disputes are creating hassles for various divisions; the opponents are California (a pollution case), the U.S. Government (a claim for back taxes), and the national oil company in Algeria (a contract dispute).

The stock has bounced around, as these uncertainties and problems are weighed against chances for a major rebound. Those chances are appealing to some speculators and investors, including Charles G. Bluhdorn, chairman of Gulf & Western Industries, which has nibbled up more than 7 percent of the stock.

The balance sheet remains in good shape: Debt was less than 20 percent of capital in early 1981. Dividends have been paid each year since 1937, and the yield recently was around 6 percent.

* * *

GENESCO INC. (GCO). Founded 1925. Headquarters: Genesco Park, Nashville TN 37202. **SHOES.** Genesco Inc. manufactures shoes and men's tailored clothing. **MAJOR SUBSIDIARIES, BRANDS:** Easy Street; Flagg Brothers; Johnston & Murphy; Wrangler Shoes for Jeans.

Sales: $662.5 million (trend −9.1% a year).
Earnings: $9.53 million (trend −28.0% a year).
What happened to a $10,000 investment

Purchase Date	*Purchase Price*	*Price on 12-31-81*	*Dividends Paid*
12-31-71	$34.50	$7.25	$640.58
12-31-76	$ 5.50	$7.25	$ 0.00

Purchase Date	*Cap. Gains (− Losses)*	*Total Return*	*Rate of Return*
12-31-71	$−7,898.55	$−7,257.97	−12.14%
12-31-76	$ 3,181.82	$ 3,181.82	5.68%

* * *

GENRAD, INC. (GEN). Founded 1915. Headquarters: 300 Baker Ave., Concord MA 01742. **ELECTRONIC TEST EQUIPMENT.** GenRad, Inc. manufactures electronic test equipment used in vibration analysis and acoustics. **MAJOR SUBSIDIARIES, BRANDS:** Future-data Computer Corp.; GenRad Semiconductor Test, Inc. (80 percent owned).

Sales: $167.7 million (trend 26.7% a year).
Earnings: $10.32 million (trend 52.5% a year).

* * *

GENSTAR LTD. (GST). Founded 1951. Headquarters: 1 Place Ville Marie, Montreal, Quebec, Canada H3B 3R1. **BUILDING MATERIALS.** Genstar Ltd. produces building materials, and is also involved in home building, land development, heavy construction, and financial services.

Sales: $1,933.8 million (trend 17.5% a year).
Earnings: $120.49 million (trend 21.7% a year).
What happened to a $10,000 investment

Purchase Date	*Purchase Price*	*Price on 12-31-81*	*Dividends Paid*
12-31-71	$ 6.56	$19.62	$12,142.10
12-31-76	$11.69	$19.62	$ 4,710.84

Purchase Date	*Cap. Gains (− Losses)*	*Total Return*	*Rate of Return*
12-31-71	$19,904.76	$32,046.86	15.44%
12-31-76	$ 6,791.44	$11,502.29	16.55%

* * *

GENUINE PARTS CO. (GPC). Founded 1928. Headquarters: 2999 Circle 75 Parkway, Atlanta GA 30339. **AUTOMOTIVE PARTS.** Genuine Parts Co. distributes automotive replacement parts. **MAJOR SUBSIDIARIES, BRANDS:** Bearing Specialty Co.; NAPA; Odell Hardware; Michigan Bearing Co.

Sales: $1,431.7 million (trend 16.4% a year).
Earnings: $67.83 million (trend 17.8% a year).
What happened to a $10,000 investment

Purchase Date	*Purchase Price*	*Price on 12-31-81*	*Dividends Paid*
12-31-71	$23.50	$31.25	$2,685.48
12-31-76	$25.00	$31.25	$1,757.33

Purchase Date	*Cap. Gains (− Losses)*	*Total Return*	*Rate of Return*
12-31-71	$3,297.87	$5,983.35	4.80%
12-31-76	$2,500.00	$4,257.33	7.35%

* * *

GEORGIA-PACIFIC CORP. (GP). Founded 1927. Headquarters: 900 S.W. Fifth Ave., Portland OR 97204; scheduled to move in 1982 to Atlanta, Georgia. **FOREST PRODUCTS.** Georgia Pacific is the nation's largest forest products company by revenues; also produces gypsum and chemicals. 44,000 employees. **MAJOR SUBSIDIARIES, BRANDS:** Exchange Oil and Gas; Coronet (paper products).

Sales: $5,016.0 million (trend 17.3% a year).
Earnings: $244.00 million (trend 11.8% a year).
What happened to a $10,000 investment

Purchase Date	*Purchase Price*	*Price on 12-31-81*	*Dividends Paid*
12-31-71	$25.24	$20.12	$3,155.46
12-31-76	$36.88	$20.12	$1,459.79

Purchase Date	*Cap. Gains (− Losses)*	*Total Return*	*Rate of Return*
12-31-71	$−2,025.68	$ 1,129.78	1.08%
12-31-76	$−4,543.83	$−3,084.05	−7.11%

PROFILE: The nation's largest forest products company is playing musical headquarters. It plans to return in 1982 to Atlanta, its original home, after excursions to Olympia, Washington, and Portland, Oregon.

Except for the headquarters, not much has been moving recently for this company. Housing was in a dreadful slump in 1980–81, which of course spells bad news for makers of plywood and lumber. The economy has been in a recession, which doesn't help sales of paper products either. So earnings of late have been going nowhere. The 1980 figure was $2.34 a share, compared with a record $3.12 a share the year before. However, investors have continued to anticipate a turnaround to come, so the p / e ratio has held up pretty well: In early 1981, when the average stock went for only 8, the stock was selling for 12 times current earnings.

Things would have been worse had not Georgia Pacific eased into chemical production, starting back in 1959. In 1980, chemicals chipped in fully 33 percent of profits, even though forest products still accounted for 86 percent of sales.

One potential problem may be management squabbling. In late 1980 *Business Week* ran a piece titled "Unrest at Georgia-Pacific." It reported a spate of defections and retirements (related in part to the impending move) and quoted an unnamed former executive as saying that "fear and politics" had infected the atmosphere at company headquarters.

Those problems may be minor to an investor who expects a housing resurgence and is looking for a fairly conservative way to participate in it. Georgia-Pacific has paid dividends each year since 1927, and yielded between 4 and 7 percent in 1980 and 1981. In its balance sheet and profitability measures, it's fairly close to the middle of the pack, both for forest products companies and for large American corporations.

* * *

GEOSOURCE INC. (GSE). Founded 1972. Headquarters: 2700 S. Post Oak Rd., Houston TX 77056. **PETROLEUM EXPLORATION.** Geosource Inc. offers products and services, particularly seismic exploration, to the petroleum industry. It is 29 percent owned by Aetna Life & Casualty, which plans to buy the rest for some $638 million.

Sales: $729.2 million (trend 34.6% a year).
Earnings: $58.55 million (trend 43.0% a year).

* * *

GERBER PRODUCTS CO. (GEB). Founded 1901. Headquarters: 445 State St., Fremont MI 49412. **BABY FOODS.** Gerber Products Co. produces baby food; also involved in life insurance and trucking. **MAJOR SUBSIDIARIES, BRANDS:** Century Products, Inc.; CW Transport.

Sales: $631.0 million (trend 11.9% a year).
Earnings: $34.47 million (trend 9.1% a year).
What happened to a $10,000 investment

Purchase Date	*Purchase Price*	*Price on 12-31-81*	*Dividends Paid*
12-31-71	$40.87	$28.62	$2,996.33
12-31-76	$25.25	$28.62	$2,479.21

Purchase Date	*Cap. Gains (− Losses)*	*Total Return*	*Rate of Return*
12-31-71	$−2,996.94	$ −.61	.00%
12-31-76	$ 1,336.63	$3,815.84	6.68%

* * *

GERBER SCIENTIFIC, INC. (GRB). Founded 1948. Headquarters: 83 Gerber Rd., PO Box 305, Hartford CT 06101. **COMPUTER SYSTEMS.** Gerber Scientific, Inc., manufactures manual and semiautomatic systems used with computers. **MAJOR SUBSIDIARIES, BRANDS:** Beta Engineering and Development of Israel (58 percent owned); Boston Digital Corp. (21 percent owned).

Sales: $93.1 million (trend 47.6% a year).
Earnings: $8.88 million (trend 74.7% a year).
What happened to a $10,000 investment

Purchase Date	*Purchase Price*	*Price on 12-31-81*	*Dividends Paid*
12-31-71	$2.71	$11.75	$ 791.08
12-31-76	$ .81	$11.75	$2,636.92

Purchase Date	*Cap. Gains (− Losses)*	*Total Return*	*Rate of Return*
12-31-71	$ 33,384.62	$ 34,175.69	16.02%
12-31-76	$134,615.38	$137,252.31	71.24%

* * *

GETTY OIL CO. (GET). Founded 1928. Headquarters: 3810 Wilshire Blvd., Los Angeles CA 90010. OIL. Getty is an international oil company, the nineteenth-largest oil producer (by revenues) in the United States. Has sidelines in chemicals, mining, agriculture, and insurance. 17,000 employees. MAJOR SUBSIDIARIES, BRANDS: ERC Corp. (insurance); Reserve Oil & Gas; Plateau Mining.

Sales: $10,150.4 million (trend 24.1% a year).
Earnings: $870.85 million (trend 28.2% a year).
What happened to a $10,000 investment

Purchase Date	*Purchase Price*	*Price on 12-31-81*	*Dividends Paid*
12-31-71	$20.94	$64.62	$4,678.21
12-31-76	$49.06	$64.62	$1,554.14

Purchase Date	*Cap. Gains (– Losses)*	*Total Return*	*Rate of Return*
12-31-71	$20,865.67	$25,543.88	13.52%
12-31-76	$ 3,171.97	$ 4,726.11	8.05%

PROFILE: Can Getty in the 1980s match its stock market performance of the 1970s? In 1970 the stock's high for the year was not quite $19. In early 1981 the price was about $70. That's a hard act to follow.

Then again, you may not need a stock that triples to be happy with your investment return. In 1981 there was a temporary glut of oil on the market. That depressed the price of all international oils, Getty included. (The 1980 high was $81 a share.) Despite its big run up, Getty was still selling at only 6 to 7 times earnings in 1981. That's a bargain price for a stock whose earnings had gone from $1.56 a share to $10.80 a share in the preceding decade.

Have the oil companies shot their wad? Wall Street seemed, in the early 1980s, to think so. Granted, oil profits will be subject to heavy tax. And granted, oil abroad will be closely guarded, taxed, and sometimes appropriated by host countries that allow foreign drilling. But in the long run, energy and oil are scarce. The political climate seems to have turned against what's viewed as excessive taxation within the United States. As for the foreign risks, Getty gets about 70 percent of its oil within the United States and another 10 percent or so from Britain's North Sea. Only about 20 percent of production comes from the strife-torn Middle East.

Getty has long been famous for its extremely strong and conservative balance sheet. In early 1981 debt was only 13 percent of total capital, and even that is more debt than the company used to carry.

Willingness to tolerate some debt, and a desire for diversification (e.g., the ERC reinsurance subsidiary) seem to be characteristic of the new management. (J. Paul Getty died in 1976.) "Political risks on top of geological risks are taking some of the romance out of (the oil) business," chairman Sidney Petersen told *Business Week* in 1980. Still, while it may plunge into new ventures (such as pay TV and cable sports TV), the company remains basically an oil company for the intermediate future. And, though neither investors nor the company's management seem quite convinced of the fact, that will probably prove a good thing to be.

* * *

GIANT PORTLAND & MASONRY CEMENT CO. (GPO). Founded 1913. Headquarters: 3006 Devine St., Columbia SC 29205. CEMENT. Giant Portland & Masonry Cement Co. produces cement in South Carolina.

Sales: $27.2 million (trend 12.3% a year).
Earnings: $–.91 million.
What happened to a $10,000 investment

Purchase Date	*Purchase Price*	*Price on 12-31-81*	*Dividends Paid*
12-31-71	$14.25	$4.50	$4,105.26
12-31-76	$10.25	$4.50	$1,609.76

Purchase Date	*Cap. Gains (– Losses)*	*Total Return*	*Rate of Return*
12-31-71	$–6,842.11	$–2,736.84	–3.15%
12-31-76	$–5,609.76	$–4,000.00	–9.71%

* * *

GIBRALTAR FINANCIAL CORP. OF CALIFORNIA (GFC). Founded 1959. Headquarters: 9111 Wilshire Blvd., Beverly Hills CA 90213. SAVINGS AND LOANS. Gibraltar Financial Corp. of California is a savings and loan holding company, parent of Gibraltar Savings and Loan Association.

Sales: $425.7 million (trend 26.1% a year).
Earnings: $–5.27 million.
What happened to a $10,000 investment

Purchase Date	*Purchase Price*	*Price on 12-31-81*	*Dividends Paid*
12-31-71	$6.07	$4.25	$3,145.89
12-31-76	$6.51	$4.25	$2,837.76

Purchase Date	*Cap. Gains (– Losses)*	*Total Return*	*Rate of Return*
12-31-71	$–3,001.06	$ 144.82	.14%
12-31-76	$–3,469.52	$–631.75	–1.30%

* * *

GIDDINGS & LEWIS, INC. (GID). Founded 1895. Headquarters: 142 Doty St., Fond du Lac WI 54935. MACHINE TOOLS. Giddings & Lewis, Inc., manufactures machine tools and industrial products.

Sales: $327.0 million (trend 26.2% a year).
Earnings: $31.36 million (trend 62.0% a year).
What happened to a $10,000 investment

Purchase Date	*Purchase Price*	*Price on 12-31-81*	*Dividends Paid*
12-31-71	$6.03	$22.25	$4,661.56
12-31-76	$3.79	$22.25	$6,405.02

Purchase Date	*Cap. Gains (– Losses)*	*Total Return*	*Rate of Return*
12-31-71	$26,919.25	$31,580.81	15.32%
12-31-76	$48,758.80	$55,163.82	45.48%

* * *

GIFFORD-HILL & CO., INC. (GFH). Founded 1926. Headquarters: 8435 Stemmons Freeway, PO Box 47127, Dallas TX 75247. CEMENT. Gifford-Hill & Company, Inc., manufactures cement, construction materials, building products, and irrigation products; also involved in trucking. MAJOR SUBSIDIARIES, BRANDS: Amcord, Inc.; Gifford-Hill Portland Cement Co.; Wales Transportation, Inc.

Sales: $560.6 million (trend 19.8% a year).
Earnings: $23.61 million (trend 32.5% a year).
What happened to a $10,000 investment

Purchase Date	*Purchase Price*	*Price on 12-31-81*	*Dividends Paid*
12-31-71	$14.83	$19.37	$3,791.91
12-31-76	$ 9.83	$19.37	$3,983.05

Purchase Date	*Cap. Gains (– Losses)*	*Total Return*	*Rate of Return*
12-31-71	$3,061.80	$ 6,853.71	5.36%
12-31-76	$9,703.39	$13,686.44	18.82%

* * *

GILLETTE CO. (GS). Founded 1917. Headquarters: Prudential Tower Building, Boston MA 02199. RAZORS, TOILETRIES. Gillette is the nation's largest maker of razors and razor blades; also produces pens, lighters, electric shavers, and toiletries. 34,000 employees. MAJOR SUBSIDIARIES, BRANDS: Trac II, Atra, Daisy, Good News, Swivel (razors); Platinum Plus, Super Stainless Steel (blades); Adorn, Dry Look, Earth Born, Foamy, Right Guard, Soft & Dri, Tame, Toni, White Rain (toiletries); Paper Mate, Flair, El Marko, Eraser Mate (pens); Liquid Paper (correcting fluid); Cricket, S. T. Dupont (lighters). A German subsidiary, Braun A. G., produces electric shavers and small household appliances.

Sales: $2,315.3 million (trend 10.3% a year).
Earnings: $123.98 million (trend 10.3% a year).
What happened to a $10,000 investment

Purchase Date	*Purchase Price*	*Price on 12-31-81*	*Dividends Paid*
12-31-71	$40.25	$33.75	$3,949.07
12-31-76	$27.87	$33.75	$3,056.50

Purchase Date	*Cap. Gains (– Losses)*	*Total Return*	*Rate of Return*
12-31-71	$–1,614.91	$2,334.16	2.12%
12-31-76	$ 2,107.62	$5,164.13	8.68%

PROFILE: After being on an earnings plateau ($2 to $3 a share) for ten years from 1968 to 1977, Gillette has finally got some momentum going. Earnings stayed in the $3 to $4 range for only two years (1978 and 1979) and hit $4.11 in 1980 and 1981, which were recession years.

In razors and blades, pens and disposable lighters, Gillette is up against arch-rival Société Bic, whose 19-cent pens almost sent Gillette's Paper Mate division down for the count in the 1960s. In toiletries and cosmetics, it is up against everybody and his brother, especially Revlon. Make no mistake, Gillette will continue to face plenty of tough competition. But recently it seems to have clear ideas on how to take on that competition. It has grown more selective in how many products it will push, and is pushing them with big ad budgets.

Gone, most likely, are the glory days of the 1950s and early 1960s, when Gillette had an almost unquestioned domination of the blade market, and a return on stockholders' equity of around 30 percent. (Return on equity fell to just over 15 percent by 1977, but had inched back up to nearly 18 percent in 1980.) But the stock sells for a lot less — both in absolute terms and in relation to earnings — than it did during those glory days. In 1967 Gillette sold for almost $63 a share, and for more than 27 times earnings. In early 1981 it sold for about $36 a share, which was approximately 9 times earnings. The stock has paid for not living up to investors' high expectations. Now it may prosper by surpassing their reduced ones.

The dividend yield in recent years has been between 5 and 7 percent; dividends have been paid each year since the company was incorporated.

* * *

GINO'S INC. (GNO). Founded 1960. Headquarters: 215 W. Church Rd., King of Prussia PA 19406. FAST FOOD. Gino's Inc. operates hamburger, chicken, and fish fast-food restaurants; also operates a steak house chain. MAJOR SUBSIDIARIES, BRANDS: Kentucky Fried Chicken (franchises); Rustler Steak House.

Sales: $320.8 million (trend 6.6% a year).
Earnings: $4.46 million (trend −6.8% a year).
What happened to a $10,000 investment

Purchase Date	*Purchase Price*	*Price on 12-31-81*	*Dividends Paid*
12-31-71	$13.87	$16.87	$ 778.38
12-31-76	$ 9.87	$16.87	$1,093.67

Purchase Date	*Cap. Gains (− Losses)*	*Total Return*	*Rate of Return*
12-31-71	$2,162.16	$2,940.54	2.61%
12-31-76	$7,088.61	$8,182.28	12.70%

* * *

GLEASON WORKS (GLE). Founded 1903. Headquarters: 100 University Ave., Rochester NY 14692. TOOLS. The Gleason Works produces machines that make gears, as well as other industrial equipment. MAJOR SUBSIDIARIES, BRANDS: Alliance Tool & Die.

Sales: $242.6 million (trend 26.9% a year).
Earnings: $16.33 million (trend 53.6% a year).
What happened to a $10,000 investment

Purchase Date	*Purchase Price*	*Price on 12-31-81*	*Dividends Paid*
12-31-71	$25.87	$11.62	$1,920.77
12-31-76	$11.25	$11.62	$3,093.33

Purchase Date	*Cap. Gains (− Losses)*	*Total Return*	*Rate of Return*
12-31-71	$−5,507.25	$−3,586.47	−4.34%
12-31-76	$ 333.33	$ 3,426.67	6.07%

* * *

GLOBAL MARINE INC. (GLM). Founded 1964. Headquarters: 811 W. Seventh St., Los Angeles CA 90017. DRILLING. Global Marine Inc. is an offshore drilling contractor for oil and gas drilling. MAJOR SUBSIDIARIES, BRANDS: Challenger Minerals; Global Marine Development; Intermarine Services; Oceanography Services.

Sales: $219.9 million (trend 18.4% a year).
Earnings: $44.88 million (trend 74.5% a year).
What happened to a $10,000 investment

Purchase Date	*Purchase Price*	*Price on 12-31-81*	*Dividends Paid*
12-31-71	$4.06	$22.87	$ 615.38
12-31-76	$2.06	$22.87	$1,212.12

Purchase Date	*Cap. Gains (− Losses)*	*Total Return*	*Rate of Return*
12-31-71	$ 46,307.69	$ 46,923.08	19.00%
12-31-76	$100,909.09	$102,121.21	62.16%

* * *

GOLDEN NUGGET, INC. (GNG). Founded 1949. Headquarters: 129 Fremont St., PO Box 610, Las Vegas NV 89101. HOTEL / CASINO. Golden Nugget, Inc., operates hotel / casino complexes in Las Vegas and Atlantic City.

Sales: $60.6 million (trend 23.0% a year).
Earnings: $−2.59 million.
What happened to a $10,000 investment

Purchase Date	*Purchase Price*	*Price on 12-31-81*	*Dividends Paid*
12-31-71	$N/A	$22.25	$ N/A
12-31-76	$ 3.42	$22.25	$234.15

Purchase Date	*Cap. Gains (− Losses)*	*Total Return*	*Rate of Return*
12-31-71	$ N/A	$ N/A	N/A%
12-31-76	$55,121.95	$55,356.10	45.57%

* * *

GOLDEN WEST FINANCIAL CORP. (GDW). Founded 1975. Headquarters: 1970 Broadway, Oakland CA 94612. SAVINGS & LOAN HOLDING COMPANY. Golden West Financial is a savings & loan holding company with offices in California and Colorado. MAJOR SUBSIDIARIES, BRANDS: World Savings and Loan Association (California); World Savings and Loan Association (Colorado).

Sales: $485.3 million (trend 36.2% a year).
Earnings: $38.06 million (trend 28.4% a year).
What happened to a $10,000 investment

Purchase Date	*Purchase Price*	*Price on 12-31-81*	*Dividends Paid*
12-31-71	$N/A	$7.87	$ N/A
12-31-76	$ 6.21	$7.87	$2,276.51

Purchase Date	*Cap. Gains (− Losses)*	*Total Return*	*Rate of Return*
12-31-71	$ N/A	$ N/A	N/A%
12-31-76	$2,684.56	$4,961.07	8.39%

* * *

B. F. GOODRICH CO. (GR). Founded 1912. Headquarters: 500 S. Main St., Akron OH 44318. **TIRES, CHEMICALS.** B. F. Goodrich is the third-largest U.S. tire manufacturer, and the largest U.S. maker of polyvinyl chloride. It also produces other chemicals and a variety of industrial products. 40,000 employees.

Sales: $3,079.6 million (trend 11.4% a year).
Earnings: $59.68 million (trend 33.4% a year).
What happened to a $10,000 investment

Purchase Date	*Purchase Price*	*Price on 12-31-81*	*Dividends Paid*
12-31-71	$28.37	$22.25	$4,401.76
12-31-76	$26.87	$22.25	$2,641.86

Purchase Date	*Cap. Gains (− Losses)*	*Total Return*	*Rate of Return*
12-31-71	$−2,158.59	$2,243.17	2.04%
12-31-76	$−1,720.93	$ 920.93	1.78%

PROFILE: At a lot of companies you have to read between the lines to figure out what's going on. Not at Goodrich. It's transforming itself right out in the open from a tire company to a diversified enterprise that will be primarily a chemical company. You can read about it in the headlines. "Goodrich: Speeding the switch from tires to industrial chemicals" (*Business Week,* 1981). "On the Rebound: Plastics Brighten B. F. Goodrich Outlook" (*Barron*'s, 1981). "Goodrich: Not Just a Tire Maker" (New York *Times,* 1981).

The reason for the change is simple, and was summed up in another headline — "Goodrich: The Industry Pessimist" (*Forbes,* 1980). The *Forbes* article quoted chairman John Ong as saying, "This [tire] industry will never again enjoy good growth." Many people agree with him, citing the trend to high gasoline prices (less driving), smaller cars (smaller, less profitable tires), and radial tires (more durable, hence fewer replacements). Based on what it saw as the handwriting on the wall, Goodrich started rewriting its script in 1971. By 1975, tires were only 53 percent of the company's sales; by 1980, only 42 percent. Meanwhile chemicals had climbed to 27 percent in 1975, 33 percent in 1980 (and that 33 percent of sales accounted for 40 percent of profits). In chemicals, Goodrich's specialty is polyvinyl chloride, which *Barron*'s describes as "a workhorse of the plastics industry . . . used in everything from pipe to packaging to floor coverings."

During the past decade, the company has struggled to trim back debt like a dieter trying to keep his weight down. As of early 1982, debt had bulged to about 40 percent of total capital. The yield on dividends (paid yearly since 1939) has recently ranged from 5 to 8 percent.

* * *

GOODYEAR TIRE & RUBBER CO. (GT). Founded 1898. Headquarters: 1144 E. Market St., Akron OH 44316. **TIRES.** Goodyear is by far the nation's largest manufacturer of auto and truck tires; also has sidelines in chemicals and industrial products. 144,000 employees.

Sales: $8,444.0 million (trend 10.1% a year).
Earnings: $206.71 million (trend 5.5% a year).
What happened to a $10,000 investment

Purchase Date	*Purchase Price*	*Price on 12-31-81*	*Dividends Paid*
12-31-71	$31.87	$19.25	$3,597.80
12-31-76	$23.75	$19.25	$2,694.74

Purchase Date	*Cap. Gains (− Losses)*	*Total Return*	*Rate of Return*
12-31-71	$−3,960.78	$−362.98	−.37%
12-31-76	$−1,894.74	$ 800.00	1.55%

PROFILE: The tire industry is sharply split between those who believe the industry has a future and those who believe it doesn't. The latter seem to include Goodrich (see preceding entry), which has diversified into plastics, and General Tire, which has diversified into almost anything that isn't round and doesn't roll. Goodyear is at the opposite extreme. Like General Motors, the nation's largest car maker, Goodyear, the nation's largest tire maker, has been pouring money into expansion during bad times for the auto industry.

The aim, in both cases, is to make number one

even bigger, to gain an even more dominant market share, and to knock some of the competitors out of the ring. Goodyear may succeed in doing that: It's quite possible that Uniroyal, Goodrich, or General Tire will give up the tire business during the coming decade.

In building big new plants, Goodyear also has a couple of other aims. One is to make a fresh start in areas where unions are less strong. The other is to produce radials, the tire that has captured the bulk of the market, contrary to Goodyear's earlier expectations.

Profits in recent years have not gone much of anywhere. Earnings were $2.34 a share in 1971. They rose gradually to $3.12 in 1978, then dropped to $2.02 in 1979. When the auto industry finally recovers, earnings will probably hit a new cyclical peak. Meantime, they're not doing badly. Partly on the strength of replacement tires, earnings hit $2.85 in 1980 and $3.36 in 1981. Meantime, they're not doing badly. Partly on the strength of replacement tires, earnings hit $2.85 in 1980 and $3.36 in 1981.

With a reputation for slow growth and cyclicality, the stock has performed poorly. However, it did seem poised for a rebound in the early 1980s.

The dividend is nothing to sneeze at. In recent years the yield has ranged from 6 to 9 percent; dividends have been paid each year since 1937.

* * *

GORDON JEWELRY CORP. (GOR). Founded 1957. Headquarters: 820 Fannin St., Houston TX 77002. **RETAIL JEWELRY.** Gordon Jewelry Corp. operates retail jewelry stores; also manufactures jewelry and paper products.

Sales: $481.5 million (trend 21.5% a year).
Earnings: $27.99 million (trend 20.4% a year).
What happened to a $10,000 investment

Purchase Date	*Purchase Price*	*Price on 12-31-81*	*Dividends Paid*
12-31-71	$18.42	$17.00	$1,552.94
12-31-76	$ 8.08	$17.00	$2,383.51

Purchase Date	*Cap. Gains (− Losses)*	*Total Return*	*Rate of Return*
12-31-71	$ −769.23	$ 783.71	.76%
12-31-76	$11,030.93	$13,414.43	18.55%

* * *

GOULD INC. (GLD). Founded 1928. Headquarters: 10 Gould Center, Rolling Meadows IL 60008. **ELECTRONICS.** Gould is a major manufacturer of electrical and electronics products, and batteries. 35,000 employees. **MAJOR SUBSIDIARIES, BRANDS:** Systems Engineering Laboratories; I-T-E Imperial Corp.; Gettys Manufacturing Co.; Taylor Electric; SRL Medical Inc.; Mark 48 (Navy torpedo); American Microsystems Inc.

Sales: $2,199.9 million (trend 21.7% a year).
Earnings: $71.94 million (trend 17.3% a year).
What happened to a $10,000 investment

Purchase Date	*Purchase Price*	*Price on 12-31-81*	*Dividends Paid*
12-31-71	$19.67	$22.62	$5,853.10
12-31-76	$30.25	$22.62	$2,585.12

Purchase Date	*Cap. Gains (− Losses)*	*Total Return*	*Rate of Return*
12-31-71	$ 1,504.24	$7,357.34	5.67%
12-31-76	$−2,520.66	$ 64.46	.13%

PROFILE: Only a decade and a half ago, Gould was a rather small battery manufacturer. Today it's among the largest 200 industrial corporations in the country, and its heart is electronics. Medical instruments and Navy weapons are a far cry from making car batteries to be sold under private labels by J. C. Penney and K mart (which Gould also continues to do).

Gould has acquired its high-tech character mainly through acquisitions. The acquisitions were funded mainly by issuing more Gould stock, so there's been a lot of dilution going on. Net income rose from about $15 million in 1970 to about $106 million in 1979 — a sevenfold increase. But earnings per share over the same period increased less than fourfold, since there were more shares outstanding. Still, that was good profit growth. Unfortunately an eight-year string of earnings gains was snapped in 1980, as the recession and labor trouble combined to dump earnings to $2.10 a share, compared to $3.78 a share (a record) the year before. In 1981 the company managed only a modest gain, to $2.42.

Another problem for Gould is management dissension. The high-energy, driving (some say abrasive) leadership style of William Ylvisaker, chairman since 1967, seems to rub a lot of people the wrong way. *Business Week* in 1980 said the company was "plagued" by an "exodus at the top" that saw five top officials leave during 1980. But Ylvisaker smoothly told *The Wall Street Journal* that the departures were merely what you'd expect when you employ "aggressive people, who want to go out and run their own businesses."

The 1981 sale of industrial operations will enable the company to concentrate on electronics, its most profitable area, and probably allow the next few acquisitions to be financed with cash, avoiding dilution of the balance sheet (debt was about 30 percent of capital in 1981).

Dividends have been increased each year from 1972 through 1980, but in the last year it took four fifths of company earnings to keep the dividend growing. The yield in recent years has ranged from 6 to 10 percent.

* * *

W. R. GRACE & CO. (GRA). Founded 1899. Headquarters: Grace Plaza, 1114 Ave. of the Americas, New York NY 10036. CHEMICALS, ENERGY, CONSUMER PRODUCTS. Grace is a conglomerate built around a steamship line that has since been sold off. Specialty chemicals, oil and gas production, specialty retailing (home improvement building supplies, sporting goods) and restaurants are the principal lines of business. 82,000 employees. MAJOR SUBSIDIARIES, BRANDS: Chemed; Channel, Handy Dan, Handy City (lumber or do-it-yourself building supply stores); Herman's (sporting goods); Del Taco (restaurants).

Sales: $6,101.3 million (trend 11.9% a year).
Earnings: $283.10 million (trend 13.5% a year).
What happened to a $10,000 investment

Purchase Date	*Purchase Price*	*Price on 12-31-81*	*Dividends Paid*
12-31-71	$28.50	$45.75	$6,342.11
12-31-76	$29.25	$45.75	$3,495.73

Purchase Date	*Cap. Gains (− Losses)*	*Total Return*	*Rate of Return*
12-31-71	$6,052.63	$12,394.74	8.40%
12-31-76	$5,641.03	$ 9,136.75	13.86%

PROFILE: Chairman Peter Grace holds the record for tenure as chief executive of one of America's biggest 500 corporations: He has been in charge of W. R. Grace since 1945. When he might retire is open to speculation. When he does, the firm's helm will probably pass from the hands of the Grace family (which owns about 3 percent of the stock) to someone selected by the Friedrich Flick Group of West Germany, which owns 27 percent of the stock.

Grace has compared himself to Babe Ruth, who was likely either to hit a home run or strike out. There have indeed been plenty of both homers (e.g., the move, in the early 1970s, into natural resources — oil, gas, and coal) and strikeouts (e.g., a massive failure in European foods companies during the 1960s). The company is certainly of Ruthian proportions. Number 51 on the *Fortune* 500 list (as of 1981), it is powerful and plump, with something around a hundred subsidiaries. The activity and subsidiary list above is only partial: it doesn't even touch on some of the smaller operations, from auto parts to cocoa, from book distribution to bull semen.

Viewed solely as a chemical company (chemicals were 53 percent of 1979 sales, 65 percent of profits), W. R. Grace ranks fifth in the United States. A fair chunk of the chemical business consists of agricultural chemicals and fertilizer, but a wide variety of specialty chemicals are produced.

Neither return on equity nor profit growth has been outstanding in the past several years. However, the company weathers recessions nicely, like an ocean liner riding out a storm.

Dividends have been paid yearly since 1934. In recent years the yield has ranged from 4 to 7 percent.

* * *

W. W. GRAINGER, INC. (GWW). Founded 1927. Headquarters: 5500 W. Howard St., Skokie IL 60077. ELECTRIC MOTORS. W. W. Grainger, Inc., distributes electric motors and related products. MAJOR SUBSIDIARIES, BRANDS: Doerr Electric Corp.

Sales: $782.6 million (trend 20.0% a year).
Earnings: $48.80 million (trend 20.7% a year).
What happened to a $10,000 investment

Purchase Date	*Purchase Price*	*Price on 12-31-81*	*Dividends Paid*
12-31-71	$20.69	$37.12	$2,708.40
12-31-76	$30.25	$37.12	$1,368.60

Purchase Date	*Cap. Gains (− Losses)*	*Total Return*	*Rate of Return*
12-31-71	$7,945.62	$10,654.02	7.52%
12-31-76	$2,272.73	$ 3,641.32	6.41%

* * *

GRANITEVILLE CO. (GVL). Founded 1845. Headquarters: Marshall St., PO Box 128, Graniteville SC 29829. TEXTILES. Graniteville Co. manufactures, dyes, and finishes cotton, synthetic, and blended fabrics. MAJOR SUBSIDIARIES, BRANDS: C. H. Patrick & Co.

Sales: $341.1 million (trend 6.6% a year).
Earnings: $11.09 million (trend −15.9% a year).
What happened to a $10,000 investment

Purchase Date	*Purchase Price*	*Price on 12-31-81*	*Dividends Paid*
12-31-71	$ 8.20	$10.25	$9,890.24
12-31-76	$14.87	$10.25	$3,310.92

Purchase Date	*Cap. Gains (− Losses)*	*Total Return*	*Rate of Return*
12-31-71	$ 2,500.00	$12,390.24	8.39%
12-31-76	$−3,109.24	$ 201.68	.40%

* * *

GREAT ATLANTIC & PACIFIC TEA CO., INC. (GAP). Founded 1925. Headquarters: 2 Paragon Dr., Montvale NJ 07645. SUPERMARKETS. Operates some 1,500 supermarkets nationwide; as of 1980 was third-largest supermarket chain in U.S., by revenues. 63,000 employees. MAJOR SUBSIDIARIES, BRANDS: A&P, PLUS, Niagara Frontier, Family Mart (supermarkets); Compass Foods (produces house brands).

Sales: $6,989.5 million (trend .3% a year).
Earnings: $−43.05 million.
What happened to a $10,000 investment

Purchase Date	*Purchase Price*	*Price on 12-31-81*	*Dividends Paid*
12-31-71	$21.12	$3.87	$591.72
12-31-76	$14.25	$3.87	$140.35

Purchase Date	*Cap. Gains (− Losses)*	*Total Return*	*Rate of Return*
12-31-71	$−8,165.68	$−7,573.96	−13.21%
12-31-76	$−7,280.70	$−7,140.35	−22.15%

PROFILE: The past decade has been full of humiliations and changes for A&P. It now has about half the number of stores it had a decade ago. It lost the number one position in the supermarket industry to Safeway in the early 1970s and slipped to third behind Kroger in the late 1970s. It is 49 percent owned by foreign interests: The Tengelmann Group of West Germany bought a controlling interest in 1979 and may have up to 65 percent of the stock before long. Its long-term debt, nonexistent as recently as 1973, had climbed to about 46 percent of capital as of late 1981. And it had lost money in five of the ten fiscal years up to February 28, 1981 — with the sum of the five losses considerably exceeding the sum of the five profits. Worse, the last three years in that period were all loss years. Dividends have been skipped the past two years, and also in 1975–76; no meaningful dividends have been paid since 1974. The company has moved to tap surplus pension funds for operating purposes. The stock, which used to fetch $25 to $40 a share in the late 1960s, went for about $6 a share in early 1981.

Do you want to buy into this disaster? Well, you might, if you relish speculation on turnarounds. Certainly the stock can't go too much lower unless the company goes bankrupt. But as of 1981 the efforts to turn A&P around had not yet shown any signs of success. One of the Tengelmann Group's main innovations has been the opening of PLUS stores — low-price, low-budget operations where the shopper chooses from a limited set of offerings, takes the merchandise straight out of cartons, and bags his or her own groceries. PLUS stores may eventually turn a profit, but it's hard to see how it could be a large one.

Unwilling to incur any more debt, the company has recently issued some additional stock, and may issue more. That will mean a dilution of per-share earnings, even when there are some earnings to dilute.

* * *

GREAT LAKES INTERNATIONAL, INC. (GL). Founded 1905. Headquarters: 2122 York Rd., Oak Brook IL 60521. DREDGING AND MARINE CONSTRUCTION. Great Lakes International, Inc., dredges rivers, harbors, channels; also involved in land reclamation, beach restoration, rock drilling. MAJOR SUBSIDIARIES, BRANDS: Henry DuBois' Sons Company, Inc.; Lydon Dredging & Construction Co.; North American Trailing Co.; Tidewater Dredging Corp.; Western Quarries and Construction Co.

Sales: $93.5 million (trend 15.7% a year).
Earnings: $8.60 million (trend 27.3% a year).
What happened to a $10,000 investment

Purchase Date	*Purchase Price*	*Price on 12-31-81*	*Dividends Paid*
12-31-71	$9.83	$32.25	$8,610.17
12-31-76	$7.75	$32.25	$7,956.99

Purchase Date	*Cap. Gains (− Losses)*	*Total Return*	*Rate of Return*
12-31-71	$22,796.61	$31,406.78	15.27%
12-31-76	$31,612.90	$39,569.89	37.73%

* * *

GREAT NORTHERN IRON ORE PROPERTIES (GNI). Founded 1906. Headquarters: W-2081 First National Bank Bldg., St. Paul MN 55101. **IRON ORE PROPERTIES.** Great Northern Iron Ore Properties is a trust that owns iron ore properties in Minnesota; income is derived from royalties from steel and mining company leases.

* * *

GREAT NORTHERN NEKOOSA CORP. (GNN). Founded 1898. Headquarters: 75 Prospect St., Stamford CT 06901. **PAPER.** Produces copier paper, newsprint, containerboard, and other paper products; also distributes paper products made by other firms. Owns 2.7 million acres of timberland; has sidelines in coal, copper, and zinc mining, mainly through leasing company land to outside mining interests. 12,000 employees. **MAJOR SUBSIDIARIES, BRANDS:** Butler Paper.

Sales: $1,373.3 million (trend 14.5% a year).
Earnings: $99.10 million (trend 17.8% a year).
What happened to a $10,000 investment

Purchase Date	*Purchase Price*	*Price on 12-31-81*	*Dividends Paid*
12-31-71	$19.70	$36.75	$5,710.66
12-31-76	$32.75	$36.75	$2,236.64

Purchase Date	*Cap. Gains (− Losses)*	*Total Return*	*Rate of Return*
12-31-71	$8,654.82	$14,365.48	9.31%
12-31-76	$1,221.37	$ 3,458.02	6.12%

PROFILE: Great Northern Nekoosa's performance has put it in the middle of the pack in recent years. However, there are some hints of qualities that could set this company apart and produce capital gains possibly in excess of the gradual ones achieved during the past decade.

One point is timberland. Great Northern Nekoosa owns 11 percent of the land in the state of Maine. This land and the timber and minerals on it have always been carried on the company's books at considerably less than their ultimate value. Partly for that reason the company might become a takeover candidate, and a bidding war could cause the price of the stock to rise substantially.

A related point is mineral recovery. Great Northern Nekoosa farms out to others the job of recovering the coal, copper, and zinc beneath its timberland. Still, it's possible that mining might be a significant contributor to profits down the road.

A third point is energy. Great Northern, more than most companies, is self-sufficient in energy: It makes about 75 percent of the power it needs, by owning its own hydroelectric dams, and plans to continue the trend by burning waste bark as boiler fuel. This could help maintain the company's profit margins, already better than most.

Finally, there's the company's strong position in copier paper — it makes about half the paper for Xerox, for example. This is a growing market.

The stock price rose from a 1971 high around $21 to a high of around $47 in 1981. The dividend yield in recent years has been between 4 and 5 percent.

If you are interested in this stock, here's a timing consideration. Unlike most stocks,. it probably shouldn't be bought near the end of a general recession. Paper sales often lag just as other segments of the economy are starting to recover.

* * *

GREAT WESTERN FINANCIAL CORP. (GWF). Founded 1955. Headquarters: 8484 Wilshire Blvd., Beverly Hills CA 90211. **SAVINGS & LOAN.** Holding company for Great Western Savings & Loan Association, the second-largest S&L in the country, with more than 100 branch offices in California. 2,000 employees. **MAJOR SUBSIDIARIES, BRANDS:** Great Western Savings & Loan Association.

Sales: $997.2 million (trend 20.6% a year).
Earnings: $39.17 million (trend 14.7% a year).
What happened to a $10,000 investment

Purchase Date	*Purchase Price*	*Price on 12-31-81*	*Dividends Paid*
12-31-71	$18.83	$14.50	$2,711.50
12-31-76	$15.67	$14.50	$2,382.98

Purchase Date	*Cap. Gains (− Losses)*	*Total Return*	*Rate of Return*
12-31-71	$−2,300.88	$ 410.62	.40%
12-31-76	$ −744.68	$1,638.30	3.08%

PROFILE: All banking institutions, and especially savings and loan associations, have been hit by pinched margins in recent years. It's particularly hard for S&Ls, since such a huge proportion of their assets is loaned out for the long term at fixed rates. Great Western, for example, has more than 80 percent of its loan portfolio in residential mortgages, many of which pay yesterday's interest rates while the S&L has to pay today's rates (mainly on six-month certificates) to attract funds.

Two developments should help, sooner or later:

A decline in interest rates, and the increasing use of adjustable mortgages. Until those occur, more tough times are in store. Great Western had record earnings of about $93 million ($4.15 a share) in 1979. In 1980, earnings plunged to about $39 million ($1.74 a share). A loss of $28 million ($1.24 a share) was suffered in 1981.

The stock market, discounting both present troubles and a future recovery, valued the stock in late 1981 at about $14 a share, which was about 8 times 1980's depressed earnings but only about 3½ times 1979's peak earnings.

This has traditionally been regarded as a growth stock, mainly because of its position in California, a growth state. As such, it sold for 16 to 19 times earnings in the late 1960s, and didn't start paying dividends until 1972. The dividend yield, traditionally modest, has recently grown into the range where it about equals the return on a passbook savings account.

* * *

GREYHOUND CORP. (G). Founded 1926. Headquarters: Greyhound Tower, Phoenix AZ 85077. **CONGLOMERATE.** Greyhound is involved in a wide range of activities including bus transportation and manufacturing, food processing, food service, consumer products, aircraft and computer leasing, and financial services. 52,000 employees. **MAJOR SUBSIDIARIES, BRANDS:** Armour & Co.; Greyhound Lines; Dial, Tone (soaps); Appian Way Pizza; Bucilla, Malina (yarns); Post House.

Sales: $4,766.1 million (trend 6.0% a year).
Earnings: $118.31 million (trend 8.8% a year).
What happened to a $10,000 investment

Purchase Date	*Purchase Price*	*Price on 12-31-81*	*Dividends Paid*
12-31-71	$21.25	$15.50	$5,087.06
12-31-76	$15.25	$15.50	$3,619.67

Purchase Date	*Cap. Gains (− Losses)*	*Total Return*	*Rate of Return*
12-31-71	$−2,705.88	$2,381.18	2.16%
12-31-76	$ 163.93	$3,783.61	6.63%

PROFILE: Greyhound has one of the most unusual earnings patterns you'll find. From 1971 through 1980 its earnings consistently went up one year and down the next.

This did not enthrall Wall Street, which likes dramatic growth best, steady growth next best, and cyclicality very little. Greyhound shares (at $13 to $20 each) fetched about 5 to 6 times earnings in 1981. They haven't commanded more than 10 times earnings since 1972.

Capital gains? Well, Greyhound's high in 1970 was $18.50 a share. In 1980 it was $18.62 a share. Dramatic capital gains would most likely require either a turnaround or a sell-off of the Armour & Co. meat operations. Food contributed only 15 percent of 1979 profits, on 52 percent of sales. In 1980 the food operation lost money. The most profitable division has been the financial group, which engages in computer and aircraft leasing, among other activities.

Give Greyhound this: It weathered the 1980–81 recession pretty well. Perhaps people trade down to hot dogs and other processed meats when times are tough. In the recent recession, Greyhound has also benefited from rising bus travel, due to high gasoline prices (which discouraged use of private cars).

Another plus is the dividend. The yield has ranged from 7 to 9 percent since 1974. And dividends have been paid each year since 1936.

Gerald Trautman, Greyhound's chairman since 1966, is due to retire in 1982. At that point, there might be some major changes in company direction.

* * *

GROW GROUP, INC. (GRO). Founded 1950. Headquarters: 200 Park Ave., New York NY 10017. **SPECIALTY CHEMICALS.** Grow Group, Inc., manufactures specialty chemicals and general purpose paints. **MAJOR SUBSIDIARIES, BRANDS:** Roy Jacobs Co.

Sales: $232.5 million (trend 15.8% a year).
Earnings: $5.91 million (trend 22.0% a year).
What happened to a $10,000 investment

Purchase Date	*Purchase Price*	*Price on 12-31-81*	*Dividends Paid*
12-31-71	$5.62	$7.26	$4,052.82
12-31-76	$6.42	$7.26	$2,227.96

Purchase Date	*Cap. Gains (− Losses)*	*Total Return*	*Rate of Return*
12-31-71	$2,914.64	$6,967.46	5.43%
12-31-76	$1,302.67	$3,530.63	6.23%

* * *

GROWTH REALTY COMPANIES (GRW). Founded 1979. Headquarters: 2029 Century Park East, Suite 2000, Los Angeles CA 90067. **REAL ESTATE INVESTMENT.** Growth Realty Companies is involved in real estate ownership, investment, and management, as well as mortgage brokerage and related financial services. **MAJOR SUBSIDIARIES, BRANDS:** Growth Realty Investment Managers; Growth Realty Financial Co.; Growth Realty National.

* * *

GRUMMAN CORP. (GQ). Founded 1929. Headquarters: Bethpage, Long Island NY 11714. **AEROSPACE.** Grumman is a major defense contractor, supplying aircraft to the Navy and Air Force. Also produces buses, fire engines, ambulances and truck bodies; makes solar heating systems and food transport equipment; manufactures canoes; and offers data processing services. 28,000 employees. **MAJOR SUBSIDIARIES, BRANDS:** F-14, A-6, EA-6B, E-2C (aircraft); Flxible (buses); Dormavac (food shipping equipment).

Sales: $1,729.3 million (trend 3.5% a year).
Earnings: $28.34 million (trend −.8% a year).
What happened to a $10,000 investment

Purchase Date	*Purchase Price*	*Price on 12-31-81*	*Dividends Paid*
12-31-71	$13.98	$27.75	$5,700.81
12-31-76	$17.87	$27.75	$3,328.67

Purchase Date	*Cap. Gains (− Losses)*	*Total Return*	*Rate of Return*
12-31-71	$9,853.65	$15,554.46	9.84%
12-31-76	$5,524.48	$ 8,853.15	13.52%

PROFILE: Lots of problems and a lot of promise: That's Grumman in a nutshell.

The positive factors are the nation's apparent commitment to stepped-up military spending, from which Grumman is almost bound to benefit, and the chance that the Flxible bus division will start chipping in a meaningful share of profits.

The negative factors include the fact that the Flxible bus division, acquired from Rohr in 1978, hadn't contributed a penny to profits through 1980. In fact, thanks in part to embarrassing cracks in the bodies of the buses, it had been a drain on profits. Yet, Grumman chairman John Bierworth was right when he thought that in the face of the energy crisis people would take the bus more. Grumman recently shared the market for U.S.-made buses about evenly with General Motors; if it can keep that much market share, it should do well.

A second negative is that Grumman reportedly had no new planes on the drawing boards, as of 1980. Although that may not matter much in the short run, it could be a long-run concern.

A third negative is the company's history of erratic earnings. It had a huge loss in 1972, a smaller loss in 1971, and three years of unimpressive profits from 1978 through 1980. In 1981 profits were down. Potential buyers should note the history of seesawing earnings. The company was in some danger of bankruptcy in the early 1970s. Debt then climbed to about 66 percent of capital; recently it was about 42 percent.

Keep a close eye on the price and the p/e ratio, both of which are volatile. In late 1981 the stock sold for about $24. That was about 12 times the most recent twelve months' earnings, but only about 6 times the company's peak earnings (1977). Since the average stock at the time was fetching about 8 times earnings, it's clear that Wall Street was carefully balancing the problems against the promise.

In 1981, Grumman fought off a determined takeover bid from LTV.

* * *

GUARDIAN INDUSTRIES CORP. (GRD). Founded 1968. Headquarters: 43043 W. Nine Mile Rd., Northville MI 48167. **GLASS.** Guardian Industries Corp. is involved in flat glass production and photofinishing services.

Sales: $299.1 million (trend 24.2% a year).
Earnings: $28.30 million (trend 31.3% a year).
What happened to a $10,000 investment

Purchase Date	*Purchase Price*	*Price on 12-31-81*	*Dividends Paid*
12-31-71	$6.33	$14.37	$2,009.42
12-31-76	$5.96	$14.37	$1,761.25

Purchase Date	*Cap. Gains (− Losses)*	*Total Return*	*Rate of Return*
12-31-71	$12,723.95	$14,733.37	9.48%
12-31-76	$14,137.13	$15,898.38	20.96%

* * *

GULF & WESTERN INDUSTRIES, INC. (GW). Founded 1958. Headquarters: 1 Gulf & Western Plaza, New York NY 10023. **CONGLOMERATE.** Movies, entertainment, publishing, sugar, auto parts, cigars, and clothing are among the major areas of operation. 110,000 employees. **MAJOR SUBSIDIARIES, BRANDS:** Paramount Pictures; Madison Square Garden Corp., New York Knickerbockers, New York Rangers (entertainment); Simon & Schuster, Pocket Books (publishing); Consolidated Cigar Corp. (Muriel, Dutch Masters, El

Producto and other brands); A.P.S. (auto parts); Associates Corp. (financial services); Kayser-Roth (clothing); New Jersey Zinc.

Sales: $5,702.5 million (trend 11.9% a year).
Earnings: $283.02 million (trend 11.7% a year).
What happened to a $10,000 investment

Purchase Date	*Purchase Price*	*Price on 12-31-81*	*Dividends Paid*
12-31-71	$ 8.25	$15.87	$5,310.84
12-31-76	$14.60	$15.87	$2,060.27

Purchase Date	*Cap. Gains (− Losses)*	*Total Return*	*Rate of Return*
12-31-71	$9,231.83	$14,542.67	9.39%
12-31-76	$ 873.29	$ 2,933.56	5.28%

PROFILE: If your taste runs to highly leveraged, highly diversified, wheeling-and-dealing conglomerates, this is a perfect stock for you.

Business Week, in 1980, called Gulf & Western "one of the first and most aggressive of the conglomerates," and quoted a company official as noting that the company ran from A to Z — auto parts to zinc. It has specialized in buying up troubled or undervalued companies and, in many cases, turning them around. The company also maintains an investment portfolio (recently over $150 million) of stock in other companies. These are a mixture of candidates for potential acquisition and stocks that will be resold later, often at a profit. When he buys in, though, chairman Charles Bluhdorn always proclaims that he's doing it simply "for investment purposes." Recently he's been buying the stocks of troubled tire companies, such as Uniroyal and General Tire. Bluhdorn, a highly controversial legend on Wall Street, also owns a fair chunk of Gulf & Western stock personally (about 6 percent, according to one recent report).

The profit trend has been erratic, but generally good. Earnings were $0.76 a share in 1971, $4.38 a share in 1980. Yet, because the company is so controversial and so diversified, the shares have never commanded a high price / earnings multiple. In 1981 the shares sold for only 4 to 6 times earnings. Since the late 1970s, the dividend yield has ranged from 4 to 6 percent.

* * *

GULF CANADA LTD. (GOC, American Stock Exchange). Founded 1909. Headquarters: 800 Bay St., Toronto, Ont. M58 1Y8, Canada. **OIL.** Gulf Canada, which is about 60 percent owned by Gulf Oil Corp., is the second-largest oil company in Canada. 11,000 employees. **MAJOR SUBSIDIARIES, BRANDS:** Gulf Minerals Canada Ltd. (10 percent owned).

Sales: $3,373.0 million (trend 13.4% a year).
Earnings: $318.00 million (trend 12.1% a year).
What happened to a $10,000 investment

Purchase Date	*Purchase Price*	*Price on 12-31-81*	*Dividends Paid*
12-31-71	$5.10	$15.62	$4,280.78
12-31-76	$5.22	$15.62	$2,633.30

Purchase Date	*Cap. Gains (− Losses)*	*Total Return*	*Rate of Return*
12-31-71	$20,637.25	$24,918.04	13.32%
12-31-76	$19,904.31	$22,537.61	26.61%

PROFILE: The year 1980 was the tenth straight year of rising earnings for Gulf Canada. In 1981 the string was snapped; still, the company had its second-best profit ever. But there's a real question whether American investors will reap the fruits of their investment, even if earnings continue to rise. The Canadian Government has been talking seriously about nationalizing or partly nationalizing the oil industry. Even if that doesn't occur, it plans to: (1) tax the oil companies heavily, (2) keep price controls on the price of oil and gas, and (3) work toward more Canadian ownership of energy-producing companies, even if ownership stays private. All of these trends introduce potential problems for U.S. investors.

And yet, the potential for growth is so vast. The company owns production rights to several promising sites both on and off shore, in such locations as the Beaufort Sea, the McKenzie River Delta, and the Hibernia Field off Newfoundland. The balance sheet is also attractive, with debt only 14 percent of capital as of early 1981.

So, it's tempting to vote (with your dollars) for the potential, and figure that the political problems may be tempered by a change in national attitude or national administration in Canada. It's a gamble, and the dividend (1½ to 3½ percent in recent years) isn't enough to lower the stakes.

Recently, investors seem more entranced by the potential than put off by the problems. The stock sold for 10 to 13 times earnings in 1981, and was the most active issue on the American Stock Exchange in 1980.

* * *

GULF OIL CORP. (GO). Founded 1922. Headquarters: Gulf Bldg., Pittsburgh PA 15230. **OIL.**

Gulf is a major international oil company, and the fifth-largest U.S. oil company. Also produces coal and uranium. 57,000 employees.

Sales: $26,483.0 million (trend 12.8% a year).
Earnings: $1,407.00 million (trend 15.3% a year).
What happened to a $10,000 investment

Purchase Date	*Purchase Price*	*Price on 12-31-81*	*Dividends Paid*
12-31-71	$28.87	$35.37	$6,523.81
12-31-76	$28.87	$35.37	$3,753.25

Purchase Date	*Cap. Gains (− Losses)*	*Total Return*	*Rate of Return*
12-31-71	$2,251.08	$8,774.89	6.50%
12-31-76	$2,251.08	$6,004.33	9.86%

PROFILE: Gulf really took its lumps during the 1970s. It was kicked out of Kuwait (where it used to get more than half its oil) in 1975. The same thing happened in Iran.

Now, Gulf is the smallest and least international of the "seven sisters," the major world oil companies (five of which are U.S.-based). It has gone from being oil rich and selling off about half its production to other companies to being oil poor; it now must buy some of the crude it refines and markets.

Accordingly, profits have gone up at Gulf more slowly than at other oil companies. And, while some oil stocks doubled and tripled from 1979 to 1981, Gulf stock didn't do as well. In fact, the late 1981 price of about $35 a share was below the 1979 high of $37.38 (though the stock did rise as high as $54.50 during 1980). In 1981, the stock commanded only a paltry 5 times earnings.

Part of that low multiple reflects the fact that about a fifth of Gulf's oil comes from Nigeria, which is one of the fiercer pricing hawks in OPEC. By contrast, the other four big U.S. internationals get at least some of their foreign crude from relatively accommodating Saudi Arabia. Having to pay more for its oil, Gulf naturally was experiencing a pinch in profits when it had to match others' prices at the gas pump, especially in a time of reduced demand for gasoline, like early 1981. Most analysts saw little or no earnings progress immediately ahead.

The long-term picture, though, looked considerably brighter. Gulf does not intend to remain a net buyer of crude for long, and is developing its abundant U.S. properties at a breakneck pace. Coal and uranium profits, depressed in recent years, may also improve. Meanwhile the stock pays a solid dividend (the yield was around 7 to 8 percent in 1981). This may be an excellent selection to buy and hold.

* * *

GULF RESOURCES & CHEMICAL CORP. (GRE). Founded 1956. Headquarters: 1100 Milam Bldg., Houston TX 77002. NATURAL RESOURCES. Gulf Resources & Chemical Corp. produces zinc, lead, silver; also mines coal and is involved in exploration for and production of oil and natural gas. **MAJOR SUBSIDIARIES, BRANDS:** Lithium Corp. of America; IRECO Chemicals; Great Salt Lake Minerals & Chemicals; Pend Oreille Oil & Gas Co.

Sales: $638.3 million (trend 16.6% a year).
Earnings: $19.77 million (trend −5.3% a year).
What happened to a $10,000 investment

Purchase Date	*Purchase Price*	*Price on 12-31-81*	*Dividends Paid*
12-31-71	$ 5.75	$14.62	$7,869.57
12-31-76	$17.25	$14.62	$1,318.84

Purchase Date	*Cap. Gains (− Losses)*	*Total Return*	*Rate of Return*
12-31-71	$ 15,434.78	$23,304.35	12.78%
12-31-76	$−1,521.74	$ −202.90	−.41%

* * *

GULF STATES UTILITIES CO. (GSU). Founded 1925. Headquarters: 285 Liberty St., PO Box 2951, Beaumont TX 77701. ELECTRICITY. Gulf States Utilities Co. generates and distributes electricity in parts of Texas and Louisiana; also distributes natural gas. **MAJOR SUBSIDIARIES, BRANDS:** Varibus Corp.

Sales: $1,005.2 million (trend 23.0% a year).
Earnings: $92.31 million (trend 14.3% a year).
What happened to a $10,000 investment

Purchase Date	*Purchase Price*	*Price on 12-31-81*	*Dividends Paid*
12-31-71	$21.75	$11.87	$5,572.41
12-31-76	$14.50	$11.87	$4,565.52

Purchase Date	*Cap. Gains (− Losses)*	*Total Return*	*Rate of Return*
12-31-71	$−4,540.23	$1,032.18	.99%
12-31-76	$−1,810.34	$2,755.17	4.99%

* * *

GULF UNITED CORP. (GHC). Founded 1968. Headquarters: Gulf Life Tower, 1301 Gulf Life Dr.,

Jacksonville FL 32207. **LIFE INSURANCE.** Gulf United Corp. is a life insurance holding company. **MAJOR SUBSIDIARIES, BRANDS:** American-Amicable Insurance; Gulf Life Group Insurance; Gulf Life Insurance; Interstate Life & Accident Insurance.

Sales: $674.4 million (trend 18.5% a year).
Earnings: $68.69 million (trend 18.3% a year).
What happened to a $10,000 investment

Purchase Date	*Purchase Price*	*Price on 12-31-81*	*Dividends Paid*
12-31-71	$15.92	$18.12	$4,516.23
12-31-76	$11.25	$18.12	$4,391.11

Purchase Date	*Cap. Gains (− Losses)*	*Total Return*	*Rate of Return*
12-31-71	$1,387.43	$ 5,903.66	4.75%
12-31-76	$6,111.11	$10,502.22	15.44%

* * *

GULTON INDUSTRIES, INC. (GUL). Founded 1942. Headquarters: 101 College Rd. East, Princeton NJ 08540. **ELECTRONICS.** Gulton Industries, Inc., manufactures electronic instruments and controls, communications equipment, and power and lighting products. **MAJOR SUBSIDIARIES, BRANDS:** Electro-Voice, Inc.; Gulton Europe Ltd.; Gulton Industries (Canada) Ltd.; Southern States, Inc.

Sales: $156.5 million (trend 11.7% a year).
Earnings: $6.32 million (trend 39.6% a year).
What happened to a $10,000 investment

Purchase Date	*Purchase Price*	*Price on 12-31-81*	*Dividends Paid*
12-31-71	$8.12	$9.50	$2,092.31
12-31-76	$4.87	$9.50	$3,384.62

Purchase Date	*Cap. Gains (− Losses)*	*Total Return*	*Rate of Return*
12-31-71	$1,692.31	$ 3,784.62	3.26%
12-31-76	$9,487.18	$12,871.79	17.99%

H

HMW INDUSTRIES, INC. (HMW). Founded 1892. Headquarters: High Ridge Park, Stamford CT 06905. **METAL PRODUCTS.** Manufactures household silverware, consumer and industrial fasteners, and fuses. Distributes electronic components. **MAJOR SUBSIDIARIES, BRANDS:** Hamilton Technology, Handi-Man Fasteners, Wallace Silversmiths; Westmoreland Products; Wallace and Tuttle; Waldom Electronics.

Sales: $101.2 million (trend 11.4% a year).
Earnings: $3.83 million (trend 16.5% a year).
What happened to a $10,000 investment

Purchase Date	*Purchase Price*	*Price on 12-31-81*	*Dividends Paid*
12-31-71	$4.12	$7.12	$0.00
12-31-76	$3.37	$7.12	$0.00

Purchase Date	*Cap. Gains (− Losses)*	*Total Return*	*Rate of Return*
12-31-71	$ 7,272.73	$ 7,272.73	5.62%
12-31-76	$11,111.11	$11,111.11	16.12%

* * *

HRT INDUSTRIES, INC. Founded 1929. Headquarters: 2525 Military Ave., Los Angeles CA 90064. **RETAILING, CLOTHING MANUFACTURE.** This company, formerly Hartfield-Zodys, Inc., operates discount department stores and shoe stores; also manufactures women's clothing. **MAJOR SUBSIDIARIES, BRANDS:** Jody-Tootique (women's clothing); Karl's Shoe Stores Ltd.; Zodys (discount department stores).

Sales: $361.1 million (trend 16.8% a year).
Earnings: $2.95 million (trend 17.5% a year).
What happened to a $10,000 investment

Purchase Date	*Purchase Price*	*Price on 12-31-81*	*Dividends Paid*
12-31-71	$12.84	$9.25	$ 906.27
12-31-76	$ 4.20	$9.25	$2,767.78

Purchase Date	*Cap. Gains (− Losses)*	*Total Return*	*Rate of Return*
12-31-71	$−2,796.46	$−1,890.20	−2.07%
12-31-76	$ 11,999.99	$ 14,767.77	19.89%

* * *

HACKENSACK WATER CO. (HWA). Founded 1869. Headquarters: 200 Old Hook Rd., Harrington Park NJ 07640. **WATER SUPPLY UTILITY.** Provides water services for municipalities in Hudson and Bergen County, New Jersey. **MAJOR SUBSIDIARIES, BRANDS:** Spring Valley Water Co., Inc.

Sales: $64.3 million (trend 11.0% a year).
Earnings: $6.67 million (trend 10.2% a year).
What happened to a $10,000 investment

Purchase Date	Purchase Price	Price on 12-31-81	Dividends Paid
12-31-71	$17.69	$17.12	$8,636.04
12-31-76	$17.75	$17.12	$5,169.01

Purchase Date	Cap. Gains (– Losses)	Total Return	Rate of Return
12-31-71	$−318.02	$8,318.02	6.24%
12-31-76	$−352.11	$4,816.90	8.18%

* * *

FRANK B. HALL & CO., INC. (FBH). Founded 1862. Headquarters: 549 Pleasantville Rd., Briarcliff Manor NY 10510. INSURANCE. A major insurance broker and agent, writing casualty and property, marine, employee benefit, life, and aviation insurance policies.

Sales: $309.6 million (trend 25.9% a year).
Earnings: $27.98 million (trend 20.0% a year).
What happened to a $10,000 investment

Purchase Date	Purchase Price	Price on 12-31-81	Dividends Paid
12-31-71	$27.37	$29.87	$2,941.55
12-31-76	$21.37	$29.87	$2,821.05

Purchase Date	Cap. Gains (– Losses)	Total Return	Rate of Return
12-31-71	$ 913.24	$3,854.79	3.31%
12-31-76	$3,976.61	$6,797.66	10.93%

* * *

HALLIBURTON CO. (HAL). Founded 1924. Headquarters: 2600 Southland Center, Dallas TX 75201. OIL FIELD SERVICES, CONSTRUCTION. Halliburton is a leading provider of oil field services, specifically cementing and stimulation. It also owns Brown & Root, the nation's second-largest engineering and construction company (by revenues) in 1980. 112,000 employees. MAJOR SUBSIDIARIES, BRANDS: Brown & Root.

Sales: $8,327.3 million (trend 15.4% a year).
Earnings: $500.30 million (trend 14.7% a year).
What happened to a $10,000 investment

Purchase Date	Purchase Price	Price on 12-31-81	Dividends Paid
12-31-71	$12.87	$52.12	$4,471.20
12-31-76	$32.56	$52.12	$1,404.99

Purchase Date	Cap. Gains (– Losses)	Total Return	Rate of Return
12-31-71	$30,485.44	$34,956.63	16.22%
12-31-76	$ 6,007.68	$ 7,412.67	11.73%

PROFILE: Strength. That's the single dominant impression Halliburton conveys as it plows into the 1980s. Profits have risen eleven years in a row through 1981 and fourteen out of the last fifteen. What's more, they've been rising at a fast clip. Return on stockholders' equity has usually been above 20 percent in recent years. That would be an outstanding performance even if it were leveraged by the use of debt. But Halliburton has almost no debt — only about 10 percent of capital, as of early 1981.

The company is among the 100 largest U.S. employers. Its sales — $8.3 billion in 1980 — would suffice to put it among the top forty of the Fortune 500 (from which it is inexplicably omitted year after year). Most of those sales (about 70 percent) come from the Brown & Root construction and engineering subsidiary. But Brown & Root has not contributed the bulk of profits: In 1979, for example, it chipped in only 27 percent of earnings. It seems to be losing ground to such hungry and top-performing competitors as Fluor and Parsons (both of which had bigger 1981 backlogs, though smaller 1980 revenues). Still, if the engineering and construction business experiences a sustained boom, Brown & Root should benefit from that.

Most of the profits come from the oil field service operations, where Halliburton enjoys a towering reputation. In cementing oil wells and in stimulating the recovery of the "last drop," it has loads of experience and a worldwide network of service facilities.

If you're going to profit in this stock, it will be through capital gains: The dividend yield was less than 2 percent in early 1981. Capital gains were certainly there during the 1970s. The 1971 high was about $13, the 1980 high $86.

Keep an eye on the price / earnings ratio. Since everybody knows that the company has an excellent record, the stock often sells at a p / e ratio considerably higher than average (e.g., 17 in early 1981 and 11 in early 1982). Expectations of good performance may already be built into the price at the time you contemplate a purchase.

* * *

HAMMERMILL PAPER CO. (HML). Founded 1916. Headquarters: PO Box 1440, Erie Lake Rd., Erie PA 16533. PAPER. Produces fine stationery and printing paper, copier paper, and industrial paper; also distributes paper and related items. Forest products operations are on a relatively small scale. 11,000 employees.

Sales: $1,182.8 million (trend 16.8% a year).
Earnings: $40.24 million (trend 19.0% a year).
What happened to a $10,000 investment

Purchase Date	*Purchase Price*	*Price on 12-31-81*	*Dividends Paid*
12-31-71	$20.37	$27.75	$5,811.04
12-31-76	$25.87	$27.75	$2,827.05

Purchase Date	*Cap. Gains (– Losses)*	*Total Return*	*Rate of Return*
12-31-71	$3,619.63	$9,430.67	6.87%
12-31-76	$ 724.64	$3,551.69	6.27%

PROFILE: Hammermill's profits have been erratic. The ten years through 1980 included seven where profits were up, three where profits were down. Hammermill ranked last in profitability (return on equity and return on total capital) among twenty-two forest products companies in the 1981 *Forbes* "Annual Report on American Industry." And the forest products industry as a whole performed slightly less well than the aggregate performance of all industries. So Hammermill was last in a slow field.

The stock market has reflected this lackluster performance by according Hammermill shares a low valuation in relation to current earnings. The p / e ratio has been 5 or less in parts of every year since 1972. The shares in early 1982 sold for $26 each, a whisker below their 1971 high of $26.88.

The balance sheet isn't strong either. Debt in early 1982 was close to 40 percent of capital.

The best thing to recommend the shares is that they've been cheap lately. That quality seems to have attracted Carl Icahn, an investor who bought up about 10 percent of the stock in 1980. Icahn had previously bought stock in two other companies whose stocks were doing poorly (Tappan Co. and Saxon Industries), snared a board seat, and fought for a sellout of the company to an acquisitor. He's tried the same thing with Hammermill, but has been unsuccessful, at least as of this writing.

* * *

JOHN HANCOCK INCOME SECURITIES CORP. (JHS). Founded 1972. Headquarters: John Hancock Place, Boston MA 02117. **INVESTING.** John Hancock Income Securities is a publicly traded investment company which invests primarily in debt securities and also holds some common and preferred stock.

* * *

JOHN HANCOCK INVESTORS INC. (JHI). Founded 1970. Headquarters: John Hancock Place, Boston MA 02117. **INVESTING.** John Hancock Investors is a publicly traded bond fund investing in bonds and other securities.

* * *

HANDLEMAN CO. (HDL). Founded 1946. Headquarters: 1055 W. Maple Rd., Clawson MI 48017. **RECORD DISTRIBUTOR.** Wholesale distributor of phonograph records and tapes, books and magazines; operates retail record outlets in major retail stores.

Sales: $217.3 million (trend 11.3% a year).
Earnings: $6.73 million (trend 27.4% a year).
What happened to a $10,000 investment

Purchase Date	*Purchase Price*	*Price on 12-31-81*	*Dividends Paid*
12-31-71	$35.75	$15.25	$1,655.94
12-31-76	$ 4.87	$15.25	$7,056.41

Purchase Date	*Cap. Gains (– Losses)*	*Total Return*	*Rate of Return*
12-31-71	$–5,734.27	$–4,078.32	–5.10%
12-31-76	$ 21,282.05	$ 28,338.46	30.84%

* * *

HANDY & HARMAN (HNH). Founded 1867. Headquarters: 850 Third Ave., New York NY 10022. **METAL FABRICATION.** Engaged in processing and fabrication of precious and non-precious metals; refining of precious metals. **MAJOR SUBSIDIARIES, BRANDS:** American Chemical & Refining Co.; Lucas-Milhaupt, Inc.; Maryland Specialty Wire, Inc.; Handy Flux, Sil-Fos, Easy Flo, Meritrol Cables.

Sales: $761.0 million (trend 18.8% a year).
Earnings: $27.75 million (trend 14.9% a year).
What happened to a $10,000 investment

Purchase Date	*Purchase Price*	*Price on 12-31-81*	*Dividends Paid*
12-31-71	$2.44	$18.25	$10,064.96
12-31-76	$5.06	$18.25	$ 3,358.02

Purchase Date	Cap. Gains (— Losses)	Total Return	Rate of Return
12-31-71	$64,871.79	$74,936.75	23.85%
12-31-76	$26,049.38	$29,407.41	31.56%

* * *

HANNA MINING CO. (HNM). Founded 1927. Headquarters: 100 Erieview Plaza, Cleveland OH 44114. **IRON ORE.** Major U.S. iron ore and ferronickel producer; also involved in exploration and oil and gas well services. **MAJOR SUBSIDIARIES, BRANDS:** WellTech, Inc. (50 percent owned).

Sales: $333.5 million (trend 1.1% a year).
Earnings: $38.69 million (trend −4.3% a year).
What happened to a $10,000 investment

Purchase Date	Purchase Price	Price on 12-31-81	Dividends Paid
12-31-71	$48.25	$30.50	$3,432.64
12-31-76	$54.25	$30.50	$1,741.94

Purchase Date	Cap. Gains (— Losses)	Total Return	Rate of Return
12-31-71	$−3,678.76	$ −246.11	−.25%
12-31-76	$−4,377.88	$−2,635.94	−5.94%

* * *

HARCOURT BRACE JOVANOVICH, INC. (HBJ). Founded 1919. Headquarters: 757 Third Ave., New York NY 10017. **PUBLISHER.** Publisher of text and trade books, professional books, and periodicals. Also involved in broadcasting, insurance, testing services, theme parks. **MAJOR SUBSIDIARIES, BRANDS:** HBJ Communications and Services; Sea World Enterprises.

Sales: $504.0 million (trend 16.5% a year).
Earnings: $24.41 million (trend 11.2% a year).
What happened to a $10,000 investment

Purchase Date	Purchase Price	Price on 12-31-81	Dividends Paid
12-31-71	$19.62	$18.12	$3,411.46
12-31-76	$16.87	$18.12	$2,305.19

Purchase Date	Cap. Gains (— Losses)	Total Return	Rate of Return
12-31-71	$−764.33	$2,647.13	2.38%
12-31-76	$ 740.74	$3,045.93	5.46%

* * *

JOHN H. HARLAND CO. (JH). Founded 1923. Headquarters: 2939 Miller Rd., Decatur GA 30035. **BANK FORMS.** Prints checks, deposit tickets, and other forms for use in banks.

Sales: $113.7 million (trend 20.3% a year).
Earnings: $11.13 million (trend 21.2% a year).
What happened to a $10,000 investment

Purchase Date	Purchase Price	Price on 12-31-81	Dividends Paid
12-31-71	$7.96	$24.50	$2,622.07
12-31-76	$6.21	$24.50	$2,759.73

Purchase Date	Cap. Gains (— Losses)	Total Return	Rate of Return
12-31-71	$20,785.34	$23,407.41	12.82%
12-31-76	$29,463.09	$32,222.82	33.39%

* * *

HARNISCHFEGER CORP. (HPH). Founded 1884. Headquarters: 13400 Bishops Lane, Brookfield WI 53005. **CAPITAL GOODS MANUFACTURER.** Designs, manufactures, and sells lifting and digging equipment for the construction industry; electric and hydraulic shovels for surface mining; overhead cranes, hoists, and materials-handling systems for industry.

Sales: $642.2 million (trend 10.2% a year).
Earnings: $4.74 million (trend −27.2% a year).
What happened to a $10,000 investment

Purchase Date	Purchase Price	Price on 12-31-81	Dividends Paid
12-31-71	$ 7.11	$11.62	$8,437.20
12-31-76	$18.25	$11.62	$2,027.40

Purchase Date	Cap. Gains (— Losses)	Total Return	Rate of Return
12-31-71	$ 6,356.78	$ 14,793.98	9.51%
12-31-76	$−3,630.14	$−1,602.74	−3.43%

* * *

HARRIS BANKCORP, INC. (HBC). Founded 1907. Headquarters: 111 W. Monroe St., Chicago IL 60603. **BANK.** Holding company for Harris Trust & Savings Bank, the third-largest commercial bank in Chicago and approximately the thirtieth-largest in the United States. 3,800 employees. **MAJOR SUBSIDIARIES, BRANDS:** Harris Trust & Savings Bank.

Sales: $725.7 million (trend 22.2% a year).
Earnings: $33.03 million (trend 2.5% a year).
What happened to a $10,000 investment

Purchase Date	*Purchase Price*	*Price on 12-31-81*	*Dividends Paid*
12-31-71	$27.19	$28.12	$5,735.17
12-31-76	$38.25	$28.12	$2,443.14

Purchase Date	*Cap. Gains (− Losses)*	*Total Return*	*Rate of Return*
12-31-71	$ 344.83	$ 6,080.00	4.86%
12-31-76	$−2,647.06	$−203.92	−.41%

PROFILE: Mention the Harris Bank in Chicago and many people will think of Hubert, the Harris lion, a mascot and advertising gimmick. An actual lion at Chicago's Lincoln Park Zoo bears that title. On recent inspection, it was looking a bit down in the tooth.

Some people might say the same about Harris Bankcorp, which suffered earnings declines in 1977 and 1980. In most industries a couple of down years wouldn't raise eyebrows, but consistent (if undramatic) gains are one of the things many investors expect from bank stocks.

Investors haven't seemed any more disenchanted with Harris than with most banks recently. But then, all bank stocks have been in the doghouse. In early 1982, for example, Harris Bankcorp shares commanded a p / e ratio of only 6, versus about 7 to 8 for the average stock. The share price, around $28, was below the stock's 1968 high — close to $30 — and well below its all-time high — about $39, in 1977.

Major areas of activity include trusts, securities underwriting, and international loans. Despite the cute lion, consumer banking activities are a relatively small part of the blend.

The return on assets has been mediocre — about 70 cents per $100 from 1971 through 1976, but only about 50 cents per $100 from 1977–80.

Management has a reputation for conservatism. There are fewer bad loans than at most banks, but there's a fairly large reserve against bad loans, just in case. Conservative investors may also like this bank for its balance sheet (debt about 13 percent of capital in 1979), and for its dividend yield (7 to 8 percent in the last couple of years, with a history of uninterrupted dividend payments going back to the time of founding).

* * *

HARRIS CORP. (HRS). Founded 1926. Headquarters: 1025 W. NASA Blvd., Melbourne FL 32919. **ELECTRONICS, COMPUTERS, PRINTING.** Harris is a major producer of electronics and communications equipment, and is the nation's largest manufacturer of printing equipment. Small computers and computer printers are a significant part of the product line; about 20 percent of the company's revenues come from government (mainly defense) work. 24,000 employees.

Sales: $1,551.5 million (trend 24.8% a year).
Earnings: $103.96 million (trend 29.4% a year).
What happened to a $10,000 investment

Purchase Date	*Purchase Price*	*Price on 12-31-81*	*Dividends Paid*
12-31-71	$12.87	$41.12	$3,427.18
12-31-76	$14.81	$41.12	$2,030.38

Purchase Date	*Cap. Gains (− Losses)*	*Total Return*	*Rate of Return*
12-31-71	$21,941.75	$25,368.93	13.47%
12-31-76	$17,763.71	$19,794.09	24.40%

PROFILE: The 1970s were a bad time for the stock market in general. They were not a bad time for people who bought Harris Corporation shares. If you'd bought at the 1971 high (about $17) and sold at the 1980 high (about $55) you would have tripled your money. If you'd bought at the 1974 low ($3.-25) and sold at the 1980 high, you'd have multiplied your original stake more than sixteen times. Harris chalked up its ninth consecutive earnings increase in 1981, and had quadrupled its earnings in eight years.

The secret has been the marriage of printing to high technology, and the adroit use of technology developed in defense work for commercial applications. In fact, according to a 1980 article in *Forbes* magazine, Harris won't take any defense work for which it doesn't foresee commercial applications, and it rewards its managers according to how well they achieve "technology transfer." It is no coincidence that the company is headquartered on NASA Boulevard. Many of its executives used to do space-program work for Radiation Inc., which was merged into Harris in 1967. Before the merger, Harris was Harris Intertype, and was based in Cleveland. The move south symbolized the change in the company from a traditional Midwestern industrial company to a new-style (and Sunbelt) technological one. Harris, for example, has provided "electronic newsrooms" to some 500 U.S. newspapers, and now hopes to hit the office word-processing market big — although it will have heavy competition from IBM, Xerox, and many others.

The main problem for investors is whether the stock has already factored the high growth potential into the price. That's a question you have to assess at the moment you're considering a purchase. In early 1981, for example, Harris's p / e was 12, close to twice that of the average stock at the time. The dividend, yielding a skimpy 2.8 percent as of early 1982, won't bail you out if you guess wrong.

* * *

HARSCO CORP. (HSC). Founded 1899. Headquarters: 350 Poplar Church Rd., Wormleysburg PA. 17043 METALS, CONSTRUCTION, DEFENSE. Harsco recovers metals from slag generated in steelmaking, fabricates metal products, and supplies materials and equipment to the building industry. Through a subsidiary, it is also a defense contractor. 16,000 employees. MAJOR SUBSIDIARIES, BRANDS: Bowen-McLaughlin-York; Broderick; Dartmouth Investments Ltd.; Fairmont Railway Motors; Heckett; Quaker Alloy Casting; Taylor-Wharton.

Sales: $1,063.2 million (trend 15.8% a year).
Earnings: $49.71 million (trend 7.9% a year).
What happened to a $10,000 investment

Purchase Date	*Purchase Price*	*Price on 12-31-81*	*Dividends Paid*
12-31-71	$ 8.36	$19.50	$8,168.68
12-31-76	$12.69	$19.50	$3,546.80

Purchase Date	*Cap. Gains (— Losses)*	*Total Return*	*Rate of Return*
12-31-71	$13,317.36	$21,486.04	12.15%
12-31-76	$ 5,369.46	$ 8,916.26	13.60%

PROFILE: Look at Harsco's list of subsidiaries, above. There's not a glamorous or well-known name in the list. For that matter, Harsco isn't exactly a household word itself. Nor should it be, for consumer products are the one element conspicuous by their absence in Harsco's diversified product blend.

Known or not, Harsco is big enough to have passed the $1 billion mark in sales in 1980, and to rank among the 300 largest industrial companies in the United States. What's more, it had put together nine straight years of rising earnings before taking a slight tumble in the recession year of 1980.

Harsco's advance has been slow and steady, like that of the heavy military equipment manufactured by its Bowen-McLaughlin-York subsidiary. For that reason, it's never sold for a high multiple: the price / earnings ratio over the last decade has never surpassed 12 and usually has been 7 or less. This, plus the regular (each year since 1939) dividend, should make the stock appealing to those who, in analyst David Dreman's phrase, like to "play it slow, play it low." The dividend yield in recent years has been in the 5-to-7 percent range. Harsco usually pays out between 30 and 40 percent of its profits in dividends.

The company's steady, unspectacular success attracted an unwelcome admirer in 1981. Crane Corp. (profiled elsewhere in this volume) tried to buy a big block of the stock, but was rebuffed as Harsco chose to purchase its own stock on the open market to compete with Crane. Further nibbles can't be ruled out.

* * *

HART SCHAFFNER & MARX (HSM). Founded 1911. Headquarters: 36 S. Franklin St., Chicago IL 60606. CLOTHING. Major manufacturer of men's clothing, operates leading men's and women's clothing stores. MAJOR SUBSIDIARIES, BRANDS: Baskin; Charles A. Stevens; Wallachs; Silverwoods; Hart Schaffner & Marx; Society; Graham & Gunn; Sterling & Hunt; Austin Reed of Regent Street; Johnny Carson; Rue Royale; Jaymar-Ruby.

Sales: $674.9 million (trend 6.5% a year).
Earnings: $22.52 million (trend 20.0% a year).
What happened to a $10,000 investment

Purchase Date	*Purchase Price*	*Price on 12-31-81*	*Dividends Paid*
12-31-71	$29.25	$23.25	$2,813.68
12-31-76	$12.62	$23.25	$3,532.67

Purchase Date	*Cap. Gains (— Losses)*	*Total Return*	*Rate of Return*
12-31-71	$−2,051.28	$ 762.39	.74%
12-31-76	$ 8,415.84	$11,948.51	17.03%

* * *

HARTE-HANKS COMMUNICATIONS, INC. (HHN). Founded 1970. Headquarters: 901 N.E. Loop 410, San Antonio TX 78209. COMMUNICATIONS. Publishes newspapers and marketing publications; owns and operates eleven radio, and four television stations, and several cable television systems, mainly in the South.

Sales: $301.9 million (trend 27.3% a year).
Earnings: $22.70 million (trend 22.8% a year).
What happened to a $10,000 investment

Purchase Date	*Purchase Price*	*Price on 12-31-81*	*Dividends Paid*
12-31-71	$ N/A	$32.25	$ N/A
12-31-76	$14.19	$32.25	$2,023.79

Purchase Date	*Cap. Gains (− Losses)*	*Total Return*	*Rate of Return*
12-31-71	$ N/A	$ N/A	N/A%
12-31-76	$12,731.28	$14,755.07	19.88%

* * *

HATTERAS INCOME SECURITIES, INC. (HAT). Founded 1973. Headquarters: 1 NCNB Plaza, Charlotte NC 28230. **INVESTMENTS.** Investment company involved in fixed-income debt securities.

* * *

HAWAIIAN ELECTRIC CO., INC. (HE). Founded 1891. Headquarters: 900 Richards St., Honolulu HI 96813. **UTILITY.** Primary electric utility in the state of Hawaii. **MAJOR SUBSIDIARIES, BRANDS:** Maui Electric; Hawaii Electric Light.

Sales: $429.9 million (trend 15.6% a year).
Earnings: $22.84 million (trend 9.4% a year).
What happened to a $10,000 investment

Purchase Date	*Purchase Price*	*Price on 12-31-81*	*Dividends Paid*
12-31-71	$28.37	$25.25	$6,903.96
12-31-76	$24.25	$25.25	$4,734.02

Purchase Date	*Cap. Gains (− Losses)*	*Total Return*	*Rate of Return*
12-31-71	$−1,101.32	$5,802.64	4.68%
12-31-76	$ 412.37	$5,146.39	8.66%

* * *

HAYES-ALBION CORP. (HAY). Founded 1935. Headquarters: 1999 Wildwood Ave., Jackson MI 49202. **METAL PRODUCTS.** Makes metal products for the passenger car and truck market, as well as for railroad and agricultural industries.

Sales: $177.2 million (trend −2.1% a year).
Earnings: $−4.01 million.
What happened to a $10,000 investment

Purchase Date	*Purchase Price*	*Price on 12-31-81*	*Dividends Paid*
12-31-71	$17.84	$6.75	$4,828.99
12-31-76	$17.25	$6.75	$2,359.42

Purchase Date	*Cap. Gains (− Losses)*	*Total Return*	*Rate of Return*
12-31-71	$−6,216.56	$−1,387.57	−1.48%
12-31-76	$−6,086.96	$−3,727.54	−8.91%

* * *

HAZELTINE CORP. (HZ). Founded 1924. Headquarters: Commack NY 11725. **ELECTRONICS.** Makes data processing and display systems and other electronic products for government and industrial markets.

Sales: $133.8 million (trend 10.2% a year).
Earnings: $4.84 million (trend 21.8% a year).
What happened to a $10,000 investment

Purchase Date	*Purchase Price*	*Price on 12-31-81*	*Dividends Paid*
12-31-71	$8.75	$26.50	$3,028.57
12-31-76	$9.12	$26.50	$2,904.11

Purchase Date	*Cap. Gains (− Losses)*	*Total Return*	*Rate of Return*
12-31-71	$20,285.71	$23,314.29	12.79%
12-31-76	$19,041.10	$21,945.21	26.15%

* * *

HECK'S, INC. (HEX). Founded 1959. Headquarters: 1012 Kahnawha Blvd. E., Charleston WV 25301. **RETAIL.** Operates retail department and shoe stores; also involved in wholesale distribution, heavy equipment sales and service. **MAJOR SUBSIDIARIES, BRANDS:** Heck's discount stores; Feldway Corp. (Shoe Town).

Sales: $432.3 million (trend 25.0% a year).
Earnings: $15.47 million (trend 24.9% a year).
What happened to a $10,000 investment

Purchase Date	*Purchase Price*	*Price on 12-31-81*	*Dividends Paid*
12-31-71	$9.42	$10.50	$1,217.70
12-31-76	$6.17	$10.50	$1,491.89

Purchase Date	*Cap. Gains (− Losses)*	*Total Return*	*Rate of Return*
12-31-71	$1,150.44	$2,368.14	2.15%
12-31-76	$7,027.03	$8,518.92	13.12%

* * *

HECLA MINING CO. (HL). Founded 1898. Headquarters: Hecla Bldg., Wallace ID 83873. MINING NONFERROUS METALS. Operates three mining properties in North Idaho and participates in a fourth. Produces silver, lead, zinc, and copper.

Sales: $77.7 million (trend 19.8% a year).
Earnings: $31.72 million (trend 40.3% a year).
What happened to a $10,000 investment

Purchase Date	*Purchase Price*	*Price on 12-31-81*	*Dividends Paid*
12-31-71	$9.10	$11.25	$457.75
12-31-76	$7.27	$11.25	$572.99

Purchase Date	*Cap. Gains (– Losses)*	*Total Return*	*Rate of Return*
12-31-71	$2,360.26	$2,818.01	2.51%
12-31-76	$5,471.90	$6,044.89	9.92%

* * *

G. HEILEMAN BREWING CO., INC. (GHB). Founded 1918. Headquarters: 100 Harborview Plaza, La Crosse WI 54601. BREWING. Major domestic beer producer, operating nine breweries. Also involved in bakery products and metal products. MAJOR SUBSIDIARIES, BRANDS: Carling Black Label; Colt 45 Malt Liquor; Blatz; Old Style; Special Export; Rainier; Schmidt.

Sales: $722.0 million (trend 34.3% a year).
Earnings: $34.68 million (trend 40.5% a year).
What happened to a $10,000 investment

Purchase Date	*Purchase Price*	*Price on 12-31-81*	*Dividends Paid*
12-31-71	$5.48	$24.25	$5,556.66
12-31-76	$4.81	$24.25	$4,738.35

Purchase Date	*Cap. Gains (– Losses)*	*Total Return*	*Rate of Return*
12-31-71	$34,239.86	$39,796.52	17.41%
12-31-76	$40,365.38	$45,103.73	40.68%

* * *

H. J. HEINZ CO. (HNZ). Founded 1900. Headquarters: 1062 Progress St., Pittsburgh PA 15212. FOODS. Heinz is a major producer of packaged and convenience foods, including ketchup, tuna, pickles, vinegar, cat food, baby food, and frozen foods (particularly potatoes and pizza). Also owns Weight Watchers International. 48,000 employees. MAJOR SUBSIDIARIES, BRANDS: Heinz; Star-Kist; 9-Lives; Ore-Ida; La Pizzeria, Mrs. Goodcookie.

Sales: $3,568.9 million (trend 14.3% a year).
Earnings: $165.26 million (trend 18.2% a year).
What happened to a $10,000 investment

Purchase Date	*Purchase Price*	*Price on 12-31-81*	*Dividends Paid*
12-31-71	$13.71	$28.25	$4,360.00
12-31-76	$16.81	$28.25	$2,325.65

Purchase Date	*Cap. Gains (– Losses)*	*Total Return*	*Rate of Return*
12-31-71	$10,607.90	$14,967.90	9.58%
12-31-76	$ 6,802.97	$ 9,128.62	13.85%

PROFILE: That red stuff you see at Heinz is definitely ketchup, not ink. Earnings have been rising each year like clockwork. (In fact, they rose a bit too regularly: the company found, in 1979, that some of its subsidiaries had been "managing" their earnings reports to keep earnings growing smoothly. The figures have since been adjusted; the irony is that no such shenanigans were necessary.)

Any company that can bring earnings in a decade from $1.87 a share (1971) to $7.10 a share (1980) deserves a reputation as a growth company. Heinz has it — and yet, Wall Street can't seem quite to believe that a company in a "mature" business like foods can really exhibit this sort of growth. So the price / earnings ratio reflects a compromise between reality and expectation. In early 1982 it was 7, about average for stocks at the time.

The formula under president A. J. (Tony) O'-Reilly, chief executive since 1973, has been straightforward. Reduce costs, increase advertising. Heinz recently had only seven plants, as opposed to fourteen a few years ago, and fewer employees than it had several years ago. But it has boosted production, sales, and earnings. The formula seems to be working. When it's time to introduce a new product, O'Reilly would rather buy a small company than start from scratch. One company recently acquired was Hubinger, which makes high-fructose corn syrup. The timing, apparently by coincidence, was perfect. Shortly after the acquisition, Coca-Cola announced that it would use high-fructose corn syrup instead of sugar in its soft drinks.

Dividends have been paid each year since 1911, and recently the stock has yielded between 5 and 6 percent.

* * *

HELENE CURTIS INDUSTRIES, INC. (HC). Founded 1928. Headquarters: 4401 W. North Ave., Chicago IL 60639. BEAUTY PRODUCTS. Manufactures consumer hair care products and toiletries, beauty salon products and equipment; also manufactures sealants and adhesives for the automotive industry. MAJOR SUBSIDIARIES, BRANDS: Spray Net; Tender Touch; King's Men; Suave; Form 3; Corto-Plex; Uniperm; Protective Treatments, Inc.

Sales: $162.5 million (trend 8.3% a year).
Earnings: $4.53 million (trend 8.0% a year).
What happened to a $10,000 investment

Purchase Date	*Purchase Price*	*Price on 12-31-81*	*Dividends Paid*
12-31-71	$7.12	$12.25	$0.00
12-31-76	$6.25	$12.25	$0.00

Purchase Date	*Cap. Gains (– Losses)*	*Total Return*	*Rate of Return*
12-31-71	$7,192.98	$7,192.98	5.57%
12-31-76	$9,600.00	$9,600.00	14.41%

* * *

WALTER E. HELLER INTERNATIONAL CORP. (HLR). Founded 1919. Headquarters: 105 W. Adams St., Chicago IL 60603. COMMERCIAL LOANS, BANKING. Heller is a major commercial lender, also active in equipment leasing, and owns American National Bank & Trust Co., approximately the ninety-seventh-largest U.S. bank and fifth-largest in Chicago. Number of employees: not available. MAJOR SUBSIDIARIES, BRANDS: Walter E. Heller Overseas Corp.; American National Bank & Trust Co.; B. B. Cohen & Co. (mortgage banking); Chandler Leasing.

Sales: $771.7 million (trend 20.0% a year).
Earnings: $42.61 million (trend 10.3% a year).
What happened to a $10,000 investment

Purchase Date	*Purchase Price*	*Price on 12-31-81*	*Dividends Paid*
12-31-71	$31.25	$19.25	$3,204.80
12-31-76	$22.50	$19.25	$2,580.00

Purchase Date	*Cap. Gains (– Losses)*	*Total Return*	*Rate of Return*
12-31-71	$ 3,840.00	$ 635.20	.65%
12-31-76	$–1,444.44	$ 1,135.56	2.17%

PROFILE: Here are the pros and cons on this stock. First the pros. The company's earnings have grown consistently, and its interest rate spread (the margin between the rate at which it borrows and the rate at which it lends), recently pinched (as at most loan companies), may widen in the coming years. The dividend yield recently has been 5 to 7 percent.

Now the cons. While earnings have been growing steadily, they've been growing slowly. And the company operates with a great deal of debt. *Business Week* in 1979 quoted analyst Stanley Iverson as saying that Heller was "under a lot of pressure to add to their credit quality" and "badly needs more equity capital." In 1981 Heller was spending about 51 percent of its gross income to pay its interest expense. Of its capital, 60 percent comes from short-term debt and 28 percent from long-term debt. It is par for the course for finance companies to carry a lot of debt. However, if you're conservative on this score, you may feel that Heller is skating on ice that's a bit thin.

The brightest spot here is the bank, which contributed 38 percent of 1979 profits on 24 percent of revenues. With profits of 95 cents per $100 of assets in 1980, American National was one of the nation's star performers among banks.

If Walter E. Heller merges into a bank, as many expect (Britain's Midland Bank Ltd. made an unsuccessful pass in 1979), American National might have to go, for antitrust reasons. Still, a merger might help the stock, which has been going nowhere.

* * *

HELMERICH & PAYNE, INC. (HP). Founded 1940. Headquarters: Utica at 21st St., Tulsa OK 74114. ENERGY. Engaged in contract oil drilling, oil and gas exploration; manufactures chemical odorants for natural gas.

Sales: $287.6 million (trend 30.4% a year).
Earnings: $75.26 million (trend 34.8% a year).
What happened to a $10,000 investment

Purchase Date	*Purchase Price*	*Price on 12-31-81*	*Dividends Paid*
12-31-71	$2.74	$36.75	$3,244.37
12-31-76	$7.48	$36.75	$ 906.85

Purchase Date	*Cap. Gains (– Losses)*	*Total Return*	*Rate of Return*
12-31-71	$124,314.72	$127,559.09	29.97%
12-31-76	$ 39,136.49	$ 40,043.34	38.00%

* * *

HEMISPHERE FUND, INC. (HEM). Founded 1967. Headquarters: 522 Fifth Ave., New York NY 10036. INVESTMENT CO. Hemisphere is a dual find; investors can choose either the income or capital-gains portion of the portfolio. Holdings are split fairly evenly between stocks and bonds.

* * *

HERCULES INC. (HPC). Founded 1912. Headquarters: 910 Market St., Wilmington DE 19899. **CHEMICALS, PLASTICS, EXPLOSIVES.** Hercules is a major chemical manufacturer with substantial business in plastics (it is the largest U.S. maker of polypropylene), explosives for mining and construction, and aerospace (including both construction and rocket fuel). 23,000 employees.

Sales: $2,485.2 million (trend 12.5% a year).
Earnings: $117.51 million (trend 27.1% a year).
What happened to a $10,000 investment

Purchase Date	*Purchase Price*	*Price on 12-31-81*	*Dividends Paid*
12-31-71	$26.12	$22.62	$3,567.46
12-31-76	$28.25	$22.62	$1,959.29

Purchase Date	*Cap. Gains (– Losses)*	*Total Return*	*Rate of Return*
12-31-71	$–1,339.71	$2,227.75	2.03%
12-31-76	$–1,991.15	$ –31.86	–.06%

PROFILE: The headlines are revealing. "Strong man at Hercules: Alexander Giacco's tough moves are paying off dramatically" (*Financial World,* 1979). "Mr. Nice Guy he wasn't" (*Forbes,* 1980). "Muscle in Chemicals: Hercules Shifts its Weight Toward Higher-Margin Products" (*Barron's,* 1980).

As you surmise, Alexander Giacco has engaged in some major cost slashing since taking over in 1977. He's shown the door to a whole squadron of middle-level executives (some 700, as of 1980), and has closed the door on a variety of relatively unprofitable operations (e.g., pigments, with intermediate chemicals for polyester fibers scheduled to go next). These major moves have freed cash to put into some of Hercules' more promising ventures, such as aerospace, which is growing by about 20 percent a year, or graphite fibers, which are useful in aerospace and defense. The company is also trying to sell more "value-added" end products instead of basic chemicals. Where it used to sell resin, for example, it's now more likely to keep the resin and make adhesives.

The effects of the restructuring can be seen both in profits and on the balance sheet. Long-term debt in early 1982 was about 25 percent of capital; it was more than 33 percent in 1974. Profits, in the recession of 1981, were the second best ever. In 1979, the best year, return on equity hit more than 19 percent.

Dividends have been paid each year since 1913. In the past couple of years the dividend yield has been 5 to 6 percent.

* * *

HERSHEY FOODS CORP. (HSY). Founded 1927. Headquarters: 100 Mansion Rd. East, Hershey PA 17033. **FOODS.** Hershey is one of the two leading U.S. chocolate and candy producers (the other being privately owned M&M Mars). Also produces pasta, offers coffee service to institutions, and owns a chain of ice cream parlor restaurants. 11,000 employees. **MAJOR SUBSIDIARIES, BRANDS:** Hershey's, Reese's, Y&S (chocolate and candy); San Giorgio, Skinner, Delmonico (pasta); Cory Food Service (coffee service); Friendly Ice Cream Corp. (restaurants).

Sales: $1,335.3 million (trend 20.7% a year).
Earnings: $62.05 million (trend 9.2% a year).
What happened to a $10,000 investment

Purchase Date	*Purchase Price*	*Price on 12-31-81*	*Dividends Paid*
12-31-71	$28.25	$36.25	$4,192.92
12-31-76	$22.37	$36.25	$3,112.85

Purchase Date	*Cap. Gains (– Losses)*	*Total Return*	*Rate of Return*
12-31-71	$2,831.86	$7,024.78	5.46%
12-31-76	$6,201.12	$9,313.97	14.07%

PROFILE: Buying stock in Hershey Foods is still a little bit like speculating in commodity futures (cocoa and sugar), though less so than a few years ago. When the company chalked up a good showing in 1979 and headed for an even better one in 1980, *Financial World* attributed the success to "diversification moves and greater leverage of Hershey's once-conservative balance sheet." That analysis is probably wrong. What produced the fine showing, primarily, was probably a lower price for sugar and a much lower price for cocoa, both coming on the heels of a price hike in Hershey's basic candy products.

Hershey is serious about diversification. Chairman William Dearden, who was raised in the Milton Hershey School for orphaned boys, has said he'd like to see the company get half its sales and earnings from products besides chocolate and candy. But the transition takes time. Hershey still gets close to three quarters of sales, and more than three quarters of profits, from chocolate and candy.

The biggest diversification move so far has been the purchase of Friendly's, a major (more than 600 stores) chain of ice cream and sandwich shops with a strong following among New England customers. It accounts for about a fifth of sales and earnings. The second-biggest diversification move has been into pasta, where Hershey's three brands add up to about 10 percent of the market (making it number two behind Mueller).

Meanwhile, in chocolate and candy Hershey continues a seesaw battle for supremacy with Mars. Aided by advertising (which it disdained until 1969), Hershey seems to have recaptured the lead it lost in the early 1970s. As in the beer business, the turf battles are all the more fierce because the total market isn't expanding much. In the case of candy, the major part of the market has historically been kids, and they aren't making as many of those as they used to.

One more factor to consider on this stock is the heavy institutional ownership. The Milton Hershey School owns 55½ percent of the stock; institutions hold another 12 percent, and individuals less than 33 percent. Thus a wave of institutional buying is unlikely, but there's a slight chance institutional selling could rock an individual investor.

Nonetheless the stock could offer a good value, based on fundamentals. The earnings trend has been up, and the stock has been quite conservatively priced in recent years, often selling for as little as 6 times earnings, and sometimes for even less.

* * *

HESSTON CORP. (HES). Founded: 1949. Headquarters: 420 W. Lincoln Blvd., Hesston KS 67062. **FARM EQUIPMENT.** Designs, manufactures, and distributes farm machinery. **MAJOR SUBSIDIARIES, BRANDS:** StakHand, StakMover, StakFeeder.

Sales: $241.4 million (trend 4.4% a year).
Earnings: $−.65 million.
What happened to a $10,000 investment

Purchase Date	*Purchase Price*	*Price on 12-31-81*	*Dividends Paid*
12-31-71	$11.50	$6.50	$2,014.49
12-31-76	$ 9.75	$6.50	$ 358.97

Purchase Date	*Cap. Gains (− Losses)*	*Total Return*	*Rate of Return*
12-31-71	$−4,347.83	$−2,333.33	−2.62%
12-31-76	$−3,333.33	$−2,974.36	−6.82%

* * *

HEUBLEIN, INC. (HBL). Founded 1915. Headquarters: Farmington CT 06032. **LIQUOR, FOODS.** Heublein is a major distiller and marketer of alcoholic beverages, and owns Kentucky Fried Chicken restaurants. It also has a sideline in grocery products. 27,000 employees. **MAJOR SUBSIDIARIES, BRANDS:** Smirnoff, Popov (vodkas); Colony, Inglenook, Lancer's, Harvey's (wines); Black Velvet (whiskey); Kentucky Fried Chicken (restaurants); A.1. Steak Sauce; Grey Poupon Dijon Mustard; Ortega (tacos and sauces).

Sales: $1,591.4 million (trend 5.3% a year).
Earnings: $88.38 million (trend 7.5% a year).
What happened to a $10,000 investment

Purchase Date	*Purchase Price*	*Price on 12-31-81*	*Dividends Paid*
12-31-71	$54.25	$34.25	$2,317.05
12-31-76	$41.75	$34.25	$1,811.98

Purchase Date	*Cap. Gains (− Losses)*	*Total Return*	*Rate of Return*
12-31-71	$−3,686.64	$−1,369.59	−1.46%
12-31-76	$−1,796.41	$ 15.57	.03%

PROFILE: This stock fell as results from the Kentucky Fried Chicken subsidiary seemed spoiled. The shares have been rebounding as the fast food chain has. The company has been putting money and time into upgrading the cleanliness and quality of outlets, redecorating them, and adding seating and drive-up windows. While a few years ago Kentucky Fried sales were falling while most fast-food places were prospering, lately KFC has been racking up increased sales and earnings while other fast-food outlets have been singing the blues. That's in part a result of the upgrading program, and in part a reflection of the chicken / beef price spread. Both trends, however, may last for some time.

Kentucky Fried Chicken is especially important to Heublein, even though wine and spirits constitute about two thirds of the company, because the market for wine and spirits in the United States lately has been a slow-growth affair. The growth hopes center on spirits abroad and chicken in the United States. The grocery products division has been doing nicely, but it's still too small (7 percent of 1979 sales, 9 percent of profits) to be a major factor.

The stock hit a peak of close to $66 a share in 1972, then sank all the way to what seems to have been a bottom — $22 in 1977. Recovery has been slow, but the stock was selling for about $35 in early 1982.

Meanwhile, it offers a good dividend yield — from 5 to 7 percent in recent years — and the company has trimmed back debt, from more than 40 percent of capital in 1974 to about 31 percent recently.

* * *

HEWLETT-PACKARD CO. (HWP). Founded 1947. Headquarters: 1501 Page Mill Rd., Palo Alto CA 94304. **ELECTRONICS, COMPUTERS.** Hewlett-Packard is a leading producer of electronic instruments and minicomputers. 52,000 employees.

Sales: $3,099.0 million (trend 26.6% a year).
Earnings: $269.00 million (trend 27.4% a year).
What happened to a $10,000 investment

Purchase Date	*Purchase Price*	*Price on 12-31-81*	*Dividends Paid*
12-31-71	$11.97	$39.62	$925.33
12-31-76	$21.81	$39.62	$375.93

Purchase Date	*Cap. Gains (– Losses)*	*Total Return*	*Rate of Return*
12-31-71	$23,107.05	$24,032.38	13.03%
12-31-76	$ 8,166.19	$ 8,542.12	13.14%

PROFILE: The 1970s were a lousy time for stocks, right? Tell it to Hewlett-Packard stockholders. But be prepared for a smug laugh in return.

In 1971 Hewlett-Packard shares hit a high of just below $25. In 1980 the high was $97. That increase in the share price wasn't the result of rising expectations fanning an expansion of the price / earnings ratio. In fact, Hewlett-Packard was already a glamour stock in 1971, when its p / e hit 54 — and in 1972, when the p / e hit a breathtaking 61. Unlike many other glamour stocks, Hewlett-Packard hasn't faltered. Its p / e has shrunk, as have those of other growth stocks, but earnings growth has been so strong that even a shrinking p / e hasn't pulled down the stock. Earnings, 44 cents a share in 1971 grew tenfold to $4.47 a share in 1980.

In early 1982, Hewlett-Packard was selling at 19 times earnings, quite a premium in a market that accorded the average stock a p / e of only 7 to 8. But if any stock deserves to sell at 2½ times the average, this one probably does. High morale, recruitment of top engineers, and a reputation for canny market research preceding product introductions are some of the hallmarks of the Hewlett-Packard reputation.

The average company spends just under 2 percent of sales on research and development. The average computer company spends about 6 percent. Hewlett-Packard spends about 9 percent — a bit more, by the way, than its rival Digital Equipment, the leader in minicomputers.

And, oh yes, the balance sheet: the company has almost no debt.

* * *

HEXCEL CORP. (HXL). Founded 1948. Headquarters: Hartford Bldg., 650 California St., San Francisco CA 94108. **HONEYCOMB CORE MATERIALS.** Manufactures honeycomb core materials for the aerospace industry; also manufactures chemicals and resins.

Sales: $146.0 million (trend 21.6% a year).
Earnings: $6.79 million (trend 23.9% a year).
What happened to a $10,000 investment

Purchase Date	*Purchase Price*	*Price on 12-31-81*	*Dividends Paid*
12-31-71	$ 8.55	$21.12	$4,730.93
12-31-76	$11.63	$21.12	$2,163.40

Purchase Date	*Cap. Gains (– Losses)*	*Total Return*	*Rate of Return*
12-31-71	$14,706.97	$19,437.90	11.40%
12-31-76	$ 8,171.58	$10,334.98	15.25%

* * *

HI-SHEAR INDUSTRIES, INC. (HSI). Founded 1976. Headquarters: 3333 New Hyde Park Rd., North Hills NY 11042. **AEROSPACE, PIPING SYSTEMS.** Manufactures fasteners and related equipment for the aerospace sector, pressure piping components and systems. **MAJOR SUBSIDIARIES, BRANDS:** Midwood Industries, Inc.; Tube-Line Corp.

Sales: $89.6 million (trend 32.1% a year).
Earnings: $9.94 million (trend 45.0% a year).
What happened to a $10,000 investment

Purchase Date	*Purchase Price*	*Price on 12-31-81*	*Dividends Paid*
12-31-71	$N/A	$11.25	$ N/A
12-31-76	$ 5.21	$11.25	$2,000.00

Purchase Date	*Cap. Gains (− Losses)*	*Total Return*	*Rate of Return*
12-31-71	$ N/A	$ N/A	N/A%
12-31-76	$11,600.00	$13,600.00	18.74%

* * *

HIGH VOLTAGE ENGINEERING CORP. (HVE). Founded 1946. Headquarters: S. Bedford St., Burlington MA 01803. ELECTRONICS. Manufactures a wide variety of components for the electric and electronics industry; also involved in industrial instruments and electrical machinery and equipment.

Sales: $88.0 million (trend 22.1% a year).
Earnings: $4.14 million (trend 39.2% a year).
What happened to a $10,000 investment

Purchase Date	*Purchase Price*	*Price on 12-31-81*	*Dividends Paid*
12-31-71	$11.25	$7.75	$560.00
12-31-76	$ 6.25	$7.75	$928.00

Purchase Date	*Cap. Gains (− Losses)*	*Total Return*	*Rate of Return*
12-31-71	$−3,111.11	$−2,551.11	−2.90%
12-31-76	$ 2,400.00	$ 3,328.00	5.91%

* * *

HILLENBRAND INDUSTRIES, INC. (HB). Founded 1969. Headquarters: Highway 46, Batesville IN 47006. CASKETS, HOSPITAL FURNITURE, LUGGAGE. Leading U.S. casket manufacturer; manufactures a variety of equipment for hospital rooms, and makes luggage. MAJOR SUBSIDIARIES, BRANDS: Batesville Casket Co.; Hill-Rom Co.; American Tourister, Inc.

Sales: $326.5 million (trend 24.3% a year).
Earnings: $25.01 million (trend 17.5% a year).
What happened to a $10,000 investment

Purchase Date	*Purchase Price*	*Price on 12-31-81*	*Dividends Paid*
12-31-71	$21.75	$50.75	$ 3,864.60
12-31-76	$21.25	$50.75	$12,625.88

Purchase Date	*Cap. Gains (− Losses)*	*Total Return*	*Rate of Return*
12-31-71	$13,333.33	$17,197.93	10.52%
12-31-76	$13,882.35	$16,508.24	21.53%

* * *

HILTON HOTELS CORP. (HLT). Founded 1946. Headquarters: 9880 Wilshire Blvd., Beverly Hills CA 90210. HOTELS, CASINOS. Hilton owns, operates, or franchises close to 200 hotels throughout the United States. 31,000 employees.

Sales: $554.3 million (trend 11.0% a year).
Earnings: $106.13 million (trend 26.6% a year).
What happened to a $10,000 investment

Purchase Date	*Purchase Price*	*Price on 12-31-81*	*Dividends Paid*
12-31-71	$13.72	$38.25	$4,943.96
12-31-76	$11.44	$38.25	$4,703.83

Purchase Date	*Cap. Gains (− Losses)*	*Total Return*	*Rate of Return*
12-31-71	$17,881.55	$22,825.51	12.62%
12-31-76	$23,442.62	$28,146.45	30.70%

PROFILE: Here's another stock that survived the 1970s with style. Hilton shares cost less than $14 each at the 1971 high, but were over $48 each at the 1980 high. Patient investors had reason to smile, but those who ran for the exit early didn't enjoy their stay. In the middle of the decade the stock took a sickening slide all the way down to $2.12 a share. In part that was a reflection of the whole stock market's doldrums in 1974, the worst year since the Great Depression. In part it was a result of the Arab oil embargo and the country's first modern energy crisis, which hit hotel stocks hard. Investors reasoned that scarce gas meant scant travel.

As it turned out, the luxury chains like Hilton were less affected by energy squeezes than the middle-class hotel chains like Ramada and Holiday Inns. Hilton has been able to raise prices repeatedly and substantially, without wrecking demand.

In recent years Hilton's profit margins have dwarfed those of competitors. The company cleared at least 9 percent of sales as profit for six years running (1975–81), and in some years much more. In 1979 Hilton racked up an incredible 20.5 percent profit margin.

In doing this, the chain relies primarily on income from the hotels it owns, some eighteen at a recent tally. Another thirty or so are managed but not owned, or they are partially owned. An additional 150 or so are franchised: They use the Hilton name and reservation service and pay Hilton a fee, but otherwise are independent. Hilton hotels abroad have nothing to do with the company, except by history; the Hilton International division was spun off to TWA in 1964.

A possible plus to this stock is the value of the company's real estate, carried on the books at substantially less than its market value. A possible minus, at least for some investors, is the stock's volatility, which reflects the fact that it is in substantial part a gambling stock. (The two Las Vegas hotel / casinos, the Las Vegas Hilton and Flamingo Hilton, probably account for more than a third of revenues. The company also plans an Atlantic City hotel / casino with MGM.)

The dividend yield is moderate; it's ranged between 3 and 5 percent in recent years.

* * *

HOLIDAY INNS, INC. (HIA). Founded 1954. Headquarters: 3742 Lamar Ave., Memphis TN 38195. HOTELS. Holiday Inns is the world's largest hotel chain, with more than 200 company-owned hotels and approximately 1,500 franchised hotels. The company also has interests in gambling, shipping, and restaurants. 32,000 employees. MAJOR SUBSIDIARIES, BRANDS: Holiday Inns; Harrah's; Perkins Cake & Steak; Delta Steamship Lines.

Sales: $1,520.5 million (trend 9.2% a year).
Earnings: $114.61 million (trend 22.2% a year).
What happened to a $10,000 investment

Purchase Date	*Purchase Price*	*Price on 12-31-81*	*Dividends Paid*
12-31-71	$45.75	$28.25	$1,043.67
12-31-76	$13.12	$28.25	$2,380.80

Purchase Date	*Cap. Gains (− Losses)*	*Total Return*	*Rate of Return*
12-31-71	$−3,825.14	$−2,781.46	−3.21%
12-31-76	$ 11,523.81	$ 13,904.61	19.04%

PROFILE: Holiday Inns posted record earnings in 1980 and again in 1981, despite a recession. However, the company's profits have been erratic, and its diversification policy has been inconsistent.

The basic idea — clean, mid-priced, standardized motels spanning the country — seems so sound and is now so ingrained in American life that it's hard to realize that the company was born only in the early 1950s. Holiday Inns was for quite a long time a growth stock, and was priced like one. From 1968 through 1972 the stock consistently commanded a price more than 25 times earnings.

Then the gas crunch hit, and the stock was never quite the same again. True, tight gas supplies and / or higher gas prices didn't by any means do the company in. But they robbed it of steady, nearly automatic growth. In early 1982, despite the company's recent good showings, the stock sold for 7 to 8 times earnings, which was an average p / e ratio at the time.

Adjusting to the altered situation, the company took several steps. It looked to urban and airport locations. It considered getting into gambling casinos, rejected that step (founder Kemmons Wilson was a devout Baptist, as were several board members), and then ultimately went into gambling anyway, acquiring Harrah's in 1980.

Meantime, the company had gotten into transportation with Trailways bus line and Delta Steamship Lines. But Trailways was sold off in 1979, and Delta was expected to follow. Now the company seems inclined to stick with three related activities — hotels, casinos, and restaurants.

The balance sheet, which had been trimmed during the 1970s, is heavy with debt again (about 45 percent of capital in 1981) as a result of the Harrah's acquisition. Dividends are modest: the yield in recent years has been 2 to 4 percent.

* * *

HOLLY SUGAR CORP. (HLY). Founded 1916. Headquarters: Holly Sugar Bldg., 100 Chase Stone Center, Colorado Springs CO 80903. SUGAR. Processes beet and cane sugar and corn syrup.

Sales: $326.6 million (trend 6.8% a year).
Earnings: $14.53 million (trend −.1% a year).
What happened to a $10,000 investment

Purchase Date	*Purchase Price*	*Price on 12-31-81*	*Dividends Paid*
12-31-71	$13.87	$44.87	$9,297.30
12-31-76	$30.25	$44.87	$ 314.05

Purchase Date	*Cap. Gains (− Losses)*	*Total Return*	*Rate of Return*
12-31-71	$22,342.34	$31,639.64	15.33%
12-31-76	$ 4,834.71	$ 5,148.76	8.66%

* * *

HOMESTAKE MINING CO. (HM). Founded 1877. Headquarters: 650 California St., San Francisco CA 94108. MINING. Homestake's primary activity is gold mining. It is also active, often through joint ventures, in mining of uranium, lead, zinc, and silver. 2,400 employees.

Sales: $302.2 million (trend 20.0% a year).
Earnings: $101.59 million (trend 34.8% a year).
What happened to a $10,000 investment

Purchase Date	*Purchase Price*	*Price on 12-31-81*	*Dividends Paid*
12-31-71	$ 5.96	$36.75	$14,327.27
12-31-76	$24.83	$36.75	$ 2,323.49

Purchase Date	*Cap. Gains (− Losses)*	*Total Return*	*Rate of Return*
12-31-71	$51,678.32	$66,005.59	22.49%
12-31-76	$ 4,798.66	$ 7,122.15	11.36%

PROFILE: At one of Homestake's gold mines in California, workers take core samples in 110-degree heat, while watching out for rattlesnakes. But the site, Lower Lake near Sacramento, appears to contain more than three million ounces of gold, making it potentially one of the nation's largest gold mines. The largest, at Lead, South Dakota, also belongs to Homestake, which is the country's leading gold producer.

The scene at Lower Lake is in some ways emblematic of the stock: high risk correlates with high potential reward. This stock is much more volatile than most, jumping up or down as it does with the changing price of gold. Would you believe a high of $88 and a low of $23.37 a share? Not over the past decade, but over just one year — 1980.

Homestake took four years of earnings gains into 1981; in the mining business, that's a streak. A good streak it was, too: earnings had progressed from $1.29 a share in 1976 up to $5.96 in 1980. But in 1981 there was a big drop in earnings, all the way down to $1.69. Investors should realize that profits are hard to predict in this business. Homestake exhibited essentially no earnings growth from 1964–71, for example.

Though it's volatile, Homestake doesn't exaggerate movements of the stock market as a whole. In fact, it's as likely as not to buck the trend either way; it marches to its own drummer.

Fans of a strong balance sheet will smile here. The company is essentially debt-free. (Long-term debt was about 1 percent of capital in early 1982.)

The dividend yield is variable. In most recent years it's been about 3 to 4 percent.

* * *

HONDA MOTOR CO., LTD. (HMC). Founded: 1948. Headquarters: 27-8, 6-chome, Jingumae, Shibuya-ku, Tokyo 150, Japan. **AUTOMOTIVE.** Major Japanese manufacturer of motorcycles and automobiles and related parts.

Sales: $7,980.0 million (trend 29.9% a year).
Earnings: $440.84 million (trend 55.8% a year).
What happened to a $10,000 investment

Purchase Date	*Purchase Price*	*Price on 12-31-81*	*Dividends Paid*
12-31-71	$ 5.17	$35.50	$4,493.50
12-31-76	$21.70	$35.50	$ 536.92

Purchase Date	*Cap. Gains (− Losses)*	*Total Return*	*Rate of Return*
12-31-71	$58,727.95	$63,221.45	22.03%
12-31-76	$ 6,356.01	$ 6,892.93	11.06%

* * *

HONEYWELL INC. (HON). Founded 1927. Headquarters: Homenwell Plaza, Minneapolis MN 55408. **ELECTRONICS, COMPUTERS.** Honeywell is a leading maker of controls for heating and cooling systems (both residential and commercial), and of industrial process control instruments. It is also a major computer manufacturer and defense contractor. 95,000 employees. **MAJOR SUBSIDIARIES, BRANDS:** CII. Honeywell Bull (20 percent owned); Micro Switch.

Sales: $4,924.7 million (trend 14.2% a year).
Earnings: $280.90 million (trend 30.4% a year).
What happened to a $10,000 investment

Purchase Date	*Purchase Price*	*Price on 12-31-81*	*Dividends Paid*
12-31-71	$133.37	$69.87	$1,443.30
12-31-76	$ 48.50	$69.87	$2,515.46

Purchase Date	*Cap. Gains (− Losses)*	*Total Return*	*Rate of Return*
12-31-71	$−4,761.01	$−3,317.71	−3.95%
12-31-76	$ 4,407.22	$ 6,922.68	11.09%

PROFILE: After an erratic profit history, and following a sickening decline in the stock price, Honeywell has been making a comeback.

As one of the "seven dwarfs" in the computer industry competing with IBM ("Snow White") in the 1960s, Honeywell used to sell for a fancy p / e multiple — more than 30 times earnings during much of the period 1968–72. The company had experienced down years in 1965, 1967, and 1970, but that didn't seem to bother investors. Then came 1974, when *everything* seemed to bother investors. Honeywell's earnings were down again in that recession year and the stock got the stuffing knocked out of it. From a high of almost $171 a share in

1972, it slid to a low of $17.50 in 1974. The person with exquisitely bad timing could have lost about 90 percent of his investment.

As of early 1981, the stock had climbed back up near $100, but in early 1982 it was back down to $70. It's true that computer operations here have never been as profitable as some competitors'. But they seem to be moving in the right direction. Meanwhile, the company maintains a reputation as a leader in the field of electronic controls. Helping make offices, factories, and homes more energy-efficient is big business for Honeywell, and the momentum shows no signs of slackening. Business is also brisk in the defense / aerospace sector, where guidance systems for missiles, aircraft, and spacecraft are a big item. (Honeywell is among the largest twenty defense contractors.) Going into 1981, the company had chalked up a string of six strong consecutive earnings gains; earnings were down a bit in 1981, a recession year.

The dividend yield in recent years has been in the 3 to 4 percent range. The p / e ratio has come way down. In early 1981, the company sold for the same multiple (8) as the average stock.

* * *

HOOVER UNIVERSAL, INC. (HVU). Founded: 1913. Headquarters: 825 Victors Way, Ann Arbor MI 48104. DIVERSIFIED MANUFACTURER. Manufacturer of auto parts, engineered plastic parts, and furniture components. MAJOR SUBSIDIARIES, BRANDS: Uniloy, AE, Franklin Aluminum, Seng, Tote, Omni, Uniloy-Springfield.

Sales: $572.8 million (trend 17.9% a year).
Earnings: $19.44 million (trend 13.1% a year).
What happened to a $10,000 investment

Purchase Date	*Purchase Price*	*Price on 12-31-81*	*Dividends Paid*
12-31-71	$15.00	$19.50	$5,427.41
12-31-76	$15.61	$19.50	$3,388.61

Purchase Date	*Cap. Gains (– Losses)*	*Total Return*	*Rate of Return*
12-31-71	$3,000.00	$8,427.41	6.30%
12-31-76	$2,491.10	$5,879.72	9.69%

* * *

HORIZON BANCORP (HZB). Founded: 1970. Headquarters: 344 Madison Ave., Morristown NJ 07960. BANK HOLDING COMPANY. Parent organization for major New Jersey banks. MAJOR SUBSIDIARIES, BRANDS: American National Bank & Trust of New Jersey; Northeastern Bank; Princeton Bank and Trust Co.; Marine National Bank of Wildwood; Horizon Creditcorp.

* * *

HORIZON CORP. (HZN). Founded: 1959. Headquarters: 4400 E. Broadway, PO Box 27324, Tucson AZ 85726. REAL ESTATE. This company owns tracts of land in New Mexico, Texas, and Arizona which it develops itself or sells to others to develop.

Sales: $34.6 million (trend 3.6% a year).
Earnings: $6.05 million (trend 65.2% a year).
What happened to a $10,000 investment

Purchase Date	*Purchase Price*	*Price on 12-31-81*	*Dividends Paid*
12-31-71	$27.98	$10.37	$0.00
12-31-76	$ 2.14	$10.37	$0.00

Purchase Date	*Cap. Gains (– Losses)*	*Total Return*	*Rate of Return*
12-31-71	$–6,291.49	$–6,291.49	–9.44%
12-31-76	$ 38,416.63	$ 38,416.63	37.09%

* * *

GEORGE A. HORMEL & CO. (HRL, AMERICAN STOCK EXCHANGE). Founded 1928. Headquarters: 510 16th Ave. N.E., Austin MN 55912. PROCESSED MEATS. Hormel is a major meat processor, specializing in pork. 8,000 employees. MAJOR SUBSIDIARIES, BRANDS: Hormel (ham); Spam; Dinty Moore; Mary Kitchen.

Sales: $1,434.0 million (trend 5.9% a year).
Earnings: $27.28 million (trend 14.4% a year).
What happened to a $10,000 investment

Purchase Date	*Purchase Price*	*Price on 12-31-81*	*Dividends Paid*
12-31-71	$11.37	$18.25	$5,200.00
12-31-76	$12.62	$18.25	$2,962.38

Purchase Date	*Cap. Gains (– Losses)*	*Total Return*	*Rate of Return*
12-31-71	$6,043.96	$11,243.96	7.83%
12-31-76	$4,455.45	$ 7,417.82	11.74%

PROFILE: If you're a frequent camper, or if you've served in the military, you're probably familiar with Spam and Dinty Moore beef stew, two well-known Hormel products. If you're a ham fancier, you've probably run into Hormel hams in the supermarket.

But though Hormel is something of a household

word, this stock hasn't been much to Wall Street's taste. It stock has sold for an average of 6 times earnings or less since 1973. One reason is the up-and-down nature of earnings here. It's bound to be that way in the meat business — particularly a specialized (pork) end of the meat business. Profits depend on the spread between the cost of pork (and labor) and the retail price pork products will fetch. The former is a function of weather and farm conditions. The latter is a function of consumer tastes and the availability and price of competing products, mainly chicken and beef. Both ends of the seesaw move; the spread, and hence the profit potential, changes from year to year and month to month.

Dividends, raised each year since 1968, have provided a 4-to-6 percent yield in recent years. The balance sheet is strong, with debt recently only about 12 percent of total capital. And the stock is, as noted above, quite reasonably priced. So if you're a patient investor looking not for a killing but for shares that may be slightly undervalued, take a careful look at Hormel.

* * *

HOSPITAL CORP. OF AMERICA (HCA). Founded 1960. Headquarters: 1 Park Plaza, Nashville TN 37203. HOSPITAL MANAGEMENT. Owns, leases, manages hospitals, primarily in Sunbelt areas.

Sales: $1,231.5 million (trend 27.4% a year).
Earnings: $80.99 million (trend 29.6% a year).
What happened to a $10,000 investment

Purchase Date	*Purchase Price*	*Price on 12-31-81*	*Dividends Paid*
12-31-71	$9.07	$34.25	$1,497.91
12-31-76	$7.00	$34.25	$1,589.68

Purchase Date	*Cap. Gains (— Losses)*	*Total Return*	*Rate of Return*
12-31-71	$27,774.77	$29,272.69	14.66%
12-31-76	$38,927.33	$40,517.01	38.26%

* * *

HOST INTERNATIONAL, INC. (HII). Founded 1897. Headquarters: Pico at 34th St., Santa Monica CA 90406. FOOD SERVICE. Operates food, beverage, and merchandise facilities at airport terminals; involved in specialty retailing; operates restaurants and airport hotels. MAJOR SUBSIDIARIES, BRANDS: Charley Brown's, Casa Maria, Joshua Tree, Phineas, Franklin Stove, JT's Place, Charley's Place, Barley Mow, Port O' Georgetown. Host International has agreed to be acquired by Marriott Corp., as of early 1982.

Sales: $356.7 million (trend 11.8% a year).
Earnings: $14.02 million (trend 16.9% a year).
What happened to a $10,000 investment

Purchase Date	*Purchase Price*	*Price on 12-31-81*	*Dividends Paid*
12-31-71	$34.87	$28.50	$1,301.79
12-31-76	$11.62	$28.50	$2,331.18

Purchase Date	*Cap. Gains (— Losses)*	*Total Return*	*Rate of Return*
12-31-71	$—1,827.96	$ —526.16	—.54%
12-31-76	$ 14,516.13	$16,847.31	21.84%

* * *

HOUGHTON MIFFLIN CO. (HTN). Founded 1908. Headquarters: 1 Beacon St., Boston MA 02107. PUBLISHER. Major U.S. book publisher, producing textbooks as well as books for general readers.

Sales: $163.9 million (trend 11.8% a year).
Earnings: $9.66 million (trend 10.7% a year).
What happened to a $10,000 investment

Purchase Date	*Purchase Price*	*Price on 12-31-81*	*Dividends Paid*
12-31-71	$23.25	$23.50	$3,987.10
12-31-76	$16.62	$23.50	$3,981.95

Purchase Date	*Cap. Gains (— Losses)*	*Total Return*	*Rate of Return*
12-31-71	$ 107.53	$4,094.62	3.49%
12-31-76	$4,135.34	$8,117.29	12.62%

* * *

HOUSE OF FABRICS, INC. (HF). Founded 1946. Headquarters: 13400 Riverside Dr., Sherman Oaks CA 91423. RETAIL FABRIC STORES. Operates large chain of retail fabric outlets.

Sales: $158.8 million (trend 7.4% a year).
Earnings: $3.70 million (trend —16.2% a year).
What happened to a $10,000 investment

Purchase Date	*Purchase Price*	*Price on 12-31-81*	*Dividends Paid*
12-31-71	$21.12	$10.87	$ 800.00
12-31-76	$ 8.87	$10.87	$1,250.70

Purchase Date	Cap. Gains (− Losses)	Total Return	Rate of Return
12-31-71	$−4,852.07	$−4,052.07	−5.06%
12-31-76	$ 2,253.52	$ 3,504.23	6.19%

* * *

HOUSEHOLD INTERNATIONAL CORP. (HI). Founded 1925. Headquarters: 2700 Sanders Rd., Prospect Heights IL 60070. FINANCE, RETAILING, LEASING. Household International (formerly Household Finance) is the second largest U.S. loan company, and is broadly diversified into retailing, consumer goods manufacturing, and leasing, particularly car rentals. 77,000 employees. MAJOR SUBSIDIARIES, BRANDS: Household Finance Co. (HFC); National Car Rental System; City Products Corp. (Ben Franklin, Coast-to-Coast, T.G.&Y., and White's stores; Huffman-Koos, American Furniture, and Barker's furniture stores; Von's grocery stores); King-Seeley Thermos; Wallace Murray Corp. (tools, engine parts, and pipe fixtures).

Sales: $959.6 million (trend 12.9% a year).
Earnings: $133.80 million (trend 6.9% a year).
What happened to a $10,000 investment

Purchase Date	Purchase Price	Price on 12-31-81	Dividends Paid
12-31-71	$34.58	$15.25	$3,536.39
12-31-76	$21.50	$15.25	$3,406.98

Purchase Date	Cap. Gains (− Losses)	Total Return	Rate of Return
12-31-71	$−5,590.36	$−2,053.98	−2.27%
12-31-76	$−2,906.98	$ 500.00	.98%

PROFILE: Household was for a long time the number one loan company in the country in consumer loans. Now it is number two to Beneficial, but the change in part is of Household's own choosing. In recent years it has emphasized diversification, and lately has formally stated that it will limit the size of the loan business. It recently changed its name from Household Finance to Household International, to reflect its diversity.

The early 1980s were a good time not to have all your eggs in the consumer-loan basket. With the cost of funds sky-high, loan companies didn't dare charge customers much more than they paid themselves, for fear of simply driving all the customers away.

Even so, the diversification program at Household was controversial, in large part because Household had yet to demonstrate that it could manage its diverse enterprises in a way that would produce steady earnings growth.

In 1981 Clifford Gridley, an analyst for Dean Witter, told the New York *Times* that it would be tough for Household to get "all the divisions to work together smoothly. When one is going well, another isn't," Gridley said. "Their performance is unpredictable and confusing to analysts and investors. Nobody knows where they're going." Of course, some of those comments could apply to any conglomerate; the test is in the management and the earnings.

One more issue here is the huge debt load: Common stock accounts for only about a quarter of capital. Towering debt is par for the course in a loan company. But now that Household is so diversified (even in 1979, loan operations were only about a sixth of revenues, and about a third of profits) it may feel pressure to pare down the debt.

* * *

HOUSTON INDUSTRIES INC. (HOU). Founded 1906. Headquarters: 611 Walker Ave., Houston TX 77002. UTILITY. Provides electricity to some 1 million customers in Houston and other Texas coastal communities. 8,000 employees. MAJOR SUBSIDIARIES, BRANDS: Houston Lighting & Power Co.; Primary Fuels, Inc.

Sales: $2,367.3 million (trend 29.8% a year).
Earnings: $183.98 million (trend 20.8% a year).
What happened to a $10,000 investment

Purchase Date	Purchase Price	Price on 12-31-81	Dividends Paid
12-31-71	$30.83	$18.12	$4,203.23
12-31-76	$21.17	$18.12	$3,782.66

Purchase Date	Cap. Gains (− Losses)	Total Return	Rate of Return
12-31-71	$−4,121.62	$ 81.61	.08%
12-31-76	$−1,437.01	$2,345.65	4.30%

PROFILE: While most utilities have been suffering from the fiscal equivalent of viral pneumonia, Houston Industries has been getting along pretty well, with not much more than a cold.

Revenues and earnings, flat at most utilities, have continued to show moderate growth here, reflecting the growth of the Houston area. Growth creates some chance for capital gains in the stock, so investors have been willing to settle for a somewhat lower dividend yield here (recently 9 to 11½ percent) than at other utilities. The company has also escaped the extreme debt levels that plague many of its competitors. There's still plenty of leverage here with long term debt recently about 41 percent of capital. But Houston Industries has actually been reducing its debt load (from 50 percent of capital in 1974), while the debt ratio at other electrical utilities has been rising.

The fuel mixture consists mainly of natural gas, and secondarily of coal; the gas is nearby and abundant. Regulators in Texas are usually viewed as pro-business, and have been relatively willing to go along with rate-increase requests. All in all, if you must own a utility stock, this is one that deserves consideration.

* * *

HOUSTON NATURAL GAS CORP. (HNG). Founded 1940. Headquarters: Houston Natural Gas Bldg., PO Box 1188, Houston TX 77001. GAS TRANSMISSION, ENERGY. The company is engaged mainly in transmission of natural gas within Texas. It also has interests in coal production, oil and gas exploration, oil field services, and chemical production. 11,000 employees. MAJOR SUBSIDIARIES, BRANDS: Ziegler Coal Co.; Pott Industries (oil field services); Liquid Carbonic (world's largest producer of carbon dioxide for industrial use).

Sales: $2,906.3 million (trend 19.4% a year).
Earnings: $238.25 million (trend 18.4% a year).
What happened to a $10,000 investment

Purchase Date	*Purchase Price*	*Price on 12-31-81*	*Dividends Paid*
12-31-71	$ 9.75	$44.50	$6,972.56
12-31-76	$34.37	$44.50	$1,520.00

Purchase Date	*Cap. Gains (− Losses)*	*Total Return*	*Rate of Return*
12-31-71	$35,641.03	$42,613.59	18.06%
12-31-76	$ 2,945.45	$ 4,465.45	7.66%

PROFILE: Houston Natural Gas has its thumbs in several profitable pies, and the results show it. The return on stockholders' equity here hasn't been below 20 percent since 1974. Profits, which amounted to $17 million in 1971, grew to $197 million by 1980, while sales advanced almost as fast. Meanwhile, debt as a percentage of total capital has been steadily reduced, from 53 percent at the start of the period to about 29 percent at its end.

All in all, a very fine record. Yet, investors haven't bid the stock up to ridiculous heights. In recent years the price / earnings ratio has varied between 6 and 13; it was recently toward the lower end of that spectrum.

The company won't gain any bonanza from the deregulation of natural gas prices, since intrastate prices were already pretty well deregulated. But the company doesn't need that boost. Chairman Robert R. (Bob) Herring, a decorated World War II Air Force pilot, has a good reputation for long-term planning and short-term execution.

Dividends have been paid each year since the company was incorporated, but the yield is low to moderate.

* * *

HOUSTON OIL ROYALTY TRUST (RTH). Founded 1980. Headquarters: c / o First City National Bank of Houston, 2 Houston Center, Houston TX 77002. TRUST. Owns 99 percent interest in royalties from oil and gas properties of Houston Oil and Minerals Corp.

* * *

HOWELL CORP. (HWL). Founded 1955. Headquarters: 1010 Lamar Bldg., Houston TX 77002. OIL REFINING. Howell is an independent refiner of petroleum products. Also, through subsidiaries, mines coal and engages in oil and gas exploration. 400 employees. MAJOR SUBSIDIARIES, BRANDS: Howell Petroleum Corp. (52 percent owned; oil and gas exploration and production); Lake Coal Co.

Sales: $284.1 million (trend 35.0% a year).
Earnings: $13.94 million (trend 15.6% a year).
What happened to a $10,000 investment

Purchase Date	*Purchase Price*	*Price on 12-31-81*	*Dividends Paid*
12-31-71	$ .94	$8.62	$20,823.88
12-31-76	$12.50	$8.62	$ 1,306.69

Purchase Date	*Cap. Gains (− Losses)*	*Total Return*	*Rate of Return*
12-31-71	$ 81,323.53	$102,147.41	27.34%
12-31-76	$−3,100.00	$−1,793.31	−3.88%

PROFILE: Howell is an extremely small (by Big Board standards), extremely volatile, and — in most years — extremely profitable energy firm. It's also quite little known. So if you buy these shares you may stand to make big profits, but you also take big risks.

As of 1981, there were only about 1,000 shareholders who owned a piece of Howell. (Chairman and President P. N. Howell owned or controlled about 44 percent of the shares.) Compare that total with, say, Mobil, which has about 271,000 shareholders. You can see that the market in these shares is thin — and that makes for big, fast price runs, either up or down. Add to this the inherent volatility of independent refining, and the feast-or-famine nature of small-scale oil exploration, and you've got a ticket to a real roller-coaster ride. Within the past couple of years the stock has been as low as $5.12, as high as $33. It had settled back to about $9 in late 1981. The p / e ratio recently has been as high as 14, as low as 1.

Dividends have been paid yearly since 1975, and provide a low to moderate yield. Most analysts expected the company to have reduced earnings in 1981; it was not known whether this would affect dividend payments.

The return on equity has been sporadic but often spectacular — for example, it was more than 66 percent in 1979, when the company registered record earnings of $5.60 a share. In 1980 it dropped to 20 percent, and was expected to drop further in 1981.

* * *

HOWELL PETROLEUM CORP. (HPT). Founded 1979. Headquarters: 1010 Lamar Bldg., Houston TX 77002. OIL, GAS. Howell explores for and produces oil and natural gas. Also collects gas from other producers and is involved in gas pipeline operation. The company is a spin-off of Howell Corp., which owns approximately 52 percent of Howell Petroleum Corp. stock. MAJOR SUBSIDIARIES, BRANDS: Mellon Energy Co.; Warrior Drilling & Engineering Co.

Sales: $26.8 million.
Earnings: $3.24 million.

* * *

HUBBARD REAL ESTATE INVESTMENTS (HRE). Founded 1969. Headquarters: 125 High St., Boston MA 02110. REAL ESTATE INVESTMENT TRUST. Manages a portfolio of real estate-oriented investments.

Sales: $10.1 million (trend 2.9% a year).
Earnings: $7.61 million (trend 8.1% a year).
What happened to a $10,000 investment

Purchase Date	*Purchase Price*	*Price on 12-31-81*	*Dividends Paid*
12-31-71	$21.25	$15.62	$7,237.65
12-31-76	$15.75	$15.62	$5,060.32

Purchase Date	*Cap. Gains (− Losses)*	*Total Return*	*Rate of Return*
12-31-71	$−2,647.06	$4,590.59	3.85%
12-31-76	$ −79.37	$4,980.95	8.42%

* * *

HUDSON BAY MINING & SMELTING CO., LTD. (HD). Founded 1927. Headquarters: PO Box 28, Toronto-Dominion Centre, Toronto, Ont. M5K 1B8 Canada. MINING. Canadian company engaged in copper, zinc, and precious metals mining; manufactures fertilizers and chemicals; involved in oil and gas.

Sales: $623.5 million (trend 18.8% a year).
Earnings: $34.69 million (trend 37.5% a year).
What happened to a $10,000 investment

Purchase Date	*Purchase Price*	*Price on 12-31-81*	*Dividends Paid*
12-31-71	$20.87	$20.87	$4,681.53
12-31-76	$17.75	$20.87	$1,770.87

Purchase Date	*Cap. Gains (− Losses)*	*Total Return*	*Rate of Return*
12-31-71	$ −.00	$4,681.53	3.91%
12-31-76	$1,760.56	$3,531.44	6.24%

* * *

HUFFY CORP. (HUF). Founded 1928. Headquarters: 7701 Byers Rd., Miamisburg OH 45342. RECREATIONAL PRODUCTS. Manufactures and sells bicycles, exercise equipment, basketball, fishing and marine equipment, gasoline containers, and automotive service equipment. MAJOR SUBSIDIARIES, BRANDS: Huffy, Frabill, Pro-Shot.

Sales: $232.0 million (trend 18.1% a year).
Earnings: $5.76 million (trend 13.9% a year).
What happened to a $10,000 investment

Purchase Date	*Purchase Price*	*Price on 12-31-81*	*Dividends Paid*
12-31-71	$5.96	$14.25	$4,452.33
12-31-76	$5.57	$14.25	$3,474.21

Purchase Date	*Cap. Gains (− Losses)*	*Total Return*	*Rate of Return*
12-31-71	$13,898.15	$18,350.48	10.98%
12-31-76	$15,587.92	$19,062.13	23.78%

* * *

HUGHES TOOL CO. (HT). Founded 1972. Headquarters: 5425 Polk Ave., Houston TX 77023. OIL FIELD SERVICES. Hughes Tool is the world's largest maker of oil drilling bits, and also provides other oil and gas drilling services and equipment. 15,000 employees. MAJOR SUBSIDIARIES, BRANDS: BJ-Hughes (formerly Byron Jackson); Regan Offshore International; Brown Oil Tools.

Sales: $1,206.2 million (trend 28.7% a year).
Earnings: $135.36 million (trend 27.2% a year).
What happened to a $10,000 investment

Purchase Date	*Purchase Price*	*Price on 12-31-81*	*Dividends Paid*
12-31-71	$ N/A	$40.12	$ N/A
12-31-76	$13.08	$40.12	$1,508.29

Purchase Date	*Cap. Gains (— Losses)*	*Total Return*	*Rate of Return*
12-31-71	$ N/A	$ N/A	N/A%
12-31-76	$20,668.79	$22,177.08	26.33%

PROFILE: The company gets its name from the storied, secretive entrepreneur Howard Hughes, who sold it to the public in 1972. Since then, sales and profits have grown more than tenfold.

Hughes bequeathed a company that was debt-free, but laden with obsolete equipment. Capital spending has been jacked up substantially to modernize the facilities — from $4 million in 1972 to $176 million in 1980. This required some debt financing, and debt rose to 27 percent of total capital in 1979. Recently, however, some debt has been retired, and the debt ratio has dropped to less than 15 percent of total capital. That's a figure that will please any conservative investor.

The return on equity has been consistently above average in recent years, ranging between 15 and 20 percent. The company supplies almost half the oil drilling bits used in the United States and also has strong sales abroad. However, it has diversified away from exclusive reliance on drill bits, in the face of increased competition in that field. Profit margins have stayed consistently in the 10-to-12 percent range.

Dividends have been paid yearly since 1973, but the yield is small.

* * *

HUMANA INC. (HUM). Founded 1964. Headquarters: 1800 First National Tower, Louisville KY 40202. HOSPITAL MANAGEMENT. Owns and operates close to 100 proprietary hospitals, mainly in the Sunbelt. 39,000 employees.

Sales: $1,342.9 million (trend 42.3% a year).
Earnings: $85.61 million (trend 61.2% a year).
What happened to a $10,000 investment

Purchase Date	*Purchase Price*	*Price on 12-31-81*	*Dividends Paid*
12-31-71	$4.21	$35.25	$3,288.76
12-31-76	$2.85	$35.25	$4,673.94

Purchase Date	*Cap. Gains (— Losses)*	*Total Return*	*Rate of Return*
12-31-71	$ 73,760.26	$ 77,049.02	24.16%
12-31-76	$113,500.53	$118,174.46	66.56%

PROFILE: This stock has been burning up the track like a sprinter, and it's kept up the performance longer than many thought possible. A quarter-miler? A miler? Could Humana possibly be a marathon performer? It might be, but there are substantial risks in the stock — as any investor who buys in, hoping for a repeat of performance to date, should be aware.

From the time it went public in 1968 through early 1982, Humana shares increased in value more than twenty-five fold. (An initial $10,000 investment would have produced a profit of more than $250,000.) The stock had split five times, as of early 1982.

Humana hospitals have plush rooms, gourmet food, and tight management. Proprietary hospitals of course remain controversial. Do they provide as good care as nonprofits? Do they "skim the cream," taking the wealthiest patients and leaving others for the nonprofits? Those questions have been the subject of hard and ongoing debate.

On Wall Street, concern is more likely to center on other factors. Can the blistering growth rate (boosted by the 1978 acquisition of American Medicorp) be sustained? What about the debt load? Humana is extremely heavily leveraged, with debt about 72 percent of capital as of early 1981. That debt has helped the company expand like a forest fire. But to conservative-minded investors, that much debt could easily end up in the company's being burned.

The company's success is, of course, far from a secret. So the stock carries a price tag as rich as the hospitals' food. In early 1982 the share price of $36 was about 15 times the previous year's earnings, or about twice the price / earnings multiple the average stock carried.

Dividends were begun in 1976, but aren't a major factor. Recently the yield was a bit under 2 percent.

* * *

PHILIP A. HUNT CHEMICAL CORP. (HCC). Founded 1963. Headquarters: Roosevelt Place, Palisades Park NJ 07650. CHEMICALS. Manufacturer of chemicals for photography, printing, electronics, and electrostatic copying.

Sales: $106.3 million (trend 14.9% a year).
Earnings: $4.03 million (trend 4.8% a year).
What happened to a $10,000 investment

Purchase Date	*Purchase Price*	*Price on 12-31-81*	*Dividends Paid*
12-31-71	$16.75	$9.62	$1,817.91
12-31-76	$13.37	$9.62	$1,428.04

Purchase Date	*Cap. Gains (– Losses)*	*Total Return*	*Rate of Return*
12-31-71	$–4,253.73	$–2,435.82	–2.75%
12-31-76	$–2,803.74	$–1,375.70	–2.92%

* * *

THE E. F. HUTTON GROUP, INC. (EFH). Founded 1904. Headquarters: 1 Battery Park Plaza, New York NY 10004. SECURITIES. Active in investment banking, stock and commodity brokerage, and life insurance.

Sales: $1,125.3 million (trend 35.0% a year).
Earnings: $82.90 million (trend 29.4% a year).
What happened to a $10,000 investment

Purchase Date	*Purchase Price*	*Price on 12-31-81*	*Dividends Paid*
12-31-71	$N/A	$39.25	$ N/A
12-31-76	$ 7.07	$39.25	$2,973.07

Purchase Date	*Cap. Gains (– Losses)*	*Total Return*	*Rate of Return*
12-31-71	$ N/A	$ N/A	N/A%
12-31-76	$45,550.08	$48,523.15	42.39%

* * *

HYDRAULIC CO. (THC). Founded 1857. Headquarters: 835 Main St., Bridgeport CT 06609. WATER SERVICES. Provides public water services in Connecticut; involved in real estate sales and management. MAJOR SUBSIDIARIES, BRANDS: Main Street South Corp.; Timco, Inc.; Bridgeport Hydraulic Co.

Sales: $25.8 million (trend 10.4% a year).
Earnings: $3.71 million (trend 20.1% a year).
What happened to a $10,000 investment

Purchase Date	*Purchase Price*	*Price on 12-31-81*	*Dividends Paid*
12-31-71	$N/A	$17.50	$ N/A
12-31-76	$16.83	$17.50	$4,569.39

Purchase Date	*Cap. Gains (– Losses)*	*Total Return*	*Rate of Return*
12-31-71	$ N/A	$ N/A	N/A%
12-31-76	$400.00	$4,969.39	8.40%

I

IC INDUSTRIES, INC. (ICX). Founded 1962. Headquarters: 1 Illinois Center, 111 East Wacker Dr., Chicago IL 60601. CONGLOMERATE. This diversified company, built around the Illinois Central Gulf Railroad, has interests in industrial equipment, real estate, auto parts, recreational vehicles, soft drinks, and foods. 62,000 employees. MAJOR SUBSIDIARIES, BRANDS: Abex Corp. (formerly American Brake Shoe & Foundry, makes transportation and industrial equipment); Bubble Up, Dad's Root Beer, Pepsi-Cola General Bottlers; Midas International (mufflers and other auto parts, recreational vehicles); Pet, Inc. (Pet evaporated milk, Old El Paso foods, Whitman's Chocolates, Sego diet foods); Illinois Central Gulf Railroad Co.

Sales: $4,141.6 million (trend 25.0% a year).
Earnings: $97.10 million (trend 23.1% a year).
What happened to a $10,000 investment

Purchase Date	*Purchase Price*	*Price on 12-31-81*	*Dividends Paid*
12-31-71	$36.37	$35.25	$4,244.67
12-31-76	$22.37	$35.25	$4,040.22

Purchase Date	*Cap. Gains (– Losses)*	*Total Return*	*Rate of Return*
12-31-71	$–309.28	$3,935.40	3.37%
12-31-76	$ 5,754.19	$9,794.41	14.63%

PROFILE: The railroad is the kernel around which this conglomerate has been built by accretion. The first diversification — Abex, in 1968 — was a natural step since it makes, among other things, couplings, brakes, and wheels for railroad cars. Since then the company has gone increasingly far afield, picking up Midas, Pepsi-Cola General Bottlers, and most recently (1978) Pet, Inc. The company has also been active in real estate development projects on the land it originally acquired for its railroad routes.

In 1979 the railroad accounted for only about a quarter of the company's sales, and only about a tenth of profits. The company has gone on record as saying it is willing to sell the railroad, which has some 8,000 miles of track in thirteen states, mainly running north-south along the Mississippi from Chicago to New Orleans. A sale would provide cash to strengthen the balance sheet (recently debt was about 46 percent of capital) and to finance other acquisitions. So, like W. R. Grace, which sloughed off the steamship line that gave it its name, this conglomerate will probably spit out its original core. In the meantime, though, railroad earnings were up in 1980 on increased grain traffic. The company has been chopping unprofitable track, and upgrading the remaining track.

Dividends have been increased each year since 1970, and the dividend yield in recent years has been 6 to 8 percent. Only investors with good timing have reaped capital gains, though, as the overall price trend in this stock for the past decade or so has been uninspiring.

* * *

ICN PHARMACEUTICALS, INC. (ICN). Founded 1960. Headquarters: 222 N. Vincent Ave., Covina CA 91722. PHARMACEUTICALS. Produces pharmaceuticals and chemicals.

Sales: $63.1 million (trend −8.4% a year).
Earnings: $.85 million.
What happened to a $10,000 investment

Purchase Date	*Purchase Price*	*Price on 12-31-81*	*Dividends Paid*
12-31-71	$23.87	$6.50	$0.00
12-31-76	$ 4.12	$6.50	$0.00

Purchase Date	*Cap. Gains (− Losses)*	*Total Return*	*Rate of Return*
12-31-71	$−7,277.49	$−7,277.49	−12.20%
12-31-76	$ 5,757.58	$ 5,757.58	9.52%

* * *

INA CORP. (INA). Founded 1968; insurance company dates to 1794. Headquarters: 1600 Arch St., Philadelphia PA 19101. INSURANCE. INA is the holding company for several insurance subsidiaries, including Insurance Co. of North America, one of the largest U.S. property and casualty insurers. Also involved in life insurance, mutual fund management, and management of hospitals and other health-care facilities. 40,000 employees. In 1981, INA announced its intention to merge with Connecticut General Corp. The combined entity would be called North American General Corp., and would be approximately the fifth-largest U.S. insurance company. **MAJOR SUBSIDIARIES, BRANDS:** Insurance Co. of North America; INA Life Insurance Co.; Horace Mann; INA Capital Management Corp.; HMO International; Ross Loos; American Health Services Inc. Owns approximately 20 percent of Paine Webber (brokerage house).

Sales: $5,254.6 million (trend 16.7% a year).
Earnings: $278.63 million (trend 37.7% a year).
What happened to a $10,000 investment

Purchase Date	*Purchase Price*	*Price on 12-31-81*	*Dividends Paid*
12-31-71	$32.83	$44.12	$4,922.03
12-31-76	$31.50	$44.12	$3,084.66

Purchase Date	*Cap. Gains (− Losses)*	*Total Return*	*Rate of Return*
12-31-71	$3,439.09	$8,361.12	6.26%
12-31-76	$4,007.94	$7,092.59	11.32%

PROFILE: Health care is a rapidly growing part of INA. It looks as if the hospital-management and related subsidiaries will soon amount to a billion-dollar business within INA. (Revenues from this segment were $782 million in 1980, and the company has been expanding rapidly in the health-care field through acquisitions.) Companies that are mainly in the hospital-management field have been fetching multiples like 20 times earnings recently — about 2½ times the multiple of the average stock. Meanwhile INA has recently sold for only 6 times earnings, a 25 percent lower multiple than that of the average stock in 1981.

Granted, health care accounted for only 15 percent of 1980 revenues, and an even smaller slice of profits. The life and health insurance operations chipped in about 20 percent, but the bulk of the company — about two thirds of revenues — is the property and casualty insurance operation. And investors know that property and casualty insurance is a notoriously cyclical business.

The cycle hit hard in 1974–75, when INA earnings dropped from a 1973 high of $3.71 a share to $1.83 a share in 1975. Presumably investors, fearing that the company may be near another cyclical peak ($7.47 a share in 1980), don't want to pay too much for earnings that may not hold up. The thought is wise and prudent. But, considering

INA's diversification, the prudence may be overdone here.

A real, but presumably temporary problem stems from INA's sale of Blyth, Eastman Dillon (in which it owned a 68 percent share) to brokerage giant Paine Webber in 1979. INA got about 20 percent of Paine Webber, but the merger brokerage ran into technical problems in combining that have proved costly. Long-term, the stake in Paine Webber should prove to INA's benefit.

INA's plans to merge with Connecticut General Corp. were announced in late 1981. If the merger comes through, the resulting firm will be one of the giants of the insurance industry. As of the time this book went to press, there was still some distance to go before the merger could be consummated.

* * *

IU INTERNATIONAL CORP. (IU) Founded 1924. Headquarters: 1105 N. Market St., Wilmington DE 19801. DIVERSIFIED TRUCKING COMPANY. IU is a major factor in the trucking market, and also has operations in several other areas, including agribusiness, environmental protection, and other industries. MAJOR SUBSIDIARIES, BRANDS: Ryder Truck Lines; Pacific Intermountain Express; Byrns Motor Express; Helms Express; C. Brewer & Co., Ltd.; Mauna Loa macadamia nuts; Unijax, Inc.; Biggers Brothers, Inc.; General Waterworks Corp.

Sales: $2,239.4 million (trend 6.6% a year).
Earnings: $73.92 million (trend −2.4% a year).
What happened to a $10,000 investment

Purchase Date	*Purchase Price*	*Price on 12-31-81*	*Dividends Paid*
12-31-71	$21.56	$13.75	$4,127.54
12-31-76	$11.87	$13.75	$4,126.32

Purchase Date	*Cap. Gains (− Losses)*	*Total Return*	*Rate of Return*
12-31-71	$−3,623.19	$ 504.35	.49%
12-31-76	$ 1,578.95	$5,705.26	9.45%

* * *

IDAHO POWER CO. (IDA). Founded 1915. Headquarters: 1220 Idaho St., Boise ID 83721. UTILITY. Provides electricity for Idaho and parts of Oregon and Nevada.

Sales: $262.6 million (trend 16.0% a year).
Earnings: $38.27 million (trend 12.2% a year).
What happened to a $10,000 investment

Purchase Date	*Purchase Price*	*Price on 12-31-81*	*Dividends Paid*
12-31-71	$34.25	$21.25	$6,227.74
12-31-76	$29.87	$21.25	$3,936.40

Purchase Date	*Cap. Gains (− Losses)*	*Total Return*	*Rate of Return*
12-31-71	$−3,795.62	$2,432.12	2.20%
12-31-76	$−2,887.03	$1,049.37	2.02%

* * *

IDEAL BASIC INDUSTRIES, INC. (IDL). Founded 1908. Headquarters: Ideal Plaza, 950 17th St., PO Box 8789, Denver, CO 80202. CEMENT PRODUCTION. A leading producer of cement and potash.

Sales: $458.9 million (trend 12.1% a year).
Earnings: $52.50 million (trend 18.3% a year).
What happened to a $10,000 investment

Purchase Date	*Purchase Price*	*Price on 12-31-81*	*Dividends Paid*
12-31-71	$16.50	$21.87	$7,424.24
12-31-76	$22.87	$21.87	$3,333.33

Purchase Date	*Cap. Gains (− Losses)*	*Total Return*	*Rate of Return*
12-31-71	$ 3,257.58	$10,681.82	7.54%
12-31-76	$−437.16	$ 2,896.17	5.22%

* * *

IDEAL TOY CORP. (ID). Founded 1912. Headquarters: 184–10 Jamaica Ave., Hollis NY 11423. TOY MANUFACTURING. Manufactures games, toys, and recreational products. In 1982, the company appeared likely to be merged into CBS.

Sales: $141.4 million (trend 2.6% a year).
Earnings: $−15.45 million.
What happened to a $10,000 investment

Purchase Date	*Purchase Price*	*Price on 12-31-81*	*Dividends Paid*
12-31-71	$17.05	$7.25	$367.10
12-31-76	$ 7.34	$7.25	$673.79

Purchase Date	*Cap. Gains (− Losses)*	*Total Return*	*Rate of Return*
12-31-71	$−5,748.78	$−5,381.68	−7.43%
12-31-76	$ −126.17	$ 547.62	1.07%

* * *

ILLINOIS POWER CO. (IPC). Founded 1923. Headquarters: 500 S. 27th St., Decatur IL 62525. UTILITY. Provides gas and electric power in major portions of Illinois.

Sales: $883.4 million (trend 17.0% a year).
Earnings: $94.49 million (trend 14.1% a year).
What happened to a $10,000 investment

Purchase Date	*Purchase Price*	*Price on 12-31-81*	*Dividends Paid*
12-31-71	$38.87	$20.62	$5,780.06
12-31-76	$27.50	$20.62	$4,170.91

Purchase Date	*Cap. Gains (− Losses)*	*Total Return*	*Rate of Return*
12-31-71	$−4,694.53	$1,085.53	1.04%
12-31-76	$−2,500.00	$1,670.91	3.14%

* * *

ILLINOIS TOOL WORKS INC. (ITW). Founded 1912. Headquarters: 8501 W. Higgins Rd., Chicago IL 60631. DIVERSIFIED MANUFACTURING. Develops and markets worldwide a broad range of products in five business segments: engineered fasteners, electronic products, packaging products, precision tools and gearing, and instruments and systems.

Sales: $401.7 million (trend 15.5% a year).
Earnings: $44.27 million (trend 24.6% a year).
What happened to a $10,000 investment

Purchase Date	*Purchase Price*	*Price on 12-31-81*	*Dividends Paid*
12-31-71	$25.12	$29.25	$2,614.13
12-31-76	$27.62	$29.25	$1,581.90

Purchase Date	*Cap. Gains (− Losses)*	*Total Return*	*Rate of Return*
12-31-71	$1,641.79	$4,255.92	3.61%
12-31-76	$ 588.24	$2,170.14	4.01%

* * *

IMPERIAL CORP. OF AMERICA (ICA). Founded 1956. Headquarters: 8787 Complex Dr., San Diego CA 92123. SAVINGS & LOANS. Imperial is a holding company for four savings & loan associations in California, Texas, Kansas, and Colorado; in 1981 it was in the process of acquiring another S&L in California. 1,500 employees. MAJOR SUBSIDIARIES, BRANDS: Imperial Savings & Loan (California); Silver State Savings & Loan (Colorado); American Savings Association (Kansas); USLIFE Savings and Loan Association (California).

Sales: $713.7 million (trend 21.8% a year).
Earnings: $40.66 million (trend 11.1% a year).
What happened to a $10,000 investment

Purchase Date	*Purchase Price*	*Price on 12-31-81*	*Dividends Paid*
12-31-71	$15.12	$11.75	$3,034.71
12-31-76	$16.37	$11.75	$2,534.35

Purchase Date	*Cap. Gains (− Losses)*	*Total Return*	*Rate of Return*
12-31-71	$−2,231.40	$ 803.31	.78%
12-31-76	$−2,824.43	$−290.08	−.59%

PROFILE: Will she or won't she? Liquidate, that is. That was the question in the summer of 1980, when Imperial announced it was considering selling off its operating units and liquidating the company. Liquidation may sound bad, but the prospects that the sum of the parts would fetch more than the whole seemed bright to investors, who bid the shares up to about $34 on the rumors.

Within a couple of weeks Imperial made its decision known: It wouldn't liquidate. Without the spur of a possible short-term gain from the sale of its units, the stock subsided; it was selling at $7 to $8 a share in early 1982. The decline reflected the miserable time that savings and loan associations all over the country are experiencing. They have to pay a lot (in interest on certificates of deposit, for example), to get money to lend. They make money mainly by mortgage lending. But many of their old mortgages bring in a return that is subpar by recent standards. And attempts to issue new mortgages at high and / or variable rates have met with heavy consumer resistance. Imperial's earnings nosedived from a record $5.24 a share in 1979 to $2.86 a share in 1980, and the company lost $2.66 a share in 1981.

Thus the stock is selling at a high multiple of recent earnings, but at only about 5 times 1979 earnings when it trades in the $25 a share range, as it did in early 1981. By early 1982 the price had plunged to around $8. The long-term prospects for recovery by the S&Ls may make this stock attractive to investors who take the long view.

Imperial's savings and loan institutions are well entrenched in their markets. Imperial Savings & Loan is approximately the ninth-largest in California, tenth-largest in the U.S.

Dividends were started in 1975 and were raised

each year through 1980. But, in light of industry conditions, dividends were suspended in mid-1981. The yield had been 4 to 5 percent.

* * *

IMPERIAL OIL LIMITED (Class A stock, **IMOA,** American Stock Exchange). Founded 1880. Headquarters: 111 St. Clair Ave. W., Toronto, Ont. M5W 1K3 Canada. OIL Imperial Oil is the largest oil company in Canada. It is 70 percent owned by Exxon Corp. Has sidelines in building materials, chemicals, and minerals. 16,000 employees.

Sales: $5,091.0 million (trend 6.7% a year).
Earnings: $503.00 million (trend 14.9% a year).
What happened to a $10,000 investment

Purchase Date	*Purchase Price*	*Price on 12-31-81*	*Dividends Paid*
12-31-71	$31.25	$21.37	$2,852.38
12-31-76	$22.25	$21.37	$2,279.28

Purchase Date	*Cap. Gains (− Losses)*	*Total Return*	*Rate of Return*
12-31-71	$−3,160.00	$−307.62	−.31%
12-31-76	$ −393.26	$ 1,886.02	3.52%

PROFILE: An analogy to three little pigs and a big bad wolf may be appropriate here. The three succulent pigs, the attractive qualities of this stock, include a good record of earnings growth, consistently fine profitability, and a nice, strong balance sheet. The wolf, at least from the standpoint of U.S. investors, is the Canadian Government. It has proposed that by 1990 any foreign oil companies operating in Canada will have to be at least 50 percent Canadian-Government owned. It taxes oil production and oil profits heavily. And its tax structure is designed to favor Canadian companies over foreign (including U.S.) ones, with proposals to go further in that regard.

Even when confronted by the specter of the wolf, investors have accorded this stock a price / earnings ratio of 7 (as of early 1981), just under the multiple of the average stock (8 at the time). That tells you something about how cute and chubby the pigs look.

But investors are jumpy, and the stock is subject to sudden price movements reflecting political developments as much as (or more than) petroleum recovery prospects. In 1979, for example, the stock ranged roughly between $20 and $40 a share, and in 1980 roughly between $25 and $50.

Dividends have been paid each year since 1891, but aren't a major reason to buy this stock. The yield in recent years has been about 4 percent. The Class A dividends are subject to a 10 percent Canadian tax on nonresidents. Canadians can buy Class B stock, with dividends that are free of that tax.

Moderate gains may be possible in this stock, even given the present political environment. If Canada elected a government in the future that was more pro-U.S. or more pro-business or both, major gains would be likely.

* * *

INCO LTD. (I). Founded 1919. Headquarters: 1 First Canadian Pl., Toronto, Ont. M5X 1C4, Canada. NICKEL. World's largest producer of nickel; also produces copper and batteries.

Sales: $3,036.1 million (trend 10.8% a year).
Earnings: $193.23 million (trend −5.1% a year).
What happened to a $10,000 investment

Purchase Date	*Purchase Price*	*Price on 12-31-81*	*Dividends Paid*
12-31-71	$32.12	$14.25	$3,374.69
12-31-76	$32.62	$14.25	$1,143.30

Purchase Date	*Cap. Gains (− Losses)*	*Total Return*	*Rate of Return*
12-31-71	$−5,564.20	$−2,189.51	−2.44%
12-31-76	$−5,632.18	$−4,488.89	−11.23%

* * *

INCOME AND CAPITAL SHARES, INC. (ICS). Founded 1966. Headquarters: 535 Boylston St., Boston MA 02116. INVESTMENT COMPANY. This is a dual-purpose investment fund; investors can choose to buy into either the capital gains portion of the portfolio or the income portion. Assets are deployed into stocks, bonds, or short-term holdings; the blend is changed in light of market conditions.

* * *

INDIANA GAS CO., INC. (IGC). Founded 1945. Headquarters: 1630 N. Meridian St., Indianapolis IN 46202. UTILITY DISTRIBUTION. Provides natural gas to residents of southern Indiana.

Sales: $302.9 million (trend 18.5% a year).
Earnings: $9.68 million (trend 9.5% a year).
What happened to a $10,000 investment

Purchase Date	Purchase Price	Price on 12-31-81	Dividends Paid
12-31-71	$25.75	$25.75	$8,431.07
12-31-76	$26.37	$25.75	$4,591.47

Purchase Date	Cap. Gains (− Losses)	Total Return	Rate of Return
12-31-71	$ −.00	$8,431.07	6.31%
12-31-76	$−236.97	$4,354.50	7.50%

* * *

INDIANAPOLIS POWER & LIGHT CO. (IPL). Founded 1926. Headquarters: 25 Monument Circle, Indianapolis IN 46202. UTILITY . Provides electric power for 528 square miles of Indiana that center on the city of Indianapolis.

Sales: $334.1 million (trend 15.4% a year).
Earnings: $48.61 million (trend 15.6% a year).
What happened to a $10,000 investment

Purchase Date	Purchase Price	Price on 12-31-81	Dividends Paid
12-31-71	$28.75	$20.75	$6,761.74
12-31-76	$24.50	$20.75	$4,361.22

Purchase Date	Cap. Gains (− Losses)	Total Return	Rate of Return
12-31-71	$−2,782.61	$3,979.13	3.41%
12-31-76	$−1,530.61	$2,830.61	5.11%

* * *

INDUSTRIAL NATIONAL CORP. (INB). Founded 1970. Headquarters: 55 Kennedy Plaza, Providence RI 02903. HOLDING COMPANY. Deals with banks and bank-related units in Rhode Island. MAJOR SUBSIDIARIES, BRANDS: Industrial National Bank of Rhode Island.

Sales: $405.2 million (trend 17.9% a year).
Earnings: $27.80 million (trend 19.8% a year).
What happened to a $10,000 investment

Purchase Date	Purchase Price	Price on 12-31-81	Dividends Paid
12-31-71	$21.25	$26.87	$6,188.24
12-31-76	$16.25	$26.87	$4,627.69

Purchase Date	Cap. Gains (− Losses)	Total Return	Rate of Return
12-31-71	$2,647.06	$ 8,835.29	6.54%
12-31-76	$6,538.46	$11,166.15	16.18%

* * *

INEXCO OIL CO. (INX). Founded 1968. Headquarters: 1100 Milam Bldg., Suite 1900, Houston TX 77002. OIL AND GAS. Involved in exploration and production of domestic oil and gas. MAJOR SUBSIDIARIES, BRANDS: Wilson Brothers Drilling Co.; Wilson Brothers Corp.

Sales: $146.6 million (trend 24.9% a year).
Earnings: $22.58 million (trend 29.4% a year).
What happened to a $10,000 investment

Purchase Date	Purchase Price	Price on 12-31-81	Dividends Paid
12-31-71	$3.37	$21.25	$1,155.56
12-31-76	$6.31	$21.25	$ 617.82

Purchase Date	Cap. Gains (− Losses)	Total Return	Rate of Return
12-31-71	$52,962.96	$54,118.52	20.42%
12-31-76	$23,663.37	$24,281.19	27.94%

* * *

INGERSOLL-RAND CO. (IR). Founded 1905. Headquarters: 200 Chestnut Ridge Rd., Woodcliff Lake NJ 07675. MACHINERY. Ingersoll-Rand is the leading U.S. maker of air compressors and related machinery for industrial, mining, and pipeline operations. Also makes other machinery and tools. 47,000 employees.

Sales: $2,971.0 million (trend 11.2% a year).
Earnings: $153.45 million (trend 8.2% a year).
What happened to a $10,000 investment

Purchase Date	Purchase Price	Price on 12-31-81	Dividends Paid
12-31-71	$56.25	$56.50	$4,871.11
12-31-76	$76.37	$56.50	$2,053.03

Purchase Date	Cap. Gains (− Losses)	Total Return	Rate of Return
12-31-71	$ 44.44	$ 4,915.56	4.08%
12-31-76	$−2,602.29	$−549.26	−1.12%

PROFILE: "What have you done for me lately?" is a question that humans are very prone to ask. That includes investors. Ingersoll-Rand long had an outstanding reputation for profitability. But in recent years it's been struggling to preserve that reputation.

A peculiarity is that many stocks, if they ran into troubles during the 1970s, were clobbered in 1974, the worst year in stock market history since the Great Depression. Ingersoll-Rand survived that debacle in style: Its 1974 range (about $50 to $98 a share) compares well with its range in the bull-market year of 1972 ($55 to $72). Yet the stock ran out of gas later in the decade, sinking to a 1978 low of $44.25 a share, and still trading below $50 a share during parts of 1979 and 1980. In early 1982 the shares were selling for about $56.

What happened? Ingersoll-Rand suffered the fate of many stocks with excellent track records: It slipped in earnings, and investors yanked away its premium price / earnings ratio. During most of the early 1970s the stock sold for around 16 times earnings. Then, in 1976, earnings dropped about 17 percent; in 1977–80 earnings grew, but not rapidly. Recently the stock has fetched only about 8 times earnings, which is about average.

Foreign currency fluctuations have accounted for part of the earnings problem. The company has expanded greatly abroad, and foreign operations have recently accounted for more than a third of earnings, but foreign demand hasn't come up to Ingersoll's expectations.

A big push into coal-mining equipment has also been part of the problem. Coal production has expanded, but more slowly than many people (apparently including Ingersoll-Rand) thought it would.

In 1980, the company acquired the oil field equipment business of Cabot Corp. (now Ingersoll-Rand Oilfield Products). That changed the balance sheet from strong to average, but gave the company a bigger stake in a business that's been booming recently.

Long-term, the outlook for capital goods looks bright, and so does the outlook for this company. Meanwhile, the dividend, paid each year since 1910 and recently yielding from 4 to 6 percent, gives stability to the stock.

* * *

INGREDIENT TECHNOLOGY CORP. (ITC). Founded 1905. Headquarters: 330 Post Rd., Darien CT 06820. **FOODS.** Produces a variety of ingredients, flavorings, and additives for the foods industry.

Sales: $105.8 million (trend −24.7% a year).
Earnings: $2.94 million (trend −4.7% a year).
What happened to a $10,000 investment

Purchase Date	*Purchase Price*	*Price on 12-31-81*	*Dividends Paid*
12-31-71	$7.75	$9.25	$5,787.10
12-31-76	$8.50	$9.25	$3,070.59

Purchase Date	*Cap. Gains (− Losses)*	*Total Return*	*Rate of Return*
12-31-71	$1,935.48	$7,722.58	5.89%
12-31-76	$ 882.35	$3,952.94	6.89%

* * *

INLAND STEEL CO. (IAD). Founded 1917. Headquarters: 30 W. Monroe St., Chicago IL 60603. **STEEL.** Inland is the nation's sixth-largest steel producer, making a wide variety of steel products for the auto, transportation, construction, and other industries. 37,000 employees. **MAJOR SUBSIDIARIES, BRANDS:** Joseph T. Ryerson & Co.; Inland Steel Urban Development Co.; Scholz Homes.

Sales: $3,255.9 million (trend 10.9% a year).
Earnings: $28.87 million (trend −10.3% a year).
What happened to a $10,000 investment

Purchase Date	*Purchase Price*	*Price on 12-31-81*	*Dividends Paid*
12-31-71	$33.12	$23.37	$7,353.96
12-31-76	$50.87	$23.37	$2,476.66

Purchase Date	*Cap. Gains (− Losses)*	*Total Return*	*Rate of Return*
12-31-71	$−2,943.40	$ 4,410.57	3.72%
12-31-76	$−5,405.41	$−2,928.75	−6.70%

PROFILE: What makes this company different from other steel companies? Location, for one thing. Most big steel companies are based in Pennsylvania. Inland has only one steel mill, the Indiana Harbor Works. From that Midwestern base, it ships to the auto industry in Michigan and to big steel users in the industrial cities of the Midwest like Chicago, Cincinnati, Cleveland, and Indianapolis. Some 75 percent of sales are to five Midwestern states. Proximity lowers the transportation costs.

Partly because of this geographical fact, Inland historically has had less volatile earnings than most diversified steelmakers. (Of course, that's a bit like saying that recreational parachute jumping is less risky than combat duty. All steel companies have cyclical earnings.) But in 1980 Inland took a classic cyclical nose dive, as earnings dropped from $6.27 in 1979 to $1.38. There was a rebound to $2.69 in 1981, but in 1982 all steelmakers were again experiencing tough times. Real growth, of course, depends on strength in the auto and construction industries.

Inland spent about $900 million to modernize its

facilities in recent years, in the process running up its debt from 27 percent of capital in 1973 to 38 percent in 1981. Now it's cutting back on capital spending, but is pretty well positioned to take an advantage of a sustained upturn in demand, if and when it comes.

Dividends have been paid each year since 1934. During 1980's woes, the dividend was chopped only moderately. But in 1982 the dividend had to be cut drastically, reducing the yield to less than 2 percent. Pay was also slashed for some four hundred executives.

* * *

INSILCO CORP. (INR). Founded 1946. Headquarters: 1000 Research Parkway, Meriden CT 06450. **CONGLOMERATE.** Diversified operations in home, commercial, and consumer products such as paint, metal parts, and electronics. **MAJOR SUBSIDIARIES, BRANDS:** Enterprise Companies (paint); International Silver Co. (tableware and silver products); Mary Carter Paint; McDonald Products (office supplies); Miles Homes Companies (supplies for build-it-yourself homes); Red Devil Paints & Chemicals; Rolodex (office supplies); Taylor Publishing (largest U.S. producer of college and high school yearbooks); Times Fiber Communications (communications equipment, 74 percent owned).

Sales: $641.8 million (trend 14.2% a year).
Earnings: $30.49 million (trend 15.1% a year).
What happened to a $10,000 investment

Purchase Date	*Purchase Price*	*Price on 12-31-81*	*Dividends Paid*
12-31-71	$13.81	$16.37	$4,788.86
12-31-76	$11.01	$16.37	$3,596.20

Purchase Date	*Cap. Gains (− Losses)*	*Total Return*	*Rate of Return*
12-31-71	$1,861.61	$6,650.47	5.23%
12-31-76	$4,877.27	$8,473.47	13.06%

* * *

INSTITUTIONAL INVESTORS TRUST (INV). Founded 1970. Headquarters: 1 Beacon St., Boston, MA 02108. **REAL ESTATE TRUST.** Real estate equity and mortgage investments.

Sales: $3.9 million (trend −6.4% a year).
Earnings: $−10.10 million.
What happened to a $10,000 investment

Purchase Date	*Purchase Price*	*Price on 12-31-81*	*Dividends Paid*
12-31-71	$ N/A	$.75	$N/A
12-31-76	$ 1.87	$.75	$ 0.00

Purchase Date	*Cap. Gains (− Losses)*	*Total Return*	*Rate of Return*
12-31-71	$ N/A	$ N/A	N/A%
12-31-76	$−6,000.00	$−6,000.00	−16.74%

* * *

INTEGRATED RESOURCES, INC. (IRE). Founded 1968. Headquarters: 666 Third Ave., New York NY 10017. **FINANCIAL SERVICES.** The company gets the largest share of its income by structuring limited partnership (tax shelter) projects in real estate, oil and gas, and other areas. Also active in insurance.

Sales: $84.3 million (trend 21.9% a year).
Earnings: $8.87 million (trend 58.4% a year).
What happened to a $10,000 investment

Purchase Date	*Purchase Price*	*Price on 12-31-81*	*Dividends Paid*
12-31-71	$10.29	$16.25	$0.00
12-31-76	$ 1.62	$16.25	$0.00

Purchase Date	*Cap. Gains (− Losses)*	*Total Return*	*Rate of Return*
12-31-71	$ 5,785.71	$ 5,785.71	4.67%
12-31-76	$90,000.00	$90,000.00	58.49%

* * *

INTER FIRST CORP. (IFC). Founded 1972; flagship bank dates to 1875. Headquarters: 1201 Elm St., Dallas TX 75270. **BANK HOLDING CO.** Holding company for thirty-three banks in Texas, including the flagship First National Bank in Dallas. 6,000 employees. **MAJOR SUBSIDIARIES, BRANDS:** First National Bank in Dallas; First International Bank in Houston.

PROFILE: Many of the fastest-growing and most profitable banks in the United States are in Texas. Of these, Inter First is the largest. It offers a good combination of safety and growth potential.

In 1981, shares of the average bank were selling for a mere 6 times earnings, an extremely small price to pay for the steady, if undramatic, growth normally associated with bank stocks. Inter First was selling at about 9 times earnings — 50 percent above the valuation of the average bank stock, but only a shade above the p / e ratio for the average stock, which was about 8 at the time.

The bank's profit performance would seem amply to justify its higher multiple. Profits have been up every year since the holding company was founded in 1972, reaching $5.66 a share in 1980 from a starting point of $1.81 a share in 1972. That smart and uninterrupted rise in profits was achieved in the face of two recessions.

Return on assets has been consistently excellent, in the range of 80 to 90 cents per $100 of assets. Return on stockholders' equity has been consistently above 15 percent. Leverage is moderate, with long-term debt about a third of total capital. And the loan portfolio is well diversified, with energy-related loans accounting for about 20 percent.

Dividends have been increased each year since 1973. The yield is moderate — about 4 percent in early 1982.

* * *

INTER-REGIONAL FINANCIAL GROUP, INC. (IFG). Founded 1973. Headquarters: 100 Dain Tower, Minneapolis MN 55402. **FINANCIAL SERVICES.** This company is active in investment banking in the Midwest and West; also has operations in equipment leasing and real estate.

Sales: $123.3 million (trend 21.7% a year).
Earnings: $7.19 million (trend 26.0% a year).
What happened to a $10,000 investment

Purchase Date	*Purchase Price*	*Price on 12-31-81*	*Dividends Paid*
12-31-71	$N/A	$21.25	$ N/A
12-31-76	$ 4.20	$21.25	$3,857.14

Purchase Date	*Cap. Gains (— Losses)*	*Total Return*	*Rate of Return*
12-31-71	$ N/A	$ N/A	N/A%
12-31-76	$40,595.24	$44,452.38	40.35%

* * *

INTERCAPITAL INCOME SECURITIES INC. (ICB). Founded 1972. Headquarters: 5 World Trade Center, New York NY 10048. **INVESTMENT FUND.** Diversified investments, almost entirely in fixed-income securities.

* * *

INTERCO INC. (ISS). Founded 1921. Headquarters: 10 Broadway, St. Louis MO 63102. **SHOES, CLOTHING, RETAILING.** Interco is a leading maker and marketer of shoes, and is also a major clothing manufacturer. In addition, it operates several regional hardware and discount store chains, and makes and sells furniture. 50,000 employees. **MAJOR SUBSIDIARIES, BRANDS:** Florsheim, Thayer McNeil (shoes); London Fog, Big Yank, Devon, Gateway Casuals, Tour de France, and other clothing brands; Eagle Family Discount, Albert's (women's specialty stores); Central Hardware; Ethan Allen, Broyhill (furniture).

Sales: $2,368.5 million (trend 10.8% a year).
Earnings: $124.40 million (trend 13.1% a year).
What happened to a $10,000 investment

Purchase Date	*Purchase Price*	*Price on 12-31-81*	*Dividends Paid*
12-31-71	$49.62	$47.25	$3,233.25
12-31-76	$46.25	$47.25	$1,932.97

Purchase Date	*Cap. Gains (— Losses)*	*Total Return*	*Rate of Return*
12-31-71	$—478.59	$2,754.66	2.46%
12-31-76	$ 216.22	$2,149.19	3.97%

PROFILE: Steady. That's been the word to describe Interco in recent years. Shoes and clothing may not be big growth businesses, but with careful cost controls Interco managed (by the skin of its teeth) to grind out the company's seventeenth consecutive increase in sales and profits in 1980. The string was snapped in 1981, a recession year, when earnings suffered a mild decline.

Interco used to be International Shoe Company, and it is still the nation's largest manufacturer of shoes. It acquired Florsheim in 1953, and bought up well over a dozen other shoe companies, clothing companies, and rural retailers during the 1960s and 1970s. In 1980, it started a push into furniture, acquiring Ethan Allen; Broyhill Furniture was added in 1981.

Shoes, clothing, and furniture are discretionary — but only up to a point. The company's past ability to ride out economic downturns is a plus. But Wall Street hasn't deemed the company's profit growth fast enough, so you may find Interco selling at a discount to the market as a whole. In early 1981, for example, Interco fetched about 7 times its previous year's earnings, while the average stock commanded 8.

Dividends have been hiked each year for the past decade and a half, but you wouldn't really classify Interco as an income stock. The dividend yield for the past five years or so has ranged from 4 to 6 percent. Still, the moderate dividend may enhance total return.

That return could use some enhancing. As of early 1982 the stock sold for about $48 a share, below its high ($50) 10 years earlier. The balance sheet is strong, with debt recently only 14 percent of capital.

* * *

INTERLAKE, INC. (IK). Founded 1905. Headquarters: Commerce Plaza, 2015 Spring Rd., Oak Brook IL 60521. SPECIALTY STEELS, METALS. Interlake produces specialty steel products, castings, metal powders, alloys, pig iron, and materials handling equipment. 13,000 employees. MAJOR SUBSIDIARIES, BRANDS: Arwood Corp. (castings); Hoeganaes Corp. (80 percent owned; metal powders).

Sales: $1,055.9 million (trend 12.1% a year).
Earnings: $13.82 million (trend −15.1% a year).
What happened to a $10,000 investment

Purchase Date	*Purchase Price*	*Price on 12-31-81*	*Dividends Paid*
12-31-71	$18.83	$35.25	$10,256.64
12-31-76	$37.75	$35.25	$ 2,966.89

Purchase Date	*Cap. Gains (− Losses)*	*Total Return*	*Rate of Return*
12-31-71	$ 8,716.81	$18,973.45	11.22%
12-31-76	$−662.25	$ 2,304.64	4.24%

PROFILE: First, the bad news. Interlake in recent years has been one of the poorer performers in a subpar industry (specialty steel). Its earnings peaked at around $7 a share in 1974–75, and didn't get that high again until 1981. What's more, earnings have been highly erratic.

Now, the good news. Interlake, facing up to tough decisions, has been transforming itself. In the last several years it has been closing down obsolete facilities and diversifying into areas requiring higher technology than the production of pig iron and flat-rolled carbon steel. In 1980 the company demanded a wage freeze at two steel plants in Kentucky. The union balked and Interlake closed the plant, resulting in the loss of more than a thousand jobs and a loss to Interlake of some $37 million even after the facilities were eventually sold to Newport Steel Corp.

The remaining, more modern facilities are running at or close to capacity, which should help the company improve its profitability. The closings also make the diversifications loom larger as a percentage of revenues and profits. The materials-handling, metal powders (Hoeganaes), and castings (Arwood) businesses have all been performing well.

The dividend, which has been flat at 55 cents a quarter from 1976–80, has provided a yield in recent years of about 7 to 8½ percent. The balance sheet is in okay shape (debt recently was about 27 percent of capital), but keep an eye on it, as the trend during the 1970s was to increase debt.

* * *

INTERNATIONAL ALUMINUM CORP. (INL). Founded 1963. Headquarters: 767 Monterey Pass Rd., Monterey Park CA 91754. ALUMINUM PRODUCTS. Manufactures aluminum and glass products for commercial and residential remodeling and construction.

Sales: $109.8 million (trend 18.8% a year).
Earnings: $7.16 million (trend 19.8% a year).
What happened to a $10,000 investment

Purchase Date	*Purchase Price*	*Price on 12-31-81*	*Dividends Paid*
12-31-71	$4.72	$13.25	$5,807.65
12-31-76	$5.62	$13.25	$4,244.44

Purchase Date	*Cap. Gains (− Losses)*	*Total Return*	*Rate of Return*
12-31-71	$18,058.82	$23,866.47	12.97%
12-31-76	$13,555.56	$17,800.00	22.69%

* * *

INTERNATIONAL BUSINESS MACHINES CORP. (IBM). Founded 1911. Headquarters: Armonk NY 10504. COMPUTERS. IBM is the world's largest supplier of computers and related equipment and services. It also makes office equipment, and does a small amount of defense contracting and educational publishing. 341,000 employees. MAJOR SUBSIDIARIES, BRANDS: IBM; Science Research Associates.

Sales: $26,213.0 million (trend 12.6% a year).
Earnings: $3,562.00 million (trend 11.2% a year).
What happened to a $10,000 investment

Purchase Date	*Purchase Price*	*Price on 12-31-81*	*Dividends Paid*
12-31-71	$67.30	$56.87	$3,404.90
12-31-76	$69.78	$56.87	$2,249.89

Purchase Date	*Cap. Gains (− Losses)*	*Total Return*	*Rate of Return*
12-31-71	$−1,549.03	$1,855.87	1.72%
12-31-76	$−1,849.53	$ 400.36	.79%

PROFILE: Suppose you could find a company that was capable of tripling its earnings in a decade. Suppose that the company could also triple its dividend payments and offer a return on stockholders' equity of better than 20 percent for four years running. Just to gild the lily, let's say the company also had very little debt.

Would you give your right arm to own such a company? You might — and a lot of people did. The company, of course, is IBM. The equivalent of giving your right arm to own a stock is paying an extremely high multiple of earnings for it. In the 1960s and early 1970s, some people paid 30 to 45 times IBM's then-current earnings to buy in.

Their reward? A stock that sold, in early 1982, for about $57 a share, as opposed to about $70 a share (adjusted for splits) ten years previously. IBM had done everything described in the first paragraph of this profile, yet its stock had dropped. Let this convince the last doubter that there is a difference between a great company and a great stock. IBM's greatness was too well known.

The stock is a much better buy now than it was a decade ago. In 1971 it sold for around 35 times earnings; in early 1982, 10 times earnings. In 1971 it yielded about 1½ percent in dividends; in early 1982 about 6 percent. True, the sales and earnings growth rates have slowed down. But the company's huge R&D budget and its marketing muscle almost assure that sales and earnings will continue to grow, even if they don't resume the red-hot pace of the 1960s.

* * *

INTERNATIONAL FLAVORS & FRAGRANCES, INC. (IFF). Founded 1909. Headquarters: 521 W. 57th St., New York NY 10019. **FRAGRANCE IMPROVEMENT.** Produces products for other manufacturers that can be used to enhance fragrances or flavors.

Sales: $448.3 million (trend 15.1% a year).
Earnings: $63.23 million (trend 20.4% a year).
What happened to a $10,000 investment

Purchase Date	*Purchase Price*	*Price on 12-31-81*	*Dividends Paid*
12-31-71	$25.52	$19.50	$1,996.55
12-31-76	$22.12	$19.50	$1,685.88

Purchase Date	*Cap. Gains (− Losses)*	*Total Return*	*Rate of Return*
12-31-71	$−2,357.73	$−361.17	−.37%
12-31-76	$−1,186.44	$ 499.44	.98%

* * *

INTERNATIONAL HARVESTER CO. (HR). Founded 1918. Headquarters: 401 N. Michigan Ave., Chicago IL 60611. **TRUCKS, FARM EQUIPMENT.** International Harvester is the leading maker of extra-large heavy-duty trucks in the United States, and a major manufacturer of farm machinery and construction equipment. 87,000 employees. **MAJOR SUBSIDIARIES, BRANDS:** Cadet, Loadstar, McCormick, Paystar, Transtar.

Sales: $6,311.8 million (trend 6.8% a year).
Earnings: $−375.43 million.
What happened to a $10,000 investment

Purchase Date	*Purchase Price*	*Price on 12-31-81*	*Dividends Paid*
12-31-71	$29.87	$7.12	$5,690.38
12-31-76	$33.25	$7.12	$2,736.84

Purchase Date	*Cap. Gains (− Losses)*	*Total Return*	*Rate of Return*
12-31-71	$−7,615.06	$−1,924.69	−2.12%
12-31-76	$−7,857.14	$−5,120.30	−13.37%

PROFILE: An extraordinary gain can be a temporary shot in the arm for a company's earnings statement. But an extraordinary earnings gain is sometimes best read as a confession of weakness. So it was with the $500 million sale by International Harvester of its turbine division in 1981.

Caterpillar Tractor was criticized for paying some 45 times earnings for the division (called Solar Turbines International, although the turbines it makes are mainly powered by gas, not solar energy). In fact, the sale fetched more than the total value of International Harvester stock at the time. But the news coverage of the sale missed one of the most significant dimensions. Harvester was selling off the only one of its four divisions that had made a profit in 1980. The fact was, this giant corporation lacked the capital to nourish the turbine business, and it was just plain strapped for cash.

Debt had climbed from about 27 percent of capital in 1971 to about 41 percent a decade later. Earnings had been erratic. Some progress seemed to be evident until a horrible strike and a recession combined to produce a loss of close to $400 million in 1980. Despite taking a six-month strike, Harvester didn't win most of the work-rule concessions it sought from unions, and it still competes at a disadvantage in that regard. After another poor year for Harvester in 1981, people were talking seriously about a possible bankruptcy here.

In 1980 Harvester paid out close to $300 million

for interest on its debt. Lower interest rates would help reduce this burden, and would also stimulate demand for Harvester's trucks, construction equipment, and farm machinery. Still, the company has a long road to hoe.

* * *

INTERNATIONAL MINERALS & CHEMICAL CORP. (IGL). Founded 1909. Headquarters: 2315 Sanders Rd., Northbrook IL 60062. **FERTILIZER.** This company is the leading U.S. producer of phosphate rock and potash, key ingredients of fertilizer. Beyond fertilizer, the company is diversified into several areas, including manufacture of industrial products (mainly for the steel and metals industries); production of veterinary medicines and animal feeds; production of chemicals; and recovery of uranium, coal, oil, and gas. 11,000 employees.

Sales: $1,984.9 million (trend 10.1% a year).
Earnings: $153.40 million (trend 4.6% a year).
What happened to a $10,000 investment

Purchase Date	*Purchase Price*	*Price on 12-31-81*	*Dividends Paid*
12-31-71	$ 8.44	$32.37	$15,239.14
12-31-76	$27.08	$32.37	$ 3,638.15

Purchase Date	*Cap. Gains (− Losses)*	*Total Return*	*Rate of Return*
12-31-71	$28,369.40	$43,608.54	18.28%
12-31-76	$ 1,953.85	$ 5,592.00	9.29%

PROFILE: In 1981 *Financial World* ran a glowing profile of the company, titled "Fertile Prospects at IMC." The gist of the piece was that worldwide demand for phosphate-based fertilizers was brisk and likely to remain so for several years. Morocco, the leading exporter of phosphate rock after the United States, was experiencing political problems that could disrupt exports. So customers all over the world were turning to the United States, where International Minerals & Chemical is the number one supplier.

The reasoning seemed sound, and probably is what investors have had in mind when they bid the price of this stock up from around $25 in the mid 1970s to about $66 in 1981. But during the recent recession fertilizer sales were disappointing, and the stock was back down to $32 or so in early 1982.

The dividend picture is encouraging. Resumed in 1972 after a two-year hiatus, dividends have increased each year since. The yield the past few years has ranged from 5 to 7 percent.

Yet the long-range investor may be given pause when he (or she) looks at the long-term earnings history of the company. It earned better than $1 a share in 1965 and 1966, only to slide below that level for the next six years. Earnings climbed to better than $6 a share in 1975, but ranged from $4.06 to $5.38 over the following five years, with no particular trend. This has not been, historically, a growth stock.

Nor (mercifully) is it priced like one. The p/e ratio was about 6 in early 1982, and has ranged from 3 to 12 in recent years. The balance sheet? Nothing to panic about; nothing to write home about either.

* * *

INTERNATIONAL MULTIFOODS CORP. (IMC). Founded 1892. Headquarters: 1200 Multifoods Bldg. 8th and Marquette, Minneapolis MN 55402. **FOODS.** International Multifoods is active in numerous aspects of the food business, including grain merchandising, bakery equipment, commercial bakery products, branded consumer foods, restaurants, animal feed, and veterinary products. 8,000 employees. **MAJOR SUBSIDIARIES, BRANDS:** Adams (peanut butter); Boston Sea Party (restaurants); Hickory Farm (cheese stores); Kaukauna Klub Cheese; Kretschmer Wheat Germ; Mister Donut (snack restaurants); Reuben (meats); Robin Hood (flour and mixes); Smoke-Craft (meats); Sun Country (granola); T-Butcher Block (restaurants).

Sales: $1,088.1 million (trend 6.5% a year).
Earnings: $27.29 million (trend 10.6% a year).
What happened to a $10,000 investment

Purchase Date	*Purchase Price*	*Price on 12-31-81*	*Dividends Paid*
12-31-71	$12.62	$22.25	$6,265.74
12-31-76	$19.25	$22.25	$2,339.22

Purchase Date	*Cap. Gains (− Losses)*	*Total Return*	*Rate of Return*
12-31-71	$7,623.76	$13,889.50	9.10%
12-31-76	$1,558.44	$ 3,897.66	6.80%

PROFILE: You're more likely to have heard of Mister Donut shops, Kretschmer wheat germ, or Sun Country granola than you are to have heard of the company that owns them all — International Multifoods. The word "International" isn't puffery: the company recently got about 40 percent of its sales from outside the United States. And although several of its consumer brands are well known, consumer foods and restaurants combined have recently accounted for only a third of sales.

The big money — almost half of sales and profits — has come from the industrial foods division, which serves the nation's (and the world's) commercial bakeries. It provides them with equipment, raw grain, flour, and mixes, among other products. About a fifth of sales come from agricultural activities, including veterinary products, animal feed, and the sale of seeds.

The balance sheet features a fair amount of leverage, with long-term debt recently about 35 percent of total capital. Despite the leverage, return on equity hasn't been outstanding; it's been around 13 or 14 percent in most recent years.

Profit margins fattened up in the late 1970s to around 2½ percent (they had been just under 2 percent early in the decade). Dividends, paid yearly since 1923, provide a substantial yield, recently a bit over 7 percent. The company usually pays out between 30 and 40 percent of profits in the form of dividends.

* * *

INTERNATIONAL PAPER CO. (IP). Founded 1941. Headquarters: 77 W. 45th St., New York NY 10036. FOREST PRODUCTS. International Paper is the largest papermaker in the world, and also has substantial operations in wood products and containers. 46,000 employees.

Sales: $5,042.9 million (trend 10.0% a year).
Earnings: $291.70 million (trend 7.1% a year).
What happened to a $10,000 investment

Purchase Date	*Purchase Price*	*Price on 12-31-81*	*Dividends Paid*
12-31-71	$35.25	$39.12	$5,673.76
12-31-76	$68.87	$39.12	$1,597.10

Purchase Date	*Cap. Gains (– Losses)*	*Total Return*	*Rate of Return*
12-31-71	$ 1,099.29	$ 6,773.05	5.31%
12-31-76	$–4,319.42	$–2,722.32	–6.16%

PROFILE: A casual glance at the record of the past decade doesn't offer many reasons why you'd want to own stock in the world's largest paper company.

Capital gains? They've certainly been possible, with astute trading. But it's hard to discern much of a fundamental uptrend in the price of the stock.

Dividends? Decent, but slow-growing. The dividend yield from 1978 through early 1981 was around 5 to 6 percent.

Management? It's been musical chairs. Profitability? Uninspiring, with return on equity under 15 percent most years, and well below that benchmark in some years.

So should you turn the page (which may be made of IP paper) and forget this stock? Not necessarily. There are some positive points that might be missed on a casual inspection. To start with, the stock has been on the bargain counter. It hasn't sold for 15 times earnings since 1973. It hasn't sold for 10 times earnings since 1978. In early 1982 it was selling at about 6 times earnings.

Management has been making some key changes. It has changed the timber growing cycle, lengthening it so as to produce more wood products, not just paper. This allows a more efficient use of resources. Likewise, old, relatively inefficient plants have been closed. Most important, the company has embarked on a major $4 billion capital spending program to upgrade its facilities.

And then there's one more fact. Even if you don't happen to be a fan of International Paper's management, the company is the leading U.S. owner of timberland (not counting the government)— some 8½ million acres of it. That's quite a resource. Liquidated, it's a good bet that this paper giant would fetch more than $50 a share, which happens to be more than its shares have sold for in most of the period from 1978 through early 1982.

* * *

INTERNATIONAL RECTIFIER CORP. (IRF). Founded 1947. Headquarters: 9220 Sunset Blvd., Los Angeles CA 90069. STEEL INDUSTRY. Manufactures metallurgical alloy liners, and power semiconductor devices for steel cylinders. A subsidiary produces animal and human antibiotics. MAJOR SUBSIDIARIES, BRANDS: Rachelle Laboratories Inc.

Sales: $126.2 million (trend 17.9% a year).
Earnings: $3.23 million (trend 47.0% a year).
What happened to a $10,000 investment

Purchase Date	*Purchase Price*	*Price on 12-31-81*	*Dividends Paid*
12-31-71	$9.25	$12.37	$1,794.59
12-31-76	$6.25	$12.37	$2,064.00

Purchase Date	*Cap. Gains (– Losses)*	*Total Return*	*Rate of Return*
12-31-71	$3,378.38	$ 5,172.97	4.26%
12-31-76	$9,800.00	$11,864.00	16.94%

* * *

INTERNATIONAL TELEPHONE & TELEGRAPH CORP. (ITT). Founded 1920. Headquarters: 320 Park Ave., New York NY 10022. **CONGLOMERATE.** ITT is the largest U.S. conglomerate, comprising more than 200 companies as of 1980. Telecommunications and insurance are the two largest business lines. 368,000 employees. **MAJOR SUBSIDIARIES, BRANDS:** Hartford Fire Insurance Co.; Sheraton Hotels; Continental Baking Co.

Sales: $18,529.7 million (trend 11.3% a year).
Earnings: $891.38 million (trend 10.2% a year).
What happened to a $10,000 investment

Purchase Date	*Purchase Price*	*Price on 12-31-81*	*Dividends Paid*
12-31-71	$58.37	$29.75	$3,143.98
12-31-76	$33.87	$29.75	$3,303.32

Purchase Date	*Cap. Gains (− Losses)*	*Total Return*	*Rate of Return*
12-31-71	$−4,903.64	$−1,759.66	−1.92%
12-31-76	$−1,217.71	$ 2,085.61	3.86%

PROFILE: Under the driving leadership of Harold Geneen, whose two decades at the helm ended in 1977, ITT was one of the first conglomerates, and one of the most successful. It was certainly the largest, gobbling up some 250 companies. Geneen was held in awe by Wall Street during the 1960s for his ability to demand and get 10 percent growth in sales and earnings, year after year. Those were the days when inflation was slight and 10 percent growth really meant something.

In more recent years, 10 percent "growth" has been a snail's pace, in light of inflation — in some years it would have amounted to a decline, in real terms. Yet, lately ITT has been growing no faster than that.

In fact, the company is deliberately shrinking, undoing part of the Geneen legacy. *Business Week* reported in late 1980 that the company had (without announcements) sold off some 33 of the 250 component companies, and planned to sell some more before it went back on the acquisition trail. A stated goal was to pare debt down below 40 percent of capital (in fact, it was down to about 30 percent in late 1981). A common belief on Wall Street was that the company was belatedly ridding itself of some dogs.

Divestiture alone won't solve the problems. In telecommunications there's a lot more competition than there used to be, worldwide. In insurance, the Hartford Fire Insurance Company fights the notorious cyclicality of the property and casualty business. ITT's return on stockholder's equity, a sparkling 24 to 26 percent early in the 1970s, has slumped fairly steadily, and in 1979 got all the way down to about 8 percent. The stock, which used to sell in the glory days for more than 20 times earnings, in early 1981 fetched a mere 5 times earnings. But it bounced back to a p / e of 9 in early 1982.

At recent levels the stock may be attractive to bargain hunters — and also to dividend fanciers. The yield in recent years has been around 8 to 9 percent.

* * *

INTERNORTH, INC. (INI). Founded 1930. Headquarters: 2223 Dodge St., Omaha NB 68102. **NATURAL GAS, PROPANE.** InterNorth supplies natural gas, propane, butane, and ethane to utilities and other customers in the North Central states. 11,000 employees. **MAJOR SUBSIDIARIES, BRANDS:** Northern Petrochemical; Peoples Natural Gas.

Sales: $3,037.8 million (trend 21.1% a year).
Earnings: $209.23 million (trend 10.0% a year).
What happened to a $10,000 investment

Purchase Date	*Purchase Price*	*Price on 12-31-81*	*Dividends Paid*
12-31-71	$11.37	$31.25	$9,931.65
12-31-76	$24.12	$31.25	$3,090.16

Purchase Date	*Cap. Gains (− Losses)*	*Total Return*	*Rate of Return*
12-31-71	$17,472.53	$27,404.18	14.10%
12-31-76	$ 2,953.37	$ 6,043.52	9.92%

PROFILE: If you believe that good investments are found by looking where everyone else isn't looking, perhaps you should take a moment to consider InterNorth. It's not well known, for two reasons. First, it serves the relatively rural North Central states. Second, it serves few consumers directly. The price / earnings ratio testifies that InterNorth isn't trendy. In late 1981 it was 7. Moreover, it's been 7 or less during parts of every year since 1972.

Yet this is a $3 billion corporation, and one with a creditable, though not spectacular, record of sales and earnings growth. Between 1971 and 1980, sales grew from less than $600 million to more than $3 billion. Profits over that same period rose from around $50 million to more than $200 million.

Keep an eye on the profit margin. It has shown some signs of shrinking. After getting as fat as 11 percent in the mid-1970s, margins had thinned out to 7 percent in 1980.

Return on stockholders' equity has been better than average here — recently around 18 percent. However, this figure was reached with the help of a fair amount of debt leverage: debt was recently about 39 percent of total capital.

Dividends have been paid here each year since 1935, and raised each year since 1972. The dividend yield is substantial — from 5 to 7½ percent in recent years.

While the company is doing okay with its present business mix, it's believed to be shopping for some faster-growth opportunities.

* * *

INTERPACE CORP. (INP). Founded 1914. Headquarters: 260 Cherry Hill Rd., Parsippany NJ 07054. UTILITY CONSTRUCTION PRODUCTS. Manufactures products for sewer, water, and electric utilities and for construction markets.

Sales: $352.0 million (trend 3.9% a year).
Earnings: $14.30 million (trend 6.7% a year).
What happened to a $10,000 investment

Purchase Date	*Purchase Price*	*Price on 12-31-81*	*Dividends Paid*
12-31-71	$19.83	$17.25	$5,278.99
12-31-76	$20.25	$17.25	$3,269.14

Purchase Date	*Cap. Gains (− Losses)*	*Total Return*	*Rate of Return*
12-31-71	$−1,302.52	$3,976.47	3.40%
12-31-76	$−1,481.48	$1,787.65	3.34%

* * *

INTERPUBLIC GROUP OF COMPANIES, INC. (IPG). Founded 1930. Headquarters: 1271 Ave. of the Americas, New York NY 10020. ADVERTISING AGENCIES. A management and holding company providing centralized financial and other services to agency subsidiaries. MAJOR SUBSIDIARIES, BRANDS: McCann-Erickson, Inc.; Campbell-Ewald Co.; SSC&B, Inc.; Marschalk Co., Inc.

Sales: $416.7 million (trend 20.1% a year).
Earnings: $19.72 million (trend 21.9% a year).
What happened to a $10,000 investment

Purchase Date	*Purchase Price*	*Price on 12-31-81*	*Dividends Paid*
12-31-71	$14.17	$32.62	$6,637.30
12-31-76	$17.29	$32.62	$4,008.07

Purchase Date	*Cap. Gains (− Losses)*	*Total Return*	*Rate of Return*
12-31-71	$13,029.40	$19,666.70	11.49%
12-31-76	$ 8,867.46	$12,875.53	18.00%

* * *

INTERSTATE BAKERIES CORP. (IBC) Founded 1961. Headquarters: 12 E. Armour Blvd., Kansas City MO 64141. BAKING. This firm, formerly involved in computer leasing, now gets the bulk of its sales and profits from making and selling bakery goods. It is the third largest U.S. wholesale baker (after ITT Continental and Campbell Taggart).

* * *

INTERSTATE POWER CO. (IPW). Founded 1925. Headquarters: 1000 Main St., Dubuque IA 52001. PUBLIC UTILITY. Distributes electricity and natural gas in portions of Minnesota, Illinois, and Iowa.

Sales: $227.4 million (trend 17.5% a year).
Earnings: $13.62 million (trend 10.7% a year).
What happened to a $10,000 investment

Purchase Date	*Purchase Price*	*Price on 12-31-81*	*Dividends Paid*
12-31-71	$18.75	$12.25	$7,686.67
12-31-76	$16.87	$12.25	$4,487.41

Purchase Date	*Cap. Gains (− Losses)*	*Total Return*	*Rate of Return*
12-31-71	$−3,466.67	$4,220.00	3.58%
12-31-76	$−2,740.74	$1,746.67	3.27%

* * *

IOWA ELECTRIC LIGHT & POWER CO. (IEL). Founded 1925. Headquarters: 200 First St. S.E., Cedar Rapids IA 52401. UTILITY. Supplies electricity and gas for agricultural communities in Iowa.

Sales: $313.6 million (trend 15.0% a year).
Earnings: $17.78 million (trend 18.5% a year).
What happened to a $10,000 investment

Purchase Date	*Purchase Price*	*Price on 12-31-81*	*Dividends Paid*
12-31-71	$19.25	$12.12	$7,462.34
12-31-76	$17.25	$12.12	$4,515.94

Purchase Date	*Cap. Gains (− Losses)*	*Total Return*	*Rate of Return*
12-31-71	$−3,701.30	$3,761.04	3.24%
12-31-76	$−2,971.01	$1,544.93	2.91%

* * *

IOWA-ILLINOIS GAS & ELECTRIC CO. (IWG). Founded 1940. Headquarters: 206 E. Second St., Davenport IA 52808. UTILITY. Supplies gas and electricity to areas in Iowa and Illinois.

Sales: $374.3 million (trend 15.4% a year).
Earnings: $26.69 million (trend 12.2% a year).
What happened to a $10,000 investment

Purchase Date	*Purchase Price*	*Price on 12-31-81*	*Dividends Paid*
12-31-71	$20.12	$18.25	$8,745.34
12-31-76	$20.62	$18.25	$4,877.58

Purchase Date	*Cap. Gains (− Losses)*	*Total Return*	*Rate of Return*
12-31-71	$ −931.68	$7,813.66	5.94%
12-31-76	$−1,151.52	$3,726.06	6.54%

* * *

IOWA PUBLIC SERVICE CO. (IPS). Founded 1901. Headquarters: 401 Douglas St., Sioux City IA 51102. UTILITIES. Provides natural gas and electricity to communities in Iowa, South Dakota, and Nebraska.

Sales: $278.7 million (trend 17.7% a year).
Earnings: $25.54 million (trend 19.3% a year).
What happened to a $10,000 investment

Purchase Date	*Purchase Price*	*Price on 12-31-81*	*Dividends Paid*
12-31-71	$22.75	$19.25	$7,894.51
12-31-76	$20.87	$19.25	$4,943.71

Purchase Date	*Cap. Gains (− Losses)*	*Total Return*	*Rate of Return*
12-31-71	$−1,538.46	$6,356.04	5.04%
12-31-76	$ −778.44	$4,165.27	7.21%

* * *

IOWA RESOURCES INC. (IOR). Founded 1926. Headquarters: 666 Grand Ave., PO Box 657, Des Moines IA 50303. UTILITY. Generates, transmits, and distributes electric energy, stores and distributes natural gas, and is involved in related construction, engineering, and transportation services. MAJOR SUBSIDIARIES, BRANDS: Iowa Power & Light Co.; Industries of Iowa Corp.; ENSERCO, Inc.; UNITRAIN, Inc.; and Iowa Computer Resources, Inc.

Sales: $297.9 million (trend 13.1% a year).
Earnings: $26.78 million (trend 14.0% a year).
What happened to a $10,000 investment

Purchase Date	*Purchase Price*	*Price on 12-31-81*	*Dividends Paid*
12-31-71	$25.12	$21.75	$8,374.13
12-31-76	$25.87	$21.75	$4,707.25

Purchase Date	*Cap. Gains (− Losses)*	*Total Return*	*Rate of Return*
12-31-71	$−1,343.28	$7,030.85	5.47%
12-31-76	$−1,594.20	$3,113.04	5.57%

* * *

IPCO CORP. (IHS). Founded 1950. Headquarters: 1025 Westchester Ave., White Plains NY 10604. HEALTH PRODUCTS. Manufactures and distributes medical, dental, and optical products. MAJOR SUBSIDIARIES, BRANDS: Sterling Optical; Sterling Dental Centers; Whitestone Products; Whaledent International; Uniforms by Gilson; Community Blood & Plasma Service.

Sales: $136.3 million (trend −4.1% a year).
Earnings: $2.35 million (trend −7.9% a year).
What happened to a $10,000 investment

Purchase Date	*Purchase Price*	*Price on 12-31-81*	*Dividends Paid*
12-31-71	$14.78	$4.50	$338.34
12-31-76	$ 5.50	$4.50	$909.09

Purchase Date	*Cap. Gains (− Losses)*	*Total Return*	*Rate of Return*
12-31-71	$−6,954.93	$−6,616.59	−10.27%
12-31-76	$−1,818.18	$ −909.09	−1.89%

* * *

IRVING BANK CORP. (V). Founded 1965; flagship bank dates to 1851. Headquarters: 1 Wall St., New York NY 10005. BANK. The corporation is a holding company for Irving Trust, the fourteenth-largest U.S. bank (by assets), and fourteen other, smaller banks in New York State. The flagship bank is active in international banking, and more than half of the corporation's earnings come from abroad. MAJOR SUBSIDIARIES, BRANDS: Irving Trust Co.; John P. Maguire & Co.

Sales: $1,740.4 million (trend 21.8% a year).
Earnings: $85.83 million (trend 14.9% a year).
What happened to a $10,000 investment

Purchase Date	Purchase Price	Price on 12-31-81	Dividends Paid
12-31-71	$34.25	$51.12	$6,586.86
12-31-76	$28.12	$51.12	$4,465.78

Purchase Date	Cap. Gains (− Losses)	Total Return	Rate of Return
12-31-71	$4,927.01	$11,513.87	7.96%
12-31-76	$8,177.78	$12,643.56	17.76%

PROFILE: This bank isn't a household word, like Citicorp or Chase Manhattan. Partly that's a matter of size. Partly it's a deliberate avoidance of the spotlight: Irving Bank Corp. officials don't make public policy pronouncements, or take the lead in adjusting the prime rate, or flaunt a million-dollar art collection.

In large part, though, this bank's low profile bespeaks its very nature. It's a banker's bank. The headquarters address, One Wall Street, suggests that Irving is out for business accounts, not ordinary consumers. That's true, although the company has made some efforts to woo high-income individuals to Irving Trust, and carries out consumer banking activities at the fourteen smaller components of the holding company. In addition, much of the company's activity is abroad, where it often carries out activities on behalf of other banks. In the jargon, it's a correspondent bank.

In 1981 a number of investment analysts were keen on Irving Bank Corp., for two reasons. First, all bank stocks had been in the doghouse in recent years, and sported p / e multiples so low as to seem almost silly. (Irving Bank Corp. went for only 5 times earnings in early 1982, for example.) Second, Irving, after several years of decidedly mediocre earnings, seemed to be growing more profitable. Return on assets, stagnant at around 40 cents per $100 for years, crept up to about 50 cents in 1980 — not great, but an improvement. Return on stockholders' equity rose from less than 10 percent early in the decade to almost 16 percent in 1980. The dividend yield has ranged from 6 to 8 percent in recent years.

* * *

ITEK CORP. (ITK). Founded 1960. Headquarters: 10 Maguire Rd., Lexington, MA 02173. **OPTICAL AND ELECTRONIC PRODUCTS.** Develops and produces graphics, defense electronics, vision and surveillance products.

Sales: $355.1 million (trend 12.9% a year).
Earnings: $9.06 million.
What happened to a $10,000 investment

Purchase Date	Purchase Price	Price on 12-31-81	Dividends Paid
12-31-71	$40.50	$18.62	$111.11
12-31-76	$16.37	$18.62	$274.81

Purchase Date	Cap. Gains (− Losses)	Total Return	Rate of Return
12-31-71	$−5,401.23	$−5,290.12	−7.25%
12-31-76	$ 1,374.05	$ 1,648.85	3.10%

J

JWT GROUP, INC. (JWT). Founded 1864. Headquarters: 420 Lexington Ave., New York NY 10017. **ADVERTISING.** The JWT Group is engaged in advertising, public relations, and related services. **MAJOR SUBSIDIARIES, BRANDS:** J. Walter Thompson Co.; Hill and Knowlton, Inc.; Euro-Advertising Holding, B.V.; Lord; Geller; Federico; Einstein, Inc.; World Wide Agency, Inc.

Sales: $341.8 million (trend 19.7% a year).
Earnings: $16.77 million (trend 39.2% a year).
What happened to a $10,000 investment

Purchase Date	Purchase Price	Price on 12-31-81	Dividends Paid
12-31-71	$28.83	$23.75	$2,821.97
12-31-76	$11.50	$23.75	$4,756.52

Purchase Date	Cap. Gains (− Losses)	Total Return	Rate of Return
12-31-71	$−1,763.01	$ 1,058.96	1.01%
12-31-76	$ 10,652.17	$15,408.70	20.50%

* * *

FRED S. JAMES & CO., INC. (JMS). Founded 1941. Headquarters: 230 W. Monroe St., Chicago IL 60606. **INSURANCE.** James is a large insurance broker, doing business for its clients with insurance companies and providing related services. **MAJOR SUBSIDIARIES, BRANDS:** Galbraith & Green, Inc.; Wigham Poland Holdings Ltd. (53 percent owned).

Sales: $205.1 million (trend 23.4% a year).
Earnings: $20.66 million (trend 26.4% a year).
What happened to a $10,000 investment

Purchase Date	Purchase Price	Price on 12-31-81	Dividends Paid
12-31-71	$25.58	$23.25	$3,031.81
12-31-76	$12.23	$23.25	$5,010.11

Purchase Date	Cap. Gains (– Losses)	Total Return	Rate of Return
12-31-71	$–909.32	$ 2,122.49	1.94%
12-31-76	$ 9,017.92	$14,028.03	19.16%

* * *

JAMES RIVER CORP. OF VIRGINIA. (JR). Founded 1969. Headquarters: Tredegar St., Richmond VA 23217. **PAPER.** James River develops, manufactures, and markets chemically treated and coated specialty papers.

Sales: $561.3 million (trend 52.9% a year).
Earnings: $18.31 million (trend 57.0% a year).
What happened to a $10,000 investment

Purchase Date	Purchase Price	Price on 12-31-81	Dividends Paid
12-31-71	$N/A	$19.75	$ N/A
12-31-76	$ 5.11	$19.75	$1,652.17

Purchase Date	Cap. Gains (– Losses)	Total Return	Rate of Return
12-31-71	$ N/A	$ N/A	N/A%
12-31-76	$28,641.30	$30,293.48	32.14%

* * *

JAMESWAY CORP. (JMY). Founded 1966. Headquarters: 40 Hartz Way, Secaucus NJ 07094. **RETAILING.** Jamesway runs approximately sixty discount department stores, mainly in Pennsylvania, New York, and New Jersey.

Sales: $273.3 million (trend 20.7% a year).
Earnings: $3.91 million (trend 17.3% a year).
What happened to a $10,000 investment

Purchase Date	Purchase Price	Price on 12-31-81	Dividends Paid
12-31-71	$13.13	$8.50	$277.22
12-31-76	$ 5.41	$8.50	$619.12

Purchase Date	Cap. Gains (– Losses)	Total Return	Rate of Return
12-31-71	$–3,524.40	$–3,247.19	–3.85%
12-31-76	$ 5,707.97	$ 6,327.09	10.30%

* * *

JAPAN FUND, INC. (JPN). Founded 1962. Headquarters: 1 Rockefeller Plaza, New York NY 10020. **INVESTING.** The Japan Fund is a closed-end investment company whose portfolio consists of Japanese common stock and debentures.

* * *

JEFFERSON-PILOT CORP. (JP). Founded 1968. Headquarters: 101 N. Elm St., Greensboro NC 27420. **LIFE INSURANCE.** Jefferson-Pilot is a holding company involved in life insurance, broadcasting, and publishing. **MAJOR SUBSIDIARIES, BRANDS:** Jefferson-Pilot Fire & Casualty; Jefferson Standard Life Insurance, Pilot Life Insurance.

Sales: $803.4 million (trend 11.2% a year).
Earnings: $91.95 million (trend 10.6% a year).
What happened to a $10,000 investment

Purchase Date	Purchase Price	Price on 12-31-81	Dividends Paid
12-31-71	$24.12	$25.75	$3,689.12
12-31-76	$32.25	$25.75	$1,829.46

Purchase Date	Cap. Gains (– Losses)	Total Return	Rate of Return
12-31-71	$ 673.58	$ 4,362.69	3.69%
12-31-76	$–2,015.50	$–186.05	–.37%

* * *

JEWEL COMPANIES, INC. (JWL). Founded 1916. Headquarters: O'Hare Plaza, 5725 N. East River Rd., Chicago IL 60631. **RETAILER.** Jewel runs the sixth-largest U.S. supermarket chain, as well as a large chain of drugstores and a sizable chain of franchised convenience stores. It has a 41.7 percent stake in Mexico's largest retailer, and sidelines in restaurants, home shopping, and food service. 33,000 employees. **MAJOR SUBSIDIARIES, BRANDS:** Jewel, Buttrey, Eisner's, Star (supermarkets); Osco and Sav-On (drugstores); White Hen Pantry (convenience food store franchises); Jewel T (discount grocery stores); Mass Feeding Corp.; Brigham's (ice cream parlors and sandwich shops); Aurrera, S.A. (41.7 percent owned).

Sales: $4,267.9 million (trend 8.5% a year).
Earnings: $62.36 million (trend 16.4% a year).
What happened to a $10,000 investment

Purchase Date	Purchase Price	Price on 12-31-81	Dividends Paid
12-31-71	$42.17	$37.87	$2,833.19
12-31-76	$23.87	$37.87	$2,575.92

Purchase Date	*Cap. Gains (— Losses)*	*Total Return*	*Rate of Return*
12-31-71	$—1,017.79	$1,815.41	1.68%
12-31-76	$ 5,863.87	$8,439.79	13.02%

PROFILE: Jewel has made so many innovations in the grocery business and in its management structure that one might expect the bottom line to look like a profit gusher. The company was first (among the major chains) to offer generic foods, unit pricing, freshness dating, and combination grocery-drugstore units. It provides young managers a shot at the top by encouraging early retirement of top executives with generous incentives. Yet, despite its tradition of innovation, Jewel's results over the years have looked fairly much like those of the average big supermarket chain. Sales and earnings have grown slowly, and erratically. Troubles lately have included unsuccessful ventures into Wisconsin and Iowa for the Chicago-area-based Jewel stores, and high start-up costs for the limited-selection Jewel T discount food stores.

A flaring bright spot is Aurrera, S.A., Mexico's largest retailer, in which Jewel owns a 41.7 percent stake. When Jewel bought in (1965), Aurrera was only the tenth-largest retailer in Mexico. The affiliation has been good for both parties. Jewel has provided Aurrera with valuable know-how, and Aurrera is providing Jewel with a big slice of its rapidly growing profits, which now probably account for about a fifth of Jewel's. Aurrera operates supermarkets, drugstores, restaurants, and discount department stores — sometimes in tandem, à la Jewel / Osco combinations. All are doing well.

As of early 1982, Jewel shares were selling at a conservative multiple (about 7 times 1981 earnings); the dividend yield in recent years has ranged from 5 to 7 percent.

* * *

JEWELCOR INC. (LC). Founded 1960. Headquarters: 72 N. Franklin St., Wilkes-Barre PA 18773. **RETAILING.** Jewelcor operates catalog showrooms for selling jewelry and general merchandise. It also manufactures jewelry and does high-speed commercial printing. **MAJOR SUBSIDIARIES, BRANDS:** Gruen Industries (59 percent owned); Robert Tabakow.

Sales: $171.6 million (trend 14.4% a year).
Earnings: $—.55 million.
What happened to a $10,000 investment

Purchase Date	*Purchase Price*	*Price on 12-31-81*	*Dividends Paid*
12-31-71	$20.92	$3.87	$0.00
12-31-76	$ 4.62	$3.87	$0.00

Purchase Date	*Cap. Gains (— Losses)*	*Total Return*	*Rate of Return*
12-31-71	$—8,147.41	$—8,147.41	—15.52%
12-31-76	$—1,621.62	$—1,621.62	—3.48%

* * *

JOHNSON & JOHNSON (JNJ). Founded 1887. Headquarters: 501 George St., New Brunswick NJ 08903. **HEALTH CARE.** Johnson & Johnson is a highly diversified company with some 150 operating subsidiaries, most of them involved in health care or toiletries. 74,000 employees. **MAJOR SUBSIDIARIES, BRANDS:** Band-Aid bandages; Johnson's baby powder, baby shampoo, and baby lotion; Ortho Pharmaceuticals (chiefly birth-control products); Janssen Pharmaceutica (large Belgium-based drug company); Modess sanitary napkins; Tylenol and Zomax pain-killers.

Sales: $4,837.4 million (trend 17.4% a year).
Earnings: $400.70 million (trend 17.7% a year).
What happened to a $10,000 investment

Purchase Date	*Purchase Price*	*Price on 12-31-81*	*Dividends Paid*
12-31-71	$32.83	$37.12	$1,368.25
12-31-76	$26.08	$37.12	$1,262.63

Purchase Date	*Cap. Gains (— Losses)*	*Total Return*	*Rate of Return*
12-31-71	$1,307.11	$2,675.36	2.40%
12-31-76	$4,233.23	$5,495.86	9.15%

PROFILE: In 1981 Johnson & Johnson notched its twenty-first consecutive year of rising earnings. It has never lost its reputation as a growth stock, though in recent years earnings growth has been considerably slower than it was in the 1960s and early 1970s.

For holders of the stock, the problem has been that growth stocks don't command the hefty (or, depending on your point of view, absurdly high) price / earnings premiums that they used to. In parts of 1972 J&J, a certified member of the "Nifty Fifty," sold at more than 60 times earnings. The market later decided that no stock deserved that much of a premium. So the stock price has come down quite a way. Though J&J earned 3 times as much in 1980 as it did in 1972, it sold in early 1982 for about $37 a share versus a 1972 peak of about $44. The p / e in early 1982 was 17, still about twice that of the average stock, but a far cry from the multiple of yore.

Two developments attracted criticism in the early 1980s. The company left the disposable-diaper business, after having had its fanny swatted by Procter & Gamble. With hindsight, everyone could see how foolhardy J&J had been to spend a lot of money trying to wriggle into that market. Also, the 1979 acquisition of Technicare, a maker of sophisticated diagnostic equipment (e.g. CT scanners), hadn't yet panned out; some analysts felt it might prove a lemon.

Countering these problems were the company's broad-based positions in many recession-resistant health-care products, plus a few new-drug successes, notably Zomax, a very strong but apparently nonaddictive pain-killer.

J&J now gets about half its sales and earnings from overseas. Sometimes this brings currency-fluctuation problems, but it's worth it: Overseas earnings are growing faster than U.S. earnings.

The dividend, though increased regularly, has been yielding a modest 2 to 3 percent in recent years.

* * *

E. F. JOHNSON CO. (JEF). Founded 1953. Headquarters: 299 Tenth Ave., Waseca MN 56093. **RADIO.** Johnson manufactures two-way radios and accessories, as well as other electronic components. **MAJOR SUBSIDIARIES, BRANDS:** Fleetcom II, PPL, and Transcom II mobile radios; Viking and Messenger CB radios.

Sales: $42.8 million (trend −12.6% a year).
Earnings: $1.82 million (trend −1.2% a year).
What happened to a $10,000 investment

Purchase Date	*Purchase Price*	*Price on 12-31-81*	*Dividends Paid*
12-31-71	$ 6.37	$24.25	$3,588.24
12-31-76	$17.12	$24.25	$ 116.79

Purchase Date	*Cap. Gains (− Losses)*	*Total Return*	*Rate of Return*
12-31-71	$28,039.22	$31,627.45	15.33%
12-31-76	$ 4,160.58	$ 4,277.37	7.38%

* * *

JOHNSON CONTROLS, INC. (JCI). Founded 1900. Headquarters: 5757 N. Green Bay Ave., Milwaukee WI 53201. **ENVIRONMENTAL CONTROLS.** Johnson Controls manufactures temperature controls for nonresidential buildings, automotive batteries, and industrial instruments and piping.

Sales: $1,128.4 million (trend 31.7% a year).
Earnings: $48.13 million (trend 21.1% a year).
What happened to a $10,000 investment

Purchase Date	*Purchase Price*	*Price on 12-31-81*	*Dividends Paid*
12-31-71	$16.19	$24.50	$4,602.32
12-31-76	$13.19	$24.50	$4,075.83

Purchase Date	*Cap. Gains (− Losses)*	*Total Return*	*Rate of Return*
12-31-71	$5,135.14	$ 9,737.45	7.04%
12-31-76	$8,578.20	$12,654.03	17.77%

* * *

JONATHAN LOGAN, INC. (JOL). Founded 1954. Headquarters: 50 Terminal Rd., Secaucus NJ 07094. **CLOTHING.** Jonathan Logan manufactures clothing, mainly for women; also produces men's and children's clothes. **MAJOR SUBSIDIARIES, BRANDS:** Butte Knit; Act III; Alice Stuart; Amy Adams; Butte Knitting Mills; Etienne Aigner; Harbor Master; Jonathan Logan; The Kollection; Lana Knit Limited; Misty Harbor; Modern Juniors; Rose Marie Reid; The Villager.

Sales: $438.7 million (trend 5.5% a year).
Earnings: $6.64 million (trend −5.1% a year).
What happened to a $10,000 investment

Purchase Date	*Purchase Price*	*Price on 12-31-81*	*Dividends Paid*
12-31-71	$59.76	$11.50	$ 994.83
12-31-76	$14.88	$11.50	$2,011.23

Purchase Date	*Cap. Gains (− Losses)*	*Total Return*	*Rate of Return*
12-31-71	$−8,075.70	$−7,080.87	−11.59%
12-31-76	$−2,272.01	$ −260.78	−.53%

* * *

EARLE M. JORGENSEN CO. (JOR). Founded 1924. Headquarters: 10700 Alameda St., Lynwood CA 90262. **STEEL AND ALUMINUM.** Jorgensen processes, warehouses, and distributes steel and aluminum in various sizes, shapes, and weights.

Sales: $356.0 million (trend 12.3% a year).
Earnings: $20.51 million (trend 10.5% a year).
What happened to a $10,000 investment

Purchase Date	*Purchase Price*	*Price on 12-31-81*	*Dividends Paid*
12-31-71	$ 4.89	$26.25	$10,550.09
12-31-76	$10.56	$26.25	$ 3,242.60

Purchase Date	*Cap. Gains (— Losses)*	*Total Return*	*Rate of Return*
12-31-71	$43,731.06	$54,281.16	20.45%
12-31-76	$14,852.07	$18,094.67	22.95%

* * *

JOSTENS, INC. (JOS). Founded 1897. Headquarters: 5501 Norman Center Dr., Minneapolis MN 55437. MANUFACTURING. Jostens produces class rings, yearbooks, graduation announcements, and diplomas. It is also active in the sale of recognition materials for schools and businesses. MAJOR SUBSIDIARIES, BRANDS: American Yearbook Co.; Artex Manufacturing Co.; Jostens; National School Services Limited; Treasurecraft.

Sales: $343.3 million (trend 15.8% a year).
Earnings: $23.73 million (trend 20.6% a year).
What happened to a $10,000 investment

Purchase Date	*Purchase Price*	*Price on 12-31-81*	*Dividends Paid*
12-31-71	$7.18	$17.37	$5,470.04
12-31-76	$7.86	$17.37	$3,594.13

Purchase Date	*Cap. Gains (— Losses)*	*Total Return*	*Rate of Return*
12-31-71	$14,213.45	$19,683.49	11.49%
12-31-76	$12,111.85	$15,705.98	20.78%

* * *

JOY MANUFACTURING CO. (JOY). Founded 1939. Headquarters: H. W. Oliver Bldg., Mellon Sq., Pittsburgh PA 15222. MINING MACHINERY. Joy is the largest U.S. producer of underground coal mining machinery. Also has major operations in oil-field equipment, air compressors, ore processing equipment, antipollution equipment, and electrical connectors. 13,000 employees.

Sales: $1,095.3 million (trend 11.5% a year).
Earnings: $87.78 million (trend 11.9% a year).
What happened to a $10,000 investment

Purchase Date	*Purchase Price*	*Price on 12-31-81*	*Dividends Paid*
12-31-71	$21.96	$35.25	$3,718.25
12-31-76	$31.17	$35.25	$1,777.43

Purchase Date	*Cap. Gains (— Losses)*	*Total Return*	*Rate of Return*
12-31-71	$6,053.13	$9,771.39	7.05%
12-31-76	$1,310.16	$3,087.59	5.53%

PROFILE: Basically, this is a vehicle for investing in coal. If you think coal mining is going to boom, sooner rather than later, and for a sustained period rather than just a brief spurt, this stock may represent a good long-term purchase. As the largest producer of underground mining equipment, Joy's fortunes rise or fall with the coal industry.

One problem is that the long-touted coal boom has been longer in coming than many people thought it would. Coal shipments have been climbing, but relatively slowly. Among the reasons: Oil price decontrol lessens the short-run economic incentives for oil users to convert to coal. Labor-management problems tend to be both acute and chronic in the coal industry. And the nation's ports can't handle as much coal as foreign buyers would like to buy.

If you think these are short-term problems, you may like Joy, primarily for its mining machinery, but also for its stake in air pollution-control equipment. Much of that coal, if burned, will produce a lot of pollution, absent extensive controls.

Joy's track record in recent years has been only fair. Earnings growth has been decent, but erratic; the same applies to profitability. However, the company definitely seemed to be on an upswing entering the 1980s.

One problem: You would not be the first investor to see the potential of what brokers call the "coal play" here. Nor the second, nor the four-hundredth. The stock, which sold for as little as 6 to 7 times earnings in parts of 1979–80, fetched 12 times earnings in 1981, when investors felt a wave of enthusiasm for coal. Recently the p / e was about 8. The dividend yield is moderate, ranging from 3 to 5½ percent in recent years. The balance sheet is very strong, with debt recently only about 13 percent of capital. Rumor has it the company is shopping for a major acquisition.

* * *

KDI CORP. (KDI). Founded 1952. Headquarters: 5721 Dragon Way, Cincinnati OH 45227. DIVERSIFIED MANUFACTURER. KDI makes electrical and electronics products, swimming pools and related equipment, and ammunition components, among other items. It also distributes scientific instruments, movies, and chemicals.

Sales: $183.0 million (trend 10.1% a year).
Earnings: $4.47 million (trend 39.3% a year).
What happened to a $10,000 investment

Purchase Date	*Purchase Price*	*Price on 12-31-81*	*Dividends Paid*
12-31-71	$2.12	$4.50	$0.00
12-31-76	$1.25	$4.50	$0.00

Purchase Date	*Cap. Gains (– Losses)*	*Total Return*	*Rate of Return*
12-31-71	$11,176.47	$11,176.47	7.79%
12-31-76	$26,000.00	$26,000.00	29.20%

* * *

KDT INDUSTRIES, INC. (KDT). Founded 1961. Headquarters: 150 California St., Newton MA 02158. DISCOUNT STORES. This organization, formerly called King's Department Stores, runs a chain of roughly 200 discount department stores. MAJOR SUBSIDIARIES, BRANDS: Barkers discount stores; King's Department Stores.

Sales: $729.7 million (trend 19.6% a year).
Earnings: $3.86 million (trend –11.1% a year).
What happened to a $10,000 investment

Purchase Date	*Purchase Price*	*Price on 12-31-81*	*Dividends Paid*
12-31-71	$20.25	$4.37	$2,471.60
12-31-76	$13.12	$4.37	$2,380.95

Purchase Date	*Cap. Gains (– Losses)*	*Total Return*	*Rate of Return*
12-31-71	$–7,839.51	$–5,367.90	–7.41%
12-31-76	$–6,666.67	$–4,285.71	–10.59%

K

KLM ROYAL DUTCH AIRLINES (KLM). Founded 1919. Headquarters: PO Box 7700, Schiphol Airport, The Netherlands. AIRLINE. KLM is one of the world's largest air carriers, transporting passengers, baggage, freight, and mail internationally. The company is owned largely by the Dutch government.

Sales: $1,602.0 million (trend 13.9% a year).
Earnings: $4.74 million (trend –41.4% a year).
What happened to a $10,000 investment

Purchase Date	*Purchase Price*	*Price on 12-31-81*	*Dividends Paid*
12-31-71	$38.21	$37.50	$1,249.14
12-31-76	$37.02	$37.50	$1,289.30

Purchase Date	*Cap. Gains (– Losses)*	*Total Return*	*Rate of Return*
12-31-71	$–186.92	$1,062.22	1.01%
12-31-76	$ 128.61	$1,417.91	2.69%

* * *

K MART CORP. (KM). Founded 1899. Headquarters: 3100 W. Big Beaver Rd., Troy MI 48084. RETAILER. K mart is the nation's second largest general retailer (by sales), with roughly 2,000 stores nationwide. 250,000 employees. MAJOR SUBSIDIARIES, BRANDS: K mart; Kresge; Jupiter; Furr's Cafeterias.

Sales: $14,342.6 million (trend 15.6% a year).
Earnings: $267.06 million (trend 6.7% a year).
What happened to a $10,000 investment

Purchase Date	*Purchase Price*	*Price on 12-31-81*	*Dividends Paid*
12-31-71	$33.42	$15.75	$1,198.38
12-31-76	$40.75	$15.75	$ 709.20

Purchase Date	*Cap. Gains (– Losses)*	*Total Return*	*Rate of Return*
12-31-71	$–5,286.78	$–4,088.40	–5.12%
12-31-76	$–6,134.97	$–5,425.77	–14.48%

PROFILE: For the past two decades, K mart has been a major success story in American retailing. It was going not much of anywhere as S. S. Kresge when, in 1962, it launched its first K mart store. The stores filled a void, apparently; there was a need for a plain, well-lighted place selling a wide range of merchandise at discount prices. As of 1977, the company changed its name to K mart; as of 1980 there were some 1,700 K marts, plus about 300 remaining Kresge and Jupiter outlets.

K mart has always seemed pretty sure of its strategy: to undercut the competition's prices on a broad range of goods and make it up on volume. Despite an unexceptional profit margin (around 2 percent in many years), the company has consistently earned more than 15 percent on stockholders' equity — and in some years, far more. Costs are kept down through management controls, small sales staffs, "no-frills" service, careful site selection (usually not in major shopping malls) to minimize real estate costs, and use of utilitarian one-story rectangles for store structures. Lately there has been an increased push towards selling branded goods rather than house brands; profit margins on the former are usually higher. Consumers have known what to expect from K mart, in contrast to certain other stores (such as Sears) that have switched their merchandising strategies back and forth over recent years.

Some analysts expect K mart to overtake Sears in retailing sales during the 1980s. It has already passed Sears in retailing profits, although Sears' total profits are larger because of its Allstate insurance subsidiary.

Both the dividend and the dividend yield have been rising each year since the early 1970s. The yield in early 1982 was about 6 percent.

One possible weak spot here is the balance sheet. Debt was 46 percent of capital recently — a hefty burden which has accumulated mainly as a result of the chain's rapid expansion (it plans 2,400 stores by 1984). Interest payments may prove a drag on profits, especially during recession years (like 1974, 1980, and 1981) when K mart earnings are down.

* * *

KAISER ALUMINUM & CHEMICAL CORP. (KLU). Founded 1940. Headquarters: 300 Lakeside Dr., Oakland CA 94643. **ALUMINUM.** Kaiser is the third largest U.S. aluminum maker; other operations include chemical production and real estate. 27,000 employees. **MAJOR SUBSIDIARIES, BRANDS:** Comalco (45 percent-owned Australian aluminum producer); Kacor Realty.

Sales: \$3,222.1 million (trend 15.6% a year).
Earnings: \$245.80 million (trend 30.1% a year).
What happened to a \$10,000 investment

Purchase Date	*Purchase Price*	*Price on 12-31-81*	*Dividends Paid*
12-31-71	\$10.06	\$15.25	\$7,416.15
12-31-76	\$18.31	\$15.25	\$2,907.85

Purchase Date	*Cap. Gains (− Losses)*	*Total Return*	*Rate of Return*
12-31-71	\$ 5,155.28	\$12,571.43	8.48%
12-31-76	\$−1,672.35	\$ 1,235.49	2.36%

PROFILE: Why would you pick this stock, rather than that of another aluminum company? After all, Alcoa and Reynolds are larger (as is Canada's Alcan); and, while Kaiser has been more profitable in recent years than Reynolds, it has not been quite as profitable as Alcoa, nor nearly so profitable as Alcan. Why not bet the favorites?

One reason may be that, as in horse racing, the favorites give the shortest odds. In the stock market, the favorites carry the highest price / earnings ratios. At a given moment, Kaiser may be selling at a p / e below that of Alcan or Alcoa. That in itself may be a legitimate consideration.

In a 1980 recommendation of the stock, R. Wayne Atwell of the brokerage firm Davis, Skaggs & Co. provided some additional reasons to consider Kaiser. "Kaiser Aluminum's cash flow has been very strong in recent years, enabling the company to significantly improve its balance sheet," Atwell wrote. (Debt had indeed been pared from 44 percent of capital in 1974 down to 29 percent in 1980; it had bounced back up to about 33 percent in late 1981.) "It is among the lowest cost aluminum producers and will be making significant capital expenditures during the next few years to reduce its energy consumption and its costs." That's a key comment, since electricity costs are crucial in aluminum production.

It does seem unlikely that the big aluminum companies will continue to sell at 4 and 5 times earnings, as they have in recent years. In 1972 Kaiser sold for 33 times earnings. Something in between seems the long-term likelihood.

The dividend yield has been increasing in recent years and was around 9 percent in early 1982. The yield may be chopped, however.

* * *

KAISER CEMENT CORP. (KCC). Founded 1939. Headquarters: 300 Lakeside Dr., Oakland CA 94612. **CEMENT.** Kaiser Cement produces and sells cement, ready-mix concrete and aggregates, and engages in related transportation and other activities. **MAJOR SUBSIDIARIES, BRANDS:** Gypsum Carrier, Inc.; Permanente; Glacier Sand and Gravel Co.

Sales: \$233.7 million (trend 4.9% a year).
Earnings: \$23.59 million (trend 73.7% a year).
What happened to a \$10,000 investment

Purchase Date	*Purchase Price*	*Price on 12-31-81*	*Dividends Paid*
12-31-71	\$15.25	\$20.87	\$5,363.93
12-31-76	\$ 9.87	\$20.87	\$5,751.90

Purchase Date	*Cap. Gains (− Losses)*	*Total Return*	*Rate of Return*
12-31-71	\$ 3,688.52	\$ 9,052.46	6.66%
12-31-76	\$11,139.24	\$16,891.14	21.88%

* * *

KAISER STEEL CORP. (KSC). Founded 1941. Headquarters: 300 Lakeside Dr., Oakland CA

94604. STEEL. This company is a major producer of steel with markets located primarily in the West.

Sales: $884.9 million (trend 6.2% a year).
Earnings: $156.98 million (trend 16.5% a year).
What happened to a $10,000 investment

Purchase Date	*Purchase Price*	*Price on 12-31-81*	*Dividends Paid*
12-31-71	$19.25	$44.37	$4,207.79
12-31-76	$32.25	$44.37	$1,279.07

Purchase Date	*Cap. Gains (– Losses)*	*Total Return*	*Rate of Return*
12-31-71	$13,051.95	$17,259.74	10.55%
12-31-76	$ 3,759.69	$ 5,038.76	8.50%

* * *

KANE-MILLER CORP. (KML). Founded 1920. Headquarters: 555 White Plains Rd., Tarrytown NY 10591. FOOD PROCESSING, PACKAGING. This company processes meat products and manufactures other food products such as margarine and cheese. It is also active in recycling food waste products into useful ingredients.

Sales: $623.1 million (trend −3.6% a year).
Earnings: $4.87 million (trend −9.9% a year).
What happened to a $10,000 investment

Purchase Date	*Purchase Price*	*Price on 12-31-81*	*Dividends Paid*
12-31-71	$ 8.13	$13.37	$2,370.49
12-31-76	$10.25	$13.37	$1,365.85

Purchase Date	*Cap. Gains (– Losses)*	*Total Return*	*Rate of Return*
12-31-71	$6,444.67	$8,815.16	6.52%
12-31-76	$3,048.78	$4,414.63	7.59%

* * *

KANEB SERVICES, INC. (KAB). Founded 1953. Headquarters: 5251 Westheimer Rd., PO Box 22029, Houston TX 77027. ENERGY, FINANCIAL SERVICES. Kaneb Services is engaged in coal production, contract drilling, and other energy-related fields. It also provides data processing services to business customers.

Sales: $488.6 million (trend 42.3% a year).
Earnings: $69.58 million (trend 47.0% a year).
What happened to a $10,000 investment

Purchase Date	*Purchase Price*	*Price on 12-31-81*	*Dividends Paid*
12-31-71	$ 6.99	$22.12	$7,644.52
12-31-76	$13.87	$22.12	$2,702.70

Purchase Date	*Cap. Gains (– Losses)*	*Total Return*	*Rate of Return*
12-31-71	$21,658.52	$29,303.04	14.67%
12-31-76	$ 5,945.95	$ 8,648.65	13.27%

* * *

KANSAS CITY POWER & LIGHT CO. (KLT). Founded 1922. Headquarters: 1330 Baltimore Ave., Kansas City MO 64141. UTILITY. Provides electricity to about 1 million customers in the Kansas City area (in both Kansas and Missouri).

Sales: $446.0 million (trend 16.2% a year).
Earnings: $56.28 million (trend 15.3% a year).
What happened to a $10,000 investment

Purchase Date	*Purchase Price*	*Price on 12-31-81*	*Dividends Paid*
12-31-71	$34.12	$22.25	$7,117.95
12-31-76	$29.62	$22.25	$4,445.57

Purchase Date	*Cap. Gains (– Losses)*	*Total Return*	*Rate of Return*
12-31-71	$−3,479.85	$3,638.10	3.15%
12-31-76	$−2,489.45	$1,956.12	3.64%

* * *

KANSAS CITY SOUTHERN INDUSTRIES, INC. (KSU). Founded 1962. Headquarters: 114 West 11th St., Kansas City MO 64105. RAILROAD. This company is primarily active as the holding company for the Kansas City Southern Railway. It is also involved in data processing and life insurance.

Sales: $323.5 million (trend 15.1% a year).
Earnings: $30.31 million (trend 48.5% a year).
What happened to a $10,000 investment

Purchase Date	*Purchase Price*	*Price on 12-31-81*	*Dividends Paid*
12-31-71	$6.23	$34.25	$2,862.88
12-31-76	$4.92	$34.25	$2,440.68

Purchase Date	*Cap. Gains (– Losses)*	*Total Return*	*Rate of Return*
12-31-71	$44,983.28	$47,846.15	19.19%
12-31-76	$59,661.02	$62,101.69	48.45%

* * *

KANSAS GAS AND ELECTRIC COMPANY (KGE). Founded 1909. Headquarters: 201 N. Market St., Wichita KS 67201. UTILITY. Provides electricity in southeastern Kansas to residential, commercial, and industrial markets.

Sales: $293.8 million (trend 18.8% a year).
Earnings: $43.21 million (trend 18.2% a year).
What happened to a $10,000 investment

Purchase Date	*Purchase Price*	*Price on 12-31-81*	*Dividends Paid*
12-31-71	$25.12	$14.87	$6,933.33
12-31-76	$21.50	$14.87	$4,432.56

Purchase Date	*Cap. Gains (– Losses)*	*Total Return*	*Rate of Return*
12-31-71	$–4,079.60	$2,853.73	2.54%
12-31-76	$–3,081.40	$1,351.16	2.57%

* * *

KANSAS-NEBRASKA NATURAL GAS COMPANY, INC. (KNB). Founded 1927. Headquarters: 300 N. St. Joseph Ave., Hastings NB 68901. NATURAL GAS. This company is primarily engaged in the wholesale sale of natural gas in the Midwest and east Texas. It also engages in oil and gas exploration, alfalfa production, and pipeline construction.

Sales: $371.6 million (trend 21.5% a year).
Earnings: $19.46 million (trend 8.4% a year).
What happened to a $10,000 investment

Purchase Date	*Purchase Price*	*Price on 12-31-81*	*Dividends Paid*
12-31-71	$13.74	$26.25	$8,524.04
12-31-76	$17.53	$26.25	$3,897.39

Purchase Date	*Cap. Gains (– Losses)*	*Total Return*	*Rate of Return*
12-31-71	$9,100.73	$17,624.77	10.70%
12-31-76	$4,972.19	$ 8,869.58	13.54%

* * *

KANSAS POWER AND LIGHT COMPANY (KAN). Founded 1924. Headquarters: 818 Kansas Ave., Topeka KS 66612. UTILITY. Kansas Power and Light services northeast and south-central Kansas with electricity and gas.

Sales: $385.4 million (trend 16.1% a year).
Earnings: $41.19 million (trend 19.8% a year).
What happened to a $10,000 investment

Purchase Date	*Purchase Price*	*Price on 12-31-81*	*Dividends Paid*
12-31-71	$27.25	$18.50	$6,352.29
12-31-76	$20.12	$18.50	$4,849.69

Purchase Date	*Cap. Gains (– Losses)*	*Total Return*	*Rate of Return*
12-31-71	$–3,211.01	$3,141.28	2.77%
12-31-76	$ –807.45	$4,042.24	7.03%

* * *

KATY INDUSTRIES, INC. (KT). Founded 1967. Headquarters: 853 Dundee Ave., Elgin IL 60120. MACHINERY, CONSUMER PRODUCTS. This diversified holding company operates businesses manufacturing a wide variety of products, such as electrical components; industrial machinery; oil-field service equipment; food; jewelry.

Sales: $293.5 million (trend 13.8% a year).
Earnings: $19.44 million (trend 27.2% a year).
What happened to a $10,000 investment

Purchase Date	*Purchase Price*	*Price on 12-31-81*	*Dividends Paid*
12-31-71	$12.62	$10.75	$0.00
12-31-76	$ 7.62	$10.75	$0.00

Purchase Date	*Cap. Gains (– Losses)*	*Total Return*	*Rate of Return*
12-31-71	$–1,485.15	$–1,485.15	–1.59%
12-31-76	$ 4,098.36	$ 4,098.36	7.11%

* * *

KAUFMAN AND BROAD, INC. (KB). Founded 1957. Headquarters: 10801 National Blvd., Los Angeles CA 90064. HOUSING, LIFE INSURANCE. Kaufman and Broad is a multinational company with operations in housing, shelter-related financial services, and life insurance. MAJOR SUBSIDIARIES, BRANDS: Sun Life Group of America, Inc.

Sales: $491.8 million (trend 11.5% a year).
Earnings: $20.89 million (trend 22.4% a year).
What happened to a $10,000 investment

Purchase Date	*Purchase Price*	*Price on 12-31-81*	*Dividends Paid*
12-31-71	$42.25	$10.50	$ 365.68
12-31-76	$ 8.75	$10.50	$1,234.29

Purchase Date	Cap. Gains (– Losses)	Total Return	Rate of Return
12-31-71	$−7,514.79	$−7,149.11	−11.79%
12-31-76	$ 2,000.00	$ 3,234.29	5.76%

* * *

KAY CORP. (**KAY,** AMERICAN STOCK EXCHANGE). Founded 1953. Headquarters: 320 King St., Alexandria VA 22314. **COMMODITY TRADING, JEWELRY.** Kay is an active international commodity trading company; also owns a chain of more than 200 jewelry stores. 2,500 employees. **MAJOR SUBSIDIARIES, BRANDS:** Kay International Trade; Kay Jewelers; DeRoy Jewelers.

Sales: $903.9 million (trend 28.6% a year).
Earnings: $5.09 million (trend 18.7% a year).
What happened to a $10,000 investment

Purchase Date	Purchase Price	Price on 12-31-81	Dividends Paid
12-31-71	$1.68	$14.50	$15,264.70
12-31-76	$3.56	$14.50	$ 6,275.00

Purchase Date	Cap. Gains (– Losses)	Total Return	Rate of Return
12-31-71	$76,317.54	$91,582.24	26.09%
12-31-76	$30,761.06	$37,036.06	36.30%

PROFILE: This is a stock that has soared like a rocket, but can fall like a jettisoned rocket engine. The unorthodox tandem company — commodity trading and jewelry stores — was put together by Anthonie van Ekris, a businessman from The Netherlands who snapped up both Kay and its name for his own corporation. Van Ekris is willing to take on a great deal more leverage than most businessmen, and his willingness to leverage Kay Corp. to the hilt is a major part of Kay's story.

Recently, the company's capitalization has been more than half debt. As every business student knows, debt magnifies your results, positive or negative. In Kay's case, the major use of leverage has turned a better-than-average performance (in terms of earnings growth and return on total capital) into a spectacular one (in terms of return on stockholders' equity). From 1977 through 1979 the return on equity ranged from 25 to 29 percent, close to double that of the average corporation.

But debt's like fire: It can provide a lot of power, but it can also burn you. In 1980, according to a 1981 article in *Forbes* magazine, Kay paid out $22 million to service its debt — eating up, in the process, two thirds of its operating earnings.

Kay stock sold for less than $2 a share in parts of 1974–75 and for less than $6 as recently as 1978. By mid-1980 it had soared to about $20, but that was still only about 8 times 1979's record earnings. In 1980, profits plummeted to about $1.39 per share, down more than 50 percent from the year before. Investors, keeping the rocket up with faith, kept the share price around $20, pushing the p / e ratio to 15. But by early 1982 the price had fallen below $10.

The dividend yield is modest — 3 to 4 percent recently.

* * *

KELLER INDUSTRIES, INC. (KEL). Founded 1951. Headquarters: 18000 State Rd. 9, Miami FL 33162. **BUILDING PRODUCTS.** Keller Industries manufactures and distributes aluminum furniture and other products for the building industry (windows, doors, carpeting, etc.). **MAJOR SUBSIDIARIES, BRANDS:** American Carpet Mills.

Sales: $167.2 million (trend 6.7% a year).
Earnings: $4.85 million (trend −10.7% a year).
What happened to a $10,000 investment

Purchase Date	Purchase Price	Price on 12-31-81	Dividends Paid
12-31-71	$24.51	$10.25	$1,256.06
12-31-76	$10.32	$10.25	$1,272.04

Purchase Date	Cap. Gains (– Losses)	Total Return	Rate of Return
12-31-71	$−5,818.81	$−4,562.76	−5.91%
12-31-76	$ −63.53	$ 1,208.51	2.31%

* * *

KELLOGG CO. (K). Founded 1922. Headquarters: 235 Porter St., Battle Creek MI 49016. **CEREAL.** Kellogg is the nation's largest maker of ready-to-eat cereal, which accounts for about 80 percent of its sales. It also produces several other food products. 21,000 employees. **MAJOR SUBSIDIARIES, BRANDS:** Kellogg's Corn Flakes, Sugar Frosted Flakes, Rice Krispies, All-Bran, Apple Jacks, Froot Loops, Frosted Mini-Wheats, Special K, and Sugar Pops cereals; Eggo waffles; Fearn International; Mrs. Smiths Pie Co.; Pure Pack Foods; Salada Foods.

Sales: $2,150.9 million (trend 11.5% a year).
Earnings: $184.80 million (trend 11.0% a year).
What happened to a $10,000 investment

Purchase Date	*Purchase Price*	*Price on 12-31-81*	*Dividends Paid*
12-31-71	$13.62	$22.50	$7,155.96
12-31-76	$27.62	$22.50	$2,307.69

Purchase Date	*Cap. Gains (− Losses)*	*Total Return*	*Rate of Return*
12-31-71	$ 6,513.76	$13,669.72	9.00%
12-31-76	$−1,855.20	$ 452.49	.89%

PROFILE: Kellogg boasts something almost unheard of in American business: an unbroken string of profit rises that looks as if it may run into a fourth decade. In 1981 Kellogg notched its thirtieth consecutive annual earnings increase.

Critics of the cereal industry say that it's unduly concentrated, with four large firms controlling the vast bulk of the business. This oligopoly, the argument runs, allows the cereal makers to charge more for their products than they normally could in a truly competitive market. That may be . . . and a long-standing antitrust investigation remains a smudge on the horizon. But even if the argument is true, it doesn't explain why Kellogg is so much more profitable than its competitors. Its profit margins usually run in the 8-to-9 percent range, more than double the recent profit margins of General Mills, Quaker Oats, or Ralston-Purina.

The recession of 1980–81 didn't hurt sales of ready-to-eat cereal, which is what economists call an "inferior good." That's not a slur; it means a good that's consumed more when times are bad (bicycles and spaghetti have been other traditional examples).

In the long run, though, Kellogg isn't confident that it can keep on pouring more cereal down the throats of American consumers, so recently it's been diversifying into other areas. It's too soon to tell whether Kellogg will market its newer lines as effectively as it has marketed cereals.

The balance sheet is as strong as rawhide, with debt a mere 10 percent of capital. Return on stockholders' equity has been extraordinary — over 25 percent in many recent years. The dividend yield is above average — 6 to 7 percent in recent years.

* * *

KELLWOOD CO. (KWD). Founded 1961. Headquarters: 600 Kellwood Parkway, Chesterfield MO 63017. **CLOTHING, RECREATIONAL GOODS, FURNITURE.** This company manufactures a variety of apparel along with furnishings for the home and camping gear. **MAJOR SUBSIDIARIES, BRANDS:** Kelty Pack, Inc.

Sales: $590.1 million (trend 6.4% a year).
Earnings: $1.30 million (trend −45.4% a year).
What happened to a $10,000 investment

Purchase Date	*Purchase Price*	*Price on 12-31-81*	*Dividends Paid*
12-31-71	$32.75	$9.25	$2,244.27
12-31-76	$15.37	$9.25	$2,256.91

Purchase Date	*Cap. Gains (− Losses)*	*Total Return*	*Rate of Return*
12-31-71	$−7,175.57	$−4,931.30	−6.57%
12-31-76	$−3,983.74	$−1,726.83	−3.72%

* * *

KENAI CORP. (KEN). Founded 1973. Headquarters: 477 Madison Ave., New York NY 10022. **OIL, GAS DRILLING.** Kenai is a contract driller; also reconditions oil-field equipment and is involved in oil and gas exploration. **MAJOR SUBSIDIARIES, BRANDS:** Equipment Renewal Co.; Hester Tool Co.; Rokk Holding Co.

Sales: $96.0 million (trend 53.3% a year).
Earnings: $7.95 million (trend 66.1% a year).
What happened to a $10,000 investment

Purchase Date	*Purchase Price*	*Price on 12-31-81*	*Dividends Paid*
12-31-71	$N/A	$15.75	$0.00
12-31-76	$ 2.25	$15.75	$0.00

Purchase Date	*Cap. Gains (− Losses)*	*Total Return*	*Rate of Return*
12-31-71	$ N/A	$ N/A	N/A%
12-31-76	$60,000.00	$60,000.00	47.58%

* * *

KENNAMETAL INC. (KMT). Founded 1943. Headquarters: 1 Lloyd Ave., Latrobe PA 15605. **METAL PRODUCTS.** Kennametal is a large manufacturer of tools and machinery used in mining and metal processing.

Sales: $379.9 million (trend 23.4% a year).
Earnings: $33.58 million (trend 24.6% a year).
What happened to a $10,000 investment

Purchase Date	*Purchase Price*	*Price on 12-31-81*	*Dividends Paid*
12-31-71	$ 5.84	$36.62	$7,871.66
12-31-76	$14.06	$36.62	$2,232.89

Purchase Date	*Cap. Gains (– Losses)*	*Total Return*	*Rate of Return*
12-31-71	$52,673.80	$60,545.45	21.58%
12-31-76	$16,044.44	$18,277.33	23.11%

* * *

KENTUCKY UTILITIES CO. (KU). Founded 1912. Headquarters: 1 Quality St., Lexington KY 40507. UTILITY. This company provides electricity to major portions of Kentucky and to parts of Virginia.

Sales: $373.3 million (trend 11.7% a year).
Earnings: $18.06 million (trend –1.0% a year).
What happened to a $10,000 investment

Purchase Date	*Purchase Price*	*Price on 12-31-81*	*Dividends Paid*
12-31-71	$28.12	$15.62	$6,725.33
12-31-76	$23.12	$15.62	$4,397.84

Purchase Date	*Cap. Gains (– Losses)*	*Total Return*	*Rate of Return*
12-31-71	$–4,444.44	$2,280.89	2.08%
12-31-76	$–3,243.24	$1,154.59	2.21%

* * *

KERR GLASS MANUFACTURING CORP. (KGM). Founded 1927. Headquarters: 501 S. Shatto Pl., Los Angeles CA 90020. GLASS CONTAINERS, PACKAGING GOODS. This organization manufactures a wide variety of glass containers, plastic bottles, and bottle caps.

Sales: $400.5 million (trend 11.8% a year).
Earnings: $6.84 million (trend –4.1% a year).
What happened to a $10,000 investment

Purchase Date	*Purchase Price*	*Price on 12-31-81*	*Dividends Paid*
12-31-71	$N/A	$13.25	$ N/A
12-31-76	$16.12	$13.25	$1,308.53

Purchase Date	*Cap. Gains (– Losses)*	*Total Return*	*Rate of Return*
12-31-71	$ N/A	$ N/A	N/A%
12-31-76	$–1,782.95	$–474.42	–.97%

* * *

KERR-MCGEE CORP. (KMG). Founded 1932. Headquarters: Kerr-McGee Center, Oklahoma City, OK 73125. OIL, URANIUM, COAL. Kerr-McGee, though primarily an integrated oil company, is also the leading supplier of uranium to nuclear power generating facilities. It also has interests in coal mining, lumber, chemicals, and fertilizer production. 11,000 employees. **MAJOR SUBSIDIARIES, BRANDS:** Kerr-McGee; Deep Rock gasoline.

Sales: $3,477.9 million (trend 12.8% a year).
Earnings: $182.22 million (trend 6.4% a year).
What happened to a $10,000 investment

Purchase Date	*Purchase Price*	*Price on 12-31-81*	*Dividends Paid*
12-31-71	$21.62	$37.37	$2,806.36
12-31-76	$34.19	$37.37	$1,155.39

Purchase Date	*Cap. Gains (– Losses)*	*Total Return*	*Rate of Return*
12-31-71	$7,283.24	$10,089.60	7.23%
12-31-76	$ 932.36	$ 2,087.75	3.86%

PROFILE: Mention Kerr-McGee and most people will think of uranium. After all, the company is the largest supplier of uranium to utilities with nuclear plants. It also was dragged through the headlines in the famous Karen Silkwood case, in which the late Ms. Silkwood (killed in 1974 in an auto accident) charged that the company's precautions against nuclear contamination were inadequate. Her estate was awarded some $10 million by a jury.

What's ironic about this is that uranium has accounted for only about 6 percent of Kerr-McGee's sales recently and none of its profits. So weak is the demand for uranium that the company closed two uranium mines in New Mexico in 1980.

More than three quarters of sales, and an even larger share of earnings, have been coming from petroleum. Kerr-McGee explores and produces crude for its own refineries, with wells in Oklahoma, Texas, Louisiana, offshore Texas and Louisiana, and Britain's North Sea. Offshore drilling is a big part of the business. Kerr-McGee, in fact, was the first company to drill offshore, back in 1947.

But not all the drilling is for Kerr-McGee's own refining operations (which, paradoxically, must sometimes buy crude on the open market). Much of it is contract drilling, in which the company sells its offshore expertise to others.

Earnings have been in an uptrend since 1969, with the exception of a setback in 1977–78. The company posted its third straight record year in 1981. The dividend yield in recent years has been between 2½ and 3½ percent.

* * *

KEYSTONE CONSOLIDATED INDUSTRIES, INC. (KES). Founded 1955. Headquarters: 7000 S.W. Adams St., Peoria IL 61641. **STEEL, WIRE, HARDWARE.** Keystone Consolidated manufactures steel and wire products, plus hinges, locks, and other hardware items for automotive, appliance, and construction markets.

Sales: $401.3 million (trend 4.7% a year).
Earnings: $−2.55 million.
What happened to a $10,000 investment

Purchase Date	*Purchase Price*	*Price on 12-31-81*	*Dividends Paid*
12-31-71	$15.50	$17.12	$3,225.81
12-31-76	$21.12	$17.12	$ 591.72

Purchase Date	*Cap. Gains (− Losses)*	*Total Return*	*Rate of Return*
12-31-71	$ 1,048.39	$ 4,274.19	3.62%
12-31-76	$−1,893.49	$−1,301.78	−2.75%

* * *

KEYSTONE FOODS CORP. (KFC). Founded 1973. Headquarters: 931 Haverford Rd., Bryn Mawr PA 19010. **FOOD PROCESSING, DISTRIBUTION.** This company is the largest producer of frozen beef patties, supplying McDonald's restaurants with these and other food products and operating supplies.

Sales: $418.7 million (trend 28.0% a year).
Earnings: $4.13 million (trend 20.3% a year).
What happened to a $10,000 investment

Purchase Date	*Purchase Price*	*Price on 12-31-81*	*Dividends Paid*
12-31-71	$N/A	$15.50	$ N/A
12-31-76	$ 4.26	$15.50	$1,353.15

Purchase Date	*Cap. Gains (− Losses)*	*Total Return*	*Rate of Return*
12-31-71	$ N/A	$ N/A	N/A%
12-31-76	$26,406.66	$27,759.81	30.44%

* * *

KEYSTONE INTERNATIONAL, INC. (KII). Founded 1947. Headquarters: 9700 W. Gulf Bank Dr., Houston TX 77040. **VALVES, TRUCK PARTS.** Keystone International is active in the manufacturing of valves and other flow-control devices, plus equipment for light trucks.

Sales: $130.6 million (trend 26.1% a year).
Earnings: $17.49 million (trend 21.8% a year).
What happened to a $10,000 investment

Purchase Date	*Purchase Price*	*Price on 12-31-81*	*Dividends Paid*
12-31-71	$1.56	$25.50	$11,560.50
12-31-76	$5.12	$25.50	$ 2,991.76

Purchase Date	*Cap. Gains (− Losses)*	*Total Return*	*Rate of Return*
12-31-71	$153,421.61	$164,982.11	33.14%
12-31-76	$ 39,804.69	$ 42,796.45	39.48%

* * *

KIDDE, INC. (KDE). Founded 1917. Headquarters: 9 Brighton Rd., Clifton NJ 07015. **CONGLOMERATE.** Kidde, a major producer of cranes and fire protection equipment, has grown into a highly diversified conglomerate with more than 100 subsidiaries producing both consumer and industrial products. 50,000 employees. **MAJOR SUBSIDIARIES, BRANDS:** Consumer products include Bear archery equipment; Cosco-Tucket plastic utensils; Daisy air rifles; Farberware cooking equipment; Jacuzzi baths; and Universal physical fitness equipment. Fire protection and security group includes Belleville Division; Globe Security Systems; LeFebure; and Sargent locks. The industrial and commercial group includes Grove cranes; American Desk; Garden State Tanning; the Input-Output Division (seismic equipment for energy exploration); Victor Comptometer (calculators, cash registers); and Weber (aircraft seats and fixtures).

Sales: $2,539.3 million (trend 18.8% a year).
Earnings: $81.84 million (trend 15.6% a year).
What happened to a $10,000 investment

Purchase Date	*Purchase Price*	*Price on 12-31-81*	*Dividends Paid*
12-31-71	$15.81	$23.25	$3,683.79
12-31-76	$14.25	$23.25	$2,894.74

Purchase Date	*Cap. Gains (− Losses)*	*Total Return*	*Rate of Return*
12-31-71	$4,703.56	$8,387.35	6.28%
12-31-76	$6,315.79	$9,210.53	13.95%

PROFILE: Balance and steadiness have been outstanding characteristics of this company, an old-time fire protection equipment manufacturer turned into a big-time conglomerate by Fred Sullivan, who has been in charge since 1964.

The balance can be demonstrated by breaking the company into four roughly equal parts: Grove cranes, other commercial-industrial lines, fire protection and security products, and consumer products. Each of these four areas chips in about a quarter of sales and earnings.

The steadiness can be demonstrated by looking at the company's record during recessions. Both 1974 and 1980–81 were times that brought many companies, moaning, to their knees. Kidde chalked up increased profits in both, and indeed had an eleven-year string of earnings increases going into 1982.

Though profits have grown consistently, they haven't been spectacular. The profit margin during the 1970s usually ran between 3.7 and 3.9 percent. Return on equity was never above 15 percent from 1970–78, though it hit 16.5 percent in 1979.

The company's original business, fire protection, will probably get more than a momentary boost as a result of disastrous hotel fires in 1980 and 1981. Not only will public awareness be heightened, but fire codes may be made more stringent in a number of cities.

Dividends were started in 1972 and have been increased each year. In recent years the yield has been at or near 5 percent.

* * *

KIMBERLY-CLARK CORP. (KMB). Founded 1928. Headquarters: N. Lake St., Neenah WI 54956. **PAPER PRODUCTS.** Kimberly-Clark makes tissues, disposable diapers, sanitary napkins, newsprint, and a variety of other paper products. Also has some operations in forest products and chemical by-products related to its basic businesses. 31,000 employees. **MAJOR SUBSIDIARIES, BRANDS:** Kleenex; Kotex; Huggies; Fems; New Freedom; Delsey; Light Days; Super Dry.

Sales: $2,600.3 million (trend 11.8% a year).
Earnings: $181.80 million (trend 18.2% a year).
What happened to a $10,000 investment

Purchase Date	*Purchase Price*	*Price on 12-31-81*	*Dividends Paid*
12-31-71	$28.37	$65.75	$7,689.87
12-31-76	$44.25	$65.75	$3,272.32

Purchase Date	*Cap. Gains (− Losses)*	*Total Return*	*Rate of Return*
12-31-71	$13,171.81	$20,861.67	11.93%
12-31-76	$ 4,858.76	$ 8,131.07	12.64%

PROFILE: As befits a company that cushions the nation's bottoms and noses, Kimberly-Clark is gentle on investors. It hasn't given them huge gains, but it hasn't dumped them for big losses either. In recent years there's been a slow but steady uptrend in earnings, with an underlying moderate uptrend in the stock price. The capital gains have been supplemented by a moderate dividend yield of from 5 to 7 percent in the last few years. Dividends have been paid each year since 1935.

Kleenex, Kotex, and Huggies are the company's best known brands. About two thirds of sales and a little more than half the profits have recently come from sales of these sorts of consumer items. Most of the rest comes from newsprint and other paper products sold in bulk to commercial and industrial users.

The company has had several good breaks lately. Johnson & Johnson gave up the ghost in disposable diapers, leaving only Kimberly-Clark and leader Procter & Gamble active in that still-growing market. Safety questions about tampons, which seem somehow to be involved in the genesis of toxic shock syndrome, have led some women to go back to the traditional sanitary napkins, of which Kimberly-Clark is the leading producer. A strike at a Canadian competitor's plants enhanced the company's market position in newsprint. And the company sold off some California timberlands in 1979, thus cushioning the effect of the 1980–81 housing slump, and giving it a pile of cash to invest. The balance sheet is healthy, with debt about 20 percent of capital.

* * *

KNIGHT-RIDDER NEWSPAPERS, INC. (KRN). Founded 1941. Headquarters: 1 Herald Plaza, Miami FL 33101. **COMMUNICATIONS.** Knight-Ridder owns approximately forty-five newspapers (more than thirty dailies), five TV stations, a business wire service, and several other news- and communication-related ventures. 15,000 employees. **MAJOR SUBSIDIARIES, BRANDS:** Philadelphia *Inquirer;* Philadelphia *Daily News;* Detroit *Free Press;* Miami *Herald;* Akron *Beacon Journal;* Charlotte *Observer;* St. Paul *Pioneer Press;* San Jose *Mercury; Journal of Commerce.*

Sales: $1,098.5 million (trend 13.2% a year).
Earnings: $92.86 million (trend 24.1% a year).
What happened to a $10,000 investment

Purchase Date	*Purchase Price*	*Price on 12-31-81*	*Dividends Paid*
12-31-71	$18.03	$30.25	$2,435.36
12-31-76	$19.19	$30.25	$1,732.90

Purchase Date	*Cap. Gains (− Losses)*	*Total Return*	*Rate of Return*
12-31-71	$6,776.43	$9,211.79	6.75%
12-31-76	$5,765.47	$7,498.37	11.84%

PROFILE: This is one of the largest newspaper chains and one of the relatively "pure plays" in the newspaper business. Unlike its larger rival chain, Gannett (also profiled in this volume), it is only ankle-deep in broadcasting and doesn't get significant revenues from outdoor advertising or satellite communications. Unlike the Washington Post Co. or the Times Mirror Co., it isn't heavily involved in magazine and book publishing. Some analysts have faulted Knight-Ridder for not diversifying and for not getting into cable television early. (The company has been trying to get into cable lately, but acquisitions of cable companies have become very expensive affairs.)

Faultfinding notwithstanding, the company is doing well in the old-fashioned field of newspapers. Its return on stockholders' equity has been between 16 and 17½ percent recently, a bit above average for a major corporation. The balance sheet is solid, with debt recently about 13 percent of total capital. Dividends have been paid each year since the company was founded in 1941. The yield, however, is modest.

The company's shares usually sell for a bit higher multiple than the average stock. In 1981, for example, the average issue had a price / earnings ratio of around 8, while Knight-Ridder commanded 13.

The stock isn't especially volatile under ordinary conditions. However, there is a potential for sudden movements in that more than half the shares are still owned by the Knight and Ridder families; institutions hold many of the remaining shares.

* * *

KOGER PROPERTIES, INC. (KOG). Founded 1969. Headquarters: 3986 Boulevard Center Dr., PO Box 4520, Jacksonville FL 32207. **OFFICE BUILDING CONSTRUCTION.** Koger Properties develops and constructs suburban office buildings in the Southeast and Southwest.

Sales: $34.4 million (trend 8.6% a year).
Earnings: $3.28 million (trend 24.9% a year).
What happened to a $10,000 investment

Purchase Date	*Purchase Price*	*Price on 12-31-81*	*Dividends Paid*
12-31-71	$13.75	$13.50	$2,680.00
12-31-76	$10.50	$13.50	$3,166.67

Purchase Date	*Cap. Gains (− Losses)*	*Total Return*	*Rate of Return*
12-31-71	$−181.82	$2,498.18	2.26%
12-31-76	$ 2,857.14	$6,023.81	9.89%

* * *

KOLLMORGEN CORP. (KOL). Founded 1916. Headquarters: 60 Washington St., Hartford CT 06106. **ELECTRONICS, OPTICS.** Kollmorgen Corp. is a leading manufacturer of printed circuit boards, direct current motors and controls, color and light measuring instruments, and electro-optical instruments. **MAJOR SUBSIDIARIES, BRANDS:** Macbeth; PMI Motors; Spectra; Multiwire.

Sales: $191.2 million (trend 22.0% a year).
Earnings: $10.59 million (trend 32.8% a year).
What happened to a $10,000 investment

Purchase Date	*Purchase Price*	*Price on 12-31-81*	*Dividends Paid*
12-31-71	$2.75	$21.37	$5,224.24
12-31-76	$5.79	$21.37	$1,876.26

Purchase Date	*Cap. Gains (− Losses)*	*Total Return*	*Rate of Return*
12-31-71	$67,727.27	$72,951.52	23.56%
12-31-76	$26,906.47	$28,782.73	31.14%

* * *

KOPPERS CO. (KOP). Founded 1944. Headquarters: 601 Koppers Bldg., Pittsburgh PA 15219. **COKE, ROAD MATERIALS.** Koppers is a highly diversified company. It produces organic materials (including coke, coal tar, polyester resins, and chemicals) and engineered metal products (including machinery, piston rings, and couplings); has major interests in forest products and road materials; and is also involved in construction, coal gasification, and (through part ownership of Genex) genetic engineering. 22,000 employees. **MAJOR SUBSIDIARIES, BRANDS:** Genex (45 percent owned).

Sales: $1,929.2 million (trend 13.3% a year).
Earnings: $54.39 million (trend 1.3% a year).
What happened to a $10,000 investment

Purchase Date	*Purchase Price*	*Price on 12-31-81*	*Dividends Paid*
12-31-71	$ 9.06	$17.25	$9,903.45
12-31-76	$25.87	$17.25	$2,367.15

Purchase Date	*Cap. Gains (− Losses)*	*Total Return*	*Rate of Return*
12-31-71	$ 9,034.48	$18,937.93	11.21%
12-31-76	$−3,333.33	$ −966.18	−2.01%

PROFILE: The recent past hasn't been shining at Koppers, but there are reasons to think the future could be better. Rather than trying to maximize profits in the short term, the company has been plowing money back into capital spending. It holds patents on a coal gasification method that has already been used commercially. And it holds a 45-percent stake in Genex, one of the leading entries in the infant but promising field of genetic engineering.

Perhaps most important, for those who take a bullish view on this stock, is the fact that it serves several fields (including the steel industry) that would benefit from incentives to industrial growth and capital spending. The recent political climate suggests that a boom in capital spending may follow the 1980–82 recessions. An exception is road building, which might be hurt by the tax-cutting movement. On the other hand, roads in many parts of the country need repair so badly that an eventual boom in that field seems likely.

Recent results have been decent, but not inspiring. Earnings first hit $1 a share in 1972, peaked at $3.27 in 1979, and declined to $2.02 in 1980 and $1.58 in 1981, both recession years. In its balance sheet, and in most measures of profitability, the company has been about average.

A bit above average is the dividend yield, which bulged to 8 percent in 1981, as the price of the stock fell.

* * *

KROEHLER MANUFACTURING COMPANY (KFM). Founded 1915. Headquarters: 222 E. Fifth Ave., Naperville IL 60540. **FURNITURE.** This company produces many different types of furniture which are distributed through independent retailers.

Sales: $45.4 million (trend −17.2% a year).
Earnings: $−8.78 million.
What happened to a $10,000 investment

Purchase Date	*Purchase Price*	*Price on 12-31-81*	*Dividends Paid*
12-31-71	$35.25	$8.37	$808.51
12-31-76	$13.75	$8.37	$181.82

Purchase Date	*Cap. Gains (− Losses)*	*Total Return*	*Rate of Return*
12-31-71	$−7,624.11	$−6,815.60	−10.81%
12-31-76	$−3,909.09	$−3,727.27	−8.91%

* * *

KROGER CO. (KR). Founded 1902. Headquarters: 1014 Vine St., Cincinnati OH 45201. **SUPERMARKETS.** Kroger is the country's second-largest food retailer. It operates some 1,200 supermarkets in twenty-one states (mainly in the Midwest and South), plus about 500 drugstores, of which about half are next to Kroger supermarkets. 63,000 employees. **MAJOR SUBSIDIARIES, BRANDS:** Kroger supermarkets; SupeRx drugstores.

Sales: $10,316.7 million (trend 14.1% a year).
Earnings: $102.79 million (trend 24.0% a year).
What happened to a $10,000 investment

Purchase Date	*Purchase Price*	*Price on 12-31-81*	*Dividends Paid*
12-31-71	$16.25	$26.25	$5,675.38
12-31-76	$11.94	$26.25	$4,925.65

Purchase Date	*Cap. Gains (− Losses)*	*Total Return*	*Rate of Return*
12-31-71	$ 6,153.85	$11,829.23	8.12%
12-31-76	$11,989.53	$16,915.18	21.90%

PROFILE: In the world of supermarket management, the traditional profit benchmark has been a penny per dollar of sales. Make more than that, and you're doing well. Make less, and you may be in trouble.

Like many rules of thumb, this one's flexible. In recent years, most chains haven't been able to make a penny per dollar, and they're still doing all right. All right — but not great. That's one reason why food retailers often sell at rather low multiples. Kroger, for example, fetched about 7 times earnings in early 1982.

What Kroger has going for it is the size of its stores, plus a fair amount of exposure to the Sunbelt. Kroger's stores average a hefty 26,300 square feet (as of 1980); the new ones being opened average more than 34,000 square feet. The significance of big stores is that they can carry an extremely comprehensive line of groceries, including specialty items, plus a lot of nonfood items, which typically have higher margins than food items.

The supermarkets have been successful enough to boost Kroger into the number-two spot in food retailing behind Safeway and to produce a long-term profit uptrend, including a six-year string of earnings increases going into 1982.

Less successful have been the company's attempts at diversification. An amusement park was bought and then sold at a loss in 1980. The SuperRx drug stores haven't been as profitable as some analysts had hoped; a major program to remodel them was underway in 1981.

The dividend yield is above average (about 7 percent in early 1982), and dividends have been paid each year since Kroger was founded in 1902.

* * *

KUBOTA LTD. (KUB). Founded 1930. Headquarters: 2-47 Shikitsuhigashi 1-chome, Naniwa-ku, Osaka, Japan. DIVERSIFIED MANUFACTURER. Kubota is the leading producer of farm equipment in Japan; also produces machinery, pipe, and building materials.

Sales: $2,648.9 million (trend 10.9% a year).
Earnings: $72.15 million (trend 1.7% a year).
What happened to a $10,000 investment

Purchase Date	*Purchase Price*	*Price on 12-31-81*	*Dividends Paid*
12-31-71	$N/A	$30.25	$ N/A
12-31-76	$24.75	$30.25	$1,149.41

Purchase Date	*Cap. Gains (− Losses)*	*Total Return*	*Rate of Return*
12-31-71	$ N/A	$ N/A	N/A%
12-31-76	$2,222.22	$3,371.64	5.98%

* * *

KUHLMAN CORP. (KUHL). Founded 1894. Headquarters: 2565 W. Maple Rd., Troy MI 48084. TRANSFORMERS, METAL, PLASTIC PRODUCTS. This company manufactures power transformers, springs, and plastic products and distributes nonferrous metals. MAJOR SUBSIDIARIES, BRANDS: Quality springs; Meier metals.

Sales: $120.5 million (trend 12.7% a year).
Earnings: $.04 million (trend −42.9% a year).
What happened to a $10,000 investment

Purchase Date	*Purchase Price*	*Price on 12-31-81*	*Dividends Paid*
12-31-71	$ 7.12	$10.50	$10,540.35
12-31-76	$11.12	$10.50	$ 4,269.66

Purchase Date	*Cap. Gains (− Losses)*	*Total Return*	*Rate of Return*
12-31-71	$ 4,736.84	$15,277.19	9.72%
12-31-76	$−561.80	$ 3,707.87	6.51%

* * *

KYOTO CERAMIC COMPANY, LTD. (KYO). Founded 1959. Headquarters: 52-11 Inoue-cho, Higashino, Yamashino-ku, Kyoto 607, Japan. CERAMIC PRODUCTS. This company manufactures ceramic materials used in the electronics industry.

Sales: $690.6 million (trend 42.1% a year).
Earnings: $68.18 million (trend 26.7% a year).
What happened to a $10,000 investment

Purchase Date	*Purchase Price*	*Price on 12-31-81*	*Dividends Paid*
12-31-71	$N/A	$34.12	$ N/A
12-31-76	$14.67	$34.12	$538.40

Purchase Date	*Cap. Gains (− Losses)*	*Total Return*	*Rate of Return*
12-31-71	$ N/A	$ N/A	N/A%
12-31-76	$13,261.52	$13,799.92	18.94%

* * *

KYSOR INDUSTRIAL CORP. (KZ). Founded 1925. Headquarters: 1 Madison Ave., Cadillac MI 49601. DIVERSIFIED PRODUCTS. Kysor Industrial provides products for commercial vehicles, home construction, and refrigeration. It also operates a trucking firm. MAJOR SUBSIDIARIES, BRANDS: Blue Arrow.

Sales: $117.5 million (trend 4.8% a year).
Earnings: $3.34 million (trend 7.8% a year).
What happened to a $10,000 investment

Purchase Date	*Purchase Price*	*Price on 12-31-81*	*Dividends Paid*
12-31-71	$8.94	$9.62	$5,886.43
12-31-76	$6.62	$9.62	$5,773.58

Purchase Date	*Cap. Gains (− Losses)*	*Total Return*	*Rate of Return*
12-31-71	$ 769.23	$ 6,655.66	5.23%
12-31-76	$4,528.30	$10,301.89	15.21%

L

LFE CORP. (LFE). Founded 1946. Headquarters: 1601 Trapelo Rd., Waltham MA 02154. INDUSTRIAL CONTROLS, ENGINEERING. LFE Corp. produces process control, fluids control, and traffic control systems; also involved in environmental consulting and urban development services.

Sales: $78.7 million (trend 6.7% a year).
Earnings: $.96 million (trend 5.5% a year).
What happened to a $10,000 investment

Purchase Date	*Purchase Price*	*Price on 12-31-81*	*Dividends Paid*
12-31-71	$7.04	$6.25	$389.43
12-31-76	$3.66	$6.25	$748.90

Purchase Date	*Cap. Gains (− Losses)*	*Total Return*	*Rate of Return*
12-31-71	$−1,126.69	$−737.26	−.76%
12-31-76	$ 7,064.06	$ 7,812.96	12.24%

* * *

LITCO BANCORPORATION OF NEW YORK, INC. (LBC). Founded 1972. Headquarters: 1401 Franklin Ave., Garden City NY 11530. BANKING LITCO Bancorporation specializes in commercial and retail banking. MAJOR SUBSIDIARIES, BRANDS: Long Island Trust Co.

* * *

LLC CORP. (LLC). Founded 1932. Headquarters: 7711 Bonhomme Ave., St. Louis MO 63105. FINANCIAL SERVICES. LLC Corp. makes personal and business loans; also operates approximately 100 restaurants (Arby's and Steak n Shake) under franchise arrangements. MAJOR SUBSIDIARIES, BRANDS: Sybra Inc.

Sales: $42.6 million (trend −8.9% a year).
Earnings: $−4.70 million.
What happened to a $10,000 investment

Purchase Date	*Purchase Price*	*Price on 12-31-81*	*Dividends Paid*
12-31-71	$13.87	$2.75	$702.70
12-31-76	$ 2.25	$2.75	$ 0.00

Purchase Date	*Cap. Gains (− Losses)*	*Total Return*	*Rate of Return*
12-31-71	$−8,018.02	$−7,315.32	−12.32%
12-31-76	$ 2,222.22	$ 2,222.22	4.10%

* * *

LTV CORP. (LTV). Founded 1958. Headquarters: 1600 Pacific Ave., Dallas TX 75222. CONGLOMERATE. LTV is active in steel making, meat packing (though this operation is scheduled to be spun off), oil drilling equipment, aerospace, and shipping. 68,000 employees. MAJOR SUBSIDIARIES, BRANDS: Jones & Laughlin Steel Corp.; Youngstown Sheet & Tube (steel); Wilson Foods Corp. (meat packing); Continental-Emsco; Wilson Oil Rig Manufacturing (oil drilling equipment); Vought Corp. (aerospace); Lykes Brothers Steamship Co. (shipping).

Sales: $8,010.0 million (trend 15.1% a year).
Earnings: $118.19 million (trend 58.8% a year).
What happened to a $10,000 investment

Purchase Date	*Purchase Price*	*Price on 12-31-81*	*Dividends Paid*
12-31-71	$10.75	$16.37	$0.00
12-31-76	$13.37	$16.37	$0.00

Purchase Date	*Cap. Gains (− Losses)*	*Total Return*	*Rate of Return*
12-31-71	$5,232.56	$5,232.56	4.30%
12-31-76	$2,242.99	$2,242.99	4.13%

PROFILE: LTV was Ling-Temco-Vought until 1972. One of the earlier conglomerates, it was put together — thrown together might be a better term — by Texas entrepreneur Jimmy Ling, who was later jettisoned by the board of directors when the company showed signs of falling apart.

Ling was never reluctant to take on debt in order to make acquisitions. During the 1960s, the company's debt came to a staggering 87 percent of its total capital. The debt load is still huge — about 54 percent of capital recently.

Many analysts thought that one of LTV's main problems in the 1970s was being in the steel business (Jones & Laughlin), a mature industry with heavy competition from the Japanese. But like the drinker who next morning takes a nip of what ailed him, LTV in 1979 bit off another steel company (Youngstown Sheet & Tube) by acquiring Lykes Corp. So far, the combination seems to have worked well, as the combined steel operation (ranking number three in steel sales) has achieved economies of scale.

Meat packing was another drag. It was long bruited on Wall Street that LTV would love to unload its Wilson Foods subsidiary, but couldn't find a buyer. In 1981 LTV announced it would simply spin Wilson Foods off as a separate company.

This, it was hoped, would help free cash for the growing businesses — oil drilling equipment and aerospace primarily. The stock rose on the news — to a price / earnings multiple of a lowly 6. In recent years it has often sold for as low as an incredible 2 times earnings. The stock pays no dividends.

In 1981 LTV made an attempt to acquire Grumman Corp., but was rebuffed.

* * *

LA QUINTA MOTOR INNS, INC. (LQM). Founded 1972. Headquarters: Century Bldg., 84 N.E. Loop 410, PO Box 32064, San Antonio TX 78216. MOTOR INNS. La Quinta Motor Inns, Inc., operates some ninety motor inns in twenty-four states.

Sales: $82.1 million (trend 27.6% a year).
Earnings: $8.61 million (trend 37.9% a year).
What happened to a $10,000 investment

Purchase Date	*Purchase Price*	*Price on 12-31-81*	*Dividends Paid*
12-31-71	$N/A	$21.50	$0.00
12-31-76	$ 1.63	$21.50	$0.00

Purchase Date	*Cap. Gains (— Losses)*	*Total Return*	*Rate of Return*
12-31-71	$ N/A	$ N/A	N/A%
12-31-76	$122,075.95	$122,075.95	67.56%

* * *

LACLEDE GAS CO. (LG). Founded 1857. Headquarters: 720 Olive St., St. Louis MO 63101. NATURAL GAS. Laclede Gas Co. distributes natural gas, operates gas storage fields and is involved in natural gas exploration.

Sales: $423.8 million (trend 18.2% a year).
Earnings: $15.25 million (trend 9.0% a year).
What happened to a $10,000 investment

Purchase Date	*Purchase Price*	*Price on 12-31-81*	*Dividends Paid*
12-31-71	$22.12	$20.25	$7,657.63
12-31-76	$20.25	$20.25	$4,553.09

Purchase Date	*Cap. Gains (— Losses)*	*Total Return*	*Rate of Return*
12-31-71	$−847.46	$6,810.17	5.33%
12-31-76	$ −.00	$4,553.09	7.79%

* * *

LAMSON & SESSIONS CO. (LMS). Founded 1883. Headquarters: 2000 Bond Court, 1300 E. Ninth St., Cleveland OH 44114. RAILROAD EQUIPMENT. Lamson & Sessions Co. manufactures equipment for the railroad and trucking industries. MAJOR SUBSIDIARIES, BRANDS: Youngstown Steel Door; United-American Car; Valley-Todeco; Midland Frame; Kent Machine; Expert Automation; RPC Corp.

Sales: $235.0 million (trend 26.5% a year).
Earnings: $−2.96 million.
What happened to a $10,000 investment

Purchase Date	*Purchase Price*	*Price on 12-31-81*	*Dividends Paid*
12-31-71	$5.36	$4.75	$8,413.93
12-31-76	$8.56	$4.75	$2,941.52

Purchase Date	*Cap. Gains (— Losses)*	*Total Return*	*Rate of Return*
12-31-71	$−1,134.64	$ 7,279.28	5.62%
12-31-76	$−4,448.05	$−1,506.53	−3.21%

* * *

LANE BRYANT, INC. (LNY). Founded 1920. Headquarters: 11 W. 42nd St., New York NY 10036. RETAIL STORES. Lane Bryant, Inc., sells special-size clothing, shoes, and accessories for women and girls. MAJOR SUBSIDIARIES, BRANDS: Smart Shops; Farr's Family Shoes; Olof Daughters.

Sales: $400.4 million (trend 4.7% a year).
Earnings: $11.13 million (trend 5.3% a year).
What happened to a $10,000 investment

Purchase Date	*Purchase Price*	*Price on 12-31-81*	*Dividends Paid*
12-31-71	$31.78	$17.25	$2,253.64
12-31-76	$12.25	$17.25	$2,979.59

Purchase Date	*Cap. Gains (— Losses)*	*Total Return*	*Rate of Return*
12-31-71	$−4,572.34	$−2,318.70	−2.60%
12-31-76	$ 4,081.63	$ 7,061.22	11.28%

* * *

LANIER BUSINESS PRODUCTS (LBP). Founded 1959. Headquarters: 1700 Chantilly Dr., N.E., Atlanta GA 30324. BUSINESS EQUIPMENT. Lanier Business Products produces word processing and dictating equipment and manufactures a video-display text-editing typewriter.

Sales: $303.1 million (trend 35.9% a year).
Earnings: $26.28 million (trend 40.2% a year).

* * *

LAWTER INTERNATIONAL, INC. (LAW). Founded 1958. Headquarters: 990 Skokie Blvd., Northbrook IL 60062. **ART PRODUCTS.** Lawter produces graphic arts products; also manufactures industrial coating and adhesives. **MAJOR SUBSIDIARIES, BRANDS:** Virkotype.

Sales: $81.5 million (trend 17.6% a year).
Earnings: $11.96 million (trend 15.3% a year).
What happened to a $10,000 investment

Purchase Date	*Purchase Price*	*Price on 12-31-81*	*Dividends Paid*
12-31-71	$12.53	$11.62	$3,069.28
12-31-76	$11.25	$11.62	$2,417.78

Purchase Date	*Cap. Gains (– Losses)*	*Total Return*	*Rate of Return*
12-31-71	$–725.05	$2,344.23	2.13%
12-31-76	$ 333.33	$2,751.11	4.98%

* * *

LEAR PETROLEUM CORP. (LPT). Founded 1968. Headquarters: Suite 950, One Energy Sq., 4925 Greenville Ave., Dallas TX 75206. **OIL EXPLORATION.** Lear Petroleum Corp. is involved in exploration for and production of oil and natural gas. **MAJOR SUBSIDIARIES, BRANDS:** LPC International Finance N.V.

Sales: $147.9 million (trend 40.4% a year).
Earnings: $4.90 million (trend 79.9% a year).
What happened to a $10,000 investment

Purchase Date	*Purchase Price*	*Price on 12-31-81*	*Dividends Paid*
12-31-71	$N/A	$18.25	$ N/A
12-31-76	$ 2.15	$18.25	$1,611.76

Purchase Date	*Cap. Gains (– Losses)*	*Total Return*	*Rate of Return*
12-31-71	$ N/A	$ N/A	N/A%
12-31-76	$74,772.68	$76,384.45	53.92%

* * *

LEAR SIEGLER, INC. (LSI). Founded 1950. Headquarters: 3171 S. Bundy Dr., Santa Monica CA 90406. **CONGLOMERATE.** Aerospace, materials-handling machinery, auto parts, heating and cooling equipment, and electronics are among the major areas of operation. 24,000 employees. **MAJOR SUBSIDIARIES, BRANDS:** Rapistan; Royal Industries; Solomon Korff.

Sales: $1,530.7 million (trend 16.7% a year).
Earnings: $74.91 million (trend 27.7% a year).
What happened to a $10,000 investment

Purchase Date	*Purchase Price*	*Price on 12-31-81*	*Dividends Paid*
12-31-71	$ 9.25	$29.25	$6,140.54
12-31-76	$14.12	$29.25	$3,100.88

Purchase Date	*Cap. Gains (– Losses)*	*Total Return*	*Rate of Return*
12-31-71	$21,621.62	$27,762.16	14.21%
12-31-76	$10,707.96	$13,808.85	18.95%

PROFILE: From a 1975 low of $3.50 a share, Lear Siegler soared to a 1980 high of $41.75. Thus it might properly be dubbed one of the stock market success stories of the 1970s. There's more to it than that, however.

What looks like a simple rise in profits, if you focus only on the 1970s, was actually a comeback. Earnings grew from 6 cents a share in 1971 to $4.71 in fiscal 1981, which was the company's tenth straight year of rising earnings. However, Lear Siegler had made $1.51 a share back in 1969, a level it didn't reach again until 1976.

The comeback and the continued progress have been the handiwork of chairman Robert Campion, an accountant who took over the reins in 1971. Prune and add, prune and add — that's been Campion's formula. And it's worked well. Each year he sells off one or two divisions that are performing relatively poorly (and fires a few managers in the bargain). Each year he takes the proceeds of the sale (plus, often, some additional cash, borrowed or internally generated) and makes another acquisition. Thus, this is a large conglomerate made up mainly of fairly small companies — some 50 of them, at a recent count.

It is also one of the most profitable of conglomerates, as measured by return on stockholders' equity, which has been consistently above 20 percent in recent years. Profit margins still aren't tops, but they're good — recently about 4½ percent, with a rising trend.

Dividends have been paid yearly since 1954; the yield is moderate.

* * *

LEASEWAY TRANSPORTATION CORP. (LTC). Founded 1960. Headquarters: 3700 Park

East Dr., Cleveland OH 44122. TRUCKING. Leaseway is the third largest U.S. trucking company. It is active in auto hauling (for General Motors), delivery service (for Sears and Whirlpool), truck leasing, and a variety of other trucking services for a wide range of customers. 16,000 employees. MAJOR SUBSIDIARIES, BRANDS: Anchor Motor Freight (car hauling); Signal Delivery Service (80 percent owned; serves Sears and Whirlpool).

Sales: $943.9 million (trend 15.1% a year).
Earnings: $43.03 million (trend 15.5% a year).
What happened to a $10,000 investment

Purchase Date	*Purchase Price*	*Price on 12-31-81*	*Dividends Paid*
12-31-71	$23.56	$26.37	$3,320.44
12-31-76	$20.17	$26.37	$2,979.34

Purchase Date	*Cap. Gains (– Losses)*	*Total Return*	*Rate of Return*
12-31-71	$1,193.90	$4,514.34	3.80%
12-31-76	$3,078.51	$6,057.85	9.94%

PROFILE: Like other big firms in the trucking industry (where Leaseway ranks number three), Leaseway hopes to benefit from deregulation. Like its competitors, it also would benefit from an economy going full throttle, instead of at half speed.

There are some things, however, that set Leaseway apart from the competition. One is its structure. Leaseway gets about two thirds of its sales from three big customers. To General Motors, Leaseway provides car hauling service, through its Anchor Motor Freight subsidiary. To Sears and Whirlpool, it provides delivery service, through its 80-percent-owned Signal Delivery Service. The company is also heavily involved in vehicle leasing, both for truck and car fleets. And it is increasingly involved in planning a total distribution package for customers, including warehousing, materials handling, and transportation.

Another thing that sets Leaseway apart from its two larger competitors is debt. Leaseway's debt is about half its total capital, and it may add a bit more. The debt load was even higher in the early 1970s. To be sure, this debt load isn't as onerous as it appears: It's secured debt, and the interest costs are not exorbitant. Still, investors who value a conservative balance sheet might prefer one of Leaseway's larger competitors. (Consolidated Freightways, the nation's second largest trucking company, has a moderate long-term debt. Roadway Express, the number-one trucker, is practically debt free.) Those investors who are believers in leverage (as Leaseway is) may prefer this company.

Dividends have been paid yearly since 1965 and raised yearly since 1970; the yield is moderate.

* * *

LEE ENTERPRISES, INC. (LEE). Founded 1950. Headquarters: 130 E. Second St., Davenport IO 52801. MEDIA. Lee Enterprises, Inc., publishes daily newspapers, operates television and radio stations. MAJOR SUBSIDIARIES, BRANDS: NAPP Systems (USA) Inc.; Lindsay-Schaub Newspapers, Inc.

Sales: $148.8 million (trend 17.4% a year).
Earnings: $19.07 million (trend 15.7% a year).
What happened to a $10,000 investment

Purchase Date	*Purchase Price*	*Price on 12-31-81*	*Dividends Paid*
12-31-71	$ 7.67	$29.25	$5,600.58
12-31-76	$16.08	$29.25	$2,105.70

Purchase Date	*Cap. Gains (– Losses)*	*Total Return*	*Rate of Return*
12-31-71	$28,152.17	$33,752.75	15.90%
12-31-76	$ 8,186.53	$10,292.23	15.20%

* * *

LEGGETT & PLATT, INC. (LEG). Founded 1901. Headquarters: 18th Rd., Carthage MO 64836. FURNITURE. Leggett & Platt, Inc., sells furniture components and finished furniture.

Sales: $229.2 million (trend 19.3% a year).
Earnings: $8.39 million (trend 17.0% a year).
What happened to a $10,000 investment

Purchase Date	*Purchase Price*	*Price on 12-31-81*	*Dividends Paid*
12-31-71	$7.83	$22.12	$4,063.22
12-31-76	$8.50	$22.12	$2,584.27

Purchase Date	*Cap. Gains (– Losses)*	*Total Return*	*Rate of Return*
12-31-71	$18,244.68	$22,307.90	12.44%
12-31-76	$16,029.41	$18,613.69	23.40%

* * *

LEHIGH VALLEY INDUSTRIES, INC. (LEH). Founded 1929. Headquarters: 200 E. 42nd St., New York NY 10017. TEXTILES. Lehigh Valley Industries manufactures textiles and industrial products. MAJOR SUBSIDIARIES, BRANDS: Blue Ridge-Winkler Textiles; Mobile Pulley and Machine Works; Dori Shoe; J&H International.

Sales: $125.1 million (trend 2.1% a year).
Earnings: $.92 million (trend −19.4% a year).
What happened to a $10,000 investment

Purchase Date	*Purchase Price*	*Price on 12-31-81*	*Dividends Paid*
12-31-71	$3.37	$1.12	$0.00
12-31-76	$1.37	$1.12	$0.00

Purchase Date	*Cap. Gains (− Losses)*	*Total Return*	*Rate of Return*
12-31-71	$−6,666.67	$−6,666.67	−10.40%
12-31-76	$−1,818.18	$−1,818.18	−3.93%

* * *

THE LEHMAN CORP. (LEM). Founded 1929. Headquarters: 55 Water St., New York NY 10041. **INVESTMENT COMPANY.** The Lehman Corp. is one of the largest publicly traded investment companies.

* * *

LENNAR CORP. (LEN). Founded 1954. Headquarters: 9555 N. Kendall Dr., Miami FL 33176. **HOUSING.** Lennar Corp. is involved in the design, building, and sale of moderately priced single-family homes, town homes and condominiums. **MAJOR SUBSIDIARIES, BRANDS:** F & R Builders, Inc.; Womack-Master Craft, Inc.; Bert L. Smokler & Company; The Dreyfus Interstate Development Corp.; Supreme Lumber & Millwork Co.; Quality Roof Truss Company; Value Realty Co.

Sales: $202.0 million (trend 35.3% a year).
Earnings: $22.02 million (trend 194.5% a year).
What happened to a $10,000 investment

Purchase Date	*Purchase Price*	*Price on 12-31-81*	*Dividends Paid*
12-31-71	$11.75	$12.75	$ 490.78
12-31-76	$ 2.17	$12.75	$2,661.54

Purchase Date	*Cap. Gains (− Losses)*	*Total Return*	*Rate of Return*
12-31-71	$ 851.06	$ 1,341.84	1.27%
12-31-76	$48,846.15	$51,507.69	43.81%

* * *

LENOX, INC. (LNX). Founded 1889. Headquarters: Old Princeton Pike, Lawrenceville NJ 08648. **CERAMICS.** Lenox, Inc., manufactures ceramics, jewelry, crystal, glassware, and candles. **MAJOR SUBSIDIARIES, BRANDS:** Lenox China, Inc.; Lenox Crystal, Inc.; Imperial Glass Corp.; Keepsake, Inc.; Rosenthal; Artcarved Class Rings; Taunton Silversmiths, Ltd.; Lenox Awards, Inc.; Lenox Candles, Inc.; Artcarved, Inc.; Eisenstadt Co.

Sales: $242.6 million (trend 15.2% a year).
Earnings: $18.78 million (trend 19.5% a year).
What happened to a $10,000 investment

Purchase Date	*Purchase Price*	*Price on 12-31-81*	*Dividends Paid*
12-31-71	$30.64	$36.25	$3,247.68
12-31-76	$23.50	$36.25	$2,782.98

Purchase Date	*Cap. Gains (− Losses)*	*Total Return*	*Rate of Return*
12-31-71	$1,831.99	$5,079.67	4.19%
12-31-76	$5,425.53	$8,208.51	12.73%

* * *

LESLIE FAY INC. (LES). Founded 1959. Headquarters: 1400 Broadway, New York NY 10018. **WOMEN'S CLOTHING.** Leslie Fay Inc. designs and manufactures women's fashions. **MAJOR SUBSIDIARIES, BRANDS:** Leslie Fay; Kasper for Joan Leslie; Leslie Pomer; L.F. Petite; Castleberry Knits Ltd.; Sassco Fashions Ltd.; Sasson; Breckenridge; Personal Sportswear; J.L. Sport.

Sales: $236.9 million (trend 9.0% a year).
Earnings: $8.21 million (trend 19.1% a year).
What happened to a $10,000 investment

Purchase Date	*Purchase Price*	*Price on 12-31-81*	*Dividends Paid*
12-31-71	$14.01	$13.87	$2,397.75
12-31-76	$ 7.12	$13.87	$2,610.53

Purchase Date	*Cap. Gains (− Losses)*	*Total Return*	*Rate of Return*
12-31-71	$ −93.25	$ 2,304.49	2.10%
12-31-76	$9,473.68	$12,084.21	17.17%

* * *

LEUCADIA NATIONAL CORP. (LUK). Founded 1968. Headquarters: 1290 Avenue of the Americas, New York NY 10019. **PERSONAL LOANS.** Leucadia National Corp. is active in consumer lending, life insurance, and property-casualty insurance. **MAJOR SUBSIDIARIES, BRANDS:** Leucadia, Inc.; American Investment Co.; City Finance; Public Finance; Domestic Finance; Charter National Life Insurance Co.

Sales: $39.1 million (trend 211.3% a year).
Earnings: $.66 million.
What happened to a $10,000 investment

Purchase Date	*Purchase Price*	*Price on 12-31-81*	*Dividends Paid*
12-31-71	$19.75	$13.12	$556.96
12-31-76	$ 5.87	$13.12	$ 0.00

Purchase Date	*Cap. Gains (− Losses)*	*Total Return*	*Rate of Return*
12-31-71	$−3,354.43	$−2,797.47	−3.23%
12-31-76	$ 12,340.43	$ 12,340.43	17.44%

* * *

LEVI STRAUSS & CO. (LVI). Founded 1850; went public in 1971. Headquarters: 2 Embarcadero Center, San Francisco CA 94106. **CLOTHING.** Levi Strauss is the world's largest clothing manufacturer and the leading manufacturer of blue jeans. 48,000 employees. **MAJOR SUBSIDIARIES, BRANDS:** Levi's; Koracorp.

Sales: $2,840.8 million (trend 21.6% a year).
Earnings: $223.69 million (trend 26.1% a year).
What happened to a $10,000 investment

Purchase Date	*Purchase Price*	*Price on 12-31-81*	*Dividends Paid*
12-31-71	$11.91	$27.25	$4,951.18
12-31-76	$13.62	$27.25	$3,844.04

Purchase Date	*Cap. Gains (− Losses)*	*Total Return*	*Rate of Return*
12-31-71	$12,887.14	$17,838.32	10.78%
12-31-76	$10,000.00	$13,844.04	18.98%

PROFILE: Reading this company's financial statistics would be enough to make you bust the buttons off your pants . . . unless you happen to be wearing the company's jeans, which feature rivets. Most amazing is the return on stockholders' equity, which has been above 30 percent in several recent years and consistently above 25 percent in the late 1970s. (The average big company manages about 15 percent.)

A gee-whiz return on equity is usually achieved (if at all) with the help of a big dollop of debt. That's not the case at Levi Strauss. The balance sheet, with debt recently only 14 percent of total capital, is as strong as double-thick denim.

Jeans, the original product of this company and its mainstay, account for about half of its sales. (The company holds about a 40-percent share of the market.) But there are signs that the jeans boom is finally ending. In recent years the company has diversified into a broad range of men's, women's, and boy's clothing. It makes some 120,000 items and is, according to Standard & Poor's, the world's largest clothing manufacturer.

It's also very much of a family corporation, in both senses of that word. The Haas family, which married into the Strauss family early this century, controls close to half the stock. Employees also own a significant number of shares; about two dozen of them became millionaires when the company went public in 1971.

The big question now is whether the company can continue the kind of earnings growth it's shown in recent years. A seven-year streak of rising earnings was snapped in 1981. Can it do, in a broad line of clothing, what it's done in jeans? Wall Street, unconvinced, accorded the stock a below-average multiple (6 times earnings) in early 1982. But the track record is sparkling.

* * *

LEVITZ FURNITURE CORP. (LEV). Founded 1965. Headquarters: 1317 N.W. 167th St., Miami FL 33169. **FURNITURE.** Levitz Furniture Corp. sells furniture in warehouse-showrooms.

Sales: $500.8 million (trend 10.3% a year).
Earnings: $13.18 million (trend 21.6% a year).
What happened to a $10,000 investment

Purchase Date	*Purchase Price*	*Price on 12-31-81*	*Dividends Paid*
12-31-71	$158.33	$34.50	$ 173.68
12-31-76	$ 25.00	$34.50	$1,100.00

Purchase Date	*Cap. Gains (− Losses)*	*Total Return*	*Rate of Return*
12-31-71	$−7,821.05	$−7,647.37	−13.47%
12-31-76	$ 3,800.00	$ 4,900.00	8.30%

* * *

LIBBEY-OWENS-FORD CO. (LOF). Founded 1916. Headquarters: 811 Madison Ave., Toledo OH 43695. **GLASS, FLUID TRANSMISSION.** Libbey-Owens-Ford is a major producer of glass and glass products and of fluid transmission equipment. Also produces plastics and plastic products. 20,000 employees. **MAJOR SUBSIDIARIES, BRANDS:** Aeroquip.

Sales: $1,159.9 million (trend 11.3% a year).
Earnings: $24.01 million (trend −1.3% a year).
What happened to a $10,000 investment

Purchase Date	*Purchase Price*	*Price on 12-31-81*	*Dividends Paid*
12-31-71	$48.37	$23.25	$4,056.85
12-31-76	$37.37	$23.25	$2,595.32

Purchase Date	*Cap. Gains (− Losses)*	*Total Return*	*Rate of Return*
12-31-71	$−5,193.80	$−1,136.95	−1.20%
12-31-76	$−3,779.26	$−1,183.95	−2.49%

PROFILE: Despite this company's name, it has no connection with Ford Motor Company; in fact, General Motors is its biggest customer. It supplies GM with close to three quarters of the glass used in GM cars. The doldrums of the auto industry in the period 1979–81 have been reflected here. The 1980 earnings ($2.17 a share) were less than half of the peak earnings ($5.50 a share) posted in 1978. The best year before that was 1973 ($5.15 a share).

If you're getting the idea that earnings are cyclical here, you're right. What else could you expect from a company that sells primarily to the auto and housing industries? However, the fluid transmission business — in other words, the Aeroquip subsidiary — has made the company less dependent on autos and housing than it used to be.

Cyclicality isn't necessarily a curse if it's cyclical growth, but growth has been slow here. Sales have risen at a rather decent clip, but the long-term upward trend in earnings has been visible only with the aid of a microscope. Yet investors haven't lost faith. In early 1982, for example, the stock was selling at 28 times the previous twelve months' meager earnings, a lofty multiple at the time. What this means is that investors were already anticipating a future rebound in housing and, particularly, autos. When such a rebound finally comes, the stock may take a brisk run up. But the long-term prospects are less clear. One development on the horizon is the company's toe-dipping into the field of solar power.

* * *

THE LIBERTY CORP. (LC). Founded 1967. Headquarters: PO Box 789, Greenville SC 29602. **FINANCIAL SERVICES, BROADCASTING.** The Liberty Corp. is involved in life insurance, broadcasting, and savings and loan operation. **MAJOR SUBSIDIARIES, BRANDS:** Liberty Life Insurance Co.; Cosmos Broadcasting Corp.; United Fidelity Life Insurance Co.; Greater Arizona Savings and Loan Association.

Sales: $300.0 million (trend 16.3% a year).
Earnings: $29.75 million (trend 15.0% a year).
What happened to a $10,000 investment

Purchase Date	*Purchase Price*	*Price on 12-31-81*	*Dividends Paid*
12-31-71	$9.94	$14.62	$3,582.39
12-31-76	$9.37	$14.62	$2,842.67

Purchase Date	*Cap. Gains (− Losses)*	*Total Return*	*Rate of Return*
12-31-71	$4,716.98	$8,299.37	6.23%
12-31-76	$5,600.00	$8,442.67	13.02%

* * *

LIBERTY NATIONAL INSURANCE HOLDING CO. (LNH). Founded 1979. Headquarters: 301 S. 20th St., Birmingham AL 35202. **INSURANCE.** Liberty National Insurance Holding Co. is the holding company for a large life insurance company; has sideline in funeral homes. **MAJOR SUBSIDIARIES, BRANDS:** Liberty National Life Insurance Co.; Rockford Life; Brown-Service Funeral Homes Co.

Sales: $475.4 million (trend 10.2% a year).
Earnings: $65.65 million (trend 9.0% a year).
What happened to a $10,000 investment

Purchase Date	*Purchase Price*	*Price on 12-31-81*	*Dividends Paid*
12-31-71	$26.06	$26.25	$2,937.48
12-31-76	$25.25	$26.25	$2,130.69

Purchase Date	*Cap. Gains (− Losses)*	*Total Return*	*Rate of Return*
12-31-71	$ 71.69	$3,009.17	2.67%
12-31-76	$396.04	$2,526.73	4.61%

* * *

LIFEMARK CORP. (LMK). Founded 1956. Headquarters: 3800 Buffalo Speedway, Houston TX 77098. **HOSPITALS.** Lifemark Corp. manages hospitals and dental laboratories.

Sales: $175.3 million (trend 23.0% a year).
Earnings: $10.06 million (trend 35.6% a year).
What happened to a $10,000 investment

Purchase Date	*Purchase Price*	*Price on 12-31-81*	*Dividends Paid*
12-31-71	$3.92	$28.25	$3,562.71
12-31-76	$2.76	$28.25	$4,491.96

Purchase Date	*Cap. Gains (– Losses)*	*Total Return*	*Rate of Return*
12-31-71	$62,064.48	$65,627.18	22.42%
12-31-76	$92,352.45	$96,844.41	60.60%

* * *

ELI LILLY AND CO. (LLY). Founded 1901. Headquarters: 307 E. McCarty St., Indianapolis IN 46225. **DRUGS.** Lilly is one of the nation's largest makers of prescription drugs and a major producer of agricultural chemicals and animal care products. Also produces over-the-counter drugs and owns a major cosmetics manufacturer. 28,000 employees. **MAJOR SUBSIDIARIES, BRANDS:** Elizabeth Arden; Darvon; Keflin; Mandol; Treflan.

Sales: $2,558.6 million (trend 16.5% a year).
Earnings: $341.97 million (trend 15.1% a year).
What happened to a $10,000 investment

Purchase Date	*Purchase Price*	*Price on 12-31-81*	*Dividends Paid*
12-31-71	$56.87	$56.25	$2,538.02
12-31-76	$47.62	$56.25	$2,014.70

Purchase Date	*Cap. Gains (– Losses)*	*Total Return*	*Rate of Return*
12-31-71	$–109.89	$2,428.13	2.20%
12-31-76	$ 1,811.02	$3,825.72	6.69%

PROFILE: Think of Lilly as a three-legged stool, but with legs of unequal thickness.

The strongest leg is the drug business. Pharmaceuticals accounted for about half of Lilly's sales and earnings in recent years. The company has a particularly strong position in broad-spectrum antibiotics. It is well known in the trade for its research efforts and for its sales force. According to *Business Week,* Lilly was recently spending about $6,600 per employee in research, the highest figure in the drug industry. Research and development spending amounted to about 7.9 percent of sales, not the highest in the industry, but close to it. The sales force consists of more than 1,000 people, 80 percent of whom are registered pharmacists, according to a 1979 report in *Business Week.* A drug analyst for Dean Witter Reynolds told the magazine that Lilly's sales force had a reputation for exploiting any advantage that could be likened to a technique in chess: "You get a pawn advantage, which is . . . minor . . . and you can parlay that into a decisive game-winning advantage."

The second leg of the business, and one that has contributed disproportionately to profits, is the agricultural area, with the herbicide Treflan being the single best-known product. This area chipped in more than 40 percent of 1979 profits.

The remainder of the company is the Elizabeth Arden cosmetics subsidiary, picked up in 1971. It has yet to be a major profit producer.

Earnings for the company have been in a long-sustained uptrend, but the stock has fluctuated erratically over the past decade. Dividends, though they've been increased regularly, remain moderate. The company has almost no long-term debt.

* * *

LINCOLN NATIONAL CORP. (LNC). Founded 1905. Headquarters: 1300 S. Clinton St., Fort Wayne IN 46801. **INSURANCE.** The corporation is a holding company for Lincoln National Life Insurance Co., which sells both life and group health insurance, and for several smaller insurance companies selling life, property and casualty, and title insurance. The company is also active in reinsurance. 8,000 employees. **MAJOR SUBSIDIARIES, BRANDS:** Lincoln National Life Insurance Co.; Chicago Title & Trust.

Sales: $2,692.9 million (trend 13.4% a year).
Earnings: $156.63 million (trend 21.5% a year).
What happened to a $10,000 investment

Purchase Date	*Purchase Price*	*Price on 12-31-81*	*Dividends Paid*
12-31-71	$N/A	$40.62	$ N/A
12-31-76	$36.25	$40.62	$3,434.48

Purchase Date	*Cap. Gains (– Losses)*	*Total Return*	*Rate of Return*
12-31-71	$ N/A	$ N/A	N/A%
12-31-76	$1,206.90	$4,641.38	7.92%

PROFILE: The company likes to point out in advertisements that it shares a name with Abraham Lincoln. It may be able to use some of old Abe's patience and fortitude in the years ahead. The insurance marketplace is full of competition. And consumers in recent years have begun to make an effort to understand the prices of insurance products and to shop for price. This may mean smaller profit margins for many insurers. Lincoln's profit margins can't stand a great deal of belt-tightening, as they're not among the fatter ones in the industry.

One thing that will help the company withstand buffeting in any one sphere is its balance. Lincoln's book of business is well distributed among life insurance, health insurance, property and casualty insurance, and title insurance. It's unlikely that all four areas would run into bad years simultaneously.

The balance is one reason why this stock may appeal to conservative investors. The dividend is another: The yield in recent years has been 6–8 percent, and dividends have been paid yearly since 1920. The solid balance sheet is a third. And the low price / earnings ratio (only 6 in early 1982) is a fourth.

But for some investors this stock may be too steady, too conservative. The stock's yearly high has been between $44 and $48 a share in 1978, 1979, 1980, and 1981, not to mention 1971–73 and 1965–66. For many investors, the dividend has been the total return.

* * *

LINCOLN NATIONAL DIRECT PLACEMENT FUND INC. (LND). Founded 1976. Headquarters: 111 W. Washington St. Chicago IL 60602. **INVESTMENT COMPANY.** Lincoln National Direct Placement Fund Inc. is designed to provide a high level of current income from interest and dividends on fixed-income securities and selected stocks.

* * *

THE LIONEL CORP. (LIO). Founded 1918. Headquarters: 9 W. 57th St., New York NY 10019. **ELECTRIC COMPONENTS, TOYS.** The Lionel Corp. sells toys and leisure products; also produces electronic components for computer, telecommunications, and aerospace industries. The company filed for protection under Chapter 11 of the Bankruptcy Code in 1982. **MAJOR SUBSIDIARIES, BRANDS:** Lionel Leisure, Inc.; Dale Electronics, Inc.

Sales: $287.4 million (trend 18.2% a year).
Earnings: $5.43 million (trend 34.1% a year).
What happened to a $10,000 investment

Purchase Date	*Purchase Price*	*Price on 12-31-81*	*Dividends Paid*
12-31-71	$5.67	$7.12	$1,136.31
12-31-76	$2.27	$7.12	$2,840.77

Purchase Date	*Cap. Gains (— Losses)*	*Total Return*	*Rate of Return*
12-31-71	$ 2,568.48	$ 3,704.79	3.20%
12-31-76	$21,421.19	$24,261.96	27.93%

* * *

LITTON INDUSTRIES, INC. (LIT). Founded 1953. Headquarters: 360 N. Crescent Dr., Beverly Hills CA 90210. **CONGLOMERATE.** Litton is a highly diversified conglomerate with more than 100 subsidiaries. Among the chief areas of operation are ship building, defense contracting, electronics, seismic exploration, microwave oven manufacture, and office equipment. Teledyne Inc. owns approximately 27 percent of the common stock. 75,000 employees. **MAJOR SUBSIDIARIES, BRANDS:** Litton; Monroe; Sweda.

Sales: $4,936.0 million (trend 8.0% a year).
Earnings: $307.19 million (trend 73.3% a year).
What happened to a $10,000 investment

Purchase Date	*Purchase Price*	*Price on 12-31-81*	*Dividends Paid*
12-31-71	$17.31	$56.37	$1,285.24
12-31-76	$13.34	$56.37	$1,666.71

Purchase Date	*Cap. Gains (— Losses)*	*Total Return*	*Rate of Return*
12-31-71	$22,575.61	$23,860.85	12.97%
12-31-76	$32,244.29	$33,911.00	34.44%

PROFILE: Litton was the first of the modern conglomerates, preceding by a few years the empire-building movements at ITT and Gulf & Western. It was founded in 1953 under the name Electro Dynamics, a name singularly appropriate for its grandiosity and bravado. Founders "Tex" Thornton (still chairman) and his right-hand man Roy Ash (later of the Nixon administration and AM International) plunged immediately into a flurry of acquisitions, including a smallish company that bequeathed this behemoth its present name.

To anyone with a truncated memory, this stock could easily be made to look like the growth stock of the century. You could have bought in for less than $3 a share in either 1974 or 1975 and ridden the stock up to a high of almost $89 a share in 1980. Some ride.

But those with memories going back to the go-go days of the 1960s may recall that Litton stock also sold for more than $88 a share back in 1967, before it began one of the more sickening slides in the modern history of the stock market. Color this one volatile. The history includes losses in 1972, 1974, and 1978, but record profits in 1979 and 1980.

Though anything but tame, Litton shares are a more conservative investment now than they were in the 1960s or early 1970s. Under President Fred O'Green, debt has been trimmed back substantially. It was about 44 percent of capital in 1974, but only about 17 percent in 1980. The price / earnings ratio is a lot more conservative these days, too. For example, it was about 7 in early 1982. Back in the 1960s the shares often fetched 30 to 40 times earnings. Litton has even settled down to paying a modest dividend, starting in 1979.

* * *

LOCKHEED CORP. (LK). Founded 1932. Headquarters: 2555 N. Hollywood Way, Burbank CA 91520. AEROSPACE. Lockheed is a major producer of aircraft, missiles, and other aerospace items and a leading defense contractor. It is involved to a relatively small extent in naval ship building. 75,000 employees. MAJOR SUBSIDIARIES, BRANDS: L-1011 (TriStar) jet (recently discontinued); C-130, C-141, CP-140, C-5N, P-3, and TR-1 military planes.

Sales: $5,395.7 million (trend 9.2% a year).
Earnings: $22.40 million (trend −11.2% a year).
What happened to a $10,000 investment

Purchase Date	*Purchase Price*	*Price on 12-31-81*	*Dividends Paid*
12-31-71	$9.75	$46.75	$0.00
12-31-76	$9.25	$46.75	$0.00

Purchase Date	*Cap. Gains (− Losses)*	*Total Return*	*Rate of Return*
12-31-71	$37,948.72	$37,948.72	16.97%
12-31-76	$40,540.54	$40,540.54	38.27%

PROFILE: At times in its history, Lockheed has been the nation's biggest defense contractor. Recently, it's been about the fifth largest.

The company has certainly had its ups and downs. The most publicized down was the near-bankruptcy in the early 1970s. Burdened by payment hassles with the military and high start-up costs for the L-1011 TriStar jet (which never made any money for the company and was reluctantly discontinued in 1981), the company skirted bankruptcy in 1971. It was bailed out by U.S. Government loan guarantees, which squeaked through the Senate by a single vote.

Lockheed lost money in 1969 and lost a lot of money ($86 million) in 1970, but has been in the black each year since. Still, earnings have continued to be highly erratic: Profits were more than $64 million in 1978 but tailed off to less than $28 million in 1980.

Balance-sheet readers who may have nearly fainted in 1974 when the company's long-term debt came to about 97 percent of total capital can breathe a little bit easier these days. But they may still bite their lips: Debt was recently (1981) about 70 percent of capital. This is no stock for people who can't afford to take a substantial amount of risk.

Yet the stock hasn't lacked for buyers, who pushed the price up from a 1973 low of $2.75 a share to a 1980 high of $48.25. Increased defense spending under the Reagan administration has been part of the appeal of these speculative shares.

Dividends were paid from 1948 through 1969, but none have been paid since.

If you buy these shares, it's a fair bet that there will always be some company activities in progress you won't know about. Over the years, the government has often turned to Lockheed for secret research performed at the company's famous "Skunk Works." Some analysts believe, for example, that the company developed prototypes of the radar-resistant "stealth" aircraft.

* * *

LOCTITE CORP. (LOC). Founded 1953. Headquarters: 705 N. Mountain Rd., Newington CT 06111. SPECIALTY CHEMICAL. Loctite Corp. produces adhesives, sealants, and other chemical specialties for industrial, consumer, and automotive repair markets. MAJOR SUBSIDIARIES, BRANDS: Loctite; Duro; Permatex; Super Glue; Gluematic; Depend.

Sales: $213.9 million (trend 21.1% a year).
Earnings: $10.38 million (trend 4.7% a year).
What happened to a $10,000 investment

Purchase Date	*Purchase Price*	*Price on 12-31-81*	*Dividends Paid*
12-31-71	$12.75	$22.75	$1,738.56
12-31-76	$19.12	$22.75	$ 983.01

Purchase Date	*Cap. Gains (− Losses)*	*Total Return*	*Rate of Return*
12-31-71	$7,843.14	$9,581.70	6.95%
12-31-76	$1,895.42	$2,878.43	5.19%

* * *

LOEWS CORP. (LTR). Founded 1954. Headquarters: 666 Fifth Ave., New York NY 10019. CONGLOMERATE. This diversified company is particularly active in insurance and cigarettes; among its other interests are hotels, theaters, lending, and watch manufacturing. 11,000 employees. MAJOR SUBSIDIARIES, BRANDS: CNA Financial Corp. (84 percent owned; includes Continental Casualty, Continental Assurance, and General Finance); Lorillard (Kent, Newport, True, Golden Lights, and Old Gold cigarettes); Loews hotels and theaters; Bulova Watch Co. (93 percent owned).

Sales: $4,266.1 million (trend 11.3% a year).
Earnings: $206.10 million (trend 27.3% a year).
What happened to a $10,000 investment

Purchase Date	*Purchase Price*	*Price on 12-31-81*	*Dividends Paid*
12-31-71	$46.37	$89.25	$2,557.41
12-31-76	$35.87	$89.25	$1,672.47

Purchase Date	*Cap. Gains (− Losses)*	*Total Return*	*Rate of Return*
12-31-71	$ 9,245.28	$11,802.70	8.11%
12-31-76	$14,878.05	$16,550.52	21.57%

PROFILE: You probably think of Loews as a company that owns theaters. After all, that's where the name comes from. And you're right — the company does own more than 100 movie theaters — but they account for only about 1 percent of the company's sales.

More than half of sales come from the 84-percent-owned CNA Financial subsidiary — mainly Continental Casualty (property and casualty insurance) and Continental Assurance (life insurance). Recently, CNA has been contributing less than half of profits, but that could change, as the property-casualty insurance cycle swings around.

The next largest chunk of sales is in the cigarette business, which in 1980 chipped in about 23 percent of sales and 34 percent of profits. Loews took over Lorillard in 1968, when it was stagnant (though much larger than Loews at the time), and breathed new life into it, as the conglomerate has done with other ailing subsidiaries. Bulova, acquired (at least 93 percent acquired) in 1979, is another company on the sick list and the latest candidate for resuscitation by the Loews managers. The managers answer to the Tisch brothers (chairman Larry and president Preston); the Tisch family owns about 43 percent of Loews.

In the early 1980s Loews was still digesting its 1979 acquisitions, Bulova and an increased stake in CNA. Debt was more than 40 percent of capital, and the Tisch brothers may choose to trim it before going after new game. But they always keep a hand in the marketplace, Charles Bluhdorn style (see Gulf & Western), buying up chunks of companies as an investment, sometimes with a future takeover in mind. Recently investment income has accounted for close to 10 percent of the company's profits.

Despite a long-term record of earnings growth, the company has had a very low p / e in recent years, often as low as 4. Keep your eye on the p / e to see if the stock remains on the bargain counter. The low multiple presumably reflects investors' distrust of conglomerates, but that sentiment may have been overdone here.

* * *

LOMAS & NETTLETON FINANCIAL CORP. (LNF). Founded 1960. Headquarters: 2001 Bryan Tower, PO Box 225644, Dallas TX 75265. **FINANCIAL SERVICES.** Lomas & Nettleton Financial Corp. is active in mortgage lending and short-term real estate lending; also provides management services and invests in securities. **MAJOR SUBSIDIARIES, BRANDS:** Lomas & Nettleton Corp.; National Homes Acceptance Corp.; Great Lakes Mortgage Corp.; Great American Funding Corp.

* * *

LOMAS & NETTLETON MORTGAGE INVESTORS (LOM). Founded 1969. Headquarters: 2001 Bryan Tower, PO Box 225644, Dallas TX 75222. **REAL ESTATE INVESTMENTS.** Lomas & Nettleton Mortgage Investors invests primarily in construction and development loans.

Sales: $44.6 million (trend 22.3% a year).
Earnings: $10.23 million (trend 19.1% a year).
What happened to a $10,000 investment

Purchase Date	*Purchase Price*	*Price on 12-31-81*	*Dividends Paid*
12-31-71	$40.25	$20.25	$6,191.30
12-31-76	$15.25	$20.25	$6,203.28

Purchase Date	*Cap. Gains (− Losses)*	*Total Return*	*Rate of Return*
12-31-71	$−4,968.94	$1,222.36	1.16%
12-31-76	$ 3,278.69	$9,481.97	14.27%

* * *

LONE STAR INDUSTRIES, INC. (LCE). Founded 1919. Headquarters: 1 Greenwich Plaza, Greenwich CT 06830. **CEMENT PRODUCTS.** Lone Star Industries produces cement, ready-mix concrete, sand, gravel aggregates, crushed stone, and concrete products. **MAJOR SUBSIDIARIES, BRANDS:** Lone Star Cement, Inc.; G. M. Stewart Lumber Co., Inc.; Lone Star Properties, Inc.

Sales: $909.3 million (trend 7.4% a year).
Earnings: $56.13 million (trend 25.9% a year).
What happened to a $10,000 investment

Purchase Date	*Purchase Price*	*Price on 12-31-81*	*Dividends Paid*
12-31-71	$25.62	$27.62	$4,770.73
12-31-76	$22.12	$27.62	$3,254.24

Purchase Date	*Cap. Gains (− Losses)*	*Total Return*	*Rate of Return*
12-31-71	$ 780.49	$5,551.22	4.51%
12-31-76	$2,485.88	$5,740.11	9.50%

* * *

LONG ISLAND LIGHTING CO. (LIL). Founded 1910. Headquarters: 250 Old Country Rd., Mineola NY 11501. UTILITIES. Long Island Lighting Co. supplies gas and electricity in Nassau and Suffolk counties in New York and in part of the New York City's Borough of Queens.

Sales: $1,276.9 million (trend 13.4% a year).
Earnings: $164.91 million (trend 17.9% a year).
What happened to a $10,000 investment

Purchase Date	*Purchase Price*	*Price on 12-31-81*	*Dividends Paid*
12-31-71	$24.75	$14.12	$6,705.05
12-31-76	$18.25	$14.12	$4,849.32

Purchase Date	*Cap. Gains (− Losses)*	*Total Return*	*Rate of Return*
12-31-71	$−4,292.93	$2,412.12	2.18%
12-31-76	$−2,260.27	$2,589.04	4.71%

* * *

LONGS DRUG STORES, INC. (LDG). Founded 1946. Headquarters: 141 N. Civic Dr., Walnut Creek CA 94596. DRUG STORES. Longs Drug Stores is a chain of more than 100 drug stores in six western states.

Sales: $893.2 million (trend 17.1% a year).
Earnings: $25.86 million (trend 13.2% a year).
What happened to a $10,000 investment

Purchase Date	*Purchase Price*	*Price on 12-31-81*	*Dividends Paid*
12-31-71	$34.37	$28.87	$1,274.18
12-31-76	$33.87	$28.87	$ 800.00

Purchase Date	*Cap. Gains (− Losses)*	*Total Return*	*Rate of Return*
12-31-71	$−1,600.00	$−325.82	−.33%
12-31-76	$−1,476.01	$−676.01	−1.39%

* * *

LORAL CORP. (LOR). Founded 1948. Headquarters: 600 Third Ave., New York NY 10016. MILITARY ELECTRONICS. Loral Corp. manufactures electronics and communications systems, primarily for military applications. MAJOR SUBSIDIARIES, BRANDS: KSW Electronics Corp.

Sales: $212.6 million (trend 22.8% a year).
Earnings: $20.55 million (trend 29.6% a year).
What happened to a $10,000 investment

Purchase Date	*Purchase Price*	*Price on 12-31-81*	*Dividends Paid*
12-31-71	$1.87	$33.50	$10,960.00
12-31-76	$6.94	$33.50	$ 2,745.95

Purchase Date	*Cap. Gains (− Losses)*	*Total Return*	*Rate of Return*
12-31-71	$168,666.67	$179,626.67	34.21%
12-31-76	$ 38,288.29	$ 41,034.23	38.54%

* * *

LOUISIANA GENERAL SERVICES, INC. (LGS). Founded 1970. Headquarters: 1233 W. Bank Expressway, Harvey LA 70058. NATURAL GAS TRANSMISSION. Distributes natural gas in suburban New Orleans and other parts of Louisiana; also explores for and produces natural gas and has a small insurance subsidiary.

Sales: $142.3 million (trend 30.8% a year).
Earnings: $6.64 million (trend 24.6% a year).
What happened to a $10,000 investment

Purchase Date	*Purchase Price*	*Price on 12-31-81*	*Dividends Paid*
12-31-71	$N/A	$15.75	$ N/A
12-31-76	$ 5.62	$15.75	$2,742.47

Purchase Date	*Cap. Gains (− Losses)*	*Total Return*	*Rate of Return*
12-31-71	$ N/A	$ N/A	N/A%
12-31-76	$18,003.02	$20,745.50	25.19%

* * *

LOUISIANA LAND & EXPLORATION CO. (LLX). Founded 1926. Headquarters: 225 Baronne St., New Orleans LA 70112. OIL, GAS. Produces oil and natural gas, mainly in the Gulf Coast area; also has copper mining subsidiary. 2,500 employees. **MAJOR SUBSIDIARIES, BRANDS:** Copper Range.

Sales: $1,036.2 million (trend 29.3% a year).
Earnings: $180.20 million (trend 16.3% a year).
What happened to a $10,000 investment

Purchase Date	*Purchase Price*	*Price on 12-31-81*	*Dividends Paid*
12-31-71	$51.12	$29.37	$2,497.80
12-31-76	$29.75	$29.37	$2,487.39

Purchase Date	*Cap. Gains (− Losses)*	*Total Return*	*Rate of Return*
12-31-71	$−4,254.28	$−1,756.48	−1.91%
12-31-76	$ −126.05	$ 2,361.34	4.33%

PROFILE: You don't see much written about Louisiana Land & Exploration. But you can read a great deal between the lines of the statistics.

This isn't an integrated oil company, nor is it an extremely large one. It ranks around 25th in oil and gas revenues, with annual sales in the $1 billion class. Since it doesn't sell its petroleum at its own gas stations, like Exxon or Mobil, it isn't a household word. In the 1980 Fortune 500 it ranked 298th. As noted above, it has relatively few employees.

Yet in the total market value of its stock, it ranked 89th in the Forbes 500 list for the same year. What did Wall Street see in the stock, to value it so highly?

The profit margin, for one thing. Of the 500 companies on the Fortune list, Louisiana Land ranked 6th in profits as a percentage of sales, making close to 18 cents on each dollar of sales.

The return on stockholders' equity is also enough to make an analyst's eyes open wide. In 1980 it was about 24 percent, in 1979 more than 28 percent. It missed 20 percent only once (and just barely) during the 1970s, and three times during that period hit a 30-percent return on equity or better. That's highly unusual.

This spectacular showing wasn't jacked up with heavy leverage: Debt has recently been around a quarter of capital.

In 1981, however, this high-flier took a tumble. The company didn't do too badly—earnings were down to $3.82 a share from $4.74 in 1980, mainly because of hitting some dry holes while increasing exploration expenses. But Wall Street doesn't like its glamour gals to have feet of clay. The stock price plunged from a 1980 high of $63.75 to a low of $25.62 and was trading near the 1981 low in early 1982. As the stock price slumped, so did the p/e (from 13 to 7), making the stock a safer buy. The dividend yield, traditionally moderate, rose to around 7 percent.

* * *

LOUISIANA-PACIFIC CORP. (LPX). Founded 1972. Headquarters: 1300 S.W. Fifth Ave., Portland OR 97201. **FOREST PRODUCTS.** Louisiana-Pacific is approximately the twelfth largest U.S. forest products company. 15,000 employees.

Sales: $1,195.6 million (trend 27.2% a year).
Earnings: $60.01 million (trend 31.6% a year).
What happened to a $10,000 investment

Purchase Date	*Purchase Price*	*Price on 12-31-81*	*Dividends Paid*
12-31-71	$N/A	$19.37	$ N/A
12-31-76	$15.72	$19.37	$1,813.66

Purchase Date	*Cap. Gains (− Losses)*	*Total Return*	*Rate of Return*
12-31-71	$ N/A	$ N/A	N/A%
12-31-76	$2,322.70	$4,136.36	7.17%

PROFILE: Louisiana-Pacific is the little brother (sister?) of Georgia-Pacific, from which it was spun off in 1972 at the behest of government antitrust authorities.

The offspring, which ranks about twelfth among U.S. forest products companies, owns more than 900,000 acres of timberland and has cutting rights on about twice again as much. Unlike many forest products companies, it has stuck closely to its original business, rather than diversifying into unrelated areas or semirelated areas like chemicals.

What really sets Louisiana-Pacific apart from its competitors, though, is its degree of specialization in building materials. A major producer of lumber, plywood, and particleboard, it gets more than 80 percent of its sales from building products. Among the major forest products companies (there were sixteen with sales over $1 billion in 1979), no other company depended on the building industry for as much as two thirds of sales. (The closest was parent Georgia-Pacific, with 64 percent.)

Naturally, then, this stock tends to rise and fall with — or in anticipation of — the trends in the housing industry. The ideal time to buy it, if you happen to own a crystal ball, is when the housing industry is at the bottom of a cyclical trough.

Dividends have been paid since the year after founding, but the yield remains modest. The balance sheet is as strong as a plank, with debt recently only about 17 percent of total capital.

* * *

LOUISVILLE GAS & ELECTRIC CO. (LOU). Founded 1913. Headquarters: 311 W. Chestnut St., PO Box 32010, Louisville KY 40232. **UTILITIES.** Louisville Gas & Electric Co. provides electric and gas service to some 800,000 people in the Louisville area.

Sales: $443.9 million (trend 17.4% a year).
Earnings: $32.65 million (trend 4.9% a year).
What happened to a $10,000 investment

Purchase Date	*Purchase Price*	*Price on 12-31-81*	*Dividends Paid*
12-31-71	$37.75	$17.37	$5,137.75
12-31-76	$26.62	$17.37	$3842.25

Purchase Date	*Cap. Gains (− Losses)*	*Total Return*	*Rate of Return*
12-31-71	$−5,397.35	$−259.60	−.26%
12-31-76	$−3,474.18	$ 368.08	.73%

* * *

LOWENSTEIN (M.) CORP. (LST). Founded 1889. Headquarters: 1430 Broadway, New York NY 10018. **TEXTILES.** Lowenstein Corp. manufactures apparel fabrics, textiles for home furnishings, and textiles for industrial use. **MAJOR SUBSIDIARIES, BRANDS:** Lowenstein, Wamsutta, and Pacific textiles.

Sales: $620.5 million (trend 6.1% a year).
Earnings: $4.87 million (trend −12.4% a year).
What happened to a $10,000 investment

Purchase Date	*Purchase Price*	*Price on 12-31-81*	*Dividends Paid*
12-31-71	$31.75	$26.37	$1,818.90
12-31-76	$14.75	$26.37	$1,355.93

Purchase Date	*Cap. Gains (− Losses)*	*Total Return*	*Rate of Return*
12-31-71	$−1,692.91	$ 125.98	.13%
12-31-76	$ 7,881.36	$9,237.29	13.98%

* * *

LOWE'S COMPANIES, INC. (LOW). Founded 1952. Headquarters: Hwy. 268 E., Box 1111, North Wilkesboro NC 28656. **BUILDING MATERIALS.** Lowe's Companies sells building materials and supplies.

Sales: $883.6 million (trend 22.3% a year).
Earnings: $18.89 million (trend 12.6% a year).
What happened to a $10,000 investment

Purchase Date	*Purchase Price*	*Price on 12-31-81*	*Dividends Paid*
12-31-71	$21.25	$12.75	$669.45
12-31-76	$20.17	$12.75	$565.29

Purchase Date	*Cap. Gains (− Losses)*	*Total Return*	*Rate of Return*
12-31-71	$−4,000.30	$−3,330.86	−3.97%
12-31-76	$−3,677.69	$−3,112.40	−7.19%

* * *

LUBRIZOL CORP. (LZ). Founded 1928. Headquarters: 29400 Lakeland Blvd., Wickliffe OH 44092. **OIL ADDITIVES.** Lubrizol Corp. supplies chemical additives to oil companies to improve the performance of lubricants. **MAJOR SUBSIDIARIES, BRANDS:** Lubrizol Enterprises Inc., the company's venture-capital arm, owns partial interests in Genentech, Inc., Altus Corp., and Greenwich Oil Corp., among others.

Sales: $902.3 million (trend 16.7% a year).
Earnings: $111.51 million (trend 19.9% a year).
What happened to a $10,000 investment

Purchase Date	*Purchase Price*	*Price on 12-31-81*	*Dividends Paid*
12-31-71	$26.94	$23.75	$2,214.20
12-31-76	$18.12	$23.75	$2,266.21

Purchase Date	*Cap. Gains (− Losses)*	*Total Return*	*Rate of Return*
12-31-71	$−1,183.29	$1,030.90	.99%
12-31-76	$ 3,103.45	$5,369.66	8.98%

* * *

LUCKY STORES, INC. (LKS). Founded 1931. Headquarters: 6300 Clark Ave., Dublin CA 94566. **RETAILING.** Lucky is the nation's eighth largest retailer and fifth largest food retailer. It operates some 1,500 stores, mainly in the West, South, and Midwest. 63,000 employees. **MAJOR SUBSIDIARIES, BRANDS:** Lucky, Eagle, Food Basket, and Kash 'N Karry food stores; Gemco and Memco discount membership department stores; Yellow Front small department stores; Checker, Dorman's, and Kragen auto parts stores; Hancock's fabric stores; Sirloin Stockade and Fred's Gang restaurants; L&G sporting goods stores; Mays and Stacey drug stores; Pic-a-Dilly women's clothing stores.

Sales: $6,468.7 million (trend 16.6% a year).
Earnings: $88.99 million (trend 17.4% a year).
What happened to a $10,000 investment

Purchase Date	*Purchase Price*	*Price on 12-31-81*	*Dividends Paid*
12-31-71	$16.06	$13.12	$3,878.43
12-31-76	$14.37	$13.12	$2,543.89

Purchase Date	*Cap. Gains (− Losses)*	*Total Return*	*Rate of Return*
12-31-71	$−1,826.82	$2,051.61	1.88%
12-31-76	$ −869.31	$1,674.57	3.15%

PROFILE: For some years, Lucky Stores had a reputation as a recession hedge. People have to eat, right? You can't trade down much further than a discount store, right? Well, right — but nevertheless, Lucky's earnings took a 10-percent tumble in the recession year of 1980 and bounced back only slightly in 1981.

Even if it's not the recession hedge some thought it was, the stock has some appealing qualities. Profitability, for one. The company has been consistently profitable in good times and bad and earns better than a 20 percent return on equity most years — often considerably better.

The dividend is also attractive. Dividends have been paid each year since 1947 and have been raised each year for more than a decade. The yield has been going up, too. It passed 5 percent in 1977, 6 percent in 1979, 7 percent in 1980, and was above 8 percent in 1981. Unfortunately, however, the rising dividend yield in part reflects a stagnation or mild decline in the stock price. The shares went to $18.62 in 1971 and haven't been higher than that since.

The company carries a fairly hefty amount of debt on its books. As of early 1982, debt was inching close to half of total capital. So keep an eye on the debt load and the trend in it.

Food accounts for close to two thirds of sales here, but less than half of earnings. The company has quite a few combination food and general merchandise stores. In these, customers have to go through the general merchandise department to get to the food section. Margins are, of course, higher on general merchandise.

Gemco and Memco are discount department stores that work on a "membership" principle. Membership costs about $1.00 and puts you on the company's extensive mailing list. These operations account for about a fourth of sales, a third of profits.

The various specialty stores listed above account for only about 10 percent of sales but close to a quarter of profits.

* * *

LUKENS STEEL CO. (LUC). Founded 1917. Headquarters: 50 S. First Ave., Coatesville PA 19320. STEEL. Lukens Steel Co. is a specialty steel-plate producer. MAJOR SUBSIDIARIES, BRANDS: Canadian Lukens Ltd.

Sales: $375.9 million (trend 7.6% a year).
Earnings: $4.70 million (trend −14.0% a year).
What happened to a $10,000 investment

Purchase Date	*Purchase Price*	*Price on 12-31-81*	*Dividends Paid*
12-31-71	$ 7.94	$13.25	$8,598.43
12-31-76	$12.94	$13.25	$3,091.79

Purchase Date	*Cap. Gains (− Losses)*	*Total Return*	*Rate of Return*
12-31-71	$6,692.91	$15,291.34	9.72%
12-31-76	$ 241.55	$ 3,333.33	5.92%

M

M / A-COM, Inc. (MAI). Founded 1950. Headquarters: 7 New England Executive Park, Burlington MA 01803. TELECOMMUNICATIONS. M / A-Com is a large manufacturer of electronic communications systems and parts for television broadcasting, cable TV, satellites, and defense operations.

Sales: $514.7 million (trend 56.6% a year).
Earnings: $40.87 million (trend 71.8% a year).
What happened to a $10,000 investment

Purchase Date	*Purchase Price*	*Price on 12-31-81*	*Dividends Paid*
12-31-71	$3.41	$25.25	$1,149.46
12-31-76	$2.53	$25.25	$1,551.87

Purchase Date	*Cap. Gains (− Losses)*	*Total Return*	*Rate of Return*
12-31-71	$63,988.32	$65,137.78	22.34%
12-31-76	$89,890.11	$91,441.98	58.94%

* * *

MCA INC. (MCA). Founded 1958. Headquarters: 100 Universal City Plaza, Universal City CA 91608. ENTERTAINMENT. MCA is a leading entertainment conglomerate, involved in movie making, TV feature production, records, music publishing, book publishing, and tourist attraction operations.

Has sidelines in mail order merchandising and banking. 19,000 employees. **MAJOR SUBSIDIARIES, BRANDS:** Universal Studios; ABC, Coral, Europa, and MCA records; Berkley, Jove, G. P. Putnam's Sons, and Coward, McCann & Geoghegan publishing houses; tourist concessions at Yosemite National Park and Mount Vernon; Spencer Gifts (mail order and retail house); Columbia Savings and Loan Association (Colorado S&L).

Sales: $1,297.1 million (trend 12.0% a year).
Earnings: $125.37 million (trend 8.8% a year).
What happened to a $10,000 investment

Purchase Date	*Purchase Price*	*Price on 12-31-81*	*Dividends Paid*
12-31-71	$10.09	$41.37	$8,117.40
12-31-76	$31.55	$41.37	$1,962.54

Purchase Date	*Cap. Gains (– Losses)*	*Total Return*	*Rate of Return*
12-31-71	$31,023.06	$39,140.46	17.26%
12-31-76	$ 3,112.69	$ 5,075.23	8.56%

PROFILE: The initials, in case you were wondering, come from Music Corporation of America, the predecessor company to the current organization. It was founded in 1924 and developed into a leading talent agency, helped in large part by the astute business and entertainment sense of one Lew Wasserman. Wasserman joined the company in 1936 at the age of twenty-two. Some forty-six years later, he is still with MCA — as chairman of a $1.3 billion operation.

The company's money today comes mainly from Universal Studios, a major maker of filmed entertainment for both big screen (e.g. *Jaws, The Sting, Close Encounters of the Third Kind)* and little (e.g. "Alfred Hitchcock Presents," "Wagon Train," "Kojak," "Quincy").

The future, in the company's opinion (shared by quite a few analysts on Wall Street), will belong to videodiscs. MCA is a leading producer of them, through a joint venture (DiscoVision Associates) with IBM. But even if MCA's attempts to provide the hardware for the videodiscs should fail, it will be almost certain to provide much of the software — i.e., the programming. Not only can it sell (to television and to the videodisc market) the output of Universal Studios; it also owns the rights to the films produced by Paramount before 1948 — some 750 films, including some highly popular ones. Filmed entertainment is by far the most profitable end of MCA's business. In 1980 it provided about 60 percent of sales, but more than 80 percent of profits.

The company's track record during the 1970s was outstanding: Earnings were up eightfold; dividends and the stock price were up about sixfold. But no company in the movie business goes straight up; 1976 and 1980, for example, were down years.

Another remarkable facet of MCA is its balance sheet. In recent years it has been absolutely debt free.

* * *

MCI COMMUNICATIONS CORP. (MCIC, Over-the-Counter). Founded 1968. Headquarters: 1150 17th St. N.W., Washington DC 20036. **COMMUNICATIONS.** Provides telephone service, mainly by microwave transmission, to some seventy-five metropolitan areas; competes on cost basis with AT&T. 1,500 employees. **MAJOR SUBSIDIARIES, BRANDS:** WUI, Inc.

Sales: $234.2 million (trend 46.2% a year).
Earnings: $6.57 million (trend 53.6% a year).
What happened to a $10,000 investment

Purchase Date	*Purchase Price*	*Price on 12-31-81*	*Dividends Paid*
12-31-71	$N/A	$34.25	$0.00
12-31-76	$ 1.87	$34.25	$0.00

Purchase Date	*Cap. Gains (– Losses)*	*Total Return*	*Rate of Return*
12-31-71	$ N/A	$ N/A	N/A%
12-31-76	$172,666.67	$172,666.67	78.79%

PROFILE: MCI is the early leader among the competitors to Ma Bell in long-distance telephone service. At first it concentrated on business users, but in recent years it has actively solicited residential business as well. (In 1981 it picked up some welcome marketing help from American Express.) Calls are transmitted via microwave relay systems owned by MCI, but are routed into this system and to the ultimate user over lines owned by American Telephone & Telegraph, MCI's giant competitor.

AT&T didn't agree to provide this service without a struggle, which lasted well into the 1970s. The outcome of the struggle was a lawsuit. In 1980 MCI won a $1.8 billion damage verdict from AT&T. Not surprisingly, the nation's largest utility is appealing.

Since it went public, MCI's sales have grown by leaps and bounds, from less than $7 million in 1975 to more than $200 million in 1980. Earnings, however, have been slippery. The company lost money

1974–76, earned a small profit in 1977, lost money 1978–79, and was profitable in 1980. The possibility of much higher profits has led investors to bid up the price of the stock. In early 1982, for example, the shares went for about $31, which was about 26 times the company's recent yearly earnings.

MCI's sales pitch is simple and direct — price. It offers long-distance calls at a cost substantially lower than that of AT&T, assuming the user makes enough calls to compensate for the monthly charge for use of the service. Several companies are taking on Ma Bell by offering similar services: Among them are ITT (CityCall) and Southern Pacific (Sprint). But those are big companies for which this activity is basically a sideline. MCI is what Wall Street calls a "pure play."

It's also a very risky stock, with chances for a big gain or a big loss. No dividends have ever been paid, and the balance sheet is freighted with a gigantic load of debt. More than two thirds of capital was recently debt, and most of the rest was preferred stock. The common stock was only about 2 percent of capital, which gives these shares an extremely large amount of leverage.

* * *

MEI CORP. (MEI). Founded 1939. Headquarters: 710 Marquette Ave., Minneapolis MN 55402. **BEVERAGES.** MEI Corp. bottles and markets soft drinks and wines, including Pepsi-Cola, 7-Up, and Dr Pepper. It also operates a bus transit company, a loan business, and a candy and nut distributorship. **MAJOR SUBSIDIARIES, BRANDS:** Minnesota Small Loan Company, West Towns Bus Company.

Sales: $349.7 million (trend 33.5% a year).
Earnings: $19.74 million (trend 38.2% a year).
What happened to a $10,000 investment

Purchase Date	*Purchase Price*	*Price on 12-31-81*	*Dividends Paid*
12-31-71	$4.50	$30.62	$4,200.00
12-31-76	$5.12	$30.62	$3,687.80

Purchase Date	*Cap. Gains (− Losses)*	*Total Return*	*Rate of Return*
12-31-71	$58,055.56	$62,255.56	21.87%
12-31-76	$49,756.10	$53,443.90	44.70%

* * *

MGIC INVESTMENT CORP. (MGI). Founded 1956. Headquarters: 600 MGIC Plaza, Milwaukee WI 53201. **INSURANCE, REAL ESTATE.** MGIC is the holding company for the country's largest mortgage insurance company. As of early 1982, MGIC had agreed to be merged into Baldwin United. **MAJOR SUBSIDIARIES, BRANDS:** Mortgage Guaranty Insurance.

Sales: $300.6 million (trend 15.3% a year).
Earnings: $81.55 million (trend 97.4% a year).
What happened to a $10,000 investment

Purchase Date	*Purchase Price*	*Price on 12-31-81*	*Dividends Paid*
12-31-71	$44.62	$48.37	$1,090.20
12-31-76	$21.25	$48.37	$2,054.12

Purchase Date	*Cap. Gains (− Losses)*	*Total Return*	*Rate of Return*
12-31-71	$ 840.34	$ 1,930.53	1.78%
12-31-76	$12,764.71	$14,818.82	19.94%

* * *

MGM GRAND HOTELS, INC. (GRH). Founded 1980; predecessor company founded in 1919. Headquarters: 3645 Las Vegas Blvd. S., Las Vegas NV 89109. **HOTELS, CASINOS.** The company owns two major hotel-casinos, one in Las Vegas and one in Reno. It plans another in Atlantic City, N.J. and possibly a fourth in Massachusetts. 8,000 employees.

Sales: $169.8 million (trend −5.2% a year).
Earnings: $29.00 million (trend −.6% a year).
What happened to a $10,000 investment

Purchase Date	*Purchase Price*	*Price on 12-31-81*	*Dividends Paid*
12-31-71	$2.85	$7.87	$12,793.08
12-31-76	$6.92	$7.87	$ 3,507.46

Purchase Date	*Cap. Gains (− Losses)*	*Total Return*	*Rate of Return*
12-31-71	$17,636.09	$30,429.17	14.99%
12-31-76	$ 1,383.11	$ 4,890.58	8.29%

PROFILE: This is a gambling stock. As such, it's likely to be volatile. In the case of this stock, there is an additional reason for uncertainty in the outlook: the parcel of lawsuits that followed a disastrous fire at the flagship hotel, the MGM Grand in Las Vegas, in the fall of 1980. More than 80 people were killed, some 500 were injured, and the lawsuit claims total a bit over $1 billion.

Through the purchase of retroactive insurance (unconventional but not unprecedented), MGM Grand has tried to minimize the damages. It bought some $170 million in retroactive coverage from a consortium of companies at an undisclosed price (widely believed to be $35 million to $37.5 million). Together with the preexisting coverage, that gives MGM $200 million of liability insurance, which might or might not be enough to cover the claims by the time the litigation, haggling, and delay are done.

In 1980, the year the original MGM split itself into MGM Grand Hotels and Metro-Goldwyn-Mayer Film, MGM Grand had sales of $307 million and profits of almost $34 million. The return on stockholders' equity in that fiscal year was 17.5 percent; this better-than-average performance was assisted a good deal by leverage. Debt recently made up between 40 and 50 percent of the company's capital.

Hotels with huge casinos, indoor tennis courts and pools, and lavish entertainment have been the approach here. Up until the fire, it was working pretty well. The stock fell from a pre-fire price of about $17 to a 1980 low of $7.12 a share. The chances of a rebound seemed pretty good, but investors seemed to have built that possibility into the stock price, since the p / e ratio in early 1982 was an above-average 11 times earnings even though the price was still below $8.

* * *

MACMILLAN BLOEDEL LIMITED (MMB). Founded 1911. Headquarters: 1075 W. Georgia St., Vancouver, B.C. V6E 3R9 Canada. FOREST PRODUCTS. This company is Canada's largest producer of newsprint, pulp, and other paper and timber products.

Sales: $2,039.3 million (trend 9.2% a year).
Earnings: $89.84 million (trend 44.1% a year).
What happened to a $10,000 investment

Purchase Date	*Purchase Price*	*Price on 12-31-81*	*Dividends Paid*
12-31-71	$N/A	$21.25	$ N/A
12-31-76	$22.50	$21.25	$2,278.44

Purchase Date	*Cap. Gains (– Losses)*	*Total Return*	*Rate of Return*
12-31-71	$ N/A	$ N/A	N/A%
12-31-76	$–555.56	$1,722.89	3.23%

* * *

MACMILLAN, INC. (MLL). Founded 1920. Headquarters: 866 Third Ave., New York NY 10022. PUBLISHING. Macmillan, Inc., is a large textbook and general publisher and also is active in home study courses, classroom tools, printing, and distribution.

Sales: $566.0 million (trend 3.3% a year).
Earnings: $9.45 million (trend –4.1% a year).
What happened to a $10,000 investment

Purchase Date	*Purchase Price*	*Price on 12-31-81*	*Dividends Paid*
12-31-71	$11.30	$16.50	$3,822.33
12-31-76	$ 9.25	$16.50	$3,572.97

Purchase Date	*Cap. Gains (– Losses)*	*Total Return*	*Rate of Return*
12-31-71	$4,604.25	$ 8,426.59	6.30%
12-31-76	$7,837.84	$11,410.81	16.45%

* * *

R. H. MACY & CO., INC. (MZ). Founded 1919. Headquarters: 151 W. 34th St., New York NY 10001. RETAILER. Macy's is approximately the twenty-fifth largest U.S. retailer, and one of the country's larger department store chains, with roughly 100 stores. 45,000 employees. MAJOR SUBSIDIARIES, BRANDS: Macy's; Bamberger's; Davison's.

Sales: $2,656.7 million (trend 12.6% a year).
Earnings: $118.98 million (trend 23.6% a year).
What happened to a $10,000 investment

Purchase Date	*Purchase Price*	*Price on 12-31-81*	*Dividends Paid*
12-31-71	$32.08	$53.25	$2,992.42
12-31-76	$23.17	$53.25	$2,604.60

Purchase Date	*Cap. Gains (– Losses)*	*Total Return*	*Rate of Return*
12-31-71	$ 6,597.40	$ 9,589.82	6.96%
12-31-76	$12,985.61	$15,590.22	20.67%

PROFILE: Macy's was a celebrated turnaround of the late 1970s. The heroes: Ed Finkelstein, who led the California stores to profitability and then was called home to do the same for the New York flagship store, and Mark Handler, who headed up the profitable Bamberger's subsidiary in New Jersey and the Philadelphia area. Now Finkelstein is chairman and Handler is president.

Macy's had seemed to be going nowhere in the early 1970s. Earnings per share were $1.69 in 1969; six years later in 1975 (admittedly a recession year) they were $1.81. Thus, for that six-year stretch, the company had a profit growth rate of barely over 1 percent.

In 1974 Finkelstein was called in from California. He turned Macy's drab, huge flagship store on 34th Street in Manhattan into a lively, flamboyant retailing space appealing to upscale buyers. Not coincidentally, the store (always a major contributor to overall company sales volume) went from being a money loser to a money maker. From 1975 to 1980 Macy's profits skyrocketed at almost a 30 percent annual rate. In 1980, a recession year, Macy's chalked up record profits of $6.48 a share.

The company's return on stockholders' equity, which had been a subpar 10 percent or so in the early 1970s, rose to an above-average 19 percent in 1980. Stores have been remodeled without any increase in the company's debt (which has stayed in the vicinity of 30 percent of total capital). The stock increased in value seven-fold between 1974 and 1980. But it was still selling for an average multiple of earnings (8) in early 1982.

Dividends are moderate. They've been paid each year since 1927, raised each year since 1975.

* * *

MADISON FUND, INC. (MAD). Founded 1929. Headquarters: Suite 608, 919 Market St., Wilmington DE 19801. **INVESTMENT COMPANY.** Madison Fund is a publicly traded investment operation with investment emphasis in industrial durables and energy.

* * *

MAGIC CHEF, INC. (MGC). Founded 1932. Headquarters: 740 King Edward Ave., Cleveland TN 37311. **APPLIANCES, HEATING / AIR CONDITIONING.** Magic Chef makes and sells household appliances, heating and air conditioning systems, and soft-drink vending machines. **MAJOR SUBSIDIARIES, BRANDS:** Magic Chef, Norge, Admiral, Johnson, and Armstrong appliances.

Sales: $674.3 million (trend 24.1% a year).
Earnings: $13.41 million (trend −2.7% a year).
What happened to a $10,000 investment

Purchase Date	*Purchase Price*	*Price on 12-31-81*	*Dividends Paid*
12-31-71	$21.06	$9.25	$1,844.51
12-31-76	$ 9.75	$9.25	$2,353.85

Purchase Date	*Cap. Gains (− Losses)*	*Total Return*	*Rate of Return*
12-31-71	$−5,608.31	$−3,763.80	−4.61%
12-31-76	$ −512.82	$ 1,841.03	3.44%

* * *

MALONE AND HYDE, INC. (MHI). Founded 1911. Headquarters: 1991 Corporate Ave., Memphis TN 38132. **FOOD DISTRIBUTION.** Malone and Hyde is a food wholesaler with interests in supermarkets, drug stores, and sporting goods stores.

Sales: $2,146.6 million (trend 16.2% a year).
Earnings: $18.39 million (trend 8.8% a year).
What happened to a $10,000 investment

Purchase Date	*Purchase Price*	*Price on 12-31-81*	*Dividends Paid*
12-31-71	$25.61	$24.37	$2,643.90
12-31-76	$25.25	$24.37	$1,932.67

Purchase Date	*Cap. Gains (− Losses)*	*Total Return*	*Rate of Return*
12-31-71	$−480.78	$2,163.13	1.98%
12-31-76	$−346.53	$1,586.14	2.99%

* * *

MANAGEMENT ASSISTANCE INC. (M). Founded 1957. Headquarters: 300 E. 44th St., New York NY 10017. **COMPUTERS.** Management Assistance manufactures and markets computers that are used in business and word processing. **MAJOR SUBSIDIARIES, BRANDS:** Basic Four; Sorbus; Wordstream.

Sales: $332.2 million (trend 23.1% a year).
Earnings: $6.81 million (trend 1.1% a year).
What happened to a $10,000 investment

Purchase Date	*Purchase Price*	*Price on 12-31-81*	*Dividends Paid*
12-31-71	$3.00	$10.87	$0.00
12-31-76	$7.50	$10.87	$0.00

Purchase Date	*Cap. Gains (− Losses)*	*Total Return*	*Rate of Return*
12-31-71	$26,250.00	$26,250.00	13.74%
12-31-76	$ 4,500.00	$ 4,500.00	7.71%

* * *

MANHATTAN INDUSTRIES, INC. (MHT). Founded 1912. Headquarters: 1271 Ave. of the Americas, New York NY 10020. **CLOTHING.** Manhattan is a manufacturer of clothing for men, women, and children; also has some retailing operations, though these have been significantly reduced.

* * *

MANHATTAN LIFE CORP. (MLC). Founded 1973. Headquarters: 111 W. 57th St., New York NY 10019. **INSURANCE.** This is the holding company for Manhattan Life Insurance. **MAJOR SUBSIDIARIES, BRANDS:** Grosten-Schlesinger Agency; Northern National Life Insurance Co.; Manhattan Life Insurance Co.

* * *

MANOR CARE, INC. (MNR). Founded 1968. Headquarters: 10750 Columbia Pike, Silver Spring MD 20901. **NURSING HOMES, HOTELS.** Manor Care runs a chain of nursing homes and a chain of hotels; also owns a hospital and two alcoholism treatment centers. **MAJOR SUBSIDIARIES, BRANDS:** Manor Healthcare; Cenco, Inc. (93 percent owned); Quality Inns.

Sales: $91.7 million (trend 23.7% a year).
Earnings: $7.63 million (trend 37.0% a year).
What happened to a $10,000 investment

Purchase Date	*Purchase Price*	*Price on 12-31-81*	*Dividends Paid*
12-31-71	$1.79	$20.62	$5,861.16
12-31-76	$1.40	$20.62	$5,773.13

Purchase Date	*Cap. Gains (− Losses)*	*Total Return*	*Rate of Return*
12-31-71	$104,962.56	$110,823.72	28.30%
12-31-76	$137,407.97	$143,181.09	72.60%

* * *

MANUFACTURERS HANOVER CORP. (MHC). Founded 1905. Headquarters: 350 Park Ave., New York NY 10022. **BANK.** The corporation is the holding company for Manufacturers Hanover Trust Co., the fourth largest U.S. commercial bank; it also owns a few smaller banks in New York State and some loan-company subsidiaries, mainly in the Sunbelt states. 21,000 employees. **MAJOR SUBSIDIARIES, BRANDS:** Manufacturers Hanover Trust Co.

Sales: $5,188.5 million (trend 24.2% a year).
Earnings: $230.18 million (trend 11.9% a year).
What happened to a $10,000 investment

Purchase Date	*Purchase Price*	*Price on 12-31-81*	*Dividends Paid*
12-31-71	$34.25	$35.62	$5,891.97
12-31-76	$39.25	$35.62	$2,998.73

Purchase Date	*Cap. Gains (− Losses)*	*Total Return*	*Rate of Return*
12-31-71	$ 401.46	$6,293.43	5.00%
12-31-76	$−923.57	$2,075.16	3.84%

PROFILE: This is, as of the early 1980s, a stock for bargain hunters.

Also for dividend fanciers. The dividend yield, which used to be only 3 to 4 percent in the 1960s, has risen steadily. From 1980 through early 1982 the dividend yield was more than 8 percent. And the company isn't straining to pay that fat dividend; the payout ratio has stayed pretty constant in recent years, at around 37 percent. From all indications the dividend is quite secure. It has been paid each year since 1852 (preceding incorporation) and raised each year since 1973.

Consistency is supposed to be a forte of banks, and "Manny Hanny," as it's known in the trade, has shown it. Earnings have been up fifteen of the sixteen years from 1966 through 1981.

Yet the stock sells at a very lowly price / earnings ratio. The p / e has been 5 or less for much of the period from 1978 to 1981. Why? Well, bank stocks in general are out of favor. And the bank's earnings rise, while steady, has been plodding. The return on assets in recent years has usually been around 50 cents per $100, certainly nothing to write home about.

Since the p / e has shrunk while earnings have risen, the stock price has basically gone nowhere. During the 1970s and in the early 1980s, the stock's high in most years was right around $40 a share and the low around $30.

One area where Manny Hanny has excelled recently has been in the performance of the trust fund, managed by a young woman named Kristin Gamble. In 1979 it was tops among common stock funds available to bank trust customers, with a 50 percent gain.

* * *

MANVILLE CORP. (JM). Founded 1926. Headquarters: Ken-Caryl Ranch, Denver CO 80217. **BUILDING MATERIALS, FOREST PRODUCTS.** Manville, formerly called Johns-Manville, has long been the leading U.S. producer of asbestos. It is also a major producer of building products (particularly insulation and roofing), fiberglass products, pipe, and forest products, and is involved in platinum mining. 31,000 employees. **MAJOR SUBSIDIARIES, BRANDS:** Olinkraft.

Sales: $2,266.8 million (trend 16.6% a year).
Earnings: $55.72 million (trend 10.9% a year).
What happened to a $10,000 investment

Purchase Date	*Purchase Price*	*Price on 12-31-81*	*Dividends Paid*
12-31-71	$40.75	$14.87	$3,737.42
12-31-76	$33.50	$14.87	$2,710.45

Purchase Date	*Cap. Gains (− Losses)*	*Total Return*	*Rate of Return*
12-31-71	$−6,349.69	$−2,612.27	−2.98%
12-31-76	$−5,559.70	$−2,849.25	−6.49%

PROFILE: There's an old saying, "Nobody wants to buy into a lawsuit." That's the woe afflicting Manville stock. Except that in Manville's case, it's that nobody wants to buy into about 3,000 lawsuits.

In June of 1980 *The Wall Street Journal* reported that the company is, "by its own calculation, one of history's most sued companies, with more than 3,000 suits pending and more pouring in." The company reported that it had already settled more than 600 lawsuits related to the health effects of asbestos, and that the average settlement was for about $7,500, with roughly an equal amount spent on legal fees. Continuation of that settlement rate would make the asbestos litigation problem a serious financial drain, but a bearable one. What terrifies the company is the possibility that it won't be able to hold the line, and some plaintiffs may start to win big damages including punitive damages. Top Manville executives are believed to spend at least half their time worrying about asbestos litigation. In 1980 the firm's auditors qualified their report on the company's annual statement, saying in essence that there was no reasonable way to estimate the size of this contingent liability. Legislators from Colorado and New Jersey, the two states where Manville facilities are biggest, have introduced legislation to get the federal government to share the burden of compensating people whose lungs have been injured by asbestos. But the chances for that sort of legislation to pass during an era of cost-cutting in government seem slight.

Meanwhile the company has been diversifying full tilt away from asbestos, notably by acquiring Olinkraft, a major paper and forest products company, in 1979. In 1980 asbestos accounted for about 7 percent of sales and 13 percent of operating income, compared with 14 percent of sales and 37 percent of earnings in 1976. "Asbestos is less and less of what we do," chairman John McKinney told *Forbes* in 1980. "The day asbestos isn't a good business for us, we'll get out of it."

The stock has yielded about 8 percent in dividends the past few years. To keep the dividend inching forward during 1980, when the housing industry was sick, the directors had to pay out 78 percent of profits in dividends. A housing rebound will help this stock, but it looks as if the litigation cloud will hover over it for a long time.

* * *

MAPCO INC. (MDA). Founded 1958. Headquarters: 1800 S. Baltimore Ave., Tulsa OK 74119. **ENERGY.** MAPCO is a diversified energy firm, producing coal, oil, and natural gas. It also operates a pipeline network, carrying natural gas liquids and ammonia, and mines precious metals. 6,000 employees. **MAJOR SUBSIDIARIES, BRANDS:** Delta Refining Co.; Delta Marketing Co.; Earth Resources; Longbranch Coal Co.; Eagle Oil Co.; Mid-America Pipeline System; DeLamar mine (52-percent-owned gold and silver mine).

Sales: $1,769.7 million (trend 34.6% a year).
Earnings: $122.26 million (trend 16.4% a year).
What happened to a $10,000 investment

Purchase Date	*Purchase Price*	*Price on 12-31-81*	*Dividends Paid*
12-31-71	$ 8.69	$30.37	$11,200.00
12-31-76	$44.25	$30.37	$ 1,627.12

Purchase Date	*Cap. Gains (− Losses)*	*Total Return*	*Rate of Return*
12-31-71	$ 24,964.03	$ 36,164.03	16.53%
12-31-76	$−3,135.59	$−1,508.47	−3.22%

PROFILE: MAPCO hit the news — well, the financial pages, at any rate — in 1980, when it doubled its size by acquiring Earth Resources, a Dallas-based oil refiner and minerals miner. That was the latest in a series of acquisitions that have helped this medium-sized energy firm achieve rapid growth over the past decade.

Growth is the first thing you notice if you take the trouble to study MAPCO. But apparently not many. people have taken that trouble. The stock hasn't moved much since 1975 even though sales and earnings have gone up substantially since then.

Look at MAPCO a bit more and the next thing you'll notice is that profitability has been outstanding — with a return on stockholders' equity above 20 percent each year since 1973 and sometimes as high as 30 percent. Look a little harder, though, and you'll see the bra under the décolletage. That return on equity looks good partly because it's propped up through liberal use of debt. Only once in the past decade did MAPCO's long-term debt dip below 40 percent of total capital. Recently, debt was fully half of capital.

All of that is no problem when things are going well. The leverage may even be viewed as an advantage by some aggressive investors. More conservative investors will note the potential for trouble inherent in such a leveraged balance sheet.

The profit gem within MAPCO is its pipeline system, connecting Kansas and New Mexico and transporting gas liquids and ammonia for fertilizer. On just 3 percent of 1980 revenues, the pipeline chipped in 17 percent of profits.

Dividends, paid yearly since 1965, provide a moderate yield.

* * *

MARINDUQUE MINING & INDUSTRIAL CORP. (**MMUB,** American Stock Exchange). Founded 1949. Headquarters: 2283 Pasong Tamo Extension, Makati, Metro Manila, Philippines. **MINING.** Marinduque mines and refines nickel, copper, gold, and silver; also produces cement. 6,000 employees.

Sales: $288.9 million (trend 37.8% a year).
Earnings: $−36.08 million.
What happened to a $10,000 investment

Purchase Date	*Purchase Price*	*Price on 12-31-81*	*Dividends Paid*
12-31-71	$ .68	$.50	$0.00
12-31-76	$1.25	$.50	$0.00

Purchase Date	*Cap. Gains (− Losses)*	*Total Return*	*Rate of Return*
12-31-71	$−2,675.78	$−2,675.78	−3.07%
12-31-76	$−6,000.00	$−6,000.00	−16.74%

PROFILE: Marinduque Mining tends to be one of the more actively traded issues on the American Stock Exchange. In 1980, for example, it was the seventh most active Amex stock.

This is a Philippine mining company — and a raw speculation. A lot of the time Marinduque is literally a penny stock. The shares went for as little as 50 cents apiece in parts of 1971–73, 1977–78, and 1981. The highest the stock has climbed to in the past two decades was $4.37 a share in 1980.

From 1976 through 1981 Marinduque lost money in five years out of the six. Only 1979 was profitable, to the tune of 24 cents a share. The five years before that were all profitable, with profits ranging from 3 cents to 30 cents a share. Thus, when an investor — to use that word loosely — pays $1.50 for Marinduque shares, he's paying roughly 6 times the average earnings in a good year for the company, by historical standards.

About two thirds of the company's sales and profits come from mining nickel and mixed sulfides. Most of the rest come from copper, gold, and silver operations.

What makes the stock interesting to speculators are the prospects for these metals, the fact that the company is spending substantially to increase production, and the fact that the stock price is so low. There's a "what've-I-got-to-lose?" flavor here.

Despite the recent losses, the balance sheet seems to be in decent shape, following a recent financial restructuring. No dividends have been paid since 1970.

* * *

MARINE MIDLAND BANKS, INC. (MM). Founded 1929. Headquarters: 1 Marine Midland Center, Buffalo NY 14240. **BANK.** Owns Marine Midland Bank, roughly the nation's fifteenth largest commercial bank, with some 300 branch offices in New York State (mainly upstate, where it is the largest bank) and several overseas. The company is 51-percent owned by Hongkong & Shanghai Banking Corp. 10,000 employees. **MAJOR SUBSIDIARIES, BRANDS:** Marine Midland Bank.

Sales: $1,859.2 million (trend 19.2% a year).
Earnings: $58.27 million (trend 38.2% a year).
What happened to a $10,000 investment

Purchase Date	*Purchase Price*	*Price on 12-31-81*	*Dividends Paid*
12-31-71	$32.62	$22.75	$3,701.15
12-31-76	$10.25	$22.75	$4,268.29

Purchase Date	*Cap. Gains (− Losses)*	*Total Return*	*Rate of Return*
12-31-71	$−3,026.82	$ 674.33	.65%
12-31-76	$ 12,195.12	$16,463.41	21.49%

PROFILE: In 1980 Marine Midland became the largest U.S. bank to pass into foreign control. The acquiring company, Hongkong & Shanghai Banking Corp., didn't come as a raider, but as a rescuer. Marine Midland had been having some very rough times during the 1970s, and the new ownership has provided a much-needed infusion of capital.

In 1978 Marine Midland owed some $389 million in long-term debt. Its stockholders' equity was only $448 million, so debt was 46 percent of total capital. That would be considered a high debt ratio for an industrial corporation, let alone a bank. Hongkong & Shanghai Banking Corp. bought 6.6 million newly issued shares at about $35 apiece, giving Marine Midland $235 million in fresh equity capital. It also tendered for 3.2 million existing shares at $25 each (a price higher than Marine Midland shares have commanded since 1974), giving some stockholders a much-appreciated exit door.

There's no question that many of this bank's stockholders had to be disappointed during the 1970s. The stock sank from a 1968 high of almost $46 a share to a 1976 low of less than $9. (It had climbed back to about $22 a share in early 1982.) Dividends were cut down in 1975, cut further in 1976, and not raised until 1980 (even then, by a token amount). Yet the shares still yielded 5 to 6 percent in the early 1980s. The bank's return on assets has been as low as a dime per $100 in some recent years and hasn't been above 50 cents per $100 since 1970.

The attraction in the shares lies in their recent low price and low multiple (a p / e of from 4 to 6 in recent years), coupled with hopes for a turnaround under new management.

* * *

MARION LABORATORIES, INC. (MKC). Founded 1952. Headquarters: 9221 Ward Parkway, Kansas City MO 64114. PHARMACEUTICALS. This company is active in pharmaceutical development, manufacturing, and marketing.

Sales: $118.6 million (trend 7.0% a year).
Earnings: $7.92 million (trend −4.6% a year).
What happened to a $10,000 investment

Purchase Date	*Purchase Price*	*Price on 12-31-81*	*Dividends Paid*
12-31-71	$29.62	$25.62	$1,597.30
12-31-76	$14.37	$25.62	$2,114.78

Purchase Date	*Cap. Gains (− Losses)*	*Total Return*	*Rate of Return*
12-31-71	$−1,350.21	$ 247.09	.24%
12-31-76	$ 7,826.09	$9,940.87	14.80%

* * *

MARK CONTROLS CORP. (MK). Founded 1931. Headquarters: 1900 Dempster St., Evanston IL 60204. CONTROL SYSTEMS. Mark Controls Corp. manufactures products that regulate temperature; also involved in ventilation, energy, and chemicals.

Sales: $263.7 million (trend 36.5% a year).
Earnings: $6.48 million (trend −6.8% a year).
What happened to a $10,000 investment

Purchase Date	*Purchase Price*	*Price on 12-31-81*	*Dividends Paid*
12-31-71	$ 4.96	$11.25	$2,807.46
12-31-76	$11.00	$11.25	$1,121.21

Purchase Date	*Cap. Gains (− Losses)*	*Total Return*	*Rate of Return*
12-31-71	$12,667.91	$15,475.37	9.80%
12-31-76	$ 227.27	$ 1,348.48	2.56%

* * *

MARRIOTT CORP. (MHS). Founded 1929. Headquarters: Marriott Dr., Washington DC 20058. HOTELS, FOOD. Marriott operates some 50 hotels and 500 restaurants; another 20 or so hotels and 1,000 or so restaurants are franchised. Also provides food service for airlines, airports, and other institutions; operates a pair of amusement parks and 3 cruise ships. 66,000 employees. MAJOR SUBSIDIARIES, BRANDS: Marriott hotels; Bob's Big Boy coffee shops; Farrell's Ice Cream Parlours; Roy Rogers fast food restaurants; Hot Shoppes cafeterias; Hogate's seafood restaurants; Great America amusement park; Host International hotels.

Sales: $1,718.7 million (trend 18.9% a year).
Earnings: $72.60 million (trend 29.2% a year).
What happened to a $10,000 investment

Purchase Date	*Purchase Price*	*Price on 12-31-81*	*Dividends Paid*
12-31-71	$22.65	$35.87	$337.77
12-31-76	$13.54	$35.87	$565.13

Purchase Date	*Cap. Gains (− Losses)*	*Total Return*	*Rate of Return*
12-31-71	$ 5,839.67	$ 6,177.43	4.93%
12-31-76	$16,502.24	$17,067.38	22.04%

PROFILE: Republican politics, Mormon religion, nonunion labor, and steady earnings increases have been some of the consistent themes at Marriott. The corporation is run and 26 percent owned by the Marriott family. J. W. (Bill) Marriott Jr., son of the founder, has been president since 1964 and chief executive officer since 1972. Founder J. W. Marriott Sr. remains chairman of the board.

Food service is the common thread holding together the various lines of business. In fact the company's first business was food (The Hot Shoppe, in Washington, D.C.), not hotels. Marriott has been selling off some hotels, but keeping its name on them, along with the right to manage them and provide the lucrative food service for them. Food is also provided for airlines, airports, schools, businesses, and the company's cruise ships and amusement parks. In fact, Marriott has denied people the right to picnic at Great America; it wants to sell the food itself.

With the exception of a single down year (1975), earnings have moved up steadily for more than a decade. The consistent gains have caused Marriott shares to command a premium multiple. In the early 1970s, when most price / earnings ratios were high, Marriott's were higher — 50 to 60 times earnings. In the early 1980s, when most p / e ratios were low, Marriott's was still a bit higher — 13 in early 1981, for example (when the average stock went for about 8). Dividends were started in 1978 but have been minuscule to date. The balance sheet is highly leveraged, with debt often more than half of total capital. The debt has been used to expand hotel capacity and (in 1980) to buy back a big chunk of the company's stock.

* * *

MARSH & MCLENNAN COMPANIES, INC. (MMC). Founded 1923. Headquarters: 1221 Ave. of the Americas, New York NY 10020. **INSURANCE BROKERAGE.** This holding company owns the largest U.S. insurance broker, a major British insurance broker, a major employee benefits consulting firm, and an investment management firm. 14,000 employees. **MAJOR SUBSIDIARIES, BRANDS:** Marsh & McLennan Inc. (largest U.S. insurance broker); C. T. Bowring & Co. (British insurance broker); William M. Mercer, Inc. (employee benefits consultant); Marsh & McLennan Management Co. (investment adviser and mutual fund manager).

Sales: $677.3 million (trend 18.2% a year).
Earnings: $100.74 million (trend 21.0% a year).
What happened to a $10,000 investment

Purchase Date	*Purchase Price*	*Price on 12-31-81*	*Dividends Paid*
12-31-71	$32.87	$33.25	$3,516.35
12-31-76	$28.37	$33.25	$2,784.14

Purchase Date	*Cap. Gains (— Losses)*	*Total Return*	*Rate of Return*
12-31-71	$ 114.07	$3,630.42	3.15%
12-31-76	$1,718.06	$4,502.20	7.72%

PROFILE: A lot of companies would give their eyeteeth to have a growth record like that of Marsh & McLennan. It has a record of uninterrupted profit rises going back well over a decade. Earnings rose from 93 cents a share in 1971 to $3.27 a share in 1981; they better than tripled in a decade.

Now you're waiting to hear the juicy tale of the fortunes people made in this stock during the 1970s, right? Keep waiting. The stock hit a high of $36.25 a share (restated for splits) in 1971 and never went higher in the following decade. In early 1982 it was selling for about $33.

Of course, there was the dividend, which has been hiked every year. The yield rose from about 2 percent at the beginning of the 1970s to about 6 percent in the early 1980s.

The lack of capital gains reflects that old sad refrain: Some people paid too much. Those who bought in during the early 1970s often paid from 25 to 40 times earnings for the stock. That proved to be an unsustainable multiple, for this stock as for many others.

In the early 1980s the shares are much more conservatively valued. (The p / e ratio in early 1982, for example, was around 11.) The company made a major move in 1980, acquiring C. T. Bowring as an entry to Lloyd's of London and the European market. The take-over involved some friction; a number of Bowring executives left. In the long run, though, it may prove to have strengthened an already strong outfit.

Weakened, though, was the balance sheet. Previously almost debt free, Marsh & McLennan took on considerable debt to finance the Bowring takeover. Recently debt was about a third of total capital.

Some two thirds of the company's sales are in the insurance brokerage realm, mainly property and casualty business and mainly for large commercial clients. About a fifth of revenues are chipped in by the William M. Mercer employee benefits consulting subsidiary.

* * *

MARSHALL FIELD AND CO. (MF). Founded 1852. Headquarters: 25 E. Washington St., Chicago IL 60602. **DEPARTMENT STORES.** Marshall Field and Co. is a large department store operation doing business primarily in the Chicago area, but expanding into the South, Pacific Northwest, and California. In 1982 Marshall Field agreed to be acquired by BATUS, Inc., a subsidiary of B.A.T. Industries, of Great Britian. **MAJOR SUBSIDIARIES, BRANDS:** Halle Brothers Co.; J. B. Ivey and Co.

Sales: $1,012.5 million (trend 12.6% a year).
Earnings: $20.68 million (trend 2.2% a year).
What happened to a $10,000 investment

Purchase Date	*Purchase Price*	*Price on 12-31-81*	*Dividends Paid*
12-31-71	$35.25	$14.25	$3,123.40
12-31-76	$22.75	$14.25	$2,180.22

Purchase Date	*Cap. Gains (– Losses)*	*Total Return*	*Rate of Return*
12-31-71	$–5,957.45	$–2,834.04	–3.28%
12-31-76	$–3,736.26	$–1,556.04	–3.33%

* * *

MARTIN MARIETTA CORP. (ML). Founded 1961. Headquarters: 6801 Rockledge Dr., Bethesda MD 20034. **AEROSPACE, ALUMINUM.** This diverse corporation gets most of its sales and earnings from aerospace, next most from aluminum operations. It is also involved in production of chemicals, aggregates, cement, and other items. 35,000 employees.

Sales: $2,619.3 million (trend 19.9% a year).
Earnings: $188.13 million (trend 28.8% a year).
What happened to a $10,000 investment

Purchase Date	*Purchase Price*	*Price on 12-31-81*	*Dividends Paid*
12-31-71	$13.42	$36.25	$8,137.14
12-31-76	$17.17	$36.25	$3,961.17

Purchase Date	*Cap. Gains (– Losses)*	*Total Return*	*Rate of Return*
12-31-71	$17,018.63	$25,155.78	13.40%
12-31-76	$11,116.50	$15,077.67	20.19%

PROFILE: "Martin Marietta moves!" That, for some time, was this company's succinct advertising slogan.

It certainly has been true in the stock market in recent years. Like most stocks, Martin Marietta hit its recent low in 1974. If you'd bought at the 1974 bottom ($12.50 a share) and sold anywhere near the 1980 high ($72.88), you would have multiplied the value of your initial investment more than fivefold.

The thrust for the gain has come from the company's big aerospace projects — work on the Titan missile, the MX missile, and the space shuttle, to name three of the most famous. Missiles and space systems accounted for more than a third of sales in 1980. Without these operations, Martin Marietta would be just another low-technology, low-multiple conglomerate, churning out aluminum, aggregates, and cement.

In the early 1980s the outlook seemed good for a continued strong showing in aerospace. The outlook for the cement and aggregates divisions seemed less rosy; no boom in road building was in sight, and a construction boom didn't seem imminent, though it seemed possible. If these basic materials divisions were to run into heavy demand and aerospace were to stay strong, the stock could make another major surge.

In early 1982 Wall Street valued this corporation as a whole about the same as any other stock, according it a p / e of about 7 times earnings. This p / e ratio didn't seem to give the company much credit for the previous decade's better-than-tripling of earnings nor for the trimming of the balance sheet, which is now excellent. Dividends have been paid since 1954; the yield is moderate.

* * *

MARY KAY COSMETICS, INC. (MKY). Founded 1963. Headquarters: 8787 Stemmons Freeway, Dallas TX 75247. **COSMETICS.** This company distributes cosmetics to consultants who then sell them to the public through in-home presentations.

Sales: $166.9 million (trend 33.3% a year).
Earnings: $15.13 million (trend 20.8% a year).
What happened to a $10,000 investment

Purchase Date	*Purchase Price*	*Price on 12-31-81*	*Dividends Paid*
12-31-71	$4.31	$16.62	$2,220.29
12-31-76	$5.09	$16.62	$1,447.85

Purchase Date	*Cap. Gains (– Losses)*	*Total Return*	*Rate of Return*
12-31-71	$28,550.72	$30,771.01	15.09%
12-31-76	$22,638.04	$24,085.89	27.80%

* * *

MARYLAND CUP CORP. (MDC). Founded 1926. Headquarters: 10100 Reisterstown Rd., Owings Mills MD 21117. **PAPER CUPS, PLATES.** Maryland Cup is the largest U.S. manufacturer of disposable paper and plastic cups for food and drink. Also makes related products. **MAJOR SUBSIDIARIES, BRANDS:** Sweetheart; Eat-It-All (ice cream cones).

Sales: $647.0 million (trend 15.8% a year).
Earnings: $30.43 million (trend 15.4% a year).
What happened to a $10,000 investment

Purchase Date	*Purchase Price*	*Price on 12-31-81*	*Dividends Paid*
12-31-71	$20.23	$34.12	$2,234.08
12-31-76	$18.61	$34.12	$1,504.87

Purchase Date	*Cap. Gains (− Losses)*	*Total Return*	*Rate of Return*
12-31-71	$6,871.39	$9,105.47	6.69%
12-31-76	$8,338.47	$9,843.34	14.69%

* * *

MASCO CORP. (MAS). Founded 1962. Headquarters: 21001 Van Born Rd., Taylor MI 48108. BUILDING PRODUCTS, ENERGY PRODUCTS, INDUSTRIAL PARTS. Masco produces faucets and other home improvement goods, as well as energy-related products and tools and valves for industry.

Sales: $766.4 million (trend 20.0% a year).
Earnings: $77.91 million (trend 17.6% a year).
What happened to a $10,000 investment

Purchase Date	*Purchase Price*	*Price on 12-31-81*	*Dividends Paid*
12-31-71	$19.62	$37.25	$1,765.61
12-31-76	$26.37	$37.25	$1,038.86

Purchase Date	*Cap. Gains (− Losses)*	*Total Return*	*Rate of Return*
12-31-71	$8,980.89	$10,746.50	7.57%
12-31-76	$4,123.22	$ 5,162.09	8.68%

* * *

MASONITE CORP. (MNC). Founded 1925. Headquarters; 29 N. Wacker Dr., Chicago IL 60606. WOOD PRODUCTS. Masonite is a leading designer, manufacturer, and marketer of wood products for construction, furniture, home improvement, and roofing.

Sales: $537.5 million (trend 6.1% a year).
Earnings: $27.11 million (trend 1.9% a year).
What happened to a $10,000 investment

Purchase Date	*Purchase Price*	*Price on 12-31-81*	*Dividends Paid*
12-31-71	$31.62	$27.50	$2,251.92
12-31-76	$24.50	$27.50	$1,983.67

Purchase Date	*Cap. Gains (− Losses)*	*Total Return*	*Rate of Return*
12-31-71	$−1,304.35	$ 947.57	.91%
12-31-76	$ 1,224.49	$3,208.16	5.72%

* * *

MASSMUTUAL CORPORATE INVESTORS INC. (MCI). Founded 1971. Headquarters: 1295 State St., Springfield MA 01111. INVESTMENT COMPANY. This investment company derives income from its interests in many areas, including metal manufacturing, machinery, and communications.

* * *

MASSMUTUAL INCOME INVESTORS, INC. (MIV). Founded 1972. Headquarters: 1295 State St., Springfield MA 01111. INVESTMENT COMPANY. This investment operation deals primarily in income-producing bonds and securities.

* * *

MASSMUTUAL MORTGAGE AND REALTY INVESTORS (MML). Founded 1970. Headquarters: 1295 State St., Springfield MA 01111. REAL ESTATE INVESTMENTS. MassMutual Mortgage and Realty invests in first-mortgage loans, construction loans, and short-term loans.

Sales: $17.8 million (trend −.9% a year).
Earnings: $7.53 million (trend 11.7% a year).
What happened to a $10,000 investment

Purchase Date	*Purchase Price*	*Price on 12-31-81*	*Dividends Paid*
12-31-71	$29.50	$13.25	$5,094.92
12-31-76	$14.12	$13.25	$5,040.71

Purchase Date	*Cap. Gains (− Losses)*	*Total Return*	*Rate of Return*
12-31-71	$−5,508.47	$−413.56	−.42%
12-31-76	$ −619.47	$ 4,421.24	7.60%

* * *

MASSEY-FERGUSON LIMITED (MSE). Founded 1891. Headquarters: 200 University Ave., Toronto, Ont. M5H 3E4 Canada. FARM MACHINERY. Massey-Ferguson is one of the world's largest manufacturers of farm and industrial machinery. MAJOR SUBSIDIARIES, BRANDS: Perkins Engines.

Sales: $3,132.1 million (trend 3.9% a year).
Earnings: $−207.84 million.
What happened to a $10,000 investment

Purchase Date	*Purchase Price*	*Price on 12-31-81*	*Dividends Paid*
12-31-71	$12.12	$1.75	$3,534.19
12-31-76	$21.75	$1.75	$ 588.69

Purchase Date	*Cap. Gains (− Losses)*	*Total Return*	*Rate of Return*
12-31-71	$−8,556.70	$−5,022.52	−6.74%
12-31-76	$−9,195.40	$−8,606.71	−32.58%

* * *

MATSUSHITA ELECTRIC INDUSTRIAL CO., LIMITED (MC). Founded 1935. Headquarters: Kadoma, Osaka, Japan. **ELECTRONICS.** This diversified enterprise is Japan's largest producer of consumer electronic products. **MAJOR SUBSIDIARIES, BRANDS:** Panasonic; Quasar; Technics.

Sales: $13,689.9 million (trend 23.4% a year).
Earnings: $584.88 million (trend 35.8% a year).
What happened to a $10,000 investment

Purchase Date	*Purchase Price*	*Price on 12-31-81*	*Dividends Paid*
12-31-71	$12.81	$54.25	$2,428.21
12-31-76	$20.00	$54.25	$ 914.19

Purchase Date	*Cap. Gains (− Losses)*	*Total Return*	*Rate of Return*
12-31-71	$32,361.15	$34,789.36	16.18%
12-31-76	$17,119.84	$18,034.03	22.90%

* * *

MATTEL, INC. (MAT). Founded 1948. Headquarters: 5150 Rosecrans Ave., Hawthorne CA 90250. **TOYS.** Mattel, with 10 percent of the highly competitive U.S. toy market, is the world's largest toy manufacturer. 17,000 employees. **MAJOR SUBSIDIARIES, BRANDS:** Western Publishing Co. (Golden Books); Barbie dolls; Hot Wheels model cars; Ice Follies; Circus World; Holiday on Ice; Monogram Models.

Sales: $915.7 million (trend 23.1% a year).
Earnings: $2.45 million (trend −19.0% a year).
What happened to a $10,000 investment

Purchase Date	*Purchase Price*	*Price on 12-31-81*	*Dividends Paid*
12-31-71	$27.25	$11.25	$ 339.45
12-31-76	$ 5.75	$11.25	$1,434.78

Purchase Date	*Cap. Gains (− Losses)*	*Total Return*	*Rate of Return*
12-31-71	$−5,871.56	$−5,532.11	−7.74%
12-31-76	$ 9,565.22	$ 11,000.00	16.00%

PROFILE: This company's history is full of chills, thrills, and spills. It's had brushes with bankruptcy and periods of prosperity. Back in 1972 a leading business newspaper reported a trade joke: "Have you heard about the new Mattel doll? Wind it up and it falls on its face." The company lost money four years running, from 1971 through 1974.

By the late 1970s Mattel seemed to be back on its feet. Arthur Spear had taken over as chairman in 1974 from the cofounders, Ruth and Elliot Handler. He had reduced the company's debt greatly — from almost 84 percent in 1974 to less than 29 percent in 1978. And he had pushed the company aggressively into the booming field of electronic games.

In 1980 Mattel's electronic games went bust, and Mattel's earnings nosedived, ending a five-year streak of rising earnings. The company stayed profitable in 1980, but just barely. Luckily, nonelectronic products, such as the ever-popular Barbie dolls and the Golden Books line (picked up through the 1979 acquisition of Western Publishing Co.) provided some stability. Western accounts for about a quarter of sales and earnings and should lessen Mattel's historic volatility. (It has profitable cookbook and commercial printing lines, in addition to Golden Books.) However, the purchase of Western raised the debt quotient again; as of early 1982 debt was about 40 percent of capital.

In 1982 the company was booming again, thanks to new hits in video and computer games. The stock remains a speculative purchase in a highly competitive industry.

* * *

MAY DEPARTMENT STORES CO. (MA). Founded 1910. Headquarters: 611 Olive St., St. Louis MO 63101. **RETAILER.** May is approximately the seventeenth largest retailing company in the United States, operating some 140 department stores, 50 discount department stores, and 1,000 shoe stores in various parts of the country. 59,000 employees. **MAJOR SUBSIDIARIES, BRANDS:** Famous-Barr, G. Fox, Hecht, Kaufmann's, May, Meier & Frank, and O'Neill department stores; Venture discount department stores; Volume Shoe; Eagle Stamp Co. (trading stamps).

Sales: $3,173.0 million (trend 10.0% a year).
Earnings: $116.56 million (trend 13.5% a year).
What happened to a $10,000 investment

Purchase Date	*Purchase Price*	*Price on 12-31-81*	*Dividends Paid*
12-31-71	$34.83	$25.25	$3,057.03
12-31-76	$32.25	$25.25	$1,635.66

Purchase Date	*Cap. Gains (− Losses)*	*Total Return*	*Rate of Return*
12-31-71	$−2,751.20	$ 305.84	.30%
12-31-76	$−2,170.54	$−534.88	−1.09%

PROFILE: This stock has been going nowhere, and in not too much of a hurry. If you'd held it for either of our sample investment periods, for example, you'd have a total return not far from zero.

Stodgy is the word that often comes to people's minds in discussing May. David Farrell, chairman since 1975, has tried to change that image, through remodeling of stores, streamlining of operations, and acquisition (in 1979) of Volume Shoe Co. Earnings held their own pretty well in the 1980 recession, but Farrell has yet to achieve results that Wall Street (or anyone else) would call really exciting. In fact, what *Forbes* magazine wrote back in 1979 still rings true: "Conservative in its history, laggard in stocking the stuff people were buying, slow in moving to where people were buying it, May for years showed profits on the low side of mediocre. David Farrell's hard work and attention to the obvious have lifted . . . profits to the point of decent mediocrity."

But May does have two strengths going for it. One is its ownership of some twenty-four shopping centers, carried on the books at far below their true worth. The other is that the shares are now very conservatively valued. In early 1982, for example, they fetched only 6 times earnings. In the late 1960s and early 1970s, the p / e ranged from 11 to 19; since then it's slowly sunk to the current low. The stock is about as out of favor as it can get. So, a turnaround seems possible, especially if a merger or an earnings upswing is in the wind.

* * *

J. W. MAYS, INC. (MJW). Founded 1924. Headquarters: 510 Fulton St., Brooklyn NY 11201. **DEPARTMENT STORES.** This company operates retail department stores in the East. It filed for protection under Chapter 11 of the bankruptcy code in 1982, and has been delisted by the New York Stock Exchange.

Sales: $180.0 million (trend 1.5% a year).
Earnings: $−1.70 million.
What happened to a $10,000 investment

Purchase Date	*Purchase Price*	*Price on 12-31-81*	*Dividends Paid*
12-31-71	$20.12	$3.37	$939.13
12-31-76	$ 3.50	$3.37	$ 0.00

Purchase Date	*Cap. Gains (− Losses)*	*Total Return*	*Rate of Return*
12-31-71	$−8,322.98	$−7,383.85	−12.55%
12-31-76	$ −357.14	$ −357.14	−.72%

* * *

MAYTAG CO. (MYG). Founded 1925. Headquarters: 403 W. Fourth St. N., Newton IA. **WASHERS AND DRYERS.** Maytag is a leading manufacturer of home laundry equipment and also produces dishwashers, food disposers, and commercial washers and dryers.

Sales: $349.2 million (trend 8.6% a year).
Earnings: $35.52 million (trend 7.6% a year).
What happened to a $10,000 investment

Purchase Date	*Purchase Price*	*Price on 12-31-81*	*Dividends Paid*
12-31-71	$39.50	$25.50	$4,362.03
12-31-76	$35.50	$25.50	$2,797.18

Purchase Date	*Cap. Gains (− Losses)*	*Total Return*	*Rate of Return*
12-31-71	$−3,544.30	$ 817.72	.79%
12-31-76	$−2,816.90	$−19.72	−.04%

* * *

MCDERMOTT INC. (MDE). Founded 1946. Headquarters: 1010 Common St., New Orleans LA 70112. **DRILLING PLATFORMS, POWER GENERATING.** McDermott is the world's largest maker of offshore oil (and gas) drilling platforms. It also is a major manufacturer of tubing and a major builder (through its Babcock & Wilcox subsidiary) of power generating plants, both conventional and nuclear, for electric utilities. 58,000 employees. **MAJOR SUBSIDIARIES, BRANDS:** Babcock & Wilcox.

Sales: $3,599.6 million (trend 32.2% a year).
Earnings: $76.41 million (trend −20.4% a year).
What happened to a $10,000 investment

Purchase Date	*Purchase Price*	*Price on 12-31-81*	*Dividends Paid*
12-31-71	$ 9.12	$38.25	$7,027.40
12-31-76	$23.19	$38.25	$1,983.83

Purchase Date	*Cap. Gains (– Losses)*	*Total Return*	*Rate of Return*
12-31-71	$31,917.81	$38,945.21	17.21%
12-31-76	$ 6,495.96	$ 8,479.78	13.07%

PROFILE: Everything about this company is related to its history as a leader in offshore drilling platforms. That includes both its periods of prosperity and its recent problems.

McDermott is the largest maker of offshore drilling platforms in the world. As such, it's made good, though cyclical, profits. In its best year, 1976, it made $192 million, cleared more than 15 cents in profit on each dollar of sales, and made more than 31 percent on stockholder's equity.

In 1977 the federal government charged that McDermott and Brown & Root had, for some two decades, conspired to fix prices of offshore drilling rigs. The two companies pleaded no contest. After that, oil companies became highly conscious of awarding contracts to the low bidder, and a number of smaller companies, both U.S. and foreign, entered the field. The heightened competition depressed profits; what's more, the period around 1980 was a cyclical trough for offshore drilling construction, despite continued demand for oil. McDermott suffered earnings declines in 1977, 1978, and 1979. In fiscal 1979–80 its offshore operations actually ran at a loss for the first time. A gradual recovery seemed to be in process in the early 1980s.

Reacting to its troubles by diversifying, McDermott acquired the major power-generating-plant construction firm Babcock & Wilcox in 1978. Unfortunately, that was just in time for the Three Mile Island disaster to hurt McDermott (Babcock & Wilcox built the plant). So, McDermott faces prolonged litigation both over that, and over civil suits relating to the antitrust infraction.

* * *

MCDONALD'S CORP. (MCD). Founded 1954; incorporated 1965. Headquarters: McDonald's Plaza, 2111 McDonald's Dr., Oak Brook IL 60521. **RESTAURANTS.** McDonald's is the world's largest fast-food restaurant chain, with more than 5,000 stores in the United States and close to 1,000 abroad. 110,000 employees.

Sales: $2,184.3 million (trend 18.6% a year).
Earnings: $220.89 million (trend 20.3% a year).
What happened to a $10,000 investment

Purchase Date	*Purchase Price*	*Price on 12-31-81*	*Dividends Paid*
12-31-71	$37.87	$65.37	$731.35
12-31-76	$53.37	$65.37	$504.92

Purchase Date	*Cap. Gains (– Losses)*	*Total Return*	*Rate of Return*
12-31-71	$7,260.73	$7,992.08	6.05%
12-31-76	$2,248.24	$2,753.16	4.98%

PROFILE: So ubiquitous are McDonald's burgers, shakes, and fries that it's hard to believe the chain was founded as recently as 1954. For investors, it's even harder to believe that the stock sold for less than $2 (adjusted for four subsequent splits) as recently as 1966. If you'd bought in at $1.75 and sold at the 1972 high of $77.36, you would have multiplied your original stake 44 times.

Latecomers, however, have gotten the bird. The stock, like many, got the stuffing knocked out of it in 1974 and since then has only gradually been approaching the 1972 high. Back in 1972 *Forbes* magazine foresaw what was coming when, in a piece that praised McDonald's management, it asked whether the stock was worth its then-current multiple and answered itself rhetorically, "Is any stock worth 60 times earnings?"

Today, as in 1972, the company is well run. But the stock today represents a much better value. In the early 1980s it was selling for only 8 to 10 times earnings, a vastly more conservative multiple than that of a decade before. Prognostications that the company couldn't keep growing haven't proved true yet; the company has continued to exhibit growth that's both rapid and steady. As the U.S. market possibly nears the saturation point, the company has begun to penetrate markets overseas.

The balance sheet carries a good deal of debt — between 46 and 50 percent of capital in recent years. That may be too much debt for those who prefer their companies without much leverage. Dividends were started in 1976, but remain quite modest.

* * *

MCDONNELL DOUGLAS CORP. (MD). Founded 1939. Headquarters: PO Box 516, St. Louis MO 63166. **AEROSPACE.** McDonnell Douglas is a leading maker of both military and commercial aircraft and of missiles and guidance systems.

Also involved in computer services. 82,000 employees. **MAJOR SUBSIDIARIES, BRANDS:** DC-9, DC-10 airliners; F-15, F / A-18A, C-9, KC-10, AV-8B military aircraft; Harpoon and Delta missiles.

Sales: $6,066.3 million (trend 13.6% a year).
Earnings: $145.80 million (trend 14.1% a year).
What happened to a $10,000 investment

Purchase Date	*Purchase Price*	*Price on 12-31-81*	*Dividends Paid*
12-31-71	$26.70	$29.75	$2,152.74
12-31-76	$23.75	$29.75	$1,604.21

Purchase Date	*Cap. Gains (− Losses)*	*Total Return*	*Rate of Return*
12-31-71	$1,142.72	$3,295.46	2.89%
12-31-76	$2,526.32	$4,130.53	7.16%

PROFILE: McDonnell Douglas has long been a successful maker of military aircraft, and it continues to be. It has long been a struggling maker of commercial aircraft, and it continues to be.

The problems in commercial aircraft include the capable competition (Boeing and Airbus) and the sales difficulties stemming from the 1979 crash of a DC-10 in Chicago. Sales of DC-10s were running at an annual rate of about forty-eight before the crash; in 1980–81 the rate had slowed to around ten a year. The company was considering trying to take up the slack by entering a joint venture with Fokker, a Dutch aerospace firm, to produce a 150-seat plane. Airlines have been clamoring for that size. However, developing any new aircraft these days requires a monstrous capital expenditure, so the project was put on ice. In 1979 and 1980 commercial aircraft accounted for more than a third of the company's sales, but the division lost money.

What's been carrying the company — and carrying it well — are military aircraft and missile sales. McDonnell Douglas ranks (in most years) as the second largest U.S. defense contractor, trailing only General Dynamics, and not by much. Demand for missiles, attack helicopters, guidance systems, and planes seems likely to continue to increase. The Reagan administration wants a continued military buildup, and the country seems in the mood to go along.

An imponderable here is what will be the long-run effect of the death of "Mr. Mac," James S. McDonnell, who founded the firm in 1939 and merged Douglas Aircraft into it in 1967. He provided strong leadership up to his death in 1980; it is not yet clear whether his successors will give the company a firm sense of direction.

A major strength is the balance sheet. Debt was recently a mere 5 percent of capital. Dividends have been paid each year since 1950, but the yield is modest.

* * *

MCGRAW-EDISON CO. (MGR). Founded 1926. Headquarters: 1701 Golf Rd., Rolling Meadows IL 60008. **ELECTRICAL, INDUSTRIAL EQUIPMENT.** McGraw-Edison is a leading manufacturer of electrical equipment for utilities and also makes a broad line of electrical and industrial process equipment. 35,000 employees. **MAJOR SUBSIDIARIES, BRANDS:** Bussman; Clarke; Masoneilan; Onan; Turbodyne; Wagner Electric; Worthington.

Sales: $2,263.6 million (trend 17.7% a year).
Earnings: $50.40 million (trend 5.7% a year).
What happened to a $10,000 investment

Purchase Date	*Purchase Price*	*Price on 12-31-81*	*Dividends Paid*
12-31-71	$34.25	$36.25	$4,613.14
12-31-76	$31.37	$36.25	$2,772.91

Purchase Date	*Cap. Gains (− Losses)*	*Total Return*	*Rate of Return*
12-31-71	$ 583.94	$5,197.08	4.27%
12-31-76	$1,553.78	$4,326.69	7.46%

PROFILE: The 1979 acquisition of Studebaker-Worthington more than doubled the size of this company, changed it from mainly an electrical equipment manufacturer to a seller of a broad line of industrial equipment, added the auto and oil industries to its customer list, and caused a radical departure from its long tradition of conservative financing.

To be sure, McGraw Electric Co., a predecessor of the current corporation, used to carry a lot of debt back in the 1920s. In 1929 founder Max McGraw decided that debt was too much of his total capital and concluded that he'd better issue a sizable chunk of new stock. He did — only eight days before the great stock market crash. With that close call in mind, McGraw determined to keep the company virtually debt free, and it stayed that way, even after the merger in the late 1950s with Thomas A. Edison Inc.

But the company hit a long stretch of flat earnings, from 1965 to 1975, and it was clear that something drastic needed to be done. The company decided that a major acquisition was the tonic needed;

it screened some seventy-five possible ones (code named for birds, to assure secrecy) before settling on Studebaker-Worthington. Since that target was larger than McGraw-Edison itself, the acquisition pumped debt up from 10 percent of capital to a whopping 63 percent. Since then the company has been trimming debt by selling off its consumer businesses (e.g. Speed Queen, Toastmaster), but it remains highly leveraged. Profitability has been mediocre in recent years, but could take off if there's a capital spending boom. The dividend yield has ranged from 4 to 7 percent in recent years.

* * *

MCGRAW-HILL, INC. (MHP). Founded 1888. Headquarters: 1221 Ave. of the Americas, New York NY 10020. **PUBLISHING.** McGraw-Hill is one of the nation's largest publishers, producing books for the general public, textbooks, scientific books, specialized trade books, magazines, and financial reference materials. It also owns four television stations. 14,000 employees. **MAJOR SUBSIDIARIES, BRANDS:** *Business Week;* Standard & Poor's Corp.; *Aviation Week & Space Technology; Engineering News-Record; Medical World News;* F. W. Dodge; Economic Models Ltd.; Data Resources, Inc.; KERO-TV (Bakersfield CA); KMGH-TV (Denver); WRTV (Indianapolis); KGTV (San Diego).

Sales: $1,000.1 million (trend 13.6% a year).
Earnings: $86.36 million (trend 21.9% a year).
What happened to a $10,000 investment

Purchase Date	*Purchase Price*	*Price on 12-31-81*	*Dividends Paid*
12-31-71	$19.25	$51.75	$4,690.91
12-31-76	$16.87	$51.75	$3,721.48

Purchase Date	*Cap. Gains (− Losses)*	*Total Return*	*Rate of Return*
12-31-71	$16,883.12	$21,574.03	12.18%
12-31-76	$20,666.67	$24,388.15	28.02%

PROFILE: Yes, McGraw-Hill is a publisher. About 80 percent of its revenues come from publishing, broadly defined. Roughly a third of revenues come from books, close to another third from magazines and newsletters, and close to a fifth from specialized, technical publishing ventures.

But you can also, quite properly, think of McGraw-Hill as an information provider. It has moved increasingly into providing information to customers through computer programs; it has acquired two economic information and forecasting firms in recent years; and it has diversified into broadcasting.

The mix has been highly successful. In 1981 McGraw-Hill was headed for its tenth straight up year in profits. During that ten-year period, profitability has been steadily increasing. In the past couple of years, the return on equity has been above 20 percent, a very nice performance indeed. (These ten years of improvement were preceded by five straight down years in the late 1960s, 1970, and 1971).

As the company's success has been increasingly noticed, the price / earnings ratio has inflated, from a low of 4 (in parts of 1974 and 1975) to a recent high of 14. Keep an eye on the p / e, since there's a limit to how much you want to pay, even for a company in top form.

The balance sheet is extremely strong here. Debt has been cut from more than 30 percent of total capital in 1972 to about 4 percent recently. Dividends have been paid yearly since 1937; the yield in recent years has been 3 to 5 percent.

* * *

MCINTYRE MINES LIMITED (MT). Founded 1911. Headquarters: 3 Calgary Pl., 355 Fourth Ave., S.W., Calgary, Alta. T2P 0J3 Canada. **COAL, NICKEL.** McIntyre Mines mines coal in Alberta and has a 37 percent interest in Falconbridge Nickel Mines, a leader in its field.

Sales: $96.5 million (trend −7.1% a year).
Earnings: $18.14 million (trend 15.6% a year).
What happened to a $10,000 investment

Purchase Date	*Purchase Price*	*Price on 12-31-81*	*Dividends Paid*
12-31-71	$75.50	$34.12	$382.77
12-31-76	$29.25	$34.12	$474.12

Purchase Date	*Cap. Gains (− Losses)*	*Total Return*	*Rate of Return*
12-31-71	$−5,480.13	$−5,097.36	−6.88%
12-31-76	$ 1,666.67	$ 2,140.79	3.96%

* * *

MCLEAN TRUCKING CO. (MLN). Founded 1940. Headquarters: 1920 W. First St., Winston-Salem NC 27102. **TRUCKING.** McLean offers trucking services in some forty-two states. It has more than 200 terminals and a fleet including more than 5,000 truck tractors. 13,000 employees. **MAJOR SUBSIDIARIES, BRANDS:** Houston Trailer & Truck Body, Inc.

Sales: $604.8 million (trend 12.4% a year).
Earnings: $−1.88 million.
What happened to a $10,000 investment

Purchase Date	*Purchase Price*	*Price on 12-31-81*	*Dividends Paid*
12-31-71	$18.59	$7.25	$2,344.87
12-31-76	$25.62	$7.25	$1,030.24

Purchase Date	*Cap. Gains (− Losses)*	*Total Return*	*Rate of Return*
12-31-71	$−6,100.84	$−3,755.97	−4.60%
12-31-76	$−7,170.73	$−6,140.49	−17.34%

PROFILE: Four times during the 1970s, McLean Trucking's earnings topped $2 a share. In three years the stock price edged over $25. But earnings haven't been above $2 a share since 1978; indeed, the company lost money in both 1980 and 1981. As for the stock price, it had fallen below $8 in 1981 and early 1982.

McLean officers probably feel as if they'd been run over by a — you should pardon the expression — truck. What really hit them? A mixture of deregulation of the trucking industry (meaning added competition) and a weak economy in 1980–81 (meaning fewer orders).

If you believe in the old adage, "Buy on a rainy day," it makes sense to acquire trucking stocks when they're chugging along in low gear. But is McLean the one you want? Don't buy these shares without also investigating the competition, including Roadway Express, Leaseway, and Yellow Freight, to name a few of the industry's most prominent players.

McLean's earnings growth in the past decade has been slow and uneven. The balance sheet has traditionally been heavy with debt. However, while long-term debt was close to half of total capital in 1980, it was chopped to around 40 percent of capital by the recent sale of the company's former refining subsidiary, Winston Refining Co. Many analysts, who viewed the refinery as an albatross, were glad to see it go. But McLean will still need to go some to prove to skeptics that it can fly on its own.

Dividends, paid yearly since 1952, provide a moderate yield.

* * *

MCNEIL CORP. (MME). Founded 1932. Headquarters: 666 W. Market St., Akron OH 44303. **DIVERSIFIED MANUFACTURING.** McNeil Corporation's products include systems for automated production and material handling, pumps, lubrication systems, heating and air conditioning, swimming pool chemicals, and beverage dispensing systems.

Sales: $222.2 million (trend 7.3% a year).
Earnings: $4.71 million (trend 5.2% a year).
What happened to a $10,000 investment

Purchase Date	*Purchase Price*	*Price on 12-31-81*	*Dividends Paid*
12-31-71	$16.37	$13.37	$4,900.76
12-31-76	$11.62	$13.37	$3,612.90

Purchase Date	*Cap. Gains (− Losses)*	*Total Return*	*Rate of Return*
12-31-71	$−1,832.06	$3,068.70	2.71%
12-31-76	$ 1,505.38	$5,118.28	8.62%

* * *

MEAD CORP. (MEA). Founded 1930. Headquarters: Courthouse Plaza N.E., Dayton OH 45463. **PAPER, PACKAGING.** Mead is a major producer of paper and packaging materials. Also has lumber operations, manufactures iron castings, and has relatively small sidelines in coal mining, pipe and valve distribution, school supplies, and parts making for oil rigs. 25,000 employees. **MAJOR SUBSIDIARIES, BRANDS:** Mead is a part owner of British Columbia Forest Products, Brunswick Pulp & Paper Co., Georgia Kraft Co., and Northwood Forest Industries Ltd.

Sales: $2,707.2 million (trend 17.2% a year).
Earnings: $127.60 million (trend 22.7% a year).
What happened to a $10,000 investment

Purchase Date	*Purchase Price*	*Price on 12-31-81*	*Dividends Paid*
12-31-71	$13.50	$23.25	$7,935.80
12-31-76	$20.75	$23.25	$3,657.83

Purchase Date	*Cap. Gains (− Losses)*	*Total Return*	*Rate of Return*
12-31-71	$7,222.22	$15,158.02	9.66%
12-31-76	$1,204.82	$ 4,862.65	8.25%

PROFILE: Mead is roughly the seventh largest U.S. forest products company. Compared to most, it is more attuned to paper and packaging sales, less attuned to lumber and building products. Thus it weathered the severe housing slump of 1979–81 fairly well, though earnings were hurt by the recession that was going on at the same time.

One thing setting Mead apart from many companies is the way its board of directors functions. Ten of its fifteen members are outsiders, and directors take a very active part in running the company. An active, outsider-dominated board has been urged by many students of corporate governance. Mead shareholders will have a good chance to see how it works in practice.

Mead's earnings have been erratic, but they've shown a definite upward trend. The dividend yield in recent years has been in the 6 to 7 percent range; dividends have been paid each year since 1940. The balance sheet is about average for a forest products company with debt around a third of capital.

The company's greatest visibility in recent years came in 1978, when it fought a bloody and publicity-grabbing battle to prevent a hostile take-over by Occidental Petroleum. Mead executives and board members used a variety of techniques to block the take-over, including strong public statements criticizing Occidental's reputation. The successful battle to preserve the company's independence buoyed morale and the stock price, at least temporarily.

* * *

MEASUREX CORP. (MX). Founded 1968. Headquarters: 1 Results Way, Cupertino CA 95014. CONTROL SYSTEMS. Measurex makes sensor-based process control systems for manufacturing operations.

Sales: $122.0 million (trend 21.8% a year).
Earnings: $7.32 million (trend 23.0% a year).
What happened to a $10,000 investment

Purchase Date	*Purchase Price*	*Price on 12-31-81*	*Dividends Paid*
12-31-71	$ N/A	$15.62	$ N/A
12-31-76	$13.87	$15.62	$1,398.20

Purchase Date	*Cap. Gains (− Losses)*	*Total Return*	*Rate of Return*
12-31-71	$ N/A	$ N/A	N/A%
12-31-76	$1,261.26	$2,659.46	4.83%

* * *

MEDTRONIC, INC. (MDT). Founded 1950. Headquarters: 3055 Old Highway Eight, Minneapolis MN 55440. MEDICAL DEVICES. Medtronic manufactures pacemakers and their components.

Sales: $313.6 million (trend 20.1% a year).
Earnings: $41.87 million (trend 29.1% a year).
What happened to a $10,000 investment

Purchase Date	*Purchase Price*	*Price on 12-31-81*	*Dividends Paid*
12-31-71	$14.81	$38.37	$ 823.63
12-31-76	$11.25	$38.37	$1,084.44

Purchase Date	*Cap. Gains (− Losses)*	*Total Return*	*Rate of Return*
12-31-71	$15,907.17	$16,730.80	10.33%
12-31-76	$24,111.11	$25,195.56	28.62%

* * *

MELLON NATIONAL CORP. (MEL). Founded 1971. Headquarters: PO Box 15629, Pittsburgh PA 15244. BANK. The corporation is the holding company for the nation's sixteenth largest commercial bank, Mellon National Bank, which has more than 100 offices in Pennsylvania (near Pittsburgh) and more than 10 abroad. 7,000 employees. MAJOR SUBSIDIARIES, BRANDS: Mellon National Bank.

Sales: $1,594.8 million (trend 18.9% a year).
Earnings: $114.17 million (trend 13.6% a year).
What happened to a $10,000 investment

Purchase Date	*Purchase Price*	*Price on 12-31-81*	*Dividends Paid*
12-31-71	$25.62	$36.75	$5,880.98
12-31-76	$29.12	$36.75	$3,002.58

Purchase Date	*Cap. Gains (− Losses)*	*Total Return*	*Rate of Return*
12-31-71	$4,341.46	$10,222.44	7.30%
12-31-76	$2,618.03	$ 5,620.60	9.33%

PROFILE: Why would anyone want to invest in a stock with a recent track record as stolid, as unexciting, as Mellon National? Well, some people have an aversion to losing their money. This stock's about as safe as they come (though *any* stock, by definition, involves risk). With the shares priced conservatively, as they were in the early 1980s, it seems likely that any surprises are more likely to be on the upside than the downside.

In four of the five years from 1976 to 1980, you could have picked up Mellon National shares for $30 a share at some point in the year. In four of the five years from 1965 to 1969, the same thing was true.

Clearly, this has not been an excellent vehicle for capital gains in recent years. Meanwhile, the dividend yield has slowly grown, from less than 3 percent in the mid-1960s to between 6 and 7 percent lately.

Profit growth has been at a walk, but steady.

Following a mild downturn in 1971–72, earnings posted their ninth straight gain in 1981.

In several ways, this is a conservative bank. Most banks don't employ much leverage; Mellon uses less than average. Loan losses have historically been lower here than at the average bank; in 1980, they were about 0.4 percent of loans. But Mellon maintains a larger than average loan loss reserve, just in case, recently about 1.5 percent of loans outstanding.

Perhaps the biggest attraction here is the very low p/e ratio. The shares, which commanded 12–19 times earnings in the late 1960s, have sold for only 4–6 times earnings in the early 1980s.

* * *

MELVILLE CORP. (MES). Founded 1914. Headquarters: 3000 Westchester Ave., Harrison NY 10528. SHOES, CLOTHING. Melville is the nation's largest shoe retailer, a major shoe manufacturer, and a leading specialty retailer of men's, women's and brand-name discount clothing. 48,000 employees. MAJOR SUBSIDIARIES, BRANDS: Thom McAn, Vanguard, Meldisco (shoe stores); Foxmoor (women's clothing); Chess King (men's clothing); Marshalls (brand-name clothing at discount—closeouts, overruns, etc.); CVS (health aids, cosmetics).

Sales: $2,332.2 million (trend 20.0% a year).
Earnings: $114.51 million (trend 20.4% a year).
What happened to a $10,000 investment

Purchase Date	*Purchase Price*	*Price on 12-31-81*	*Dividends Paid*
12-31-71	$30.87	$37.75	$3,045.86
12-31-76	$26.75	$37.75	$2,586.92

Purchase Date	*Cap. Gains (— Losses)*	*Total Return*	*Rate of Return*
12-31-71	$2,226.72	$5,272.58	4.33%
12-31-76	$4,112.15	$6,699.07	10.80%

PROFILE: Francis (Frank) Rooney, chairman since 1964, has provided Melville with firm, innovative leadership, sales flair, and an increasingly broad sales base. What was once simply a shoe company has become a leading specialty retailer, deriving only about half of sales and profits from shoe sales.

Rooney likes stores with clear, specialized concepts. Chess King, for example, is clearly aimed at male teenagers and young adults. Marshalls is a place for brand-name clothing at bargain prices. Thom McAn sells only shoes; Foxmoor only women's clothing. Rooney figures that a store selling a single type of item (or a single concept) is likely to inspire consumer loyalty. That's why Melville will often have several stores under different names in the same shopping center.

When you put these discrete operations together, you get the nation's twenty-seventh largest retailer and one with a good growth rate. Melville's earnings have moved up smartly in fourteen of the fifteen years from 1965 to 1980, with only a slight stumble in recession-plagued 1974. Return on stockholders' equity has been outstanding—above 25 percent in many recent years. The number of stores has been growing fast, yet the company hasn't resorted to much debt to fuel the expansion: Debt recently has been a mere 15 to 17 percent of capital.

Shoes, though they're far from the whole story now, aren't being neglected; the company continues to add outlets. Thom McAn now has more than 1,200; and Meldisco (the shoe department in K mart) more than 1,500.

A moderate dividend adds stability to the stock price; dividends have been paid yearly since 1916.

* * *

MERCANTILE STORES CO., INC. (MST). Founded 1919. Headquarters: 100 W. 10th St., Wilmington DE 19899. DEPARTMENT STORES. This retailer operates a large chain of department stores under a variety of trade names in the United States and Canada. MAJOR SUBSIDIARIES, BRANDS: McAlpin's; Jones Stores; Gayfer's; Lion Stores.

Sales: $1,108.1 million (trend 12.9% a year).
Earnings: $42.45 million (trend 8.6% a year).
What happened to a $10,000 investment

Purchase Date	*Purchase Price*	*Price on 12-31-81*	*Dividends Paid*
12-31-71	$63.25	$55.87	$1,338.02
12-31-76	$45.37	$55.87	$1,011.13

Purchase Date	*Cap. Gains (— Losses)*	*Total Return*	*Rate of Return*
12-31-71	$−1,166.01	$ 172.02	.17%
12-31-76	$ 2,314.05	$3,325.18	5.91%

* * *

MERCANTILE TEXAS CORP. (MTD). Founded 1975. Headquarters: PO Box 225415, Dallas TX 75265. BANKING. Mercantile Texas Corp. is a holding company for several banks in Texas. MAJOR SUBSIDIARIES, BRANDS: Mercantile National Bank; Capital National Bank; Corpus Christi National

Bank; Alamo National Bank; American National Bank.

Sales: $554.5 million (trend 54.2% a year).
Earnings: $49.56 million (trend 37.7% a year).
What happened to a $10,000 investment

Purchase Date	*Purchase Price*	*Price on 12-31-81*	*Dividends Paid*
12-31-71	$11.62	$30.12	$5,677.51
12-31-76	$12.75	$30.12	$3,078.38

Purchase Date	*Cap. Gains (− Losses)*	*Total Return*	*Rate of Return*
12-31-71	$15,934.35	$21,611.86	12.20%
12-31-76	$13,626.85	$16,705.23	21.71%

* * *

MERCK & CO., INC. (MRK). Founded 1934. Headquarters: 125 E. Lincoln Ave., Rahway NJ 07065. DRUGS. Merck is one of the leading prescription drug companies in the world. It has sidelines in animal health products, and in pollution control products and services. 31,000 employees. MAJOR SUBSIDIARIES, BRANDS: Aldomet; Blocadren; Clinoril; Elavil; Indocin; Mefoxin; Timoptic; Calgon Corp.

Sales: $2,734.0 million (trend 12.9% a year).
Earnings: $415.35 million (trend 13.0% a year).
What happened to a $10,000 investment

Purchase Date	*Purchase Price*	*Price on 12-31-81*	*Dividends Paid*
12-31-71	$62.12	$84.75	$2,721.13
12-31-76	$68.12	$84.75	$1,515.60

Purchase Date	*Cap. Gains (− Losses)*	*Total Return*	*Rate of Return*
12-31-71	$3,641.85	$6,362.98	5.05%
12-31-76	$2,440.37	$3,955.96	6.89%

PROFILE: Merck is a powerhouse with a magnificent track record. When you buy the stock, you understandably have to pay a premium for this: Often the stock will sell at twice the price / earnings multiple of the average stock. For example, in early 1982 Merck sold at 16 times earnings, while the shares of the average company fetched only 7 to 8. It's the price you pay for buying into an enterprise with a string of more than two decades of uninterrupted earnings rises and a reputation for outstanding research.

Shareholders who bought in during the early 1970s have probably been feeling that they paid *too* high a price, in retrospect. The shares have declined from a peak of $101.50 in 1973 to around $85 in early 1982, with some dips along the way. But then, most people who bought in 1973 were paying 30 to 40 times earnings. Those sorts of multiples are probably best reserved for companies that can coin money.

Merck doesn't coin money, but it has created a stream of new drug successes in recent years, after a dry spell (roughly from 1965 to 1975) during which it depended on established drugs like Aldomet (for high blood pressure) and Indocin (an antiinflammatory). Recent successes include Clinoril (for arthritis), Timoptic (for glaucoma), and Mefoxin (an antibiotic). On the horizon is Blocadren, a new drug for high blood pressure. Most Merck drugs are for combating chronic conditions, allowing for repeat sales.

Dividends have been paid since 1935, but the yield has only recently crept up as high as 3 percent. The balance sheet is very strong, with debt a mere 10 percent or so of capital.

* * *

MEREDITH CORP. (MDP). Founded 1905. Headquarters: 1716 Locust St., Des Moines IA 50336. MEDIA. Meredith Corp. is engaged in printing, publishing, broadcasting, and real estate franchising. MAJOR SUBSIDIARIES, BRANDS: *Better Homes and Gardens; Successful Farming; Metropolitan Home.*

Sales: $403.4 million (trend 15.4% a year).
Earnings: $25.57 million (trend 15.6% a year).
What happened to a $10,000 investment

Purchase Date	*Purchase Price*	*Price on 12-31-81*	*Dividends Paid*
12-31-71	$23.25	$63.25	$3,858.06
12-31-76	$19.25	$63.25	$2,841.56

Purchase Date	*Cap. Gains (− Losses)*	*Total Return*	*Rate of Return*
12-31-71	$17,204.30	$21,062.37	12.00%
12-31-76	$22,857.14	$25,698.70	28.98%

* * *

MERRILL LYNCH & CO., INC. (MER). Founded 1914. Headquarters: 165 Broadway, New York NY 10080. BROKERAGE. Merrill Lynch is the parent to the nation's largest brokerage firm and offers a diversified and expanding range of financial services. These include insurance, investment banking, real estate brokerage, executive relocation, and "cash management," which verges on banking. 27,000 employees. **MAJOR SUBSIDIARIES, BRANDS:** Merrill Lynch, Pierce, Fenner & Smith (brokerage and investment banking); Merrill Lynch Realty Associates (real estate brokerage); Merrill Lynch Relocation Management (employee relocation); Merrill Lynch, Hubbard (real estate financing); Family Life Insurance (mortgage life, mortgage disability, and conventional life and disability insurance); AMIC Corp. (mortgage default insurance); Advance Mortgage Co. Ltd. (mortgage servicing).

Sales: $3,022.5 million (trend 24.8% a year).
Earnings: $204.12 million (trend 14.0% a year).
What happened to a $10,000 investment

Purchase Date	*Purchase Price*	*Price on 12-31-81*	*Dividends Paid*
12-31-71	$34.12	$33.12	$2,320.88
12-31-76	$25.25	$33.12	$1,940.59

Purchase Date	*Cap. Gains (− Losses)*	*Total Return*	*Rate of Return*
12-31-71	$−293.04	$2,027.84	1.86%
12-31-76	$ 3,118.81	$5,059.41	8.53%

PROFILE: Merrill Lynch has long been the nation's largest brokerage firm, dwarfing its nearest competitors (several of whom scramble for the title of distant second). But Merrill Lynch doesn't just want to be your stock broker. In its heart, it wants to be your bank, insurance company, and real estate broker, too. In short, Merrill Lynch (following a blueprint laid down by its former chairman, Donald Regan, now U.S. Treasury Secretary) wants to bring the concept of "one-stop shopping" to financial services.

So far, the insurance operations are small; the growing real estate operations are not established as profitable. But Merrill Lynch runs the nation's largest money market fund. And its incursion into the world of banking — the so-called Cash Management Account (CMA) is enjoying rapid growth and has bankers both scared and angry. The mechanics of the account are too complicated to go into here; suffice it to say that it allows a customer with $20,000 or more to open a margin account and write checks (or use a Visa card) against the credit balance in the account. Any loose money in the account is funneled, at least once a week, into a money market fund.

Despite its controversial and potentially lucrative diversification, Merrill Lynch's best returns for now are coming from its traditional business, brokerage. Stock trading boomed in the late 1970s and early 1980s, bringing in a tide of commissions. (Commissions account for only about a third of profits here, less than at most brokerage houses, but still a big chunk.) Investment banking (managing stock and bond issues) is doing well and is likely to do even better in the years ahead. And Merrill Lynch has been making money from its huge inventory of bonds.

As do most brokerage stocks, these shares tend to fluctuate wildly and erratically. That's how brokerage earnings go. (In 1971–80 Merrill Lynch's earnings doubled, but by a dipsy-doodle path, including five up years, three down years, and one where earnings were unchanged.) The lack of predictability causes investors to grant Merrill Lynch shares only a low p / e multiple — 6 in early 1982. Dividends have been paid each year since the predecessor company went public in 1971, but the yield is slight.

* * *

MESA PETROLEUM CO. (MSA). Founded 1964. Headquarters: 1 Mesa Sq., PO Box 2009, Amarillo TX 79189. **OIL.** Mesa explores for and produces oil and natural gas, mainly in Texas, Louisiana, Oklahoma, the Rocky Mountain Overthrust Belt, and the Gulf of Mexico. It also owns minority interests in several other oil companies. 700 employees. **MAJOR SUBSIDIARIES, BRANDS:** Owns fractional interest (from 1 to 15 percent) in Cities Service, Equity Oil, General American Oil, Sunlite Oil.

Sales: $328.3 million (trend 37.8% a year).
Earnings: $95.24 million (trend 58.7% a year).
What happened to a $10,000 investment

Purchase Date	*Purchase Price*	*Price on 12-31-81*	*Dividends Paid*
12-31-71	$5.13	$20.37	$1,008.10
12-31-76	$9.06	$20.37	$ 488.28

Purchase Date	*Cap. Gains (− Losses)*	*Total Return*	*Rate of Return*
12-31-71	$29,734.05	$30,742.15	15.08%
12-31-76	$12,482.76	$12,971.03	18.10%

PROFILE: Is this a big company or a tiny one? It depends on how you measure. Certainly, no one would pay any attention to Mesa if it were judged by the number of its employees (roughly some 700). And in sales, Mesa isn't big enough to make the Fortune 500.

Profits, though, are something else. Mesa's 1980 profits (around $95 million) would have landed it among the top 200 industrial companies if *Fortune* ranked by profits instead of sales. In 1979 the gushing $286 million profit would have put it among the country's 100 most profitable companies — in fact, seventy-seventh, according to *Forbes* magazine.

How can this relatively small company be so profitable? There are lots of answers. The super profits of 1979 came in part from selling off properties in Canada and the North Sea — moves that look smart in light of political developments (particularly in Canada) since. The company is known for innovative financial techniques — many of them cooked up by chairman and founder T. Boone Pickens, whose stock options were worth an estimated $110 million as of early 1981. (Pickens is also paid some $365,000 a year. One stockholder has sued the company, claiming that Pickens is compensated too well.) Among his moves was the 1980 spin-off of many older producing oil and gas wells into a royalty trust owned by shareholders. The benefit: Income from the wells goes directly to the shareholders and is thus taxed only once (personal income tax) rather than twice (corporate and personal). According to *Time* magazine, other firms may copy this tactic.

Some caveats: The shares are volatile. Dividends, though paid each year since founding, are hardly worth mentioning. The company carries a lot of debt — about half of its capital, as of the early 1980s. And the shares sell for an above-average multiple of earnings — about 14 times earnings in early 1982. Keep an eye on the p / e, and think carefully about how much you're willing to pay.

* * *

MESA ROYALTY TRUST (MTR). Founded 1979. Headquarters: c / o Texas Commerce Bank National Association, 712 Main St., Houston TX 77002. OIL. Mesa Royalty Trust serves to collect and distribute certain revenues from Mesa Petroleum (see that entry).

Sales: $33.9 million.
Earnings: $33.39 million.

* * *

MESABI TRUST (MSB). Founded 1961. Headquarters: Bankers Trust Co., 16 Wall St., New York NY 10015. MINING. This trust receives income from iron ore production done on land it leases to Republic Steel and Armco Steel.

* * *

MESTA MACHINE CO. (MCC). Founded 1898. Headquarters: PO Box 1466, Pittsburgh PA 15230. STEEL INDUSTRY PRODUCTS. This company designs and manufactures heavy machinery used for forming various types of metals.

Sales: $103.2 million (trend 1.1% a year).
Earnings: $−12.11 million.
What happened to a $10,000 investment

Purchase Date	*Purchase Price*	*Price on 12-31-81*	*Dividends Paid*
12-31-71	$26.25	$6.25	$2,361.90
12-31-76	$29.37	$6.25	$ 731.91

Purchase Date	*Cap. Gains (− Losses)*	*Total Return*	*Rate of Return*
12-31-71	$−7,619.05	$−5,257.14	−7.19%
12-31-76	$−7,872.34	$−7,140.43	−22.15%

* * *

METRO-GOLDWYN-MAYER FILM CO. (MGM). Founded 1980; predecessor company was founded in 1919. Headquarters: 10202 W. Washington Blvd., Culver City CA 90230. MOVIES, TV. The company is a major producer of filmed entertainment, mainly motion pictures. Also produces TV shows and runs a film processing laboratory. 2,000 employees. MAJOR SUBSIDIARIES, BRANDS: In 1981 the company acquired United Artists from Transamerica Corp.

Sales: $298.3 million.
Earnings: $23.16 million.

PROFILE: This stock is an interesting but risky speculation. As *Business Week* put it, the company is "bringing the semiretired lion back into the movie business" and "the MGM lion is roaring again."

MGM was one of the largest movie studios for many years, boasting "more stars than there are in heaven" and producing as many as thirty movies a year in its heyday. *The Wizard of Oz, Gone With the Wind,* and *2001: A Space Odyssey* are among its best-known hits. But by the early 1970s that heyday was passed. The movie business in general wasn't doing too well, and MGM was doing worse. Financier Kirk Kerkorian, who bought a 47-percent interest in MGM in the late 1960s, steered the company away from movies and into hotel-casinos (notably the MGM Grand Hotel in Las Vegas). In 1972 thousands of props, including Judy Garland's famed "ruby slippers" from *The Wizard of Oz,* were auctioned off. MGM gave up its film distribution operations (farming the task out, at a fee, to United Artists) and dropped production to about five or six movies a year.

By the late 1970s the movie business looked better again, and MGM enjoyed a couple of hits. Kirkorian decided to reemphasize movies. MGM was split into two companies, MGM Grand Hotels and Metro-Goldwyn-Mayer Films. In 1981 the fledgling (or reborn) film company took over United Artists from Transamerica Corp.

The company had to borrow big to finance the take-over. To restabilize the balance sheet, it will probably have to sell more stock. That, in turn, could dilute per-share earnings for several years and put a damper on the price of the shares. Still, speculators may like the possibility, always present in the movie business, of hitting it big. They also have one eye on MGM's film library of 1,600 past productions, which can be licensed to TV stations and video cassette producers.

Dividends have been paid since the inception (spin-off) of the company, but are too modest to be a factor in the buying decision.

* * *

METROMEDIA, INC. (MET). Founded 1955. Headquarters: 1 Harmon Plaza, Secaucus NJ 07094. **BROADCASTING, BILLBOARDS.** Metromedia owns seven TV and thirteen radio stations, is a major seller of outdoor advertising (billboard and transit), and owns several entertainment attractions. It is also involved in mail-order marketing. 5,000 employees. **MAJOR SUBSIDIARIES, BRANDS:** Foster & Kleiser (outdoor advertising); Harlem Globetrotters; Ice Capades. Broadcasting affiliates are WNEW TV and radio in New York; WMET radio in Chicago; KTTV-TV, KLAC, and KMET radio in Los Angeles; WOMC radio in Detroit; WTTG-TV and WASH radio in the District of Columbia; WCBM radio in Baltimore; WIP and WMMR radio in Philadelphia; KSAN radio in San Francisco; KMBC-TV in Kansas City; KTCN-TV in Minneapolis; KRLD radio in Dallas; WXIX-TV in Cincinnati; KRIV-TV in Houston; and KJR radio in Seattle.

Sales: $453.9 million (trend 16.4% a year).
Earnings: $54.80 million (trend 25.1% a year).
What happened to a $10,000 investment

Purchase Date	*Purchase Price*	*Price on 12-31-81*	*Dividends Paid*
12-31-71	$26.07	$160.25	$5,949.26
12-31-76	$27.75	$160.25	$4,612.61

Purchase Date	*Cap. Gains (− Losses)*	*Total Return*	*Rate of Return*
12-31-71	$51,465.02	$57,414.28	21.03%
12-31-76	$47,747.75	$52,360.36	44.21%

PROFILE: The Federal Communications Commission (FCC) allows any single company to own no more than seven stations in each of three major categories — TV, AM radio, and FM radio. By 1979, as *Financial World* observed, Metromedia had "assembled almost a full deck." In the early 1980s the company had seven TV stations, seven FM radio stations, and six AM radio stations.

Broadcasting accounts for about half of the company's sales and more than half of its profits. The next biggest part of Metromedia is billboards. Foster & Kleiser is the second largest seller of outdoor advertising in the United States, following Gannett. Billboards and ads on buses, subways, and railroad trains account for close to a quarter of sales and close to a third of earnings.

The rest of the company is a grab bag that includes the Harlem Globetrotters, the Ice Capades, and a mail-order marketing operation. Put it all together and you've got a mix that was quite profitable during the 1970s. Profits rose in eight of the ten years from 1971 to 1980 (1973–74 was the down period) and bounded up from $2.15 a share in 1975 to $12.36 in 1980. A fair part of that increase was due to the company's borrowing money to buy back its own stock (reducing the number of shares outstanding, and thus improving the per-share results). That left Metromedia with a highly leveraged balance sheet in the early 1980s (debt was close to half of total capital in 1981), making this stock perhaps unsuitable for risk-averse investors, but more attractive to investors who will accept some risk in hopes of higher return. The stock price zoomed from a 1974 low of $4.25 a share to a 1980 high of $107. (On the other hand, it had fallen to its 1974 low from a 1968 high of almost $54 a share.)

Dividends have been paid each year since 1962, increased each year since 1971. The dividend yield is moderate — about 4 to 5 percent in most periods during recent years.

* * *

MEXICO FUND, INC. (MXF). Founded 1981. Headquarters: 1 Liberty Plaza, 165 Broadway, New York NY 10080. **INVESTMENT CO.** Invests almost exclusively in Mexican financial instruments (mainly stocks, some debt securities and bank paper).

* * *

MICHIGAN ENERGY RESOURCES (MCG). Founded 1928. Headquarters: 899 S. Telegraph Rd., Monroe MI 48161. NATURAL GAS. Michigan Energy Resources is the holding company for Michigan Gas Utilities, which distributes natural gas in southern and western Michigan.

Sales: $123.8 million (trend 18.7% a year).
Earnings: $2.58 million (trend −2.4% a year).
What happened to a $10,000 investment

Purchase Date	*Purchase Price*	*Price on 12-31-81*	*Dividends Paid*
12-31-71	$13.83	$11.25	$7,913.20
12-31-76	$12.93	$11.25	$4,763.25

Purchase Date	*Cap. Gains (− Losses)*	*Total Return*	*Rate of Return*
12-31-71	$−1,866.82	$6,046.39	4.84%
12-31-76	$−1,296.07	$3,467.19	6.13%

* * *

MID-CONTINENT TELEPHONE CORP. (MID). Founded 1960. Headquarters: 100 Executive Parkway, Hudson OH 44236. TELEPHONE. Mid-Continent Telephone is a large independent phone system operating in thirteen states. MAJOR SUBSIDIARIES, BRANDS: Buckeye Telephone and Supply.

Sales: $253.9 million (trend 15.6% a year).
Earnings: $27.97 million (trend 16.8% a year).
What happened to a $10,000 investment

Purchase Date	*Purchase Price*	*Price on 12-31-81*	*Dividends Paid*
12-31-71	$17.50	$17.75	$7,257.14
12-31-76	$17.12	$17.75	$4,432.12

Purchase Date	*Cap. Gains (− Losses)*	*Total Return*	*Rate of Return*
12-31-71	$142.86	$7,400.00	5.70%
12-31-76	$364.96	$4,797.08	8.15%

* * *

MIDCON CORP. (MCN). Founded 1981. Headquarters: 122 S. Michigan Ave., Chicago Il 60603. ENERGY. This company is a spin-off of the unregulated and less regulated divisions of Peoples Energy Corp. (see that entry). Its main business is natural gas transmission from the Gulf states and southwest to Chicago and surrounding areas. It is also involved in gas and oil explorations, contract drilling, and coal mining. MAJOR SUBSIDIARIES, BRANDS: Natural Gas Pipeline Co. of America; Exeter Co. (contact drilling); Industrial Fuels Corp. (coal mining); Buckhorn Petroleum Co.; Harper Oil Co.

* * *

MIDDLE SOUTH UTILITIES, INC. (MSU). Founded 1949. Headquarters: 225 Baronne St., New Orleans LA 70112. UTILITY. This holding company, with five major operating subsidiaries, provides electricity to portions of Arkansas, Missouri, Louisiana, and Mississippi. Also distributes natural gas in New Orleans and operates transit services there. 12,000 employees. MAJOR SUBSIDIARIES, BRANDS: Arkansas-Missouri Power; Arkansas Power & Light; Louisiana Power & Light; Mississippi Power & Light; New Orleans Public Service.

Sales: $2,342.2 million (trend 19.3% a year).
Earnings: $195.91 million (trend 18.6% a year).
What happened to a $10,000 investment

Purchase Date	*Purchase Price*	*Price on 12-31-81*	*Dividends Paid*
12-31-71	$24.75	$12.62	$5,523.23
12-31-76	$16.75	$12.62	$4,543.28

Purchase Date	*Cap. Gains (− Losses)*	*Total Return*	*Rate of Return*
12-31-71	$−4,898.99	$ 624.24	.61%
12-31-76	$−2,462.69	$2,080.60	3.85%

PROFILE: In the early 1980s about the only reason why investors would buy shares in this (or almost any other) utility was for dividends. The yield in early 1981 was a whopping 14 percent, quite close to the yield on AAA-rated bonds at the time. What's more, in some years the dividends (or a major portion of them) are officially considered a "return of capital," and as such aren't subject to ordinary income tax. Rather, they reduce your original cost basis on the stock and affect the amount of the capital gain (if any) you eventually report. (This is a special tax break available only to struggling companies, and generally only to utilities.)

Profits have been essentially flat here for about a decade. As a result, capital gains have been elusive, to say the least. The 1980 high of $14.25 a share was less than half of the 1971 high, $28.62. Because no one can see any reason why the stock should go up, it sells at a low multiple — only 6 to 8 times earnings in the last few years. About the only thing going for the capital-gains-oriented investor here is the low p / e and the unpredictability of the world (including the stock market). Also, utility stocks—because of their high dividends—tend to go up when interest rates go down.

The company is spending heavily on converting from natural gas and oil as energy sources (recently gas supplied 63 percent of the company's energy for electricity generation, oil another 18 percent) to coal and nuclear power. That drains off profits in the short run, but may help in the long run.

Keep an eye on the payout ratio. In 1980 the company had to pay out 79 percent of profits to keep the dividend rising modestly.

* * *

MIDLAND-ROSS CORP. (MLR). Founded 1923. Headquarters: 20600 Chagrin Blvd., Cleveland OH 44122. INDUSTRIAL GOODS. Midland-Ross manufactures furnaces, industrial castings, truck brakes, and air-conditioning systems, as well as electronic products for the construction industry.

Sales: $908.4 million (trend 19.2% a year).
Earnings: $43.58 million (trend 17.7% a year).
What happened to a $10,000 investment

Purchase Date	*Purchase Price*	*Price on 12-31-81*	*Dividends Paid*
12-31-71	$ 8.12	$17.50	$10,230.77
12-31-76	$14.62	$17.50	$ 3,991.45

Purchase Date	*Cap. Gains (– Losses)*	*Total Return*	*Rate of Return*
12-31-71	$11,538.46	$21,769.23	12.25%
12-31-76	$ 1,965.81	$ 5,957.26	9.80%

* * *

MILLER-WOHL CO. (MLW). Founded 1932. Headquarters: 915 Secaucus Rd., Secaucus NJ 07094. RETAIL CLOTHES. Miller-Wohl operates a large chain of women's apparel stores in thirty-two states. MAJOR SUBSIDIARIES, BRANDS: Three Sisters; Jean Nicole.

Sales: $201.7 million (trend 18.8% a year).
Earnings: $19.33 million (trend 25.3% a year).
What happened to a $10,000 investment

Purchase Date	*Purchase Price*	*Price on 12-31-81*	*Dividends Paid*
12-31-71	$ 1.27	$26.37	$28,014.81
12-31-76	$11.62	$26.37	$ 2,800.00

Purchase Date	*Cap. Gains (– Losses)*	*Total Return*	*Rate of Return*
12-31-71	$198,395.06	$226,409.88	37.20%
12-31-76	$ 12,688.17	$ 15,488.17	20.58%

* * *

MILTON BRADLEY CO. (MB). Founded 1860. Headquarters: 1500 Main St., Springfield MA 01115. TOYS. Milton Bradley develops, manufactures, and distributes toys, games, and educational materials. MAJOR SUBSIDIARIES, BRANDS: Playskool; South Bend; MB Electronics.

Sales: $420.7 million (trend 20.6% a year).
Earnings: $29.91 million (trend 30.1% a year).
What happened to a $10,000 investment

Purchase Date	*Purchase Price*	*Price on 12-31-81*	*Dividends Paid*
12-31-71	$26.93	$21.25	$2,478.64
12-31-76	$14.75	$21.25	$3,145.76

Purchase Date	*Cap. Gains (– Losses)*	*Total Return*	*Rate of Return*
12-31-71	$–2,108.03	$ 370.61	.36%
12-31-76	$ 4,406.78	$7,552.54	11.91%

* * *

MILTON ROY CO. (MRC). Founded 1946. 1 Plaza Pl. N.E., St. Petersburg FL 33701. PUMPS, LABORATORY PRODUCTS. This company designs and manufactures controlled-volume pumps, combustion control equipment, and laboratory instruments.

Sales: $55.1 million (trend 2.0% a year).
Earnings: $3.37 million (trend 10.9% a year).
What happened to a $10,000 investment

Purchase Date	*Purchase Price*	*Price on 12-31-81*	*Dividends Paid*
12-31-71	$22.17	$18.87	$ 897.76
12-31-76	$10.17	$18.87	$1,416.43

Purchase Date	*Cap. Gains (– Losses)*	*Total Return*	*Rate of Return*
12-31-71	$–1,484.96	$–587.20	–.60%
12-31-76	$ 8,565.57	$9,982.00	14.85%

* * *

MINNESOTA GAS CO. (MNG). Founded 1928. Headquarters: 733 Marquette Ave., Minneapolis MN 55402. NATURAL GAS. Minnesota Gas supplies natural gas to parts of Minnesota, Iowa, South

Dakota, and Nebraska. It also markets gas appliances and provides a customer appliance service program. **MAJOR SUBSIDIARIES, BRANDS:** Bruest Industries, Inc.

Sales: $435.1 million (trend 21.1% a year).
Earnings: $15.79 million (trend 10.8% a year).
What happened to a $10,000 investment

Purchase Date	*Purchase Price*	*Price on 12-31-81*	*Dividends Paid*
12-31-71	$24.17	$19.37	$7,203.19
12-31-76	$23.62	$19.37	$4,038.10

Purchase Date	*Cap. Gains (— Losses)*	*Total Return*	*Rate of Return*
12-31-71	$−1,982.76	$5,220.43	4.29%
12-31-76	$−1,798.94	$2,239.15	4.12%

* * *

MINNESOTA MINING & MANUFACTURING CO. (MMM). Founded 1929. Headquarters: 3M Center, St. Paul MN 55144. **MULTI-INDUSTRY.** The company sells thousands of products to a wide range of industries; most products are related in some way to coating and bonding technology. Among the major products are photocopying machines, tape, adhesives, photographic film, recording tape, microfilm, abrasives, protective coatings and sealants, insulating materials, and reflective materials. 87,000 employees. **MAJOR SUBSIDIARIES, BRANDS:** Scotch brand tape; Tartan recording tape; 3M copiers.

Sales: $6,079.5 million (trend 14.7% a year).
Earnings: $678.03 million (trend 22.3% a year).
What happened to a $10,000 investment

Purchase Date	*Purchase Price*	*Price on 12-31-81*	*Dividends Paid*
12-31-71	$67.62	$54.50	$2,656.12
12-31-76	$56.62	$54.50	$2,101.55

Purchase Date	*Cap. Gains (— Losses)*	*Total Return*	*Rate of Return*
12-31-71	$−1,940.85	$ 715.27	.69%
12-31-76	$ −375.28	$1,726.27	3.24%

PROFILE: When 1981's earnings showed a tiny downturn, it marked only the second profit decline in thirty years at 3M. The company's consistent success has come from an extremely active and prestigious research and development program, on which the company now spends around $300 million a year.

The other down year in the last thirty was 1975, when earnings fell from $2.66 to $2.29. It wasn't unusual for companies to have down years in 1975: The first wave of Arab oil price increases was pulsing through the economy (hitting 3M hard, since it uses petroleum in many of its products), and the country was just coming out of a recession. Nevertheless, Wall Street reacted like a nineteenth-century Latin-American male who had discovered that his girl friend wasn't a virgin. The stock price dropped from a 1973 high of $91.62 and didn't get much above $66 a share from 1975 through early 1981.

In the early 1980s the shares were trading at 8 to 11 times earnings, a bit above the average multiple, but certainly a modest p / e for a stock with a track record like 3M's. If the company has a weakness, it's probably lack of aggressiveness in using the technology it develops to make consumer sales. (Consumer products are only about a tenth of sales.) On the other hand, the emphasis on commercial and industrial markets may save on advertising, marketing, and distribution costs.

The company's return on equity has been above 20 percent in most recent years. The balance sheet is quite strong, with debt recently less than 10 percent of capital. Dividends have been paid each year since 1916 and provide a moderate yield.

* * *

MINNESOTA POWER AND LIGHT CO. (MPL). Founded 1906. Headquarters: 30 W. Superior St., Duluth MN 55802. **ELECTRICITY.** Minnesota Power and Light distributes electricity to northeastern Minnesota. **MAJOR SUBSIDIARIES, BRANDS:** Superior Water, Light, and Power (SWL&P); Energy Land, Inc.; Topeka Land Co.

Sales: $330.6 million (trend 25.1% a year).
Earnings: $27.68 million (trend 24.9% a year).
What happened to a $10,000 investment

Purchase Date	*Purchase Price*	*Price on 12-31-81*	*Dividends Paid*
12-31-71	$23.12	$17.87	$7,410.16
12-31-76	$21.25	$17.87	$4,564.71

Purchase Date	*Cap. Gains (— Losses)*	*Total Return*	*Rate of Return*
12-31-71	$−2,270.27	$5,139.89	4.23%
12-31-76	$−1,588.24	$2,976.47	5.35%

* * *

MIRRO CORP. (MIR). Founded 1909. Headquarters: 1512 Washington St., Manitowoc WI 54220. ALUMINUM PRODUCTS. Mirro produces aluminum cooking utensils, table appliances; aluminum siding; aluminum and fiber-glass boats.

Sales: $147.0 million (trend 8.8% a year).
Earnings: $3.49 million (trend 4.6% a year).
What happened to a $10,000 investment

Purchase Date	*Purchase Price*	*Price on 12-31-81*	*Dividends Paid*
12-31-71	$18.69	$10.87	$5,116.25
12-31-76	$12.37	$10.87	$3,878.79

Purchase Date	*Cap. Gains (— Losses)*	*Total Return*	*Rate of Return*
12-31-71	$—4,180.60	$ 935.65	.90%
12-31-76	$—1,212.12	$2,666.67	4.84%

* * *

MISSION INSURANCE GROUP, INC. (MEQ). Founded 1960. Headquarters: 2600 Wilshire Blvd., Los Angeles CA 90057. INSURANCE. Mission is a holding company for five major subsidiaries dealing in property and casualty insurance. Virtually all of its business is with commercial clients; the bulk of it is workmen's compensation insurance. 2,000 employees. MAJOR SUBSIDIARIES, BRANDS: Mission Insurance Co.; Holland-American Insurance Co.; Sayre & Toso; Pacific Reinsurance Management Co.; Mission Re Management Co.

Sales: $402.0 million (trend 36.0% a year).
Earnings: $40.49 million (trend 59.5% a year).
What happened to a $10,000 investment

Purchase Date	*Purchase Price*	*Price on 12-31-81*	*Dividends Paid*
12-31-71	$N/A	$35.87	$ N/A
12-31-76	$7.94	$35.87	$3,823.85

Purchase Date	*Cap. Gains (— Losses)*	*Total Return*	*Rate of Return*
12-31-71	$ N/A	$ N/A	N/A%
12-31-76	$35,157.34	$38,981.19	37.41%

PROFILE: Mission is the largest writer of workmen's compensation insurance in California. It also writes a good deal of workmen's compensation coverage in several other states in the Southwest, West, and Southeast. This line accounts for more than half of the company's sales and profits. In some states, notably California, premiums for the insurance (paid by employers) are fixed by state regulators. Insurers compete by the loss-prevention (safety) services they offer and the dividends (in effect, rebates) they pay back to employers. Mission has done well in the competition. From 1970 to 1980 its revenues grew tenfold, from just under $32 million to almost $330 million. Profits over the same period grew twentyfold, from just under $2 million to about $40 million.

The political movement toward more comprehensive workmen's compensation benefits, mandated by state law, has been incomplete and sporadic. But the general tendency has been to mandate more benefits. This naturally raises the price of coverage and increases Mission's premium income.

Other lines of business include placement of excess and surplus risks (mainly large or unusual risks) with out-of-state insurers, commercial multiperil insurance (the business equivalent of a homeowner's policy — and, incidentally, a money loser recently), and liability insurance.

Despite its history of rapid growth, the company sported only an average multiple (about 8 times earnings) in the early 1980s. That's pretty cheap for a company that's grown like Mission. Dividends, paid since 1967, are modest.

* * *

MISSOURI PACIFIC CORP. (MIS). Founded 1928; railroad dates to 1851. Headquarters: 9900 Clayton Rd., St. Louis MO 63124. RAILROAD, NATURAL GAS. This holding company owns Missouri Pacific Railroad, the nation's fifth largest railroad, with some 11,500 miles of track in the Midwest and South. Also owns Mississippi River Transmission Corp., which operates a natural gas pipeline and explores for and produces natural gas and oil. 21,000 employees. MAJOR SUBSIDIARIES, BRANDS: Missouri Pacific Railroad; Mississippi River Transmission Corp.

Sales: $2,237.4 million (trend 15.0% a year).
Earnings: $166.06 million (trend 26.9% a year).
What happened to a $10,000 investment

Purchase Date	*Purchase Price*	*Price on 12-31-81*	*Dividends Paid*
12-31-71	$16.87	$82.25	$11,816.30
12-31-76	$40.87	$82.25	$ 3,519.27

Purchase Date	*Cap. Gains (− Losses)*	*Total Return*	*Rate of Return*
12-31-71	$38,740.74	$50,557.04	19.73%
12-31-76	$10,122.32	$13,641.59	18.78%

PROFILE: Who would have thought in the early 1970s that this would have turned out to be one of the best performing stocks of the decade? Very few people — which is one reason it *was* one of the best performing stocks; expectations of great performance weren't built into the stock price. In the stock market, what matters most isn't doing well, it's doing better than expected.

Missouri Pacific has done both. From about 1965 to 1972 earnings were growing very slowly, and the stock wasn't going much of anywhere. Earnings began to accelerate around 1973, but the stock market didn't take much notice at first. Around 1976 the whole rail group began to move up, as people realized that railroads were an energy-related triple play. (They have extensive natural resource holdings; they transport coal; and they are an energy-efficient form of transportation.) Deregulation helped, too. Through the late 1970s the rail group thrived, and Missouri Pacific did particularly well. From a 1975 high of $23.25, the shares soared to a 1980 high of $115.

Missouri Pacific ranked first among ten railroads in return on total capital in the Forbes 1981 *Annual Report on American Industry.* In return on equity, it ranked second, behind the Chicago & Northwestern, but only because the latter was extremely leveraged. Despite the big run-up in the stock price, Missouri Pacific was still selling for a modest multiple (around 8 to 10 times earnings) in the early 1980s. Dividends are moderate and have been paid each year since 1936.

Part of the stock's rise was due to plans for the railroad to be merged into the Union Pacific. Federal regulators were expected to give their final word on the merger in 1982 or early 1983. (Competitors, predictably, attacked the merger on antitrust grounds.) Some analysts viewed Missouri Pacific shares as a cheap way to buy into Union Pacific. If you are thinking of buying these shares, stay tuned to your newspaper (or your local library) for the latest on the merger.

* * *

MISSOURI PUBLIC SERVICE CO. (MPV). Founded 1950. Headquarters: 10700 E. 350 Highway, Kansas City MO 64138. **ELECTRICITY.** Provides electricity, as well as some gas and water, to northern and central Missouri.

Sales: $153.2 million (trend 15.8% a year).
Earnings: $9.30 million (trend 5.6% a year).
What happened to a $10,000 investment

Purchase Date	*Purchase Price*	*Price on 12-31-81*	*Dividends Paid*
12-31-71	$12.71	$11.25	$6,074.39
12-31-76	$13.02	$11.25	$3,448.79

Purchase Date	*Cap. Gains (− Losses)*	*Total Return*	*Rate of Return*
12-31-71	$−1,147.39	$4,927.00	4.09%
12-31-76	$−1,361.49	$2,087.30	3.86%

* * *

MITCHELL ENERGY & DEVELOPMENT CORP. (MND, American Stock Exchange). Founded 1946; went public 1972. Headquarters: 2001 Timberloch Pl., The Woodlands TX 77380. **GAS, OIL, REAL ESTATE.** Mitchell explores for and produces natural gas and its by-products (propane, butane) and oil; also develops real estate in the Houston-Galveston area, particularly the Woodlands planned community. 3,000 employees.

Sales: $696.0 million (trend 37.2% a year).
Earnings: $100.83 million (trend 32.9% a year).
What happened to a $10,000 investment

Purchase Date	*Purchase Price*	*Price on 12-31-81*	*Dividends Paid*
12-31-71	$N/A	$21.12	$ N/A
12-31-76	$ 5.57	$21.12	$436.74

Purchase Date	*Cap. Gains (− Losses)*	*Total Return*	*Rate of Return*
12-31-71	$ N/A	$ N/A	N/A%
12-31-76	$27,908.08	$28,344.82	30.84%

PROFILE: Of the 1,029 stocks ranked in the 1981 edition of Forbes's *Annual Report on American Industry,* there were only three that had multiplied investors' stake more than twentyfold in the previous five years. Mitchell Energy & Development was one of them, having provided a titanic 2,422 percent increase in the share price (behind only Resorts International and Wang Laboratories).

Since it went public in 1972, the former Roxoil Drilling Inc. (renamed after chairman George Mitchell) has certainly burned up the track. Profits were up for nine straight years through 1981. They had grown from 13 cents a share in 1972 to $2.10 a share in 1981.

The phenomenal growth was not all attributable

to operating results. As *Forbes* pointed out, Mitchell's average return on capital for the five-year period was less than 12 percent, placing it only twenty-ninth among forty-three domestic oil and gas companies ranked. In return on stockholders' equity, it did much better (fifth), with an average annual return of about 36½ percent. Clearly, it was bold use of leverage as much as operating skill that helped George Mitchell produce stratospheric per-share growth. With debt close to two thirds of capital in the early 1980s, this was no stock for conservative investors. Adding to the risk is the relatively high price / earnings ratio (a recent development) — about 13 to 19 in the early 1980s.

Mitchell has been taking the profits from gas and gas by-products (more highly margined) as well as oil and putting them into his pet project, The Woodlands, a large planned community some twenty-five miles from downtown Houston and about fifteen miles from Houston's Intercontinental Airport. The location and the attractiveness of the development itself have caused land and property values to boom.

If you think you might fancy this stock, be aware of one other factor that could heighten its volatility: George Mitchell personally owns about 61 percent of the outstanding shares.

* * *

MITEL CORP. (MLT). Founded 1971. Headquarters: 350 Leggett Dr., Kanata, Ont. K2K 1X3 Canada. **TELECOMMUNICATIONS EQUIPMENT.** Mitel makes electronic equipment, primarily advanced switching equipment for telephone and other telecommunications systems.

* * *

MOBIL CORP. (MOB). Founded 1882. Headquarters: 150 E. 42nd St., New York NY 10017. **OIL.** Mobil is the second largest U.S. oil company, after Exxon, and the country's second largest industrial corporation. It also has interests in retailing, chemicals, and containers. 212,000 employees. **MAJOR SUBSIDIARIES, BRANDS:** Mobil Oil Corp.; Montgomery Ward & Co.; Container Corp. of America; Mobil Chemicals.

Sales: $59,510.0 million (trend 22.1% a year).
Earnings: $2,813.00 million (trend 27.9% a year).
What happened to a $10,000 investment

Purchase Date	*Purchase Price*	*Price on 12-31-81*	*Dividends Paid*	*Cap. Gains (— Losses)*	*Total Return*	*Rate of Return*
12-31-71	$13.66	$24.12	$8,009.15	$7,665.90	$15,675.06	9.89%
12-31-76	$16.31	$24.12	$4,321.84	$4,789.27	$ 9,111.11	13.83%

PROFILE: Mobil's reputation as an exploration company has risen greatly in recent years. From being what some considered the weakest of the five big U.S. international oil companies in exploration, it has gone to being one of the strongest. But investors are worried that politics may undo what a mixture of science and money has accomplished. Much of Mobil's oil is in the Middle East; another big share is off the shore of Newfoundland. Expropriation and excessive taxation are always worries.

Lately those worries have depressed the shares of all the big international oils, Mobil among them. In one sense, investors are on target in Mobil's case: More than 80 percent of its crude is found outside the United States. But investors may have gone overboard in their concern. In the early 1980s Mobil shares were going for only 4 to 7 times earnings. That's a real bargain-basement ratio.

Some other factors have been depressing the shares, too. In 1981 a worldwide oil glut developed, driving down the price of oil, at least temporarily, for the first time in eight years. Montgomery Ward, the nation's fifth largest single-name department store chain (behind Sears, K mart, Penney, and Woolworth) has been a drain on capital lately and a negative contributor to profits. Ward, acquired in 1974 to give Mobil some diversity and a hedge against bad times in oil, has chipped in about an eighth of Mobil's sales. But given the lack of profits, Mobil executives aren't saying they'd buy it again. A 1981 pass at Marathon Oil failed.

Still, long-term investors are often advised to buy on bad news. Mobil's balance sheet is healthy; its dividend is moderate and has been paid each year since 1902. It's doubtful that oil will be in oversupply for the long term.

* * *

MOBILE HOME INDUSTRIES, INC. (MH). Founded 1968. Headquarters: 1309 Thomasville Rd., Tallahassee FL 32304. **HOUSING.** This organization builds and sells mobile homes. **MAJOR SUBSIDIARIES, BRANDS:** Housing by Tiffany; Housing by Vogue.

Sales: $58.4 million (trend .3% a year).
Earnings: $ — .50 million.
What happened to a $10,000 investment

Purchase Date	*Purchase Price*	*Price on 12-31-81*	*Dividends Paid*
12-31-71	$18.12	$2.50	$220.69
12-31-76	$ 4.37	$2.50	$ 0.00

Purchase Date	*Cap. Gains (− Losses)*	*Total Return*	*Rate of Return*
12-31-71	$−8,620.69	$−8,400.00	−16.74%
12-31-76	$−4,285.71	$−4,285.71	−10.59%

* * *

MODERN MERCHANDISING, INC. (MOM). Founded 1968. Headquarters: 5101 Shady Oak Rd., Minnetonka MN 55343. **CATALOG SHOWROOMS.** Operates more than 200 catalog showrooms in some eighteen states, mainly in the Midwest and West. 5,000 employees. **MAJOR SUBSIDIARIES, BRANDS:** Anchor, Dolgin's, Great Western, Jafco, LaBelle's, Miller Sales, Rogers, and Standard Sales catalog showrooms; Creative Merchandising & Publishing (publishes catalogs for other catalog showroom companies, as well as for Modern Merchandising).

Sales: $678.8 million (trend 34.7% a year).
Earnings: $1.31 million (trend −10.6% a year).
What happened to a $10,000 investment

Purchase Date	*Purchase Price*	*Price on 12-31-81*	*Dividends Paid*
12-31-71	$ 8.90	$9.37	$764.04
12-31-76	$13.37	$9.37	$478.50

Purchase Date	*Cap. Gains (− Losses)*	*Total Return*	*Rate of Return*
12-31-71	$ 533.71	$ 1,297.75	1.23%
12-31-76	$−2,990.65	$−2,512.15	−5.62%

PROFILE: Modern Merchandising is the second largest catalog showroom chain, after Best Products Co. Compared to other such chains, Modern tends to carry somewhat more upscale merchandise, particularly in cameras and consumer electronics. According to a 1980 article in *Barron's,* those items make up about 30 percent of the company's sales mix. About 30 percent comes from housewares and gifts, 20 percent from jewelry and silver, 10 percent from sporting goods, and 10 percent from toys. Unlike some catalog showroom chains, Modern will take credit cards; about 30 percent of sales are charged on Visa or MasterCards.

Discounting is an important part of the appeal of catalog showrooms, so profit margins tend to be fairly thin. In recent years, Modern's margins have generally ranged between 2 to 4 percent of sales. Comes a recession, the store is likely to be pinched — and it was, in 1980, with a vengeance. That year, sales rose just a bit, to about $680 million, but profits plummeted to 20 cents a share, compared to $1.52 the year before and $1.67 in the company's best previous year, 1978. In 1981 earnings bounced back, but only a bit.

The majority of catalog showroom operators had poor results in 1980–81, but Modern nosedived worse than most. The stock reacted to the decline by retreating modestly; up until 1978 it had been a sizzling gainer, but extremely volatile. For example, in 1973 the price ranged from $1.75 to $10.75 a share.

Investors' expectations for a recovery were buoying the stock in the early 1980s. The dividend is tiny, the p / e ratio tends to be high, and the balance sheet labors under a lot of debt — more than half of capital in the early 1980s. If you think you might want to invest in these shares, check also the stocks of leading competitors (e.g. Best Products, Service Merchandise) before deciding which horse you want to bet on in the fast but bumpy track of catalog showroom merchandising.

* * *

MODULAR COMPUTER SYSTEMS, INC. (MSY). Founded 1970. Headquarters: 1650 W. McNab Rd., Fort Lauderdale FL 33309. **COMPUTERS.** Modular Computer is involved in the design, manufacturing, marketing, and servicing of high-speed computers.

Sales: $81.1 million (trend 18.2% a year).
Earnings: $3.81 million (trend 14.0% a year).
What happened to a $10,000 investment

Purchase Date	*Purchase Price*	*Price on 12-31-81*	*Dividends Paid*
12-31-71	$N/A	$9.37	$0.00
12-31-76	$ 5.25	$9.37	$0.00

Purchase Date	*Cap. Gains (− Losses)*	*Total Return*	*Rate of Return*
12-31-71	$ N/A	$ N/A	N/A%
12-31-76	$7,857.14	$7,857.14	12.30%

* * *

MOHASCO CORP. (MOH). Founded 1873. Headquarters: 57 Lyon St., Amsterdam NY 12010. **FURNISHINGS.** Mohasco is a major manufacturer and retailer of furniture and carpeting. 16,000 employees. **MAJOR SUBSIDIARIES, BRANDS:** Chromcraft, Futorian, Liberty, and Monarch furniture; Alexander Smith, Firth, and Mohawk carpeting; Cort Furniture Rental; William Volker (wholesale furniture distribution).

Sales: $745.2 million (trend 6.0% a year).
Earnings: $−2.24 million.
What happened to a $10,000 investment

Purchase Date	*Purchase Price*	*Price on 12-31-81*	*Dividends Paid*
12-31-71	$42.25	$12.37	$1,905.33
12-31-76	$18.87	$12.37	$1,549.67

Purchase Date	*Cap. Gains (− Losses)*	*Total Return*	*Rate of Return*
12-31-71	$−7,071.01	$−5,165.68	−7.01%
12-31-76	$−3,443.71	$−1,894.04	−4.11%

PROFILE: The question is whether things could possibly get any worse at Mohasco. For a long time, investors have been waiting for a turnaround here. That expectation has kept the stock price from scraping the floor, but it's a long time since the price was more than a carpet's breadth away.

In parts of 1979 and 1980 the shares traded at less than $8 apiece, compared to a 1972 high of $48.62. From 1973 through 1980 the company had more years when earnings went down than years when earnings went up. The slide finally culminated in a loss of about $2 million (or 34 cents a share) in 1980.

For the last decade, the company has been earning less than 10 percent on stockholders' equity, sometimes a lot less. Even that miserable showing would have been worse if per-share results hadn't been buoyed by a bit of leverage. Debt recently was about 41 percent of capital.

Both dividends and the dividend yield reached a peak in 1974, when the $1.20 per share dividend provided a yield of 8.2 percent. But that was achieved only by paying out more in dividends than the company earned in profits for the year. After 1974 the dividend was chopped, raised a little, held constant, chopped again, and finally, in spring of 1980, eliminated altogether. (Before that, dividends had been paid yearly since 1958.)

A turnaround in home building would help Mohasco. So would the sale of its William Volker furniture wholesaling division, which is on the block. But a merger or a change of management may be necessary to get the company going again.

* * *

MOHAWK DATA SCIENCES CORP. (MDS). Founded 1964. Headquarters: 7 Century Dr., Parsippany NJ 07054. **DATA PROCESSING.** This company is a major producer of systems for data processing, data entry, and word processing.

Sales: $287.4 million (trend 12.6% a year).
Earnings: $18.28 million (trend 59.4% a year).
What happened to a $10,000 investment

Purchase Date	*Purchase Price*	*Price on 12-31-81*	*Dividends Paid*
12-31-71	$21.50	$14.50	$0.00
12-31-76	$ 6.25	$14.50	$0.00

Purchase Date	*Cap. Gains (− Losses)*	*Total Return*	*Rate of Return*
12-31-71	$−3,255.81	$−3,255.81	−3.86%
12-31-76	$ 13,200.00	$ 13,200.00	18.33%

* * *

MOHAWK RUBBER CO. (MWK). Founded 1913. Headquarters: 50 Executive Parkway, Hudson OH 44236. **RUBBER PRODUCTS.** Mohawk Rubber manufactures and sells automobile tires and other rubber products. **MAJOR SUBSIDIARIES, BRANDS:** Friend Tire Service, Inc.

Sales: $180.7 million (trend 4.6% a year).
Earnings: $4.71 million (trend −9.0% a year).
What happened to a $10,000 investment

Purchase Date	*Purchase Price*	*Price on 12-31-81*	*Dividends Paid*
12-31-71	$14.83	$15.37	$5,061.80
12-31-76	$14.92	$15.37	$2,731.84

Purchase Date	*Cap. Gains (− Losses)*	*Total Return*	*Rate of Return*
12-31-71	$365.17	$5,426.97	4.43%
12-31-76	$307.26	$3,039.11	5.45%

* * *

MONARCH MACHINE TOOL CO. (MMO). Founded 1909. Headquarters: 615 N. Oak St., Sidney OH 45365. **MACHINE TOOLS.** This organization produces tools used for milling, drilling, boring, etc.; also manufactures equipment for the manipulation of sheet metal.

Sales: $130.0 million (trend 10.7% a year).
Earnings: $12.15 million (trend 26.5% a year).
What happened to a $10,000 investment

Purchase Date	*Purchase Price*	*Price on 12-31-81*	*Dividends Paid*
12-31-71	$4.81	$19.25	$8,348.05
12-31-76	$6.12	$19.25	$4,783.67

Purchase Date	*Cap. Gains (— Losses)*	*Total Return*	*Rate of Return*
12-31-71	$30,000.00	$38,348.05	17.07%
12-31-76	$21,428.57	$26,212.24	29.35%

* * *

MONOGRAM INDUSTRIES, INC. (MG). Founded 1947. Headquarters: 100 Wilshire Blvd., Santa Monica CA 90401. MANUFACTURING, REAL ESTATE. This diversified company manufactures industrial fasteners, aircraft landing gear, sanitation systems, and sheet metal; also designs and constructs houses, condominiums, and commercial buildings.

Sales: $262.6 million (trend 10.2% a year).
Earnings: $12.84 million (trend 15.0% a year).
What happened to a $10,000 investment

Purchase Date	*Purchase Price*	*Price on 12-31-81*	*Dividends Paid*
12-31-71	$12.25	$49.50	$2,316.73
12-31-76	$12.50	$49.50	$2,150.40

Purchase Date	*Cap. Gains (— Losses)*	*Total Return*	*Rate of Return*
12-31-71	$30,408.16	$32,724.90	15.63%
12-31-76	$29,600.00	$31,750.40	33.09%

* * *

MONSANTO CO. (MTC). Founded 1933. Headquarters: 800 N. Lindbergh Blvd., St. Louis MO 63166. CHEMICALS. Monsanto is the fourth largest U.S. chemical producer, with a specialty in agricultural chemicals. Also produces plastics, textiles, and industrial process control machinery. 62,000 employees. MAJOR SUBSIDIARIES, BRANDS: Fisher Controls.

Sales: $6,573.6 million (trend 12.7% a year).
Earnings: $148.70 million (trend −10.1% a year).
What happened to a $10,000 investment

Purchase Date	*Purchase Price*	*Price on 12-31-81*	*Dividends Paid*
12-31-71	$48.87	$70.12	$5,759.59
12-31-76	$88.12	$70.12	$1,912.06

Purchase Date	*Cap. Gains (— Losses)*	*Total Return*	*Rate of Return*
12-31-71	$ 4,347.83	$10,107.42	7.23%
12-31-76	$−2,042.55	$ −130.50	−.26%

PROFILE: Watching Monsanto in recent years has been like watching a tug of war between the money-making divisions and the money-losing ones. In 1980, for example, agricultural chemicals accounted for only 15 percent of sales, but that division's operating income ($401 million) was greater than the company's after-tax profit for the year. Reason: Good results in agricultural and industrial chemicals were partly offset by big losses in plastics and textiles.

Now Monsanto is implementing a divestiture program to rid itself of operations that have been a drag on profits. First to go (in 1980) was the polyester filament business; without it, it appeared that Monsanto's textile division could operate in the black.

After showing excellent profit growth from 1973 to 1976, culminating in record earnings of $10.05 per share in 1976, the company has been struggling. Recession-burdened 1980 earnings were only $4.06 a share, but in 1981 earnings rebounded to $11.50. The streamlining should help in the short run. Long run, some substantial profit momentum may come from genetic engineering. Monsanto has a minority stake in Genentech, Genex, and Biogen N.V., three of the four best-known gene-splicing specialists. Despite this touch of glamour, Monsanto shares fetched only 8 times earnings in early 1982.

Dividends have been paid each year since 1925. The yield in recent years has been in the 5–7 percent range. The balance sheet's in decent shape, and the future for agricultural chemicals looks bright.

* * *

MONTANA-DAKOTA UTILITIES CO. (MDK). Founded 1924. Headquarters: 400 N. Fourth St., Bismarck ND 58501. ELECTRICITY, NATURAL GAS. Montana-Dakota services communities in North Dakota, South Dakota, eastern Montana, and parts of Wyoming with electricity and natural gas.

Sales: $181.6 million (trend 16.8% a year).
Earnings: $15.19 million (trend 10.7% a year).
What happened to a $10,000 investment

Purchase Date	*Purchase Price*	*Price on 12-31-81*	*Dividends Paid*
12-31-71	$16.62	$18.25	$7,825.56
12-31-76	$17.81	$18.25	$4,407.02

Purchase Date	*Cap. Gains (— Losses)*	*Total Return*	*Rate of Return*
12-31-71	$977.44	$8,803.01	6.52%
12-31-76	$245.61	$4,652.63	7.94%

* * *

MONTANA POWER CO. (MTP). Founded 1961. Headquarters: 40 E. Broadway, Butte MT 59701. ELECTRICITY, NATURAL GAS. Montana Power provides electricity and natural gas to more than half of Montana. Also involved in nonutility resource development.

Sales: $342.5 million (trend 18.7% a year).
Earnings: $37.75 million (trend 5.2% a year).
What happened to a $10,000 investment

Purchase Date	*Purchase Price*	*Price on 12-31-81*	*Dividends Paid*
12-31-71	$30.25	$25.50	$6,332.23
12-31-76	$27.50	$25.50	$3,730.91

Purchase Date	*Cap. Gains (— Losses)*	*Total Return*	*Rate of Return*
12-31-71	$−1,570.25	$4,761.98	3.97%
12-31-76	$ −727.27	$3,003.64	5.39%

* * *

MONTGOMERY STREET INCOME SECURITIES, INC. (MTS). Founded 1972. Headquarters: 315 Montgomery St., Suite 1608, San Francisco CA 94104. INVESTMENT COMPANY. This organization invests in corporate and government debt securities.

* * *

MONY MORTGAGE INVESTORS (MYM). Founded 1970. Headquarters: 1740 Broadway, New York NY 10019. REAL ESTATE. Acquires property throughout the United States; makes construction loans; and holds long-term first mortgages.

Sales: $25.8 million (trend 2.0% a year).
Earnings: $7.61 million (trend 2.2% a year).
What happened to a $10,000 investment

Purchase Date	*Purchase Price*	*Price on 12-31-81*	*Dividends Paid*
12-31-71	$13.62	$5.87	$5,820.18
12-31-76	$11.50	$5.87	$3,286.96

Purchase Date	*Cap. Gains (— Losses)*	*Total Return*	*Rate of Return*
12-31-71	$−5,688.07	$ 132.11	.13%
12-31-76	$−4,891.30	$−1,604.35	−3.44%

* * *

MOORE CORP. (MCL). Founded 1938. Headquarters: 1 First Canadian Place, Toronto, Ont. M5G 1S3 Canada. BUSINESS FORMS. Produces and distributes business forms internationally; also provides small-business computer services.

Sales: $1,804.8 million (trend 12.7% a year).
Earnings: $110.72 million (trend 12.1% a year).
What happened to a $10,000 investment

Purchase Date	*Purchase Price*	*Price on 12-31-81*	*Dividends Paid*
12-31-71	$38.25	$33.25	$3,296.94
12-31-76	$36.25	$33.25	$2,041.38

Purchase Date	*Cap. Gains (— Losses)*	*Total Return*	*Rate of Return*
12-31-71	$−1,307.19	$1,989.75	1.83%
12-31-76	$ −827.59	$1,213.79	2.32%

* * *

MOORE MCCORMACK RESOURCES, INC. (MMR). Founded 1913. Headquarters: 1 Landmark Sq., Stamford CT 06901. SHIPPING, CEMENT, OIL. This is a miniconglomerate built around a shipping line. Major activities includes ocean and Great Lakes shipping, cement making, oil and gas exploration, coal mining, and iron ore mining and pelletizing. 4,000 employees. MAJOR SUBSIDIARIES, BRANDS: Picklands Mather; McCormack Lines; Moore McCormack Cement.

Sales: $641.1 million (trend 18.8% a year).
Earnings: $47.05 million (trend 9.4% a year).
What happened to a $10,000 investment

Purchase Date	*Purchase Price*	*Price on 12-31-81*	*Dividends Paid*
12-31-71	$ 2.72	$29.12	$16,563.22
12-31-76	$20.83	$29.12	$ 1,774.93

Purchase Date	*Cap. Gains (— Losses)*	*Total Return*	*Rate of Return*
12-31-71	$96,989.80	$113,553.02	28.58%
12-31-76	$ 3,980.00	$ 5,754.93	9.52%

PROFILE: Moore McCormack was running ads in 1981 proclaiming that the company is "more than oil and gas." That's very true — in fact, oil and gas accounted for less than 15 percent of the company's 1980 sales. More significant were cargo shipping (28 percent) and cement (22 percent). But perhaps the company didn't want to stress these divisions, figuring that they were less glamorous and less likely to give a shot in the arm to the company's p / e multiple, then an unexciting 7.

When chairman James Barker took over in 1971, the company was basically a shipping company, with sales of about $64 million and no profits (it had lost $12 million in 1970). Barker diversified the company into a variety of areas. His first big move was acquiring Picklands Mather & Co., which mines, ships, and pelletizes iron ore. (It also mines coal.) He strengthened shipping operations by negotiating long-term contracts, mainly for iron and steel (Bethlehem, Republic) shipping. In 1979 he acquired Florida Mining & Materials for $88 million, thus bringing the company into the cement business. With its "dry process" plants and position in the fast-growing Florida market, the acquisition proved a plum. Cement, concrete, and aggregates provided a third of the company's 1980 profits. Barker also pulled Moore McCormack into oil and gas, mainly through buying some Gulf Coast properties from Shenandoah Oil.

This growth and diversification plan swelled the company's debt load. Debt was recently more than half of capital. The dividend yield has hovered around 3 percent in recent years.

* * *

MORAN ENERGY, INC. (MOE). Founded 1935. Headquarters: 262 N. Belt, Suite 300, Houston TX 77060. GAS AND OIL DRILLING. Moran Energy is a contract drilling firm operating in Texas, Oklahoma, New Mexico, Arkansas, and Louisiana.

Sales: $60.9 million (trend 19.2% a year).
Earnings: $13.12 million (trend 45.9% a year).
What happened to a $10,000 investment

Purchase Date	*Purchase Price*	*Price on 12-31-81*	*Dividends Paid*
12-31-71	$N/A	$18.25	$ N/A
12-31-76	$ 3.33	$18.25	$894.75

Purchase Date	*Cap. Gains (− Losses)*	*Total Return*	*Rate of Return*
12-31-71	$ N/A	$ N/A	N/A%
12-31-76	$44,739.63	$45,634.38	40.95%

* * *

J. P. MORGAN & CO. INC. (JPM). Founded 1969; bank dates to 1864. Headquarters: 23 Wall St., New York NY 10015. BANK. J. P. Morgan is the holding company for Morgan Guaranty Trust, the fifth largest U.S. bank. It operates the largest trust department in the United States and is a major factor in commercial, industrial, and international lending. 11,000 employees. MAJOR SUBSIDIARIES, BRANDS: Morgan Guaranty Trust Co.

Sales: $5,173.4 million (trend 22.8% a year).
Earnings: $371.39 million (trend 13.6% a year).
What happened to a $10,000 investment

Purchase Date	*Purchase Price*	*Price on 12-31-81*	*Dividends Paid*
12-31-71	$37.44	$53.75	$5,652.09
12-31-76	$56.25	$53.75	$2,302.22

Purchase Date	*Cap. Gains (− Losses)*	*Total Return*	*Rate of Return*
12-31-71	$ 4,357.26	$10,009.35	7.18%
12-31-76	$−444.44	$ 1,857.78	3.47%

PROFILE: The cachet of the Morgan name has survived from the turn-of-the-century days when the great entrepreneur (or robber baron, depending on your point of view) reigned supreme. Here are a few sentences from a recent *Wall Street Journal* portrait: "Inside the marble-faced building, the desks are mahogany, the chairs are covered with leather, and the draperies are silk. . . . The overall image is prestige. Although Morgan is only the nation's fifth-largest bank, it has long been regarded as the *ne plus ultra* of banking names."

Morgan today boasts a few superlatives. Its trust department is the nation's largest, managing some $30 billion for pension funds, universities, and other clients. The bank is not in the habit of making bad loans. In 1980 net charge-offs were only 0.1 percent of loans, the lowest percentage among the nation's thirty largest banks. Morgan is the largest single holder of the stock of numerous major corporations, including several other banks. And Morgan is the world's largest transfer agent, keeping stockholder records for more than 1,000 companies.

Despite the superlatives and a creditable return on assets (usually around 70 cents per $100 in recent years), there have been some problems. The trust department (which provides only about 5 percent of earnings, but much of the bank's prestige) has been underperforming the market averages in several recent years. A shake-up was in progress in the early 1980s.

Despite a steady stream of earnings rises, going back well over a decade, Morgan stock hasn't gone much of anywhere in the period 1970–80. In the early 1980s it was selling at only around 5 to 7 times earnings, historically an extremely low p / e for this stock.

The dividend, raised each year since 1966, has recently provided about a 6 percent yield. Dividends have been paid every year since 1892.

* * *

MORRISON-KNUDSEN CO., INC. (MRN). Founded 1932. Headquarters: 1 Morrison-Knudsen Plaza, Boise ID 83729. **GENERAL CONTRACTOR.** Morrison-Knudsen is a large international contractor with interests in heavy construction, mining, engineering, commercial building, and shipbuilding.

Sales: $1,735.4 million (trend 11.7% a year).
Earnings: $30.61 million (trend 23.5% a year).
What happened to a $10,000 investment

Purchase Date	*Purchase Price*	*Price on 12-31-81*	*Dividends Paid*
12-31-71	$5.82	$26.25	$8,177.30
12-31-76	$6.83	$26.25	$5,321.74

Purchase Date	*Cap. Gains (– Losses)*	*Total Return*	*Rate of Return*
12-31-71	$35,102.21	$43,279.51	18.21%
12-31-76	$28,459.27	$33,781.01	34.36%

* * *

MORSE SHOE, INC. (MRS). Founded 1961. Headquarters: 555 Turnpike St., Canton MA 02021. **SHOES.** Morse is a major retailer of footwear; also manufactures footwear. Retailing is done both through freestanding stores and leased shoe departments in department stores and supermarkets. 5,600 employees. **MAJOR SUBSIDIARIES, BRANDS:** Morse, Fayva, Upstage, and Jack & Jill stores; Bendey Shoe; Jo-Gal Shoe; Isabela Shoe; Limerick Footwear; Lowell Shoe; Milford Shoe; White Cap Footwear; Soft Spots; Nurse Mates.

Sales: $437.1 million (trend 16.4% a year).
Earnings: $15.86 million (trend 17.0% a year).
What happened to a $10,000 investment

Purchase Date	*Purchase Price*	*Price on 12-31-81*	*Dividends Paid*
12-31-71	$10.90	$13.87	$4,077.18
12-31-76	$ 9.47	$13.87	$3,383.48

Purchase Date	*Cap. Gains (– Losses)*	*Total Return*	*Rate of Return*
12-31-71	$2,730.53	$6,807.71	5.33%
12-31-76	$4,653.10	$8,036.57	12.52%

PROFILE: Morse, after stumbling badly early in the 1970s, regained its stride and turned in several impressive earnings gains late in the decade. It was one of the hot stocks of the latter 1970s, rising from a 1975 low of $1.25 a share to a 1980 high of $29 a share, thanks both to rising profits and to takeover rumors.

The rumors continued into the early 1980s, causing the stock to be volatile. Management has hinted that it wouldn't mind being taken over.

Fayva shoe stores are the fastest growing part of the business and are expanding rapidly. There were more than 400 Fayva stores in 1978, more than 500 in 1979, and more than 600 in 1980; analysts expect continued rapid expansion of this division at about the same pace. Leased shoe departments in discount department stores are expanding much more slowly and recently totaled around 500. Following a trend in retailing toward more specialized stores, Morse has started up a couple of new chains: Jack & Jill for children's shoes and Upstage for women's shoes.

Keep an eye on the balance sheet. As recently as 1976, debt was less than 10 percent of total capital. But partly to fuel the expansion of Fayva, whose high-fashion and imported shoes at discount prices have proved popular, the company has been borrowing more than it used to. Debt recently was about a third of capital.

The p / e ratio has ranged from 6 to 9 in the early 1980s. Dividends are moderate and have been paid each year since 1965.

* * *

MORTON-NORWICH PRODUCTS, INC. (MNP). Founded 1969. Headquarters: 110 N. Wacker Dr., Chicago IL 60606. **SALT, CHEMICAL PRODUCTS.** Morton-Norwich manufactures and sells salt, pharmaceuticals, and household and specialty chemical products. **MAJOR SUBSIDIARIES, BRANDS:** Morton Salt; Spray 'n Wash; Fantastik; Pepto-Bismol.

Sales: $957.6 million (trend 11.3% a year).
Earnings: $53.01 million (trend 36.5% a year).
What happened to a $10,000 investment

Purchase Date	*Purchase Price*	*Price on 12-31-81*	*Dividends Paid*
12-31-71	$27.75	$34.12	$3,765.77
12-31-76	$20.75	$34.12	$2,973.49

Purchase Date	*Cap. Gains (– Losses)*	*Total Return*	*Rate of Return*
12-31-71	$2,297.30	$6,063.06	4.85%
12-31-76	$6,445.78	$9,419.28	14.19%

* * *

MOTOROLA INC. (MOT). Founded 1928. Headquarters: 1303 E. Algonquin Rd., Schaumburg IL 60196. SEMICONDUCTORS, ELECTRONICS. Motorola is a major manufacturer of semiconductors, mobile communications equipment, electronics for cars (including electronic ignition systems, car radios, etc.), and data communications equipment. 71,000 employees. **MAJOR SUBSIDIARIES, BRANDS:** Codex Corp.

Sales: $3,098.8 million (trend 19.6% a year).
Earnings: $186.08 million (trend 30.8% a year).
What happened to a $10,000 investment

Purchase Date	*Purchase Price*	*Price on 12-31-81*	*Dividends Paid*
12-31-71	$42.69	$57.75	$2,114.67
12-31-76	$57.25	$57.75	$1,088.21

Purchase Date	*Cap. Gains (– Losses)*	*Total Return*	*Rate of Return*
12-31-71	$3,528.55	$5,643.22	4.58%
12-31-76	$ 87.34	$1,175.55	2.25%

PROFILE: This company ain't what it used to be — it's better. Old timers may remember that the company's name stems from its original mission, to provide radios for the "motor cars" of the late 1920s and early 1930s. People over thirty will recall that Motorola used to be a big factor in television sets. The TV division was sold off to Matsushita Electric (Quasar) in 1974.

Chairman Robert Galvin, son of the founder, has redirected the company's energy into advanced electronics. Semiconductors, which used to be a small slice of the business, now loom large: They provided half the company's profits and more than a third of its sales in 1980. In fact, Motorola has become the second largest U.S. semiconductor manufacturer, after Texas Instruments. The man on the street doesn't know this, but Wall Street does. That's why Motorola stock carried a price / earnings multiple of 12 in the early 1980s, when the average stock fetched only 8.

The company is in two other growth businesses, as well. One is mobile communications, a field it has been in for a long time but which is now taking off. Portable two-way radios and paging equipment provided another 40 percent or so of 1980 sales and earnings.

Finally, there's the Codex Corp. subsidiary, which makes data communications equipment that enhances the functioning of the increasingly popular distributed data systems. This is a small but very rapidly growing end of the business.

Motorola has paid dividends each year since 1942, but the yield has traditionally been modest. One caveat: Institutions and the Galvin family own about three quarters of the stock. Should the institutions for some reason sour on Motorola, the price could drop a large amount at a crack. In view of the company's recent track record, though, there's not much reason why that should happen.

* * *

MOUNTAIN FUEL SUPPLY CO. (MFS). Founded 1935. Headquarters: 180 E. First South St., Salt Lake City UT 84139. NATURAL GAS. Mountain Fuel Supply is involved in all aspects of natural gas production in Utah and Wyoming. **MAJOR SUBSIDIARIES, BRANDS:** Entrada Industries.

Sales: $399.6 million (trend 22.9% a year).
Earnings: $28.11 million (trend 7.5% a year).
What happened to a $10,000 investment

Purchase Date	*Purchase Price*	*Price on 12-31-81*	*Dividends Paid*
12-31-71	$19.31	$32.25	$8,978.64
12-31-76	$44.50	$32.25	$2,516.85

Purchase Date	*Cap. Gains (– Losses)*	*Total Return*	*Rate of Return*
12-31-71	$ 6,699.03	$15,677.67	9.89%
12-31-76	$–2,752.81	$ –235.96	–.48%

* * *

MUNFORD, INC. (MFD). Founded 1968. Headquarters: 1860–74 Peachtree St. N.E., Atlanta GA 30309. FOOD STORES. Munford operates a large chain of convenience food stores and is also involved in warehousing and import stores. **MAJOR SUBSIDIARIES, BRANDS:** Majik Market; World Bazaar.

Sales: $314.0 million (trend .1% a year).
Earnings: $.43 million (trend −33.6% a year).
What happened to a $10,000 investment

Purchase Date	*Purchase Price*	*Price on 12-31-81*	*Dividends Paid*
12-31-71	$17.37	$10.62	$1,266.19
12-31-76	$ 8.75	$10.62	$ 685.71

Purchase Date	*Cap. Gains (− Losses)*	*Total Return*	*Rate of Return*
12-31-71	$−3,884.89	$−2,618.71	−2.99%
12-31-76	$ 2,142.86	$ 2,828.57	5.11%

* * *

MUNSINGWEAR, INC. (MUN). Founded 1923. Headquarters: 718 Glenwood Ave., Minneapolis MN 55405. **CLOTHING.** Munsingwear is a major manufacturer of men's and boy's sportswear and underwear, as well as women's lingerie and sleepwear. **MAJOR SUBSIDIARIES, BRANDS:** Vassarette.

Sales: $133.5 million (trend 6.7% a year).
Earnings: $−.64 million.
What happened to a $10,000 investment

Purchase Date	*Purchase Price*	*Price on 12-31-81*	*Dividends Paid*
12-31-71	$30.50	$14.75	$3,108.20
12-31-76	$16.12	$14.75	$2,567.44

Purchase Date	*Cap. Gains (− Losses)*	*Total Return*	*Rate of Return*
12-31-71	$−5,163.93	$−2,055.74	−2.28%
12-31-76	$ −852.71	$ 1,714.73	3.22%

* * *

(G. C.) MURPHY CO. (MPH). Founded 1919. Headquarters: 531 Fifth Ave., McKeesport PA 15132. **DEPARTMENT STORES.** G. C. Murphy operates a chain of department stores throughout the United States, primarily in the east. **MAJOR SUBSIDIARIES, BRANDS:** Murphy's Mart; Terry Farris; Bruners; Cobbs.

Sales: $803.7 million (trend 7.5% a year).
Earnings: $9.47 million (trend −11.6% a year).
What happened to a $10,000 investment

Purchase Date	*Purchase Price*	*Price on 12-31-81*	*Dividends Paid*
12-31-71	$26.37	$14.62	$4,216.11
12-31-76	$19.25	$14.62	$2,659.74

Purchase Date	*Cap. Gains (− Losses)*	*Total Return*	*Rate of Return*
12-31-71	$−4,454.98	$−238.86	−.24%
12-31-76	$−2,402.60	$ 257.14	.51%

* * *

MURPHY OIL CORP. (MUR). Founded 1950. Headquarters: 200 Jefferson Ave., El Dorado AR 71730. **OIL.** Murphy is an integrated international oil company with a major ocean drilling subsidiary. Has a small sideline in farming and timber. 4,000 employees. **MAJOR SUBSIDIARIES, BRANDS:** Ocean Drilling & Exploration Co. (53 percent owned); Murphy Oil Co. Ltd. (Canadian, 77 percent owned); Deltic Farm & Timber; Spur gasoline stations.

Sales: $1,966.7 million (trend 16.0% a year).
Earnings: $150.55 million (trend 28.8% a year).
What happened to a $10,000 investment

Purchase Date	*Purchase Price*	*Price on 12-31-81*	*Dividends Paid*
12-31-71	$5.58	$30.75	$5,232.84
12-31-76	$7.75	$30.75	$2,731.18

Purchase Date	*Cap. Gains (− Losses)*	*Total Return*	*Rate of Return*
12-31-71	$45,074.63	$50,307.46	19.68%
12-31-76	$29,677.42	$32,408.60	33.50%

PROFILE: This stock shot up like a rocket in the 1970s. If you'd bought at the 1970 high ($5.12 a share) and sold at the 1980 high ($64), you'd have multiplied your original stake more than twelvefold, disregarding dividends and taxes.

During those years the company's sales grew from about $270 million to almost $2 billion. Profits grew even more dramatically, from about $9 million to about $150 million.

The stock gave up a lot of its gains in the early 1980s, as did many oil stocks. In early 1982 the shares were going for around $30, which was about 7 times earnings (the same multiple as the average stock). That seems quite a reasonable price for a company that's shown Murphy's kind of growth.

True, there were some clouds on the horizon. Oil prices were falling significantly in 1981, for the first time since 1973. And Murphy faces political problems on its Canadian holdings. However, those holdings constitute less than 10 percent of Murphy's proved reserves. (Most of its oil is in the North Sea.) And the falling prices, while they may persist for a while, are unlikely to persist over the long term. Thus, the early 1980s may be a good time to pick up the stock at a reasonable p/e ratio.

The company's gasoline is sold at more than 1,000 Spur stations in the United States, Canada, and Britain. The Ocean Drilling & Exploration Co. (ODECO) subsidiary has done well and may have skirted an overcapacity problem that will afflict some other drilling contractors in the next few years. The dividend, paid since 1961, is modest.

* * *

MURRAY OHIO MANUFACTURING CO. (MYO). Founded 1919. Headquarters: 219 Franklin Rd., Brentwood TN 37027. LEISURE AND LAWN EQUIPMENT. Murray is a manufacturer of bicycles (often sold under house brands), lawn and garden equipment, and mopeds.

Sales: $294.7 million (trend 21.2% a year).
Earnings: $8.47 million (trend 14.4% a year).
What happened to a $10,000 investment

Purchase Date	*Purchase Price*	*Price on 12-31-81*	*Dividends Paid*
12-31-71	$22.96	$19.25	$3,615.56
12-31-76	$12.17	$19.25	$4,397.26

Purchase Date	*Cap. Gains (– Losses)*	*Total Return*	*Rate of Return*
12-31-71	$–1,615.79	$ 1,999.77	1.84%
12-31-76	$ 5,821.92	$10,219.18	15.12%

* * *

MUTUAL OF OMAHA INTEREST SHARES, INC. (MUO). Founded 1971. Headquarters: 3102 Farnam St., Omaha NE 68131. INVESTMENT COMPANY. Mutual of Omaha Interest Shares is a publicly traded investment group fund dealing in both high- and low-grade bonds.

* * *

MYERS (L. E.) CO. GROUP (MYR). Founded 1914. Headquarters: 550 W. Jackson Blvd., Chicago IL 60606. ELECTRICAL CONTRACTOR. This firm is one of the country's largest contractors of electrical transmission systems.

Sales: $190.3 million (trend 19.3% a year).
Earnings: $2.85 million (trend 38.5% a year).
What happened to a $10,000 investment

Purchase Date	*Purchase Price*	*Price on 12-31-81*	*Dividends Paid*
12-31-71	$33.50	$9.25	$1,686.57
12-31-76	$ 9.50	$9.25	$2,736.84

Purchase Date	*Cap. Gains (– Losses)*	*Total Return*	*Rate of Return*
12-31-71	$–7,238.81	$–5,552.24	–7.78%
12-31-76	$ –263.16	$ 2,473.68	4.52%

N

NBD BANCORP, INC. (NBD). Founded 1972. Headquarters: 611 Woodward Ave., Detroit MI 48226. BANKING. Owns and operates some fourteen banks in the state of Michigan. MAJOR SUBSIDIARIES, BRANDS: National Bank of Detroit.

Sales: $1,023.5 million (trend 17.4% a year).
Earnings: $79.96 million (trend 10.8% a year).
What happened to a $10,000 investment

Purchase Date	*Purchase Price*	*Price on 12-31-81*	*Dividends Paid*
12-31-71	$24.12	$24.25	$6,375.13
12-31-76	$27.87	$24.25	$3,271.75

Purchase Date	*Cap. Gains (– Losses)*	*Total Return*	*Rate of Return*
12-31-71	$ 51.81	$6,426.94	5.09%
12-31-76	$–1,300.45	$1,971.30	3.66%

* * *

NBI, INC. (NBI). Founded 1973. Headquarters: 1695 38th St., Boulder CO 80301. WORD PROCESSORS. Produces office automation equipment, primarily word processors and related products.

Sales: $57.6 million.
Earnings: $7.16 million.

* * *

NCH CORP. (NCH). Founded 1965. Headquarters: 2727 Chemsearch Blvd., Irving TX 75061. MAINTENANCE PRODUCTS. Distributes specialty chemicals, fasteners, welding supplies, and electrical and plumbing parts.

Sales: $356.1 million (trend 14.5% a year).
Earnings: $26.81 million (trend 9.4% a year).
What happened to a $10,000 investment

Purchase Date	*Purchase Price*	*Price on 12-31-81*	*Dividends Paid*
12-31-71	$27.44	$14.87	$1,409.38
12-31-76	$22.87	$14.87	$1,075.41

Purchase Date	*Cap. Gains (− Losses)*	*Total Return*	*Rate of Return*
12-31-71	$−4,578.59	$−3,169.20	−3.74%
12-31-76	$−3,497.27	$−2,421.86	−5.40%

* * *

NCNB CORP. (NCB). Founded 1968. Headquarters: 1 NCNB Plaza, Box 120, Charlotte NC 28255. **BANKING, FINANCE.** Company owns North Carolina National Bank, the largest commercial bank in North Carolina; also has consumer finance and mortgage lending subsidiaries. 5,000 employees. **MAJOR SUBSIDIARIES, BRANDS:** North Carolina National Bank; TranSouth Financial; Atlantic Discount Co.; NCNB Mortgage Group.

Sales: $741.9 million (trend 22.1% a year).
Earnings: $47.70 million (trend 23.7% a year).
What happened to a $10,000 investment

Purchase Date	*Purchase Price*	*Price on 12-31-81*	*Dividends Paid*
12-31-71	$24.12	$14.87	$2,393.78
12-31-76	$12.12	$14.87	$2,721.65

Purchase Date	*Cap. Gains (− Losses)*	*Total Return*	*Rate of Return*
12-31-71	$−3,834.20	$−1,440.41	−1.54%
12-31-76	$ 2,268.04	$ 4,989.69	8.43%

PROFILE: NCNB had gotten a little bit too go-go for its own good in the mid-1970s. Since then, like a girl watching her reputation and staying out of back seats, this bank holding company has been acting more conservatively.

The back seats were a lot of fun, though. In the early 1970s the stock used to sell for more than 20 times earnings. The p / e ratio actually hit a high of 38 in 1974. But then came a severe earnings decline, triggered in part by aggressive lending to real estate investment trusts, construction ventures, mobile home makers, and textile firms that ran into problems.

Today, risky loans have been reduced. Construction loans, for example, are a mere bite of the pie, versus a chunk back in the mid-1970s. Long-term debt has also been pared back a bit, though the company remains more leveraged than most banks. The dividend, frozen at 52 cents a share from 1974 to 1977, has been raised each year since 1977 and provides a moderate yield. (Dividends have been paid yearly since 1903.)

The stock has been trading in the $10–16 range the last few years, after going as high as $42 in 1973. The once-lofty p / e ratio was only around 6 in the early 1980s, a shadow of its former self and around the bargain-basement average for bank stocks in a time when the whole banking group was out of favor.

The possibility of a reversal of opinion on the bank group, aided by a possible decline in interest rates in the early 1980s, makes these shares of possible interest. In addition, NCNB is in the forefront of the challenge to laws that prohibit interstate banking. In 1981 it bought a controlling interest in a small Florida bank and then made headlines by offering to buy outright for some $210 million a larger Florida bank, Florida National Banks of Florida Inc. That move was highly controversial and was later dropped. But NCNB said it might go after some other Florida bank. Meanwhile it has been positioning itself more quietly to be ready when interstate banking comes, by snapping up loan company offices in Georgia and Florida. These could quickly be converted to banking offices if and when regulations permit.

* * *

NCR CORP. (NCR). Founded 1926. Headquarters: 1700 S. Patterson Blvd., Dayton OH 45479. **COMPUTERS.** NCR is a leading maker of computers, electronic cash registers, and related equipment. 68,000 employees.

Sales: $3,322.4 million (trend 8.8% a year).
Earnings: $254.86 million (trend 32.7% a year).
What happened to a $10,000 investment

Purchase Date	*Purchase Price*	*Price on 12-31-81*	*Dividends Paid*
12-31-71	$29.37	$43.62	$3,622.13
12-31-76	$37.50	$43.62	$2,026.67

Purchase Date	*Cap. Gains (− Losses)*	*Total Return*	*Rate of Return*
12-31-71	$4,851.06	$8,473.19	6.33%
12-31-76	$1,633.33	$3,660.00	6.44%

PROFILE: Until 1974 NCR was the National Cash Register Co., and that name still gives an insight into the company. True, NCR happens to be the largest U.S. computer maker after IBM. But competing against that giant almost requires a company to pick a niche; NCR's niche has been its old familiar territory, the point of sale. NCR is a leading maker of supermarket electronic scanners, electronic cash registers for retail stores, electronic banking terminals, and bank cash-dispensing machines.

A 1972 deficit of $60 million woke NCR from a semislumber and induced it to bring in a new chairman (William Anderson, who has held the job since) and enter the electronic age with both feet. Besides sounding the death knell for the production of mechanical cash registers, Anderson chopped both blue-collar and white-collar work forces dramatically and put increased emphasis on foreign sales. This last aspect seems natural if one reflects that Anderson was born in China and came to prominence as the highly successful head of NCR's operations in Japan. Recently about half of the company's sales and earnings have come from abroad.

Wall Street, which had bestowed a price-earnings ratio above 30 on this stock in the late 1960s, seems reluctant to repeat a past mistake and has valued it quite conservatively in recent years. In the late 1970s and early 1980s NCR sold for 5 to 9 times earnings, quite a conservative multiple for a leading computer company. The balance sheet is strong, and the dividends, paid yearly since 1934, provide a moderate yield.

* * *

NL INDUSTRIES, INC. (NL). Founded 1891. Headquarters: 1230 Ave. of the Americas, New York NY 10020. **OIL-FIELD SERVICES.** The company is a major supplier of oil-field products and services, particularly drilling muds (lubricants). It also makes pigments and other specialty chemicals and fabricated metal products. 22,000 employees. **MAJOR SUBSIDIARIES, BRANDS:** Baroid; Rucker Co.; Sperry-Sun Inc.; Titanium Metals Corp. (50 percent owned).

Sales: $2,117.6 million (trend 11.2% a year).
Earnings: $163.36 million (trend 27.9% a year).
What happened to a $10,000 investment

Purchase Date	*Purchase Price*	*Price on 12-31-81*	*Dividends Paid*
12-31-71	$ 7.19	$39.75	$8,069.57
12-31-76	$10.31	$39.75	$3,175.76

Purchase Date	*Cap. Gains (− Losses)*	*Total Return*	*Rate of Return*
12-31-71	$45,304.35	$53,373.91	20.28%
12-31-76	$28,545.45	$31,721.21	33.07%

PROFILES: Since the days of Cinderella and the pumpkin coach, there have been few transformations more complete than the one NL (formerly National Lead) has undergone in the past decade. Once a leading producer of lead and of paint (Dutch Boy), the company has all but abandoned those fields and has gradually built itself into a major supplier of oil-field products and services, including drilling muds (which clean and lubricate drill bits underground and also help prevent blowouts) and drilling equipment. To make sure that all this didn't go unnoticed by investors, NL has taken the trouble to place ads in national publications calling attention to the transformation. It was rewarded with a multiple (about 12 times earnings in mid-1981) considerably above that of the average stock. But in late 1981 oil and oil-service stocks sank and NL's multiple dropped all the way to 6 in early 1982.

The company has divested itself of close to fifty operations that it judged to have limited prospects. These divestitures have provided cash to cover most of the tab for the company's push into oil-field services. From its original base (Baroid), NL added Rucker Co. (1977) and Sperry-Sun (1981), creating a likelihood that oil-field services will account for more than three quarters of profits in the mid- and late 1980s.

Some of the older operations that have, at least to date, been retained (e.g. titanium pigments, magnesium die castings) help to generate cash which can be redeployed into the fast-growing areas of the company's business mix.

As the stock price has risen and the company has acquired something of a glamorous tinge, the dividend yield has dropped. It was more than 7 percent in the mid-1970s, but less than 3 percent in 1981. In early 1982 it was just under 4 percent.

* * *

NLT CORP. (NLT). Founded 1968; insurance company dates to 1900. Headquarters: National Life Center, Nashville TN 37250. **INSURANCE.** NLT is a holding company for four insurance companies and four other significant subsidiaries. Life insurance is the company's principal business; property and casualty insurance the other major line. Company also has sidelines in computer services, broadcasting, savings and loan operation, and real estate. 14,000 employees. **MAJOR SUBSIDIARIES, BRANDS:** National Life and Accident Insurance Co.; Great Southern Life Insurance Co.; Guardsman Life Insurance Co.; U.S. National Property Owners Insurance Co.; State Savings and Loan Association (Hawaii and Utah); NLT Computer Services Corp.; Intereal Co. (real estate).

Sales: $748.2 million (trend 9.5% a year).
Earnings: $132.91 million (trend 8.4% a year).
What happened to a $10,000 investment

Purchase Date	*Purchase Price*	*Price on 12-31-81*	*Dividends Paid*
12-31-71	$16.81	$22.75	$4,642.38
12-31-76	$24.25	$22.75	$2,276.29

Purchase Date	*Cap. Gains (− Losses)*	*Total Return*	*Rate of Return*
12-31-71	$ 3,531.60	$8,173.98	6.16%
12-31-76	$−618.56	$1,657.73	3.12%

PROFILE: Growth in premium volume at NLT has been extremely slow over the past decade. The company is struggling to stay even with inflation, never mind showing sales and earnings increases in real terms. Investment income has been keeping the company afloat, but skeptics may question whether interest rates can rise indefinitely. Merger rumors have periodically buoyed the stock, but by and large the shares haven't gone much of anywhere for the past several years.

The company's main business, insurance, is extremely competitive. According to one count, for example, there are some 1,800 life insurance companies in the United States. While this tally can be questioned, the fact remains that competition is likely to keep price competition fierce over the next decade and force some mergers and consolidations. A major part of the competition is from mutual companies which, as nonprofit organizations, do not have to provide a return to shareholders.

When in trouble, diversify. That's an adage some in the business community subscribe to. NLT's diversity is evident (see above), but the diversification is less significant than it may appear. Insurance and investment income account for about 90 percent of earnings here. The savings and loan subsidiary, like most S&Ls, has encountered rocky times recently. Computer services and real estate have shown promise. WSM television in Nashville was sold by NLT in 1981.

Dividends, paid since 1920 and increased regularly in recent years, provide a moderate yield.

In April 1982 American General Corp. said it wanted to acquire NLT through a $1.1 billion stock swap. However, the bid was expected to be opposed both by NLT and by regulators.

* * *

NVF CO. (NVF). Founded 1904. Headquarters: Yorklyn Rd., Yorklyn DE 19736. **STEEL.** Active in steel and coal production; also manufactures vulcanized fiber, laminated plastics, paper, and materials handling machinery. **MAJOR SUBSIDIARIES, BRANDS:** Sharon Steel Corp.; Parsons Paper.

Sales: $885.9 million (trend 19.3% a year).
Earnings: $14.46 million (trend 17.1% a year).
What happened to a $10,000 investment

Purchase Date	*Purchase Price*	*Price on 12-31-81*	*Dividends Paid*
12-31-71	$ .22	$3.10	$6,161.36
12-31-76	$1.21	$3.10	$1,094.02

Purchase Date	*Cap. Gains (− Losses)*	*Total Return*	*Rate of Return*
12-31-71	$133,647.25	$139,808.61	31.09%
12-31-76	$ 15,506.28	$ 16,600.30	21.61%

* * *

NABISCO BRANDS, INC. (NB). Founded 1981. Headquarters: 9 W. 57th St., New York NY 10019. **FOODS.** The company, formed by the 1981 merger of Nabisco and Standard Brands, is a major marketer of processed, branded foods. It has sidelines in drugs, toiletries, food ingredients, and household goods. 61,000 employees. **MAJOR SUBSIDIARIES, BRANDS:** Food brands include Nabisco crackers, cookies, and cereals; Planters peanuts and snack foods; Blue Bonnet and Fleischmann's margarine; Royal gelatin and desserts; Blue Mountain Burgerbits, Fives, Milk-Bone, and Walter Kendall pet foods; Oreo cookies; Ritz crackers; Baby Ruth and Butterfinger candy bars. Other subsidiaries include J. B. Williams, a maker of over-the-counter drugs and toiletries (Geritol, Sominex, Aqua Velva, Lectric Shave); Clinton Corn Processing; Fleischmann Bakery Ingredients; and Life Savers, Inc.

Sales: $3,018.5 million (trend 10.2% a year).
Earnings: $103.94 million (trend 9.2% a year).
What happened to a $10,000 investment

Purchase Date	*Purchase Price*	*Price on 12-31-81*	*Dividends Paid*
12-31-71	$23.31	$31.12	$5,280.86
12-31-76	$30.25	$31.12	$2,441.32

Purchase Date	*Cap. Gains (− Losses)*	*Total Return*	*Rate of Return*
12-31-71	$3,351.21	$8,632.06	6.42%
12-31-76	$ 289.26	$2,730.58	4.95%

PROFILE: Most analysts viewed the 1981 merger of Nabisco with Standard Brands as a marriage made in, if not heaven, at least someplace sensible. Standard Brands was known for its marketing strength abroad, particularly in Britain and Latin America. Nabisco was known for its marketing apparatus in the United States, where it had something like 3,000 salespeople and 12,000 delivery trucks capable of visiting every supermarket in the nation twice a month. Both had a large pantry of well-known brand names. A good fit.

At the time of the merger, Standard Brands was the larger (about $3 billion to Nabisco's $2.6 billion) but Nabisco was somewhat more profitable and growing faster. At first, the two companies said they would "keep their separate identities." But by fall, the company was consolidating and streamlining formerly separate operations that overlapped.

Sales and earnings growth at both companies have been respectable, yet the shares have carried a dull price / earnings ratio (often well below 10 in recent years, and 6–7 in 1981), probably because investors are inclined to regard branded foods as a mature industry.

With a low p / e, long-term debt less than 30 percent of capital, more than $200 million of cash on hand, and a high dividend yield, this stock is well positioned to appeal to conservative investors. Both Nabisco and Standard Brands had paid dividends each year from 1899 to 1980. The merged company was offering a dividend yield around 6 percent in early 1982.

* * *

NALCO CHEMICAL CO. (NLC). Founded 1928. Headquarters: 2901 Butterfield Rd., Oak Brook IL 60521. **CHEMICALS.** Manufacturer of specialty chemicals for oil production, water treatment, and industrial processes.

Sales: $616.7 million (trend 14.2% a year).
Earnings: $72.26 million (trend 16.2% a year).
What happened to a $10,000 investment

Purchase Date	*Purchase Price*	*Price on 12-31-81*	*Dividends Paid*
12-31-71	$30.12	$50.25	$3,352.37
12-31-76	$34.25	$50.25	$2,121.17

Purchase Date	*Cap. Gains (− Losses)*	*Total Return*	*Rate of Return*
12-31-71	$6,680.50	$10,032.86	7.19%
12-31-76	$4,671.53	$ 6,792.70	10.92%

* * *

NAPCO INDUSTRIES, INC. (NAP). Founded 1933. Headquarters: 1600 Second St. S., Hopkins MN 55343. **NONFOOD CONSUMABLES.** Supplies nonfood items to grocery and other retail stores; distributes parts for military vehicles.

Sales: $224.1 million (trend 38.4% a year).
Earnings: $6.12 million (trend 31.3% a year).
What happened to a $10,000 investment

Purchase Date	*Purchase Price*	*Price on 12-31-81*	*Dividends Paid*
12-31-71	$1.69	$17.50	$4,044.73
12-31-76	$3.02	$17.50	$2,072.06

Purchase Date	*Cap. Gains (− Losses)*	*Total Return*	*Rate of Return*
12-31-71	$93,618.35	$97,663.09	26.83%
12-31-76	$47,904.37	$49,976.43	43.09%

* * *

NAPLES FEDERAL SAVINGS & LOAN ASSN. (NAF). Founded 1953. Headquarters: 900 Fifth Avenue S., Naples FL 33940. **SAVINGS AND LOAN.** Savings and loan association with some sixteen branches in Florida.

* * *

NARCO SCIENTIFIC, INC. (NAO). Founded 1945. Headquarters: 455 Pennsylvania Ave., Fort Washington PA 19034. **MEDICAL EQUIPMENT AND DEVICES.** Manufacturer of medical products used in infant care, surgery, intensive care, diagnosis, life-science teaching, and research. **MAJOR SUBSIDIARIES, BRANDS:** Air-Shields; Pilling; Telecare.

Sales: $69.5 million (trend .1% a year).
Earnings: $.42 million (trend −27.1% a year).
What happened to a $10,000 investment

Purchase Date	*Purchase Price*	*Price on 12-31-81*	*Dividends Paid*
12-31-71	$27.12	$14.62	$2,337.33
12-31-76	$12.62	$14.62	$2,645.54

Purchase Date	*Cap. Gains (– Losses)*	*Total Return*	*Rate of Return*
12-31-71	$–4,608.29	$–2,270.97	–2.54%
12-31-76	$ 1,584.16	$ 4,229.70	7.31%

* * *

NASHUA CORP. (NSH). Founded 1957. Headquarters: 44 Franklin St., Nashua NH 03061. COPIER SYSTEMS AND SUPPLIES. Manufactures copy machines and related supplies, coated paper products, and computer and photo products. MAJOR SUBSIDIARIES, BRANDS: Nashua 2210; Davac.

Sales: $671.1 million (trend 17.9% a year).
Earnings: $21.45 million (trend 64.2% a year).
What happened to a $10,000 investment

Purchase Date	*Purchase Price*	*Price on 12-31-81*	*Dividends Paid*
12-31-71	$48.12	$17.37	$1,865.97
12-31-76	$18.25	$17.37	$3,402.74

Purchase Date	*Cap. Gains (– Losses)*	*Total Return*	*Rate of Return*
12-31-71	$–6,389.61	$–4,523.64	–5.84%
12-31-76	$ –479.45	$ 2,923.29	5.26%

* * *

NATIONAL CAN CORP. (NAC). Founded 1929. Headquarters: 8101 Higgins Rd., Chicago IL 60631. CANS. National Can is the third largest U.S. can manufacturer (after American Can and Continental Group). It also makes plastic and glass containers, bottle caps, and food flavorings. 12,000 employees.

Sales: $1,550.9 million (trend 11.8% a year).
Earnings: $53.66 million (trend 23.6% a year).
What happened to a $10,000 investment

Purchase Date	*Purchase Price*	*Price on 12-31-81*	*Dividends Paid*
12-31-71	$16.62	$21.25	$3,769.92
12-31-76	$13.87	$21.25	$2,736.94

Purchase Date	*Cap. Gains (– Losses)*	*Total Return*	*Rate of Return*
12-31-71	$2,781.95	$6,551.88	5.17%
12-31-76	$5,315.32	$8,052.25	12.54%

PROFILE: For years, the return on stockholders' equity at National Can piddled along at between 9 and 14 percent. Suddenly, in 1979 and 1980, it surged above 19 percent. At the same time, long-term debt was sliced to less than 30 percent of capital for the first time since the beginning of the 1970s.

What happened? Did the company reach outside of its traditional can business for a new and different — and highly profitable — product?

Quite the contrary. While its larger can-making rivals, American Can and Continental Group (both profiled elsewhere in this volume), have been looking for ways to diversify, National Can has been putting money into modernizing and expanding its can-making plants. Metal containers (meaning, for all practical purposes, cans) accounted for more than 80 percent of 1980 sales and more than 90 percent of profits.

The company is consistently profitable; its growth rates are steady though not spectacular (can making is a mature business); and dividends have been paid each year since 1963 (the yield is moderate). All of this should add up to a safe, steady, conservative stock. But things aren't quite so simple. The stock price moves around a fair amount in response to merger rumors.

The merger talk is natural since big chunks of the stock are owned by NVF Corp. (recently 32 percent) and Teledyne (recently 14 percent). The former is controlled by controversial wheeler-dealer Victor Posner, the latter by the famed Henry Singleton. Neither appears to want to take over the company, but either could help tip control to a potential acquisitor.

* * *

NATIONAL CONVENIENCE STORES INC. (NCS). Founded 1959. Headquarters: 3200 Travis St., Houston TX 77006. FOOD STORES. Runs several chains of convenience food stores, mainly in Texas and California. MAJOR SUBSIDIARIES, BRANDS: Shop N Go; Super Duper; Stop N Go; Mr. M. Food Stores; Hot Stop.

Sales: $527.4 million (trend 20.8% a year).
Earnings: $10.14 million (trend 30.7% a year).
What happened to a $10,000 investment

Purchase Date	*Purchase Price*	*Price on 12-31-81*	*Dividends Paid*
12-31-71	$N/A	$16.46	$ N/A
12-31-76	$ 2.29	$16.46	$6,286.32

Purchase Date	*Cap. Gains (– Losses)*	*Total Return*	*Rate of Return*
12-31-71	$ N/A	$ N/A	N/A%
12-31-76	$61,738.61	$68,024.93	50.82%

* * *

NATIONAL DISTILLERS & CHEMICAL CORP. (DR). Founded 1924. Headquarters: 99 Park Ave., New York NY 10016. **CHEMICALS, METALS, LIQUOR.** The company has diversified widely from its original base in the liquor industry. It is a major producer of specialty chemicals, brass, titanium, liquor, and wine. Also owns a pair of small property and casualty insurance companies. 14,000 employees. **MAJOR SUBSIDIARIES, BRANDS:** Old Grand-Dad; Gilbey's gin; Vat 69 scotch; Almadén Vineyards; Old Taylor; Old Crow; Windsor Supreme; De Kuyper; Holland House; Sunny Brook; U.S.I. Chemicals; Emery Industries (specialty chemicals); Bridgeport Brass Co.; Indiana Group; Elkhorn Insurance. Owns 11 percent of Cetus Corp. Is 10 percent owned by Panhandle Eastern Pipe Line Co.

Sales: $1,709.8 million (trend 13.8% a year).
Earnings: $101.23 million (trend 8.1% a year).
What happened to a $10,000 investment

Purchase Date	*Purchase Price*	*Price on 12-31-81*	*Dividends Paid*
12-31-71	$15.87	$23.87	$9,275.59
12-31-76	$25.12	$23.87	$3,701.49

Purchase Date	*Cap. Gains (– Losses)*	*Total Return*	*Rate of Return*
12-31-71	$ 5,039.37	$14,314.96	9.29%
12-31-76	$–497.51	$ 3,203.98	5.72%

PROFILE: Ups and downs have been par for the course at National Distillers. In the past decade there have been down years in 1975, 1977, and 1980. However, even in the down years, the company hasn't come close to taking a loss.

Furthermore, a look at the earnings statement alone may cause you to miss some important changes that have been going on here since Drummond Bell took over as chairman in 1970. The company has been cutting back on less-profitable operations (notably brass) and adding capacity in its most profitable line — specialty chemicals, particularly those not based on petroleum. The 1978 acquisition of Emery Industries gave the company a big stake in oleochemicals, which are produced from tallow and vegetable oils. The company also has a big stake in chemicals made from grain and a new, efficient process for producing grain alcohol. In addition the company picked up an early 11-percent stake in Cetus, one of the four best-known genetic engineering firms. While all this was going on, debt was trimmed from about 35 percent of capital in 1971 to about 20 percent in 1981.

Dividends have been paid yearly since 1935 and increased yearly since 1973. In recent years the dividend yield has been a hefty 7 to 8 percent.

The stock's multiple was below that for the average stock for much of the 1970s. In the early 1980s, investors, taking note of some of the developments described above, bid the stock up a bit and raised its multiple to 9, which was just above average at the time.

* * *

NATIONAL EDUCATION CORP. (NEC). Founded 1954. Headquarters: 4361 Birch St., Newport Beach CA 92660. **VOCATIONAL TRAINING.** Provides career training through vocational schools, home study courses, and publishing. **MAJOR SUBSIDIARIES, BRANDS:** RETS Electronic Schools; Spartan School of Aeronautics; Brown Institute; Vale Technical Institute; Bryman Schools; Steck-Vaughan; Intext Communications Systems; International Correspondence School.

Sales: $89.3 million (trend 49.6% a year).
Earnings: $4.04 million (trend 50.9% a year).
What happened to a $10,000 investment

Purchase Date	*Purchase Price*	*Price on 12-31-81*	*Dividends Paid*
12-31-71	$11.08	$15.37	$149.15
12-31-76	$ 3.94	$15.37	$419.05

Purchase Date	*Cap. Gains (– Losses)*	*Total Return*	*Rate of Return*
12-31-71	$ 3,873.95	$ 4,023.10	3.44%
12-31-76	$28,979.18	$29,398.23	31.55%

* * *

NATIONAL FUEL GAS CO. (NFG). Founded 1902. Headquarters: 30 Rockefeller Plaza, New York NY 10020. **UTILITY.** Natural gas utility serving the Buffalo, New York, area.

Sales: $723.4 million (trend 15.2% a year).
Earnings: $22.00 million (trend 6.5% a year).
What happened to a $10,000 investment

Purchase Date	*Purchase Price*	*Price on 12-31-81*	*Dividends Paid*
12-31-71	$24.87	$29.62	$8,854.27
12-31-76	$28.25	$29.62	$4,378.76

Purchase Date	*Cap. Gains (− Losses)*	*Total Return*	*Rate of Return*
12-31-71	$1,909.55	$10,763.82	7.58%
12-31-76	$ 486.73	$ 4,865.49	8.25%

* * *

NATIONAL GYPSUM CO. (NG). Founded 1925. Headquarters: 4100 First International Bldg., Dallas TX 75270. GYPSUM BUILDING PRODUCTS. Manufacturer of gypsum building products, ceramic tiles, and other building products.

Sales: $834.5 million (trend 10.2% a year).
Earnings: $47.46 million (trend 22.6% a year).
What happened to a $10,000 investment

Purchase Date	*Purchase Price*	*Price on 12-31-81*	*Dividends Paid*
12-31-71	$19.62	$21.50	$6,038.47
12-31-76	$17.12	$21.50	$3,854.01

Purchase Date	*Cap. Gains (− Losses)*	*Total Return*	*Rate of Return*
12-31-71	$ 955.41	$6,993.89	5.45%
12-31-76	$2,554.74	$6,408.76	10.41%

* * *

NATIONAL HOMES CORP. (NHX). Founded 1940. Headquarters: 401 S. Earl Ave., Lafayette IN 47904. PREFABRICATED HOUSING. Manufactures prefabricated single- and multi-family homes and commercial structures. Active in sale of resort homesites and other real estate. MAJOR SUBSIDIARIES, BRANDS: NRC, Inc.; National Homes Mortgage Services Corp.

Sales: $83.5 million (trend −3.5% a year).
Earnings: $−6.60 million.
What happened to a $10,000 investment

Purchase Date	*Purchase Price*	*Price on 12-31-81*	*Dividends Paid*
12-31-71	$32.25	$2.37	$93.02
12-31-76	$ 5.25	$2.37	$ 0.00

Purchase Date	*Cap. Gains (− Losses)*	*Total Return*	*Rate of Return*
12-31-71	$−9,263.57	$−9,170.54	−22.04%
12-31-76	$−5,476.19	$−5,476.19	−14.67%

* * *

NATIONAL MEDICAL CARE, INC. (NMD). Founded 1968. Headquarters: 200 Clarendon St., Boston MA 02116. HEALTH CARE SERVICES. Operates out-patient dialysis centers and obesity facilities; distributes respiratory therapy supplies. MAJOR SUBSIDIARIES, BRANDS: Erika, Inc.; Consolidated Medical Corp.

Sales: $245.6 million (trend 24.6% a year).
Earnings: $24.94 million (trend 33.1% a year).
What happened to a $10,000 investment

Purchase Date	*Purchase Price*	*Price on 12-31-81*	*Dividends Paid*
12-31-71	$4.13	$9.62	$3,362.10
12-31-76	$5.30	$9.62	$2,591.82

Purchase Date	*Cap. Gains (− Losses)*	*Total Return*	*Rate of Return*
12-31-71	$13,286.29	$16,648.39	10.30%
12-31-76	$ 8,160.38	$10,752.20	15.72%

* * *

NATIONAL MEDICAL ENTERPRISES, INC. (NME). Founded 1968. Headquarters: 11620 Wilshire Blvd., Los Angeles CA 90025. HOSPITAL MANAGEMENT. Owns some thirty-four hospitals and manages twenty-two more, as of mid-1981. Also owns more than a hundred nursing homes, provides respiratory therapy equipment and services, and owns a subsidiary that makes telephone-answering devices. 25,000 employees. MAJOR SUBSIDIARIES, BRANDS: Hillhaven Corp. (nursing homes); Livingston Medical Products Co.; Hospital Pulmonary Services; Oxygen Emergency Supply, Inc.; Uniservice, Inc. (respiratory therapy); T.A.D. Avanti (telephone-answering machines).

Sales: $881.0 million (trend 52.4% a year).
Earnings: $51.30 million (trend 57.4% a year).
What happened to a $10,000 investment

Purchase Date	*Purchase Price*	*Price on 12-31-81*	*Dividends Paid*
12-31-71	$2.84	$17.37	$3,131.55
12-31-76	$1.92	$17.37	$3,972.16

Purchase Date	*Cap. Gains (− Losses)*	*Total Return*	*Rate of Return*
12-31-71	$51,107.18	$54,238.73	20.44%
12-31-76	$80,532.89	$84,505.05	56.71%

PROFILE: Hospital management stocks were Wall Street's darlings during the past decade, and National Medical Enterprises was among the sexiest of all. In recent years there have been three major splits and several smaller splits and stock dividends. From a 1970 high of $3.62, the shares shimmied to a 1980 high of $23.25.

Had you bought at the 1974–75 low, during the worst bear market since the depression, you could have picked these shares up for 50 cents apiece and turned a $10,000 stake into $460,000, disregarding taxes and dividends.

The dividends should, indeed, be disregarded in deciding whether to buy this stock. Though paid since 1973, they're negligible, as befits a red-hot growth stock. The recent yield has ranged between 1½ and 3 percent.

The company's biggest markets have been California, where most of its wholly owned hospitals are located, and Saudi Arabia, where it has close to $200 million of contract work building and managing hospitals. The company's growth has been spectacular — from $26 million in sales in 1970 to more than $610 million in 1980. Profits over that period grew from $1.6 million to almost $30 million. And there's no sign of any slackening in the momentum.

There is danger in investing in this stock, however. Part of the problem is that nobody can see a cloud on the horizon. When that's the case, investors bid a stock up to a relatively high multiple. The higher the multiple, the more chance investors' expectations won't be met. A glamour stock can drop when earnings slow down, even if the company's still making good money. The recent multiple of 13 isn't outrageous, but keep an eye on it.

The other danger is the highly leveraged balance sheet. Recently, debt was about half of total capital. In most years it's been even more. The company believes in borrowing to finance rapid expansion. That produces fine results when things are going well, but if the company encounters reverses, the heavy debt load could become a crushing burden.

* * *

NATIONAL MINE SERVICE CO. (NMS). Founded 1919. Headquarters: 4900 / 600 Grant St., Pittsburgh PA 15219. **MINING EQUIPMENT.** Manufactures underground mining equipment, distributes mine supplies, rebuilds hydraulic equipment.

Sales: $133.5 million (trend 4.5% a year).
Earnings: $1.16 million (trend −31.0% a year).
What happened to a $10,000 investment

Purchase Date	*Purchase Price*	*Price on 12-31-81*	*Dividends Paid*
12-31-71	$ 6.31	$11.12	$5,940.59
12-31-76	$24.25	$11.12	$1,072.16

Purchase Date	*Cap. Gains (− Losses)*	*Total Return*	*Rate of Return*
12-31-71	$ 7,623.76	$ 13,564.36	8.95%
12-31-76	$−5,412.37	$−4,340.21	−10.76%

* * *

NATIONAL PRESTO INDUSTRIES (NPK). Founded 1905. Headquarters: 3925 N. Hastings Way, Eau Claire WI 54701. **CONSUMER APPLIANCES.** Manufactures small household appliances. **MAJOR SUBSIDIARIES, BRANDS:** Presto; Pop Corn-Now; GranCookerie; ChicknFryer; Liddle Griddle.

Sales: $118.0 million (trend −1.8% a year).
Earnings: $17.46 million (trend 3.8% a year).
What happened to a $10,000 investment

Purchase Date	*Purchase Price*	*Price on 12-31-81*	*Dividends Paid*
12-31-71	$13.12	$31.37	$8,174.60
12-31-76	$23.25	$31.37	$3,349.46

Purchase Date	*Cap. Gains (− Losses)*	*Total Return*	*Rate of Return*
12-31-71	$13,904.76	$22,079.37	12.36%
12-31-76	$ 3,494.62	$ 6,844.09	10.99%

* * *

NATIONAL SEMICONDUCTOR CORP. (NSM). Founded 1959. Headquarters: 2900 Semiconductor Dr., Santa Clara CA 95051. **SEMICONDUCTORS.** The company is the nation's third largest producer of semiconductors (after Texas Instruments and Motorola). It also makes computers, markets its own computers and those made by Japan's Hitachi, Ltd., and makes electronic checkout equipment for supermarkets. 40,000 employees. **MAJOR SUBSIDIARIES, BRANDS:** Advanced Systems.

Sales: $1,110.1 million (trend 30.4% a year).
Earnings: $52.96 million (trend 34.9% a year).
What happened to a $10,000 investment

Purchase Date	*Purchase Price*	*Price on 12-31-81*	*Dividends Paid*
12-31-71	$ 4.47	$19.12	$0.00
12-31-76	$18.58	$19.12	$0.00

Purchase Date	*Cap. Gains (– Losses)*	*Total Return*	*Rate of Return*
12-31-71	$32,763.98	$32,763.98	15.64%
12-31-76	$ 291.48	$ 291.48	.58%

PROFILE: For years this was a glamour stock and had a soaring price / earnings multiple to prove it. In the late 1960s and early 1970s it was common for investors to pay 30 to 40 times the company's earnings to buy in. Most of them weren't sorry. From a high of $4.50 a share in 1971, the stock rose to a 1980 high of $51.50.

But the stock is volatile: People who don't plan to hold it for the long haul should check their timing extremely carefully. In early 1982 the stock sold for around $20, down 61 percent from the 1980 high. In 1975 the price range was from $6.12 to $32.25, and there have been several other years in which the low for the year was only half the high.

The volatility reflects conditions in the semiconductor industry, which is commonly described as cutthroat. National Semiconductor cuts throats — and prices — with the best of them. It's one of the lowest-cost producers and has often slashed prices to gain market share. The industry tends to run hot and cold, with periods of furious demand alternating with periods of overcapacity.

The company has been consistently successful in its basic business, semiconductors. Over the years it's tried several diversification efforts, most of them unsuccessful. Digital watches and pocket calculators were discontinued recently. The latest push is into computers, but the company has yet to prove it can succeed in that tough market, where competition is as fierce as in National's home ground. Recently, semiconductors accounted for about three quarters of sales and an even greater proportion of earnings.

The balance sheet here is very strong, with debt recently only 11 percent of capital. The company has never paid any dividends.

In the late 1970s and early 1980s the p / e ratio had dropped into the 8–12 range, making this stock cheap by historical standards.

* * *

NATIONAL SERVICE INDUSTRIES, INC. (NAS). Founded 1928. Headquarters: 1180 Peachtree St. N.E., Atlanta GA 30309. **MANUFACTURING AND SERVICE.** Manufactures lighting equipment and chemicals; provides linen and uniform service; and engages in other diversified activities.

Sales: $853.4 million (trend 12.9% a year).
Earnings: $50.09 million (trend 16.4% a year).
What happened to a $10,000 investment

Purchase Date	*Purchase Price*	*Price on 12-31-81*	*Dividends Paid*
12-31-71	$27.62	$25.37	$3,180.09
12-31-76	$15.25	$25.37	$3,419.67

Purchase Date	*Cap. Gains (– Losses)*	*Total Return*	*Rate of Return*
12-31-71	$–814.48	$ 2,365.61	2.15%
12-31-76	$ 6,639.34	$10,059.02	14.94%

* * *

NATIONAL-STANDARD CO. (NSD). Founded 1955. Headquarters: 601 N. Eighth St., Niles MI 49120. **WIRE PRODUCTS.** Produces steel wire and wire products, machinery, strip steel, and hot and cold forgings.

Sales: $309.3 million (trend 6.7% a year).
Earnings: $1.11 million (trend –30.5% a year).
What happened to a $10,000 investment

Purchase Date	*Purchase Price*	*Price on 12-31-81*	*Dividends Paid*
12-31-71	$35.62	$14.37	$2,810.53
12-31-76	$16.62	$14.37	$3,536.84

Purchase Date	*Cap. Gains (– Losses)*	*Total Return*	*Rate of Return*
12-31-71	$–5,964.91	$–3,154.39	–3.72%
12-31-76	$–1,353.38	$ 2,183.46	4.03%

* * *

NATIONAL STEEL CORP. (NS). Founded 1929. Headquarters: 2800 Brant Bldg., Pittsburgh PA 15219. **STEEL.** National is the nation's fourth largest steel company. It also produces aluminum and owns a large savings and loan association. 36,000 employees. **MAJOR SUBSIDIARIES, BRANDS:** National Aluminum Corp.; First Nationwide Savings.

Sales: $3,706.7 million (trend 11.8% a year).
Earnings: $83.76 million (trend 10.9% a year).
What happened to a $10,000 investment

Purchase Date	*Purchase Price*	*Price on 12-31-81*	*Dividends Paid*
12-31-71	$44.75	$23.12	$5,575.42
12-31-76	$45.12	$23.12	$2,648.20

Purchase Date	*Cap. Gains (− Losses)*	*Total Return*	*Rate of Return*
12-31-71	$−4,832.40	$ 743.02	.72%
12-31-76	$−4,875.35	$−2,227.15	−4.91%

PROFILE: The steel industry in the United States seems to have become chronically ill. Is the disease the patient's fault? Or would a good boom cure most of what's ailing the industry? That's the question investors must ask.

National Steel, the country's fourth largest steel firm, is a case in point. It specializes in flat-rolled steel. Its major customers are the auto industry, can industry, and appliance industry, in roughly that order most years. (The auto industry was in such bad shape in 1980 that National sold more steel for containers than for autos that year.)

Clearly, without a rebound in those basic industries, National can't prosper. The next best course is to diversify. National has done that by expanding its aluminum operations (which accounted for close to 20 percent of profits recently, though a much smaller percentage of sales) and by moving heavily into the savings and loan business. In 1980 it acquired United Financial Corp. of California. In 1981 it added West Side Federal Savings & Loan Association of New York City and Washington Savings & Loan Association of Miami. They were, in *The Wall Street Journal*'s words, "two of the biggest and sickest thrift institutions in the country." Those three institutions have been combined into First Nationwide Savings, which is the country's fourth biggest savings and loan association. The savings and loan industry is one of the few in the county in as bad shape as . . . well, the steel industry. But falling interest rates could bring a big rebound.

Earnings at National have been on a plateau since the 1960s. If you take inflation into account, real earnings have been falling. Of late, sales volume has just been keeping pace with inflation. These facts contribute to a lack of esteem for the stock on Wall Street: The shares in the last few years have sold for 4–7 times earnings.

However, the balance sheet remains healthy, and the stock has recently yielded 6–8 percent in dividends. Those who think the U.S. steel industry has a future probably can't buy in too much cheaper.

* * *

NATIONAL TEA CO. (NTY). Founded 1902. Headquarters: 9701 W. Higgins Rd., Rosemont IL 60018. **SUPERMARKETS.** Operates a chain of grocery stores in the Midwest and south-central United States. In 1982 National Tea was acquired by Loblaw Companies Ltd., a Canadian firm, and was delisted by the New York Stock Exchange.

Sales: $1,219.3 million (trend −4.8% a year).
Earnings: $8.65 million (trend 9.2% a year).
What happened to a $10,000 investment

Purchase Date	*Purchase Price*	*Price on 12-31-81*	*Dividends Paid*
12-31-71	$13.37	$7.62	$299.07
12-31-76	$ 3.75	$7.62	$ 0.00

Purchase Date	*Cap. Gains (− Losses)*	*Total Return*	*Rate of Return*
12-31-71	$−4,299.07	$−4,000.00	−4.98%
12-31-76	$ 10,333.33	$ 10,333.33	15.25%

* * *

NATOMAS CO. (NOM). Founded 1928. Headquarters: 601 California St., San Francisco CA 94108. **ENERGY.** Natomas is active in oil and natural gas production, geothermal energy, and coal mining; also owns American President shipping lines. 4,500 employees. **MAJOR SUBSIDIARIES, BRANDS:** American President Lines.

Sales: $1,315.6 million (trend 41.4% a year).
Earnings: $208.37 million (trend 35.6% a year).
What happened to a $10,000 investment

Purchase Date	*Purchase Price*	*Price on 12-31-81*	*Dividends Paid*
12-31-71	$9.68	$24.25	$4,304.41
12-31-76	$8.27	$24.25	$4,148.46

Purchase Date	*Cap. Gains (− Losses)*	*Total Return*	*Rate of Return*
12-31-71	$15,061.18	$19,365.59	11.37%
12-31-76	$19,333.32	$23,481.78	27.34%

PROFILE: Most of the news stories you'll read about Natomas concern such exotic enterprises as geothermal energy. Natomas is a big factor in it and is also involved in coal mining (having taken over Brown Badgett Inc. and expanded it), oil recovery from tar sands, and other alternative energy sources. When news regarding any of these projects hits the papers (or the Dow Jones news ticker known as the "broad tape"), Natomas stock is likely to spurt up like a geyser or sink like a prehistoric tiger caught in a tar pit.

All of which is testimony to the semirationality of the stock market. Energy alternatives, intriguing as they are, accounted for less than 10 percent of Natomas's 1980 profits. The shipping line, American President, accounted for a bit less than 20 percent. About three quarters of profits came from oil and gas, and most of that came from the company's traditional mainstay, Indonesian oil.

The company's profit history has been erratic, but there has been no denying the uptrend that capped the 1970s and continued into the early 1980s. The stock enjoyed a major surge in 1980, rising from a 1979 high of about $17 to a 1980 peak of more than $45, before it, like most oil stocks, settled back in 1981. (In early 1982 the price was back down to $24.) The p / e ratio in recent years has been volatile, ranging from 3 to 11. Dividends have been paid each year since 1964 and raised each year since 1974; they provide a moderate yield.

Chairman Dorman Commons, who has been praised by some and damned by others for diversifying the company, seems determined to continue the trend, putting oil money into shipping, geothermal ventures, and coal (another small coal company, Trail Mountain, was picked up in 1981). In 1980 he even considered making a bid for the Southern Pacific railroad, indicating that nonenergy acquisitions are a possibility in the future.

* * *

NEVADA POWER CO. (NVP). Founded 1929. Headquarters: Fourth & Stewart Sts., Las Vegas NV 89101. ELECTRIC UTILITY. Provides electricity for southern Nevada.

Sales: $221.3 million (trend 18.7% a year).
Earnings: $12.41 million (trend 13.6% a year).
What happened to a $10,000 investment

Purchase Date	*Purchase Price*	*Price on 12-31-81*	*Dividends Paid*
12-31-71	$20.07	$21.75	$6,325.38
12-31-76	$13.47	$21.75	$6,629.21

Purchase Date	*Cap. Gains (− Losses)*	*Total Return*	*Rate of Return*
12-31-71	$ 838.87	$ 7,164.25	5.55%
12-31-76	$6,150.99	$12,780.20	17.90%

* * *

NEW ENGLAND ELECTRIC SYSTEM (NES). Founded 1926. Headquarters: 20 Turnpike Rd., Westborough MA 01581. ELECTRIC UTILITY. Provides electric power to portions of Massachusetts, Rhode Island, and New Hampshire.

Sales: $1,090.1 million (trend 9.6% a year).
Earnings: $76.36 million (trend 11.8% a year).
What happened to a $10,000 investment

Purchase Date	*Purchase Price*	*Price on 12-31-81*	*Dividends Paid*
12-31-71	$23.87	$24.75	$8,374.87
12-31-76	$23.25	$24.75	$4,827.96

Purchase Date	*Cap. Gains (− Losses)*	*Total Return*	*Rate of Return*
12-31-71	$366.49	$8,741.36	6.48%
12-31-76	$645.16	$5,473.12	9.12%

* * *

NEW YORK STATE ELECTRIC & GAS CORP. (NGE). Founded 1852. Headquarters: 4500 Vestal Parkway E., Binghamton NY 13902. UTILITY. Provides electric and gas service in New York State.

Sales: $645.3 million (trend 13.5% a year).
Earnings: $73.64 million (trend 18.3% a year).
What happened to a $10,000 investment

Purchase Date	*Purchase Price*	*Price on 12-31-81*	*Dividends Paid*
12-31-71	$21.92	$15.25	$7,364.26
12-31-76	$20.17	$15.25	$4,343.80

Purchase Date	*Cap. Gains (− Losses)*	*Total Return*	*Rate of Return*
12-31-71	$−3,041.83	$4,322.43	3.66%
12-31-76	$−2,438.02	$1,905.79	3.55%

* * *

NEWELL COMPANIES, INC. (NWL). Founded 1970. Headquarters: 29 E. Stephenson St., Freeport IL 61032. HOME IMPROVEMENT PRODUCTS. Manufactures drapery hardware, painting products, shelving systems, hobby and craft products.

Sales: $138.5 million (trend 10.3% a year).
Earnings: $7.82 million (trend 20.3% a year).
What happened to a $10,000 investment

Purchase Date	Purchase Price	Price on 12-31-81	Dividends Paid
12-31-71	$N/A	$14.50	$ N/A
12-31-76	$ 9.25	$14.50	$3,783.78

Purchase Date	Cap. Gains (− Losses)	Total Return	Rate of Return
12-31-71	$ N/A	$ N/A	N/A%
12-31-76	$5,675.68	$9,459.46	14.24%

* * *

THE NEWHALL LAND AND FARMING CO. (NHL). Founded 1976. Headquarters: 23823 Valencia Blvd., Valencia CA 91355. **REAL ESTATE.** Owns agricultural property; involved in real estate development, oil, and natural gas.

Sales: $120.9 million (trend 5.3% a year).
Earnings: $20.56 million (trend 22.2% a year).
What happened to a $10,000 investment

Purchase Date	Purchase Price	Price on 12-31-81	Dividends Paid
12-31-71	$10.75	$29.87	$2,309.30
12-31-76	$ 8.25	$29.87	$1,890.91

Purchase Date	Cap. Gains (− Losses)	Total Return	Rate of Return
12-31-71	$17,790.70	$20,100.00	11.65%
12-31-76	$26,212.12	$28,103.03	30.67%

* * *

NEWMONT MINING CORP. (NEM). Founded 1921. Headquarters: 300 Park Ave., New York NY 10022. **NATURAL RESOURCES.** Leading copper producer; active in exploration and production of nonferrous metals and minerals; interests in oil and gas operations. **MAJOR SUBSIDIARIES, BRANDS:** Magma Copper Co.; Foote Mineral Co.; Carlin Gold Mining Co.

Sales: $881.6 million (trend 11.9% a year).
Earnings: $196.00 million (trend 45.7% a year).
What happened to a $10,000 investment

Purchase Date	Purchase Price	Price on 12-31-81	Dividends Paid
12-31-71	$28.37	$43.12	$5,355.07
12-31-76	$28.25	$43.12	$2,929.20

Purchase Date	Cap. Gains (− Losses)	Total Return	Rate of Return
12-31-71	$5,198.24	$10,553.30	7.47%
12-31-76	$5,265.49	$ 8,194.69	12.72%

* * *

NEWPARK RESOURCES (NP). Founded 1932. Headquarters: 1 Shell Square, Suite 5120, New Orleans LA 70139. **ENERGY PRODUCTS AND SERVICES.** Oil-field products and services; offshore marine services; supplier of drilling fluids; mineral interests. **MAJOR SUBSIDIARIES, BRANDS.** South Louisiana Contractors Inc. (SOLOCO); George W. Townsend Lease Service; LOR Inc.; Newpark Shipbuilding and Repair.

Sales: $186.6 million (trend 39.5% a year).
Earnings: $10.89 million (trend 48.5% a year).
What happened to a $10,000 investment

Purchase Date	Purchase Price	Price on 12-31-81	Dividends Paid
12-31-71	$2.75	$19.25	$1,045.45
12-31-76	$2.44	$19.25	$1,179.49

Purchase Date	Cap. Gains (− Losses)	Total Return	Rate of Return
12-31-71	$60,000.00	$61,045.45	21.66%
12-31-76	$68,974.36	$70,153.85	51.63%

* * *

NIAGARA MOHAWK POWER CORP. (NMK). Founded 1937. Headquarters: 300 Erie Blvd., Syracuse NY 13202. **UTILITY.** Provides electric and gas service in upstate New York and (through a subsidiary) in southern Ontario, Canada. **MAJOR SUBSIDIARIES, BRANDS:** St. Lawrence Power Co.; NM Uranium, Inc.

Sales: $1,777.1 million (trend 12.4% a year).
Earnings: $133.20 million (trend 9.1% a year).
What happened to a $10,000 investment

Purchase Date	Purchase Price	Price on 12-31-81	Dividends Paid
12-31-71	$16.75	$12.37	$7,838.81
12-31-76	$14.37	$12.37	$5,029.57

Purchase Date	Cap. Gains (− Losses)	Total Return	Rate of Return
12-31-71	$−2,611.94	$5,226.87	4.29%
12-31-76	$−1,391.30	$3,638.26	6.40%

* * *

NIAGARA SHARE CORP. (NGS). Founded 1929. Headquarters: 70 Niagara St., Buffalo NY 14202. INVESTMENT COMPANY. Diversified investment company with emphasis on petroleum, metals, and mining.

* * *

NICOR INC. (GAS). Founded 1953. Headquarters: 1700 W. Ferry Rd., PO Box 200, Naperville IL 60566. ENERGY. NICOR is a holding company engaged in the purchase, storage, distribution, and sale of natural gas; oil and gas exploration and development; contract drilling; barge and marine operations; and coal mining. MAJOR SUBSIDIARIES, BRANDS: Northern Illinois Gas Co.; Mid-Continent Gas Storage Co.; Mid-Continent Gasification Co.; NI-Gas Exploration Inc.; National Marine Service Inc.; Acadian Marine Service Inc.; NICOR Mining Inc.; Cardinal Mining Inc.; Eagle Mining Inc.; Lark Mining Inc.

Sales: $1,740.4 million (trend 20.0% a year).
Earnings: $95.27 million (trend 16.7% a year).
What happened to a $10,000 investment

Purchase Date	*Purchase Price*	*Price on 12-31-81*	*Dividends Paid*
12-31-71	$27.50	$33.37	$7,752.73
12-31-76	$30.87	$33.37	$4,132.79

Purchase Date	*Cap. Gains (– Losses)*	*Total Return*	*Rate of Return*
12-31-71	$2,136.36	$9,889.09	7.12%
12-31-76	$ 809.72	$4,942.51	8.36%

* * *

NOBLE AFFILIATES, INC. (NBL). Founded 1969. Headquarters: 330 Neustadt Plaza, Ardmore OK 73401. OIL AND GAS. Active in exploration, production, and sale of oil and natural gas; contract drilling; transport; real estate; and coal mining. MAJOR SUBSIDIARIES, BRANDS: Noble Drilling Corp.; Samedan Oil Corp.; B. F. Walker.

Sales: $271.2 million (trend 21.8% a year).
Earnings: $49.19 million (trend 33.1% a year).
What happened to a $10,000 investment

Purchase Date	*Purchase Price*	*Price on 12-31-81*	*Dividends Paid*
12-31-71	$N/A	$16.75	$ N/A
12-31-76	$ 3.26	$16.75	$941.55

Purchase Date	*Cap. Gains (– Losses)*	*Total Return*	*Rate of Return*
12-31-71	$ N/A	$ N/A	N/A%
12-31-76	$41,319.14	$42,260.69	39.20%

* * *

NORFOLK & WESTERN RAILWAY CO. (NFK). Founded 1896. Headquarters: 8 N. Jefferson St., Roanoke VA 24042. RAILROAD. Norfolk & Western is approximately the nation's sixth largest railroad, with some 7,500 miles of track in the eastern half of the United States and Canada. 24,000 employees. MAJOR SUBSIDIARIES, BRANDS: Norfolk & Western Railway; Delaware & Hudson Railway; Erie Lackawana Railway. Also owns 20% of Piedmont Aviation, Inc.

Sales: $1,576.3 million (trend 7.2% a year).
Earnings: $232.42 million (trend 19.2% a year).
What happened to a $10,000 investment

Purchase Date	*Purchase Price*	*Price on 12-31-81*	*Dividends Paid*
12-31-71	$25.08	$51.87	$7,455.14
12-31-76	$31.62	$51.87	$3,263.24

Purchase Date	*Cap. Gains (– Losses)*	*Total Return*	*Rate of Return*
12-31-71	$10,681.06	$18,136.20	10.90%
12-31-76	$ 6,403.16	$ 9,666.40	14.48%

PROFILE: To be educated about this railroad, you have to learn not about the three Rs but the three Cs — coal, cars, and chemicals. Those are three major categories of freight here, with coal by far the biggest. Coal is what Norfolk & Western has traditionally been known for hauling; it accounts for more than 40 percent of revenues most years.

The presumably bright outlook for coal use helped to trigger an upward movement in the price of most railroad shares around 1980, and Norfolk & Western was certainly no exception. It more than doubled from a 1979 low of about $22 to a 1980 high of about $46. Still, the stock remained quite conservatively valued, at around 6 to 7 times earnings in the early 1980s.

Questions about how much coal the railroad can haul in the future relate chiefly to the coal industry's perennially poor labor relations (frequent strikes) and to inefficiency in U.S. ports (since exports are a growing share of the coal market).

The other big question in the early 1980s for this railroad was when it would merge with Southern Railway to form the nation's third largest road. The combined railroad would have some 18,000 miles of track, would serve the eastern half of the country, and would go head-to-head against CSX. Approval of the merger by regulators was obtained in 1982 so the merger may already have occurred when you read this. (Both companies' shareholders have already approved an arrangement under which each Norfolk & Western share would command one share of "NWS Enterprises," while each Southern share would be worth 1.9 shares in the new company.)

Norfolk & Western is one of the stronger U.S. railroads financially, with debt only about a quarter of capital. It also enjoys a reputation for good on-time performance. Dividends have been paid each year since 1901. In recent years the dividend yield has ranged around 5 to 7 percent.

* * *

NORLIN CORP. (NRL). Founded 1937. Headquarters: Westchester One, White Plains NY 10601. **MUSICAL INSTRUMENTS.** Manufactures musical instruments and technical products; also owns brewery in Ecuador. **MAJOR SUBSIDIARIES, BRANDS:** Gibson and Epiphone (guitars and other string instruments); Lowrey (pianos and organs); Story & Clark (pianos); Pearl (drums); Moog (synthesizers).

Sales: $275.5 million (trend 8.1% a year).
Earnings: $−3.87 million.
What happened to a $10,000 investment

Purchase Date	*Purchase Price*	*Price on 12-31-81*	*Dividends Paid*
12-31-71	$21.25	$14.25	$4,888.24
12-31-76	$17.62	$14.25	$3,042.55

Purchase Date	*Cap. Gains (− Losses)*	*Total Return*	*Rate of Return*
12-31-71	$−3,294.12	$1,594.12	1.49%
12-31-76	$−1,914.89	$1,127.66	2.16%

* * *

NORTEK, INC. (NTK). Founded 1967. Headquarters: 815 Reservoir Ave., Cranston RI 02910. **CONGLOMERATE.** Through various subsidiaries, Nortek manufactures wire and cable; textiles; and pipe. Also produces granite; ventilating and heating equipment; and interior walls. **MAJOR SUBSIDIARIES, BRANDS:** American Flexible Conduit (wire and cable); Whitney Blake Co. (telephone and electrical wire); Duro (textiles); Tooltech (piping, primarily for oil and gas drilling); Rock of Ages Corp. (granite); Broan Manufacturing (ventilation and heating); Glassalum Engineering Corp. (interior walls).

Sales: $143.8 million (trend 18.0% a year).
Earnings: $4.20 million (trend 65.2% a year).
What happened to a $10,000 investment

Purchase Date	*Purchase Price*	*Price on 12-31-81*	*Dividends Paid*
12-31-71	$7.50	$9.25	$ 453.33
12-31-76	$2.75	$9.25	$1,127.27

Purchase Date	*Cap. Gains (− Losses)*	*Total Return*	*Rate of Return*
12-31-71	$ 2,333.33	$ 2,786.67	2.49%
12-31-76	$23,636.36	$24,763.64	28.30%

* * *

THE NORTH AMERICAN COAL CORP. (NC). Founded 1913. Headquarters: 12800 Shaker Blvd., Cleveland OH 44120. **COAL.** Independent coal producer with long-term contract sales of coal to utilities.

Sales: $443.8 million (trend 10.9% a year).
Earnings: $10.25 million (trend 10.0% a year).
What happened to a $10,000 investment

Purchase Date	*Purchase Price*	*Price on 12-31-81*	*Dividends Paid*
12-31-71	$ 9.31	$26.25	$5,159.73
12-31-76	$21.62	$26.25	$1,389.60

Purchase Date	*Cap. Gains (− Losses)*	*Total Return*	*Rate of Return*
12-31-71	$18,187.92	$23,347.65	12.80%
12-31-76	$ 2,138.73	$ 3,528.32	6.23%

* * *

NORTH AMERICAN PHILIPS CORP. (NPH). Founded 1959. Headquarters: 100 E. 42nd St., New York NY 10017. **ELECTRONICS.** This company is a major producer of electrical and electronic components, consumer products, and medical diagnostic equipment. 37,000 employees. **MAJOR SUBSIDIARIES, BRANDS:** Magnavox; Sylvania; Philco; Norelco; Philips.

Sales: $2,658.4 million (trend 13.1% a year).
Earnings: $74.49 million (trend 17.2% a year).
What happened to a $10,000 investment

Purchase Date	*Purchase Price*	*Price on 12-31-81*	*Dividends Paid*
12-31-71	$26.50	$39.25	$5,150.94
12-31-76	$36.25	$39.25	$2,220.69

Purchase Date	*Cap. Gains (– Losses)*	*Total Return*	*Rate of Return*
12-31-71	$4,811.32	$9,962.26	7.16%
12-31-76	$ 827.59	$3,048.28	5.47%

PROFILE: This company is almost two thirds controlled by Philips N.V., a Dutch colossus with more than $18 billion in annual sales. The stories you see in the financial pages about North American Philips are as likely as not to concern alleged friction between the American company and its Dutch parent, or the degree of independence the U.S. firm has, or the size of the latest infusion of technology or capital from the parent. Security analysts argue at length over whether the Dutch connection is an advantage to the U.S. investor. The flow of money and know-how is a plus (the parent gets some benefits, too, for example from the U.S. firm's advanced technology in medical diagnostic equipment), but the lack of total independence is often seen as a minus.

The Dutch control is indirect. It's exercised through a trust (established in 1939 to prevent the possibility of Hitler's gaining control of the company's U.S. operations). The trust owns some 62 percent of the shares. Its stated goal is to represent the interests of the shareholders of the parent corporation.

In part through acquisitions (Magnavox in 1974, the Sylvania and Philco components businesses from General Telephone & Electronics in 1981), the company has shown rapid growth in sales. Profit growth, though, has been erratic and generally trailed that of most U.S. electronics companies during the 1970s. For most of the past decade, the stock had a lowly p / e ratio, ranging from 4 to 8. However, investor interest in the stock seemed to be rising in the early 1980s. The dividend yield is moderate, and dividends have been paid each year since 1960.

* * *

NORTH EUROPEAN OIL ROYALTY TRUST (NET). Founded 1975. Headquarters: 43 W. Front St., Red Bank NJ 07701. **OIL, GAS.** Provides royalties from oil and natural gas production in West Germany.

Sales: $14.0 million (trend 27.8% a year).
Earnings: $13.70 million (trend 29.2% a year).
What happened to a $10,000 investment

Purchase Date	*Purchase Price*	*Price on 12-31-81*	*Dividends Paid*
12-31-71	$N/A	$15.87	$ N/A
12-31-76	$10.08	$15.87	$5,874.38

Purchase Date	*Cap. Gains (– Losses)*	*Total Return*	*Rate of Return*
12-31-71	$ N/A	$ N/A	N/A%
12-31-76	$5,743.80	$11,618.18	16.67%

* * *

NORTHEAST UTILITIES (NU). Founded 1927. Headquarters: Selden St., Berlin CT 06037. **UTILITY.** Subsidiaries provide gas and electric service in Connecticut and Massachusetts. **MAJOR SUBSIDIARIES, BRANDS:** Connecticut Light & Power; Hartford Electric Light; Western Massachusetts Electric; Holyoke Water Power.

Sales: $1,324.5 million (trend 12.6% a year).
Earnings: $88.75 million (trend 2.6% a year).
What happened to a $10,000 investment

Purchase Date	*Purchase Price*	*Price on 12-31-81*	*Dividends Paid*
12-31-71	$14.25	$9.12	$7,307.93
12-31-76	$10.87	$9.12	$4,938.85

Purchase Date	*Cap. Gains (– Losses)*	*Total Return*	*Rate of Return*
12-31-71	$–3,596.49	$3,711.44	3.21%
12-31-76	$–1,609.20	$3,329.66	5.92%

* * *

NORTHERN CALIFORNIA SAVINGS & LOAN ASSOCIATION (NCX). Founded 1892. Headquarters: 300 Hamilton Ave., Palo Alto CA 94301. **SAVINGS & LOAN.** This large savings and loan association agreed in 1982 to be merged into Great Western Financial Corp. The merger had not yet been approved by stockholders or regulators when this book went to press.

* * *

NORTHERN INDIANA PUBLIC SERVICE CO. (NI). Founded 1912. Headquarters: 5265 Hohman Ave., Hammond IN 46320. **UTILITY.** Provides electricity and gas service to northern Indiana. **MAJOR SUBSIDIARIES, BRANDS:** Shore Line Shops,

Inc.; NIPSCO Exploration Co., Inc.; NIPSCO Fuel Co., Inc.

Sales: $1,366.5 million (trend 21.0% a year).
Earnings: $55.03 million (trend 2.8% a year).
What happened to a $10,000 investment

Purchase Date	*Purchase Price*	*Price on 12-31-81*	*Dividends Paid*
12-31-71	$26.87	$11.25	$5,302.33
12-31-76	$19.87	$11.25	$3,743.40

Purchase Date	*Cap. Gains (− Losses)*	*Total Return*	*Rate of Return*
12-31-71	$−5,813.95	$−511.63	−.52%
12-31-76	$−4,339.62	$−596.23	−1.22%

* * *

NORTHERN TELECOM LTD. (NT). Founded 1914. Headquarters: 1600 Dorchester Blvd. W., Montreal P.Q., H3H 1R1 Canada. TELECOMMUNICATIONS EQUIPMENT. Largest Canadian telecommunications equipment manufacturer. Also manufactures computer terminals and related equipment. MAJOR SUBSIDIARIES, BRANDS: Data 100 Corp.; Sycor, Inc.

Sales: $1,719.7 million (trend 12.0% a year).
Earnings: $−17.91 million.
What happened to a $10,000 investment

Purchase Date	*Purchase Price*	*Price on 12-31-81*	*Dividends Paid*
12-31-71	$N/A	$48.50	$ N/A
12-31-76	$31.50	$48.50	$1,169.11

Purchase Date	*Cap. Gains (− Losses)*	*Total Return*	*Rate of Return*
12-31-71	$ N/A	$ N/A	N/A%
12-31-76	$5,396.83	$6,565.94	10.62%

* * *

NORTHERN STATES POWER CO. (NSP). Founded 1909. Headquarters: 414 Nicollet Mall, Minneapolis MN 55401. UTILITY. Provides electricity and gas (and, to a minor extent, steam, heating service, and telephone service) to customers in portions of Minnesota, Wisconsin, North Dakota, and South Dakota.

Sales: $1,159.1 million (trend 11.3% a year).
Earnings: $97.25 million (trend 6.2% a year).
What happened to a $10,000 investment

Purchase Date	*Purchase Price*	*Price on 12-31-81*	*Dividends Paid*
12-31-71	$27.25	$24.12	$7,547.52
12-31-76	$29.50	$24.12	$3,838.98

Purchase Date	*Cap. Gains (− Losses)*	*Total Return*	*Rate of Return*
12-31-71	$−1,146.79	$6,400.73	5.07%
12-31-76	$−1,822.03	$2,016.95	3.74%

* * *

NORTHGATE EXPLORATION LTD. (NGX). Founded 1919. Headquarters: Suite 3140, PO Box 143, 1 First Canadian Pl., Toronto, Ont. M5X 1C7 Canada. MINING. Northgate is involved in exploration and development of mining properties in Canada.

Sales: $25.9 million (trend 3.1% a year).
Earnings: $3.68 million (trend 36.3% a year).
What happened to a $10,000 investment

Purchase Date	*Purchase Price*	*Price on 12-31-81*	*Dividends Paid*
12-31-71	$5.12	$4.62	$2,384.98
12-31-76	$5.25	$4.62	$ 476.19

Purchase Date	*Cap. Gains (− Losses)*	*Total Return*	*Rate of Return*
12-31-71	$ −975.61	$ 1,409.37	1.33%
12-31-76	$−1,190.48	$−714.29	−1.47%

* * *

NORTHROP CORP. (NOC). Founded 1939. Headquarters: 1800 Century Park E., Los Angeles CA 90067. AEROSPACE. Northrop is a leading maker of military aircraft for export (the F-5 series); chief contractor for development of "stealth" (radar-resistant) aircraft; a major subcontractor on the F-18 fighter plane; and a subcontractor for Boeing in production of fuselages for 747 jets. It is also active in military electronics, including guidance systems for the MX missile. 29,000 employees.

Sales: $1,655.4 million (trend 10.2% a year).
Earnings: $86.10 million (trend 30.6% a year).
What happened to a $10,000 investment

Purchase Date	*Purchase Price*	*Price on 12-31-81*	*Dividends Paid*
12-31-71	$ 7.21	$52.37	$14,420.81
12-31-76	$24.12	$52.37	$ 3,336.79

Purchase Date	*Cap. Gains (− Losses)*	*Total Return*	*Rate of Return*
12-31-71	$62,658.96	$77,079.77	24.16%
12-31-76	$11,709.84	$15,046.63	20.16%

PROFILE: The backbone of this company has been the F-5 tactical fighter plane. As of early 1981 Northrop had sold some 2,300 F-5s over the years to twenty-five countries. (The plane isn't used by the U.S. armed forces, though Northrop is also a major subcontractor on the F-18, which is.) The F-5 has gone through six versions (A–F), and the company is now pouring money into development of the F-5G.

Forbes magazine characterized that step, together with other major research and development and capital spending, as a "$500 million gamble by a company with a total net worth of only $480 million." But the magazine also noted that chairman Thomas Jones has taken major gambles before, and they've paid off. What makes the F-5G spending a gamble is that no orders had been received for the plane in advance, and no prototype was built. That's not how things are usually done in the aircraft business. But it's how the original F-5 was built. If it works, it results in bigger profits and faster delivery of the planes. If it doesn't work, the company could be in big trouble.

The heavy spending (on expansion, the F-5G, and the guidance system for the MX missile) is proving a drag on earnings for the time being. Profits hit a peak of more than $90 million in 1979, fell a bit in 1980, and were off substantially in 1981, reflecting development costs on the F-5G. But if Jones's bold step works, the payoff for stockholders could be a big advance in the share price during the middle 1980s.

The company's balance sheet is one of the strongest in the industry, with debt a mere wisp (2 percent of capital) as of late 1981 and a pile of cash on hand. That situation may change some because of the heavy spending in the early 1980s, but the trend throughout the 1970s was to pare debt and strengthen the balance sheet. Dividends, paid each year since 1951, provide a moderate yield in most years.

The company got a boost in 1981, when it was selected by the Air Force as chief contractor to develop the top-secret "stealth" radar-resistant bomber.

* * *

NORTHWEST AIRLINES, INC. (NWA). Founded 1934. Headquarters: Minneapolis-St. Paul International Airport, St. Paul MN 55111. **AIRLINE.** Northwest is approximately the seventh largest U.S. airline. It carries passengers, cargo, and mail to some twenty-three states and about twelve foreign countries. 13,000 employees.

Sales: $1,639.3 million (trend 12.8% a year).
Earnings: $7.08 million (trend −21.5% a year).
What happened to a $10,000 investment

Purchase Date	*Purchase Price*	*Price on 12-31-81*	*Dividends Paid*
12-31-71	$38.62	$27.25	$1,527.51
12-31-76	$29.75	$27.25	$1,226.89

Purchase Date	*Cap. Gains (− Losses)*	*Total Return*	*Rate of Return*
12-31-71	$−2,944.98	$−1,417.48	−1.52%
12-31-76	$ −840.34	$ 386.55	.76%

PROFILE: Tightfistedness was Northwest's hallmark throughout the 1970s. That quality, a reflection of the predilections of longtime chairman Donald Nyrup, who retired in 1979, accounted for many other things. One was a balance sheet that remains superb. While competitors like Pan American and TWA have had more debt than equity, Northwest's balance sheet at the start of 1982 showed debt at a mere 1 percent of total capital.

Labor costs here were the lowest in the industry during the 1970s. That fact reflected Nyrup's hard line, which cost Northwest a bundle of strikes but earned it high marks on Wall Street for productivity and efficiency. Nyrup's replacement, M. Joseph Lapensky, has been more conciliatory toward labor, avoiding strife and strikes but incurring higher costs on a regular basis.

Customers were never quite as impressed with Northwest's spartan operation as Wall Street analysts were. Poor service, late flights, and slow baggage handling were chronic complaints. Lapensky has acted to ease these complaints. (He probably had little choice, since Northwest faced increased competition on its major routes as a result of deregulation.) The result: better prospects for volume growth, but a probable shrinkage in Northwest's traditionally high profit margins.

A major strength here is the fleet, large (both in number and size of planes) and owned virtually outright. In 1981 Lapensky said the airline had enough excess capacity to allow two years of route expansion with no purchases of planes. However, planes may need to be bought anyway, to make aircraft fit routes that are likely to be rejuggled.

Most analysts predict that Northwest will use its jumbo jets to expand its international operations.

While most airlines had dipped into and out of red ink in recent years, Northwest had stayed consistently profitable (though, in 1980, barely so). However, like other airlines, Northwest lost money in early 1982. Earnings show a definite, though erratic, long-term uptrend. Dividends have been paid yearly since 1955, but provide only a modest yield.

* * *

NORTHWEST BANCORPORATION (NOB). Founded 1929. Headquarters: 1200 Northwestern Bank Bldg., Minneapolis MN 55480. **BANKING.** Northwest is a holding company for close to ninety banks in seven midwestern states and is approximately the eighteenth largest banking company in the U.S. Also active in consumer lending. 13,000 employees. **MAJOR SUBSIDIARIES, BRANDS:** Dial Corp. (consumer lending) acquired in 1981.

Sales: $1,477.7 million (trend 23.1% a year).
Earnings: $116.69 million (trend 16.0% a year).
What happened to a $10,000 investment

Purchase Date	*Purchase Price*	*Price on 12-31-81*	*Dividends Paid*
12-31-71	$19.19	$23.75	$5,420.20
12-31-76	$28.62	$23.75	$2,235.81

Purchase Date	*Cap. Gains (− Losses)*	*Total Return*	*Rate of Return*
12-31-71	$ 2,377.85	$7,798.05	5.93%
12-31-76	$−1,703.06	$ 532.75	1.04%

PROFILE: While other banks drool at the prospect of interstate banking, Northwest Bancorporation already enjoys it. The company owns close to ninety banks in Minnesota, North and South Dakota, Montana, Iowa, Nebraska, and Wisconsin. It enjoys a "grandfather clause" exemption from the 1933 prohibitions against interstate banking.

And if Northwest's experience is a valid indication, interstate banking can be consistently profitable. In fact, Northwest had a string of thirty-four consecutive profit rises through 1981, a record matched by few banks — or, for that matter, corporations of any stripe.

The profits haven't been spectacular. Many banks do better in any given year. But Northwest's record for consistency is hard to match. Year after year, it has achieved a return of about 80 to 90 cents per $100 of assets, a record many major money-center banks would love to match.

You can probably buy this stock cheap. The price / earnings ratio rose to a peak of 17 during the boom years of the early 1970s, but in recent years the stock has sold for only 4 to 10 times current earnings.

Dividends have been paid each year since 1939, and it's the company's habit to raise them a bit each year. They provide a moderate yield.

Besides straight banking (with a specialty in agricultural loans), the company has strong sidelines in mortgage banking and venture capital operations.

* * *

NORTHWEST ENERGY CO. (NWP). Founded 1974. Headquarters: 315 E. 200 South, Salt Lake City UT 84110. **OIL AND GAS.** Holding company for various energy-related subsidiaries. **MAJOR SUBSIDIARIES, BRANDS:** Northwest Pipeline Corp.; Northwest Alaskan Pipeline Co.; Northwest Coal Corp.; Northwest Exploration Co.

Sales: $1,323.4 million (trend 21.6% a year).
Earnings: $51.35 million (trend 18.4% a year).
What happened to a $10,000 investment

Purchase Date	*Purchase Price*	*Price on 12-31-81*	*Dividends Paid*
12-31-71	$ N/A	$20.87	$ N/A
12-31-76	$11.12	$20.87	$4,000.00

Purchase Date	*Cap. Gains (− Losses)*	*Total Return*	*Rate of Return*
12-31-71	$ N/A	$ N/A	N/A%
12-31-76	$8,764.04	$12,764.04	17.88%

* * *

NORTHWEST INDUSTRIES (NWT). Founded 1967. Headquarters: 6300 Sears Tower, Chicago IL 60606. **CONGLOMERATE.** Northwest is a holding company for ten operating subsidiaries, the largest being Lone Star Steel. It is highly diversified and ranks approximately 136th among U.S. industrial firms, by sales. 44,000 employees. **MAJOR SUBSIDIARIES, BRANDS:** Lone Star Steel; Union Underwear Co. (Fruit of the Loom); Acme Boot Co.; General Battery; Microdot; Universal Manufacturing; Velsicol Chemical; NWT Natural Resources Co.

Sales: $2,876.4 million (trend 19.2% a year).
Earnings: $151.60 million (trend 12.9% a year).
What happened to a $10,000 investment

Purchase Date	Purchase Price	Price on 12-31-81	Dividends Paid
12-31-71	$16.87	$71.50	$7,608.86
12-31-76	$23.12	$71.50	$4,236.19

Purchase Date	Cap. Gains (– Losses)	Total Return	Rate of Return
12-31-71	$32,370.37	$39,979.23	17.46%
12-31-76	$20,918.92	$25,155.11	28.59%

PROFILE: Northwest is the handiwork of gruff, forceful Chicago entrepreneur Ben Heineman. It is one of that peculiar modern breed, a conglomerate that has grown out of a transportation company and then shed its parent.

The parent was the Chicago & North Western Railway, a road that has had its ups and downs. Heineman took over the railroad's management in 1956, built Northwest Industries around it, and then sold off the railroad in 1968, while it was in a downslide period. Northwest came away with lots of cash and $260 million in tax-loss carry-forwards to shield the earnings of the companies it proceeded to acquire.

Those companies are often in the forefront of their industry, like Acme Boot, the leading seller of Western-style boots, or Union Underwear, whose Fruit of the Loom brand is the best seller among men and boys. "There's nothing particularly novel about Heineman's standards" for acquisitions, one analyst told *Financial World* recently. "The novelty is his strict adherence to them."

The results of this strategy have generally been good. Northwest has been among the most profitable of conglomerates, and among the faster-growing. It does experience earnings fluctuations, both in line with the general economy and in line with interest rates. (The company's medium-sized debt is in substantial part tied to the prime rate.) But the company showed rising profits in ten of the twelve years following its founding and predicted record profits for 1981.

Despite its good record, the stock hasn't usually sold for a high multiple. In recent years the p / e ratio has been between 4 and 8. Dividends are moderate and have been paid each year since 1972.

The biggest money-maker here is Lone Star Steel, the largest of Northwest's ten subsidiaries. It recently has kicked in close to half of the company's profits, riding a boom in the oil-tubing market. There have been rumors that the company will sell Lone Star while things are going great, generating a new pile of money for acquisitions. But the firm has said Lone Star's not for sale and has hinted it may instead divest its controversy-plagued Velsicol chemical subsidiary.

* * *

NORTHWESTERN MUTUAL LIFE MORTGAGE & REALTY INVESTORS (NML). Founded 1971. Headquarters: 720 E. Wisconsin Ave., Milwaukee WI 53202. **REAL ESTATE.** Real estate investment trust, investing in short- and long-term mortgage loans and real estate equities.

Sales: $24.5 million (trend 2.3% a year).
Earnings: $5.74 million (trend 8.0% a year).
What happened to a $10,000 investment

Purchase Date	Purchase Price	Price on 12-31-81	Dividends Paid
12-31-71	$25.37	$10.37	$4,425.62
12-31-76	$13.37	$10.37	$3,267.29

Purchase Date	Cap. Gains (– Losses)	Total Return	Rate of Return
12-31-71	$–5,911.33	$–1,485.71	–1.60%
12-31-76	$–2,242.99	$ 1,024.30	1.97%

* * *

NORTHWESTERN STEEL AND WIRE CO. (NSW). Founded 1879. Headquarters: 121 Wallace St., Sterling IL 61081. **STEEL PRODUCTS.** Makes steel wire, bar, rod, and structural products.

Sales: $468.5 million (trend 14.3% a year).
Earnings: $28.13 million (trend 13.5% a year).
What happened to a $10,000 investment

Purchase Date	Purchase Price	Price on 12-31-81	Dividends Paid
12-31-71	$28.75	$25.12	$5,000.00
12-31-76	$30.25	$25.12	$2,330.58

Purchase Date	Cap. Gains (– Losses)	Total Return	Rate of Return
12-31-71	$–1,260.87	$3,739.13	3.23%
12-31-76	$–1,694.21	$ 636.36	1.24%

* * *

NORTON COMPANY (NRT). Founded 1885. Headquarters: 1 New Bond St., Worcester MA 01606. **ABRASIVES.** Norton remains the world's largest manufacturer of abrasives and has diversified into other areas, including oil-drilling equipment, industrial ceramics, safety products, and chemical process products. 25,000 employees. **MAJOR SUBSIDIARIES, BRANDS:** Christensen, Inc.

Sales: $1,281.8 million (trend 19.1% a year).
Earnings: $87.13 million (trend 36.0% a year).
What happened to a $10,000 investment

Purchase Date	*Purchase Price*	*Price on 12-31-81*	*Dividends Paid*
12-31-71	$16.12	$43.12	$6,728.68
12-31-76	$19.25	$43.12	$3,558.44

Purchase Date	*Cap. Gains (− Losses)*	*Total Return*	*Rate of Return*
12-31-71	$16,744.19	$23,472.87	12.84%
12-31-76	$12,402.60	$15,961.04	21.02%

PROFILE: Norton is no longer a diamond in the rough. It's been discovered, and the stock price enjoyed a brisk run-up in 1979–80. The increased popularity of the stock stems from two things. One is the widespread belief that industrial equipment is due for a boom in the 1980s. The other is the company's 1977 acquisition of Christensen, Inc., a leading maker of diamond oil-drilling and coring bits. Oil-drilling equipment has been highly popular on Wall Street, and the company itself has done its share of crowing about the acquisition. With reason: Christensen contributed 30 percent of the company's 1980 profits on only 17 percent of sales.

But all of this good news got pretty well reflected in the price of the stock in 1979–80. The stock rose from a 1979 low of $22 to a 1980 high of $61. The p / e ratio rose from a 1979 low of 4 to a 1980 high of 12. Check to see what the p / e ratio is now, before you invest. If it's too high, think twice.

Despite this caution, the stock has several advantages going for it, not the least of which is that its abrasive products enjoy a constant demand but a limited life-span. According to *Barron's,* abrasives still make up nearly two thirds of sales, despite the company's considerable diversification effort in recent years. Norton supplies about a quarter of the world market for industrial abrasives (twice the market share of its nearest competitor), sells worldwide, and has some 115 plants in 27 countries. The geographical balance gives the company stability, though it also means that currency fluctuations affect the earnings.

* * *

NORTON SIMON, INC. (NSI). Founded 1968. Headquarters: 277 Park Ave., New York NY 10017. **CONSUMER PRODUCTS.** Norton Simon is a food-products-based conglomerate, with operations in branded foods, car rental, cosmetics, liquor, soft drinks, fashions, and packaging. 38,000 employees.

MAJOR SUBSIDIARIES, BRANDS: Hunt-Wesson (Hunt tomato products, Wesson cooking oils); Avis, Inc., car rental; Somerset Importers (imports liquors, including Johnnie Walker scotch and Alexis Lichine wines); Max Factor cosmetics; McCall Pattern and Halston fashion products; Glass Containers Corp. and United Can container manufacturing.

Sales: $3,191.9 million (trend 14.3% a year).
Earnings: $102.71 million (trend 5.0% a year).
What happened to a $10,000 investment

Purchase Date	*Purchase Price*	*Price on 12-31-81*	*Dividends Paid*
12-31-71	$25.75	$19.25	$2,092.59
12-31-76	$19.04	$19.25	$2,198.42

Purchase Date	*Cap. Gains (− Losses)*	*Total Return*	*Rate of Return*
12-31-71	$−2,524.58	$−431.99	−.44%
12-31-76	$ 112.25	$ 2,310.67	4.25%

PROFILE: Disappointment and frustration. Those have been the emotions attached to Norton Simon in recent years. Earnings have been inching up, but barely enough to keep pace with inflation. The Max Factor cosmetics division, acquired at a cost of more than $400 million, has been an albatross. Avis, usually one of the stronger divisions, has recently been battered by recession-dampened rental demand and by price wars in the car-rental industry. And managers at the company's cash cow, the Hunt-Wesson division, have groused to *Business Week* that they are forced to maximize short-term profits at the expense of building for the long term. The magazine reported in 1980 that Norton Simon's "market shares in food, cosmetics, and beverages are declining, and the company suffers from a dearth of successful new products. Its management ranks are wracked by turmoil and defections."

In response to the problems, chairman David Mahoney has talked about resigning. He's also talked about restructuring the company by selling off one or more divisions and making a new, major acquisition. So far, neither shoe has dropped.

The company's eight operating divisions (see above) grew out of a sequence of eight acquisitions and twenty-two divestitures by Mahoney, who took over the reins when founder and art patron Norton Simon walked away from the company he created, only shortly after its birth in 1968. Hunt, Wesson, and Canada Dry (recently sold to Dr Pepper) were part of Simon's original empire. Max Factor was added in 1973, Avis in 1977. Food and beverages account for almost half of company earnings and Avis for about another 30 percent.

Despite all the publicity about problems, the stock has continued to sell at fairly near the average p / e multiple. Bargain hunters and turnaround prospectors should keep an eye on the p / e, which has ranged from about 4 to 8 in recent years. Dividend-conscious investors may like the stock's yield, which was above 7 percent in 1981. Dividends have been paid (and raised) each year since 1972.

* * *

NOVO INDUSTRI A / S (NVO). Founded 1940. Headquarters: Novo Alle DK-2880 Bagsvaerd, Denmark. DRUGS, ENZYMES. Novo is a major producer of insulin; it is also the world's largest producer of enzymes for use in the drug industry, baking, brewing, tanning, detergents, and various other industrial processes.

* * *

NUCOR CORP. (NUE). Founded 1958. Headquarters: 4425 Randolph Rd., Charlotte NC 28211. STEEL. Nucor is the leading company among the "mini-mill" producers of steel. It is a major producer of joists and other structural steel products for the building industry, and is among the twenty largest U.S. steelmakers. 3,000 employees.

Sales: $482.4 million (trend 32.8% a year).
Earnings: $45.06 million (trend 50.8% a year).
What happened to a $10,000 investment

Purchase Date	*Purchase Price*	*Price on 12-31-81*	*Dividends Paid*
12-31-71	$4.93	$59.75	$4,003.45
12-31-76	$8.93	$59.75	$1,834.29

Purchase Date	*Cap. Gains (– Losses)*	*Total Return*	*Rate of Return*
12-31-71	$111,148.18	$115,151.63	28.75%
12-31-76	$ 56,919.95	$ 58,754.23	47.05%

PROFILE: Everybody knows that steel companies have fallen on hard times. Saddled with huge and often old-fashioned plants, faced with stiff low-cost competition from the Japanese, and hurt by a recession in autos and housing, the big U.S. steel firms limped into the 1980s. In 1981, stocks of the giants like U.S. Steel and Bethlehem Steel were selling for a mere 4 to 6 times earnings. Clearly, Wall Street had little confidence in the future of the American steel industry.

But what's this? Little Nucor has been one of the hottest stocks, and one of the most profitable companies, in the country. Its return on stockholders' equity in recent years has been consistently more than 20 percent and sometimes more than 30 percent. Its earnings grew during the late 1970s at better than a 30-percent-a-year clip. Its profit margins are high, yet its steel costs less than that imported from Japan. And the stock, which you could have snatched up for $5 or less in parts of each year from 1971 to 1976, hit $82 in 1981, with a p / e around 14. (In early 1982 the price had retreated below $50, but the p / e was still a healthy 10.)

How can a U.S. steel company buck the trend so successfully? Nucor thrives in the shadow of the giants. It relies on mini-mills, which cost less to build than conventional ones, use scrap steel as their raw material (and thus cost less to run than big mills that need coke ovens and blast furnaces to create steel out of iron ore), and ship specialized products (especially joists and other structural steel items) to nearby customers. The mini-mills are in small towns scattered around the country, and the nonunion labor force is paid under a highly unusual incentive pay system that encourages maximum productivity. Managers are paid under a similar system, geared to the company's profits.

Despite the company's rapid growth and the use of the latest technology in its mini-mills, it has managed to keep debt down to below the average for U.S. corporations. Dividends were started in 1973, but still provide only a tiny yield; this is definitely a capital-gains stock. Watch the p / e: Since Nucor's success has become widely known, the stock's price and p / e have soared, making it a riskier, and possibly less canny, investment than it would have been a few years ago.

O

OAK INDUSTRIES, INC. (OAK). Founded 1932. Headquarters: 16935 W. Bernardo Dr., Rancho Bernardo CA 92128. COMMUNICATIONS. Oak Industries and its subsidiaries provide subscription television services and manufacture components for subscription and cable television systems. They also manufacture a line of components sold to electronic-, industrial-, and consumer-product manufacturers. MAJOR SUBSIDIARIES, BRANDS: ON-TV; Unidex; Harper-Wyman Co.; Oak Communications, Inc.; Oak Materials Group, Inc.; Oak Systems, Inc.; Oak Switch Systems, Inc.; Oak Technology, Inc.; OAK; Diminsion II; Oak Tip; Total Control; Video-Text.

Sales: $385.6 million (trend 27.1% a year).
Earnings: $20.02 million (trend 93.7% a year).
What happened to a $10,000 investment

Purchase Date	*Purchase Price*	*Price on 12-31-81*	*Dividends Paid*
12-31-71	$3.17	$32.25	$4,868.42
12-31-76	$3.17	$32.25	$3,100.00

Purchase Date	*Cap. Gains (− Losses)*	*Total Return*	*Rate of Return*
12-31-71	$91,842.11	$96,710.53	26.71%
12-31-76	$91,842.11	$94,942.11	60.03%

* * *

OAKITE PRODUCTS, INC. (OKT). Founded 1909. Headquarters: 50 Valley Rd., Berkeley Heights NJ 07922. **SPECIALTY CHEMICALS.** Oakite Products, Inc., manufactures chemical products for industrial cleaning and metal treating. **MAJOR SUBSIDIARIES, BRANDS:** Oakite Products of Canada, Ltd.; Solventol Chemical Products, Inc.; Claire Manufacturing Co.; Sprayway, Inc.

Sales: $67.7 million (trend 8.3% a year).
Earnings: $4.37 million (trend 9.3% a year).
What happened to a $10,000 investment

Purchase Date	*Purchase Price*	*Price on 12-31-81*	*Dividends Paid*
12-31-71	$14.75	$23.37	$7,064.41
12-31-76	$17.37	$23.37	$3,528.06

Purchase Date	*Cap. Gains (− Losses)*	*Total Return*	*Rate of Return*
12-31-71	$5,847.46	$12,911.86	8.64%
12-31-76	$3,453.24	$ 6,981.29	11.17%

* * *

OCCIDENTAL PETROLEUM CORP. (OXY). Founded 1920. Headquarters: 10889 Wilshire Blvd., Los Angeles CA 90024. **OIL.** Occidental is approximately the twelfth largest U.S.-based oil company. It is also active in coal mining, chemical manufacturing, and mining of uranium and precious metals. In 1981 it acquired Iowa Beef, a major meat-packer. 35,000 employees. **MAJOR SUBSIDIARIES, BRANDS:** Hooker Chemical; Island Creek Coal; Iowa Beef Processors.

Sales: $12,476.1 million (trend 18.4% a year).
Earnings: $680.07 million (trend 39.8% a year).
What happened to a $10,000 investment

Purchase Date	*Purchase Price*	*Price on 12-31-81*	*Dividends Paid*
12-31-71	$11.87	$24.25	$8,715.79
12-31-76	$24.25	$24.25	$3,340.21

Purchase Date	*Cap. Gains (− Losses)*	*Total Return*	*Rate of Return*
12-31-71	$10,421.05	$19,136.84	11.29%
12-31-76	$ −.00	$ 3,340.21	5.93%

PROFILE: Any securities analyst could give you at least half a dozen reasons not to invest in Occidental Petroleum. The company is the fiefdom of international entrepreneur Armand Hammer, who is in his eighties and who is notorious for hiring and firing executives. What happens after Hammer goes is uncertain. Earnings have been extremely unpredictable. Much of the company's oil production comes from Libya, a radical, anti-American, and potentially unstable country. The company is lawsuit prone; in particular, it faces a mountain of litigation over the liability of its Hooker Chemical subsidiary for pollution at Love Canal, in northwestern New York State. The acquisition of Iowa Beef, though it may bring a highly successful company into Oxy's fold, is hard to understand in terms of how the meat-packer would fit with the oil company's other businesses. Hammer made illegal contributions to President Richard M. Nixon's 1972 campaign and has signed three consent decrees with the Securities and Exchange Commission. Oil prices in the early 1980s were soft.

All these negatives have so pressed on the stock that in 1981 it was selling for 3 times current earnings — record earnings, by the way. If the multiple stays that low, or anywhere near that low, the stock will get deserved attention from bargain hunters. In 1981 the depressed stock was yielding 9 percent in dividends. (Dividends were resumed in 1974 after a two-year dry spell.)

People who believe that international oil companies have a future may find this stock attractive on fundamentals. The company has reduced its dependence on Libya and has taken on big stakes in ventures in Peru and offshore Britain. To boot, it has a strong position in uranium and coal; Island Creek Coal is the nation's third largest coal company. A big plus is the 1981 acquisition of Iowa Beef; that subsidiary will provide close to a quarter of revenues. Though it may not "fit" with Oxy's other holdings, it has an admirable record for fast growth and technological innovation and may be ready to revolutionize the pork business as it did the beef business in the past decade.

* * *

OCEAN DRILLING & EXPLORATION CO. (ODR). Founded 1953. Headquarters: 1600 Canal St., New Orleans LA 70161. OFFSHORE DRILLING. Ocean Drilling & Exploration Co. operates the world's largest fleet of offshore drilling rigs and explores for and produces oil and natural gas. The company is 54 percent owned by Murphy Oil Corp. MAJOR SUBSIDIARIES, BRANDS: Ocean Oil & Gas; Sub Sea International (50 percent owned).

Sales: $697.2 million (trend 29.1% a year).
Earnings: $135.48 million (trend 24.0% a year).
What happened to a $10,000 investment

Purchase Date	*Purchase Price*	*Price on 12-31-81*	*Dividends Paid*
12-31-71	$9.37	$27.87	$1,906.67
12-31-76	$6.87	$27.87	$2,254.55

Purchase Date	*Cap. Gains (– Losses)*	*Total Return*	*Rate of Return*
12-31-71	$19,733.33	$21,640.00	12.21%
12-31-76	$30,545.45	$32,800.00	33.75%

* * *

OGDEN CORP. (OG). Founded 1939. Headquarters: 277 Park Ave., New York NY 10172. CONGLOMERATE. Ogden's largest area of operation is shipbuilding and shipping; it is also involved in foods, food service, security service, racetrack operation, scrap metal, railroad car manufacturing, and other industrial operations. 30,000 employees. MAJOR SUBSIDIARIES, BRANDS: Avondale Shipyards; Ogden Marine; International Terminal Operating Co.; Ogden Services; Ogden Food Products (Progresso, Las Palmas, Ramirez & Feraud, Tasti-Diet).

Sales: $2,187.3 million (trend 9.4% a year).
Earnings: $56.63 million (trend 5.4% a year).
What happened to a $10,000 investment

Purchase Date	*Purchase Price*	*Price on 12-31-81*	*Dividends Paid*
12-31-71	$10.17	$26.12	$8,918.03
12-31-76	$14.83	$26.12	$4,224.72

Purchase Date	*Cap. Gains (– Losses)*	*Total Return*	*Rate of Return*
12-31-71	$15,696.72	$24,614.75	13.22%
12-31-76	$ 7,612.36	$11,837.08	16.91%

PROFILE: *Financial World* has called Ogden "the thinking man's conglomerate." *Forbes* describes its chairman, Ralph Ablon, as "not your typical blunt-talking industrial manager," noting that he "has a penchant for quoting Shakespeare while puffing professorially on his pipe." (Favorite quote: "Lilies that fester smell far worse than weeds.")

Is Ogden, for investors, a lily or a weed? The answer isn't entirely clear. Certainly, investors who bought the stock below $10 early in the 1970s have little to complain about: The stock was above $25 a share in early 1982. A moderate dividend (about 5 percent in 1981) adds to total return and has been paid since 1972. The p / e ratio ranged from 4 to 8 in the period 1973–80, so the buyer isn't paying for glamour.

Still, there are some negatives to consider. While per-share results have shown good progress, raw after-tax profits were inching upward at a puny rate of less than 4 percent a year in 1974–80. The per-share results look better than that because the company has from time to time bought in chunks of its own stock. Few would fault Ogden for that strategy —but neither would many people be impressed with the growth rate. Also, debt has at times sloshed past 50 percent of capital, a potentially worrisome fact, even though less so than it might be at other firms (much of the debt is tied to the shipping operation and is fairly short term).

Although it's highly diversified, Ogden still has as its mainstay Avondale Shipyards, the nation's fourth largest shipbuilder. Avondale boasts modern facilities, a nonunion work force, and an aversion to fixed-cost military contracts. The various industrial operations provide about 40 percent of revenues and profits; of these, one of the most successful divisions is the one that builds coal-hauling railroad cars.

* * *

OHIO EDISON CO. (OEC). Founded 1930. Headquarters: 76 S. Main St., Akron OH 44308. ELECTRIC UTILITY. Ohio Edison provides electricity to 552 communities and rural areas in Ohio. Its subsidiary, the Pennsylvania Power Co., provides service to nearby areas of Pennsylvania. MAJOR SUBSIDIARIES, BRANDS: Pennsylvania Power Co.

Sales: $1,080.9 million (trend 13.3% a year).
Earnings: $101.40 million (trend 7.0% a year).
What happened to a $10,000 investment

Purchase Date	*Purchase Price*	*Price on 12-31-81*	*Dividends Paid*
12-31-71	$24.50	$11.62	$6,879.59
12-31-76	$20.87	$11.62	$4,194.01

Purchase Date	*Cap. Gains (− Losses)*	*Total Return*	*Rate of Return*
12-31-71	$−5,255.10	$ 1,624.49	1.52%
12-31-76	$−4,431.14	$−237.13	−.48%

* * *

OKLAHOMA GAS AND ELECTRIC CO. (OGE). Founded February 27, 1902. Headquarters: 321 N. Harvey Ave., Oklahoma City OK 73101. ELECTRIC UTILITY. Oklahoma Gas and Electric provides electricity to approximately 520,000 customers in Oklahoma and Arkansas.

Sales: $709.1 million (trend 19.8% a year).
Earnings: $53.34 million (trend 7.6% a year).
What happened to a $10,000 investment

Purchase Date	*Purchase Price*	*Price on 12-31-81*	*Dividends Paid*
12-31-71	$26.75	$14.12	$5,495.33
12-31-76	$19.62	$14.12	$4,025.48

Purchase Date	*Cap. Gains (− Losses)*	*Total Return*	*Rate of Return*
12-31-71	$−4,719.63	$ 775.70	.75%
12-31-76	$−2,802.55	$1,222.93	2.33%

* * *

OLIN CORP. (OLN). Founded 1892. Headquarters: 120 Long Ridge Rd., Stamford CT 06904. CHEMICALS. Olin's main line of business is the production of bulk and specialty chemicals. It is also involved in firearms and ammunition making; paper and packaging production; brass and alloy fabrication; and a few miscellaneous manufacturing operations (skis, flares, construction fasteners). 21,000 employees. MAJOR SUBSIDIARIES, BRANDS: Winchester (ammunition); Ecusta (cigarette paper and packaging).

Sales: $1,852.9 million (trend 8.2% a year).
Earnings: $33.93 million (trend −8.4% a year).
What happened to a $10,000 investment

Purchase Date	*Purchase Price*	*Price on 12-31-81*	*Dividends Paid*
12-31-71	$17.50	$24.25	$4,928.57
12-31-76	$21.25	$24.25	$2,277.65

Purchase Date	*Cap. Gains (− Losses)*	*Total Return*	*Rate of Return*
12-31-71	$3,857.14	$8,785.71	6.51%
12-31-76	$1,411.76	$3,689.41	6.48%

PROFILE: Olin has been sputtering along for the past decade. The annual return on stockholders' equity has only sporadically been above 10 percent. The stock price has gone nowhere overall, though you could have hit a fairly sharp profit or loss on the fluctuations.

"The fact is," the editors of *Financial World* said in 1979, "that Olin is simply not a very highly regarded company." Commenting on take-over rumors (and an aborted take-over by Celanese), the magazine sniped that maybe chairman John Henske "has nothing to fear. Maybe nobody wants Olin."

In a more positive vein, *Barron's* in 1981 commented, "The reason it has taken so long for the huge . . . diversified chemicals producer to get back to its winning ways is that for the past few years Olin has been busily doing what many other concerns are just now getting around to — that is, divesting themselves of unprofitable or unpromising units." Olin in 1981 sold the firearms segment of Winchester, while keeping the profitable ammunition segment. Expenses connected with that move hurt 1980 earnings, which were the lowest in some years.

A more serious long-term concern is Olin's dependence on bulk chemicals with low profit margins. The other parts of the business (see above) don't particularly excite investors. Barring occasional statistical quirks, Olin shares usually fetch a fairly low multiple of earnings. Dividends have been paid each year since 1926; the yield is moderate.

* * *

OMARK INDUSTRIES, INC. (OMK). Founded 1953. Headquarters: 2100 S.E. Milport Rd., Portland OR 97222. MANUFACTURING. Omark Industries is a manufacturer of metal products, including chain for power saws, sporting ammunition, and industrial fasteners. MAJOR SUBSIDIARIES, BRANDS: Oregon Saw Chain; Speer; Prentice; KSM Fastening Systems; Mesabi Drill and Tool Co.; Lifetime Carbide Co.; Credo; Omark.

Sales: $280.1 million (trend 20.3% a year).
Earnings: $23.04 million (trend 27.3% a year).
What happened to a $10,000 investment

Purchase Date	*Purchase Price*	*Price on 12-31-81*	*Dividends Paid*
12-31-71	$6.36	$18.75	$5,616.45
12-31-76	$7.06	$18.75	$3,985.84

Purchase Date	Cap. Gains (− Losses)	Total Return	Rate of Return
12-31-71	$19,498.17	$25,114.63	13.38%
12-31-76	$16,548.67	$20,534.51	25.01%

* * *

OMNICARE, INC. (OCR). Founded 1981. Headquarters: 511 Walnut St., Cincinnati OH 45202. **HEALTH CARE.** Omnicare runs respiratory therapy units and pharmacies for hospitals; also produces medical supplies.

* * *

ONEIDA LIMITED. (OCQ). Founded 1880. Headquarters: Kenwood Ave., Oneida NY 13421. **MANUFACTURING.** Oneida produces tableware, stainless steel flatware, industrial wire, and jewelry. Through a subsidiary, Oneida distributes cookware to be sold door-to-door. **MAJOR SUBSIDIARIES, BRANDS:** Camden Wire Co., Inc.; Leavens Manufacturing Co., Inc.; Oneida Canada, Ltd.; Rena Ware Distributors, Inc.; Community; Heirloom.

Sales: $368.7 million (trend 35.1% a year).
Earnings: $22.38 million (trend 57.3% a year).
What happened to a $10,000 investment

Purchase Date	Purchase Price	Price on 12-31-81	Dividends Paid
12-31-71	$4.54	$22.50	$5,254.93
12-31-76	$4.74	$22.50	$3,017.57

Purchase Date	Cap. Gains (− Losses)	Total Return	Rate of Return
12-31-71	$39,515.85	$44,770.77	18.54%
12-31-76	$37,508.45	$40,526.01	38.26%

* * *

ONEOK, INC. (OKE). Founded 1906. Headquarters: PO Box 871, Tulsa OK 74102. **ENERGY.** ONEOK, formerly Oklahoma Natural Gas, retails natural gas to approximately 583,000 customers in 209 communities in Oklahoma. The company is involved in certain nonutility businesses, including exploration, drilling, and production of oil and gas. **MAJOR SUBSIDIARIES, BRANDS:** ONEOK Exploration Co.; ONEOK Resources Co.; ONG Red Oak Transmission; ONG Sayre Storage; ONG Western, Inc.; Ringwood Gathering Co.; Smart Drilling Co.; Thermal Systems, Inc.

Sales: $1,085.3 million (trend 20.4% a year).
Earnings: $46.27 million (trend 6.4% a year).
What happened to a $10,000 investment

Purchase Date	Purchase Price	Price on 12-31-81	Dividends Paid
12-31-71	$13.67	$27.62	$9,711.95
12-31-76	$23.00	$27.62	$3,683.91

Purchase Date	Cap. Gains (− Losses)	Total Return	Rate of Return
12-31-71	$10,213.41	$19,925.37	11.58%
12-31-76	$ 2,010.87	$ 5,694.78	9.43%

* * *

OPELIKA MANUFACTURING CORP. (OPK). Founded 1946. Headquarters: 361 W. Chestnut St., Chicago IL 60610. **TEXTILE MANUFACTURING.** Opelika manufactures textiles, towels, and service apparel for rental laundries; makes garments and specialty textiles for hospitals and institutions; and operates a textile machinery business. **MAJOR BRANDS, SUBSIDIARIES:** M. Snower & Co.; Sew Simple Systems; Snowflake; Whitehouse; Wolf.

* * *

ORANGE AND ROCKLAND UTILITIES, INC. (ORU). Founded 1926. Headquarters: 1 Blue Hill Plaza, Pearl River NY 10965. **ELECTRIC-GAS UTILITY.** Provides electric and gas service to more than 600,000 customers in Orange and Rockland counties near New York City, in northern New Jersey, and in northeast Pennsylvania.

Sales: $373.7 million (trend 11.3% a year).
Earnings: $23.52 million (trend 7.0% a year).
What happened to a $10,000 investment

Purchase Date	Purchase Price	Price on 12-31-81	Dividends Paid
12-31-71	$18.25	$13.37	$7,484.93
12-31-76	$15.87	$13.37	$4,762.20

Purchase Date	Cap. Gains (− Losses)	Total Return	Rate of Return
12-31-71	$−2,671.23	$4,813.70	4.01%
12-31-76	$−1,574.80	$3,187.40	5.69%

* * *

ORANGE-CO, INC. (OJ). Founded 1969. Headquarters: 1328 Dublin Rd., Columbus OH 43215. **CITRUS FRUIT.** Orange-co produces frozen orange juice concentrate; also grows and markets fresh citrus fruits.

Sales: $76.2 million (trend −2.8% a year).
Earnings: $3.75 million (trend −1.0% a year).
What happened to a $10,000 investment

Purchase Date	*Purchase Price*	*Price on 12-31-81*	*Dividends Paid*
12-31-71	$N/A	$9.62	$ N/A
12-31-76	$ 8.12	$9.62	$984.62

Purchase Date	*Cap. Gains (− Losses)*	*Total Return*	*Rate of Return*
12-31-71	$ N/A	$ N/A	N/A%
12-31-76	$1,846.15	$2,830.77	5.11%

* * *

ORION CAPITAL CORP. (OC). Founded 1976. Headquarters: 30 Rockefeller Plaza, New York NY 10020. **INSURANCE.** Orion (formerly Equity Funding) is an insurance holding company whose business consists mainly of life insurance; also has a property and casualty group. **MAJOR SUBSIDIARIES, BRANDS:** Security Insurance Co. of Hartford; EFC Property Management; Employees Benefits, Inc.

* * *

OUTBOARD MARINE CORP. (OM). Founded 1936. Headquarters: 100 Sea-Horse Dr., Waukegan IL 60085. **ENGINE MANUFACTURING.** Outboard Marine is the world's largest producer of outboard motors and also manufactures inboard-outboard motors, lawn mowers, and light industrial vehicles. **MAJOR SUBSIDIARIES, BRANDS:** Evinrude; Johnson; Lawn-Boy; Cushman; OMC Stern Drive.

Sales: $795.6 million (trend 5.5% a year).
Earnings: $26.95 million (trend −20.7% a year).
What happened to a $10,000 investment

Purchase Date	*Purchase Price*	*Price on 12-31-81*	*Dividends Paid*
12-31-71	$46.62	$20.25	$2,456.84
12-31-76	$27.50	$20.25	$2,045.45

Purchase Date	*Cap. Gains (− Losses)*	*Total Return*	*Rate of Return*
12-31-71	$−5,656.84	$−3,200.00	−3.78%
12-31-76	$−2,636.36	$ −590.91	−1.21%

* * *

THE OUTLET CO. (OTU). Founded 1894. Headquarters: 176 Weybosset St., Providence RI 02902. **BROADCASTING AND RETAILING.** The Outlet is a northeastern retail firm which has expanded into broadcasting. It operates five television and seven radio stations across the country. In 1982 it agreed to be acquired by the Coca-Cola Co. **MAJOR SUBSIDIARIES, BRANDS:** Outlet Specialty Stores, Inc.; KOVR-TV (Sacramento); WDBO-TV (Orlando); KSAT-TV (San Antonio); KCMH-TV (Columbus, Ohio); KJAR-TV (Providence); WTOP-AM (Washington, D.C.); WIOQ-FM (Philadelphia); KIQQ-FM (Los Angeles); WQRS-FM (Detroit).

Sales: $132.3 million (trend 8.7% a year).
Earnings: $−1.60 million.
What happened to a $10,000 investment

Purchase Date	*Purchase Price*	*Price on 12-31-81*	*Dividends Paid*
12-31-71	$ 9.67	$38.25	$5,862.07
12-31-76	$12.25	$38.25	$2,693.88

Purchase Date	*Cap. Gains (− Losses)*	*Total Return*	*Rate of Return*
12-31-71	$29,568.97	$35,431.03	16.34%
12-31-76	$21,224.49	$23,918.37	27.67%

* * *

OVERHEAD DOOR CORP. (OHD). Founded 1923. Headquarters: 6750 LBJ Freeway, Dallas TX 75240. **DOOR MANUFACTURING.** Overhead Door is the largest U.S. manufacturer of overhead sectional doors and electric door operators for use in residential, commercial, and industrial buildings. The company also makes similar doors for trucks and trailers.

Sales: $235.0 million (trend 21.4% a year).
Earnings: $4.48 million (trend 7.9% a year).
What happened to a $10,000 investment

Purchase Date	*Purchase Price*	*Price on 12-31-81*	*Dividends Paid*
12-31-71	$17.37	$10.75	$3,437.70
12-31-76	$12.62	$10.75	$3,239.60

Purchase Date	*Cap. Gains (− Losses)*	*Total Return*	*Rate of Return*
12-31-71	$−3,812.95	$−375.25	−.38%
12-31-76	$−1,485.15	$ 1,754.46	3.29%

* * *

OVERNITE TRANSPORTATION CO. (OVT). Founded 1947. Headquarters: 1000 Semmes Ave., Richmond VA 23224. **TRUCKING.** Overnite is a common carrier of general freight and the largest nonunion motor carrier in the U.S. **MAJOR SUBSIDIARIES, BRANDS:** Foremost Warehouse Corp.

Sales: $242.6 million (trend 21.6% a year).
Earnings: $18.00 million (trend 23.2% a year).
What happened to a $10,000 investment

Purchase Date	*Purchase Price*	*Price on 12-31-81*	*Dividends Paid*
12-31-71	$16.56	$27.50	$2,997.74
12-31-76	$10.94	$27.50	$2,818.29

Purchase Date	*Cap. Gains (− Losses)*	*Total Return*	*Rate of Return*
12-31-71	$ 6,603.77	$ 9,601.51	6.96%
12-31-76	$15,142.86	$17,961.14	22.83%

* * *

OVERSEAS SHIPHOLDING GROUP, INC. (OSG). Founded 1969. Headquarters: 1114 Ave. of the Americas, New York NY 10036. **BULK SHIPPING.** The Overseas Shipping Group ships liquid and dry bulk cargoes in U.S. and international shipping markets. The company also charters its ships for medium- and long-term use.

Sales: $298.5 million (trend 17.9% a year).
Earnings: $79.06 million (trend 17.1% a year).
What happened to a $10,000 investment

Purchase Date	*Purchase Price*	*Price on 12-31-81*	*Dividends Paid*
12-31-71	$4.88	$16.25	$2,972.80
12-31-76	$9.63	$16.25	$1,281.02

Purchase Date	*Cap. Gains (− Losses)*	*Total Return*	*Rate of Return*
12-31-71	$23,329.54	$26,302.35	13.76%
12-31-76	$ 6,872.95	$ 8,153.96	12.67%

* * *

OWENS-CORNING FIBERGLAS CORP. (OCF). Founded 1938. Headquarters: Fiberglas Tower, Toledo OH 43659. **GLASS FIBER PRODUCTS.** The company is the world's largest seller of glass fiber products, including insulation and roofing. Also manufactures a variety of other products, primarily for the construction industry. 24,000 employees. **MAJOR SUBSIDIARIES, BRANDS:** Fiberglas.

Sales: $2,285.1 million (trend 22.7% a year).
Earnings: $54.32 million (trend 8.1% a year).
What happened to a $10,000 investment

Purchase Date	*Purchase Price*	*Price on 12-31-81*	*Dividends Paid*
12-31-71	$26.37	$22.50	$2,732.23
12-31-76	$33.37	$22.50	$1,505.62

Purchase Date	*Cap. Gains (− Losses)*	*Total Return*	*Rate of Return*
12-31-71	$−1,469.19	$ 1,263.03	1.20%
12-31-76	$−3,258.43	$−1,752.81	−3.78%

PROFILE: Like Kleenex and Xerox, Fiberglas has been a product so successful that its name has verged on becoming a generic term. The company that made it so used to be regarded as a growth company. In the late 1960s it commanded a price / earnings multiple of 20 to 30.

Now, Owens-Corning is more of a blue-chip than a growth stock. On the evidence of its severe earnings decline in 1979–80, it must be regarded as cyclical. Good as the product and company may be, they can't create a market out of thin air when the housing industry is sick. It was hard to predict, in the early 1980s, when the housing industry might revive. But Wall Street apparently had faith that it would: in early 1982, Owens-Corning shares were selling at 11 times the company's recently depressed earnings.

Under pressure from antitrust regulators, the two companies that gave Owens-Corning its name have been selling off their major holdings. Owens-Illinois recently owned only 2 percent of the common stock; Corning Glass still had a significant minority holding (24 percent) in 1981, but was moving to dispose of it. Institutions also have large chunks of the stock, making it possibly vulnerable to a rapid fall if analysts sour on the stock.

However, the company has a lot of fundamental factors in its favor, including a recognized product, a big market share in a market expected to revive some day, and a history of profitability. (Return on stockholders' equity is usually about 10 percent and has been above 20 percent in good years.) Dividends are moderate and have been paid yearly since 1950.

* * *

OWENS-ILLINOIS, INC. (OI). Founded 1907. Headquarters: 405 Madison Ave., Toledo OH 43666. **GLASS, CONTAINERS.** Owens-Illinois is the nation's largest producer of glass containers. Also makes a variety of other glass products, container products (including corrugated packaging), and other manufactured items. 58,000 employees. **MAJOR SUBSIDIARIES, BRANDS:** Plasti-Shield bottles; Kimble scientific glass; Libbey glass tableware; Lily paper and plastic cups and dishes.

Sales: $3,905.7 million (trend 11.3% a year).
Earnings: $146.10 million (trend 11.1% a year).
What happened to a $10,000 investment

Purchase Date	*Purchase Price*	*Price on 12-31-81*	*Dividends Paid*
12-31-71	$23.25	$29.62	$4,472.69
12-31-76	$28.12	$29.62	$2,272.00

Purchase Date	*Cap. Gains (− Losses)*	*Total Return*	*Rate of Return*
12-31-71	$2,741.94	$7,214.62	5.58%
12-31-76	$ 533.33	$2,805.33	5.07%

PROFILE: Glass and containers are Owens-Illinois's two specialties. Combine them and you get glass containers, in which the company is the industry leader.

Since 1971 the company has been concentrating increasingly on Plasti-Shield bottles, compact glass bottles with a plastic wraparound shield that also serves as a label. Using this design, the company can plan on gargantuan production runs, since the bottle is the same whether it's for Pepsi or 7-Up; only the label is different. In an effort to improve profit margins, which had been squeezed in recent years, the company has been increasingly turning away custom orders and smaller orders, to concentrate on fewer products and big-volume production. *Business Week* wrote in 1981 that the company had reduced its number of molds from 2,912 to 1,226 between 1973 and 1980. The magazine quoted an analyst as summing up, "They're no longer willing to make a couple of dozen gross for Uncle Elmer's pickles."

While glass is primary, the company also owns more than a million acres of timberland and has a strong position in paper products, especially corrugated containers. Playing both sides of the glass / plastic fence, it also makes plastic containers. Still, it's clear that the company has harnessed its capital spending wagon to glass, not plastic. By spending heavily on new equipment, it hopes to keep glass containers cost-competitive with, or lower in cost than, metal and plastic containers. The heavy capital spending has helped keep earnings down in recent years. The company has also been working at trimming its debt load. (In 1981 debt was about 31 percent of capital, down from about 38 percent in 1974.) For all these reasons, the low p / e Wall Street has given Owens-Illinois (4 to 7 in recent years) may mask a company with substantial strength and a chance for good earnings gains. The dividend yield is moderate, and dividends have been paid since 1907.

* * *

OXFORD INDUSTRIES, INC. (OXM). Founded 1960. Headquarters: 222 Piedmont Ave. N.E., Atlanta GA 30308. **CLOTHING.** Oxford is a manufacturer of popularly priced clothing. The company sells large amounts of its production to J. C. Penney Co. and Sears, Roebuck & Co. **MAJOR SUBSIDIARIES, BRANDS:** Oxford Apparel; Oxford Products Limited; Cos Cob; Lanier Clothes; OSA; Holbrook.

Sales: $333.7 million (trend 3.3% a year).
Earnings: $8.77 million (trend −3.1% a year).
What happened to a $10,000 investment

Purchase Date	*Purchase Price*	*Price on 12-31-81*	*Dividends Paid*
12-31-71	$22.08	$22.37	$2,601.51
12-31-76	$20.25	$22.37	$1,338.27

Purchase Date	*Cap. Gains (− Losses)*	*Total Return*	*Rate of Return*
12-31-71	$ 132.07	$2,733.58	2.45%
12-31-76	$1,049.38	$2,387.65	4.38%

P

PHH GROUP, INC. (PHH). Founded 1953. Headquarters: 11333 McCormick Rd., Hunt Valley MD 21031. **RELOCATION SERVICES.** PHH Group, Inc., assists corporations in personnel relocation, automobile leasing and truck-fleet services. **MAJOR SUBSIDIARIES, BRANDS:** Homequity, Inc.

Sales: $388.8 million (trend 73.6% a year).
Earnings: $22.57 million (trend 26.8% a year).
What happened to a $10,000 investment

Purchase Date	*Purchase Price*	*Price on 12-31-81*	*Dividends Paid*
12-31-71	$16.62	$24.25	$1,353.68
12-31-76	$ 6.62	$24.25	$2,135.85

Purchase Date	*Cap. Gains (− Losses)*	*Total Return*	*Rate of Return*
12-31-71	$ 4,586.47	$ 5,940.15	4.77%
12-31-76	$26,603.77	$28,739.62	31.11%

* * *

PNB MORTGAGE & REALTY INVESTORS (PNI). Founded 1970. Headquarters: 7320 Old York Rd., Melrose Park PA 19126. **REALTY IN-**

VESTMENTS. PNB Mortgage & Realty invests in long-term and short-term realty investments and mortgages. **MAJOR SUBSIDIARIES, BRANDS:** Sutro Mortgage Investment Trust.

* * *

PPG INDUSTRIES, INC. (PPG). Founded 1883. Headquarters: 1 Gateway Center, Pittsburgh PA 15222. **GLASS, CHEMICALS, COATINGS.** PPG is the largest U.S. maker of flat glass and the leading producer of construction glass, particularly insulating glass. It also produces chemicals, especially chlorine and caustic soda, and makes coatings and resins, particularly automobile primers and paints. Recently it has diversified into natural gas exploration. 37,000 employees.

Sales: $3,158.4 million (trend 10.9% a year).
Earnings: $209.20 million (trend 17.8% a year).
What happened to a $10,000 investment

Purchase Date	*Purchase Price*	*Price on 12-31-81*	*Dividends Paid*
12-31-71	$29.50	$37.75	$5,159.33
12-31-76	$38.33	$37.75	$2,495.66

Purchase Date	*Cap. Gains (− Losses)*	*Total Return*	*Rate of Return*
12-31-71	$ 2,796.61	$7,955.94	6.03%
12-31-76	$−152.17	$2,343.49	4.30%

PROFILE: With the housing and auto markets making up close to half its market, it's small wonder that PPG is cyclical. In recent years, both housing and autos have been depressed. PPG has nevertheless managed to stay on its feet and even maintain some modest earnings momentum.

For the longer term, PPG has shown consistent profitability, but the return on stockholders' equity has been nothing better than average. It remains to be seen whether chairman L. Stanton Williams can achieve his goal of bringing the return on equity up to 18 percent a year before he retires in 1984.

In the attempt to improve profitability from its decent but just-like-the-guy-next-door showing, PPG has two tactics. One is to use more modern, efficient production methods. Capital spending has been hiked (from historically low levels), and the company boasts new, energy-efficient methods for producing both glass and chlorine. The other tactic is to expand cautiously into new business areas that show promise of greater profitability than PPG's traditional lines. The company's small natural gas exploration program is an example. (In 1981, it made a promising find in Michigan.)

PPG began life as Pittsburgh Plate Glass almost 100 years ago. It has a long string of yearly dividend payments dating back to 1899. In recent years the dividend yield has been in the range of 5 to 7 percent.

* * *

PSA, INC. (PSA). Founded 1945. Headquarters: 3225 N. Harbor Dr., San Diego CA 92101. **AVIATION.** PSA, Inc., the holding company for Pacific Southwest Airlines, also operates aviation maintenance services. **MAJOR SUBSIDIARIES, BRANDS:** Pacific Southwest Airlines.

Sales: $370.2 million (trend 21.1% a year).
Earnings: $12.65 million (trend 60.4% a year).
What happened to a $10,000 investment

Purchase Date	*Purchase Price*	*Price on 12-31-81*	*Dividends Paid*
12-31-71	$20.20	$19.75	$ 519.80
12-31-76	$ 6.00	$19.75	$1,750.00

Purchase Date	*Cap. Gains (− Losses)*	*Total Return*	*Rate of Return*
12-31-71	$ −222.77	$ 297.03	.29%
12-31-76	$22,916.67	$24,666.67	28.23%

* * *

PACCAR INC. (PCAR, Over-the-Counter). Founded 1971. Headquarters: 777 106th Ave. N.E., Bellevue WA 98004. **TRUCKS, RAILROAD CARS.** PACCAR is a major producer of heavy-duty trucks and hauling equipment and is also a significant factor in the production of railroad cars. 12,000 employees. **MAJOR SUBSIDIARIES, BRANDS:** Peterbilt and Kenworth trucks; Pacific Car and Foundry Division; Wagner Mining Equipment Division; Dart Truck Co.

Sales: $1,673.7 million (trend 20.1% a year).
Earnings: $81.09 million (trend 31.5% a year).
What happened to a $10,000 investment

Purchase Date	*Purchase Price*	*Price on 12-31-81*	*Dividends Paid*
12-31-71	$30.76	$73.86	$5,758.52
12-31-76	$42.95	$73.86	$3,047.62

Purchase Date	*Cap. Gains (− Losses)*	*Total Return*	*Rate of Return*
12-31-71	$14,014.78	$19,773.30	11.53%
12-31-76	$ 7,195.77	$10,243.39	15.15%

PROFILE: Let's face it: The man on the street has never heard of PACCAR, even though the firm ranks about 200th on the Fortune 500 list of major industrial corporations.

But there are even better reasons to be interested in PACCAR than its size. Profitability, foremost. PACCAR consistently earns close to 20 percent on stockholders' equity, sometimes 25 percent or better. That's an outstanding performance. If you don't like figures, look at it this way: In 1980, a poor year for the transportation industry, PACCAR was the only major truck manufacturer that was making money making trucks. Its Kenworth and Peterbilt trucks enjoy an excellent reputation among truck users.

There's also growth. PACCAR's profits have grown better than 20 percent a year from 1970 to 1980 and about 25 percent a year for the latter half of the decade. That's the kind of record you might expect from a small maker of specialized computer peripherals, not from an established maker of large vehicles used in mining, logging, and trucking.

Was it done, then, with mirrors — i.e. with debt? Nope. PACCAR hasn't achieved fast growth by playing with other people's money; its growth has been internally financed. As of 1981, there was barely a hint of debt on the books — about 3 percent of capital.

What keeps this stock from looking perfect is that it is, after all, cyclical. Recessions and high interest rates will set back earnings, as they did in 1980. But the stock has one more thing going for it — its lack of glamour. This equity has never commanded a high p / e. In recent years, the multiple has ranged from 4 to 8. If you invest here, your dollars buy a solid track record for growth at a cheap price.

* * *

PACIFIC AMERICAN INCOME SHARES, INC. (PAI). Founded 1972. Headquarters: 707 Wilshire Blvd., Los Angeles CA 90017. **INVESTMENTS.** Pacific American Income Shares, Inc., invests in government and corporate debt securities.

* * *

PACIFIC GAS & ELECTRIC CO. (PCG). Founded 1905. Headquarters: 77 Beale St., San Francisco CA 94106. **UTILITY.** The company supplies electricity and natural gas to some 9 million people in the northern two thirds of California. 27,000 employees.

Sales: $5,258.9 million (trend 17.9% a year).
Earnings: $415.60 million (trend 15.3% a year).
What happened to a $10,000 investment

Purchase Date	*Purchase Price*	*Price on 12-31-81*	*Dividends Paid*
12-31-71	$32.37	$21.25	$6,486.49
12-31-76	$23.12	$21.25	$5,128.65

Purchase Date	*Cap. Gains (− Losses)*	*Total Return*	*Rate of Return*
12-31-71	$−3,436.29	$3,050.19	2.70%
12-31-76	$ −810.81	$4,317.84	7.44%

PROFILE: No one currently expects capital gains in utility stocks. That's why they command such miserly multiples. Pacific Gas & Electric sold for 5 to 8 times earnings from 1976 through early 1982. On the basis of the record, the investor pessimism is justified. For the ten years ending in 1980, the annual growth in earnings was less than 4 percent and the total return to investors was about 3 percent — worse, in other words, than putting your money in a passbook savings account.

That poor return was the result of capital losses offsetting a high and growing dividend. The dividend yield in early 1981 was a striking 13 percent. And a portion of that dividend, in many years, was wholly or partially tax exempt (because it counted as a return of capital).

People close to retirement age who want a portion of their portfolio in utility stocks may find these shares attractive. Based on recent history, it's hard to see who else would, though.

Granted, the future is impossible to predict. That's why unpopular stocks (those with low p / e ratios) do better, on the average and in the long run, than popular ones (those with high p / e ratios). It's hard to see what unexpected event could make this stock soar, though. A drop in interest rates would help. The long-awaited start up of the Diablo Canyon nuclear plant would help, by reducing dependence on purchased power, which recently was almost a quarter of the company's power. But, in the wake of allegations about design flaws, the plant might not open for years. More favorable regulation would help, though California of late has been more accommodating than many states. But even if all of these happened, a speculator's lips would remain dry.

On the plus side, besides the low price and the high dividend yield, note that the company's debt load isn't high for a utility. It was recently about 43 percent of capital, down from about 50 percent in 1975.

* * *

PACIFIC LIGHTING CORP. (PLT). Founded 1886. Headquarters: 810 S. Flower St., Los Angeles CA 90017. NATURAL GAS. Pacific Lighting is the parent corporation of Southern California Gas, the nation's largest natural gas distributor, which provides natural gas to some 4 million customers in Los Angeles and other parts of southern California. Has sidelines in real estate, liquefied natural gas handling, and the Alaska Highway Pipeline Project. 9,000 employees. MAJOR SUBSIDIARIES, BRANDS: Southern California Gas.

Sales: $3,328.1 million (trend 24.4% a year).
Earnings: $101.13 million (trend 18.9% a year).
What happened to a $10,000 investment

Purchase Date	*Purchase Price*	*Price on 12-31-81*	*Dividends Paid*
12-31-71	$24.75	$27.25	$7,632.32
12-31-76	$19.37	$27.25	$5,424.52

Purchase Date	*Cap. Gains (− Losses)*	*Total Return*	*Rate of Return*
12-31-71	$1,010.10	$8,642.42	6.43%
12-31-76	$4,064.52	$9,489.03	14.28%

PROFILE: Natural gas companies are aligned on a continuum, from those that emphasize exploration and production, through those that emphasize pipeline operations, to those that emphasize simple delivery of gas to customers. Pacific Lighting is on this last end of the continuum. It is, in essence, a utility.

A little more than a quarter of its gas (which is bought on the open market, in large part from El Paso Co., also profiled in this book) goes for power generation. More than another quarter goes directly to industrial and commercial users. Just over another quarter goes to residential users, and most of the residual is sold to other utilities.

Pacific Lighting will probably be classified as a utility for tax purposes, meaning that you may be able to reinvest your dividends in newly issued common stock, and pay capital-gains rates instead of full tax rates. But the company also has many of the disadvantages that have been plaguing most utilities: It's highly regulated, and its growth rate (though better than some) is nothing to write home about. It also resembles most other utilities in carrying a good deal of debt; long-term debt was recently about 44 percent of total capital. The return on stockholders' equity has been unexciting, but it has been improving steadily, partly as a result of increased sympathy from rate regulators.

The dividend yield is high — 9 to 11 percent in recent years. Dividends have been paid every year since 1909.

* * *

THE PACIFIC LUMBER CO. (PL). Founded 1905. Headquarters: 1111 Columbus Ave., San Francisco CA 94133. LUMBER. The Pacific Lumber Co. produces redwood lumber and plywood and manufactures welding equipment.

Sales: $289.5 million (trend 18.7% a year).
Earnings: $42.08 million (trend 16.2% a year).
What happened to a $10,000 investment

Purchase Date	*Purchase Price*	*Price on 12-31-81*	*Dividends Paid*
12-31-71	$ 5.58	$24.75	$12,717.94
12-31-76	$19.56	$24.75	$ 2,670.93

Purchase Date	*Cap. Gains (− Losses)*	*Total Return*	*Rate of Return*
12-31-71	$34,328.36	$47,046.30	19.02%
12-31-76	$ 2,651.76	$ 5,322.68	8.91%

* * *

PACIFIC POWER & LIGHT CO. (PPW). Founded 1910. Headquarters: Public Service Bldg., Portland OR 97204. UTILITY. Pacific Power & Light Co. provides electric, water, and steam-heat services in six western states; also involved in telecommunications services and coal mining. MAJOR SUBSIDIARIES, BRANDS: NERCO, Inc.

Sales: $975.4 million (trend 25.2% a year).
Earnings: $110.72 million (trend 10.8% a year).
What happened to a $10,000 investment

Purchase Date	*Purchase Price*	*Price on 12-31-81*	*Dividends Paid*
12-31-71	$23.75	$17.87	$7,290.53
12-31 76	$24.12	$17.87	$3,842.49

Purchase Date	*Cap. Gains (− Losses)*	*Total Return*	*Rate of Return*
12-31-71	$−2,473.68	$4,816.84	4.01%
12-31-76	$−2,590.67	$1,251.81	2.39%

* * *

PACIFIC SCIENTIFIC CO. (PSX). Founded 1937. Headquarters: 1350 S. State College Blvd.,

Anaheim CA 92803. **ELECTRONIC INSTRUMENTS.** Pacific Scientific Co. manufactures, sells, and services electronic instruments. **MAJOR SUBSIDIARIES, BRANDS:** Gardner Laboratory; Kin-Tech; Royco Instruments.

Sales: $62.8 million (trend 28.4% a year).
Earnings: $7.15 million (trend 69.2% a year).
What happened to a $10,000 investment

Purchase Date	*Purchase Price*	*Price on 12-31-81*	*Dividends Paid*
12-31-71	$ .74	$14.75	$12,229.06
12-31-76	$1.11	$14.75	$ 7,639.70

Purchase Date	*Cap. Gains (− Losses)*	*Total Return*	*Rate of Return*
12-31-71	$189,124.86	$201,353.91	35.68%
12-31-76	$122,750.00	$130,389.70	69.62%

* * *

PACIFIC TELEPHONE & TELEGRAPH CO. (PAC). Founded 1906. Headquarters: 140 New Montgomery St., San Francisco CA 94105. **COMMUNICATIONS SERVICES.** Pacific Telephone & Telegraph provides communications service primarily in California and Nevada. The company is 91 percent owned by American Telephone & Telegraph Co., which plans to acquire the remainder (and later to spin it off along with other operating subsidiaries). **MAJOR SUBSIDIARIES, BRANDS:** Bell Telephone Co. of Nevada.

Sales: $5,782.3 million (trend 11.6% a year).
Earnings: $316.20 million (trend −1.1% a year).
What happened to a $10,000 investment

Purchase Date	*Purchase Price*	*Price on 12-31-81*	*Dividends Paid*
12-31-71	$18.75	$19.87	$6,960.00
12-31-76	$18.25	$19.87	$3,835.62

Purchase Date	*Cap. Gains (− Losses)*	*Total Return*	*Rate of Return*
12-31-71	$600.00	$7,560.00	5.79%
12-31-76	$890.41	$4,726.03	8.05%

* * *

PACIFIC TIN CONSOLIDATED CORP. (PTC). Founded 1907. Headquarters: 280 Park Ave., New York NY 10017. **TIN.** Pacific Tin Consolidated Corp. produces feldspar and iron powders; also dredges tin in Southeast Asia. **MAJOR SUBSIDIARIES, BRANDS:** The Feldspar Corp.; The Pyron Corp.

Sales: $35.1 million (trend 19.4% a year).
Earnings: $2.37 million (trend 16.2% a year).
What happened to a $10,000 investment

Purchase Date	*Purchase Price*	*Price on 12-31-81*	*Dividends Paid*
12-31-71	$10.25	$17.12	$8,000.00
12-31-76	$ 9.37	$17.12	$4,800.00

Purchase Date	*Cap. Gains (− Losses)*	*Total Return*	*Rate of Return*
12-31-71	$6,707.32	$14,707.32	9.47%
12-31-76	$8,266.67	$13,066.67	18.19%

* * *

PAINE WEBBER INC. (PWJ). Founded 1973. Headquarters: 140 Broadway, New York NY 10005. **BROKERAGE FIRM.** Paine Webber Inc. aids clients in the sale and purchase of securities; deals in corporate and government securities; also offers investment banking services. **MAJOR SUBSIDIARIES, BRANDS:** Blyth Eastman Dillon & Co.; Paine Webber Mitchell Hutchins Inc.; Paine Webber Real Estate Securities.

Sales: $1,027.1 million (trend 38.9% a year).
Earnings: $13.96 million (trend 8.4% a year).
What happened to a $10,000 investment

Purchase Date	*Purchase Price*	*Price on 12-31-81*	*Dividends Paid*
12-31-71	$N/A	$25.25	$ N/A
12-31-76	$ 8.50	$25.25	$2,670.59

Purchase Date	*Cap. Gains (− Losses)*	*Total Return*	*Rate of Return*
12-31-71	$ N/A	$ N/A	N/A%
12-31-76	$19,705.88	$22,376.47	26.49%

* * *

PALM BEACH INC. (PMB). Founded 1931. Headquarters: 400 Pike St., Cincinnati OH 45202. **APPAREL.** Palm Beach Inc. designs, manufactures, and sells clothing for men, women, and boys. **MAJOR SUBSIDIARIES, BRANDS:** Evan-Picone; Gant; Pierre Cardin; Rugger.

Sales: $407.8 million (trend 27.5% a year).
Earnings: $13.00 million (trend 32.4% a year).
What happened to a $10,000 investment

Purchase Date	Purchase Price	Price on 12-31-81	Dividends Paid
12-31-71	$8.30	$25.12	$7,109.40
12-31-76	$8.10	$25.12	$6,024.69

Purchase Date	Cap. Gains (− Losses)	Total Return	Rate of Return
12-31-71	$20,271.08	$27,380.48	14.09%
12-31-76	$21,018.52	$27,043.21	29.94%

* * *

PAN AMERICAN BANKS, INC. (PAB). Founded 1968. Headquarters: 150 S.E. Third Ave., Miami FL 33131. BANKING. Pan American owns seven banks in Florida, including Pan American Bank in Miami; also has international banking operations.

* * *

PAN AMERICAN WORLD AIRWAYS, INC. (PN). Founded 1927. Headquarters: Pan Am Bldg., 200 Park Ave., New York NY 10166. AIRLINE. Pan Am is the nation's third largest airline and the largest primarily international U.S. airline. 32,000 employees. MAJOR SUBSIDIARIES, BRANDS: Pan American World Airways.

Sales: $4,016.1 million (trend 18.5% a year).
Earnings: $80.27 million (trend 13.8% a year).
What happened to a $10,000 investment

Purchase Date	Purchase Price	Price on 12-31-81	Dividends Paid
12-31-71	$15.25	$2.75	$0.00
12-31-76	$ 5.25	$2.75	$0.00

Purchase Date	Cap. Gains (− Losses)	Total Return	Rate of Return
12-31-71	$−8,196.72	$−8,196.72	−15.74%
12-31-76	$−4,761.90	$−4,761.90	−12.13%

PROFILE: It's hard to operate an airline in a hole. That's what Pan Am is trying to do these days.

Its fleet is old, and it lacks money to replace it. Its fuel costs are high, partly because it must buy much of its fuel abroad, partly because its planes are old. It can't modernize its fleet because no one will lend to an airline that already has far more debt than equity capital. It can't get money by issuing new stock because the stock has already shrunk to a share price only a fraction of what it was in years past.

Pan Am lost money on its airline operations in eight of the eleven years from 1970 to 1980. The loss in 1980 was the worst ever, almost a quarter of a billion dollars. One result: While the company still boasts the Pan Am Building in New York City as an address, the building now belongs to Metropolitan Life. Even the almost $300-million gain from selling the building was barely enough to give the corporation a gain, on paper, for 1980. And the troubles looked as if they would continue on into the 1980s.

The company blames many of its troubles on subsidized foreign competition, and the excuse has merit. Unsolved problems from the merger with National airlines are playing a part, too. So has the recession. Whatever the causes or excuses, the airline is sinking under its own debt load. In 1981 the long-term debt was approaching $1.5 billion. Debt was about two thirds of total capital. Interest on the debt in 1980 was $144 million. No dividends have been paid since 1969, and none are likely in the foreseeable future. Firings and resignations among top managers come with popcorn-popper frequency.

Airline stocks tend to be volatile, and speculators often get a ride in Pan Am, as the price bounces on the air currents of hope or despair. Some combination of government help, an improved economy, and lower (or stable) fuel prices might save Pan Am or restore it to black ink. If the airline is nursed back to health, speculators could reap a huge profit. But Wall Street, in pricing this stock at bargain-basement levels, has correctly perceived that bankruptcy is a very real possibility. In its latest desperation move, Pan Am sold its Intercontinental Hotels subsidiary (which, unlike the airline, had been profitable recently), for $500 million in 1981 to Grand Metropolitan, Ltd.

* * *

PANHANDLE EASTERN PIPE LINE CO. (PEL). Founded 1929. Headquarters: 3000 Bissonnet Ave., Houston TX 77005. OIL PIPELINES. Panhandle Eastern Pipe Line Co. operates interstate natural gas pipelines; also involved in oil and gas exploration. MAJOR SUBSIDIARIES, BRANDS: Anadarko Production; Pan Eastern Exploration; Trunkline Gas.

Sales: $2,472.2 million (trend 30.7% a year).
Earnings: $181.96 million (trend 20.5% a year).
What happened to a $10,000 investment

Purchase Date	Purchase Price	Price on 12-31-81	Dividends Paid
12-31-71	$16.12	$36.75	$7,939.53
12-31-76	$23.87	$36.75	$3,268.06

Purchase Date	Cap. Gains (− Losses)	Total Return	Rate of Return
12-31-71	$12,790.70	$20,730.23	11.88%
12-31-76	$ 5,392.67	$ 8,660.73	13.29%

* * *

PAPERCRAFT CORP. (PCT). Founded 1945. Headquarters: Papercraft Park, Pittsburgh PA 15238. **GIFT WRAPS.** Papercraft Corp. manufactures gift wrappings, ribbons, cellophane tape and adhesives. **MAJOR SUBSIDIARIES, BRANDS:** American Technical Industries; Barth & Dreyfuss of California; Kim Color Corp.; Knomark Inc.; LePage (adhesives).

Sales: $147.4 million (trend 15.1% a year).
Earnings: $11.60 million (trend 14.7% a year).
What happened to a $10,000 investment

Purchase Date	Purchase Price	Price on 12-31-81	Dividends Paid
12-31-71	$20.39	$20.12	$3,113.19
12-31-76	$ 9.49	$20.12	$4,590.31

Purchase Date	Cap. Gains (− Losses)	Total Return	Rate of Return
12-31-71	$ −128.42	$ 2,984.77	2.65%
12-31-76	$11,209.38	$15,799.69	20.87%

* * *

PARADYNE CORP. (PDN). Founded 1969. Headquarters: 8550 Ulmerton Rd., Largo FL 33541. **DATA COMMUNICATIONS.** Paradyne produces a variety of products that allow communication by phone line or similar means of computer-generated data.

Sales: $75.9 million (trend 71.2% a year).
Earnings: $8.25 million (trend 126.5% a year).

* * *

PARGAS, INC. (PAG). Founded 1946. Headquarters: PO Box 67, Waldorf MD 20601. **LIQUID PROPANE GAS.** Pargas, Inc., distributes propane gas and related appliances. **MAJOR SUBSIDIARIES, BRANDS:** River Processing, Inc.

Sales: $237.7 million (trend 15.2% a year).
Earnings: $10.89 million (trend 18.2% a year).
What happened to a $10,000 investment

Purchase Date	Purchase Price	Price on 12-31-81	Dividends Paid
12-31-71	$17.38	$18.25	$5,757.26
12-31-76	$16.07	$18.25	$3,447.11

Purchase Date	Cap. Gains (− Losses)	Total Return	Rate of Return
12-31-71	$ 499.99	$6,257.25	4.98%
12-31-76	$1,355.55	$4,802.66	8.16%

* * *

PARKER DRILLING CO. (PKD). Founded 1954. Headquarters: Parker Bldg., 8 E. Third St., Tulsa OK 74103. **OIL DRILLING.** Parker is a leading drilling contractor, specializing in remote area and deep land drilling. 6,000 employees. **MAJOR SUBSIDIARIES, BRANDS:** Perry Gas Companies.

Sales: $582.3 million (trend 35.0% a year).
Earnings: $78.89 million (trend 39.5% a year).
What happened to a $10,000 investment

Purchase Date	Purchase Price	Price on 12-31-81	Dividends Paid
12-31-71	$2.31	$21.12	$2,024.50
12-31-76	$5.21	$21.12	$ 882.88

Purchase Date	Cap. Gains (− Losses)	Total Return	Rate of Return
12-31-71	$81,351.35	$83,375.86	25.03%
12-31-76	$30,560.00	$31,442.88	32.89%

PROFILE: Each of the highly successful oil drilling firms has its specialty. Parker leaves the offshore business to others. Its specialty is land drilling, in places (remote) or at depths (more than 15,000 feet) that others find hard to reach.

In 1981 Parker was turning away business, so great was the demand for its services. Some analysts anticipated that the trend would continue, as Parker turned its attention increasingly to overseas markets with untapped potential.

An investor who found this stock at the beginning of the 1970s did the equivalent of striking oil. With perfect timing, a $10,000 investment at the beginning of that decade would have been worth about $340,000 at decade's end. Parker was among the 25 top-performing stocks in a field of more than 1,000 equities monitored by *Forbes* magazine.

If it's hard to quarrel with success, let's make an effort. There must be *some* argument against this stock. Well . . . to begin with, the company's success is widely enough recognized so you can't buy in cheap. The stock usually sells at a premium to the market. The p / e ratio ranged from 10 to 23 in 1980. And, as that variation indicates, the stock is volatile. It pays only a token dividend. And the company has more debt than a debt-averse investor might wish — recently about a third of total capital.

Despite such objections, this is a stock worth watching and perhaps accumulating on market dips. If you believe that oil gluts are transitory and the oil shortage is lasting, you can expect Parker's services will be in great demand.

* * *

PARKER-HANNIFIN CORP. (PH). Founded 1938. Headquarters: 17325 Euclid Ave., Cleveland OH 44112. FLUID CONTROLS. Parker-Hannifin is a leading maker of fluid power systems, flow control systems, and flow measuring devices. It is also a factor in the auto parts and aerospace markets. 20,000 employees.

Sales: $1,105.9 million (trend 23.2% a year).
Earnings: $64.06 million (trend 26.1% a year).
What happened to a $10,000 investment

Purchase Date	*Purchase Price*	*Price on 12-31-81*	*Dividends Paid*
12-31-71	$13.56	$22.92	$4,475.41
12-31-76	$15.22	$22.92	$2,417.52

Purchase Date	*Cap. Gains (— Losses)*	*Total Return*	*Rate of Return*
12-31-71	$6,905.74	$11,381.15	7.90%
12-31-76	$5,054.74	$ 7,472.26	11.81%

PROFILE: If it has to do with the movement of fluids, there's a good chance Parker-Hannifin has a hand in it. The company makes fluid-control equipment ranging from simple hoses, valves, and pumps to air-conditioning equipment and complicated hydraulic power systems.

About half the company's business is in replacement parts, giving it some buffer against earnings fluctuations due to recession-induced cutbacks on capital spending. About a fifth of sales are outside the United States, so there's some geographic balance, too.

These factors had helped Parker-Hannifin to chalk up ten years of consecutive earnings gains through fiscal 1981, despite a couple of nasty recessions. In 1981 the company also announced that it planned to use its knowledge of fluid technology in the medical field, possibly for the treatment of arthritis or diabetes. This aspect of the stock must be viewed as speculative, pending further developments.

Profitability here has been a bit above that achieved by the average corporation. Profit margins have been trending upward and have been above 5 percent since 1977. The debt load is manageable (debt was recently about a quarter of total capital). Dividends have been paid each year since 1949 and have provided a yield in the neighborhood of 4 percent the past few years.

* * *

THE PARKER PEN CO. (PKR). Founded 1892. Headquarters: 219 E. Court St., Janesville WI 53545. PENS. Parker Pen Co. manufactures pens and operates a temporary help firm, Manpower, Inc. MAJOR SUBSIDIARIES, BRANDS: Manpower, Inc.; Eversharp; Parker; Super Quink.

Sales: $723.3 million (trend 34.6% a year).
Earnings: $37.68 million (trend 33.0% a year).
What happened to a $10,000 investment

Purchase Date	*Purchase Price*	*Price on 12-31-81*	*Dividends Paid*
12-31-71	$2.84	$14.25	$6,538.47
12-31-76	$6.24	$14.25	$2,052.25

Purchase Date	*Cap. Gains (— Losses)*	*Total Return*	*Rate of Return*
12-31-71	$40,140.21	$46,678.68	18.94%
12-31-76	$12,843.49	$14,895.75	20.01%

* * *

PARSONS CORP. (RMP). Founded 1944. Headquarters: 100 W. Walnut St., Pasadena CA 91124. ENGINEERING, CONSTRUCTION. Parsons is one of the world's largest engineering and construction firms, serving the petroleum, synthetic fuels, chemical, mining, metallurgical, power generation, transportation, and defense industries. 14,000 employees. MAJOR SUBSIDIARIES, BRANDS: Ralph M. Parsons Co.; De Leuw, Cather & Co.; S.I.P. Engineering, Inc.; Parsons Constructors Inc.; Engineering-Science, Inc.

Sales: $773.1 million (trend −2.9% a year).
Earnings: $26.78 million (trend 20.3% a year).
What happened to a $10,000 investment

Purchase Date	*Purchase Price*	*Price on 12-31-81*	*Dividends Paid*
12-31-71	$5.09	$34.25	$7,048.06
12-31-76	$6.41	$34.25	$4,722.43

Purchase Date	*Cap. Gains (— Losses)*	*Total Return*	*Rate of Return*
12-31-71	$57,336.17	$64,384.22	22.22%
12-31-76	$43,453.76	$48,176.19	42.22%

PROFILE: This firm is a powerhouse, with a big order backlog, a good growth record, and a strong financial position. It's a class outfit and the market knows it, according the stock a price / earnings ratio of 16 in early 1981, when the average stock fetched only 8.

If you prefer low p / e stocks, Parsons may not be your cup of tea. However, if you allot a portion of your portfolio to recognized high achievers, you may want to look at Parsons's report card. It includes a profit growth rate of more than 20 percent in recent years, a solid balance sheet (debt recently only 15 percent of capital and more than $100 million of cash on hand), and a reputation for providing good service to the varied clients who buy its engineering services.

In revenues, Parsons isn't a giant — yet. It ranked last in 1980 revenues ($773 million) among ten construction firms profiled in 1981 by *Financial World* magazine. But new orders are another story. Ranked by dollar value of 1980 contracts (according to *Engineering News-Record),* Parsons was third among all construction firms, just a bit behind Bechtel Group and Brown & Root and a whisker ahead of Fluor.

Financial World wrote recently that Parsons has broken away from its former image as a "mini-Fluor." It is less concentrated in energy projects than Fluor is, has a broader base, and does a lot of defense work, particularly missile engineering.

Dividend payments were started in 1972 and provide a modest yield, around 2½ to 4 percent in recent years.

* * *

PATRICK PETROLEUM CO. (PPC). Founded 1970. Headquarters: 744 W. Michigan Ave., Jackson MI 49201. **OIL.** Patrick Petroleum Co. produces oil and natural gas; also involved in onshore exploration.

Sales: $77.7 million (trend 10.5% a year).
Earnings: $6.23 million (trend −7.3% a year).
What happened to a $10,000 investment

Purchase Date	*Purchase Price*	*Price on 12-31-81*	*Dividends Paid*
12-31-71	$4.81	$13.87	$0.00
12-31-76	$7.58	$13.87	$0.00

Purchase Date	*Cap. Gains (− Losses)*	*Total Return*	*Rate of Return*
12-31-71	$18,852.35	$18,852.35	11.18%
12-31-76	$ 8,296.70	$ 8,296.70	12.84%

* * *

PAY LESS DRUG STORES NORTHWEST, INC. (PAY). Founded 1967. Headquarters: 9275 S.W. Peyton Lane, Wilsonville OR 97070. **DRUG STORES.** Pay Less Drug Stores Northwest, Inc., operates approximately 150 drug stores in 5 western states.

Sales: $750.9 million (trend 26.5% a year).
Earnings: $14.32 million (trend 19.6% a year).
What happened to a $10,000 investment

Purchase Date	*Purchase Price*	*Price on 12-31-81*	*Dividends Paid*
12-31-71	$5.81	$16.25	$2,631.40
12-31-76	$6.80	$16.25	$1,510.29

Purchase Date	*Cap. Gains (− Losses)*	*Total Return*	*Rate of Return*
12-31-71	$17,952.98	$20,584.38	11.83%
12-31-76	$13,897.06	$15,407.35	20.50%

* * *

PAYLESS CASHWAYS, INC. (PCI). Founded 1968. Headquarters: 2301 Main, Kansas City MO 64108. **BUILDING SUPPLIES.** Payless Cashways runs a chain of approximately 100 building supply stores, catering primarily to do-it-yourselfers. The stores are scattered throughout the Midwest, Southwest, and West.

Sales: $382.7 million (trend 31.1% a year).
Earnings: $11.00 million (trend 24.4% a year).
What happened to a $10,000 investment

Purchase Date	*Purchase Price*	*Price on 12-31-81*	*Dividends Paid*
12-31-71	$7.84	$16.25	$1,077.29
12-31-76	$7.62	$16.25	$ 780.33

Purchase Date	*Cap. Gains (− Losses)*	*Total Return*	*Rate of Return*
12-31-71	$10,717.13	$11,794.42	8.10%
12-31-76	$11,311.48	$12,091.80	17.18%

* * *

PEABODY INTERNATIONAL CORP. (PBD). Founded 1946. Headquarters: 4 Landmark Sq., Stamford CT 06901. **ENVIRONMENTAL PROTECTION.** Peabody International Corp. manufactures equipment and offers services related to energy and environmental protection.

Sales: $423.9 million (trend 9.3% a year).
Earnings: $3.40 million (trend −16.0% a year).
What happened to a $10,000 investment

Purchase Date	*Purchase Price*	*Price on 12-31-81*	*Dividends Paid*
12-31-71	$24.74	$6.50	$594.74
12-31-76	$19.76	$6.50	$588.83

Purchase Date	*Cap. Gains (− Losses)*	*Total Return*	*Rate of Return*
12-31-71	$−7,372.79	$−6,778.05	−10.71%
12-31-76	$−6,710.58	$−6,121.76	−17.26%

* * *

PEAVEY CO. (PV). Founded 1922. Headquarters: 730 Second Ave. S., Minneapolis MN 55402. **FOOD.** Peavey Co. produces food products, merchandises grain and agricultural commodities, and manages retail farm stores. **MAJOR SUBSIDIARIES, BRANDS:** Northwest Fabrics; Steamex.

Sales: $820.9 million (trend 11.3% a year).
Earnings: $23.22 million (trend 15.1% a year).
What happened to a $10,000 investment

Purchase Date	*Purchase Price*	*Price on 12-31-81*	*Dividends Paid*
12-31-71	$ N/A	$21.25	$ N/A
12-31-76	$16.62	$21.25	$2,790.98

Purchase Date	*Cap. Gains (− Losses)*	*Total Return*	*Rate of Return*
12-31-71	$ N/A	$ N/A	N/A%
12-31-76	$2,781.95	$5,572.93	9.26%

* * *

PENGO INDUSTRIES, INC. (PGO). Founded 1977. Headquarters: 1400 Everman Parkway, PO Box 40530, Fort Worth TX 76140. **OIL SERVICES.** Pengo Industries provides services and equipment to the petroleum industry. **MAJOR SUBSIDIARIES, BRANDS:** Chaparral Transports, Inc.; East Texas Swabbing, Inc.

Sales: $182.2 million (trend 144.3% a year).
Earnings: $15.81 million (trend 512.1% a year).

* * *

PENN CENTRAL CORP. (PC). Founded 1978; predecessor company (railroad) dated to 1846. Headquarters: 245 Park Ave., New York NY 10017. **CONGLOMERATE.** Penn Central, emerged from both bankruptcy and the railroad business, is active in energy production and distribution, industrial equipment, electronics, auto parts, real estate, and other fields. 41,000 employees. **MAJOR SUBSIDIARIES, BRANDS:** GK Technologies; Marathon Manufacturing; Butler-Johnson Inc.; Cubby Drilling; Buckeye Energy Co.; Edgington Oil Co.; Arvida Corp.

Sales: $2,013.7 million.
Earnings: $58.60 million.

PROFILE: There's nary a train in sight at Penn Central these days, but there's plenty of movement. After bankruptcy proceedings that stretched through almost eight years, the conglomerate that succeeded the old railroad company emerged from bankruptcy in 1978. Armed with hundreds of millions of dollars of tax loss carry-forwards, it has gone on an acquisition binge, concentrating mainly on companies involved in energy or industrial process equipment.

One booming subsidiary is Marathon Manufacturing, the world's largest manufacturer of moveable "jackup" offshore drilling rigs. It is part of Penn Central's energy group, which also includes Edgington Oil, Buckeye Energy Co., Cubby Drilling, and Butler-Johnson, another drilling firm. In 1981 Penn Central moved to acquire Colt Industries, but the merger attempt fell through when some major Penn Central Stockholders felt that the company was going to pay too much for Colt. (Colt is profiled elsewhere in this volume.)

Holders in the old Penn Central Co. got one share of the new Penn Central Corp. for each 25 shares they held previously. On a restated basis, the stock hit bottom at around $14 a share in 1978–79 and was selling for about $41 in early 1982. A nice profit . . . but it would have taken a burglar's guts to buy at the low. A person who purchased the old Penn Central shares in the late 1960s and sold at the end of 1978 could easily have seen a $10,000 investment melt down to $100.

No dividends are yet being paid on the new Penn Central shares.

* * *

PENNCORP FINANCIAL, INC. (PCF). Founded 1968. Headquarters: 3130 Wilshire Blvd., Santa Monica CA 90406. **INSURANCE.** PennCorp Financial, Inc., underwrites and sells life, accident and health, and property and casualty insurance; also operates a savings and loan association. **MAJOR SUBSIDIARIES, BRANDS:** Bankers and Shippers Insurance Co. of New York; Houston First Savings Association; Massachusetts Indemnity and

Life Insurance Co.; Pennsylvania Life Insurance Co.

Sales: $479.0 million (trend 21.3% a year).
Earnings: $21.67 million (trend 32.9% a year).
What happened to a $10,000 investment

Purchase Date	*Purchase Price*	*Price on 12-31-81*	*Dividends Paid*
12-31-71	$28.69	$5.62	$ 156.86
12-31-76	$ 2.87	$5.62	$1,565.22

Purchase Date	*Cap. Gains (– Losses)*	*Total Return*	*Rate of Return*
12-31-71	$–8,039.27	$–7,882.41	–14.38%
12-31-76	$ 9,565.22	$ 11,130.43	16.14%

* * *

J. C. PENNEY CO. INC. (JCP). Founded 1924. Headquarters: 1301 Ave. of the Americas, New York NY 10019. **RETAILER.** Penney is the nation's third largest general merchandise retailer. 194,000 employees. **MAJOR SUBSIDIARIES, BRANDS:** Treasury and Thrift drug stores; Sarma general merchandise stores in Belgium.

Sales: $11,353.0 million (trend 9.0% a year).
Earnings: $268.37 million (trend 5.5% a year).
What happened to a $10,000 investment

Purchase Date	*Purchase Price*	*Price on 12-31-81*	*Dividends Paid*
12-31-71	$73.25	$28.62	$1,720.14
12-31-76	$52.62	$28.62	$1,299.76

Purchase Date	*Cap. Gains (– Losses)*	*Total Return*	*Rate of Return*
12-31-71	$–6,092.15	$–4,372.01	–5.59%
12-31-76	$–4,560.57	$–3,260.81	–7.59%

PROFILE: Perhaps it doesn't come as a shock to say that the fortunes of retailers rise and fall with consumer spending. That makes for a lot of ups and downs — seven ups and three downs, from year to year, in the decade recently completed, for example.

Penney's is known for soft goods — clothing and linens. Originally, its stores carried soft goods almost exclusively, and about half of its more than 2,000 stores still do. In the full-line stores, soft goods usually take up more than half the selling space.

Unfortunately, soft is also the word for the results the chain has achieved in recent years. Sales have barely been keeping up with inflation, and profits have been rising more slowly than sales.

As a result, a lot of people have lost a good deal of money in this stock, which declined from a 1973 high of $101 a share to a 1980 low of about $20 a share, before staging a moderate comeback. In early 1982 the stock was selling at around $29, or 6 times earnings. The dividend yield was around 5 percent.

Any stock that's fallen as far as this one deserves scrutiny as a possible bargain. Like many equities, Penney would benefit from a decline in interest rates, and an upturn in general economic activity. The short-term price action might be fairly dramatic. However, there are many other stocks that would similarly benefit. Among them are Sears, long the nation's largest retailer, and K mart, which in recent years has passed Penney as number two.

* * *

PENNSYLVANIA POWER & LIGHT CO. (PPL). Founded 1920. Headquarters: 2 N. Ninth St., Allentown PA 18101. **ELECTRIC UTILITY.** Pennsylvania Power & Light Co. provides central-eastern Pennsylvania with electricity.

Sales: $885.5 million (trend 10.1% a year).
Earnings: $120.38 million (trend 12.2% a year).
What happened to a $10,000 investment

Purchase Date	*Purchase Price*	*Price on 12-31-81*	*Dividends Paid*
12-31-71	$25.25	$17.12	$7,485.15
12-31-76	$22.25	$17.12	$4,588.76

Purchase Date	*Cap. Gains (– Losses)*	*Total Return*	*Rate of Return*
12-31-71	$–3,217.82	$4,267.33	3.62%
12-31-76	$–2,303.37	$2,285.39	4.20%

* * *

PENNWALT CORP. (PSM). Founded 1850. Headquarters: Pennwalt Bldg., 3 Parkway, Philadelphia PA 19102. **CHEMICALS, DRUGS, DENTAL SUPPLIES.** Pennwalt is a major chemical manufacturer, and the nation's largest maker of dental health products. Also produces pharmaceuticals and precision equipment. 13,000 employees. **MAJOR SUBSIDIARIES, BRANDS:** Allerest; Cruex; Desenex; Sinarest; J. F. Jelenko, S. S. White (dental supplies); Sharples; Wallace & Tiernan.

Sales: $1,188.7 million (trend 10.9% a year).
Earnings: $43.29 million (trend 8.1% a year).
What happened to a $10,000 investment

Purchase Date	*Purchase Price*	*Price on 12-31-81*	*Dividends Paid*
12-31-71	$26.87	$27.25	$6,489.30
12-31-76	$32.75	$27.25	$3,328.24

Purchase Date	*Cap. Gains (− Losses)*	*Total Return*	*Rate of Return*
12-31-71	$ 139.53	$6,628.84	5.22%
12-31-76	$−1,679.39	$1,648.85	3.10%

PROFILE: To the extent the public knows Pennwalt at all, it's mainly for the company's leading position in dental supplies. The J. F. Jelenko division makes dental laboratory equipment and tooth filling alloys. The S. S. White division makes a variety of dental equipment.

Some investors may have found these shares to bear some resemblance to a trip to the dentist—leaving them with, if not a pain, at least a funny taste in the mouth. The 1970 high was around $36 a share, the 1980 high a bit below $35.

Indeed, Pennwalt's long-term price chart looks pretty flat. What movement there was could be attributed in large part to market movements, although Pennwalt tends to swing less than the average stock.

Dental products account for only about a fifth of sales. Chemicals loom largest, with about half of sales. These range from bulk chemicals, through organics, to specialty chemicals. In 1980 the firm sold a bit more than $600-million worth of chemicals, out of total sales of almost $1.2 billion.

Smaller, but slated to grow, is the pharmaceuticals end of the business, which recently accounted for less than a tenth of sales (about $82 million in 1980). The company has said it plans to parlay its small stable of known brands (Allerest, Desenex, etc.) into a $250-million division by 1985, both through internal growth and through take-overs.

The dividend yield, recently in the 7-to-8 percent area, is one of the stock's more attractive features. Dividends have been paid each year since 1863 at this slow-growing but consistently profitable firm.

* * *

PENNZOIL CO. (PZL). Founded 1889. Headquarters: Pennzoil Pl., PO Box 2967, Houston TX 77001. **OIL, MINING.** Pennzoil is a major oil company, approximately the twenty-first largest in the United States. It explores for and produces oil and natural gas; markets petroleum products, including Pennzoil motor oil; and through a subsidiary is active in mining molybdenum, copper, sulfur, and potash. 10,000 employees. **MAJOR SUBSIDIARIES, BRANDS:** Pennzoil; Duval (mining).

Sales: $2,483.0 million (trend 20.3% a year).
Earnings: $304.08 million (trend 22.8% a year).
What happened to a $10,000 investment

Purchase Date	*Purchase Price*	*Price on 12-31-81*	*Dividends Paid*
12-31-71	$16.17	$48.25	$7,177.34
12-31-76	$22.17	$48.25	$3,682.72

Purchase Date	*Cap. Gains (− Losses)*	*Total Return*	*Rate of Return*
12-31-71	$19,845.36	$27,022.70	13.98%
12-31-76	$11,766.92	$15,449.64	20.54%

PROFILE: Ah yes, Pennzoil, says the average investor. They make the motor oil in those little green cans. Name stands for Pennsylvania-grade crude oil. Slightly quaint flavor to the enterprise. Probably a fairly small outfit.

In contrast to the image, some facts: First, Pennzoil is already a $2-billion (annual sales) corporation, and may be a $3-billion one before too long. Second, the well-known motor oil, while an important part of the company, is less important than natural gas production or mining. Third, the company has spread far beyond Pennsylvania and gets the biggest share of its natural gas and petroleum from the Gulf Coast area.

Pennzoil has also been a very successful stock. Had you bought it in 1970 and held it for ten years, you would have roughly tripled your money. With perfect timing (buying at the 1974 low, selling at the 1980 high), you could have multiplied your money six times.

The company hasn't been shy about using debt to leverage the return on stockholders' equity and to finance expansion. Recently, debt was more than 40 percent of capital. However, that's down from more than 60 percent in 1970 and more than 50 percent as recently as 1975. Dividends have been paid each year since 1925 and provide a moderate yield, recently around 5 percent.

Much of the activity in this stock tends to be speculative and based on merger rumors. Even though Pennzoil is a big outfit, it's a "second tier" oil company. As such, it's a natural take-over candidate in the recent merger wave. The mining segment adds to the firm's attractiveness to potential acquisitors.

* * *

PEOPLES DRUG STORES, INC. (PDG). Founded 1905. Headquarters: 6315 Bren Mar Dr., Alexandria VA 22312. **DRUG STORES.** Peoples Drug Stores, Inc., operates drug stores, dental and optical centers, and convenience stores. **MAJOR SUBSIDIARIES, BRANDS:** B. H. Krueger, Inc.; Lane Drug Co.; Haag Drug Co.; Reed Drug Co.

Sales: $634.3 million (trend 27.3% a year).
Earnings: $9.30 million (trend 24.9% a year).
What happened to a $10,000 investment

Purchase Date	*Purchase Price*	*Price on 12-31-81*	*Dividends Paid*
12-31-71	$12.62	$15.75	$2,035.64
12-31-76	$ 8.87	$15.75	$1,374.65

Purchase Date	*Cap. Gains (− Losses)*	*Total Return*	*Rate of Return*
12-31-71	$2,475.25	$4,510.89	3.79%
12-31-76	$7,746.48	$9,121.13	13.84%

* * *

PEOPLES ENERGY CORP. (PGL). Founded 1850. Headquarters: 122 S. Michigan Ave., Chicago IL 60603. **GAS PIPELINES, DISTRIBUTION.** Peoples Energy transports natural gas interstate — primarily from the Southwest to the Chicago area. It also distributes natural gas in the Chicago metropolitan region; explores for and produces natural gas, oil, and coal; and provides contract drilling services. 7,000 employees. **MAJOR SUBSIDIARIES, BRANDS:** Peoples Gas, Light and Coke; North Shore Gas; Buckhorn Petroleum; Exeter Co.; Harper Oil; IFC; Texoma.

Sales: $3,403.2 million (trend 23.3% a year).
Earnings: $156.96 million (trend 6.6% a year).
What happened to a $10,000 investment

Purchase Date	*Purchase Price*	*Price on 12-31-81*	*Dividends Paid*
12-31-71	$26.16	$8.25	$9,078.00
12-31-76	$36.38	$8.25	$3,962.79

Purchase Date	*Cap. Gains (− Losses)*	*Total Return*	*Rate of Return*
12-31-71	$−6,845.96	$ 2,232.04	2.04%
12-31-76	$−7,732.02	$−3,769.23	−9.03%

PROFILE: Despite its countercultural-sounding name, Peoples Energy is, by and large, a conventional natural gas utility. It gets most of its money by moving gas through interstate pipelines and most of the rest by selling gas in the Chicago area.

However, Peoples has acquired quite a parcel of promising little exploration and production companies. There's Buckhorn Petroleum, which drills in the Rocky Mountains; Harper Oil, which drills in Oklahoma and Texas; IFC, which mines coal; and Texoma, which drills in the Gulf of Mexico. Like many utilities, Peoples Energy has found it unwieldy to try to give these subsidiaries freedom to grow while operating as a heavily regulated utility.

The proposed solution — not unprecedented, but still unusual — was to spin off the unregulated businesses (those just mentioned, plus Exeter contract drilling and the interstate pipeline) to a new corporation, named MidCon Corp. What's left of Peoples Energy would be a pure utility, with a high dividend (probably) and low growth prospects (most likely). MidCon would be where the action is.

The company went ahead with the spin-off in late 1981.

The company has had a low growth rate and a mediocre return on equity. Its debt burden is fairly high, recently more than 40 percent of capital (though this represents a trimming of the balance sheet from a few years back, when debt was more than half of capital). Dividends have been paid each year since 1937, and the yield is substantial — recently from 6 to 8½ percent.

* * *

PEPSICO, INC. (PEP). Founded 1919. Headquarters: Purchase NY 10577. **SOFT DRINKS, SNACK FOODS.** PepsiCo is the number-two soft drink producer in the United States. Through subsidiaries, it has major interests in snack foods, trucking, fast-food restaurants, and sporting goods. 111,000 employees. **MAJOR SUBSIDIARIES, BRANDS:** Pepsi-Cola, Mountain Dew, Patio, and Teem soft drinks; Frito-Lay snack foods; Pizza Hut and Taco Bell fast-food restaurants; Lee Way Motor Freight; North American Van Lines; Wilson Sporting Goods.

Sales: $5,975.2 million (trend 21.4% a year).
Earnings: $291.75 million (trend 23.2% a year).
What happened to a $10,000 investment

Purchase Date	*Purchase Price*	*Price on 12-31-81*	*Dividends Paid*
12-31-71	$23.42	$36.37	$3,358.72
12-31-76	$26.54	$36.37	$2,104.24

Purchase Date	Cap. Gains (– Losses)	Total Return	Rate of Return
12-31-71	$5,533.81	$8,892.53	6.57%
12-31-76	$3,704.87	$5,809.11	9.59%

PROFILE: It's a cinch to tell what Pepsi makes, right? Wrong. Stop a man or woman on the street and they'll tell you that PepsiCo makes Pepsi-Cola. What they won't know is that soft drinks recently have accounted for only about 40 percent of the company's sales.

Pepsi, in fact, is diverse — more diverse than Coca-Cola, which is both good and bad for PepsiCo shareholders. It's good in that diversification provides stability and a hedge against bad times in any single business. It's not so good in that few of Pepsi's acquisitions outside soft drinks (see list above) can match the high profit margins of the original business. As one Pepsi official told *Forbes* in 1981, "We sell concentrate, and the only things more profitable than concentrate are rock music and prostitution."

But one of Pepsi's diversifications, Frito-Lay, does match (and sometimes exceed) the profitability of soft drinks. Frito-Lay, which makes about 40 percent of the salted snacks Americans love to gobble up, chipped in 39 percent of Pepsi's profits in 1980 (on 31 percent of sales), not far behind the 44 percent of profits contributed by soft drinks.

Both Coke and Pepsi have been growing during the past decade, at the expense of the competition. Between them, they had 51 percent of the soft drink market (Coke 31, Pepsi 20) as of 1968. By 1980 they had 59 percent (Coke 34, Pepsi 25). However, that trend may change during the 1980s, as tough competitors Philip Morris and Procter & Gamble move into the arena. And the arena is changing, too. In the next decade or two, foreign markets will be increasingly important, as soft drink growth is petering out in the United States.

Pepsi's earnings growth has been uninterrupted through the last few recessions, and it's quite profitable (return on equity is often above 20 percent). With this track record, the stock usually commands a price / earnings multiple somewhat above that of the average stock. In 1981, for example, Pepsi's p / e was 11, when the average stock went for 8. Dividends are moderate and have been paid since 1952.

* * *

THE PERKIN-ELMER CORP. (PKN). Founded 1939. Headquarters: Main Ave., Norwalk CT 06856. ELECTRONIC INSTRUMENTS. Perkin-Elmer Corp. manufactures analytical instruments, precision optical instruments, computers, and related products.

Sales: $1,115.8 million (trend 27.8% a year).
Earnings: $78.17 million (trend 32.6% a year).
What happened to a $10,000 investment

Purchase Date	Purchase Price	Price on 12-31-81	Dividends Paid
12-31-71	$14.56	$27.25	$1,339.74
12-31-76	$10.62	$27.25	$1,268.24

Purchase Date	Cap. Gains (– Losses)	Total Return	Rate of Return
12-31-71	$ 8,712.45	$10,052.19	7.21%
12-31-76	$15,647.06	$16,915.29	21.90%

* * *

PERMIAN BASIN ROYALTY TRUST (PBT). Founded 1980. Headquarters: c / o The First National Bank of Fort Worth, 1 Burnett Plaza, Fort Worth TX 76102. OIL AND GAS DRILLING INCOME. Provides income from oil and natural gas production at several producing facilities in Texas.

* * *

PETRIE STORES CORP. (PST). Founded 1932. Headquarters: 70 Enterprise Ave., Secaucus NJ 07094. WOMEN'S CLOTHING RETAILER. Sells women's and girls' clothing at some 800 specialty stores throughout most of the United States. 7,000 employees. MAJOR SUBSIDIARIES, BRANDS: Petrie's; David's; Franklin; G&G; Marianne; Stuarts. Owns 22 percent of Toys 'R' Us.

Sales: $479.5 million (trend 11.3% a year).
Earnings: $46.29 million (trend 11.7% a year).
What happened to a $10,000 investment

Purchase Date	Purchase Price	Price on 12-31-81	Dividends Paid
12-31-71	$18.62	$20.75	$3,064.16
12-31-76	$25.17	$20.75	$1,655.63

Purchase Date	Cap. Gains (– Losses)	Total Return	Rate of Return
12-31-71	$ 1,140.94	$4,205.10	3.57%
12-31-76	$–1,754.97	$ –99.34	–.20%

PROFILE: This has been one of the most shrewdly run, and one of the most profitable, of American corporations. Among retailers, it stands out most for its high profit margin — in recent years, above

10 percent. But there are quite a few other unusual things about Petrie.

It disdains debt. Despite rapid growth, including lately some growth by acquisition (e.g. Franklin; G&G), the company has not one penny of long-term debt. Recently, it had more than $100 million of cash on hand.

Petrie doesn't like to encourage debt among its customers, either. Bowing to the times, it has recently allowed the use of bank cards, but still makes the vast majority of its sales for cash. This lowers costs by keeping operations simple. In the same vein (simplicity, low costs, high profit margin), the company does not deliver goods or do alterations, and — strange as this may sound these days — it does not advertise.

How can Petrie be so different from most other companies? In large part its style reflects the judgment of one man, founder and chairman Milton Petrie, who owns a whopping 62 percent of the stock. Since institutions hold another 28 percent, there's very little individual ownership, and the stock could be in for some violent swings some year if the Petrie estate (Mr. Petrie is nearing eighty) sells or if institutions sour on the stock.

The recession of 1980 brought the first dip in Petrie's earnings since it went public . . . but it was a mild dip. The shares offer a moderate dividend yield. In light of Petrie's solid record of profit growth and high return on stockholders' equity, the stock usually commands a multiple higher than that of the average stock. In the early 1980s, though, Petrie's p / e was only slightly higher than that of the market as a whole.

Petrie also owns a minority interest (recently about 22 percent) in Toys 'R' Us, a highly successful "toy supermarket" chain. Since the company is known to be on the prowl for acquisitions, one possibility is that it will expand that stake.

* * *

PETROLANE INC. (PTO). Founded 1930. Headquarters: 1600 E. Hill St., Long Beach CA 90806. **DIVERSIFIED OIL DRILLER.** Petrolane provides drilling and other services for the petroleum industry. It is also a major distributor of propane and other liquid petroleum gases, and has diversified into a number of other activities including the operation of alcoholism rehabilitation clinics, hospitals, and supermarkets.

Sales: $1,877.3 million (trend 23.1% a year).
Earnings: $99.27 million (trend 26.3% a year).
What happened to a $10,000 investment

Purchase Date	*Purchase Price*	*Price on 12-31-81*	*Dividends Paid*
12-31-71	$7.06	$17.12	$2,777.95
12-31-76	$6.34	$17.12	$2,260.10

Purchase Date	*Cap. Gains (— Losses)*	*Total Return*	*Rate of Return*
12-31-71	$14,247.79	$17,025.73	10.45%
12-31-76	$16,995.07	$19,255.17	23.95%

* * *

PETROLEUM & RESOURCES CORP. (PEO). Founded 1977. Headquarters: 201 N. Charles St., Baltimore MD 21201. **OIL INVESTMENT.** Petroleum & Resources Corp. invests in oil and gas securities.

* * *

PFIZER INC. (PFE). Founded 1849. Headquarters: 235 E. 42nd St., New York NY 10017. **DRUGS.** Pfizer is a major producer of prescription drugs, including antibiotics and drugs for cardiovascular health. Also produces specialty chemicals (many of them drug-related), agricultural products (including animal health products), over-the-counter drugs, cosmetics, pigments, specialty metals, and magnetic oxides for coating audio- and videotapes. 41,000 employees. **MAJOR SUBSIDIARIES, BRANDS:** Feldene (antiarthritic); Minipress (antihypertensive); Vibramycin, Terramycin, Spectrobid (antibiotics); Ben-Gay and Desitin ointments; Visine eyedrops; Emeraude, Coty (cosmetics).

Sales: $3,029.3 million (trend 13.0% a year).
Earnings: $254.80 million (trend 12.4% a year).
What happened to a $10,000 investment

Purchase Date	*Purchase Price*	*Price on 12-31-81*	*Dividends Paid*
12-31-71	$41.87	$53.25	$2,471.64
12-31-76	$29.37	$53.25	$2,219.57

Purchase Date	*Cap. Gains (— Losses)*	*Total Return*	*Rate of Return*
12-31-71	$2,716.42	$ 5,188.06	4.27%
12-31-76	$8,127.66	$10,347.23	15.27%

PROFILE: Pfizer ranks approximately fifth in size among U.S. drug and health-care companies. In profitability, it has not traditionally been among the industry leaders, though its results have been more than respectable. For example, the company has consistently earned more than 15 percent on stockholders' equity. And it had achieved thirteen straight yearly earnings increases before the string was snapped in 1981.

This performance doesn't satisfy the company's critics, because Pfizer travels in fast company. Good performance and good growth are expected from drug companies. Among the eight big drug companies profiled in *Forbes* magazine's 1981 *Annual Report on American Industry,* Pfizer ranked sixth in return on equity and seventh in return on total capital — well behind such profit synthesizers as SmithKline and Merck.

However, Pfizer stock fetched 19 times the company's earnings in early 1982, more than double the average p / e ratio at the time. The stock had a brisk run-up in 1980, based mainly on published reports about several new drugs (some named in the introductory section above). *Barron's* in late 1980 reported that the company was ready to launch "no fewer than seven of what [Chairman Edmund] Pratt, with a wry allusion to Wall Street, calls 'those new blockbusters that analysts love to see.' "

One question critics raise about Pfizer is whether its nonprescription-drug divisions (which chipped in only 22 percent of 1980 profits on 46 percent of sales) eat up too much of the company's capital.

Dividends have been paid each year since 1901 and raised regularly. But they provide only a moderate yield, 3 to 4 percent in recent years.

* * *

PHELPS DODGE CORP. (PD). Founded 1885. Headquarters: 300 Park Ave., New York NY 10022. **COPPER.** Phelps Dodge is the second largest U.S. copper producer (after Kennecott). It explores for, mines, and smelts copper, and also produces copper products. Through a subsidiary, it mines uranium; as a by-product of copper operations, it also produces some gold, silver, and molybdenum. 15,000 employees. **MAJOR SUBSIDIARIES, BRANDS:** Western Nuclear Inc.; Black Mountain Ltd. (49 percent owned); Southern Peru Copper (16¼ percent owned).

Sales: $1,440.1 million (trend 12.2% a year).
Earnings: $87.28 million (trend 20.3% a year).
What happened to a $10,000 investment

Purchase Date	*Purchase Price*	*Price on 12-31-81*	*Dividends Paid*	*Cap. Gains (− Losses)*	*Total Return*	*Rate of Return*
12-31-71	$37.62	$33.62	$4,684.39	$−1,063.12	$ 3,621.26	3.14%
12-31-76	$41.25	$33.62	$1,636.36	$−1,848.48	$−212.12	−.43%

PROFILE: "Been down so long it looks like up to me" was the title of a popular novel some years back, but may be even more apt as a description of the copper industry. Copper prices have been in a prolonged slump. Those prices — and industry profits — have been historically volatile. Lately, they've been as volatile as ever, but the underlying trend for the past decade has been more down than up. Thus, the profits of leading copper producers, Phelps Dodge included, have barely inched ahead, failing to keep pace with inflation.

With wild swings in copper prices and with puny profits, the companies have been unable or unwilling to spend heavily on new production equipment. However, using old equipment tends to raise the cost of production (per ton) and thus squeezes profit margins. It's a vicious cycle.

Phelps Dodge has increased its capital spending in recent years, but the $124 million budgeted for capital expenditures in 1980 was still far below the spending levels of 1974 and 1975 ($289 million and $223 million, respectively), and the gap is even greater when the effect of inflation is considered.

The industry is about due for a boom. (It's been down so long, etc.) One may not come too soon, though, so shares in this stock are for the patient. A moderate dividend yield will ease the wait only slightly. If you contemplate buying, watch the p / e ratio like a hawk to see to what extent investors have already factored a potential recovery into the price of the shares.

* * *

PHIBRO CORP. (PB). Founded 1981; predecessor company founded 1960. Headquarters: 1221 Ave. of the Americas, New York NY 10020. **COMMODITIES TRADING, SECURITIES BROKERAGE.** Phibro is a leading worldwide dealer in minerals, metals, petrochemicals, and agricultural commodities. Through the 1981 acquisition of Salomon Brothers, it is also a major factor in the securities industry. The company is approximately 27 percent owned by The Minerals & Resources Corp. (Minorco), which in turn is associated with Anglo American Corp. of South Africa. **MAJOR SUBSIDIARIES, BRANDS:** Philipp Brothers (commodities trading); Salomon Brothers (securities brokerage).

Sales: $26,570.0 million (trend 37.4% a year).
Earnings: $532.74 million (trend 36.7% a year).
What happened to a $10,000 investment

Purchase Date	*Purchase Price*	*Price on 12-31-81*	*Dividends Paid*
12-31-71	$11.18	$26.25	$5,091.63
12-31-76	$16.26	$26.25	$2,501.70

Purchase Date	*Cap. Gains (− Losses)*	*Total Return*	*Rate of Return*
12-31-71	$13,470.82	$18,562.45	11.07%
12-31-76	$ 6,141.78	$ 8,643.48	13.27%

PROFILE: Paradoxes. This company is almost legendary in the international financial community, yet is little known to the public. The company is practically brand-new, yet has a track record going back two decades. The company is extraordinarily profitable, yet the stock sells at a puny multiple of earnings.

Phibro is one of two companies to emerge from the 1981 breakup of Engelhard Minerals & Chemicals Corp. (The other, Engelhard Corp., is also profiled in this volume.) The mining and metal refining businesses went to Engelhard; the commodities trading business went to Phibro. The name Phibro is a contraction of Philipp Brothers, which for years has had a reputation as one of the world's largest and shrewdest commodity trading organizations.

People are scared — and rightly so — of commodity trading and its attendant volatility. That's surely one reason why this stock sold in the early 1980s for a mere 6 times earnings. Yet Philipp Brothers trades so many commodities (about 150) in so many markets, and has such a good long-term record, that one shouldn't put undue weight on the risks. Return on equity has been astonishingly high — usually above 20 percent, and sporadically above 40 percent.

In late 1981, only a few months after its creation, Phibro scored a coup by acquiring Salomon Brothers, another firm with a towering reputation, and one of the world's leading investment banking and brokerage firms. Since Salomon Brothers was previously a private partnership, numbers aren't available on its past performance, but it has a reputation on Wall Street for astuteness and profitability.

The balance sheet is slightly on the conservative side, with debt recently about 25 percent of total capital. It's too early to tell what the firm's dividend policies will be. In the early going, the dividend provided a moderate yield; the dividend payout was about a sixth of profits.

* * *

PHILADELPHIA ELECTRIC CO. (PE). Founded 1929. Headquarters: 2301 Market St., Philadelphia PA 19101. UTILITY. Supplies electricity to Philadelphia and portions of adjoining southeast Pennsylvania. Also provides gas to most of its service area (but not Philadelphia). 9,000 employees.

Sales: $2,123.4 million (trend 11.9% a year).
Earnings: $174.95 million (trend 9.0% a year).
What happened to a $10,000 investment

Purchase Date	*Purchase Price*	*Price on 12-31-81*	*Dividends Paid*
12-31-71	$23.87	$13.62	$7,229.32
12-31-76	$17.87	$13.62	$5,068.53

Purchase Date	*Cap. Gains (− Losses)*	*Total Return*	*Rate of Return*
12-31-71	$−4,293.19	$2,936.13	2.61%
12-31-76	$−2,377.62	$2,690.91	4.88%

PROFILE: How can you go wrong buying a stock that yields (as of early 1982) more than 15 percent a year in dividends?

Easily. The sky-high dividend, while a legitimate attraction, is also a measure of the company's desperation. Why else would anyone buy these shares? Growth has been unspectacular, profitability poor. And in truth, the dividend yield is high in large part because the price of the stock has shrunk to fit — not because the dividend itself has been growing much. Watching Philadelphia Electric increase its dividend has been like watching a blade of grass grow. Yearly dividends were $1.48 a share in 1966 and $2.00 a share in 1980, which works out to a compound annual rate of increase of 2.2 percent.

Even achieving that slow rate of dividend growth is straining Philadelphia Electric's resources. The company paid out from 93 to 98 percent of its profits in dividends each year from 1977 to 1980. Yet it faces big expenditures on its planned Limerick nuclear plant, twenty-one miles from Philadelphia. After repeated delays, the plant is due to come in at between $3 and $4 billion — or about half of Philadelphia Electric's total capital. Well over $1 billion has already been spent. But to scrape up the rest, the company will presumably have to go further into debt, an unpleasant choice for a company whose long-term debt was already 51 percent of capital in the late 1970s and early 1980s.

* * *

PHILADELPHIA SUBURBAN CORP. (PSC). Founded 1905. Headquarters: 2 Radnor Corporate Center, 100 Matsonford Rd., PO Box 26, Radnor PA 19087. UTILITY. Philadelphia Suburban Corp. designs and manufactures pipeline equipment and provides water service to suburban Philadelphia.

* * *

PHILIP MORRIS INC. (MO). Founded 1919. Headquarters: 100 Park Ave., New York NY 10017. **CIGARETTES, BEER, SOFT DRINKS.** Philip Morris derives most of its sales and earnings from cigarettes. In recent years, it has diversified into beer, soft drinks, and real estate development. 60,000 employees. **MAJOR SUBSIDIARIES, BRANDS:** Marlboro, Benson & Hedges, Cambridge, Merit, and Parliament cigarettes; Miller and Lowenbrau beers; 7-Up soft drinks; Mission Viejo real estate development.

Sales: $7,328.3 million (trend 24.0% a year).
Earnings: $576.80 million (trend 22.7% a year).
What happened to a $10,000 investment

Purchase Date	*Purchase Price*	*Price on 12-31-81*	*Dividends Paid*
12-31-71	$17.56	$48.75	$4,972.95
12-31-76	$30.87	$48.75	$2,155.87

Purchase Date	*Cap. Gains (− Losses)*	*Total Return*	*Rate of Return*
12-31-71	$17,758.01	$22,730.96	12.59%
12-31-76	$ 5,789.47	$ 7,945.34	12.41%

PROFILE: Marketing, marketing, marketing. That's what Philip Morris is known for — indeed, famed for. One of its greatest successes has been Marlboro cigarettes, which shot past Winston in the mid-1970s to become America's (and the world's) best-selling cigarette. Led by Marlboro, Philip Morris's cigarette group recently commanded 29 percent of the U.S. market, about double its share a decade earlier and close on the heels of industry leader R. J. Reynolds, whose share has been stagnant at around 33 percent.

Another success has been Miller beer, acquired in 1969 (for $130 million from W. R. Grace). At the time, Miller was the seventh-ranked U.S. beer in sales, with about 5 percent of the market. Today, it's number two (behind Anheuser-Busch's Budweiser), with about 20 percent of the market.

That triumph hasn't (at least yet) been duplicated with Seven-Up, for which Philip Morris shelled out more than $500 million in 1978. Seven-Up lost money in 1980 and was passed as the third largest seller in the United States soft-drink market by Dr Pepper.

The fact is that neither beer nor soft drinks has been providing Philip Morris with the kind of profitability that the cigarette business has. So, in 1981, Philip Morris "undiversified," as *Fortune* magazine put it, by paying some $350 million for a 22 percent stake in Rothmans International, a major British cigarette company.

Philip Morris's operating results have been outstanding. The company has consistently earned around 20 percent a year on stockholders' equity (with the help of some leverage — debt in recent years has been about 45 percent of capital). Its string of uninterrupted earnings gains goes back through several recessions.

The stock has done well, but not so well as the company itself. Investors never quite believe that Philip Morris can continue to show the kind of gains that it has in mature industries. For that reason, the stock in recent years has sold at only a modest premium over the market multiple, fetching from 8 to 12 times earnings. Dividends have been paid yearly since 1928 and provide a moderate yield.

* * *

PHILIPS INDUSTRIES INC. (PHL). Founded 1957. Headquarters: 4801 Springfield St., Dayton OH 45401. **HOUSING.** Philips Industries manufactures and sells housing components, including windows, doors, and axles for manufactured housing; fans and blowers; fiber-glass tubs / showers. **MAJOR SUBSIDIARIES, BRANDS:** Philips-Lau Products Limited.

Sales: $229.1 million (trend 7.1% a year).
Earnings: $7.84 million (trend 15.3% a year).
What happened to a $10,000 investment

Purchase Date	*Purchase Price*	*Price on 12-31-81*	*Dividends Paid*
12-31-71	$21.75	$14.12	$ 800.00
12-31-76	$ 8.62	$14.12	$1,333.33

Purchase Date	*Cap. Gains (− Losses)*	*Total Return*	*Rate of Return*
12-31-71	$−3,505.75	$−2,705.75	−3.11%
12-31-76	$ 6,376.81	$ 7,710.14	12.11%

* * *

PHILLIPS PETROLEUM CO. (P). Founded 1917. Headquarters: Phillips Bldg., Bartlesville OK 74004. **OIL.** Phillips is a major oil company, with both domestic and international operations; also produces chemicals. It is approximately the sixteenth largest industrial firm in the United States and approximately the tenth largest oil company. 32,000 employees. **MAJOR SUBSIDIARIES, BRANDS:** Phillips 66 gasoline; Trop-Artic motor oil.

Sales: $13,376.6 million (trend 20.2% a year).
Earnings: $1,069.61 million (trend 26.9% a year).
What happened to a $10,000 investment

Purchase Date	*Purchase Price*	*Price on 12-31-81*	*Dividends Paid*
12-31-71	$15.31	$40.50	$7,330.61
12-31-76	$33.06	$40.50	$2,275.99

Purchase Date	*Cap. Gains (– Losses)*	*Total Return*	*Rate of Return*
12-31-71	$16,448.98	$23,779.59	12.94%
12-31-76	$ 2,249.53	$ 4,525.52	7.75%

PROFILE: Phillips had traditionally been known as a stay-at-home oil company. It surprised both competitors and analysts with a huge find in the North Sea off Norway in the early 1970s. Throughout the past decade, that find provided a fair part of the company's crude and an even larger portion of its profits. But now the Ekofisk field seems to be getting depleted.

Some of the slack may be taken up by a promising find off the shore of the Ivory Coast. Phillips stock in recent months has bobbed up and down with rumors as to how huge that find really is. The oil there is believed to be high-quality and low in sulfur. But the bulk of Phillips's production remains in the United States and the company is spending heavily on domestic exploration.

The company has experienced outstanding results for the past ten years or so, with profit growth at the rate of around 20 percent a year and return on stockholders' equity sometimes passing that mark. Yet the stock has sold in recent years at a conservative multiple of earnings, with a p / e of from 5 to 10.

Dividends have been paid each year since 1934 and raised each year since 1972. In the late 1970s, the yield was 3 to 4 percent; but in the early 1980s, the general slide in the price of oil stocks raised the yield close to 6 percent. The balance sheet is strong, with debt less than 15 percent of capital.

Those who believe that the oil surplus of the early 1980s is more likely to be temporary than permanent may well want to make room in their portfolios for this stock.

* * *

PHILIPS-VAN HEUSEN CORP. (PVH). Founded 1919. Headquarters: 1290 Ave. of the Americas, New York NY 10019. **CLOTHING.** Philips-Van Heusen manufactures and sells clothing for men and boys. **MAJOR SUBSIDIARIES, BRANDS:** Men's Wear International.

Sales: $419.4 million (trend 6.9% a year).
Earnings: $5.36 million (trend 8.9% a year).
What happened to a $10,000 investment

Purchase Date	*Purchase Price*	*Price on 12-31-81*	*Dividends Paid*
12-31-71	$24.25	$15.75	$1,901.03
12-31-76	$10.50	$15.75	$2,285.71

Purchase Date	*Cap. Gains (– Losses)*	*Total Return*	*Rate of Return*
12-31-71	$–3,505.15	$–1,604.12	–1.73%
12-31-76	$ 5,000.00	$ 7,285.71	11.57%

* * *

PIEDMONT AVIATION, INC. (PIE). Founded 1940. Headquarters: Smith Reynolds Airport, Winston-Salem NC 27102. **AIRLINE.** Piedmont Aviation operates Piedmont Airlines, which serves approximately ninety cities, mostly connecting various cities with points in Virginia and the Carolinas. The company also sells small aircraft and services them. Piedmont is approximately 20-percent-owned by Norfolk & Western. 6,000 employees. **MAJOR SUBSIDIARIES, BRANDS:** Piedmont Airlines.

Sales: $473.4 million (trend 23.4% a year).
Earnings: $16.06 million (trend 100.4% a year).
What happened to a $10,000 investment

Purchase Date	*Purchase Price*	*Price on 12-31-81*	*Dividends Paid*
12-31-71	$7.29	$27.25	$1,824.00
12-31-76	$4.06	$27.25	$2,453.33

Purchase Date	*Cap. Gains (– Losses)*	*Total Return*	*Rate of Return*
12-31-71	$27,371.39	$29,195.39	14.64%
12-31-76	$57,076.91	$59,530.25	47.38%

PROFILE: Look at the ticker symbol. Reflect on what business the company is in. Do you see the pun coming? What we have here is PIE in the sky.

Well, egregious puns can be forgiven when things are going well — as they have for Piedmont lately. Lots of airlines have experienced losses in recent years. Piedmont, by contrast, has been racking up record earnings. In 1980 its profits were $3.32 a share, breaking the previous record of $2.86, set the year before. Results for 1981 were better yet, at $4.41 a share.

Lots of airlines these days have balance sheets top-heavy with debt. Piedmont carries a lot of debt, too, but the trend is favorable. Whereas an incredible 93 percent of total capital was in the form of debt in 1971, recently debt has been trimmed to around 58 percent of capital. (A conversion of some convertible preferred stock helped.)

Return on stockholders' equity is volatile, but has been above 20 percent seven times in the ten years from 1971 to 1980 and above 30 percent twice during that period. One reason for the airline's profitability: It has had relatively little competition in the Carolinas-Virginia area, an area with expanding industry.

Despite a rapid rise in the stock price — from less than $3 a share during parts of each year from 1973 to 1976 to more than $25 during much of 1981 — the price / earnings ratio hasn't been exorbitant recently. (It was only 6 in early 1982.) However, there are more shares outstanding now than there were a couple of years ago, so earnings will have to continue to soar for per-share earnings to look good.

While more than four fifths of the company's sales come from the airline, it has a sideline in selling and servicing small planes, chiefly Beech and Piper aircraft.

Dividends have been paid each year since 1974, but the yield is small.

* * *

PIEDMONT NATURAL GAS CO., INC. (PNY). Founded 1950. Headquarters: 4301 Yancey Rd., Charlotte NC 28233. NATURAL GAS DISTRIBUTOR. Piedmont Natural Gas Co. distributes natural gas in North and South Carolina; also involved in exploration activities.

Sales: $222.2 million (trend 22.0% a year).
Earnings: $8.99 million (trend 5.6% a year).
What happened to a $10,000 investment

Purchase Date	*Purchase Price*	*Price on 12-31-81*	*Dividends Paid*
12-31-71	$16.70	$17.37	$8,029.06
12-31-76	$15.68	$17.37	$4,749.80

Purchase Date	*Cap. Gains (− Losses)*	*Total Return*	*Rate of Return*
12-31-71	$ 401.36	$8,430.42	6.30%
12-31-76	$1,079.70	$5,829.50	9.62%

* * *

PIER 1. IMPORTS, INC. (PIR). Founded 1970. Headquarters: 2520 West Freeway, Fort Worth TX 76102. RETAILING, REAL ESTATE. Operates some 300 Pier 1. retail stores nationwide, selling primarily craft, decorative, and novelty items (most of them imported). Also owns and manages real estate, and operates a chain of tree and plant nurseries.

Sales: $156.5 million.
Earnings: $3.42 million.

* * *

PILLSBURY CO. (PSY). Founded 1923. Headquarters: 608 Second Ave. S., Minneapolis MN 55402. FOOD PRODUCTS, RESTAURANTS. Pillsbury produces a wide variety of food products, many bearing well-known brands; owns several restaurant chains; and supplies grain and flour to commercial customers. 59,000 employees. MAJOR SUBSIDIARIES, BRANDS: Pillsbury flour; Green Giant vegetables; Fox Deluxe and Totino's frozen pizzas; Burger King; Poppin Fresh Pie Shops; and Steak and Ale restaurants.

Sales: $3,301.7 million (trend 20.9% a year).
Earnings: $119.60 million (trend 19.9% a year).
What happened to a $10,000 investment

Purchase Date	*Purchase Price*	*Price on 12-31-81*	*Dividends Paid*
12-31-71	$24.62	$39.62	$4,402.03
12-31-76	$41.12	$39.62	$1,534.35

Purchase Date	*Cap. Gains (− Losses)*	*Total Return*	*Rate of Return*
12-31-71	$ 6,091.37	$10,493.40	7.44%
12-31-76	$−364.74	$ 1,169.60	2.24%

PROFILE: Pillsbury has shown steady but unspectacular earnings increases. That's about what you'd expect from a company its size, with its blend of businesses. Earnings can't fall too far during a recession, since people do, after all, have to eat. When times are good, the restaurant end of the business (Burger King, Steak and Ale, Poppin Fresh Pie Shops), which accounts for a bit over a third of sales and earnings, can be expected to show brisk results. The least-known operations (grain merchandising, rice milling, and supplying flour to commercial customers) are perhaps the most profitable, but they make up only around a quarter of the business.

The acquisitions of Green Giant and the restaurant chains have pushed volume way up: Pillsbury now has more than $3 billion in annual sales, versus less than $1 billion as recently as 1972. However, the acquisitions have strained the debt-to-equity ratio a bit. In the mid-1970s, debt was down to about a third of capital; in 1981 it was back up to 42 percent. The company recently trimmed debt by selling some new stock; this helps the balance sheet, but may dilute per-share earnings for a while.

It's difficult to see reasons for this stock either to soar or plummet. It carries a price / earnings ratio about average for large corporations (around 8 in the early 1980s). Dividends have been paid each year since 1927 and are raised a bit each year. The moderate yield (4 to 5 percent in recent years) is well covered by earnings.

* * *

PIONEER CORP. (PNA). Founded 1928. Headquarters: 301 Taylor St., Box 511, Amarillo TX 79163. **ENERGY.** Pioneer Corp. is involved in the exploration and production of oil, gas, and uranium; transmission and distribution of natural gas; and sale of heavy construction equipment. **MAJOR SUBSIDIARIES, BRANDS:** Amarillo Oil Co.; Pioneer Gas Products Co.; Plains Machinery Co.; Sharp Drilling Co.

Sales: $912.0 million (trend 20.9% a year).
Earnings: $90.56 million (trend 24.2% a year).
What happened to a $10,000 investment

Purchase Date	*Purchase Price*	*Price on 12-31-81*	*Dividends Paid*
12-31-71	$3.07	$29.87	$13,233.90
12-31-76	$9.06	$29.87	$ 3,280.00

Purchase Date	*Cap. Gains (— Losses)*	*Total Return*	*Rate of Return*
12-31-71	$87,220.32	$100,454.22	27.15%
12-31-76	$22,965.52	$ 26,245.52	29.38%

* * *

PIONEER ELECTRONIC CORP. (PIO). Founded 1947. Headquarters: 4–1 Meguro 1-chome, Meguro-ku, Tokyo 153 Japan. **STEREO EQUIPMENT.** Pioneer Electronic manufactures audio equipment and other electronic products.

Sales: $1,407.9 million (trend 16.7% a year).
Earnings: $63.85 million (trend 7.5% a year).
What happened to a $10,000 investment

Purchase Date	*Purchase Price*	*Price on 12-31-81*	*Dividends Paid*
12-31-71	$N/A	$16.50	$ N/A
12-31-76	$13.80	$16.50	$793.74

Purchase Date	*Cap. Gains (— Losses)*	*Total Return*	*Rate of Return*
12-31-71	$ N/A	$ N/A	N/A%
12-31-76	$1,956.52	$2,750.26	4.98%

* * *

PITNEY-BOWES, INC. (PBI). Founded 1920. Headquarters: Walter H. Wheeler Jr. Dr., Stamford CT 06926. **OFFICE EQUIPMENT.** Pitney-Bowes is the world's largest supplier of mailing equipment; also markets copiers, word processors, dictating equipment, and price marking equipment. 25,000 employees. **MAJOR SUBSIDIARIES, BRANDS:** Dictaphone Corp.; Artec International Corp.; Monarch Marking Systems.

Sales: $1,257.3 million (trend 22.5% a year).
Earnings: $75.14 million (trend 25.1% a year).
What happened to a $10,000 investment

Purchase Date	*Purchase Price*	*Price on 12-31-81*	*Dividends Paid*
12-31-71	$24.50	$25.25	$3,742.86
12-31-76	$15.75	$25.25	$3,936.51

Purchase Date	*Cap. Gains (— Losses)*	*Total Return*	*Rate of Return*
12-31-71	$ 306.12	$4,048.98	3.46%
12-31-76	$6,031.75	$9,968.25	14.83%

PROFILE: Prosaic? Maybe. But there are often better things to have going for you in the stock market than glamour.

What Pitney-Bowes has is a foot in the door — at least the mail-room door. Lately, it's been methodically building a wider line of products to take advantage of the entry its mailing equipment gives it. In 1979 it acquired Dictaphone, another firm with a fat customer list and a lot of sales and service people. More recently, it picked up a hot little word processing outfit, Artec International. (Artec cost only $10 million while Dictaphone had cost more than $100 million.) Meanwhile, Pitney-Bowes has gradually been expanding its line of copiers, mainly by winning marketing rights to a couple of Japanese brands, notably Ricoh.

So, the company can now supplement its line of mailing equipment (in which it remains the dominant firm) with copiers, dictating machines, and word processors. Not a bad line. And all can be sold to the small- and medium-sized businesses Pitney-Bowes specializes in servicing.

The stock's high in 1980, about $40 a share, was no higher than its peak in 1970, a full decade earlier. However, in 1970 that price represented about 30 times earnings. In 1980 it was only about 8 times earnings. Less glamour, more value.

The dividend yield (dividends have been paid every year since 1934) was around 4 to 5 percent in most recent years, but broke above 6 percent in the early 1980s when the stock's price dipped below $30 a share. Investors were probably discouraged by the wet blanket a recession could throw on earnings. The long-term outlook, though, appears brighter.

* * *

THE PITTSTON CO. (PCO). Founded 1930. Headquarters: 1 Pickwick Plaza, Greenwich CT 06830. COAL. The Pittston Co. produces coal, and is also involved in oil distribution, trucking, and armored car services. In 1982 it announced plans to acquire Burlington Northern's air freight business for some $177 million. MAJOR SUBSIDIARIES, BRANDS: Brink's Inc.

Sales: $2,051.6 million (trend 5.9% a year).
Earnings: $77.41 million (trend −22.4% a year).
What happened to a $10,000 investment

Purchase Date	*Purchase Price*	*Price on 12-31-81*	*Dividends Paid*
12-31-71	$18.63	$25.12	$4,532.89
12-31-76	$34.93	$25.12	$1,743.72

Purchase Date	*Cap. Gains (− Losses)*	*Total Return*	*Rate of Return*
12-31-71	$ 3,488.03	$ 8,020.92	6.07%
12-31-76	$−2,806.32	$−1,062.60	−2.22%

* * *

PLANNING RESEARCH CORP. (PLN). Founded 1954. Headquarters: 1850 K St. N.W., International Sq., Washington DC 20006. INFORMATIONAL SERVICES. Planning Research Corp. is involved in data processing, management consulting, computer systems, and construction management.

Sales: $314.4 million (trend 15.9% a year).
Earnings: $−1.39 million.
What happened to a $10,000 investment

Purchase Date	*Purchase Price*	*Price on 12-31-81*	*Dividends Paid*
12-31-71	$14.37	$6.25	$0.00
12-31-76	$ 4.12	$6.25	$0.00

Purchase Date	*Cap. Gains (− Losses)*	*Total Return*	*Rate of Return*
12-31-71	$−5,652.17	$−5,652.17	−7.99%
12-31-76	$ 5,151.52	$ 5,151.52	8.67%

* * *

PLANTRONICS, INC. (PLX). Founded 1961. Headquarters: 1762 Technology Dr., Suite 225, Cupertino CA 95110. TELECOMMUNICATIONS. Plantronics, Inc., produces telecommunications equipment, telephone answering systems, and test equipment. MAJOR SUBSIDIARIES, BRANDS: Eltex V telex switching systems; Roadrunner communications management systems.

Sales: $95.5 million (trend 23.7% a year).
Earnings: $8.36 million (trend 15.3% a year).
What happened to a $10,000 investment

Purchase Date	*Purchase Price*	*Price on 12-31-81*	*Dividends Paid*
12-31-71	$ 8.03	$16.25	$859.14
12-31-76	$12.25	$16.25	$448.98

Purchase Date	*Cap. Gains (− Losses)*	*Total Return*	*Rate of Return*
12-31-71	$10,233.46	$11,092.61	7.75%
12-31-76	$ 3,265.31	$ 3,714.29	6.52%

* * *

PLAYBOY ENTERPRISES, INC. (PLA). Founded 1953. Headquarters: 919 N. Michigan Ave., Chicago IL 60611. PUBLISHING. Playboy Enterprises, Inc., is involved in magazine publishing, casino gambling, and club management. MAJOR SUBSIDIARIES, BRANDS: *Playboy* magazine; *Oui* magazine; Playboy Clubs International, Inc.

Sales: $388.9 million (trend 15.4% a year).
Earnings: $14.34 million (trend 47.1% a year).
What happened to a $10,000 investment

Purchase Date	*Purchase Price*	*Price on 12-31-81*	*Dividends Paid*
12-31-71	$19.87	$8.25	$ 603.77
12-31-76	$ 5.75	$8.25	$1,043.48

Purchase Date	*Cap. Gains (− Losses)*	*Total Return*	*Rate of Return*
12-31-71	$−5,849.06	$−5,245.28	−7.16%
12-31-76	$ 4,347.83	$ 5,391.30	9.01%

* * *

THE PLESSEY COMPANY LIMITED. (PLY). Founded 1925. Headquarters: 2–60 Vicarage Lane, Ilford, Essex 1G1 4AQ England. TELECOMMUNICATIONS. The Plessey Company Limited manufactures electronic systems, including office, data, and control systems; also radio communications equipment.

Sales: $1,553.9 million (trend 13.1% a year).
Earnings: $99.26 million (trend 25.6% a year).
What happened to a $10,000 investment

Purchase Date	*Purchase Price*	*Price on 12-31-81*	*Dividends Paid*
12-31-71	$26.25	$67.50	$3,767.54
12-31-76	$10.75	$67.50	$4,667.07

Purchase Date	*Cap. Gains (− Losses)*	*Total Return*	*Rate of Return*
12-31-71	$15,714.28	$19,481.82	11.42%
12-31-76	$52,790.70	$57,457.77	46.49%

* * *

PNEUMO CORP. (PNC). Founded 1959. Headquarters: 4800 Prudential Tower, Boston MA 02199. AEROSPACE. Pneumo is one of the two leading U.S. makers of aircraft landing gear and makes a variety of other aerospace equipment. It also has subsidiaries that produce industrial electrical equipment and that sell food and drugs; the latter are being sold. 6,000 employees. MAJOR SUBSIDIARIES, BRANDS: Cleveland Pneumatic; Numerical Control Inc.; National Water Lift; Claud S. Gordon; P & C Food Markets; Carls Drug Co.

Sales: $983.8 million (trend 16.0% a year).
Earnings: $13.53 million (trend 8.3% a year).
What happened to a $10,000 investment

Purchase Date	*Purchase Price*	*Price on 12-31-81*	*Dividends Paid*
12-31-71	$ 4.92	$27.50	$9,355.93
12-31-76	$10.58	$27.50	$3,307.09

Purchase Date	*Cap. Gains (− Losses)*	*Total Return*	*Rate of Return*
12-31-71	$45,932.20	$55,288.14	20.64%
12-31-76	$15,984.25	$19,291.34	23.98%

PROFILE: The investing public probably best knows Pneumo as the company Harold Geneen bought a chunk of, after he retired from active duty as chairman of ITT. So imposing is Geneen's reputation that his purchase of close to 1 percent of Pneumo's shares (as part of a consortium that holds about 16 percent) probably did a good deal to boost the share price to its peak of nearly $37 in 1980. As recently as 1975, it was possible to pick up Pneumo shares for less than $3, so some lucky souls multiplied their money more than ten times.

The stock has backed off its 1980 peak (it was selling below $30 in early 1982), mainly because of recession-induced softness in orders for aircraft landing gear. All of the major commercial aircraft companies are Pneumo customers, and Pneumo has about a 40 percent share of that market. (So does the other leader, Menasco, which is part of Colt Industries.) Indeed, Pneumo (then Cleveland Pneumatic) had the first patents on pneumatic aircraft landing gear, but lost its monopoly during World War II when the United States needed a lot of planes fast and forced the company to share its patents.

In 1981 Pneumo announced it would sell P&C Food Markets and Carls Drug Co. (to Triton Group for $65 million in cash). This came as a surprise, since Pneumo had used those businesses as cash cows, throwing off funds to reinvest in aerospace. But the cows apparently hadn't been giving enough milk and were worth more as beef. Pneumo said it would reinvest the $65 million in aerospace, probably by acquiring another aerospace company. The deal with Triton later fell through, but Pneumo may try again to sell these subsidiaries. Pneumo itself has been an acquisition target, and its price will fluctuate with merger rumors.

* * *

POGO PRODUCING CO. (PPP). Founded 1970. Headquarters: 707 McKinney, PO Box 2504, Houston TX 77001. OIL EXPLORATION. Pogo Producing Co. is active in oil exploration and production in the Gulf of Mexico and Alaska.

Sales: $220.4 million (trend 10.2% a year).
Earnings: $54.03 million (trend 6.2% a year).
What happened to a $10,000 investment

Purchase Date	Purchase Price	Price on 12-31-81	Dividends Paid
12-31-71	$ N/A	$28.75	$ N/A
12-31-76	$14.37	$28.75	$911.30

Purchase Date	Cap. Gains (— Losses)	Total Return	Rate of Return
12-31-71	$ N/A	$ N/A	N/A%
12-31-76	$10,000.00	$10,911.30	15.90%

* * *

POLAROID CORP. (PRD). Founded 1937. Headquarters: 549 Technology Sq., Cambridge MA 02139. CAMERAS. Polaroid is the leading maker of instant photography equipment. 17,000 employees. MAJOR SUBSIDIARIES, BRANDS: SX-70; Instant 600; Pronto!; OneStep; Polavision.

Sales: $1,450.8 million (trend 12.9% a year).
Earnings: $85.41 million (trend −1.6% a year).
What happened to a $10,000 investment

Purchase Date	Purchase Price	Price on 12-31-81	Dividends Paid
12-31-71	$89.25	$20.50	$ 699.16
12-31-76	$38.87	$20.50	$1,170.42

Purchase Date	Cap. Gains (— Losses)	Total Return	Rate of Return
12-31-71	$−7,703.08	$−7,003.92	−11.35%
12-31-76	$−4,726.69	$−3,556.27	−8.41%

PROFILE: This company has always ridden on the vision and innovation of one man, Edwin Land, and his era is just beginning to end. Land stepped down as chief executive officer in 1980, but he retained the title of chairman, owns the largest block of stock in the company (about 12½ percent), and continues to do research for Polaroid.

His successor as president, William McCune, Jr., has already broken Land's tradition of keeping the company debt free (debt was recently about 11 percent of capital) and seems determined to make it less of a one-product company than it always has been. Instant photography for the amateur market has always been the focus here. But in light of recent setbacks — demand has fallen off for instant cameras, and the Polavision instant movie system was a flop — the company now feels it can't afford to keep all its eggs in one basket.

From the late 1960s to the early 1970s, Polaroid stock usually sold for more than $100 a share. Investors were entranced with the company's brilliant record for innovation, dazzled by its rapid growth. But the stock's multiple got ridiculous: The stock's all-time high of $149.50, achieved in 1972, was 115 times the company's earnings that year. No wonder, then, that when the bubble of unrelenting growth burst, the stock plummeted. It hit bottom at around $14 in 1974 and was selling in the early 1980s for around $20 to $35.

Dividends have been paid each year since 1952. In recent years, the yield has ranged between 2 and 4 percent.

* * *

PONDEROSA SYSTEM, INC. (PON). Founded 1968. Headquarters: PO Box 578, Dayton OH 45401. RESTAURANTS. Ponderosa System, Inc., manages a chain of more than 450 company-operated and more than 230 licensee-operated steakhouses in the United States and Canada. MAJOR SUBSIDIARIES, BRANDS: ESI Meats, Inc.

Sales: $334.0 million (trend 20.3% a year).
Earnings: $2.57 million (trend 17.7% a year).
What happened to a $10,000 investment

Purchase Date	Purchase Price	Price on 12-31-81	Dividends Paid
12-31-71	$34.12	$13.62	$ 322.34
12-31-76	$ 7.12	$13.62	$1,543.86

Purchase Date	Cap. Gains (— Losses)	Total Return	Rate of Return
12-31-71	$−6,007.33	$−5,684.98	−8.06%
12-31-76	$ 9,122.81	$ 10,666.67	15.63%

* * *

POPE & TALBOT, INC. (POP). Founded 1940. Headquarters: 1700 S.W. Fourth Ave., Portland OR 97201. WOOD. Pope & Talbot, Inc., produces wood products, including lumber, pulp, and logs; also involved in real estate development.

Sales: $210.3 million (trend 23.7% a year).
Earnings: $11.09 million (trend 31.7% a year).
What happened to a $10,000 investment

Purchase Date	Purchase Price	Price on 12-31-81	Dividends Paid
12-31-71	$8.82	$17.62	$4,794.01
12-31-76	$9.62	$17.62	$3,096.10

Purchase Date	Cap. Gains (— Losses)	Total Return	Rate of Return
12-31-71	$9,992.31	$14,786.32	9.50%
12-31-76	$8,311.69	$11,407.79	16.44%

* * *

PORTEC, INC. (POR). Founded 1928. Headquarters: 300 Windsor Dr., Oak Brook IL 60521. RAILROAD EQUIPMENT. Portec, Inc., manufactures railroad, mining, quarrying, and road-building equipment.

Sales: $250.8 million (trend 21.1% a year).
Earnings: $8.92 million (trend 12.5% a year).
What happened to a $10,000 investment

Purchase Date	*Purchase Price*	*Price on 12-31-81*	*Dividends Paid*
12-31-71	$ 5.50	$11.25	$10,315.10
12-31-76	$17.96	$11.25	$ 2,030.37

Purchase Date	*Cap. Gains (− Losses)*	*Total Return*	*Rate of Return*
12-31-71	$ 10,459.68	$ 20,774.78	11.90%
12-31-76	$−3,737.46	$−1,707.09	−3.67%

* * *

PORTLAND GENERAL ELECTRIC CO. (PGN). Founded 1930. Headquarters: 121 S.W. Salmon St., Portland OR 97204. UTILITY. Portland General Electric Co. is engaged in the generation, purchase, transmission, distribution, and sale of electricity in Oregon. MAJOR SUBSIDIARIES, BRANDS: The Boardman Power Co.; Energy Resources Group of Oregon, Inc.; Miracel Mine Operations, Inc.; Portland General Electric N.V.

Sales: $490.2 million (trend 20.8% a year).
Earnings: $72.59 million (trend 9.6% a year).
What happened to a $10,000 investment

Purchase Date	*Purchase Price*	*Price on 12-31-81*	*Dividends Paid*
12-31-71	$21.12	$12.50	$7,644.97
12-31-76	$20.37	$12.50	$4,176.69

Purchase Date	*Cap. Gains (− Losses)*	*Total Return*	*Rate of Return*
12-31-71	$−4,082.84	$3,562.13	3.09%
12-31-76	$−3,865.03	$ 311.66	.62%

* * *

POTLATCH CORP. (PCH). Founded 1903. Headquarters: 1 Maritime Plaza, 24th Fl., San Francisco CA 94111. FOREST PRODUCTS. Potlatch Corp. produces lumber, wood products, paperboard, paper, tissue, toweling, and containers. MAJOR SUBSIDIARIES, BRANDS: Townsend Decorative Hardwood Paneling.

Sales: $819.6 million (trend 10.0% a year).
Earnings: $49.41 million (trend 7.8% a year).
What happened to a $10,000 investment

Purchase Date	*Purchase Price*	*Price on 12-31-81*	*Dividends Paid*
12-31-71	$12.37	$29.75	$7,284.85
12-31-76	$34.62	$29.75	$1,698.19

Purchase Date	*Cap. Gains (− Losses)*	*Total Return*	*Rate of Return*
12-31-71	$ 14,040.40	$21,325.25	12.10%
12-31-76	$−1,407.94	$ 290.25	.57%

* * *

POTOMAC ELECTRIC POWER CO. (POM). Founded 1896. Headquarters: 1900 Pennsylvania Ave. N.W., Washington DC 20068. ELECTRIC UTILITY. Potomac Electric Power Co. provides electricity in the Washington metropolitan area.

Sales: $856.1 million (trend 11.4% a year).
Earnings: $88.77 million (trend 13.4% a year).
What happened to a $10,000 investment

Purchase Date	*Purchase Price*	*Price on 12-31-81*	*Dividends Paid*
12-31-71	$15.50	$14.50	$8,125.81
12-31-76	$14.37	$14.50	$4,880.00

Purchase Date	*Cap. Gains (− Losses)*	*Total Return*	*Rate of Return*
12-31-71	$−645.16	$7,480.65	5.74%
12-31-76	$ 86.96	$4,966.96	8.40%

* * *

PREMIER INDUSTRIAL CORP. (PRE). Founded 1940. Headquarters: 4415 Euclid Ave., Cleveland OH 44103. INDUSTRIAL PRODUCTS. Premier Industrial Corp. distributes electronic and electrical components; makes and distributes industrial maintenance products, and fire fighting equipment. MAJOR SUBSIDIARIES, BRANDS: D-A Lubricant Company, Inc.; Premier Industrial Export Corp.; Premier Energy Corp.; Newark Electronics; Cadillac Electric; Akron Brass; Western Fire Equipment.

Sales: $317.5 million (trend 16.7% a year).
Earnings: $32.45 million (trend 24.2% a year).
What happened to a $10,000 investment

Purchase Date	Purchase Price	Price on 12-31-81	Dividends Paid
12-31-71	$5.71	$20.75	$2,728.76
12-31-76	$4.12	$20.75	$2,366.06

Purchase Date	Cap. Gains (– Losses)	Total Return	Rate of Return
12-31-71	$26,350.36	$29,079.12	14.60%
12-31-76	$40,303.03	$42,669.09	39.42%

* * *

THE PRESLEY COS. (PDC). Founded 1956. Headquarters: 4600 Campus Dr., PO Box 2200, Newport Beach CA 92660. HOUSING. Builds mass-produced single-family homes.

Sales: $126.4 million (trend 5.2% a year).
Earnings: $10.83 million (trend 74.8% a year).
What happened to a $10,000 investment

Purchase Date	Purchase Price	Price on 12-31-81	Dividends Paid
12-31-71	$16.92	$9.37	$ 680.47
12-31-76	$ 6.66	$9.37	$1,727.35

Purchase Date	Cap. Gains (– Losses)	Total Return	Rate of Return
12-31-71	$–4,458.49	$–3,778.02	–4.63%
12-31-76	$ 4,066.92	$ 5,794.27	9.57%

* * *

PRIMARK CORP. (PMK) Founded 1981. Headquarters: 500 Griswold St., Detroit MI 48226. GAS DISTRIBUTION. Distributes natural gas in major portions of Michigan, including the Detroit area. Company was spun off in 1981 from American Natural Resources Co. MAJOR SUBSIDIARIES, BRANDS: Michigan Consolidated Gas Co.

* * *

PRIME COMPUTER INC. (PRM): Founded 1972. Headquarters: Prime Park, Natick MA 01760. COMPUTERS. Prime Computer Inc. produces, designs, and services digital computers. MAJOR SUBSIDIARIES, BRANDS: All Prime computers.

Sales: $267.6 million (trend 88.1% a year).
Earnings: $31.22 million (trend 146.8% a year).
What happened to a $10,000 investment

Purchase Date	Purchase Price	Price on 12-31-81	Dividends Paid
12-31-71	$N/A	$23.62	$0.00
12-31-76	$ 1.92	$23.62	$0.00

Purchase Date	Cap. Gains (– Losses)	Total Return	Rate of Return
12-31-71	$ N/A	$ N/A	N/A%
12-31-76	$113,260.87	$113,260.87	65.26%

* * *

PRIME MOTOR INNS, INC. (PDQ). Founded 1968. Headquarters: 1030 Clifton Ave., Clifton NJ 07013. MOTOR INNS, RESTAURANTS. Prime Motor Inns, Inc., operates motor inns catering primarily to commercial travelers and corporate accounts. MAJOR SUBSIDIARIES, BRANDS: Prime Management; Prime-O-Lene; operates selected Ramada Inns, Howard Johnsons, and Sheraton Motor Inns, and Sandalwood Restaurants.

Sales: $42.4 million (trend 15.5% a year).
Earnings: $6.48 million (trend 56.6% a year).
What happened to a $10,000 investment

Purchase Date	Purchase Price	Price on 12-31-81	Dividends Paid
12-31-71	$6.21	$17.75	$215.10
12-31-76	$1.81	$17.75	$ 0.00

Purchase Date	Cap. Gains (– Losses)	Total Return	Rate of Return
12-31-71	$18,583.21	$18,798.30	11.16%
12-31-76	$88,307.65	$88,307.65	57.95%

* * *

PROCTER & GAMBLE CO. (PG). Founded 1837, incorporated 1905. Headquarters: 301 E. 6th St., Cincinnati OH 45202. CONSUMER PRODUCTS. Procter & Gamble is the country's largest supplier of household products, particularly soap, laundry detergent, and disposable diapers. 61,000 employees. MAJOR SUBSIDIARIES, BRANDS: Pampers disposable diapers; Ivory soap and dishwashing liquid; Crest toothpaste; Tide, Cheer, Era, Dash, and Downy laundry products; Charmin bathroom tissue; Bounty paper towels; Comet cleanser; Cascade dishwasher detergent; Zest and Camay soaps; Puffs tissues; Folger's coffee; Duncan Hines baking mixes; Crisco cooking oil; Pringle's potato chips; Jif peanut butter; Scope mouthwash; Rely tampons (discontinued in 1980); Prell and Head & Shoulders shampoos; Secret and Sure deodorants; Crush International (Orange Crush; Hires root beer).

Sales: $11,416.0 million (trend 12.5% a year).
Earnings: $667.97 million (trend 11.0% a year).
What happened to a $10,000 investment

Purchase Date	*Purchase Price*	*Price on 12-31-81*	*Dividends Paid*
12-31-71	$78.50	$80.37	$3,084.08
12-31-76	$93.62	$80.37	$1,644.86

Purchase Date	*Cap. Gains (− Losses)*	*Total Return*	*Rate of Return*
12-31-71	$ 238.85	$3,322.93	2.91%
12-31-76	$−1,415.22	$ 229.64	.46%

PROFILE: The colossus of Cincinnati is the nation's largest advertiser, spending about 20 percent more per year to advertise its products than the number-two advertiser — which happens to be Sears, Roebuck, the nation's largest retailer. As the country's largest maker of household products, Procter & Gamble boasts a stable of household names — Crest, Ivory, Pampers, and the like — many of which are the leaders in their market segment. In fact, according to survey results published by *Fortune* in 1981, P&G makes four of the five top-selling household products. (They're Pampers, Tide, Charmin, and Bounty. The intruder is Glad bags — from Union Carbide.)

But Procter & Gamble doesn't pour its advertising money into a product until the product has been thoroughly tested, first in-house and then through marketing surveys. It normally will not launch a product unless it thinks the item can be number one in its market niche.

Staying in close touch with consumers' wants and feelings is vital to a business like P&G's. Besides doing market research, the company encourages consumers to write or phone by putting its name and address — and lately a toll-free phone number — on almost all of its products. According to *The Wall Street Journal,* P&G as of 1980 was getting about 250,000 calls and letters per year. About half were questions, a third complaints, and a sixth praise. With the publicizing of the toll-free number, the company expects annual call-and-letter volume to go up to around 500,000 a year.

Procter & Gamble carried a twenty-four-year streak of increases (in sales, earnings, and dividends) into fiscal 1981. Because of a $75-million write-off connected with the withdrawal of Rely tampons from the market (after they were suspected of being involved in causing toxic shock syndrome), the company's streak was snapped (unless you disregard "extraordinary items"). Recessions in the United States and Europe didn't help either. But the long-term record of the company is remarkable.

The stock usually sells at a premium to the market multiple, but recently only a slight one. Dividends (paid each year since 1891) provide a moderate yield.

* * *

PRODUCTS RESEARCH & CHEMICAL CORP. (PRC). Founded 1945. Headquarters: 5430 San Fernando Rd., Glendale CA 91203. **SEALANTS, COATINGS.** Products Research & Chemical Corp. develops and manufactures sealants, coatings, and adhesives for the defense, transportation, insulation, construction, and telecommunications industries. **MAJOR SUBSIDIARIES, BRANDS:** PRC Insulating Glass Sealant; PRC Rubber Calk; Thermal Brake.

Sales: $54.7 million (trend 3.7% a year).
Earnings: $3.28 million (trend 13.9% a year).
What happened to a $10,000 investment

Purchase Date	*Purchase Price*	*Price on 12-31-81*	*Dividends Paid*
12-31-71	$3.52	$9.25	$3,872.98
12-31-76	$2.70	$9.25	$3,939.80

Purchase Date	*Cap. Gains (− Losses)*	*Total Return*	*Rate of Return*
12-31-71	$16,278.41	$20,151.39	11.67%
12-31-76	$24,231.09	$28,170.89	30.72%

* * *

PROLER INTERNATIONAL CORP. (PS). Founded 1925. Headquarters: 7501 Wallisville Rd., PO Box 286, Houston TX 77001. **METALS RECYCLING.** Proler International Corp. acquires and processes ferrous and nonferrous scrap metals.

Sales: $105.7 million (trend 7.6% a year).
Earnings: $7.22 million (trend .8% a year).
What happened to a $10,000 investment

Purchase Date	*Purchase Price*	*Price on 12-31-81*	*Dividends Paid*
12-31-71	$16.93	$31.75	$6,005.37
12-31-76	$30.75	$31.75	$1,382.11

Purchase Date	Cap. Gains (− Losses)	Total Return	Rate of Return
12-31-71	$8,751.67	$14,757.04	9.49%
12-31-76	$ 325.20	$ 1,707.32	3.20%

* * *

PUBLIC SERVICE CO. OF COLORADO (PSR). Founded 1924. Headquarters: 550 15th St., Denver CO 80202. UTILITY. Provides electric and gas service in the Denver area.

Sales: $1,155.6 million (trend 20.2% a year).
Earnings: $70.01 million (trend 5.8% a year).
What happened to a $10,000 investment

Purchase Date	Purchase Price	Price on 12-31-81	Dividends Paid
12-31-71	$23.75	$14.25	$5,724.21
12-31-76	$19.25	$14.25	$4,059.74

Purchase Date	Cap. Gains (− Losses)	Total Return	Rate of Return
12-31-71	$−4,000.00	$1,724.21	1.60%
12-31-76	$−2,597.40	$1,462.34	2.77%

* * *

PUBLIC SERVICE CO. OF INDIANA, INC. (PIN). Founded 1941. Headquarters: 1000 E. Main St., Plainfield IN 46168. UTILITY. Public Service Co. of Indiana provides electric energy to major portions of the state of Indiana.

Sales: $645.7 million (trend 16.2% a year).
Earnings: $100.61 million (trend 15.3% a year).
What happened to a $10,000 investment

Purchase Date	Purchase Price	Price on 12-31-81	Dividends Paid
12-31-71	$26.33	$20.25	$7,494.92
12-31-76	$31.62	$20.25	$3,614.23

Purchase Date	Cap. Gains (− Losses)	Total Return	Rate of Return
12-31-71	$−2,310.13	$5,184.80	4.27%
12-31-76	$−3,596.84	$ 17.39	.03%

* * *

PUBLIC SERVICE CO. OF NEW HAMPSHIRE (PNH). Founded 1926. Headquarters: 1000 Elm St., Manchester NH 03105. UTILITY. Public Service Co. of New Hampshire provides electric power to New Hampshire and, to a limited extent, to surrounding states.

Sales: $351.2 million (trend 13.9% a year).
Earnings: $45.82 million (trend 24.2% a year).
What happened to a $10,000 investment

Purchase Date	Purchase Price	Price on 12-31-81	Dividends Paid
12-31-71	$26.12	$14.87	$7,150.24
12-31-76	$21.50	$14.87	$4,734.88

Purchase Date	Cap. Gains (− Losses)	Total Return	Rate of Return
12-31-71	$−4,306.22	$2,844.02	2.53%
12-31-76	$−3,081.40	$1,653.49	3.11%

* * *

PUBLIC SERVICE CO. OF NEW MEXICO (PNM). Founded 1917. Headquarters: Alvarado Sq., Albuquerque NM 87158. UTILITY. Provides electric service to north-central New Mexico. MAJOR SUBSIDIARIES, BRANDS: Paragon Resources, Inc.; Sunbelt Mining Company, Inc.

Sales: $277.9 million (trend 29.1% a year).
Earnings: $53.60 million (trend 40.0% a year).
What happened to a $10,000 investment

Purchase Date	Purchase Price	Price on 12-31-81	Dividends Paid
12-31-71	$23.25	$23.75	$6,877.42
12-31-76	$24.25	$23.75	$4,094.85

Purchase Date	Cap. Gains (− Losses)	Total Return	Rate of Return
12-31-71	$ 215.05	$7,092.47	5.51%
12-31-76	$−206.19	$3,888.66	6.79%

* * *

PUBLIC SERVICE ELECTRIC AND GAS CO. (PEG). Founded 1924. Headquarters: 80 Park Plaza, Newark NJ 07101. UTILITY. Supplying electricity and gas to more than 5 million people in northern New Jersey, this company ranks as approximately the tenth largest U.S. utility. 12,000 employees.

Sales: $2,994.1 million (trend 11.8% a year).
Earnings: $229.06 million (trend 10.9% a year).
What happened to a $10,000 investment

Purchase Date	Purchase Price	Price on 12-31-81	Dividends Paid
12-31-71	$27.50	$18.25	$7,116.36
12-31-76	$23.25	$18.25	$4,701.08

Purchase Date	Cap. Gains (− Losses)	Total Return	Rate of Return
12-31-71	$−3,363.64	$3,752.73	3.24%
12-31-76	$−2,150.54	$2,550.54	4.65%

PROFILE: Like most utilities, this stock went nowhere during the past decade. A sinking stock price counterbalanced the big dividend yield, leaving investors with a total return a bit below what they could have gotten by putting their money in a passbook savings account.

The company has an unusually diverse power-source mix. As of 1980, it got about 22 percent of its power from nuclear plants, but this percentage can be expected to increase as new ones Salem #2 and Hope Creek #1 and #2 come on stream during the 1980s. Coal was 29 percent and may also increase. Oil was 18 percent, natural gas 17 percent, and purchased power 14 percent; all of these may fall.

Among the many reasons investors have been sour on utilities is that they're subject to strict and detailed state regulation. Any price increases granted are sure to provoke protests and must be squeezed out through hearings and deliberations. Merrill Lynch rates the regulatory climate in New Jersey as "average."

The dividend yield is large (above 13 percent in 1981) but dividend payments have been growing only slowly. In recent years, the company has usually distributed about three quarters of its profits in the form of dividends.

One reason some investors may be interested in utility stocks is because they anticipate a long-term decline in interest rates. Since utility stocks compete with bonds for a place in conservative portfolios, falling interest rates will boost the price of these stocks. That's probably why these shares, which could be had in 1981 for only 5 times earnings, went for 7 times earnings in early 1982. A tax break for investing in utility stocks has also sweetened the pot.

* * *

PUBLICKER INDUSTRIES, INC. (PUL). Founded 1913. Headquarters: 777 W. Putnam Ave., Greenwich CT 06830. **ALCOHOL.** Publicker Industries, Inc., produces industrial alcohols and alcoholic beverages in the United Kingdom. **MAJOR SUBSIDIARIES, BRANDS:** Garnhealth Grain; Inver House; MacArthur's; Kulov vodka.

Sales: $134.9 million (trend 2.4% a year).
Earnings: $.71 million.
What happened to a $10,000 investment

Purchase Date	Purchase Price	Price on 12-31-81	Dividends Paid
12-31-71	$3.92	$2.87	$0.00
12-31-76	$5.48	$2.87	$0.00

Purchase Date	Cap. Gains (− Losses)	Total Return	Rate of Return
12-31-71	$−2,661.43	$−2,661.43	−3.05%
12-31-76	$−4,750.00	$−4,750.00	−12.09%

* * *

PUEBLO INTERNATIONAL, INC. (PII). Founded 1970. Headquarters: Loiza Expressway & Campo Rico Ave., Carolina PR 00630. **SUPERMARKETS.** Pueblo International, Inc., operates Pueblo supermarkets; also own several bakeries and two Puerto Rican radio stations.

Sales: $396.6 million (trend −10.6% a year).
Earnings: $3.37 million (trend 10.6% a year).
What happened to a $10,000 investment

Purchase Date	Purchase Price	Price on 12-31-81	Dividends Paid
12-31-71	$12.87	$3.62	$803.88
12-31-76	$ 2.75	$3.62	$ 0.00

Purchase Date	Cap. Gains (− Losses)	Total Return	Rate of Return
12-31-71	$−7,184.47	$−6,380.58	−9.66%
12-31-76	$ 3,181.82	$ 3,181.82	5.68%

* * *

PUERTO RICAN CEMENT COMPANY, INC. (PRN). Founded 1938. Headquarters: GPO Box 4487, San Juan PR 00936. **CEMENT.** Puerto Rican Cement Company, Inc., manufactures cement; also involved in realty sale and leasing. **MAJOR SUBSIDIARIES, BRANDS:** Caribbean Cement Carriers; St. Regis Paper and Bags; Desarrollos Multiples Insulares, Inc.

Sales: $78.2 million (trend 6.3% a year).
Earnings: $3.74 million (trend 7.0% a year).
What happened to a $10,000 investment

Purchase Date	Purchase Price	Price on 12-31-81	Dividends Paid
12-31-71	$12.50	$3.37	$864.00
12-31-76	$ 3.37	$3.37	$ 0.00

Purchase Date	*Cap. Gains (– Losses)*	*Total Return*	*Rate of Return*
12-31-71	$–7,300.00	$–6,436.00	–9.80%
12-31-76	$ –.00	$ –.00	0.00%

* * *

PUGET SOUND POWER & LIGHT CO. (PSD). Founded 1960. Headquarters: Puget Power Bldg., Bellevue WA 98009. UTILITY. Puget Sound Power & Light Co. produces electricity for western Washington and portions of central Washington.

Sales: $358.3 million (trend 16.5% a year).
Earnings: $38.64 million (trend 10.3% a year).
What happened to a $10,000 investment

Purchase Date	*Purchase Price*	*Price on 12-31-81*	*Dividends Paid*
12-31-71	$14.81	$13.25	$8,740.93
12-31-76	$16.81	$13.25	$4,624.54

Purchase Date	*Cap. Gains (– Losses)*	*Total Return*	*Rate of Return*
12-31-71	$–1,054.85	$7,686.08	5.87%
12-31-76	$–2,118.96	$2,505.58	4.57%

* * *

PUREX INDUSTRIES, INC. (PRX). Founded 1927. Headquarters: 5101 Clark Ave., Lakewood CA 90712. CLEANING PRODUCTS. Purex Industries, Inc., manufactures household cleaning products; also produces fire fighting equipment, drugs, and operates an aviation service company.

Sales: $650.2 million (trend 7.8% a year).
Earnings: $28.31 million (trend 6.5% a year).
What happened to a $10,000 investment

Purchase Date	*Purchase Price*	*Price on 12-31-81*	*Dividends Paid*
12-31-71	$17.75	$24.12	$5,836.62
12-31-76	$19.25	$24.12	$3,101.30

Purchase Date	*Cap. Gains (– Losses)*	*Total Return*	*Rate of Return*
12-31-71	$3,591.55	$9,428.17	6.87%
12-31-76	$2,532.47	$5,633.77	9.35%

* * *

PURITAN FASHIONS, CORP. (PFC). Founded 1961. Headquarters: 1400 Broadway, New York NY 10018. APPAREL. Puritan Fashions, Corp., manufactures women's clothing; also textile products. MAJOR SUBSIDIARIES, BRANDS: Calvin Klein; Diane von Furstenberg.

Sales: $162.2 million (trend –4.4% a year).
Earnings: $–3.44 million.
What happened to a $10,000 investment

Purchase Date	*Purchase Price*	*Price on 12-31-81*	*Dividends Paid*
12-31-71	$12.98	$14.12	$491.74
12-31-76	$ 3.33	$14.12	$ 0.00

Purchase Date	*Cap. Gains (– Losses)*	*Total Return*	*Rate of Return*
12-31-71	$ 885.31	$ 1,377.06	1.30%
12-31-76	$32,374.97	$32,374.97	33.48%

* * *

PUROLATOR, INC. (PPD). Founded 1923. Headquarters: 255 Old New Brunswick Rd., Piscataway NJ 08854. AUTOMOTIVE SUPPLIES. Purolator, Inc., produces automotive filters and runs a courier service; also provides armored car service and chartered aircraft.

Sales: $561.3 million (trend 13.3% a year).
Earnings: $13.48 million (trend 4.6% a year).
What happened to a $10,000 investment

Purchase Date	*Purchase Price*	*Price on 12-31-81*	*Dividends Paid*
12-31-71	$28.17	$36.25	$2,676.91
12-31-76	$18.92	$36.25	$2,329.50

Purchase Date	*Cap. Gains (– Losses)*	*Total Return*	*Rate of Return*
12-31-71	$2,869.82	$ 5,546.73	4.51%
12-31-76	$9,163.00	$11,492.49	16.54%

* * *

PYRO ENERGY CORP. (BTU). Founded 1969. Headquarters: 653 S. Hebron Ave., Evansville IN 47715. COAL, OIL, GAS. Pyro mines coal in several states; also produces oil and natural gas. Company's name was changed in 1981 from R. L. Burns Corp.

Sales: $118.1 million (trend 29.0% a year).
Earnings: $1.80 million (trend –21.6% a year).
What happened to a $10,000 investment

Purchase Date	*Purchase Price*	*Price on 12-31-81*	*Dividends Paid*
12-31-71	$ N/A	$5.75	$ N/A
12-31-76	$12.62	$5.75	$297.03

Purchase Date	*Cap. Gains (− Losses)*	*Total Return*	*Rate of Return*
12-31-71	$ N/A	$ N/A	N/A%
12-31-76	$−5,445.54	$−5,148.51	−13.47%

Q

QUAKER OATS CO. (OAT). Founded 1901. Headquarters: Merchandise Mart Plaza, Chicago IL 60654. **FOODS, TOYS.** Quaker is a major producer of cereal and other foods, including pet food. Also owns a major toy company, produces a limited line of chemicals, and owns three restaurant chains. 31,000 employees. **MAJOR SUBSIDIARIES, BRANDS:** Fisher-Price Toys; Quaker Oats, Shredded Wheat, Corn Bran, Quaker 100% Natural, Life, and Cap'n Crunch cereals; Aunt Jemima syrups; Flako pie crusts; Celeste frozen pizzas; Ken-L Ration and Puss'n Boots pet foods; Magic Pan, Engine House Pizza, and Proud Popover restaurants; Ciari & Forti (Italy) and Pampas Sales (Australia) food companies; Brookstone mail-order tools; Herrschners mail-order knitting products.

Sales: $2,599.5 million (trend 13.1% a year).
Earnings: $100.60 million (trend 15.4% a year).
What happened to a $10,000 investment

Purchase Date	*Purchase Price*	*Price on 12-31-81*	*Dividends Paid*
12-31-71	$33.58	$35.75	$2,965.76
12-31-76	$26.12	$35.75	$2,357.89

Purchase Date	*Cap. Gains (− Losses)*	*Total Return*	*Rate of Return*
12-31-71	$ 645.16	$3,610.92	3.13%
12-31-76	$3,684.21	$6,042.11	9.91%

PROFILE: Quaker is the small guy on the block in the tough cereal marketplace, competing with the likes of Kellogg, General Mills, and General Foods. In pet foods, it must tangle with Ralston Purina, among others. In this company, Quaker doesn't shine, but it has survived and, in recent years, shown some progress in its earnings and balance sheets.

Profitability has been inching up. In 1978–81 return on equity was above 16 percent. Meanwhile, the balance sheet has been trimmed, with debt dropping from more than 30 percent of capital in the early 1970s to less than 20 percent in the early 1980s.

In a 1980 article called "Quaker Oats retreats to its food lines," *Business Week* said that Quaker had tried to "perk up a lethargic earnings and growth record" in the early 1970s through a "hectic drive to diversify." Many of the fruits of that diversification effort turned sour. All the restaurants are rumored to be for sale. Marx toys has already been sold. But Fisher-Price, acquired in 1969, has been highly successful selling durable, medium-priced toys for preschoolers and has chipped in about a quarter of Quaker's profits recently, on just under a fifth of sales.

While concentrating on diversification, Quaker had been losing shelf space in supermarkets. It is trying to correct that by beefing up its sales force, spending more on advertising, and generally re-emphasizing food.

Dividends, which have been paid each year since 1906, provide a moderate yield.

* * *

QUAKER STATE OIL REFINING CORP. (KSF). Founded 1931. Headquarters: 255 Elm St., Oil City PA 16301. **OIL.** Quaker State Oil Refining Corp. manufactures lubricants; also operates a coal mining subsidiary and is involved in oil and natural gas exploration and production. **MAJOR SUBSIDIARIES, BRANDS:** Valley Camp Coal Co.

Sales: $832.5 million (trend 21.3% a year).
Earnings: $25.77 million (trend 3.8% a year).
What happened to a $10,000 investment

Purchase Date	*Purchase Price*	*Price on 12-31-81*	*Dividends Paid*
12-31-71	$24.05	$12.37	$2,528.73
12-31-76	$15.80	$12.37	$2,354.43

Purchase Date	*Cap. Gains (− Losses)*	*Total Return*	*Rate of Return*
12-31-71	$−4,854.47	$−2,325.74	−2.61%
12-31-76	$−2,167.72	$ 186.71	.37%

* * *

QUANEX CORP. (NX). Founded 1927. Headquarters: 4801 Woodway, Suite 280 W., Houston TX 77056. **METAL FABRICATING.** Quanex Corp. produces seamless and welded specialty tubing, steel bars, and other fabricated metal products serving the oil and gas machinery and transportation industries. **MAJOR SUBSIDIARIES, BRANDS:** Arbuckle Corp.; Pipe Specialties, Inc.; Quanex Management Sciences Corp.; Quanexport, Inc.; Vicking Metallurgical Corp.

Sales: $416.8 million (trend 25.3% a year).
Earnings: $31.44 million (trend 29.7% a year).
What happened to a $10,000 investment

Purchase Date	*Purchase Price*	*Price on 12-31-81*	*Dividends Paid*
12-31-71	$3.01	$20.50	$11,170.08
12-31-76	$7.26	$20.50	$ 3,084.18

Purchase Date	*Cap. Gains (− Losses)*	*Total Return*	*Rate of Return*
12-31-71	$58,053.28	$69,223.36	22.99%
12-31-76	$18,239.80	$21,323.98	25.65%

* * *

QUESTOR CORP. (IQ). Founded 1923. Headquarters: 1 John Goerlich Sq., Toledo OH 43691. **AUTO PRODUCTS.** Questor Corp. manufactures automotive products, as well as recreational, juvenile, and building products. **MAJOR SUBSIDIARIES, BRANDS:** AP Parts; Baby Line; Leslie-Locke; Spalding.

R

RB INDUSTRIES, INC. (RBI). Founded 1956. Headquarters: 2323 S.E. Main St., Irvine CA 92714. **FURNITURE SALES.** This company controls a group of retail furniture showrooms in the western United States.

Sales: $90.3 million (trend 12.9% a year).
Earnings: $.65 million (trend −8.7% a year).
What happened to a $10,000 investment

Purchase Date	*Purchase Price*	*Price on 12-31-81*	*Dividends Paid*
12-31-71	$4.73	$5.62	$2,154.39
12-31-76	$4.73	$5.62	$2,154.45

Purchase Date	*Cap. Gains (− Losses)*	*Total Return*	*Rate of Return*
12-31-71	$1,904.15	$4,058.55	3.47%
12-31-76	$1,904.46	$4,058.90	7.05%

* * *

RCA CORP. (RCA). Founded 1919. Headquarters: 30 Rockefeller Plaza, New York NY 10020. **ELECTRONICS, COMMUNICATIONS.** RCA is a major maker of televisions and other consumer electronics items and owns the NBC television and radio network. Also is involved in satellite communications, commercial electronics, rent-a-cars, records, consumer and industrial lending and insurance, and defense electronics. 133,000 employees. **MAJOR SUBSIDIARIES, BRANDS:** NBC; Hertz; C.I.T. Financial.

Sales: $8,011.3 million (trend 11.1% a year).
Earnings: $251.60 million (trend 18.5% a year).
What happened to a $10,000 investment

Purchase Date	*Purchase Price*	*Price on 12-31-81*	*Dividends Paid*
12-31-71	$37.12	$18.25	$3,447.81
12-31-76	$26.87	$18.25	$2,902.33

Purchase Date	*Cap. Gains (− Losses)*	*Total Return*	*Rate of Return*
12-31-71	$−5,084.18	$−1,636.36	−1.77%
12-31-76	$−3,209.30	$ −306.98	−.62%

PROFILE: RCA's financial results have been up and down. Its managers have been in and out. In the six years ending in 1981, the corporation has had four chairmen. *Time* magazine in 1981 quoted one insider as saying, "If you put two people together at this company, you will have three factions." It quoted a board member as saying that the company's officers were "the most highly politicized group you can imagine, and the infighting was absolutely terrible." Infighting has also been fierce at RCA's NBC broadcasting subsidiary, where there have been several management changes recently.

However, as the Oakland A's and New York Yankees have proved, infighting doesn't necessarily mean bad results. Of greater concern to Wall Street has been the slow long-term growth rate in earnings. RCA needs new products, goes the conventional wisdom, particularly in consumer electronics. It needs to get back to its roots in high technology and away from diversifications like Hertz rent-a-car and C.I.T. Financial. In early 1982 RCA said it would spin off Hertz; some expected C.I.T. to follow.

That conventional wisdom may evaporate like the dew when boom times come or interest rates drop. In any case, RCA may be near a high-tech market success with videotape recorders (imported) and videocassette players (manufactured). Early sales have been sluggish, but the products were, after all, launched into a recession.

All the bad publicity RCA has gotten in the last few years may be a spur to the investor who likes to march counter to the crowd. However, those who like a clean balance sheet may be given pause by the fact that RCA recently had a bit over 40 percent of its capital in the form of debt and only about 40 percent in common stock (the rest was in preferred stock).

The silver lining in the stock's poor market performance is an above-average dividend yield. The stock has been yielding more than 6 percent since 1979 and around 8 percent in 1980–81. Dividends have been paid yearly since 1940.

* * *

RLC CORP. (RLC). Founded 1954. Headquarters: 1 Rollins Plaza, Wilmington DE 19899. TRUCKING. RLC is the nation's largest hauler of bulk cargo via tank trucks. Also engages in truck leasing and in hazardous waste disposal. 4,000 employees. MAJOR SUBSIDIARIES, BRANDS: Matlack, Inc. (tank truck hauling); Rollins Leasing Corp. (truck rentals and maintenance); Rollins Environmental Services.

Sales: $360.7 million (trend 14.5% a year).
Earnings: $14.37 million (trend 8.1% a year).
What happened to a $10,000 investment

Purchase Date	*Purchase Price*	*Price on 12-31-81*	*Dividends Paid*
12-31-71	$7.67	$12.12	$2,513.33
12-31-76	$4.78	$12.12	$3,977.21

Purchase Date	*Cap. Gains (− Losses)*	*Total Return*	*Rate of Return*
12-31-71	$ 5,815.22	$ 8,328.55	6.25%
12-31-76	$15,377.91	$19,355.12	24.03%

PROFILE: RLC has several aspects that should intrigue investors. It also has some aspects that should scare them. In some cases, they're the same aspects.

Begin with size. The firm is relatively small: Sales in 1981, for example, were about $360 million. That leaves plenty of room for growth. But small firms are also more likely to be tossed by unexpected waves than larger firms are.

Next, consider debt, or leverage if you prefer the more positive term. In 1980 RLC reduced its long-term debt to the lowest level in a decade, in percentage terms — and yet, debt was still a whopping 56 percent of capital. (In 1975 debt was more than three quarters of capital.) Leverage like this gives a big kick to return on equity — which, indeed, has been outstanding in recent years (better than 22 percent in 1980 and better than 30 percent the previous four years). But that much debt can also be dangerous — very dangerous, should the economy get stuck in a long and deep recession.

Some of RLC's special characteristics include its position as one of two U.S. firms licensed to incinerate PCBs and its position (through the Matlack subsidiary) as the only currently licensed coast-to-coast tank truck hauler. More competition may come in both areas, but RLC clearly has a head start.

Recently, tank truck hauling has accounted for most of sales and profits, truck leasing for most of the rest. The relatively small environmental services sector is the only one whose fortunes aren't tied closely to the state of the economy.

Dividends were started in 1976 and provide a moderate yield.

* * *

RTE CORP. (RTE). Founded 1955. Headquarters: 1900 E. North St., Waukesha WI 53186. ELECTRICAL EQUIPMENT. RTE is engaged in the manufacturing of electrical transformers, fuses, connectors, switches, and related equipment.

Sales: $207.5 million (trend 28.8% a year).
Earnings: $2.08 million (trend −.6% a year).
What happened to a $10,000 investment

Purchase Date	*Purchase Price*	*Price on 12-31-81*	*Dividends Paid*
12-31-71	$8.37	$7.12	$3,820.90
12-31-76	$9.12	$7.12	$2,783.56

Purchase Date	*Cap. Gains (− Losses)*	*Total Return*	*Rate of Return*
12-31-71	$−1,492.54	$2,328.36	2.12%
12-31-76	$−2,191.78	$ 591.78	1.16%

* * *

RALSTON PURINA CO. (RAL). Founded 1894. Headquarters: Checkerboard Sq., St. Louis MO 63188. ANIMAL FEED. Ralston Purina is the world's largest producer of dog food, cat food, and livestock feed. The company also operates restaurants and produces tuna and cereals. MAJOR SUBSIDIARIES, BRANDS: Jack in the Box; Purina; Chicken of the Sea; Chex.

Sales: $5,224.7 million (trend 9.2% a year).
Earnings: $184.30 million (trend 6.2% a year).
What happened to a $10,000 investment

Purchase Date	*Purchase Price*	*Price on 12-31-81*	*Dividends Paid*
12-31-71	$11.79	$12.25	$3,478.16
12-31-76	$17.71	$12.25	$1,548.99

Purchase Date	*Cap. Gains (− Losses)*	*Total Return*	*Rate of Return*
12-31-71	$ 388.69	$ 3,866.86	3.32%
12-31-76	$−3,082.35	$−1,533.36	−3.27%

PROFILE: Think of Ralston Purina, and what do you think of? Chex cereals? Jack in the Box restaurants? Perhaps the St. Louis Blues hockey team? Ralston Purina owns or produces all of these. It also produces Chicken of the Sea, a leading brand of canned tuna. But all of these products and brands put together account for less than 15 percent of the company's sales and earnings.

The driving engines of this company are animals and agriculture — pet food, farm animal feed, animal health products, soy protein, grain merchandising. Those are what Ralston Purina is really made of. While agricultural products supply the bulk (almost half) of the revenues, grocery products, mainly pet foods, supply the bulk (almost half) of the profits.

It's appropriate, then, that William Stiritz, who holds the reins here, came up through the grocery division and won his position as chief executive (jumping over eight more senior candidates) by directing the company's defense in the pet food wars of 1977–80. Ralston is traditionally the holder of the largest share of the pet food market; in dry dog food, for example, it had a 50-percent market share. In the late 1970s, that share came under attack as four major competitors — General Foods, Kal Kan, Liggett, and Quaker Oats — all stepped up advertising and cut prices. Stiritz responded by pouring on the advertising and introducing several new pet food products, but leaving prices pretty much alone. Result: Ralston lost some market share, but held on to most of its profits. The others gained some market share, but didn't make much money and finally had to back down.

Dividends, paid since 1934, have produced a yield above 5 percent in recent years.

* * *

RAMADA INNS, INC. (RAM). Founded 1961. Headquarters: 3838 E. Van Buren St., Phoenix AZ 85008. **MOTELS, GAMBLING.** Ramada has more than 600 owned or franchised hotels throughout the United States and in 17 foreign countries. Also operates a hotel / casino in Las Vegas and plans to operate one in Atlantic City. 17,000 employees.

Sales: $366.1 million (trend 11.5% a year).
Earnings: $15.07 million (trend 62.7% a year).
What happened to a $10,000 investment

Purchase Date	*Purchase Price*	*Price on 12-31-81*	*Dividends Paid*	*Cap. Gains (– Losses)*	*Total Return*	*Rate of Return*
12-31-71	$15.11	$6.12	$ 665.88	$–5,947.37	$–5,281.49	–7.24%
12-31-76	$ 4.37	$6.12	$1,302.86	$ 4,000.00	$ 5,302.86	8.88%

PROFILE: More than two thirds of Ramada Inns' capital recently consisted of debt. In 1980 Ramada spent some $42 million to pay interest on its debt, a sum approximately equal to the company's after-tax profits for the years 1978–80. Ramada has not had a loss year since it went public, but it's had some close scrapes, and profitability has been nothing to write home about — even on hotel stationary. In recent years its return on stockholders' equity has been around 10 percent, a mediocre showing that would have been worse without the leverage from all that debt. Fiscal 1981 was so poor that the company discontinued its dividend.

How does the company propose to pull out of this hole? Through gambling, in large part. Founder Marion Isbell rejected gambling as unsavory, but his son, M. William Isbell, helped lead Ramada into gambling by buying the big Tropicana Hotel in Las Vegas and rebuilding the former Ambassador Hotel in Atlantic City. In 1981 M. William Isbell resigned as chairman and president in the wake of cost overruns in Atlantic City and alleged thefts at the Las Vegas facility. The company will probably press ahead into gambling though; in 1980 a Ramada official predicted that gambling would account for 55 percent of company revenues by 1982.

Besides gambling, the company hopes for good results from its four-year program of refurbishing facilities that had become run-down. *Business Week* reported in 1980 that an internal Ramada study showed that "one third of the travelers who have slept in Ramada's beds indicate they are shunning the chain vs. one fifth for arch-rival Holiday Inns."

Dividends had been paid each year from the time the company went public until 1981, but the yield had always been modest.

Ramada is often among the most actively traded issues on the Big Board, partly because the extreme volatility of the stock makes it of interest to speculators. For example, in 1973 the shares ranged between $4 and $20. In 1974 the range was roughly from $2 to $9 and in 1980 roughly $5.50 to $11.50.

* * *

RAMPAC (RPC). Formerly Realty and Mortgage Investors of the Pacific. Founded 1971. Headquarters: 7700 Edgewater Dr., Oakland CA 94621. **REAL ESTATE INVESTMENTS.** This firm invests in real estate through construction loans and mortgages.

Sales: $14.8 million (trend 14.1% a year).
Earnings: $3.54 million (trend 12.1% a year).
What happened to a $10,000 investment

Purchase Date	*Purchase Price*	*Price on 12-31-81*	*Dividends Paid*
12-31-71	$N/A	$26.37	$ N/A
12-31-76	$10.37	$26.37	$7,171.08

Purchase Date	*Cap. Gains (− Losses)*	*Total Return*	*Rate of Return*
12-31-71	$ N/A	$ N/A	N/A%
12-31-76	$15,421.69	$22,592.77	26.66%

* * *

RANCO, INC. (RNI). Founded 1913. Headquarters: 701 W. Fifth Ave., Columbus OH 43201. **CONTROL DEVICES.** This firm manufactures products that regulate temperature, time, and electricity in furnaces, air-conditioners, cars, stoves, and refrigerators. **MAJOR SUBSIDIARIES, BRANDS:** Teccor Electronics.

Sales: $179.4 million (trend 11.1% a year).
Earnings: $1.94 million (trend −17.0% a year).
What happened to a $10,000 investment

Purchase Date	*Purchase Price*	*Price on 12-31-81*	*Dividends Paid*
12-31-71	$12.83	$12.25	$4,831.17
12-31-76	$ 9.00	$12.25	$4,014.81

Purchase Date	*Cap. Gains (− Losses)*	*Total Return*	*Rate of Return*
12-31-71	$−454.55	$4,376.62	3.70%
12-31-76	$ 3,611.11	$7,625.93	12.00%

* * *

RAYBESTOS-MANHATTAN, INC. (RAY). Founded 1929. Headquarters: 100 Oakview Dr., Trumbull CT 06611. **INDUSTRIAL GOODS, BRAKE PARTS.** Raybestos-Manhattan makes linings and pads for automotive brakes, as well as rivets, plastics, and fibers. **MAJOR SUBSIDIARIES, BRANDS:** Milford Rivet and Machine.

Sales: $274.4 million (trend 6.1% a year).
Earnings: $−6.27 million.
What happened to a $10,000 investment

Purchase Date	*Purchase Price*	*Price on 12-31-81*	*Dividends Paid*
12-31-71	$18.08	$17.50	$5,866.04
12-31-76	$23.48	$17.50	$2,730.19

Purchase Date	*Cap. Gains (− Losses)*	*Total Return*	*Rate of Return*
12-31-71	$ −320.03	$5,546.01	4.51%
12-31-76	$−2,546.42	$ 183.77	.36%

* * *

RAYMOND INTERNATIONAL, INC. (RII). Founded 1902. Headquarters: 1225 Galleria Tower E., Houston TX 77056. **ENGINEERING, CONSTRUCTION.** Raymond International is involved in construction and engineering worldwide. One of its specialties is marine engineering. 5,000 employees. **MAJOR SUBSIDIARIES, BRANDS:** Kaiser Engineers; Raymond International Builders; Raymond Offshore Constructors.

Sales: $653.0 million (trend 24.7% a year).
Earnings: $6.11 million (trend −4.7% a year).
What happened to a $10,000 investment

Purchase Date	*Purchase Price*	*Price on 12-31-81*	*Dividends Paid*
12-31-71	$ 6.83	$22.25	$8,917.07
12-31-76	$18.58	$22.25	$2,647.53

Purchase Date	*Cap. Gains (− Losses)*	*Total Return*	*Rate of Return*
12-31-71	$22,560.98	$31,478.05	15.29%
12-31-76	$ 1,973.09	$ 4,620.63	7.89%

PROFILE: Engineering and construction companies lately have had order backlogs bulging like the wad of chewing tobacco in the cheek of an old-fashioned baseball player.

In this league, Raymond International has to tangle with some seasoned major leaguers—Fluor, Parsons, and Brown & Root (Halliburton), to name only a few. All are much bigger than Raymond, whose revenues are still less than $1 billion, and whose order backlog ($3.8 billion as of early 1981) ranked approximately tenth among engineering and construction firms.

Being smaller, Raymond has fewer projects than the very largest firms, and this in turn makes earnings more variable from quarter to quarter and from year to year. In 1980, for example, the firm had just finished a major pipeline job in Saudi Arabia and hadn't yet begun receiving major profits from several of its newer projects. Earnings in 1980 were only $1.23, down for the third year in a row from a 1977 peak of around $4.00 a share. But Raymond had experienced down years before and come back strong. A solid growth trend seems to underlie the erratic year-to-year results.

As you might guess, these shares are volatile. In 1980, for example, the price ranged from $13 to $33. As with most major construction companies, the balance sheet is strong. Dividends have been paid each year since 1936; the yield is moderate.

* * *

RAYTHEON CO. (RTN). Founded 1928. Headquarters: 141 Spring St., Lexington MA 02173. AEROSPACE. Raytheon is a major producer of defense electronics and missile systems. Also produces small aircraft, computer systems, word processors, and appliances; builds utility and chemical plants; provides oil and gas exploration services; and publishes textbooks. 78,000 employees. MAJOR SUBSIDIARIES, BRANDS: Hawk, Patriot, Sidewinder, and Sparrow missiles; Beech Aircraft Corp.; Amana, Caloric (appliances); Badger Co. (chemical plant engineering); Seismograph Service Corp. (oil and gas exploration); United Engineers (power plant construction); D. C. Heath (textbooks).

Sales: $5,002.1 million (trend 16.6% a year).
Earnings: $282.26 million (trend 31.9% a year).
What happened to a $10,000 investment

Purchase Date	*Purchase Price*	*Price on 12-31-81*	*Dividends Paid*
12-31-71	$ 9.87	$37.37	$5,101.27
12-31-76	$15.12	$37.37	$2,661.16

Purchase Date	*Cap. Gains (− Losses)*	*Total Return*	*Rate of Return*
12-31-71	$27,848.10	$32,949.37	15.69%
12-31-76	$14,710.74	$17,371.90	22.31%

PROFILE: As a company, Raytheon has taken off as swiftly and unerringly as one of its missiles. During the 1970s, sales quadrupled. Income quintupled. Dividends sextupled. And the price of the stock didn't do badly either. If you'd bought anytime at the beginning of the decade, you'd have multipled your money at least four to six times by the early 1980s.

Raytheon is no Johnny-come-lately growth company, playing with a lot of borrowed money and flirting with investors' farfetched hopes. It's a solid, $5-billion (sales) operation, with a balance sheet as hard as a fuselage. Some 95 percent of the company's capital recently consisted of equity; only about 5 percent was debt.

The combination of extraordinary growth with a conservative balance sheet is unusual and hasn't gone unnoticed on Wall Street, where Raytheon carries an above-average price tag — 10 times earnings, for example, in early 1982, when the average stock was good only for 7 or 8. It's hard to argue that the premium is excessive for a stock with this kind of track record.

Raytheon traded some 20.6 million shares for Beech Aircraft Corp. in 1980, increasing the number of shares outstanding to about 83 million. Dilution, worried some. But despite the dilution, Raytheon continued its long-standing record of uninterrupted earnings growth. Beech, for its part, contributed close to a fifth of Raytheon's earnings (on about 15 percent of sales) in 1980.

Dividends have been paid since 1964, but the yield is usually in the 2-to-3½ percent range.

* * *

READING AND BATES CORP. (RB). Founded 1955. Headquarters: 3800 First National Tower, Tulsa OK 74103. OIL, COAL. Reading and Bates is active in the contracting of offshore drilling sites, onshore pipelines, and oil and coal production.

Sales: $407.4 million (trend 13.6% a year).
Earnings: $70.29 million (trend 16.0% a year).
What happened to a $10,000 investment

Purchase Date	*Purchase Price*	*Price on 12-31-81*	*Dividends Paid*
12-31-71	$7.93	$25.37	$3,102.87
12-31-76	$5.11	$25.37	$3,855.18

Purchase Date	*Cap. Gains (− Losses)*	*Total Return*	*Rate of Return*
12-31-71	$22,015.19	$25,118.06	13.38%
12-31-76	$39,646.74	$43,501.92	39.85%

* * *

REALTY REFUND TRUST (RRF). Founded 1971. Headquarters: 1101 Euclid Ave., Cleveland OH 44115. REAL ESTATE INVESTMENTS. This company refinances existing property through mortgage loans.

* * *

RECOGNITION EQUIPMENT INC. (REC). Founded 1962. Headquarters: 2701 E. Grauwyler Rd., Irving TX 75061. DATA PROCESSING. This company manufactures information processing systems used most often for bank check processing and credit card operations.

Sales: $113.1 million (trend 14.1% a year).
Earnings: $4.89 million (trend 9.9% a year).
What happened to a $10,000 investment

Purchase Date	*Purchase Price*	*Price on 12-31-81*	*Dividends Paid*
12-31-71	$13.50	$6.62	$0.00
12-31-76	$10.12	$6.62	$0.00

Purchase Date	*Cap. Gains (− Losses)*	*Total Return*	*Rate of Return*
12-31-71	$−5,092.59	$−5,092.59	−6.87%
12-31-76	$−3,456.79	$−3,456.79	−8.13%

* * *

REDMAN INDUSTRIES, INC. (RE). Founded 1937. Headquarters: 2550 Walnut Hill Lane, Dallas TX 75229. MOBILE HOMES. Redman manufactures and sells mobile homes.

Sales: $241.9 million (trend 19.5% a year).
Earnings: $7.19 million (trend 19.9% a year).
What happened to a $10,000 investment

Purchase Date	*Purchase Price*	*Price on 12-31-81*	*Dividends Paid*
12-31-71	$25.50	$12.87	$ 250.98
12-31-76	$ 3.37	$12.87	$1,096.30

Purchase Date	*Cap. Gains (− Losses)*	*Total Return*	*Rate of Return*
12-31-71	$−4,950.98	$−4,700.00	−6.15%
12-31-76	$ 28,148.15	$ 29,244.44	31.45%

* * *

REECE CORP. (RCE). Founded 1948. Headquarters: 200 Prospect St., Waltham MA 02154. INDUSTRIAL APPAREL MACHINERY. Reece Corp. produces machines for sewing buttonholes and pockets.

Sales: $46.4 million (trend 6.8% a year).
Earnings: $2.23 million (trend −2.8% a year).
What happened to a $10,000 investment

Purchase Date	*Purchase Price*	*Price on 12-31-81*	*Dividends Paid*
12-31-71	$31.25	$5.25	$2,190.40
12-31-76	$12.25	$5.25	$2,355.10

Purchase Date	*Cap. Gains (− Losses)*	*Total Return*	*Rate of Return*
12-31-71	$−8,320.00	$−6,129.60	−9.06%
12-31-76	$−5,714.29	$−3,359.18	−7.86%

* * *

REEVES BROTHERS, INC. (RVS). Founded 1922. Headquarters: 1271 Ave. of the Americas, New York NY 10020. TEXTILES, FOAM, UNDERWEAR. This diversified manufacturer produces textiles for sportswear, foam for furniture, and men's and boys' underwear. MAJOR SUBSIDIARIES, BRANDS: Comfy Home Furnishings; Coverlight.

Sales: $353.2 million (trend 7.6% a year).
Earnings: $18.94 million (trend 16.0% a year).
What happened to a $10,000 investment

Purchase Date	*Purchase Price*	*Price on 12-31-81*	*Dividends Paid*
12-31-71	$21.75	$48.37	$6,724.46
12-31-76	$21.52	$48.37	$4,199.77

Purchase Date	*Cap. Gains (− Losses)*	*Total Return*	*Rate of Return*
12-31-71	$12,238.03	$18,962.50	11.22%
12-31-76	$12,481.32	$16,681.09	21.69%

* * *

REICHHOLD CHEMICALS, INC. (RCI). Founded 1930. Headquarters: 525 N. Broadway, White Plains NY 10603. CHEMICAL PRODUCTS. Reichhold Chemicals produces synthetic resins and industrial chemicals.

Sales: $885.1 million (trend 16.0% a year).
Earnings: $13.17 million (trend −7.8% a year).
What happened to a $10,000 investment

Purchase Date	*Purchase Price*	*Price on 12-31-81*	*Dividends Paid*
12-31-71	$ 9.25	$11.37	$6,421.62
12-31-76	$19.12	$11.37	$1,730.72

Purchase Date	*Cap. Gains (− Losses)*	*Total Return*	*Rate of Return*
12-31-71	$ 2,297.30	$ 8,718.92	6.47%
12-31-76	$−4,052.29	$−2,321.57	−5.15%

* * *

REPUBLIC AIRLINES, INC. (RAI). Founded 1979. Headquarters: 7500 Airline Dr., Minneapolis MN 55450. AIRLINE. Republic is approximately the seventh largest U.S. airline, serving some thirty-three states, Canada, Mexico, and the Caribbean. 14,000 employees. **MAJOR SUBSIDIARIES, BRANDS:** Republic was formed in 1979 by the merger of North Central Airlines and Southern Airways. It absorbed Hughes Airwest in 1980.

Sales: $916.7 million (trend 42.4% a year).
Earnings: $−24.66 million.
What happened to a $10,000 investment

Purchase Date	*Purchase Price*	*Price on 12-31-81*	*Dividends Paid*
12-31-71	$4.12	$4.12	$2,739.39
12-31-76	$3.87	$4.12	$2,012.90

Purchase Date	*Cap. Gains (− Losses)*	*Total Return*	*Rate of Return*
12-31-71	$ −.00	$2,739.39	2.45%
12-31-76	$645.16	$2,658.06	4.83%

PROFILE: Republic's Minneapolis headquarters aren't far from those of Northwest Airlines, a rival carrier. The financial situations of the two airlines, though, are worlds apart. Northwest has escaped the debt-plagued status of most airlines, while Republic exemplifies that status in spades. A towering 85 percent of Republic's capital is in the form of long-term debt. While Northwest has almost always remained profitable, Republic, like many airlines, has had its share of losses recently. It lost almost $25 million in 1980 and more than $46 million in 1981.

As at several other troubled lines, management has asked the employees to take pay cuts. Union members agreed in the summer of 1981 to take part of their salaries in the form of company stock, instead of cash.

That stock is risky — for the employees and other investors alike. But the potential gains are large, if and when the airline industry rebounds. In early 1982 the stock was going for less than $5 a share. North Central alone sold for more than $10 a share during parts of 1978.

Dividends have been paid each year since 1973, but lately have been of almost token size.

* * *

REPUBLIC CORP. (REP). Founded 1927. Headquarters: 1900 Ave. of the Stars, Los Angeles CA 90067. **DIVERSIFIED MANUFACTURING.** This firm is involved in steel, aviation, film, videotape, printing, and fabricated building products. **MAJOR SUBSIDIARIES, BRANDS:** Kentucky Electric Steel.

Sales: $300.3 million (trend 7.8% a year).
Earnings: $11.88 million (trend 49.1% a year).
What happened to a $10,000 investment

Purchase Date	*Purchase Price*	*Price on 12-31-81*	*Dividends Paid*
12-31-71	$21.35	$23.25	$ 786.34
12-31-76	$ 6.35	$23.25	$2,642.62

Purchase Date	*Cap. Gains (− Losses)*	*Total Return*	*Rate of Return*
12-31-71	$ 887.80	$ 1,674.14	1.56%
12-31-76	$26,590.16	$29,232.78	31.44%

* * *

REPUBLIC FINANCIAL SERVICES (RFS). Founded 1969. Headquarters: 2727 Turtle Creek Blvd., Dallas TX 75219. **INSURANCE.** This operation is a holding company for a group of insurance companies. **MAJOR SUBSIDIARIES, BRANDS:** Republic Insurance Co.; Republic-Vanguard Life Insurance Co.; Allied Finance Co.

* * *

REPUBLIC NEW YORK CORP. (RNB). Founded 1965. Headquarters: 452 Fifth Ave., New York NY 10018. **BANK.** Republic New York is involved in international banking, precious metals trading, and retail banking. 2,000 employees. **MAJOR SUBSIDIARIES, BRANDS:** Republic National Bank of New York.

Sales: $771.0 million (trend 45.1% a year).
Earnings: $68.90 million (trend 30.3% a year).
What happened to a $10,000 investment

Purchase Date	*Purchase Price*	*Price on 12-31-81*	*Dividends Paid*
12-31-71	$8.83	$38.25	$4,709.43
12-31-76	$9.04	$38.25	$4,033.18

Purchase Date	*Cap. Gains (− Losses)*	*Total Return*	*Rate of Return*
12-31-71	$33,301.89	$38,011.32	16.99%
12-31-76	$32,304.15	$36,337.33	35.89%

PROFILE: This has been one of the most consistently and dramatically profitable of all U.S. banks. If, that is, you wish to call it a U.S. bank. International entrepreneur Edmond Safra owns about 61 percent of the stock and controls the company in all but name.

Perhaps investors are scared by having a man from the Middle East in charge of a major bank.

Perhaps they don't know how to evaluate a bank that depends so much on gold trading and international finance and so little on the domestic economy. Or perhaps they're nervous at any individual, whatever his origin, controlling so large a block of stock. These may be some of the reasons why Republic New York sells at a price / earnings ratio ridiculous in the light of its outstanding operating results. Recently the p / e has ranged between 2 and 7.

The return on stockholders' equity in 1980 was an amazing 33 percent and in most other recent years has been in the 17-to-23 percent range. The company often earns more than $1 for each $100 in assets — a ratio that most banks would give their eyeteeth to have (some banks would be willing to settle for half that). The results have been achieved without piling on debt, but with a generous helping of unconventional tactics.

In 1980 *The Insiders' Chronicle,* a stock market newsletter, noted that "Republic has been a maverick since its inception." It "makes no pretense of offering full-service banking," but selects services on which it expects it can make a good profit. The gold buying and selling operations, in which the bank typically acts as an arbitrageur, are of course unusual. But they're not as risky as an uninitiated observer might think, since Republic can make money whether gold is headed up or down. Another unusual aspect of Republic's operation is the way in which it attracts time deposits through unconventional premiums (TV sets, pianos, and the like). It may seem hokey, but so far it has proven a cost-efficient way to attract money to lend out at a higher rate. In its loans, Republic often prefers to lend to safe clients, such as foreign governments and other banks.

Dividends, started in 1975, have provided a modest yield.

* * *

REPUBLIC STEEL CORP. (RS). Founded 1899. Headquarters: Republic Bldg., Cleveland OH 44101. STEEL. Republic is approximately the fifth largest U.S. steel firm. It makes steel for machinery, construction, autos, and other uses. 41,000 employees. MAJOR SUBSIDIARIES, BRANDS: Mooney Aircraft Corp.; Reserve Mining (50 percent owned).

Sales: $3,760.0 million (trend 11.8% a year).
Earnings: $50.98 million (trend 3.1% a year).
What happened to a $10,000 investment

Purchase Date	*Purchase Price*	*Price on 12-31-81*	*Dividends Paid*
12-31-71	$20.62	$24.50	$9,551.52
12-31-76	$32.75	$24.50	$3,145.04

Purchase Date	*Cap. Gains (— Losses)*	*Total Return*	*Rate of Return*
12-31-71	$ 1,878.79	$11,430.30	7.92%
12-31-76	$—2,519.08	$ 625.95	1.22%

PROFILE: What would you think of a company with this sequence of earnings figures: $0.09, $2.54, $2.66, $3.15, $4.07, $4.46, $5.36, $6.86, $7.49, and $10.55? Sound good? The numbers are indeed Republic Steel's for the period 1971–80, but the sequence is not. The $10.55 figure, for example, was for 1974, while the $3.15 was for 1980.

Cyclical is the classic description of steel companies, and few are more cyclical than Republic. Unfortunately, it's been difficult to discern any underlying uptrend beneath the cycles for the past decade or so. Like most steel companies, Republic has been hard hit both by a lackluster economy and by fierce, efficient competition from abroad (mainly Japan). Depending on the years you select for comparison, you may find that the long-term trend in both earnings and dividends is slightly up, or slightly down.

At the start of the 1980s, the steel industry was in an upswing, and so was Republic. The uptick didn't last long, however, times were bad for steel in 1981–82. There is some reason for optimism long-term. Republic has lately been spending heavily on new equipment to upgrade antiquated facilities. And the Reagan administration's avowed intention to stimulate capital spending would be good news here, since much of Republic's output goes into machinery and construction.

The balance sheet remains in acceptable shape (debt recently was about 30 percent of capital), and the stock offers a substantial yield (6 to 9 percent in recent years). Dividends have been paid every year since 1940.

* * *

REPUBLIC OF TEXAS CORP. (RPT). Founded 1920. Headquarters: 1800 Republic National Bank Bldg., Dallas TX 75222. BANKING This is a holding company for several Texas banks, including Republic National Bank of Dallas, the largest in the state.

Sales: $1,246.3 million (trend 31.5% a year).
Earnings: $87.69 million (trend 17.3% a year).
What happened to a $10,000 investment

Purchase Date	Purchase Price	Price on 12-31-81	Dividends Paid
12-31-71	$16.53	$36.62	$4,546.55
12-31-76	$18.47	$36.62	$2,446.92

Purchase Date	Cap. Gains (− Losses)	Total Return	Rate of Return
12-31-71	$12,159.65	$16,706.21	10.32%
12-31-76	$ 9,827.06	$12,273.98	17.37%

* * *

RESEARCH-COTTRELL, INC. (RC). Founded 1954. Headquarters: PO Box 1500, Somerville NJ 08876. **POLLUTION CONTROL, OIL EQUIPMENT.** Research-Cottrell produces pollution control equipment, cooling towers, and equipment for the production and transmission of petroleum products. Also does contract engineering. **MAJOR SUBSIDIARIES, BRANDS:** Metcalf & Eddy (engineering, particularly water treatment); Hamon Cooling Tower; Custodis Construction; Flex-Kleen Corp.

Sales: $379.6 million (trend 10.2% a year).
Earnings: $7.53 million (trend 16.1% a year).
What happened to a $10,000 investment

Purchase Date	Purchase Price	Price on 12-31-81	Dividends Paid
12-31-71	$59.12	$15.25	$250.32
12-31-76	$18.75	$15.25	$576.00

Purchase Date	Cap. Gains (− Losses)	Total Return	Rate of Return
12-31-71	$−7,420.72	$−7,170.40	−11.86%
12-31-76	$−1,866.67	$−1,290.67	−2.73%

* * *

RESORTS INTERNATIONAL, INC. (RTA, AMERICAN STOCK EXCHANGE). Founded 1957. Headquarters: 915 N.E. 125th St., North Miami FL 33161. **GAMBLING.** Resorts International operates a large hotel casino in Atlantic City, New Jersey, and additional hotel casinos in the Bahamas at Freeport and at Paradise Island. Also involved in security services and charter airline service. 8,000 employees. **MAJOR SUBSIDIARIES, BRANDS:** Resorts International hotels; Intertel (security); Chalk's International (airline charters).

Sales: $349.6 million (trend 62.7% a year).
Earnings: $45.25 million (trend 138.3% a year).
What happened to a $10,000 investment

Purchase Date	Purchase Price	Price on 12-31-81	Dividends Paid
12-31-71	$2.12	$16.62	$0.00
12-31-76	$3.54	$16.62	$0.00

Purchase Date	Cap. Gains (− Losses)	Total Return	Rate of Return
12-31-71	$68,235.29	$68,235.29	22.84%
12-31-76	$36,941.18	$36,941.18	36.24%

PROFILE: Anticipating the approval of casino gambling in Atlantic City in 1976, Resorts International bought extensive holdings in the Boardwalk area and other parts of the city, including the city's largest hotel. Bingo. The timing proved perfect, and the company's hotel casino in Atlantic City proved the largest money-maker ever among U.S. casinos. From $0.26 a share in 1977, earnings jumped to $4.57 in 1978 and to a peak of $6.84 in 1979.

Unfortunately for the company, it couldn't play "Monopoly" forever. It still may have the biggest casino in Atlantic City, but far from the only one. As the increased competition has been felt, earnings have declined. In 1980 the company earned $3.85 a share, and it was struggling in the early 1980s, though some analysts were optimistic about the longer term.

Resorts International's other businesses, Intertel (security) and Chalk's International (charter flights), have an insignificant effect on earnings. The stock remains pretty much a straight gambling play.

No dividends have been paid on these shares. With a zero yield, the whole story is capital gains (or losses). The balance sheet is leveraged, with debt recently about 42 percent of total capital.

The Atlantic City facility, which is being made still larger, recently accounted for about 80 percent of profits, with about 15 of the remaining 20 percent coming from the two hotel casinos in the Bahamas.

* * *

REVCO D. S., INC. (RDS). Founded 1956. Headquarters: 1925 Enterprise Parkway, Twinsburg OH 44087. **DRUG STORES.** Revco is a large national chain of retail drug stores. The company is also involved in some vitamin and drug manufacturing.

Sales: $1,310.4 million (trend 18.7% a year).
Earnings: $45.13 million (trend 18.2% a year).
What happened to a $10,000 investment

Purchase Date	*Purchase Price*	*Price on 12-31-81*	*Dividends Paid*
12-31-71	$13.50	$24.12	$1,777.78
12-31-76	$17.83	$24.12	$1,016.82

Purchase Date	*Cap. Gains (– Losses)*	*Total Return*	*Rate of Return*
12-31-71	$7,870.37	$9,648.15	6.99%
12-31-76	$3,528.04	$4,544.86	7.78%

* * *

REVERE COPPER AND BRASS (RVB). Founded 1928. Headquarters: 605 Third Ave., New York NY 10016. **COPPER, BRASS PRODUCTS.** Revere produces copper, brass, and aluminum in sheets, rolls, tubes, etc.; also involved in the production of cookware and electrical parts. **MAJOR SUBSIDIARIES, BRANDS:** Revere Ware.

Sales: $748.1 million (trend 14.9% a year).
Earnings: $21.78 million (trend 85.7% a year).
What happened to a $10,000 investment

Purchase Date	*Purchase Price*	*Price on 12-31-81*	*Dividends Paid*
12-31-71	$13.12	$14.75	$514.29
12-31-76	$ 9.62	$14.75	$311.69

Purchase Date	*Cap. Gains (– Losses)*	*Total Return*	*Rate of Return*
12-31-71	$1,238.10	$1,752.38	1.63%
12-31-76	$5,324.68	$5,636.36	9.35%

* * *

REVLON, INC. (REV). Founded 1955. Headquarters: 767 Fifth Ave., New York NY 10022. **COSMETICS, HEALTH CARE.** Revlon is the leading U.S. maker of cosmetics, and has also become, through acquisitions, a major producer of health-care products. 37,000 employees. **MAJOR SUBSIDIARIES, BRANDS:** Revlon; Charlie; Jontue; Flex; Milk Plus 6; Mitchum; Oxy; Technicon; USV (formerly U. S. Vitamin and Pharmaceutical Corp.); Norcliff Laboratories; Meloy Laboratories; Coburn Optical Industries; Barnes-Hind; Armour Pharmaceutical Co.; Lewis-Howe Co. (Tums); Continuous Curve Contact Lenses Inc.; Thompson Medical Co.

Sales: $2,203.3 million (trend 23.4% a year).
Earnings: $174.79 million (trend 23.2% a year).
What happened to a $10,000 investment

Purchase Date	*Purchase Price*	*Price on 12-31-81*	*Dividends Paid*
12-31-71	$34.81	$30.62	$2,960.14
12-31-76	$44.37	$30.62	$1,625.92

Purchase Date	*Cap. Gains (– Losses)*	*Total Return*	*Rate of Return*
12-31-71	$–1,202.87	$ 1,757.27	1.63%
12-31-76	$–3,098.59	$–1,472.68	–3.14%

PROFILE: If you have to describe Revlon briefly, you could do it with three *S*'s — secretive, savvy, and successful. Based on past advertising, some would add a fourth *S*, for sexy. Revlon had the marketing flair to produce ads in the 1950s that were risqué for their time. But during the 1970s, when women were more career oriented, the advertising (particularly for Charlie, now the nation's number-one perfume) turned more in that direction.

To all the *S*'s, add a *T*, for tough. Revlon's rivals know it as the most respected, and sometimes feared, factor in the fiercely competitive cosmetics business. Revlon leads the field with about a 19-percent market share and is gaining about 1 percent a year, according to a 1980 report in *Financial World*.

Less well known, and not publicized by the company, is its massive plunge into the health-care field. In the early 1980s, health-care products from a slew of acquisitions (see above) were already providing about 45 percent of sales. They may soon be the heart of the company. Among Revlon's catches were major producers of contact lens products (Barnes-Hind and Continuous Curve Contact Lens Inc.); a leading producer of interferon (Meloy Laboratories); and a promising maker of blood-analysis equipment (Technicon). Yet the stock's price / earnings ratio (7 to 12 recently) is more that of a solid cosmetics company than a successful drug company.

Earnings have grown strongly and consistently for the past decade. Dividends, paid since the year after incorporation, provide a moderate yield.

* * *

REXHAM CORP. (RXH). Founded 1971. Headquarters: 90 Park Ave., New York NY 10016. **PAPER, FILM.** Rexham manufactures paper and film products for packaging.

Sales: $168.9 million (trend 14.8% a year).
Earnings: $7.29 million (trend 18.2% a year).
What happened to a $10,000 investment

Purchase Date	Purchase Price	Price on 12-31-81	Dividends Paid
12-31-71	$ N/A	$15.25	$ N/A
12-31-76	$10.62	$15.25	$2,635.29

Purchase Date	Cap. Gains (− Losses)	Total Return	Rate of Return
12-31-71	$ N/A	$ N/A	N/A%
12-31-76	$4,352.94	$6,988.24	11.18%

* * *

REXNORD INC. (REX). Founded 1892. Headquarters: 777 E. Wisconsin Ave., Milwaukee WI 53202. **HEAVY MACHINERY.** Rexnord is a leading maker of power transmission equipment. It also makes rock crushing and mineral processing equipment, sewage treatment equipment, cement mixers, fasteners, and other products for heavy industry. 18,000 employees. **MAJOR SUBSIDIARIES, BRANDS:** Nordberg (rock and mineral crushing and handling equipment).

Sales: $1,130.0 million (trend 12.7% a year).
Earnings: $38.42 million (trend 1.5% a year).
What happened to a $10,000 investment

Purchase Date	Purchase Price	Price on 12-31-81	Dividends Paid
12-31-71	$13.37	$15.37	$5,381.93
12-31-76	$17.25	$15.37	$2,652.17

Purchase Date	Cap. Gains (− Losses)	Total Return	Rate of Return
12-31-71	$ 1,495.33	$6,877.26	5.37%
12-31-76	$−1,086.96	$1,565.22	2.95%

PROFILE: Throughout much of 1979–81, the economy was either clearly in a recession, anticipating a recession, or wondering whether or not it was in a recession. That sort of climate isn't conducive to capital spending, particularly on big-budget items. The capital goods companies, like Rexnord, have been languishing.

This situation won't last forever. The revised tax structure, with decreased business taxes and accelerated depreciation for new equipment, is designed to encourage industry in the long run to take on both new equipment and new workers. Businesses won't take those steps until the outlook is brighter, until recently idle production capacity is tapped, and until inventories are reduced. When it finally comes, the long-bruited capital goods boom may come with a rush.

Rexnord will unquestionably benefit when the boom arrives. But whether it's the best stock in which to ride the long-awaited wave is another question. Its history has been one of markedly cyclical earnings, fairly slow earnings growth, and unspectacular profitability. On the other hand, the company has weathered a lot of storms, paid dividends each year since 1894, and shown consistent profitability. The dividend yield is substantial — recently in the 6-to-7 percent range. The balance sheet shows about the average amount of debt, with long-term debt recently just under a third of total capital.

* * *

R. J. REYNOLDS INDUSTRIES, INC. (RJR). Founded 1899. Headquarters: Reynolds Blvd., Winston-Salem NC 27102. **TOBACCO.** R. J. Reynolds is the largest U.S. cigarette manufacturer. Also has major subsidiaries in foods, shipping, and energy. 83,000 employees. **MAJOR SUBSIDIARIES, BRANDS:** Winston, Salem, Camel, and Vantage cigarettes; Del Monte foods (including Chun King); Sea-Land Service shipping; Aminoil oil and gas.

Sales: $8,449.0 million (trend 18.4% a year).
Earnings: $639.80 million (trend 14.2% a year).
What happened to a $10,000 investment

Purchase Date	Purchase Price	Price on 12-31-81	Dividends Paid
12-31-71	$29.12	$47.12	$5,850.99
12-31-76	$33.81	$47.12	$2,981.15

Purchase Date	Cap. Gains (− Losses)	Total Return	Rate of Return
12-31-71	$6,180.26	$12,031.24	8.22%
12-31-76	$3,937.15	$ 6,918.30	11.09%

PROFILE: R. J. Reynolds owns three companies each big enough to merit potential listing on the Big Board, were they independent. One is Del Monte, which produces canned fruits under that well-known name, as well as Hawaiian Punch, Chun King, Morton Frozen Foods, and other food products. A second is Sea-Land Service, a large but struggling shipping concern which is the world's biggest containerized shipping firm. A third is Aminoil, formerly American Independent Oil Co., which probably ranks among the forty largest oil companies in the United States, and perhaps in the top thirty. Put these three substantial firms together and you'd have a sizable conglomerate, even without the tobacco business. Yet the fact is that the three big diversifications contribute a bit less than half of sales and barely a quarter of earnings.

Tobacco still accounts for almost three quarters of profits. Like several other tobacco firms, Reynolds is finding that its diversifications aren't as profitable as its original business. To the dismay of some analysts, who see cigarettes as a no-growth market, Reynolds has embarked on a $1-billion expansion program for cigarette production. Presumably, it's banking on exports for growth. In the United States, Reynolds has about one third of a stable market.

So strong is the company's financial condition that the heavy expenditures may be financed entirely from cash flow. The balance sheet is strong, with debt recently (and traditionally) around 20 percent of capital. Return on equity has been consistently in the 17-to-20 percent range. Dividends have been paid each year since 1900; the yield in recent years has been from 5 to 6½ percent.

* * *

REYNOLDS METALS CO. (RLM). Founded 1928. Headquarters: Reynolds Metals Bldg., 6601 Broad St. Rd., Richmond VA 23261. ALUMINUM. Reynolds is the second largest U.S. aluminum company. 37,000 employees. MAJOR SUBSIDIARIES, BRANDS: Robertshaw Controls Co. (30 percent owned).

Sales: $3,653.2 million (trend 16.9% a year).
Earnings: $178.20 million (trend 28.2% a year).
What happened to a $10,000 investment

Purchase Date	*Purchase Price*	*Price on 12-31-81*	*Dividends Paid*
12-31-71	$17.87	$24.25	$7,566.43
12-31-76	$40.25	$24.25	$2,378.88

Purchase Date	*Cap. Gains (− Losses)*	*Total Return*	*Rate of Return*
12-31-71	$ 3,566.43	$ 11,132.87	7.77%
12-31-76	$−3,975.16	$−1,596.27	−3.42%

PROFILE: Cars and houses are the outlets for a major slice of every aluminum maker's production. However, the auto industry and housing industry have been in a slump. The can industry, another major customer, hasn't exactly been booming. And the cost of electricity, a major raw material in the production of aluminum, has been rising. With all these negative factors, it's little wonder that the stocks of all the major aluminum companies are hiding in the basement.

They may be found there by bargain hunters who like their low price / earnings ratios. Reynolds, for example, was selling for as little as 4 times earnings during much of the period from 1978 to 1981. It also offers a substantial dividend yield — around 6 to 8 percent in recent years. Dividends have been paid yearly since 1942, raised yearly since 1975, and are well covered by earnings. The balance sheet is about average, with debt recently about 35 percent of capital. But that's an improvement; debt has been gradually paired from about 53 percent of capital in the early 1970s.

On fundamentals, then, this stock might be a good value. To boot, there's the possibility that the need for lighter cars will cause car makers to step up their use of the lightweight metal. However, you shouldn't necessarily choose this stock if you want to invest in the aluminum industry. According to *Forbes* magazine's *Annual Report on American Industry,* published in 1981, Reynolds was the least profitable of the four major aluminum makers (the other three are Alcan, Alcoa, and Kaiser), and had the lowest sales growth rate of the four.

* * *

RICHARDSON CO. (RDS). Founded 1898. Headquarters: 2400 E. Devon Ave., Des Plains IL 60018. INDUSTRIAL GOODS, CHEMICALS. This company manufactures materials for industry, such as cases, fabrics, and seals; also makes chemicals for detergents, insecticides, and personal products. In 1982 Witco Chemical Corp. acquired a controlling interest in Richardson, and the stock was delisted by the New York Stock Exchange.

* * *

RICHARDSON-VICKS INC. (RVI). Founded 1933. Headquarters: 10 Westport Rd., Wilton CT 06897. HEALTH CARE, COSMETICS. Richardson-Vicks is a major manufacturer of over-the-counter medications and toiletries. 15,000 employees. MAJOR SUBSIDIARIES, BRANDS: Vicks VapoRub, cough drops, and cough syrup; Oil of Olay; Clearasil; Lavoris; Baker Diagnostics, J. T. Baker Chemical Co.

Sales: $1,088.1 million (trend 9.4% a year).
Earnings: $83.20 million (trend 11.5% a year).
What happened to a $10,000 investment

Purchase Date	*Purchase Price*	*Price on 12-31-81*	*Dividends Paid*
12-31-71	$33.75	$27.50	$2,389.63
12-31-76	$25.75	$27.50	$2,011.65

Purchase Date	*Cap. Gains (– Losses)*	*Total Return*	*Rate of Return*
12-31-71	$–1,851.85	$ 537.78	.53%
12-31-76	$ 679.61	$2,691.26	4.88%

PROFILE: When the woman down the street gets a divorce and changes her name, one is never quite sure whether congratulations are in order. But when Richardson-Merrell decided to sell its Merrell prescription drug division, nearly everybody was happy. *Fortune* magazine quipped, while the deal was pending, that any Richardson shareholder tempted to vote against it "should perhaps consider applying Vicks VapoRub to his person. He would appear to need a little something to clear his head." Wall Street greeted the sale by pushing the price of Richardson shares up substantially, though the price later retreated.

The trouble with Merrell was that it was lawsuit prone. It has been involved in litigation over thalidomide, Mer-29, and Bendectin. Also, many drug industry observers thought Merrell was simply too small to generate an adequate budget for long-term research. Dow Chemical was glad to add Merrell to its growing pharmaceutical holdings for $260 million in stock.

Richardson didn't simply resume its maiden name. Rather, it added Vicks after the hyphen, in honor of its best-known and best-selling product. But there's — excuse the expression — the rub. Vicks is an old product; so are most of Richardson-Vicks's other offerings. Perhaps for this reason, the shares command only an average price / earnings multiple (8 in early 1982). The balance sheet is extremely strong, with debt less than 5 percent of capital recently. Dividends provide a moderate yield. The company is known to be looking for a major acquisition.

* * *

RIEGEL TEXTILE CORP. (RTX). Founded 1946. Headquarters: Green Gate Park, Suite 800, 25 Woods Lake Rd., Greenville SC 29607. **TEXTILES.** This firm produces textiles for the clothing, industrial, home furnishings, and baby products markets.

Sales: $455.3 million (trend 8.6% a year).
Earnings: $16.73 million (trend 2.8% a year).
What happened to a $10,000 investment

Purchase Date	*Purchase Price*	*Price on 12-31-81*	*Dividends Paid*
12-31-71	$11.42	$20.62	$10,087.88
12-31-76	$20.62	$20.62	$ 3,769.70

Purchase Date	*Cap. Gains (– Losses)*	*Total Return*	*Rate of Return*
12-31-71	$8,065.69	$18,153.58	10.91%
12-31-76	$ –.00	$ 3,769.70	6.61%

* * *

RIO GRANDE INDUSTRIES, INC. (RGI). Founded 1920. Headquarters: 1 Park Central, 1515 Arapahoe St., Denver CO 80217. **RAILROADS, TRUCKING.** This holding company controls a medium-sized railroad and a small trucking company; also provides computer services. **MAJOR SUBSIDIARIES, BRANDS:** Denver and Rio Grande Western Railroad; Rio Grande Motor Way.

Sales: $349.9 million (trend 14.0% a year).
Earnings: $29.62 million (trend 27.5% a year).
What happened to a $10,000 investment

Purchase Date	*Purchase Price*	*Price on 12-31-81*	*Dividends Paid*
12-31-71	$24.25	$34.12	$3,195.88
12-31-76	$21.25	$34.12	$2,211.76

Purchase Date	*Cap. Gains (– Losses)*	*Total Return*	*Rate of Return*
12-31-71	$4,072.16	$7,268.04	5.61%
12-31-76	$6,058.82	$8,270.59	12.81%

* * *

RITE AID CORP. (RAD). Founded 1968. Headquarters: Trindle Rd. and Railroad Ave., Shiremanstown PA 17011. **DRUG STORES.** Rite Aid operates a large chain of drug stores in the eastern portion of the United States.

Sales: $944.2 million (trend 19.4% a year).
Earnings: $35.88 million (trend 24.7% a year).
What happened to a $10,000 investment

Purchase Date	*Purchase Price*	*Price on 12-31-81*	*Dividends Paid*
12-31-71	$20.81	$28.62	$1,018.97
12-31-76	$13.03	$28.62	$1,218.79

Purchase Date	*Cap. Gains (– Losses)*	*Total Return*	*Rate of Return*
12-31-71	$ 3,753.41	$ 4,772.38	3.98%
12-31-76	$11,965.87	$13,184.66	18.32%

* * *

ROADWAY EXPRESS, INC. (ROAD, Over-the-Counter). Founded 1930. Headquarters: 1077 George Blvd., Akron OH 44309. **TRUCKING.** Roadway is the nation's largest trucking firm, operating more than 23,000 trucks, tractors, and trailers, and more than 400 depots. 23,000 employees.

Sales: $1,154.9 million (trend 19.0% a year).
Earnings: $69.66 million (trend 13.5% a year).
What happened to a $10,000 investment

Purchase Date	*Purchase Price*	*Price on 12-31-81*	*Dividends Paid*
12-31-71	$17.43	$38.25	$2,962.52
12-31-76	$45.25	$38.25	$ 864.64

Purchase Date	*Cap. Gains (− Losses)*	*Total Return*	*Rate of Return*
12-31-71	$ 11,947.59	$14,910.11	9.56%
12-31-76	$−1,546.96	$ −682.32	−1.40%

PROFILE: Roadway's orange trucks and trailers are ubiquitous on America's highways. Almost anyone who's ridden on an interstate highway lately can discern that Roadway is a big company. What's less well known is that it's an extraordinarily successful one.

The company maintains a low profile, following the dictum of founder Galen Roush, who said, "A whale would never be harpooned if he didn't swim to the surface." Roadway has never been listed on the New York Stock Exchange, although its revenues are now more than $1 billion a year. It avoids interviews and publicity.

But the figures have all the force of a semi at full throttle. It's likely that the company will chalk up its thirtieth straight year of record sales and profits in 1982, an incredible record of defying recessions in an industry noted for its vulnerability to them. In an age when leverage and debt are the norm, Roadway's capitalization consists of 100 percent common stock — no debt, no preferred. Earnings growth and return on equity are both in the 20-percent range.

It would take quite a bushel to hide these lights under. And so, despite its penchant for secrecy, Roadway's success has not exactly gone unnoticed. Wall Street has dished out a multiple of about 12 to 14 for this stock, as of the early 1980s, when the average stock traded at about 8 times earnings. Descendents of Galen Roush own more than a quarter of the stock, and institutions also own a fair amount.

The company's success is due in large part to top-notch planning and local autonomy for depot managers. The company specializes in "less than truckload" shipments, which competitors used to disdain. But Roadway can charge a higher price per pound for these, making up for the need for frequent stops. Cramming up to twenty-eight loads into a truck, the company keeps careful track of its paperwork and plans loading and unloading for maximum efficiency.

The dividend yield is modest, but dividends have been raised each year since 1967.

* * *

ROBERTSHAW CONTROLS CO. (ROF). Founded 1926. Headquarters: 1701 Byrd Ave., Richmond VA 23261. **CONTROL DEVICES.** Robertshaw produces automatic control units for heating, cooling, electricity, and industrial processes.

Sales: $349.0 million (trend 11.8% a year).
Earnings: $10.18 million (trend 22.4% a year).
What happened to a $10,000 investment

Purchase Date	*Purchase Price*	*Price on 12-31-81*	*Dividends Paid*
12-31-71	$37.87	$18.50	$2,773.60
12-31-76	$23.12	$18.50	$2,767.57

Purchase Date	*Cap. Gains (− Losses)*	*Total Return*	*Rate of Return*
12-31-71	$−5,115.51	$−2,341.91	−2.63%
12-31-76	$−2,000.00	$ 767.57	1.49%

* * *

ROBERTSON (H. H.) CO. (RHH). Founded 1916. Headquarters: 2 Gateway Center, Pittsburgh PA 15222. **BUILDING PRODUCTS.** This company makes and installs building products for business and industry and is also a manufacturer of synthetic resins.

Sales: $571.2 million (trend 11.5% a year).
Earnings: $19.60 million (trend 9.5% a year).
What happened to a $10,000 investment

Purchase Date	*Purchase Price*	*Price on 12-31-81*	*Dividends Paid*
12-31-71	$11.69	$30.62	$6,973.26
12-31-76	$12.75	$30.62	$3,901.96

Purchase Date	*Cap. Gains (− Losses)*	*Total Return*	*Rate of Return*
12-31-71	$16,203.21	$23,176.47	12.74%
12-31-76	$14,019.61	$17,921.57	22.80%

* * *

ROBINS (A. H.) CO., INC. (RAH). Founded 1948. Headquarters: 1407 Cummings Dr., Richmond VA 23220. **HEALTH-CARE PRODUCTS.** A. H. Robins manufactures health-care and consumer products. **MAJOR SUBSIDIARIES, BRANDS:** Robitussin; ChapStick; Sergeant's; Dalkon Shield (discontinued).

Sales: $432.3 million (trend 12.1% a year).
Earnings: $25.47 million (trend 2.8% a year).
What happened to a $10,000 investment

Purchase Date	*Purchase Price*	*Price on 12-31-81*	*Dividends Paid*
12-31-71	$22.12	$12.25	$1,435.03
12-31-76	$12.25	$12.25	$1,567.35

Purchase Date	*Cap. Gains (− Losses)*	*Total Return*	*Rate of Return*
12-31-71	$−4,463.28	$−3,028.25	−3.54%
12-31-76	$ −.00	$ 1,567.35	2.95%

* * *

ROCHESTER GAS AND ELECTRIC CORP. (RGS). Founded 1904. Headquarters: 89 East Ave., Rochester NY 14649. **ELECTRICITY, GAS.** This company supplies electricity and gas to the city of Rochester, New York, using primarily nuclear and coal generators.

Sales: $502.4 million (trend 12.4% a year).
Earnings: $34.72 million (trend 9.2% a year).
What happened to a $10,000 investment

Purchase Date	*Purchase Price*	*Price on 12-31-81*	*Dividends Paid*
12-31-71	$17.70	$14.32	$6,488.42
12-31-76	$16.65	$14.32	$3,975.00

Purchase Date	*Cap. Gains (− Losses)*	*Total Return*	*Rate of Return*
12-31-71	$−1,909.13	$4,579.29	3.84%
12-31-76	$−1,396.61	$2,578.39	4.69%

* * *

ROCHESTER TELEPHONE CORP. (RTC). Founded 1920. Headquarters: 100 Midtown Plaza, Rochester NY 14646. **TELEPHONE.** This is an independent telephone company that services the city of Rochester and the surrounding areas.

Sales: $180.2 million (trend 9.9% a year).
Earnings: $28.47 million (trend 18.4% a year).
What happened to a $10,000 investment

Purchase Date	*Purchase Price*	*Price on 12-31-81*	*Dividends Paid*
12-31-71	$22.25	$28.12	$4,959.55
12-31-76	$15.50	$28.12	$4,767.74

Purchase Date	*Cap. Gains (− Losses)*	*Total Return*	*Rate of Return*
12-31-71	$2,640.45	$ 7,600.00	5.82%
12-31-76	$8,145.16	$12,912.90	18.04%

* * *

ROCKWELL INTERNATIONAL CORP. (ROK). Founded 1928. Headquarters: 600 Grant St., Pittsburgh PA 15219. **AEROSPACE, ELECTRONICS, AUTOMOTIVE.** Rockwell is a major aerospace company and prime contractor for the Space Shuttle program. It is a major supplier of defense electronics, truck and auto parts, and printing presses, and has sidelines in several other industrial products. **MAJOR SUBSIDIARIES, BRANDS:** Space Shuttle Orbiter; B-1 bomber.

Sales: $7,039.7 million (trend 6.2% a year).
Earnings: $290.00 million (trend 22.5% a year).
What happened to a $10,000 investment

Purchase Date	*Purchase Price*	*Price on 12-31-81*	*Dividends Paid*
12-31-71	$15.31	$32.75	$7,030.20
12-31-76	$15.37	$32.75	$4,042.28

Purchase Date	*Cap. Gains (− Losses)*	*Total Return*	*Rate of Return*
12-31-71	$11,387.76	$18,417.96	11.01%
12-31-76	$11,300.81	$15,343.09	20.44%

PROFILE: Rockwell's prestige is flying high as a result of the Space Shuttle, on which it is prime contractor. Still, it remains remarkably little known for a company that employs more than 100,000 people, and that is among the 50 largest industrial corporations in this country.

More than two thirds of this nation's daily newspapers use presses made by Rockwell. But in those papers, you'll rarely find much about the company. The reason isn't hard to find: Rockwell doesn't make consumer products. It used to make several — Admiral radios, for example — but consumer products were never highly successful here, and they've been gradually phased out in recent years.

Rockwell is among the country's largest defense contractors. Besides the Space Shuttle, it is prime contractor for the B-1 bomber and a major subcontractor on the proposed MX missile. Aerospace and electronics account for a bit more than half of sales and profits.

About another quarter of sales comes from automotive parts, mainly truck parts. In this sector, the company is trying to emphasize sales to foreign manufacturers to lessen its dependence on Detroit, which hasn't been a great customer of late.

In recent years, Rockwell has boosted return on equity to more than 17 percent, while trimming debt to less than 20 percent of capital. The stock market expressed its appreciation by upping the price / earnings ratio from the 4 to 9 range, where it was stuck for most of the 1970s, into the 10 to 12 range in the early 1980s. Dividends, paid yearly since 1948, provide a moderate yield.

* * *

ROHM AND HAAS CO. (ROH). Founded 1917. Headquarters: Independence Mall W., Philadelphia PA 19105. **CHEMICALS.** The company is a major producer of specialty chemicals, including herbicides, plastics, and ingredients for paint and floor polish. 13,000 employees. **MAJOR SUBSIDIARIES, BRANDS:** Plexiglas; Blazer herbicide.

Sales: $1,725.3 million (trend 11.6% a year).
Earnings: $93.74 million (trend 30.8% a year).
What happened to a $10,000 investment

Purchase Date	*Purchase Price*	*Price on 12-31-81*	*Dividends Paid*
12-31-71	$55.25	$61.25	$2,659.73
12-31-76	$48.25	$61.25	$1,898.45

Purchase Date	*Cap. Gains (− Losses)*	*Total Return*	*Rate of Return*
12-31-71	$1,085.97	$3,745.70	3.23%
12-31-76	$2,694.30	$4,592.75	7.85%

PROFILE: It's hard to win a race when you've tripped in the middle. That's something like the problem that faced Rohm and Haas in the 1970s. After achieving peak earnings of more than $74 million in 1974, the company slid to $23 million in 1975 and lost almost $12 million the following year. A large part of the trouble was the company's attempt to go head on with such giants as DuPont and Celanese in the fibers field.

Rohm and Haas has since given up fibers. It gradually built earnings back up to a new peak of more than $95 million in 1979, then slipped to just under $94 million in the recession years of 1980 and 1981. For the decade as a whole, its growth rates and profitability weren't impressive. *Forbes* ranked Rohm and Haas thirteenth in profitability among fourteen major diversified chemical firms, in the magazine's *Annual Report on American Industry,* published in 1981.

Recently, the biggest selling point for the stock has been the development of Blazer, a herbicide that kills broad-leafed weeds in soybean fields. Some analysts think this product could capture about a third of this large market.

The stock carried an average price / earnings ratio (around 8) in the early 1980s. The balance sheet is also roughly average, with debt around a quarter of total capital. Dividends have been paid here each year since 1927, have been rising about in pace with inflation, and provide a moderate yield.

* * *

ROHR INDUSTRIES, INC. (RHR). Founded 1949. Headquarters: Chula Vista CA 92012. **AIRCRAFT COMPONENTS.** Rohr Industries is a leading supplier of parts and assemblies for aircraft, marine vessels, and rockets.

Sales: $543.9 million (trend 10.7% a year).
Earnings: $6.09 million (trend 17.2% a year).
What happened to a $10,000 investment

Purchase Date	*Purchase Price*	*Price on 12-31-81*	*Dividends Paid*
12-31-71	$16.37	$12.50	$1,984.73
12-31-76	$ 6.25	$12.50	$ 0.00

Purchase Date	*Cap. Gains (− Losses)*	*Total Return*	*Rate of Return*
12-31-71	$−2,366.41	$ −381.68	−.39%
12-31-76	$ 10,000.00	$10,000.00	14.87%

* * *

ROLLINS, INC. (ROL). Founded 1948. Headquarters: 2170 Piedmont Rd. N.E., Atlanta GA 30324. **INSECT CONTROL, OIL, BROADCASTING.** Rollins, Inc., is a diversified company with interests in termite and pest control; oil and gas production; and TV and radio broadcasting. **MAJOR SUBSIDIARIES, BRANDS:** Rollins-Orkin; Patterson Services; Rollins Protective Services.

Sales: $454.6 million (trend 15.3% a year).
Earnings: $44.44 million (trend 14.0% a year).
What happened to a $10,000 investment

Purchase Date	*Purchase Price*	*Price on 12-31-81*	*Dividends Paid*
12-31-71	$16.31	$17.50	$1,305.29
12-31-76	$12.06	$17.50	$1,347.15

Purchase Date	Cap. Gains (— Losses)	Total Return	Rate of Return
12-31-71	$ 727.97	$2,033.26	1.87%
12-31-76	$4,507.77	$5,854.92	9.66%

* * *

ROLM CORP. (RM). Founded 1969. Headquarters: 4900 Old Ironsides Dr., Santa Clara CA 95050. **COMPUTERS.** Rolm Corp. is involved in the design and production of computers and telecommunications systems based on computers.

Sales: $294.6 million (trend 81.4% a year).
Earnings: $23.78 million (trend 93.1% a year).
What happened to a $10,000 investment

Purchase Date	Purchase Price	Price on 12-31-81	Dividends Paid
12-31-71	$N/A	$32.25	$0.00
12-31-76	$ 1.70	$32.25	$0.00

Purchase Date	Cap. Gains (— Losses)	Total Return	Rate of Return
12-31-71	$ N/A	$ N/A	N/A%
12-31-76	$179,357.80	$179,357.80	80.08%

* * *

RONSON CORP. (RON). Founded 1928. Headquarters: 1 Ronson Rd., Bridgewater NJ 08807. **CIGARETTE LIGHTERS, APPLIANCES.** This diversified company manufactures cigarette lighters, food preparation appliances, and gas appliances. Ronson is also active in the production of aerospace items.

Sales: $142.9 million (trend 2.7% a year).
Earnings: $−5.60 million.
What happened to a $10,000 investment

Purchase Date	Purchase Price	Price on 12-31-81	Dividends Paid
12-31-71	$5.89	$2.37	$1,276.30
12-31-76	$4.25	$2.37	$ 0.00

Purchase Date	Cap. Gains (— Losses)	Total Return	Rate of Return
12-31-71	$−5,968.97	$−4,692.66	−6.14%
12-31-76	$−4,411.76	$−4,411.76	−10.99%

* * *

ROPER CORP. (ROP). Founded 1963. Headquarters: 1905 W. Court St., Kankakee IL 60901. **POWER EQUIPMENT, APPLIANCES.** Roper is a diversified firm that is a major supplier to Sears. The company produces cooking ranges, lawn mowers, chain saws, and other goods for the home.

Sales: $427.5 million (trend 3.2% a year).
Earnings: $6.30 million (trend −14.1% a year).
What happened to a $10,000 investment

Purchase Date	Purchase Price	Price on 12-31-81	Dividends Paid
12-31-71	$16.94	$13.50	$3,948.34
12-31-76	$11.75	$13.50	$3,361.70

Purchase Date	Cap. Gains (— Losses)	Total Return	Rate of Return
12-31-71	$−2,029.52	$1,918.82	1.77%
12-31-76	$ 1,489.36	$4,851.06	8.23%

* * *

RORER GROUP, INC. (ROR). Founded 1968. Headquarters: 500 Virginia Dr., Fort Washington PA 19034. **PHARMACEUTICALS.** Rorer Group is active in the production of drugs — mostly antacids — and surgical products. **MAJOR SUBSIDIARIES, BRANDS:** Maalox.

Sales: $312.5 million (trend 1.9% a year).
Earnings: $32.28 million (trend 2.8% a year).
What happened to a $10,000 investment

Purchase Date	Purchase Price	Price on 12-31-81	Dividends Paid
12-31-71	$34.75	$18.12	$2,345.32
12-31-76	$19.50	$18.12	$2,030.77

Purchase Date	Cap. Gains (— Losses)	Total Return	Rate of Return
12-31-71	$−4,784.17	$−2,438.85	−2.76%
12-31-76	$ −705.13	$ 1,325.64	2.52%

* * *

ROUSE CO. (ROUS, Over-the-Counter). Founded 1956. Headquarters: Rouse Co. Bldg., Columbia MD 21044. **REAL ESTATE DEVELOPMENT.** Rouse is a major developer of regional shopping centers and, in particular, of downtown urban centers. 3,000 employees.

PROFILE: Flair, innovation, even genius: It's fair to apply those words to the outstanding efforts this company (under founder James Rouse) has put into the conception and execution of its developments, such as Harbor Place in Baltimore or Faneuil Hall Marketplace in Boston. But that doesn't necessarily make this a good stock.

A high quotient of admiration for Mr. Rouse and

his company is built into the price of the stock. In 1968 the stock sold for close to 100 times earnings. After dipping for a time into the more realistic territory between 10 and 20, the p / e had again soared to around 40 in the early 1980s. A 1981 cover story on Rouse in *Time* magazine may have helped to feed investor enthusiasm.

In the early 1970s, *Forbes* magazine ran a flattering piece on McDonald's, then selling at 60 times earnings, but asked whether the company could really be worth that multiple. It answered its own question rhetorically: "Is any stock worth 60 times earnings?" In the case of McDonald's, earnings went up but the stock went down. The same could happen to Rouse.

Evaluated from the point of view of its financial statistics, rather than the beauty and imagination of its architecture, Rouse presents a less than engaging vista. To start with, leverage is extremely high, debt recently constituting about 94 percent of capital. The company lost money four years running from 1972 to 75. Earnings peaked at $0.44 a share in 1978 before declining to $0.24 in 1979 and rebounding to $0.29 in 1980 and $0.37 in 1981. Yet the stock in early 1982 was selling for about $16 a share. Clearly, people are buying the sizzle and not the steak.

* * *

ROWAN COMPANIES, INC. (RDC). Founded 1947. Headquarters: 1900 Oak Tower Bldg., 5051 Westheimer, Houston TX 77056. OIL AND GAS DRILLING. This company is primarily a contract drilling operation for onshore and offshore sites in the United States and abroad.

Sales: $255.2 million (trend 33.0% a year).
Earnings: $68.62 million (trend 31.4% a year).
What happened to a $10,000 investment

Purchase Date	*Purchase Price*	*Price on 12-31-81*	*Dividends Paid*
12-31-71	$ .95	$16.50	$2,105.99
12-31-76	$1.77	$16.50	$ 870.80

Purchase Date	*Cap. Gains (— Losses)*	*Total Return*	*Rate of Return*
12-31-71	$163,929.29	$166,035.28	33.22%
12-31-76	$ 83,451.33	$ 84,322.12	56.65%

* * *

ROYAL CROWN COMPANIES, INC. (RCC). Founded 1928. Headquarters: 41 Perimeter Center East, N.E., Atlanta GA 30346. SOFT DRINKS, FAST FOOD, HOME FURNISHINGS. This company is a major producer of soft drinks, as well as the operator of the Arby's restaurant chain. It is also active in home decor products and citrus juices.

Sales: $438.1 million (trend 12.0% a year).
Earnings: $10.17 million (trend −11.0% a year).
What happened to a $10,000 investment

Purchase Date	*Purchase Price*	*Price on 12-31-81*	*Dividends Paid*
12-31-71	$35.25	$14.37	$2,353.19
12-31-76	$17.62	$14.37	$2,859.57

Purchase Date	*Cap. Gains (— Losses)*	*Total Return*	*Rate of Return*
12-31-71	$−5,921.99	$−3,568.79	−4.32%
12-31-76	$−1,843.97	$ 1,015.60	1.95%

* * *

ROYAL DUTCH PETROLEUM CO. (RD). Founded 1890. Headquarters: 30 Carel van Bylandtlaan, The Hague, The Netherlands. OIL. Royal Dutch owns 60 percent of the Royal Dutch-Shell Group, a leading international oil producer. For further details, see Shell Oil Company.

Sales: $47,352.0 million (trend 21.7% a year).
Earnings: $2,972.13 million (trend 24.5% a year).
What happened to a $10,000 investment

Purchase Date	*Purchase Price*	*Price on 12-31-81*	*Dividends Paid*
12-31-71	$17.37	$34.87	$12,165.70
12-31-76	$26.19	$34.87	$ 5,037.06

Purchase Date	*Cap. Gains (— Losses)*	*Total Return*	*Rate of Return*
12-31-71	$10,071.94	$22,237.64	12.42%
12-31-76	$ 3,317.42	$ 8,354.48	12.91%

* * *

RUBBERMAID, INC. (RBD). Founded 1920. Headquarters: 1147 Akron Rd., Wooster OH 44691. PLASTIC, RUBBER PRODUCTS. Rubbermaid produces and markets plastic and rubber products for the home and car. It also manufactures a line of similar goods for commercial and institutional use.

Sales: $308.9 million (trend 15.7% a year).
Earnings: $20.10 million (trend 15.3% a year).
What happened to a $10,000 investment

Purchase Date	*Purchase Price*	*Price on 12-31-81*	*Dividends Paid*
12-31-71	$31.31	$36.87	$1,884.23
12-31-76	$26.37	$36.87	$1,569.67

Purchase Date	*Cap. Gains (– Losses)*	*Total Return*	*Rate of Return*
12-31-71	$1,776.45	$3,660.68	3.17%
12-31-76	$3,981.04	$5,550.71	9.23%

* * *

RUSS TOGS, INC. (RTS). Founded 1946. Headquarters: 1411 Broadway, New York NY 10018. APPAREL. Russ Togs manufactures a variety of garments for women and children, along with shirts for men and women. MAJOR SUBSIDIARIES, BRANDS: Russ; Crazy Horse; Sutton.

Sales: $190.4 million (trend 7.2% a year).
Earnings: $8.67 million (trend 7.5% a year).
What happened to a $10,000 investment

Purchase Date	*Purchase Price*	*Price on 12-31-81*	*Dividends Paid*
12-31-71	$21.25	$14.50	$3,331.76
12-31-76	$11.12	$14.50	$3,056.18

Purchase Date	*Cap. Gains (– Losses)*	*Total Return*	*Rate of Return*
12-31-71	$–3,176.47	$ 155.29	.15%
12-31-76	$ 3,033.71	$6,089.89	9.98%

* * *

RYAN HOMES, INC. (RYN). Founded 1948. Headquarters: 100 Ryan Court, Pittsburgh PA 15205. HOMEBUILDER. Ryan Homes is one of the country's most active homebuilders, constructing single-family homes, townhouses, and apartments.

Sales: $425.9 million (trend 20.6% a year).
Earnings: $15.51 million (trend 11.6% a year).
What happened to a $10,000 investment

Purchase Date	*Purchase Price*	*Price on 12-31-81*	*Dividends Paid*
12-31-71	$28.50	$18.75	$2,035.09
12-31-76	$19.87	$18.75	$2,415.09

Purchase Date	*Cap. Gains (– Losses)*	*Total Return*	*Rate of Return*
12-31-71	$–3,421.05	$–1,385.96	–1.48%
12-31-76	$ –566.04	$ 1,849.06	3.45%

* * *

RYDER SYSTEM, INC. (RDR). Founded 1955. Headquarters: 3600 N.W. 82nd Ave., Miami FL 33166. TRUCK LEASING AND SERVICES. This company is involved in the leasing and rentals of trucks, along with the operation of truckstops and transportation services. MAJOR SUBSIDIARIES, BRANDS: Truckstops of America; The Automotive Carrier.

Sales: $1,694.1 million (trend 23.3% a year).
Earnings: $56.52 million (trend 37.0% a year).
What happened to a $10,000 investment

Purchase Date	*Purchase Price*	*Price on 12-31-81*	*Dividends Paid*
12-31-71	$29.92	$29.37	$1,536.32
12-31-76	$12.18	$29.37	$3,129.98

Purchase Date	*Cap. Gains (– Losses)*	*Total Return*	*Rate of Return*
12-31-71	$ –182.76	$ 1,353.56	1.28%
12-31-76	$14,108.72	$17,238.70	22.19%

S

SCA SERVICES, INC. (SCV). Founded 1969. Headquarters: 60 State St., Boston MA 02109. WASTE MANAGEMENT. Major factor in chemical and liquid waste disposal and recovery.

Sales: $269.1 million (trend 12.9% a year).
Earnings: $16.56 million (trend 68.0% a year).
What happened to a $10,000 investment

Purchase Date	*Purchase Price*	*Price on 12-31-81*	*Dividends Paid*
12-31-71	$16.48	$16.12	$0.00
12-31-76	$ 2.27	$16.12	$0.00

Purchase Date	*Cap. Gains (– Losses)*	*Total Return*	*Rate of Return*
12-31-71	$ –218.35	$ –218.35	–.22%
12-31-76	$61,111.03	$61,111.03	48.04%

* * *

SCM CORP. (SCM). Founded 1958. Headquarters: 299 Park Ave., New York NY 10017. CONGLOMERATE. SCM, formerly Smith-Corona, produces typewriters, paint, paper, chemicals, food, titanium dioxide and other pigments, copiers, and small appliances. 27,000 employees. MAJOR SUBSIDIARIES, BRANDS: Smith-Corona (typewriters); Glidden Coatings and Resins (paint); Allied Paper; Durkee Foods; Proctor-Silex (small appliances).

Sales: $1,938.4 million (trend 8.9% a year).
Earnings: $56.51 million (trend 13.5% a year).
What happened to a $10,000 investment

Purchase Date	*Purchase Price*	*Price on 12-31-81*	*Dividends Paid*
12-31-71	$17.87	$21.87	$4,475.52
12-31-76	$21.75	$21.87	$2,896.55

Purchase Date	*Cap. Gains (− Losses)*	*Total Return*	*Rate of Return*
12-31-71	$2,237.76	$6,713.29	5.27%
12-31-76	$ 57.47	$2,954.02	5.31%

PROFILE: SCM's typewriters have been a favorite graduation gift for years. But SCM's stock hasn't been a favorite. The shares have never regained the favor they enjoyed in the late 1960s (when they sold for around $40 to $75, versus around $15 to $32 recently), and the stock price has been fairly flat for the past decade.

The firm has spent a lot of time and money fighting off stockholders' suits (first from N. Norman Muller, then from the more formidable Willard F. Rockwell). The gist of the dissidents' demands was that SCM should spin off unprofitable divisions and split the remaining divisions into two or more companies. Their reasoning: As a conglomerate, SCM had engendered little enthusiasm and was undervalued by the stock market. Splitting the company, the argument goes, would force a more realistic valuation. Even though the dissidents haven't yet prevailed (SCM bought back Rockwell's stock from him), their plan may come to pass.

It's true that SCM shares have been in the doghouse. The stock carried a lowly p / e of 5 in the early 1980s. Gradual increases in the dividend, coupled with stagnation in the stock price, has created a rising dividend yield — over 7 percent in 1981. Dividends were resumed in 1973 after a hiatus when the company stumbled badly in the early 1970s. The problems were generally blamed by analysts on indiscriminate expansion and acquisition. Lately, SCM's strategy seems to be to concentrate increasingly on chemicals and office equipment. It has introduced an electronic office typewriter to supplement its well-known line of personal portables.

* * *

SFN COMPANIES, INC. (SFN). Founded 1896. Headquarters: 1900 E. Lake Ave., Glenview IL 60025. **BOOK PUBLISHING.** Diversified publishing holding company. **MAJOR SUBSIDIARIES, BRANDS:** Scott, Foresman and Co.; South-Western Publishing Co.; Silver Burdett Co.; Fleming H. Revell Co.; University Park Press, Inc.

Sales: $270.8 million (trend 10.8% a year).
Earnings: $36.05 million (trend 20.5% a year).
What happened to a $10,000 investment

Purchase Date	*Purchase Price*	*Price on 12-31-81*	*Dividends Paid*
12-31-71	$ 9.69	$20.25	$4,560.00
12-31-76	$11.62	$20.25	$2,352.69

Purchase Date	*Cap. Gains (− Losses)*	*Total Return*	*Rate of Return*
12-31-71	$10,903.23	$15,463.23	9.80%
12-31-76	$ 7,419.35	$ 9,772.04	14.61%

* * *

SPS TECHNOLOGIES, INC. (ST). Founded 1903. Headquarters: Jenkintown PA 19046. **INDUSTRIAL FASTENERS.** Major producer of industrial fasteners. Also manufactures steel shelving, storage systems, and handling systems.

Sales: $341.1 million (trend 17.3% a year).
Earnings: $21.81 million (trend 69.5% a year).
What happened to a $10,000 investment

Purchase Date	*Purchase Price*	*Price on 12-31-81*	*Dividends Paid*
12-31-71	$6.59	$22.87	$5,969.64
12-31-76	$7.16	$22.87	$3,718.08

Purchase Date	*Cap. Gains (− Losses)*	*Total Return*	*Rate of Return*
12-31-71	$24,706.88	$30,676.52	15.06%
12-31-76	$21,952.36	$25,670.45	28.96%

* * *

SABINE CORP. (SAB). Founded 1933. Headquarters: 1200 Mercantile Bank Bldg., Dallas TX 75201. **OIL AND NATURAL GAS.** Explores and develops oil, gas, and uranium producing properties. **MAJOR SUBSIDIARIES, BRANDS:** Sarkeys, Inc.

Sales: $119.6 million (trend 24.1% a year).
Earnings: $25.54 million (trend 1.8% a year).
What happened to a $10,000 investment

Purchase Date	*Purchase Price*	*Price on 12-31-81*	*Dividends Paid*
12-31-71	$ 5.24	$35.62	$3,877.64
12-31-76	$11.82	$35.62	$1,210.43

Purchase Date	*Cap. Gains (− Losses)*	*Total Return*	*Rate of Return*
12-31-71	$57,976.67	$61,854.31	21.80%
12-31-76	$20,140.23	$21,350.67	25.68%

* * *

SAFEGUARD BUSINESS SYSTEMS, INC. (SGB). Founded: 1967. Headquarters: 400 Maryland Dr., Fort Washington PA 19034. ACCOUNTING SYSTEMS. Designs and manufactures business forms and manual bookkeeping systems, as well as data processing systems for small business.

Sales: $112.9 million.
Earnings: $7.25 million.

* * *

SAFEGUARD SCIENTIFICS, INC. (SFE). Founded 1953. Headquarters: 630 Park Ave., King of Prussia PA 19406. POWER EQUIPMENT. Safeguard makes power transmission equipment for industrial, automotive, and agricultural markets. Also produces auto parts and is involved in metal finishing and several miscellaneous activities.

Sales: $45.6 million (trend −13.5% a year).
Earnings: $.63 million (trend −15.1% a year).
What happened to a $10,000 investment

Purchase Date	*Purchase Price*	*Price on 12-31-81*	*Dividends Paid*
12-31-71	$7.37	$9.25	$1,044.07
12-31-76	$5.25	$9.25	$1,352.38

Purchase Date	*Cap. Gains (− Losses)*	*Total Return*	*Rate of Return*
12-31-71	$2,542.37	$3,586.44	3.11%
12-31-76	$7,619.05	$8,971.43	13.66%

* * *

SAFEWAY STORES, INC. (SA). Founded 1926. Headquarters: 4th and Jackson Sts., Oakland CA 94660. SUPERMARKETS. Safeway is the largest supermarket chain in the United States and also has substantial foreign operations. Owns approximately 2,000 U.S. supermarkets and close to 500 abroad. 150,000 employees.

Sales: $15,102.7 million (trend 9.4% a year).
Earnings: $119.37 million (trend .5% a year).
What happened to a $10,000 investment

Purchase Date	*Purchase Price*	*Price on 12-31-81*	*Dividends Paid*
12-31-71	$35.87	$26.50	$5,797.91
12-31-76	$50.12	$26.50	$2,453.87

Purchase Date	*Cap. Gains (− Losses)*	*Total Return*	*Rate of Return*
12-31-71	$−2,613.24	$ 3,184.67	2.80%
12-31-76	$−4,713.22	$−2,259.35	−4.99%

PROFILE: During the past decade, Safeway passed A&P to become the largest U.S. supermarket chain, in both sales and profits. (A&P later dropped to third, behind Kroger, but Safeway has solidified its grip on first place.) That was a milestone for this chain. But, on Wall Street (among other places), the motto is, "What have you done for me lately?"

Lately, Safeway hasn't been doing too hot. While it managed to maintain a profit margin of about 1½ percent in the early 1970s and sporadically in the mid-1970s (in the supermarket industry, believe it or not, that's fat), it has recently struggled to try to keep margins consistently over 1 percent. Price cutting has been part of the problem. A weak economy has made consumers more price conscious. Safeway has also been trying to hold onto market share in the face of increased competition in the western half of the country (where Safeway has some 1,700 of its roughly 2,000 U.S. stores).

In recent years, Safeway's sales have been growing only slightly faster than inflation. Earnings have been growing, but slower than inflation, so a case can be made that real earnings have been down. At the same time, debt has soared, in part to finance an ambitious program of enlarging and modernizing stores. At the beginning of the 1970s, Safeway's capital was less than 10 percent debt; at the beginning of the 1980s, debt was about half of total capital. As a result of all this, the stock sells for a low multiple, ranging in recent years from about 6 to 8.

Dividends, paid each year since 1927, are substantial — recently in the 6-to-9 percent range.

* * *

SAGA CORP. (SGA). Founded 1957. Headquarters: 1 Saga Lane, Menlo Park CA 94025. INSTITUTIONAL CATERING, RESTAURANTS. Provides contract food services for educational institutions, businesses and hospitals; operates three restaurant chains. MAJOR SUBSIDIARIES, BRANDS: Stuart Anderson's Black Angus / Cattle Company; Straw Hat Pizza and Velvet Turtle restaurant chains.

Sales: $819.0 million (trend 14.7% a year).
Earnings: $11.56 million (trend 3.5% a year).
What happened to a $10,000 investment

Purchase Date	*Purchase Price*	*Price on 12-31-81*	*Dividends Paid*
12-31-71	$28.37	$19.25	$ 768.28
12-31-76	$12.25	$19.25	$1,665.31

Purchase Date	*Cap. Gains (– Losses)*	*Total Return*	*Rate of Return*
12-31-71	$–3,215.86	$–2,447.58	–2.77%
12-31-76	$ 5,714.29	$ 7,379.59	11.69%

* * *

ST. JOSEPH LIGHT & POWER CO. (SAJ). Founded 1895. Headquarters: 520 Francis St., St. Joseph MO 64502. UTILITY. Missouri gas and electric utility.

Sales: $66.7 million (trend 15.3% a year).
Earnings: $4.74 million (trend 16.1% a year).
What happened to a $10,000 investment

Purchase Date	*Purchase Price*	*Price on 12-31-81*	*Dividends Paid*
12-31-71	$16.87	$10.50	$6,968.89
12-31-76	$13.37	$10.50	$4,628.04

Purchase Date	*Cap. Gains (– Losses)*	*Total Return*	*Rate of Return*
12-31-71	$–3,777.78	$3,191.11	2.81%
12-31-76	$–2,149.53	$2,478.50	4.53%

* * *

ST. PAUL SECURITIES, INC. (SPI). Founded 1972. Headquarters: 500 Bielenberg Dr., Woodbury MN 55164. DEBT SECURITIES. Investment company with primary holdings in investment-grade debt securities.

* * *

ST. REGIS PAPER CO. (SRT). Founded 1899. Headquarters: 150 E. 42nd St., New York NY 10017. FOREST PRODUCTS. St. Regis is among the ten largest U.S. forest products firms. It produces packaging; various grades of paper, including newsprint; lumber and plywood. Also has interests in oil, gas, and sulfur production and in publishing. 30,000 employees. MAJOR SUBSIDIARIES, BRANDS: Southland Paper.

Sales: $2,714.2 million (trend 14.5% a year).
Earnings: $170.49 million (trend 14.5% a year).
What happened to a $10,000 investment

Purchase Date	*Purchase Price*	*Price on 12-31-81*	*Dividends Paid*
12-31-71	$24.25	$31.50	$6,526.46
12-31-76	$38.62	$31.50	$2,441.42

Purchase Date	*Cap. Gains (– Losses)*	*Total Return*	*Rate of Return*
12-31-71	$ 2,989.69	$9,516.15	6.92%
12-31-76	$–1,844.66	$ 596.76	1.17%

PROFILE: Watching St. Regis is a bit like watching a homely but extremely rich girl. You figure it's only a matter of time before somebody makes his move. The homeliness lies in St. Regis's operating results. Growth in both sales and earnings has been no better than average. Return on stockholders' equity has been uninspiring. Nothing to excite investors here; that's why the stock sold in the early 1980s for only 5 to 7 times earnings, a very modest multiple.

But ah, the wilderness. More specifically, the timberlands. St. Regis owns outright well over three million acres, scattered throughout various parts of the United States. It owns cutting rights on more than another two million acres, here and in Canada. For several years, analysts have been saying that the value of the owned timber alone works out to well above the price of the outstanding common stock. A tender offer seems possible, even likely. And a take-over would stand a good chance of success, in light of the stock's depressed price / earnings multiple. Someone could buy the company cheap and still give an attractive deal to current stockholders.

That shoe hadn't dropped as of the time this book went to press. Perhaps it never will. Meanwhile, management is trying to improve on the company's admittedly mediocre track record by concentrating in areas where the company has been most successful, such as printing paper and lumber.

The balance sheet is average. The dividend yield is moderate to substantial — in recent years, around 5 to 7 percent. Dividends have been paid since 1947 and are well covered by earnings.

* * *

SALANT CORP. (SLT). Founded 1919. Headquarters: 330 Fifth Ave., New York NY 10001. CLOTHING. Manufactures clothing, primarily distributed under private labels.

Sales: $280.7 million (trend 9.5% a year).
Earnings: $.64 million (trend −25.6% a year).
What happened to a $10,000 investment

Purchase Date	*Purchase Price*	*Price on 12-31-81*	*Dividends Paid*
12-31-71	$11.79	$10.50	$2,413.15
12-31-76	$ 7.28	$10.50	$2,469.25

Purchase Date	*Cap. Gains (− Losses)*	*Total Return*	*Rate of Return*
12-31-71	$−1,097.64	$1,315.51	1.24%
12-31-76	$ 4,420.00	$6,889.25	11.05%

* * *

SAN DIEGO GAS & ELECTRIC CO. (SDO). Founded 1881. Headquarters: 101 Ash St., San Diego CA 92112. UTILITY. Generates and distributes electricity; distributes gas.

Sales: $960.4 million (trend 20.2% a year).
Earnings: $34.40 million (trend 14.8% a year).
What happened to a $10,000 investment

Purchase Date	*Purchase Price*	*Price on 12-31-81*	*Dividends Paid*
12-31-71	$21.25	$12.50	$6,258.82
12-31-76	$14.62	$12.50	$5,032.48

Purchase Date	*Cap. Gains (− Losses)*	*Total Return*	*Rate of Return*
12-31-71	$−4,117.65	$2,141.18	1.96%
12-31-76	$−1,452.99	$3,579.49	6.31%

* * *

SAN JUAN BASIN ROYALTY TRUST (SJT). Founded 1980. Headquarters: c/o The Fort Worth National Bank, 500 Throckmorton, Fort Worth TX 76102. GAS, OIL. Provides royalties from gas- and oil-producing properties in New Mexico.

* * *

SAN JUAN RACING ASSOCIATION, INC. (SJR). Founded 1954. Headquarters: PO Box 29500, Sixty-fifth Infantry Station, Rio Piedras PR 00929. HORSE RACING. Operates Puerto Rican race track; owns ten small U.S. radio stations.

Sales: $32.4 million (trend 20.3% a year).
Earnings: $4.28 million (trend 2.9% a year).
What happened to a $10,000 investment

Purchase Date	*Purchase Price*	*Price on 12-31-81*	*Dividends Paid*
12-31-71	$14.15	$7.25	$0.00
12-31-76	$ 5.81	$7.25	$0.00

Purchase Date	*Cap. Gains (− Losses)*	*Total Return*	*Rate of Return*
12-31-71	$−4,877.90	$−4,877.90	−6.47%
12-31-76	$ 2,487.87	$ 2,487.87	4.54%

* * *

SANDERS ASSOCIATES, INC. (SAA). Founded 1951. Headquarters: Daniel Webster Highway S., Nashua NH 03061. ELECTRONICS. Develops, manufactures, and sells advanced technology electronic systems. MAJOR SUBSIDIARIES, BRANDS: California Computer Products, Inc.; Talos Systems, Inc.; Sanders Graphic; CalComp; Talos Digitizer.

Sales: $364.5 million (trend 15.8% a year).
Earnings: $21.87 million (trend 40.2% a year).
What happened to a $10,000 investment

Purchase Date	*Purchase Price*	*Price on 12-31-81*	*Dividends Paid*
12-31-71	$15.75	$45.87	$ 939.68
12-31-76	$10.50	$45.87	$1,409.52

Purchase Date	*Cap. Gains (− Losses)*	*Total Return*	*Rate of Return*
12-31-71	$19,126.98	$20,066.67	11.64%
12-31-76	$33,690.48	$35,100.00	35.16%

* * *

SANTA ANITA COMPANIES (SAR). Founded 1979. Headquarters: see description following. REAL ESTATE, RACING. This is a single stock issued on behalf of two cooperating companies, Santa Anita Realty Enterprises and Santa Anita Operating Co. The former is a real estate investment trust (REIT); its headquarters are at 1 Wilshire Bldg., Suite 2303, Los Angeles CA 90017. The latter operates the Santa Anita Racetrack and also develops commercial real estate; it is headquartered at 285 W. Huntington Dr., Arcadia CA 91006.

Sales: $9.1 million (trend −29.5% a year).
Earnings: $8.32 million (trend 22.4% a year).
What happened to a $10,000 investment

Purchase Date	*Purchase Price*	*Price on 12-31-81*	*Dividends Paid*
12-31-71	$14.37	$15.75	$3,640.00
12-31-76	$ 4.62	$15.75	$8,070.27

Purchase Date	*Cap. Gains (− Losses)*	*Total Return*	*Rate of Return*
12-31-71	$ 956.52	$ 4,596.52	3.85%
12-31-76	$24,054.05	$32,124.32	33.32%

* * *

SANTA FE INDUSTRIES, INC. (SFF). Founded 1895. Headquarters: 224 S. Michigan Ave., Chicago IL 60604. **RAILROAD, NATURAL RESOURCES.** Santa Fe is the holding company for the Atchison, Topeka & Santa Fe Railway, which runs from the Midwest to the Southwest. It is also active in natural resource recovery (including oil, gas, minerals, and forest products) and in real estate development. 40,000 employees. **MAJOR SUBSIDIARIES, BRANDS:** Atchison, Topeka & Santa Fe Railway; Santa Fe Energy Co.; Kirby Forest Products.

Sales: $3,215.0 million (trend 17.3% a year).
Earnings: $301.60 million (trend 22.4% a year).
What happened to a $10,000 investment

Purchase Date	*Purchase Price*	*Price on 12-31-81*	*Dividends Paid*
12-31-71	$10.96	$21.12	$6,357.41
12-31-76	$13.17	$21.12	$3,088.61

Purchase Date	*Cap. Gains (− Losses)*	*Total Return*	*Rate of Return*
12-31-71	$9,277.57	$15,634.98	9.87%
12-31-76	$6,044.30	$ 9,132.91	13.86%

PROFILE: You can probably think of certain athletes who are always described as "underrated." After a while, one thinks that if the underrating is so well known, the player can't really be underrated any more. So it was with Santa Fe, which for several years has been described as a hidden energy play.

It's not hidden any more. By 1980 every more-than-casual investor knew that Santa Fe had extensive natural resources, and that, in particular, it was making a barrel of money from oil. *The Value Line Investment Survey* once quipped that Santa Fe was "an oil company which happens to own a railroad. . . ."

That's poetic license. In 1980 the railroad accounted for almost three quarters of sales here, and more than half of profits. Natural resources — mainly oil, but also gas, forest products, and minerals — chipped in a bit less than 20 percent of sales, but a solid 36 percent of profits. A little less than a tenth of the profit pie came from real estate development.

The stock price soared from about $10 in early 1979 to a high of around $36 in 1980–81, as investors lapped up the "hidden assets" idea. Then the price fell back into the mid-20s, amid general market weakness and a falling out of fashion among the energy issues. Both may well be temporary negatives.

The balance sheet here is strong; the dividend yield moderate. Dividends have been paid yearly since 1940.

* * *

SARGENT-WELCH SCIENTIFIC CO. (SWS). Founded 1852. Headquarters: 7300 N. Linder Ave., Skokie IL 60077. **SCIENTIFIC APPARATUS.** Manufactures and distributes scientific equipment for research, education and applied science. Also has graphics and printing operations. **MAJOR SUBSIDIARIES, BRANDS:** CryoSource; Densichron; Millikan; Polarograph; Inter-Collegiate Press, Inc.

Sales: $99.5 million (trend 8.8% a year).
Earnings: $6.17 million (trend 4.7% a year).
What happened to a $10,000 investment

Purchase Date	*Purchase Price*	*Price on 12-31-81*	*Dividends Paid*
12-31-71	$ 9.75	$24.12	$6,297.44
12-31-76	$13.25	$24.12	$3,260.38

Purchase Date	*Cap. Gains (− Losses)*	*Total Return*	*Rate of Return*
12-31-71	$14,743.59	$21,041.03	11.99%
12-31-76	$ 8,207.55	$11,467.92	16.51%

* * *

B. F. SAUL REAL ESTATE INVESTMENT TRUST (BFS). Founded 1962. Headquarters: 8401 Connecticut Ave., Chevy Chase MD 20015. **REAL ESTATE INVESTMENT TRUST.** Owns and develops investment properties; involved in condominium conversions.

Sales: $81.3 million (trend 21.2% a year).
Earnings: $2.17 million.
What happened to a $10,000 investment

Purchase Date	*Purchase Price*	*Price on 12-31-81*	*Dividends Paid*
12-31-71	$21.87	$7.37	$2,162.29
12-31-76	$ 4.12	$7.37	$ 606.06

Purchase Date	*Cap. Gains (− Losses)*	*Total Return*	*Rate of Return*
12-31-71	$−6,628.57	$−4,466.29	−5.75%
12-31-76	$ 7,878.79	$ 8,484.85	13.07%

* * *

SAV-A-STOP INC. (SVS). Founded 1953. 2055 Reyko Rd., Jacksonville FL 32207. **DISTRIBUTION.** Markets and distributes health and beauty aids and other nonfood merchandise to retail stores. As of early 1982 the company had agreed in principle to be acquired by Consolidated Foods.

Sales: $289.1 million (trend 7.0% a year).
Earnings: $5.14 million (trend 46.9% a year).
What happened to a $10,000 investment

Purchase Date	*Purchase Price*	*Price on 12-31-81*	*Dividends Paid*
12-31-71	$14.25	$11.87	$568.42
12-31-76	$ 3.62	$11.87	$413.79

Purchase Date	*Cap. Gains (− Losses)*	*Total Return*	*Rate of Return*
12-31-71	$−1,666.67	$−1,098.25	−1.16%
12-31-76	$ 22,758.62	$ 23,172.41	27.10%

* * *

SAVANNAH ELECTRIC AND POWER CO. (SAV). Founded 1866. Headquarters: 600 Bay St. E., Savannah GA 31401. **UTILITY.** Generates and distributes electricity in southeastern Georgia.

Sales: $122.2 million (trend 13.3% a year).
Earnings: $4.24 million (trend −3.0% a year).
What happened to a $10,000 investment

Purchase Date	*Purchase Price*	*Price on 12-31-81*	*Dividends Paid*
12-31-71	$16.53	$10.25	$5,611.46
12-31-76	$ 9.76	$10.25	$5,510.29

Purchase Date	*Cap. Gains (− Losses)*	*Total Return*	*Rate of Return*
12-31-71	$−3,798.40	$1,813.06	1.68%
12-31-76	$ 499.99	$6,010.29	9.87%

* * *

SAVIN CORP. (SVB). Founded 1959. Headquarters: Columbus Ave., Valhalla NY 10595. **COPIERS.** Savin is a major seller of copying machines and is developing a capacity to manufacture its own machines. 2,500 employees. **MAJOR SUBSIDIARIES, BRANDS:** Magnetic Laboratories, Inc.

Sales: $434.7 million (trend 47.2% a year).
Earnings: $−3.20 million.
What happened to a $10,000 investment

Purchase Date	*Purchase Price*	*Price on 12-31-81*	*Dividends Paid*
12-31-71	$11.12	$8.12	$1,997.75
12-31-76	$ 9.44	$8.12	$2,262.25

Purchase Date	*Cap. Gains (− Losses)*	*Total Return*	*Rate of Return*
12-31-71	$−2,696.63	$−698.88	−.72%
12-31-76	$−1,390.73	$ 871.52	1.69%

PROFILE: Savin was one of the great success stories of the 1970s, but it's fighting for its life now. The reason: Never has the company made its own copiers, but now it must. Its agreement with Ricoh to market the Japanese firm's copiers in the United States is running out.

The old formula worked marvelously during the 1970s, as Savin caught Xerox and other competitors off guard with its attractively cheap imports and its aggressive marketing. Sales soared from $37 million in fiscal 1970 to almost $435 million in fiscal 1980. Profits leaped from less than $3 million to more than $65 million over the same period.

In 1980, though, the company lost money, as it incurred huge start-up costs for its own manufacturing facilities, which it was building in upstate New York. The company claimed to be confident that it would not only survive, but thrive. It boasted of a new copying technology. Most Wall Street analysts, however, were taking a wait-and-see attitude about the technique. It's clear that any investment in Savin in the early 1980s must be speculative, since the company is entering territory previously foreign to it.

The shares are all the more speculative because the new ball game has forced Savin into heavy debt financing. Debt recently made up about 60 percent of total capital. In conjunction with this, the dividend, started in 1976, was cut in 1980 and suspended in 1981. The yield is modest. In 1982 Savin, in effect, sold a 57-percent interest in itself to Canada Development Corp. for about $75 million.

The stock has a history of jumping around wildly. (For example: above $18 in 1971, below $1 in 1974–75, up to $25 in 1977, below $12 in 1980.) The gyrations aren't likely to stop now.

* * *

SAXON INDUSTRIES, INC. (SXP). Founded 1924. Headquarters: 1230 Ave. of the Americas,

New York NY 10020. **PAPER.** Manufactures and distributes paper products, copy machines, and supplies. Also designs and produces promotional items, such as calendars that feature advertising. In 1982 Saxon filed for protection under Chapter 11 of the federal bankruptcy code.

Sales: $709.6 million (trend 10.6% a year).
Earnings: $5.37 million (trend 3.7% a year).
What happened to a $10,000 investment

Purchase Date	*Purchase Price*	*Price on 12-31-81*	*Dividends Paid*
12-31-71	$20.50	$4.62	$ 73.17
12-31-76	$ 4.75	$4.62	$315.79

Purchase Date	*Cap. Gains (− Losses)*	*Total Return*	*Rate of Return*
12-31-71	$−7,743.90	$−7,670.73	−13.56%
12-31-76	$ −263.16	$ 52.63	.11%

* * *

SCHERING-PLOUGH CORP. (SGP). Founded 1970. Headquarters: 2000 Galloping Hill Rd., Kenilworth NJ 07033. **DRUGS.** Schering-Plough is a leading maker of prescription drugs and over-the-counter medications; also has interests in footwear, broadcasting, and home repair products. Owns 16 percent of Biogen, S. A., the Swiss genetic engineering firm. 27,000 employees. **MAJOR SUBSIDIARIES, BRANDS:** Garamycin; Coppertone suntan lotion; Solarcaine sunburn lotion; St. Joseph aspirin; Di-Gel antacid, Scholl sandals; Maybelline cosmetics; Afrin nose spray; Chlor-Trimeton; Biogen, S. A. (16 percent owned); Unifa; Wesley-Jessen; Kirby Pharmaceuticals.

Sales: $1,740.4 million (trend 17.2% a year).
Earnings: $236.00 million (trend 11.5% a year).
What happened to a $10,000 investment

Purchase Date	*Purchase Price*	*Price on 12-31-81*	*Dividends Paid*
12-31-71	$42.94	$28.25	$2,436.68
12-31-76	$44.75	$28.25	$1,544.13

Purchase Date	*Cap. Gains (− Losses)*	*Total Return*	*Rate of Return*
12-31-71	$−3,420.67	$ −983.99	−1.03%
12-31-76	$−3,687.15	$−2,143.02	−4.71%

PROFILE: Riddle: Why would the stock of a company with two decades of uninterrupted earnings increases sell for only 8 times earnings? That riddle applied to Schering-Plough in the early 1980s, a time when 8 times earnings was the average multiple in a depressed market.

Answer: Wall Street expected the string to be snapped in 1981 — as indeed it was. The double-decade string had gone back to the days before Schering merged with Plough. That merger combined two strong entities into a stronger one. The combined company never racked up less than a 20 percent return on stockholders' equity from 1971 to 1980.

The reason "the street" correctly predicted the 1981 earnings decline was that anyone familiar with the company could see it coming. Schering-Plough had for years gotten a quarter of sales and more than 40 percent of earnings from Garamycin, a powerful antibiotic. When Garamycin's seventeen-year patent finally ran out in 1980, the company lost some sales and had to cut prices to keep from losing more. Improvements in the company's other segments, including the strong consumer lines acquired through the Plough merger (Maybelline, St. Joseph, Coppertone, etc.) weren't enough to offset the blow.

Schering-Plough nonetheless remains a very strong company and quite possibly a bargain at the prices prevailing recently. The company has barely a trace of debt (recently only about 3 percent of capital). Dividends, paid yearly since 1952, provide a moderate yield. And at around 8 times earnings for an established drug company (an industry resistant to recession), how can you go far wrong?

* * *

SCHLITZ (JOS.) BREWING CO. (SLZ). Founded 1920. Headquarters: 235 W. Galena St., Milwaukee WI 53212. **BREWERY.** Major U.S. brewery. **SUBSIDIARIES, BRANDS:** Old Milwaukee; Schlitz; Erlanger.

Sales: $896.7 million (trend −1.4% a year).
Earnings: $26.99 million (trend −10.4% a year).
What happened to a $10,000 investment

Purchase Date	*Purchase Price*	*Price on 12-31-81*	*Dividends Paid*
12-31-71	$36.42	$10.87	$1,246.96
12-31-76	$18.12	$10.87	$ 744.83

Purchase Date	*Cap. Gains (− Losses)*	*Total Return*	*Rate of Return*
12-31-71	$−7,013.73	$−5,766.77	−8.24%
12-31-76	$−4,000.00	$−3,255.17	−7.57%

* * *

SCHLUMBERGER LIMITED (SLB). Founded 1956. Headquarters: 277 Park Ave., New York NY 10017. **OILFIELD SERVICES.** Schlumberger is the world's leading company in providing "logging" services (analyses of well shaft contents and hydrocarbon potential) to oil drillers. Also provides other oilfield services; produces a variety of instruments and semiconductors; and is becoming increasingly involved in the computer field. 81,000 employees. **MAJOR SUBSIDIARIES, BRANDS:** Fairchild Camera and Instrument Corp.; Sangamo Western; Manufacturing Data Systems Inc.; Measurement & Control — Europe; Applicon Inc.

Sales: $4,883.9 million (trend 25.3% a year).
Earnings: $994.35 million (trend 33.9% a year).
What happened to a $10,000 investment

Purchase Date	*Purchase Price*	*Price on 12-31-81*	*Dividends Paid*
12-31-71	$ 6.79	$55.87	$4,531.77
12-31-76	$19.04	$55.87	$1,331.15

Purchase Date	*Cap. Gains (— Losses)*	*Total Return*	*Rate of Return*
12-31-71	$72,255.40	$76,787.17	24.12%
12-31-76	$19,350.68	$20,681.83	25.13%

PROFILE: This company is a legend. Though the man on the street knows little about Schlumberger, people in the oil industry regard it with awe. People on Wall Street have usually regarded it with an even stronger emotion — greed.

Their feelings have so far been rewarded. Schlumberger shares tripled (from around $6 to around $18) from 1971 to 1973. After a period of slow growth to around $21 in 1977, the shares tripled again between 1978 and the early 1980s.

Meanwhile, the return on equity has surged like magma from a volcano. It has been above 15 percent each year since 1972, above 25 percent each year since 1976, and above 30 percent in 1979–80. Leverage contributed not a whit to this eruption, for the company has virtually no debt.

The engine that produces these profits is the wireline, or logging, business — a sophisticated process for measuring the probable hydrocarbon content of a well. As *Business Week* explained recently, "little is known about what is going on inside a hole that is several thousand feet deep and only a few inches in diameter." To find out, "a series of torpedo-shaped tools is lowered on a wire-wrapped cable called a wireline. As each device is pulled up, it determines how the formation reacts to electric, acoustic, or other types of stimuli. These readings are . . . recorded on . . . photographic film — called a log — that resembles an electrocardiogram printout." The wireline business has recently provided more than half of sales, and more than three quarters of profits. The rest of the business — several instrumentation firms, notably Fairchild Camera and Instrument — provide balance and diversity. Since its acquisition in 1979, Fairchild has been more of a profit drag than a help. But management changes and — even more important — changes in the economy could make the acquisition look good.

The potential drawback of buying Schlumberger shares is the price / earnings ratio. You may pay filet mignon prices here — in recent years, anywhere from 11 to 25 times earnings. When the p / e is high, the company must continue to perform spectacularly for your investment to pan out. The dividend, paid yearly since 1957, provides only a modest yield.

* * *

SCIENTIFIC-ATLANTA, INC. (SFA). Founded 1951. Headquarters: 3845 Pleasantdale Rd., Atlanta GA 30340. **ELECTRONICS.** Manufactures electronic communication and instrumentation equipment for cable television; also cast and machined parts.

Sales: $277.3 million (trend 46.3% a year).
Earnings: $19.00 million (trend 59.1% a year).
What happened to a $10,000 investment

Purchase Date	*Purchase Price*	*Price on 12-31-81*	*Dividends Paid*
12-31-71	$1.06	$27.25	$1,987.55
12-31-76	$3.37	$27.25	$ 622.22

Purchase Date	*Cap. Gains (— Losses)*	*Total Return*	*Rate of Return*
12-31-71	$247,908.78	$249,896.33	38.51%
12-31-76	$ 70,740.74	$ 71,362.96	52.08%

* * *

SCOA INDUSTRIES, INC. (SOA). Founded 1920. Headquarters: 155 E. Broad St., Columbus OH 43215. **RETAILING.** SCOA owns and operates discount department stores, shoe stores, appliance stores, and operates leased shoe departments in other companies' department stores. 16,000 employees. **MAJOR SUBSIDIARIES, BRANDS:** Hills discount department stores; Gallenkamp shoe stores;

Duet shoe stores; Kelly & Cohen appliance stores; The Dry Goods (promotional department stores).

Sales: $941.7 million (trend 13.2% a year).
Earnings: $28.12 million (trend 32.2% a year).
What happened to a $10,000 investment

Purchase Date	*Purchase Price*	*Price on 12-31-81*	*Dividends Paid*
12-31-71	$3.24	$20.12	$6,331.99
12-31-76	$3.27	$20.12	$4,068.23

Purchase Date	*Cap. Gains (– Losses)*	*Total Return*	*Rate of Return*
12-31-71	$52,063.12	$58,395.11	21.20%
12-31-76	$51,523.44	$55,591.67	45.67%

PROFILE: SCOA's earnings slipped a bit in 1980 after seven straight years of growth and were fairly flat in 1981. During those seven good years, profits grew from about $2.4 million in 1971 to about $30.4 million in 1979. The company, which until recently made shoes as well as sold them, had acquired something of a reputation as a growth issue.

But the seven good years (to continue the biblical phrasing) were preceded by seven lean years, during which SCOA's earnings didn't grow much. The gains of 1973–79 look less impressive when you realize that 1972 profits represented a seven-year low. Growth rates are a tricky thing, and an artificially low base can make a company's performance look better than it was.

With good timing, you could have made a lot of money in SCOA. The stock sold for less than $2 a share during much of 1973, 1974, and 1975. In 1980 it hit a high of more than $20, and in 1981 it was flirting with the $30 mark. Throughout most of this time, SCOA shares have not been highly regarded; they sold for 8 times earnings or less until late 1981, when the p / e hit 9.

The return on equity has been handsome—above 20 percent each year from 1976 through 1980. But this showing was helped by a high degree of leverage. Debt has usually been more than 40 percent of capital and was recently 45 percent.

Shoes have become progressively less important over the years. Recently, shoe retailing has accounted for less than a quarter of sales and profits, even though the company still has more than 700 shoe stores and outlets. General merchandising, particularly the Hills discount department store chain, is now the mainstay of the company.

Dividends have been paid each year since 1929; the yield is moderate.

* * *

SCOT LAD FOODS, INC. (SLF). Founded 1961. 1 Scot Lad Lane, Lansing IL 60438. **FOOD DISTRIBUTOR.** Food processor and distributor; also distributes nonfood items to food retailers; operates retail outlets. **MAJOR SUBSIDIARIES, BRANDS:** Scot Lad; Queen of Scott; Bonnie; Mister Industries; Convenient Food Mart, Inc. (50 percent owned).

Sales: $879.0 million (trend 2.3% a year).
Earnings: $5.33 million (trend 5.6% a year).
What happened to a $10,000 investment

Purchase Date	*Purchase Price*	*Price on 12-31-81*	*Dividends Paid*
12-31-71	$15.12	$4.25	$1,344.60
12-31-76	$ 5.60	$4.25	$1,007.74

Purchase Date	*Cap. Gains (– Losses)*	*Total Return*	*Rate of Return*
12-31-71	$–7,188.98	$–5,844.38	–8.41%
12-31-76	$–2,404.26	$–1,396.52	–2.96%

* * *

THE SCOTT & FETZER CO. (SFZ). Founded 1917. Headquarters: 14600 Detroit Ave., Lakewood OH 44107. **CONGLOMERATE.** Diversified manufacturer and door-to-door marketer of consumer and industrial products. **MAJOR SUBSIDIARIES, BRANDS.** World-Book-Childcraft International, Inc.; Kirby; World Book Encyclopedia.

Sales: $632.4 million (trend 20.2% a year).
Earnings: $23.07 million (trend 8.4% a year).
What happened to a $10,000 investment

Purchase Date	*Purchase Price*	*Price on 12-31-81*	*Dividends Paid*
12-31-71	$28.25	$28.50	$4,644.25
12-31-76	$26.25	$28.50	$3,085.71

Purchase Date	*Cap. Gains (– Losses)*	*Total Return*	*Rate of Return*
12-31-71	$ 88.50	$4,732.74	3.95%
12-31-76	$857.14	$3,942.86	6.87%

* * *

SCOTT PAPER CO. (SPP). Founded 1922. Headquarters: 1 Scott Plaza, Philadelphia PA 19113. **PAPER PRODUCTS.** Scott is a leading maker of paper towels, napkins, and tissues. Also makes printing and specialty papers, lighting products, furniture, and polyurethane foam. 20,000 employees. **MAJOR SUBSIDIARIES, BRANDS:** Scott; Scotties; Viva; Waldorf; Brunswick Pulp & Paper Co. (50 percent owned).

Sales: $2,083.2 million (trend 11.8% a year).
Earnings: $133.25 million (trend 18.4% a year).
What happened to a $10,000 investment

Purchase Date	*Purchase Price*	*Price on 12-31-81*	*Dividends Paid*
12-31-71	$16.25	$16.25	$4,630.77
12-31-76	$20.75	$16.25	$2,149.40

Purchase Date	*Cap. Gains (− Losses)*	*Total Return*	*Rate of Return*
12-31-71	$ −.00	$4,630.77	3.88%
12-31-76	$−2,168.67	$ −19.28	−.04%

PROFILE: Sometimes this long-established company seems as old and used as one of its . . . well, we'll forgo the analogy. Anyway, the dividend in 1980 was the same as that paid in the late 1960s. Both sales and earnings have grown slowly — in many years, more slowly than inflation. And the stock price is less than it was a dozen years ago.

Much of what's wrong with Scott can be summed up in two and a half words: Procter & Gamble. Scott's profits looked better in the old days when it pretty much had the soft paper markets to itself. Along came Procter & Gamble with its Charmin bathroom tissue, Bounty paper towels, and big advertising budgets. Things have never been the same since, though Scott has managed to recapture a narrow lead in the toilet tissue market from P&G's Charmin. The recent recession helped Scott some, as people traded down from P&G's more expensive brands to Scott's cheaper ones. But now Procter & Gamble has announced plans to go after the cheaper end of the market too. Other prominent competitors to Scott's lines include Georgia Pacific and Fort Howard Paper.

Another part of Scott's troubles has been that its plants haven't been modern enough. Obsolete plants lead to higher production costs, hence lower profit margins. To fix things, better late than never, Scott embarked recently on an ambitious $2-billion capital spending program. The program is expected to require at least $1 billion in borrowing, which will push long-term debt up substantially from its recent level of around 28 percent of capital.

Dividends have been paid every year since 1915; the yield is moderate.

* * *

SCOTTY'S, INC. (SHB). Founded 1924. Headquarters: PO Box 939, Winter Haven FL 33880. **RETAIL BUILDING SUPPLY CHAIN.** Sells building supplies to consumers and professional builders through eighty retail outlets.

Sales: $294.4 million (trend 29.4% a year).
Earnings: $11.26 million (trend 43.1% a year).
What happened to a $10,000 investment

Purchase Date	*Purchase Price*	*Price on 12-31-81*	*Dividends Paid*
12-31-71	$15.58	$19.25	$1,084.28
12-31-76	$ 6.33	$19.25	$2,299.47

Purchase Date	*Cap. Gains (− Losses)*	*Total Return*	*Rate of Return*
12-31-71	$ 2,352.94	$ 3,437.22	3.00%
12-31-76	$20,394.74	$22,694.21	26.73%

* * *

SCOVILL INC. (SCO). Founded 1802. Headquarters: 500 Chase Parkway, Waterbury CT 06720. **DIVERSIFIED MANUFACTURER.** Manufactures machinery; automotive, housing, housewares, and security products. **MAJOR SUBSIDIARIES, BRANDS:** Hamilton Beach (housewares); Yale (locks); Schrader Bellows (machinery); NuTone (door chimes and other home products).

Sales: $900.4 million (trend 15.5% a year).
Earnings: $24.83 million (trend 18.1% a year).
What happened to a $10,000 investment

Purchase Date	*Purchase Price*	*Price on 12-31-81*	*Dividends Paid*
12-31-71	$27.12	$18.62	$4,302.67
12-31-76	$21.75	$18.62	$3,273.56

Purchase Date	*Cap. Gains (− Losses)*	*Total Return*	*Rate of Return*
12-31-71	$−3,133.64	$1,169.03	1.11%
12-31-76	$−1,436.78	$1,836.78	3.43%

* * *

SCUDDER DUO-VEST INC. (SDV). Founded 1966. Headquarters: 345 Park Ave., New York NY 10022. **INVESTMENT COMPANY.** Invests in securities for growth and income; portfolio is divided so that investors can choose either "growth" or "income" shares.

* * *

SEA CONTAINERS GROUP (SCN). Founded 1965. Headquarters: 1 World Trade Center, New York NY 10048. **MARINE CONTAINERS.** Leases marine container equipment to transportation companies, including cargo containers, chassis, and cranes; charters containerships.

Sales: $180.7 million (trend 35.3% a year.)
Earnings: $35.07 million (trend 24.4% a year).
What happened to a $10,000 investment

Purchase Date	*Purchase Price*	*Price on 12-31-81*	*Dividends Paid*
12-31-71	$ 2.84	$21.25	$7,191.21
12-31-76	$12.81	$21.25	$1,430.24

Purchase Date	*Cap. Gains (− Losses)*	*Total Return*	*Rate of Return*
12-31-71	$64,725.27	$71,916.48	23.41%
12-31-76	$ 6,585.37	$ 8,015.61	12.49%

* * *

SEAFIRST CORP. (SFC). Founded 1929. Headquarters: 1001 Fourth Ave., Seattle WA 98124. **BANK.** Seafirst is the holding company for Seattle-First National Bank, which is approximately the twenty-sixth largest U.S. bank and the largest in the state of Washington. 6,000 employees. **MAJOR SUBSIDIARIES, BRANDS:** Seattle-First National Bank.

Sales: $1,036.5 million (trend 25.8% a year).
Earnings: $69.78 million (trend 18.1% a year).
What happened to a $10,000 investment

Purchase Date	*Purchase Price*	*Price on 12-31-81*	*Dividends Paid*
12-31-71	$18.08	$28.50	$4,916.13
12-31-76	$22.83	$28.50	$2,411.68

Purchase Date	*Cap. Gains (− Losses)*	*Total Return*	*Rate of Return*
12-31-71	$5,760.37	$10,676.50	7.53%
12-31-76	$2,481.75	$ 4,893.43	8.29%

PROFILE: Seafirst has built a record of steady growth by exploiting the resources of its region. Many of its loans are to agriculture or aerospace businesses, which are among the major enterprises in the Northwest. More than 10 percent of the loan portfolio is foreign loans, and this percentage is growing. Most of these are to the Pacific Basin countries — Japan and Taiwan, for example.

The company has raised its dividend payment each year since 1965, but the yield remains moderate, as profits have more than kept pace with the dividend increases. In the early 1970s, the company was paying out more than a third of earnings in dividends; in the early 1980s, it was paying out a little more than a quarter.

Going into 1982, profits had grown steadily, if not spectacularly, for more than a decade. From 1971 through 1980, profits grew from about $22 million to about $68 million, while assets grew from $2.8 billion to $9.6 billion. The return on assets has been remarkably consistent at $0.70 to $0.80 per $100. That's not superb, but it's a tidy return. A lot of better-known banks wouldn't mind trading return on assets figures with Seafirst.

The return on stockholders' equity has been only a bit better than average for a bank. But the return on total capital has been considerably better than the norm. The difference reflects the fact that Seafirst hasn't resorted to much leverage; the balance sheet is kept clean.

Seafirst has some 170 offices in Washington State, and another 8 or so abroad.

* * *

SEAGRAM CO. LTD. (VO). Founded 1928. Headquarters: 1430 Peel St., Montreal, PQ H3A 1S9 Canada. **LIQUOR.** Seagram is the world's largest distiller and seller of liquor and wine. It sells about 150 brands of liquor and some 300 brands of wine in roughly 175 countries. Production facilities were recently maintained in 26 countries. Also has interests in oil and gas. 15,000 employees. **MAJOR SUBSIDIARIES, BRANDS:** 7 Crown, V.O., and Chivas Regal whiskeys; Wolfschmidt vodka; Seagram's gin; Ronrico rum; Paul Masson wines; Christian Brothers brandy. Owns approximately 20% of E. I. Du Pont de Nemours.

Sales: $1,789.7 million (trend 10.2% a year).
Earnings: $330.33 million (trend 20.7% a year).
What happened to a $10,000 investment

Purchase Date	*Purchase Price*	*Price on 12-31-81*	*Dividends Paid*
12-31-71	$34.12	$57.62	$2,554.11
12-31-76	$23.50	$57.62	$2,108.47

Purchase Date	*Cap. Gains (− Losses)*	*Total Return*	*Rate of Return*
12-31-71	$ 6,886.45	$ 9,440.56	6.87%
12-31-76	$14,521.28	$16,629.74	21.64%

PROFILE: Founder and longtime chairman Sam Bronfman made a fortune in the liquor business worldwide and passed the gargantuan business on to his sons. Bronfman family trusts own about a third of the stock, and Sam's son Edgar is now chairman of the board.

Much of the money from the liquor business was invested in oil and gas. Seagram bought Texas Pacific Oil Co. in 1963 for $256 million. In 1980 Seagram sold Texas Pacific to the Sun Co. for $2.3 billion. (Oil and gas properties abroad, notably in Canada and Thailand, were kept.) Invested at high interest rates, the $2.3 billion from the sale had grown to more than $3 billion in 1981. Edgar Bronfman made no secret of the fact that the company planned to use the money for a big acquisition. "There are a lot of willing brides," he told *Time* magazine, "but the boy still has to make up his mind."

In 1981 Seagram made a $2.1-billion offer for St. Joe Minerals. It was rebuffed, and St. Joe eventually was merged into Fluor Corp. Later in 1981, Seagram made a $2.5-billion offer for Conoco. Again it was rebuffed, and Conoco eventually merged into DuPont. Was Seagram upset, and did these developments show a clumsy touch on its part in the acquisition game? Not likely. In both cases, Seagram came away with large profits from selling the stock it had acquired in the process of its take-over attempts. Seagram also ended up owning about 20% of DuPont, since it took DuPont stock in exchange for its Conoco shares.

The acquisitions game has made Seagram interesting to business writers and investors. However, its underlying results in the liquor business haven't been spectacular. Return on stockholders' equity was less than 10 percent most years during the past decade. Dividends, which have been paid each year since 1937, provide only a modest yield.

* * *

SEAGULL PIPELINE CORP. (SGO). Founded 1973. Headquarters: 1100 Louisiana, Houston TX 77002. GAS TRANSMISSION. Seagull's main activity is gathering and distribution of natural gas in Texas; also has some interstate gas pipeline operations and gas processing operations.

* * *

SEALED AIR CORP. (SEE). Founded 1969. Headquarters: Park 80 Plaza E., Saddle Brook NJ 07662. PACKAGING PRODUCTS. Makes air cellular plastic packaging materials, foam-in-place packaging systems, and solar swimming pool products. MAJOR SUBSIDIARIES, BRANDS: Instapak Corp.; AirCap.

Sales: $88.6 million (trend 36.0% a year).
Earnings: $6.41 million (trend 35.0% a year).
What happened to a $10,000 investment

Purchase Date	*Purchase Price*	*Price on 12-31-81*	*Dividends Paid*
12-31-71	$ 6.50	$27.12	$3,692.31
12-31-76	$10.25	$27.12	$2,048.78

Purchase Date	*Cap. Gains (— Losses)*	*Total Return*	*Rate of Return*
12-31-71	$31,730.77	$35,423.08	16.34%
12-31-76	$16,463.41	$18,512.20	23.31%

* * *

SEALED POWER CORP. (SPW). Founded 1912. Headquarters: 100 Terrace Plaza, Muskegon MI 49443. PISTON RINGS. Manufactures engine parts for auto and truck manufacturers, and for replacement markets.

Sales: $257.9 million (trend 13.5% a year).
Earnings: $11.77 million (trend 15.9% a year).
What happened to a $10,000 investment

Purchase Date	*Purchase Price*	*Price on 12-31-81*	*Dividends Paid*
12-31-71	$13.94	$32.25	$6,287.67
12-31-76	$16.25	$32.25	$3,581.54

Purchase Date	*Cap. Gains (— Losses)*	*Total Return*	*Rate of Return*
12-31-71	$13,135.85	$19,423.52	11.40%
12-31-76	$ 9,846.15	$13,427.69	18.56%

* * *

G. D. SEARLE & CO. (SRL). Founded 1888. Headquarters: 4711 Gold Rd., Skokie IL 60076. DRUGS. Searle is a major manufacturer of prescription drugs. Also owns more than 800 retail optical stores in the United States, Canada, Mexico, and Europe. 18,000 employees. MAJOR SUBSIDIARIES, BRANDS: Aldactazide, Aldactone (high blood pressure drugs); Enovid, Demulen, and Ovulen 21 (oral contraceptives); Flagyl (vaginitis medication); Aspartame (artificial sweetener); Lomotil (antidiarrhea medication); Dramamine (antinausea medication); Pearle Vision Centers.

Sales: $1,081.6 million (trend 8.1% a year).
Earnings: $94.64 million (trend 7.6% a year).
What happened to a $10,000 investment

Purchase Date	*Purchase Price*	*Price on 12-31-81*	*Dividends Paid*
12-31-71	$24.58	$31.37	$2,019.67
12-31-76	$13.12	$31.37	$1,980.95

Purchase Date	*Cap. Gains (− Losses)*	*Total Return*	*Rate of Return*
12-31-71	$ 2,762.71	$ 4,782.39	3.99%
12-31-76	$13,904.76	$15,885.71	20.95%

PROFILE: For a company with headquarters in Illinois, Searle seems to make a lot of news that has to do with Washington, D.C. On the negative side, it had a fierce run-in with the Food and Drug Administration, which charged that animal tests on various Searle drugs had been conducted incorrectly and made the company go back to the drawing board (or the lab) for a redo of numerous tests. The FDA also held up for years approval of the artificial sweetener Aspartame. And a nongovernmental but Washington-based group — the Health Research Group, affiliated with Ralph Nader — has criticized another major Searle drug, Flagyl, saying its cancer risk is too high to justify its use in treating vaginitis.

Searle has fought back against the allegations and the setbacks. And Washington, D.C., has also brought it some positive developments. Searle's highly regarded chairman, Donald Rumsfeld, was Secretary of Defense in the Nixon administration. Under the Reagan administration, the FDA reversed its earlier decisions and approved the use of Aspartame, a development that some analysts think could significantly help Searle's bottom line.

Profits have seesawed here and so has the stock price, which entered the 1980s at about the same level it entered the 1970s. Return on equity has generally been good. The balance sheet has been strengthened lately, in part through the sale of poorly performing divisions; debt was recently only about 14 percent of total capital. Dividends have been paid each year since 1935, but as with most drug companies the yield is small and the stock's multiple is usually high.

* * *

SEARS, ROEBUCK AND CO. (S). Founded 1906. Headquarters: Sears Tower, Chicago IL 60684. **RETAILING, INSURANCE.** Sears is the nation's largest retailer, with more than 800 department stores and the nation's largest catalog operation. Also owns Allstate, the nation's second largest property and casualty insurer, and is becoming increasingly involved in real estate and financial services. 390,000 employees. **MAJOR SUBSIDIARIES, BRANDS:** Sears; Allstate Insurance Co.; Seraco (financial services); PMI (mortgage insurance); Allstate Savings & Loan Association; Homart Development Co. (shopping center development); Dean Witter Reynolds Organization Inc. (securities brokerage); Coldwell, Banker (real estate brokerage).

Sales: $25,194.9 million (trend 10.8% a year).
Earnings: $606.00 million (trend 3.8% a year).
What happened to a $10,000 investment

Purchase Date	*Purchase Price*	*Price on 12-31-81*	*Dividends Paid*
12-31-71	$51.25	$16.12	$2,083.90
12-31-76	$34.62	$16.12	$1,833.94

Purchase Date	*Cap. Gains (− Losses)*	*Total Return*	*Rate of Return*
12-31-71	$−6,853.66	$−4,769.76	−6.28%
12-31-76	$−5,342.96	$−3,509.03	−8.28%

PROFILE: How the mighty have fallen. The nation's largest retailer earned profits of only $606 million in 1980, less than it earned in 1972. In 1981 profits were down further, to $592 million. For the past decade, earnings have been struggling to keep pace with inflation — and often losing.

Performance of retailing operations has been even worse than the overall corporate figures indicate: Allstate's profits have been compensating for lackluster retail earnings. In 1980, for example, Allstate chipped in close to two thirds of profits on about a quarter of sales.

Like a ballplayer in a slump who fiddles with his stance, Sears has been trying one strategy after another. First it tried to go "upscale," appealing to more affluent consumers by adding more expensive merchandise to its traditional middle-of-the-road lines. When that flopped, Sears tried to regain market share by slashing prices. Sales rose, but profits kept going down. Now, somewhat by default, Sears is back in the middle of the road, but faces heavy competition from discount stores, snazzier stores, and specialized retailers — all of which have gained in popularity.

The fall from grace has brought the stock down from a 1973 peak above $60 a share to a level around $15 to $20 in the early 1980s. The dividend yield is substantial — above 7 percent in 1981 — but it took 71 percent of 1980 earnings to keep the dividend inching up. The balance sheet's still not bad, with debt recently about 28 percent of capital. A decade earlier, debt was only about half that proportion of total capital.

The newest development at Sears is the push into financial services. Sears has owned Allstate for many years, but only recently has it taken the plunge and decided to offer the full range of items that compose what analysts call the "financial supermarket." In short order, it opened a money market fund, acquired Dean Witter (a major securities brokerage house), and acquired Coldwell, Banker (a large national real estate brokerage firm).

Some say the move into finance shows that Sears figures it can't squeeze growth out of retailing any more. However, it's more likely that Sears thinks the two can work together — that people who are used to buying their washing machines and hammers at Sears may buy their investments there too.

* * *

SECURITY PACIFIC CORP. (SPC). Founded 1971; bank dates to 1871. Headquarters: 333 S. Hope St., Los Angeles CA 90071. **BANK.** The corporation is the holding company for Security Pacific National Bank, second largest in California and approximately tenth largest in the United States. 24,000 employees. **MAJOR SUBSIDIARIES, BRANDS:** Security Pacific National Bank; A. J. Armstrong Co.

Sales: $3,116.7 million (trend 23.9% a year).
Earnings: $181.89 million (trend 24.6% a year).
What happened to a $10,000 investment

Purchase Date	*Purchase Price*	*Price on 12-31-81*	*Dividends Paid*
12-31-71	$24.48	$40.75	$5,857.02
12-31-76	$22.19	$40.75	$3,900.47

Purchase Date	*Cap. Gains (− Losses)*	*Total Return*	*Rate of Return*
12-31-71	$6,646.81	$12,503.83	8.45%
12-31-76	$8,366.19	$12,266.66	17.36%

PROFILE: A few years back, the wags took to calling Security Pacific "Security Pathetic." You don't hear that joke much any more.

From 1972 through 1976, this bank holding company managed to earn less than $0.50 per $100 of assets, an unimpressive showing, indeed. But in the last few years, it's upped the return to about $0.66 per $100, which is considered pretty good. Return on stockholders' equity in recent years has been around 16 percent, which is a shade better than average. In 1981 the corporation, still feeling its oats at age one hundred and ten, acquired the A. J. Armstrong Co., a commercial finance company. It also owns a good chunk of the Bank of Canton.

A California location has been an advantage for this banking outfit and should continue to be. Electronics, defense, and other nonsmokestack industries are big in the Golden State, and the population is growing. Security Pacific has been concentrating on lending money to medium-sized, growing businesses.

To expand its range of services to customers, the bank recently entered an arraangement with Fidelity Brokerage Services Inc., that would enable Security Pacific customers to buy and sell stocks and bonds.

Despite its improved performance and favorable location, this stock, like many bank stocks, was dirt cheap in the early 1980s. In 1981 it was selling for only about 5 times earnings, a low multiple even in a depressed stock market. In 1980 it sold, at times, for as little as 3 times earnings. The p / e is one of the chief recommendations for the stock.

The dividend yield is moderate. Dividends are well covered by earnings. The payout has been raised each year since 1976, and dividends have been paid each year since 1881.

* * *

SEDCO, INC. (SED). Founded 1950. Headquarters: 1901 N. Akard., Dallas TX 75201. **OFFSHORE OIL DRILLING.** Major offshore drilling contractor; also active in pipeline construction and land drilling.

Sales: $362.6 million (trend 1.9% a year).
Earnings: $57.20 million (trend −3.5% a year).
What happened to a $10,000 investment

Purchase Date	*Purchase Price*	*Price on 12-31-81*	*Dividends Paid*
12-31-71	$15.42	$37.25	$740.43
12-31-76	$ 9.83	$37.25	$975.93

Purchase Date	*Cap. Gains (− Losses)*	*Total Return*	*Rate of Return*
12-31-71	$14,162.16	$14,902.59	9.55%
12-31-76	$27,881.36	$28,857.29	31.19%

* * *

SELIGMAN & LATZ, INC. (SAL). Founded 1953. Headquarters: 666 Fifth Ave., New York NY 10019. **BEAUTY SALONS.** Operates beauty salons in major department stores; manufactures cosmetics; operates retail jewelry departments. **MAJOR SUBSIDIARIES, BRANDS:** Adrien Arpel; "The Trimmers"; "Soul Scissors".

Sales: $263.6 million (trend 15.1% a year).
Earnings: $1.62 million (trend −23.9% a year).
What happened to a $10,000 investment

Purchase Date	*Purchase Price*	*Price on 12-31-81*	*Dividends Paid*
12-31-71	$ 6.26	$16.87	$12,190.38
12-31-76	$15.99	$16.87	$ 3,289.61

Purchase Date	*Cap. Gains (— Losses)*	*Total Return*	*Rate of Return*
12-31-71	$16,953.40	$29,143.78	14.62%
12-31-76	$ 555.83	$ 3,845.44	6.72%

* * *

SERVICE CORP. INTERNATIONAL (SRV). Founded 1962. Headquarters: 1929 Allen Parkway, PO Box 13548, Houston TX 77019. **FUNERAL SERVICES.** Owns and operates funeral homes, cemeteries, and related businesses.

Sales: $134.8 million (trend 11.3% a year).
Earnings: $9.30 million (trend 15.8% a year).
What happened to a $10,000 investment

Purchase Date	*Purchase Price*	*Price on 12-31-81*	*Dividends Paid*
12-31-71	$13.13	$24.75	$1,022.86
12-31-76	$ 3.94	$24.75	$2,476.19

Purchase Date	*Cap. Gains (— Losses)*	*Total Return*	*Rate of Return*
12-31-71	$ 8,856.67	$ 9,879.52	7.11%
12-31-76	$52,855.55	$55,331.74	45.55%

* * *

SERVICE MERCHANDISE CO., INC. (SMCH, Over-the-Counter). Founded 1960. Headquarters: 2968 Foster Creighton Dr., Nashville TN 37204. **CATALOG SHOWROOMS.** Service Merchandise is one of the three largest catalog showroom chains in the United States (along with Best Products and Modern Merchandising). 10,000 employees.

PROFILE: Time out. In 1981 Service Merchandise added only about half a dozen stores to its set of 113 catalog showrooms, scattered over some 25 states. That was quite a decrease from the breakneck expansion of recent years, which saw the chain double the number of its outlets between 1978 and 1980.

Service Merchandise, like other catalog showroom operators, has been among the fastest growing of all U.S. businesses (never mind retailers). And, like its compatriots in the catalog showroom biz, it has financed its furious expansion with debt, debt, and more debt. Each of the big three catalog showroom chains (Best Products, Service Merchandise, and Modern Merchandising) recently had more debt than equity. In Service's case, debt recently accounted før about 59 percent of capital.

Forbes reported in 1980 that the company had recently taken on another $41 million of long-term debt tied to the prime rate, "part of which is helping to pay down [the company's] first loan." The combination of high interest rates and a recession can be expected to put a squeeze on operations like Service Merchandise, which is why the stock, despite its phenomenal growth record, was selling at only about 8 times earnings (an average multiple) in 1981.

Dividends were started in 1977, but provide only a modest yield.

* * *

SHAKLEE CORP. (SHC). Founded 1962. Headquarters: 444 Market St., San Francisco CA 94111. **VITAMINS.** Shaklee is the country's largest maker and seller of vitamins and nutrition supplements; these and selected household products are sold door to door. 1,000 full-time employees; 11,000 independent salespersons. **MAJOR SUBSIDIARIES, BRANDS:** Instant Protein; Liquid-Lea; NPS; Vita-Lea.

Sales: $454.5 million (trend 20.8% a year).
Earnings: $24.54 million (trend 8.0% a year).
What happened to a $10,000 investment

Purchase Date	*Purchase Price*	*Price on 12-31-81*	*Dividends Paid*
12-31-71	$N/A	$23.75	$ N/A
12-31-76	$21.50	$23.75	$1,648.06

Purchase Date	*Cap. Gains (— Losses)*	*Total Return*	*Rate of Return*
12-31-71	$ N/A	$ N/A	N/A%
12-31-76	$1,046.51	$2,694.57	4.89%

PROFILE: Shaklee makes and sells more vitamins than Squibb (Theragran) or Miles Laboratories (One-A-Day Brand). In fact, according to *Business Week*, analysts' best guesses about the fragmented vitamin market are that Shaklee sells about four times the volume of any single competitor.

Selling vitamins door to door may strike you as the sort of thing that would only work in California. Well, Shaklee is headquartered there, all right, but it sells nationwide — and in Canada, England, and Japan as well. Foreign sales recently accounted for about an eighth of sales and more than a third of profits.

The profitability of selling abroad suggests that foreign buyers may not yet be picking from as wide a range of competing vitamin and nutrition products as U.S. buyers have available. The competition in the U.S. market has forced Shaklee to slow down its price increases and accept a lower profit margin than it used to. Still, the company boasts an outstanding growth record. Sales were about $62 million in 1972, when the company went public. In 1980 they were $411 million. Profits have been erratic, but over the years have shown an equally dramatic uptrend. The 1980 earnings were hurt by expenses of closing down two older factories to open a new, highly efficient plant in Norman, Oklahoma; by trimming the product line (eliminating most household products to concentrate on vitamins); and by expenses for the opening of the company's lavish San Francisco headquarters, a skyscraper with a terraced roof topped by Australian trees.

The stock's growth record earned it a p / e (in the early 1980s) of about 16, or twice that for the average stock at the time. The balance sheet is solid, with debt recently about 17 percent of capital. The dividend yield is modest.

* * *

SHAPELL INDUSTRIES, INC. (SHA). Founded 1969. Headquarters: 8383 Wilshire Blvd., Suite 700, Beverly Hills CA 90211. REAL ESTATE. Real estate developer and builder, active in California.

Sales: $308.1 million (trend 26.7% a year).
Earnings: $14.13 million (trend 22.3% a year).
What happened to a $10,000 investment

Purchase Date	*Purchase Price*	*Price on 12-31-81*	*Dividends Paid*
12-31-71	$25.50	$36.25	$406.86
12-31-76	$19.25	$36.25	$279.22

Purchase Date	*Cap. Gains (− Losses)*	*Total Return*	*Rate of Return*
12-31-71	$4,215.69	$4,622.55	3.87%
12-31-76	$8,831.17	$9,110.39	13.83%

* * *

SHAW INDUSTRIES, INC. (SHX). Founded 1967. Headquarters: 616 E. Walnut Ave., Dalton GA 30720. CARPETING. Produces carpeting under several brand names for home and office use. MAJOR SUBSIDIARIES, BRANDS: Magee, Philadelphia, and Sabre carpeting.

Sales: $250.6 million (trend 19.8% a year).
Earnings: $8.42 million (trend 9.9% a year).
What happened to a $10,000 investment

Purchase Date	*Purchase Price*	*Price on 12-31-81*	*Dividends Paid*
12-31-71	$10.13	$5.75	$3,374.00
12-31-76	$ 8.68	$5.75	$2,499.51

Purchase Date	*Cap. Gains (− Losses)*	*Total Return*	*Rate of Return*
12-31-71	$−4,324.57	$−950.57	−.99%
12-31-76	$−3,373.81	$−874.30	−1.81%

* * *

SHELL OIL CO. (SUO). Founded 1922. Headquarters: 1 Shell Plaza, PO Box 2463, Houston TX 77001. OIL. Shell is approximately the eighth largest U.S. oil company, and the twelfth largest U.S. industrial corporation. It is 69 percent owned by Royal Dutch Shell Group, the Netherlands-based international oil giant. 26,000 employees.

Sales: $19,830.0 million (trend 18.3% a year).
Earnings: $1,542.00 million (trend 22.1% a year).
What happened to a $10,000 investment

Purchase Date	*Purchase Price*	*Price on 12-31-81*	*Dividends Paid*
12-31-71	$11.81	$44.25	$7,756.61
12-31-76	$19.72	$44.25	$3,042.79

Purchase Date	*Cap. Gains (− Losses)*	*Total Return*	*Rate of Return*
12-31-71	$27,460.32	$35,216.93	16.29%
12-31-76	$12,440.57	$15,483.36	20.57%

PROFILE: Even though Shell Oil sells around $20-billion worth of oil products and petrochemicals each year, even though it's among the dozen largest industrial firms in this country, even though it's the eighth largest U.S. oil enterprise, it is still a baby compared to its parents.

Daddy is Royal Dutch Petroleum of the Netherlands, which owns 60 percent of the Royal Dutch Shell Group, the giant international operating company that in turn owns 69 percent of Shell Oil Co., the U.S. firm. Mommy is Shell Transport & Trading, a British enterprise that owns 40 percent of Royal Dutch Shell. The 1980 sales of the operating company (Daddy and Mommy together) were about $92 billion. Royal Dutch Shell is the second largest worldwide oil company after Exxon, measured by sales. In profits, it's hard on Exxon's heels.

Shell Oil, the U.S. company, has a good track record of sales, earnings, and dividend growth. In 1980 it sold more gasoline than any other U.S. company. But it isn't self-sufficient in petroleum.

(Neither are its parents.) It has a good record for finding oil and gas in the Gulf of Mexico and is also a significant factor in petrochemicals (about 8 percent of 1980 profits). The stock has paid dividends every year since 1936 and offers a moderate yield. The p / e ratio in recent years has gyrated between 4 and 13, with 6 to 8 being the usual multiple.

If you're interested in Shell, consider a direct investment in Daddy or Mommy (ticker symbols RD or SC), both traded on the New York Stock Exchange. Owning foreign stocks makes your tax return more complicated, and has certain adverse tax consequences (you may be taxed on earnings in both countries, and you lose the U.S. dividend exemption.) However, Royal Dutch and Shell Transport usually sell for a lower multiple than Shell Oil, offer a higher dividend yield, are spending heavily on new production facilities, and have big stakes in the North Sea. They are also slightly less leveraged than Shell Oil (about 27 percent recently vs. 37 percent for the U.S. company).

* * *

SHELL TRANSPORT & TRADING CO., LTD. (SC). Founded 1897. Headquarters: Hell Centre, London SE1 7NA, England. **OIL.** Shell Transport owns 40 percent of the Royal Dutch Shell Group, the world's second largest oil company (after Exxon). The other 60 percent is owned by Royal Dutch Petroleum, whose shares are also traded on the New York Stock Exchange. The Royal Dutch Shell Group is the parent corporation to Shell Oil Co., which is profiled in the previous entry.

Sales: $31,568.0 million (trend 21.7% a year).
Earnings: $2,054.40 million (trend 30.1% a year).
What happened to a $10,000 investment

Purchase Date	*Purchase Price*	*Price on 12-31-81*	*Dividends Paid*
12-31-71	$ N/A	$30.12	$ N/A
12-31-76	$15.25	$30.12	$6,061.15

Purchase Date	*Cap. Gains (− Losses)*	*Total Return*	*Rate of Return*
12-31-71	$ N/A	$ N/A	N/A%
12-31-76	$9,754.10	$15,815.25	20.89%

* * *

SHELLER-GLOBE CORP. (SHG). Founded 1929. Headquarters: 1505 Jefferson Ave., PO Box 962, Toledo OH 43697. **AUTOMOTIVE AND OFFICE PRODUCTS.** Diversified manufacturer of automotive parts, office supplies and accessories, and radiation detection instruments. **MAJOR SUBSIDIARIES, BRANDS:** Globe-Weis; Leece-Neville; Kralinator; Red Rope; Victoreen; Smokador.

Sales: $512.1 million (trend −.3% a year).
Earnings: $15.44 million (trend −3.5% a year).
What happened to a $10,000 investment

Purchase Date	*Purchase Price*	*Price on 12-31-81*	*Dividends Paid*
12-31-71	$13.83	$12.25	$3,997.08
12-31-76	$14.32	$12.25	$1,967.82

Purchase Date	*Cap. Gains (− Losses)*	*Total Return*	*Rate of Return*
12-31-71	$−1,145.62	$2,851.46	2.54%
12-31-76	$−1,445.76	$ 522.06	1.02%

* * *

SHERWIN-WILLIAMS CO. (SHW). Founded 1884. Headquarters: 101 Prospect Ave. N.W., Cleveland OH 44115. **PAINT.** Sherwin-Williams is the world's largest manufacturer of paint and is also a major marketer of paint and wallpaper through some 1,400 stores. Also makes specialty chemicals and containers. 16,000 employees. **MAJOR SUBSIDIARIES, BRANDS:** Sherwin-Williams; Martin Senour; Dutch Boy; Gray Drug Stores Inc.

Sales: $1,263.7 million (trend 7.9% a year).
Earnings: $23.81 million (trend −5.9% a year).
What happened to a $10,000 investment

Purchase Date	*Purchase Price*	*Price on 12-31-81*	*Dividends Paid*
12-31-71	$23.94	$22.25	$3,248.04
12-31-76	$20.62	$22.25	$1,248.48

Purchase Date	*Cap. Gains (− Losses)*	*Total Return*	*Rate of Return*
12-31-71	$−704.96	$2,543.08	2.29%
12-31-76	$ 787.88	$2,036.36	3.78%

PROFILE: Let's be blunt. Sherwin-Williams Company's performance during the 1970s was one of the most lackluster in American industry. But look at this sampling of headlines and comments from 1980.

From *Barron's:* "Cleaning up . . . Sherwin-Williams Co. is recovering from its spill."

From *Financial World:* "John Breen puts long-ailing Sherwin-Williams on the turnaround trail."

From *Forbes:* "Sherwin-Williams, near collapse three years ago, still needs refurbishing, but John Breen is already laying on a solid coat of primer."

Breen, brought in from Gould Inc. to head the company in 1979, has fired half the top managers, changed the accounting system, and required the retail stores to pull their own weight. (Previously, they were treated as factory outlets for the paint and allowed to lose money, on the theory that a manufacturing profit had already been logged when the paint was delivered to the stores.)

In 1981 the company spent around $55 million (a bit more than the three previous years' slim profits) to pick up Gray Drug Stores, which in turn had recently acquired Drug Fair Inc. This was the first in what may be a series of diversification moves.

The balance sheet is freighted with a good share of debt, with debt recently composing about 40 percent of total capital. Dividends were started up again in 1979, after a one-year hiatus followed a 1977 loss. The yield is moderate.

* * *

SIERRA PACIFIC POWER CO. (SRP). Founded 1912. Headquarters: PO Box 10100, Reno NV 89520. UTILITY. Provides electric, gas, and water service in parts of western Nevada and eastern California. MAJOR SUBSIDIARIES, BRANDS: Lands of Sierra, Inc.; Sierra Energy Co.

Sales: $233.9 million (trend 17.4% a year).
Earnings: $16.62 million (trend 20.2% a year).
What happened to a $10,000 investment

Purchase Date	*Purchase Price*	*Price on 12-31-81*	*Dividends Paid*
12-31-71	$17.87	$11.12	$6,064.34
12-31-76	$14.25	$11.12	$4,477.19

Purchase Date	*Cap. Gains (− Losses)*	*Total Return*	*Rate of Return*
12-31-71	$−3,776.22	$2,288.11	2.08%
12-31-76	$−2,192.98	$2,284.21	4.20%

* * *

SIGNAL COMPANIES, INC. (SGN). Founded 1928. Headquarters: 11255 N. Torrey Pines Rd., La Jolla CA 92037. CONGLOMERATE. Signal is involved in aerospace, truck manufacturing, petrochemical processing, audiovisual equipment, and other areas. 50,000 employees. MAJOR SUBSIDIARIES, BRANDS: Garrett Corp. (aerospace); Mack Trucks (90 percent owned); UOP Inc. (petrochemical processes); Ampex Corp. (audiovisual equipment and computer peripherals); Natomas Co. (energy — 13 percent owned); Unitrode Corp. (semiconductors and electronics — 24 percent owned); Golden West Broadcasters (includes KTLA TV, Channel 5 in Los Angeles, and the California Angels baseball team — 49.9 percent owned).

Sales: $4,285.3 million (trend 16.3% a year).
Earnings: $152.40 million (trend 34.2% a year).
What happened to a $10,000 investment

Purchase Date	*Purchase Price*	*Price on 12-31-81*	*Dividends Paid*
12-31-71	$5.40	$25.37	$7,667.53
12-31-76	$8.42	$25.37	$3,483.17

Purchase Date	*Cap. Gains (− Losses)*	*Total Return*	*Rate of Return*
12-31-71	$36,947.53	$44,615.06	18.50%
12-31-76	$20,148.51	$23,631.68	27.45%

PROFILE: The heart of this conglomerate is Garrett Corp., which makes engines and other parts for jet aircraft, both commercial and military, and turbochargers for cars. In 1980 Garrett contributed two thirds of Signal's profits, though only about 40 percent of the company's sales.

Most of the rest of sales — but lately hardly any profits recently — come from Mack Trucks, a leading producer of heavy-duty diesel trucks. Signal owns 90 percent of Mack, whose fortunes tend to rise and fall with the economy.

A big chunk of the company used to be Signal Oil. No more; the oil properties were sold off in 1974. Instead, the company now has a framed check on the wall for $420 million. That money did not go to trim debt, which Signal likes to maintain at around 30 percent of capital. Instead, much of it went into acquisitions, notably UOP (formerly Universal Oil Products Corp.) and the fractional positions in Natomas, Golden West Broadcasters, and Unitrode, all fast-growing, successful outfits. In 1981 Signal acquired Ampex, which makes computer memory products and other computer products, plus video recording tape and magnetic tape for professional broadcasts. For Ampex, Signal shelled out roughly $415 million.

There have been rumors that Signal plans to sell Mack Trucks, which lost money in 1980 and made a modest profit in 1981. At the least, it apparently plans to de-emphasize the division by surrounding it with higher-tech, faster-growing businesses. Excluding Mack, Signal's entourage has shown rapid growth, hence the p / e ratio of 9 for the stock in early 1982, when the average equity was valued at only 7 to 8 times earnings.

* * *

SIGNODE CORP. (SGS). Founded 1928. Headquarters: 3600 W. Lake Ave., Glenview IL 60025. **STRAPPING AND FASTENERS.** Manufactures and markets steel and plastic strapping and fasteners, and related products. **MAJOR SUBSIDIARIES, BRANDS:** Reichel & Drews, Inc.; Product Identification Corp.; Minigrip, Inc.; TrusWal Systems Corp.; Angleboard, Inc.; Signode Wrapping Systems Inc.; J. D. Adams Co.

Sales: $695.5 million (trend 14.9% a year).
Earnings: $38.56 million (trend 18.5% a year).
What happened to a $10,000 investment

Purchase Date	*Purchase Price*	*Price on 12-31-81*	*Dividends Paid*
12-31-71	$35.08	$36.25	$3,597.34
12-31-76	$40.25	$36.25	$1,977.64

Purchase Date	*Cap. Gains (− Losses)*	*Total Return*	*Rate of Return*
12-31-71	$ 332.54	$3,929.88	3.37%
12-31-76	$−993.79	$ 983.85	1.89%

* * *

SIMMONDS PRECISION PRODUCTS, INC. (SP). Founded 1936. Headquarters: 150 White Plains Rd., Tarrytown NY 10591. **AEROSPACE.** Makes high-technology products and systems for the aerospace industry.

Sales: $132.0 million (trend 24.3% a year).
Earnings: $8.46 million (trend 32.2% a year).
What happened to a $10,000 investment

Purchase Date	*Purchase Price*	*Price on 12-31-81*	*Dividends Paid*
12-31-71	$5.25	$14.25	$3,200.00
12-31-76	$6.50	$14.25	$2,015.38

Purchase Date	*Cap. Gains (− Losses)*	*Total Return*	*Rate of Return*
12-31-71	$17,142.86	$20,342.86	11.74%
12-31-76	$11,923.08	$13,938.46	19.07%

* * *

SIMPLICITY PATTERN CO., INC. (SYP). Founded 1927. Headquarters: 200 Madison Ave., New York NY 10016. **DRESSMAKING PATTERNS.** Manufactures paper patterns for women's and children's clothing.

Sales: $86.8 million (trend −3.7% a year).
Earnings: $10.25 million (trend −6.2% a year).
What happened to a $10,000 investment

Purchase Date	*Purchase Price*	*Price on 12-31-81*	*Dividends Paid*
12-31-71	$46.91	$10.37	$ 839.89
12-31-76	$15.62	$10.37	$1,376.00

Purchase Date	*Cap. Gains (− Losses)*	*Total Return*	*Rate of Return*
12-31-71	$−7,788.35	$−6,948.46	−11.19%
12-31-76	$−3,360.00	$−1,984.00	−4.33%

* * *

SINGER CO. (SMF). Founded 1873. Headquarters: 8 Stamford Forum, Stamford CT 06904. **SEWING MACHINES, DEFENSE ELECTRONICS.** Singer remains the largest U.S. maker of sewing machines, but has diversified into a number of areas including defense electronics, power tools, heating and air conditioning, industrial controls and meters, and educational materials. 70,000 employees.

Sales: $2,786.6 million (trend 6.5% a year).
Earnings: $33.10 million (trend −13.7% a year).
What happened to a $10,000 investment

Purchase Date	*Purchase Price*	*Price on 12-31-81*	*Dividends Paid*
12-31-71	$77.25	$13.87	$1,216.83
12-31-76	$20.12	$13.87	$ 844.72

Purchase Date	*Cap. Gains (− Losses)*	*Total Return*	*Rate of Return*
12-31-71	$−8,203.88	$−6,987.06	−11.31%
12-31-76	$−3,105.59	$−2,260.87	−5.00%

PROFILE: More than a stitch has been dropped here. The stock, which hit a high above $93 in 1972, plunged to a low of just above $6 in 1980 before rebounding. In the past decade, the stock has bounced around quite a bit, as news of disasters alternates with feelings that a comeback is in the works.

The sewing machine business is in sad shape, both in the United States and Europe, and the reasons are now well enough known to be inscribed on a sampler. Women work more. They haven't time to sew, aren't interested in sewing. Higher family incomes, coupled with less leisure time, mean that clothing will be bought at the store, not made at home.

Luckily for Singer, these facts of life aren't true in Asia and Latin America the way they are in Europe and the United States. Sewing machines sales in the Third World are still pretty good. And Singer does get a big share of its money (43 percent of 1980 sales and 66 percent of 1980 profits) from abroad. Foreign sales buy time for Singer to complete its program of diversifying away from dependence on sewing machines, which recently accounted for about half of sales and earnings.

The booming part of the business is electronics — in particular, defense electronics. Missile guidance systems and flight simulators are among the products Singer has been selling successfully.

But the company has been riding a roller coaster. It took big losses in 1975 and 1979, slashing the dividend in each of the following years to a dime per share. As with many stocks seen on Wall Street as "turnaround plays," it's a risky investment.

* * *

SKYLINE CORP. (SKY). Founded 1951. Headquarters: 2520 By-Pass Rd., Elkhart IN 46514. **MOBILE HOMES.** Manufactures mobile homes and recreational vehicles. **MAJOR SUBSIDIARIES, BRANDS:** Skyline Homes, Inc.; Homette Corp.; Layton Homes Corp.; Hillcrest; Buddy; Ramada; Nomad; Aly; Lindy.

Sales: $276.6 million (trend 2.2% a year).
Earnings: $6.68 million (trend −5.6% a year).
What happened to a $10,000 investment

Purchase Date	*Purchase Price*	*Price on 12-31-81*	*Dividends Paid*
12-31-71	$53.87	$14.87	$567.98
12-31-76	$18.62	$14.87	$966.44

Purchase Date	*Cap. Gains (− Losses)*	*Total Return*	*Rate of Return*
12-31-71	$−7,238.98	$−6,671.00	−10.42%
12-31-76	$−2,013.42	$−1,046.98	−2.19%

* * *

A. O. SMITH CORP. (SMC). Founded 1916. Headquarters: 3533 N. 27th St., Milwaukee WI 43216. **AUTOMOTIVE PRODUCTS.** Manufactures structural parts and other items for cars and trucks; electric motors for refrigeration and jet pumps; water heaters and boilers; agricultural storage systems, and other products. **MAJOR SUBSIDIARIES, BRANDS:** AgriStor Credit Corp.; Harvestore.

Sales: $693.7 million (trend 9.4% a year).
Earnings: $−1.70 million.
What happened to a $10,000 investment

Purchase Date	*Purchase Price*	*Price on 12-31-81*	*Dividends Paid*
12-31-71	$24.12	$12.12	$3,980.52
12-31-76	$15.87	$12.12	$3,779.53

Purchase Date	*Cap. Gains (− Losses)*	*Total Return*	*Rate of Return*
12-31-71	$−4,974.09	$−993.58	−1.04%
12-31-76	$−2,362.20	$ 1,417.32	2.69%

* * *

SMITH INTERNATIONAL, INC. (SII). Founded 1937. Headquarters: 4343 Von Karman Ave., Newport Beach CA 92660. **MINING TOOLS.** Supplies drilling and boring tools to the oil well and mining industries. **MAJOR SUBSIDIARIES, BRANDS:** Drilco; Dyna-Drill; Smith Tool.

Sales: $784.1 million (trend 21.7% a year).
Earnings: $79.07 million (trend 17.6% a year).
What happened to a $10,000 investment

Purchase Date	*Purchase Price*	*Price on 12-31-81*	*Dividends Paid*
12-31-71	$ 6.56	$45.87	$5,154.29
12-31-76	$20.12	$45.87	$1,334.16

Purchase Date	*Cap. Gains (− Losses)*	*Total Return*	*Rate of Return*
12-31-71	$59,904.76	$65,059.05	22.33%
12-31-76	$12,795.03	$14,129.19	19.26%

* * *

SMITHKLINE CORP. (SKL). Founded 1929. Headquarters: 1 Franklin Plaza, PO Box 7929, Philadelphia PA 19101. **DRUGS.** SmithKline is approximately the eleventh largest U.S. drug manufacturer. It produces prescription and over-the-counter drugs, diagnostic products, and animal health products. 21,000 employees. **MAJOR SUBSIDIARIES, BRANDS:** Tagamet (antiulcer drug); Contac (cold remedy); Dyazide (diuretic); Sine-Off (sinus medicine). In 1982 SmithKline acquired Beckman Instruments, Inc.

Sales: $1,771.9 million (trend 25.5% a year).
Earnings: $307.99 million (trend 41.0% a year).
What happened to a $10,000 investment

Purchase Date	*Purchase Price*	*Price on 12-31-81*	*Dividends Paid*
12-31-71	$14.31	$67.62	$6,275.98
12-31-76	$19.84	$67.62	$3,266.77

Purchase Date	*Cap. Gains (— Losses)*	*Total Return*	*Rate of Return*
12-31-71	$37,248.91	$43,524.89	18.26%
12-31-76	$24,078.74	$27,345.51	30.15%

PROFILE: The company has been radically transformed by Tagamet, the first drug that produces a cure (rather than merely symptomatic relief) for stomach ulcers. In a 1980 profile, *Fortune* magazine observed that in the company's "dingy yellow-brick headquarters on the edge of a Philadelphia slum . . . the lobby is swarming with prospective suppliers, prospective distributors, prospective employees, and prospective dealmakers, not to mention Wall Street analysts. . . . Most of them wouldn't have gone near the place a few years ago."

As recently as 1973, SmithKline's sales were less than half a million dollars a year. In 1980 sales were $1.7 billion and profits a hefty $308 million. Tagamet accounted for more than a third of sales and about 60 percent of profits. Its success has allowed the company to more than double its research budget (recently $170 million) and to trim debt to a mere 12 percent of capital. The return on stockholders' equity, which was quite decent before Tagamet, averaged around 35 percent in 1978–80. *Fortune* called Tagamet "one of the most stunningly successful products in the history of American business," along with the Xerox 914 copier and the Ford Mustang. It is the second largest selling prescription drug, after Valium (made by Hoffman LaRoche).

The stock's multiple hasn't changed much. It used to sell for about 10 to 20 times earnings in the early 1970s, and it still does. (Meanwhile, most stock's multiples have declined.) What's changed are earnings — up from $1.07 a share in 1975 to $4.65 in 1980.

Over the same period, the dividend has jumped from $0.50 to $1.72. But the yield remains moderate, since the stock price has soared. The 1975 high was just under $15, the 1980 high just above $80. The outlook for both drug and company remains good, but watch the p / e ratio closely to make sure you're not paying in advance for all the success that can be expected.

* * *

J. M. SMUCKER CO. (SJM). Founded 1921. Headquarters: Strawberry Lane, Orrville OH 44667. **JAMS, JELLIES.** Smucker is a leading U.S. producer of jams and jellies; also sells other retail food products and wholesales fruit.

Sales: $169.4 million (trend 8.6% a year).
Earnings: $7.70 million (trend 12.1% a year).
What happened to a $10,000 investment

Purchase Date	*Purchase Price*	*Price on 12-31-81*	*Dividends Paid*
12-31-71	$25.12	$36.25	$3,194.03
12-31-76	$18.75	$36.25	$2,173.33

Purchase Date	*Cap. Gains (— Losses)*	*Total Return*	*Rate of Return*
12-31-71	$4,427.86	$ 7,621.89	5.83%
12-31-76	$9,333.33	$11,506.67	16.55%

* * *

SNAP-ON TOOL CORP. (SNA). Founded 1920. Headquarters: 2801 80th St., Kenosha WI 53140. **TOOLS.** Major manufacturer and distributor of automotive tools and equipment.

Sales: $401.8 million (trend 19.3% a year).
Earnings: $38.32 million (trend 25.3% a year).
What happened to a $10,000 investment

Purchase Date	*Purchase Price*	*Price on 12-31-81*	*Dividends Paid*
12-31-71	$14.54	$21.12	$3,182.23
12-31-76	$16.87	$21.12	$2,002.96

Purchase Date	*Cap. Gains (— Losses)*	*Total Return*	*Rate of Return*
12-31-71	$4,527.22	$7,709.46	5.88%
12-31-76	$2,518.52	$4,521.48	7.75%

* * *

SONY CORP. (SNE). Founded 1946. Headquarters: 7–35 Kitashinagawa 6-chome, Shinagawa-ku, Tokyo 141 Japan. **CONSUMER ELECTRONICS.** Sony is one of the world's leading producers of consumer electronic products, including televisions, radios, tape recorders, and videocassette recorders. It is also diversifying into office products and miscellaneous other areas. 32,000 employees. **MAJOR SUBSIDIARIES, BRANDS:** Trinitron color televisions; Betamax video recorders; Walkman portable stereos.

Sales: $4,266.5 million (trend 24.4% a year).
Earnings: $325.32 million (trend 25.3% a year).
What happened to a $10,000 investment

Purchase Date	*Purchase Price*	*Price on 12-31-81*	*Dividends Paid*
12-31-71	$5.82	$17.50	$1,444.03
12-31-76	$9.25	$17.50	$ 671.57

Purchase Date	*Cap. Gains (− Losses)*	*Total Return*	*Rate of Return*
12-31-71	$20,048.08	$21,492.10	12.16%
12-31-76	$ 8,918.92	$ 9,590.49	14.40%

PROFILE: When one household in twenty had a black-and-white TV set, sales started to take off. When one household in twenty had a color TV, the same thing happened. Today almost every household in the United States has a TV; most have color. Borrowing a phrase from physics, marketers call the 5-percent threshold a "critical mass," after the amount of fissionable material needed to start a chain reaction.

In 1981 about 4 percent of householders in the United States and Europe had video recorders. In Japan the 5-percent threshold has already been reached. Sony is one of the two largest producers of video recording equipment in the world. (The other is Matsushita, which Americans know as Panasonic.) Its Betamax system is getting a good reception.

That's probably the main reason why Sony is once again (as it was about a decade ago, after the success of its Trinitron color TVs) a hot stock. From a 1979 low of less than $7 a share, Sony ADRs (American depository receipts) rose to $16.75 in 1980 and almost $25 in mid-1981. In the last year or two, it has been among the most actively traded stocks on the New York Stock Exchange.

Sony has other things going for it besides Betamax. Its long-term record shows steady earnings growth (though growth appears deceptively erratic, due to currency fluctuations). Its balance sheet is as clean as the inside of one of its electronic devices: Debt hasn't edged above 3 percent of capital since 1971. And it's truly an international company. Less than half its factories are in Japan; about two thirds of sales come from outside Japan.

An oddity is the recent diversification program, which has seen Sony venture into such unfamiliar areas as cosmetics, importing sporting goods (from PepsiCo's Wilson), selling insurance (with Prudential), marketing records (with CBS), importing whiskey and aircraft, and even manufacturing spaghetti. *Business Week* in 1980 reported that both U.S. and Japanese security analysts were puzzled by the diversification program. However, all of these sidelines account for less than 15 percent of sales and are considered likely to stay in that proportion. Consumer electronics remains the heart of Sony's activity.

Dividends have been paid each year since 1947, but are, and always have been, tiny.

* * *

SOO LINE RAILROAD CO. (SOO). Founded 1961. Headquarters: Box 530, Minneapolis MN 55440. **TRANSPORTATION.** Interstate carrier of freight by rail.

Sales: $314.3 million (trend 14.6% a year).
Earnings: $34.04 million (trend 24.7% a year).
What happened to a $10,000 investment

Purchase Date	*Purchase Price*	*Price on 12-31-81*	*Dividends Paid*
12-31-71	$ 8.56	$29.62	$15,342.09
12-31-76	$13.42	$29.62	$ 6,551.55

Purchase Date	*Cap. Gains (− Losses)*	*Total Return*	*Rate of Return*
12-31-71	$24,598.54	$39,940.63	17.45%
12-31-76	$12,080.75	$18,632.30	23.42%

* * *

SOURCE CAPITAL, INC. (SOR). Founded 1968. Headquarters: 1888 Century Park E., Los Angeles CA 90067. **INVESTMENTS.** Closed-end investment company with a portfolio consisting mainly of common stock and convertible debentures.

* * *

SOUTH ATLANTIC FINANCIAL CORP. (SAT). Founded 1979. Headquarters: 150 S.E. Third Ave., Miami FL 33131. **REAL ESTATE.** Manages investments in real estate; markets condominiums.

* * *

SOUTH CAROLINA ELECTRIC & GAS CO. (SCG). Founded 1924. Headquarters: 328 Main St., Columbia SC 29218. **UTILITY.** Sells electricity and natural gas in major portions of South Carolina. Also provides urban bus service. **MAJOR SUBSIDIARIES, BRANDS:** Energy Subsidiary, Inc.; South Carolina LNG Co., Inc.; South Carolina Fuel Co., Inc.

Sales: $630.7 million (trend 14.9% a year).
Earnings: $50.75 million (trend 9.9% a year).
What happened to a $10,000 investment

Purchase Date	*Purchase Price*	*Price on 12-31-81*	*Dividends Paid*
12-31-71	$24.75	$15.25	$6,347.47
12-31-76	$19.37	$15.25	$4,345.81

Purchase Date	*Cap. Gains (− Losses)*	*Total Return*	*Rate of Return*
12-31-71	$−3,838.38	$2,509.09	2.26%
12-31-76	$−2,129.03	$2,216.77	4.09%

* * *

SOUTH JERSEY INDUSTRIES, INC. (SJI). Founded 1969. Headquarters: 1 S. Jersey Plaza, Route 54, Folsom NJ 08037. **UTILITY.** Provides natural gas to customers in southern New Jersey. Also distributes heating oil; mines and processes sand and gravel. **MAJOR SUBSIDIARIES, BRANDS:** South Jersey Gas Co.; Energy & Minerals, Inc.

Sales: $219.2 million (trend 23.4% a year).
Earnings: $9.46 million (trend 19.6% a year).
What happened to a $10,000 investment

Purchase Date	*Purchase Price*	*Price on 12-31-81*	*Dividends Paid*
12-31-71	$24.25	$16.75	$6,841.24
12-31-76	$18.50	$16.75	$4,778.38

Purchase Date	*Cap. Gains (− Losses)*	*Total Return*	*Rate of Return*
12-31-71	$−3,092.78	$3,748.45	3.23%
12-31-76	$ −945.95	$3,832.43	6.70%

* * *

SOUTHDOWN, INC. (SDW). Founded 1930. Headquarters: Suite 2200, 2 Allen Center, Houston TX 77002. **CEMENT.** Manufactures and distributes Portland cement; also active in exploration for gas and oil. **MAJOR SUBSIDIARIES, BRANDS:** Southwestern Portland Cement Co.; Pelto Oil Co.; Judson Candies, Inc.

Sales: $240.4 million (trend −3.0% a year).
Earnings: $31.62 million (trend 32.1% a year).
What happened to a $10,000 investment

Purchase Date	*Purchase Price*	*Price on 12-31-81*	*Dividends Paid*
12-31-71	$11.06	$39.25	$1,966.10
12-31-76	$ 7.12	$39.25	$2,526.32

Purchase Date	*Cap. Gains (− Losses)*	*Total Return*	*Rate of Return*
12-31-71	$25,480.23	$27,446.33	14.11%
12-31-76	$45,087.72	$47,614.04	41.94%

* * *

SOUTHEASTERN PUBLIC SERVICE CO. (SPV). Founded 1947. Headquarters: 6917 Collins Ave., Miami Beach FL 33141. **DIVERSIFIED SERVICES.** Performs various services for utility companies in the South, including tree trimming, pole setting, and line installation. Also involved in refrigeration, food processing, distribution of liquid petroleum gas, and natural gas and oil production.

Sales: $150.5 million (trend 16.8% a year).
Earnings: $10.29 million (trend 46.3% a year).
What happened to a $10,000 investment

Purchase Date	*Purchase Price*	*Price on 12-31-81*	*Dividends Paid*
12-31-71	$4.69	$9.62	$1,902.69
12-31-76	$2.64	$9.62	$ 0.00

Purchase Date	*Cap. Gains (− Losses)*	*Total Return*	*Rate of Return*
12-31-71	$10,522.35	$12,425.04	8.41%
12-31-76	$26,478.58	$26,478.58	29.54%

* * *

SOUTHEAST BANKING CORP. (STB). Founded 1967. Headquarters: 100 S. Biscayne Blvd., Miami FL 33131. **BANK HOLDING COMPANY.** Parent company for Southeast First National Bank of Miami and numerous other Florida banks. **MAJOR SUBSIDIARIES, BRANDS:** Southeast Mortgage; Southeast First National Bank of Miami.

Sales: $603.4 million (trend 20.4% a year).
Earnings: $47.91 million (trend 35.2% a year).
What happened to a $10,000 investment

Purchase Date	*Purchase Price*	*Price on 12-31-81*	*Dividends Paid*
12-31-71	$26.56	$18.37	$2,650.95
12-31-76	$11.12	$18.37	$3,307.87

Purchase Date	*Cap. Gains (− Losses)*	*Total Return*	*Rate of Return*
12-31-71	$−3,082.35	$−431.40	−.44%
12-31-76	$ 6,516.85	$ 9,824.72	14.67%

* * *

SOUTHERN CALIFORNIA EDISON CO. (SCE). Founded 1909. Headquarters: 2244 Walnut Grove Ave., Rosemead CA 91770. UTILITY. Supplies gas, water, and electricity in central and southern California (excluding Los Angeles and San Diego). It is the fifth largest U.S. electric utility company. 14,000 employees. MAJOR SUBSIDIARIES, BRANDS: Associated Southern Investment Co.; Calabasas Park Co.; Mono Power Co.; Southern Surplus Realty Co.; Energy Services, Inc.; Electric Systems Co.

Sales: $3,661.7 million (trend 15.6% a year).
Earnings: $256.59 million (trend 12.8% a year).
What happened to a $10,000 investment

Purchase Date	*Purchase Price*	*Price on 12-31-81*	*Dividends Paid*
12-31-71	$29.50	$28.75	$7,138.98
12-31-76	$22.87	$28.75	$5,639.34

Purchase Date	*Cap. Gains (− Losses)*	*Total Return*	*Rate of Return*
12-31-71	$−254.24	$6,884.75	5.38%
12-31-76	$ 2,568.31	$8,207.65	12.73%

PROFILE: Most of what you'll read in the papers about Southern California Edison concerns the company's commitment to alternative energy sources, like solar energy, wind, and biomass. The company is more serious about these energy sources than most utilities are. It has, for example, constructed a working solar generating plant in the Mojave Desert. And in 1980 it announced that a third of future generating capacity would use alternative energy sources.

This goes over big, especially in California, but it ought to be put in perspective. In the early 1980s, the company had the capacity to generate more than 13,000 megawatts of electricity daily. It expected to add about 5,500 megawatts of capacity in the 1980s. That would make a total of around 18,-500 megawatts, of which only 2,000 or so would come from the new-style sources.

Meanwhile, as of 1980, the power mix was about 30 percent gas, 28 percent oil, 20 percent purchased power, 12 percent hydroelectric, 9 percent coal, and 1 percent nuclear — anything but newfangled. The pledge to emphasize renewable power sources in the future may be of value in getting political help (or, at least, leniency) from state regulators, whose aid the company (like almost all utilities) desperately needs.

The balance sheet, with debt a bit less than half of capital, is better than that of most utilities. Growth, though not inspiring, is also better than typical for a utility — mainly because the service area has a growing population. The dividend yield in the early 1980s was around 12 percent — high, but less than what some competitors must offer to attract capital in a landscape barren of prospects for capital gains.

Is the dividend covered by earnings? That depends on how you account. Even as the company counts it, more than 80 percent of 1980 profits were needed to pay the 1980 dividend.

* * *

SOUTHERN CO. (SO). Founded 1945. Headquarters: 64 Perimeter Center E., PO Box 720071, Atlanta GA 30346. UTILITY. Through four operating subsidiaries, this holding company supplies electricity to more than nine million people in portions of Georgia, Alabama, Florida, and Mississippi. It is the largest electrical utility holding company in the United States. 28,000 employees. MAJOR SUBSIDIARIES, BRANDS: Alabama Power; Georgia Power; Gulf Power; Mississippi Power.

Sales: $3,763.5 million (trend 13.1% a year).
Earnings: $344.39 million (trend 5.7% a year).
What happened to a $10,000 investment

Purchase Date	*Purchase Price*	*Price on 12-31-81*	*Dividends Paid*
12-31-71	$22.25	$12.25	$6,557.30
12-31-76	$16.37	$12.25	$4,726.72

Purchase Date	*Cap. Gains (− Losses)*	*Total Return*	*Rate of Return*
12-31-71	$−4,494.38	$2,062.92	1.89%
12-31-76	$−2,519.08	$2,207.63	4.07%

PROFILE: Coal is far and away the dominant power source for the collection of four utilities that make up the Southern Co. You could build a case that this augurs well for the company's future. Coal in the long run may be less expensive than oil or gas and hence give a competitive advantage to the utilities that use it.

The case has some weak points, though. In the short run, hydroelectric power is certainly cheaper than coal. In the long run, perhaps nuclear power will be cheaper. Most important, the electric utility industry isn't a competitive one, but a series of local regulated monopolies. It's not likely that Southern will be granted fatter operating margins by regulators as a result of its fuel mix, which was recently

84 percent coal, 9 percent nuclear, 6 percent hydro, and 1 percent oil and gas.

Sales have grown steadily, as the South has experienced both residential and industrial growth. From less than $1 billion in 1972, revenues grew to close to $4 billion a year in the early 1980s. Over the same period, profits grew from less than $150 million to more than $400 million. But profits per share have hardly budged, as the number of shares outstanding have ballooned. At the same time, the company has taken on more than $5 billion in long-term debt. For several years now, debt has been well over half of total capital (recently 58 percent).

Like most utilities, Southern can attract investment money only by offering a big dividend—and in Southern's case, it's a whopper. The yield in 1981 was around 13 to 14 percent. Most (and, in some years, all) of the company's earnings are required to make that hefty payout.

* * *

SOUTHERN INDIANA GAS AND ELECTRIC CO. (SIG). Founded 1912. Headquarters: 20–24 N.W. Fourth St., Evansville IN 47741. UTILITY. Provides electric and gas service in southwestern Indiana.

Sales: $205.0 million (trend 19.9% a year).
Earnings: $18.25 million (trend 11.2% a year).
What happened to a $10,000 investment

Purchase Date	*Purchase Price*	*Price on 12-31-81*	*Dividends Paid*
12-31-71	$16.62	$18.75	$7,939.85
12-31-76	$20.62	$18.75	$3,781.82

Purchase Date	*Cap. Gains (– Losses)*	*Total Return*	*Rate of Return*
12-31-71	$ 1,278.20	$9,218.05	6.75%
12-31-76	$–909.09	$2,872.73	5.18%

* * *

SOUTHERN NATURAL RESOURCES, INC. (NRG). Founded 1935. Headquarters: First National-Southern Natural Bldg., Birmingham AL 35203. NATURAL GAS. Operates interstate natural gas pipeline; active in contract drilling and exploration for gas and oil. MAJOR SUBSIDIARIES, BRANDS. SONAT Exploration; The Offshore Co.; Boise Southern Co. (60 percent owned).

* * *

THE SOUTHERN NEW ENGLAND TELEPHONE CO. (SNG). Founded 1882. Headquarters: 227 Church St., New Haven CT 06506. TELEPHONE UTILITY. Provides telephone service for most of the state of Connecticut.

Sales: $825.0 million (trend 11.7% a year).
Earnings: $71.80 million (trend 13.1% a year).
What happened to a $10,000 investment

Purchase Date	*Purchase Price*	*Price on 12-31-81*	*Dividends Paid*
12-31-71	$39.12	$43.75	$8,148.24
12-31-76	$39.12	$43.75	$4,529.07

Purchase Date	*Cap. Gains (– Losses)*	*Total Return*	*Rate of Return*
12-31-71	$1,182.11	$9,330.35	6.81%
12-31-76	$1,182.11	$5,711.18	9.46%

* * *

SOUTHERN PACIFIC CO. (SX). Founded 1947. Headquarters: Southern Pacific Bldg., 1 Market Plaza, San Francisco CA 94105. RAILROAD. Southern Pacific is the fourth largest U.S. railroad, ranked by sales. It has some 13,000 miles of track in fifteen western and midwestern states. The company has sidelines in pipeline operations, forest products, real estate, microwave telecommunications, trucking, and insurance. 54,000 employees. MAJOR SUBSIDIARIES, BRANDS: Southern Pacific Transportation Co.; Southern Pacific Communications (Sprint); Ticor (largest U.S. writer of title insurance).

Sales: $2,859.7 million (trend 11.6% a year).
Earnings: $155.90 million (trend 15.8% a year).
What happened to a $10,000 investment

Purchase Date	*Purchase Price*	*Price on 12-31-81*	*Dividends Paid*
12-31-71	$45.75	$40.75	$5,099.45
12-31-76	$35.87	$40.75	$3,459.23

Purchase Date	*Cap. Gains (– Losses)*	*Total Return*	*Rate of Return*
12-31-71	$–1,092.90	$4,006.56	3.43%
12-31-76	$ 1,358.89	$4,818.12	8.18%

PROFILE: This is one of the nation's largest, but least profitable railroads. Profits have followed an erratic course, wending their way up from $102 million in 1971 to $156 million in 1980. The return on stockholders' equity has been poor for years (lately in the 6-to-9 percent range), even though it's hyped by a big dollop of debt (recently about 37 percent of capital).

As always, when a railroad isn't burning up the track, the fancy of stockholders and analysts turns to the road's real estate. "Sell it off," is the cry. "Or develop it. Or cut the timber. Or mine the minerals." In Southern Pacific's case, it's the timber that attracts the most attention. The railroad just happens to be the biggest landowner in California. Much of its land is timberland, and the company let it be known in 1981 that it was willing to part with some. *The Value Line Investment Survey* estimated that 115,000 acres of timberland and mountain property might bring in as much as $460 million, or more than twice as much as the company has ever earned in a year. (No sales had yet been reported as of early 1982.)

Among the company's diversifications is Sprint, a microwave telecommunications service that competes with Ma Bell for the long-distance-call business of firms and individuals. Both Sprint and the fledgling trucking business show promise, but, as yet, few profits.

Another avenue the company has been pursuing is a possible merger with Santa Fe, a slightly larger and considerably more prosperous road. But merger talks have been on again, off again, under the skeptical eye of the Justice Department, which can't help but notice the similarity in the service area of the two railroads.

* * *

SOUTHERN RAILWAY CO. (SR). Founded 1894. Headquarters: 920 15th St. N.W., Washington DC 20005. RAILROAD. Southern is the sixth largest U.S. railroad, with some 10,000 miles of track in thirteen southern and midwestern states. 30,000 employees.

Sales: $1,637.7 million (trend 13.3% a year).
Earnings: $178.07 million (trend 20.0% a year).
What happened to a $10,000 investment

Purchase Date	*Purchase Price*	*Price on 12-31-81*	*Dividends Paid*
12-31-71	$43.06	$95.25	$6,091.15
12-31-76	$62.25	$95.25	$2,632.93

Purchase Date	*Cap. Gains (– Losses)*	*Total Return*	*Rate of Return*
12-31-71	$12,119.01	$18,210.16	10.93%
12-31-76	$ 5,301.20	$ 7,934.14	12.39%

PROFILE: Read the other entries for railroads in this book and you'll find a lot of subsidiaries and brand names that have little or nothing to do with railroading. You'll find a lot of the railroad companies are holding companies that have removed any reference to railroading from the corporate name. Not so with Southern. It keeps the word "railway" in its name, and sticks to its game. Does pretty well, too.

Between 1971 and 1980, Southern managed to increase the return on stockholders' equity from around 7 percent to around 14 percent. This was done while simultaneously whittling down the company's debt load a few percentage points; recently, it was about 34 percent of capital. The company has spent substantial sums to keep its track and rolling stock in good repair. It has an extremely diversified cargo mix, with coal the single biggest element (about 16 percent of revenues). The railroad is lean, both in its track structure and in its labor costs; it's been practicing automation for a long time.

Southern plans to merge with Norfolk & Western, forming a new road under the name NWS Enterprises. Each Southern shareholder would get shares in the new outfit on a 1.9-for-1 basis. (Norfolk and Western shareholders would get shares on a straight 1-for-1 basis.) Both companies have approved the plan. The major remaining step, approval from the Interstate Commerce Commission (ICC), was accomplished in early 1982. The merger should be consummated soon, probably by the time you read this.

From 1978 through mid-1981, these shares sold for less than 8 times earnings, a bargain multiple for a stock with the steady growth record Southern has posted.

* * *

SOUTHERN UNION CO. (SUG). Founded 1932. Headquarters: First International Bldg., Dallas TX 75270. NATURAL GAS. Distributes natural gas; also involved in gas processing and oil refining and marketing. MAJOR SUBSIDIARIES, BRANDS: Supron Energy Corp.

Sales: $553.7 million (trend 19.4% a year).
Earnings: $37.59 million (trend 18.0% a year).
What happened to a $10,000 investment

Purchase Date	*Purchase Price*	*Price on 12-31-81*	*Dividends Paid*
12-31-71	$13.07	$22.25	$7,835.20
12-31-76	$18.93	$22.25	$3,231.34

Purchase Date	*Cap. Gains (– Losses)*	*Total Return*	*Rate of Return*
12-31-71	$7,028.06	$14,863.27	9.54%
12-31-76	$1,751.76	$ 4,983.10	8.42%

* * *

SOUTHLAND CORP. (SLC). Founded 1961. Headquarters: 2828 N. Haskell Ave., Dallas TX 75204. **CONVENIENCE STORES.** Southland operates some 7,000 7-Eleven convenience stores; also runs four other retail chains, a dairy business, and an ice business. 44,000 employees. **MAJOR SUBSIDIARIES, BRANDS:** 7-Eleven; Gristede's; Charles & Co.; Chief Auto Parts; and R. S. McColl (British tobacco, confectionary and newsstand chain).

Sales: $4,758.7 million (trend 21.8% a year).
Earnings: $77.67 million (trend 18.1% a year).
What happened to a $10,000 investment

Purchase Date	*Purchase Price*	*Price on 12-31-81*	*Dividends Paid*
12-31-71	$24.72	$31.75	$2,143.77
12-31-76	$24.21	$31.75	$1,602.77

Purchase Date	*Cap. Gains (– Losses)*	*Total Return*	*Rate of Return*
12-31-71	$2,845.37	$4,989.14	4.13%
12-31-76	$3,113.69	$4,716.46	8.03%

PROFILE: As you pulled away from a 7-Eleven convenience store one warm evening, a six-pack on the seat next to you, you may have wondered why the corporation that owns this massive chain of quick-stop convenience stores is named Southland. The name comes from the Southland Ice Company, the predecessor of the current corporation. While working for Southland Ice in the 1920s, Joe C. Thompson suggested selling bread, milk, and eggs at the ice docks, since they were open late anyway. The idea caught on, and convenience foods quickly bypassed ice as the company's staple. (The company still has an ice business, though it probably accounts for less than one percent of revenues.)

Today, Southland, according to *Financial World,* is "the largest operator and franchiser of convenience stores in the world" (42 states, 5 foreign countries) and "the nation's largest retailer of candy, soda, canned beer, single packs of cigarettes, and *Playboy* magazine."

Financial World saw growth slowing "from super to merely excellent," but *Forbes,* in a gloomy 1980 profile, declared that "the giant of convenience stores has lost its way." Among *Forbes*'s gripes: too much of recent growth has come from gasoline (pumps have been added to about 40 percent of stores); the diversifications haven't been notably successful; and the company faces increased competition from imitators and from conventional supermarkets, which are keeping longer hours.

In the early 1980s, the stock has sold in the same $20-to-$30 range as in the early 1970s. But whereas a decade ago the p / e was 20 to 30, lately it's been around — well, 7 to 11. That's a much more conservative multiple — a low one, in fact, for a company that's shown the kind of steady earnings growth Southland has.

Not so conservative is the balance sheet. Debt sloshed above 50 percent of capital in 1978–79, and was still close to that mark in 1980–81. The dividend yield is moderate; dividends have been paid yearly since 1957, and it's company policy to pay out roughly a quarter of earnings.

* * *

SOUTHLAND ROYALTY CO. (SRO). Founded 1924. Headquarters: 1000 Fort Worth Club Tower, Fort Worth TX 76102. **OIL AND GAS.** Explores for and produces oil and gas.

Sales: $363.8 million (trend 35.6% a year).
Earnings: $62.29 million (trend 24.6% a year).
What happened to a $10,000 investment

Purchase Date	*Purchase Price*	*Price on 12-31-81*	*Dividends Paid*
12-31-71	$ 2.46	$26.25	$6,394.18
12-31-76	$10.72	$26.25	$ 998.25

Purchase Date	*Cap. Gains (– Losses)*	*Total Return*	*Rate of Return*
12-31-71	$96,586.03	$102,980.20	27.44%
12-31-76	$14,489.80	$ 15,488.05	20.58%

* * *

SOUTHMARK PROPERTIES (SM). Founded 1970. Headquarters: 3300 Holcomb Bridge Rd., Norcross GA 30092. **REAL ESTATE.** Active in acquisition, leasing, sale, management, and development of real estate.

Sales: $39.0 million (trend 7.2% a year).
Earnings: $3.54 million.
What happened to a $10,000 investment

Purchase Date	*Purchase Price*	*Price on 12-31-81*	*Dividends Paid*
12-31-71	$31.87	$5.25	$2,861.18
12-31-76	$ 1.87	$5.25	$ 0.00

Purchase Date	*Cap. Gains (– Losses)*	*Total Return*	*Rate of Return*
12-31-71	$–8,352.94	$–5,491.76	–7.66%
12-31-76	$ 18,000.00	$ 18,000.00	22.87%

* * *

SOUTHWEST AIRLINES CO. (LUV). Founded 1967. Headquarters: Aviation Pl., PO Box 37611, Dallas TX 75235. AIRLINE. Operates single-class airline, primarily serving Texas.

Sales: $213.0 million (trend 58.6% a year).
Earnings: $28.45 million (trend 63.9% a year).
What happened to a $10,000 investment

Purchase Date	*Purchase Price*	*Price on 12-31-81*	*Dividends Paid*
12-31-71	$ .64	$28.87	$12,491.34
12-31-76	$4.22	$28.87	$ 1,866.66

Purchase Date	*Cap. Gains (− Losses)*	*Total Return*	*Rate of Return*
12-31-71	$441,171.88	$453,663.22	46.76%
12-31-76	$ 58,436.18	$ 60,302.85	47.70%

* * *

SOUTHWEST BANCSHARES, INC. (SWB). Founded 1970. Headquarters: 707 McKinney St., Houston TX 77002. BANK HOLDING COMPANY. Parent company of numerous Texas banks, including Bank of the Southwest, in Houston. MAJOR SUBSIDIARIES, BRANDS: Bank of the Southwest.

Sales: $378.0 million (trend 24.0% a year).
Earnings: $30.86 million (trend 16.2% a year).
What happened to a $10,000 investment

Purchase Date	*Purchase Price*	*Price on 12-31-81*	*Dividends Paid*
12-31-71	$15.42	$30.25	$4,871.35
12-31-76	$15.17	$30.25	$2,857.14

Purchase Date	*Cap. Gains (− Losses)*	*Total Return*	*Rate of Return*
12-31-71	$9,621.62	$14,492.97	9.37%
12-31-76	$9,945.05	$12,802.20	17.92%

* * *

SOUTHWEST FLORIDA BANKS, INC. (SFB). Founded 1972. Headquarters: 2400 First St., Fort Myers FL 33901. BANK HOLDING COMPANY. Parent to some thirteen banks in southwest Florida. MAJOR SUBSIDIARIES, BRANDS: Southwest Financial Services; Southwest Mortgage Services; First National Bank & Trust Co. of Naples; First National Bank in Fort Myers.

* * *

SOUTHWEST FOREST INDUSTRIES, INC. (SWF). Founded 1917. Headquarters: 3443 N. Central Ave., Phoenix AZ 85012. FOREST PRODUCTS. Manufacturer of paper, packaging, and building products.

Sales: $737.9 million (trend 10.7% a year).
Earnings: $25.96 million (trend 112.0% a year).
What happened to a $10,000 investment

Purchase Date	*Purchase Price*	*Price on 12-31-81*	*Dividends Paid*
12-31-71	$17.50	$15.50	$1,485.71
12-31-76	$ 9.62	$15.50	$1,974.03

Purchase Date	*Cap. Gains (− Losses)*	*Total Return*	*Rate of Return*
12-31-71	$−1,142.86	$ 342.86	.34%
12-31-76	$ 6,103.90	$8,077.92	12.57%

* * *

SOUTHWEST GAS CORP. (SWX). Founded 1931. Headquarters: 5241 Spring Mountain Rd., Las Vegas NV 89114. UTILITY. Provides natural gas in Nevada and parts of California and Arizona. MAJOR SUBSIDIARIES, BRANDS: Energy Increments.

Sales: $317.5 million (trend 28.5% a year).
Earnings: $6.63 million (trend 19.9% a year).
What happened to a $10,000 investment

Purchase Date	*Purchase Price*	*Price on 12-31-81*	*Dividends Paid*
12-31-71	$14.50	$8.50	$7,186.21
12-31-76	$10.75	$8.50	$5,041.86

Purchase Date	*Cap. Gains (− Losses)*	*Total Return*	*Rate of Return*
12-31-71	$−4,137.93	$3,048.28	2.70%
12-31-76	$−2,093.02	$2,948.84	5.30%

* * *

SOUTHWESTERN ENERGY CO. (SWN). Founded 1929. Headquarters: 1001 Sain St., Fayetteville AR 72701. NATURAL GAS. Distributes natural gas within Arkansas; also explores for and produces natural gas and oil.

* * *

SOUTHWESTERN PUBLIC SERVICE CO. (SPS). Founded 1942. Headquarters: SPS Tower, Tyler at Sixth, Amarillo TX 79170. UTILITY. Supplies electricity in the Texas Panhandle and adjacent areas.

Sales: $533.9 million (trend 16.9% a year).
Earnings: $56.15 million (trend 6.8% a year).
What happened to a $10,000 investment

Purchase Date	*Purchase Price*	*Price on 12-31-81*	*Dividends Paid*
12-31-71	$13.12	$13.25	$8,015.24
12-31-76	$15.12	$13.25	$4,125.62

Purchase Date	*Cap. Gains (− Losses)*	*Total Return*	*Rate of Return*
12-31-71	$ 95.24	$8,110.48	6.12%
12-31-76	$−1,239.67	$2,885.95	5.20%

* * *

SPARTON CORP. (SPA). Founded 1919. Headquarters: 2400 E. Ganson St., Jackson MI 49202. ELECTRONICS. Manufacturer of electronics products for military applications. Also produces auto parts and marine accessories and conveyor systems; involved in oil exploration.

Sales: $132.6 million (trend 15.4% a year).
Earnings: $7.30 million (trend 12.5% a year).
What happened to a $10,000 investment

Purchase Date	*Purchase Price*	*Price on 12-31-81*	*Dividends Paid*
12-31-71	$3.37	$13.87	$6,992.59
12-31-76	$6.62	$13.87	$2,588.68

Purchase Date	*Cap. Gains (− Losses)*	*Total Return*	*Rate of Return*
12-31-71	$31,111.11	$38,103.70	17.01%
12-31-76	$10,943.40	$13,532.08	18.67%

* * *

SPECTRA-PHYSICS, INC. (SPY). Founded 1961. Headquarters: 1250 W. Middlefield Rd., Mountain View CA 94042. LASERS. Developer and producer of laser and chromatography products and related systems.

Sales: $135.7 million (trend 29.9% a year).
Earnings: $2.52 million (trend 5.2% a year).
What happened to a $10,000 investment

Purchase Date	*Purchase Price*	*Price on 12-31-81*	*Dividends Paid*
12-31-71	$ 5.04	$21.25	$0.00
12-31-76	$15.25	$21.25	$0.00

Purchase Date	*Cap. Gains (− Losses)*	*Total Return*	*Rate of Return*
12-31-71	$32,148.76	$32,148.76	15.47%
12-31-76	$ 3,934.43	$ 3,934.43	6.86%

* * *

SPERRY CORP. (SY). Founded 1955. Headquarters: 1290 Ave. of the Americas, New York NY 10104. COMPUTERS, AEROSPACE. Sperry's main lines of business are computer manufacturing and guidance systems for missiles and aircraft. It is also a major producer of farm machinery and of fluid power transmission equipment. 92,000 employees. MAJOR SUBSIDIARIES, BRANDS: Univac computers; Sperry guidance systems; New Holland farm machinery; Vickers fluid power transmission equipment.

Sales: $5,427.2 million (trend 11.8% a year).
Earnings: $313.00 million (trend 18.0% a year).
What happened to a $10,000 investment

Purchase Date	*Purchase Price*	*Price on 12-31-81*	*Dividends Paid*
12-31-71	$30.75	$35.25	$2,933.33
12-31-76	$42.75	$35.25	$1,244.44

Purchase Date	*Cap. Gains (− Losses)*	*Total Return*	*Rate of Return*
12-31-71	$ 1,463.41	$ 4,396.75	3.71%
12-31-76	$−1,754.39	$−509.94	−1.04%

PROFILE: Sperry boasts a balanced product line in four major areas, each of which has good long-term growth prospects. The revolution in computer use is by no means over. Aerospace will get a boost from planned increases in defense spending. Farm machinery should be strong as America continues its role as breadbasket to the world. And fluid power transmission equipment stands to benefit from the increase in capital spending that the Reagan administration hopes will result from its economic policies.

Thus, the long term holds opportunities for Sperry, and the past makes a good prologue. From 1971 (admittedly a down year) to 1980, earnings marched up from $1.77 a share to $7.68. Earnings were flat in 1981, but the overall trend has been clearly up. At about 5 to 8 times earnings recently, the stock offers you this growth record quite cheap.

There has to be a catch, given the world's notorious shortage of true free lunches. And there is. The catch is that Sperry faces tough competition in most of its product lines, and especially in computers, which have recently accounted for just over half of sales and profits. In large computers, a Univac specialty, IBM has recently made aggressive product-design and pricing moves. Computer analysts also fault Univac for failing to use the latest technology, and for missing the boat in minicomputers. So the low multiple to a large extent reflects Wall Street's worries over whether Sperry Univac can hold its computer market share.

The balance sheet is in good shape, with debt recently around 20 to 25 percent of capital. The dividend yield is moderate; dividends have been paid each year since 1967.

* * *

SPRINGS MILLS, INC. (SMI). Founded 1888. Headquarters: PO Box 70, No. White St., Fort Mill SC 29715. **TEXTILES.** Manufactures and markets fabrics, consumer textiles, drapery and window furnishing products, and frozen foods. **MAJOR SUBSIDIARIES, BRANDS:** Seabrook Foods; Lawtex Industries; Graber Industries; Springmaid; Skinner; Ultrasuede; Pequot; Wondercale; Morgan Jones; Seabrook Farms; Gold King.

Sales: $794.5 million (trend 8.4% a year).
Earnings: $32.16 million (trend 28.0% a year).
What happened to a $10,000 investment

Purchase Date	*Purchase Price*	*Price on 12-31-81*	*Dividends Paid*
12-31-71	$16.12	$23.50	$5,688.99
12-31-76	$13.12	$23.50	$4,236.19

Purchase Date	*Cap. Gains (− Losses)*	*Total Return*	*Rate of Return*
12-31-71	$4,573.64	$10,262.64	7.32%
12-31-76	$7,904.76	$12,140.95	17.23%

* * *

SQUARE D CO. (SQD). Founded 1903. Executive Plaza, Palatine IL 60067. **ELECTRICAL PRODUCTS.** Manufacturer of varied electrical products for home and industry. **MAJOR SUBSIDIARIES, BRANDS:** Square D; Yates; GSI; Bell; Rodale; Sun Dial; Trine.

Sales: $999.0 million (trend 16.6% a year).
Earnings: $83.04 million (trend 18.0% a year).
What happened to a $10,000 investment

Purchase Date	*Purchase Price*	*Price on 12-31-81*	*Dividends Paid*
12-31-71	$31.12	$28.87	$4,146.18
12-31-76	$27.87	$28.87	$2,712.11

Purchase Date	*Cap. Gains (− Losses)*	*Total Return*	*Rate of Return*
12-31-71	$−722.89	$3,423.29	2.99%
12-31-76	$ 358.74	$3,070.85	5.50%

* * *

SQUIBB CORP. (SQB). Founded 1968. Headquarters: 40 W. 57th St., New York NY 10019. **DRUGS.** Squibb is a major producer of prescription medications. Also makes medical diagnostic equipment, over-the-counter drugs, candy, and cosmetics. 27,000 employees. **MAJOR SUBSIDIARIES, BRANDS:** Capoten blood pressure drug; Theragran vitamins; Charles of the Ritz Group Ltd. (Jean Naté, Yves Saint Laurent perfumes and colognes); Advanced Technology Labs; Spacelabs; Vita-Stat.

Sales: $1,675.8 million (trend 8.1% a year).
Earnings: $123.89 million (trend 3.9% a year).
What happened to a $10,000 investment

Purchase Date	*Purchase Price*	*Price on 12-31-81*	*Dividends Paid*
12-31-71	$43.75	$32.75	$2,199.43
12-31-76	$29.50	$32.75	$1,855.93

Purchase Date	*Cap. Gains (− Losses)*	*Total Return*	*Rate of Return*
12-31-71	$−2,514.29	$−314.86	−.32%
12-31-76	$ 1,101.69	$ 2,957.63	5.32%

PROFILE: Among the billion-dollar drug companies, Squibb has been among the least profitable in recent years. Return on stockholders' equity has ranged from 12 to 16½ percent — not bad, but bad for a drug company. Profit margins have been in the 7-to-9 percent range; the same comment applies. Unable to build up solid earnings momentum, Squibb has been outspent by rivals in the crucial research and development area.

A drug that many analysts hope will give Squibb some needed earnings momentum is Capoten, a high blood pressure drug the company has touted as a breakthrough. In 1981 the Food and Drug Administration approved its use to treat patients on whom older drugs have failed.

The company derives about two thirds of its profits from the drug business. Until recently, about two thirds of the remainder came from candy. Bubble Yum and Care*Free were recent hits; Life Savers and Beech-Nut were steady sellers. In 1981 Squibb sold its candy operations to Nabisco Brands for $250 million. The last slice of earnings is contributed by cosmetics, notably Jean Naté and Yves Saint Laurent.

Though profitability has sagged some in recent years, the balance sheet has been kept in trim. Debt was recently about 28 percent of capital. Dividends have been paid yearly since 1902 and provide a moderate yield. Ranging from about 10 to 16 recently, the p / e ratio is higher than for most stocks, but lower than it used to be and lower than that of several competitors.

* * *

STA-RITE INDUSTRIES, INC. (SRE). Founded 1934. Headquarters: 777 E. Wisconsin Ave., Milwaukee WI 53202. **PUMPS.** Sta-Rite produces pumps and other fluid handling equipment for use in irrigation, swimming pools, industrial processes, and other applications.

Sales: $146.4 million (trend 12.1% a year).
Earnings: $−.57 million.
What happened to a $10,000 investment

Purchase Date	*Purchase Price*	*Price on 12-31-81*	*Dividends Paid*
12-31-71	$ 8.60	$10.75	$5,827.08
12-31-76	$11.44	$10.75	$2,393.39

Purchase Date	*Cap. Gains (− Losses)*	*Total Return*	*Rate of Return*
12-31-71	$ 2,494.00	$8,321.08	6.24%
12-31-76	$−601.33	$1,792.06	3.35%

* * *

A. E. STALEY MANUFACTURING CO. (STA). Founded 1906. Headquarters: 2200 Eldorado St., Decatur IL 62525. **GRAIN PROCESSING.** Staley is a leading wet-corn miller and soybean crusher. Close to half of its production goes into food ingredients (starch, vegetable oil, corn sweetener, etc.), and another 40 percent or so goes into animal feeds. 4,000 employees.

Sales: $2,006.2 million (trend 18.1% a year).
Earnings: $103.55 million (trend 28.2% a year).
What happened to a $10,000 investment

Purchase Date	*Purchase Price*	*Price on 12-31-81*	*Dividends Paid*
12-31-71	$ 5.04	$22.25	$10,280.99
12-31-76	$14.42	$22.25	$ 2,404.62

Purchase Date	*Cap. Gains (− Losses)*	*Total Return*	*Rate of Return*
12-31-71	$34,132.23	$44,413.22	18.46%
12-31-76	$ 5,433.53	$ 7,838.15	12.27%

PROFILE: The Chicago Bears, back in 1920–21, used to be the Decatur Staleys. Company founder "Gus" Staley founded the football team also. He hired George Halas to coach, then paid Halas to take the team off his hands — and to give Staley free advertising in the programs.

Forbes magazine related that story in a 1980 profile that said Staley "has a habit of snatching defeat from the jaws of victory." It's true that earnings here are (choose your own adjective) cyclical . . . volatile . . . unstable. But there's been an underlying uptrend through the past decade.

Volatile? You haven't seen volatile until you've seen Staley. In 1975, for example, Staley shares sold for less than $7 and for more than $21. Between the start of 1980 and the middle of 1981, you could have tripled your money in Staley — or lost more than half of it, depending on your timing. One reason for the wild gyrations: One of Staley's main products is high-fructose corn syrup, a sugar substitute. Its price moves up and down with the price of sugar (Staley keep the HFCS price 15 to 30 percent below that of sugar), and the stock moves with the HFCS price.

The gyrations may be tamed a little bit in the future as Staley expands its processing capacity in grains other than corn (notably soybeans and sunflower seeds). A major capital spending program is underway. The dividend yield is moderate, and dividends have been paid yearly since 1935.

* * *

STANDARD BRANDS PAINT CO. (SBP). Founded 1961. Headquarters: 4300 W. 190th St., Torrance CA 90509. **PAINT STORES.** Operates a chain of paint stores in California and southwestern states; manufactures 80 percent of paint sold in its own retail outlets.

Sales: $220.0 million (trend 10.3% a year).
Earnings: $15.13 million (trend 8.6% a year).
What happened to a $10,000 investment

Purchase Date	*Purchase Price*	*Price on 12-31-81*	*Dividends Paid*
12-31-71	$38.44	$25.50	$1,137.95
12-31-76	$42.50	$25.50	$ 710.59

Purchase Date	*Cap. Gains (– Losses)*	*Total Return*	*Rate of Return*
12-31-71	$–3,365.85	$–2,227.90	–2.49%
12-31-76	$–4,000.00	$–3,289.41	–7.67%

* * *

STANDARD MOTOR PRODUCTS, INC. (SMP). Founded 1926. Headquarters: 37–18 Northern Blvd., Long Island City NY 11101. **AUTOMOTIVE PARTS.** Manufacturers replacement parts for automotive, marine, and industrial engines. **MAJOR SUBSIDIARIES, BRANDS:** Blue Streak; Champ; Hygrade; Standard.

Sales: $125.9 million (trend 9.4% a year).
Earnings: $3.29 million (trend 2.7% a year).
What happened to a $10,000 investment

Purchase Date	*Purchase Price*	*Price on 12-31-81*	*Dividends Paid*
12-31-71	$14.78	$21.12	$1,957.89
12-31-76	$ 6.78	$21.12	$2,862.30

Purchase Date	*Cap. Gains (– Losses)*	*Total Return*	*Rate of Return*
12-31-71	$ 4,295.11	$ 6,253.01	4.98%
12-31-76	$21,168.03	$24,030.33	27.75%

* * *

STANDARD OIL CO. OF CALIFORNIA (SD). Founded 1926. Headquarters: 225 Bush St., San Francisco CA 94104. **OIL.** Standard Oil of California is the fourth largest U.S. oil company and fifth largest U.S. industrial corporation. In addition to oil production, refining, and marketing, it owns 20 percent of AMAX, a major mining concern, and is active in geothermal energy, coal, and uranium. 38,000 employees. **MAJOR SUBSIDIARIES, BRANDS:** Chevron, Standard (gasoline stations, in Southeast only).

Sales: $40,479.0 million (trend 18.0% a year).
Earnings: $2,401.00 million (trend 25.2% a year).
What happened to a $10,000 investment

Purchase Date	*Purchase Price*	*Price on 12-31-81*	*Dividends Paid*
12-31-71	$14.34	$42.87	$8,671.02
12-31-76	$20.62	$42.87	$3,830.30

Purchase Date	*Cap. Gains (– Losses)*	*Total Return*	*Rate of Return*
12-31-71	$19,891.07	$28,562.09	14.45%
12-31-76	$10,787.88	$14,618.18	19.74%

PROFILE: How many companies do you know that have $2 to $3 billion of cash — that's right, *cash,* not assets — on hand? Standard of California does. How many big companies do you know where long-term debt is only around 14 percent of total capital? That was recently the figure for Standard of California. How many companies have earnings that grew from $1.51 a share in 1971 to $7.02 a share in 1980? And finally, how many major international oil companies do you know that get more than half their profits from U.S. oil operations? Standard of California does.

All of these attributes make the stock interesting, and it becomes more interesting still at the bargain multiples (5 to 8 times earnings) that have prevailed for the international oil companies for the past few years. Why such low multiples? Well, they're huge companies, so they're not about to double their size overnight. Standard of California may have looked indecisive in its on-again, off-again pursuit of AMAX (in which it holds a 20-percent stake). The company has been involved in a number of pollution suits. Most important, the price of oil recently stopped going up, and some analysts think it may be soft for years. Standard of California thinks the price will rise or at least stay constant. That's why it put about $4.6 billion into capital spending in 1981, most of it for domestic exploration and production.

Balancing the negatives against the positives, the company looks strong. The dividend yield — 4½ to 7 percent in recent years — adds to total return potential. Dividends have been paid yearly since 1912, fourteen years before incorporation.

* * *

STANDARD OIL CO. (INDIANA). (SN). Founded 1889. Headquarters: 200 E. Randolph Dr., Chicago IL 60601. **OIL.** Standard Oil of Indiana is the sixth largest U.S. oil company and ninth largest U.S. industrial firm. It is active in oil production, refining, and marketing in the United States and abroad; also produces petrochemicals. Through partly owned companies, has sidelines in solar energy, genetic engineering, and industrial controls. 56,000 employees. **MAJOR SUBSIDIARIES, BRANDS:** Amoco, Standard (oil, and gasoline stations); Solarex (solar energy — 20 percent owned); Analog Devices (computerized industrial controls — 16 percent owned); Cetus Corp. (genetic engineering — 21 percent owned).

Sales: $26,133.1 million (trend 20.1% a year).
Earnings: $1,915.31 million (trend 19.0% a year).
What happened to a $10,000 investment

Purchase Date	*Purchase Price*	*Price on 12-31-81*	*Dividends Paid*
12-31-71	$17.37	$52.25	$7,492.95
12-31-76	$29.81	$52.25	$2,951.78

Purchase Date	*Cap. Gains (– Losses)*	*Total Return*	*Rate of Return*
12-31-71	$20,071.94	$27,564.89	14.15%
12-31-76	$ 7,526.21	$10,477.99	15.41%

PROFILE: A comparison between this company and Standard Oil Co. of California (see entry above) is on point. While Standard of California is an international oil firm that's going increasingly domestic, Standard of Indiana is a domestic firm that's been going international. Recently, just about half of Indiana Standard's profits came from U.S. oil operations (petrochemicals chipped in another 7 percent or so). Sources outside the United States and Canada recently accounted for more than a third of oil production, with Egypt and South America being the chief foreign locales.

In drilling methods, the two companies differ substantially. Yet both have towering reputations for drilling success. California Standard prefers exhaustive seismic tests before it starts drilling. As a result, its percentage of successes is a wonder in the industry. Indiana Standard buys or leases lots of land and drills lots of wells. But the amount of oil it finds draws *oohs* and *aahs* from competitors and analysts alike.

The past decade was kind to Indiana Standard, as to most oil companies. Here, earnings shot up from $1.24 a share in 1971 to $6.54 in 1980. Oil shares took a tumble in 1981, on anticipation of an extended glut. But Indiana Standard isn't planning on one: It's spending some $35 billion from 1981 to 85 for exploration and capital projects.

The balance sheet is solid, the p / e ratio highly variable (so watch it closely), and the dividend yield moderate. Dividends have been paid each year since 1894.

* * *

STANDARD OIL CO. (OHIO) (SOH). Founded 1870. Headquarters: Midland Bldg., Cleveland OH 44115. **OIL, COPPER.** Standard of Ohio is a major oil company, the largest producer of domestic crude in the United States. In 1981 it acquired Kennecott Corp., the nation's largest copper producer. 60,000 employees. **MAJOR SUBSIDIARIES, BRANDS:** Sohio, Boron, William Penn gasoline stations; Kennecott Corp. Standard Oil Co. of Ohio is 53 percent owned by British Petroleum.

Sales: $11,023.2 million (trend 36.3% a year).
Earnings: $1,810.92 million (trend 80.8% a year).
What happened to a $10,000 investment

Purchase Date	*Purchase Price*	*Price on 12-31-81*	*Dividends Paid*
12-31-71	$10.23	$41.50	$6,556.95
12-31-76	$19.19	$41.50	$2,613.68

Purchase Date	*Cap. Gains (– Losses)*	*Total Return*	*Rate of Return*
12-31-71	$30,549.62	$37,106.56	16.76%
12-31-76	$11,628.66	$14,242.35	19.38%

PROFILE: Alaskan oil turned this David into a Goliath. In 1969–1970, this was a small midwestern company, chiefly a refiner, and an also-ran in the oil business. That was when Sohio decided to sell 53 percent of its stock to British Petroleum in exchange for some promising Alaskan interests of the British firm.

As it turned out: (a) there was more oil there than anyone had thought; (b) it could be recovered faster than anyone had thought; and (c) due to OPEC and price decontrol, the value of each barrel was far greater than anyone had thought. Thus did Sohio get turned, overnight, from a pipsqueak to a colossus.

But Sohio was not prepared, by experience or structure, to reinvest its huge profits in further exploration. As a result, its cash coffers got fatter and fatter. By the middle of 1980, it was sitting on about $2.5 billion in cash and marketable securities. The whole world knew that it would soon have to make a major acquisition.

In 1981 it announced that acquisition: Kennecott, for $1.8 billion. Besides being the largest copper producer in the country, Kennecott also mines molybdenum, gold, silver, zinc, lead, iron, and titanium. The copper business was down in 1981, so the purchase won't pay in the short run. In the long run, it might.

In recent years, Sohio trimmed its debt from almost 72 percent of capital in 1977 down to about 40 percent in 1980 (still high, but not horrendous). The company has been paying dividends each year since 1936 and offers a moderate yield.

* * *

STANDARD-PACIFIC CORP. (SPF). Founded 1961. Headquarters: 1565 W. MacArthur Blvd., Costa Mesa CA 92626. **CONSTRUCTION.** Builds medium-priced single-family homes; manufactures office partitions, aircraft components. **MAJOR SUB-**

SIDIARIES, BRANDS: Panel-Air Corp.; Panel Concepts, Inc.

Sales: $120.7 million (trend 20.9% a year).
Earnings: $8.46 million (trend 34.7% a year).
What happened to a $10,000 investment

Purchase Date	*Purchase Price*	*Price on 12-31-81*	*Dividends Paid*
12-31-71	$4.09	$10.37	$6,339.07
12-31-76	$5.91	$10.37	$4,183.46

Purchase Date	*Cap. Gains (– Losses)*	*Total Return*	*Rate of Return*
12-31-71	$15,361.09	$21,700.16	12.23%
12-31-76	$ 7,557.68	$11,741.14	16.80%

* * *

STANDEX INTERNATIONAL CORP. (SXI). Founded 1955. Headquarters: Manor Parkway, Salem NH 03079. DIVERSIFIED MANUFACTURER. Manufactures and markets consumer, institutional and industrial products, including furniture, housewares, refrigeration equipment, electronics products. Graphics segment is involved in publishing, printing, binding, producing specialized business forms, and other related areas. MAJOR SUBSIDIARIES, BRANDS: Club Aluminum Cookware; Yield House Furniture; Frank Lewis Grapefruit Club; Dresher; Roehlen; Woodside.

Sales: $369.9 million (trend 15.7% a year).
Earnings: $15.21 million (trend 21.9% a year).
What happened to a $10,000 investment

Purchase Date	*Purchase Price*	*Price on 12-31-81*	*Dividends Paid*
12-31-71	$8.31	$13.50	$5,212.03
12-31-76	$8.44	$13.50	$3,816.30

Purchase Date	*Cap. Gains (– Losses)*	*Total Return*	*Rate of Return*
12-31-71	$6,240.60	$11,452.63	7.93%
12-31-76	$6,000.00	$ 9,816.30	14.66%

* * *

THE STANLEY WORKS (SWK). Founded 1852. Headquarters: 195 Lake St., New Britain CT 06050. TOOLS. Manufactures hand tools; builders' and household hardware; and industrial products. MAJOR SUBSIDIARIES, BRANDS: Stanley; Mac Tools, Inc.

Sales: $939.8 million (trend 15.4% a year).
Earnings: $50.37 million (trend 23.7% a year).
What happened to a $10,000 investment

Purchase Date	*Purchase Price*	*Price on 12-31-81*	*Dividends Paid*
12-31-71	$10.44	$17.50	$4,282.02
12-31-76	$10.83	$17.50	$2,656.92

Purchase Date	*Cap. Gains (– Losses)*	*Total Return*	*Rate of Return*
12-31-71	$6,767.44	$11,049.46	7.73%
12-31-76	$6,153.85	$ 8,810.77	13.47%

* * *

THE L. S. STARRETT CO. (SCX). Founded 1929. Headquarters: Crescent St., Athol MA 01331. TOOLS. Internationally active manufacturer of hand tools and measuring devices, especially for the metalworking industry.

Sales: $122.5 million (trend 16.7% a year).
Earnings: $13.79 million (trend 21.2% a year).
What happened to a $10,000 investment

Purchase Date	*Purchase Price*	*Price on 12-31-81*	*Dividends Paid*
12-31-71	$ 8.31	$26.25	$7,464.66
12-31-76	$11.44	$26.25	$3,353.01

Purchase Date	*Cap. Gains (– Losses)*	*Total Return*	*Rate of Return*
12-31-71	$21,578.95	$29,043.61	14.59%
12-31-76	$12,950.82	$16,303.83	21.34%

* * *

STATE MUTUAL SECURITIES, INC. (SMS). Founded 1972. Headquarters: 440 Lincoln St., Worcester MA 01605. INVESTMENTS. A closed-end bond fund, investing in fixed-income securities.

* * *

STAUFFER CHEMICAL CO. (STF). Founded 1953. Headquarters: Westport CT 06880. CHEMICALS. Stauffer is a major producer of both bulk and specialty chemicals and does a large part of its business in agricultural chemicals. 13,000 employees.

Sales: $1,695.2 million (trend 12.0% a year).
Earnings: $136.57 million (trend 6.8% a year).
What happened to a $10,000 investment

Purchase Date	*Purchase Price*	*Price on 12-31-81*	*Dividends Paid*
12-31-71	$ 9.81	$22.25	$8,226.75
12-31-76	$24.87	$22.25	$2,158.79

Purchase Date	*Cap. Gains (− Losses)*	*Total Return*	*Rate of Return*
12-31-71	$ 12,675.16	$20,901.91	11.94%
12-31-76	$−1,055.28	$ 1,103.52	2.12%

PROFILE: Stauffer ranks only about eighteenth in the chemical industry, by size. But in profitability it is among the top few.

One reason is that its agricultural chemicals, particularly weed killers and insecticides to aid the growing of corn, are in demand. Two big sellers (both weed killers) are Sutan-plus and Eradicane. Agricultural chemicals accounted for about 40 percent of the company's profits recently, though only about 25 percent of sales.

In its *Annual Report on American Industry* published in 1981, *Forbes* magazine ranked Stauffer first among fourteen broad-gauge chemical companies in return on total capital, and third in return on equity. (The difference in the two measures reflects the fact that Stauffer doesn't rely on debt too much; debt was recently about a quarter of total capital, down from about 37 percent in 1976.) In recent years, the company has consistently managed a return on equity of better than 15 percent. Profits inched ahead, even during the recession of 1980 and 1981.

The weak spot is plastics, a division that lost money in 1980. Some plastics-making facilities have been sold off, but the company invested heavily in a big plant in South Carolina, only to find that there simply wasn't enough demand to use the plant effectively. A pickup in the economy will help that problem — and help a lot of chemical companies with a lot of problems, for that matter.

The dividend yield recently was in the 5-to-6 percent range, and dividends are well covered by earnings.

* * *

STEEGO CORP. (STG). Founded 1955. Headquarters: 319 Clematis St., West Palm Beach FL 33401. **AUTOMOTIVE PARTS.** Distributes automotive and agricultural replacement parts; manufactures metal working equipment and other industrial equipment.

Sales: $249.0 million (trend 10.8% a year).
Earnings: $3.03 million (trend −5.4% a year).
What happened to a $10,000 investment

Purchase Date	*Purchase Price*	*Price on 12-31-81*	*Dividends Paid*
12-31-71	$3.36	$3.50	$1,373.32
12-31-76	$5.00	$3.50	$ 830.75

Purchase Date	*Cap. Gains (− Losses)*	*Total Return*	*Rate of Return*
12-31-71	$ 404.61	$ 1,777.93	1.65%
12-31-76	$−2,993.00	$−2,162.25	−4.76%

* * *

STERCHI BROS. STORES, INC. (SBI). Founded 1888. Headquarters: 114 S. Gay St., Knoxville TN 37901. **FURNITURE STORES.** Operates a chain of retail furniture stores in eight southeastern states.

Sales: $46.4 million (trend 8.5% a year).
Earnings: $2.47 million (trend 15.4% a year).
What happened to a $10,000 investment

Purchase Date	*Purchase Price*	*Price on 12-31-81*	*Dividends Paid*
12-31-71	$9.89	$12.25	$4,982.08
12-31-76	$8.62	$12.25	$2,991.30

Purchase Date	*Cap. Gains (− Losses)*	*Total Return*	*Rate of Return*
12-31-71	$2,390.80	$7,372.87	5.68%
12-31-76	$4,202.90	$7,194.20	11.45%

* * *

STERLING BANCORP (STL). Founded 1966. Headquarters: 540 Madison Ave., New York NY 10022. **BANK HOLDING COMPANY.** Involved in banking and commercial financial services. **MAJOR SUBSIDIARIES, BRANDS:** Standard Financial Corp.; Sterling National Bank & Trust Co. of New York; Sterling Banking Corp.

* * *

STERLING DRUG INC. (STY). Founded 1932. Headquarters: 90 Park Ave., New York NY 10016. **DRUGS, HOUSEHOLD PRODUCTS, TOILETRIES.** Sterling is a major marketer of over-the-counter drugs, prescription drugs, and household products; has sidelines in chemical production and waste-treatment facilities. 26,000 employees. **MAJOR SUBSIDIARIES, BRANDS:** Over-the-counter drugs include Bayer aspirin, Haley's M-O laxative, Midol pain-killer, Neo-Synephrine nasal spray, and Phillips' Milk of Magnesia. Prescription drugs include Demerol and Talwin pain-killers, and Inocor, an experimental drug for heart failure. Household products include Lysol cleaning fluids, d-Con insecticides, and Minwax waxes and stains. Toiletries are sold under the Dorothy Gray, Ogilvie, and Tussy labels.

Sales: $1,701.4 million (trend 11.9% a year).
Earnings: $123.34 million (trend 9.0% a year).
What happened to a $10,000 investment

Purchase Date	*Purchase Price*	*Price on 12-31-81*	*Dividends Paid*
12-31-71	$32.17	$22.25	$2,292.03
12-31-76	$16.75	$22.25	$2,480.60

Purchase Date	*Cap. Gains (– Losses)*	*Total Return*	*Rate of Return*
12-31-71	$–3,082.90	$–790.87	–.82%
12-31-76	$ 3,283.58	$ 5,764.18	9.53%

PROFILE: If you haven't heard Sterling's ads for Bayer aspirin or Phillips' Milk of Magnesia, you're an unusual (if not lucky) person. Sterling has been big on advertising since its inception. Research is not its long suit; marketing is. Thus, Sterling, despite its name, isn't really a drug company in the sense that companies like Merck, Upjohn, and Lilly are. Rather, it's in a class with such companies as American Home Products and Bristol-Myers.

Competing in that class can be tough. American Home Products is remarkably profitable and financially strong. Bristol-Myers is no slouch either. While Sterling rarely matches these two in profitability, it doesn't do badly. Return on stockholders' equity has usually been above 15 percent in recent years.

Sterling bears some similarity to arch-rival American Home Products. Both companies are an ad agency's delight, spending big bucks to push their products. But each product is advertised separately; little or nothing is done to promote a sense of corporate identity. Both companies are also rather secretive. And both have extremely strong balance sheets. In Sterling's case, debt was recently a mere 5½ percent of capital.

Based on its record of steady, though not spectacular, earnings growth, Sterling will normally sell at a premium to the market. In the early 1980s, when the average stock commanded about 8 times earnings, Sterling's p / e was about 11.

The moderate dividend yield is nicely covered by earnings; the company usually pays out a little less than half of profits in dividends.

* * *

J. P. STEVENS & CO., INC. (STN). Founded 1923. Headquarters: 1185 Ave. of the Americas, New York NY 10036. **TEXTILES.** Stevens is the nation's second largest textile manufacturer (after Burlington). Through subsidiaries, it is also involved in commercial printing and aircraft maintenance. 41,000 employees.

Sales: $1,916.0 million (trend 10.5% a year).
Earnings: $20.32 million (trend 1.7% a year).
What happened to a $10,000 investment

Purchase Date	*Purchase Price*	*Price on 12-31-81*	*Dividends Paid*
12-31-71	$11.21	$16.25	$8,275.85
12-31-76	$16.12	$16.25	$3,364.94

Purchase Date	*Cap. Gains (– Losses)*	*Total Return*	*Rate of Return*
12-31-71	$4,497.67	$12,773.53	8.58%
12-31-76	$ 83.32	$ 3,448.25	6.10%

PROFILE: Ask any union friend of yours what company union people hate most. He or she will probably answer J. P. Stevens. The company has a long record of bitter feuding with the Amalgamated Clothing & Textile Workers Union. The company has been sharply criticized by the National Labor Relations Board for bargaining in bad faith; it has been called an "embarrassment to the business community" in *Fortune* magazine; and it has been the target of a nationwide boycott led by organized labor.

In 1980 the hatchet was buried at least part way. J. P. Stevens agreed to let the union represent some of the workers at some of its plants. The boycott was called off. Was the hard-line stance worth it? Not judging by some of Stevens's bottom-line results. Unlike some nonunionized companies, Stevens has no special reputation for profitability. Earnings, for the past decade, have crept up slowly and erratically. The stock price has been close to stagnant.

In the early 1980s, the dividend yield was one of the more attractive features of this stock. It was yielding between 7½ and 9½ percent (depending on the stock price when you measured). But this attraction may be snatched away. In 1980 it took 83 percent of earnings to pay the dividend. In 1981 the company lost more than $22 million, or $1.59 a share.

Return on stockholders' equity has been poor, inching above 10 percent only once in the 1971–81 period, and sporadically dipping below 5 percent. In short, you don't have to be liberal or pro-union to avoid J. P. Stevens.

* * *

STEWART-WARNER CORP. (STX). Founded 1912. Headquarters: 1826 Diversey Parkway, Chicago IL 60614. DIVERSIFIED MANUFACTURER. Manufactures electronic and electromechanical systems, metal products and hardware, vehicular service equipment, and specialty products for industrial and military applications.

Sales: $336.2 million (trend 7.9% a year).
Earnings: $18.59 million (trend 7.1% a year).
What happened to a $10,000 investment

Purchase Date	*Purchase Price*	*Price on 12-31-81*	*Dividends Paid*
12-31-71	$22.48	$23.62	$5,889.41
12-31-76	$22.24	$23.62	$3,211.24

Purchase Date	*Cap. Gains (− Losses)*	*Total Return*	*Rate of Return*
12-31-71	$509.34	$6,398.75	5.07%
12-31-76	$622.75	$3,833.99	6.71%

* * *

STOKELY-VAN CAMP, INC. (SVC). Founded 1936. Headquarters: 941 N. Meridian St., Indianapolis IN 46206. FOOD PROCESSOR. Producer of canned and frozen food products. MAJOR SUBSIDIARIES, BRANDS: Stokely's; Van Camp's; Gatorade; Picktsweet.

Sales: $565.0 million (trend 4.5% a year).
Earnings: $8.27 million (trend 5.2% a year).
What happened to a $10,000 investment

Purchase Date	*Purchase Price*	*Price on 12-31-81*	*Dividends Paid*
12-31-71	$18.50	$31.75	$5,870.27
12-31-76	$20.37	$31.75	$2,655.21

Purchase Date	*Cap. Gains (− Losses)*	*Total Return*	*Rate of Return*
12-31-71	$7,162.16	$13,032.43	8.70%
12-31-76	$5,582.82	$ 8,238.04	12.77%

* * *

STONE & WEBSTER, INC. (SW). Founded 1929. Headquarters: 90 Broad St., New York NY 10004. ENGINEERING. Designs and builds electrical power plants; international consultants on civil and industrial projects.

Sales: $229.6 million (trend 7.9% a year).
Earnings: $37.21 million (trend .9% a year).
What happened to a $10,000 investment

Purchase Date	*Purchase Price*	*Price on 12-31-81*	*Dividends Paid*
12-31-71	$23.87	$37.25	$4,044.50
12-31-76	$28.56	$37.25	$2,199.12

Purchase Date	*Cap. Gains (− Losses)*	*Total Return*	*Rate of Return*
12-31-71	$5,602.09	$9,646.60	6.99%
12-31-76	$3,041.58	$5,240.70	8.79%

* * *

STONE CONTAINER CORP. (STO). Founded 1945. Headquarters: 360 N. Michigan Ave., Chicago IL 60601. PACKAGING. Manufactures corrugated packaging and paperboard.

Sales: $379.2 million (trend 11.0% a year).
Earnings: $21.31 million (trend 10.1% a year).
What happened to a $10,000 investment

Purchase Date	*Purchase Price*	*Price on 12-31-81*	*Dividends Paid*
12-31-71	$ 3.50	$16.62	$9,415.87
12-31-76	$10.17	$16.62	$2,281.97

Purchase Date	*Cap. Gains (− Losses)*	*Total Return*	*Rate of Return*
12-31-71	$37,500.00	$46,915.87	18.99%
12-31-76	$ 6,352.46	$ 8,634.43	13.26%

* * *

STOP & SHOP COMPANIES INC. (SHP). Founded 1925. Headquarters: PO Box 369, Boston MA 02101. RETAILING. Stop & Shop operates Boston's largest supermarket chain. In addition to supermarkets, it operates discount department stores, women's clothing stores, tobacco shops, and drug stores throughout the Northeast. 28,000 employees. MAJOR SUBSIDIARIES, BRANDS: Stop & Shop supermarkets; Bradlees discount department stores; Off the Rax women's clothing stores; Perkins tobacco shops; Medi Mart drug stores.

Sales: $2,059.2 million (trend 8.6% a year).
Earnings: $16.27 million (trend 4.8% a year).
What happened to a $10,000 investment

Purchase Date	Purchase Price	Price on 12-31-81	Dividends Paid
12-31-71	$18.60	$22.25	$4,561.83
12-31-76	$15.50	$22.25	$2,854.84

Purchase Date	Cap. Gains (− Losses)	Total Return	Rate of Return
12-31-71	$1,962.37	$6,524.19	5.15%
12-31-76	$4,354.84	$7,209.68	11.47%

PROFILE: In recent years, Stop & Shop has been paying out about as much in interest on its debt as it's been making in profits. In the last few years, long-term debt has been around $170 to $180 million and has composed 50 to 60 percent of the company's capital.

That's the kind of financial structure you might expect — and shrug off — in a small, young, fast-growing firm. But do you really want this much leverage in an established retailer?

If you do, look at this stock in depth. It's one of the most leveraged of the major supermarket chains. But even with the benefit of leverage, return on stockholders' equity has been only middling here. So if you seek an outstanding record for profitability or if you abhor debt, look elsewhere.

On the other hand, you might be a bargain hunter, and Stop & Shop may have some appeal in this light. The price / earnings ratio has usually been 5 or below the past few years — and they don't come much lower than that. The dividend yield in recent years has generally ranged from 6 to 8 percent, which is substantial. And the dividend is well covered by earnings. It's rare for the company to pay out more than a third of profits in dividends. Thus, if you can stomach the balance sheet, you may be able to make a good case that the stock is undervalued.

The stock market hasn't bought that argument for the past several years, however. Though the company has shown fairly consistent, if moderate, earnings increases, the stock in the early 1980s was selling below its highs in the early 1970s.

Apparently one of the brightest spots here is the Off the Rax women's clothing division; it's been expanding rapidly. Meanwhile, the number of supermarkets has been trimmed. (The company pulled out of the New Jersey supermarket derby, for example.)

One more caveat: The Rabb family owns about a fifth to a quarter of the stock. This could cause a sudden price movement some time in the future.

* * *

STORAGE TECHNOLOGY CORP. (STK). Founded 1969. Headquarters: 2270 S. 88th St., Louisville CO 80027. **COMPUTER PRODUCTS.** Storage Technology is a leading supplier of computer tape, tape drives, and disc drives. It recently acquired Documation, which makes computer printers and related products, and it is working, through a subsidiary, on developing its own mainframe computers. 11,000 employees. **MAJOR SUBSIDIARIES, BRANDS:** Documation Inc.; STC Computer Research Corp.

Sales: $603.5 million (trend 48.2% a year).
Earnings: $45.40 million (trend 58.7% a year).
What happened to a $10,000 investment

Purchase Date	Purchase Price	Price on 12-31-81	Dividends Paid
12-31-71	$3.52	$35.25	$0.00
12-31-76	$2.74	$35.25	$0.00

Purchase Date	Cap. Gains (− Losses)	Total Return	Rate of Return
12-31-71	$ 90,059.36	$ 90,059.36	25.90%
12-31-76	$118,567.68	$118,567.68	66.66%

PROFILE: Storage Technology is a bit like a crocodile bird, which gets its food from between that beast's teeth. It has found a profitable niche, but lives in constant danger.

The crocodile, of course, is IBM. Storage Technology has created an admirable growth record selling tape, tape drives, and disc drives compatible with IBM equipment. But there's always the danger that IBM, through breakthroughs, price cutting, or other market tactics, will flatten the intruder.

Meanwhile, the gutsy upstart (formed in 1969 by several engineers who broke away from IBM, notably chairman Jesse Aweida) has shown an earnings trajectory resembling a rocket. The company experienced its first black ink in 1972. From then through 1981, earnings climbed from $0.16 a share to $2.61 a share, with only one down year (1975, when earnings were down $0.01) along the way.

Like many young, fast-growing firms, Storage Technology has used a lot of debt. Recently, debt was a bit more than half of total capital. That adds to the risk, and perhaps makes these shares unsuitable for conservative accounts. Also (again like many young, fast-growing firms) the company pays no dividends. To boot (to complete the fast-growth syndrome) the price / earnings ratio is high, often about twice the market multiple. But the stock has "earned" its multiple with a return on stockholders' equity that has been above 20 percent most years and approaching 30 percent in good years.

After a 1980 attempt at a merger with Amdahl fell through, Storage Technology decided to try making mainframe computers on its own. It set up a subsidiary for the purpose, structured so that not much of the company's own capital is at risk. It's too early to tell whether this venture will pay off.

* * *

STORER BROADCASTING CO. (SBK). Founded 1927. Headquarters: 1177 Kane Concourse, Miami Beach FL 33154. **BROADCASTING.** Operates seven television stations and one radio station; active in cable TV.

Sales: $197.1 million (trend 13.4% a year).
Earnings: $25.24 million (trend 21.0% a year).
What happened to a $10,000 investment

Purchase Date	*Purchase Price*	*Price on 12-31-81*	*Dividends Paid*
12-31-71	$12.50	$26.87	$4,098.00
12-31-76	$12.94	$26.87	$2,517.87

Purchase Date	*Cap. Gains (− Losses)*	*Total Return*	*Rate of Return*
12-31-71	$11,500.00	$15,597.99	9.86%
12-31-76	$10,772.95	$13,290.82	18.42%

* * *

THE STRIDE RITE CORP. (SRR). Founded 1919. Headquarters: 960 Harrison Ave., Boston MA 02118. **SHOES.** Manufactures children's and adults' shoes. **MAJOR SUBSIDIARIES, BRANDS:** Stride Rite; Weber; Herman; Sperry Top-Sider, Inc.; KEDS Corp.

Sales: $166.0 million (trend 14.0% a year).
Earnings: $6.32 million (trend .7% a year).
What happened to a $10,000 investment

Purchase Date	*Purchase Price*	*Price on 12-31-81*	*Dividends Paid*
12-31-71	$21.37	$19.37	$4,126.32
12-31-76	$12.62	$19.37	$4,277.23

Purchase Date	*Cap. Gains (− Losses)*	*Total Return*	*Rate of Return*
12-31-71	$−935.67	$3,190.64	2.81%
12-31-76	$ 5,346.53	$9,623.76	14.43%

* * *

SUAVE SHOE CORP. (SWV). Founded 1960. Headquarters: 14100 N.W. 60th Ave., Miami Lakes FL 33014. **SHOES.** Manufactures and distributes casual footwear for men, women, and children. Also manufactures women's clothing.

Sales: $117.0 million (trend 13.0% a year).
Earnings: $5.72 million (trend 22.7% a year).
What happened to a $10,000 investment

Purchase Date	*Purchase Price*	*Price on 12-31-81*	*Dividends Paid*
12-31-71	$15.00	$10.25	$ 721.27
12-31-76	$ 4.77	$10.25	$1,924.00

Purchase Date	*Cap. Gains (− Losses)*	*Total Return*	*Rate of Return*
12-31-71	$−3,166.67	$−2,445.40	−2.77%
12-31-76	$ 11,476.18	$ 13,400.18	18.53%

* * *

SUBARU OF AMERICA, INC. (SBRU, Over-the-Counter). Founded 1967. Headquarters: 7040 Central Hwy., Pennsauken NJ 08109. **AUTOS.** Subaru is the fifth largest importer of cars to the United States, marketing vehicles produced by Fuji Heavy Industries of Japan. Has fewer than 500 direct employees. **MAJOR SUBSIDIARIES, BRANDS:** Subaru; Brat. Company is approximately 49 percent owned by Fuji Heavy Industries.

PROFILE: No, this is not a foreign stock. It's the stock of an American company that sells foreign cars. The difference is much more than semantic. First, you don't go through the red tape of owning a foreign stock, and you're entitled to the standard dividend exclusion on your income tax form. Second, since the company imports Japanese cars, but makes nothing, its fixed costs are very small. It does not have to make the kind of massive investments in manufacturing equipment that the big car makers do, nor does it have to pay union wages to a huge work force. (In fact, its work force is tiny.) Thus, the company has been able to earn a tremendous return on capital — consistently better than 50 percent and often above 75 percent — even though its profit margin isn't great. The company is also debt free.

Subaru is the only major importer that is independent and publicly traded. It ranks fifth in import volume, behind Toyota, Nissan (Datsun), Honda, and Volkswagen. Recently, Subaru had a bit more than 5 percent of the imported-car market. (That share was earned almost entirely in the late 1970s.

The company got off to a slow start in the 1960s and for a while teetered on the brink of bankruptcy.)

Despite the company's phenomenal success in recent years, investors haven't bid the stock up to the skies. In the early 1980s, it was selling for barely more than the average price / earnings ratio (then 8). Apparently, Wall Street isn't convinced that Subaru can keep its momentum going. Fuel economy and optional four-wheel drive have been the company's big selling points. But the competition is getting more crowded in both fuel-efficient and four-wheel-drive cars.

* * *

SUBURBAN PROPANE GAS CORP. (SPG). Founded 1945. Headquarters: 334 Madison Ave., Morristown NJ 07960. **LIQUID PROPANE GAS.** Markets liquefied petroleum gas; active in gas and oil exploration and production. **MAJOR SUBSIDIARIES, BRANDS:** The Plateau, Inc.

Sales: $738.0 million (trend 20.6% a year).
Earnings: $23.15 million (trend 16.5% a year).
What happened to a $10,000 investment

Purchase Date	*Purchase Price*	*Price on 12-31-81*	*Dividends Paid*
12-31-71	$23.00	$29.62	$4,812.74
12-31-76	$21.75	$29.62	$3,080.46

Purchase Date	*Cap. Gains (– Losses)*	*Total Return*	*Rate of Return*
12-31-71	$2,880.43	$7,693.17	5.87%
12-31-76	$3,620.69	$6,701.15	10.80%

* * *

SULLAIR CORP. (SUL). Founded 1965. Headquarters: 3700 E. Michigan Blvd., Michigan City IN 46360. **COMPRESSORS.** Manufactures rotary screw air compressors and related products for construction, mining, and industrial applications.

Sales: $154.9 million (trend 26.1% a year).
Earnings: $9.70 million (trend 38.3% a year).
What happened to a $10,000 investment

Purchase Date	*Purchase Price*	*Price on 12-31-81*	*Dividends Paid*
12-31-71	$N/A	$12.75	$ N/A
12-31-76	$ 2.67	$12.75	$4,149.85

Purchase Date	*Cap. Gains (– Losses)*	*Total Return*	*Rate of Return*
12-31-71	$ N/A	$ N/A	N/A%
12-31-76	$37,744.66	$41,894.51	39.00%

* * *

SUN BANKS OF FLORIDA, INC. (SU). Founded 1966. Headquarters: 200 S. Orange Ave., Orlando FL 32802. **BANKING.** Holding company for some fifteen Florida banks, including Sun Bank, Orlando, which is the second largest commercial bank in Florida. **MAJOR SUBSIDIARIES, BRANDS:** Sun Bank, Orlando.

Sales: $326.1 million (trend 21.4% a year).
Earnings: $27.63 million (trend 41.7% a year).
What happened to a $10,000 investment

Purchase Date	*Purchase Price*	*Price on 12-31-81*	*Dividends Paid*
12-31-71	$24.25	$18.50	$2,643.30
12-31-76	$10.62	$18.50	$3,482.35

Purchase Date	*Cap. Gains (– Losses)*	*Total Return*	*Rate of Return*
12-31-71	$–2,371.13	$ 272.16	.27%
12-31-76	$ 7,411.76	$10,894.12	15.88%

* * *

SUN CHEMICAL CORP. (SNL). Founded 1929. Headquarters: 200 Park Ave., New York NY 10166. **INKS, PIGMENTS.** Sun's principal business is manufacturing printing ink (of which it is the world's largest supplier) and organic pigments (of which it is the largest U.S. supplier). The company also has operations in electronics, specialty chemicals, graphic equipment, and other areas. 6,000 employees. **MAJOR SUBSIDIARIES, BRANDS:** Standard Kollsman; Chromalloy American (34 percent owned).

Sales: $514.0 million (trend 15.3% a year).
Earnings: $31.44 million (trend 29.0% a year).
What happened to a $10,000 investment

Purchase Date	*Purchase Price*	*Price on 12-31-81*	*Dividends Paid*
12-31-71	$9.92	$23.87	$2,416.78
12-31-76	$9.42	$23.87	$1,837.14

Purchase Date	*Cap. Gains (– Losses)*	*Total Return*	*Rate of Return*
12-31-71	$14,075.02	$16,491.79	10.23%
12-31-76	$15,353.34	$17,190.47	22.15%

PROFILE: Chairman Norman Alexander would like to rule a larger empire than his medium-sized, profitable producer of printing ink. For more than a decade, he has made unsuccessful passes at a number of companies, some of them larger than Sun Chemical. Among those that got away were Walter Kidde, Chemetron, Lily-Tulip Cup, and Harshaw Chemical. The largest fish he landed was the electronics firm Standard Kollsman.

As of 1981, another fish was on the line, and it looked probable that this one wouldn't get away. Sun had gradually acquired about 34 percent of the stock of Chromalloy American, a highly (some say ridiculously) diversified firm some three times Sun's size. Since Alexander boasts a good record for trimming less profitable operations and achieving a good return on stockholders' equity at Sun, some Chromalloy shareholders would probably be glad to see a take-over. However, Chromalloy's management had been resisting a take-over and, according to some reports, shopping for a "white knight" acquirer who might grant more autonomy to Chromalloy.

Sun's return on stockholders' equity has been consistently above 20 percent in recent years. Though dividends have been paid each year since 1929, the yield is tiny — less than 2 percent recently. The debt load tends to be on the high side — recently close to half of capital. And the stock's multiple tends to be low — in recent years, from 3 to 7.

* * *

SUN ELECTRIC CORPORATION (SE). Founded 1946. Headquarters: 1 Sun Parkway, Crystal Lake IL 60014. **TEST EQUIPMENT.** Designs, manufactures, and markets diagnostic test and service equipment for the transportation industry.

Sales: $177.4 million (trend 19.1% a year).
Earnings: $—.74 million.
What happened to a $10,000 investment

Purchase Date	*Purchase Price*	*Price on 12-31-81*	*Dividends Paid*
12-31-71	$ 8.98	$12.25	$4,509.90
12-31-76	$12.17	$12.25	$2,443.84

Purchase Date	*Cap. Gains (— Losses)*	*Total Return*	*Rate of Return*
12-31-71	$3,644.80	$8,154.70	6.14%
12-31-76	$ 68.49	$2,512.33	4.58%

* * *

SUN CO., INC. (SUN). Founded 1901. Headquarters: 100 Matsonford Rd., Radnor PA 19087. **OIL.** Sun is approximately the tenth largest oil company and the eighteenth largest industrial firm in the United States. In addition to conventional oil and gas operations, it has interests in tar sands, coal, and uranium. 48,000 employees. **MAJOR SUBSIDIARIES, BRANDS:** Sunoco; DX.

Sales: $12,945.0 million (trend 24.3% a year).
Earnings: $717.00 million (trend 29.9% a year).
What happened to a $10,000 investment

Purchase Date	*Purchase Price*	*Price on 12-31-81*	*Dividends Paid*
12-31-71	$19.60	$45.50	$5,205.48
12-31-76	$24.12	$45.50	$3,200.00

Purchase Date	*Cap. Gains (— Losses)*	*Total Return*	*Rate of Return*
12-31-71	$13,212.90	$18,418.39	11.01%
12-31-76	$ 8,860.10	$12,060.10	17.14%

PROFILE: Among major oil companies, Sun is one of the handful that has virtually all of its reserves in North America. Most of its production comes from U.S. sites; a significant chunk also comes from Canada — in particular, the Athabasca tar sands field in Alberta. Sun's chairman Theodore Burtis is proud of that project, which Sun initiated about twenty years ago. "That was long before the current experts even heard of an energy shortage or knew what oil sands were or where Athabasca was," he told *Forbes* magazine in 1980.

But if Sun was innovative then, it has seemed a bit cautious of late, spending less on exploration than some of its competitors. On the other hand, Sun picked up a lot of producing properties in 1980 when it bought Texas Pacific Oil Co. for $2.3 billion from Seagram. That move created a lot of ripples in the balance sheet, as debt shot up to about 35 percent of capital, versus only about 17 percent in 1979. Based on its past track record, it won't take too long for Sun to trim that debt load back: The company has a history of financial strength.

A diversification effort several years ago saw Sun pick up 34 percent of the stock of Becton, Dickinson, a health products company. In 1981 the company essentially divested itself of that holding, by issuing some $389 million in bonds convertible into the Becton, Dickinson shares.

Dividends have been paid every year since 1904, and the moderate yield is well covered by earnings.

* * *

SUNDSTRAND CORP. (SNS). Founded 1966. Headquarters: 4751 Harrison Ave., Rockford IL 61101. **AEROSPACE.** Producer of components for jet aircraft, construction, and agricultural equipment. Involved in power transmission and fluid and heat transfer equipment.

Sales: $926.0 million (trend 12.6% a year).
Earnings: $77.30 million (trend 31.6% a year).
What happened to a $10,000 investment

Purchase Date	*Purchase Price*	*Price on 12-31-81*	*Dividends Paid*
12-31-71	$13.62	$42.25	$5,614.68
12-31-76	$17.81	$42.25	$3,129.82

Purchase Date	*Cap. Gains (− Losses)*	*Total Return*	*Rate of Return*
12-31-71	$21,009.17	$26,623.85	13.86%
12-31-76	$13,719.30	$16,849.12	21.84%

* * *

SUNSHINE MINING CO. (SSC). Founded 1918. Headquarters: 500 Plaza of the Americas (South Tower), Dallas TX 75201. **SILVER MINING.** Sunshine is a leading U.S. silver mining company and has a majority interest in the country's largest silver mine, in Idaho. 1,400 employees. **MAJOR SUBSIDIARIES, BRANDS:** Sunshine Mine.

Sales: $7.2 million (trend −29.2% a year).
Earnings: $−4.96 million.
What happened to a $10,000 investment

Purchase Date	*Purchase Price*	*Price on 12-31-81*	*Dividends Paid*
12-31-71	$3.17	$8.25	$4,767.55
12-31-76	$4.50	$8.25	$2,222.22

Purchase Date	*Cap. Gains (− Losses)*	*Total Return*	*Rate of Return*
12-31-71	$16,009.97	$20,777.52	11.90%
12-31-76	$ 8,333.33	$10,555.56	15.50%

PROFILE: This is not a penny stock, but it resembles some popular penny stocks in being: (1) a natural resource issue; (2) active in the western states; (3) volatile; and (4) relatively low-priced. In 1980 Sunshine hit an all-time high of $26.25 a share. But the stock traded as low as $9.00 that year, and sold below $5.00 a share in at least parts of every year during the 1970s.

The 1980 high was brought on in large part by a high price of silver. The price of the stock has since subsided, with the price of the metal. Buying shares of Sunshine is a bit like speculating in commodities, since the price will react violently to the changes (and there will be plenty) in silver quotes. But the company doesn't change strategy from day to day. Like any mining company, it must plan years in advance, based on a reasonable hope or expectation about future prices. Under chairman Michael Boswell, Sunshine has bet heavily that silver has a glistening future. It has trimmed nonsilver subsidiaries (electronics, oil, gas, fencemaking) and moved to expand operations both at the famous Sunshine Mine in Idaho and elsewhere. The Sunshine Mine, the country's largest, is owned 57 percent by Sunshine, 33 percent by Hecla Mining, and 10 percent by Silver Dollar Mining Co. Sunshine has tried, at various times, to take over both Hecla and Silver Dollar. At least up to the time this book went to press, it had succeeded in taking over neither.

The stock often sells for a high price / earnings ratio, and the dividend yield is small to moderate, so this is an issue for the speculative part of your portfolio. If you buy it, try to do so when the price of silver is low; you'll get a lot more bang for your buck that way.

* * *

SUNSTATES CORP. (SST). Founded 1969. Headquarters: 4300 Six Forks Rd., Suite 324, Raleigh NC 27609. **REAL ESTATE DEVELOPMENT.** Holding company for Sunstates Properties, a real estate firm.

* * *

SUPER VALU STORES, INC. (SVU). Founded 1925. Headquarters: 11840 Valley View Rd., Eden Prairie MN 55344. **FOODS WHOLESALER.** Super Valu is the nation's largest food wholesaler, providing food distribution and other support services to some 2,000 grocery stores and supermarkets unaffiliated with large chains. The company also owns more than 100 food stores; more than 200 casual clothing stores; and a small chain of department stores in the Midwest. 18,000 employees. **MAJOR SUBSIDIARIES, BRANDS:** County Seat (casual clothing); ShopKo (department stores).

Sales: $4,203.7 million (trend 18.0% a year).
Earnings: $55.58 million (trend 29.7% a year).
What happened to a $10,000 investment

Purchase Date	*Purchase Price*	*Price on 12-31-81*	*Dividends Paid*
12-31-71	$3.61	$19.62	$4,830.48
12-31-76	$6.06	$19.62	$1,975.67

Purchase Date	*Cap. Gains (– Losses)*	*Total Return*	*Rate of Return*
12-31-71	$44,372.29	$49,202.77	19.46%
12-31-76	$22,371.13	$24,346.80	27.99%

PROFILE: This huge, successful company—which, let's face it, you have probably never heard of—is among the 150 largest firms in the United States and has been one of the more profitable stocks you could have held during the past decade. The stock price, less than $2 a share during parts of 1973–75, has been $16 or more during much of 1980–81. Eight times your money isn't bad.

The reason few people have heard of Super Valu is that it isn't a supermarket; it's a foods distributor. Independent grocery stores—those unaffiliated with the large national and regional chains—buy their groceries from outfits like Super Valu, rather than dealing directly with the numerous manufacturers. As *Forbes* magazine pointed out in 1981, the wholesalers have an advantage during periods of inflation, since they are usually paid within ten days by the grocery stores, but may take thirty days or so to pay the food producers. However, it is a low-margin business; in a good year, Super Valu's profit margin is less than 1½ percent.

Debt here was recently about a third of capital. Return on equity has been outstanding—consistently better than 25 percent in the years from 1977 to 1980. Profit growth has been fast, but the price / earnings ratio hasn't gotten far out of line: It was around 10 recently. Dividends have been paid each year since 1936, but offer only a modest-to-moderate yield.

* * *

SUPERIOR OIL CO. (SOC). Founded 1963. Headquarters: First City National Bank Bldg., Houston TX 77002. **OIL.** Superior is a major producer of oil and natural gas in the United States and Canada. Also involved in mining, through subsidiaries. 3,700 employees. **MAJOR SUBSIDIARIES, BRANDS:** Canadian Superior Oil Ltd.; McIntyre Mines (53 percent owned); Falconbridge Nickel (42 percent owned); Western Platinum Ltd. (24 percent owned).

Sales: $1,497.7 million (trend 32.4% a year).
Earnings: $334.46 million (trend 43.9% a year).
What happened to a $10,000 investment

Purchase Date	*Purchase Price*	*Price on 12-31-81*	*Dividends Paid*
12-31-71	$7.49	$36.87	$1,196.26
12-31-76	$9.49	$36.87	$ 623.81

Purchase Date	*Cap. Gains (– Losses)*	*Total Return*	*Rate of Return*
12-31-71	$39,232.31	$40,428.57	17.56%
12-31-76	$28,856.69	$29,480.51	31.61%

PROFILE: For years, Superior Oil was best known as the highest-priced stock on the New York Stock Exchange. It held that position (occasionally yielding to IBM) for some years, until the departure of the founding family from a central role in the corporation led to a desire for a stock price individual investors might find more affordable. Two 5-for-1 stock splits followed (in 1979 and 1981), bringing Superior down from the $200-to-$300 range to the $25-to-$50 range.

Disregarding the splits, Superior has performed very well indeed. This has been a stock in which it's been possible to double or triple your money—and, with nice timing, to quadruple it or more.

Superior is involved in exploring for and producing oil and gas, but not refining it or marketing it. At times, this structure might have seemed a weakness. But in the early 1980s, production was where the money was, so Superior was sitting pretty. The only cloud on the horizon was that a major part of the company's reserves (about half the oil and more than a third of the gas) are in Canada. The Canadian government has been taxing oil companies, especially foreign ones, heavily, and talking about nationalizing oil and gas properties. Most analysts figure Superior can ride out this political storm.

They also figure it can weather a recent spate of executive departures. The exits were ironic, since Superior has had a reputation for luring top-notch operating people away from such rivals as Mobil and Exxon.

The price / earnings ratio tends to be high, and the dividend yield has always been small. It's purely a capital-gains stock.

* * *

SUPERMARKETS GENERAL CORP. (SGL). Founded 1966. Headquarters: 301 Blair Rd., Woodbridge NJ 07095. **RETAILER.** Supermarkets General operates more than 100 Pathmark supermarkets (many of them large and combined with drug stores); also runs 2 small department store chains and a chain of home improvement centers. 30,000 employees. **MAJOR SUBSIDIARIES, BRANDS:** Pathmark (supermarkets); Hochschild, Kohn (department stores); Howland-Steinbach (department stores); Rickel (home improvement).

Sales: $2,628.8 million (trend 11.8% a year).
Earnings: $26.07 million (trend 26.5% a year).
What happened to a $10,000 investment

Purchase Date	*Purchase Price*	*Price on 12-31-81*	*Dividends Paid*
12-31-71	$21.25	$19.25	$1,315.29
12-31-76	$ 7.50	$19.25	$2,320.00

Purchase Date	*Cap. Gains (− Losses)*	*Total Return*	*Rate of Return*
12-31-71	$ −941.18	$ 374.12	.37%
12-31-76	$15,666.67	$17,986.67	22.85%

PROFILE: Pathmark has a reputation for innovation in the supermarket field. It was one of the first chains, for example, to stock generic foods. And it has been in the forefront of the movement toward large stores (Super Centers, in Pathmark's terms) combining food and general merchandise—"one-stop shopping," to use the jargon.

As a result, Supermarkets General has shown a good profit trend over the years. After some up-and-down years in the early 1970s, the company put together a skein of consecutive earnings gains in the latter half of the 1970s. Even though margins are low (1 percent is a good margin for Pathmark), the company has been among the more profitable of supermarket operators.

Contributing to the rapid expansion of the chain (starting in the late 1960s, it has grown to be about the tenth largest supermarket chain in the United States) has been a heavy debt load—recently about 56 percent of capital. The debt factor enhances the company's return on stockholders' equity, but it's something to be careful of. Those who dislike leverage may want to avoid this issue.

Dividends have been paid each year since incorporation, but the yield ranges from small to moderate. Most of the action here is capital gains.

Pathmark's reputation used to attract this stock a keen following, and a high (10 to 20) price / earnings ratio, back in the late 1960s and early 1970s. Lately, though, its p / e has sagged, with those of retailers in general. That might represent a buying opportunity.

* * *

SUPERSCOPE, INC. (SSP). Founded 1954. Headquarters: 20525 Nordhoff St., Chatsworth CA 91311. **STEREO EQUIPMENT.** Manufacturer and distributor of electronic home entertainment equipment. **MAJOR SUBSIDIARIES, BRANDS:** Marantz; Pianocorder; Superscope.

Sales: $153.7 million (trend .8% a year).
Earnings: $−13.07 million.
What happened to a $10,000 investment

Purchase Date	*Purchase Price*	*Price on 12-31-81*	*Dividends Paid*
12-31-71	$12.25	$3.25	$816.33
12-31-76	$22.12	$3.25	$451.98

Purchase Date	*Cap. Gains (− Losses)*	*Total Return*	*Rate of Return*
12-31-71	$−7,346.94	$−6,530.61	−10.05%
12-31-76	$−8,531.07	$−8,079.10	−28.10%

* * *

SWANK, INC. (SNK). Founded 1936. Headquarters: 6 Hazel St., Attleboro MA 02703. **FASHION ACCESSORIES.** Manufactures and distributes men's and ladies' jewelry, men's belts, men's and ladies' personal leather goods, fragrances, and gift items. **MAJOR SUBSIDIARIES, BRANDS:** Swank; Prince Gardner; Princess Gardner; Royal Copenhagen; Flora Danica; Pierre Cardin; L'Aiglon; Biagi.

Sales: $137.1 million (trend 11.7% a year).
Earnings: $7.56 million (trend 9.8% a year).
What happened to a $10,000 investment

Purchase Date	*Purchase Price*	*Price on 12-31-81*	*Dividends Paid*
12-31-71	$15.80	$14.62	$6,837.40
12-31-76	$16.70	$14.62	$4,337.41

Purchase Date	*Cap. Gains (− Losses)*	*Total Return*	*Rate of Return*
12-31-71	$ −741.01	$6,096.39	4.88%
12-31-76	$−1,244.90	$3,092.51	5.54%

* * *

SYBRON CORP. (SYB). Founded 1965. Headquarters: 1100 Midtown Tower, Rochester NY 14604. **HEALTH PRODUCTS.** Manufacturer of hospital, dental and laboratory products, instruments, process equipment, and specialty chemicals.

Sales: $792.9 million (trend 7.4% a year).
Earnings: $23.45 million (trend −2.7% a year).
What happened to a $10,000 investment

Purchase Date	*Purchase Price*	*Price on 12-31-81*	*Dividends Paid*
12-31-71	$34.62	$19.25	$2,506.86
12-31-76	$19.25	$19.25	$2,618.18

Purchase Date	*Cap. Gains (− Losses)*	*Total Return*	*Rate of Return*
12-31-71	$−4,440.43	$−1,933.57	−2.13%
12-31-76	$ −.00	$ 2,618.18	4.76%

* * *

SYNTEX CORP. (SYN). Founded 1957. Headquarters: 3401 Hillview Ave., Palo Alto CA 94304. **DRUGS.** Syntex derives most of its income from the sale of prescription drugs, particularly an antiarthritis medication. Also involved in the manufacture of animal pharmaceuticals, dental products, contact lenses, beauty products, and diagnostic products. **MAJOR SUBSIDIARIES, BRANDS:** Naprosyn (antiarthritic).

Sales: $710.9 million (trend 21.3% a year).
Earnings: $97.66 million (trend 18.7% a year).
What happened to a $10,000 investment

Purchase Date	*Purchase Price*	*Price on 12-31-81*	*Dividends Paid*
12-31-71	$41.62	$61.62	$1,453.45
12-31-76	$23.12	$61.62	$1,956.76

Purchase Date	*Cap. Gains (− Losses)*	*Total Return*	*Rate of Return*
12-31-71	$ 4,804.80	$ 6,258.26	4.98%
12-31-76	$16,648.65	$18,605.41	23.39%

* * *

SYSCO CORP. (SYY). Founded 1969. Headquarters: 1177 W. Loop S., Houston TX 77027. **FOOD SERVICE.** Distributes food and other products and services to the food service and retail food industries.

Sales: $1,382.2 million (trend 18.3% a year).
Earnings: $26.81 million (trend 30.0% a year).
What happened to a $10,000 investment

Purchase Date	*Purchase Price*	*Price on 12-31-81*	*Dividends Paid*
12-31-71	$11.24	$39.50	$1,519.66
12-31-76	$ 7.17	$39.50	$1,726.98

Purchase Date	*Cap. Gains (− Losses)*	*Total Return*	*Rate of Return*
12-31-71	$25,128.46	$26,648.12	13.87%
12-31-76	$45,116.28	$46,843.26	41.56%

T

TECO ENERGY, INC. (TE). Founded 1899. Headquarters: 702 N. Franklin St., Tampa FL 33602. **UTILITY.** Holding company for Tampa Electric, which provides electricity to customers on Florida's west coast. Has sidelines in coal mining, transportation, and real estate development.

Sales: $509.3 million (trend 14.6% a year).
Earnings: $47.83 million (trend 11.8% a year).
What happened to a $10,000 investment

Purchase Date	*Purchase Price*	*Price on 12-31-81*	*Dividends Paid*
12-31-71	$26.25	$20.25	$4,487.62
12-31-76	$20.25	$20.25	$3,481.48

Purchase Date	*Cap. Gains (− Losses)*	*Total Return*	*Rate of Return*
12-31-71	$−2,285.71	$2,201.90	2.01%
12-31-76	$ −.00	$3,481.48	6.16%

* * *

TRE CORP. (TRE). Founded 1959. Headquarters: 9460 Wilshire Blvd., Beverly Hills CA 90212. **DIVERSIFIED MANUFACTURER.** TRE manufactures components for the aircraft, aerospace, and shipbuilding industries. It also produces locksets and specialty plumbing for the homebuilding industry. **MAJOR SUBSIDIARIES, BRANDS:** Astech; Modern Faucet; TRE Semiconductor Equipment Corp.; Weslock.

Sales: $127.6 million (trend 11.3% a year).
Earnings: $17.68 million (trend 45.8% a year).
What happened to a $10,000 investment

Purchase Date	*Purchase Price*	*Price on 12-31-81*	*Dividends Paid*
12-31-71	$19.95	$18.25	$1,535.46
12-31-76	$ 6.42	$18.25	$4,774.03

Purchase Date	*Cap. Gains (− Losses)*	*Total Return*	*Rate of Return*
12-31-71	$ −852.41	$ 683.05	.66%
12-31-76	$18,441.56	$23,215.58	27.14%

* * *

TRW INC. (TRW). Founded 1916. Headquarters: 23555 Euclid Ave., Cleveland OH 44117. AUTO PARTS, AEROSPACE. This conglomerate is a major worldwide supplier of auto and truck parts, has major operations in electronics and aerospace, and diversified operations in industrial equipment with an emphasis on energy-related equipment. 94,000 employees.

Sales: $4,984.0 million (trend 14.6% a year).
Earnings: $200.31 million (trend 17.6% a year).
What happened to a $10,000 investment

Purchase Date	*Purchase Price*	*Price on 12-31-81*	*Dividends Paid*
12-31-71	$30.37	$54.75	$5,099.59
12-31-76	$36.75	$54.75	$2,653.06

Purchase Date	*Cap. Gains (— Losses)*	*Total Return*	*Rate of Return*
12-31-71	$8,024.69	$13,124.28	8.74%
12-31-76	$4,897.96	$ 7,551.02	11.91%

PROFILE: TRW is so diversified that you might think investing in it would be like investing in an index fund — a simple cross-section of the American economy. Not so. The company's operating results have been better than those of the economy. Return on stockholders' equity has usually been around 20 percent in recent years (15 percent is about average for major corporations). And TRW has a remarkable record of consistency in earnings gains — twenty out of the last twenty-one years, through 1981.

If the gains have been steady, they haven't been spectacular. Wall Street, which likes a bit of show and a "story," has bestowed on TRW a multiple of only 5 to 10 in recent years. Not until 1980 (when the "story" of many favored stocks was "high technology," or, in jargon, "high tech") did the stock break out of a long rut and gain some ground, rising from a 1979 low around $33 to a 1980 high of more than $61.

TRW escaped the red ink that bathed the U.S. auto manufacturers (its customers) for several reasons. It sells auto parts worldwide, not just in the United States. In fact, it sells more auto parts abroad than domestically, and in the United States sells more truck parts than auto parts. Also, it wisely specialized in high-demand components, notably rack-and-pinion steering for small cars — the coming demand for which it saw years in advance.

The company also does a fair amount of defense work, and may profit from the anticipated military buildup. Dividends, paid yearly since 1936, provide a moderate yield.

* * *

TAFT BROADCASTING CO. (TFB). Founded 1959. Headquarters: 1718 Young St., Cincinnati OH 45210. BROADCASTING. Taft Broadcasting is a group broadcaster with seven television stations, six AM radio stations, and six FM radio stations. Taft is also involved in movie and television program production and operates several amusement parks. MAJOR SUBSIDIARIES, BRANDS: WTAF-TV (UHF), Philadelphia; WKRC-TV & AM, WKRQ-FM, Cincinnati; WDCA-TV (UHF), Washington, D.C.

Sales: $239.9 million (trend 22.9% a year).
Earnings: $28.46 million (trend 21.9% a year).
What happened to a $10,000 investment

Purchase Date	*Purchase Price*	*Price on 12-31-81*	*Dividends Paid*
12-31-71	$21.69	$32.75	$2,024.21
12-31-76	$15.12	$32.75	$1,778.51

Purchase Date	*Cap. Gains (— Losses)*	*Total Return*	*Rate of Return*
12-31-71	$ 5,100.86	$ 7,125.07	5.53%
12-31-76	$11,652.89	$13,431.40	18.57%

* * *

TALLEY INDUSTRIES, INC. (TAL). Founded 1960. Headquarters: 3500 N. Greenfield Rd., Mesa AZ 85201. DIVERSIFIED MANUFACTURING. Talley Industries is the manufacturer and distributor of many consumer products, principally clocks and watches. It also produces a variety of technical products for government and industry. MAJOR SUBSIDIARIES, BRANDS: Big Ben; Westclox; Adorence Co., Inc.; General Time Corp.; Seth Thomas; Talley Industries of Arizona; Quartzmatic.

Sales: $376.8 million (trend 2.0% a year).
Earnings: $—6.36 million.
What happened to a $10,000 investment

Purchase Date	*Purchase Price*	*Price on 12-31-81*	*Dividends Paid*
12-31-71	$10.83	$3.62	$4,823.07
12-31-76	$ 9.50	$3.62	$2,657.89

Purchase Date	*Cap. Gains (– Losses)*	*Total Return*	*Rate of Return*
12-31-71	$–6,653.85	$–1,830.78	–2.00%
12-31-76	$–6,184.21	$–3,526.32	–8.33%

* * *

TANDY CORP. (TAN). Founded 1899. Headquarters: 1800 One Tandy Center, Fort Worth TX 76102. **CONSUMER ELECTRONICS.** Tandy operates the nation's largest chain of consumer electronics stores, with roughly 4,000 stores in the United States and an approximately equal number abroad. It manufactures about half the products sold in its outlets. 20,000 employees. **MAJOR SUBSIDIARIES, BRANDS:** Tandy; Radio Shack.

Sales: $1,691.4 million (trend 16.7% a year).
Earnings: $169.60 million (trend 20.5% a year).
What happened to a $10,000 investment

Purchase Date	*Purchase Price*	*Price on 12-31-81*	*Dividends Paid*
12-31-71	$2.60	$33.75	$0.00
12-31-76	$5.27	$33.75	$0.00

Purchase Date	*Cap. Gains (– Losses)*	*Total Return*	*Rate of Return*
12-31-71	$119,729.73	$119,729.73	29.21%
12-31-76	$ 54,094.96	$ 54,094.96	45.00%

PROFILE: Tandy was growing by leaps and bounds in the early 1970s as a marketer of consumer electronic products, from tape recorders to telephone answering devices. Consumers were familiar with the company's Radio Shack stores, which blanket the United States. Then Tandy decided to make and sell personal computers. The result: Now the company is growing even faster.

Tandy is one of the most profitable of all American companies. In recent years, it has been earning more than 40 percent on stockholders' equity. (A return of half that percentage is considered very good.) Besides being extremely profitable, it has been growing extremely fast. Profits, $11 million in 1971, were up more than tenfold by 1980, to $112 million. Sales had jumped from $357 million to $1.4 billion over the same period.

The stock has had some ups and downs. In 1978 it dropped from $8.75 to just below $4.00 when the bottom fell out of the CB radio market. In 1981 it dropped from $38 to $30 when IBM entered the personal computers market. Such upsets are accentuated by the fact that investors have high expectations of Tandy: In 1981 it sold for more than 20 times earnings. But the overall trend in the stock has been pleasant for all long-term stockholders. Early in the 1970s, Tandy was practically a penny stock. In 1980–81, it traded between $20 and $40.

No dividends are paid here. The balance sheet has traditionally been leveraged, but recently debt was trimmed to less than 30 percent of capital.

* * *

TANDYCRAFTS, INC. (TAC). Founded 1975. Headquarters: 1700 One Tandy Center, Fort Worth TX 76102. **LEATHER.** Tandycrafts, a spin-off of Tandy Corp., operates retail handicraft stores. It is the nation's largest manufacturer of do-it-yourself leather products. **MAJOR SUBSIDIARIES, BRANDS:** Bona Allen Tannery; American Handicrafts; Merribee; The Magee Company, Inc.; Tandy Leather.

Sales: $82.2 million (trend –16.9% a year).
Earnings: $3.86 million (trend –25.9% a year).
What happened to a $10,000 investment

Purchase Date	*Purchase Price*	*Price on 12-31-81*	*Dividends Paid*
12-31-71	$ N/A	$10.62	$0.00
12-31-76	$15.12	$10.62	$0.00

Purchase Date	*Cap. Gains (– Losses)*	*Total Return*	*Rate of Return*
12-31-71	$ N/A	$ N/A	N/A%
12-31-76	$–2,975.21	$–2,975.21	–6.82%

* * *

TANNETICS, INC. (TNT). Founded 1969. Headquarters: 700 First National Bank Bldg., Erie PA 16501. **REFRIGERATION EQUIPMENT.** Tannetics' single largest line is commercial beverage refrigerators. It is also involved in packaging and paper products; manufacture of valves and gaskets; and oil and gas drilling.

Sales: $84.8 million (trend 12.4% a year).
Earnings: $2.86 million (trend 15.4% a year).
What happened to a $10,000 investment

Purchase Date	*Purchase Price*	*Price on 12-31-81*	*Dividends Paid*
12-31-71	$N/A	$9.32	$ N/A
12-31-76	$ 4.90	$9.32	$1,921.46

Purchase Date	*Cap. Gains (– Losses)*	*Total Return*	*Rate of Return*
12-31-71	$ N/A	$ N/A	N/A%
12-31-76	$9,028.08	$10,949.54	15.94%

* * *

TECHNICOLOR, INC. (TK). Founded 1922. Headquarters: 2049 Century Park E., Los Angeles CA 90067. **FILM PROCESSING LABORATORY.** Technicolor is the largest independent processor of professional movie film and is involved in consumer photofinishing. **MAJOR SUBSIDIARIES, BRANDS:** Technicolor Graphic Services, Inc.; The Vidtronics Company, Inc.

Sales: $237.2 million (trend 14.5% a year).
Earnings: $17.22 million (trend 57.9% a year).
What happened to a $10,000 investment

Purchase Date	*Purchase Price*	*Price on 12-31-81*	*Dividends Paid*
12-31-71	$9.58	$14.62	$2,017.39
12-31-76	$3.58	$14.62	$5,395.35

Purchase Date	*Cap. Gains (− Losses)*	*Total Return*	*Rate of Return*
12-31-71	$ 5,260.87	$ 7,278.26	5.62%
12-31-76	$30,813.95	$36,209.30	35.81%

* * *

TEKTRONIX, INC. (TEK). Founded 1946. Headquarters: 14150 S.W. Karl Braun Dr., Beaverton OR 97077. **INSTRUMENT MANUFACTURING.** Tektronix is the largest manufacturer of cathode ray oscilloscopes, and makes other test and measurement instruments. It also manufactures information displays, such as graphic computer terminals, display monitors, and digital plotters.

Sales: $1,061.8 million (trend 25.2% a year).
Earnings: $80.17 million (trend 22.8% a year).
What happened to a $10,000 investment

Purchase Date	*Purchase Price*	*Price on 12-31-81*	*Dividends Paid*
12-31-71	$16.25	$55.25	$2,101.54
12-31-76	$34.25	$55.25	$ 808.76

Purchase Date	*Cap. Gains (− Losses)*	*Total Return*	*Rate of Return*
12-31-71	$24,000.00	$26,101.54	13.70%
12-31-76	$ 6,131.39	$ 6,940.15	11.12%

* * *

TELECOM CORP. (TEL). Founded 1958. Headquarters: 2424 Houston Natural Gas Bldg., Houston TX 77002. **TRUCKING.** TeleCom is a holding company involved in trucking, wholesale distribution, and manufacturing. **MAJOR SUBSIDIARIES, BRANDS:** Comfort Supply; Meyer Machine; Meyer Systems; Spector Red Ball, Inc.

Sales: $466.9 million (trend 41.7% a year).
Earnings: $−3.33 million.
What happened to a $10,000 investment

Purchase Date	*Purchase Price*	*Price on 12-31-81*	*Dividends Paid*
12-31-71	$7.37	$3.50	$3,742.37
12-31-76	$7.37	$3.50	$3,240.68

Purchase Date	*Cap. Gains (− Losses)*	*Total Return*	*Rate of Return*
12-31-71	$−5,254.24	$−1,511.86	−1.63%
12-31-76	$−5,254.24	$−2,013.56	−4.40%

* * *

TELEDYNE, INC. (TDY). Founded 1960. Headquarters: 1901 Ave. of the Stars, Los Angeles CA 90067. **CONGLOMERATE.** Teledyne is a diversified conglomerate with operations primarily in four broad areas: industrial products, specialty metals, aviation and electronic products, and consumer products. 48,000 employees. **MAJOR SUBSIDIARIES, BRANDS:** Curtiss-Wright (54 percent owned); Litton Industries (25 percent owned); Brockway Glass Co. (29 percent owned); Reichhold Chemicals (21 percent owned); Argonaut Insurance Co. (property and casualty insurance); Unicoa Corp. (life insurance); Water Pik (dental hygiene products); Acoustic Research (stereo components). Also owns fractions of Walter Kidde; International Harvester; H. J. Heinz; and National Can.

Sales: $2,926.4 million (trend 11.4% a year).
Earnings: $343.80 million (trend 31.3% a year).
What happened to a $10,000 investment

Purchase Date	*Purchase Price*	*Price on 12-31-81*	*Dividends Paid*
12-31-71	$ 9.17	$138.50	$0.00
12-31-76	$30.15	$138.50	$0.00

Purchase Date	*Cap. Gains (− Losses)*	*Total Return*	*Rate of Return*
12-31-71	$141,052.81	$141,052.81	31.19%
12-31-76	$ 35,933.02	$ 35,933.02	35.65%

PROFILE: Teledyne means, roughly, "force applied at a distance." The description is singularly apt.

Narrowly, it's apt because some of Teledyne's main products are engines — gas, diesel, and, especially, aircraft engines. More profoundly, it's apt because Teledyne's strategy has been to acquire a large number of small and medium-sized companies and to give them considerable operating autonomy. Managers who produce good profit margins are rewarded with more capital and with bonuses. But the "force" moves across the distance from headquarters on occasion: When a division isn't performing well, it's apt to end up with new officers and a radically changed mix of operations.

So ably has founder and chairman Henry Singleton managed this unusual conglomerate that it's common to find virtually all of Teledyne's 130 or so operating divisions making money in any given year. The company's return on equity in recent years has been consistently above 20 percent and sometimes above 30 percent — an outstanding record.

Several hallmarks of Singleton's managerial method set this company apart from most others. The company is well known for buying shares of its own stock when the price dips. This lessens the number of shares outstanding and improves profits per share. Singleton often buys a significant fraction of another company (see above) without trying to take over the whole company. Once a company is acquired, in whole or in part, Teledyne is unlikely to part with it: Singleton is a collector of undervalued assets, not a wheeler-dealer. And, no matter how well Teledyne does, it doesn't pay dividends (except for stock dividends). Partly because dividends are taxable as ordinary income, Singleton doesn't believe in them.

The fruit of all this unorthodoxy? It's been a record of steady growth and profitability matched by few companies in this country. The stock, with quite a few dips and spurts along the way, has performed extremely well over the long haul. A lot of investors here have seen their money grow tenfold within the past decade.

* * *

THE TELEX CORP. (TC). Founded 1963. Headquarters: 6422 E. 41 St., Tulsa OK 74135. **COMPUTER AND COMMUNICATIONS PRODUCTS.** Telex manufactures equipment for computer systems, tape recorders and players, headphones, microphones, and other communications products. **MAJOR SUBSIDIARIES, BRANDS:** Telex Communications; Telex Computer Products.

Sales: $178.5 million (trend 11.8% a year).
Earnings: $8.08 million (trend 2.1% a year).
What happened to a $10,000 investment

Purchase Date	*Purchase Price*	*Price on 12-31-81*	*Dividends Paid*
12-31-71	$12.25	$6.50	$0.00
12-31-76	$ 3.12	$6.50	$0.00

Purchase Date	*Cap. Gains (— Losses)*	*Total Return*	*Rate of Return*
12-31-71	$−4,693.88	$−4,693.88	−6.14%
12-31-76	$ 10,800.00	$ 10,800.00	15.77%

* * *

TENNECO INC. (TGT). Founded 1947. Headquarters: Tenneco Bldg., PO Box 2511, Houston TX 77001. **CONGLOMERATE.** Tenneco was originally and primarily a gas pipeline company, but has diversified extensively into a variety of fields, including oil and gas production, refining and marketing; farm equipment; shipbuilding; chemicals; agriculture; auto parts; and insurance. 106,000 employees. **MAJOR SUBSIDIARIES, BRANDS:** Houston Oil & Minerals Corp.; J. I. Case farm equipment; Walker Manufacturing (mufflers and other auto parts); Monroe Auto Equipment (shock absorbers and other auto parts); Newport News Shipbuilding; Tennessee Gas Transmission; Sun Giant (raisins, dried fruits, and almonds); Philadelphia Life Insurance Co.; Tenneco, Red Diamond, U Fill 'em, and Direct gasoline.

Sales: $13,226.0 million (trend 19.1% a year).
Earnings: $674.00 million (trend 15.7% a year).
What happened to a $10,000 investment

Purchase Date	*Purchase Price*	*Price on 12-31-81*	*Dividends Paid*
12-31-71	$25.50	$33.50	$7,458.82
12-31-76	$36.75	$33.50	$3,072.11

Purchase Date	*Cap. Gains (— Losses)*	*Total Return*	*Rate of Return*
12-31-71	$ 3,137.25	$10,596.08	7.49%
12-31-76	$−884.35	$ 2,187.76	4.04%

PROFILE: This is an energy-oriented conglomerate. Built originally around a pipeline system, Tenneco has moved increasingly into oil and gas production. In 1980 production, refining, and marketing of petroleum products accounted for more than half of profits and a bit more than a quarter of revenues. Another quarter of revenues (but less than a fifth of profits) came from the pipeline business. Thus, together these two main business lines account for more than half of revenues and more than three quarters of profits.

The other lines of business are small only in percentage terms. Newport News, for example, is among the nation's largest shipbuilding companies. Philadelphia Life, Sun Giant, Monroe, J. I. Case, and Walker (see above) are all big companies. Put the whole thing together (more than 300 companies acquired by Tenneco over the years) and you've got what was recently the seventeenth largest U.S. industrial corporation.

Tenneco's profit performance has been steady, though not spectacular. Investors have achieved only a moderate total return, with few capital gains but moderate-to-substantial dividend yield. In most recent years, the yield has been around 6 percent. To pay it, the company disperses a bit less than half of earnings.

The company has not been reluctant to take on debt, which recently amounted to about 42 percent of capital. Partly because it's so diversified, the company usually carries a middling price / earnings ratio, recently 5 to 10.

The 1981 acquisition of Houston Oil & Minerals Corp. (for Tenneco stock worth somewhere around $2 billion) will dilute per-share earnings a bit temporarily. But Houston is known as a premiere wildcatter, and the purchase was generally considered a plum on Wall Street.

* * *

TERADYNE, INC. (TER). Founded 1960. Headquarters: 183 Essex St., Boston MA 02111. ELECTRONICS. Teradyne manufactures automatic test equipment and connection systems for the electronics and telecommunications industries. MAJOR SUBSIDIARIES, BRANDS: 4-TEL.

Sales: $165.0 million (trend 33.6% a year).
Earnings: $11.37 million (trend 82.4% a year).
What happened to a $10,000 investment

Purchase Date	*Purchase Price*	*Price on 12-31-81*	*Dividends Paid*
12-31-71	$14.75	$35.25	$0.00
12-31-76	$14.25	$35.25	$0.00

Purchase Date	*Cap. Gains (– Losses)*	*Total Return*	*Rate of Return*
12-31-71	$13,898.31	$13,898.31	9.10%
12-31-76	$14,736.84	$14,736.84	19.86%

* * *

TESORO PETROLEUM CORP. (TSO). Founded 1968. Headquarters: 8700 Tesoro Dr., San Antonio TX 78286. OIL. Tesoro is a medium-sized international oil company that gets most of its oil from Trinidad and Indonesia. 5,000 employees. MAJOR SUBSIDIARIES, BRANDS: Trinidad-Tesoro Petroleum Co. (49.9 percent owned); Commonwealth Oil Refining Co. (37 percent owned).

Sales: $3,034.8 million (trend 29.8% a year).
Earnings: $73.39 million (trend 37.0% a year).
What happened to a $10,000 investment

Purchase Date	*Purchase Price*	*Price on 12-31-81*	*Dividends Paid*
12-31-71	$19.25	$20.25	$1,638.96
12-31-76	$16.25	$20.25	$ 938.46

Purchase Date	*Cap. Gains (– Losses)*	*Total Return*	*Rate of Return*
12-31-71	$ 519.48	$2,158.44	1.97%
12-31-76	$2,461.54	$3,400.00	6.03%

PROFILE: This has been a wild, volatile, up-and-down stock. In 1974, a year many companies would prefer to forget, Tesoro posted then-record earnings of $5.55 a share. In 1977, a year many companies remember fondly, Tesoro lost money. In 1980 the company finally broke 1974's record.

If earnings have seesawed, the stock price has too — with a vengeance. It's been a rare year when Tesoro's high for the year hasn't been at least 100 percent above its low. It's not a stock for people who have trouble sleeping at night.

One reason for the volatility has been Tesoro's part ownership of Commonwealth Oil (Corco, as it's often called), which plunged into bankruptcy in 1978 and was recently trying to emerge. Another reason for it has been that Tesoro's balance sheet has traditionally been highly leveraged. Recently, though, management has decided (with some help from Tesoro's banks) to be more conservative. Debt has been trimmed and was recently less than 20 percent of capital for the first time in more than a decade. Management also said it would pay more attention to long-range planning. (*Business Week,* for one, has twitted the company for a "penchant for fast, but haphazard, growth.") However, in early 1982 company officials said that the best plan might be to voluntarily liquidate the company (sell off its components), and that they were considering that course.

Due to its history of uncertainty and to the fact that it gets very little of its oil in the politically safe (relatively speaking) United States, Tesoro usually sells for a low multiple of earnings — in recent years, 2 to 7. It can be a bargain stock, as well as a hot potato.

Dividends, resumed in 1980 after a two-year lapse, provide a small yield.

* * *

TEXACO INC. (TX). Founded 1902. Headquarters: 2000 Westchester Ave., White Plains NY 10650. **OIL.** Texaco is the third largest U.S.-based oil company and the fourth largest U.S. industrial corporation. 66,000 employees.

Sales: $51,195.8 million (trend 14.8% a year).
Earnings: $2,240.24 million (trend 22.1% a year).
What happened to a $10,000 investment

Purchase Date	*Purchase Price*	*Price on 12-31-81*	*Dividends Paid*
12-31-71	$34.37	$33.25	$6,068.36
12-31-76	$27.75	$33.25	$4,097.30

Purchase Date	*Cap. Gains (− Losses)*	*Total Return*	*Rate of Return*
12-31-71	$−327.27	$5,741.09	4.64%
12-31-76	$ 1,981.98	$6,079.28	9.96%

PROFILE: Texaco saw its profits rise in recent years, as did virtually all oil companies. But Texaco prospered less than most, because its basic strategy historically has been to emphasize refining and marketing, rather than exploration and production. In *Forbes* magazine's 1981 *Annual Report on American Industry,* Texaco ranked last among eight major international oil companies in return on total capital, in profit margin, and in profit growth.

Business Week, in a 1980 article called "Restoring Luster to the Star," analyzed the reasons behind the giant company's malaise. Back in the 1950s, the analysis went, Texaco "had set in place a long-range strategy centered on a key assumption — that crude oil supplies would remain cheap and plentiful forever. . . . Exploration was minimized, while enormous efforts went into acquiring strong market positions in all fifty states. To service those markets, Texaco built a network of regional refineries . . ." But in the late 1970s and early 1980s, the money in oil was not in refining and marketing, but in finding and selling crude.

Texaco's new strategy is to explore more heavily and to diversify into some non-oil areas. It has barely begun this new approach, so it's too early to make informed judgments about how the company will do. But it has the financial strength to give it a running start. Profits are solid, the balance sheet is strong (less than 20 percent debt recently), and the company recently had some $3.5 billion in cash and equivalents.

The stock, out of favor, has sold for less than 7 times earnings since 1978 and sometimes as low as 3 to 4 times earnings. Dividends have been paid since 1903, and the yield is substantial — 6 to 8 percent in recent years.

* * *

TEXAS AIR CORP. (TEX, American Stock Exchange). Founded 1968. Headquarters: 2 Allen Center, Houston TX 77002. **AIRLINE.** Texas Air Corp. is an airline holding company. It owns a Southwest regional carrier, a shuttle plane operator between Boston and Washington, and a majority interest in Continental Air Lines, which it acquired in 1981. 14,000 employees. **MAJOR SUBSIDIARIES, BRANDS:** Continental Air Lines (51 percent owned); New York Air; Texas International Airlines.

Sales: $291.5 million (trend 28.5% a year).
Earnings: $4.67 million (trend 31.1% a year).
What happened to a $10,000 investment

Purchase Date	*Purchase Price*	*Price on 12-31-81*	*Dividends Paid*
12-31-71	$N/A	$5.62	$ N/A
12-31-76	$ 3.25	$5.62	$1,846.15

Purchase Date	*Cap. Gains (− Losses)*	*Total Return*	*Rate of Return*
12-31-71	$ N/A	$ N/A	N/A%
12-31-76	$7,307.69	$9,153.85	13.88%

PROFILE: Talk about high-flying speculations! This is one if there ever was one. Through its subsidiaries — Texas International Airlines and New York Air — Texas Air in the late 1970s exemplified the new breed of successful regional carriers. Then in 1981 Texas Air made a startlingly successful bid to take control of Continental Air Lines, which at the time was the nation's ninth largest airline and three times the size of Texas Air. President Reagan approved the 51-percent take-over in October 1981.In 1982 the two airlines anounced that a total merger would follow.

At the time of the take-over, Continental had more than 10,000 employees and close to $1 billion in revenues. Texas Air had about 3,500 employees and less than $300 million in revenues. But there was another major difference that helped explain the merger: Texas Air was profitable. Continental was not.

It took an eight-month battle for Texas Air to win Continental. The other would-be acquirers were Western Airlines (profiled elsewhere in this volume) and Continental's own employees. When the battle was done, many analysts feared that what Texas Air had won was an albatross, albeit a big one.

One thing Texas Air and Continental had in common was a huge debt load. Preceeding the takeover, Texas Air had 76 percent of its capital in the form of debt, while Continental had 72 percent. Both figures are extraordinarily high. The stock of the new, larger Texas Air Corp. must be considered extremely risky. But there is a speculative chance for a very large return.

Dividends were started in 1978, but the yield is small.

* * *

TEXAS COMMERCE BANCSHARES, INC. (TCB). Founded 1970 (bank dates to 1912). Headquarters: 712 Main St., Houston TX 77002. BANKING. Texas Commerce Bancshares is a holding company that owns more than forty banks in Texas, including Texas Commerce Bank, the state's fourth largest. MAJOR SUBSIDIARIES, BRANDS: Texas Commerce Bank; Texas Commerce Funding Co.; Texas Commerce Leasing Co.; TCB Leasing Co.

Sales: $1,028.6 million (trend 32.2% a year).
Earnings: $102.95 million (trend 25.3% a year).
What happened to a $10,000 investment

Purchase Date	*Purchase Price*	*Price on 12-31-81*	*Dividends Paid*
12-31-71	$10.90	$38.62	$5,339.45
12-31-76	$18.87	$38.62	$1,969.54

Purchase Date	*Cap. Gains (− Losses)*	*Total Return*	*Rate of Return*
12-31-71	$25,435.78	$30,775.23	15.09%
12-31-76	$10,463.58	$12,433.11	17.54%

* * *

TEXAS EASTERN CORP. (TET). Founded 1947. Headquarters: 1 Houston Center, Houston TX 77001. NATURAL GAS. Texas Eastern transports natural gas through pipelines in the United States and explores for natural gas and oil, primarily in the North Sea. It is also involved in oil production, refining, pipeline transportation of petroleum products, and some other energy-related ventures. 5,000 employees.

Sales: $4272.9 million (trend 25.1% a year).
Earnings: $219.76 million (trend 16.3% a year).
What happened to a $10,000 investment

Purchase Date	*Purchase Price*	*Price on 12-31-81*	*Dividends Paid*
12-31-71	$44.62	$52.50	$4,803.81
12-31-76	$40.87	$52.50	$3,211.01

Purchase Date	*Cap. Gains (− Losses)*	*Total Return*	*Rate of Return*
12-31-71	$1,764.71	$6,568.52	5.18%
12-31-76	$2,844.04	$6,055.05	9.93%

PROFILE: "How do you get from here to there?" asks an old song. In Texas Eastern's case, the question might be rephrased: "How do you get natural gas from the places where it's abundant, such as Texas, Louisiana, and Alaska, to the places where it's not, such as New York, New Jersey, and California?" The answer might be given briefly thus: "With consistent profitability."

For the past decade, Texas Eastern's profits have not only been consistent, they've been growing fast. Profits were $68 million ($2.89 a share) in 1971; they were $220 million ($8.72 a share) in 1980. Over that same period, return on equity has advanced from around 15 percent to around 20 percent, while debt as a percentage of total capital has been slashed from almost 60 percent down to around 32 percent.

For this bravura performance, what is Texas Eastern's reward? A stock that sold in early 1982 for a miserly 6 times earnings. Perhaps that low p / e can be best understood as an expression of pessimism over profit prospects in light of the fact that pipeline operations are government-regulated. Indeed, while Texas Eastern's profits have gone up, its profit *margins* have gone down.

However, though Texas Eastern is indeed a pipeline company (getting more than half of revenues from that source), it is also a gas and oil exploration and production company (getting more than half of recent profits from that source). Oil prices were down in the early 1980s and gas prices weren't soaring either. But experts differed over how long this pricing trend could last. In any case, oil and gas should be at least a solid business for years to come. At recent prices, this stock looked like a bargain.

The dividend yield is substantial — around 7 percent in early 1982. Dividends have been paid each year since 1950.

* * *

TEXAS GAS TRANSMISSION CORP. (TXG). Founded 1945. Headquarters: 3800 Frederica St., Owensburg KY 42301. ENERGY AND TRANSPORTATION. Texas Gas Transmission operates an interstate natural gas pipeline, produces oil and gas, and is involved in trucking. It also owns the largest inland shipyard in the United States and operates an inland waterways barge company. **MAJOR SUBSIDIARIES, BRANDS:** American Commercial Barging Line; American Commercial Terminals, Inc.

Sales: $2,230.1 million (trend 24.9% a year).
Earnings: $92.76 million (trend 14.7% a year).
What happened to a $10,000 investment

Purchase Date	*Purchase Price*	*Price on 12-31-81*	*Dividends Paid*
12-31-71	$16.62	$35.25	$6,933.83
12-31-76	$23.94	$35.25	$2,991.12

Purchase Date	*Cap. Gains (− Losses)*	*Total Return*	*Rate of Return*
12-31-71	$11,203.01	$18,136.84	10.90%
12-31-76	$ 4,725.85	$ 7,716.97	12.12%

* * *

TEXAS INDUSTRIES, INC. (TXI). Founded 1951. Headquarters: 8100 Carpenter Freeway, Dallas TX 75247. **CONCRETE.** Texas Industries manufactures and sells concrete products and is also engaged in construction. **MAJOR SUBSIDIARIES, BRANDS:** Brookhollow Corp.; Chaparral Steel Co.; Southwestern Financial Corp.; TXI Cement Co.; United Cement Co.

* * *

TEXAS INSTRUMENTS (TXN). Founded 1938. Headquarters: 13500 North Central Expressway, Dallas TX 75265. **SEMICONDUCTORS, ELECTRONICS.** Texas Instruments is the nation's largest maker of semiconductors and produces a variety of other electronic products. It is also involved in seismic exploration for petroleum companies and, to a lesser extent, in specialty metals. 89,000 employees.

Sales: $4074.7 million (trend 24.5% a year).
Earnings: $212.20 million (trend 25.8% a year).
What happened to a $10,000 investment

Purchase Date	*Purchase Price*	*Price on 12-31-81*	*Dividends Paid*
12-31-71	$ 62.69	$80.50	$2,135.99
12-31-76	$102.62	$80.50	$ 893.54

Purchase Date	*Cap. Gains (− Losses)*	*Total Return*	*Rate of Return*
12-31-71	$ 2,841.48	$ 4,977.47	4.12%
12-31-76	$−2,155.91	$−1,262.36	−2.66%

PROFILE: Texas Instruments has been a successful company in a brutal field. Most long-term holders of this stock have reason to be pleased with their gains. But it's a stock in which you can lose quite a bit of money, with bad timing.

Say you jumped on at the 1980 high of $150 and lost your nerve in mid-1981, selling at $88. Or you could have bought in 1973 at $138 and sold in 1974 at $59. The problem is that the semiconductor industry, in which Texas Instruments is the leading player, is subject to waves of high demand and waves of overcapacity. Catch these tides when the current is going the right way and you'll be happier than a surfer in the curl. But time the waves wrong and you can be — to borrow a term where surfers' and brokers' parlance coincide — wiped out.

The company has traditionally spent heavily on research and development, and on capital expenditures. This has helped it maintain rapid sales and earnings growth. Fast growth, in turn, has caused the shares to command a high p / e, relative to the average stock. You'll often find Texas Instruments selling at around twice the market multiple.

If the company has a weak point (other than the cyclical nature of its chief business) it's probably marketing. But many companies would be glad to have one of Texas Instruments' bad years: Return on equity here is usually 15 to 20 percent. The balance sheet looks good too, with debt recently around 15 percent of total capital.

The stock may be a shade less good than the company, basically because of the high multiple. This is no little-known treasure, but it can be a good long-term investment — especially if you buy in when semiconductor stocks are out of favor.

* * *

TEXAS INTERNATIONAL CO. (TEI). Founded 1930. Headquarters: 3545 N.W. 58th St., Oklahoma City, OK 73112. **OIL.** Texas International is a relatively small oil and gas exploration and production company. **MAJOR SUBSIDIARIES, BRANDS:** Phoenix Resources Co. (51 percent owned).

Sales: $80.5 million (trend 2.0% a year).
Earnings: $14.80 million (trend 14.7% a year).
What happened to a $10,000 investment

Purchase Date	*Purchase Price*	*Price on 12-31-81*	*Dividends Paid*
12-31-71	$2.62	$38.25	$190.48
12-31-76	$4.69	$38.25	$106.67

Purchase Date	Cap. Gains (– Losses)	Total Return	Rate of Return
12-31-71	$135,714.29	$135,904.76	30.74%
12-31-76	$ 71,600.00	$ 71,706.67	52.21%

* * *

TEXAS-NEW MEXICO POWER CO. (TNP). Founded 1963. Headquarters: 501 W. Sixth St., Fort Worth TX 76102. **UTILITY.** Provides electricity to approximately half a million customers in portions of Texas and New Mexico.

Sales: $216.4 million (trend 23.1% a year).
Earnings: $6.02 million (trend 10.1% a year).
What happened to a $10,000 investment

Purchase Date	Purchase Price	Price on 12-31-81	Dividends Paid
12-31-71	$24.77	$16.62	$6,868.79
12-31-76	$19.12	$16.62	$4,844.44

Purchase Date	Cap. Gains (– Losses)	Total Return	Rate of Return
12-31-71	$–3,288.99	$3,579.80	3.11%
12-31-76	$–1,307.19	$3,537.25	6.24%

* * *

TEXAS OIL & GAS CORP. (TXO). Founded 1955. Headquarters: Fidelity Union Tower, Dallas TX 75201. **GAS, OIL.** Buys, sells, and transports natural gas; also produces and processes natural gas and oil. 2,600 employees. **MAJOR SUBSIDIARIES, BRANDS:** FWA Drilling Co.

Sales: $1,433.9 million (trend 29.5% a year).
Earnings: $191.92 million (trend 30.7% a year).
What happened to a $10,000 investment

Purchase Date	Purchase Price	Price on 12-31-81	Dividends Paid
12-31-71	$4.54	$35.25	$1,244.48
12-31-76	$5.63	$35.25	$ 913.39

Purchase Date	Cap. Gains (– Losses)	Total Return	Rate of Return
12-31-71	$67,589.97	$68,834.46	22.93%
12-31-76	$52,609.13	$53,522.52	44.74%

PROFILE: This has been one of the fastest-growing companies in the country, as well as one of the most profitable. Return on stockholders' equity has been better than 20 percent every year since 1974 and broke 30 percent in fiscal 1980. The company has an uninterrupted string of substantial earnings gains each year, from the time it was founded through 1981. Sales first hit $100 million in 1974 and broke $1 billion in 1980. Margins are high — in recent years, around 10 to 13 percent.

The goose that lays these golden eggs? Gas gathering. Somebody has to get natural gas from small producers, process it, and resell it in larger quantities to big users (large industrial customers and utilities). That somebody — in major parts of Texas, Oklahoma, and other states — is Texas Oil & Gas Corp.

Had you bought this stock at its 1971 high and sold at its 1980 high, you would have multiplied your money about eight-fold, not counting the modest dividend. Had you bought at a market nadir in 1974, you could have multiplied your money more than twenty-fold.

Decontrol of natural gas prices should help the company to some more fine years. The question is whether it will also help the stock. Has the market already discounted the company's bright future? At least to some extent, yes. The p / e recently was 11, at a time when the average stock was going for about 7 or 8.

* * *

TEXAS PACIFIC LAND TRUST. (TPL). Founded 1888. Headquarters: 61 Broadway, New York NY 10006. **REAL ESTATE.** Texas Pacific makes over half of its income from land sales and also receives royalties from oil and natural gas wells.

* * *

TEXAS UTILITIES CO. (TXU). Founded 1945. Headquarters: 2001 Bryan Tower, Dallas TX 75201. **UTILITY.** Provides electricity to some four million customers in Texas through three major operating subsidiaries. 14,000 employees. **MAJOR SUBSIDIARIES, BRANDS:** Dallas Power & Light; Texas Electric Service; Texas Power & Light.

Sales: $2,174.6 million (trend 19.0% a year).
Earnings: $297.84 million (trend 18.3% a year).
What happened to a $10,000 investment

Purchase Date	Purchase Price	Price on 12-31-81	Dividends Paid
12-31-71	$30.81	$19.62	$4,517.65
12-31-76	$21.75	$19.62	$3,770.11

Purchase Date	*Cap. Gains (— Losses)*	*Total Return*	*Rate of Return*
12-31-71	$−3,630.83	$ 886.82	.85%
12-31-76	$ −977.01	$2,793.10	5.05%

PROFILE: If you must own a utility stock, this one merits consideration. For one thing, instead of watching your company get pilloried in the press, you may be able to watch it get some good publicity from time to time. Chairman T. L. Austin, Jr., has a flair for public relations. Example: He once had the power turned off in the home office in sympathy for customers during a storm-induced power outage.

Austin is an articulate proponent of the need for greater use of coal. And he's put that belief into practice at his own utilities, where coal recently supplied a bit over half the power generated.

Texas is still a growing market, which is both good news and bad news. The good news is that revenue growth provides a basis for profit growth. The bad news is that the company has needed to build lots of new power-generating facilities, which cost money. It's turned to both the bond markets (about $2.5 billion in long-term debt), and to the stock market (lots of dilution) to raise this money. Between 1974 and 1980, total earnings more than doubled, but per-share earnings were up only about 57 percent.

Still, lots of utilities would love to see *any* per-share earnings progress. The stock price has declined a bit (a lower multiple offsetting higher earnings), but not as much as at most utilities. It's hard to see the p / e going much lower than it has recently (6), and the stock in recent years has yielded 8 to 10 percent.

* * *

TEXFLI INDUSTRIES, INC. (TXF). Founded 1963. Headquarters: 1400 Battleground Ave., Greensboro NC 27420. **TEXTILES.** Texfli designs, produces, and sells clothing fabrics for men's wear and women's wear.

Sales: $144.5 million (trend −4.9% a year).
Earnings: $−21.50 million.
What happened to a $10,000 investment

Purchase Date	*Purchase Price*	*Price on 12-31-81*	*Dividends Paid*
12-31-71	$31.50	$4.25	$0.00
12-31-76	$ 4.12	$4.25	$0.00

Purchase Date	*Cap. Gains (— Losses)*	*Total Return*	*Rate of Return*
12-31-71	$−8,650.79	$−8,650.79	−18.15%
12-31-76	$ 303.03	$ 303.03	.60%

* * *

TEXTRON INC. (TXT). Founded 1928. Headquarters: 40 Westminster St., Providence RI 02903. **CONGLOMERATE.** Textron is a widely diversified conglomerate and a major producer of helicopters, which account for about a quarter of sales and profits. 61,000 employees. **MAJOR SUBSIDIARIES, BRANDS:** Bell Helicopter; Talon (zippers); Homelite (chainsaws); Shaeffer (pens); Eaton (paper); Jacobson (lawn mowers, snow blowers); Speidel (watch bands); Bridgeport Machines (machine tools); Dalmo Victor (radar); Bostitch (stapling equipment); Camcar (fasteners); Fafnir (bearings).

Sales: $3376.7 million (trend 7.4% a year).
Earnings: $169.40 million (trend 12.3% a year).
What happened to a $10,000 investment

Purchase Date	*Purchase Price*	*Price on 12-31-81*	*Dividends Paid*
12-31-71	$30.50	$26.62	$4,486.89
12-31-76	$27.50	$26.62	$3,054.55

Purchase Date	*Cap. Gains (— Losses)*	*Total Return*	*Rate of Return*
12-31-71	$−1,270.49	$3,216.39	2.83%
12-31-76	$ −318.18	$2,736.36	4.96%

PROFILE: Textron is generally considered the first of the major modern conglomerates, having beaten the likes of IT&T and LTV to the punch in the early 1950s. In recent years, it's gained a reputation for achieving consistently good profitability (usually 16 to 19 percent on stockholders' equity), but only slow growth. Hence, a 1980 *Business Week* headline: "Textron: Shaking up the Divisions to Enliven a Sluggish Conglomerate."

Textron has some twenty-five divisions. As *Business Week* pointed out, the heads of at least eight of them were replaced in 1979–80. Among those divisions the magazine said had turned in a subpar performance were Jacobson Manufacturing (lawn mowers, snow blowers) and Talon (zippers, sewing supplies). It quoted Bear, Stearns analyst Robert Sussman as saying, "There have been a lot of sleepy and unaggressive people there," and it quoted Robert Straetz, the new chief executive, as saying, "We plan to coach the team a little closer than in the past."

Shareholders will probably be glad to see tighter control from headquarters, since the price per share has stayed virtually unchanged for a decade. (The 1971 high was $32.75, the 1980 high $32.37.)

Although it's been consistently profitable, Textron represents a possible "turnaround" situation. The p / e has gradually sunk; recently it's been 5 to 7. A profit upturn would presumably hike the p / e, along with earnings. Meanwhile, the stock provides a consistent dividend yield (recently 5 to 7 percent), well covered by earnings. Dividends have been paid each year since 1942.

* * *

THACKERAY CORP. (THK). Founded 1968. Headquarters: 2401 Douglas Rd., Miami FL 33145. **REAL ESTATE.** Manages properties acquired (mainly through foreclosure) during the company's previous incarnation (as Republic Mortgage Investors) as a real estate investment trust.

* * *

THERMO ELECTRON CORP. (TMO). Founded 1956. Headquarters: 101 First Ave., Waltham MA 02154. **MANUFACTURING.** Thermo Electron produces manufacturing equipment, energy recovery and conversion equipment, and monitoring instruments; also provides research and development services. **MAJOR SUBSIDIARIES, BRANDS:** Van Hengel Instruments B.V.

Sales: $210.0 million (trend 35.1% a year).
Earnings: $8.21 million (trend 52.0% a year).
What happened to a $10,000 investment

Purchase Date	*Purchase Price*	*Price on 12-31-81*	*Dividends Paid*
12-31-71	$21.42	$21.25	$0.00
12-31-76	$ 7.67	$21.25	$0.00

Purchase Date	*Cap. Gains (− Losses)*	*Total Return*	*Rate of Return*
12-31-71	$ −77.82	$ −77.82	−.08%
12-31-76	$17,717.39	$17,717.39	22.62%

* * *

THIOKOL CORP. (THI). Founded 1930. Headquarters: Newton-Yardley Rd., Route No. 332, Newton PA 18940. **SPECIALTY CHEMICALS.** Thiokol's revenues are divided between government contracts for solid-fuel rocket engines and ordnance, and specialty chemicals manufacturing. **MAJOR SUBSIDIARIES, BRANDS:** Cincinnati Milacron Chemicals.

Sales: $622.7 million (trend 13.6% a year).
Earnings: $30.75 million (trend 17.2% a year).
What happened to a $10,000 investment

Purchase Date	*Purchase Price*	*Price on 12-31-81*	*Dividends Paid*
12-31-71	$8.25	$31.87	$6,315.15
12-31-76	$9.62	$31.87	$3,880.52

Purchase Date	*Cap. Gains (− Losses)*	*Total Return*	*Rate of Return*
12-31-71	$28,636.36	$34,951.52	16.22%
12-31-76	$23,116.88	$26,997.40	29.91%

* * *

THOMAS & BETTS CORP. (TNB). Founded 1895. Headquarters: 920 Route 202, Raritan NJ 08869. **MANUFACTURING.** Thomas & Betts manufactures electrical and electronic components; also designs and manufactures systems for connecting, fastening, protecting, and identifying wires and conduits. **MAJOR SUBSIDIARIES, BRANDS:** Thomas & Betts International, Inc.; Thomas & Betts Limited; T & B / Ansley Corp.

Sales: $254.0 million (trend 18.9% a year).
Earnings: $32.50 million (trend 20.1% a year).
What happened to a $10,000 investment

Purchase Date	*Purchase Price*	*Price on 12-31-81*	*Dividends Paid*
12-31-71	$25.62	$58.25	$4,230.24
12-31-76	$40.25	$58.25	$1,843.48

Purchase Date	*Cap. Gains (− Losses)*	*Total Return*	*Rate of Return*
12-31-71	$12,731.71	$16,961.95	10.43%
12-31-76	$ 4,472.05	$ 6,315.53	10.29%

* * *

THOMAS INDUSTRIES, INC. (TII). Founded 1928. Headquarters: 207 E. Broadway, Louisville KY 40202. **ELECTRICAL PRODUCTS.** Thomas Industries manufactures and sells lighting fixtures, home accessories, tools, and hardware. **MAJOR SUBSIDIARIES, BRANDS:** Abbott; Benjamin; Builders Brass Works; C & M Products Limited; Colonial; Fastway Fasteners; Hit; Jackson Exit; Jet Line; Oliver MacLeod; Pouliot Designs; Sprayit; Star Light; Thomas.

Sales: $227.1 million (trend 18.0% a year).
Earnings: $10.74 million (trend 29.4% a year).
What happened to a $10,000 investment

Purchase Date	*Purchase Price*	*Price on 12-31-81*	*Dividends Paid*
12-31-71	$14.99	$15.37	$2,140.05
12-31-76	$ 7.92	$15.37	$2,592.60

Purchase Date	*Cap. Gains (− Losses)*	*Total Return*	*Rate of Return*
12-31-71	$ 253.95	$ 2,394.00	2.17%
12-31-76	$9,420.77	$12,013.38	17.09%

* * *

THOMPSON MEDICAL CO., INC. (TM). Founded 1954. Headquarters: 919 Third Ave., New York NY 10022. **NONPRESCRIPTION DRUGS.** Thompson Medical sells nonprescription healthcare products, with the largest share of its revenues coming from the sale of appetite suppressants. **MAJOR SUBSIDIARIES, BRANDS:** Dexatrim; Prolamine; Appedrine; Coffee, Tea & A New Me; Aspercreme.

Sales: $95.3 million.
Earnings: $10.03 million.

* * *

THRIFTY CORP. (TFD). Founded 1929. Headquarters: 5051 Rodeo Rd., Los Angeles CA 90016. **SPECIALTY RETAILER.** Thrifty operates the largest drug and discount store chain in California and also runs a chain of sporting goods stores. **MAJOR SUBSIDIARIES, BRANDS:** Big 5 Sporting Goods Stores; Thrifty Drug and Discount Stores; Broun Brothers; Discount Drug Stores; Newman Importing Co., Inc.; Thrifty Realty Co.; United Merchandising Corp.; Wonder World Co.

Sales: $1,054.4 million (trend 11.4% a year).
Earnings: $17.75 million (trend 18.6% a year).
What happened to a $10,000 investment

Purchase Date	*Purchase Price*	*Price on 12-31-81*	*Dividends Paid*
12-31-71	$11.44	$12.62	$4,331.37
12-31-76	$ 8.87	$12.62	$3,419.72

Purchase Date	*Cap. Gains (− Losses)*	*Total Return*	*Rate of Return*
12-31-71	$1,038.25	$5,369.62	4.39%
12-31-76	$4,225.35	$7,645.07	12.03%

* * *

TI-CARO, INC. (TCX). Founded 1931. Headquarters: Bessemer City Rd., Gastonia NC 28052. **TEXTILES.** Ti-Caro manufactures industrial threads and yarns for use by garment manufacturers; also makes knit fabrics. **MAJOR SUBSIDIARIES, BRANDS:** Caro-Knit; Clyde Fabrics; Spun-Lo Eiderlon.

Sales: $271.8 million (trend 9.7% a year).
Earnings: $17.32 million (trend 7.6% a year).
What happened to a $10,000 investment

Purchase Date	*Purchase Price*	*Price on 12-31-81*	*Dividends Paid*
12-31-71	$7.25	$15.75	$9,352.58
12-31-76	$7.12	$15.75	$6,561.40

Purchase Date	*Cap. Gains (− Losses)*	*Total Return*	*Rate of Return*
12-31-71	$11,709.44	$21,062.02	12.00%
12-31-76	$12,105.26	$18,666.67	23.45%

* * *

TIDEWATER INC. (TDW). Founded 1956. Headquarters: 1440 Canal St., New Orleans LA 70112. **OFFSHORE DRILLING SUPPORT.** Tidewater provides support to the offshore drilling industry, ranging from light construction to exploration and development. **MAJOR SUBSIDIARIES, BRANDS:** Dental Insurance Co., Limited; Hilliard Oil & Gas, Inc.; Tidewater Compression, Inc.; Tidewater Contractor Services, Inc.; Tidewater Marine Services, Inc.; Tidewater Realty, Inc.

Sales: $341.1 million (trend 21.3% a year).
Earnings: $53.45 million (trend 15.7% a year).
What happened to a $10,000 investment

Purchase Date	*Purchase Price*	*Price on 12-31-81*	*Dividends Paid*
12-31-71	$10.50	$42.62	$3,246.35
12-31-76	$12.17	$42.62	$1,912.60

Purchase Date	*Cap. Gains (− Losses)*	*Total Return*	*Rate of Return*
12-31-71	$30,595.24	$33,841.59	15.93%
12-31-76	$25,034.25	$26,946.85	29.87%

* * *

TIGER INTERNATIONAL, INC. (TGR). Founded 1945. Headquarters: 1888 Century Park E., Los Angeles CA 90067. **FREIGHT TRANSPORTATION.** Tiger is a major U.S. and international air freight company. It is also active in railroad car leasing and in trucking; and is trying to enter the courier business. 10,000 employees. **MAJOR SUBSIDIARIES, BRANDS:** Flying Tiger Lines; Seaboard World Airways; North American Car (railroad car leasing); Hall's Motor Transport; Warrent Transport. Owns 12½ percent of Purolator.

Sales: $1,528.0 million (trend 32.8% a year).
Earnings: $42.37 million (trend 22.1% a year).
What happened to a $10,000 investment

Purchase Date	*Purchase Price*	*Price on 12-31-81*	*Dividends Paid*
12-31-71	$23.51	$13.50	$2,073.83
12-31-76	$12.25	$13.50	$2,836.73

Purchase Date	*Cap. Gains (– Losses)*	*Total Return*	*Rate of Return*
12-31-71	$–4,257.08	$–2,183.25	–2.43%
12-31-76	$ 1,020.41	$ 3,857.14	6.74%

PROFILE: The "first U.S. intermodal transportation company." Is it a pipe dream or a valid plan? Tiger is trying to cover the waterfront — or, more exactly, everything but the waterfront. While continuing as a major air freight hauler (in fact, acquiring Seaboard World Airways in 1980), Tiger has snapped up three trucking companies and is trying to shove its nose into the courier business by buying into Purolator. (Should that fail, management has said it might try to buy another courier company.) All this and railcar leasing, too.

The concept may be sound. And now — with deregulation coming to the fore — is the time to try it. Credit chairman Wayne Hoffman with vision.

But don't credit him with credit. This company's balance sheet is a mess, and that could create some problems down the road. Recently, debt was a whopping 72 percent of total capital. In 1980 the company paid out some $153 million to service its debt, a sum more than 3 times profits for the year. Margins lately have been low (due partly to airfare wars), and return on stockholders' equity has been nothing to brag about.

All this could change: In a highly leveraged company, it's possible to go quickly from a bad year to a very good one. But certainly conservative investors will shy away from Tiger because of its balance sheet.

Dividends have been paid yearly since 1973 and increased yearly since 1976. The yield is modest to moderate.

* * *

TIME INC. (TL). Founded 1922. Headquarters: Time & Life Bldg., Rockefeller Center, New York NY 10020. **PUBLISHING, BROADCASTING, FOREST PRODUCTS.** Time is the country's leading magazine publisher and largest pay cable television operator. It is also a major book publisher and forest products company. 26,000 employees. **MAJOR SUBSIDIARIES, BRANDS:** *Time, Life, Sports Illustrated, Fortune, People,* and *Money* magazines; Book-of-the-Month Club; Little, Brown & Co.; Time-Life Books; Home Box Office (cable TV); Temple-Eastex, Inland Container (forest products).

Sales: $2,881.8 million (trend 28.2% a year).
Earnings: $141.20 million (trend 26.6% a year).
What happened to a $10,000 investment

Purchase Date	*Purchase Price*	*Price on 12-31-81*	*Dividends Paid*
12-31-71	$14.56	$38.25	$4,454.08
12-31-76	$18.62	$38.25	$2,146.98

Purchase Date	*Cap. Gains (– Losses)*	*Total Return*	*Rate of Return*
12-31-71	$16,266.09	$20,720.17	11.88%
12-31-76	$10,536.91	$12,683.89	17.80%

PROFILE: You think of Time as a magazine publisher. That's reasonable — it *is* the largest and best-known magazine publisher in the country. But Wall Street doesn't think of it that way. It thinks of Time as the leading factor in the red-hot cable television industry. That's why Time shares were recently selling at about 14 times earnings when the average stock fetched about 8.

In a cogent and pithy 1981 *Forbes* magazine article, writer Allan Sloan argued that "Time is now a cable television company, with trees in second place and magazines only third." That case can certainly be made, though publishing operations contributed more revenues and profits in 1980 than did forest products or video. (Sloan may merely have jumped the gun a trifle.) The case can also be made — and Sloan made it — that the stock is undervalued on an assets basis, with the cable and forest properties alone worth more than the recent price of the stock.

The Value Line Investment Survey, however, argues that Time shares tend to be perenially undervalued on an assets basis, and that this factor alone doesn't justify buying the stock. *Value Line* also pointed out that Time's return on stockholders' equity has been only about average.

The bottom line? If you like asset plays, have lots of patience, think cable will stay hot, and don't mind a fairly ample price / earnings ratio, this may be a stock for you.

Though dividends have been paid every year since 1930, the dividend yield remains small.

* * *

TIMES MIRROR CO. (TMC). Founded 1884. Headquarters: Times Mirror Sq., Los Angeles CA 90053. NEWSPAPERS, BROADCASTING, FOREST PRODUCTS. Times Mirror is the nation's largest newspaper chain, measured by sales (though not by number of papers). The company is also active in cable TV and commercial broadcasting, forest products, book publishing, and magazine publishing; it has sidelines in art and graphics supplies, telephone book printing, road maps, real estate, and recording charts. 27,000 employees. MAJOR SUBSIDIARIES, BRANDS: Los Angeles *Times;* Hartford *Courant;* Dallas *Times Herald*; *Newsday;* Denver *Post; The Sporting News;* New American Library (paperback books); *Popular Science, Golf,* and *Outdoor Life* magazines; KTBC-TV (Austin, Texas); WVTM-TV (Birmingham, Alabama); KDFW-TV (Dallas, Texas); WETM-TV (Elmira, New York); WHTM-TV (Harrisburg, Pennsylvania); KTVI-TV (St. Louis, Missouri); WSTM-TV (Syracuse, New York); Videotex interactive cable TV system; M. Grumbacher art supplies; Graphic Controls recording charts.

Sales: $1,857.3 million (trend 18.8% a year).
Earnings: $139.22 million (trend 25.8% a year).
What happened to a $10,000 investment

Purchase Date	*Purchase Price*	*Price on 12-31-81*	*Dividends Paid*
12-31-71	$25.75	$45.75	$3,186.41
12-31-76	$23.25	$45.75	$2,627.96

Purchase Date	*Cap. Gains (− Losses)*	*Total Return*	*Rate of Return*
12-31-71	$7,766.99	$10,953.40	7.68%
12-31-76	$9,677.42	$12,305.38	17.40%

PROFILE: Hold on to your hats! This media conglomerate has been expanding fast. In the past few years, it's picked up the Hartford *Courant,* the Denver *Post, The Sporting News,* five regular TV stations, and two cable TV stations, among other sundries. The tab: around $480 million.

You might expect a buying binge like that would require a company either to issue more stock or to take on more debt. Times Mirror has so far chosen the latter. It could afford to, since debt in the mid-1970s was well under 10 percent of total capital. Recently, it's up to about 34 percent of total capital. That's still well within reason, but keep an eye on the debt ratio.

In taking on more debt, the company may give a boost to return on stockholders' equity. That figure is already good — better than 15 percent just about every year in the past decade, and better than 20 percent occasionally. The company enjoys a reputation for taking over big metropolitan papers that aren't highly profitable and improving both their quality and their profitability.

Newspapers account for about half of sales and profits. Like Time Inc., Times Mirror is also involved in forest products, cable TV (it's roughly the sixth largest U.S. operator), book publishing, and magazine publishing. It's also involved in conventional commercial television, having bought five stations from Newhouse Broadcasting in 1978. The diversity gives the company some balance, although earnings from many of the subsidiaries can be expected to rise and fall in synchronization.

With its rapid growth, the company lately commands a stock multiple above that of the average stock. The p / e tends to fluctuate a good deal, though. The dividend, paid yearly since 1892, affords a small-to-moderate yield.

* * *

TIMKEN CO. (TKR). Founded 1904. Headquarters: 1835 Dueber Ave. S.W., Canton OH 44706. BEARINGS, STEEL. Timken is the world's largest maker of tapered roller bearings and a supplier of specialty steel products. 22,000 employees. MAJOR SUBSIDIARIES, BRANDS: Latrobe Steel.

Sales: $1,338.5 million (trend 11.4% a year).
Earnings: $92.63 million (trend 11.4% a year).
What happened to a $10,000 investment

Purchase Date	*Purchase Price*	*Price on 12-31-81*	*Dividends Paid*
12-31-71	$44.25	$64.75	$5,801.13
12-31-76	$53.25	$64.75	$2,910.80

Purchase Date	*Cap. Gains (− Losses)*	*Total Return*	*Rate of Return*
12-31-71	$4,632.77	$10,433.90	7.41%
12-31-76	$2,159.62	$ 5,070.42	8.55%

PROFILE: Visit an efficiently run factory. If the assembly lines and machine tools are running well, you won't notice the bearings. You just notice that everything's going smoothly.

Timken is the leading maker of tapered roller bearings, and its role in the economy parallels the role of its bearings in a well-run plant. Timken doesn't attract much attention, but its products help keep things running smoothly in hundreds of industries, from autos and railroads to construction and mining.

As you might expect, Timken's earnings tend to rise and fall with the economy. After a good year in 1979, it saw an earnings decline in 1980, but bounced back pretty well in 1981, another recession-shaded year. Wall Street expects the company to bounce back from its off years, and the stock's price / earnings ratio generally edges up a bit when earnings go down, as investors anticipate the recovery to follow. In recent years, the p / e has ranged from 5 to 9.

The 1975 acquisition of Latrobe Steel has proved a profitable one. In fact, specialty steel accounted for more than half of 1980 earnings, on only 28 percent of sales. Timken has been mulling over plans for a new, advanced steelmaking facility with an estimated price tag of $500 million. If it decides to go ahead, the company will have to borrow. But it can afford to — debt has traditionally been less than 5 percent of total capital.

Dividends have been paid each year since 1921. In recent years, the yield has been moderate — about 4½ to 6 percent.

* * *

TODD SHIPYARDS CORP. (TOD). Founded 1916. Headquarters: 1 State St. Plaza, New York NY 10004. SHIPBUILDING. Todd Shipyards is the largest independent shipbuilder and ship repair company in the United States. It serves domestic and foreign ship owners and the U. S. Navy from seven different shipyards.

Sales: $610.5 million (trend 24.2% a year).
Earnings: $20.22 million (trend 104.2% a year).
What happened to a $10,000 investment

Purchase Date	*Purchase Price*	*Price on 12-31-81*	*Dividends Paid*
12-31-71	$8.31	$28.25	$1,112.78
12-31-76	$4.12	$28.25	$1,272.73

Purchase Date	*Cap. Gains (− Losses)*	*Total Return*	*Rate of Return*
12-31-71	$23,984.96	$25,097.74	13.38%
12-31-76	$58,484.85	$59,757.58	47.47%

* * *

TOKHEIM CORP. (TOK). Founded 1901. Headquarters: 1602 Wabash Ave., Fort Wayne IN 46801. MANUFACTURING. Tokheim produces systems for the movement and measurement of liquids, principally gasoline. MAJOR SUBSIDIARIES, BRANDS: Central Die Casting & Manufacturing, Co., Inc.; National Controls Corp.

Sales: $134.8 million (trend 16.7% a year).
Earnings: $8.92 million (trend 22.9% a year).
What happened to a $10,000 investment

Purchase Date	*Purchase Price*	*Price on 12-31-81*	*Dividends Paid*
12-31-71	$4.35	$14.25	$5,977.42
12-31-76	$6.58	$14.25	$3,098.73

Purchase Date	*Cap. Gains (− Losses)*	*Total Return*	*Rate of Return*
12-31-71	$22,727.27	$28,704.69	14.49%
12-31-76	$11,645.57	$14,744.30	19.87%

* * *

TOLEDO EDISON CO. (TED). Founded 1901. Headquarters: 300 Madison Ave., Toledo OH 43652. ELECTRIC UTILITY. Toledo Edison supplies electricity to the city of Toledo and surrounding areas in Ohio.

Sales: $401.9 million (trend 16.6% a year).
Earnings: $49.16 million (trend 11.7% a year).
What happened to a $10,000 investment

Purchase Date	*Purchase Price*	*Price on 12-31-81*	*Dividends Paid*
12-31-71	$31.75	$16.50	$6,554.33
12-31-76	$26.50	$16.50	$4,113.21

Purchase Date	*Cap. Gains (− Losses)*	*Total Return*	*Rate of Return*
12-31-71	$−4,803.15	$1,751.18	1.63%
12-31-76	$−3,773.58	$ 339.62	.67%

* * *

TONKA CORP. (TKA). Founded 1946. Headquarters: 4144 Shoreline Blvd., Spring Park MN 55384. TOYS. Tonka manufactures a broad line of steel toys, primarily trucks, along with plastic preschool toys. MAJOR SUBSIDIARIES, BRANDS: Gresen Manufacturing; Mighty Tonka; Mini Tonka; Tonka; Tiny Tonka.

Sales: $101.1 million (trend 4.0% a year).
Earnings: $3.91 million (trend 9.7% a year).
What happened to a $10,000 investment

Purchase Date	*Purchase Price*	*Price on 12-31-81*	*Dividena Paid*
12-31-71	$14.52	$32.25	$2,531.15
12-31-76	$11.55	$32.25	$1,484.54

Purchase Date	*Cap. Gains (– Losses)*	*Total Return*	*Rate of Return*
12-31-71	$12,204.90	$14,736.05	9.48%
12-31-76	$17,927.81	$19,412.35	24.08%

* * *

TOOTSIE ROLL INDUSTRIES, INC. (TR). Founded 1919. Headquarters: 7401 S. Cicero Ave., Chicago IL 60629. **CANDY.** Tootsie Roll makes and distributes candy. **MAJOR SUBSIDIARIES, BRANDS:** Tootsie Roll; Tootsie Roll Pops; Tootsie Pop Drops; Caramel Tootsie Pops; Tootsie Roll Flavor Rolls; Tootsie Squares; Bonomo; Mason.

Sales: $72.3 million (trend 11.2% a year).
Earnings: $3.17 million (trend 31.0% a year).
What happened to a $10,000 investment

Purchase Date	*Purchase Price*	*Price on 12-31-81*	*Dividends Paid*
12-31-71	$9.86	$11.87	$3,538.68
12-31-76	$6.15	$11.87	$3,047.72

Purchase Date	*Cap. Gains (– Losses)*	*Total Return*	*Rate of Return*
12-31-71	$2,044.46	$ 5,583.14	4.54%
12-31-76	$9,321.17	$12,368.89	17.47%

* * *

THE TORO CO. (TTC). Founded 1935. Headquarters: 8009 34th Ave., S., Minneapolis MN 55420. **LAWN MOWERS, SNOW EQUIPMENT.** Toro produces lawn mowers and snow removal equipment. It also manufactures other lawn maintenance and irrigation equipment. **MAJOR SUBSIDIARIES, BRANDS:** Toro.

Sales: $247.0 million (trend 19.1% a year).
Earnings: $–14.29 million.
What happened to a $10,000 investment

Purchase Date	*Purchase Price*	*Price on 12-31-81*	*Dividends Paid*
12-31-71	$17.37	$7.50	$2,125.18
12-31-76	$ 7.12	$7.50	$3,592.98

Purchase Date	*Cap. Gains (– Losses)*	*Total Return*	*Rate of Return*
12-31-71	$–5,683.45	$–3,558.27	–4.30%
12-31-76	$ 526.32	$ 4,119.30	7.14%

* * *

TOSCO CORP. (TOS). Founded 1955. Headquarters: 10100 Santa Monica Blvd., Los Angeles CA 90067. **OIL SHALE, REFINING.** Tosco is a large independent gasoline refiner and a leader in the development of energy recovery from oil shale. 3,000 employees. **MAJOR SUBSIDIARIES, BRANDS:** Colony Shale Oil Project (40 percent owned; Exxon holds a 60-percent share).

Sales: $2,387.2 million (trend 37.0% a year).
Earnings: $46.52 million (trend 84.5% a year).
What happened to a $10,000 investment

Purchase Date	*Purchase Price*	*Price on 12-31-81*	*Dividends Paid*
12-31-71	$3.25	$16.25	$0.00
12-31-76	$4.62	$16.25	$0.00

Purchase Date	*Cap. Gains (– Losses)*	*Total Return*	*Rate of Return*
12-31-71	$40,000.00	$40,000.00	17.46%
12-31-76	$25,135.14	$25,135.14	28.57%

PROFILE: First, let's unravel the name. Tosco stems from an abbreviation of The Oil Shale Corp., which was the firm's name until 1976. Tosco was a pioneer in the development of technology to recover crude from oil shale, but it has yet to see the payoff. While waiting . . . and waiting and waiting . . . for its ship to come in, Tosco bought refineries from other producers, and recently was the second largest independent U.S. refiner, after Ashland Oil.

Being a refiner without your own solid supply of crude is a ticklish position to be in these days. (See the entry on Ashland.) Tosco's margins have been slim, and occasionally nonexistent. Earnings have been volatile and are likely to remain so. By entering a joint venture with Tosco (The Colony Shale Oil Project), Exxon temporarily put a stamp of industry approval on shale oil. And Tosco holds a nice handful of patents on a variety of processes for recovering crude from shale. It all looked good—until 1982, when Exxon yanked the rug out from under the project. Tosco had the bulk of its expenses reimbursed by Exxon. But that giant's determination that shale oil wasn't yet economically viable represented a blow to Tosco's future.

The stock bobs up and down like a swallow on a summer evening. It's not unheard of for the yearly high to be four times above the yearly low — that happened in 1974 and 1979 — and it's common for the high / low spread to involve a factor of 2 or 3. The p / e is volatile, too — in the past few years, it's ranged from 2 to 21. No dividends have ever been paid on the stock. And the company is heavily debt financed. Recently, debt was almost three quarters of total capital — an extremely high percentage.

In short, this stock may be an interesting speculation. But make no bones about it, a speculation is exactly what it is.

* * *

TOWLE MANUFACTURING CO. (TOW). Founded 1880. Headquarters: 144 Addison St., Boston MA 02128. **GIFTWARE.** Towle manufactures, imports and sells giftware, primarily sterling silver and silver-plated tableware. **MAJOR SUBSIDIARIES, BRANDS:** Holloware; Leonard Silver.

Sales: $166.2 million (trend 49.1% a year).
Earnings: $9.26 million (trend 41.2% a year).
What happened to a $10,000 investment

Purchase Date	*Purchase Price*	*Price on 12-31-81*	*Dividends Paid*
12-31-71	$7.62	$19.50	$5,186.89
12-31-76	$5.12	$19.50	$4,292.68

Purchase Date	*Cap. Gains (– Losses)*	*Total Return*	*Rate of Return*
12-31-71	$15,573.77	$20,760.66	11.89%
12-31-76	$28,048.78	$32,341.46	33.46%

* * *

TOYS 'R' US, INC. (TOY). Founded 1948. Headquarters: 395 W. Passaic St., Rochelle Park NJ 07662. **TOY RETAILING.** The company is the leading operator of "toy supermarkets," which carry a large assortment of toys and virtually no other merchandise. Also owns several conventional department stores. 9,000 employees.

Sales: $597.3 million (trend 30.4% a year).
Earnings: $28.71 million (trend 47.0% a year).

PROFILE: Toys 'R' Us (the 'R' is printed forwards here, but backwards in the stores and company literature) has the unusual distinction of having been a star performer in a company (Interstate Stores) that went bankrupt. Toys 'R' Us was founded in 1948 by Charles Lazarus, who still heads the firm and who is widely regarded as a retailing genius. In 1966 Lazarus sold out to Interstate Stores for $7½ million. He continued to run Toys 'R' Us, which continued to grow by leaps and bounds. But Interstate's other divisions were flopping, and the whole company went under in 1974. Through a 1978 reorganization, holders of Interstate debts were given shares in a new corporation named — you guessed it — Toys 'R' Us. Since then, earnings have gone up each year through 1981. Debt of the corporation was recently a fairly conservative 21 percent of total capital, and Lazarus is taking care to finance expansion mainly out of current earnings.

As of 1981, there were 101 Toys 'R' Us toy supermarkets nationwide, each one boasting the same 18,000 items, in virtually the same shelf locations. The huge variety and low prices have lured a large and loyal clientele to the chain. But in the toy business, low prices are relative to the competition. Markups on selected items are high enough so that profit margins have recently been around 5 percent. Since the reorganization, return on stockholders' equity has been consistently better than 20 percent, sometimes much better. Lazarus maintains a reputation for spotting the toys that are hot and for purchasing them in huge quantities from suppliers whose good will is cultivated year-round — a rarity in the toy business.

No dividends are being paid, and the price / earnings ratio was recently a heady 18. Keep an eye on the p / e, which from time to time may fan out on the basis of merger rumors. (Petrie Stores owns 22 percent of Toys 'R' Us, but says it plans no take-over.)

* * *

TRACOR, INC. (TRR). Founded 1955. Headquarters: 6500 Tracor Lane, Austin TX 78721. **ELECTRONICS.** Tracor designs and produces electronic and electromechanical components, and radar-confusing devices for the U.S. military; also does contract research and development work.

Sales: $295.1 million (trend 23.4% a year).
Earnings: $13.25 million (trend 33.4% a year).
What happened to a $10,000 investment

Purchase Date	*Purchase Price*	*Price on 12-31-81*	*Dividends Paid*
12-31-71	$3.25	$26.87	$3,400.10
12-31-76	$5.23	$26.87	$1,993.94

Purchase Date	*Cap. Gains (– Losses)*	*Total Return*	*Rate of Return*
12-31-71	$72,607.58	$76,007.68	24.01%
12-31-76	$41,419.01	$43,412.95	39.81%

* * *

THE TRANE CO. (TRA). Founded 1913. Headquarters: 3600 Pammel Creek Rd., La Crosse WI 54601. **AIR CONDITIONING.** Trane manufactures and markets a variety of heating, air-conditioning, ventilating, and specialized heat transfer products.

Sales: $764.8 million (trend 13.1% a year).
Earnings: $38.22 million (trend 18.2% a year).
What happened to a $10,000 investment

Purchase Date	*Purchase Price*	*Price on 12-31-81*	*Dividends Paid*
12-31-71	$36.25	$29.37	$1,885.52
12-31-76	$18.19	$29.37	$2,446.74

Purchase Date	*Cap. Gains (− Losses)*	*Total Return*	*Rate of Return*
12-31-71	$−1,896.55	$ −11.03	−.01%
12-31-76	$ 6,151.20	$8,597.94	13.21%

* * *

TRANS WORLD CORP. (TW). Founded 1934. Headquarters: 605 Third Ave., New York NY 10158. **AIRLINE, FOOD, HOTELS.** The company is the parent to Trans World Airlines, the nation's fifth largest airline. It also has activities in food service, restaurants, hotels, and real estate. 35,000 employees. **MAJOR SUBSIDIARIES, BRANDS:** Trans World Airlines; Canteen Corp. (food service, vending machines); Spartan Food Systems (Hardee's and Quincy's restaurants); Hilton International hotels; Century 21 Real Estate.

Sales: $5,018.3 million (trend 13.5% a year).
Earnings: $−.76 million.
What happened to a $10,000 investment

Purchase Date	*Purchase Price*	*Price on 12-31-81*	*Dividends Paid*
12-31-71	$41.25	$15.25	$0.00
12-31-76	$11.37	$15.25	$0.00

Purchase Date	*Cap. Gains (− Losses)*	*Total Return*	*Rate of Return*
12-31-71	$−6,303.03	$−6,303.03	−9.47%
12-31-76	$ 3,406.59	$ 3,406.59	6.04%

PROFILE: Imagine a conglomerate consisting of Canteen Corp., Spartan Food Systems, Hilton International hotels, and Century 21 Real Estate. It would be quite a sizable enterprise — more than 75 hotels, 300 restaurants, and 7,500 real estate brokerage outlets. It would also have a pretty good profit margin.

That hypothetical conglomerate is, of course, part of Trans World Corp. — and in the last couple of years provided most of its profits. However, all of these operations in 1980 accounted for only about a third of the corporation's revenues. That means that TWA is more diversified than any other U.S. airline. But it also means that Trans World Corp., barring even further diversification, will continue to rise and fall with its airline.

In the ten years from 1971 through 1980, Trans World lost money four times. It has not paid a dividend since 1969. Long-term debt was recently more than 63 percent of capital, an undesirably high percentage. The airline's fleet is relatively old and not very fuel-efficient, but TWA lacks capital to replace planes rapidly. The stock's 1980 high was about half the 1971 high.

There are certainly trading opportunities here, since the stock is highly volatile. And there may be fundamental opportunities as well, if the corporation can overcome the airline's serious and entrenched problems. But the stock has a relatively high degree of risk.

* * *

TRANSAMERICA CORP. (TA). Founded 1928. Headquarters: 600 Montgomery St., San Francisco CA 94111. **FINANCIAL SERVICES.** Transamerica is active in insurance (life, credit, title, and property-casualty); loans; transportation (rental cars, truck leasing, aircraft chartering); and industrial machinery. 29,000 employees. **MAJOR SUBSIDIARIES, BRANDS:** Transamerica Occidental Life Insurance Co.; Transamerica Financial; Budget Rent-A-Car; Transamerica Airlines; Transamerica Delaval (industrial machinery).

Sales: $4,384.1 million (trend 13.0% a year).
Earnings: $244.98 million (trend 27.5% a year).
What happened to a $10,000 investment

Purchase Date	*Purchase Price*	*Price on 12-31-81*	*Dividends Paid*
12-31-71	$17.91	$23.37	$4,564.83
12-31-76	$14.37	$23.37	$3,638.26

Purchase Date	*Cap. Gains (− Losses)*	*Total Return*	*Rate of Return*
12-31-71	$3,052.35	$7,617.18	5.83%
12-31-76	$6,260.87	$9,899.13	14.75%

PROFILE: During the 1960s and 1970s, the corporate trend in the United States was toward diversification. Under John R. Beckett, Transamerica flowed with that tide, engulfing Delaval Turbine (1963), United Artists (1967), Trans International Airlines (1968), and Budget Rent-A-Car (1968).

In the early 1980s, there was a tendency for companies to trim deadwood, to retrench a bit, to sharpen their images, and to specialize a bit more than previously. Transamerica was part of this trend, too, under a new head, James R. Harvey. The biggest change was the jettisoning of United Artists, the big film company, whose profits had been weak and inconsistent. (It was sold to Metro-Goldwyn-Mayer Film Co. for about $380 million.)

Harvey has said that the company will stay in three "core businesses" — financial services, transportation, and machinery. But the emphasis clearly is on financial services, which happens to be the company's original business. (Beckett built the conglomerate around Occidental Life of California.) Insurance has contributed well over half of sales and earnings recently, and Transamerica has made no secret of the fact that it would like to add a large property-and-casualty insurer to the fold.

Budget Rent-A-Car (the only major subsidiary that doesn't have Transamerica tacked onto its name, because it was already a well-known company when it was acquired) is the third largest U.S. rental car firm, after Hertz (RCA) and Avis (Norton Simon). Even so, it accounts for less than 10 percent of sales and earnings.

In recent years, conglomerates in general and Transamerica in particular have been out of favor on Wall Street. The price / earnings ratio has been only 4 to 7, while the dividend yield has been about 5 to 7 percent.

* * *

TRANSAMERICA INCOME SHARES, INC. (TAI). Founded 1972. Headquarters: PO Box 2438, Los Angeles CA 90051. INVESTMENT CO. Transamerica Income shares is a management company that invests in fixed-income debt securities.

* * *

TRANSAMERICA REALTY INVESTORS (TAR). Founded 1969. Headquarters: 600 Montgomery St., San Francisco CA 94111. REAL ESTATE. Formerly a real estate investment trust (then called Mortgage Trust of America), this company owns real estate and makes commercial mortgage loans. About a quarter of the company's shares are held by Transamerica Corp.

Sales: $13.3 million (trend 1.2% a year).
Earnings: $3.54 million (trend −13.4% a year).
What happened to a $10,000 investment

Purchase Date	*Purchase Price*	*Price on 12-31-81*	*Dividends Paid*
12-31-71	$24.25	$9.62	$2,028.87
12-31-76	$ 4.62	$9.62	$ 0.00

Purchase Date	*Cap. Gains (− Losses)*	*Total Return*	*Rate of Return*
12-31-71	$−6,030.93	$−4,002.06	−4.98%
12-31-76	$ 10,810.81	$ 10,810.81	15.79%

* * *

TRANSCO ENERGY COMPANY (E). Founded 1948. Headquarters: 2700 S. Post Oak Rd., Houston TX 77056. ENERGY. Transco is a holding company that is involved, through its subsidiaries, in the sale and transmission of natural gas. It is also involved in exploration for and production of oil and natural gas. MAJOR SUBSIDIARIES, BRANDS: Transco Exploration Co.; Transcontinental Gas Pipe Line Corp.; Transco Coal Co.; Transco Coal Gas Co. (22.5 percent owned).

Sales: $2,627.8 million (trend 33.2% a year).
Earnings: $120.29 million (trend 18.1% a year).
What happened to a $10,000 investment

Purchase Date	*Purchase Price*	*Price on 12-31-81*	*Dividends Paid*
12-31-71	$17.25	$46.25	$6,539.13
12-31-76	$19.37	$46.25	$3,249.03

Purchase Date	*Cap. Gains (− Losses)*	*Total Return*	*Rate of Return*
12-31-71	$16,811.59	$23,350.72	12.80%
12-31-76	$13,870.97	$17,120.00	22.08%

* * *

TRANSCON LINES (TCL). Founded 1946. Headquarters 101 Continental Blvd., El Segundo CA 90245. TRUCKING. Transcon is a common carrier of general freight, operating through a network of 112 terminals in 38 states.

Sales: $229.5 million (trend 12.0% a year).
Earnings: $.06 million (trend −44.8% a year).
What happened to a $10,000 investment

Purchase Date	*Purchase Price*	*Price on 12-31-81*	*Dividends Paid*
12-31-71	$24.12	$5.62	$1,738.86
12-31-76	$11.37	$5.62	$1,745.05

Purchase Date	*Cap. Gains (− Losses)*	*Total Return*	*Rate of Return*
12-31-71	$−7,668.39	$−5,929.53	−8.60%
12-31-76	$−5,054.95	$−3,309.89	−7.72%

* * *

TRANSOHIO FINANCIAL CORP. (TFC). Founded 1970. Headquarters: 1 Penton Plaza, Cleveland OH 44114. **FINANCIAL SERVICES.** Transohio Financial is approximately the ninth largest savings and loan holding company in the country, and operates the largest savings and loan in Ohio. **MAJOR SUBSIDIARIES, BRANDS:** Transohio Savings; Cincinnati Savings; County Savings; Newark Savings.

* * *

TRANSWAY INTERNATIONAL CORP. (TNW). Founded 1925. Headquarters: 747 Third Ave., New York NY 10017. **DIVERSIFIED TRANSPORTATION.** Transway is a major freight forwarder, consolidating less-than-carload amounts of freight for shipment by truck, rail, steamship, or air. It also manufactures trailers for trucking and distributes liquid propane gas in the Southeast. **MAJOR SUBSIDIARIES, BRANDS:** Coordinated Caribbean Transport; Great Dane Trailers; Tropigas International Corp.; Transway.

Sales: $738.2 million (trend 9.1% a year).
Earnings: $27.66 million (trend 11.1% a year).
What happened to a $10,000 investment

Purchase Date	*Purchase Price*	*Price on 12-31-81*	*Dividends Paid*
12-31-71	$31.25	$23.37	$4,960.00
12-31-76	$23.12	$23.37	$3,675.68

Purchase Date	*Cap. Gains (− Losses)*	*Total Return*	*Rate of Return*
12-31-71	$−2,520.00	$2,440.00	2.21%
12-31-76	$ 108.11	$3,783.78	6.63%

* * *

TRAVELERS CORP. (TIC). Founded 1863. Headquarters: 1 Tower Sq., Hartford CT 06115. **INSURANCE.** Travelers is a broad-spectrum insurance company, selling life, health, and property and casualty insurance. It is the second largest stock (as opposed to mutual) insurance company. 30,000 employees.

Sales: $8,722.2 million (trend 9.6% a year).
Earnings: $364.90 million (trend 32.3% a year).
What happened to a $10,000 investment

Purchase Date	*Purchase Price*	*Price on 12-31-81*	*Dividends Paid*
12-31-71	$37.12	$43.87	$4,099.66
12-31-76	$36.75	$43.87	$2,789.12

Purchase Date	*Cap. Gains (− Losses)*	*Total Return*	*Rate of Return*
12-31-71	$1,818.18	$5,917.85	4.76%
12-31-76	$1,938.78	$4,727.89	8.05%

PROFILE: In parts of 1971, Travelers shares were going for just under $40 apiece. The same was true in parts of 1981, a decade later. But the underlying values for this second largest (after Aetna) U.S. stock insurance company had changed significantly. In 1971 the price represented about 16 times earnings. In 1981 it was about 6. The dividend yield back in 1971 was around 2 percent; in 1981 it was around 6 percent. Even long-term debt had been pared. Recently, debt was an insignificant 3 percent of total capital.

So — was the stock overvalued in 1971 or undervalued in 1981? Probably a little of both. Travelers has not been burning up the track: Return on stockholders' equity the past few years has averaged around 16 percent — certainly respectable, but not great. And investors remember the poorer years of the mid-1970s, when return on equity fell below 10 percent. The property and casualty insurance business (which provides about half of Travelers' profits) is notoriously cyclical.

But with a decent dividend (paid each year since 1864 — Civil War days — and well covered by earnings), a low p / e, and practically no debt, Travelers deserves consideration for conservative, value-oriented portfolios.

The company has considerable diversity. It sells life insurance, health insurance (group, mainly), car insurance, property insurance (commercial and homeowners' multiperil), workmen's compensation coverage, and annuities, along with a few other coverages. It is large, moderately recession resistant, and relatively safe.

* * *

TRI-CONTINENTAL CORP. (TY). Founded 1929. Headquarters: 1 Bankers Trust Plaza, New York NY 10006. **INVESTMENT CO.** Tri-Continental is a large publicly held investment company. The bulk of its portfolio is in common stocks, widely diversified by industry.

* * *

TRI-SOUTH INVESTMENTS INC. (TSI). Founded 1970. Headquarters: 1532 Dunwoody Village Parkway, Atlanta GA 30338. **REAL ESTATE.** Owns and manages properties acquired, mainly through foreclosure, when the company was a real estate investment trust (Tri-South Mortgage Investors). Also continues to receive funds from some mortgages made during its days as a REIT. Most of the company's properties are in the Southeast.

Sales: $11.6 million (trend 5.2% a year).
Earnings: $2.80 million.
What happened to a $10,000 investment

Purchase Date	*Purchase Price*	*Price on 12-31-81*	*Dividends Paid*
12-31-71	$N/A	$3.50	$N/A
12-31-76	$ 1.37	$3.50	$ 0.00

Purchase Date	*Cap. Gains (− Losses)*	*Total Return*	*Rate of Return*
12-31-71	$ N/A	$ N/A	N/A%
12-31-76	$15,454.55	$15,454.55	20.55%

* * *

TRIANGLE INDUSTRIES, INC. (TRI). Founded 1916. Headquarters: Route 520, Holmdel NJ 07733. DIVERSIFIED MANUFACTURER. Triangle manufactures electrical products for the construction, utility, and equipment manufacturing industries. It also produces vending machines, music systems, phonographs, currency changers, and preinsulated pipe and panels. MAJOR SUBSIDIARIES, BRANDS: Rowe International, Inc.; TPCO, Inc.; Triangle Finance Co., Inc.; Triangle PWC, Inc.

Sales: $296.3 million (trend 12.3% a year).
Earnings: $4.04 million (trend 7.7% a year).
What happened to a $10,000 investment

Purchase Date	*Purchase Price*	*Price on 12-31-81*	*Dividends Paid*
12-31-71	$15.53	$11.37	$3,139.83
12-31-76	$ 8.39	$11.37	$1,488.61

Purchase Date	*Cap. Gains (− Losses)*	*Total Return*	*Rate of Return*
12-31-71	$−2,676.84	$ 462.99	.45%
12-31-76	$ 3,557.75	$5,046.35	8.51%

* * *

TRIANGLE PACIFIC CORP. (TPC). Founded 1943. Headquarters: 4255 LBJ Freeway, Dallas TX 75234. CABINET MANUFACTURING. Triangle Pacific is the leading producer of kitchen and bathroom cabinets in the United States and also manufactures hardwood flooring and other building products. MAJOR SUBSIDIARIES, BRANDS: Beauty Queen; Bruce; Del Mar; IXL; Mutschler; Tri Pac.

Sales: $207.7 million (trend 11.0% a year).
Earnings: $2.90 million (trend −15.0% a year).
What happened to a $10,000 investment

Purchase Date	*Purchase Price*	*Price on 12-31-81*	*Dividends Paid*
12-31-71	$12.62	$15.87	$3,568.32
12-31-76	$ 7.31	$15.87	$5,152.14

Purchase Date	*Cap. Gains (− Losses)*	*Total Return*	*Rate of Return*
12-31-71	$ 2,574.26	$ 6,142.57	4.91%
12-31-76	$11,709.40	$16,861.54	21.85%

* * *

TRICENTROL LTD. (TCT). Founded 1917. Headquarters: Chapel House, New Broad St., London EC2M 1JS England. OIL AND GAS. Tricentrol engages in oil and gas exploration and production in the British North Sea, Canada, and the United States.

Sales: $660.8 million (trend 46.1% a year).
Earnings: $37.77 million (trend 93.9% a year).

* * *

TRICO INDUSTRIES, INC. (TRO). Founded 1934. Headquarters: 15707 S. Main St., Gardena CA 90248. PETROLEUM EQUIPMENT. Trico manufactures and services equipment for the petroleum industry and also for agricultural applications.

Sales: $82.5 million (trend 26.3% a year).
Earnings: $6.07 million (trend 22.6% a year).
What happened to a $10,000 investment

Purchase Date	*Purchase Price*	*Price on 12-31-81*	*Dividends Paid*
12-31-71	$ .62	$14.25	$7,520.00
12-31-76	$3.06	$14.25	$1,453.06

Purchase Date	*Cap. Gains (− Losses)*	*Total Return*	*Rate of Return*
12-31-71	$218,000.00	$225,520.00	37.15%
12-31-76	$ 36,530.61	$ 37,983.67	36.84%

* * *

TRINITY INDUSTRIES, INC. (TRN). Founded 1933. Headquarters: 4001 Irving Blvd., Dallas TX 75207. MANUFACTURING. Trinity Industries manufactures metal products, such as railcars and metal containers. It also produces structural products and metal components for other industries. MAJOR SUBSIDIARIES, BRANDS: Ingalls Industries.

Sales: $736.1 million (trend 25.9% a year).
Earnings: $47.16 million (trend 24.2% a year).
What happened to a $10,000 investment

Purchase Date	*Purchase Price*	*Price on 12-31-81*	*Dividends Paid*
12-31-71	$2.09	$16.25	$7,629.85
12-31-76	$5.31	$16.25	$2,047.06

Purchase Date	*Cap. Gains (− Losses)*	*Total Return*	*Rate of Return*
12-31-71	$67,611.94	$75,241.79	23.90%
12-31-76	$20,588.24	$22,635.29	26.69%

* * *

TUCSON ELECTRIC POWER CO. (TEP). Founded 1963. Headquarters: 220 W. Sixth St., Tucson AZ 85702. ELECTRIC UTILITY. Tucson Electric supplies electricity to the city of Tucson and nearby areas in Arizona.

Sales: $320.1 million (trend 12.2% a year).
Earnings: $49.54 million (trend 16.6% a year).
What happened to a $10,000 investment

Purchase Date	*Purchase Price*	*Price on 12-31-81*	*Dividends Paid*
12-31-71	$15.12	$18.25	$7,600.66
12-31-76	$15.50	$18.25	$4,593.55

Purchase Date	*Cap. Gains (− Losses)*	*Total Return*	*Rate of Return*
12-31-71	$2,066.12	$9,666.78	7.00%
12-31-76	$1,774.19	$6,367.74	10.36%

* * *

TWIN DISC, INC. (TDI). Founded 1918. Headquarters: 1318 Racine St., Racine WI 53403. MANUFACTURING. Twin Disc manufactures and sells power transmission equipment, such as torque converters, power-shift transmissions, universal joints and clutches.

Sales: $210.3 million (trend 14.3% a year).
Earnings: $8.58 million (trend 7.1% a year).
What happened to a $10,000 investment

Purchase Date	*Purchase Price*	*Price on 12-31-81*	*Dividends Paid*
12-31-71	$ 9.80	$16.50	$7,147.35
12-31-76	$11.00	$16.50	$4,127.64

Purchase Date	*Cap. Gains (− Losses)*	*Total Return*	*Rate of Return*
12-31-71	$6,836.73	$13,984.08	9.14%
12-31-76	$5,000.00	$ 9,127.64	13.85%

* * *

TYCO LABORATORIES, INC. (TYC). Founded 1962. Headquarters: Tyco Park, Exeter NH 03833. MANUFACTURING. Tyco manufactures fire protection and safety equipment; electrical and electronic components; and packaging and consumer materials. It is also involved in the development of solar energy. MAJOR SUBSIDIARIES, BRANDS: Grinnel Fire Protection Systems; Japan Solar Energy Corp. (19.5 percent owned); Mobil Tyco Solar Energy Corp. (20 percent owned); Simplex Wire and Cable; Ludlow Corp.

Sales: $360.9 million (trend 29.7% a year).
Earnings: $22.52 million (trend 42.6% a year).
What happened to a $10,000 investment

Purchase Date	*Purchase Price*	*Price on 12-31-81*	*Dividends Paid*
12-31-71	$5.56	$12.37	$3,460.67
12-31-76	$9.62	$12.37	$1,688.31

Purchase Date	*Cap. Gains (− Losses)*	*Total Return*	*Rate of Return*
12-31-71	$12,247.19	$15,707.87	9.90%
12-31-76	$ 2,857.14	$ 4,545.45	7.78%

* * *

TYLER CORP. (TYL). Founded 1966. Headquarters: 3100 Southland Center, Dallas TX 75201. INDUSTRIAL GOODS AND SERVICES. Through four operating companies, Tyler provides pipe and fittings, industrial explosives, and trucking services to industrial customers. MAJOR SUBSIDIARIES, BRANDS: Atlas Powder Co.; C & H Transportation Co.; Thurston Motor Lines, Inc.; Tyler Pipe Industries.

Sales: $563.8 million (trend 14.2% a year).
Earnings: $23.84 million (trend 8.9% a year).
What happened to a $10,000 investment

Purchase Date	*Purchase Price*	*Price on 12-31-81*	*Dividends Paid*
12-31-71	$ 6.62	$23.50	$4,094.34
12-31-76	$11.37	$23.50	$1,912.09

Purchase Date	*Cap. Gains (– Losses)*	*Total Return*	*Rate of Return*
12-31-71	$25,471.70	$29,566.04	14.74%
12-31-76	$10,659.34	$12,571.43	17.68%

* * *

TYMSHARE, INC. (TYM). Founded 1966. Headquarters: 20705 Valley Green Dr., Cupertino CA 95014. **COMPUTER SERVICES.** Tymshare provides computer services to businesses in such areas as corporate planning, financial and accounting services, manufacturing and production control, and administrative management. **MAJOR SUBSIDIARIES, BRANDS:** Tymnet, Inc.; Tymshare Transaction Services.

Sales: $235.3 million (trend 33.5% a year).
Earnings: $18.74 million (trend 31.7% a year).
What happened to a $10,000 investment

Purchase Date	*Purchase Price*	*Price on 12-31-81*	*Dividends Paid*
12-31-71	$4.25	$28.62	$0.00
12-31-76	$9.75	$28.62	$0.00

Purchase Date	*Cap. Gains (– Losses)*	*Total Return*	*Rate of Return*
12-31-71	$57,352.94	$57,352.94	21.01%
12-31-76	$19,358.97	$19,358.97	24.04%

U

UAL, INC. (UAL). Founded 1934. Headquarters: 1200 Algonquin Rd., Elk Grove IL 60606. **AIRLINE.** UAL runs the nation's largest airline (by revenues) and also has interests in hotels and insurance adjusting. 52,000 employees. **MAJOR SUBSIDIARIES, BRANDS:** United Airlines; Westin Hotels; GAB Business Services.

Sales: $5,041.3 million (trend 14.3% a year).
Earnings: $20.62 million (trend −3.1% a year).
What happened to a $10,000 investment

Purchase Date	*Purchase Price*	*Price on 12-31-81*	*Dividends Paid*
12-31-71	$41.25	$16.50	$1,090.91
12-31-76	$26.87	$16.50	$ 986.05

Purchase Date	*Cap. Gains (– Losses)*	*Total Return*	*Rate of Return*
12-31-71	$−6,000.00	$−4,909.09	−6.53%
12-31-76	$−3,860.47	$−2,874.42	−6.55%

PROFILE: If anyone needs proof of the airline industry's cyclicality, let him look at United Airlines. In 1978 it earned more than $300 million, with a whopping 28-percent return on stockholders' equity. In 1979 it lost $73 million. The same sort of up-and-down results have obtained for years: There were deficits in 1971 and 1975, pretty good years (though not nearly so good as 1978) in 1974 and 1977.

Lately, of course, the airline industry has been in for a rough ride, due mainly to high fuel costs and a lackluster economy that dampens demand for travel. UAL has withstood the blows better than many — though not as well as, say, Delta. It eked out a small profit in 1980 but lost $70 million in 1981. Its balance sheet, with debt recently just over 50 percent of total capital, is less debt-laden than those of Eastern and Pan Am. Its average fleet age (about 8 years) isn't too bad.

The 1980 profit was made in spite of the airline, whose $15-million loss was outweighed by a $31-million profit at Westin Hotels. GAB Business Services chipped in another $4.6 million. Though the diversifications have proved helpful, the airline still accounts for close to 90 percent of company revenues. GAB is the biggest U.S. insurance adjuster; Westin runs some 50 hotels in 15 countries.

The next few years should be challenging ones for United, as deregulation exposes it to tougher competition from small airlines on selected routes. Partly to meet such challenges and to take advantage of opportunities in a deregulated environment, United has been tinkering extensively with its route structure, dropping more than 100 routes and adding close to 100 others.

Dividends had been paid each year from 1974 through 1979, but the dividend was eliminated in the second quarter of 1980.

* * *

UGI CORP. (UGI). Founded 1882. Headquarters: 460 N. Gulph Rd., Valley Forge PA 19482. **NATURAL GAS.** UGI distributes natural gas and electricity in eastern and central Pennsylvania. It is also involved in oil and gas production and the manufacturing of welding equipment. **MAJOR SUBSIDIARIES, BRANDS:** AmeriGas; Triad Drilling.

Sales: $420.9 million (trend 20.0% a year).
Earnings: $16.46 million (trend 12.5% a year).
What happened to a $10,000 investment

Purchase Date	*Purchase Price*	*Price on 12-31-81*	*Dividends Paid*
12-31-71	$22.50	$26.12	$6,640.00
12-31-76	$18.87	$26.12	$4,376.16

Purchase Date	*Cap. Gains (− Losses)*	*Total Return*	*Rate of Return*
12-31-71	$1,611.11	$8,251.11	6.20%
12-31-76	$3,841.06	$8,217.22	12.74%

* * *

UMC INDUSTRIES, INC. (UMT). Founded 1937. Headquarters: High Ridge Park, Stamford CT 06904. **MANUFACTURING.** UMC is a manufacturer of a diverse line of products in three main groups: merchandising equipment, industrial products, and engineered plastics. **MAJOR SUBSIDIARIES, BRANDS:** Kemlite Corp.; National Rejectors, Inc.; National Vendors; NRI; Cor Tec; Resistoflex Corp.; Unidynamics, Inc.; Universal Match; Zallea Brothers, Inc.

Sales: $318.3 million (trend 13.7% a year).
Earnings: $7.99 million (trend 10.8% a year).
What happened to a $10,000 investment

Purchase Date	*Purchase Price*	*Price on 12-31-81*	*Dividends Paid*
12-31-71	$21.75	$11.50	$4,822.07
12-31-76	$14.87	$11.50	$3,966.39

Purchase Date	*Cap. Gains (− Losses)*	*Total Return*	*Rate of Return*
12-31-71	$−4,712.64	$ 109.43	.11%
12-31-76	$−2,268.91	$1,697.48	3.19%

* * *

UMET TRUST (UAT). Founded 1969. Headquarters: 9595 Wilshire Blvd., Beverly Hills CA 90212. **REAL ESTATE.** UMET owns and sells real estate gained through foreclosures or lease terminations.

* * *

UNC RESOURCES (UNC). Founded 1954. Headquarters: 7700 Leesburg Pike, Falls Church VA 22043. **MINING.** UNC is a holding company dealing in the mining and milling of uranium and coal. It also is active in manufacturing nuclear fuel and related components for the U. S. Navy. **MAJOR SUBSIDIARIES, BRANDS:** United Nuclear Corp.; UNC Nuclear Industries, Inc.; UNC Teton (50 percent owned).

Sales: $259.6 million (trend 19.6% a year).
Earnings: $17.42 million (trend −8.5% a year).
What happened to a $10,000 investment

Purchase Date	*Purchase Price*	*Price on 12-31-81*	*Dividends Paid*
12-31-71	$ 9.14	$6.62	$1,066.46
12-31-76	$21.93	$6.62	$ 444.69

Purchase Date	*Cap. Gains (− Losses)*	*Total Return*	*Rate of Return*
12-31-71	$−2,753.54	$−1,687.08	−1.83%
12-31-76	$−6,978.42	$−6,533.73	−19.10%

* * *

UNR INDUSTRIES, INC. (UNR). Founded 1970. Headquarters: 332 S. Michigan Ave., Chicago IL 60604. **MANUFACTURING.** UNR manufactures products primarily made from steel, for industry and the home. **MAJOR SUBSIDIARIES, BRANDS:** Buddy's; Unarco-Midwest Corp.

Sales: $316.4 million (trend 21.6% a year).
Earnings: $−4.42 million.
What happened to a $10,000 investment

Purchase Date	*Purchase Price*	*Price on 12-31-81*	*Dividends Paid*
12-31-71	$10.28	$6.25	$5,155.33
12-31-76	$11.12	$6.25	$2,943.82

Purchase Date	*Cap. Gains (− Losses)*	*Total Return*	*Rate of Return*
12-31-71	$−3,918.92	$ 1,236.41	1.17%
12-31-76	$−4,382.02	$−1,438.20	−3.06%

* * *

US F&G CORP. (FG). Founded 1896. Headquarters: 100 Light St., Baltimore MD 21202. **INSURANCE.** U. S. Fidelity & Guaranty is the eleventh largest property-casualty insurer in the United States. Other subsidiaries sell life insurance. **MAJOR SUBSIDIARIES, BRANDS:** Fidelity & Guaranty Life; Thomas Jefferson Life; U.S. Fidelity & Guaranty.

Sales: $2,252.9 million (trend 15.8% a year).
Earnings: $228.50 million (trend 40.7% a year).
What happened to a $10,000 investment

Purchase Date	*Purchase Price*	*Price on 12-31-81*	*Dividends Paid*
12-31-71	$ N/A	$41.37	$ N/A
12-31-76	$33.18	$41.37	$3,638.35

Purchase Date	Cap. Gains (− Losses)	Total Return	Rate of Return
12-31-71	$ N/A	$ N/A	N/A%
12-31-76	$2,469.17	$6,107.52	10.00%

* * *

UNILEVER N.V. (UN). Founded 1927. Headquarters: Museumpark, Rotterdam 1 The Netherlands. **CONSUMER GOODS.** Unilever N.V. is a part of an international organization with Unilever PLC. It produces a broad line of consumer goods, primarily foods, detergents, and toiletries. For further details, see Unilever PLC.

Sales: $13,818.0 million (trend 13.7% a year).
Earnings: $308.00 million (trend 17.4% a year).
What happened to a $10,000 investment

Purchase Date	Purchase Price	Price on 12-31-81	Dividends Paid
12-31-71	$36.25	$59.50	$9,514.81
12-31-76	$49.75	$59.50	$4,326.23

Purchase Date	Cap. Gains (− Losses)	Total Return	Rate of Return
12-31-71	$6,413.79	$15,928.61	10.00%
12-31-76	$1,959.80	$ 6,286.03	10.25%

* * *

UNILEVER PLC (UL). Founded 1894. Headquarters: Unilever House, London EC4P 4BQ England. **CONSUMER PRODUCTS.** Unilever is a huge worldwide enterprise producing primarily foods, detergents, household products, chemicals, animal feeds, and packaging. Among its other interests are the operation of plantations in Africa, and transportation. 300,000 employees. **MAJOR SUBSIDIARIES, BRANDS:** Lever Brothers; Thomas J. Lipton Inc. (Lipton tea); Lawry's Foods, Inc.; UAC International; National Starch and Chemical. Unilever PLC functions, in effect, as a joint operation with Unilever N.V. of the Netherlands. Among the U.S. brands are Imperial margarine; All dishwasher detergent; Dove and Lifebuoy soaps; Aim and Pepsodent toothpastes; Wisk detergent.

Sales: $10,343.0 million (trend 12.0% a year).
Earnings: $359.00 million (trend 16.6% a year).
What happened to a $10,000 investment

Purchase Date	Purchase Price	Price on 12-31-81	Dividends Paid
12-31-71	$32.25	$47.25	$4,744.84
12-31-76	$28.50	$47.25	$3,831.79

Purchase Date	Cap. Gains (− Losses)	Total Return	Rate of Return
12-31-71	$4,651.16	$ 9,396.00	6.85%
12-31-76	$6,578.95	$10,410.74	15.34%

PROFILE: Think of Unilever as the Procter & Gamble of Europe. Both Unilever and Procter & Gamble are international giants (sales in the neighborhood of $10 billion), with a big stable of well-established brand-name consumer products. Both have shown steady, moderate growth. Unilever's growth has been a shade faster; Procter & Gamble has been a shade more profitable. While Procter & Gamble gets two thirds of its sales in the United States, Unilever gets more than two thirds in Europe and only about 10 percent in America. (Even so, Lever Brothers, Unilever's wholly owned U.S. subsidiary, ranks among the largest 300 industrial corporations in America.) Unilever puts greater emphasis on food, Procter & Gamble on household products.

You can buy the shares of either Unilever PLC (of Britain) or Unilever N.V., its Dutch partner, on the New York Stock Exchange. Both are subject to foreign tax; dividend yield after foreign taxes has recently been higher on the Dutch shares (around 8 percent) than on the British shares (around 5 percent). The Dutch half of the partnership shows a higher percentage of debt (around 25 percent of capital, versus around 10 percent for the British arm), but both balance sheets are sound. Both stocks have recently been selling for a low multiple — about 5 to 6 as of early 1982.

* * *

UNION CAMP CORP. (UCC). Founded 1956. Headquarters: 1600 Valley Rd., Wayne NJ 07470. **PAPER.** Union Camp is a major producer of paper and packaging, with sidelines in retailing and chemicals. 16,000 employees. **MAJOR SUBSIDIARIES, BRANDS:** Moore Handley (Homecrafters, Hardware House retail outlets).

Sales: $1,574.8 million (trend 12.9% a year).
Earnings: $165.13 million (trend 11.8% a year)
What happened to a $10,000 investment

Purchase Date	Purchase Price	Price on 12-31-81	Dividends Paid
12-31-71	$25.67	$49.62	$6,741.56
12-31-76	$66.62	$49.62	$1,763.60

Purchase Date	*Cap. Gains (– Losses)*	*Total Return*	*Rate of Return*
12-31-71	$ 9,334.42	$16,075.97	10.06%
12-31-76	$–2,551.59	$ –787.99	–1.63%

PROFILE: Union Camp has been among the more profitable paper companies for a number of years. It deserves credit for that, but it may not deserve your investment dollars. The paper business is a tricky one (because of the risk of industry overcapacity and price cutting), so even though Union Camp has walked the tightrope very well in the past (adding capacity at the right times in the right places) there's always a risk that the tightrope walker will fall. More important, it's a bulk commodity business with plenty of competition, so the profits of even the best companies (like Union Camp), while good, haven't been spectacular.

That said, there are several points in favor of this stock. The company has reduced long-term debt from 40 percent of capital in 1971 to only about 23 percent recently, while maintaining a good rate of return (recently 17 to 18 percent) on stockholders' equity. Profits have risen fairly consistently with a solid underlying uptrend. The dividend, paid yearly since 1940, provides a moderate yield, with a payout ratio of 35–40 percent in recent years. The p / e ratio doesn't tend to get too high. It's not a stock that will take you out too far on a limb.

Speaking of limbs, the company is moving closer to self-sufficiency in timber supply and has a highly regarded program of forest management. It owns about 1.7 million acres.

* * *

UNION CARBIDE CORP. (UK). Founded 1917. Headquarters: 270 Park Ave., New York NY 10017. **CHEMICALS.** The company is one of the largest U.S. chemical manufacturers, producing a wide variety of chemicals, industrial gases, and consumer products. 116,000 employees. **MAJOR SUBSIDIARIES, BRANDS:** Glad bags; Eveready batteries; Prestone antifreeze; Simoniz car wax.

Sales: $9,994.0 million (trend 12.3% a year).
Earnings: $673.00 million (trend 10.7% a year).
What happened to a $10,000 investment

Purchase Date	*Purchase Price*	*Price on 12-31-81*	*Dividends Paid*
12-31-71	$42.25	$51.37	$6,165.68
12-31-76	$61.87	$51.37	$2,408.08

Purchase Date	*Cap. Gains (– Losses)*	*Total Return*	*Rate of Return*
12-31-71	$ 2,159.76	$8,325.44	6.24%
12-31-76	$–1,696.97	$ 711.11	1.38%

PROFILE: Among the three giants of the chemical industry, Union Carbide ranks third in size, a shade behind Dow Chemical and a few billion dollars behind DuPont. In profitability, Dow has usually been the leader in recent years, but in 1980 Union Carbide topped both of its major rivals in return on equity. In growth, Dow again has been the leader, though none of the three has burned up the track; Carbide's profit growth has been sluggish in recent years.

Wall Street now scorns this slightly sleepy giant, according it a price / earnings multiple of only 4 to 7 in recent years. That's a puny evaluation. If the stock returns to favor (it sold for 15 to 20 times earnings in the late 1960s and early 1970s), the widening of the multiple could lead to some substantial profits. Adding to the stock's attractiveness is a solid dividend yield (5 to 7 percent in recent years), well covered by earnings. The company hasn't missed a dividend since it was incorporated. And another plus: the balance sheet is in good shape, with debt recently less than 30 percent of total capital.

One reason investors have been sour on the stock is that the company's stock in trade is bulk commodity chemicals, on which margins are traditionally thin due to heavy competition in the United States and abroad. Carbide has been resolutely trimming diversifications (from brain scanners to shrimp); it intends to stick to its traditional business. This damn-the-torpedoes strategy could backfire if the U.S. economy hits a long period of stagnation, or if the Germans, Japanese, or OPEC chemical producers flood the market with low-priced offerings. But if the economy revives and sustains a boom, the company might be sitting pretty.

* * *

UNION COMMERCE CORP. (UCM). Founded 1970. Headquarters: 300 Union Commerce Bldg., Cleveland OH 44115. **BANKING.** Union Commerce is a holding company which owns four banks in Ohio. **MAJOR SUBSIDIARIES, BRANDS:** Union Commerce Bank; Southern Ohio Bank.

Sales: $169.2 million (trend 9.3% a year).
Earnings: $4.82 million (trend 31.6% a year).
What happened to a $10,000 investment

Purchase Date	Purchase Price	Price on 12-31-81	Dividends Paid
12-31-71	$29.50	$13.12	$1,856.61
12-31-76	$ 7.12	$13.12	$ 842.11

Purchase Date	Cap. Gains (– Losses)	Total Return	Rate of Return
12-31-71	$–5,550.85	$–3,694.24	–4.51%
12-31-76	$ 8,421.05	$ 9,263.16	14.01%

* * *

THE UNION CORP. (UCO). Founded 1938. Headquarters: Jones St., Verona PA 15147. **DIVERSIFIED MANUFACTURING.** Union is a diversified company active in manufacturing and services. The company is involved in recovering resources from scrap metal and used oil; manufacturing industrial equipment; manufacturing electrical components; and producing contact lenses. **MAJOR SUBSIDIARIES, BRANDS:** Capital Credit Corp.; Prinair (98 percent owned).

Sales: $205.9 million (trend 13.3% a year).
Earnings: $4.41 million (trend 14.0% a year).
What happened to a $10,000 investment

Purchase Date	Purchase Price	Price on 12-31-81	Dividends Paid
12-31-71	$10.18	$4.40	$0.00
12-31-76	$ 5.19	$4.40	$0.00

Purchase Date	Cap. Gains (– Losses)	Total Return	Rate of Return
12-31-71	$–5,671.01	$–5,671.01	–8.03%
12-31-76	$–1,515.18	$–1,515.18	–3.23%

* * *

UNION ELECTRIC CO. (UEP). Founded September 21, 1922. Headquarters: 1901 Gratiot St., St. Louis MO 63103. **PUBLIC UTILITY.** Union Electric supplies electricity in St. Louis and nearby areas of Missouri and also supplies natural gas and water in Missouri, Illinois, and Iowa. **MAJOR SUBSIDIARIES, BRANDS:** Missouri Edison Co.; Missouri Power & Light Co.; Missouri Utilities Co.; Union Colliery Co.

Sales: $1,077.9 million (trend 12.8% a year).
Earnings: $125.04 million (trend 12.0% a year).
What happened to a $10,000 investment

Purchase Date	Purchase Price	Price on 12-31-81	Dividends Paid
12-31-71	$18.50	$10.87	$7,383.78
12-31-76	$15.75	$10.87	$4,571.43

Purchase Date	Cap. Gains (– Losses)	Total Return	Rate of Return
12-31-71	$–4,121.62	$3,262.16	2.86%
12-31-76	$–3,095.24	$1,476.19	2.79%

* * *

UNION OIL CO. OF CALIFORNIA (UCL). Founded 1890. Headquarters: Union Oil Center, 461 S. Boylston St., Los Angeles CA 90017. **OIL.** Union is a major oil company, with sidelines in mining and chemical production. 18,000 employees.

Sales: $9,984.1 million (trend 13.6% a year).
Earnings: $647.00 million (trend 24.4% a year).
What happened to a $10,000 investment

Purchase Date	Purchase Price	Price on 12-31-81	Dividends Paid
12-31-71	$ 8.47	$37.62	$6,645.02
12-31-76	$14.81	$37.62	$2,248.95

Purchase Date	Cap. Gains (– Losses)	Total Return	Rate of Return
12-31-71	$34,428.04	$41,073.06	17.71%
12-31-76	$15,400.84	$17,649.79	22.56%

PROFILE: Union has a highly regarded exploration program. In one recent study by Petroleum Analysts Ltd., it topped fifteen oil companies in "new reserves per well drilled." Its balance between domestic and foreign reserves (about two-thirds domestic) strikes many as a good one. Production abroad is in large part from the North Sea and from Thailand; the company has been withdrawing from Canada, where (as noted in several other entries) the political climate has been hostile.

In 1981 Merrill Lynch circulated a favorable report on the company, which it described as "extremely well balanced . . . with excellent exploratory and development prospects in a number of important areas." Union, the brokerage firm said, "also has well-positioned operations in fertilizers, molybdenum, and rare earths. Because of excellent success in the Gulf of Mexico, onshore Gulf Coast, onshore and offshore California, and California heavy oil properties, UCL appears to be on the verge of stabilizing and even increasing both domestic liquids and natural gas output over the next five years."

If one wished to quarrel with the nation's largest brokerage firm, one could point out that the company's return on equity, while good in the past couple of years, has been unimpressive during much of the past decade. The price / earnings ratio has been volatile, ranging from 6 to 15 in 1980, for example. Keep an eye on it. With a variety of bargains recently available in the oil stocks, you may prefer one with a lower p / e, particularly if Union's multiple shoots upward.

Dividends have been paid each year here since 1916. The yield ranges from modest (recently) to moderate (during most of the 1970s). The payout is amply covered by earnings.

* * *

UNION PACIFIC CORP. (UNP). Founded 1897. Headquarters: 345 Park Ave., New York NY 10154. RAILROAD, OIL. Union Pacific is a holding company for one of the nation's largest railroads (with more than 9,000 miles of track connecting the Midwest and West), and three energy and natural resources development companies. 32,000 employees. MAJOR SUBSIDIARIES, BRANDS: Union Pacific Railroad; Champlin Petroleum Co.; Rocky Mountain Energy Co.; Upland Industries.

Sales: $4,831.7 million (trend 23.0% a year).
Earnings: $404.50 million (trend 23.3% a year).
What happened to a $10,000 investment

Purchase Date	*Purchase Price*	*Price on 12-31-81*	*Dividends Paid*
12-31-71	$15.31	$52.25	$6,128.98
12-31-76	$25.62	$52.25	$2,434.15

Purchase Date	*Cap. Gains (– Losses)*	*Total Return*	*Rate of Return*
12-31-71	$24,122.45	$30,251.43	14.94%
12-31-76	$10,390.24	$12,824.39	17.95%

PROFILE: Shareholders at several railroads are always urging management to do more to develop natural resources on company land. No one has to push for that at Union Pacific. Natural resource development has always been part of this railroad — and has been so with a vengeance since the early 1960s. In 1979 Champlin Petroleum, an integrated oil company acquired in 1970, outearned the railroad. In 1980 railroad earnings were only about 41 percent of total company earnings; oil and gas chipped in 52 percent, mining 5 percent, and real estate 2 percent. Besides Champlin, there's Upland Industries, essentially a land management arm, and Rocky Mountain Energy, which mines some of the riches on the company's 7½ million acres.

Business Week sniffed in 1980 that it would be "superficial" to attribute the company's success to the nineteenth-century land giveaway pushed through Congress and signed by President Abraham Lincoln. The generous land grants were intended to encourage entrepreneurs to take the risks involved in building a transcontinental railroad and to help them attract capital. It's hardly superficial to note that the 7½ million acres the company has now are largely left over from some 18 million it was given then.

The company recently has enjoyed a good press. It's been praised for farsighted strategic planning, for keeping its track upgraded, and for its bold proposal to merge with Missouri Pacific (see that entry). However, return on stockholders' equity, while it's improved over the past decade, has never been much better than average. Dividends, paid yearly since 1900, have recently provided a yield of around 3 percent.

* * *

UNIROYAL, INC. (R). Founded 1892. Headquarters: Middlebury CT 06749. TIRES, CHEMICALS. Uniroyal is one of the major U.S. tire manufacturers. It has been deemphasizing tires and expanding operations in chemicals and industrial products. 34,000 employees. MAJOR SUBSIDIARIES, BRANDS: Steeler brand tires.

Sales: $2,299.5 million (trend 1.8% a year).
Earnings: $–7.84 million.
What happened to a $10,000 investment

Purchase Date	*Purchase Price*	*Price on 12-31-81*	*Dividends Paid*
12-31-71	$18.25	$6.87	$2,260.27
12-31-76	$ 9.62	$6.87	$ 909.09

Purchase Date	*Cap. Gains (– Losses)*	*Total Return*	*Rate of Return*
12-31-71	$–6,232.88	$–3,972.60	–4.94%
12-31-76	$–2,857.14	$–1,948.05	–4.24%

PROFILE: In 1981, Uniroyal turned in its best year in a decade — which was saying very little. Uniroyal's most profitable year during the 1970s was 1972, when it earned a puny 8.2 percent on stockholders' equity. Earnings ranged from $0.57 (1976) to $1.65 a share (1974) in the period from 1971 to 77, then fell off the plateau into the abyss. There was a $0.04-a-share profit in 1978, a big loss in 1979, and a smaller loss in 1980 before a $1.76-a-share profit in 1981.

Contributing to the 1981 rebound was some major surgery. The company closed a fair number of its tire plants, sold some non-tire operations, laid off a number of workers, and persuaded remaining workers to accept wage cuts. These drastic moves seemed to have restored profitability to the tire line (which was also helped by good public reception of the new Steeler line of tires). But the company is putting very little money into tires, preferring to expand its chemical and industrial-products businesses, which contributed almost half of 1980 sales.

Uniroyal's lenders have it on a tight leash — not surprisingly, since debt is about half of capital. The company promised its lenders not to pay any dividends until June 1982 at the earliest, and to consult with them about asset sales. Meanwhile, Uniroyal is paying 10 percent above the prime rate on some of its debt.

* * *

UNIT DRILLING AND EXPLORATION CO. (UDE). Founded 1963. Headquarters: 1101 Petroleum Club Bldg., Tulsa OK 74119. **OIL, GAS.** Unit Drilling is a contract driller for oil and natural gas; also does a limited amount of oil and gas exploration and production on its own.

Sales: $29.9 million.
Earnings: $5.15 million.

* * *

UNITED BRANDS CO. (UB). Founded 1899. Headquarters: 1271 Ave. of the Americas, New York NY 10020. **BANANAS, MEAT.** The company is a major banana importer and meat packer; it has diversifications chiefly in fast food and telecommunications. 52,000 employees. **MAJOR SUBSIDIARIES, BRANDS:** United Fruit (Chiquita bananas); John Morrell & Co. (meat packing); A&W root beer; TRT Telecommunications Corp.

Sales: $4,058.4 million (trend 13.4% a year).
Earnings: $27.61 million (trend 31.5% a year).
What happened to a $10,000 investment

Purchase Date	*Purchase Price*	*Price on 12-31-81*	*Dividends Paid*
12-31-71	$10.75	$12.25	$930.23
12-31-76	$10.50	$12.25	$952.38

Purchase Date	*Cap. Gains (– Losses)*	*Total Return*	*Rate of Return*
12-31-71	$1,395.35	$2,325.58	2.11%
12-31-76	$1,666.67	$2,619.05	4.76%

PROFILE: "Meat and bananas are a perfectly crappy business, about the worst combination I can think of," a former United Brands executive told *Forbes* magazine in 1980. "If you don't move your inventory, it *rots,* for crissakes. The weaknesses reinforce each other."

That succinct statement can be attacked as an oversimplification (after all, Iowa Beef, for one, has bucked the trend and made money in meat packing). But you can't disprove it by looking at United Brands' operating results. From 1971 through 1980, the best return on equity the company ever earned was the 1980 return — a measly 5.6 percent.

The company's management has long promised to pursue diversification efforts — but somehow the other shoe never drops. "It's still *mañana* for getting off the banana boat," wrote *Business Week* in 1981. The company's most promising diversification now is TRT Telecommunications, which has about 20 percent of the U.S. telex market. TRT and A&W root beer contributed close to 20 percent of company earnings in fiscal 1980, on a tiny slice (about 3 percent) of sales. The company used to have a couple of other promising diversifications — Foster Grant (sunglasses) and Baskin-Robbins (ice cream). But it had to sell them for cash.

The balance sheet has been improved in recent years, and the p / e ratio is nice and low (recently about 5). Dividends, resumed in 1978 after a long dry spell, provide a modest-to-moderate yield. But there's little in the track record to encourage optimism. Adding to the risk is the fact that slightly over 50 percent of the shares are held by a few individuals.

* * *

UNITED CABLE TELEVISION CORP. (UCT). Founded 1969. Headquarters: 4700 S. Syracuse Parkway, Denver CO 80237. **CABLE TV.** Owns and runs close to forty cable TV systems in sixteen states.

Sales: $62.8 million (trend 34.2% a year).
Earnings: $7.90 million (trend 183.5% a year).
What happened to a $10,000 investment

Purchase Date	*Purchase Price*	*Price on 12-31-81*	*Dividends Paid*
12-31-71	$2.81	$26.25	$1,048.89
12-31-76	$1.06	$26.25	$2,776.47

Purchase Date	Cap. Gains (− Losses)	Total Return	Rate of Return
12-31-71	$ 83,333.33	$ 84,382.22	25.17%
12-31-76	$237,058.82	$239,835.29	90.34%

* * *

UNITED ENERGY RESOURCES, INC. (UER). Founded 1974. Headquarters: 700 Milam, Houston TX 77001. GAS PIPELINES. United Energy Resources is one of the country's larger natural gas pipeline operators, with both intrastate (Texas) and interstate (serving chiefly the Southeast) operations. It also explores for and produces natural gas and oil, operates storage terminals, and sells natural gas liquids. 4,000 employees. **MAJOR SUBSIDIARIES, BRANDS:** United Gas Pipe Line; Cotton Petroleum; United Texas Transmission; PetroUnited; United Energy Services.

Sales: $4,135.3 million (trend 36.8% a year).
Earnings: $165.45 million (trend 32.7% a year).
What happened to a $10,000 investment

Purchase Date	Purchase Price	Price on 12-31-81	Dividends Paid
12-31-71	$ N/A	$41.25	$ N/A
12-31-76	$13.94	$41.25	$4,721.08

Purchase Date	Cap. Gains (− Losses)	Total Return	Rate of Return
12-31-71	$ N/A	$ N/A	N/A%
12-31-76	$19,596.41	$24,317.49	27.97%

PROFILE: A hot stock? They don't get too much hotter than United Energy Resources has been. Suppose you'd bought some shares here in 1974, when the company was spun off from Pennzoil. It might have cost you around $2 a share. In 1980 you could have sold for $56 a share. You would have multiplied your money twenty-eight times.

In retrospect, the spin-off from Pennzoil looks ironic. Pennzoil was apparently concerned at owning a mixture of regulated and unregulated businesses. However, its child, United Energy Resources, has done just that. Much of the interstate pipeline business is regulated (though this hasn't depressed profit margins unduly); the company's other businesses — including the promising Cotton Petroleum subsidiary — largely aren't.

Long-term debt is a relatively conservative share of total capital — recently about 22 percent. One risk element is the existence of several large and long-pending suits for damages from customers whose gas allocations were chopped during shortages in the 1970s.

The stock has cooled off some recently, along with other energy issues. From its 1980 high of $56, it bobbed down to around $45, before bouncing back to $54 in early 1982. The price-earnings ratio was recently a downright prosaic 5.

Dividends, paid yearly since the company was spun off from Pennzoil, provide a moderate yield.

* * *

THE UNITED ILLUMINATING CO. (UIL). Founded 1899. Headquarters: 80 Temple St., New Haven CT 06506. ELECTRICITY. United Illuminating produces and distributes electricity in southern Connecticut.

Sales: $364.1 million (trend 13.4% a year).
Earnings: $25.17 million (trend 8.8% a year).
What happened to a $10,000 investment

Purchase Date	Purchase Price	Price on 12-31-81	Dividends Paid
12-31-71	$29.12	$18.62	$8,412.02
12-31-76	$26.37	$18.62	$4,963.03

Purchase Date	Cap. Gains (− Losses)	Total Return	Rate of Return
12-31-71	$−3,605.15	$4,806.87	4.00%
12-31-76	$−2,938.39	$2,024.64	3.76%

* * *

UNITED INDUSTRIAL CORP. (UIC). Founded 1959. Headquarters: 18 E. 48th St., New York NY 10017. MANUFACTURING. United Industrial is active in research and development and military-equipment manufacturing for the government. It also manufatures hospital supplies and equipment and industrial equipment. **MAJOR SUBSIDIARIES, BRANDS:** AAI Corp.; Affiliated Hospital Products, Inc.; Detroit Stoker Co.; Neo Products; Perry Surgical Gloves; Shampaine Hospital Equipment.

Sales: $165.5 million (trend 16.1% a year).
Earnings: $8.27 million (trend 22.2% a year).
What happened to a $10,000 investment

Purchase Date	Purchase Price	Price on 12-31-81	Dividends Paid
12-31-71	$ 6.59	$35.57	$6,539.82
12-31-76	$13.41	$35.57	$2,489.43

Purchase Date	Cap. Gains (– Losses)	Total Return	Rate of Return
12-31-71	$43,977.41	$50,517.23	19.73%
12-31-76	$16,530.91	$19,020.34	23.75%

* * *

UNITED INNS, INC. (UI). Founded 1956. Headquarters: 2300 Clark Tower, Memphis TN 38137. MOTELS. United Inns runs thirty-four Holiday Inns in the South and Southwest. It also operates a chain of car washes and a furniture manufacturer. MAJOR SUBSIDIARIES, BRANDS: Gaines Manufacturing Co.; Mr. Pride.

Sales: $135.9 million (trend 9.9% a year).
Earnings: $9.20 million (trend 20.8% a year).
What happened to a $10,000 investment

Purchase Date	Purchase Price	Price on 12-31-81	Dividends Paid
12-31-71	$26.25	$18.50	$ 560.00
12-31-76	$ 5.12	$18.50	$1,892.68

Purchase Date	Cap. Gains (– Losses)	Total Return	Rate of Return
12-31-71	$–2,952.38	$–2,392.38	–2.70%
12-31-76	$ 26,097.56	$ 27,990.24	30.60%

* * *

UNITED JERSEY BANKS (UJB). Founded 1969. Headquarters: 90 Nassau St., Princeton NJ 08540. BANKING. United Jersey Banks is a holding company that owns eight banks operating in approximately seventy New Jersey communities. MAJOR SUBSIDIARIES, BRANDS: United Jersey Bank; Gibraltar Corp. of America; United Jersey Leasing; United Jersey Mortgage.

Sales: $236.6 million (trend 13.1% a year).
Earnings: $14.93 million (trend 14.7% a year).
What happened to a $10,000 investment

Purchase Date	Purchase Price	Price on 12-31-81	Dividends Paid
12-31-71	$23.12	$12.62	$4,549.19
12-31-76	$13.87	$12.62	$4,050.45

Purchase Date	Cap. Gains (– Losses)	Total Return	Rate of Return
12-31-71	$–4,540.54	$ 8.65	.01%
12-31-76	$ –900.90	$3,149.55	5.63%

* * *

UNITED MERCHANTS & MANUFACTURERS, INC. (UMM). Founded 1928. Headquarters: 1407 Broadway, New York NY 10018. TEXTILES. United Merchants is a diversified textile company which makes wearing apparel, decorative fabric for home furnishings, and glass fiber products for industry. MAJOR SUBSIDIARIES, BRANDS: Con-Tact.

Sales: $669.6 million (trend –7.1% a year).
Earnings: $–7.29 million.
What happened to a $10,000 investment

Purchase Date	Purchase Price	Price on 12-31-81	Dividends Paid
12-31-71	$ N/A	$4.25	$ N/A
12-31-76	$11.50	$4.25	$260.87

Purchase Date	Cap. Gains (– Losses)	Total Return	Rate of Return
12-31-71	$ N/A	$ N/A	N/A%
12-31-76	$–6,304.35	$–6,043.48	–16.93%

* * *

UNITED PARK CITY MINES (UPK). Founded 1953. Headquarters: 309 Kearns Bldg., Salt Lake City UT 84101. METAL MINING. Mines silver, zinc, and lead in Utah. MAJOR SUBSIDIARIES, BRANDS: The Weber Coal Co.

Sales: $.9 million (trend 17.8% a year).
Earnings: $.79 million (trend 244.8% a year).
What happened to a $10,000 investment

Purchase Date	Purchase Price	Price on 12-31-81	Dividends Paid
12-31-71	$2.25	$2.25	$0.00
12-31-76	$3.12	$2.25	$0.00

Purchase Date	Cap. Gains (– Losses)	Total Return	Rate of Return
12-31-71	$ –.00	$ –.00	0.00%
12-31-76	$–2,800.00	$–2,800.00	–6.36%

* * *

U. S. & FOREIGN SECURITIES CORP. (UFO). Founded 1924. Headquarters: 767 Fifth Ave., New York NY 10022. INVESTING. U. S. & Foreign Securities Corp. is a publicly traded investment company, offering participation in a portfolio of growth oriented stocks. The company's largest investments are in oil and gas.

* * *

U. S. AIR, INC. (U). Founded 1937. Headquarters: Washington National Airport, Washington DC 20001. AIRLINE. U. S. Air, formerly Allegheny Airlines, serves some fifty to sixty airports in the Northeast and connects the Northeast (principally Pittsburgh) with the South and Southwest. 10,000 employees.

Sales: $971.8 million (trend 20.2% a year).
Earnings: $56.78 million (trend 80.9% a year).
What happened to a $10,000 investment

Purchase Date	*Purchase Price*	*Price on 12-31-81*	*Dividends Paid*
12-31-71	$13.87	$11.87	$151.35
12-31-76	$ 5.25	$11.87	$400.00

Purchase Date	*Cap. Gains (− Losses)*	*Total Return*	*Rate of Return*
12-31-71	$−1,441.44	$−1,290.09	−1.37%
12-31-76	$ 12,619.05	$ 13,019.05	18.15%

PROFILE: When it was Allegheny Airlines, U. S. Air was the butt of some cruel jibes. It was called "the Willy Loman of the skies," or worse (and often), Agony Airlines. "People thought we were a little airline flying little propeller planes to little cities," one company official told *Fortune* in 1980.

But U. S. Air has become one of the success stories of the late 1970s and early 1980s. While many airlines have been taking losses, U. S. Air racked up five straight profits and showed a strong earnings uptrend from 1976 to 1980. The company made money again in 1981, a terrible year for most airlines, though profits were down from 1980. Its jets (the company belatedly switched to jets from propeller planes in the mid-1970s) are generally smaller and more fuel-efficient than those of competitors. Its hub-and-spoke system is highly efficient. It is the dominant airline for flights in and out of Pittsburgh and has recently added profitable Sun Belt routes from Pittsburgh to Florida, Phoenix, New Orleans, and Houston. At the same time, it has resisted the temptation to overexpand in response to deregulation. "Our basic decision was not to get a bellyache from sticking our hand in the cookie jar too often," Chairman Ed Colodny told *Fortune.* While the larger airlines have been caught in costly fare wars on transcontinental flights, U. S. Air has stuck mainly to the more profitable medium-haul routes.

Debt has been pared from close to 80 percent of capital at the beginning of the 1970s to around 44 percent at the beginning of the 1980s. Dividends were resumed in 1980, following a thirteen-year dry spell. The yield is modest. Despite the line's success, Wall Street is still fearful that the whole thing may be a flash in the pan. The stock has been selling for extremely low earnings multiples, ranging recently from 1 to 5.

* * *

U. S. GYPSUM CO. (USG). Founded 1920. Headquarters: 101 S. Wacker Dr., Chicago IL 60606. BUILDING SUPPLIES. U. S. Gypsum is one of the largest U.S. building supply companies, with gypsum board the main product. 18,000 employees.

Sales: $1,474.4 million (trend 13.7% a year).
Earnings: $93.32 million (trend 35.2% a year).
What happened to a $10,000 investment

Purchase Date	*Purchase Price*	*Price on 12-31-81*	*Dividends Paid*
12-31-71	$32.37	$33.50	$5,644.79
12-31-76	$26.37	$33.50	$3,924.17

Purchase Date	*Cap. Gains (− Losses)*	*Total Return*	*Rate of Return*
12-31-71	$ 347.49	$5,992.28	4.81%
12-31-76	$2,701.42	$6,625.59	10.70%

PROFILE: Can the building industry stay depressed forever? If you think not, U. S. Gypsum deserves serious consideration as a long-term investment. In the last few years, the company's profits have been decent, though certainly nothing to write home about. Despite horrendous conditions in the housing industry, the company turned in fairly decent years in 1980 and 1981. If it can do that when housing is down, what happens when housing finally takes off?

Much of what's been depressing housing is high interest rates, and those, while stubborn, won't persist indefinitely. To a degree, then, this stock is likely to prove interest-rate sensitive, rising faster than most when interest rates decline.

The stock is conservative in terms of downside risk. Dividends have been paid every year since the company was incorporated, and have provided a solid 6-to-8 percent yield the past few years. The balance sheet is in excellent shape, with debt recently less than 15 percent of total capital.

The stock's price has showed no net progress for a decade. But the shares have recently sold for a mere 4 to 7 times earnings, whereas a decade ago they sold for more than twice that. Patience is likely to be rewarded here.

* * *

U. S. HOME CORP. (UH). Founded 1959. Headquarters: 1177 W. Loop S., Houston TX 77001. HOUSING. U. S. Home manufactures single-family houses, largely in the Sun Belt area. It is the largest manufacturer of on-site homes (as opposed to mobile homes) in the country. MAJOR SUBSIDIARIES, BRANDS: Clearwater Concrete; Dee Wood Industries; U. S. Home Mortgage Corp.; U. S. Home Finance Co.

Sales: $1,080.9 million (trend 29.0% a year).
Earnings: $44.30 million (trend 60.9% a year).
What happened to a $10,000 investment

Purchase Date	*Purchase Price*	*Price on 12-31-81*	*Dividends Paid*
12-31-71	$22.21	$13.75	$1,121.36
12-31-76	$ 6.82	$13.75	$2,937.75

Purchase Date	*Cap. Gains (− Losses)*	*Total Return*	*Rate of Return*
12-31-71	$−3,809.31	$−2,687.95	−3.08%
12-31-76	$ 10,166.65	$ 13,104.40	18.23%

* * *

U. S. INDUSTRIES, INC. (USI). Founded 1898. Headquarters: 250 Park Ave., New York NY 10177. CONGLOMERATE. U. S. Industries is a conglomerate comprising some twenty-eight subsidiary companies, all relatively small. Businesses include oil field equipment, fasteners, machinery, agricultural irrigation equipment, poultry farming, furniture, and building materials. 20,000 employees.

Sales: $1,144.7 million (trend −2.6% a year).
Earnings: $17.72 million (trend 23.4% a year).
What happened to a $10,000 investment

Purchase Date	*Purchase Price*	*Price on 12-31-81*	*Dividends Paid*
12-31-71	$23.18	$9.50	$2,336.86
12-31-76	$ 8.25	$9.50	$3,842.42

Purchase Date	*Cap. Gains (− Losses)*	*Total Return*	*Rate of Return*
12-31-71	$−5,901.57	$−3,564.71	−4.31%
12-31-76	$ 1,515.15	$ 5,357.58	8.96%

PROFILE: Call it the case of the shrinking conglomerate. U. S. Industries used to be among the largest 100 industrial companies in the country. Now it's hanging by its fingernails to a spot in the top 300. The company, which had accumulated more than 100 wildly diverse and unrelated subsidiaries by the late 1960s, had divested all but 28 by 1981. The latest to go were 14 subsidiaries that made up most of the "consumer products and services" division. Total company sales shrunk from $1.4 billion in 1971 to $1.1 billion in 1980.

In retreat, the company has kept its mouth closed. Most companies these days toot their own horns or at least make a show of openness in dealing with the press and public. But U. S. Industries is about as secretive as it's possible for a publicly owned company to be.

Profits have been poor. In 1980, for example, the profit margin was under 2 percent, and the return on stockholders' equity was under 4 percent. Granted, that was an especially bad year—but there have been several. Even in 1979, the company's best recent year, the return on equity was an uninspiring 10.2 percent.

A detailed article on the company in *Financial World* back in 1979 said that U. S. Industries had an interesting concept in trying to put together a highly diverse conglomerate of small companies. But it starved the component companies of capital and gave little freedom to the entrepreneurs who had started them. Total capital expenditures have never exceeded $50 million since 1973.

Dividends have been paid each year since 1965. In recent years, the yield has usually been above 6 percent.

* * *

U. S. LEASING INTERNATIONAL, INC. (USL). Founded 1952. Headquarters: 633 Battery St., San Francisco CA 94111. EQUIPMENT LEASING. U. S. Leasing operates leasing programs for manufacturers, leases and manages commercial auto fleets, and rents and leases computer peripherals, electronic test equipment, and railroad cars. MAJOR SUBSIDIARIES, BRANDS. Home Savings Association; U. S. Fleet Leasing; U. S. Lease Financing; U. S. Instrument Leasing; U. S. Portfolio Leasing; U. S. Rail Services.

Sales: $196.4 million (trend 23.7% a year).
Earnings: $15.60 million (trend 14.4% a year).
What happened to a $10,000 investment

Purchase Date	*Purchase Price*	*Price on 12-31-81*	*Dividends Paid*
12-31-71	$24.33	$25.75	$1,539.74
12-31-76	$10.87	$25.75	$2,317.24

Purchase Date	*Cap. Gains (− Losses)*	*Total Return*	*Rate of Return*
12-31-71	$ 582.19	$ 2,121.93	1.94%
12-31-76	$13,678.16	$15,995.40	21.05%

* * *

U. S. REALTY INVESTMENTS (UTY). Founded 1961. Headquarters: 1020 Terminal Tower, Cleveland OH 44113. **REAL ESTATE.** U. S. Realty finances, develops, and owns office buildings, motels, and shopping centers. **MAJOR SUBSIDIARIES, BRANDS:** Terminal Management, Inc.; Tower City Corp.

* * *

UNITED STATES SHOE CORP. (USR). Founded 1931. Headquarters: 1658 Herald Ave., Cincinnati OH 45212. **SHOES.** U. S. Shoe manufactures, imports and retails footware. The company also operates a string of specialty apparel stores. **MAJOR SUBSIDIARIES, BRANDS:** Amalfi; August Max; Casual Corner; Cobbies; French Shriner; J. Riggings; Miss Capezio; Papagallo; Red Cross; Texas Boot.

Sales: $973.6 million (trend 15.3% a year).
Earnings: $45.55 million (trend 21.6% a year).
What happened to a $10,000 investment

Purchase Date	*Purchase Price*	*Price on 12-31-81*	*Dividends Paid*
12-31-71	$15.00	$33.37	$4,504.89
12-31-76	$17.17	$33.37	$2,106.02

Purchase Date	*Cap. Gains (− Losses)*	*Total Return*	*Rate of Return*
12-31-71	$12,250.00	$16,754.89	10.34%
12-31-76	$ 9,441.75	$11,547.77	16.60%

* * *

U. S. STEEL CORP. (X) Founded 1901. Headquarters: 600 Grant St., Pittsburgh PA 15230. **STEEL.** U. S. Steel is the nation's largest steelmaker. It also has operations in construction, chemicals, oil field equipment, and transportation, and recently acquired Marathon, a major oil company. 149,000 employees.

Sales: $12,492.1 million (trend 10.5% a year).
Earnings: $458.90 million (trend −3.8% a year).
What happened to a $10,000 investment

Purchase Date	*Purchase Price*	*Price on 12-31-81*	*Dividends Paid*
12-31-71	$20.17	$29.87	$8,223.16
12-31-76	$49.75	$29.87	$1,809.05

Purchase Date	*Cap. Gains (− Losses)*	*Total Return*	*Rate of Return*
12-31-71	$ 4,814.05	$ 13,037.21	8.70%
12-31-76	$−3,994.97	$−2,185.93	−4.81%

PROFILE: They call it "big steel" or, simply, "the company." It is a classic blue-chip, smokestack, Dow-Jones-Industrial stock. It is, of course, cyclical. And it has just come through several lean years.

But look at the headlines now. "Back from the slag heap; melted down and remolded, it's almost a new company," said *Financial World* in 1981. "Big Steel Recasts Itself," wrote *Fortune.* The New York *Times* cited "The Turnaround at U. S. Steel." And the *Wall Street Journal* headlined, "U. S. Steel's Long Decline May Be Over."

Once one of the nation's worst polluters, U. S. Steel has made substantial cleanup steps. Those have cost lots of money, but the outlay per year is now declining. Once a producer that relied heavily on old, sometimes antiquated plants, U. S. Steel has closed several such facilities and modernized others in an effort (which will continue to be a tough struggle) to compete with efficient Japanese producers and U.S. mini-mills.

Granted, the appeal of these shares lies in the direction the company has been going lately, not in its recent results. Return on stockholders' equity never broke 10 percent from 1976 to 1980. But the stock is conservatively valued (recently 5 times earnings), and dividends (paid yearly since 1940) have recently afforded a yield of 6 to 8 percent.

The acquisition of Marathon Oil, which had been more profitable in recent years than U. S. Steel, will give the company additional earning power and balance. U. S. Steel paid some $6 billion to win Marathon, which had also been sought by Mobil. In the merged corporation, steel and petroleum will each account for about 40 percent of sales; chemicals will account for much of the rest.

* * *

UNITED STATES TOBACCO CO. (UBO). Founded 1911. Headquarters: 100 W. Putnam Ave., Greenwich CT 06830. **TOBACCO.** U. S. Tobacco manufactures and sells tobacco products, including smokeless tobacco, pipe tobacco, and cigars. It also makes smoking accessories and cat food, and operates a television station. **MAJOR SUB-**

SIDIARIES, BRANDS: Copenhagen; Happy Days; Skoal; House of Windsor, Inc.; Ste. Michelle Vintners Inc.; WPBN-TV, Inc. (Traverse City, Michigan); WTOM-TV, Inc. (Cheboygan, Michigan).

Sales: $265.8 million (trend 13.3% a year).
Earnings: $37.69 million (trend 18.6% a year).
What happened to a $10,000 investment

Purchase Date	*Purchase Price*	*Price on 12-31-81*	*Dividends Paid*
12-31-71	$19.75	$47.37	$6,800.00
12-31-76	$25.62	$47.37	$3,637.07

Purchase Date	*Cap. Gains (— Losses)*	*Total Return*	*Rate of Return*
12-31-71	$13,987.34	$20,787.34	11.90%
12-31-76	$ 8,487.80	$12,124.88	17.21%

* * *

UNITED TECHNOLOGIES CORP. (UTX). Founded 1934. Headquarters: United Technologies Bldg., Hartford CT 06101. CONGLOMERATE. The company is chiefly involved in aerospace products, but is widely diversified in such areas as elevators, semiconductors, and wire and cable. 200,000 employees. MAJOR SUBSIDIARIES, BRANDS: Pratt & Whitney (jet engines); Hamilton Standard (flight controls); Norden Systems (radar and minicomputers); Sikorsky (helicopters); Ambac Industries (diesel engine systems); Carrier Corp. (cooling and heating equipment); Essex (wire and cable); Mostek (semiconductors); Otis (elevators).

Sales: $12,324.0 million (trend 24.2% a year).
Earnings: $312.14 million (trend 27.6% a year).
What happened to a $10,000 investment

Purchase Date	*Purchase Price*	*Price on 12-31-81*	*Dividends Paid*
12-31-71	$14.69	$41.75	$10,493.62
12-31-76	$38.87	$41.75	$ 2,688.10

Purchase Date	*Cap. Gains (— Losses)*	*Total Return*	*Rate of Return*
12-31-71	$18,425.53	$28,919.15	14.56%
12-31-76	$ 739.55	$ 3,427.65	6.07%

PROFILE: This is a high-technology conglomerate. As A. F. Ehrbar noted in *Fortune* in 1980, much of the technology is developed by Hamilton Standard, a flight-control systems company that is less known than many of United Technologies' subsidiaries. Another source of technology to be spread around the company is Mostek, the fast-growing semiconductor manufacturer, acquired in 1979.

Most of the companies joined together under the United Technologies banner are leaders in their respective fields. For the corporation as a whole, growth has been steady. Despite a bad recession, earnings were up slightly in 1981; the last previous down year was 1971. As Ehrbar pointed out, it is "a giant in R and D," spending some $625 million in 1980 on research and development: "Only five companies spend more . . . and none of them spends as high a percentage of sales."

Two minor drawbacks to this stock are that institutions hold about 40 percent of the shares (thus there's not much chance of an upward move from institutions "discovering" the stock) and that there's a fair amount of preferred stock outstanding, soaking up cash that might otherwise go to common stockholders. The dividend yield is moderate; dividends have been paid yearly since 1936. The p / e has ranged in recent years between 5 and 9.

* * *

UNITRODE CORP. (UTR). Founded 1960. Headquarters: 5 Forbes Rd., Lexington MA 02173. ELECTRONICS. Unitrode manufactures semiconductor components, sold mainly to defense and aerospace customers. MAJOR SUBSIDIARIES, BRANDS: Micro Networks; High Voltage Devices; Schottky; Unitrode Computer Products Corp.

Sales: $103.6 million (trend 32.1% a year).
Earnings: $10.31 million (trend 46.4% a year).
What happened to a $10,000 investment

Purchase Date	*Purchase Price*	*Price on 12-31-81*	*Dividends Paid*
12-31-71	$5.62	$30.50	$1,244.44
12-31-76	$3.81	$30.50	$1,704.92

Purchase Date	*Cap. Gains (— Losses)*	*Total Return*	*Rate of Return*
12-31-71	$44,222.22	$45,466.67	18.69%
12-31-76	$70,000.00	$71,704.92	52.21%

* * *

UNIVAR CORP. (UVX). Founded 1966. Headquarters: 1600 Norton Bldg., Seattle WA 98104. CHEMICALS. Univar distributes industrial chemicals and specialty chemicals. The company also distributes scientific and graphic arts products and produces and distributes food products. MAJOR SUBSIDIARIES, BRANDS: Great Western Malting;

Pacific Resins & Chemicals; Penick & Ford; Van Waters & Rogers; VWR Scientific.

Sales: $970.2 million (trend 10.7% a year).
Earnings: $17.06 million (trend 5.9% a year).
What happened to a $10,000 investment

Purchase Date	*Purchase Price*	*Price on 12-31-81*	*Dividends Paid*
12-31-71	$ 4.37	$27.75	$9,020.95
12-31-76	$10.87	$27.75	$2,151.72

Purchase Date	*Cap. Gains (– Losses)*	*Total Return*	*Rate of Return*
12-31-71	$53,428.57	$62,449.52	21.90%
12-31-76	$15,517.24	$17,668.97	22.57%

* * *

UNIVERSAL FOODS CORP. (UFC). Founded 1882. Headquarters: 433 E. Michigan St., Milwaukee WI 53202. FOODS. Universal Foods is a diversified food company, producing yeast and cheese; bottling soft drinks and importing gourmet foods. MAJOR SUBSIDIARIES, BRANDS: Ile De France; Mid-Continent Bottlers, Inc.; Red Star; Stella.

Sales: $434.4 million (trend 21.4% a year).
Earnings: $13.66 million (trend 10.6% a year).
What happened to a $10,000 investment

Purchase Date	*Purchase Price*	*Price on 12-31-81*	*Dividends Paid*
12-31-71	$11.78	$15.37	$5,797.92
12-31-76	$14.58	$15.37	$3,044.57

Purchase Date	*Cap. Gains (– Losses)*	*Total Return*	*Rate of Return*
12-31-71	$3,054.25	$8,852.17	6.55%
12-31-76	$ 542.86	$3,587.43	6.32%

* * *

UNIVERSAL LEAF TOBACCO CO., INC. (UVV). Founded 1918. Headquarters: Hamilton St. at Broad, Richmond VA 23230. TOBACCO. Universal Leaf Tobacco buys, stores, and sells leaf tobacco and processes tobacco for others. MAJOR SUBSIDIARIES, BRANDS: Royster Co.

Sales: $1,039.7 million (trend 8.9% a year).
Earnings: $31.26 million (trend 12.3% a year).
What happened to a $10,000 investment

Purchase Date	*Purchase Price*	*Price on 12-31-81*	*Dividends Paid*
12-31-71	$ 7.87	$24.25	$10,066.67
12-31-76	$15.37	$24.25	$ 3,655.28

Purchase Date	*Cap. Gains (– Losses)*	*Total Return*	*Rate of Return*
12-31-71	$20,793.65	$30,860.32	15.11%
12-31-76	$ 5,772.36	$ 9,427.64	14.20%

* * *

UPJOHN CO. (UPJ). Founded 1886. Headquarters: 7000 Portage Rd., Kalamazoo MI 49001. DRUGS. Upjohn is a major producer of prescription drugs. It also has operations in agriculture, chemicals, and over-the-counter drugs. 22,000 employees. MAJOR SUBSIDIARIES, BRANDS: Asgrow Seed Co.; Cleocin (antibiotic); Motrin (anti-inflammatory); Cheracol (cough syrup); Unicap (vitamins).

Sales: $1,760.6 million (trend 14.4% a year).
Earnings: $170.37 million (trend 22.1% a year).
What happened to a $10,000 investment

Purchase Date	*Purchase Price*	*Price on 12-31-81*	*Dividends Paid*
12-31-71	$36.37	$53.75	$3,413.06
12-31-76	$38.50	$53.75	$2,041.56

Purchase Date	*Cap. Gains (– Losses)*	*Total Return*	*Rate of Return*
12-31-71	$4,776.63	$8,189.69	6.17%
12-31-76	$3,961.04	$6,002.60	9.86%

PROFILE: In recent years, Upjohn has been no more profitable than the average drug company—which is to say it's been very profitable. Return on equity has been remarkably steady—for example, it was between 21 and 22 percent each year from 1978 to 1980.

Upjohn's growth has been nothing to sneeze at, either. Profits rose from $40 million in 1971 to $170 million in 1980. With a solid growth record, Upjohn sells for a higher multiple than the average stock, but a lower one than the average drug company. (Recently, the multiple has ranged from 7 to 12.) Why?

One reason is that this isn't a pure drug company. A third of its sales (and about a fifth of its profits) come from chemicals (mainly urethane products and isocyanates) and agriculture (Asgrow Seed Co.). Many drug companies have experimented with, but subsequently retreated from, diversification, having found no other area so profitable as drugs. Upjohn has given no indication it will change course, and some investors may prefer to have this counterbalance.

Dividends have been paid each year since 1909, and in recent years have consumed about a third of profits. The yield the past few years has been between 3 and 4 percent.

The company's research and development program is well regarded in the industry, and Upjohn spends 8 to 9 percent of revenues on research—considerably more than the 5 to 6 percent spent by most drug companies.

* * *

USLIFE CORP. (USH). Founded 1850. Headquarters: 125 Maiden Lane, New York NY 10038. LIFE INSURANCE. USLIFE is an insurance holding company with subsidiaries providing life insurance, title insurance, and financial services. MAJOR SUBSIDIARIES, BRANDS: USLIFE Credit Corp.

Sales: $788.5 million (trend 12.9% a year).
Earnings: $92.82 million (trend 14.2% a year).
What happened to a $10,000 investment

Purchase Date	*Purchase Price*	*Price on 12-31-81*	*Dividends Paid*
12-31-71	$23.25	$23.25	$2,058.06
12-31-76	$17.25	$23.25	$1,895.65

Purchase Date	*Cap. Gains (− Losses)*	*Total Return*	*Rate of Return*
12-31-71	$ .00	$2,058.06	1.89%
12-31-76	$3,478.26	$5,373.91	8.98%

* * *

USLIFE INCOME FUND, INC. (UIF). Founded 1972. Headquarters: 125 Maiden Lane, New York NY 10038. INVESTING. USLIFE Income Fund is a publicly traded investment company that invests primarily in bonds.

* * *

UTAH POWER & LIGHT CO. (UTP). Founded 1912. Headquarters: 1407 W. North Temple St., Salt Lake City UT 84110. ELECTRIC UTILITY. Utah Power & Light provides electricity in Salt Lake City, Ogden, and surrounding areas in Utah, Idaho, and Wyoming.

Sales: $609.2 million (trend 24.2% a year).
Earnings: $85.63 million (trend 18.2% a year).
What happened to a $10,000 investment

Purchase Date	*Purchase Price*	*Price on 12-31-81*	*Dividends Paid*
12-31-71	$17.19	$17.87	$8,659.49
12-31-76	$22.31	$17.87	$4,051.54

Purchase Date	*Cap. Gains (− Losses)*	*Total Return*	*Rate of Return*
12-31-71	$ 400.00	$9,059.49	6.66%
12-31-76	$−1,988.80	$2,062.75	3.82%

V

V. F. CORP. (VFC). Founded 1899. Headquarters: 1047 N. Park Rd., Wyomissing PA 19610. CLOTHING. V. F. Corp. is a holding company whose subsidiaries produce leisure wear and women's clothing. MAJOR SUBSIDIARIES, BRANDS: Lee; H. D. Lee; Kay Windsor; Vanity Fair.

Sales: $633.8 million (trend 8.9% a year).
Earnings: $45.89 million (trend 14.1% a year).
What happened to a $10,000 investment

Purchase Date	*Purchase Price*	*Price on 12-31-81*	*Dividends Paid*
12-31-71	$26.62	$40.75	$4,408.26
12-31-76	$21.62	$40.75	$3,526.01

Purchase Date	*Cap. Gains (− Losses)*	*Total Return*	*Rate of Return*
12-31-71	$5,305.16	$ 9,713.43	7.02%
12-31-76	$8,843.93	$12,369.94	17.47%

* * *

VALERO ENERGY CORP. (VLO). Founded 1955. Headquarters: 530 McCullough Ave., San Antonio TX 78215. NATURAL GAS. Valero Energy operates natural gas systems in Texas, including purchasing, transporting, and selling; also active in oil and gas exploration. MAJOR SUBSIDIARIES, BRANDS: Valero Transmission Co.; Saber Energy, Inc. (50 percent owned).

Sales: $1,702.0 million.
Earnings: $54.42 million.

* * *

VALLEY INDUSTRIES, INC. (VI). Founded 1961. Headquarters: 105 S. Ninth St., St. Louis MO 63166. STEEL PRODUCTS. Valley Industries processes, markets, and distributes a variety of steel products and is also active in coal mining. Steel products are sold to industry and offshore drillers. MAJOR SUBSIDIARIES, BRANDS: Dredgemasters International.

Sales: $166.5 million (trend 8.5% a year).
Earnings: $6.36 million (trend −13.4% a year).
What happened to a $10,000 investment

Purchase Date	*Purchase Price*	*Price on 12-31-81*	*Dividends Paid*
12-31-71	$N/A	$10.25	$ N/A
12-31-76	$ 7.25	$10.25	$2,758.62

Purchase Date	*Cap. Gains (− Losses)*	*Total Return*	*Rate of Return*
12-31-71	$ N/A	$ N/A	N/A%
12-31-76	$4,137.93	$6,896.55	11.06%

* * *

VAN DORN CO. (VDC). Founded 1872. Headquarters: 2700 E. 79th St., Cleveland OH 44104. MANUFACTURING. Van Dorn produces aluminum cans for paint, chemical, petroleum, and household products; also produces plastic molding equipment. MAJOR SUBSIDIARIES, BRANDS: Central States Can Co.; Davies Can Co.; George A. Milton Can Co.; Ohio Paper Products Co.; Van Dorn Heat Treating Co.; Van Dorn Machinery Co.

Sales: $172.4 million (trend 11.8% a year).
Earnings: $6.12 million (trend 19.3% a year).
What happened to a $10,000 investment

Purchase Date	*Purchase Price*	*Price on 12-31-81*	*Dividends Paid*
12-31-71	$16.30	$15.25	$3,566.87
12-31-76	$10.25	$15.25	$4,107.32

Purchase Date	*Cap. Gains (− Losses)*	*Total Return*	*Rate of Return*
12-31-71	$−644.17	$2,922.70	2.60%
12-31-76	$ 4,878.05	$8,985.37	13.68%

* * *

VARCO INTERNATIONAL, INC. (VRC). Founded 1911. Headquarters: 800 N. Eckhoff St., Orange CA 92668. OIL EQUIPMENT. Varco makes drilling equipment and equipment used in pipelines for the petroleum industry. MAJOR SUBSIDIARIES, BRANDS: Best Industries.

Sales: $108.1 million (trend 38.2% a year).
Earnings: $11.90 million (trend 27.7% a year).
What happened to a $10,000 investment

Purchase Date	*Purchase Price*	*Price on 12-31-81*	*Dividends Paid*
12-31-71	$N/A	$18.37	$ N/A
12-31-76	$ 3.19	$18.37	$580.39

Purchase Date	*Cap. Gains (− Losses)*	*Total Return*	*Rate of Return*
12-31-71	$ N/A	$ N/A	N/A%
12-31-76	$47,647.06	$48,227.45	42.24%

* * *

VARIAN ASSOCIATES, INC. (VAR). Founded 1948. Headquarters: 611 Hansen Way, Palo Alto CA 94303. HIGH TECHNOLOGY MANUFACTURING. Varian produces a broad line of equipment, including electron tubes, analytical instruments, industrial equipment, and medical equipment.

Sales: $620.9 million (trend 14.4% a year).
Earnings: $21.65 million (trend 22.9% a year).
What happened to a $10,000 investment

Purchase Date	*Purchase Price*	*Price on 12-31-81*	*Dividends Paid*
12-31-71	$13.87	$30.25	$1,881.08
12-31-76	$15.25	$30.25	$1,318.03

Purchase Date	*Cap. Gains (− Losses)*	*Total Return*	*Rate of Return*
12-31-71	$11,801.80	$13,682.88	9.00%
12-31-76	$ 9,836.07	$11,154.10	16.17%

* * *

VARO, INC. (VRO). Founded 1946. Headquarters: 2203 W. Walnut St., Garland TX 75040. ELECTRONICS. Varo manufactures and sells electronic and electro-optical equipment to military and commercial markets. MAJOR SUBSIDIARIES, BRANDS: Varo Semiconductor, Inc.

Sales: $83.3 million (trend 3.5% a year).
Earnings: $6.58 million (trend −7.2% a year).
What happened to a $10,000 investment

Purchase Date	*Purchase Price*	*Price on 12-31-81*	*Dividends Paid*
12-31-71	$2.25	$8.25	$6,888.89
12-31-76	$8.75	$8.25	$1,657.14

Purchase Date	*Cap. Gains (− Losses)*	*Total Return*	*Rate of Return*
12-31-71	$26,666.67	$33,555.56	15.85%
12-31-76	$ −571.43	$ 1,085.71	2.08%

* * *

VEECO INSTRUMENTS INC. (VEE). Founded 1951. Headquarters: 515 Broad Hollow Rd., Melville NY 11747. ELECTRONICS. Veeco manufactures electronic power supplies, specialty power semiconductors, and industrial equipment. MAJOR SUBSIDIARIES, BRANDS: Lambda.

Sales: $111.1 million (trend 26.5% a year).
Earnings: $10.17 million (trend 33.8% a year).
What happened to a $10,000 investment

Purchase Date	*Purchase Price*	*Price on 12-31-81*	*Dividends Paid*
12-31-71	$2.16	$14.25	$4,292.57
12-31-76	$1.85	$14.25	$4,080.00

Purchase Date	*Cap. Gains (− Losses)*	*Total Return*	*Rate of Return*
12-31-71	$55,957.14	$60,249.71	21.52%
12-31-76	$66,950.00	$71,030.00	51.96%

* * *

THE VENDO CO. (VEN). Founded 1937. Headquarters: 10500 Barkley St., Overland Park KA 66212. VENDING MACHINES. Vendo manufactures and sells coin-operated vending machines; also produces some metal products. MAJOR SUBSIDIARIES, BRANDS: VCF Acceptance Corp.

Sales: $71.7 million (trend 1.4% a year).
Earnings: $−15.50 million.
What happened to a $10,000 investment

Purchase Date	*Purchase Price*	*Price on 12-31-81*	*Dividends Paid*
12-31-71	$12.25	$2.12	$816.33
12-31-76	$ 5.50	$2.12	$ 0.00

Purchase Date	*Cap. Gains (− Losses)*	*Total Return*	*Rate of Return*
12-31-71	$−8,265.31	$−7,448.98	−12.77%
12-31-76	$−6,136.36	$−6,136.36	−17.32%

* * *

VESTAUR SECURITIES, INC. (VES). Founded 1972. Headquarters: 1500 Chestnut St., Philadelphia PA 19102. INVESTMENT CO. Vestaur is a publicly traded bond fund.

* * *

VIACOM INTERNATIONAL INC. (VIA). Founded 1971. Headquarters: 1211 Ave. of the Americas, New York NY 10036. TELEVISION. Viacom is a communications company that distributes television programs and movies and also has interests in cable TV. MAJOR SUBSIDIARIES, BRANDS: Showtime (50 percent owned); Sonderling Broadcasting Corp.

Sales: $160.1 million (trend 32.7% a year).
Earnings: $15.03 million (trend 37.1% a year).
What happened to a $10,000 investment

Purchase Date	*Purchase Price*	*Price on 12-31-81*	*Dividends Paid*
12-31-71	$7.94	$24.25	$ 894.49
12-31-76	$5.12	$24.25	$1,385.37

Purchase Date	*Cap. Gains (− Losses)*	*Total Return*	*Rate of Return*
12-31-71	$20,551.18	$21,445.67	12.14%
12-31-76	$37,317.07	$38,702.44	37.25%

* * *

VIRGINIA ELECTRIC & POWER CO. (VEL). Founded 1909. Headquarters: 1 James River Plaza, Richmond VA 23261. UTILITY. Virginia Electric supplies electricity to the major portion of Virginia and to small parts of West Virginia and North Carolina. 10,000 employees.

Sales: $2,119.8 million (trend 15.3% a year).
Earnings: $184.33 million (trend 7.9% a year).
What happened to a $10,000 investment

Purchase Date	*Purchase Price*	*Price on 12-31-81*	*Dividends Paid*
12-31-71	$20.50	$11.75	$6,153.66
12-31-76	$15.37	$11.75	$4,386.99

Purchase Date	*Cap. Gains (− Losses)*	*Total Return*	*Rate of Return*
12-31-71	$−4,268.29	$1,885.37	1.74%
12-31-76	$−2,357.72	$2,029.27	3.76%

PROFILE: Here's the story of Virginia Electric's last decade in a nutshell. Earnings have been as flat as a pancake (a thin pancake at that). The stock price has been chopped in half. Return on equity has been pitiful, often in the neighborhood of 5 percent.

Some analysts saw reason for optimism entering the 1980s. Their hopes are based primarily on the company's changing fuel mix. While it once relied mainly on oil and paid OPEC through the nose for it, Virginia Electric now has brought four nuclear plants on-stream and reduced its dependence on oil. Regulators have also become more receptive to hearing about — and acting to ameliorate — the company's plight.

All that makes only a medium-sized reed to support hopes for substantial capital gains. However, one would need only a moderate capital gain to achieve a good total return in this stock, which was recently offering an 11-to-13 percent yield through annual dividends. Dividends have been paid each year since 1925. Lately, they have consumed well over half the company's profits.

The price / earnings ratio in recent months has been around 5 or 6. If you think the utilities, or Virginia Electric in particular, are due for a turnaround, you probably can't buy in much cheaper.

* * *

VISTA RESOURCES, INC. (SVE). Founded 1965. Headquarters: 350 Fifth Ave., New York NY 10001. **LEATHER.** Vista manufactures, distributes, and sells leather products.

Sales: $37.2 million (trend −10.7% a year).
Earnings: $.25 million (trend −16.4% a year).
What happened to a $10,000 investment

Purchase Date	*Purchase Price*	*Price on 12-31-81*	*Dividends Paid*
12-31-71	$12.13	$18.50	$1,520.04
12-31-76	$ 7.25	$18.50	$1,641.38

Purchase Date	*Cap. Gains (− Losses)*	*Total Return*	*Rate of Return*
12-31-71	$ 5,249.87	$ 6,769.91	5.31%
12-31-76	$15,517.24	$17,158.62	22.12%

* * *

VORNADO, INC. (VNO). Founded 1965. Headquarters: 174 Passaic St., Garfield NJ 07026. **RETAILING.** Vornado operates discount department stores in the eastern United States. It also runs three catalog showrooms. Since 1980 the company has closed forty-eight of its sixty Two Guys discount department stores. As of early 1982 twelve are still in operation. **MAJOR SUBSIDIARIES, BRANDS:** Sutton Place; Two Guys.

Sales: $591.5 million (trend −10.0% a year).
Earnings: $−3.56 million.
What happened to a $10,000 investment

Purchase Date	*Purchase Price*	*Price on 12-31-81*	*Dividends Paid*
12-31-71	$26.40	$12.12	$ 284.07
12-31-76	$ 5.75	$12.12	$1,304.35

Purchase Date	*Cap. Gains (− Losses)*	*Total Return*	*Rate of Return*
12-31-71	$−5,407.52	$−5,123.45	−6.93%
12-31-76	$ 11,086.96	$ 12,391.30	17.49%

* * *

VULCAN, INC. (VX). Founded 1923. Headquarters: Avenue E, Latrobe PA 15650. **FOUNDRY.** Vulcan produces molds for making ingots from molten metal. Through a subsidiary, Vulcan also designs and manufactures cranes. **MAJOR SUBSIDIARIES, BRANDS:** Hydro Carbide; Shepard Niles Crane & Hoist; Vulcan Engineering; Vulcan Mold and Iron; Westmoreland Plastics.

Sales: $121.6 million (trend 7.9% a year).
Earnings: $3.45 million (trend .9% a year).
What happened to a $10,000 investment

Purchase Date	*Purchase Price*	*Price on 12-31-81*	*Dividends Paid*
12-31-71	$4.75	$18.25	$10,836.84
12-31-76	$9.50	$18.25	$ 3,723.68

Purchase Date	*Cap. Gains (− Losses)*	*Total Return*	*Rate of Return*
12-31-71	$28,421.05	$39,257.89	17.29%
12-31-76	$ 9,210.53	$12,934.21	18.06%

* * *

VULCAN MATERIALS CO. (VMC). Founded 1910. Headquarters: 1 Metroplex Dr., Birmingham AL 35209. **CONSTRUCTION, CHEMICALS & METALS.** Vulcan Materials produces, distributes, and sells construction materials, industrial and agricultural chemicals, recovered metals, steel and aluminum scrap.

Sales: $754.0 million (trend 17.8% a year).
Earnings: $69.86 million (trend 20.6% a year).
What happened to a $10,000 investment

Purchase Date	*Purchase Price*	*Price on 12-31-81*	*Dividends Paid*
12-31-71	$12.75	$54.25	$9,443.14
12-31-76	$26.50	$54.25	$3,094.34

Purchase Date	*Cap. Gains (− Losses)*	*Total Return*	*Rate of Return*
12-31-71	$32,549.02	$41,992.16	17.92%
12-31-76	$10,471.70	$13,566.04	18.70%

W

WICOR, INC. (WIC). Founded 1852. Headquarters: 626 E. Wisconsin Ave., Milwaukee WI 53202. GAS. WICOR is the largest natural gas distributor in Wisconsin. MAJOR SUBSIDIARIES, BRANDS: WEXCO.

Sales: $450.3 million (trend 17.9% a year).
Earnings: $11.45 million (trend 7.5% a year).
What happened to a $10,000 investment

Purchase Date	*Purchase Price*	*Price on 12-31-81*	*Dividends Paid*
12-31-71	$N/A	$18.50	$ N/A
12-31-76	$20.50	$18.50	$4,741.46

Purchase Date	*Cap. Gains (– Losses)*	*Total Return*	*Rate of Return*
12-31-71	$ N/A	$ N/A	N/A%
12-31-76	$–975.61	$3,765.85	6.60%

* * *

WACHOVIA CORP. (WACHOV). Founded 1968. Headquarters: 301 N. Main St., Winston-Salem NC 27101. BANKING. Wachovia Corp. is the holding company for Wachovia Bank and Trust Co., a national banking association with close to 200 offices in various communities in North Carolina. Engaged in retail, commercial, and corporate banking.

Sales: $551.7 million (trend 17.6% a year).
Earnings: $54.25 million (trend 9.4% a year).
What happened to a $10,000 investment

Purchase Date	*Purchase Price*	*Price on 12-31-81*	*Dividends Paid*
12-31-71	$32.25	$26.25	$2,293.02
12-31-76	$21.25	$26.25	$1,854.12

Purchase Date	*Cap. Gains (– Losses)*	*Total Return*	*Rate of Return*
12-31-71	$–1,860.47	$ 432.56	.42%
12-31-76	$ 2,352.94	$4,207.06	7.28%

* * *

WACHOVIA REALTY INVESTMENTS (WRI). Founded 1969. Headquarters: 301 N. Main St., Winston-Salem NC 27102. REAL ESTATE. Wachovia is a former real estate investment trust (REIT); in recent years it has owned and managed certain real estate properties acquired during its years as a REIT. Wachovia has agreed to be acquired by Old Stone Corp. but the merger had not yet taken place as of early 1982.

Sales: $11.1 million (trend –2.0% a year).
Earnings: $1.25 million.
What happened to a $10,000 investment

Purchase Date	*Purchase Price*	*Price on 12-31-81*	*Dividends Paid*
12-31-71	$32.12	$7.50	$2,244.36
12-31-76	$ 4.12	$7.50	$ 0.00

Purchase Date	*Cap. Gains (– Losses)*	*Total Return*	*Rate of Return*
12-31-71	$–7,665.37	$–5,421.01	–7.51%
12-31-76	$ 8,181.82	$ 8,181.82	12.70%

* * *

WACKENHUT CORP. (WAK). Founded 1954. Headquarters: 3280 Ponce De Leon Blvd., Coral Gables FL 33134. SECURITY. This organization is involved in security and investigations operations worldwide.

Sales: $177.5 million (trend 11.3% a year).
Earnings: $3.86 million (trend 9.7% a year).
What happened to a $10,000 investment

Purchase Date	*Purchase Price*	*Price on 12-31-81*	*Dividends Paid*
12-31-71	$12.01	$12.75	$2,232.71
12-31-76	$ 4.61	$12.75	$3,585.06

Purchase Date	*Cap. Gains (– Losses)*	*Total Return*	*Rate of Return*
12-31-71	$ 616.21	$ 2,848.92	2.54%
12-31-76	$17,655.13	$21,240.19	25.59%

* * *

WAINOCO OIL CORP. (WOL). Founded 1949. Headquarters: 1200 Smith St., Houston TX 77002. OIL, GAS. Wainoco is a small international oil company formerly headquartered in Canada. It explores for and produces oil and natural gas in the United States, Canada and Australia.

Sales: $33.5 million (trend 60.9% a year).
Earnings: $7.05 million (trend 63.9% a year).
What happened to a $10,000 investment

Purchase Date	*Purchase Price*	*Price on 12-31-81*	*Dividends Paid*
12-31-71	$3.12	$20.25	$1,088.00
12-31-76	$3.12	$20.25	$1,088.00

Purchase Date	*Cap. Gains (− Losses)*	*Total Return*	*Rate of Return*
12-31-71	$54,800.00	$55,888.00	20.75%
12-31-76	$54,800.00	$55,888.00	45.80%

* * *

WAL-MART STORES, INC. (WMT). Founded 1969. Headquarters: 702 S.W. Eighth St., PO Box 116, Bentonville AR 72712. **RETAILER.** Wal-Mart operates a chain of discount department stores, recently totaling almost 500 stores in 13 states. It plans to have some 700 stores by 1986. 22,000 employees. **MAJOR SUBSIDIARIES, BRANDS:** Wal-Mart Discount City.

Sales: $1,643.2 million (trend 37.0% a year).
Earnings: $55.68 million (trend 36.6% a year).
What happened to a $10,000 investment

Purchase Date	*Purchase Price*	*Price on 12-31-81*	*Dividends Paid*
12-31-71	$5.03	$42.50	$1,296.89
12-31-76	$7.75	$42.50	$ 696.77

Purchase Date	*Cap. Gains (− Losses)*	*Total Return*	*Rate of Return*
12-31-71	$74,472.05	$75,768.94	23.97%
12-31-76	$44,838.71	$45,535.48	40.90%

PROFILE: Wal-Mart has been one of the skyrocket success stories among retailers in recent years. From nowhere, it's jumped to thirty-third (in 1980) among retailers, by *Fortune*'s tally. Its return on equity has been spectacular, often above 25 percent. And its growth has been red-hot.

What's the secret of all this success? Big stores (often the biggest in their communities) and a fast-growing market (the South), in part. But it goes beyond that. *The Wall Street Journal* described the revival-meeting spirit of a Wal-Mart corporate gathering. Part of the picture was Chairman Sam Walton jumping up and bellowing, "Who's number one?" in cheerleader fashion. (The answer, of course: Wal-Mart.) Walton's personal involvement in visiting stores and listening to employees' gripes and suggestions is another factor. "Some of our best ideas have come from clerks and stockboys," Walton told the *Journal.*

Beyond these intangibles, Wal-Mart has prospered by locating its stores primarily in small towns, thus avoiding the heavy competition that keeps profit margins very slim in more urban areas. Wal-Mart's margin is usually above 3 percent, eye-poppingly high for a retailer, particularly a discount retailer.

* * *

WALGREEN CO. (WAG). Founded 1909. Headquarters: 200 Wilmot Rd., Deerfield IL 60015. **DRUG STORES.** Walgreen is a large, well-known drug store chain, with more than 900 stores, mainly in the Midwest and South. It has diversified into restaurant operations, and — in Mexico — into retailing and manufacturing as well. **MAJOR SUBSIDIARIES, BRANDS:** Walgreen drug stores; Wag's restaurants; Sanborns (47-percent-owned Mexican subsidiary involved in restaurants, manufacturing, and retailing.)

Sales: $1,743.5 million (trend 8.3% a year).
Earnings: $42.13 million (trend 25.0% a year).
What happened to a $10,000 investment

Purchase Date	*Purchase Price*	*Price on 12-31-81*	*Dividends Paid*
12-31-71	$26.87	$48.62	$4,450.23
12-31-76	$17.87	$48.62	$3,893.71

Purchase Date	*Cap. Gains (− Losses)*	*Total Return*	*Rate of Return*
12-31-71	$ 8,093.02	$12,543.26	8.47%
12-31-76	$17,202.80	$21,096.50	25.47%

* * *

HIRAM WALKER RESOURCES LTD. (HWR). Founded 1955. Headquarters: 1 First Canadian Pl., Toronto, Ont. M5X 1C5 Canada. **LIQUOR, NATURAL GAS.** Hiram Walker derives most of its revenues from liquor sales, but is also actively engaged in natural gas (and to a lesser extent, oil) production and distribution. **MAJOR SUBSIDIARIES, BRANDS:** Ballantine's (scotch); Canadian Club; Courvoisier (cognac); Kahlua (liqueur); Consumers' Gas (distributes natural gas in parts of southern Ontario, southern Quebec, and northern New York state); Home Oil.

Sales: $2,386.0 million (trend 39.2% a year).
Earnings: $184.29 million (trend 31.9% a year).
What happened to a $10,000 investment

Purchase Date	*Purchase Price*	*Price on 12-31-81*	*Dividends Paid*
12-31-71	$15.32	$19.37	$4,250.83
12-31-76	$10.41	$19.37	$3,538.38

Purchase Date	*Cap. Gains (– Losses)*	*Total Return*	*Rate of Return*
12-31-71	$2,648.37	$ 6,899.20	5.39%
12-31-76	$8,613.54	$12,151.92	17.24%

* * *

WALLACE COMPUTER SERVICES, INC. (WCS). Founded 1908. Headquarters: 4600 W. Roosevelt Rd., Hillside IL 60162. **BUSINESS FORMS, PRINTING.** Wallace is a leading supplier of business forms, particularly those designed for computer use. Also prints catalogs, manuals, textbooks, and other materials. Changed name in 1981 from Wallace Business Forms.

Sales: $166.2 million (trend 18.2% a year).
Earnings: $12.81 million (trend 23.5% a year).
What happened to a $10,000 investment

Purchase Date	*Purchase Price*	*Price on 12-31-81*	*Dividends Paid*
12-31-71	$11.81	$33.25	$2,830.90
12-31-76	$10.56	$33.25	$2,026.04

Purchase Date	*Cap. Gains (– Losses)*	*Total Return*	*Rate of Return*
12-31-71	$18,148.15	$20,979.05	11.97%
12-31-76	$21,479.29	$23,505.33	27.36%

* * *

JIM WALTER CORP. (JWC). Founded 1955. Headquarters: 1500 N. Dale Mabry Hwy., Tampa FL 33607. **BUILDING MATERIALS.** Jim Walter is a major supplier of building materials and is also a homebuilder. It has diversified into coal mining, other mining, operation of a savings and loan, and jewelry wholesaling and retailing, among other operations. 23,000 employees. **MAJOR SUBSIDIARIES, BRANDS:** Brentwood Savings and Loan Association.

Sales: $2,017.1 million (trend 10.2% a year).
Earnings: $18.82 million (trend −17.4% a year).
What happened to a $10,000 investment

Purchase Date	*Purchase Price*	*Price on 12-31-81*	*Dividends Paid*
12-31-71	$37.25	$19.37	$3,177.18
12-31-76	$39.12	$19.37	$2,063.90

Purchase Date	*Cap. Gains (– Losses)*	*Total Return*	*Rate of Return*
12-31-71	$−4,798.66	$−1,621.48	−1.75%
12-31-76	$−5,047.92	$−2,984.03	−6.84%

PROFILE: This company bears the name of its founder and still chairman, who first got into business by borrowing $500 from his father in 1946 to buy an uncompleted house and reselling the building to a passerby three days later.

A lot of houses have come and gone since then, but the company seems still to bear the stamp of some impulsiveness on Walter's part. What he has put together looks like a hodgepodge. It was, though, a very profitable hodgepodge in the early 1970s, when return on equity used to be consistently above 25 percent.

Lately, return on equity has deteriorated (it was about 11 percent in 1980), but that's not surprising, considering that the company's main field — building and building materials — has been in a prolonged and severe slump. Aggravating the problem has been the poor performance of coal mining operations. That segment of the business, while still not good, is improving, and many analysts remain optimistic about the outlook for coal (notwithstanding the fact that they were prematurely optimistic, beginning in 1973).

Through its bad times, the company has remained profitable, and has paid dividends every year since incorporation. The yield has recently been in the 5-to-8 percent range. The stock price was down in the early 1980s, but the p / e ratio was still around 11; check it before you consider a purchase here.

* * *

WANG LABORATORIES, INC. (WAN, American Stock Exchange). Founded 1955. Headquarters: 1 Industrial Ave., Lowell MA 01851. **WORD PROCESSORS, MINICOMPUTERS.** Wang is a leading manufacturer of word processors and other advanced office equipment, minicomputers, and medium-sized computers. 12,000 employees.

Sales: $856.4 million (trend 56.1% a year).
Earnings: $78.07 million (trend 70.1% a year).
What happened to a $10,000 investment

Purchase Date	*Purchase Price*	*Price on 12-31-81*	*Dividends Paid*
12-31-71	$4.22	$33.25	$ 779.29
12-31-76	$1.53	$33.25	$2,008.16

Purchase Date	*Cap. Gains (– Losses)*	*Total Return*	*Rate of Return*
12-31-71	$ 68,698.22	$ 69,477.51	23.03%
12-31-76	$207,142.86	$209,151.02	85.42%

PROFILE: Genius. That's the only appropriate word to describe An Wang, the company's founder, president, and chairman; born in China, educated at Harvard and M.I.T., and credited with a long list of innovations in computer and word-processor technology.

Investing in a company founded and run by a genius can involve risks (ask people who invested in Polaroid at its height). What happens after Dr. Wang retires? Will his son and the many talented people he has gathered around him be able to maintain that special spark? Another issue is that the Wang family owns close to half the stock. A big outstanding block like that always creates the potential for volatility. Institutions own a major portion of the remaining shares, creating further risk of an individual being buffeted in the winds generated by big block trades.

A further drawback to this stock is the high price / earnings ratio, recently 20 or a bit above. When a company's excellence is this well recognized, you pay a price predicated on the general expectation of success. The company must do even better than expected for you to make a significant profit.

One more factor adding to volatility is the fact that the company is highly leveraged — though not so highly as it was a few years ago. Debt recently was a bit under half of total capital.

Against all these factors that add to risk, you must weigh the company's absolutely splendid record for financial growth and technological innovation. Revenues, less than $50 million a year in the early 1970s, should surpass $1 billion in the early 1980s. Profits were about $3 million in 1972, about $78 million in 1980. Most people who bought the stock a decade ago have about a sevenfold gain on their holdings. Some, who exercised perfect timing and bought in the market slump of 1974, have seen the value of their shares go up by a factor close to 50.

* * *

WARNACO INC. (WRC). Founded 1893. Headquarters: 350 Lafayette St., Bridgeport CT 06602. **CLOTHING.** Warnaco produces men's and women's clothing under a number of well-known labels; also has a sideline in sporting goods. **MAJOR SUBSIDIARIES, BRANDS:** Warner's undergarments; White Stag sportswear; Hathaway, Puritan, and Thane (men's shirts); Edelweiss ski clothing; Speedo swim suits; Hirsch Weis sports equipment.

Sales: $465.0 million (trend 6.0% a year).
Earnings: $16.23 million (trend 57.3% a year).
What happened to a $10,000 investment

Purchase Date	*Purchase Price*	*Price on 12-31-81*	*Dividends Paid*
12-31-71	$18.57	$27.25	$2,901.28
12-31-76	$ 6.90	$27.25	$3,113.79

Purchase Date	*Cap. Gains (− Losses)*	*Total Return*	*Rate of Return*
12-31-71	$ 4,673.07	$ 7,574.35	5.80%
12-31-76	$29,465.49	$32,579.28	33.61%

* * *

WARNER COMMUNICATIONS, INC. (WCI). Founded 1961. Headquarters: 75 Rockefeller Plaza, New York NY 10019. **ENTERTAINMENT.** Warner is a major factor in several phases of entertainment, including movies, home video, records, tapes, books, toys, and games. 8,000 employees. **MAJOR SUBSIDIARIES, BRANDS:** Warner Brothers (movies and records); Elektra, Asylum, Atlantic (records); Warner-Amex (cable television — joint venture with American Express); Warner Books; Atari (electronic games); Franklin Mint (memorabilia); Knickerbocker Toy Co.; *Mad Magazine;* Independent News (distributor of paperbacks and magazines); Cosmos soccer team. Owns about 8 percent of Harcourt Brace Jovanovich (diversified publishing company).

Sales: $2,059.4 million (trend 25.0% a year).
Earnings: $137.09 million (trend 29.4% a year).
What happened to a $10,000 investment

Purchase Date	*Purchase Price*	*Price on 12-31-81*	*Dividends Paid*
12-31-71	$8.79	$54.87	$2,890.95
12-31-76	$7.52	$54.87	$2,629.61

Purchase Date	*Cap. Gains (− Losses)*	*Total Return*	*Rate of Return*
12-31-71	$52,432.39	$55,323.33	20.64%
12-31-76	$62,935.03	$65,564.64	49.85%

PROFILE: From Bugs Bunny to Linda Ronstadt, from cable TV to big-grossing pictures like *The Exorcist* and *Superman II,* Warner Communications has the entertainment world covered. Like Columbia Pictures and MCA, it has been riding high in recent years. Profit margins in this business can be high. Warner's return on equity was above 20 percent every year from 1976 to 1979 (it was above 30 percent in 1979), and it just missed the 20 percent mark in 1980. The trend in profits has generally been upward, though with slips in 1975 and 1980.

This entertainment conglomerate was fashioned out of humble roots. Entrepreneur Steve Ross started in his father-in-law's funeral parlor business. He built that into a conglomerate of funeral homes, parking lots, and building maintenance operations, most of which survives under the name National Kinney. The big jump came in 1969, when Kinney scooped up the moribund Warner Brothers. Ross started accumulating more glamorous businesses to go with Warner, and in 1971 he split the corporation in two, shucking off the less glamorous parts to Kinney. A series of acquisitions has given the conglomerate its present glossy appearance; the latest hit was Atari, maker of the popular Asteroids video game.

The balance sheet here is strong, with debt recently only about 20 percent of capital. (It's been trimmed substantially since the mid-1970s.) Dividends have been paid every year, but afford only a modest yield. The p / e ratio tends to be high; recently, it surged above 20. The p / e tends to be volatile, though (it was as low as 3 in 1979, when investors correctly anticipated that the company couldn't duplicate the great year it was having). So, keep an eye on the p / e. Timing is especially important in buying stocks in a volatile field like entertainment.

* * *

WARNER-LAMBERT CO. (WLA). Founded 1920. Headquarters: 201 Tabor Rd., Morris Plains NJ 07950. **DRUGS, CONSUMER PRODUCTS.** Warner-Lambert is a major producer of prescription and over-the-counter drugs. Also makes medical instruments and a variety of consumer products, including gum, shaving supplies, pet food, and bakery goods. 61,000 employees. **MAJOR SUBSIDIARIES, BRANDS:** Parke-Davis, Deseret, Warner / Chilcott, and Texas Pharmacal (prescription drugs); Listerine, Bromo-Seltzer (over-the-counter drugs); American Chicle (Chiclets, Dentyne, Trident gums); Schick razors and blades; Tetra fish food; Entenmann's bakery.

Sales: $3,479.2 million (trend 10.3% a year).
Earnings: $193.40 million (trend .4% a year).
What happened to a $10,000 investment

Purchase Date	*Purchase Price*	*Price on 12-31-81*	*Dividends Paid*
12-31-71	$39.87	$22.25	$2,584.95
12-31-76	$30.87	$22.25	$2,008.10

Purchase Date	*Cap. Gains (− Losses)*	*Total Return*	*Rate of Return*
12-31-71	$−4,420.06	$−1,835.11	−2.01%
12-31-76	$−2,793.52	$ −785.43	−1.62%

PROFILE: While the profits of pure pharmaceutical companies tend to go up in an unbroken straight line, Warner-Lambert's tend to bump and run with the economy. The company has a long list of consumer products (see above), constituting about 44 percent of sales in 1980. Over-the-counter remedies like Bromo-Seltzer and Listerine accounted for another 22 percent of sales, leaving the prescription drug business as barely over a third of the total.

Now, hankering after higher profit margins, Warner-Lambert plans to re-emphasize prescription drugs. But analysts aren't sure whether the company will be able to pull off that change of emphasis. Major research and development efforts in the pharmaceutical field certainly can't be mounted overnight.

Accordingly, the stock sells at a multiple (from 7 to 10 in 1980) more typical of a consumer-products company than a drug company. (The p / e multiple for 1981 wasn't meaningful, since earnings were depressed, in part by the sale of American Optical, a lackluster producer of vision-care equipment.)

The dividend yield in recent years has ranged from 5 to 8 percent. Dividends have been paid yearly since 1926.

* * *

WASHINGTON GAS LIGHT CO. (WGL). Founded 1848. Headquarters: 1100 H St. N.W., Washington DC 20080. **NATURAL GAS.** This gas distributor services Washington, D.C., and some surrounding areas in Maryland and Virginia.

Sales: $464.0 million (trend 14.6% a year).
Earnings: $15.42 million (trend 12.0% a year).
What happened to a $10,000 investment

Purchase Date	*Purchase Price*	*Price on 12-31-81*	*Dividends Paid*
12-31-71	$25.75	$32.25	$8,166.99
12-31-76	$21.75	$32.25	$5,393.10

Purchase Date	*Cap. Gains (− Losses)*	*Total Return*	*Rate of Return*
12-31-71	$2,524.27	$10,691.26	7.54%
12-31-76	$4,827.59	$10,220.69	15.12%

* * *

WASHINGTON NATIONAL CORP. (WNT). Founded 1969. Headquarters: 1630 Chicago Ave., Evanston IL 60201. INSURANCE. This corporation is the parent company to Washington National Insurance Co., a seller of life and health insurance and annuities.

Sales: $857.6 million (trend 14.9% a year).
Earnings: $34.31 million (trend 21.3% a year).
What happened to a $10,000 investment

Purchase Date	*Purchase Price*	*Price on 12-31-81*	*Dividends Paid*
12-31-71	$18.80	$19.62	$3,566.67
12-31-76	$12.83	$19.62	$3,412.99

Purchase Date	*Cap. Gains (− Losses)*	*Total Return*	*Rate of Return*
12-31-71	$ 438.83	$4,005.50	3.43%
12-31-76	$5,292.21	$8,705.19	13.34%

* * *

WASHINGTON WATER POWER CO. (WWP). Founded 1889. Headquarters: E. 1411 Mission Ave., Spokane WA 99202. UTILITY. Provides electricity and gas to north-central and eastern Washington, and to parts of northern Idaho.

Sales: $290.5 million (trend 17.1% a year).
Earnings: $23.62 million (trend 6.5% a year).
What happened to a $10,000 investment

Purchase Date	*Purchase Price*	*Price on 12-31-81*	*Dividends Paid*
12-31-71	$21.87	$17.50	$8,100.57
12-31-76	$25.62	$17.50	$3,988.29

Purchase Date	*Cap. Gains (− Losses)*	*Total Return*	*Rate of Return*
12-31-71	$−2,000.00	$6,100.57	4.88%
12-31-76	$−3,170.73	$ 817.56	1.58%

* * *

WASTE MANAGEMENT, INC. (WMX). Founded 1968. Headquarters: 900 Jorie Blvd., Oak Brook IL 60521. GARBAGE DISPOSAL. Waste Management is an industry leader in the disposal of conventional garbage and of toxic wastes (not including nuclear wastes). It also provides street-cleaning and sanitation services abroad, particularly to Saudi Arabia and Argentina. 5,000 employees.

Sales: $560.1 million (trend 28.9% a year).
Earnings: $54.85 million (trend 44.7% a year).
What happened to a $10,000 investment

Purchase Date	*Purchase Price*	*Price on 12-31-81*	*Dividends Paid*
12-31-71	$4.47	$33.87	$2,582.61
12-31-76	$4.50	$33.87	$2,455.56

Purchase Date	*Cap. Gains (− Losses)*	*Total Return*	*Rate of Return*
12-31-71	$65,745.34	$68,327.95	22.85%
12-31-76	$65,277.78	$67,733.33	50.70%

PROFILE: Waste Management is what Wall Street calls a "concept stock." The concept, in this case, is simple: The disposal of solid wastes, and toxic wastes in particular, will continue to be a thorn in society's side. As the problem becomes more acute, the companies that have the facilities to solve (or at least deal with) the problem will experience a continuing surge in demand.

Responding to this logic, several waste disposal firms had big run-ups in their stock prices at the end of the past decade. As the largest and most profitable firm in the field, Waste Management did particularly well. The stock took off from a 1978 low of less than $6 to reach $41 a share in 1981, before settling back. The price / earnings ratio recently has been a whistle-provoking 15 to 25.

Is the stock really worth that much? Two diametrically opposed views appeared recently in *Financial World* and *Forbes.* Enthused *Financial World:* "As the world turns increasingly to Waste Management for help cleaning up everyone's foul and poisonous act, Wall Street's optimism seems fully warranted." But Jeff Blyskal, writing in *Forbes,* took a more jaundiced view, pointing out that recycling of chemicals will take away some of the projected market, and arguing that Waste Management's technology is, as one analyst put it, "on the technological bottom rung." Most of the waste, suggests Blyskal, goes into landfills.

Buying stocks with high p / e ratios can be risky, as has been stressed throughout this book. It's arguable that a company with special, advanced technology (e.g., Schlumberger) deserves a premium ratio. But it would seem to be straining to make that argument for Waste Management.

Dividends were started in 1976, but the yield remains small.

* * *

WATKINS-JOHNSON CO. (WJ). Founded 1957. Headquarters: 3333 Hillview Ave., Palo Alto CA 94304. ELECTRONICS. Watkins-Johnson designs and manufactures advanced electronics systems and devices.

Sales: $132.8 million (trend 14.1% a year).
Earnings: $7.09 million (trend .7% a year).
What happened to a $10,000 investment

Purchase Date	*Purchase Price*	*Price on 12-31-81*	*Dividends Paid*
12-31-71	$34.25	$29.25	$817.52
12-31-76	$23.87	$29.25	$871.20

Purchase Date	*Cap. Gains (− Losses)*	*Total Return*	*Rate of Return*
12-31-71	$−1,459.85	$−642.34	−.66%
12-31-76	$ 2,251.31	$ 3,122.51	5.59%

* * *

WAYNE-GOSSARD CORP. (WKT). Founded 1891. Headquarters: 701 Market St., Suite 922, Chattanooga TN 37402. APPAREL. Wayne-Gossard is a manufacturer of underwear, sportswear, knitwear, and hosiery. MAJOR SUBSIDIARIES, BRANDS: G's; Signal Knitting Mills; Heritage Sportswear.

Sales: $59.8 million (trend 3.3% a year).
Earnings: $1.50 million (trend 23.8% a year).
What happened to a $10,000 investment

Purchase Date	*Purchase Price*	*Price on 12-31-81*	*Dividends Paid*
12-31-71	$10.37	$9.25	$4,240.96
12-31-76	$ 7.37	$9.25	$2,115.25

Purchase Date	*Cap. Gains (− Losses)*	*Total Return*	*Rate of Return*
12-31-71	$−1,084.34	$3,156.63	2.78%
12-31-76	$ 2,542.37	$4,657.63	7.95%

* * *

WEAN UNITED, INC. (WID). Founded 1929. Headquarters: 948 Fort Duquesne Blvd., Pittsburgh PA 15222. INDUSTRIAL MACHINERY. Wean produces heavy machinery for the steel industry.

Sales: $262.1 million (trend −3.2% a year).
Earnings: $2.14 million (trend −29.3% a year).
What happened to a $10,000 investment

Purchase Date	*Purchase Price*	*Price on 12-31-81*	*Dividends Paid*
12-31-71	$5.50	$4.62	$1,545.45
12-31-76	$4.62	$4.62	$1,837.84

Purchase Date	*Cap. Gains (− Losses)*	*Total Return*	*Rate of Return*
12-31-71	$−1,590.91	$ −45.45	−.05%
12-31-76	$ .00	$1,837.84	3.43%

* * *

WEBB (DEL E.) CORP. (WBB). Founded 1946. Headquarters: 3800 N. Central Ave., Phoenix AZ 85012. HOTELS, CASINOS. This organization owns and operates hotels and casinos in Nevada and is also involved in real estate development. MAJOR SUBSIDIARIES, BRANDS: Sahara Hotel; Mint Hotel.

Sales: $486.0 million (trend 11.2% a year).
Earnings: $4.05 million (trend 5.1% a year).
What happened to a $10,000 investment

Purchase Date	*Purchase Price*	*Price on 12-31-81*	*Dividends Paid*
12-31-71	$8.50	$6.87	$882.35
12-31-76	$8.87	$6.87	$845.07

Purchase Date	*Cap. Gains (− Losses)*	*Total Return*	*Rate of Return*
12-31-71	$−1,911.76	$−1,029.41	−1.08%
12-31-76	$−2,253.52	$−1,408.45	−2.99%

* * *

WEIS MARKETS, INC. (WMK). Founded 1924. Headquarters: 1000 S. Second St., Sunbury PA 17801. SUPERMARKETS. Weis Markets operates a chain of supermarkets in the Northeast.

Sales: $684.8 million (trend 13.5% a year).
Earnings: $33.09 million (trend 16.8% a year).
What happened to a $10,000 investment

Purchase Date	*Purchase Price*	*Price on 12-31-81*	*Dividends Paid*
12-31-71	$16.83	$37.50	$3,401.19
12-31-76	$17.00	$37.50	$2,266.67

Purchase Date	*Cap. Gains (− Losses)*	*Total Return*	*Rate of Return*
12-31-71	$12,277.23	$15,678.42	9.89%
12-31-76	$12,058.82	$14,325.49	19.46%

* * *

WELLS FARGO & CO. (WFC). Founded 1852, bank incorporated in 1899, current corporation incorporated in 1968. Headquarters: 420 Montgomery St., San Francisco CA 94104. **BANK.** Wells Fargo is a holding company for the Wells Fargo Bank, approximately the twelfth largest bank in the United States and the third largest in California. The parent corporation has sidelines in insurance, equipment leasing, and financial services. 17,000 employees. **MAJOR SUBSIDIARIES, BRANDS:** Wells Fargo Bank, N.A.

Sales: $2,545.5 million (trend 24.1% a year).
Earnings: $121.74 million (trend 19.8% a year).
What happened to a $10,000 investment

Purchase Date	*Purchase Price*	*Price on 12-31-81*	*Dividends Paid*
12-31-71	$20.69	$25.50	$6,160.73
12-31-76	$27.25	$25.50	$2,965.14

Purchase Date	*Cap. Gains (– Losses)*	*Total Return*	*Rate of Return*
12-31-71	$ 2,326.28	$8,487.01	6.34%
12-31-76	$ –642.20	$2,322.94	4.27%

PROFILE: Wells Fargo gets the prize for most romantic name among American banks. It hasn't gotten top prizes in too many other banking categories, though.

A strong point here is consumer recognition; the bank's stagecoach symbol is well known, and its name is instantly recognizable. Capitalizing on this asset, the bank has done well at attracting consumer deposits, including savings accounts. Further along this line, it made something of a specialty of mortgage lending — until recently. High interest rates have recently burned those institutions (such as the savings and loans, and, to a lesser extent, Wells Fargo) that had a high proportion of their assets invested in long-term fixed-return vehicles like mortgages. Now Wells Fargo has de-emphasized mortgages and re-emphasized commercial loans. But in that field it faces tough regional competition from Bank of America and Security Pacific, among others.

Wells Fargo's growth rates have been somewhat above average for a bank, but profitability has been no better than average. Return on assets over the past decade has ranged from about $0.40 to about $0.70 per $100.

Dividends have been paid yearly since 1936. The yield in recent years has ranged from about 5 to 7½ percent.

* * *

WELLS FARGO MORTGAGE & EQUITY TRUST (WFM). Founded 1970. Headquarters: 475 Sansome St., San Francisco CA 94111. **REAL ESTATE.** This real estate investment trust (REIT) mixes debt (mortgage) and equity (participation) investments in fairly equal proportions. The majority of investments are in office buildings or industrial buildings.

Sales: $37.1 million (trend 19.8% a year).
Earnings: $11.94 million (trend 46.3% a year).
What happened to a $10,000 investment

Purchase Date	*Purchase Price*	*Price on 12-31-81*	*Dividends Paid*
12-31-71	$22.25	$22.37	$5,748.31
12-31-76	$ 9.62	$22.37	$6,742.86

Purchase Date	*Cap. Gains (– Losses)*	*Total Return*	*Rate of Return*
12-31-71	$ 56.18	$ 5,804.49	4.68%
12-31-76	$13,246.75	$19,989.61	24.56%

* * *

WENDY'S INTERNATIONAL, INC. (WEN). Founded 1969. Headquarters: 4288 W. Dublin-Granville Rd., Dublin OH 43017. **FAST FOOD RESTAURANTS.** Wendy's owns roughly 500 Wendy's Old Fashioned Hamburgers restaurants in the United States and abroad; receives franchise revenue from approximately 1,500 more such outlets.

Sales: $347.0 million (trend 63.4% a year).
Earnings: $30.10 million (trend 58.7% a year).
What happened to a $10,000 investment

Purchase Date	*Purchase Price*	*Price on 12-31-81*	*Dividends Paid*
12-31-71	$N/A	$14.12	$ N/A
12-31-76	$ 6.91	$14.12	$1,433.45

Purchase Date	*Cap. Gains (– Losses)*	*Total Return*	*Rate of Return*
12-31-71	$ N/A	$ N/A	N/A%
12-31-76	$10,451.97	$11,885.42	16.96%

* * *

WEST CO. (WST). Founded 1923. Headquarters: W. Bridge St., Phoenixville PA 19460. **PHARMACEUTICAL PACKAGING.** West Co. manufactures packaging parts and machinery for the pharmaceutical, hospital supply, cosmetics, and beverage industries.

Sales: $148.2 million (trend 23.2% a year).
Earnings: $9.88 million (trend 27.0% a year).
What happened to a $10,000 investment

Purchase Date	*Purchase Price*	*Price on 12-31-81*	*Dividends Paid*
12-31-71	$11.62	$38.25	$2,209.03
12-31-76	$11.50	$38.25	$1,747.83

Purchase Date	*Cap. Gains (– Losses)*	*Total Return*	*Rate of Return*
12-31-71	$22,903.23	$25,112.26	13.38%
12-31-76	$23,260.87	$25,008.70	28.48%

* * *

WEST POINT-PEPPERELL, INC. (WPM). Founded 1955. Headquarters: 400 W. Tenth St., West Point GA 31833. **TEXTILES.** The company makes fabrics for sheets, towels, clothing, carpeting, and rugs. 23,000 employees. **MAJOR SUBSIDIARIES, BRANDS:** Alamac; Cabin Crafts; Georgian; Martex; Lady Pepperell; Pepperell; Vellux; Walter.

Sales: $1,221.5 million (trend 12.4% a year).
Earnings: $41.05 million (trend 10.0% a year).
What happened to a $10,000 investment

Purchase Date	*Purchase Price*	*Price on 12-31-81*	*Dividends Paid*
12-31-71	$11.31	$22.87	$9,812.15
12-31-76	$20.37	$22.87	$3,386.50

Purchase Date	*Cap. Gains (– Losses)*	*Total Return*	*Rate of Return*
12-31-71	$10,220.99	$20,033.15	11.62%
12-31-76	$ 1,226.99	$ 4,613.50	7.88%

PROFILE: West Point-Pepperell is one of the country's larger fabric makers and one of the fastest-growing. It had a record year in 1980, and a decent year in 1981. Why, then, was its stock selling in 1980 and 1981 for a miserable 3 to 5 times earnings?

Short answer: Wall Street just doesn't have much enthusiasm for this company or its industry. Textile and apparel companies in general can't help but bend with the winds of the economy. And profit margins in this industry, while fatter than in retailing, still aren't large. Fabric users always have plenty of suppliers to choose from — and to haggle over price with.

If you chart the return on equity at West Point-Pepperell over the last few years, the chart will look like a zigzag stitch. Some years it rises above 10 percent, and some years it falls below. That's not a very exciting performance.

The attractions here are well-known brand names (Georgian carpets, Martex towels, etc.), a high dividend (with a yield recently up around 8 percent), and the simple fact that the stock is cheap. Dividends have been paid by this company or its predecessor companies each year since 1888, and have been increased each year since 1977.

Household fabrics (mainly towels, sheets, and carpeting) account for more than half of sales and profits; competition is tougher, and margins slimmer, in industrial fabrics and fabrics for the clothing industry.

* * *

WESTCOAST TRANSMISSION CO. LTD. (WTC). Founded 1949. Headquarters: 1333 W. Georgia St., Vancouver, B.C. V6E 3K9 Canada. **GAS TRANSMISSION.** Operates gas pipelines that distribute natural gas in western Canada and the northwest United States. Also has (relatively small) gas and oil production activities. **MAJOR SUBSIDIARIES, BRANDS:** Westcoast Petroleum (58 percent owned).

Sales: $1,019.3 million (trend 18.7% a year).
Earnings: $40.73 million (trend 5.5% a year).
What happened to a $10,000 investment

Purchase Date	*Purchase Price*	*Price on 12-31-81*	*Dividends Paid*
12-31-71	$N/A	$11.25	$ N/A
12-31-76	$ 9.08	$11.25	$3,769.91

Purchase Date	*Cap. Gains (– Losses)*	*Total Return*	*Rate of Return*
12-31-71	$ N/A	$ N/A	N/A%
12-31-76	$2,385.32	$6,155.23	10.07%

* * *

WESTERN AIR LINES, INC. (WAL). Founded 1928. Headquarters: 6060 Avion Dr., Los Angeles CA 90045. **AIRLINE.** Western Air Lines connects various cities in the western United States with each other and with Canada, Mexico, Hawaii, and Britain. 9,000 employees.

Sales: $995.8 million (trend 14.5% a year).
Earnings: $–32.03 million.
What happened to a $10,000 investment

Purchase Date	*Purchase Price*	*Price on 12-31-81*	*Dividends Paid*
12-31-71	$12.39	$4.87	$2,435.55
12-31-76	$10.25	$4.87	$1,414.63

Purchase Date	*Cap. Gains (− Losses)*	*Total Return*	*Rate of Return*
12-31-71	$−6,064.87	$−3,629.33	−4.41%
12-31-76	$−5,243.90	$−3,829.27	−9.20%

PROFILE: In the airline business, the big fish sometimes swallow the little fish — but sometimes it goes the other way around. At times, lately, the business has looked like the classic cartoon in which a chain of assorted-sized fish are about to serially swallow one another.

Western, the ninth largest U.S. airline, had been trying for a long time to acquire troubled Continental Air Lines, the tenth largest. But it was unable to bring off the merger and comparatively small Texas International Airlines (owned by Texas Air Corp., profiled elsewhere in this volume) flew off with that prize (assuming you can call a money-losing airline with a huge debt a prize).

Failing to grab Continental left Western just small enough to be vulnerable to a take-over bid itself from another comparative small fry, Air Florida. (Both Texas Air and Air Florida have been prospering as regional airlines.) In the fall of 1981, Air Florida had already bought more than 11 percent of Western Air Lines' stock, and had acquired tentative government approval to bring off a merger — friendly or otherwise. However, at the time this book went to press in mid-1982, Air Florida had a 12 percent share in Western and wasn't pushing for more.

Western lost $29 million in 1980, and many analysts expected it to continue losing money into the early 1980s. Long-term debt recently had climbed to a record $435 million, which worked out to more than 65 percent of capital. Dividends, which had been moderate in recent years, were suspended in 1980. Some routes have been dropped, some plane orders canceled, and union workers have accepted a wage freeze. Interest in the stock mainly reflects people's speculation on how much the company would be worth to Air Florida or another potential acquirer.

* * *

WESTERN CO. OF NORTH AMERICA (WSN). Founded 1950. Headquarters: 6000 Western Pl., Fort Worth TX 76116. **OIL SERVICES.** Western is active in well stimulation, flow control, offshore drilling, and other services for the oil industry.

Sales: $448.1 million (trend 32.6% a year).
Earnings: $52.27 million (trend 25.1% a year).
What happened to a $10,000 investment

Purchase Date	*Purchase Price*	*Price on 12-31-81*	*Dividends Paid*
12-31-71	$ .49	$23.75	$11,071.03
12-31-76	$2.03	$23.75	$ 2,352.42

Purchase Date	*Cap. Gains (− Losses)*	*Total Return*	*Rate of Return*
12-31-71	$475,703.65	$486,774.69	47.78%
12-31-76	$106,803.28	$109,155.70	64.14%

* * *

WESTERN PACIFIC INDUSTRIES, INC. (WPI). Founded 1970. Headquarters: 345 Park Ave., New York NY 10022. **INDUSTRIAL PRODUCTS.** Western Pacific Industries manufactures counting machines, precision fasteners and precision components.

Sales: $249.3 million (trend 2.0% a year).
Earnings: $28.89 million (trend 47.8% a year).
What happened to a $10,000 investment

Purchase Date	*Purchase Price*	*Price on 12-31-81*	*Dividends Paid*
12-31-71	$20.25	$51.50	$12,345.68
12-31-76	$14.12	$51.50	$17,699.12

Purchase Date	*Cap. Gains (− Losses)*	*Total Return*	*Rate of Return*
12-31-71	$15,432.10	$27,777.78	14.22%
12-31-76	$26,460.18	$44,159.29	40.20%

* * *

WESTERN UNION CORP. (WU). Founded 1851. Headquarters: 1 Lake St., Upper Saddle River NJ 07458. **TELECOMMUNICATIONS.** Western Union operates the Western Union Telegraph Co., an international communications network.

Sales: $794.2 million (trend 6.6% a year).
Earnings: $28.58 million (trend −.6% a year).
What happened to a $10,000 investment

Purchase Date	*Purchase Price*	*Price on 12-31-81*	*Dividends Paid*
12-31-71	$43.75	$36.50	$3,200.00
12-31-76	$20.25	$36.50	$3,456.79

Purchase Date	*Cap. Gains (− Losses)*	*Total Return*	*Rate of Return*
12-31-71	$−1,657.14	$ 1,542.86	1.45%
12-31-76	$ 8,024.69	$11,481.48	16.52%

* * *

WESTINGHOUSE ELECTRIC CORP. (WX). Founded 1886. Headquarters: Gateway Center, Pittsburgh PA 15222. ELECTRICAL EQUIPMENT, GENERATING. Westinghouse is the second largest maker of electrical equipment in the United States (after General Electric). It is the largest U.S. manufacturer of nuclear generating equipment and a major maker of conventional generating equipment. It has also diversified into broadcasting and a variety of industrial operations. 145,000 employees. MAJOR SUBSIDIARIES, BRANDS: Teleprompter Corp. (nation's largest cable TV system).

Sales: $8,514.3 million (trend 7.3% a year).
Earnings: $402.30 million (trend 16.7% a year).
What happened to a $10,000 investment

Purchase Date	*Purchase Price*	*Price on 12-31-81*	*Dividends Paid*
12-31-71	$45.87	$25.50	$2,384.74
12-31-76	$17.62	$25.50	$3,470.07

Purchase Date	*Cap. Gains (− Losses)*	*Total Return*	*Rate of Return*
12-31-71	$−4,441.42	$−2,056.68	−2.28%
12-31-76	$ 4,468.09	$ 7,938.16	12.40%

PROFILE: Read the business pages, and you may get the impression that Westinghouse is stumbling from crisis to crisis. For years, you'd read stories about the lawsuits involving the company's failure to deliver uranium, as agreed, to nuclear utilities at a fixed price that turned out to be ridiculously low when the price soared. (Westinghouse in turn sued uranium suppliers with some success, charging that they had fixed prices.)

Now all the suits have been settled. But some analysts say that in the meantime the company, having tied up its cash in litigation, has neglected capital spending. They say, too, that relations between Westinghouse and its customers have been damaged.

The latest controversy is whether Westinghouse, in its eagerness to explore new and more profitable territory, grossly overpaid for Teleprompter (about $646 million in cash, plus assumption of perhaps $200 million in debts).

There's a lot of substance to the criticisms, but in an enterprise as large as Westinghouse, some of these problems are mere barnacles on a whale. Look at the operating results: Westinghouse has been steadily improving return on equity, from less than 8 percent in 1974 to more than 16 percent in 1980. At the same time, debt has been trimmed from more than 28 percent of capital to less than 12 percent recently. Profit margins are trending up. The company recently had more cash than long-term debt. And the shares, disdained by Wall Street, have recently gone for only 4 to 7 times earnings. In short, the bad news has been amply publicized, the good news has not, and the stock may represent a good value at its levels of the past couple of years.

* * *

WESTVACO CORP. (W). Founded 1899. Headquarters: 299 Park Ave., New York NY 10171. PAPER. Westvaco is a major producer of paper products and corrugated packaging. 15,000 employees. MAJOR SUBSIDIARIES, BRANDS: Rigesa (Brazilian paper products company); U. S. Envelope.

Sales: $1,550.5 million (trend 11.1% a year).
Earnings: $100.78 million (trend 12.4% a year).
What happened to a $10,000 investment

Purchase Date	*Purchase Price*	*Price on 12-31-81*	*Dividends Paid*
12-31-71	$ 9.06	$23.62	$8,202.82
12-31-76	$21.00	$23.62	$2,214.44

Purchase Date	*Cap. Gains (− Losses)*	*Total Return*	*Rate of Return*
12-31-71	$16,088.96	$24,291.78	13.11%
12-31-76	$ 1,250.00	$ 3,464.44	6.13%

PROFILE: Are you looking for a superlative to apply to Westvaco? Well, its U. S. Envelope subsidiary is probably the largest maker of envelopes in the country. Other than that, it's hard to find areas where the company stands out. Its financial results, by and large, have been run-of-the-paper-mill.

Take return on equity. In recent years, it's been consistently in the 13-to-15 percent range. That's nothing to be ashamed of (it's a bit below average for major U.S. corporations, and a whisker below average for forest products companies), but it's nothing to write home about either.

Take the balance sheet. It's average. Take the dividend yield. It's moderate, staying between 4½ and 5 percent in recent years with remarkable consistency.

The stock, in keeping with the company's unexceptional performance, has sold for 5 to 8 times earnings in recent years, which is just a bit below average. The company, having been burned badly in an overambitious expansion about a decade ago, seems to be playing it safe. It's trying to improve profitability by cost-cutting measures, such as revamping existing production equipment (rather than purchasing expensive new equipment), and taking steps to make its plants more energy-efficient.

* * *

WEYERHAEUSER CO. (WY). Founded 1900. Headquarters: Tacoma Building, Tacoma WA 98401. **FOREST PRODUCTS.** Weyerhaeuser is one of the largest U.S. forest products companies, producing building materials, paper, and packaging. It owns close to 6 million acres of forests in the United States, and has timber cutting rights on more than 10 million more acres in the United States and abroad. 45,000 employees.

Sales: $4,535.8 million (trend 14.0% a year).
Earnings: $310.33 million (trend 13.2% a year).
What happened to a $10,000 investment

Purchase Date	*Purchase Price*	*Price on 12-31-81*	*Dividends Paid*
12-31-71	$23.12	$29.25	$3,723.24
12-31-76	$46.50	$29.25	$1,145.16

Purchase Date	*Cap. Gains (– Losses)*	*Total Return*	*Rate of Return*
12-31-71	$ 2,648.65	$ 6,371.89	5.05%
12-31-76	$–3,709.68	$–2,564.52	–5.75%

PROFILE: Weyerhaeuser's massive forest holdings make it one of the biggest U.S. landowners, and the only one of the major forest products companies that is totally self-sufficient in timber. The land is carried on the company's books at a relatively low value (recently $641 million) but may in fact be worth close to $10 billion, according to a recent estimate by the brokerage firm Morgan, Stanley. If you accept this estimate, it works out to about $78 per share of common stock. Yet in the early 1980s, Weyerhaeuser shares were going for less than half that. Is this an asset play? You bet.

The contrast between the forest land's book value and its real value also explains the heavy sighs at Weyerhaeuser headquarters following the eruption of Mount Saint Helens. For accounting purposes, Weyerhaeuser's loss was about $36 million. Yet the true value of the flattened forests may have been about ten times that.

Weyerhaeuser concentrates on the building supplies end of the forest products business, rather than the comparatively stable paper products side. That renders the stock subject to swings, depending on how the building industry is doing. Lately, of course, it's been doing terribly, and Weyerhaeuser shares had dropped from a 1976 high near $50 to a mid-1981 price in the $30 to $35 range. Good times for the building industry could do a great deal for this stock.

Dividends have been paid here each year since 1933 and provide a moderate yield.

* * *

WHEELABRATOR-FRYE INC. (WFI). Founded 1935. Headquarters: Liberty Lane, Hampton NH 03842. **ENGINEERING, POLLUTION CONTROL.** Wheelabrator-Frye is a diversified supplier of engineering services, antipollution equipment, fluid measuring systems, chemicals, and other products. Railroad car manufacturing operations (Pullman Standard) spun off in early 1982. 25,000 employees. **MAJOR SUBSIDIARIES, BRANDS:** M. W. Kellogg; Neptune International Corp.; Rust Engineering Corp.; Conap.

Sales: $1,299.7 million (trend 32.0% a year).
Earnings: $52.34 million (trend 29.6% a year).
What happened to a $10,000 investment

Purchase Date	*Purchase Price*	*Price on 12-31-81*	*Dividends Paid*
12-31-71	$20.63	$44.12	$4,050.50
12-31-76	$25.62	$44.12	$2,372.68

Purchase Date	*Cap. Gains (– Losses)*	*Total Return*	*Rate of Return*
12-31-71	$11,391.80	$15,442.30	9.79%
12-31-76	$ 7,219.51	$ 9,592.20	14.40%

PROFILE: Wheelabrator-Frye is the canary that swallowed the cat. In 1980 it acquired Pullman, Inc., for $600 million in cash and stock. At that time, Wheelabrator's annual sales were less than $1 billion; Pullman's were more than $3 billion.

In 1982 Wheelabrator spun off Pullman's railroad car operations to a newly formed company (in which Wheelabrator retained preferred stock). This may help bring the cat down to a size Wheelabrator can more effectively manage.

But Wheelabrator has grown fast — and through acquisitions — all of its life. Though the company often describes itself as being in the energy and environmental fields, its operations are considerably more various than that. As one analyst told *The*

Insiders' Chronicle, it's "an amalgamation of assets that Mike Dingman [the company's promotional-minded chairman] has been trying to sell as a pollution play." Still, the fact is that antipollution equipment, garbage recycling for energy, and synfuels are among the major areas of operation.

Return on equity has been erratic, but on the average better than the typical major corporation's. Dividends, paid yearly since 1951, provide a moderate yield.

Finally, in case you've always wondered, a Wheelabrator is a giant scrubbing device, used primarily in steel furnaces.

* * *

WHEELING & LAKE ERIE RAILWAY CO. (WLE). Founded 1916. Headquarters: 8 N. Jefferson St., Roanoke VA 24042. **RAILROAD.** This small railroad operates under a lease arrangement with the Norfolk & Western Railway.

* * *

WHEELING-PITTSBURGH STEEL CORP. (WHX). Founded 1920. Headquarters: 4 Gateway Center, Pittsburgh PA 15230. **STEEL.** Wheeling-Pittsburgh is approximately the eighth largest U.S. steel company. 12,000 employees.

Sales: $1,054.1 million (trend 6.7% a year).
Earnings: $11.03 million (trend 228.7% a year).
What happened to a $10,000 investment

Purchase Date	*Purchase Price*	*Price on 12-31-81*	*Dividends Paid*
12-31-71	$17.75	$30.50	$1,352.11
12-31-76	$18.50	$30.50	$ 540.54

Purchase Date	*Cap. Gains (− Losses)*	*Total Return*	*Rate of Return*
12-31-71	$7,183.10	$8,535.21	6.37%
12-31-76	$6,486.49	$7,027.03	11.23%

PROFILE: Think of all the signs of a troubled company you can. You could probably find all of them in recent years at Wheeling-Pittsburgh. There were losses in 1975 and 1977 (the latter one huge); in other years, profits have been wildly erratic. There have been executive changes, pleas for government help, talk of mergers, and a search for a foreign buyer to supply the company with fresh capital.

Yet a lot of brokers and analysts think the stock — speculative though it certainly is — looks attractive for the 1980s. Under Chairman Dennis Carney, the company has become much leaner, with higher productivity, a smaller work force, and some modernized facilities. In 1981 it opened a major plant to produce steel for railroad track, which is generally a more profitable product than the sheet and strip steel that have been Wheeling-Pittsburgh's traditional specialties. The big users of flat-rolled steel are the auto, housing, and appliance industries — all of them cyclical customers whose demand has recently been down.

But the same factors that make this stock cyclical in the extreme can make it an attractive investment if you pick it up in the trough of a down cycle.

About 40 percent of the company's capital was recently in the form of debt. Potential investors here should keep an eye on the debt ratio. Dividends have been paid irregularly during the past decade, with no payment in most years.

* * *

WHIRLPOOL CORP. (WHR). Founded 1911. Headquarters: Benton Harbor MI 49022. **APPLIANCES.** Whirlpool is one of the nation's largest makers of washers, dryers, refrigerators, freezers, air-conditioners, ranges, and other appliances. 23,000 employees. **MAJOR SUBSIDIARIES, BRANDS:** Whirlpool; Kenmore (sold through Sears, Roebuck & Co.).

Sales: $2,243.2 million (trend 9.7% a year).
Earnings: $101.70 million (trend 10.1% a year).
What happened to a $10,000 investment

Purchase Date	*Purchase Price*	*Price on 12-31-81*	*Dividends Paid*
12-31-71	$32.75	$25.37	$3,123.30
12-31-76	$27.37	$25.37	$2,410.96

Purchase Date	*Cap. Gains (− Losses)*	*Total Return*	*Rate of Return*
12-31-71	$−2,251.91	$ 871.39	.84%
12-31-76	$ −730.59	$1,680.37	3.16%

PROFILE: Like clothes in a dryer, Whirlpool earnings have tumbled up, down, and around during the past decade. The overall trend has been up, but only moderately so.

In the 1980s, demographics should favor somewhat faster growth for this manufacturer, which along with General Electric dominates the appliance market (each has about a 30 percent market share). There will be a lot of people in the baby boom generation starting families, probably buying houses, and buying major appliances. Even so, you can't look for red-hot growth here. The appliance business is a mature one. What Whirlpool offers is a chance for fairly steady growth, with considerable safety. It's a stock that has appeal for conservative investors.

In part, that's because of the balance sheet. Debt has gradually been pared down during the past decade; recently, it accounted for less than 10 percent of total capital. In that light, the company's return on equity (14 to 21 percent in recent years) looks impressive, as it was achieved with very little help from leverage.

Conservative investors will also like the dividend situation. Dividends have been paid each year since 1929 and have been raised each year since 1976. The yield recently has been in the 6-to-8 percent range, with a third to a half of profits paid out as dividends.

Since its birth, Whirlpool has had a special relationship with Sears, Roebuck. It used to sell exclusively through Sears until 1956. Lately, close to half of Whirlpool's output has been sold through the nation's largest retailer, mainly under the Sears Kenmore brand name.

* * *

WHITE CONSOLIDATED INDUSTRIES, INC. (WSW). Founded 1926. Headquarters: 11770 Berea Rd., Cleveland OH 44111. **APPLIANCES, MACHINERY.** White is the third largest U.S. appliance maker (after Whirlpool and General Electric). Among the other products it produces are machine tools, printing presses, tank armor, conveyor belt systems, and industrial controls. 28,000 employees. **MAJOR SUBSIDIARIES, BRANDS:** Frigidaire; Kelvinator; White-Westinghouse; Gibson; American Tool.

Sales: $2,057.3 million (trend 12.7% a year).
Earnings: $52.37 million (trend 5.6% a year).
What happened to a $10,000 investment

Purchase Date	*Purchase Price*	*Price on 12-31-81*	*Dividends Paid*
12-31-71	$19.29	$27.25	$5,309.63
12-31-76	$26.87	$27.25	$2,465.12

Purchase Date	*Cap. Gains (− Losses)*	*Total Return*	*Rate of Return*
12-31-71	$4,129.62	$9,439.25	6.87%
12-31-76	$ 139.53	$2,604.65	4.74%

PROFILE: In the appliance business, there used to be about thirty major manufacturers. Today there are only about four or five. White is one of the survivors, and its brand names include several that it took over from companies getting out of the business, such as General Motors (Frigidaire), American Motors (Kelvinator), and Westinghouse (White-Westinghouse).

In a cyclical industry, White has ground out fairly steady earnings increases. Partly, this is because the company is balanced: About a third of its sales come not from appliances but from capital goods, ranging from tank armor to conveyor belts. Partly, it's a result of the way White has used acquisitions. It has tended to acquire new brands at times when factory capacity was underutilized. The recent acquisition of Frigidaire, for example, allowed White to run several plants at 80 to 100 percent of capacity, instead of 60 to 80 percent.

The balance sheet, heavy with debt a decade ago, is about average now. Dividends, paid each year since 1967 and increased every year, provide a moderate yield.

White's growth rates have been subpar in recent years, but may pick up some during the next decade because (as explained in the Whirlpool entry) demographics seem to favor increased consumption of home appliances during the 1980s.

* * *

WHITTAKER CORP. (WKR). Founded 1947. Headquarters: 10880 Wilshire Blvd., Los Angeles CA 90024. **CONGLOMERATE.** Whittaker is a conglomerate with an emphasis on health-care products and services. It is also involved in railroad car making, metal processing, industrial equipment, boat making, and chemical manufacturing. 16,000 employees. **MAJOR SUBSIDIARIES, BRANDS:** General Medical Corp.; Medicus Systems; Spectra Medical; Trojan Yacht.

Sales: $1,396.2 million (trend 15.9% a year).
Earnings: $56.90 million (trend 54.2% a year).
What happened to a $10,000 investment

Purchase Date	*Purchase Price*	*Price on 12-31-81*	*Dividends Paid*
12-31-71	$10.37	$33.50	$2,915.66
12-31-76	$ 6.25	$33.50	$4,840.00

Purchase Date	*Cap. Gains (− Losses)*	*Total Return*	*Rate of Return*
12-31-71	$22,289.16	$25,204.82	13.41%
12-31-76	$43,600.00	$48,440.00	42.34%

PROFILE: This corporation has had a checkered career, with frequent changes in the complexion of the game. It started in the 1940s (under founder William Whittaker) as a maker of aircraft valves. By the end of the 1960s, it was a conglomerate comprising some 150 companies. During the 1970s, about 100 subsidiaries were sold off, as the company tried to rationalize its operations, improve operating results, and reduce its debt. (Debt was more than 50 percent of capital as recently as 1973.)

Now the company has proclaimed that its primary emphasis will be on health-care products and services, including hospital management and hospital supplies. This business segment, which provided about a third of 1980 revenues and a somewhat larger chunk of profits, is heavily dependent on contracts in Saudi Arabia and Abu Dhabi.

In early 1982 Whittaker moved to acquire Brunswick (profiled elsewhere in this volume). But Brunswick seems to have wriggled away by selling off Sherwood Laboratories — generally believed by analysts to be the part of Brunswick Whittaker really wanted.

The company, under chairman Joseph Alibrandi, a former Raytheon executive brought in in 1970, has pared down debt to around 30 percent of capital and has improved the return on stockholders' equity from less than 10 percent in the early 1970s to more than 20 percent in 1979 and 1980. Dividends were started in 1978 and have recently provided a moderate yield. Both the p / e ratio and the stock price tend to be volatile.

* * *

WICKES COMPANIES, INC. (WIX). Founded 1947. Headquarters: 1010 Second Ave., San Diego CA 92101. **RETAILING.** Wickes is a major diversified retailer, with particular emphasis on lumber and building supplies. Nonretail operations include dealing in agricultural commodities, financial services, and manufacturing of golf equipment, furniture, and industrial equipment. In 1982 it sought protection under Chapter 11 of the bankruptcy code. 43,000 employees. **MAJOR SUBSIDIARIES, BRANDS:** Wickes Lumber; Wickes Furniture; Gambles; Gamble Department Stores; Alden's mail-order house; Builders Emporium; Country Store; Double Up; Fashion Crossroads; Howard Brothers; Leath-Maxwell; J. M. McDonald Co.; Mode O'Day; Rasco-Temp; Red Owl; Sequoia Supply; Sarco; Snyder's; Toy World.

Sales: $2,877.0 million (trend 21.0% a year).
Earnings: $13.79 million (trend 23.6% a year).
What happened to a $10,000 investment

Purchase Date	*Purchase Price*	*Price on 12-31-81*	*Dividends Paid*
12-31-71	$47.06	$9.37	$1,504.42
12-31-76	$13.54	$9.37	$2,652.25

Purchase Date	*Cap. Gains (− Losses)*	*Total Return*	*Rate of Return*
12-31-71	$−8,008.07	$−6,503.65	−9.98%
12-31-76	$−3,074.33	$ −422.07	−.86%

PROFILE: In 1980 Wickes roughly doubled its size by acquiring Gamble-Skogmo, the big Minneapolis-based retailer. In the process, Wickes became much more diverse — no longer mainly a building-supplies firm, it now is a highly diversified retailer, with operations in general merchandise, food, drugs, and catalog sales.

In its new shape, Wickes — if it survives and reemerges from bankruptcy — will tend to mirror the general economy, and will reflect trends in consumer spending generally. It will remain disproportionately influenced by the state of the building industry, which is bad news in the short run (that industry has been in a horrible slump), but may be good news in the long run (homebuilding has to recover some year, right?).

Holders of Wickes shares have had little to be happy about, either lately or during the past decade. From a 1971 high of almost $50, the shares have declined to a 1980 high of $18, and were selling for around $15 in mid-1981. The above-average dividend yield (recently close to 7 percent) hasn't been sufficient consolation.

The balance sheet is enough to scare off almost any conservative investor, and many middle-of-the-roaders. Debt has recently amounted to almost two thirds of total capital. In 1980 the company paid about $117 million in interest, roughly equal to profits for the four preceding years. In 1982 it entered a bankruptcy reorganization.

* * *

WIEBOLDT STORES, INC. (WIE). Founded 1883. Headquarters: 1 N. State St., Chicago IL 60602. **DEPARTMENT STORES.** Wieboldt's is a chain of department stores operating in and around Chicago.

Sales: $164.9 million (trend 2.1% a year).
Earnings: $1.69 million (trend −11.2% a year).
What happened to a $10,000 investment

Purchase Date	*Purchase Price*	*Price on 12-31-81*	*Dividends Paid*
12-31-71	$8.05	$5.12	$3,692.27
12-31-76	$6.50	$5.12	$2,507.69

Purchase Date	Cap. Gains (− Losses)	Total Return	Rate of Return
12-31-71	$−3,633.46	$ 58.80	.06%
12-31-76	$−2,115.38	$392.31	.77%

* * *

WILLIAMS COMPANIES (WMB). Founded 1949. Headquarters: 1 Williams Center, Tulsa OK 74172. **FERTILIZER.** This major fertilizer manufacturer has diversified into oil exploration, metal processing, and (through partly owned Peabody Coal) coal mining. It also remains active in its original business, pipeline operation. 7,000 employees. **MAJOR SUBSIDIARIES, BRANDS:** Agrico Chemical Co. (fertilizer); Edgcomb Metals Co. (metal processing); Peabody Coal Co. (27.5 percent owned — nation's largest coal mining company); Williams Exploration Co. (oil and gas exploration); Williams Pipe Line Co. (pipeline transport of petroleum products and fertilizer).

Sales: $2,072.7 million (trend 19.7% a year).
Earnings: $138.70 million (trend 1.2% a year).
What happened to a $10,000 investment

Purchase Date	Purchase Price	Price on 12-31-81	Dividends Paid
12-31-71	$21.25	$27.37	$3,364.71
12-31-76	$25.62	$27.37	$2,068.29

Purchase Date	Cap. Gains (− Losses)	Total Return	Rate of Return
12-31-71	$2,882.35	$6,247.06	4.97%
12-31-76	$ 682.93	$2,751.22	4.98%

PROFILE: You can expect a lot of ups and downs in the stock of this leading fertilizer maker. But if you can stand the sleepless nights, the long-term trends look pretty good.

The company, new to oil and gas exploration, has done well drilling in the Overthrust Belt of the Rocky Mountains. Its investment in Peabody Coal was made at a time when that company was in a down phase. Coal production hasn't come along as fast as some have hoped, and production remains crippled by sporadic strikes. Yet there seems little reason to doubt that the nation will be both using and exporting more coal in the future than it does today.

In its main business, fertilizer, Williams has a solid position. The main contributor to volatility here is the changing (usually rising) cost of phosphates, the main ingredient. Also, weather, politics, and exports help determine the supply / demand ratio in any given year. But again, looking at the long run, the United States seems destined to play bread basket to the world and to use a great deal of fertilizer.

The company's return on equity has been wildly erratic. The balance sheet shows a fair amount of debt — recently about 40 percent of capital. Dividends have been paid each year since 1974 and provide a moderate yield.

* * *

WILSHIRE OIL COMPANY OF TEXAS (WOC). Founded 1951. Headquarters: 921 Bergen Ave., Jersey City NJ 07306. **OIL, GAS, BANKING.** This company is involved in oil and natural gas exploration and production, and has a large interest in the Trust Company of New Jersey.

Sales: $12.2 million (trend −5.3% a year).
Earnings: $2.30 million (trend −19.8% a year).
What happened to a $10,000 investment

Purchase Date	Purchase Price	Price on 12-31-81	Dividends Paid
12-31-71	$4.17	$9.22	$1,341.34
12-31-76	$5.82	$9.22	$ 577.78

Purchase Date	Cap. Gains (− Losses)	Total Return	Rate of Return
12-31-71	$12,131.51	$13,472.85	8.91%
12-31-76	$ 5,840.47	$ 6,418.25	10.42%

* * *

WINN-DIXIE STORES, INC. (WIN). Founded 1928. Headquarters: 5050 Edgewood Court, Jacksonville FL 32203. **SUPERMARKETS.** Winn-Dixie is approximately the fourth largest U.S. supermarket chain, with more than 1,200 stores in 13 Southern states. 63,000 employees.

Sales: $6,200.2 million (trend 12.8% a year).
Earnings: $95.39 million (trend 8.9% a year).
What happened to a $10,000 investment

Purchase Date	Purchase Price	Price on 12-31-81	Dividends Paid
12-31-71	$25.13	$30.62	$4,877.56
12-31-76	$34.03	$30.62	$2,195.00

Purchase Date	Cap. Gains (− Losses)	Total Return	Rate of Return
12-31-71	$ 2,188.75	$7,066.31	5.49%
12-31-76	$−1,001.15	$1,193.86	2.28%

PROFILE: Consistent? It's hard to believe how consistent Winn-Dixie has been. During the decade 1971–80, its return on stockholders' equity fell below 20 percent only once (1977), and then missed only by a hair (19.8 percent). The highest return on equity during that decade was 21.5 percent in 1974.

That's a record most corporations would envy, since a 15 percent on equity is about average. What's more, most corporations make it to 15 percent only with the help of some leverage, but Winn-Dixie has very little leverage — in other words, very little debt. Debt has recently been only about 16 percent of total capital. While many companies (including quite a few supermarket chains) stagger under a burden of heavy interest payments, Winn-Dixie pays relatively little interest. In fact, it has more cash than it has debt, so it can earn more interest than it pays.

Add a substantial dividend yield (recently 6 to 7 percent) to this equation and you can see why the stock has appeal for conservative investors. You can also see why *The Insiders' Chronicle* was moved to describe Winn-Dixie a few years ago as the "strongman in [the] weak supermarket industry." The description still holds. While most supermarket chains command low p / e ratios, Winn-Dixie commands a better one (recently 9, a bit better than the average stock at the time). The chain's growth has been good (being in the Sun Belt helps) but not spectacular. So, if you fancy these relatively low-risk shares, keep an eye on the p / e to make sure you don't pay a high-growth multiple for a shares in moderate-growth company.

* * *

WINNEBAGO INDUSTRIES, INC. (WGO). Founded 1958. Headquarters: Junction Hwys. 9 and 69, PO Box 152, Forest City IO 50436. **RECREATIONAL VEHICLES.** Winnebago is the leading U.S. manufacturer of motor homes. The company also manufactures travel trailers, aluminum products, and plastic and glass-fiber products.

Sales: $143.0 million (trend −12.2% a year).
Earnings: $4.62 million (trend −4.4% a year).
What happened to a $10,000 investment

Purchase Date	*Purchase Price*	*Price on 12-31-81*	*Dividends Paid*
12-31-71	$24.25	$3.75	$0.00
12-31-76	$ 6.50	$3.75	$0.00

Purchase Date	*Cap. Gains (− Losses)*	*Total Return*	*Rate of Return*
12-31-71	$−8,453.61	$−8,453.61	−17.03%
12-31-76	$−4,230.77	$−4,230.77	−10.42%

* * *

JACK WINTER (JWI). Founded 1936. Headquarters: 8100 N. Teutonia Ave., Milwaukee WI 53209. **APPAREL.** Jack Winter produces a large line of women's apparel. **MAJOR SUBSIDIARIES, BRANDS:** Wendy Winter; Generation '79; Clothesworks.

Sales: $37.7 million (trend −12.0% a year).
Earnings: $−1.84 million.
What happened to a $10,000 investment

Purchase Date	*Purchase Price*	*Price on 12-31-81*	*Dividends Paid*
12-31-71	$ 4.67	$4.25	$11,578.57
12-31-76	$18.87	$4.25	$ 2,092.72

Purchase Date	*Cap. Gains (− Losses)*	*Total Return*	*Rate of Return*
12-31-71	$ −892.86	$ 10,685.71	7.54%
12-31-76	$−7,748.34	$−5,655.63	−15.36%

* * *

WISCONSIN ELECTRIC POWER CO. (WPC). Founded 1896. Headquarters: 231 W. Michigan St., Milwaukee WI 53201. **UTILITY.** Provides electricity to customers in Milwaukee, other portions of Wisconsin, and parts of Michigan; also furnishes natural gas to residents of southern Wisconsin. **MAJOR SUBSIDIARIES, BRANDS:** Wisconsin Natural Gas.

Sales: $1,007.1 million (trend 14.4% a year).
Earnings: $68.97 million (trend 10.1% a year).
What happened to a $10,000 investment

Purchase Date	*Purchase Price*	*Price on 12-31-81*	*Dividends Paid*
12-31-71	$24.25	$27.25	$8,519.18
12-31-76	$31.37	$27.25	$3,751.39

Purchase Date	*Cap. Gains (− Losses)*	*Total Return*	*Rate of Return*
12-31-71	$ 1,237.11	$9,756.29	7.05%
12-31-76	$−1,314.74	$2,436.65	4.46%

* * *

WISCONSIN POWER AND LIGHT CO. (WPL). Founded 1924. Headquarters: 222 W. Washington Ave., Madison WI 53701. **UTILITY.**

Wisconsin Power and Light provides basic electric, water, or gas service to more than 300,000 homes in Wisconsin. **MAJOR SUBSIDIARIES, BRANDS:** South Beloit Water, Gas and Electric Co.

Sales: $404.1 million (trend 15.1% a year).
Earnings: $29.93 million (trend 11.5% a year).
What happened to a $10,000 investment

Purchase Date	*Purchase Price*	*Price on 12-31-81*	*Dividends Paid*
12-31-71	$21.25	$19.25	$7,736.47
12-31-76	$22.25	$19.25	$4,071.91

Purchase Date	*Cap. Gains (− Losses)*	*Total Return*	*Rate of Return*
12-31-71	$ −941.18	$6,795.29	5.32%
12-31-76	$−1,348.31	$2,723.60	4.94%

* * *

WISCONSIN PUBLIC SERVICE CORP. (WPS). Founded 1883. Headquarters: 700 N. Adams St., PO Box 700, Green Bay WI 54305. **UTILITY.** Furnishes northeastern Wisconsin and parts of upper Michigan with electricity and gas.

Sales: $436.4 million (trend 14.0% a year).
Earnings: $30.81 million (trend 10.1% a year).
What happened to a $10,000 investment

Purchase Date	*Purchase Price*	*Price on 12-31-81*	*Dividends Paid*
12-31-71	$17.87	$18.62	$8,313.29
12-31-76	$21.62	$18.62	$3,889.02

Purchase Date	*Cap. Gains (− Losses)*	*Total Return*	*Rate of Return*
12-31-71	$ 419.58	$8,732.87	6.48%
12-31-76	$−1,387.28	$2,501.73	4.57%

* * *

WITCO CHEMICAL CORP. (WIT). Founded 1958. Headquarters: 277 Park Ave., New York NY 10017. **CHEMICALS.** Witco is a producer of a variety of specialty chemicals. 7,000 employees. **MAJOR SUBSIDIARIES, BRANDS:** Kendall motor oil; Amalie motor oil; Beam Oil Co.; Humko Chemical; Pearsall Chemical; Richardson Co.

Sales: $1,175.7 million (trend 18.0% a year).
Earnings: $41.08 million (trend 25.1% a year).
What happened to a $10,000 investment

Purchase Date	*Purchase Price*	*Price on 12-31-81*	*Dividends Paid*
12-31-71	$19.58	$24.25	$5,365.09
12-31-76	$19.58	$24.25	$3,445.09

Purchase Date	*Cap. Gains (− Losses)*	*Total Return*	*Rate of Return*
12-31-71	$2,382.98	$7,748.07	5.90%
12-31-76	$2,382.98	$5,828.07	9.62%

PROFILE: William (Billy) Wishnick is one of the few corporate chairmen around who have been known to grow beards and race stock cars. Perhaps the confidence to do these things comes in part from heading what used to be a family business. (Recently, the Wishnick family still owned 11 percent of the stock.) Be that as it may, Wishnick was confident enough to go out on a limb in a 1978 interview with *Forbes* magazine.

Witco's 3.9-percent profit margin in 1977, Wishnick told *Forbes,* was "really very low." His target was a 5-percent margin, not an unreasonable goal for a specialty chemical producer. Wishnick said he was confident the target could be met in short order. However, the 1981 margin was 2.9 percent, and the highest it had gotten in the interim was 4.5 percent in 1978.

Witco's margins have been modest partly because it doesn't dominate its markets. That fact, in turn, is due partly to the fact that the company started out as a marketer, not a producer, of chemicals. Despite the modest margins, growth and profitability have been respectable here. Several acquisitions have been financed without putting much strain on the balance sheet. Dividends have been paid each year since 1950, preceding the company's incorporation in its current form. The moderate dividend yield has been remarkably consistent over the past eight years — between 5 and 6 percent every year. Most holders of these shares have also been rewarded with modest capital gains.

* * *

WOLVERINE WORLD WIDE INC. (WWW). Founded 1906. Headquarters: 9341 Courtland Dr., Rockford MI 49351. **SHOES.** This company is a major manufacturer of casual shoes. **MAJOR SUBSIDIARIES, BRANDS:** Hush Puppies.

Sales: $253.3 million (trend 14.1% a year).
Earnings: $13.56 million (trend 47.9% a year).
What happened to a $10,000 investment

Purchase Date	Purchase Price	Price on 12-31-81	Dividends Paid
12-31-71	$6.75	$14.25	$2,412.35
12-31-76	$3.17	$14.25	$4,036.84

Purchase Date	Cap. Gains (− Losses)	Total Return	Rate of Return
12-31-71	$11,111.11	$13,523.46	8.93%
12-31-76	$35,000.00	$39,036.84	37.44%

* * *

WOMETCO ENTERPRISES, INC. (WOM). Founded 1925. Headquarters: 306 N. Miami Ave., Miami FL 33128. **BROADCASTING, SOFT DRINKS, VENDING, ENTERTAINMENT.** This company is active in leisure-time businesses through television and radio stations, Coca-Cola bottling franchises, vending, motion picture theaters, and cable television systems. **MAJOR SUBSIDIARIES, BRANDS:** WTVJ-TV (Miami); the Miami Seaquarium.

Sales: $349.0 million (trend 16.9% a year).
Earnings: $20.80 million (trend 13.5% a year).
What happened to a $10,000 investment

Purchase Date	Purchase Price	Price on 12-31-81	Dividends Paid
12-31-71	$8.33	$20.25	$3,877.40
12-31-76	$8.50	$20.25	$2,399.02

Purchase Date	Cap. Gains (− Losses)	Total Return	Rate of Return
12-31-71	$14,300.00	$18,177.40	10.91%
12-31-76	$13,823.53	$16,222.55	21.26%

* * *

WOODS PETROLEUM CORP. (WOG). Founded 1954. Headquarters: Suite 500, National Foundation West Bldg., 3555 N.W. 58th St., Oklahoma City OK 73112. **OIL, GAS.** This company is an independent oil and gas explorer, working mostly in the Midwest and Rocky Mountains.

Sales: $54.0 million (trend 20.0% a year).
Earnings: $22.57 million (trend 18.0% a year).
What happened to a $10,000 investment

Purchase Date	Purchase Price	Price on 12-31-81	Dividends Paid
12-31-71	$ N/A	$25.62	$ N/A
12-31-76	$10.31	$25.62	$1,270.30

Purchase Date	Cap. Gains (− Losses)	Total Return	Rate of Return
12-31-71	$ N/A	$ N/A	N/A%
12-31-76	$14,848.48	$16,118.79	21.17%

* * *

F. W. WOOLWORTH CO. (Z). Founded 1911. Headquarters: 233 Broadway, New York NY 10279. **RETAILING.** Woolworth operates more than 1,700 variety stores, close to 3,000 shoe stores (or leased departments), more than 400 discount department stores, and more than 300 clothing stores in the United States, Canada, Mexico, and West Germany. Also owns 52 percent of F. W. Woolworth Ltd. in Great Britain. 200,000 employees. **MAJOR SUBSIDIARIES, BRANDS:** Woolworth variety stores; Woolco discount department stores; Kinney shoe stores; Foot Locker; J. Brannam; Richman; Shirt Closet; Susie's Casuals.

Sales: $7,218.0 million (trend 9.3% a year).
Earnings: $158.50 million (trend 13.6% a year).
What happened to a $10,000 investment

Purchase Date	Purchase Price	Price on 12-31-81	Dividends Paid
12-31-71	$45.12	$18.25	$2,714.68
12-31-76	$25.75	$18.25	$2,407.77

Purchase Date	Cap. Gains (− Losses)	Total Return	Rate of Return
12-31-71	$−5,955.68	$−3,241.00	−3.84%
12-31-76	$−2,912.62	$ −504.85	−1.03%

PROFILE: A staid, stodgy retailer of five-and-dime items in old-fashioned, wood-floored stores: That's your image of Woolworth, isn't it? No? Well, somebody out there still thinks that's what Woolworth is, and the price / earnings multiple shows it. In recent years, Woolworth shares have gone for only 3 to 6 times earnings.

True, the company hasn't been burning up the track. But earnings have been growing decently, if unspectacularly, and the very low value Wall Street has put on this stock may be an underestimate. The shares, which reached $55 in 1971, were selling for less than half that in 1981.

One of the major attractions here is the high dividend yield. Since 1977, the yield has been above 6 percent. Recently, it's crept up near 9 percent. Yet, unlike many utilities (which people buy as income stocks), Woolworth isn't straining every financial muscle to pay its dividends. Only in 1974 during the past decade did the company pay out more than half of earnings.

In an effort to improve margins (traditionally around 2 to 2½ percent), management has recently emphasized clothing retailing, both in Woolworth's and Woolco outlets and through specialty stores.

The substantial foreign interests (Britain, Germany, Canada, Mexico) give the company some balance when conditions in the United States are adverse. But they also make for substantial short-term volatility of earnings because of currency fluctuations.

* * *

WORLD AIRWAYS, INC. (WOA). Founded 1948. Headquarters: Oakland International Airport, Oakland CA 94614. CHARTER AIRLINE. This airline is a large charter carrier for commercial, military, and cargo use in the United States.

Sales: $247.8 million (trend 19.5% a year).
Earnings: $−28.22 million.
What happened to a $10,000 investment

Purchase Date	*Purchase Price*	*Price on 12-31-81*	*Dividends Paid*
12-31-71	$11.50	$4.50	$0.00
12-31-76	$ 4.75	$4.50	$0.00

Purchase Date	*Cap. Gains (− Losses)*	*Total Return*	*Rate of Return*
12-31-71	$−6,086.96	$−6,086.96	−8.96%
12-31-76	$ −526.32	$ −526.32	−1.08%

* * *

WM. WRIGLEY JR. CO. (WWY). Founded 1892. Headquarters: 410 N. Michigan Ave., Chicago IL 60611. CHEWING GUM. Wm. Wrigley is the leading producer of chewing gum in the United States and many foreign markets. MAJOR SUBSIDIARIES, BRANDS: Doublemint; Juicy Fruit; Big Red; Freedent; Hubba Bubba Bubble Gum.

Sales: $557.6 million (trend 10.6% a year).
Earnings: $30.69 million (trend 3.3% a year).
What happened to a $10,000 investment

Purchase Date	*Purchase Price*	*Price on 12-31-81*	*Dividends Paid*
12-31-71	$34.87	$35.25	$5,293.91
12-31-76	$36.75	$35.25	$2,829.93

Purchase Date	*Cap. Gains (− Losses)*	*Total Return*	*Rate of Return*
12-31-71	$ 107.53	$5,401.43	4.41%
12-31-76	$−408.16	$2,421.77	4.43%

* * *

WURLITZER CO. (WUR). Founded 1890. Headquarters: 403 E. Gurler Rd., DeKalb IL 60115. PIANOS, ORGANS. Wurlitzer is a major producer of pianos, electronic organs, and electronic pianos. It also has interests in vending machines and jukeboxes.

Sales: $84.8 million (trend 2.7% a year).
Earnings: $−6.09 million.
What happened to a $10,000 investment

Purchase Date	*Purchase Price*	*Price on 12-31-81*	*Dividends Paid*
12-31-71	$9.83	$5.25	$2,345.76
12-31-76	$7.12	$5.25	$1,740.35

Purchase Date	*Cap. Gains (− Losses)*	*Total Return*	*Rate of Return*
12-31-71	$−4,661.02	$−2,315.25	−2.60%
12-31-76	$−2,631.58	$ −891.23	−1.85%

* * *

WYLE LABORATORIES (WYL). Founded 1949. Headquarters: 128 Maryland St., El Segundo CA 90245. ELECTRONICS DISTRIBUTION. Wyle Laboratories is primarily active in the distribution of electronics parts. It also owns a trucking line and manufactures industrial products. MAJOR SUBSIDIARIES, BRANDS: Redwing Carriers (trucking).

Sales: $252.9 million (trend 16.5% a year).
Earnings: $6.59 million (trend 28.5% a year).
What happened to a $10,000 investment

Purchase Date	*Purchase Price*	*Price on 12-31-81*	*Dividends Paid*
12-31-71	$2.08	$8.12	$7,769.23
12-31-76	$3.92	$8.12	$2,946.94

Purchase Date	*Cap. Gains (− Losses)*	*Total Return*	*Rate of Return*
12-31-71	$29,062.50	$36,831.73	16.70%
12-31-76	$10,727.04	$13,673.98	18.81%

* * *

WYLY CORP. (WLY). Founded 1963. Headquarters: UCC Tower, Exchange Park, Dallas TX

75235. COMPUTERS. Wyly offers computer services, software, and equipment.

Sales: $117.8 million (trend 13.0% a year).
Earnings: $6.63 million (trend 60.1% a year).
What happened to a $10,000 investment

Purchase Date	*Purchase Price*	*Price on 12-31-81*	*Dividends Paid*
12-31-71	$81.50	$8.12	$0.00
12-31-76	$ 7.00	$8.12	$0.00

Purchase Date	*Cap. Gains (− Losses)*	*Total Return*	*Rate of Return*
12-31-71	$−9,003.07	$−9,003.07	−20.59%
12-31-76	$ 1,607.14	$ 1,607.14	3.03%

* * *

WYNN'S INTERNATIONAL INC. (WN). Founded 1947. Headquarters: 2600 E. Nutwood Ave., Fullerton CA 92631. AUTOMOTIVE PARTS, PETROCHEMICALS. This company manufactures automotive parts and petrochemical-based car care products. Also owns a lock-making subsidiary. MAJOR SUBSIDIARIES, BRANDS: Frostemp; Mopar; American Air; Husky; Robert Skeels & Co. (locks).

Sales: $173.7 million (trend 21.2% a year).
Earnings: $7.61 million (trend 24.0% a year).
What happened to a $10,000 investment

Purchase Date	*Purchase Price*	*Price on 12-31-81*	*Dividends Paid*
12-31-71	$13.44	$20.37	$1,755.37
12-31-76	$ 7.50	$20.37	$2,813.33

Purchase Date	*Cap. Gains (− Losses)*	*Total Return*	*Rate of Return*
12-31-71	$ 5,154.96	$ 6,910.33	5.39%
12-31-76	$17,166.67	$19,980.00	24.56%

X

XEROX CORP. (XRX). Founded 1906. Headquarters: Stamford CT 06904. COPIERS. Xerox is the world's leading producer of copying equipment. It also makes computer printers, word processors, and other office equipment. Through subsidiaries it is involved in educational publishing, data processing, and telecommunications. 120,000 employees. MAJOR SUBSIDIARIES, BRANDS: Rank Xerox (50-percent-owned European subsidiary); WUI, Inc. (international telecommunications); R. R. Bowker (educational publishing); University Microfilms.

Sales: $8,196.5 million (trend 15.6% a year).
Earnings: $619.20 million (trend 13.6% a year).
What happened to a $10,000 investment

Purchase Date	*Purchase Price*	*Price on 12-31-81*	*Dividends Paid*
12-31-71	$125.25	$40.50	$1,320.56
12-31-76	$ 58.50	$40.50	$2,000.00

Purchase Date	*Cap. Gains (− Losses)*	*Total Return*	*Rate of Return*
12-31-71	$−6,766.47	$−5,445.91	−7.56%
12-31-76	$−3,076.92	$−1,076.92	−2.25%

PROFILE: In 1972 Xerox's sales were $2.4 billion, on which it earned profits of $250 million, which was $3.16 a share. By 1980, sales had grown to more than $8 billion, profits to more than $600 million, and profits per share to $7.33. You would think, then, that Xerox shares would have sold for substantially more in 1980 than in 1972.

But if you're at all familiar with the stock market, you already know that this isn't so. In 1972 Xerox shares hit an all-time high of nearly $172. In 1980 the high was just under $72. The stock price had been clipped by an even $100, even as sales and profits were rising. How can this be?

In part, this sad tale is simply a result of the fact that the stock market back in 1972 was manic and overheated. Xerox shares sold that year for as much as 54 times earnings, a multiple virtually unheard of today.

Then, too, there has been a change in the competitive situation. Back in the early 1970s, Xerox had a near monopoly of the world copier market. Competition from Japanese manufacturers and from IBM has sliced Xerox's share of the market from 97 percent in 1970 to about 47 percent recently. And that competition has forced Xerox to narrow its profit margins, which were around 10 percent at the beginning of the decade and around 7½ percent at the decade's end.

No, Xerox is not likely to become again the fireworks type of stock it was during the 1960s, when the company was riding a new product to astonishing growth. But it's still a fine company. And so devastating has the market's correction been that Xerox may now be undervalued. Its balance sheet is strong, with debt recently around 17 percent of total capital. Its dividend yield has risen steadily in recent years and lately has been above 6 percent. Return on equity has been a healthy 17 to 18½ percent in recent years. This is by no means a sick company, yet it has recently sold at a price/earnings ratio as weak as 6.

* * *

XTRA CORP. (XTR). Founded 1957. Headquarters: 2625 Concord Pike, Wilmington DE 19803. **TRANSPORTATION.** XTRA owns and leases transportation equipment, such as trailers and containers. It is also active in trucking. **MAJOR SUBSIDIARIES, BRANDS:** Mercury Motor Express; AJF Industries; Dunham Manufacturing Co.; MOTAC; Rowland Truck Equipment; X-L-CO, Inc.

Sales: $206.0 million (trend 17.2% a year).
Earnings: $3.54 million (trend −7.6% a year).
What happened to a $10,000 investment

Purchase Date	*Purchase Price*	*Price on 12-31-81*	*Dividends Paid*
12-31-71	$8.95	$14.25	$2,369.01
12-31-76	$8.06	$14.25	$2,629.46

Purchase Date	*Cap. Gains (− Losses)*	*Total Return*	*Rate of Return*
12-31-71	$5,923.79	$ 8,292.81	6.23%
12-31-76	$7,674.42	$10,303.88	15.22%

Y

YELLOW FREIGHT SYSTEM, INC. (YELL, Over-the-Counter). Founded 1950. Headquarters: 10990 Roe Ave., Overland Park, KS 66207. **TRUCKING.** Yellow Freight is one of the nation's largest trucking companies, with nationwide routes, and some 300 terminals in some 40 states. 13,000 employees.

Sales: $776.5 million (trend 14.9% a year).
Earnings: $21.05 million (trend −6.0% a year).
What happened to a $10,000 investment

Purchase Date	*Purchase Price*	*Price on 12-31-81*	*Dividends Paid*
12-31-71	$17.25	$15.75	$2,958.55
12-31-76	$42.75	$15.75	$ 809.36

Purchase Date	*Cap. Gains (− Losses)*	*Total Return*	*Rate of Return*
12-31-71	$ −869.57	$ 2,088.99	1.92%
12-31-76	$−6,315.79	$−5,506.43	−14.78%

PROFILE: You could have bought shares in Yellow Freight for $17 apiece in 1971 and sold them ten years later for . . . exactly the same price. In between, the stock climbed as high as $46 (in 1976) and sank as low as $12 (in 1980). What accounts for the recent decline?

In fair part, deregulation of the trucking industry. While its leading competitor, Roadway Express, has always specialized in partial-truckload shipments, Yellow used to go in mainly for full loads. But most firms moving into the trucking industry in the wake of deregulation went in for full-load hauling (it's easiest), and many of them were cutting prices to gain business. This forced Yellow to move increasingly to partial-truckload business, an area where its experience and big network of terminals give it an edge over the upstarts. However, the company has been caught between a rock and a hard place, because in partial-truckload shipments, it has to compete with other topnotch trucking firms, most notably Roadway. Yellow decided to distinguish itself by cutting prices on partial-truckload shipments — a tactic that has gained it business, but cut into its profit margins. As a result, profit growth in recent years has been slow, and return on equity mediocre.

Yellow's balance sheet is quite strong, with long-term debt recently less than 15 percent of total capital. The stock offers a moderate dividend yield; dividends have been increased each year since 1967.

Z

ZALE CORP. (ZAL). Founded 1924. Headquarters: 3000 Diamond Park Dr., Dallas TX 75247. **JEWELRY.** Zale operates retail jewelry stores across the country. **MAJOR SUBSIDIARIES, BRANDS:** Zale; Butler Shoe Corp.; Aeroplex Stands, Inc.

Sales: $828.7 million (trend 8.2% a year).
Earnings: $36.24 million (trend 7.0% a year).
What happened to a $10,000 investment

Purchase Date	*Purchase Price*	*Price on 12-31-81*	*Dividends Paid*
12-31-71	$41.75	$21.25	$1,885.03
12-31-76	$16.25	$21.25	$2,516.92

Purchase Date	*Cap. Gains (− Losses)*	*Total Return*	*Rate of Return*
12-31-71	$−4,910.18	$−3,025.15	−3.54%
12-31-76	$ 3,076.92	$ 5,593.85	9.29%

* * *

ZAPATA CORP. (ZOS). Founded 1954. Headquarters: Zapata Tower, 711 Louisiana St., Houston TX 77002. **OFFSHORE DRILLING.** Zapata is a natural resources company active in offshore drilling, dredging, fishing, and coal mining. **MAJOR**

SUBSIDIARIES, BRANDS: Zapata Exploration Co.; Zapata Marine Services, Inc.; Zapata Off-Shore Co.

Sales: $463.0 million (trend 6.6% a year).
Earnings: $72.03 million (trend 47.4% a year).
What happened to a $10,000 investment

Purchase Date	*Purchase Price*	*Price on 12-31-81*	*Dividends Paid*
12-31-71	$6.32	$28.25	$2,025.21
12-31-76	$5.33	$28.25	$1,820.13

Purchase Date	*Cap. Gains (− Losses)*	*Total Return*	*Rate of Return*
12-31-71	$34,723.59	$36,748.80	16.67%
12-31-76	$43,007.03	$44,827.16	40.54%

* * *

ZAYRE CORP. (ZY). Founded 1962. Headquarters: 770 Cochituate Rd., Framingham MA 01701. **DISCOUNT RETAILING.** Zayre operates nearly 250 discount department stores, a roughly equal number of discount women's clothing stores, and a smaller chain of family discount clothing stores. 28,000 employees. **MAJOR SUBSIDIARIES, BRANDS:** Zayre (discount department stores); Hit or Miss (discount women's clothing); T. J. Maxx (discount family clothing).

Sales: $1,594.2 million (trend 8.6% a year).
Earnings: $17.86 million (trend 20.1% a year).
What happened to a $10,000 investment

Purchase Date	*Purchase Price*	*Price on 12-31-81*	*Dividends Paid*
12-31-71	$36.62	$28.75	$ 65.53
12-31-76	$ 7.62	$28.75	$314.75

Purchase Date	*Cap. Gains (− Losses)*	*Total Return*	*Rate of Return*
12-31-71	$−2,150.17	$−2,084.64	−2.31%
12-31-76	$ 27,704.92	$ 28,019.67	30.62%

PROFILE: "We're not trying to be Saks Fifth Avenue," Zayre President Maurice Segall told *Financial World* in 1981. "We make no bones about the fact that we're a discount department store."

Until recently, many Zayre stores looked as cheap as their merchandise, if not downright scuzzy. Believing that the unappetizing appearance of the stores was contributing to a slow growth rate, management embarked on an expensive program of upgrading the stores, now close to complete. However, the program added to an already substantial level of corporate debt at Zayre. Recently, long-term debt was around 60 percent of total capital.

That debt level alone is enough to discourage some investors. Other negatives include an uninspiring record for profitability (from 1972 to 1980, return on equity never broke 12 percent) and low profit margins. Zayre's margins resemble those of a supermarket chain — barely above 1 percent. It's hard to build up profit momentum on such slim margins.

Positive factors include seven straight years of rising earnings from 1975 through 1981, despite a nasty recession. Recessions usually hit discount retailers less hard than other retailers.

Dividends were started in 1980; the yield is small. The founding family (the Feldbergs) still owned more than 30 percent of the shares recently.

* * *

ZENITH RADIO CORP. (ZE). Founded 1918. Headquarters: 1000 Milwaukee Ave., Glenview IL 60025. **TELEVISIONS.** Zenith is a leading maker of color television sets. Also makes minicomputers, radios, videocassette recorders, and other consumer electronics products. 25,000 employees. **MAJOR SUBSIDIARIES, BRANDS:** Heath Co. (minicomputers, electronic hobby kits).

Sales: $1,185.9 million (trend 4.9% a year).
Earnings: $26.40 million (trend −2.6% a year).
What happened to a $10,000 investment

Purchase Date	*Purchase Price*	*Price on 12-31-81*	*Dividends Paid*
12-31-71	$42.25	$11.12	$2,439.05
12-31-76	$27.87	$11.12	$1,443.95

Purchase Date	*Cap. Gains (− Losses)*	*Total Return*	*Rate of Return*
12-31-71	$−7,366.86	$−4,927.81	−6.56%
12-31-76	$−6,008.97	$−4,565.02	−11.48%

PROFILE: In 1981 *Business Week* ran an upbeat article about Zenith, pointing out that the company had a strong position in the videocassette recorder market, and speculating that it "may lead the way in the video revolution" including interactive systems. Zenith, the magazine said, "did well to survive a decade in which so many competitors sold out or closed up shop. Although Zenith emerged with shabby earnings and wounded pride, it hung on to top billing in the highly competitive TV business — even though it is by far the smallest company in an industry of diversified giants and the only major player dedicated primarily to this market."

That sanguine view contains interesting points to think about, including the fact that Zenith is indeed a "pure play" in TV and TV-related technology. But the fact remains that Zenith has been going downhill. Earnings peaked in 1973 at $2.90 a share, and haven't come close since. What's more, earnings were growing slowly for several years before 1973. The company has blamed many of its problems on what it considers unfair competition from Japan, but this is scant comfort to an investor who saw the shares slide from more than $50 a share a decade ago to less than $20 recently. Meanwhile, long-term debt has steadily crept up from about 3 percent of capital a decade ago to around 34 percent now.

The company has paid dividends each year since 1939 and the dividend still provides a modest yield. But dividends haven't been increased since 1973; they were chopped in 1974, 1975, 1979, 1980, and 1981.

* * *

ZERO CORP. (ZRO). Founded 1952. Headquarters: 777 Front St., Burbank CA 91503. ELECTRONICS HOUSING. Zero produces and designs cabinets, cases, cooling equipment, and other electronic packaging for the electronic and computer industries. MAJOR SUBSIDIARIES, BRANDS: McLean Midwest; Ocean Technology, Inc. (39 percent owned); Zero Halliburton.

Sales: $79.3 million (trend 19.5% a year).
Earnings: $5.88 million (trend 25.0% a year).
What happened to a $10,000 investment

Purchase Date	*Purchase Price*	*Price on 12-31-81*	*Dividends Paid*
12-31-71	$1.02	$25.12	$11,782.62
12-31-76	$3.43	$25.12	$ 2,850.93

Purchase Date	*Cap. Gains (– Losses)*	*Total Return*	*Rate of Return*
12-31-71	$235,361.33	$247,143.95	38.36%
12-31-76	$ 63,242.19	$ 66,093.12	50.06%

* * *

ZURN INDUSTRIES, INC. (ZRN). Founded 1932. Headquarters: 1 Zurn Place, Box 2000, Erie PA 16512. POLLUTION CONTROL. Zurn is active in controlling water, air, and land pollution. It also produces energy systems and golf clubs. MAJOR SUBSIDIARIES, BRANDS: Lynx golf clubs.

Sales: $364.1 million (trend 9.9% a year).
Earnings: $18.19 million (trend 22.0% a year).
What happened to a $10,000 investment

Purchase Date	*Purchase Price*	*Price on 12-31-81*	*Dividends Paid*
12-31-71	$25.50	$25.25	$1,858.82
12-31-76	$14.62	$25.25	$2,133.33

Purchase Date	*Cap. Gains (– Losses)*	*Total Return*	*Rate of Return*
12-31-71	$ –98.04	$1,760.78	1.64%
12-31-76	$7,264.96	$9,398.29	14.17%

Appendix I

INDEX OF SUBSIDIARIES AND BRAND NAMES: WHO OWNS WHAT, WHO MAKES WHAT

Note: Subsidiaries less than 50 percent owned are not included here.

A

A-6 Grumman Corp.
A-10 Fairchild Industries, Inc.
A & P Great Atlantic & Pacific Tea Co.
A&W United Brands Co.
A. J. Armstrong Co. Security Pacific Corp.
A.M. General American Motors Corp.
A.1. Steak Sauce Heublein, Inc.
A.P.S. Gulf & Western Industries, Inc.
AA Development American Airlines, Inc.
AA Energy Corp. American Airlines, Inc.
AAI Corp. United Industrial Corp.
AAR Del Monte AAR Corp.
AAR Western Skyways AAR Corp.
ABC MCA Inc.
ACF Petroleum Co. ACF Industries, Inc.
AE Hoover Universal, Inc.
AFCO Credit Corp. Continental Corp.
AJF Industries XTRA Corp.
AMF AMF Inc.
AMIC Corp. Merrill Lynch & Co., Inc.
AP Parts Questor Corp.
AV-8B McDonnell Douglas Corp.
Abbott Thomas Industries, Inc.
Abby Michael Bobbie Brooks, Inc.
Abex Corp. IC Industries, Inc.
Abraham & Straus Federated Department Stores, Inc.
Acadian Marine Service Inc. NICOR Inc.
Aceros Anglos Continental Copper & Steel Industries, Inc.
Acme (office supplies) American Brands, Inc.
Acme (supermarkets) American Stores, Co.
Acme Boot Co. Northwest Industries
Acoustic Research Teledyne, Inc.
Act III Jonathan Logan, Inc.
Acushnet American Brands, Inc.
Adams International Multifoods Corp.
Admiral Magic Chef, Inc.
Adobe Oil & Gas AMAX Inc.
Adolph's Chesebrough-Pond's Inc.
Adorence Co., Inc. Talley Industries, Inc.
Adorn Gillette Co.
Adrien Arpel Seligman & Latz, Inc.
Advance Mortage Co. Ltd. Merrill Lynch & Co., Inc.
Advanced Systems National Semiconductor Corp.
Advanced Technology Labs Squibb Corp.
Aero-Shave American Home Products Corp.
Aerojet-General General Tire & Rubber Co.
Aeroplex Stands, Inc. Zale Corp.
Aeroquip Libbey-Owens-Ford Co.
Aerostyle Ltd. Basic Resources Corp.
Aetna Casualty & Surety Co. Aetna Life and Casualty Co.
Aetna Insurance Co. Connecticut General Insurance Corp.
Aetna Life Insurance Co. Aetna Life and Casualty Co.
Affiliated Hospital Products, Inc. United Industrial Corp.
Afrin Schering-Plough Corp.
Agrico Chemical Co. Williams Companies
AgriStor Credit Corp. A. O. Smith Corp.
Aileen Aileen, Inc.
Aileen Girl Aileen, Inc.
Aileen Sport Aileen, Inc.
Aileen Teen Aileen, Inc.
Aim Unilever PLC
Air Asia E-Systems, Inc.
AirCap Sealed Air Corp.
Air Service, Inc. Piedmont Aviation, Inc.
Air-Shields Narco Scientific, Inc.
Air Step Brown Group, Inc.
Airtemp Fedders Corp.
Ajax Colgate-Palmolive Co.
Akron *Beacon Journal* Knight-Ridder Newspapers, Inc.
Akron Brass Premier Industrial Corp.
Alabama Power Southern Co.
Aladdin's Castle Bally Manufacturing Corp.
Alamac West Point-Pepperell, Inc.
Alamo Enterprises Evans Products Co.
Alamo National Bank Mercantile Texas Corp.
Alaska Gas and Service Co. Alaska Interstate Co.
Alaska Pipeline Co. Alaska Interstate Co.

Alberto Balsam Alberto-Culver Co.
Alberto VO5 Alberto-Culver Co.
Albert's Interco Inc.
Alco Electronic Products, Inc. Augat, Inc.
Alcon Data Corp. Dun & Bradstreet Corp.
Alcort AMF, Inc.
Aldactazide G. D. Searle & Co.
Aldactone G. D. Searle & Co.
Alden Press John Blair & Co.
Alden's Wickes Companies, Inc.
Aldomet Merck & Co., Inc.
Alexander Smith Mohasco Corp.
Alexander's Alexander's, Inc.
Alhambra Foremost-McKesson, Inc.
Alice Stuart Jonathan Logan, Inc.
All Unilever PLC
All-Bran Kellogg Co.
All Prime Prime Computer Inc.
The Allen Manufacturing Co. Chicago Pneumatic Tool Co.
Allerest Pennwalt Corp.
Allied Finance Co. Republic Financial Services
Alliance Tool & Die Gleason Works
Allied Paper SCM Corp.
Allied Steel & Tractor Products Chicago Pneumatic Tool Co.
Allstate Insurance Co. Sears, Roebuck and Co.
Allstate Savings & Loan Association Sears, Roebuck and Co.
Almadén National Distillers & Chemical Corp.
Almond Instruments Co. EG & G, Inc.
Alpha/Beta American Stores Co.
Alum A Form Elixir Industries
Alumax AMAX Inc.
Aly Skyline Corp.
Amalfi United States Shoe Corp.
Amalie Witco Chemical Corp.
Amana Raytheon Co.
Amarillo Oil Co. Pioneer Corp.
Ambac Industries United Technologies Corp.
Amcar ACF Industries, Inc.
Amcord, Inc. Gifford-Hill & Co., Inc.
Amercoat Protective Coatings Ameron, Inc.
American Air Wynn's International Inc.
American Air Filter Allis-Chalmers Corp.
American-Amicable Insurance Gulf United Corp.
American Carpet Mills Keller Industries, Inc.
American Century Advisors American Heritage Life Investment Corp.
American Chemical & Refining Co. Handy & Harman
American Chicle Warner-Lambert Co.
American Commercial Barging Line Texas Gas Transmission Corp.
American Commercial Terminals, Inc. Texas Gas Transmission Corp.
American Desk Kidde, Inc.
American Enka Akzona Inc.
American Family Life Assurance Co. American Family Corp.
American Flexible Conduit Nortek, Inc.
American Founders Life Insurance Co. Anderson, Clayton & Co.
American Furniture Household International Corp.
American General Bond Fund American General Corp.
American General Convertible Securities American General Corp.
American General Life Insurance Co. American General Corp.
American Handicrafts Tandycrafts, Inc.
American Health Services Inc. INA Corp.
American Heritage Life Insurance Co. American Heritage Life Investment Corp.
American Hoist of Canada, Ltd. American Hoist & Derrick Co.
American Home Insurance Group American International Group, Inc.
American Home Video Corp. Jack Eckerd Corp.
American International Pictures Filmways, Inc.
American Investment Co. Leucadia National Corp.
American LaFrance Figgie International
American Learning Systems, Inc. American Family Corp.
American National Bank Mercantile Texas Corp.
American National Bank & Trust Co. Walter E. Heller International Corp.
American National Bank & Trust of New Jersey Horizon Bancorp.
American Orange Corp. American Agronomics Corp.
American Pipe and Construction International Ameron, Inc.
American President Lines Natomas Co.
American Printers and Lithographers John Blair & Co.
American Reinsurance Co. Aetna Life and Casualty Co.
American Satellite Corp. Continental Telephone Corp. (50%) and Fairchild Industries, Inc. (50%)
American Savings & Loan Association First Charter Financial Corp.
American Savings Association (Kansas) Imperial Corp. of America
American Technical Industries Papercraft Corp.

American Telecommunications General Dynamics Corp.
American Tool White Consolidated Industries, Inc.
American Tourister, Inc. Hillenbrand Industries, Inc.
American Wells Corp. American Hospital Supply Co.
American Yearbook Co. Jostens, Inc.
AmeriGas UGI Corp.
Amerock Corp. Anchor Hocking Corp.
Ames Taping Tool Systems Axia Inc.
Aminoil R. J. Reynolds Industries, Inc.
Amoco Standard Oil Co. (Indiana)
Ampex Corp. Signal Companies, Inc.
Amphenol Bunker Ramo Corp.
Amship The American Ship Building Co.
AmTote General Instrument Corp.
Amy Adams Jonathan Logan, Inc.
Anacin American Home Products Corp.
Anaconda Co. Atlantic Richfield Co.
Anadarko Production Panhandle Eastern Pipe Line Co.
Anamas AMAX Inc.
Anchor Motor Freight Leaseway Transportation Corp.
Anchor Modern Merchandising, Inc.
The Anderson Co. Champion Spark Plug Co.
Anderson Hosiery Collins & Aikman Corp.
Andrew Jergens American Brands, Inc.
Angleboard, Inc. Signode Corp.
Aphrodesia Fabergé, Inc.
Appalachian Power American Electric Power Co., Inc.
Appedrine The Thompson Medical Co., Inc.
Appian Way Pizza Greyhound Corp.
Apple Jacks Kellogg Co.
Applicon Inc. Schlumberger Ltd.
Aqua Velva Nabisco Brands, Inc.
Arbuckle Corp. Quanex Corp.
Arby's Royal Crown Companies, Inc.
Arco Atlantic Richfield Co.
Arco Wheel The Armstrong Rubber Co.
Argo CPC International Inc.
Argonaut Insurance Co. Teledyne, Inc.
Aritech Corp. American District Telegraph Co.
Arkansas-Missouri Power Middle South Utilities, Inc.
Arkansas Power & Light Co. Middle South Utilities, Inc.
Armak Akzona Inc.
Armco Finance Corp. Armco Inc.
Armira Corp. Akzona Inc.
Armour & Co. Greyhound Corp.
Armour Pharmaceutical Co. Revlon, Inc.
Armstrong (appliances) Magic Chef, Inc.
Armstrong (flooring) Armstrong World Industries, Inc.
Arnel Celanese Corp.
Arrid Carter-Wallace, Inc.
The Arrow Co. Cluett, Peabody & Co., Inc.
Artcarved Class Rings Lenox, Inc.
Artcarved, Inc. Lenox, Inc.
Artec International Corp. Pitney-Bowes, Inc.
Artex Manufacturing Co. Jostens, Inc.
Arvida Corp. Penn Central Corp.
Arwood Corp. Interlake, Inc.
Asgrow Seed Co. Upjohn Co.
Aslesen Co. Chicago Milwaukee Corp.
Aspartame G. D. Searle & Co.
Aspercreme The Thompson Medical Co., Inc.
Associated Southern Investment Co. Southern California Edison Co.
Associates Corp. Gulf & Western Industries, Inc.
Astech TRE Corp.
Asylum Warner Communications, Inc.
Atari Warner Communications, Inc.
Atchison, Topeka & Santa Fe Railway Santa Fe Industries, Inc.
Atlantic Warner Communications, Inc.
Atlantic Discount Co. NCNB Corp.
Atlas Powder Co. Tyler Corp.
Atra Gillette Co.
August Max United States Shoe Corp.
Aunt Jemima Quaker Oats Co.
Aurora American Can Co.
Aurrera, S.A. Jewel Companies, Inc.
Austin Reed of Regent Street Hart Schaffner & Marx
Autolite Bendix Corp.
Automated Screening Devices, Inc. Bard (C.R.), Inc.
Automatic Sprinkler Corp. Figgie International
Automobile Insurance Co. of Hartford Aetna Life and Casualty Co.
The Automotive Carrier Ryder System, Inc.
Avco Financial Services Avco Corp.
Aviance Chesebrough-Pond's Inc.
Aviation Week & Space Technology McGraw-Hill, Inc.
Avis, Inc. Norton Simon, Inc.
Avon Fashions Avon Products, Inc.
Avondale Shipyards Ogden Corp.
Avoset Food Corp. Anderson, Clayton & Co.
Ayerst American Home Products Corp.

B

B-1 Rockwell International Corp.
B & B The Clorox Co.

B. B. Cohen & Co. Walter E. Heller International Corp.
B. Dalton Dayton-Hudson Corp.
B. F. Walker Noble Affiliates Inc.
B. H. Krueger, Inc. Peoples Drug Stores, Inc.
BJ-Hughes Hughes Tool Co.
BLK Steel Inc. Axia Inc.
Babcock & Wilcox McDermott Inc.
Babe Fabergé, Inc.
Baby Line Questor Corp.
Baby Ruth Nabisco Brands, Inc.
Bache Halsey Stuart Shields, Inc. Bache Group Inc.
Badger Co. Raytheon Co.
Baggies Colgate-Palmolive Co.
Baker Diagnostics Richardson-Vicks Inc.
Bakers Edison Brothers Stores, Inc.
Baldwin Fun Machine Baldwin-United Corp.
Baltimore & Ohio CSX Corp.
Ballantine's Hiram Walker Resources Ltd.
Bama Borden, Inc.
Bamberger's R. H. Macy & Co., Inc.
Ban Bristol-Myers Co.
Bancroft Colgate-Palmolive Co.
Band-Aid Johnson & Johnson
Bank of America BankAmerica Corp.
The Bank of California, N.A. Bancal Tri-State Corp.
Bank of the Southwest Southwest Bancshares, Inc.
Bank of Virginia Bank of Virginia Co.
Bank of Virginia International Bank of Virginia Co.
Bankers and Shippers Insurance Co. of New York PennCorp Financial, Inc.
Bankers National Life Insurance Co. H. F. Ahmanson & Co.
Banquet ConAgra, Inc.
Barbie Mattel, Inc.
Bard Parker Becton, Dickinson and Co.
Barker's Household International Corp.
Barkers KDT Industries, Inc.
Barley Mow Host International, Inc.
Barnes & Tucker Alco Standard Corp.
Barnes-Hind Revlon, Inc.
Baroid NL Industries, Inc.
Baron Drawn Steel Corp. Champion Spark Plug Co.
Barron's Dow Jones & Co., Inc.
Barth & Dreyfuss of California Papercraft Corp.
Basic Four Management Assistance Inc.
Baskin Hart Schaffner & Marx
Bass Ale Carling O'Keefe Ltd.
Batesville Casket Co. Hillenbrand Industries, Inc.
Bauer & Black Becton, Dickinson and Co.
Bay State Exploration, Inc. Bay State Gas Co.
Bayer Sterling Drug Inc.
Beacon Manufacturing Co. Cannon Mills Co.
Beam Oil Co. Witco Chemical Corp.
Bear Kidde, Inc.
Bearing Specialty Co. Genuine Parts Co.
Beaumont Well Works Combustion Engineering, Inc.
Beauty Queen Triangle Pacific Corp.
Beckman Instruments, Inc. SmithKline Corp.
Beech Aircraft Corp. Raytheon Co.
Beech-Nut Nabisco Brands, Inc.
Belding Corticelli Belding Heminway Company, Inc.
Belding Lily Belding Heminway Company, Inc.
Bell Square D Co.
Bell Helicopter Textron Inc.
Bell Telephone Co. of Nevada Pacific Telephone & Telegraph Co.
Bell Telephone Laboratories American Telephone and Telegraph Co.
Belleville Division Kidde, Inc.
Belwin-Mills Publishing Corp. Esquire, Inc.
Ben Franklin (stores) Household International Corp.
Ben Franklin Life Insurance Co. Continental Corp.
Ben-Gay Pfiza Inc.
Ben Hogan AMF, Inc.
Bendey Shoe Morse Shoe, Inc.
Benguet Management Corp. Benguet Corp.
Benguet Gold Benguet Corp.
Benjamin Thomas Industries, Inc.
Benson & Hedges Philip Morris Inc.
Bentley Laboratories American Hospital Supply Co.
Berco Manufacturing Co. Burndy Corp.
Bergdorf Goodman Carter Hawley Hale Stores, Inc.
Berkley MCA Inc.
Bert L. Smokler & Company Lennar Corp.
Best Industries Varco International, Inc.
Beta Engineering and Development of Israel Gerber Scientific, Inc.
Betamax Sony Corp.
Better Homes and Gardens Meredith Corp.
Betty Crocker General Mills, Inc.
Biagi Swank, Inc.
BIC/Avnet Avnet, Inc.
Big Ben (clocks) Talley Industries, Inc.
Big Ben (clothing) Blue Bell, Inc.
Big 5 Sporting Goods Stores Thrifty Corp.
Big Red Wm. Wrigley Jr. Co.
Big Yank Interco Inc.

Bigelow Carpets Baldwin-United Corp.
Biggers Brothers, Inc. IU International Corp.
Billups Petroleum Charter Co.
Bimbo Campbell Taggart, Inc.
Bing Crosby Productions Cox Broadcasting Corp.
Binney & Smith Ltd. Binney & Smith Inc.
Bio Logicals Allied Corp.
Birds Eye General Foods Corp.
Bisquick General Mills, Inc.
Black & Decker Black & Decker Manufacturing Co.
Black Flag American Home Products Corp.
Black Velvet Heublein, Inc.
Blackfield Hawaii Corp. Pacific Lighting Corp.
Blairsat, Inc. John Blair & Co.
Blatz G. Heileman Brewing Co., Inc.
Blazer Rohm and Haas Co.
Blendex Borg-Warner Corp.
Blevins Popcorn Co. Conwood Corp.
Blocadren Merck & Co., Inc.
Block Management Co. Block (H & R), Inc.
Block's Allied Stores Corp.
Bloomingdale's Federated Department Stores, Inc.
Blue Arrow Kysor Industrial Corp.
Blue Bonnet Nabisco Brands, Inc.
Blue Mountain Nabisco Brands, Inc.
Blue Ribbon Insurance Emery Air Freight Corp.
The Blue Ridge-Winkler Textiles Lehigh Valley Industries, Inc.
Blue Streak Standard Motor Products, Inc.
Blyth Eastman Dillon & Co. Paine Webber Inc.
The Boardman Power Co. Portland General Electric Co.
Boardwalk Regency Caesars World, Inc.
Bobbie Brooks Bobbie Brooks, Inc.
Bob's Big Boy Marriott Corp.
Boeing 727, 737, 747, 757, 767 The Boeing Co.
Boise Southern Co. Southern Natural Resources, Inc.
Boker Tree Cooper Industries, Inc.
Bolt American Can Co.
Bon Marche Allied Stores Corp.
Bona Allen Tannery Tandycrafts, Inc.
Bondstrand Ameron, Inc.
Bonnie Scot Lad Foods, Inc.
Bonomo Tootsie Roll Industries, Inc.
Bonray Drilling Anta Corp.
Bonwit Teller Allied Stores Corp.
Book-of-the-Month Club Time Inc.
BookCrafters American Business Products, Inc.
Booth Consolidated Foods Corp.
Borax Colgate-Palmolive Co.
Borden Borden, Inc.
Borg Textile Bunker Ramo Corp.
Boron Standard Oil Co. (Ohio)
Borrego Springs Airline Di Giorgio Corp.
Borun Brothers Thrifty Corp.
Bosco CPC International Inc.
Bostitch Textron Inc.
The Boston Company American Express Co.
Boston Sea Party International Multifoods Corp.
BottomHalf Brown Group, Inc.
Bounty (frozen foods) Campbell Soup Co.
Bounty (paper towels) Procter & Gamble Co.
Bow Wow ConAgra, Inc.
Bowen-McLaughlin-York Harsco Corp.
Bower/BCA Bearings Federal-Mogul Corp.
Bradfoote Gear Works, Inc. Bucyrus-Erie Co.
Bradlees Stop & Shop Companies Inc.
Bradley Elgin National Industries, Inc.
Braeburn Alloy Steel Continental Copper & Steel Industries, Inc.
Brand-Rex Akzona Inc.
Braniff Airways Braniff International Corp.
Brat Subaru of America, Inc.
Braun A. G. Gillette Co.
Breakstone Dart & Kraft, Inc.
Breck American Cyanamid Co.
Breckenridge Leslie Fay Inc.
Brentwood Savings and Loan Association Jim Walter Corp.
Breyers Dart & Kraft, Inc.
Bridgeport Brass Co. National Distillers & Chemical Corp.
Bridgeport Hydraulic Co. The Hydraulic Co.
Bridgeport Machines Textron Inc.
Briggs & Stratton Disc Inc. Briggs & Stratton Corp.
Briggs & Stratton Export Corp. Briggs & Stratton Corp.
Brigham's Jewel Companies, Inc.
Bright Eyes Carnation Co.
Brim General Foods Corp.
Brink's Inc. The Pittston Co.
British Columbia Forest Products Mead Corp.
Broadcast Electronics Filmways, Inc.
The Broadway Carter Hawley Hale Stores, Inc.
Broan Manufacturing Nortek, Inc.
Brocton Sole & Plastics Atlas Corp.
Brockway Glass Co. Teledyne, Inc.
Broderick Harsco Corp.
Brohltal-Deumang A.G. General Refractories Co.
Bromo-Seltzer Warner-Lambert Co.
Brookhollow Corp. Texas Industries, Inc.
Brooks (drug stores) Adams Drug Co.
'Brooks Brothers Allied Stores Corp.
Brooks-Scanlon Diamond International Corp.

Brookstone Quaker Oats Co.
Brown & Root Halliburton Co.
Brown Institute National Education Corp.
Brown Oil Tools, Inc. Hughes Tool Co.
Brown-Service Funeral Homes Co. Liberty National Insurance Holding Co.
Brown Shoe Co. Brown Group, Inc.
Broyhill Interco Inc.
Bruce Triangle Pacific Corp.
Bruest Industries, Inc. Minnesota Gas Co.
Bruners (G. C.) Murphy Co.
Brunswick Brunswick Corp.
Brunswick Pulp & Paper Co. Mead Corp. (50%), Scott Paper Co. (50%)
Brut Fabergé, Inc.
Bryman Schools National Education Corp.
Bryn Mawr Bobbie Brooks, Inc.
Bubble Up IC Industries, Inc.
Bubble Yum Nabisco Brands, Inc.
Bucilla Greyhound Corp.
Buckeye Energy Co. Penn Central Corp.
Buckeye Telephone and Supply Mid-Continent Telephone Corp.
Buckhorn Petroleum Co. MidCon Corp.
Buckingham Corp. Beatrice Foods Co.
Bud Antle, Inc. Castle & Cooke, Inc.
Bud of California Castle & Cooke, Inc.
Buddy Skyline Corp.
Buddy's UNR Industries, Inc.
Budget Rent-A-Car Transamerica Corp.
Budweiser Anheuser-Busch Companies, Inc.
Bufferin Bristol-Myers Co.
Buffet Chef's Blend Carnation Co.
Buick General Motors Corp.
Builders Brass Works Thomas Industries, Inc.
Builders Emporium Wickes Companies, Inc.
Bull of the Woods Conwood Corp.
Bullock's Federated Department Stores, Inc.
Bulova Watch Co. Loews Corp.
Bumble Bee Castle & Cooke, Inc.
Bundy of Canada Bundy Corp.
Bunker Ramo Corp. Allied Corp.
Burdines Federated Department Stores, Inc.
Burger Chef General Foods Corp.
Burger King Pillsbury Co.
Burgerbits Nabisco Brands, Inc.
Burlington County Trust Co. Fidelity Union Bancorporation
Burlington Northern Air Freight Burlington Northern Inc.
Burlington-Northern Railroad Burlington Northern Inc.
Busch Anheuser-Busch Companies, Inc.
Bush Hog Allied Products Corp.
Business Week McGraw-Hill, Inc.
Bussman McGraw-Edison Co.
Buster Brown Brown Group, Inc.
Busy Beaver Building Centers Cyclops Corp.
Butler Aviation International, Inc. Butler International, Inc.
Butler-Johnson Inc. Penn Central Corp.
Butler Paper Great Northern Nekoosa Corp.
Butler Service Group, Inc. Butler International, Inc.
Butler Shoe Corp. Zale Corp.
Butte Knit Jonathan Logan, Inc.
Butte Knitting Mills Jonathan Logan, Inc.
Butterfinger Nabisco Brands, Inc.
Butterick Co. American Can Co.
Buttes Resources Co. Buttes Gas & Oil Co.
Buttrey Jewel Companies, Inc.
Byrns Motor Express IU International Corp.

C

C9 McDonnell Douglas Corp.
C-5N Lockheed Corp.
C-47 The Boeing Co.
C-130 Lockheed Corp.
C-141 Lockheed Corp.
C & D Batteries Allied Corp.
C & H Transportation Co. Tyler Corp.
C & M Products Limited Thomas Industries, Inc.
C. Brewer & Co., Ltd. IU International Corp.
C. H. Patrick & Co. Graniteville Co.
C.I.T. Financial RCA Corp.
CATV Anixter Bros., Inc.
CBS CBS Inc.
CF Air Consolidated Freightways, Inc.
CF & I Steel Crane Co.
CLC Barge Line CLC of America, Inc.
CNA Financial Corp. Loews Corp.
CNA Realty Corp. CNA Financial Corp.
CNG Realty Corp. Connecticut Natural Gas Corp.
CP-140 Lockheed Corp.
C. T. Bowring & Co. Marsh & McLennan Companies, Inc.
CTI International, Inc. Gelco Corp.
CTS Knights CTS Corp.
CTS Microelectronics CTS Corp.
CVS Melville Corp.
CW Transport Gerber Products Co.
Cab-O-Sil Cabot Corp.
Cabin Crafts West Point-Pepperell, Inc.
Cachet Chesebrough-Pond's Inc.
Cadet International Harvester Co.
Cadillac General Motors Corp.
Cadillac Electric Premier Industrial Corp.
Cadillac Pet Foods United States Tobacco Co.
Caesars Palace Caesars World, Inc.

Caesars Tahoe Caesars World, Inc.
Cain's Marcelle Potato Chip Co. Culbro Corp.
CalComp Sanders Associates, Inc.
Cal-Fact, Inc. Facet Enterprises, Inc.
Calabasas Park Co. Southern California Edison Co.
Caladay Project Callahan Mining Corp.
Calgon Corp. Merck & Co., Inc.
Calhoun's Dillon Companies, Inc.
California Computer Products, Inc. Sanders Associates, Inc.
California Liquid Gas Corp. Dillingham Corp.
Caloric Raytheon Co.
Calspan Corp. Arvin Industries, Inc.
Calvin Klein Puritan Fashions, Corp.
Camay Procter & Gamble Co.
Cambell Filter Co. Facet Enterprises, Inc.
Cambridge Philip Morris Inc.
Cambridge Electric Light Commonwealth Energy System
Camcar Textron Inc.
Camden Lime Atlas Corp.
Camden Wire Co., Inc. Oneida Limited
Camel R. J. Reynolds Industries, Inc.
Campbell-Ewald Co. Interpublic Group of Companies, Inc.
Campbell Red Lake Mines Dome Mines Limited
Campbell's Campbell Soup Co.
Canada Dry Dr Pepper Co.
Canadian Club Hiram Walker Resources Ltd.
Canadian Lukens Ltd. Lukens Steel Co.
Canadian Superior Oil Ltd. Superior Oil Co.
Canal Electric Commonwealth Energy System
Cannon Cannon Mills Co.
Canteen Corp. Trans World Corp.
Capital National Bank Mercantile Texas Corp.
Capital Credit Corp. The Union Corp.
Cap'n Crunch Quaker Oats Co.
Capoten Squibb Corp.
Captainer Plastics Corp. Brockway Glass Company, Inc.
Caramel Tootsie Pops Tootsie Roll Industries, Inc.
Cardiac Resuscitator Corp. Emerson Radio Corp.
Cardinal Contract Carriers, Inc. Carolina Freight Carriers Corp.
Cardinal Mining Inc. NICOR Inc.
Care Free Nabisco Brands, Inc.
Caribbean Cement Carriers Puerto Rican Cement Company, Inc.
Carlin Gold Mining Co. Newmont Mining Corp.
Carling Black Label (Canada) G. Heileman Brewing Co., Inc.
Carling Black Label (United States) Carling O'Keefe Ltd.
Carls Drug Co. Pneumo Corp.
Carlsberg Carling O'Keefe Ltd.
Carlton American Brands, Inc.
Carnation Carnation Co.
Caro-Knit Ti-Caro, Inc.
Carolina Rice Colgate-Palmolive Co.
Carrier Corp. United Technologies Corp.
Carson International Inc. Carson Pirie Scott & Co.
Carte Blanche Citicorp
Carter Automotive Group ACF Industries, Inc.
Casa Maria Host International, Inc.
Cascade Procter & Gamble Co.
Cascade Land Leasing Co. Cascade Natural Gas Corp.
Castleberry Knits Ltd. Leslie Fay Inc.
Casual Corner United States Shoe Corp.
Celeste Quaker Oats Co.
Cenco, Inc. Manor Care, Inc.
Central Die Casting & Manufacturing Co., Inc. Tokheim Corp.
Central Hardware Interco Inc.
Central Louisiana Electric Central Louisiana Energy Corp.
Central Metal Products Co. Barnes Groups, Inc.
Central Power & Light Central & South West Corp.
Central States Can Co. Van Dorn Co.
Centurion Computer Corp. Electronic Data Systems Corp.
Centurion Life Insurance Co. Dial Corp.
Century Products, Inc. Gerber Products Co.
Century 21 Real Estate Trans World Corp.
Cessna Finance Corp. The Cessna Aircraft Co.
Cessna Fluid Power, Ltd. The Cessna Aircraft Co.
Chalk's International Resorts International, Inc.
Challenge Minerals Global Marine Inc.
Chamberlain Group Ltd. Brown & Sharpe Manufacturing Co.
Champ Standard Motor Products, Inc.
Champlin Petroleum Co. Union Pacific Corp.
Chandler Leasing Walter E. Heller International Corp.
Chandlers Edison Brothers Stores, Inc.
Channel W. R. Grace & Co.
Channel Master Avnet, Inc.
ChapStick Robins (A. H.) Co., Inc.
Chaparral Steel Co. Texas Industries, Inc.
Chaparral Transports, Inc. Pengo Industries, Inc.
Charles A. Stevens Hart Schaffner & Marx
Charles & Co. Southland Corp.
Charles of the Ritz Group Ltd. Squibb Corp.

Charles Schwab BankAmerica Corp.
Charley Brown's Host International, Inc.
Charley's Place Host International, Inc.
Charlie Revlon, Inc.
Charlotte *Observer* Knight-Ridder Newspapers, Inc.
Charmin Procter & Gamble Co.
Charter Distributing Co. American Agronomics Corp.
Charter National Life Insurance Co. Leucadia National Corp.
Charter Oil Charter Co.
Checker Lucky Stores, Inc.
Cheer Procter & Gamble Co.
Cheerios General Mills, Inc.
Chef Boy-ar-dee American Home Products Corp.
Chef Saluto General Mills, Inc.
Chemed W. R. Grace & Co.
Chemetron Corp. Allegheny International, Inc.
Chemical Bank Chemical New York Corp.
Cheracol Upjohn Co.
Chesapeake & Ohio CSX Corp.
Chess King Melville Corp.
Chevrolet General Motors Corp.
Chevron Standard Oil Co. of California
Chex Ralston Purina Co.
Chicago Bridge & Iron Co. CBI Industries, Inc.
Chicago Title & Trust Lincoln National Corp.
Chicken of the Sea Ralston Purina Co.
Chiclets Warner-Lambert Co.
ChicknFryer National Presto Industries
Chief Auto Parts Southland Corp.
Chiffon Anderson, Clayton & Co.
Child Guidance CBS Inc.
Child World Cole National Corp.
Children's Place Federated Department Stores, Inc.
Chinet Arcata Corp.
Chinook The Boeing Co.
Chivas Regal Seagram Co. Ltd.
Chlor-Trimeton Schering-Plough Corp.
Christensen, Inc. Norton Company
Christian Brothers Seagram Co. Ltd.
Chromcraft Mohasco Corp.
Chromium Corp. Elcor Corp.
Chrysler Chrysler Corp.
Chrysler Defense Chrysler Corp.
Chun King R. J. Reynolds Industries, Inc.
Church's Fried Chicken Church's Fried Chicken, Inc.
Ciari & Forti (Italy) Quaker Oats Co.
CIE American Cyanamid Co.
Cincinnati *Enquirer* Gannett Co., Inc.
Cincinnati Milacron Chemicals Thiokol Corp.
Cincinnati Savings Transohio Financial Corp.
Circle Bar Drilling Co. CBI Industries, Inc.
Circus World Mattel, Inc.
Citibank Citicorp
Cities Service Gas Co. Cities Service Co.
City Finance Leucadia National Corp.
City Market Dillon Companies, Inc.
City Products Corp. Household International Corp.
Claire Manufacturing Co. Oakite Products, Inc.
Clairol Bristol-Myers Co.
Clark Clark Oil & Refining Corp.
Clarke McGraw-Edison Co.
Clark's Cook United Inc.
Classic Dark Anheuser-Busch Companies, Inc.
Claud S. Gordon Pneumo Corp.
Clearasil Richardson-Vicks Inc.
Clearwater Concrete U. S. Home Corp.
Cleocin Upjohn Co.
Cleveland Pneumatic Pneumo Corp.
Cleveland Twist Drill Acme-Cleveland Corp.
Climatrol Fedders Corp.
Clinchfield Railroad CSX Corp.
Clinch River Corp. Elgin National Industries, Inc.
Clinoril Merck & Co., Inc.
Clinton Corn Processing Nabisco Brands, Inc.
Clorox The Clorox Co.
Cloth World Brown Group, Inc.
Clothesworks Jack Winter
Club Aluminum Cookware Standex International Corp.
Clyde Fabrics Ti-Caro, Inc.
Coast-to-Coast Household International Corp.
Cobbies United States Shoe Corp.
Cobbs (G. C.) Murphy Co.
Coburn Optical Industries Revlon, Inc.
Coca-Cola Coca-Cola Co.
Coca-Cola Bottling Co. of Los Angeles Beatrice Foods Co.
Codex Corp. Motorola Inc.
Coffee, Tea & A New Me The Thompson Medical Co., Inc.
Coffee-mate Carnation Co.
Coldwell, Banker Sears, Roebuck and Co.
Colgate Colgate-Palmolive Co.
Colonial (breads) Campbell Taggart, Inc.
Colonial (lighting fixtures) Thomas Industries, Inc.
Colonial (sugar) Borden, Inc.
Colonial First National Bank Fidelity Union Bancorporation
Colony Heublein, Inc.
Colorburst Eastman Kodak Co.
Colortex APL Corp.
Colt Colt Industries Inc.

Colt 45 Malt Liquor G. Heileman Brewing Co., Inc.
Columbia Pictures Industries, Inc. Coca-Cola Co.
Columbia CBS Inc.
Columbia Savings and Loan Association MCA Inc.
Comalco Kaiser Aluminum & Chemical Corp.
Combined Communications Gannett Co., Inc.
Com/Energy Exploration Commonwealth Energy System
Com/Energy Steam Commonwealth Energy System
Comet Procter & Gamble Co.
Comfort Supply Telecom Corp.
Comfy Home Furnishings Reeves Brothers, Inc.
Commercial Credit Co. Control Data Corp.
Commercial Lovelace Motor Freight, Inc. Banner Industries, Inc.
Commonwealth Electric Commonwealth Energy System
Commonwealth Gas Commonwealth Energy System
Commonwealth Life Insurance Co. Capital Holding Corp.
Commonwealth Water Co. American Water Works Company, Inc.
Community Oneida Limited
Community Blood & Plasma Service Ipco Corp.
Compass Foods Great Atlantic & Pacific Tea Co.
Computalog Gearhart, Ltd. Gearhart Industries, Inc.
Computer Accounting Management, Inc. Di Giorgio Corp.
COMSAT General Corp. Communications Satellite Corp.
Con-Tact United Merchants & Manufacturers, Inc.
Conap Wheelabrator-Frye Corp.
Concord American Motors Corp.
Connecticut General Life Insurance Co. Connecticut General Insurance Corp.
Connecticut Light & Power Northeast Utilities
Connolly Tool & Engineering Co. Ennis Business Forms, Inc.
Conoco Inc. E. I. du Pont de Nemours & Co.
Conrel Albany International Corp.
Consolidated Cigar Corp. Gulf & Western Industries, Inc.
Consolidated Leasing Corp. CLC of America, Inc.
Consolidated Sales Co. Cook United Inc.
Constitution Reinsurance Corp. Crum and Forster
Consumers' Gas Hiram Walker Resources Ltd.
Contac SmithKline Corp.
Container Carrier Corp. Arkansas Best Corp.
Container Corp. of America Mobil Corp.
Contempo Casuals Carter Hawley Hale Stores, Inc.
Continental Air Lines Texas Air Corp.
Continental American Life Insurance Co. Crown Central Petroleum Corp.
Continental Assurance Loews Corp.
Continental Baking Co. International Telephone & Telegraph Corp.
Continental Can Co. Continental Group, Inc.
Continental Casualty Loews Corp.
Continental-Emsco LTV Corp.
Continental Forest Industries Continental Group, Inc.
Continental Illinois National Bank & Trust Co. Continental Illinois Corp.
Continental Insurance Co. Continental Corp.
Continental Plastics Co. Carlisle Corp.
Continuous Curve Contact Lenses Inc. Revlon, Inc.
Convenient Food Mart, Inc. Scot Lad Foods, Inc.
Cook's Cook United Inc.
Cookbook American Bakeries Co.
Cooper Cooper Tire & Rubber Co.
CooperVision Cooper Laboratories, Inc.
CooperCare Cooper Laboratories, Inc.
Coordinated Caribbean Transport Transway International Corp.
Copenhagen United States Tobacco Co.
Copper Range Louisiana Land & Exploration Co.
Coppertone Schering-Plough Corp.
Cor Tec UMC Industries, Inc.
Coral MCA Inc.
Corelle Corning Glass Works
Corinthian Broadcasting Dun & Bradstreet Corp.
Corn Bran Quaker Oats Co.
Corning Ware Corning Glass Works
Coronet Georgia-Pacific Corp.
Corpus Christi National Bank Mercantile Texas Corp.
Cort Furniture Rental Mohasco Corp.
Corto-Plex Helene Curtis Industries, Inc.
Cory Food Service Hershey Foods Corp.
Cos Cob Oxford Industries, Inc.
Cosco-Tucket Kidde, Inc.
Cosden Oil & Chemical Co. American Petrofina, Inc.
Cosmos (soccer team) Warner Communications, Inc.
Cosmos Broadcasting Corp. The Liberty Corp.
Cotton Petroleum United Energy Resources, Inc.
Coty Pfizer Inc.

Country Kitchen American Home Products Corp.
County Savings Transohio Financial Corp.
County Seat Super Valu Stores, Inc.
Country Store Wickes Companies, Inc.
Courvoisier Hiram Walker Resources Ltd.
Coverlight Reeves Brothers, Inc.
Coward, McCann & Geoghegan MCA Inc.
Cracker Jack Borden, Inc.
Craft Master General Mills, Inc.
Craft Showcase Cole National Corp.
Craftlite Esquire, Inc.
Crane Canada Ltd. Crane Co.
Crane Carrier Company CCI Corp.
Crayola Binney & Smith Inc.
Crazy Horse Russ Togs, Inc.
Creative Merchandising & Publishing Modern Merchandising, Inc.
Creative Playthings CBS Inc.
Credo Omark Industries, Inc.
Crescent Cooper Industries, Inc.
Crest (publishing) CBS Inc.
Crest (toothpaste) Procter & Gamble Co.
Crestliner AMF, Inc.
Cricket Gillette Co.
Crisco Procter & Gamble Co.
Criterion Insurance Co. GEICO Corp.
Crocker National Bank Crocker National Corp.
Crometrics American Home Products Corp.
Crosman Coleman Co., Inc.
Crouse-Hinds Cooper Industries, Inc.
Crown Airways Brockway Glass Company, Inc.
Crown Financial Corp. Crown Cork & Seal Co., Inc.
Crucible Steel Colt Industries Inc.
Cruex Pennwalt Corp.
Cruise The Boeing Co.
Crush International Procter & Gamble Co.
CryoSource Sargent-Welch Scientific Co.
Crystal Foremost-McKesson, Inc.
Cubby Drilling Penn Central Corp.
Cudahy Co. General Host Corp.
Cuno AMF, Inc.
Curad Colgate-Palmolive Co.
Curtis Circulation Co. Cadence Industries Corp.
Curtis 1000 American Business Products, Inc.
Curtiss-Wright Teledyne, Inc.
Curwood, Inc. Bemis Company, Inc.
Cushman Outboard Marine Corp.
Custodis Construction Research-Cottrell, Inc.
Cutco Aluminum Co. of America
Cutex Chesebrough-Pond's Inc.
Cutler-Hammer Eaton Corp.
Cycle General Foods Corp.
Cycopac Borg-Warner Corp.

D

D-A Lubricant Company, Inc. Premier Industrial Corp.
D. C. Heath Raytheon Co.
DC-9 McDonnell Douglas Corp.
DC-10 McDonnell Douglas Corp.
DX Sun Co., Inc.
Dacron E. I. du Pont de Nemours & Co.
Dad's Root Beer IC Industries, Inc.
Daisy (air rifles) Kidde, Inc.
Daisy (razors) Gillette Co.
Dale Electronics, Inc. The Lionel Corp.
Dalkon Shield Robins (A. H.) Co., Inc.
Dalmo Victor Textron Inc.
Dallas Power & Light Texas Utilities Co.
Dallas *Times Herald* Times Mirror Co.
Dan River Dan River Inc.
Daniel International Fluor Corp.
Daniel Oil Tools Co. Daniel Industries, Inc.
Daniel Valve Co. Daniel Industries, Inc.
Dart Truck Co. PACCAR Inc.
Dartmouth Investments Ltd. Harsco Corp.
Darvon Eli Lilly and Co.
Dash Procter & Gamble Co.
Data 100 Corp. Northern Telecom Ltd.
Data Resources, Inc. McGraw-Hill, Inc.
Dataservice Co. Bergen Brunswig Corp.
Davac Nashua Corp.
David Crystal General Mills, Inc.
David's Petrie Stores Corp.
Davies Can Co. Van Dorn Co.
Davis & Geck American Cyanamid Co.
Davison's R. H. Macy & Co., Inc.
Davol Inc. Bard (C. R.), Inc.
Dayton-Hudson Jewelers Dayton-Hudson Corp.
Dayton's Dayton-Hudson Corp.
d-Con Sterling Drug Inc.
De Kuyper National Distillers & Chemical Corp.
De Leuw, Cather & Co. Parsons Corp.
DeLiso Brown Group, Inc.
DeRoy Jewelers Kay Corp.
DeSoto Coatings Ltd. DeSoto, Inc.
Dean Witter Reynolds Organization Inc. Sears, Roebuck and Co.
Decimus Corp. BankAmerica Corp.
Dee Wood Industries U. S. Home Corp.
Deep Rock Kerr-McGee Corp.
Del Mar Triangle Pacific Corp.
Del Monte R. J. Reynolds Industries, Inc.
Del Taco W. R. Grace & Co.
DeLamar MAPCO Inc.
Delaware & Hudson Railway Norfolk & Western Railway Co.
Delmonico Hershey Foods Corp.

Delsey Kimberly-Clark Corp.
Delta McDonnell Douglas Corp.
Delta Engineering Alaska Interstate Co.
Delta Marketing Co. MAPCO Inc.
Delta Refining Co. MAPCO Inc.
Delta Steamship Lines Holiday Inns, Inc.
Deltic Farm & Timber Murphy Oil Corp.
Demerol Sterling Drug Inc.
Demulen G. D. Searle & Co.
Denny's Denny's Inc.
Densichron Sargent-Welch Scientific Co.
Dental Conwood Corp.
Dental Insurance Co., Ltd. Tidewater Inc.
Dentyne Warner-Lambert Co.
Denver and Rio Grande Western Railroad Rio Grande Industries, Inc.
Denver Dry Goods Associated Dry Goods Corp.
Denver *Post* Times Mirror Co.
Depend Loctite Corp.
Dermassage Colgate-Palmolive Co.
Desarrollos Multiples Insulares, Inc. Puerto Rican Cement Company, Inc.
Desenex Pennwalt Corp.
Deseret Warner-Lambert Co.
Desitin Pfizer Inc.
Detroit *Free Press* Knight-Ridder Newspapers, Inc.
Detroit Stoker Co. United Industrial Corp.
The DeVilbiss Co. Champion Spark Plug Co.
Devon Interco Inc.
Dexatrim The Thompson Medical Co., Inc.
Di-Gel Schering-Plough Corp.
Di Giorgio Development Corp. Di Giorgio Corp.
Dial Greyhound Corp.
Dial Corp. Northwest Bancorporation
The Diamond Associated Dry Goods Corp.
Diamond Financial Holdings Inc. Dana Corp.
Diamond's Dayton-Hudson Corp.
Diana Fruit Preserving Federal Co.
Diane von Furstenberg Puritan Fashions, Corp.
Dictaphone Corp. Pitney-Bowes, Inc.
Dillon's Dillon Companies, Inc.
Diminsion II Oak Industries, Inc.
Dinty Moore George A. Hormel & Co.
Direct Tenneco Inc.
Discount Drug Stores Thrifty Corp.
Disneyland Walt Disney Productions
Dixie American Can Co.
Dixie Vim Charter Co.
Dixon Industries Bundy Corp.
Dobbs Houses, Inc. Carson Pirie Scott & Co.
Documation Inc. Storage Technology Corp.
Dodge Chrysler Corp.
Doerr Electric Corp. W. W. Grainger, Inc.
Dole Castle & Cooke, Inc.
Dolgin's Modern Merchandising, Inc.
Dolly Madison (ice cream) Foremost-McKesson, Inc.
Dolly Madison (paper products) Fort Howard Paper Co.
Dominick's Finer Foods Fisher Foods, Inc.
Domestic Finance Leucadia National Corp.
Domino Amstar Corp.
Donaldson, Lufkin & Jenrette Securities Donaldson, Lufkin & Jenrette, Inc.
Donaldson's Allied Stores Corp.
Donmoor Cluett, Peabody & Co., Inc.
Dori Shoe Lehigh Valley Industries, Inc.
Doric Co. Esmark, Inc.
Dorman's Lucky Stores, Inc.
Dormavac Grumman Corp.
Dorothy Gray Sterling Drug Inc.
Double Up Wickes Companies, Inc.
Doublemint Wm. Wrigley Jr. Co.
Douwe Egberts B.V. Consolidated Foods Corp.
Dove Unilever PLC
Dow Dow Chemical Co.
Dow Corning Corning Glass Works
Downy Procter & Gamble Co.
Drake's Borden, Inc.
Dramamine G. D. Searle & Co.
Drano Bristol-Myers Co.
Dredgemasters International Valley Industries, Inc.
Dresher Standex International Corp.
Dressel's American Bakeries Co.
The Dreyfus Interstate Development Corp. Lennar Corp.
Drilco Smith International, Inc.
Dristan American Home Products Corp.
The Dry Goods SCOA Industries, Inc.
Dry Look Gillette Co.
Duet SCOA Industries, Inc.
Duff-Norton Amstar Corp.
Duffy-Mott American Brands, Inc.
Duncan Hines Procter & Gamble Co.
Dunham Manufacturing Co. XTRA Corp.
Dunn Properties Corp. Pacific Lighting Corp.
Duofold Cluett, Peabody & Co., Inc.
Duracell Dart & Kraft, Inc.
Duraflame The Clorox Co.
Durkee Foods SCM Corp.
Duro (adhesives) Loctite Corp.
Duro (textiles) Nortek, Inc.
Dutch Boy Sherwin-Williams Co.
Dutch Masters Gulf & Western Industries, Inc.
Duval Pennzoil Co.
Dyazide SmithKline Corp.
Dyna-Drill Smith International, Inc.
Dynamo Colgate-Palmolive Co.

Dynapar Corp. Chicago Pneumatic Tool Co.
Dynatech Corp. Craig Corp.

E

E-2C Grumman Corp.
E. J. Brach American Home Products Corp.
EA-6B Grumman Corp.
ECRM AM International
EFC Property Management Orion Capital Corp.
ERC Corp. Getty Oil Co.
ESI Meats, Inc. Ponderosa System, Inc.
Eagle (automobiles) American Motors Corp.
Eagle (food) Lucky Stores, Inc.
Eagle Family Discount Interco, Inc.
Eagle Mining Inc. NICOR Inc.
Eagle Oil Co. MAPCO Inc.
Eagle Rubber Brown Group, Inc.
Eagle Stamp Co. May Department Stores Co.
Earth Born Gillette Co.
Earth Grains Campbell Taggart, Inc.
Earth Resources MAPCO Inc.
East Texas Swabbing, Inc. Pengo Industries, Inc.
Eastman Chemicals Eastman Kodak Co.
Easy Flo Handy & Harman
Easy-Off American Home Products Corp.
Easy Street Genesco Inc.
Eat-It-All Maryland Cup Corp.
Eaton Textron Inc.
Ebasco Services Enserch Corp.
Eckerd Drug Jack Eckerd Corp.
Eckerd's Apparel Jack Eckerd Corp.
Eclipse Data General Corp.
Economic Models Ltd. McGraw-Hill, Inc.
Ecusta Olin Corp.
Edelweiss Warnaco Inc.
Edgcomb Metals Co. Williams Companies
Edgington Oil Co. Penn Central Corp.
Edon Fort Howard Paper Co.
Edward Phillips Alco Standard Corp.
Effects Technology, Inc. Flow General Inc.
Eggo Kellogg Co.
Eisenstadt Co. Lenox, Inc.
Eisner's Jewel Companies, Inc.
Ekco American Home Products Corp.
Ektachrome Eastman Kodak Co.
Ektra Eastman Kodak Co.
El Charrito Campbell Taggart, Inc.
El Chico Campbell Taggart, Inc.
El Marko Gillette Co.
El Producto Gulf & Western Industries, Inc.
Elavil Merck & Co., Inc.
Elektra Warner Communications, Inc.
Electric Systems Co. Southern California Edison Co.
Electro-Voice, Inc. Gulton Industries, Inc.
Electrolux Consolidated Foods Corp.
Elgin Elgin National Industries, Inc.
Elizabeth Arden Eli Lilly and Co.
Elk Corporation of America Elcor Corp.
Elkhorn Insurance National Distillers & Chemical Corp.
Elmer's Borden, Inc.
Elox Colt Industries Inc.
Eltex V Plantronics, Inc.
Eltra Corp. Allied Corp.
Emeraude Pfizer Inc.
Emerson Plastronics Basic Resources Corp.
Emery Industries National Distillers & Chemical Corp.
Emery Ocean Freight Emery Air Freight Corp.
Empire Machinery Corp. Empire Inc.
Employees Benefits, Inc. Orion Capital Corp.
Emporium Capwell Carter Hawley Hale Stores, Inc.
Energy & Minerals, Inc. South Jersey Industries, Inc.
Energy Increments Southwest Gas Corp.
Energy Land, Inc. Minnesota Power and Light Co.
Energy Resources Group of Oregon, Inc. Portland General Electric Co.
Energy Services, Inc. Southern California Edison Co.
Energy Subsidiary, Inc. South Carolina Electric & Gas Co.
Enfamil Bristol-Myers Co.
Engine House Pizza Quaker Oats Co.
Engineering Equipment, Inc. Berguet Corp.
Engineering News-Record McGraw-Hill, Inc.
Engineering-Science, Inc. Parsons Corp.
Enline Ennis Business Forms, Inc.
Enovid G. D. Searle & Co.
ENSERCO, Inc. Iowa Resources, Inc.
Entenmann's Warner-Lambert Co.
Enterprise Companies Insilco Corp.
Entrada Industries Mountain Fuel Supply Co.
Environmental Research & Technology, Inc. Communications Satellite Corp.
Environmentals and Southern Service Co. Angelica Corp.
Epic CBS Inc.
Epiphone Norlin Corp.
Equibank Equimark Corp.
Equipment Renewal Co. Kenai Corp.
Equitable Gas-Energy Equitable Gas Co.
Era Procter & Gamble Co.
Eraser Mate Gillette Co.
Erector CBS Inc.
Erie Lackawanna Railway Norfolk & Western Railway Co.

Erika, Inc. National Medical Care, Inc.
Erlanger Schlitz (Jos.) Brewing Co.
Erythrocin Abbott Laboratories
Essex United Technologies Corp.
Essex Frank Essex Chemical Corp.
Estech Inc. Esmark, Inc.
Ethan Allen Interco Inc.
Etienne Aigner Jonathan Logan, Inc.
Euro-Advertising Holding, B.V. JWT Group, Inc.
Europa MCA Inc.
Europate Campbell Taggart, Inc.
Evan-Picone Palm Beach Inc.
Evans-Black Armstrong World Industries, Inc.
Evansville Morris Plan Co., Inc. Credithrift Financial, Inc.
Eveready Union Carbide Corp.
Eversharp The Parker Pen Co.
Evinrude Outboard Marine Corp.
Excedrin Bristol-Myers Co.
Exchange Oil and Gas Georgia-Pacific Corp.
Executone, Inc. Continental Telephone Corp.
Exeter Co. MidCon Corp.
Expert Automation Lamson & Sessions Co.
Exxon Exxon Corp.
Exxon Enterprises Exxon Corp.
Exxon Office Systems Exxon Corp.

F

F-15 McDonnell Douglas Corp.
F-14 Grumman Corp.
F-16 General Dynamics Corp.
F & R Builders, Inc. Lennar Corp.
F. W. Dodge McGraw-Hill, Inc.
F/A-18A McDonnell Douglas Corp.
FDS Alberto-Culver Co.
FWA Drilling Co. Texas Oil & Gas Corp.
Fab Colgate-Palmolive Co.
FabricsAmerica Allied Products Corp.
Fafnir Textron Inc.
Fairbanks Morse Colt Industries Inc.
Fairchild Camera and Instrument Corp. Schlumberger Limited
Fairchild Publications Capital Cities Communications, Inc.
Fairmac Realty Corp. CBI Industries, Inc.
Fairmont Food Co. Culbro Corp.
Fairmont Railway Motors Harsco Corp.
Falcon Seaboard Diamond Shamrock Corp.
Falls Cooper Tire & Rubber Co.
Family Life Insurance Merrill Lynch & Co., Inc.
Family Mart Great Atlantic & Pacific Tea Co.
Famous-Barr May Department Stores Co.
Fan Coach Coachmen Industries, Inc.
Fanta Coca-Cola Co.
Fantastik Morton-Norwich Products, Inc.
Far West Savings and Loan Association Far West Financial Corp.
Farberware Kidde, Inc.
Farmer Jack Borman's Inc.
Farrell, Ozmun, Kirk & Co. American Hoist & Derrick Co.
Farrell's Ice Cream Parlours Marriott Corp.
Farr's Family Shoes Lane Bryant, Inc.
Farymann Diesel GmbH Briggs & Stratton Corp.
Fashion Crossroads Wickes Companies, Inc.
Fastway Fasteners Thomas Industries, Inc.
Fawcett CBS Inc.
Fayva Morse Shoe, Inc.
Fazio's Albertson's, Inc.
Fazio's (Ohio) Fisher Foods, Inc.
Fearn International Kellogg Co.
Fedders Fedders Corp.
Feld Truck Leasing Division Gelco Corp.
Feldene Pfizer Inc.
The Feldspar Corp. Pacific Tin Consolidated Corp.
Felsway Corp. Heck's, Inc.
Fems Kimberly-Clark Corp.
Fender-Rhodes CBS Inc.
Fiat-Allis Allis-Chalmers Corp.
Fiberglas Owens-Corning Fiberglas Corp.
Fidelity & Guaranty Life USF & G Corp.
Fidelity Union Trust Co. Fidelity Union Bancorporation
Field & Stream CBS Inc.
Fieldcrest Fieldcrest Mills, Inc.
Filene's Federated Department Stores, Inc.
FINA American Petrofina, Inc.
Finance-America Corp. BankAmerica Corp.
Fingerhut American Can Co.
Fireman's Fund Insurance Co. American Express Co.
First Atlanta Factors Inc. First Atlanta Corp.
First Bank of Savannah First Atlanta Corp.
First Chicago Leasing Corp. First Chicago Corp.
First Chicago Realty Services First Chicago Corp.
First City National Bank of Houston First City Bancorp of Texas, Inc.
First Colony Life Insurance Co. Ethyl Corp.
First Financial Life Insurance Co. First Atlanta Corp.
First International Bank in Houston First International Bancshares, Inc.
First Interstate Bank of (California, Oregon, etc.) First Interstate Bancorp
First National Bank and Trust Co. of Naples Southwest Florida Banks, Inc.

First National Bank in Dallas First International Bancshares, Inc.
First National Bank in Fort Meyers Southwest Florida Banks, Inc.
First National Bank of Atlanta First Atlanta Corp.
First National Bank of Birmingham AmSouth Corp.
First National Bank of Boston First National Boston Corp.
First National Bank of Chicago First Chicago Corp.
First National Bank of Dalton First Atlanta Corp.
First National Bank of New Jersey Fidelity Union Bancorporation
First National Bank of Savannah First Atlanta Corp.
First National State Bank of New Jersey First National State Bancorporation
First Nationwide Savings National Steel Corp.
First Pennsylvania Bank First Pennsylvania Corp.
First Texas Financial Corp. Beneficial Corp.
First Wisconsin National Bank of Milwaukee First Wisconsin Corp.
Firth Mohasco Corp.
Fischbach and Moore Fischbach Corp.
Fisher Controls Monsanto Co.
Fisher Beatrice Foods Co.
Fisher-Price Toys Quaker Oats Co.
Fisher Scientific Allied Corp.
Fives Nabisco Brands, Inc.
Flagg Brothers Genesco Inc.
Flagyl G. D. Searle & Co.
Flair Gillette Co.
Flako Quaker Oats Co.
Fleetcom II Johnson (E. F.) Co.
Fleischmann Bakery Ingredients Nabisco Brands, Inc.
Fleischmann's Nabisco Brands, Inc.
Fleming H. Revell Co. SFN Companies, Inc.
Flex Revlon, Inc.
Flex-Kleen Corp. Research-Cottrell, Inc.
Flex-O-Lite General Steel Industries, Inc.
Flora Danica Swank, Inc.
Florida Associated Services American Heritage Life Investment Corp.
Florsheim Interco Inc.
Flow Laboratories Flow General Inc.
Flxible Grumman Corp.
Flying Tiger Lines Tiger International, Inc.
Foamy Gillette Co.
Foley's Federated Department Stores, Inc.
Folger's Procter & Gamble Co.
Food Basket Lucky Stores, Inc.
Food Fair Mini Mart Borman's Inc.
Foods Plus APL Corp.
Foot Locker F. W. Woolworth Co.
Foote Mineral Co. Newmont Mining Corp.
Ford Ford Motor Co.
Ford Motor Credit Co. Ford Motor Co.
Foremost Foremost-McKesson, Inc.
Foremost Warehouse Corp. Overnite Transportation Co.
Form 3 Helene Curtis Industries, Inc.
Formica American Cyanamid Co.
Formula 409 The Clorox Co.
Fort Dodge American Home Products Corp.
Fortrel Celanese Corp.
Fortune Time Inc.
Foss Launch & Tug Co. Dillingham Corp.
Foster & Kleiser Metromedia, Inc.
Four Seasons Nursing Centers Anta Corp.
4-TEL Teradyne, Inc.
Fox Deluxe Pillsbury Co.
Fox Valley Instrument Co. Chicago Pneumatic Tool Co.
Foxmoor Melville Corp.
Frabill Huffy Corp.
Fram Bendix Corp.
Franco-American Campbell Soup Co.
Frank Lewis Grapefruit Club Standex International Corp.
Franklin (stores) Petrie Stores Corp.
Franklin Aluminum Hoover Universal, Inc.
Franklin Life Insurance Co. American Brands, Inc.
Franklin Mint Warner Communications, Inc.
Franklin Stove Host International, Inc.
Fred Perry Sportswear Figgie International
Fred's Gang Lucky Stores, Inc.
Freedent Wm. Wrigley Jr. Co.
Freeport Minerals Co. Freeport-McMoRan Inc.
French Shriner United States Shoe Corp.
Freon E. I. Du Pont de Nemours & Co.
Fresca Coca-Cola Co.
Fresh Start Colgate-Palmolive Co.
Friend Tire Service, Inc. Mohawk Rubber Co.
Friendly Ice Cream Corp. Hershey Foods Corp.
Friendship Regional Airport Piedmont Aviation, Inc.
Frigidaire White Consolidated Industries, Inc.
Friskies Carnation Co.
First Interstate Bank of . . . (California, Oregon, etc.) First Interstate Bancorp
Frito-Lay PepsiCo, Inc.
Frontier Airlines General Tire & Rubber Co.
Froot Loops Kellogg Co.
Frosted Mini-Wheats Kellogg Co.

Frostemp Wynn's International Inc.
Fruit of the Loom Northwest Industries
Fry's Gerbes Dillon Companies, Inc.
Frye Alberto-Culver Co.
Frye Copysystems Wheelabrator-Frye Inc.
Fuel Resources Inc. The Brooklyn Union Gas Co.
Fuels, Inc. Connecticut Natural Gas Corp.
Full Course General Foods Corp.
Fuller Brush Consolidated Foods Corp.
Fuller Co. GATX Corp.
Funk & Wagnalls Dun & Bradstreet Corp.
Funk Cooper Industries, Inc.
Furr's Cafeterias K mart Corp.
Futorian Mohasco Corp.
Future-data Computer Corp. GenRad, Inc.

G

G&G Petrie Stores Corp.
G's Wayne-Gossard Corp.
G. Fox May Department Stores Co.
G. H. Bass & Co. Chesebrough-Pond's Inc.
G. M. Stewart Lumber Co., Inc. Lone Star Industries, Inc.
G. P. Putnam's Sons MCA Inc.
G.W. Jr. Hamburgers Church's Fried Chicken, Inc.
GAB Business Services UAL, Inc.
GATX Tank Erection GATX Corp.
GCA/Burlington Division GCA Corp.
GDV Inc. City Investing Co.
GE General Electric Co.
GES EG & G, Inc.
GK Technologies Penn Central Corp.
GMC General Motors Corp.
GSC/Six Flags Corp. Penn Central Corp.
GSI Square D Co.
GTE Communications Products General Telephone & Electronics Corp.
GTE Electrical Products General Telephone & Electronics Corp.
Gabriel CBS Inc.
Gaftemp GAF Corp.
Gaido-Lingle Division General Steel Industries, Inc.
Gaines Manufacturing Co. United Inns, Inc.
Gaines (pet food) General Foods Corp.
Gala American Can Co.
Galbraith & Green, Inc. Fred S. James & Co., Inc.
Gallagher Ltd. American Brands, Inc.
Gallenkamp SCOA Industries, Inc.
Gamble Department Stores Wickes Companies, Inc.
Gambles Wickes Companies, Inc.
Gant Palm Beach Inc.
Garamycin Schering-Plough Corp.
Garcia Y Vega Bayuk Cigars Inc.
Garden State National Bank Fidelity Union Bancorporation
Garden State Tanning Kidde, Inc.
Gardner-Denver Cooper Industries, Inc.
Gardner Laboratory Pacific Scientific Co.
Garfinkel, Brooks Brothers, Miller & Rhoads, Inc. Allied Stores Corp.
Garland E-Systems, Inc.
Garlock Inc. Colt Industries Inc.
Garnhealth Grain Publicker Industries, Inc.
Garrett Corp. Signal Companies, Inc.
Gas Energy Inc. The Brooklyn Union Gas Co.
Gateway Casuals Interco Inc.
Gatorade Stokely-Van Camp, Inc.
Gayfer's Mercantile Stores Co., Inc.
Gelco Fleet and Management Services Division Gelco Corp.
Gemco Lucky Stores, Inc.
Gemeinhardt CBS Inc.
GenRad Semiconductor Test, Inc. GenRad, Inc.
General American Advisers, Inc. General American Investors Co., Inc.
General American Transportation Corp. GATX Corp.
General Battery Northwest Industries
General DataComm Systems, Inc. General DataComm Industries, Inc.
General Defense Corp. Clabir Corp.
General Development Corp. City Investing Co.
General Finance Loews Corp.
General Finance Service Corp. Bank of Virginia Co.
General Medical Corp. Whittaker Corp.
General Motors Acceptance Corp. General Motors Corp.
General Nutrition Centers General Nutrition, Inc.
General Ohio S&L Corp. Dana Corp.
General Refractories Co. of Canada, Ltd. General Refractories Co.
General Reinsurance Corp. General Reinsurance Corp.
General Time Corp. Talley Industries, Inc.
General Waterworks Corp. IU International Corp.
Generation '79 Jack Winter
Genex Koppers Co.
Geni Avon Products, Inc.
Geo Churchill, Inc. GEO International Corp.
Geo Drilling Fluids GEO International Corp.
Geo Vann, Inc. GEO International Corp.
George A. Milton Can Co. Van Dorn Co.

George W. Townsend Lease Service Newpark Resources
Georgia International Life Capital Holding Corp.
Georgia Kraft Co. Mead Corp.
Georgia Power Southern Co.
Georgian West Point-Pepperell, Inc.
Geotex Corp. Gearhart Industries, Inc.
Geriatrics Inc. ARA Services, Inc.
Geritol Nabisco Brands, Inc.
Gertz Allied Stores Corp.
Gettys Manufacturing Co. Gould Inc.
Giant Cooper Tire & Rubber Co.
Gibraltar Corp. of America United Jersey Banks
Gibraltar Savings and Loan Association Gibraltar Financial Corp. of California
Gibson (appliances) White Consolidated Industries, Inc.
Gibson (instruments) Norlin Corp.
Gifford-Hill Portland Cement Co. Gifford-Hill & Co., Inc.
Gilbey's National Distillers & Chemical Corp.
Glacier Sand and Gravel Co. Kaiser Cement Corp.
Glad bags Union Carbide Corp.
Glass Containers Corp. Norton Simon, Inc.
Glassalium Engineering Corp. Nortek, Inc.
Glidden Coatings and Resins SCM Corp.
Global Associates Atlas Corp.
Global Marine Development Global Marine Inc.
Globe Book Co. Esquire, Inc.
Globe Security Systems Kidde, Inc.
Globe-Weis Sheller-Globe Corp.
Gluematic Loctite Corp.
Godiva Campbell Soup Co.
Gold Circle Federated Department Stores, Inc.
Gold King Springs Mills, Inc.
Gold Medal General Mills, Inc.
Gold Toe Cluett, Peabody & Co., Inc.
Goldblatt Tool Co. Axia Inc.
Golden Books Mattel, Inc.
Golden Griddle CPC International Inc.
Golden Grove Management American Agronomics Corp.
Golden Lights Loews Corp.
Goldwaters Associated Dry Goods Corp.
Golf Times Mirror Co.
Good News Gillette Co.
Gordon H. Ball Inc. Dillingham Corp.
Gory Associated Industries, Inc. Elcor Corp.
Government Employees Financial Corp. GEICO Corp.
Government Employees Insurance Co. GEICO Corp.
Government Employees Life Insurance Co. GEICO Corp.
Graber Industries Springs Mills, Inc.
Graham & Gunn Hart Schaffner & Marx
Graham Magnetics Inc. Carlisle Corp.
GranCookerie National Presto Industries
Graphic Controls Times Mirror Co.
Gravy Train General Foods Corp.
Gray Drug Stores Inc. Sherwin-Williams Co.
Gray Tool Co. Combustion Engineering, Inc.
Great America Marriott Corp.
Great American Funding Corp. Lomas & Nettleton Financial Corp.
Great Dane Trailers Transway International Corp.
Great Falls Insurance Co. Credithrift Financial, Inc.
Great Lakes Mortgage Corp. Lomas & Nettleton Financial Corp.
Great Lakes Transmission Co. American Natural Resources Co.
Great Salt Lake Minerals & Chemicals Gulf Resources & Chemical Corp.
Great Southern Life Insurance Co. NLT Corp.
Great Western Modern Merchandising, Inc.
Great Western Malting Univar Corp.
Great Western Savings & Loan Association Great Western Financial Corp.
Greater Arizona Savings and Loan Association The Liberty Corp.
Green Giant Pillsbury Co.
Green River Steel Corp. Athlone Industries, Inc.
Grefco, Inc. General Refractories Co.
Gresen Manufacturing Tonka Corp.
Gretsch Baldwin-United Corp.
Grey Poupon Dijon Mustard Heublein, Inc.
Greyhound Lines Greyhound Corp.
Grinnel Fire Protection Systems Tyco Laboratories, Inc.
Gristede's Southland Corp.
Grosset & Dunlap Filmways, Inc.
Grossman's Evans Products Co.
Grosten-Schlesinger Agency Manhattan Life Corp.
Grove Kidde, Inc.
Growth Realty Financial Co. Growth Realty Companies
Growth Realty Investment Managers Growth Realty Companies
Growth Realty National Growth Realty Companies
Gruen Industries Jewelcor Inc.
Guardsman Life Insurance Co. NLT Corp.
Guild Musical Instruments Avnet, Inc.
Gulbransen CBS Inc.
Gulden's American Home Products Corp.
Gulf Finance Corp. First Atlanta Corp.

Gulf Life Group Insurance Gulf United Corp.
Gulf Life Insurance Gulf United Corp.
Gulf Minerals Canada Ltd. Gulf Canada Ltd.
Gulf Power Southern Co.
Gulton Europe Ltd. Gulton Industries, Inc.
Gulton Industries (Canada) Ltd. Gulton Industries, Inc.
Gypsum Carrier, Inc. Kaiser Cement Corp.
Gyrex Corp. Allied Corp.

H

H & S Pogue Associated Dry Goods Corp.
H. D. Lee V. F. Corp.
HBJ Communications and Services Harcourt Brace Jovanovich, Inc.
HFC Household International Corp.
Haag Drug Co. Peoples Drug Stores, Inc.
Hahne & Co. Associated Dry Goods Corp.
Haley's M-O Sterling Drug Inc.
Halle Brothers Co. Marshall Field and Co.
Hall's Motor Transport Tiger International, Inc.
Halston Norton Simon, Inc.
Hamilton Beach Scovill Inc.
Hamilton Standard United Technologies Corp.
Hamilton Technology HMW Industries Inc.
Hamon Cooling Tower Research-Cottrell, Inc.
Hancock's Lucky Stores, Inc.
Handi-Man Fasteners HMW Industries Inc.
Handi Wrap Dow Chemical Co.
Handy City W. R. Grace & Co.
Handy Dan W. R. Grace & Co.
Handy Flux Handy & Harman
Handy Wipes Colgate-Palmolive Co.
Hanes Group Consolidated Foods Corp.
Hanover Wire Cloth Continental Copper & Steel Industries, Inc.
Hanson Allegheny International, Inc.
Happy Days United States Tobacco Co.
Harbor Master Jonathan Logan, Inc.
Hardware House Union Camp Corp.
Hardy Boys Filmways, Inc.
Harlem Globetrotters Metromedia, Inc.
Harper Oil Co. MidCon Corp.
Harper-Wyman Co. Oak Industries, Inc.
Harpoon McDonnell Douglas Corp.
Harrah's Holiday Inns, Inc.
Harris Trust & Savings Bank Harris Bankcorp, Inc.
Hart Schaffner & Marx Hart Schaffner & Marx
Hartford *Courant* Times Mirror Co.
Hartford Electric Light Northeast Utilities
Hartford Fire Insurance Co. International Telephone & Telegraph Corp.
Hartford Steam Service Co. Connecticut Natural Gas Corp.
Harvel Industries Corp. ARTRA Group, Inc.
Harvestore A. O. Smith Corp.
Harvey's Heublein, Inc.
Hatfield Wire & Cable Continental Copper & Steel Industries, Inc.
Hathaway Warnaco Inc.
Hatteras AMF, Inc.
Hawaii Electric Light Hawaiian Electric Co., Inc.
Hawk Raytheon Co.
Hawley Fuel Corp. Belco Petroleum Corp.
Hayssen Manufacturing Bemis Company, Inc.
Head AMF, Inc.
Head & Shoulders Procter & Gamble Co.
Head to Head Coleco Industries, Inc.
Health-tex Chesebrough-Pond's Inc.
Heath Co. Zenith Radio Corp.
Hecht May Department Stores Co.
Heckett Harsco Corp.
Heck's Heck's, Inc.
Hecla Mining AMAX Inc.
Hedstrom Co. Brown Group, Inc.
Heinz H. J. Heinz Co.
Heirloom Oneida Limited
Hellman's CPC International Inc.
Helms Express IU International Corp.
Henco Coachmen Industries, Inc.
Hennessy Industries Chicago Pneumatic Tool Co.
Henry DuBois' Sons Company, Inc. Great Lakes International, Inc.
Hensley Industries, Inc. Galveston-Houston Co.
Hercofina American Petrofina, Inc.
Herff Jones Carnation Co.
Heritage Sportswear Wayne-Gossard Corp.
Herman The Stride Rite Corp.
Herman's W. R. Grace & Co.
Herrschners Quaker Oats Co.
Hershey's Hershey Foods Corp.
Hertz RCA Corp.
Hess Amerada Hess Corp.
Hester Tool Co. Kenai Corp.
Hi-C Coca-Cola Co.
Hickory Farm International Multifoods Corp.
Hickory Farms Sales Corp. General Host Corp.
Hidden Valley Ranch The Clorox Co.
High Fidelity American Broadcasting Companies, Inc.
High Voltage Devices Unitrode Corp.
Hill and Knowlton, Inc. JWT Group, Inc.
Hill-Rom Co. Hillenbrand Industries, Inc.
Hillcrest Skyline Corp.
Hillhaven Corp. National Medical Enterprises, Inc.
Hilliard Oil & Gas, Inc. Tidewater, Inc.

Hills SCOA Industries, Inc.
Hilton Athletic Apparel Anthony Industries, Inc.
Hilton International Trans World Corp.
Hires Procter & Gamble Co.
Hirsch Weis Warnaco Inc.
Hit Thomas Industries, Inc.
Hit or Miss Zayre Corp.
HMO International INA Corp.
Hobie Cat Coleman Co., Inc.
Hochschild, Kohn Supermarkets General Corp.
Hoeganaes Corp. Interlake, Inc.
Hoerner Waldorf Champion International Corp.
Hogate's Marriott Corp.
Holbrook Oxford Industries, Inc.
Holden General Motors Corp. (import)
Holiday Inns Holiday Inns, Inc.
Holiday on Ice Mattel, Inc.
Holland-American Insurance Co. Mission Insurance Group, Inc.
Holland House National Distillers & Chemical Corp.
Holley Carburetor Colt Industries Inc.
Holloware Towle Manufacturing Co.
Holt, Renfrew Carter Hawley Hale Stores, Inc.
Holt, Rinehart & Winston CBS Inc.
Holyoke Water Power Northeast Utilities
Homart Development Co. Sears, Roebuck and Co.
Home Box Office Time Inc.
The Home Group City Investing Co.
The Home Insurance Co. City Investing Co.
Home Life Insurance of America Capital Holding Corp.
Home Oil Hiram Walker Resources Ltd.
Home Savings & Loan Association H. F. Ahmanson & Co.
Home Savings Association U. S. Leasing International, Inc.
Home Security Life Capital Holding Corp.
Homecrafters Union Camp Corp.
Homelite Textron Inc.
Homequity, Inc. PHH Group, Inc.
Homes American Broadcasting Companies, Inc.
Hometté Corp. Skyline Corp.
Honest Conwood Corp.
Honey Bear Farm Carson Pirie Scott & Co.
Hooker Chemical Occidental Petroleum Corp.
Horace Mann INA Corp.
Horizon Creditcorp Horizon Bancorp
Hormel George A. Hormel & Co.
Hoskin's Brookfield Wire Co. Armada Corp.
Hoskins Manufacturing Co. Armada Corp.
Hospital Pulmonary Services National Medical Enterprises, Inc.
Host International Marriott Corp.
Hot Sam General Host Corp.
Hot Shoppes Marriott Corp.
Hot Shot Conwood Corp.
Hot Stop National Convenience Stores Inc.
Hot Wheels Mattel, Inc.
Hotpoint General Electric Co.
House of Fine Fabrics Fabri-Centers of America, Inc.
House of Windsor, Inc. United States Tobacco Co.
Household Finance Co. Household International Corp.
Housing by Tiffany Mobile Home Industries, Inc.
Housing by Vogue Mobile Home Industries, Inc.
Houston First Savings Association PennCorp Financial, Inc.
Houston Lighting & Power Co. Houston Industries Inc.
Houston Oil & Minerals Corp. Tenneco Inc.
Houston Trailer and Truck Body, Inc. McLean Trucking Co.
Howard Brothers Wickes Companies, Inc.
Howell Petroleum Corp. Howell Corp.
Howland-Steinbach Supermarkets General Corp.
Hubba Bubba Bubble Gum Wm. Wrigley Jr. Co.
Hubbard & Johnson Evans Products Co.
Huck Manufacturing Co. Federal-Mogul Corp.
Hudson Pharmaceutical Cadence Industries Corp.
Hudson Vitamins Cadence Industries Corp.
Hudson's Dayton-Hudson Corp.
Huffman-Koos Household International Corp.
Huffy Huffy Corp.
Huggies Kimberly-Clark Corp.
Hughes Tool Co. Borg-Warner Corp.
Humko Chemical Witco Chemical Corp.
Hunt Norton Simon, Inc.
Hunt-Wesson Norton Simon, Inc.
Hush Puppies Wolverine World Wide Inc.
Husky Wynn's International Inc.
Husky Products Inc. Burndy Corp.
Huttig Sash & Door Crane Co.
Hy-Lo American Stores Co.
Hyatt Medical Enterprises American Medical International, Inc.
Hydro Carbide Vulcan, Inc.
Hydro-Tech Hughes Tool Co.
Hygrade Standard Motor Products, Inc.

I

I-T-E Imperial Corp. Gould Inc.
I. Magnin Federated Department Stores, Inc.
IBM Science Research Associates International Business Machines Corp.

IDS Alleghany Corp.
IFC Peoples Energy Corp.
INA Capital Management Corp. INA Corp.
INA Life Insurance Co. INA Corp.
INA Reinsurance Co. INA Corp.
IRECO Chemicals Gulf Resources & Chemical Corp.
IXL Triangle Pacific Corp.
Ice Capades Metromedia, Inc.
Ice Follies Mattel, Inc.
Icy Hot G. D. Searle & Co.
Ideal Publishing Co. Filmways, Inc.
Igloo Corp. Anderson, Clayton & Co.
Ile De France Universal Foods Corp.
Illinois Bell Telephone Co. American Telephone and Telegraph Co.
Illinois Central Gulf Railroad Co. IC Industries, Inc.
Imperial Unilever PLC
Imperial Glass Corp. Lenox, Inc.
Imperial Lumber Deltona Corp.
Imperial Oil Exxon Corp.
Imperial Paper Co. Collins & Aikman Corp.
Imperial Savings & Loan (California) Imperial Corp. of America
Inco Bay State Gas Co.
Independent News Warner Communications, Inc.
Indiana & Michigan Electric American Electric Power Co., Inc.
Indiana Group National Distillers & Chemical Corp.
Indocin Merck & Co., Inc.
Industrial Fuels Corp MidCon Corp.
Industrial Indemnity Co. Crum and Forster
Industrial National Bank of Rhode Island Industrial National Corp.
Industries of Iowa Corp. Iowa Resources Inc.
Infonet Computer Sciences Corp.
Ingalls Industries Trinity Industries, Inc.
Inglenook Heublein, Inc.
Inland Container Time Inc.
Inland Steel Urban Development Co. Inland Steel Co.
Inocor Sterling Drug Inc.
Input-Output Division Kidde, Inc.
Instant Protein Shaklee Corp.
Instant 600 Polaroid Corp.
Instapak Corp. Sealed Air Corp.
Insurance Co. of North America INA Corp.
Integon Life Insurance Co. Ashland Oil, Inc.
Inter-Collegiate Press, Inc. Sargent-Welch Scientific Co.
Intereal Co. NLT Corp.
Intermarine Services Global Marine Inc.
International Correspondence School National Education Corp.
International Jensen Esmark, Inc.
International Salt Akzona Inc.
International Silver Co. Insilco Corp.
International Terminal Operating Co. Ogden Corp.
International Transport, Inc. Butler International, Inc.
Interstate Life & Accident Insurance Gulf United Corp.
Intertel Resorts International, Inc.
Intext Communications Systems National Education Corp.
Inver House Publicker Industries, Inc.
Investors Diversified Services, Inc. Alleghany Corp.
Iowa Beef Processors Occidental Petroleum Corp.
Iowa Computer Resources, Inc. Iowa Resources Inc.
Iowa Power & Light Co. Iowa Resources Inc.
Irish Spring Colgate-Palmolive Co.
Irving Trust Co. Irving Bank Corp.
Isabela Shoe Morse Shoe, Inc.
Isaly Co., Inc. Clabir Corp.
Island Creek Coal Occidental Petroleum Corp.
Isomil Abbott Laboratories
Isotronics Inc. Augat, Inc.
Ives American Home Products Corp.
Ivory Procter & Gamble Co.
Izod General Mills, Inc.

J

J&H International Lehigh Valley Industries, Inc.
J. B. Ivey and Co. Marshall Field and Co.
J. B. Williams Nabisco Brands, Inc.
J. Brannam F. W. Woolworth Co.
JByrons Jack Eckerd Corp.
J. D. Adams Co. Signode Corp.
J. F. Jelenko Pennwalt Corp.
J. I. Case Tenneco Inc.
J.L. Sport Leslie Fay Inc.
J. M. McDonald Co. Wickes Companies, Inc.
J. P. Snodgrass Cook United Inc.
J. Riggings United States Shoe Corp.
J. Schoeneman Cluett, Peabody & Co.
J. T. Baker Chemical Co. Richardson-Vicks Inc.
J. W. Bateson Co. Centex Corp.
J. W. Robinson Associated Dry Goods Corp.
J. Walter Thompson Co. JWT Group, Inc.
JT's Place Host International, Inc.
Jack and Jill Morse Shoe, Inc.
Jack in the Box Ralston Purina Co.
Jackson Exit Thomas Industries, Inc.

Jackson's Ice Cream Co. Dillon Companies, Inc.
The Jacobs Manufacturing Co. Chicago Pneumatic Tool Co.
Jacobson Textron Inc.
Jacquard Systems AM International
Jacuzzi Kidde, Inc.
Jafco Modern Merchandising, Inc.
Janssen Pharmaceutica Johnson & Johnson
Jantzen Inc. Blue Bell, Inc.
Jaymar-Ruby Hart Schaffner & Marx
Jean Naté Squibb Corp.
Jean Nicole Miller-Wohl Co.
Jeans West Edison Brothers Stores, Inc.
Jeep American Motors Corp.
Jefferson-Pilot Fire & Casualty Jefferson-Pilot Corp.
Jefferson Standard Life Insurance Jefferson-Pilot Corp.
Jell-O General Foods Corp.
Jensen Tools Inc. Axia Inc.
Jerrold Electronics General Instrument Corp.
Jersey Central Power & Light Co. General Public Utilities Corp.
Jessop Steel Co. Athlone Industries, Inc.
Jet CBS Inc.
Jet Line Thomas Industries, Inc.
Jewel Jewel Companies, Inc.
Jewel T Jewel Companies, Inc.
Jif Procter & Gamble Co.
Jim Beam American Brands, Inc.
Jo-Ann Fabrics Fabri-Centers of America, Inc.
Jo-Gal Shoe Morse Shoe, Inc.
Jody-Tootique HRT Industries, Inc.
John A. Brown Dayton-Hudson Corp.
John Morrell & Co. United Brands Co.
John P. Maguire & Co. Irving Trust Corp.
John Wanamaker Carter Hawley Hale Stores, Inc.
Johnny Carson Hart Schaffner & Marx
Johnson (engines) Outboard Marine Corp.
Johnson Corp. Magic Chef, Inc.
Johnson's Johnson & Johnson
Johnston & Murphy Genesco Inc.
Jonathan Logan Jonathan Logan, Inc.
Jones & Laughlin Steel Corp. LTV Corp.
Jones Motor Co. Alleghany Corp.
Jones Stores Mercantile Stores Co., Inc.
Jontue Revlon, Inc.
Jordan Marsh Allied Stores Corp.
Joseph Horne Associated Dry Goods Corp.
Joseph T. Ryerson & Co. Inland Steel Co.
Joshua Tree Host International, Inc.
Joske's Allied Stores Corp.
Jostens Jostens, Inc.
Journal of Commerce Knight-Ridder Newspapers, Inc.
Jove MCA Inc.
Judson Candies, Inc. Southdown, Inc.
Juice Tree Inc. American Agronomics Corp.
Juicy Fruit Wm. Wrigley Jr. Co.
Jupiter K mart Corp.

K

K mart K mart Corp.
KC-10 McDonnell Douglas Corp.
K.R.M. Petroleum Corp. Callahan Mining Corp.
KABC American Broadcasting Companies, Inc.
KAUM American Broadcasting Companies, Inc.
KCBS CBS Inc.
KCCI-TV Cowles Communications, Inc.
KCMH-TV The Outlet Co.
KCOP Chris-Craft Industries Inc.
KDFW-TV Times Mirror Co.
KEDS Corp. The Stride Rite Corp.
KERO-TV McGraw-Hill, Inc.
KGO American Broadcasting Companies, Inc.
KFI-AM Cox Broadcasting Corp.
KGTV McGraw-Hill, Inc.
KIQQ-FM The Outlet Co.
KJAR-TV The Outlet Co.
KJR Metromedia, Inc.
KLAC Metromedia, Inc.
KLOS American Broadcasting Companies, Inc.
KMBC-TV Metromedia, Inc.
KMGH-TV McGraw-Hill, Inc.
KMET Metromedia, Inc.
KMOX TV, Radio CBS Inc.
KNX CBS Inc.
KNXT-TV CBS Inc.
KOST-FM Cox Broadcasting Corp.
KOVR-TV The Outlet Co.
KPTV Chris-Craft Industries Inc.
KRIV-TV Metromedia, Inc.
KRLD Metromedia, Inc.
KSAN Metromedia, Inc.
KSAT-TV The Outlet Co.
KSFX American Broadcasting Companies, Inc.
KSM Fastening Systems Omark Industries, Inc.
KSW Electronics Corp. Loral Corp.
KTBC-TV Times Mirror Co.
KTCN-TV Metromedia, Inc.
KTLA-TV Signal Companies, Inc.
KTTV-TV Metromedia, Inc.
KTVU Cox Broadcasting Corp.
KTVI-TV Times Mirror Co.
Kable News Co. AMREP Corp.
Kacor Realty Kaiser Aluminum & Chemical Corp.
Kahlua Hiram Walker Resources Ltd.

Kaiser Engineers Raymond International, Inc.
Karastan Fieldcrest Mills, Inc.
Karl's Shoe Stores Ltd. HRT Industries, Inc.
Karo CPC International Inc.
Kash 'N Karry Lucky Stores, Inc.
Kasper for Joan Leslie Leslie Fay Inc.
Kaufmann's May Department Stores Co.
Kaukauna Klub Cheese International Multifoods Corp.
Kava Borden, Inc.
Kawecki Berylco Cabot Corp.
Kay International Trade Kay Corp.
Kay Jewelers Kay Corp.
Kay Windsor V. F. Corp.
Kayex General Signal Corp.
Kayser-Roth Gulf & Western Industries, Inc.
Keene Corp. Bairnco Corp.
Keene Products, Inc. CTS Corp.
Keepsake, Inc. Lenox, Inc.
Keflin Eli Lilly and Co.
M. W. Kellogg Wheelabrator-Frye Inc.
Kellogg's Corn Flakes Kellogg Co.
Kelly & Cohen SCOA Industries, Inc.
Kelsey-Hayes Co. Fruehauf Corp.
Kelty Pack, Inc. Kellwood Co.
Kelvinator White Consolidated Industries, Inc.
Kemlite Corp. UMC Industries, Inc.
Ken-L Ration Quaker Oats Co.
Kenco Coachmen Industries, Inc.
Kendall (motor oil) Witco Chemical Corp.
Kendall (specialty fabrics) Colgate-Palmolive Co.
Kenmore Whirlpool Corp.
Kennecott Corp. Standard Oil Co. (Ohio)
Kenner General Mills, Inc.
Kent Loews Corp.
Kent Machine Lamson & Sessions Co.
Kentucky Electric Steel Republic Corp.
Kentucky Fried Chicken Heublein, Inc.
Kentucky Hydrocarbon Co. Equitable Gas Co.
Kentucky Power American Electric Power Co., Inc.
Kenworth PACCAR Inc.
Kerr-McGee Kerr-McGee Corp.
Kevlar E. I. Du Pont de Nemours & Co.
Keyes Fibre Co. Arcata Corp.
Kilpatrick's Bakeries Campbell Taggart, Inc.
Kim Color Corp. Papercraft Corp.
Kimble Owens-Illinois, Inc.
Kin-Tech Pacific Scientific Co.
King-Seeley Thermos Household International Corp.
King Soopers Dillon Companies, Inc.
King's Department Stores KDT Industries, Inc.
King's Men Helene Curtis Industries, Inc.
Kingsford The Clorox Co.
Kingsford (corn starch) CPC International Inc.
Kingsport Power American Electric Power Co., Inc.
Kinney F. W. Woolworth Co.
Kirby The Scott & Fetzer Co.
Kirby Forest Products Santa Fe Industries, Inc.
Kirby Pharmaceuticals Schering-Plough Corp.
Kirsch Cooper Industries, Inc.
Kleenex Kimberly-Clark Corp.
Klondike Clabir Corp.
Knickerbocker Toy Co. Warner Communications, Inc.
Knomark Inc. Papercraft Corp.
Knorr CPC International Inc.
Kodachrome Eastman Kodak Co.
Kodak Eastman Kodak Co.
The Kollection Jonathan Logan, Inc.
Kool-Aid General Foods Corp.
Koracorp Levi Strauss & Co.
Kotex Kimberly-Clark Corp.
Kraft Dart & Kraft, Inc.
Kraft Systems, Inc. Carlisle Corp.
Kragen Lucky Stores, Inc.
Kralinator Sheller-Globe Corp.
Kresge K mart Corp.
Kretschmer Wheat Germ International Multifoods Corp.
Kroger Kroger Co.
Kulov Publicker Industries, Inc.
Kwik Shops Dillon Companies, Inc.

L

L-1011 (TriStar) Lockheed Corp.
L&G Lucky Stores, Inc.
L.F. Petite Leslie Fay Inc.
L. S. Ayres Associated Dry Goods Corp.
LOR Inc. Newpark Resources
LPC International Finance N.V. Lear Petroleum Corp.
LRC Electronics Inc. Augat, Inc.
L'Aiglon Swank, Inc.
La Choy Beatrice Foods Co.
La Mode Belding Heminway Company, Inc.
La Pizzeria H. J. Heinz Co.
LaBelle's Modern Merchandising, Inc.
Lacoste General Mills, Inc.
Ladies' Home Journal Charter Co.
Ladish Co. Armco Inc.
Lady Arrow Cluett, Peabody & Co., Inc.
Lady Pepperell West Point-Pepperell, Inc.
Lake Coal Co. Howell Corp.
Lakeside Press R. R. Donnelley & Sons Co.
Lambda Veeco Instruments Inc.
Lana Knit Limited Jonathan Logan, Inc.

Lancer's Heublein, Inc.
Lands of Sierra, Inc. Sierra Pacific Power Co.
Lane Drug Co. Peoples Drug Stores, Inc.
Langendorf American Bakeries Co.
Lanier Clothes Oxford Industries, Inc.
Lark Mining Inc. NICOR Inc.
Larry's Food Products Campbell Taggart, Inc.
LaSalle Machine Tool Acme-Cleveland Corp.
Las Palmas Ogden Corp.
Latrobe Steel Timken Co.
Lavoris Richardson-Vicks Inc.
Lawn-Boy Outboard Marine Corp.
Lawry's Foods, Inc. Unilever PLC
Lawson's Consolidated Foods Corp.
Lawtex Industries Springs Mills, Inc.
Layton Homes Corp. Skyline Corp.
Lazarus Federated Department Stores, Inc.
Le Chic Belding Heminway Company, Inc.
LeFebure Kidde, Inc.
LePage Papercraft Corp.
Leath-Maxwell Wickes Companies, Inc.
Leavens Manufacturing Co., Inc. Oneida Limited
Lechmere Dayton-Hudson Corp.
Lectric Shave Nabisco Brands, Inc.
Lederle American Cyanamid Co.
Lee V. F. Corp.
Lee Way Motor Freight PepsiCo, Inc.
Leece-Neville Sheller-Globe Corp.
Leeds & Northrup Co. General Signal Corp.
Lenox Awards, Inc. Lenox, Inc.
Lenox Candles, Inc. Lenox, Inc.
Lenox China, Inc. Lenox, Inc.
Lenox Crystal, Inc. Lenox, Inc.
Leonard Silver Towle Manufacturing Co.
Leslie Fay Leslie Fay Inc.
Leslie-Locke Questor Corp.
Leslie Pomer Leslie Fay Inc.
Leslie CBS Inc.
Leucadia, Inc. Leucadia National Corp.
Lever Brothers Unilever PLC
Levi Garrett Conwood Corp.
Levi's Levi Strauss & Co.
Levi's For Feet Brown Group, Inc.
Lewis-Howe Co. Revlon, Inc.
Libbey Owens-Illinois, Inc.
Liberty Mohasco Corp.
Liberty Life Insurance Co. The Liberty Corp.
Liberty National Life Insurance Co. Liberty National Insurance Holding Co.
Liddle Griddle National Presto Industries
Liederkranz Borden, Inc.
Life (cereal) Quaker Oats Co.
***Life* (magazine)** Time Inc.
Life & Casualty of Tennessee American General Corp.
Life Insurance Co. of Virginia Continental Group, Inc.
Life Savers, Inc. Nabisco Brands, Inc.
Life Uniform Shops Angelica Corp.
Lifebuoy Unilever PLC
Lifetime Carbide Co. Omark Industries, Inc.
Light Days Kimberly-Clark Corp.
Light 'N Lively Dart & Kraft, Inc.
Li'l General General Host Corp.
Lil Genius Coleco Industries, Inc.
Lily Owens-Illinois, Inc.
Limerick Footwear Morse Shoe, Inc.
Lincoln Ford Motor Co.
Lincoln National Life Insurance Co. Lincoln National Corp.
Lindsay-Schaub Newspapers, Inc. Lee Enterprises, Inc.
Lindsley Evans Products Co.
Lindy Skyline Corp.
Lion Stores Mercantile Stores Co., Inc.
Lionel General Mills, Inc.
Lionel Leisure, Inc. The Lionel Corp.
Lipton Unilever PLC
Liquid Carbonic Houston Natural Gas Corp.
Liquid-Lea Shaklee Corp.
Liquid Paper Gillette Co.
Liquid-plumr The Clorox Co.
Liquitex Binney & Smith Inc.
Listerine Warner-Lambert Co.
Lite-Line Borden, Inc.
Lithium Corp. of America Gulf Resources & Chemical Corp.
Litter Green The Clorox Co.
Little, Brown & Co. Time Inc.
Litton Litton Industries, Inc.
Litton Industries Teledyne, Inc.
Livingston Medical Products Co. National Medical Enterprises, Inc.
Loadstar International Harvester Co.
Loctite Loctite Corp.
Loews Loews Corp.
Lomas & Nettleton Corp. Lomas & Nettleton Financial Corp.
Lomotil G. D. Searle & Co.
London Fog Interco Inc.
Lone Star Cement, Inc. Lone Star Industries, Inc.
Lone Star Gas Enserch Corp.
Lone Star Properties, Inc. Lone Star Industries, Inc.
Lone Star Steel Northwest Industries
Long Island Trust Co. LITCO Bancorporation of New York, Inc.
Longbranch Coal Co. MAPCO Inc.
Lord & Taylor Associated Dry Goods Corp.

Lord, Geller, Federico, Einstein, Inc. JWT Group, Inc.
Lorillard Loews Corp.
Los Angeles Angels Signal Companies, Inc.
Los Angeles American Broadcasting Companies, Inc.
Los Angeles ***Times*** Times Mirror Co.
Louis Sherry Beatrice Foods Co.
Louisiana Intrastate Gas Central Louisiana Energy Corp.
Louisiana Power & Light Co. Middle South Utilities, Inc.
Louisville & Nashville CSX Corp.
Lowell Shoe Morse Shoe, Inc.
Lowenbrau Philip Morris Inc.
Lowenstein Lowenstein (M.) Corp.
Lowrey Norlin Corp.
Lubrizol Enterprises Inc. Lubrizol Corp.
Lucas-Milhaupt, Inc. Handy & Harman
Lucite E. I. Du Pont de Nemours & Co.
Lucky Lucky Stores, Inc.
Lucky Strike American Brands, Inc.
Ludlow Corp. Tyco Laboratories, Inc.
Ludlow-Saylor General Steel Industries, Inc.
Lufkin Cooper Industries, Inc.
Lummus Co. Combustion Engineering, Inc.
Lux Co. Coachmen Industries, Inc.
Lycoming Stratford Avco Corp.
Lydon Dredging & Construction Co. Great Lakes International, Inc.
Lykes Brothers Steamship Co. LTV Corp.
Lynx Zurn Industries, Inc.
Lyon & Healy CBS Inc.
Lyon's Restaurants Consolidated Foods Corp.
Lysol Sterling Drug Inc.

M

M. Grumbacher Times Mirror Co.
M. Snower & Co. Opelika Manufacturing Corp.
M. W. Kellogg Co. Wheelabrator-Frye Inc.
MB Electronics Milton Bradley Co.
MCA MCA Inc.
MX The Boeing Co.
Maalox Rorer Group, Inc.
Maas Brothers Allied Stores Corp.
Mac Tools, Inc. The Stanley Works
MacArthur's Publicker Industries, Inc.
Macbeth Kollmorgen Corp.
Mack Trucks Signal Companies, Inc.
Macy's R. H. Macy & Co., Inc.
Mad Magazine Warner Communications, Inc.
Madison Square Garden Corp. Gulf & Western Industries, Inc.
Magee (carpeting) Shaw Industries, Inc.
The Magee Company, Inc. Tandycrafts, Inc.
Magic Chef Magic Chef, Inc.
Magic Pan Quaker Oats Co.
Magma Copper Co. Newmont Mining Corp.
Magnaflux Corp. GEO International Corp.
Magnasync/Moviola Craig Corp.
Magnavox North American Philips Corp.
Magnetic Laboratories, Inc. Savin Corp.
Maiden Knitting Mills Cannon Mills Co.
Main Street South Corp. The Hydraulic Co.
Majik Market Munford, Inc.
Malina Greyhound Corp.
Mallory Components Group Emhart Corp.
Malsbary Manufacturing Co. Carlisle Corp.
Mandol Eli Lilly and Co.
Manhattan Life Insurance Co. Manhattan Life Corp.
Mann GCA Corp.
Manor Campbell Taggart, Inc.
Manor Healthcare Manor Care, Inc.
Manpower, Inc. The Parker Pen Co.
Manufacturers Hanover Trust Co. Manufacturers Hanover Corp.
Manufacturing Data Systems Inc. Schlumberger Limited
Marantz Superscope, Inc.
Marathon Manufacturing Penn Central Corp.
Marathon Oil Co. U. S. Steel Corp.
Mardi-Gras Fort Howard Paper Co.
Margo's La Mode Alexander's, Inc.
Marianne Petrie Stores Corp.
Marine Midland Bank Marine Midland Banks, Inc.
Marine National Bank of Wildwood Horizon Bancorp
Mariner Brunswick Corp.
Mark 48 Gould Inc.
Marlboro Philip Morris Inc.
The Marquardt Co. CCI Corp.
Marriott Marriott Corp.
Marschalk Co. Inc. Interpublic Group of Companies, Inc.
Marsh & McLennan Inc. Marsh & McLennan Companies, Inc.
Marsh & McLennan Management Co. Marsh & McLennan Companies, Inc.
Marshalls Melville Corp.
Martex West Point-Pepperell, Inc.
Martin Senour Sherwin-Williams Co.
Marvel Comics Cadence Industries Corp.
Mary Carter Paint Insilco Corp.
Mary Kitchen George A. Hormel & Co.
Maryland Casualty American General Corp.
Maryland Specialty Wire, Inc. Handy & Harman
Mason Tootsie Roll Industries, Inc.
Masoneilan McGraw-Edison Co.

Mass Feeding Corp. Jewel Companies, Inc.
Massachusetts Indemnity and Life Insurance Co. PennCorp Financial, Inc.
Master Lock American Brands, Inc.
Mastercraft Corp. Collins & Aikman Corp.
Masury-Columbia Co. Alberto-Culver Co.
Matlack, Inc. RLC Corp.
Maui Electric Hawaiian Electric Co., Inc.
Mauna Loa IU International Corp.
Maverick Blue Bell, Inc.
Max Factor Norton Simon, Inc.
Max-Pax General Foods Corp.
Maxim General Foods Corp.
Maxwell House General Foods Corp.
May May Department Stores Co.
Maybelline Schering-Plough Corp.
Mays Lucky Stores, Inc.
Mazola CPC International Inc.
McAlester Fuel Alaska Interstate Co.
McAlpin's Mercantile Stores Co., Inc.
McCall Pattern Norton Simon, Inc.
McCann-Erickson, Inc. Interpublic Group of Companies, Inc.
McCormack Lines Moore McCormack Resources, Inc.
McCormick International Harvester Co.
McCulloch Corp. Black & Decker Manufacturing Co.
McDonald Products Insilco Corp.
McGaw Supply Ltd. American Hospital Supply Co.
McIntyre Mines Superior Oil Co.
McLean Midwest Zero Corp.
McMoRan Oil and Gas Co. Freeport-McMoRan Inc.
Meadow Gold Beatrice Foods Co.
Measurement & Control—Europe Schlumberger Limited
Mechanix Illustrated CBS Inc.
Medesonics Colgate-Palmolive Co.
Medi Mart Stop & Shop Companies Inc.
Medical World News McGraw-Hill, Inc.
Medicus Systems Whittaker Corp.
Medusa Corp. Crane Co.
Mefoxin Merck & Co., Inc.
Meier & Frank May Department Stores Co.
Meier (metals) Kuhlman Corp.
Meisel Music Co. Avnet, Inc.
Meldisco Melville Corp.
Mellon Energy Co. Howell Petroleum Corp.
Mellon National Bank Mellon National Corp.
Meloy Laboratories Revlon, Inc.
Melpar E-Systems, Inc.
Memco Lucky Stores, Inc.
Memorex Burroughs Corp.
Menasco Inc. Colt Industries Inc.
Men's Wear International Philips-Van Heusen Corp.
Mercantile National Bank Mercantile Texas Corp.
Mercury Ford Motor Co.
Mercury Motor Express XTRA Corp.
Mercury (outboard motors) Brunswick Corp.
Merico, Inc. Campbell Taggart, Inc.
Merit Philip Morris Inc.
Merita American Bakeries Co.
Meritrol Cables Handy & Harman
Merlin Fairchild Industries, Inc.
Merrell Dow Chemical Co.
Merribee Tandycrafts, Inc.
Merrill Lynch, Hubbard Merrill Lynch & Co., Inc.
Merrill Lynch, Pierce, Fenner & Smith Merrill Lynch & Co., Inc.
Merrill Lynch Realty Associates Merrill Lynch & Co., Inc.
Merrill Lynch Relocation Management Merrill Lynch & Co., Inc.
Mervyn's Dayton-Hudson Corp.
Mesabi Drill and Tool Co. Omark Industries, Inc.
Messenger Johnson (E. F.) Co.
Metalsource Alco Standard Corp.
Metamucil G. D. Searle & Co.
Metcalf & Eddy Research-Cottrell, Inc.
Metro Fairchild Industries, Inc.
Metropolitan Edison Co. General Public Utilities Corp.
Metropolitan Home Meredith Corp.
Mexico Desarrollo Industrial Minero, S.A. ASARCO Inc.
Meyer Machine Telecom Corp.
Meyer Systems Telecom Corp.
Miami *Herald* Knight-Ridder Newspapers, Inc.
Miami Seaquarium Wometco Enterprises, Inc.
Michelob Anheuser-Busch Companies, Inc.
Michigan Bearing Co. Genuine Parts Co.
Michigan Consolidated Gas Co. Primark Corp.
Michigan Power American Electric Power Co., Inc.
Michigan Wisconsin Pipe Line Co. American Natural Resources Co.
Mickey American Bakeries Co.
Micro-Data AM International
Micro Networks Unitrode Corp.
Micro Switch Honeywell, Inc.
Microdot Northwest Industries
microNOVA Data General Corp.
Mid-America Pipeline System MAPCO Inc.
Mid-Continent Bottlers, Inc. Universal Foods Corp.

Mid-Continent Gas Storage Co. NICOR Inc.
Mid-Continent Gasification Co. NICOR Inc.
Mid Louisiana Gas Co. Central Louisiana Energy Corp.
Midas International IC Industries, Inc.
Midland Frame Lamson & Sessions Co.
Midland International Beneficial Corp.
Midol Sterling Drug Inc.
Midway Manufacturing Bally Manufacturing Corp.
Midwest Charter Express Airborne Freight Corp.
Midwood Industries, Inc. Hi-Shear Industries, Inc.
Mighty Dog Carnation Co.
Mighty Tonka Tonka Corp.
Milchem Baker International Corp.
Miles Homes Companies Insilco Corp.
Milford Rivet and Machine Raybestos-Manhattan, Inc.
Milford Shoe Morse Shoe, Inc.
Milk Plus 6 Revlon, Inc.
Milk-Bone Nabisco Brands, Inc.
Miller Philip Morris Inc.
Miller Sales Modern Merchandising, Inc.
Millikan Sargent-Welch Scientific Co.
Milwaukee Electric Tool Amstar Corp.
The Milwaukee Road Chicago Milwaukee Corp.
Minerec Corp. Essex Chemical Corp.
Mini Tonka Tonka Corp.
Minigrip, Inc. Signode Corp.
Minipress Pfizer Inc.
Minnesota Small Loan Company MEI Corp.
Mint Hotel Webb (Del E.) Corp.
Minute Maid Coca-Cola Co.
Minute Rice General Foods Corp.
Minwax Sterling Drug Inc.
Miracel Mine Operations, Inc. Portland General Electric Co.
Miracle Whip Dart & Kraft, Inc.
Miss Capezio United States Shoe Corp.
Mission Insurance Co. Mission Insurance Group, Inc.
Mission Re Management Co. Mission Insurance Group, Inc.
Mission Viejo Philip Morris Inc.
Mississippi Power Southern Co.
Mississippi Power & Light Co. Middle South Utilities, Inc.
Mississippi River Transmission Corp. Missouri Pacific Corp.
Missouri Edison Co. Union Electric Co.
Missouri Pacific Railroad Missouri Pacific Corp.
Missouri Power & Light Co. Union Electric Co.
Missouri Utilities Co. Union Electric Co.
Mister Donut International Multifoods Corp.
Mister Industries Scot Lad Foods, Inc.
Mr. M. Food Stores National Convenience Stores Inc.
Mr. Mushroom The Clorox Co.
Mr. Pride United Inns, Inc.
Misty Harbor Jonathan Logan, Inc.
Mitchum Revlon, Inc.
Mobil Chemicals Mobil Corp.
Mobil Oil Corp. Mobil Corp.
Mobile Pulley and Machine Works Lehigh Valley Industries, Inc.
Mode O'Day Wickes Companies, Inc.
Modern Faucet TRE Corp.
Modern Juniors Jonathan Logan, Inc.
Modern Photography American Broadcasting Companies, Inc.
Modess Johnson & Johnson
Mohawk Mohasco Corp.
Monarch Mohasco Corp.
Monarch Marking Systems Pitney-Bowes, Inc.
Monet General Mills, Inc.
Money Time Inc.
Mono Power Co. Southern California Edison Co.
Monogram Models Mattel, Inc.
Monroe Litton Industries, Inc.
Monroe Auto Equipment Tenneco Inc.
Montgomery Ward & Co. Mobil Corp.
Montrose Chemical Corp. of California Chris-Craft Industries Inc.
Moody's Investor Service Dun & Bradstreet Corp.
Moog Norlin Corp.
Mooney Aircraft Corp. Republic Steel Corp.
Moore Handley Union Camp Corp.
Moore McCormack Cement Moore McCormack Resources, Inc.
Moore's Evans Products Co.
Mopar Wynn's International Inc.
Morgan Adhesives Co. Bemis Company, Inc.
Morgan Drive Away CLC of America, Inc.
Morgan Guaranty Trust Co. J. P. Morgan & Co. Inc.
Morgan Jones Springs Mills, Inc.
The Morris Plan Co. of California Credithrift Financial, Inc.
Morse Morse Shoe, Inc.
Mortgage Guarantee Insurance MGIC Investment Corp.
Morton Salt Morton-Norwich Products, Inc.
Mosely Associates, Inc. Flow General Inc.
Mosley Machinery Company, Inc. Elcor Corp.
Mostek United Technologies Corp.
MOTAC XTRA Corp.
Motel 6 City Investing Co.

Motor Carrier Insurance, Ltd. Carolina Freight Carriers Corp.
Motrin Upjohn Co.
Mountain Dew PepsiCo, Inc.
Mrs. Goodcookie H. J. Heinz Co.
Mrs. Smiths Pie Co. Kellogg Co.
Mueller Foremost-McKesson, Inc.
Mueller Engineering and Manufacturing ARTRA Group, Inc.
Multiwire Kollmorgen Corp.
Muriel Gulf & Western Industries, Inc.
Murine Abbott Laboratories
Murphy Oil Co. Ltd. Murphy Oil Corp.
Murphy's Mart (G. C.) Murphy Co.
Mutschler Triangle Pacific Corp.
Mylar E. I. Du Pont de Nemours & Co.

N

NBC RCA Corp.
NCNB Mortgage Group NCNB Corp.
NDM Colgate-Palmolive Co.
NEC Gas Analytical Services Ltd. Gearhart Industries, Inc.
NLT Computer Services Corp. NLT Corp.
NM Uranium, Inc. Niagara Mohawk Power Corp.
NN Corp. Armco Inc.
NPS Shaklee Corp.
NRC, Inc. National Homes Corp.
NRI UMC Industries, Inc.
NWT Natural Resources Co. Northwest Industries
Nabisco Nabisco Brands, Inc.
NABRICO The American Ship Building Co.
Namco Controls Acme-Cleveland Corp.
Nancy Drew Filmways, Inc.
NAPA Genuine Parts Co.
NAPP Systems (USA) Inc. Lee Enterprises, Inc.
Naprosyn Syntex Corp.
Nashua 2210 Nashua Corp.
Natco Combustion Engineering, Inc.
National Aluminum Corp. National Steel Corp.
National Bank of Commerce Commerce Southwest Inc.
National Bank of Detroit NBD Bancorp, Inc.
National By-Products Federal Co.
National Car Rental System Household International Corp.
National Controls Corp. Tokheim Corp.
National Homes Acceptance Corp. Lomas & Nettleton Financial Corp.
National Homes Mortgage Services Corp. National Homes Corp.
National Life and Accident Insurance Co. NLT Corp.
National Living Centers ARA Services, Inc.
National Marine Service Inc. NICOR Inc.
National Oil Seals Federal-Mogul Corp.
National Papaya Co. American Agronomics Corp.
National Rejectors, Inc. UMC Industries, Inc.
National School Services Limited Jostens, Inc.
National Standard Life Capital Holding Corp.
National Starch and Chemical Unilever PLC
National Trust Life Capital Holding Corp.
National Union Insurance Group American International Group, Inc.
National Vendors UMC Industries, Inc.
National Water Lift Pneumo Corp.
Natkin & Co. Fischbach Corp.
Natural Gas Pipeline Co. of America MidCon Corp.
Natural Light Anheuser-Busch Companies, Inc.
Naturalizer Brown Group, Inc.
Neiman-Marcus Carter Hawley Hale Stores, Inc.
Neo Products United Industrial Corp.
Neo-Synephrine Sterling Drug Inc.
Neptune International Corp. Wheelabrator-Frye Inc.
NERCO, Inc. Pacific Power & Light Co.
Nescott Adams Drug Co.
Network Analysis Corp. Continental Telephone Corp.
New American Library Times Mirror Co.
New England Bell Telephone Co. American Telephone and Telegraph Co.
New Freedom Kimberly-Clark Corp.
New Hampshire Insurance Group American International Group, Inc.
New Holland Sperry Corp.
New Jersey Zinc Gulf & Western Industries, Inc.
New Orleans Public Service, Inc. Middle South Utilities, Inc.
New York Air Texas Air Corp.
New York Bell Telephone Co. American Telephone and Telegraph Co.
New York Knickerbockers Gulf & Western Industries, Inc.
New York Rangers Gulf & Western Industries, Inc.
Newark Electronics Premier Industrial Corp.
Newark Savings Transohio Financial Corp.
Newman Importing Co., Inc. Thrifty Corp.
Newpark Shipbuilding and Repair Newpark Resources
Newport Loews Corp.
Newport News Shipbuilding Tenneco Inc.
Newsday Times Mirror Co.
NI-Gas Exploration Inc. NICOR Inc.

Niagara CPC International Inc.
Niagara Frontier Great Atlantic & Pacific Tea Co.
Nichols-Homeshield Anta Corp.
Nicholson Cooper Industries, Inc.
NICOR Mining Inc. NICOR Inc.
Nina Ricci American Cyanamid Co.
9-Lives H. J. Heinz Co.
NIPSCO Exploration Co., Inc. Northern Indiana Public Service Co.
NIPSCO Fuel Co., Inc. Northern Indiana Public Service Co.
Noble Drilling Corp. Noble Affiliates, Inc.
Nobur Acme-Cleveland Corp.
Nomad Skyline Corp.
Norcliff Laboratories Revlon, Inc.
Nordberg Rexnord Inc.
Norden Systems United Technologies Corp.
Nordic Hills Country Club Carson Pirie Scott & Co.
Norelco North American Philips Corp.
Norfolk & Western Railway Norfolk & Western Railway Co.
Norford Corp. Chicago Pneumatic Tool Co.
Norge Magic Chef, Inc.
Norpace G. D. Searle & Co.
North American Car Tiger International, Inc.
North American Trailing Co. Great Lakes International, Inc.
North American Van Lines PepsiCo, Inc.
North Carolina National Bank NCNB Corp.
North Shore Gas Peoples Energy Corp.
North Star Reinsurance Corp. General Reinsurance Corp.
Northeastern Bank Horizon Bancorp
Northern American Can Co.
Northern Electric Allegheny International, Inc.
Northern Illinois Gas Co. NICOR Inc.
Northern National Life Insurance Co. Manhattan Life Corp.
Northern Petrochemical InterNorth, Inc.
Northern Telecom Ltd. Bell Canada
Northern Utilities, Inc. Bay State Gas Co.
Northwest Alaskan Pipeline Co. Northwest Energy Co.
Northwest Coal Corp. Northwest Energy Co.
Northwest Exploration Co. Northwest Energy Co.
Northwest Fabrics Peavey Co.
Northwest Pipeline Corp. Northwest Energy Co.
Northwood Forest Industries Ltd. Mead Corp.
Nottingham Corp. Equimark Corp.
NOVA Data General Corp.
Novo Script Ennis Business Forms, Inc.
NuTone Scovill Inc.
Nukem Ameron, Inc.
Numerical Control Inc. Pneumo Corp.
Nurse Mates Morse Shoe, Inc.

O

OMC Stern Drive Outboard Marine Corp.
ONG Red Oak Transmission ONEOK, Inc.
ONG Sayre Storage ONEOK, Inc.
ONG Western, Inc. ONEOK, Inc.
ON-TV Oak Industries, Inc.
OSA Oxford Industries, Inc.
OAK Oak Industries, Inc.
Oak Communications, Inc. Oak Industries, Inc.
Oak Materials Group, Inc. Oak Industries, Inc.
Oak Switch Systems, Inc. Oak Industries, Inc.
Oak Systems, Inc. Oak Industries, Inc.
Oak Technology, Inc. Oak Industries, Inc.
Oak Tip Oak Industries, Inc.
Oakite Products of Canada, Ltd. Oakite Products, Inc.
Oakland *Tribune* Gannett Co., Inc.
O'Brien Coleman Co., Inc.
Ocean Drilling & Exploration Co. Murphy Oil Corp.
Ocean Oil & Gas Murphy Oil Corp.
Oceanic Properties, Inc. Castle & Cooke, Inc.
Oceanography Services Global Marine Inc.
Odell Hardware Genuine Parts Co.
Odyssey CBS Inc.
Off the Rax Stop & Shop Companies Inc.
The Offshore Co. Southern Natural Resources, Inc.
Ogden Food Products Ogden Corp.
Ogden Marine Ogden Corp.
Ogden Services Ogden Corp.
Ogilvie Sterling Drug Inc.
Ohio-American Water Co. American Water Works Company, Inc.
Ohio Paper Products Co. Van Dorn Co.
Ohio Power American Electric Power Co., Inc.
Ohio Scientific Co. Control Data Corp.
Oil of Olay Richardson-Vicks Inc.
Old Crow National Distillers & Chemical Corp.
Old El Paso IC Industries, Inc.
Old English American Home Products Corp.
Old Gold Loews Corp.
Old Grand-Dad National Distillers & Chemical Corp.
Old London Borden, Inc.
Old Milwaukee Schlitz (Jos.) Brewing Co.
Old Style G. Heileman Brewing Co., Inc.
Old Taylor National Distillers & Chemical Corp.
Old Taylor (tobacco) Conwood Corp.
Oldsmobile General Motors Corp.

Olinkraft Manville Corp.
Oliver MacLeod Thomas Industries, Inc.
Olof Daughters Lane Bryant, Inc.
Omark Omark Industries, Inc.
Omni Hoover Universal, Inc.
Onan McGraw-Edison Co.
Oneida Canada, Limited Oneida Limited
O'Neill May Department Stores Co.
ONEOK Exploration Co. ONEOK, Inc.
ONEOK Resources Co. ONEOK, Inc.
OneStep Polaroid Corp.
Ontario Cook's United Inc.
Opco Oil Development Inc. Ensource Inc.
Opel General Motors Corp.
Optel Adams Drug Co.
Orange Crush Procter & Gamble
Orchid APL Corp.
Ore-Ida H. J. Heinz Co.
Oregon Saw Chain Omark Industries, Inc.
Oreo Nabisco Brands, Inc.
Organon Akzona Inc.
Ortega Heublein, Inc.
Ortho Pharmaceuticals Johnson & Johnson
Oscar Mayer General Foods Corp.
Osco Jewel Companies, Inc.
Oster Allegheny International, Inc.
Otis United Technologies Corp.
Ottaway Newspapers Inc. Dow Jones & Company, Inc.
Oui Playboy Enterprises, Inc.
Outdoor Life Times Mirror Co.
Outdoor Sports Industries Brown Group, Inc.
Outlet Specialty Stores, Inc. The Outlet Co.
Ovulen 21 G. D. Searle & Co.
Owens Clark Oil & Refining Corp.
Oxford Apparel Oxford Industries, Inc.
Oxford Consolidated Foods Corp.
Oxford Products Limited Oxford Industries, Inc.
Oxy Revlon, Inc.
Oxygen Emergency Supply, Inc. National Medical Enterprises, Inc.

P

P-3 Lockheed Corp.
P & C Food Markets Pneumo Corp.
P. R. Mallory Dart & Kraft, Inc.
PMI Sears, Roebuck and Co.
PMI Motors Kollmorgen Corp.
PPL Johnson (E. F.) Co.
PRC Insulating Glass Sealant Products Research & Chemical Corp.
PRC Rubber Calk Products Research & Chemical Corp.
PYA/Monarch Consolidated Foods Corp.
Pacific Lowenstein (M.) Corp.
Pacific Car and Foundry Division PACCAR Inc.
Pacific Coast Properties Cenvill Communities, Inc.
Pacific Intermountain Express IU International Corp.
Pacific International American Hospital Supply Co.
Pacific Reinsurance Management Co. Mission Insurance Group, Inc.
Pacific Resins & Chemicals Univar Corp.
Pacific Southwest Airlines PSA, Inc.
Pacific Stereo CBS Inc.
Pacific Telephone Co. American Telephone and Telegraph Co.
Page Fort Howard Paper Co.
Paine Webber Mitchell Hutchins Inc. Paine Webber Inc.
Paine Webber Real Estate Securities Paine Webber Inc.
Pall Mall American Brands, Inc.
Palmolive Colgate-Palmolive Co.
Palo Petroleum Inc. Ensource Inc.
Pampas Sales (Australia) Quaker Oats Co.
Pampers Procter & Gamble Co.
Pan-Alaska Fisheries, Inc. Castle & Cooke, Inc.
Pan American World Airways Pan American World Airways, Inc.
Pan Eastern Exploration Panhandle Eastern Pipe Line Co.
Panasonic Matsushita Electric Industrial Co., Limited
Panel-Air Corp. Standard-Pacific Corp.
Panel Concepts, Inc. Standard-Pacific Corp.
Papagallo United States Shoe Corp.
Paper Mate Gillette Co.
Paragon AMF, Inc.
Paragon Resources, Inc. Public Service Company of New Mexico
Paramount Pictures Gulf & Western Industries, Inc.
Parkay Dart & Kraft, Inc.
Park Place Bally Manufacturing Corp.
Parke-Davis Warner-Lambert Co.
Parker The Parker Pen Co.
Parker Brothers General Mills, Inc.
Parliament Philip Morris Inc.
Parsons Constructors Inc. Parsons Corp.
Parsons Paper NVF Co.
The Partlow Corp. Chicago Pneumatic Tool Co.
Pathmark Supermarkets General Corp.
Patio PepsiCo, Inc.
Patriot Raytheon Co.
Patterson Services Rollins, Inc.
Paul Masson Seagram Co. Ltd.

Paul Revere Avco Corp.
Paystar International Harvester Co.
Peabody Coal Fluor Corp.
Peabody Coal Co. Williams Companies
Pearl Norlin Corp.
Pearle Vision Centers G. D. Searle & Co.
Pearsall Chemical Witco Chemical Corp.
Pelto Oil Co. Southdown, Inc.
Pend Oreille Oil & Gas Co. Gulf Resources & Chemical Corp.
Penick & Ford Univar Corp.
Penn Belding Heminway Company, Inc.
Pennsylvania Electric Co. General Public Utilities Corp.
Pennsylvania Life Insurance Co. PennCorp Financial, Inc.
Pennsylvania Power Co. Ohio Edison Co.
Pennzoil Pennzoil Co.
People Time Inc.
Peoples Life Capital Holding Corp.
Peoples Gas, Light and Coke Peoples Energy Corp.
Peoples Natural Gas InterNorth, Inc.
Pepperell West Point-Pepperell, Inc.
Pepperidge Farm Campbell Soup Co.
Pepsi-Cola PepsiCo, Inc.
Pepsi-Cola General Bottlers IC Industries, Inc.
Pepsodent Unilever PLC
Pepto-Bismol Morton-Norwich Products, Inc.
Pequot Springs Mills, Inc.
Perception Bobbie Brooks, Inc.
Perfect Subscription Co. Cadence Industries Corp.
Perkins (tobacco shops) Stop & Shop Companies Inc.
Perkins Cake & Steak Holiday Inns, Inc.
Perkins Engines Massey-Ferguson Limited
Permanente Kaiser Cement Corp.
Permatex Loctite Corp.
Perry Gas Companies Parker Drilling Co.
Perry Surgical Gloves United Industrial Corp.
Pershing & Co., Inc. Donaldson, Lufkin & Jenrette, Inc.
Personal Sportswear Leslie Fay Inc.
Personnel Pool of America Block (H & R), Inc.
Pertussin Chesebrough-Pond's Inc.
Pervel Industries Bemis Company, Inc.
Pet (evaporated milk) IC Industries, Inc.
Pet Inc. IC Industries, Inc.
Peterbilt PACCAR Inc.
Petrie's Petrie Stores Corp.
Petro Data, Ltd. Gearhart Industries, Inc.
PetroUnited United Energy Resources, Inc.
Peugeot Chrysler Corp.
Philadelphia Shaw Industries, Inc.
Philadelphia *Daily News* Knight-Ridder Newspapers, Inc.
Philadelphia *Inquirer* Knight-Ridder Newspapers, Inc.
Philadelphia Life Insurance Co. Tenneco Inc.
Philadelphia Oil Equitable Gas Co.
Philadelphia Printing Properties Basic Resources Corp.
Philco North American Philips Corp.
Philipp Brothers Engelhard Minerals & Chemicals Corp.
Philips North American Philips Corp.
Philips-Lau Products Limited Philips Industries Inc.
Phillies Bayuk Cigars Inc.
Philipp Brothers Phibro Corp.
Phillips' Milk of Magnesia Sterling Drug Inc.
Phillips 66 Phillips Petroleum Co.
Phineas Host International, Inc.
Phoenix Glass Anchor Hocking Corp.
Phoenix Resources Co. Texas International Co.
Pianocorder Superscope, Inc.
Pic-a-Dilly Lucky Stores, Inc.
Picklands Mather Moore McCormack Resources, Inc.
Picktsweet Stokely-Van Camp, Inc.
Pic-Mount Filmways, Inc.
Pickwick International American Can Co.
Piedmont Airlines Piedmont Aviation, Inc.
Pierre Cardin (accessories) Swank, Inc.
Pierre Cardin (clothes) Palm Beach Inc.
Pierre Cardin (toiletries) American Cyanamid Co.
Pietro's Campbell Soup Co.
Piggly Wiggly Fleming Cos., Inc.
Pilling Narco Scientific, Inc.
Pillsbury Pillsbury Co.
Pilot Life Insurance Jefferson-Pilot Corp.
Pine-Sol American Cyanamid Co.
Pinnacle Exploration Callahan Mining Corp.
Pioneer Gas Products Co. Pioneer Corp.
Pipe Specialties, Inc. Quanex Corp.
Piper Aircraft Bangor Punta Corp.
Pittsburgh Corning Corning Glass Works
Pittsburgh Forgings Co. Ampco-Pittsburgh Corp.
Pizza Hut PepsiCo, Inc.
Plains Machinery Co. Pioneer Corp.
Planters Nabisco Brands Inc.
Plas-T-Cote Elixir Industries
Plasti-Shield Owens-Illinois, Inc.
The Plateau, Inc. Suburban Propane Gas Corp.
Plateau Mining Getty Oil Co.
Platinol Bristol-Myers Co.
Platinum Plus Gillette Co.

Playboy Playboy Enterprises, Inc.
Playboy Clubs International, Inc. Playboy Enterprises, Inc.
Playskool Milton Bradley Co.
Playtex International Esmark, Inc.
Plexiglas Rohm and Haas Co.
PLUS Great Atlantic & Pacific Tea Co.
Plus Vita Campbell Taggart, Inc.
Plymouth Chrysler Corp.
Plymouth Shops Allied Stores Corp.
Pocket Books Gulf & Western Industries, Inc.
Polarograph Sargent-Welch Scientific Co.
Polavision Polaroid Corp.
Polymer Corp. ACF Industries, Inc.
Pomeroy's Allied Stores Corp.
Pond's Chesebrough-Pond's Inc.
Pontiac General Motors Corp.
Pool Co. Enserch Corp.
Pop CornNow National Presto Industries
Popov Heublein, Inc.
Poppin Fresh Pie Shops Pillsbury Co.
Popsicle Consolidated Foods Corp.
Popular Library CBS Inc.
Popular Science Times Mirror Co.
Port O' Georgetown Host International, Inc.
Portland General Electric N.V. Portland General Electric Co.
Post General Foods Corp.
Post House Greyhound Corp.
Pott Industries Houston Natural Gas Corp.
Potter & Brumfield AMF, Inc.
Pouliot Designs Thomas Industries, Inc.
Powers Dry Goods Associated Dry Goods Corp.
Prairie Farmer American Broadcasting Companies, Inc.
Pratt & Whitney United Technologies Corp.
Precision Scientific GCA Corp.
Prell Procter & Gamble Co.
Premier Energy Corp. Premier Industrial Corp.
Premier Industrial Export Corp. Premier Industrial Corp.
Prentice Omark Industries, Inc.
Preparation H American Home Products Corp.
Presto National Presto Industries
Prestolite Allied Chemical Corp.
Prestone Union Carbide Corp.
Primary Fuels, Inc. Houston Industries Inc.
Prime Management Prime Motor Inns, Inc.
Prime-O-Lene Prime Motor Inns, Inc.
Prinair The Union Corp.
Prince Gardner Swank, Inc.
Prince Matchabelli Chesebrough-Pond's Inc.
Princess Gardner Swank, Inc.
Princeton Bank and Trust Co. Horizon Bancorp
Pringle's Procter & Gamble Co.
Pro-Banthine G. D. Searle & Co.
Pro-Shot Huffy Corp.
Proctor-Silex SCM Corp.
Product Identification Corp. Signode Corp.
Progress Drilling & Marine, Inc. Buttes Gas & Oil Co.
Progresso Ogden Corp.
Prolamine The Thompson Medical Co., Inc.
Prologue Perception Bobbie Brooks, Inc.
Pronto! Polaroid Corp.
Protective Treatments, Inc. Helene Curtis Industries, Inc.
Proud Popover Quaker Oats Co.
Public Finance Leucadia National Corp.
Public Service of Oklahoma Central & South West Corp.
Puffs Procter & Gamble Co.
Pure Pack Foods Kellogg Co.
Purina Ralston Purina Co.
Puritan Warnaco Inc.
Puss'n Boots Quaker Oats Co.
Pyrex Corning Glass Works
The Pyron Corp. Pacific Tin Consolidated Corp.

Q

Q-Tips Chesebrough-Pond's Inc.
Qiana E. I. Du Pont de Nemours & Co.
Quaker Alloy Casting Harsco Corp.
Quaker Oats Quaker Oats Co.
Quaker 100% Natural Quaker Oats Co.
Qualitrol Corp. Chicago Pneumatic Tool Co.
Quality Inns Manor Care, Inc.
Quality Roof Truss Company Lennar Corp.
Quality (springs) Kuhlman Corp.
Quanex Management Sciences Corp. Quanex Corp.
Quanexport, Inc. Quanex Corp.
Quartzmatic Talley Industries, Inc.
Quasar Matsushita Electric Industrial Co., Limited
Queen of Scott Scot Lad Foods, Inc.
Quik Stop Markets Dillon Companies, Inc.
Quincy Compressor Colt Industries Inc.
Quiz Wiz Coleco Industries, Inc.

R

R. E. Harrington Cordura Corp.
R. R. Bowker Xerox Corp.
R. S. McColl Southland Corp.
RETS Electronic Schools National Education Corp.
RKO General General Tire & Rubber Co.
RPC Corp. Lamson & Sessions Co.
Rachelle Laboratories Inc. International Rectifier Corp.

Racon Inc. Essex Chemical Corp.
Radio Shack Tandy Corp.
Ragu Chesebrough-Pond's Inc.
Rainbo Campbell Taggart, Inc.
Rainier G. Heileman Brewing Co., Inc.
Ralph M. Parsons Co. Parsons Corp.
Ralphs Grocery Federated Department Stores, Inc.
Ram Colgate-Palmolive Co.
Ramada Skyline Corp.
Ramirez & Feraud Ogden Corp.
Ranger Insurance Co. Anderson, Clayton & Co.
Rank Xerox Xerox Corp.
Rapistan Lear Siegler, Inc.
Rasco-Temp Wickes Companies, Inc.
Rawlings Sporting Goods Figgie International
Raymond Offshore Constructors Raymond International, Inc.
Raymond International Builders Raymond International, Inc.
Rea & Derick American Stores Co.
ReaLemon Borden, Inc.
Recipe Campbell Soup Co.
Red Barn City Investing Co.
Red Cross United States Shoe Corp.
Red Devil Paints & Chemicals Insilco Corp.
Red Diamond Tenneco Inc.
Red i Aileen, Inc.
Red Kap Blue Bell, Inc.
Red Lobster Inns General Mills, Inc.
Red Owl Wickes Companies, Inc.
Red Rope Sheller-Globe Corp.
Red Star Universal Foods Corp.
Redbook Charter Co.
Redwing Carriers Wyle Laboratories
Reed Drug Co. Peoples Drug Stores, Inc.
Reed Tool Baker International Corp.
Reese's Hershey Foods Corp.
Regal Brown Group, Inc.
Regan Offshore International Hughes Tool Co.
Reichel & Drews, Inc. Signode Corp.
Reliance Electric Exxon Corp.
Remington E. I. Du Pont de Nemours & Co.
Rena Ware Distributors, Inc. Oneida Limited
Republic Insurance Co. Republic Financial Services
Republic National Bank of New York Republic New York Corp.
Republic-Vanguard Life Insurance Co. Republic Financial Services
Reserve Mining Republic Steel Corp.
Reserve Oil & Gas Getty Oil Co.
Resistoflex Corp. UMC Industries, Inc.
Resorts International Resorts International, Inc.
Respiratory Care Colgate-Palmolive Co.
Reuben International Multifoods Corp.
Revere Copper & Brass ASARCO Inc.
Revere Ware Revere Copper and Brass
Revlon Revlon, Inc.
Reynolds Electrical & Engineering EG & G, Inc.
Rheem City Investing Co.
Rhodes Plastics Corp. ARTRA Group, Inc.
Rice Krispies Kellogg Co.
Richard D. Irwin Inc. Dow Jones & Company, Inc.
Richardson Co. Witco Chemical Corp.
Richman F. W. Woolworth Co.
Richmond Converters, Inc. The Armstrong Rubber Co.
Rich's Federated Department Stores, Inc.
Richway Federated Department Stores, Inc.
Rickel Supermarkets General Corp.
Riekes Group Alco Standard Corp.
Rigesa Westvaco Corp.
Right Guard Gillette Co.
Ringwood Gathering Co. ONEOK Inc.
Rink's Cook United Inc.
Rio Grande Motor Way Rio Grande Industries, Inc.
Rise Carter-Wallace, Inc.
Rit CPC International Inc.
Ritz Nabisco Brands, Inc.
River Processing, Inc. Pargas, Inc.
Riverside Furniture Corp. Arkansas Best Corp.
Riviana Foods Colgate-Palmolive Co.
Roadrunner Plantronics, Inc.
Robert Burns Culbro Corp.
Robert Tabakow Jewelcor Inc.
Roberts & Schaefer Co. Elgin National Industries, Inc.
Robin Hood International Multifoods Corp.
Robinson's of Florida Associated Dry Goods Corp.
Robitussin Robins (A. H.) Co., Inc.
Rochlen Standex International Corp.
Rock of Ages Corp. Nortek, Inc.
Rockford Life Liberty National Insurance Holding Co.
Rocky Mountain Energy Co. Union Pacific Corp.
Rodale Square D Co.
Rod's Food Products Campbell Taggart, Inc.
Roehlen Standex International Corp.
Rogers (musical instruments) CBS Inc.
Rogers (showrooms) Modern Merchandising, Inc.
Rokk Holding Co. Kenai Corp.
Roll Coater, Inc. Arvin Industries, Inc.
Rollins Environmental Services RLC Corp.
Rollins Leasing Corp. RLC Corp.
Rollins-Orkin Rollins, Inc.

Rollins Protective Services Rollins, Inc.
Rolodex Insilco Corp.
Ronrico Seagram Co. Ltd.
Rosario Resources AMAX Inc.
Rose Marie Reid Jonathan Logan, Inc.
Rosenthal Lenox, Inc.
Ross Loos INA Corp.
Rotor Tool Cooper Industries, Inc.
Rowe International, Inc. Triangle Industries, Inc.
Rowena Allegheny International, Inc.
Rowland Truck Equipment XTRA Corp.
Roy Jacobs Co. Grow Group, Inc.
Roy Rogers Marriott Corp.
Royal Nabisco Brands, Inc.
Royal Alaskan Castle & Cooke, Inc.
Royal Copenhagen Swank, Inc.
Royal Industries Lear Siegler, Inc.
Royco Instruments Pacific Scientific Co.
Royster Co. Universal Leaf Tobacco Co., Inc.
Rucker Co. NL Industries, Inc.
Rue Royale Hart Schaffner & Marx
Rugger Palm Beach Inc.
Rusco Electronic Systems Figgie International
Russ Russ Togs, Inc.
Rust Engineering Corp. Wheelabrator-Frye Corp.
Rustler Steak House Gino's Inc.
Ruston-Bucyrus Limited Bucyrus-Erie Co.
Ryder Truck Lines IU International Corp.

S

S & H Green Stamps Baldwin-United Corp.
S.I.P. Engineering, Inc. Parsons Corp.
S. K. Wellman Brush Wellman Inc.
S. S. White Pennwalt Corp.
S. T. Dupont Gillette Co.
SRL Medical Inc. Gould Inc.
SSC&B, Inc. Interpublic Group of Companies, Inc.
SSN-688 General Dynamics Corp.
STC Computer Research Corp. Storage Technology Corp.
STP Corp. Esmark, Inc.
SWL&P Minnesota Power and Light Co.
SX-70 Polaroid Corp.
Saber Energy, Inc. Valero Energy Corp.
Sabre Shaw Industries, Inc.
Sacramento Borden, Inc.
Safetran Systems Corp. CCI Corp.
Sahara Hotel Webb (Del E.) Corp.
St. Joseph Schering-Plough Corp.
St. Lawrence Power Co. Niagara Mohawk Power Corp.
Saint Louis-San Francisco Railway Co. Burlington Northern Inc.
St. Marys Fieldcrest Mills, Inc.
Ste. Michelle Vintners United States Tobacco Co.
St. Paul *Pioneer Press* Knight-Ridder Newspapers, Inc.
St. Regis Paper and Bags Puerto Rican Cement Company, Inc.
Salada Foods Kellogg Co.
Salem R. J. Reynolds Industries, Inc.
Salomon Brothers Phibro Corp.
Samedan Oil Corp. Noble Affiliates, Inc.
Samsonite Beatrice Foods Co.
San Jose *Mercury* Knight-Ridder Newspapers, Inc.
Sanders Graphic Sanders Associates, Inc.
Sandra Lou Blue Bell, Inc.
Sanfor-Set Cluett, Peabody & Co., Inc.
Sanforized Cluett, Peabody & Co., Inc.
The Sanforized Co. Cluett, Peabody & Co., Inc.
Sangamo Western Schlumberger Limited
Sanger-Harris Federated Department Stores, Inc.
San Giorgio Hershey Foods Corp.
Sani-Flush American Home Products Corp.
Sanka General Foods Corp.
Santa Fe Energy Co. Santa Fe Industries, Inc.
Sara Lee Consolidated Foods Corp.
Saran Wrap Dow Chemical Co.
Sarco Wickes Companies, Inc.
Sargent Kidde, Inc.
Sarkeys, Inc. Sabine Corp.
Sarma (Belgium) J. C. Penney Co. Inc.
Sassco Fashions Ltd. Leslie Fay Inc.
Sasson Leslie Fay Inc.
Satellite Television Corp. Communications Satellite Corp.
Saturdays in California Cluett, Peabody & Co., Inc.
Sav-On Jewel Companies, Inc.
Saxon Theatre Corp. Cadence Industries Corp.
Sayre & Toso Mission Insurance Group, Inc.
Schick Warner-Lambert Co.
Schlitz Schlitz (Jos.) Brewing Co.
Schmidt G. Heileman Brewing Co., Inc.
Scholl Schering-Plough Corp.
Scholz Homes Inland Steel Co.
Schottky Unitrode Corp.
Schrader Bellows Scovill Inc.
Schuylkill Metals Corp. Arrow Electronics
Science Research Associates International Business Machines Corp.
Scope Procter & Gamble Co.
Scorpion Facet Enterprises, Inc.
Scot Lad Scot Lad Foods, Inc.
Scotch Minnesota Mining & Manufacturing Co.

Scott Scott Paper Co.
Scott, Foresman and Co. SFN Companies, Inc.
Scotties Scott Paper Co.
Scripto Allegheny International, Inc.
Sea & Ski Carter-Wallace, Inc.
Sea-Con Services CBI Industries, Inc.
Sea-Land Service R. J. Reynolds Industries, Inc.
Sea World Enterprises Harcourt Brace Jovanovich, Inc.
Seaboard CSX Corp.
Seaboard World Airways Tiger International, Inc.
Seabrook Farms Springs Mills, Inc.
Seabrook Foods Springs Mills, Inc.
Seagram's Seagram Co. Ltd.
Sealtest Dart & Kraft, Inc.
Sears Sears, Roebuck and Co.
Seattle-First National Bank Seafirst Corp.
Secret Procter & Gamble Co.
Security Insurance Co. of Hartford Orion Capital Corp.
Security Pacific National Bank Security Pacific Corp.
Sedgefield Blue Bell, Inc.
Sego IC Industries, Inc.
Seismograph Service Corp. Raytheon Co.
Seng Hoover Universal, Inc.
Sentinel GAF Corp.
Sequoia Supply Wickes Companies, Inc.
Seraco Sears, Roebuck and Co.
Sergeant's Robins (A. H.) Co., Inc.
Serv-Air E-Systems, Inc.
Servomation City Investing Co.
Seth Thomas Talley Industries, Inc.
7 Crown Seagram Co. Ltd.
7-Eleven Southland Corp.
Seven Seas Anderson, Clayton & Co.
Seven-Up Philip Morris Inc.
Sew Simple Systems Opelika Manufacturing Corp.
Shadow Interiors Parts and Accessories Co. Coachmen Industries, Inc.
Shaeffer Textron Inc.
Shakespeare Co. Anthony Industries, Inc.
Shampaine Hospital Equipment United Industrial Corp.
Sharon Steel Corp. NVF Co.
Sharp Drilling Co. Pioneer Corp.
Sharples Pennwalt Corp.
Shasta (soft drinks) Consolidated Foods Corp.
Shasta (recreational vehicles) Coachmen Industries, Inc.
Shearson Loeb Rhodes Inc. American Express Co.
Shepard Niles Crane & Hoist Vulcan, Inc.
Sheraton Hotels International Telephone & Telegraph Corp.
Sherwin-Williams Sherwin-Williams Co.
Shillito's Federated Department Stores, Inc.
Ship 'n Shore General Mills, Inc.
Shirt Closet F. W. Woolworth Co.
Shoe Town Heck's, Inc.
ShopKo Super Valu Stores, Inc.
Shop N Go National Convenience Stores Inc.
Shore Line Shops, Inc. Northern Indiana Public Service Co.
Show-Biz Pizza Place Brock Hotel Corp.
Showcase of Fine Fabrics Fabri-Centers of America, Inc.
Showtime Viacom International Inc.
Shredded Wheat Quaker Oats Co.
Shulton's Old Spice American Cyanamid Co.
Sibley, Lindsay & Curr Associated Dry Goods Corp.
Sidewinder Raytheon Co.
Siemens-Allis Allis-Chalmers Corp.
Sierra Energy Co. Sierra Pacific Power Co.
Sigma Mines Dome Mines Limited
Signal Delivery Service Leaseway Transportation Corp.
Signal Knitting Mills Wayne-Gossard Corp.
Signode Wrapping Systems, Inc. Signode Corp.
Sikorsky United Technologies Corp.
Sil-Fos Handy & Harman
Silo, Inc. Cyclops Corp.
Silver Burdett Co. SFN Companies, Inc.
Silver State Savings & Loan (Colorado) Imperial Corp. of America
Silverwoods Hart Schaffner & Marx
Similac Abbott Laboratories
Simon & Schuster Gulf & Western Industries, Inc.
Simoniz Union Carbide Corp.
Simplex Industries Anthony Industries, Inc.
Simplex Wire and Cable Tyco Laboratories, Inc.
Sinarest Pennwalt Corp.
Sine-Off SmithKline Corp.
Sirloin Stockade Lucky Stores, Inc.
Six Flags Bally Manufacturing Corp.
Size 5-7-9 Shops Edison Brothers Stores, Inc.
Sizzler Family Steak Houses Collins Foods International, Inc.
Skaggs American Stores Co.
Robert Skeels & Co. Wynn's International Inc.
Skinner Springs Mills, Inc.
Skinner (pasta) Hershey Foods Corp.
Skippy CPC International Inc.
Skoal United States Tobacco Co.
Skram Conwood Corp.

Skyline Homes, Inc. Skyline Corp.
Slickcraft AMF, Inc.
Smart Drilling Co. ONEOK, Inc.
Smart Shops Lane Bryant, Inc.
Smith Tool Smith International, Inc.
Smirnoff Heublein, Inc.
Smith & Wesson Bangor Punta Corp.
Smith-Corona SCM Corp.
Smith's Transfer Corp. ARA Services, Inc.
Smokador Sheller-Globe Corp.
Smoke-Craft International Multifoods Corp.
Snow Crop Coca-Cola Co.
Snowflake Opelika Manufacturing Corp.
Snyder's Wickes Companies, Inc.
So-Dri Fort Howard Paper Co.
Society Hart Schaffner & Marx
SOFLENS Bausch & Lomb Inc.
Soft & Dri Gillette Co.
Soft Scrub The Clorox Co.
Soft-Shoes Hughes Tool Co.
Soft Spots Morse Shoe, Inc.
Sohio Standard Oil Co. (Ohio)
Solar Turbines International Caterpillar Tractor Co.
Solarcaine Schering-Plough Corp.
SOLOCO Newpark Resources
Solomon Korff Lear Siegler, Inc.
Solventol Chemical Products, Inc. Oakite Products, Inc.
Somerset Importers Norton Simon, Inc.
Sominex Nabisco Brands, Inc.
Sonapco Belco Petroleum Corp.
SONAT Exploration Southern Natural Resources, Inc.
Sonderling Broadcasting Corp. Viacom International Inc.
The Soo Line Railroad Canadian Pacific Ltd.
Sorbus Management Assistance Inc.
"Soul Scissors" Seligman & Latz, Inc.
SoundWorks CBS Inc.
South Beloit Water, Gas & Electric Co. Wisconsin Power & Light Co.
South Bend Milton Bradley Co.
South Carolina Fuel Co., Inc. South Carolina Electric & Gas Co.
South Carolina LNG Co. South Carolina Electric & Gas Co.
South Jersey Gas Co. South Jersey Industries, Inc.
South Louisiana Contractors Inc. Newpark Resources
South Louisiana Production Co. Central Louisiana Energy Corp.
South-Western Publishing Co. SFN Companies, Inc.
Southco Albertson's, Inc.
Southeast First National Bank of Miami Southeast Banking Corp.
Southeast Mortgage Southeast Banking Corp.
Southern Boiler & Tank Works Chicago Milwaukee Corp.
Southern California Savings & Loan Association City Investing Co.
Southern California Gas Pacific Lighting Corp.
Southern Ohio Bank Union Commerce Corp.
Southern Pacific Communications Southern Pacific Co.
Southern Pacific Transportation Co. Southern Pacific Co.
Southern States, Inc. Gulton Industries, Inc.
Southern Surplus Realty Co. Southern California Edison Co.
Southern Telephone Supply Co. Allied Telephone Co.
Southland Paper St. Regis Paper Co.
Southwest Financial Services Southwest Florida Banks, Inc.
Southwest Mortgage Services Southwest Florida Banks, Inc.
Southwestern Bell Telephone Co. American Telephone and Telegraph Co.
Southwestern Electric Power Central & South West Corp.
Southwestern Financial Corp. Texas Industries, Inc.
Southwestern Portland Cement Co. Southdown, Inc.
Space Shuttle Orbiter Rockwell International Corp.
Spacelabs Squibb Corp.
Spalding Questor Corp.
Spam George A. Hormel & Co.
Sparklett Foremost-McKesson, Inc.
Sparrow Raytheon Co.
Spartan Food Systems (Hardee's and Quincy's restaurants) Trans World Corp.
Spartan School of Aeronautics National Education Corp.
Special Export G. Heileman Brewing Co., Inc.
Special K Kellogg Co.
Spector Red Ball, Inc. Telecom Corp.
Spectra Kollmorgen Corp.
Spectra Medical Whittaker Corp.
Spectrobid Pfizer Inc.
Speedi-Print American Business Products, Inc.
Speedo Warnaco Inc.
Speer Omark Industries, Inc.
Speidel Textron Inc.
Spencer Gifts MCA Inc.
Sperry (guidance systems) Sperry Corp.

Sperry & Hutchinson Co. Baldwin-United Corp.
Sperry-Sun Inc. NL Industries, Inc.
Sperry Top-Sider, Inc. The Stride Rite Corp.
Spiegel Beneficial Corp.
Spirit American Motors Corp.
Sport Charter Co.
The Sporting News Times Mirror Co.
Sports Illustrated Time Inc.
Sportscoach Coachmen Industries, Inc.
Spray 'n Wash Morton-Norwich Products, Inc.
Spray Net Helene Curtis Industries, Inc.
Sprayit Thomas Industries, Inc.
Sprayway, Inc. Oakite Products, Inc.
Spreckels Amstar Corp.
Spring City Knitting Co. Cluett, Peabody & Co., Inc.
Spring Valley Water Co., Inc. Hackensack Water Co.
Springmaid Springs Mills, Inc.
Sprint Southern Pacific Co.
Sprite Coca-Cola Co.
Spun-Lo Eiderlon Ti-Caro, Inc.
Spur Murphy Oil Corp.
Square D Square D Co.
Stacey Lucky Stores, Inc.
StakFeeder Hesston Corp.
StakHand Hesston Corp.
StakMover Hesston Corp.
Standard (oil) Standard Oil Co. of Indiana
Standard (engine parts) Standard Motor Products, Inc.
Standard (gasoline stations, Midwest) Standard Oil Co. of Indiana
Standard (gasoline stations, Southeast) Standard Oil Co. of California
Standard & Poor's Corp. McGraw-Hill, Inc.
Standard Financial Corp. Sterling Bancorp.
Standard Fire Insurance Co. Aetna Life and Casualty Co.
Standard Fruit & Steamship Co. Castle & Cooke, Inc.
Standard Kollsman Sun Chemical Corp.
Standard Pipeprotection General Steel Industries, Inc.
Standard Sales Modern Merchandising, Inc.
Standard-Thomson Corp. Allegheny International, Inc.
Stanley The Stanley Works
Star Jewel Companies, Inc.
Star-Kist H. J. Heinz Co.
Star Light Thomas Industries, Inc.
Starcraft Bangor Punta Corp.
Static Guard Alberto-Culver Co.
State Savings and Loan Association NLT Corp.
Steak and Ale Pillsbury Co.
Steamex Peavey Co.
Steck-Vaughan National Education Corp.
Steeler Uniroyal, Inc.
Steinway CBS Inc.
Stella Universal Foods Corp.
Stellite Cabot Corp.
Sterling & Hunt Hart Schaffner & Marx
Sterling Banking Corp. Sterling Bancorp.
Sterling Dental Centers Ipco Corp.
Sterling National Bank & Trust Co. of New York Sterling Bancorp.
Sterling Optical Ipco Corp.
Stern's Allied Stores Corp.
Steuben Glass Corning Glass Works
Stewart & Co. Associated Dry Goods Corp.
Stewart Dry Goods Associated Dry Goods Corp.
Stix, Baer & Fuller Associated Dry Goods Corp.
Stockton, Whatley, Davin & Co. General American Oil Co. of Texas
Stokely's Stokely-Van Camp, Inc.
Stop & Shop Stop & Shop Companies Inc.
Stop N Go National Convenience Stores Inc.
Story & Clark Norlin Corp.
Stratford Jewelers and Distributors Cook United Inc.
Straw Hat Pizza Saga Corp.
Stride Rite The Stride Rite Corp.
Stromberg-Carlson General Dynamics Corp.
Stuart Anderson's Black Angus/Cattle Company Saga Corp.
Stuarts Petrie Stores Corp.
Suave Helene Curtis Industries, Inc.
Sub Sea International Murphy Oil Corp.
Subaru Subaru of America, Inc.
Sucaryl Abbott Laboratories
Successful Farming Meredith Corp.
Sugar Frosted Flakes Kellogg Co.
Sugar Pops Kellogg Co.
Sugartwin Alberto-Culver Co.
Sun Adams Drug Co.
Sun Bank, Orlando Sun Banks of Florida, Inc.
Sun Country International Multifoods Corp.
Sun Dial Square D Co.
Sun Life Group of America, Inc. Kaufman and Broad, Inc.
Sun Giant Tenneco Inc.
Sunbeam Allegheny International, Inc.
Sunbelt Mining Company, Inc. Public Service Company of New Mexico
Sunkist Soft Drinks General Cinema Corp.
Sunny Brook National Distillers & Chemical Corp.
Sunoco Sun Co., Inc.
Sunshine American Brands, Inc.
Sunshine Mine Sunshine Mining Co.

SupeRx Kroger Co.
Super Duper National Convenience Stores Inc.
Super Dry Kimberly-Clark Corp.
Super Glue Loctite Corp.
Super Quink The Parker Pen Co.
Super Saver American Stores Co.
Super Stainless Steel Gillette Co.
Super Valu Super Valu Stores, Inc.
Superior Water, Light, and Power Minnesota Power and Light Co.
Superscope Superscope, Inc.
Supersweet Feeds International Multifoods Corp.
Supertest Charter Co.
Supreme Lumber & Millwork Co. Lennar Corp.
Supron Energy Corp. Southern Union Co.
Sure Procter & Gamble Co.
Surety Life Insurance Co. Dean Witter Reynolds Organization Inc.
Susie's Casuals F. W. Woolworth Co.
Sutro Mortgage Investment Trust PNB Mortgage & Realty Investors
Sutton Russ Togs, Inc.
Sutton Place Vornado, Inc.
Swank Swank, Inc.
Swanson Campbell Soup Co.
Swearingen Aircraft Fairchild Industries, Inc.
Sweda Litton Industries, Inc.
Sweet William Clabir Corp.
Sweetheart Maryland Cup Corp.
Swift & Co. Esmark, Inc.
Swingline American Brands, Inc.
Swivel Gillette Co.
Sybra Inc. LLC Corp.
Sycor, Inc. Northern Telecom Ltd.
Sylvania North American Philips Co.
Syncrude Canada Ltd. Cities Service Co.
Syndyne Corp. American Agronomics Corp.
Systems Engineering Laboratories Gould Inc.

T

T-Butcher Block International Multifoods Corp.
T & B/Ansley Corp. Thomas & Betts Corp.
T.A.D. Avanti National Medical Enterprises, Inc.
T.G.&Y. Household International Corp.
T. J. Maxx Zayre Corp.
TCB Leasing Co. Texas Commerce Bancshares, Inc.
TPCO, Inc. Triangle Industries, Inc.
TR-1 Lockheed Corp.
TRE Semiconductor Equipment Corp. TRE Corp.
TRT Telecommunications Corp. United Brands Co.
TUCO Cabot Corp.
TXI Cement Co. Texas Industries, Inc.
Tab Coca-Cola Co.
Taco Bell PepsiCo, Inc.
Taco Plaza ConAgra, Inc.
Tagamet SmithKline Corp.
Talley Industries of Arizona Talley Industries, Inc.
Talon Textron Inc.
Talos Digitizer Sanders Associates, Inc.
Talos Systems, Inc. Sanders Associates, Inc.
Talwin Sterling Drug Inc.
Tame Gillette Co.
Tandy Tandy Corp.
Tandy Leather Tandycrafts, Inc.
Tareyton American Brands, Inc.
Target Dayton-Hudson Corp.
Tartan Minnesota Mining & Manufacturing Co.
Tasti-Diet Ogden Corp.
Taunton Silversmiths, Ltd. Lenox, Inc.
Taylor (food products) American Brands, Inc.
Taylor (wines) Coca-Cola Co.
Taylor Electric Gould Inc.
Taylor Publishing Insilco Corp.
Taylor-Wharton Harsco Corp.
Taystee American Bakeries Co.
Teccor Electronics Ranco, Inc.
Technicolor Graphic Services, Inc. Technicolor, Inc.
Technicon Revlon, Inc.
Technics Matsushita Electric Industrial Co., Ltd.
Teem PepsiCo, Inc.
Teflon E. I. Du Pont de Nemours & Co.
Telecare Narco Scientific, Inc.
Telenet General Telephone & Electronics Corp.
Teleprompter Corp. Westinghouse Electric Corp.
Telex Communications The Telex Corp.
Telex Computer Products The Telex Corp.
Telstar Colortron Electronic Learning Machine Coleco Industries, Inc.
Temple-Eastex Time Inc.
Tender Touch Helene Curtis Industries, Inc.
Tenneco Tenneco Inc.
Tennessee Gas Transmission Tenneco Inc.
Tennessee Tufting Collins & Aikman Corp.
Terminal Management, Inc. U. S. Realty Investments
Terramycin Pfizer Inc.
Terry Farris (G. C.) Murphy Co.
Tetra Warner-Lambert Co.
Texas Boot United States Shoe Corp.
Texas Commerce Bank Texas Commerce Bancshares, Inc.
Texas Commerce Funding Co. Texas Commerce Bancshares, Inc.
Texas Commerce Leasing Co. Texas Commerce Bancshares, Inc.

Texas Electric Service Texas Utilities Co.
Texas International Airlines Texas Air Corp.
Texas Pharmacal Warner-Lambert Co.
Texas Power & Light Texas Utilities Co.
Texas Reamer Co. Galveston-Houston Co.
TexElastic Corp. Adams-Millis Corp.
TexElectric Corp. Adams-Millis Corp.
Texoma Peoples Energy Corp.
Thalhimer's Carter Hawley Hale Stores, Inc.
Thane Warnaco Inc.
Tharpe & Brooks First Atlanta Corp.
Thatcher Glass Dart & Kraft, Inc.
Thayer McNeil Interco Inc.
Theragran Squibb Corp.
Thermal Brake Products Research & Chemical Corp.
Thermal Systems, Inc. ONEOK, Inc.
Thermometer Corp. of America Figgie International
Things Remembered Stores Cole National Corp.
Thom McAn Melville Corp.
Thomas Thomas Industries, Inc.
Thomas & Betts International, Inc. Thomas & Betts Corp.
Thomas & Betts Limited Thomas & Betts Corp.
Thomas' English Muffins CPC International Inc.
Thomas J. Lipton Inc. Unilever PLC
Thomas Jefferson Life USF&G Corp.
Thomasville Armstrong World Industries, Inc.
Thompson Medical Co. Revlon, Inc.
3M Minnesota Mining & Manufacturing Co.
Three Sisters Miller-Wohl Co.
Thrift J. C. Penney Co. Inc.
Thrift, Inc. Credithrift Financial, Inc.
Thrifty Drug and Discount Stores Thrifty Corp.
Thrifty Realty Co. Thrifty Corp.
Thurston Motor Lines Tyler Corp.
Ticor Southern Pacific Co.
Tide Procter & Gamble Co.
Tidewater Compression, Inc. Tidewater Inc.
Tidewater Contractor Services, Inc. Tidewater Inc.
Tidewater Dredging Corp. Great Lakes International, Inc.
Tidewater Marine Services, Inc. Tidewater Inc.
Tidewater Realty, Inc. Tidewater Inc.
Tiffany & Co. Avon Products, Inc.
Tiger Insurance Group Tiger International, Inc.
Tiger Leasing Group Tiger International, Inc.
Tigress Fabergé, Inc.
Timberline GAF Corp.
Timco, Inc. The Hydraulic Co.
Time Time Inc.
Time-Life Books Time Inc.
Time Saver Dillon Companies, Inc.
Times Fiber Communications Insilco Corp.
Timoptic Merck & Co., Inc.
Tinkertoy CBS Inc.
Tiny Tonka Tonka Corp.
Titanium Metals Corp. NL Industries, Inc.
Titanium Metals Corp. of America Allegheny International, Inc.
Tomahawk General Dynamics Corp.
Tone Greyhound Corp.
Toni Gillette Co.
Tonka Tonka Corp.
Tooltech Nortek, Inc.
Tootsie Pop Drops Tootsie Roll Industries, Inc.
Tootsie Roll Tootsie Roll Industries, Inc.
Tootsie Roll Flavor Rolls Tootsie Roll Industries, Inc.
Tootsie Roll Pops Tootsie Roll Industries, Inc.
Tootsie Squares Tootsie Roll Industries, Inc.
Top Choice General Foods Corp.
Topeka Land Co. Minnesota Power and Light Co.
Toro The Toro Co.
Total General Mills, Inc.
Total Control Oak Industries, Inc.
Tote Hoover Universal, Inc.
Totino's Pillsbury Co.
Tour de France Interco Inc.
Tower City Corp. U. S. Realty Investments
Town Pride Borman's Inc.
Townsend Decorative Hardwood Paneling Potlatch Corp.
Toy World Wickes Companies, Inc.
Trac II Gillette Co.
Trans World Airlines Trans World Corp.
Transamerica Airlines Transamerica Corp.
Transamerica Delaval Transamerica Corp.
Transamerica Financial Transamerica Corp.
Transamerica Occidental Life Insurance Co. Transamerica Corp.
Transco Coal Co. Transco Energy Co.
Transco Coal Gas Co. Transco Energy Co.
Transco Exploration Co. Transco Energy Co.
Transcom II Johnson (E. F.) Co.
Transcontinental Gas Pipe Line Corp. Transco Energy Co.
Transohio Savings Transohio Financial Corp.
TranSouth Financial NCNB Corp.
Transport International Pool, Inc. Gelco Corp.
Transtar International Harvester Co.
Transway Transway International Corp.
Travel Trim Elixir Industries
Treasurecraft Jostens, Inc.
Treasury J. C. Penney Co., Inc.
Treflan Eli Lilly and Co.
Trent Tube Colt Industries Inc.

Tri Pac Triangle Pacific Corp.
Triad Drilling UGI Corp.
Triangle Finance Co., Inc. Triangle Industries, Inc.
Triangle PWC, Inc. Triangle Industries, Inc.
Tricone Hughes Tool Co.
Trident (gum) Warner-Lambert Co.
Trident (submarines) General Dynamics Corp.
The Trident Group General Reinsurance Corp.
"The Trimmers" Seligman & Latz, Inc.
Trine Square D Co.
Trinitron Sony Corp.
Trojan Yacht Whittaker Corp.
Trop-Artic Phillips Petroleum Co.
Tropicana Beatrice Foods Co.
Tropigas International Corp. Transway International Corp.
Tru-Form Plastics Elixir Industries
Truckstops of America Ryder System, Inc.
True Loews Corp.
True Temper Allegheny International, Inc.
Trunkline Gas Panhandle Eastern Pipe Line Co.
TrusWal Systems Corp. Signode Corp.
Tube-Line Corp. Hi-Shear Industries, Inc.
Tuboscope AMF, Inc.
Tums Revlon, Inc.
Tupperware Dart & Kraft, Inc.
Turbodyne McGraw-Edison Co.
Tussy Sterling Drug Inc.
Twice as Fresh The Clorox Co.
Two Guys Vornado, Inc.
Tylenol Johnson & Johnson
Tyler Pipe Industries Tyler Corp.
Tymnet, Inc. Tymshare, Inc.
Tymshare Transaction Services Tymshare, Inc.

U

U Fill 'em Tenneco Inc.
U. S. Envelope Westvaco Corp.
U. S. Fidelity & Guaranty USF&G Corp.
U. S. Filter Corp. Ashland Oil, Inc.
U. S. Fleet Leasing U. S. Leasing International, Inc.
U. S. Home Finance Co. U. S. Home Corp.
U. S. Home Mortgage Corp. U. S. Home Corp.
U. S. I. Chemicals National Distillers & Chemical Corp.
U. S. Investment Leasing U. S. Leasing International, Inc.
U. S. Lease Financing U. S. Leasing International, Inc.
U. S. National Property Owners Insurance Co. NLT Corp.
U. S. Pencil & Stationery Cadence Industries Corp.
U. S. Portfolio Leasing U. S. Leasing International, Inc.
U. S. Rail Services U. S. Leasing International, Inc.
UAC International Unilever PLC
UNC Nuclear Industries, Inc. UNC Resources
UNC Teton UNC Resources
UOP Inc. Signal Companies, Inc.
USLIFE Credit Corp. USLIFE Corp.
USLIFE Savings and Loan Association Imperial Corp. of America
USM Corp. Emhart Corp.
USV Revlon, Inc.
Ultra Brite Colgate-Palmolive Co.
Ultrasuede Springs Mills, Inc.
Unarco-Midwest Corp. UNR Industries, Inc.
Uncle Bill's Cook United Inc.
Unicap Upjohn Co.
Unicoa Corp. Teledyne, Inc.
Unidex Oak Industries, Inc.
Unidynamics, Inc. UMC Industries, Inc.
Unifa Schering-Plough Corp.
Uniforms by Gilson Ipco Corp.
Unijax, Inc. IU International Corp.
Uniloy Hoover Universal, Inc.
Uniloy-Springfield Hoover Universal, Inc.
Union Colliery Co. Union Electric Co.
Union Commerce Bank Union Commerce Corp.
The Union Light, Heat and Power Co. The Cincinnati Gas & Electric Co.
Union Pacific Railroad Union Pacific Corp.
Union Texas Petroleum Allied Chemical Corp.
Union Underwear Co. Northwest Industries
Uniperm Helene Curtis Industries, Inc.
Uniservice, Inc. National Medical Enterprises, Inc.
Unisource Alco Standard Corp.
United Agri Products ConAgra, Inc.
United Airlines UAL, Inc.
United-American Car Lamson & Sessions Co.
United Artists Metro-Goldwyn-Mayer Film Co.
United Can Norton Simon, Inc.
United Cement Co. Texas Industries, Inc.
United Energy Services United Energy Services, Inc.
United Engineers Raytheon Co.
United Fidelity Life Insurance Co. The Liberty Co.
United Fruit United Brands Co.
United Gas Pipe Line United Energy Resources, Inc.
United Jersey Bank United Jersey Banks
United Jersey Leasing United Jersey Banks
United Jersey Mortgage United Jersey Banks
United Merchandising Corp. Thrifty Corp.

United Nuclear Corp. UNC Resources
United Offshore United Energy Resources, Inc.
United Stockyards Canal-Randolph Corp.
United Supply Century Telephone Enterprises, Inc.
United Texas Transmission United Energy Resources, Inc.
UNITRAIN, Inc. Iowa Resources Inc.
Unitrode Computer Products Corp. Unitrode Corp.
Univac Sperry Corp.
Universal (physical fitness equipment) Kidde, Inc.
Universal Manufacturing Northwest Industries
Universal Match UMC Industries, Inc.
Universal Studios MCA Inc.
University Microfilms Xerox Corp.
University Park Press, Inc. SFN Companies, Inc.
University Savings Association of Houston Entex, Inc.
Upland Industries Union Pacific Corp.
Upshur Coals Alco Standard Corp.
Upstage Morse Shoe, Inc.
Utah International General Electric Co.
Utility Fuels, Inc. Houston Industries, Inc.

V

V-8 Campbell Soup Co.
V.O. Seagram Co. Ltd.
VCF Acceptance Corp. The Vendo Co.
VSI Corp. Fairchild Industries, Inc.
VWR Scientific Univar Corp.
Vale Technical Institute National Education Corp.
Valero Transmission Co. Valero Energy Corp.
Valley Camp Coal Co. Quaker State Oil Refining Corp.
Valley-Todeco Lamson & Sessions Co.
Value Realty Co. Lennar Corp.
Van Camp's Stokely-Van Camp, Inc.
Van de Kamp's General Host Corp.
Van Dorn Heat Treating Co. Van Dorn Co.
Van Dorn Machinery Co. Van Dorn Co.
Van Hengel Instruments B.V. Thermal Electron Corp.
Van Waters & Rogers Univar Corp.
Vanguard Melville Corp.
Vanish Bristol-Myers Co.
Vanity Fair V. F. Corp.
Vantage R. J. Reynolds Industries, Inc.
Varibus Corp. Gulf States Utilities Co.
Varo Semiconductor, Inc. Varo, Inc.
Vaseline Chesebrough-Pond's Inc.
Vassarette Munsingwear, Inc.
Vat 69 National Distillers & Chemical Corp.
Vauxhall General Motors Corp. (import)
Vellux West Point-Pepperell, Inc.
Velsicol Chemical Northwest Industries
Velvet Turtle Saga Corp.
Venture May Department Stores Co.
Vetco Combustion Engineering, Inc.
Vibramycin Pfizer Inc.
Vickers Sperry Corp.
Vicking Metallurgical Corp. Quanex Corp.
Vicks Richardson-Vicks Inc.
Victa Allegheny International, Inc.
Victor Comptometer Kidde, Inc.
Victoreen Sheller-Globe Corp.
Videotex Times Mirror Co.
Video-Text Oak Industries, Inc.
The Vidtronics Company, Inc. Technicolor, Inc.
Viking Johnson (E. F.) Co.
Viking Boat Coachmen Industries, Inc.
The Villager Jonathan Logan, Inc.
Virkotype Lawter International, Inc.
Visine Pfizer Inc.
Vita-Lea Shaklee Corp.
Vita-Stat Squibb Corp.
Viva Scott Paper Co.
Vlasic Campbell Soup Co.
Voit AMF, Inc.
Volume Shoe May Department Stores Co.
Von's Household International Corp.
Vought Corp. LTV Corp.
Vulcan Engineering Vulcan, Inc.
Vulcan-Hart Corp. Chicago Milwaukee Corp.
Vulcan Mold and Iron Vulcan, Inc.
Vydec Exxon Corp.

W

WABC American Broadcasting Companies, Inc.
WAIA-FM Cox Broadcasting Corp.
WASH Metromedia, Inc.
WBBM TV, Radio CBS Inc.
WCAU TV, Radio CBS Inc.
WCBM Metromedia, Inc.
WCBS TV, Radio CBS Inc.
WDAI American Broadcasting Companies, Inc.
WDBO-TV The Outlet Co.
WDCA-TV Taft Broadcasting Co.
WEEI CBS Inc.
WESH-TV Cowles Communications, Inc.
WETM-TV Times Mirror Co.
WEXCO WICOR, Inc.
WHIO Cox Broadcasting Corp.
WHTM-TV Times Mirror Co.
WIOD-AM Cox Broadcasting Corp.
WIOQ-FM The Outlet Co.
WIP Metromedia, Inc.
WKM Valve ACF Industries, Inc.

WKRC-TV & AM Taft Broadcasting Co.
WKRQ-FM Taft Broadcasting Co.
WLIF-FM Cox Broadcasting Corp.
WLS American Broadcasting Companies, Inc.
WMAL American Broadcasting Companies, Inc.
WMET Metromedia, Inc.
WMMR Metromedia, Inc.
WNEW Metromedia, Inc.
WOMC Metromedia, Inc.
WPBN-TV, Inc. United States Tobacco Co.
WPLJ American Broadcasting Companies, Inc.
WPVI-TV Capital Cities Broadcasting
WPXI Cox Broadcasting Corp.
WQRS-FM The Outlet Co.
WRIF American Broadcasting Companies, Inc.
WRQX American Broadcasting Companies, Inc.
WRTV McGraw-Hill, Inc.
WSB Cox Broadcasting Corp.
WSOC Cox Broadcasting Corp.
WSTM-TV Times Mirror Co.
WTAF-TV Taft Broadcasting Co.
WTOM-TV United States Tobacco Co.
WTOP-AM The Outlet Co.
WTRK-TV Capital Cities Broadcasting
WTTG-TV Metromedia, Inc.
WTVJ-TV Wometco Enterprises, Inc.
WUI, Inc. MCI Communications Corp.
WVTM-TV Times Mirror Co.
WWSH-FM Cox Broadcasting Corp.
WXIX-TV Metromedia, Inc.
WXYZ American Broadcasting Companies, Inc.
Wagner Electric McGraw-Edison Co.
Wagner Mining Equipment Division PACCAR Inc.
Wag's Walgreen Co.
Waialua Sugar Co. Castle & Cooke Inc.
Waldenbook Carter Hawley Hale Stores, Inc.
Waldom Electronics HMW Industries Inc.
Waldorf Scott Paper Co.
Wales Transportation, Inc. Gifford-Hill Co., Inc.
Walgreen Walgreen Co.
Walker Manufacturing Tenneco Inc.
Walkman Sony Corp.
The Wall Street Journal Dow Jones & Co., Inc.
Wallace & Tiernan Pennwalt Corp.
Wallace and Tuttle HMW Industries Inc.
Wallace Murray Corp. Household International Corp.
Wallace Silversmiths HMW Industries Inc.
Wallaces Farmer American Broadcasting Companies, Inc.
Wallachs Hart Schaffner & Marx
Wallpapers To Go General Mills, Inc.
Wal-Mart Discount City Wal-Mart Stores, Inc.
Walt Disney World Walt Disney Productions
Walter West Point-Pepperell, Inc.
Walter E. Heller Overseas Corp. Walter E. Heller International Corp.
Walter Kendall Nabisco Brands, Inc.
Wamsutta Lowenstein (M.) Corp.
Warner-Amex Warner Communications Inc. (50%), American Express Co. (50%)
Warner Books Warner Communications, Inc.
Warner Brothers Warner Communications, Inc.
Warner/Chilcott Warner-Lambert Co.
Warner & Swasey Bendix Corp.
Warner's Warnaco Inc.
Warrent Transport Tiger International, Inc.
Warrior Drilling & Engineering Co. Howell Petroleum Corp.
Water Pik Teledyne, Inc.
Waterous American Hoist & Derrick Co.
Wear-Ever Aluminum Co. of America
Weber (aircraft fixtures) Kidde, Inc.
Weber (shoes) The Stride Rite Corp.
The Weber Coal Co. United Park City Mines
Webster Bayuk Cigars Inc.
Weight Watchers International H. J. Heinz Co.
Weinstock's Carter Hawley Hale Stores, Inc.
Welby Elgin National Industries, Inc.
Weller Cooper Industries, Inc.
Wells Fargo Bank, N.A. Wells Fargo & Co.
WellTech, Inc. Hanna Mining Co.
Wendy Winter Jack Winter
Wesley-Jessen Schering-Plough Corp.
Wesley's Quaker Maid Borman's Inc.
Weslock TRE Corp.
Wesson Norton Simon, Inc.
West Bend Dart & Kraft, Inc.
West Chemical Co. American Sterilizer Co.
West Texas Utilities Central & South West Corp.
West Towns Bus Company MEI Corp.
West Virginia Gas Co. Equitable Gas Co.
Westclox Talley Industries, Inc.
Westcoast Petroleum Westcoast Transmission Co. Ltd.
Western Auto Supply Co. Beneficial Corp.
Western Electric American Telephone and Telegraph Co.
Western Fire Equipment Premier Industrial Corp.
Western Litho Bemis Company, Inc.
Western Maryland CSX Corp.
Western Massachusetts Electric Northeast Utilities
Western Nuclear Inc. Phelps Dodge Corp.
Western Pennsylvania Water Co. American Water Works Company, Inc.

Western Platinum Ltd. Superior Oil Co.
Western Publishing Co. Mattel, Inc.
Western Quarries and Construction Co. Great Lakes International, Inc.
Western Sky Industries Atlas Corp.
Westin Hotels UAL, Inc.
Westmoreland Plastics Vulcan, Inc.
Westmoreland Products HMW Industries Inc.
Weston Borg-Warner Corp.
Whaledent International Ipco Corp.
Wheaties General Mills, Inc.
Wheeling Electric American Electric Power Co., Inc.
Whelan Adams Drug Co.
Whirlpool Whirlpool Corp.
White Cap Footwear Morse Shoe, Inc.
White Hen Pantry Jewel Companies, Inc.
White Lily Foods Federal Co.
White Owl Culbro Corp.
White Rain Gillette Co.
White Stag Warnaco Inc.
White-Westinghouse White Consolidated Industries, Inc.
Whitehouse Opelika Manufacturing Corp.
White's Household International Corp.
Whitestone Products Ipco Corp.
Whitman Chocolates IC Industries, Inc.
Whitney Blake Co. Nortek, Inc.
Wickes Furniture Wickes Companies, Inc.
Wickes Lumber Wickes Companies, Inc.
Wide-Lite Corp. Esquire, Inc.
Wigham Poland Holdings Ltd. Fred S. James & Co., Inc.
The Wild Pair Edison Brothers Stores, Inc.
Wilkinson Allegheny International, Inc.
Wilkinson Match Co. Allegheny International, Inc.
William M. Mercer, Inc. Marsh & McLennan Companies, Inc.
William Penn (cigars) Culbro Corp.
William Penn (gasoline stations) Standard Oil Co. (Ohio)
William Volker Mohasco Corp.
Williams Exploration Co. Williams Companies
Williams Pipe Line Co. Williams Companies
Wilson Brothers Corp. Inexco Oil Co.
Wilson Brothers Drilling Co. Inexco Oil Co.
Wilson Foods Corp. LTV Corp.
Wilson Jones American Brands, Inc.
Wilson Oil Rig Manufacturing LTV Corp.
Wilson Sporting Goods PepsiCo, Inc.
Wilsonart Dart & Kraft, Inc.
Winchell's Donut House Denny's Inc.
Winchester Olin Corp.
Wind Song Chesebrough-Pond's Inc.
Windex Bristol-Myers Co.
Windsor Supreme National Distillers & Chemical Corp.
Winston R. J. Reynolds Industries, Inc.
Wisconsin Barge Line CLC of America, Inc.
Wisconsin Natural Gas Wisconsin Electric Power Co.
Wise Borden, Inc.
Wisk Unilever PLC
Wiss Cooper Industries, Inc.
Wizard American Home Products Corp.
Wohl Shoe Co. Brown Group, Inc.
Wolf Opelika Manufacturing Corp.
Wolfschmidt Seagram Co. Ltd.
Womack-Master Craft, Inc. Lennar Corp.
Woman's Day CBS Inc.
Wonder CBS Inc.
Wonder World Co. Thrifty Corp.
Wondercale Springs Mills, Inc.
Wood, Struthers & Winthrop, Inc. Donaldson, Lufkin & Jenrette, Inc.
Woodside Standex International Corp.
Woolco F. W. Woolworth Co.
Woolite American Home Products Corp.
Woolworth F. W. Woolworth Co.
Wordstream Management Assistance Inc.
Work Wear ARA Services, Inc.
World Bazaar Munford, Inc.
World-Book-Childcraft International, Inc. The Scott & Fetzer Co.
World Book Encyclopedia The Scott & Fetzer Co.
World Color Press City Investing Co.
World Savings and Loan Association (California) Golden West Financial Corp.
World Savings and Loan Association (Colorado) Golden West Financial Corp.
World Wide Agency, Inc. JWT Group, Inc.
Worthington McGraw-Edison Co.
Wrangler Blue Bell, Inc.
Wrangler Shoes for Jeans Genesco Inc.
Wright Line Inc. Barry Wright Corp.
Wunda Weve Dan River Inc.
Wurzburger Anheuser-Busch Companies, Inc.
Wyeth American Home Products Corp.
Wyler's Borden, Inc.

X

X-L-CO, Inc. XTRA Corp.
Xcelite Cooper Industries, Inc.
Xynetics General Signal Corp.

Y

Y & S Hershey Foods Corp.
Yale Scovill Inc.

Yates Square D Co.
Yellow Front Lucky Stores, Inc.
Yield House Furniture Standex International Corp.
York Air Conditioning Borg-Warner Corp.
York Steak House General Mills, Inc.
Yosemite Insurance Co. Credithrift Financial, Inc.
You and i Aileen, Inc.
Youngstown Sheet & Tube LTV Corp.
Youngstown Steel Door Lamson & Sessions Co.
Yuban General Foods Corp.

Z

Zale Zale Corp.
Zallea Brothers, Inc. UMC Industries
Zapata Exploration Co. Zapata Corp.
Zapata Marine Services, Inc. Zapata Corp.
Zapata Off Shore Co. Zapata Corp.
Zayre Zayre Corp.
Zero Halliburton Zero Corp.
Zest Procter & Gamble Co.
Ziegler Coal Co. Houston Natural Gas Corp.
Zodys HRT Industries, Inc.
Zomax Johnson & Johnson

Appendix II

COMPANIES GROUPED BY INDUSTRY

Here are all New York Stock Exchange Companies (as of 1980) arranged in industry groups. Thoughtful investors often decide first which industry they wish to invest in, and only after that, which stock to pick within the industry. The purpose of this appendix is to facilitate that approach.

The list is adapted from "Common Stocks Listed" (December 1980 edition) published by the New York Stock Exchange Inc. Companies that are no longer on the New York Stock Exchange (as of February 1982) are not listed here.

The stocks fall into four broad groupings:

1. Industrials
2. Transportation
3. Utilities
4. Finance, Real Estate

1. INDUSTRIALS

AIRCRAFT

AAR CORP.
BENDIX CORP.
BOEING CO., THE
CCI CORP.
CESSNA AIRCRAFT CO.
CURTISS-WRIGHT CORP.
FAIRCHILD INDUSTRIES, INC.
GENERAL DYNAMICS CORP.
GRUMMAN CORP.
HI-SHEAR INDUSTRIES INC.
LOCKHEED CORP.
MARTIN MARIETTA CORP.
MCDONNELL DOUGLAS CORP.
NORTHROP CORP.
PARKER-HANNIFIN CORP.
PNEUMO CORP.
ROHR INDUSTRIES, INC.
TRW, INC.
TALLEY INDUSTRIES, INC.
UNITED TECHNOLOGIES CORP.

AMUSEMENT

AMERICAN BROADCASTING COMPANIES, INC.
CBS INC.
CAPITAL CITIES COMMUNICATIONS, INC.
COX BROADCASTING CORP.
DISNEY (WALT) PRODUCTIONS
FILMWAYS, INC.
GENERAL CINEMA CORP.
LOEWS CORP.
MCA INC.
METRO-GOLDWYN-MAYER FILM CO.
METROMEDIA, INC.
STORER BROADCASTING CO.
TAFT BROADCASTING CO.
TELEPROMPTER CORP.
TWENTIETH CENTURY-FOX FILM CORP.
VIACOM INTERNATIONAL INC.
WOMETCO ENTERPRISES, INC.

AUTOMOTIVE

AMERICAN MOTORS CORP.
ARVIN INDUSTRIES, INC.
BEARINGS, INC.
BORG-WARNER CORP.
CHAMPION SPARK PLUG CO.
CHRIS-CRAFT INDUSTRIES INC.
CHRYSLER CORP.
CORE INDUSTRIES INC.
DANA CORP.
EATON CORP.
ECHLIN MANUFACTURING CO.
FACET ENTERPRISES, INC.
FEDERAL-MOGUL CORP.
FORD MOTOR CO.
FRUEHAUF CORP.
GATEWAY INDUSTRIES, INC.
GENERAL MOTORS CORP.
GENUINE PARTS CO.
GULF & WESTERN INDUSTRIES, INC.
HAYES-ALBION CORP.
HONDA MOTOR CO., LTD.
HOOVER UNIVERSAL, INC.
LEHIGH VALLEY INDUSTRIES, INC.
PUROLATOR INC.
RAYBESTOS-MANHATTAN, INC.
SIGNAL COMPANIES, INC.
A. O. SMITH CORP.
SPARTON CORP.
STANDARD MOTOR PRODUCTS, INC.
STEEGO CORP.
STEWART-WARNER CORP.
SUN ELECTRIC CORP.
TIMKEN CO.
WYNN'S INTERNATIONAL INC.

BUILDING

ALPHA PORTLAND INDUSTRIES, INC.
ANTHONY INDUSTRIES, INC.
ARMSTRONG WORLD INDUSTRIES, INC.
CENTEX CORP.
CENVILL COMMUNITIES, INC.
CERTAIN-TEED CORP.

CHAMPION INTERNATIONAL CORP.
DILLINGHAM CORPORATION
ELCOR CORP.
EVANS PRODUCTS CO.
FISCHBACH CORP.
FLUOR CORP.
FUQUA INDUSTRIES, INC.
GENERAL PORTLAND INC.
GENERAL REFRACTORIES CO.
GENSTAR LTD.
GIANT PORTLAND & MASONRY CEMENT CO.
GIFFORD-HILL & CO., INC.
GREAT LAKES INTERNATIONAL, INC.
IDEAL BASIC INDUSTRIES, INC.
INTERNATIONAL ALUMINUM CORP.
INTERPACE CORP.
JIM WALTER CORP.
JOHNS-MANVILLE CORP.
KAISER CEMENT CORP.
KAUFMAN AND BROAD, INC.
KEENE CORP.
KELLER INDUSTRIES, INC.
LENNAR CORP.
LONE STAR INDUSTRIES, INC.
MASONITE CORP.
MCDERMOTT INC.
MORRISON-KNUDSEN CO., INC.
NATIONAL GYPSUM CO.
OKC CORP.
OVERHEAD DOOR CORP.
PARSONS CORP.
PRESLEY COS.
PUERTO RICAN CEMENT CO., INC.
RAYMOND INTERNATIONAL, INC.
ROBERTSON (H. H.) CO.
RYAN HOMES, INC.
SHAPELL INDUSTRIES, INC.
SOUTHWEST FOREST INDUSTRIES, INC.
STANDARD-PACIFIC CORP.
STONE & WEBSTER, INC.
TEXAS INDUSTRIES, INC.
UNR INDUSTRIES, INC.
U. S. GYPSUM CO.
U. S. HOME CORP.
VULCAN MATERIALS CO.
WICKES COMPANIES, INC.

CHEMICALS

AIR PRODUCTS & CHEMICALS, INC.
ALLIED CHEMICAL CORP.
AMERICAN CYANAMID CO.
ANCHOR HOCKING CORP.
AVERY INTERNATIONAL CORP.
BALL CORP.
BAUSCH & LOMB INC.
BEKER INDUSTRIES CORP.
BIG THREE INDUSTRIES, INC.
BROCKWAY GLASS COMPANY, INC.
CABOT CORP.
CELANESE CORP.
CLOROX CO.
COLGATE-PALMOLIVE CO.
CORNING GLASS WORKS
DESOTO, INC.
DEXTER CORP.
DIAMOND SHAMROCK CORP.
DORSEY CORP.
DOW CHEMICAL CO.
DRAVO CORP.
DU PONT DE NEMOURS (E. I.) & CO.
EASTMAN KODAK CO.
ESSEX CHEMICAL CORP.
ETHYL CORP.
FMC CORP.
FERRO CORP.
FIRST MISSISSIPPI CORP.
FREEPORT MINERALS CO.
FRIGITRONICS, INC.
GAF CORP.
GRACE (W. R.) & CO.
GROW GROUP, INC.
GUARDIAN INDUSTRIES CORP.
HERCULES INC.
HEXCEL CORP.
HUNT (PHILIP A.) CHEMICAL CORP.
INTERNATIONAL MINERALS & CHEMICAL CORP.
KERR GLASS MANUFACTURING CORP.
KOPPERS CO.
KYOTO CERAMIC COMPANY, LTD.
LAWTER CHEMICALS, INC.
LENOX, INC.
LIBBEY-OWENS-FORD CO.
LOCTITE CORP.
LUBRIZOL CORP.
MINNESOTA MINING & MANUFACTURING CO.
MONSANTO CO.
NCH CORP.
NL INDUSTRIES, INC.
NALCO CHEMICAL CO.
NVF CO.
NEW ENGLAND NUCLEAR CORP.
NORTON COMPANY
OAKITE PRODUCTS, INC.
OLIN CORP.
OWENS-CORNING FIBERGLAS CORP.
OWENS-ILLINOIS, INC.
PPG INDUSTRIES, INC.

PENNWALT CORP.
PROCTER & GAMBLE CO.
PRODUCTS RESEARCH & CHEMICAL CORP.
PUREX INDUSTRIES, INC.
REICHHOLD CHEMICALS, INC.
RICHARDSON-VICKS INC.
ROHM AND HAAS CO.
SHERWIN-WILLIAMS CO.
STANDARD BRANDS PAINT COMPANY
STAUFFER CHEMICAL CO.
SUN CHEMICAL CORP.
TECHNICOLOR, INC.
TEXASGULF INC.
THIOKOL CORP.
UNION CARBIDE CORP.
UNIVAR CORP.
WILLIAMS COMPANIES
WITCO CHEMICAL CORP.

DRUGS, COSMETICS

ABBOTT LABORATORIES
ALBERTO-CULVER CO.
AMERICAN HOME PRODUCTS CORP.
AVON PRODUCTS, INC.
BAXTER TRAVENOL LABORATORIES, INC.
BRISTOL-MYERS CO.
CARTER-WALLACE, INC.
CHESEBROUGH-POND'S INC.
COOPER LABORATORIES, INC.
ECKERD (JACK) CORP.
ELI LILLY AND COMPANY
FABERGÉ, INC.
FOREMOST-MCKESSON, INC.
GENERAL NUTRITION, INC.
HELENE CURTIS INDUSTRIES, INC.
ICN PHARMACEUTICALS, INC.
INTERNATIONAL FLAVORS & FRAGRANCES, INC.
JOHNSON & JOHNSON
MARION LABORATORIES, INC.
MARY KAY COSMETICS, INC.
MERCK & CO., INC.
MORTON-NORWICH PRODUCTS, INC.
PFIZER INC.
REVLON, INC.
RICHARDSON-VICKS INC.
ROBINS (A. H.) COMPANY, INC.
RORER GROUP INC.
SCHERING-PLOUGH CORP.
G. D. SEARLE & CO.
SHAKLEE CORP.
SMITHKLINE CORP.
STERLING DRUG INC.
UPJOHN CO.
WARNER-LAMBERT CO.

ELECTRONICS, ELECTRICAL

AVX CORP.
ADVANCED MICRO DEVICES, INC.
ALLEN GROUP INC.
ALLIS-CHALMERS CORP.
AMP INC.
AMPEX CORP.
ANALOG DEVICES, INC.
ANIXTER BROS., INC.
APPLIED MAGNETICS CORP.
ARROW ELECTRONICS
AUGAT, INC.
AVNET, INC.
AYDIN CORP.
BALDOR ELECTRIC CO.
BALLY MANUFACTURING CORP.
BARRY WRIGHT CORP.
BECKMAN INSTRUMENTS, INC.
BELL INDUSTRIES, INC.
BLACK & DECKER MANUFACTURING CO.
BURNDY CORP.
CTS CORP.
CENCO INC.
CENTRONICS DATA COMPUTER CORP.
COMDISCO, INC.
COMPUTERVISION CORP.
CONRAC CORP.
CONTROL DATA CORP.
CRAIG CORP.
CRAY RESEARCH, INC.
CRITON CORP.
CROUSE-HINDS CO.
DATA GENERAL CORP.
DATA TERMINAL SYSTEMS, INC.
DATAPOINT CORP.
DIGITAL EQUIPMENT CORP.
DYNAMICS CORP. OF AMERICA
EG & G, INC.
ELECTRONIC ASSOCIATES, INC.
ELECTRONIC MEMORIES & MAGNETICS CORP.
EMERSON ELECTRIC CO.
EMERSON RADIO CORP.
E-SYSTEMS, INC.
FOUR-PHASE SYSTEMS, INC.
GK TECHNOLOGIES, INC.
GENERAL ELECTRIC CO.
GENERAL INSTRUMENT CORP.
GENRAD, INC.
GERBER SCIENTIFIC, INC.
GOULD INC.
GRAINGER (W. W.), INC.

GULTON INDUSTRIES, INC.
HAZELTINE CORP.
HEWLETT-PACKARD CO.
HIGH VOLTAGE ENGINEERING CORP.
INTERNATIONAL BUSINESS MACHINES CORP.
INTERNATIONAL RECTIFIER CORP.
INTERNATIONAL TELEPHONE & TELEGRAPH CORP.
ITEK CORP.
JOHNSON (E. F.) COMPANY
KOLLMORGEN CORP.
LEAR SIEGLER, INC.
LFE CORP.
LTV CORP.
LITTON INDUSTRIES, INC.
LORAL CORP.
LYNCH COMMUNICATION SYSTEMS, INC.
M/A-COM, INC.
MANAGEMENT ASSISTANCE INC.
MATSUSHITA ELECTRIC INDUSTRIAL CO., LIMITED
MAYTAG CO.
MCGRAW-EDISON CO.
MEASUREX CORP.
MEDTRONIC, INC.
MODULAR COMPUTER SYSTEMS, INC.
MOHAWK DATA SCIENCES CORP.
MOTOROLA INC.
MYERS (L. E.) CO. GROUP
NARCO SCIENTIFIC, INC.
NATIONAL PRESTO INDUSTRIES
NATIONAL SEMICONDUCTOR CORP.
NORLIN CORP.
NORTH AMERICAN PHILLIPS CORP.
NORTHERN TELECOM LTD.
OAK INDUSTRIES, INC.
PERKIN-ELMER CORP.
PIONEER ELECTRONIC CORP.
PLANTRONICS, INC.
PLESSEY COMPANY LIMITED, THE
PRIME COMPUTER, INC.
RCA CORP.
RTE CORP.
RAYTHEON CO.
RECOGNITION EQUIPMENT INC.
ROLM CORP.
SANDERS ASSOCIATES, INC.
SARGENT-WELCH SCIENTIFIC CO.
SCIENTIFIC-ATLANTA, INC.
SCOTT & FETZER CO., THE
SONY CORP.
SPECTRA-PHYSICS, INC.
SPERRY CORP.
SQUARE D CO.
STORAGE TECHNOLOGY CORP.
SUPERSCOPE, INC.
TANDY CORP.
TEKTRONIX, INC.
TELEDYNE, INC.
TELEX CORP., THE
TERADYNE, INC.
TEXAS INSTRUMENTS, INC.
THOMAS & BETTS CORP.
THOMAS INDUSTRIES, INC.
TRACOR, INC.
TRIANGLE INDUSTRIES, INC.
TYCO LABORATORIES, INC.
TYMSHARE, INC.
UNITRODE CORP.
VARIAN ASSOCIATES, INC.
VARO, INC.
VEECO INSTRUMENTS INC.
WABASH, INC.
WATKINS-JOHNSON CO.
WESTINGHOUSE ELECTRIC CORP.
WHIRLPOOL CORP.
WHITTAKER CORP.
WURLITZER CO.
WYLE LABORATORIES
ZENITH RADIO CORP.

FOODS, COMMODITIES

AMALGAMATED SUGAR CO.
AMERICAN BAKERIES CO.
AMSTAR CORP.
ANDERSON, CLAYTON & CO.
ANHEUSER-BUSCH COMPANIES, INC.
ARCHER-DANIELS-MIDLAND CO.
ARMADA CORP.
BEATRICE FOODS CO.
BORDEN, INC.
CPC INTERNATIONAL INC.
CAMPBELL SOUP CO.
CAMPBELL TAGGART, INC.
CARLING O'KEEFE LTD.
CARNATION CO.
CASTLE & COOKE, INC.
CENTRAL SOYA CO. INC.
CHOCK FULL O'NUTS CORP.
COCA-COLA BOTTLING CO. OF N.Y., INC.
COCA-COLA CO.
CONAGRA, INC.
CONSOLIDATED FOODS CORP.
DART & KRAFT, INC.
DI GIORGIO CORP.
DR PEPPER CO.
ESMARK, INC.
FEDERAL CO.
GENERAL FOODS CORP.

GENERAL HOST CORP.
GENERAL MILLS, INC.
GERBER PRODUCTS CO.
HEILEMAN (G.) BREWING CO., INC.
HEINZ (H. J.) CO.
HERSHEY FOODS CORP.
HEUBLEIN, INC.
HIRAM WALKER-CONSUMERS HOME LTD.
HOLLY SUGAR CORP.
INGREDIENT TECHNOLOGY CORP.
INTERNATIONAL MULTIFOODS CORP.
IOWA BEEF PROCESSORS, INC.
KANE-MILLER CORP.
KELLOGG CO.
KEYSTONE FOODS CORP.
MAYER (OSCAR) & CO., INC.
NABISCO BRANDS, INC.
NATIONAL DISTILLERS & CHEMICAL CORP.
NEWHALL LAND AND FARMING CO., THE
NORTON SIMON, INC.
ORANGE-CO, INC.
PEPSICO, INC.
PILLSBURY CO.
PUBLICKER INDUSTRIES, INC.
QUAKER OATS CO.
RALSTON PURINA CO.
ROYAL CROWN COMPANIES, INC.
SCHAEFER (F. & M.) CORP.
SCHLITZ (JOS.) BREWING CO.
SCOT LAD FOODS, INC.
SEAGRAM CO. LTD.
SMUCKER (J. M.) CO.
SQUIBB CORP.
A. E. STALEY MANUFACTURING CO.
STANDARD BRANDS INC.
STOKELY-VAN CAMP, INC.
TOOTSIE ROLL INDUSTRIES, INC.
UNILEVER LTD.
UNILEVER N.V.
UNITED BRANDS CO.
UNIVERSAL FOODS CORP.
WARD FOODS, INC.
WM. WRIGLEY JR. CO.

FURNITURE, OFFICE EQUIPMENT

AM INTERNATIONAL
BURROUGHS CORP.
DIEBOLD, INC.
GF BUSINESS EQUIPMENT, INC.
KROEHLER MANUFACTURING COMPANY
LANIER BUSINESS PRODUCTS
LEGGETT & PLATT, INC.
NCR CORP.
PITNEY-BOWES, INC.
SCM CORP.
SAVIN CORP.
SHELLER-GLOBE CORP.
XEROX CORP.
ZERO CORP.

LEATHER, SHOES

BROWN GROUP, INC.
GENESCO INC.
INTERCO INC.
MCDONOUGH CO.
MELVILLE CORP.
MORSE SHOE, INC.
SCOA INDUSTRIES, INC.
STRIDE RITE CORP.
UNITED STATES SHOE CORP.
VISTA RESOURCES, INC.
WOLVERINE WORLD WIDE INC.

MACHINERY, METALS

AMF, INC.
ACME-CLEVELAND CORP.
ALBANY INTERNATIONAL CORP.
ALCO STANDARD CORP.
ALLIED PRODUCTS CORP.
AMERICAN CAN CO.
AMERICAN DISTRICT TELEGRAPH CO.
AMERICAN HOIST & DERRICK CO.
AMERICAN HOSPITAL SUPPLY CO.
AMERICAN STANDARD INC.
AMERICAN STERILIZER CO.
AMETEK, INC.
AMPCO-PITTSBURGH CORP.
AMSTED INDUSTRIES, INC.
ARO CORP.
ATO INC.
BAKER INTERNATIONAL CORP.
BARD (C. R.), INC.
BARNES GROUP, INC.
BECTON, DICKINSON AND CO.
BELL & HOWELL CO.
BERKEY PHOTO, INC.
BRIGGS & STRATTON CORP.
BROWN & SHARPE MANUFACTURING CO.
BRUNSWICK CORP.
BRUSH WELLMAN INC.
BUCYRUS-ERIE CO.
BUFFALO FORGE CO.
CBI INDUSTRIES, INC.
CADENCE INDUSTRIES CORP.
CAMERON IRON WORKS, INC.
CATERPILLAR TRACTOR CO.
CHICAGO PNEUMATIC TOOL CO.
CHROMALLOY AMERICAN CORP.
CINCINNATI MILACRON INC.

CLARK EQUIPMENT CO.
COLECO INDUSTRIES, INC.
COLT INDUSTRIES INC.
COMBUSTION ENGINEERING, INC.
COMPUGRAPHIC CORP.
CONTINENTAL COPPER & STEEL INDUSTRIES, INC.
CONTINENTAL GROUP, INC.
COOPER INDUSTRIES, INC.
COPELAND CORP.
CRANE CO.
CROMPTON & KNOWLES CORP.
CROWN CORK & SEAL CO., INC.
CUMMINS ENGINE COMPANY, INC.
DAMON CORP.
DANIEL INDUSTRIES, INC.
DEERE & CO.
DENTSPLY INTERNATIONAL, INC.
DONALDSON CO. INC.
DOVER CORP.
DRESSER INDUSTRIES, INC.
DUTCH BOY INC.
ELGIN NATIONAL INDUSTRIES, INC.
EMHART CORP.
ENVIROTECH CORP.
ESTERLINE CORP.
EX-CELL-O CORP.
FEDDERS CORP.
FOSTER WHEELER CORP.
FOX-STANLEY PHOTO PRODUCTS, INC.
FOXBORO CO.
GALVESTON-HOUSTON CO.
GCA CORP.
GEARHART INDUSTRIES, INC.
GIDDINGS & LEWIS, INC.
GILLETTE CO.
GLEASON WORKS
HMW INDUSTRIES, INC.
HANDY & HARMAN
HARNISCHFEGER CORP.
HARRIS CORP.
HESSTON CORP.
HILLENBRAND INDUSTRIES, INC.
HOBART CORP.
HONEYWELL INC.
HUFFY CORP.
HUGHES TOOL CO.
IDEAL TOY CORP.
ILLINOIS TOOL WORKS INC.
INGERSOLL-RAND CO.
INSILCO CORP.
INTERNATIONAL HARVESTER CO.
IPCO CORP.
JOHNSON CONTROLS, INC.
JOY MANUFACTURING CO.
KENNAMETAL INC.
KEYSTONE CONSOLIDATED INDUSTRIES, INC.
KEYSTONE INTERNATIONAL, INC.
KIDDE, INC.
KIRSCH CO.
KUBOTA, LTD.
KUHLMAN CORP.
KYSOR INDUSTRIAL CORP.
LAMSON & SESSIONS CO.
LIONEL CORP., THE
MAGIC CHEF, INC.
MARK CONTROLS CORP.
MARLEY CO.
MASCO CORP.
MASSEY-FERGUSON LTD.
MATTEL, INC.
MCNEIL CORP.
MESTA MACHINE CO.
MIDLAND ROSS CORP.
MILTON BRADLEY CO.
MILTON ROY CO.
MIRRO CORP.
MONARCH MACHINE TOOL CO.
MONOGRAM INDUSTRIES, INC.
MURRAY OHIO MANUFACTURING CO.
NATIONAL CAN CORP.
NATIONAL MINE SERVICE CO.
NATIONAL-STANDARD CO.
NEWELL COMPANIES, INC.
NORRIS INDUSTRIES, INC.
OMARK INDUSTRIES, INC.
ONEIDA LTD.
OUTBOARD MARINE CORP.
PACIFIC SCIENTIFIC CO.
PARKER PEN CO., THE
PEABODY INTERNATIONAL CORP.
PENGO INDUSTRIES, INC.
POLAROID CORP.
PREMIER INDUSTRIAL CORP.
PROLER INTERNATIONAL CORP.
QUESTOR CORP.
RANCO INC.
REECE CORP.
REVERE COPPER AND BRASS INC.
REXNORD INC.
ROBERTSHAW CONTROLS CO.
ROCKWELL INTERNATIONAL CORP.
RONSON CORP.
ROPER CORP.
SPS TECHNOLOGIES, INC.
SCOVILL INC.
SEALED POWER CORP.
SIGNODE CORP.
SIMMONDS PRECISION PRODUCTS, INC.

SINGER CO.
SMITH INTERNATIONAL, INC.
SNAP-ON TOOL CORP.
STANLEY WORKS, THE
STA-RITE INDUSTRIES, INC.
L. S. STARRETT CO., THE
SUNDSTRAND CORP.
SWANK, INC.
SYBRON CORP.
TRE CORP.
TEXTRON INC.
THERMO ELECTRON CORP.
TOKHEIM CORP.
TONKA CORP.
TORO CO., THE
TOWLE MANUFACTURING CO.
TRANE CO., THE
TRICO INDUSTRIES, INC.
TRINITY INDUSTRIES, INC.
TWIN DISC, INC.
UNION CORP., THE
UNITED INDUSTRIAL CORP.
U. S. INDUSTRIES, INC.
VAN DORN CO.
VENDO CO., THE
VULCAN, INC.
WALLACE-MURRAY CORP.
WEAN UNITED, INC.
WHEELABRATOR-FRYE INC.
WHITE CONSOLIDATED INDUSTRIES, INC.
ZURN INDUSTRIES, INC.

MINING

ALCAN ALUMINUM LTD.
ALUMINUM CO. OF AMERICA
AMAX INC.
ASARCO INC.
ATLAS CORP.
BENGUET CORP.
CALLAHAN MINING CORP.
CAMPBELL RED LAKE MINES LTD.
CLEVELAND-CLIFFS IRON CO., THE
DOME MINES LTD.
EAGLE-PICHER INDUSTRIES, INC.
EASTERN GAS & FUEL ASSOCIATES
GULF RESOURCES & CHEMICAL CORP.
HANNA MINING CO.
HECLA MINING CO.
HOMESTAKE MINING CO.
HUDSON BAY MINING & SMELTING CO., LTD.
INCO LTD.
KAISER ALUMINUM & CHEMICAL CORP.
KENNECOTT CORP.
MCINTYRE MINES LIMITED
NEWMONT MINING CORP.
NORTH AMERICAN COAL CORP., THE
NORTHGATE EXPLORATION LTD.
PACIFIC TIN CONSOLIDATED CORP.
PHELPS DODGE CORP.
REYNOLDS METALS CO.
SUNSHINE MINING CO.
UNC RESOURCES
UNITED PARK CITY MINES

PAPER, PUBLISHING

AMERICAN BUSINESS PRODUCTS, INC.
ARCATA CORP.
BEMIS CO., INC.
BOISE CASCADE CORP.
CHESAPEAKE CORP. OF VIRGINIA, THE
CLEVEPAK CORP.
COWLES COMMUNICATIONS, INC.
CROWN ZELLERBACH CORP.
DELUXE CHECK PRINTERS, INC.
DENNISON MANUFACTURING CO.
DIAMOND INTERNATIONAL CORP.
DONNELLEY (R. R.) & SONS CO.
DOW JONES & CO., INC.
ENNIS BUSINESS FORMS, INC.
ESQUIRE, INC.
FEDERAL PAPER BOARD CO., INC.
FORT HOWARD PAPER CO.
GANNETT CO., INC.
GEORGIA-PACIFIC CORP.
GREAT NORTHERN NEKOOSA CORP.
HAMMERMILL PAPER CO.
HARCOURT BRACE JOVANOVICH, INC.
HARLAND (JOHN H.) CO.
HARTE-HANKS COMMUNICATIONS, INC.
HOUGHTON MIFFLIN CO.
INTERNATIONAL PAPER CO.
JAMES RIVER CORP. OF VIRGINIA
JOSTENS, INC.
KIMBERLY-CLARK CORP.
KNIGHT-RIDDER NEWSPAPERS, INC.
LEE ENTERPRISES, INC.
LOUISIANA-PACIFIC CORP.
MACMILLAN BLOEDEL LIMITED
MARYLAND CUP CORP.
MCGRAW-HILL, INC.
MEAD CORP.
MEREDITH CORP.
MOORE CORP.
PACIFIC LUMBER CO., THE
PAPERCRAFT CORP.
PLAYBOY ENTERPRISES, INC.
POPE & TALBOT, INC.
POTLATCH CORP.
REXHAM CORP.

SFN COMPANIES, INC.
ST. REGIS PAPER CO.
SCOTT PAPER CO.
SEALED AIR CORP.
SIMPLICITY PATTERN CO., INC.
STANDEX INTERNATIONAL CORP.
STONE CONTAINER CORP.
TIME, INC.
TIMES MIRROR CO.
TRIANGLE PACIFIC CORP.
UMC INDUSTRIES, INC.
UNION CAMP CORP.
WALLACE BUSINESS FORMS
WESTVACO CORP.
WEYERHAEUSER CO.

PETROLEUM, NATURAL GAS

AMERADA HESS CORP.
APACHE CORP.
ASHLAND OIL, INC.
ATLANTIC RICHFIELD CO.
BARBER OIL CORP.
BASIC RESOURCES CORP.
BELCO PETROLEUM CORP.
BRITISH PETROLEUM CO. LTD.
BURNS (R. L.) CORP.
BUTTES GAS & OIL CO.
CHARTER CO.
CITIES SERVICE CO.
EXXON CORP.
FREEPORT-MCMORAN, INC.
GENERAL AMERICAN OIL CO. OF TEXAS
GEOSOURCE INC.
GETTY OIL CO.
GLOBAL MARINE INC.
GULF OIL CORP.
HELMERICH & PAYNE, INC.
HOWELL CORP.
HOWELL PETROLEUM CORP.
INEXCO OIL CO.
KANEB SERVICES, INC.
KERR-MCGEE CORP.
LEAR PETROLEUM CORP.
LOUISIANA LAND & EXPLORATION CO.
MESA PETROLEUM CO.
MOBIL CORP.
MORAN ENERGY, INC.
MURPHY OIL CORP.
NEWPARK RESOURCES
NOBLE AFFILIATES, INC.
OCCIDENTAL PETROLEUM CORP.
OCEAN DRILLING & EXPLORATION CO.
PARKER DRILLING CO.
PATRICK PETROLEUM CO.
PENN CENTRAL CORP.
PENNZOIL CO.
PHILLIPS PETROLEUM CO.
POGO PRODUCING CO.
QUAKER STATE OIL REFINING CORP.
READING & BATES CORP.
ROWAN COMPANIES, INC.
ROYAL DUTCH PETROLEUM CO.
SABINE CORP.
SCHLUMBERGER LIMITED
SEDCO, INC.
SHELL OIL CO.
SHELL TRANSPORT & TRADING CO., LTD.
SOUTHLAND ROYALTY CO.
STANDARD OIL CO. (INDIANA)
STANDARD OIL CO. (OHIO)
STANDARD OIL CO. OF CALIFORNIA
SUN CO., INC.
SUPERIOR OIL CO.
TESORO PETROLEUM CORP.
TEXACO INC.
TEXAS INTERNATIONAL CO.
TEXAS OIL & GAS CORP.
TIDEWATER INC.
TOSCO CORP.
TRICENTROL LTD.
UNION OIL CO. OF CALIFORNIA
UNITED REFINING CO.
WESTERN CO. OF NORTH AMERICA
WILSHIRE OIL COMPANY OF TEXAS
WOODS PETROLEUM CORP.
ZAPATA CORP.

RETAIL TRADE

ADAMS DRUG CO., INC.
ALBERTSON'S, INC.
ALEXANDER'S, INC.
ALLIED STORES CORP.
AMERICAN STORES CO.
AMES DEPARTMENT STORES, INC.
AMFAC, INC.
ARLEN REALTY & DEVELOPMENT CORP.
ASSOCIATED DRY GOODS CORP.
BEST PRODUCTS CO., INC.
BORMAN'S INC.
CAESARS WORLD, INC.
CARSON PIRIE SCOTT & CO.
CARTER HAWLEY HALE STORES, INC.
CHURCH'S FRIED CHICKEN, INC.
COLE NATIONAL CORP.
COLLINS FOODS INTERNATIONAL, INC.
COOK UNITED INC.
CUNNINGHAM DRUG STORES, INC.
DAYTON-HUDSON CORP.
DENNY'S, INC.
DILLON COMPANIES, INC.

EDISON BROTHERS STORES, INC.
FABRI-CENTERS OF AMERICA, INC.
FAMILY DOLLAR STORES, INC.
FEDERATED DEPARTMENT STORES, INC.
FISHER FOODS, INC.
FOTOMAT CORP.
GAP STORES, INC.
GARFINCKEL, BROOKS BROS., MILLER & RHOADS
GINO'S INC.
GOLDEN NUGGET, INC.
GORDON JEWELRY CORP.
GREAT ATLANTIC & PACIFIC TEA CO., INC.
HARDEE'S FOOD SYSTEMS, INC.
HARTFIELD-ZODYS, INC.
HECK'S, INC.
HILTON HOTELS CORP.
HOLIDAY INNS, INC.
HOST INTERNATIONAL, INC.
HOUSE OF FABRICS, INC.
JAMESWAY CORP.
JEWEL COMPANIES, INC.
JEWELCOR INC.
K MART CORP.
KING'S DEPARTMENT STORES, INC.
KROGER CO.
LA QUINTA MOTOR INNS, INC.
LANE BRYANT, INC.
LEVITZ FURNITURE CORP.
LONGS DRUG STORES, INC.
LOWE'S COMPANIES, INC.
LUCKY STORES, INC.
MGM GRAND HOTELS, INC.
MACY (R. H.) & CO., INC.
MARRIOTT CORP.
MARSHALL FIELD AND CO.
MAY DEPARTMENT STORES CO.
MAYS (J. W.), INC.
MCDONALD'S CORP.
MERCANTILE STORES CO., INC.
MILLER-WOHL CO.
MODERN MERCHANDISING, INC.
MUNFORD, INC.
MURPHY (G. C.) CO.
NASHUA CORP.
NATIONAL TEA CO.
OUTLET CO., THE
PAMIDA, INC.
PAY LESS DRUG STORES NORTHWEST, INC.
J. C. PENNEY CO., INC.
PEOPLES DRUG STORES, INC.
PETRIE STORES CORP.
PONDEROSA SYSTEM, INC.
PRIME MOTOR INNS, INC.
PUEBLO INTERNATIONAL, INC.
RB INDUSTRIES, INC.
RAMADA INNS, INC.
RAPID-AMERICAN CORP.
REVCO D. S., INC.
RITE AID CORP.
SAFEWAY STORES, INC.
SAV-A-STOP INC.
SCOTTY'S, INC.
SEARS, ROEBUCK AND CO.
SELIGMAN & LATZ, INC.
SOUTHLAND CORP.
STERCHI BROS. STORES, INC.
STOP & SHOP COMPANIES, INC.
SUAVE SHOE CORP.
SUPER VALU STORES, INC.
SUPERMARKETS GENERAL CORP.
THRIFTY CORP.
TOYS 'R' US, INC.
UNITED INNS, INC.
VORNADO, INC.
WALGREEN CO.
WAL-MART STORES, INC.
WEIS MARKETS, INC.
WIEBOLDT STORES, INC.
WINN-DIXIE STORES, INC.
F. W. WOOLWORTH CO.
ZALE CORP.
ZAYRE CORP.

RUBBER

AMERACE CORP.
ARMSTRONG RUBBER CO., THE
BANDAG INC.
CARLISLE CORP.
COOPER TIRE & RUBBER CO.
DAYCO CORP.
FIRESTONE TIRE & RUBBER CO.
GENERAL TIRE & RUBBER CO.
GOODRICH (B. F.) CO.
GOODYEAR TIRE & RUBBER CO.
MOHAWK RUBBER CO.
RUBBERMAID INC.
UNIROYAL, INC.

STEEL

ALLEGHENY LUDLUM INDUSTRIES, INC.
AMERON, INC.
ARMCO INC.
ATHLONE INDUSTRIES, INC.
AXIA INC.
BETHLEHEM STEEL CORP.
BUNDY CORP.
CANADIAN PACIFIC ENTERPRISES LTD.

CARPENTER TECHNOLOGY CORP.
CECO CORP., THE
COPPERWELD CORP.
CYCLOPS CORP.
DIVERSIFIED INDUSTRIES, INC.
EASCO CORP.
FLORIDA STEEL CORP.
GENERAL STEEL INDUSTRIES, INC.
HAJOCA CORP.
HARSCO CORP.
INLAND STEEL CO.
INTERLAKE, INC.
JORGENSEN (EARLE M.) CO.
KAISER STEEL CORP.
LUKENS STEEL CO.
NATIONAL STEEL CORP.
NORTHWESTERN STEEL AND WIRE CO.
NUCOR CORP.
OGDEN CORP.
QUANEX CORP.
REPUBLIC CORP.
REPUBLIC STEEL CORP.
TYLER CORP.
U. S. STEEL CORP.
VALLEY INDUSTRIES, INC.
WHEELING-PITTSBURGH STEEL CORP.

TEXTILES

ADAMS-MILLIS CORP.
AILEEN, INC.
AKZONA INC.
ANGELICA CORP.
BELDING HEMINWAY COMPANY, INC.
BLUE BELL, INC.
BOBBIE BROOKS, INC.
BURLINGTON INDUSTRIES, INC.
CANNON MILLS CO.
CHELSEA INDUSTRIES, INC.
CLUETT, PEABODY & CO., INC.
COLLINS & AIKMAN CORP.
CONE MILLS CORP.
DAN RIVER INC.
FARAH MANUFACTURING CO., INC.
FIELDCREST MILLS, INC.
GRANITEVILLE CO.
HART SCHAFFNER & MARX
JONATHAN LOGAN, INC.
KELLWOOD CO.
LESLIE FAY INC.
LEVI STRAUSS & CO.
LOWENSTEIN (M.) CORP.
MANHATTAN INDUSTRIES, INC.
MOHASCO CORP.
MUNSINGWEAR, INC.
OPELIKA MANUFACTURING CORP.
OXFORD INDUSTRIES, INC.
PALM BEACH INC.
PHILIPS-VAN HEUSEN CORP.
PURITAN FASHIONS, CORP.
REEVES BROTHERS, INC.
RIEGEL TEXTILE CORP.
RUSS TOGS, INC.
SALANT CORP.
SPRINGS MILLS, INC.
J. P. STEVENS & CO., INC.
TEXFI INDUSTRIES, INC.
TI-CARO, INC.
UNITED MERCHANTS & MANUFACTURERS, INC.
V. F. CORP.
WARNACO INC.
WAYNE-GOSSARD CORP.
WEST POINT-PEPPERELL, INC.
JACK WINTER

TOBACCO

AMERICAN BRANDS, INC.
BAYUK CIGARS INC.
CONWOOD CORP.
CULBRO CORP.
PHILIP MORRIS INC.
R. J. REYNOLDS INDUSTRIES, INC.
UNITED STATES TOBACCO CO.
UNIVERSAL LEAF TOBACCO CO., INC.

OTHER

ACF INDUSTRIES, INC.
APL CORP.
ALLIED MAINTENANCE CORP.
ALLRIGHT AUTO PARKS, INC.
AMERICAN BUILDING MAINTENANCE INDUSTRIES
AMERICAN MEDICAL INTERNATIONAL, INC.
AMERICAN SHIP BUILDING CO.
ARA SERVICES, INC.
ARCTIC ENTERPRISES, INC.
AUTOMATIC DATA PROCESSING, INC.
BANGOR PUNTA CORP.
BINNEY & SMITH INC.
BLAIR (JOHN) & CO.
BLOCK (H & R), INC.
BROWNING-FERRIS INDUSTRIES, INC.
CLC OF AMERICA, INC.
COACHMEN INDUSTRIES, INC.
COMMUNITY PSYCHIATRIC CENTERS
COMPUTER SCIENCES CORP.
CORDURA CORP.
DPF INC.
DUN & BRADSTREET CORP.

ELECTRONIC DATA SYSTEMS CORP.
ELIXIR INDUSTRIES
EQUIFAX INC.
FEDERAL SIGNAL CORP.
FLEETWOOD ENTERPRISES, INC.
FLEMING COS., INC.
FLIGHTSAFETY INTERNATIONAL, INC.
FOOTE, CONE & BELDING COMM., INC.
FRANKLIN MINT CORP.
GATX CORP.
GELCO CORP.
GENERAL SIGNAL CORP.
HALLIBURTON CO.
HANDLEMAN CO.
HOSPITAL CORP. OF AMERICA
HUMANA INC.
INTERPUBLIC GROUP OF COMPANIES, INC.
JWT GROUP, INC.
LIFEMARK CORP.
MACKE COMPANY
MALONE AND HYDE, INC.
MOBILE HOME INDUSTRIES, INC.
NAPCO INDUSTRIES, INC.
NATIONAL EDUCATION CORP.
NATIONAL HOMES CORP.
NATIONAL MEDICAL CARE, INC.
NATIONAL MEDICAL ENTERPRISES, INC.
NATIONAL SERVICE INDUSTRIES, INC.
NORTHWEST INDUSTRIES
PHILIPS INDUSTRIES INC.
PITTSTON CO., THE
PLANNING RESEARCH CORP.
PORTEC, INC.
REDMAN INDUSTRIES, INC.
RELIANCE GROUP, INC.
ROLLINS, INC.
SAFEGUARD BUSINESS SYSTEMS, INC.
SAFEGUARD INDUSTRIES, INC.
SAGA CORP.
SAN JUAN RACING ASSOCIATION, INC.
SAXON INDUSTRIES, INC.
SCA SERVICES, INC.
SERVICE CORP. INTERNATIONAL
SKYLINE CORP.
SOUTHDOWN, INC.
SPERRY AND HUTCHINSON CO.
TANDYCRAFTS, INC.
TODD SHIPYARDS CORP.
U. S. LEASING INTERNATIONAL, INC.
WACKENHUT CORP.
WARNER COMMUNICATIONS INC.
WASTE MANAGEMENT, INC.
WEST CO.
WINNEBAGO INDUSTRIES, INC.
WYLY CORP.
XTRA CORP.

2. TRANSPORTATION

AIR

AIRBORNE FREIGHT CORP.
AMERICAN AIRLINES, INC.
BRANIFF INTERNATIONAL CORP.
CONTINENTAL AIR LINES, INC.
DELTA AIR LINES, INC.
EASTERN AIR LINES, INC.
EMERY AIR FREIGHT CORP.
FEDERAL EXPRESS CORP.
KLM ROYAL DUTCH AIRLINES
NORTHWEST AIRLINES, INC.
PSA, INC.
PAN AMERICAN WORLD AIRWAYS, INC.
PIEDMONT AVIATION, INC.
REPUBLIC AIRLINES, INC.
SOUTHWEST AIRLINES CO.
TIGER INTERNATIONAL, INC.
TRANS WORLD CORP.
UAL, INC.
U.S. AIR, INC.
WESTERN AIR LINES, INC.
WORLD AIRWAYS, INC.

AUTO, BUS, TRUCK

ARKANSAS BEST CORP.
BANNER INDUSTRIES, INC.
BUTLER INTERNATIONAL, INC.
CAROLINA FREIGHT CARRIERS CORP.
CONSOLIDATED FREIGHTWAYS, INC.
FLEXI-VAN CORP.
GREYHOUND CORP.
LEASEWAY TRANSPORTATION CORP.
MEI CORP.
MCLEAN TRUCKING CO.
OVERNITE TRANSPORTATION CO.
PHH GROUP, INC.
RLC CORP.
RYDER SYSTEM, INC.
TELECOM CORP.
TRANSCON LINES
TRANSWAY INTERNATIONAL CORP.

RAIL

BURLINGTON NORTHERN INC.
CSX CORP.
CANADIAN PACIFIC LTD.
CHICAGO MILWAUKEE CORP.
FLORIDA EAST COAST RAILWAY CO.
IC INDUSTRIES, INC.

KANSAS CITY SOUTHERN INDUSTRIES INC.
KATY INDUSTRIES, INC.
MISSOURI PACIFIC CORP.
NORFOLK & WESTERN RAILWAY CO.
RIO GRANDE INDUSTRIES, INC.
SANTA FE INDUSTRIES, INC.
SOO LINE RAILROAD CO.
SOUTHERN PACIFIC CO.
SOUTHERN RAILWAY CO.
TRANS UNION CORP.
UNION PACIFIC CORP.
WESTERN PACIFIC INDUSTRIES, INC.

SHIP

MOORE MCCORMACK RESOURCES, INC.
NATOMAS CO.
OVERSEAS SHIPHOLDING GROUP, INC.
SEA CONTAINERS GROUP
SEATRAIN LINES, INC.

3. UTILITIES

ELECTRIC, GAS, WATER

ALAGASCO, INC.
ALASKA INTERSTATE CO.
ALLEGHENY POWER SYSTEM, INC.
AMERICAN ELECTRIC POWER CO., INC.
AMERICAN NATURAL RESOURCES CO.
AMERICAN WATER WORKS CO. INC.
ARIZONA PUBLIC SERVICE CO.
ARKANSAS LOUISIANA GAS CO.
ATLANTIC CITY ELECTRIC CO.
BALTIMORE GAS & ELECTRIC
BAY STATE GAS CO.
BLACK HILLS POWER & LIGHT CO.
BOSTON EDISON CO.
BROOKLYN UNION GAS CO., THE
CP NATIONAL CORP.
CAROLINA POWER & LIGHT CO.
CASCADE NATURAL GAS CORP.
CENTRAL & SOUTH WEST CORP.
CENTRAL HUDSON GAS & ELECTRIC CORP.
CENTRAL ILLINOIS LIGHT CO.
CENTRAL ILLINOIS PUBLIC SERVICE CO.
CENTRAL LOUISIANA ENERGY CORP.
CENTRAL MAINE POWER CO.
CINCINNATI GAS & ELECTRIC CO.
CLEVELAND ELECTRIC ILLUMINATING CO., THE
COASTAL CORP.
COLUMBIA GAS SYSTEM, INC.
COLUMBUS & SOUTHERN OHIO ELECTRIC CO.
COMMONWEALTH EDISON CO.
COMMUNITY PUBLIC SERVICE CO.
CONNECTICUT NATURAL GAS CORP.
CONSOLIDATED EDISON CO. OF N.Y., INC.
CONSOLIDATED NATURAL GAS CO.
CONSUMERS POWER CO.
DAYTON POWER & LIGHT CO.
DELMARVA POWER & LIGHT CO.
DETROIT EDISON CO.
DUKE POWER CO.
DUQUESNE LIGHT CO.
EASTERN UTILITIES ASSOCIATES
EL PASO CO.
EMPIRE DISTRICT ELECTRIC CO.
EMPIRE INC.
ENSERCH CORP.
ENTEX, INC.
EQUITABLE GAS CO.
FLORIDA POWER & LIGHT CO.
FLORIDA POWER CORP.
GAS SERVICE CO.
GENERAL PUBLIC UTILITIES CORP.
GULF STATES UTILITIES CO.
HACKENSACK WATER CO.
HAWAIIAN ELECTRIC CO., INC.
HOUSTON INDUSTRIES INC.
HOUSTON NATURAL GAS CORP.
HYDRAULIC CO.
IU INTERNATIONAL CORP.
IDAHO POWER CO.
ILLINOIS POWER CO.
INDIANA GAS CO., INC.
INDIANAPOLIS POWER & LIGHT CO.
INTERNORTH, INC.
INTERSTATE POWER CO.
IOWA ELECTRIC LIGHT & POWER CO.
IOWA-ILLINOIS GAS & ELECTRIC CO.
IOWA PUBLIC SERVICE CO.
IOWA RESOURCES INC.
KANSAS CITY POWER & LIGHT CO.
KANSAS GAS AND ELECTRIC COMPANY
KANSAS-NEBRASKA NATURAL GAS COMPANY, INC.
KANSAS POWER AND LIGHT CO.
KENTUCKY UTILITIES CO.
LACLEDE GAS CO.
LONG ISLAND LIGHTING CO.
LOUISVILLE GAS & ELECTRIC CO.
MAPCO INC.
MICHIGAN ENERGY RESOURCES
MIDDLE SOUTH UTILITIES, INC.
MINNESOTA GAS CO.
MINNESOTA POWER AND LIGHT CO.
MISSOURI PUBLIC SERVICE CO.
MONTANA POWER CO.
MONTANA-DAKOTA UTILITIES CO.
MOUNTAIN FUEL SUPPLY CO.

NATIONAL FUEL GAS CO.
NEVADA POWER CO.
NEW ENGLAND ELECTRIC SYSTEM
NEW ENGLAND GAS AND ELECTRIC ASSOCIATION
NEW YORK STATE ELECTRIC & GAS CORP.
NIAGARA MOHAWK POWER CORP.
NICOR INC.
NORTHEAST UTILITIES
NORTHERN INDIANA PUBLIC SERVICE CO.
NORTHERN STATES POWER CO.
NORTHWEST ENERGY CO.
OHIO EDISON CO.
OKLAHOMA GAS AND ELECTRIC CO.
ONEOK, INC.
ORANGE AND ROCKLAND UTILITIES, INC.
PACIFIC GAS & ELECTRIC CO.
PACIFIC LIGHTING CORP.
PACIFIC POWER & LIGHT CO.
PANHANDLE EASTERN PIPE LINE CO.
PARGAS, INC.
PENNSYLVANIA POWER & LIGHT CO.
PEOPLES ENERGY CORP.
PETROLANE INC.
PHILADELPHIA ELECTRIC CO.
PHILADELPHIA SUBURBAN CORP.
PIEDMONT NATURAL GAS CO., INC.
PIONEER CORP.
PORTLAND GENERAL ELECTRIC CO.
POTOMAC ELECTRIC POWER CO.
PUBLIC SERVICE COMPANY OF COLORADO
PUBLIC SERVICE COMPANY OF INDIANA, INC.
PUBLIC SERVICE COMPANY OF NEW HAMPSHIRE
PUBLIC SERVICE COMPANY OF NEW MEXICO
PUBLIC SERVICE ELECTRIC & GAS CO.
PUGET SOUND POWER & LIGHT CO.
ROCHESTER GAS & ELECTRIC CORP.
ST. JOSEPH LIGHT & POWER CO.
SAN DIEGO GAS & ELECTRIC CO.
SAVANNAH ELECTRIC AND POWER CO.
SIERRA PACIFIC POWER CO.
SOUTH CAROLINA ELECTRIC & GAS CO.
SOUTH JERSEY INDUSTRIES, INC.
SOUTHEASTERN PUBLIC SERVICE CO.
SOUTHERN CALIFORNIA EDISON CO.
SOUTHERN CO.
SOUTHERN INDIANA GAS AND ELECTRIC CO.
SOUTHERN NATURAL RESOURCES, INC.
SOUTHERN UNION CO.
SOUTHWEST GAS CORP.
SOUTHWESTERN PUBLIC SERVICE CO.
SUBURBAN PROPANE GAS CORP.
TAMPA ELECTRIC COMPANY
TENNECO INC.
TEXAS EASTERN CORP.
TEXAS GAS TRANSMISSION CORP.
TEXAS UTILITIES CO.
TOLEDO EDISON CO.
TRANSCO COMPANIES, INC.
TUCSON ELECTRIC POWER CO.
UGI CORP.
UNION ELECTRIC CO.
UNITED ENERGY RESOURCES, INC.
UNITED ILLUMINATING CO., THE
UTAH POWER & LIGHT CO.
VALERO ENERGY CORP.
VIRGINIA ELECTRIC & POWER CO.
WASHINGTON GAS LIGHT CO.
WASHINGTON WATER POWER CO.
WESTCOAST TRANSMISSION CO. LTD.
WICOR, INC.
WISCONSIN ELECTRIC POWER CO.
WISCONSIN POWER AND LIGHT CO.
WISCONSIN PUBLIC SERVICE CORP.

COMMUNICATION

AMERICAN TELEPHONE AND TELEGRAPH CO.
BELL CANADA
CENTRAL TELEPHONE & UTILITIES CORP.
CENTURY TELEPHONE ENTERPRISES, INC.
CINCINNATI BELL INC.
COMMUNICATIONS SATELLITE CORP.
CONTINENTAL TELEPHONE CORP.
GENERAL TELEPHONE & ELECTRONICS CORP.
MID-CONTINENT TELEPHONE CORP.
PACIFIC TELEPHONE & TELEGRAPH CO.
ROCHESTER TELEPHONE CORP.
SOUTHERN NEW ENGLAND TELEPHONE CO.
UNITED TELECOMMUNICATIONS, INC.
WESTERN UNION CORP.

4. FINANCE, REAL ESTATE

BANKING

AHMANSON (H. F.) & CO.
AMERICAN SAVINGS & LOAN ASSOCIATION OF FLORIDA
BALDWIN-UNITED CORP.
BANCAL TRI-STATE CORP.

BANK OF NEW YORK COMPANY, INC., THE
BANK OF VIRGINIA CO.
BANKAMERICA CORP.
BANKERS TRUST NEW YORK CORP.
BARNETT BANKS OF FLORIDA, INC.
BISCAYNE FEDERAL SAVINGS & LOAN ASSOCIATION
CHASE MANHATTAN CORP.
CHEMICAL NEW YORK CORP.
CITICORP
CONTINENTAL ILLINOIS CORP.
CROCKER NATIONAL CORP.
EQUIMARK CORP.
FAR WEST FINANCIAL CORP.
FIDELITY FINANCIAL CORP.
FIDELITY UNION BANCORPORATION
FINANCIAL CORP. OF SANTA BARBARA
FINANCIAL FEDERATION, INC.
FIRST CHARTER FINANCIAL CORP.
FIRST CHICAGO CORP.
FIRST CITY BANCORP. OF TEXAS, INC.
FIRST INTERNATIONAL BANCSHARES, INC.
FIRST NATIONAL BOSTON CORP.
FIRST NATIONAL STATE BANCORPORATION
FIRST PENNSYLVANIA CORP.
FIRST VIRGINIA BANKS, INC.
FIRST WISCONSIN CORP.
GENERAL BANCSHARES CORP.
GIBRALTAR FINANCIAL CORP. OF CALIFORNIA
GOLDEN WEST FINANCIAL CORP.
GREAT WESTERN FINANCIAL CORP.
HARRIS BANKCORP, INC.
HORIZON BANCORP
IMPERIAL CORP. OF AMERICA
INDUSTRIAL NATIONAL CORP.
IRVING BANK CORP.
LITCO BANCORPORATION OF NEW YORK, INC.
MANUFACTURERS HANOVER CORP.
MARINE MIDLAND BANKS, INC.
MERCANTILE TEXAS CORP.
MORGAN (J. P.) & CO. INC.
NAPLES FEDERAL SAVINGS & LOAN ASSN.
NATIONAL DETROIT CORPORATION
NCNB CORP.
NORTHERN CALIFORNIA SAVINGS & LOAN ASSN.
NORTHWEST BANCORPORATION
REPUBLIC NEW YORK CORP.
REPUBLIC OF TEXAS CORP.
SEAFIRST CORP.
SECURITY PACIFIC CORP.
SOUTHEAST BANKING CORP.
SOUTHWEST BANCSHARES, INC.
SOUTHWEST FLORIDA BANKS, INC.
TEXAS COMMERCE BANCSHARES, INC.
TRANSOHIO FINANCIAL CORP.
UNION COMMERCE CORP.
UNITED JERSEY BANKS
WACHOVIA CORP.
WELLS FARGO & CO.
WESTERN BANCORPORATION

INSURANCE

AETNA LIFE AND CASUALTY CO.
AMERICAN EXPRESS CO.
AMERICAN FAMILY CORP.
AMERICAN GENERAL CORP.
AMERICAN HERITAGE LIFE INVESTMENT CORP.
CNA FINANCIAL CORP.
CAPITAL HOLDING CORP.
COLONIAL PENN GROUP, INC.
COMBINED INTERNATIONAL CORP.
CONNECTICUT GENERAL INSURANCE CORP.
CONTINENTAL CORP.
CORROON & BLACK CORP.
CRUM AND FORSTER
GEICO CORP.
GENERAL REINSURANCE CORP.
GULF UNITED CORP.
HALL (FRANK B.) & CO., INC.
INA CORP.
INTEGON CORP.
JAMES (FRED S.) & CO., INC.
JEFFERSON-PILOT CORP.
LIBERTY CORP., THE
LIBERTY NATIONAL HOLDING INSURANCE CO.
LINCOLN NATIONAL CORP.
MGIC INVESTMENT CORP.
MANHATTAN LIFE CORP.
MARSH & MCLENNAN COMPANIES, INC.
MISSION INSURANCE GROUP, INC.
NLT CORP.
NATIONAL LIBERTY CORP.
ORION CAPITAL CORP.
PENNCORP FINANCIAL, INC.
REPUBLIC FINANCIAL SERVICES, INC.
TRANSAMERICA CORP.
TRAVELERS CORP.
U. S. FIDELITY AND GUARANTY CO.
USLIFE CORP.
WASHINGTON NATIONAL CORP.

INVESTMENT COMPANIES

ADAMS EXPRESS CO.
ALLEGHANY CORP.
AMERICAN GENERAL BOND FUND, INC.
AMERICAN GENERAL CONVERTIBLE SECURITIES, INC.
ASA LIMITED
BUNKER HILL INCOME SECURITIES, INC.
CNA INCOME SHARES, INC.
CAMERON-BROWN INVESTMENT GROUP
CARRIERS & GENERAL CORP.
CHASE CONVERTIBLE FUND OF BOSTON, INC.
CURRENT INCOME SHARES, INC.
DREXEL BOND-DEBENTURE TRADING FUND
EXCELSIOR INCOME SHARES, INC.
FORT DEARBORN INCOME SECURITIES, INC.
GEMINI FUND, INC.
GENERAL AMERICAN INVESTORS CO., INC.
HATTERAS INCOME SECURITIES, INC.
HEMISPHERE FUND, INC.
INA INVESTMENT SECURITIES, INC.
INCOME AND CAPITAL SHARES, INC.
INTERCAPITAL INCOME SECURITIES INC.
JAPAN FUND, INC.
JOHN HANCOCK INCOME SECURITIES CORP.
JOHN HANCOCK INVESTORS INC.
LEHMAN CORP., THE
LEVERAGE FUND OF BOSTON, INC.
LINCOLN NATIONAL DIRECT PLACEMENT FUND INC.
MADISON FUND, INC.
MASSMUTUAL CORPORATE INVESTORS INC.
MASSMUTUAL INCOME INVESTORS, INC.
MONTGOMERY STREET INCOME SECURITIES, INC.
MUTUAL OF OMAHA INTEREST SHARES, INC.
NIAGARA SHARE CORP.
PACIFIC AMERICAN INCOME SHARES, INC.
PETROLEUM & RESOURCES CORP.
ST. PAUL SECURITIES, INC.
SCUDDER DUO-VEST INC.
SOURCE CAPITAL, INC.
STATE MUTUAL SECURITIES, INC.
TRANSAMERICA INCOME SHARES, INC.
TRI-CONTINENTAL CORP.
U. S. & FOREIGN SECURITIES CORP.
USLIFE INCOME FUND, INC.
VESTAUR SECURITIES, INC.

OTHER FINANCIAL

AMERICAN CENTURY TRUST
AVCO CORP.
BT MORTGAGE INVESTORS
BACHE GROUP INC.
BANKAMERICA REALTY INVESTORS
BAY FINANCIAL CORP.
BENEFICIAL CORP.
CONN. GENERAL MORTGAGE & REALTY INVESTMENTS
CREDITHRIFT FINANCIAL, INC.
DMG, INC.
DIAL CORP.
DONALDSON, LUFKIN & JENRETTE, INC.
DREYFUS CORP.
EDWARDS (A. G.) & SONS, INC.
EQUITABLE LIFE MORTGAGE & REALTY INVESTORS
FEDERAL NATIONAL MORTGAGE ASSOCIATION
FINANCIAL CORP. OF AMERICA
FIRST PENNSYLVANIA MORTGAGE TRUST
FIRST UNION REAL ESTATE EQUITY & MORTGAGE INVESTMENTS
GMR PROPERTIES
GENERAL GROWTH PROPERTIES
GREAT NORTHERN IRON ORE PROPERTIES
GROWTH REALTY COMPANIES
HELLER (WALTER E.) INTERNATIONAL CORP.
HOUSEHOLD FINANCE CORP.
HOUSTON OIL ROYALTY TRUST
HUBBARD REAL ESTATE INVESTMENTS
HUTTON (E. F.) GROUP, INC.
INSTITUTIONAL INVESTORS TRUST
KENILWORTH REALTY TRUST
LLC CORP.
LEUCADIA NATIONAL CORP.
LOMAS & NETTLETON FINANCIAL CORP.
LOMAS & NETTLETON MORTGAGE INVESTORS
MASSMUTUAL MORTGAGE AND REALTY INVESTORS
MERRILL LYNCH & CO., INC.
MESA ROYALTY TRUST
MESABI TRUST
MONY MORTGAGE INVESTORS
NORTH AMERICAN MORTGAGE INVESTORS

NORTHWESTERN MUTUAL LIFE MORTGAGE & REALTY INVESTORS
PAINE WEBBER INC.
PERMIAN BASIN ROYALTY TRUST
PIER 1. IMPORTS, INC.
PNB MORTGAGE & REALTY INVESTORS
REALTY & MORTGAGE INVESTORS OF THE PACIFIC
REALTY REFUND TRUST
REPUBLIC MORTGAGE INVESTORS
SAN JUAN BASIN ROYALTY TRUST
B. F. SAUL REAL ESTATE INVESTMENT TRUST
SHEARSON LOEB RHOADES INC.
SOUTH ATLANTIC FINANCIAL CORP.
SOUTHMARK PROPERTIES
STATE MUTUAL SECURITIES, INC.
STERLING BANCORP
TRANSAMERICA REALTY INVESTORS
TRI-SOUTH INVESTMENTS INC.
UMET TRUST
U. S. REALTY INVESTMENTS
WACHOVIA REALTY INVESTMENTS
WELLS FARGO MORTGAGE & EQUITY TRUST
WITTER (DEAN) REYNOLDS ORGANIZATION INC.

REAL ESTATE

AMREP CORP.
CANAL-RANDOLPH CORP.
CHRISTIANA COMPANIES, INC., THE
CITY INVESTING CO.
DELTONA CORP.
HORIZON CORP.
KOGER PROPERTIES, INC.
TEXAS PACIFIC LAND TRUST
WEBB (DEL E.) CORP.

Appendix III

STOCK MARKET AVERAGES

Was the stock market up or down today? Was it up or down for the past year?

Easy questions, you might think. But really, they're not so easy to answer as you might think. Roughly speaking, there are 40,000 companies in the United States whose stock is owned, in major part, by the public. Yet when most people talk about whether "the market" was up or down, they are usually referring to a mere thirty stocks, those that compose the Dow Jones Industrial Average. It is possible for the Dow Industrials to be down on a day when most stocks advanced. Likewise, it's possible for the Dow Jones Industrial Average to show a decline for a year in which most stocks registered gains. Lately, both events have happened with some frequency. It's also possible, though it hasn't happened much lately, for the Dow Jones Industrial Average to be up, when most stocks are down.

On most days, and in most years, the Dow Jones Industrials serve as a decent, though crude, proxy for the stock market as a whole. Here are the thirty stocks whose prices are averaged (after adjustment for splits) to make up the Dow Jones Industrial Average:

Allied Corp.
Aluminum Co. of America
American Brands
American Can
American Telephone and Telegraph
Bethlehem Steel
Du Pont
Eastman Kodak
Exxon
General Electric
General Foods
General Motors
Goodyear
International Business Machines
Inco
International Harvester
International Paper
Manville Corp.
Merck
Minnesota Mining & Manufacturing
Owens-Illinois
Procter & Gamble
Sears, Roebuck
Standard Oil of California
Texaco
Union Carbide
U. S. Steel
United Technologies
Westinghouse
Woolworth

If you want to look at a broader, more representative sampling of stocks, you have several choices. Among the major stock market averages are:

- The Standard & Poor's 500. This is an average of prices for 500 stocks of large corporations.
- The New York Stock Exchange (NYSE) Index. This average includes all the 1,500 or so stocks listed on the nation's biggest stock exchange.
- The American Stock Exchange Index. This one includes about 1,000 companies, listed on the nation's second largest stock exchange. Most of them are companies somewhat smaller than those listed on the "Big Board," or NYSE. This index is known for short as the "Amex Index."
- The NASDAQ Index. The initials stand for National Association of Securities Dealers Automated Quotations. The index includes some 2,350 stocks traded over the counter. By and large, these are smaller companies than those listed on either the New York Stock Exchange or the American Stock Exchange.
- The Wilshire 5000 Index. As its name implies, this index (put out by the financial advisory firm Wilshire Associates) includes 5,000 stocks. They are a blend of companies listed on the New York Stock Exchange, American Stock Exchange, regional stock exchanges, and the over-the-counter market.

Most of the time, the various averages move more or less in concert. But the exceptions are significant. Between early 1977 and mid-1978, for example, the

American Stock Exchange index rose more than 20 percent while the Dow Jones Industrial Average dropped about 20 percent. Watching the performance of the various indexes gives you an idea of which groups of stocks are hot. If you want to compare the performances of the stocks you hold with the performance of "the stock market" in general, knowing about the various yardsticks available will help you make a more thorough and appropriate comparison.

NOTES

NOTES

NOTES

NOTES

NOTES

NOTES

NOTES

NOTES

NOTES

NOTES